# THE RED SHIRT

## AND

# THE CROSS OF SAVOY

Also by George Martin

THE OPERA COMPANION:
*A Guide for the Casual Operagoer*

THE BATTLE OF THE FROGS AND THE MICE:
*An Homeric Fable*

VERDI: HIS MUSIC, LIFE AND TIMES

# THE RED SHIRT

## *AND*

# THE CROSS OF SAVOY

The Story of Italy's Risorgimento (1748–1871)

GEORGE Whitney MARTIN

*Illustrated with Photographs,*
*and with Maps by James MacDonald*

DODD, MEAD & COMPANY

*NEW YORK*

# Acknowledgments

I am grateful to the following for permission to use quotations or trans-
lations: to Farrar, Straus & Giroux, Inc., New York, for the quotation from
Alberto Moravia's essay "The Vulgarity of Giuseppe Verdi" which ap-
peared in his book *Man as an End;* to the Agenzia Letteraria Inter-
nazionale, Milano, for the quotation from Benedetto Croce's *History of
Europe in the Nineteenth Century* as translated by Henry Furst; to G.
Bell and Sons, London, for the translations by Bertha Pritchard and Lily
C. Freeman of two documents published in Guglielmo Ferrero's *The
Gamble;* to G. Scalabrini Editore for the translations from Leopardi's
*Canti* by John Humphreys Whitfield; and to Doubleday & Co., Inc., New
York, for the quotation from E. E. Y. Hales' *Napoleon and the Pope,*
also published under the title *The Emperor and the Pope.*

With regard to the illustrations, I am grateful to the following for permission to reproduce portraits: to the Soprintendenza alle Gallerie, Napoli,
for the portrait of Carlo III by Francesco Liani, of Maria Carolina by
Landini, and of Ferdinando I by Gennaro Maldarelli; to the Lord Chamberlain, London, for the portrait of Pius VII by Sir Thomas Lawrence,
copyright reserved to H. M. the Queen; to the Radio Times Hulton Picture Library for the portrait of Pio Nono, of Francesco II of The Two
Sicilies, and of Cardinal Antonelli; to the Pinacoteca di Brera, Milano, for
the portrait of Massimo d'Azeglio by Francesco Hayez; to the Casa del
Manzoni, Milano, for the drawing of Manzoni by Stefano Stampa; to the
Gabinetto Fotografico Nazionale, Roma, for the portrait of Alfieri by an
unknown artist; and to the Soprintendenza alle Gallerie, Firenze for the
portrait of Ugo Foscolo by Antonio Fabre.

In the course of writing the book I have used the facilities of many
libraries and museums and would like to mention two whose staffs, in
various ways, have given me special assistance: The New York Public
Library, New York City, and the Biblioteca del Museo Correr, Venice.
I want to thank Delight Ansley for the useful index. I am grateful, also,

to the following individuals who have read the book in typescript or proof and made suggestions for improving it: Charles F. Delzell, of Vanderbilt University, Allen T. Klots, Jr., of Dodd, Mead, and two friends, Elliott B. Nixon and Arthur K. Satz.

—GEORGE MARTIN

*New York City*

# *Preface*

I have tried in this book simply to present a narrative history of the Risorgimento in the light of present scholarship; I have not tried to bring new facts to light or to offer a unique interpretation of past events. Foolishly, perhaps, I think a narrative history, by which I mean one that proceeds chronologically with its emphasis on plot, setting and characterization, is needed.

The Risorgimento is a vast subject, and English and American scholars in the last fifty years generally have dealt only with parts of it. Even G. M. Trevelyan, in his tetralogy on it, limited himself to Garibaldi, Manin and what he called its "central period." Since then the specialization has increased, and the scholars have produced some fascinating studies which have changed men's ideas about the history of Italy in the nineteenth century. But no scholar, alas, has taken the time to write a general account of the Risorgimento which would lead the amateurs of Italy and its history into the events, problems and personalities of the period.

Meanwhile, of course, the older general histories, such as Bolton King's published in 1899, or W. J. Stillman's published in 1909, have gone out of print and, because of the changes in point of view caused by the new works, are unlikely to be reissued. A. J. Whyte's *Evolution of Modern Italy,* published in 1944, is still available but compresses two hundred years of history into only a few more pages and presupposes, as he suggests in the preface, familiarity with the story. Anyone searching for a more recent general account of the Risorgimento will not find one.

I hope this book will fill that need, whether for a student just approaching the history of modern Italy, for an enterprising tourist about to visit the country, or for the armchair historian who is looking for an introduction to the more specialized studies and biographies. But, of course, regardless of the need, I wrote the book out of enthusiasm for the subject, and I hope, too, that the reader will come to share it.

—GEORGE MARTIN

# Contents

*Preface*                                                                     *vii*

## PROLOGUE

1. The Spanish Habsburgs in Italy. Carlos II. His Will. The War
   of the Spanish Succession. Treaties of Utrecht and their effect
   on the Risorgimento.                                                          3
2. The Austrian Habsburgs in Italy. End of the Medici and Far-
   nese; Elisabetta Farnese establishes her sons in Italy. Maria
   Theresa in Milan and Tuscany. The political frontiers and
   dynasties of the Risorgimento period are set.                                 9
3. Intellectual developments. The attraction of England and
   France. Voltaire. Montesquieu. The Church and Galileo. Freemasonry and Jansenism. The *Encyclopédie*.                                   18

## PART I

4. Feudalism in Italy; in Naples, Savoy and Venice. Carlo Gozzi.
   Lucca. Genoa and its republican legacy to the Risorgimento.
   The position of the Church. The renaissance in Naples.                       27
5. Parma's renaissance and its collapse. Carlo III of The Two
   Sicilies leaves for Spain. Ferdinando and Maria Carolina. The
   decline of the renaissance at Naples.                                        37
6. Maria Theresa and the Habsburg family in Italy. The family's
   concept of itself. Changes in the concept. The Duchy of Milan.
   The spirit of reform. *Il Caffè*. Habsburg reforms in Milan and
   their consequences.                                                          45
7. The unpolitical temper of the eighteenth-century in Italy.

Metastasio. Alfieri. His plays. His *Vita* and *Della tirannide.*
The new spirit.                                                                52

 8. The decline of faith. Suppression of the Jesuits. Pius VI. The
    Papal States. Religious reforms of Joseph II, of the French
    Revolution. The French deputies and the Papacy.                            60

 9. The French Revolution. Its four periods. The principle of
    monarchy. The rejection of feudalism. The Directory. The
    Consulate.                                                                 72

10. The war in Italy. Napoleon. Political settlements and difficul-
    ties. Tolentino. To Vienna. Preliminaries of Leoben. Collapse
    of Venice. Gozzi. Foscolo. Cisalpine Republic. Campoformio.
    Effects of the war in Italy.                                               78

11. 18th Fructidor (4 September 1797). Revolution in Rome. Pius
    expelled. Loot of Rome. Revolution to Naples. Nelson. Battle
    of the Nile. Neapolitan invasion of Rome. Disaster. Flight to
    Palermo. France's position in Italy.                                      101

12. Ferdinando and Maria Carolina in Palermo. Ruffo's campaign
    in Calabria. The capture of Naples. Nelson. Caracciolo. Bour-
    bon cruelty. The decline of Naples under Ferdinando.                      116

13. Death of Pius VI at Valence. Napoleon returns from Egypt.
    18 and 19 Brumaire (9 and 10 November 1799) First Consul.
    Conclave at Venice. Pius VII and his Christmas homily. Ma-
    rengo.                                                                     131

14. Napoleon in Italy. The Concordat. The Cisalpine Republic.
    Napoleon's despotism. The Civil Code. He becomes Emperor.
    Pius VII goes to Paris. Francis becomes Emperor Franz of
    Austria. Napoleon's reforms in Italy.                                     140

15. Opposition in Italy to Napoleonic regimes. By the peasants in
    Calabria. By Foscolo and the republicans in the Kingdom of
    Italy. "Dei Sepolcri." By the Pope at Rome. His kidnapping
    and imprisonment.                                                         156

16. Wagram. The Treaty of Schönbrunn. Metternich. Marie
    Louise. The black cardinals. Napoleon and Pius. The Pope
    returns to Rome.                                                          172

17. Franz regains Milan and Venice. Genoa given to Sardinia.
    Congress of Vienna. Form of the treaty. Napoleon's Hundred
    Days. Murat's attempt to make a united Italy. Maria Caro-
    lina exiled. Her death. Ferdinando restored to Naples. The
    Habsburg settlement of Italy.                                             182

## PART II

18. Reactionary government at Rome and Turin. Naples, Murat and the Carbonaro revolution. Ferdinando calls in Austria. Revolution at Turin. Lombardo-Veneto. Franz's personality. Metternich's philosophy. Carbonaro trials. Pellico and Confalonieri.     195
19. Mazzini's family and youth. Leopardi. His patriotic poems. Censorship. Manzoni's novel. Its importance for the development of a national language.     212
20. Francesco I of The Two Sicilies. Ferdinando II and his saintly Queen. His character. Carlo Alberto. Mazzini's Open Letter. Papal rule at Ravenna. The Sanfedisti. The problem of Temporal Power. The Carbonaro revolution of 1831.     224
21. Mazzini in exile. His influence. La Giovine Italia. The invasion of Savoy. Garibaldi at Genoa. Mazzini in London.     235
22. The Bandiera brothers. Garibaldi in Brazil. Anita. In Montivideo and the Italian Legion. The "red shirt." The Manifesto of Rimini. Massimo d'Azeglio. His journey through the Papal States and his interview with Carlo Alberto. The election of a liberal Pope.     248
23. Effects of Pio Nono's reforms. Manin and the Venetians. Milan. Catholic tradition in the Po valley. Carlo Alberto's reforms. Cavour. His politics, his farming, his unpopularity. His newspaper. Death of Marie Louise in Parma. Metternich's opposition to reform.     264
24. The year 1848. Communications. Tobacco Riots in Milan. *I Lutti di Lombardia*. Manin arrested in Venice. The effect on Venetians. Revolution in Palermo. The Genovesi and the Jesuits. The *Benedite* of Pio Nono. Carlo Alberto grants a constitution. The parade in Turin.     276
25. The revolution in Paris and the Second Republic. The students in Vienna. Manin, the Arsenal and the Venetian Republic. The "Cinque Giornate" of Milan.     288
26. Sardinia declares war. *L'Italia farà da sè*. Pastrengo. Carlo Alberto. Political confusion. The Allocution. The problems facing the Papacy. The Sardinian army. Carlo Alberto's military and political decisions. The battle of Custoza. Carlo Alberto in Milan. The armistice.     307

27. The armistice in Venice. Manin as dictator. Military occupation of Lombardia. Garibaldi in the Alps. His judgment of Carlo Alberto. The armistice in Piedmont. Republican revolution in Rome. The murder of Rossi. The Pope flees. Reaction in Naples. Leopoldo flees from Tuscany. The new Habsburg Emperor, Franz Josef. Barricades in Paris. Louis Napoleon elected Prince-President. The armistice ends. Novara. Vittorio Emanuele becomes King.                                         327

28. Republicans at Florence and Rome. Guerrazzi. The Grand Duke returns. Verdi and *La Battaglia di Legnano*. The Roman Republic proclaimed. The French support the Pope. Mazzini, Garibaldi and the defense of the Roman Republic. Manara's Bersaglieri Lombardi. Garibaldi's retreat from Rome. San Marino. Death of Anita. Garibaldi's escape.                    345

29. The siege of Venice. Manin and resistance at any cost. The assault on Malghera. The railway bridge. The bombardment. Cholera. The failure of the fleet and surrender. Manin's departure. The end of the liberal movements of 1848–49. The settlement of Italy.                                            367

## PART III

30. Changes in life and attitudes after 1848. King *Bomba*. His increasing autocracy. Vittorio Emanuele. His liberalism. The Proclamation of Moncalieri. The Siccardi Laws. Cavour's speech. Santa Rosa's death. Cavour enters the ministry.          379

31. Franz Josef's character. Radetzky's attitude. Austrian occupation of Lombardo-Veneto. Mazzini's National Italian Committee. Contessa Maffei's salon. *Crepuscolo*. The lesser Habsburgs. Pio Nono and the hierarchy for Britain. Ferdinando and Poerio. Gladstone's *Letters to Lord Aberdeen*. Ferdinando's character and its effect on his Kingdom. Pio Nono's government. Its failings. His relations with his people and with the rest of Europe.                                     392

32. Cavour and Sardinia's economic revolution. Louis Napoleon's *coup d'état* and reactions to it. Increasing pressure on Sardinia. The *Connubio*. Cavour resigns from d'Azeglio's ministry. His trip abroad. The Civil Marriage bill. Cavour becomes Prime Minister. Napoleon proclaims the Second Empire.       407

33. Mazzini's committees and the trials at Mantua. Mazzini's rising

in Milan, 6 February 1853. The sequestration decree. Sardinia's response. The character of Franz Josef and Count Buol. Sardinia as "Piedmont."    420

34. The Crimean War begins. Cavour's vision of its effects in Europe. Franz Josef and Nicholas. Duke of Parma assassinated. The Law on the Convents. The State's position. The Church's position. The constitutional crisis. D'Azeglio's letter to the King. The bill passes. Its significance.    428

35. The Crimean expedition. The battle of Tchernaja. Manin's letter: "If not, no!" Vittorio Emanuele's visit to Paris and London. The Congress of Paris. Cavour's maneuvering. Lord Clarendon's speech. Cavour's success.    446

36. Significance of Cavour's success. Manin's letters. Franz Josef starts a policy of conciliation. His tour of Lombardia and the Veneto. Mazzini's expedition to Sapri. Pisacane. La Farina, Manin, Pallavicino and the *Società Nazionale Italiana*.    457

37. Orsini attempts to assassinate Napoleon III. His trial. His letters. Cavour and Vittorio Emanuele resist pressure from France. Mazzini's attack on Cavour. The meeting at Plombières. Clotilde. Napoleon's greeting to the Austrian Ambassador. The King's speech: *il grido di dolore*. Efforts for peace. Verdi's name and Dandolo's funeral. Napoleon hesitates. Cavour's collapse and victory. Austria declares war.    472

38. Gyulai's slow advance. Metternich and Ferdinando of Naples die. Napoleon's war. Magenta. Proclamation of Milan. Revolution in Tuscany. Italian patriots cheer Napoleon but turn to Cavour. Papal forces retake Perugia. Garibaldi and the *Cacciatori delle Alpi*. Solferino. Peace of Villafranca. Cavour and the King. Napoleon returns to France. Cavour resigns.    492

39. Italian resistance to the terms of Villafranca. Ricasoli. Tuscany and Emilia offer to unite with Sardinia. Murder of Anviti. Garibaldi and the Papal States. Treaty of Zurich. Napoleon's maneuvers toward a Congress. His pamphlet *Le Pape et le Congrès*. The Congress postponed. Plebiscites in Tuscany and Emilia. What the votes represented. Plebiscites in Nice and Savoy. Garibaldi's anger. Cavour's defense of his actions. Italian attitude toward Napoleon.    509

40. The Sicilian expedition. Mazzini's preparations. His letter of

2 March. The rising on 4 April at the Gancia Convent. Rosolino Pilo. Garibaldi decides to go. Cavour and Vittorio Emanuele. The stop at Talamone. The landing at Marsala. Abba's
description of Sicily. Calatafimi. Republican misgivings. The
taking of Palermo.                                                    532

41. Francesco's need for aid and his decision to appeal to France.
Its significance. Vittorio Emanuele's letter to him. He revives
the Constitution of 1848. Its effect on the Kingdom. Garibaldi's columns into the interior of Sicily. Abba's description
of the march and of events at Bronte. The problem of annexation. Crispi and La Farina. La Farina deported. The battle of
Milazzo. The Bourbon government disintegrating. Garibaldi
reaches the Strait.                                                   551

42. The Strait of Messina. Garibaldi urged on by the King. Cavour's actions to stop Garibaldi. First attempt to cross fails.
Bertani's volunteers. Cavour stops further re-enforcements.
Origin of plan to invade the Papal States. Garibaldi's second
attempt to cross succeeds. Collapse of the Neapolitan army in
Calabria. Cavour clears his plan for the Papal States with Napoleon. Garibaldi decides against annexation for Sicily. Francesco abandons Naples. Garibaldi enters.                             568

43. Pio Nono's view of the invasion of the Papal States. His volun-
teer army. Its defeat at Castelfidardo. Garibaldi asks for
Cavour's dismissal. Cavour's estimate of Garibaldi. The repub-
lican dream of Rome. The volunteers and the Bandiera
Brothers at Cosenza. Garibaldi again postpones annexation of
Sicily. Failure of his government at Naples. Mazzini, Pallavi-
cino, Cavour, and the threat of civil war. Garibaldi's reception
of the Sardinian army. Battle of the Volturno. Cavour declares
Rome to be the capital. Annexation by plebiscite or assembly.
Pallavicino asks Mazzini to leave Naples. The plebiscites and
their significance. Garibaldi meets the King at Teano. Lord
John Russell's dispatch. The regular army and the volunteers.    590

## PART IV

44. Failures of the King and Farini with the volunteers and southerners. The first Italian Parliament and the franchise upon

which it was based. Francesco abandons Gaeta. Cavour's negotiations with the Papacy. The Pantaleone Memorandum. Pio
Nono's Allocution and Cavour's speech on the Roman Question. Parliament resolves Rome to be the capital. Garibaldi
attacks Cavour in the Chamber. Cavour's last speech. His
death.  629

45. Italy's loss in Cavour's death. The division of allegiance be-
tween the government and a concept of Italy. Ricasoli as Prime
Minister. The war in the south. Rattazzi succeeds Ricasoli. The
Constitutional question. Garibaldi's tour of northern Italy. His
technique of speaking. His speech at Marsala. He crosses the
Strait. Aspromonte. The government's complicity.  654

46. Rattazzi resigns. Farini. Minghetti. Resentment of Piedmont.
The September convention and the move to Florence. The
Turin riots. The Southern problem. The "Liberal Catholic"
movement. Montalembert. Döllinger. The Syllabus of Errors.
The Civil Marriage Bill. *Non expedit.* The problems prove the
strength of the Risorgimento's basic ideas.  667

47. Garibaldi's visit to England. The Galician scheme. The Prussian alliance and third war against Austria. Custoza. Lissa.
The Veneto annexed. The failure of the Venetians to rise.  682

48. Ricasoli's effort to negotiate the Roman Question. Garibaldi's
election campaign. His preparations for a march on Rome.
Mentana. The French back in Rome.  695

49. Results of Mentana. Religious events under Pio Nono. The
Vatican Council in prospect. Manin's return to Venice. The
Kingdom's economic problems. Its desire for a large army.
Lanza replaces Menabrea. Franco-Prussian war. The min-
istry's plan for Rome. Its execution. Pio Nono's last act in a
Papal Rome. Rome taken. The Romans don't rise. The
plebiscite. The Law of Guarantees. *Roma capitale* realized.
The Risorgimento ends. Was it a success?  706

EPILOGUE

50. The deaths or burials of Foscolo, Mazzini, Napoleon, Manzoni, Vittorio Emanuele, Pio Nono and Garibaldi.  727

APPENDIX: *The Lateran Pacts and the Law of Guarantees*      733

BIBLIOGRAPHICAL NOTES                                        735

SUGGESTIONS FOR FURTHER READING                              745

TABLES OF SUCCESSION                                         755

INDEX                                                        761

# Illustrations

## PHOTOGRAPHS

*Following page 110*

| | |
|---|---|
| Carlo III | Pio Nono |
| Maria Carolina | Massimo d'Azeglio |
| Ferdinando I | Francesco II |
| Pius VII | Cardinal Antonelli |
| Vittorio Alfieri | Camillo Cavour |
| Ugo Foscolo | Bettino Ricasoli |
| Alessandro Manzoni | Giorgio Pollavieino |
| Giacomo Leopardi | Giuseppe La Farina |
| Giuseppe Mazzini | Giuseppe Cesare Abba |
| Carlo Alberto | Giuseppe Verdi |
| Leopoldo II | Giuseppe Garibaldi, Naples 1860 |
| Ferdinando II | Garibaldi in old age |
| Daniele Manin | Vittorio Emanuele II |

Pio Nono, "Prisoner in the Vatican"

## MAPS AND TABLES

The Spanish Empire in the Mediterranean under Carlos II, 1665–1700    5
Habsburg Holdings in Italy after the Treaties of Utrecht, 1713    10
Italy in 1780, at the death of Maria Theresa    46
Italy in 1813, at the height of Napoleon's expansion of France    173
Italy in 1815, after the treaties of the Congress of Vienna    189
Milan in 1848, during the Cinque Giornate    302
The Po valley, with its principal rivers and cities    309
Rome in 1849, during the defense of The Roman Republic    356
Garibaldi's Retreat from Rome and his Escape from the Austrians, in
     July and August 1849    363
The Campaign of 1859 in the Po valley    495
Western Sicily: Route of Garibaldi and The Thousand from Marsala
     to Palermo    543
The Strait of Messina and Garibaldi's Crossing    574

Garibaldi's Route to Naples 19 August–7 September 1860            583
Route of Vittorio Emanuele to meet Garibaldi, 2–26 October 1860   594
Environs of Naples, 1860                                          620
The Unification of Italy, 1859–60                                 630
The Northeastern Boundary of Italy, with Note on Venice and
    the Veneto                                                    689
Mentana, 3 November 1867                                          703
Tables of Succession:
    Habsburg-Lorraine                                             756
    House of Savoy                                                758
    Bourbons of Naples                                            758
    Duchies of Parma, Modena and Tuscany                          759
    Popes                                                         760
    Prime Ministers of Italy                                      760

# PROLOGUE

PROLOGUE

# CHAPTER 1

The Spanish Habsburgs in Italy. Carlos II. His Will. The War of the
Spanish Succession. Treaties of Utrecht and their effect on the Risorgimento.

THE RISORGIMENTO was both a period in Italian political history, roughly
the nineteenth century, and a spiritual movement that profoundly influenced Italian art, letters, music, social and economic life and even, by
reaction to it, the Church. Like all such movements its beginnings are
obscure, and its end merges imperceptibly into something quite different.
Those at the start of it were certainly unaware of the forces that history
and themselves let loose in Italian life, and many at its end regretted that
they had missed the best of it. For at full flood the Risorgimento was one
of those periods in history in which the actors, caught up in a movement,
an idea, however imperfectly understood, seem to have experienced life
more fully and intensely than most men; they burned with a flame more
fierce and, perhaps, more pure. The issues of the time have largely faded
into dispassionate history, but the glow of the men's vitality, their faith,
passion and commitment to life, even if it meant to die, still catches the
eye and heart of later men; it is a testament of life itself.

The background in Italy against which the spirit of the Risorgimento
first appeared was partly determined by the deaths of three ruling princes,
each of whom was the last of his line to rule and who, dying childless,
left a kingdom or duchy over which survivors squabbled and went to
war. Two of the princes were Italians, the last of distinguished Renaissance dynasties, Gian Gastone de' Medici and Antonio Farnese, the
Dukes of Tuscany and Parma. The third prince, the most important and
first to die, in 1700, was Carlos II, the sixth Habsburg to be King of
Spain. Among his great predecessors were the Emperor Charles V and
Philip II of the Armada who, through two more generations, had be-
queathed to Carlos a collection of kingdoms, duchies, counties, palatines,
cities and towns, which a later age has called collectively the Spanish Empire. On it, truly, the sun never set. Overseas there were the Philippines,
the Canaries, Cuba, Mexico, Florida, California, Panama and all of South

3

America except the Guianas and Portuguese Brazil. In Europe besides Spain and the Balearic Isles there were the Spanish Netherlands, corresponding roughly to modern Belgium and Luxembourg, and about half of modern Italy: the Duchy of Milan, the Kingdoms of Naples, Sicily, and Sardinia, and the two best ports in Tuscany known as the Tuscan Presidii. Since that day in 1530 when the pope at Bologna had crowned Charles V and proclaimed him Holy Roman Emperor, Spanish Habsburg power had been dominant in Italy.

For most of the period it had been exercised directly by viceroys in Naples, Sicily and Sardinia, by a governor in Milan, and indirectly by cardinals and ambassadors at Rome and the ducal courts. The positions of the duchies were often particularly delicate in that the Spanish kings claimed them, or large parts of them, as fiefs of the Spanish Crown. The theory was that the Emperor Charles V or Philip II, in capturing a city during any of several military sweeps through Italy, had returned it to its duke or ruling body to be held as a fief. The Spanish kings constantly invoked the theory to keep the duchies neutral in times of war or even to claim them outright when the local dynasties lapsed. But then so did the emperors at Vienna and the popes at Rome, for, over the years, most of the cities had been captured two or three times by troops of the various forces. In the seventeenth century, however, the serious claim was Spain's, for it had military garrisons in many of the cities. Only the Republic of Venice, still strong in itself, and the Duchy of Savoy, bordering on France, could maintain an independent policy.

But with the accession of Carlos II to the Spanish throne that country's dominance in Italy seemed certain soon to end. He succeeded his father, Philip IV, in 1665, less than a month before his fourth birthday, and the foreign ambassadors at the Spanish court at once reported home that the new king was physically weak, malformed and possibly mentally deficient. At four he could not stand alone and was carried everywhere by a nurse. At six he could stand but still not walk. He had the Habsburg protruding lower jaw to such an extent that he could not chew and had to swallow his food in indigestible lumps, and he suffered constantly with fevers, giddiness, rashes. It seemed unlikely that he would survive for long.

A monarchy, at the time, was still regarded as family property to be disposed of by gift or will, and the other monarchs of Europe, most of whom were related to Carlos, followed his health with interest, continually calculating their consanguinity and intriguing to better their positions with him and with the ministers who dominated his court. The Italian princes had little hope that on Carlos' death they would gain much for themselves; they hoped merely that the transfer to a successor of Spanish power and holdings in Italy could be managed peaceably with perhaps a slight terri-

**THE SPANISH EMPIRE ~**
*IN THE MEDITERRANEAN UNDER CARLOS II, 1665-1700*

**THE ITALIAN STATES ARE...**

| | |
|---|---|
| 1. Duchy of Savoy | 6. Duchy of Modena |
| 2. Marquisate of Montferrat | 7. Duchy of Mantua |
| 3. Republic of Genoa | 8. Republic of Venice |
| 4. Duchy of Parma | 9. Papal States |
| 5. Republic of Lucca | 10. Grand Duchy of Tuscany |

**THE SPANISH HOLDINGS IN ITALY ARE...**

| | |
|---|---|
| 11. Duchy of Milan | 13. Kingdom of Sardinia |
| 12. The Presidii | 14. Kingdom of Sicily |
| 15. Kingdom of Naples | |

torial adjustment here and there or the dropping of a claim of feudal right or duty.

Meanwhile Carlos, against all probability, survived in a pathetic half-life for almost forty years, and when, in 1700, he finally died childless, by his will he gave the entire Spanish Empire, including all its Italian parts, to Philippe de Bourbon, the grandson of Louis XIV of France. The bequest, not unexpectedly, outraged Leopold I, the Archduke of Austria, who as a Habsburg and Holy Roman Emperor wanted the entire inheritance for *his* heir, and soon thereafter began the War of the Spanish Succession in which France fought, with some aid from Spain, against England, Holland and Austria.

In Italy the fighting was almost entirely in the Po valley where Leopold's armies, led by Prince Eugene of Savoy, drove the French out of Milan and then, in a famous battle at Turin, which the basilica at Superga commemorates, out of Piedmont. The Italians, except for the Piemontesi under Vittorio Amedeo II, the Duke of Savoy, were not directly involved in the fighting. They suffered, however, all the woes of being occupied: incidents with arrogant soldiers, shortages of food and heavy extra taxation imposed at gun-point. The Dukes of Parma, Mantua and Modena protested their neutrality and did their best to protect themselves and their people, but with only diplomacy to oppose to the Imperial armies from Austria their protests were either ignored or answered by claims of feudal rights.

The war ended with a congress of the powers at Utrecht and a series of treaties, most of which were signed there in March and April of 1713. The dominant power was England, relatively more important in the world then than at any time since. She alone of all the powers had emerged from the war stronger than when she entered it. Spain's weakness had been wholly revealed; France, exhausted and defeated; Holland and Austria, exhausted though victorious. But England's fields and towns had not been trampled and bombarded, and her navy and merchant marine had been greatly expanded. To match these she had a small but experienced army led by a general of genius, Marlborough. Working largely with her enemy, France, and betraying her ally, Holland, England imposed a peace on the world which was to have great consequences for Italians in the next two centuries.

By the terms of the treaties Louis' grandson, who had renounced any right he might inherit to the throne of France, was to continue on the Spanish throne, as Philip V, and to keep for Spain all its overseas colonies. This Bourbon dynasty, started by Philip, continued to rule in Spain, despite an occasional interruption, until 1931. Leopold's younger son, Charles, who by deaths in the family had become the Archduke of Austria and Holy Roman Emperor, was to have the Spanish Netherlands, the Kingdom of Sardinia and, on the Italian mainland, the Duchy of Milan, the Tuscan Presidii and the Kingdom of Naples. In addition he was to merge into the Duchy of Milan the eastern portion of the Duchy of Mantua which his father had occupied with his troops and claimed as a lapsed fief when the last Gonzaga had died childless in 1708. He was to hold directly, therefore, even more of the Italian mainland than had his Spanish cousin, Carlos. The dominance of Spanish Habsburgs in Italian affairs had lasted 150 years; that of the Austrian Habsburgs would last as long, and driving the Austrians out of Italy would be one of the chief goals and achievements of the Risorgimento.

Only one Italian prince gained something from the treaties for himself: Vittorio Amedeo II, Duke of Savoy, who had, depending on the point of view, the courage of a lion or the duplicity of a fox. He had started the war fighting for Louis and then, most opportunely, changed sides. As his reward he received the Marquisate of Montferrat, a small part of the Duchy of Mantua which was separate from the rest and bordered on Piedmont. He also received—for at the peace conferences he emerged as the pet of the all-powerful English—the Kingdom of Sicily. But seven years later he gave this to Charles of Austria in return for the Kingdom of Sardinia which lay closer to Savoy and which, although more backward than Sicily, would prove far less difficult to rule.

Vittorio Amedeo's success irritated and alarmed the other Italian princes. After the war and the exchange of the island kingdoms he was styled, by agreement of the great powers, King of Sardinia, and was granted royal honors. His ambassadors now walked ahead of those of mere dukes, which caused Cosimo, Grand Duke of Tuscany, nearly to expire with rage. More serious, because lasting down to and even adversely affecting the development of the Risorgimento, was the mistrust of Savoy engendered in the other Italian princes by the absorption of the tiny Marquisate of Montferrat.

In times past, the House of Savoy had held in its duchy as much land on the French and Swiss slopes of the Alps as on the Italian. The family spoke French as did all the duchy's aristocrats and their retainers and all the peasants on the French and Swiss slopes. Only on the Italian side, in Piedmont, was an Italian dialect spoken and then only by the lowest classes. Turin, the duchy's capital, although in Piedmont was a French rather than Italian city. Yet gradually, over hundreds of years, this French orientation was changing. The dukes could not expand their holdings down the French slopes into the heart of France, and the Swiss Confederation blocked them to the north; but to the east, down the Po valley from Turin, there were many tiny principalities. To the rulers of these and, to some extent, even to their people Savoy seemed a close and dangerous enemy; particularly after Vittorio Amedeo was widely quoted as saying that Italy was like an artichoke: to be eaten leaf by leaf. Montferrat was a leaf, and before the horrified eyes of the other Italian princes, it was pulled off and digested with the blessings of the great powers.

By the treaties of Utrecht, England took very little for herself, at least in the way of land. But part of what she took in the Mediterranean and, even more, what she prevented France and Spain from taking was to have great importance for Italians. England kept for herself Gibraltar and the Balearic island of Minorca with its excellent harbor of Port Mahon, thus insuring her naval supremacy in the western Mediterranean. In the coming years, in the wake of Napoleon, she would pick up Malta and Corfu and then, much later, Cyprus. Meanwhile, by passing the harbors of Sicily, Sardinia and southern Italy to the non-naval powers of Savoy and Austria, she had made it difficult for France or Spain to challenge her supremacy in the Mediterranean.

As the Risorgimento developed, as Italians began to unite to drive the Austrians out of the peninsula, it was to be important to them that the undisputed naval power along their flanks and in their rear was Great Britain, a country with no holdings in Italy and no desire for any. To some immeasurable extent the fact that the enemy, Austria, and the fight against it were largely restricted to land made the work of the Risorgimento easier and perhaps even possible.

In the same way when the drive for unity on the peninsula began to collide with the Papacy over the fate of the Papal States, it was important that Great Britain was a Protestant power whose people had no great desire to support the pope. Often in the nineteenth century Britain would aid the Italian patriots by doing nothing at moments when the Catholic powers were inclined to act but lacked the naval means.

The diplomats at the conferences in Utrecht in 1713 might well have been astonished, and even amused, if they could have seen these results of their work. But for their own generation they did their work well. Dividing the immense holdings of the Spanish Habsburgs among eager heirs cannot have been easy, yet the peace which they devised, in the opinion of such a historian as G. M. Trevelyan, "proved more suited to the needs of the new century than the post-Napoleonic treaties of Vienna or the Versailles Treaty of our own day." In the concepts of the time the gift of half of Italy to an Austrian Habsburg, Charles VI, was not unreasonable, and no Italian, either prince or poet, seriously protested it.

# CHAPTER 2

The Austrian Habsburgs in Italy. End of the Medici and Farnese; Elisabetta Farnese establishes her sons in Italy. Maria Theresa in Milan and Tuscany. The political frontiers and dynasties of the Risorgimento period are set.

THE AUSTRIAN HABSBURG, Charles VI, ruled his new Italian possessions in much the same manner as his Spanish predecessors. He continued the system of viceroys and governors, bolstering each with some troops and a small staff, but, as before, much of the government was managed by local lords who considered that they owed allegiance directly to Charles as emperor and over whom the viceroys had little real control. There was much regulation of life, such as nobles being required to appear at certain functions, but little government in the larger sense of a policy being consciously adopted and applied over a period of years. The one exception, of course, was taxation which, whether imposed from Madrid or Vienna, was always unpopular.

On the whole, perhaps, Charles was more successful than the Spanish in Milan and less so in Naples; but the difference was as much a matter of temperament and geography as of policy. Vienna was closer than Madrid to Milan, and the Milanesi felt, with justice, that the Austrians rather than the Spanish had the greater interest in them. The situation, considering the difficulties of travel, was reversed in Naples and aggravated by the difference in temperament. The Spanish, being a Mediterranean people, had instinctively understood the Neapolitans' mixture of pride and poverty, their love of display and gaudy religiosity. The Austrians were less successful in their contacts with the people, and to most Neapolitans their rule seemed more hostile and foreign. But no one, in the south or north of Italy, thought of contesting Charles' rule, and what political excitement there was now turned on the fate of the Duchies of Tuscany and Parma.

In each, by 1730, an ancient and glorious dynasty seemed about to expire and, as with Carlos in Spain, the would-be heirs protested their devotion to the two dukes while suggesting far more openly that, if disappointed in the wills, they would take by force what they considered to be

9

HABSBURG HOLDINGS ~
*IN ITALY AFTER THE TREATIES OF UTRECHT, 1713,*
*WHICH ENDED THE WAR OF THE SPANISH SUCCESSION*

### THE ITALIAN STATES ARE:

1. *Duchy of Savoy~Kingdom of Sicily*
2. *Republic of Genoa*
3. *Duchy of Parma*
4. *Republic of Lucca*
5. *Duchy of Modena*
6. *Republic of Venice*
7. *Papal States*
8. *Grand Duchy of Tuscany*

### THE HABSBURG HOLDINGS ARE:

9. *Duchy of Milan*
10  *The Presidii*
11. *Kingdom of Sardinia*
12. *Kingdom of Naples*

theirs by right. Meanwhile the dukes, hoping to preserve their duchies from a war in which their subjects would gain nothing, struggled to find some solution that the more powerful Bourbons and Habsburgs surrounding them would respect.

In Tuscany, the larger duchy, the grand duke who seemed certain to be the last Medici was Gian Gastone, a strange, almost tragic figure. In his youth he had been handsome, but a life of debauchery, occasioned by genuine unhappiness, had turned him by sixty into a slobbering, stinking mound of flesh. Few persons, however, saw him. His last public appearance in Florence, in 1729, had been a disaster. He had never liked appearances and had always overfortified himself with wine. On this occasion, as the carriage had jolted him through the streets, he had been forced every now and again to lean out the window and vomit, while his unsuspecting people, on seeing his face at the window, had dropped to their knees below it.

Since then Gian Gastone had remained in bed where he received all ambassadors and transacted all the duchy's business. The sheets were filthy, the room stank of wine and snuff, and its most frequent visitors were a gang of ruffians hired to keep the duke amused. Yet in most ways Gian Gastone was a better duke for his people than his father, Cosimo, whose morals had been unimpeachable but who had been a puritan and a bigot. Strangely, out of that fetid room in the Palazzo Pitti there blew an air of intellectual freedom and common sense about government which the duchy sorely needed.

The situation at Parma was happier. Francesco Farnese, the last duke but one, had died childless in 1727 and had been succeeded by his brother, Antonio, the last male Farnese. Antonio, at the time, was a bachelor, forty-seven years old and, like Gian Gastone, monstrously fat. But unlike Gian Gastone he had swelled not from the disappointments of life but from its enjoyments. In the words of Ferdinando Bernini, a historian of Parma, Antonio "passed his days in elegant conversations with knights and ladies, foppish assignations, late suppers, drives in a carriage, long sleeps and delicious siestas."

It had been a complete and perfect life for a bachelor; but still, as duke, Antonio had to make room in it somewhere for a duchess and an heir. Within a year he married Enrichetta, a daughter of the neighboring Duke of Modena, and although Enrichetta seems to have been perfectly amenable to his embraces, after two years there was still no child.

Parma was not a large duchy, but its flat, fertile fields and its two large, energetic towns, Parma and Piacenza, exerted a strong appeal on its neighbors. To the north and west was the Duchy of Milan where Charles VI, with an occasional flourish of his Habsburg troops, claimed that, if Antonio died without male issue, then the Duchy of Parma as a lapsed fief should revert to himself as Holy Roman Emperor. To the south and east was Modena where Duke Rinaldo hoped to acquire at least some part of Parma through his daughter's rights as a widow. And from Rome the pope pressed a historical claim, for in 1545 Pope Paul III, Alessandro Farnese, had formed the duchy by carving it out of the Papal States to give his natural son, Pierluigi. By a peaceful return of the duchy now, argued Pope Clement XII, an old Church scandal would be quieted, to the greater glory of all the Christian princes.

In the end, however, all were defeated by a woman, Elisabetta Farnese, who devoted all her mature life to the single purpose of advancing her two sons. She was Antonio's niece, the daughter of an elder brother who had died young. As a female member of a minor dynasty about to expire her prospects as a young girl had been dismal, either spinsterhood or marriage with some second son who could not demand a dowry of lands and titles. Then, incredibly, by a course of events over which she had no control, she had been married to Louis XIV's grandson, Philip V of Spain (Philippe de Bourbon), and had become Queen of Spain.

It had been an extraordinary step forward for an unlikely princess, even when all the circumstances were considered. She was to be Phillip's second queen; his first, Maria Louisa of Savoy, had died but only after bearing two sons. Both boys were alive and healthy and would succeed to the Spanish throne before any sons Elisabetta might bear. Furthermore she had been chosen partly because she was so insignificant that her elevation would not unsettle any of Spain's alliances. She was expected to be Phillip's companion in bed and by the fire and nothing more.

At first, as expected, she had been queen merely in name, but when Philip began to suffer increasingly from melancholia, she had become, through her domination of his mind, the actual sovereign of Spain. Working closely with Philip's prime minister, Cardinal Alberoni, who himself came from Parma, she negotiated constantly to procure duchies in Italy for the two sons she had borne Philip. The elder of these was Don Carlos or, as he was known in Italy, Carlo di Borbone.

Her claim to Parma on his behalf, should Antonio die without issue, was clear and appealing. If successful, it would have the virtue, at least for the Parmigiani, of continuing a popular dynasty. Also on Carlo's behalf she claimed Tuscany; or if the two duchies were too much for Carlo, then Tuscany for him and Parma for her younger son, Filippo. In her heart, however, she wanted both duchies for Carlo and then later, perhaps, something else for Filippo.

Her claim to Tuscany was by reason of being the great-granddaughter of Margherita de' Medici, a sister of an earlier grand duke. Technically, her claim was weak, and if Elisabetta had not been a queen with troops at her command, the great powers would have ignored it. But further, besides what she could bring from Spain to back her claims, she had a natural ally in Louis XV of France, who did not want the Habsburgs of Austria to become too powerful in Italy, and she had also a weakness in Austria: Charles, who had no sons, was willing to make concessions to obtain recognition of his daughter, Maria Theresa, as heiress to the Habsburg lands.

The negotiations between the powers were endless, and treaties were at best only temporary pauses of agreement. But by 1731 all, including even the dukes whose lands were being disposed of, were settled on the plan that, the dukes lacking issue, Elisabetta's son, Carlo, should inherit Parma and Tuscany. Still uncertain, however, was whether Carlo should hold them independently or as fiefs of Charles as Holy Roman Emperor. Both Elisabetta and Gian Gastone in Tuscany were strongly opposed to this condition, for it would give Charles a residual claim to the duchies.

Then suddenly one day in Parma in 1731 the enormously fat Antonio, who had overeaten every day of his life, died of indigestion. He had always enjoyed the lighter side of life, and he swept the Farnese out of history with a true comic opera finale. Some weeks before his death and during a party he had seen his Duchess Enrichetta, when heated with dancing, suddenly call for a cup of iced chocolate. In a purely personal vision Antonio saw in his wife's appearance and simple request evidence that she was three months gone with child. Accordingly in his will he left all his possessions, including the duchy, "al ventre pregnante della Serenissima Signora Duchessa" and named her regent. In default of any issue the duchy was to go to the male descendants of his niece, Elisabetta.

As no one else, not even the duchess herself, had seen the evidence so plain to Antonio, there was a startled pause in the expected chain of events while the eyes of the diplomatic world focused on Enrichetta's belly. She arranged to have her person examined by a jury of five midwives which proclaimed, unanimously, that she was with child. A special service was held in the cathedral to help along the gestation, and the head of St. Bernard was exposed. Elisabetta's representatives, however, continued politely skeptical, remarking on the size of the late duke and hinting that about the palace there was a gardener's wife in a condition to provide a supposititious child at the right moment. Charles, meanwhile, ordered Habsburg troops from Milan to occupy the duchy; later, if necessary, they could be withdrawn.

Finally, in what would have been the twelfth month, Enrichetta formally announced that the pregnancy was false. From Spain, Carlo, bearing a jeweled sword given to his father by Louis XIV, started for Parma. He was fifteen and, during his minority in Italy, was to have as his guardians, Grand Duke Gian Gastone and his grandmother, the Dowager Duchess of Parma.

He stopped first in Tuscany for a long visit with the grand duke, whose appearance and behavior must have startled him, but undoubtedly he had been warned in advance what he would find and kept his thoughts about it to himself. No one expected him, at fifteen, to be politically wise; that was left to his mother and Gian Gastone. It was sufficient that he was healthy, vigorous and, as everyone remarked, more Italian than Spanish. His youth charmed the Tuscans. He loved horses and hunting, and whenever he passed a tapestry with a horse in it, he would raise his leg as if to mount. He practiced archery on the tapestries in his suite, shooting at the woolen birds, until one day, while he was out hunting, Gian Gastone had all the Gobelins taken down and replaced with plain damask. Then he explained to the astonished Carlo that, with the hot weather coming, the rooms would be cooler.

More important he allowed Carlo to receive homage from the Tuscan provinces without first consulting Charles in Vienna or having any ceremony of investiture to show that Carlo held the duchy as a vassal of the

Holy Roman Emperor. Soon after, Carlo, preceded by Spanish troops, made a formal entry into Parma, again without any Imperial investiture. Charles was furious and a serious quarrel threatened, only to be absorbed in the larger, European disagreement known as the War of the Polish Succession.

The war, in which the Bourbons of France and Spain fought Habsburg Austria, lasted only two summers, but it made several important changes in the political hierarchy of Italy. At its start Elisabetta correctly guessed that Charles, in Vienna, would be unable to defend his distant Kingdoms of Naples and Sicily, and she wrote to the eighteen-year-old Carlo, who was at Parma, urging him to conquer the combined crowns "which elevated into a free kingdom, will be yours. Go forth and win: the most beautiful crown in Italy awaits you." A kingdom, of course, was better than a duchy, and best of all was a kingdom taken in war and "free" of all feudal ties to Charles or anyone else.

Carlo moved quickly and while the Austrians, French and Spanish fought the main war in the Po valley, he in the south took one Austrian fort after another and successfully established himself in Naples. In theory he was reconquering the former Spanish possessions for his father, Philip. But from the start everyone understood that Philip, guided by Elisabetta, had seen the truth of an idea then becoming current: that the kingdoms of Italy, united to Spain, enfeebled the latter; and he was expected to give Naples and Sicily to Carlo outright. This he did by public proclamation, and for the first time in almost 250 years Naples was once again the capital of an independent state.

Carlo then went to Sicily where, in the cathedral at Palermo, he was crowned "King of The Two Sicilies." The title was an ancient one, stretching back to the eleventh century when the Normans conquered Sicily and southern Italy. They made their capital in Palermo and referred to "Sicily this side of the Strait of Messina," which was the island proper, and to "Sicily that side of Messina," the mainland. But thereafter the island and the mainland, the "Two Sicilies," frequently had a different history, and the mainland, when referred to alone, was conventionally called the Kingdom of Naples. The older title, however, was constantly revived, and the memory of a time when the island dominated the mainland and the king lived in Palermo rather than Naples kept Sicilians irritated with the later, reversed position.

For the moment, however, both the Neapolitans and the Sicilians rejoiced in their independence and their young, vigorous king. Carlo had an auspicious start, and the Bourbon dynasty he founded in Naples in 1734 continued to rule there until, in 1860, Garibaldi and his red shirts unseated it.

Carlo's success, however, distressed the Florentines, particularly Gian Gastone over whose exhausted body the great powers began again to thrash out the fate of Tuscany. This time, however, Elisabetta lost; for France, to gain the Duchy of Lorraine on its border, made a separate treaty with Austria, which Spain, in the end, was forced to accept. France, by the terms, received Lorraine immediately, and Francis, Duke of Lorraine, was to have Tuscany on Gian Gastone's death. As Francis was married to Charles' daughter, Maria Theresa, the Habsburgs had, in effect, added Tuscany to their holdings in Italy.

The Tuscans were not happy with the solution, but Gian Gastone was unable to change it. The only modification he could achieve was a stipulation that the duchy would not be merged with any other Habsburg holdings in Italy and would always be governed directly by its own duke, some Habsburg younger son, rather than indirectly by a viceroy of the head of the house in Vienna.

Besides gaining Tuscany, Charles, in return for acknowledging Carlo's right to Naples and Sicily, received Parma, which he absorbed into the Duchy of Milan. Carlo, however, was allowed to take all the personal property of the Farnese to Naples. He stripped the ducal palaces, as the Parmigiani still sigh, "down to the nail," taking besides a marble staircase, furniture and tapestries, the entire library and some four hundred pictures and statues, among which was the famous Farnese Bull, now in the National Museum in Naples.

There was one other change of territory as a result of the war, and a most characteristic one. Carlo Emanuele III, King of Sardinia and Duke of Savoy, had joined the French with his Piemontesi troops and helped to overrun much of the Duchy of Milan. He would have liked the city itself, but at the close of the war Milan with the bulk of its duchy was returned to Charles. Carlo Emanuele was allowed, however, to keep two of its provinces which bordered on Piedmont and which lay west of the Ticino river, one of the Po's tributaries. The amount of land involved was not large, only two small leaves of the Italian artichoke, but the absorption of them by the Sardinian House of Savoy further irritated the less successful Italian princes and increased the mistrust with which they and their people viewed Sardinia. For Sardinia itself the acquisition still further inclined the kingdom's interest to the Italian rather than the French or Swiss slopes of the Alps.

Ten years later, in 1748, at the conclusion of still another war Carlo Emanuele received as a reward, this time for aiding Austria, the balance of the Milanese provinces west of the Ticino. This war, known as the War of the Austrian Succession, followed the death of Charles VI and the succession of his daughter, Maria Theresa, to the Habsburg lands. In Europe it was a complicated, desultory dynastic war in which Maria Theresa success-fully advanced her husband, Francis, to the position of Holy Roman Emperor. In doing so she lost her province of Silesia to Frederick the Great of Prussia and was forced to reward Sardinia and placate Spain with bits of her Italian holdings. But considering the difficulties of her situation —for a brief period, and for the first time in hundreds of years, a non-Habsburg German prince held the Imperial title in opposition to her—she emerged from the struggle remarkably well. At the end of it she was still only thirty-one, handsome, and had demonstrated her competence to rule. Her husband, Francis, who in 1737 had succeeded Gian Gastone as Grand Duke of Tuscany, was a support to her personal life and of almost no im-portance publicly. His marriage to her, however, when combined with the failure of male heirs to her father, technically changed the title of the House from Habsburg to Habsburg-Lorraine. (See Genealogical Table, pages 756-757).

In Italy the war was restricted almost entirely to the Po valley and was another round in the continuous struggle there between Bourbon France and Habsburg Austria for position and influence. Generally the Habsburgs had more titles and military power while France had the greater cultural and intellectual influence. But at the conclusion of this war France, allied with Spain, forced Maria Theresa to give up the Duchy of Parma, which her father had absorbed into Milan. At Parma the combined Bourbon powers installed as duke and duchess, Filippo, Elisabetta Farnese's second son, and his wife, Louise, who was the eldest and favorite daughter of Louis XV of France. With Carlo reigning in Naples and his brother in Parma, Elisabetta finally had achieved her ambition.

Further, with the close of this war, in 1748, the political frontiers of the Italian states, except for a few minor adjustments, now were set on lines which, with the exception of the temporary dislocation caused by Napo-leon, would continue to exist for more than a hundred years, until they were all erased by the patriots of the Risorgimento in favor of a united Italy.

The ruling houses of the various states also now were set. In 1860 the patriots, in order to unite the country under the House of Savoy, would dispossess the Bourbon descendants of Carlo and Filippo in The Two Sicilies and Parma and the Habsburg descendants of Maria Theresa in Milan and Tuscany.

More immediately, however, the peninsula enjoyed a long period of peace, almost fifty years, during which the peoples of the eight Italian states, as well as their leaders, adjusted, sometimes slowly and sometimes swiftly, to a new age and new ideas. During this period in Italy, in the broadest terms, the age of faith was giving way to the age of reason, and feudalism, to a new concept of the state.

For these reasons historians, trying to fix for laymen some date when the Risorgimento could be said to begin, sometimes have selected 1748 and the peace which closed the War of the Austrian Succession. But, of course, the date is arbitrary and unsatisfactory, for the Risorgimento began, not with an event, which can be dated, but with ideas, which are dateless. Nevertheless, if a date must be fixed, there at least are good reasons for selecting 1748.

# CHAPTER 3

Intellectual developments. The attraction of England and France. Voltaire. Montesquieu. The Church and Galileo. Freemasonry and Jansenism. The *Encyclopédie.*

THE DYNASTIC ISSUES of these wars of succession, however important they may have seemed to the princes and peoples involved, were relatively unimportant. Outside of Austria and Italy the issues were not dynastic but colonial, and each war was another round in a continuous struggle between France and England to wrest lands overseas from an exhausted Spain and to exclude each other, wherever possible, from enormous areas of trade. Between 1688 and 1815 England, with Austria as its ally on the continent, fought France in seven major wars which consumed sixty of the 127 years. At issue were the control and development of North America, India and many of the great islands of the world. The religion, the language and the political system of millions of people today were determined by the fortunes of that struggle.

On the whole, England had the best of it, and her success was immediately apparent and caused an intellectual revolution among political thinkers. All through the seventeenth century, in the years while Europe waited for poor Carlos II of Spain to die, France under Louis XIV, *le roi soleil,* had been universally considered the example of a State in its most perfect form, an unlimited monarchy ruled by a strong, central bureaucracy owing allegiance solely to the king. In the same period, England, on the other hand, with its revolution ending in the beheading of its king, its period of dictatorship under Cromwell, its restoration of the Stuart line and, finally, its supplanting of the Stuarts with the Hanoverians, seemed to be the example of all to be avoided. Yet England, not France, had won the War of the Spanish Succession, imposed the Peace of Utrecht, and thereafter enjoyed the greater prosperity. The paradox disturbed men, and they pondered it.

Voltaire visited England from 1726 to 1729 and in his *Letters Concerning the English* praised the country's atmosphere of freedom and tolerance. As if to prove his point the *parlement* of Paris ordered the work to be burnt as scandalous and disrespectful and the author to be arrested. Voltaire judiciously retired for a time, while in Paris almost everyone who could read hurried to borrow or to buy a copy of the book.

But even before Voltaire men had begun to wonder if tolerance of sects dissenting from the state-supported religion was not only better for the dissenters but for everyone else, too. They had begun to argue that when Louis XIV, in 1685, revoked the Edict of Nantes, driving many Protestants from France, the country had lost more, in the skills of the displaced, than it had gained in the religious unity of those who remained. For the unity had been specious; the country was soon torn in two by the differences between two Catholic groups, Jesuits and Jansenists, and then the leading Jansenists had been driven from France.

In 1729 Montesquieu followed Voltaire to England and, perhaps because of Voltaire's experience, in the first instance, in 1748, published his *De l'Esprit des lois* anonymously. Possibly because the work was more scholarly and less sprightly than Voltaire's it escaped the ban of *parlement,* although not that of the Roman Church. It was, however, even more successful than Voltaire's work, going through twenty-one editions in eighteen months.

In it Montesquieu compared three kinds of government, a republic, a constitutional monarchy and an absolute monarchy or despotism. He recognized the ideal superiority of a republic but feared the form lacked stability. He preferred, therefore, a constitutional monarchy, and he particularly recommended the English constitution in which he felt the independence of the executive, legislative and judicial arms of the government secured a high degree of liberty.

Others attacked the theories of the prevailing mercantile system of commerce, which was highly protective both in tariffs to keep goods of other nations out and in government subsidies of new industries at home. The system undoubtedly helped to start industries, but it also seemed, on occasion, to impede them with too much regulation. The same seemed true of trade. The British and Dutch overseas trading companies were independent of their governments and prospered, while the French companies, government-controlled in every detail, languished. In Italy, with its many small states and semi-independent cities, the tariff barriers could have ludicrous and stifling results. In Tuscany eight duties had to be paid on a bale of wool passing from the port of Livorno to Cortona, sixty miles inland. Merchants and thinkers increasingly questioned the tariff system. They also began to challenge the system of monopolies, whether exercised by a government, an independent trading company, or a guild of craftsmen.

Probably both the intellectual ferment in France and the freedom and prosperity of the average man in England were different expressions of the same vigor that impelled the people of the two countries to colonize and fight over the world. But whatever the reason behind the explosions of thought and energy, the excitement of them attracted the attention of educated men everywhere.

Of those in Italy many were aware that this excitement and energy somehow, in the last two hundred years, had deserted Italians, and they were inclined, in casting about for the reason, to find it in the Church's attitude toward education, particularly in its attitude toward science. It was an attitude which cost the Church the support and sympathy of many men, and in the story of Galileo and his teaching lies both the seed and an example of it.

He had been born in Pisa on 15 February 1564, a time when the artistic period of the Renaissance was closing and when the scientific period was just beginning. Columbus, seventy-two years earlier, had discovered a new world, and Magellan had later shown it to be round. Men were thrilled by the enormous expansion of their world and ripe for new explanations of it.

Galileo taught at the University of Pisa, in the Grand Duchy of Tuscany, and at the University of Padua, in the Republic of Venice. He contributed enormously to the prestige of both. His work attracted other scientists to them, and his lectures, which he delivered with wit and charm, attracted all kinds of men as well as students. He wrote several of his tracts in Italian for the many people who, as he described them, "cannot read Latin . . . (and) believe that in 'those awful books' . . . there are things way above their heads," and thousands of Italians repeated the simple experiments, were convinced and looked at nature or the universe with fresh, excited eyes.

But it all ended unhappily. Looking through his telescope, which he had introduced to Italy, Galileo became convinced that the sun and not the earth was the center of the universe and that the earth moved round the sun. This belief was contrary to the teaching of Aristotle which the Church had adopted as its own. Did not the scripture state that Joshua commanded the sun to stand still, and not the earth? And therefore was it not clear that the sun moved, and not the earth?

The clash between science and theology was more fundamental than Galileo perhaps realized. He was a devout Catholic and found in the wonderful universe an exciting revelation of God. What he possibly did not fully grasp was that his telescope had made God's universe an object of direct human observation, which could be interpreted without the help of the scripture or of religion. Probably even his enemies in the Church did not fully grasp this either, for, as far as can be judged, he was brought before the Inquisition as much to soothe the wounded pride and vanities of men as for teaching heretical doctrine about God.

After a five months trial he was found guilty, and, although seventy years old and Europe's most distinguished scientist, was made to kneel before his judges while his sentence was read. And there, still kneeling, he denied that the earth moved, and stated: "I Galileo . . . swear that I have always believed, do believe, and by God's help will in future believe all that is held, preached and taught by the Holy Catholic and Apostolic Church . . ."

According to a legend, the old man, on the way back to his rooms that were his prison, sighed and said: *"Eppur si muove"* ("And yet it does move"). The legend is almost certainly not true; the earliest appearance of the phrase is said to be 1761. Yet legends reflect popular belief and this one suggests that, by the middle of the eighteenth century, popular feeling was for Galileo.

Probably the clash between science and the Church was inevitable. Objective observation is, for most men, an irresistibly persuasive argument, particularly when opposed to one that relies simply on the weight of authority and tradition. But it was unfortunate for Italians that the clash came so soon, over the very founder of modern science, for it excited the Jesuits and others in the Church who were interested in education to throw all their weight against any change in curriculum or, indeed, anything new. Grand Duke Cosimo of Tuscany (1670–1723), influenced by his priests, forbade the professors at the University of Pisa "to read or teach, in public or in private, by writing or by voice, the philosophy of Democritus, or of atoms, or any save that of Aristotle." Anyone opposing the ruling could "consider himself dismissed from his chair," and Cosimo backed the Inquisition in its prosecution for heresy of any violators. Galileo's disciple, Viviani, at one time became so alarmed that he hid his master's manuscripts, several of which were still unpublished, in a haystack.

But Cosimo went even further. He revived an old, forgotten law requiring Tuscan students to study solely at the University of Pisa; under no circumstances would he give permission to study abroad.

The result of such a policy when continued for fifty years was to create an intellectual backwater of Tuscany, which had been one of the great intellectual centers of Europe. Tuscans might know their Latin and Greek, their Dante and Ariosto, but they knew almost nothing outside the medieval curriculum. The same was true of Italians generally, for the same pressures had been exerted by Church and State on all the universities.

It was not just a question of book-learning; agriculture, commerce and navigation all suffered because of it. Elsewhere, because of the needs of sailors, great strides were made in the studies of tides, the stars, magnetism and of optics. Almost none of it penetrated Italy because the conduits through which the theoretical information should have passed, the universities, were blocked. It is a reason why Italian navigation, from its great days of Columbus, Verrazano, Vespucci and the Cabots, father and son, declined into mere coastal trading with ignorant captains proceeding timidly from one landfall to the next. Even in the Mediterranean the better trained, more adventurous English and Dutch captured most of the trade.

In much the same fashion other Italian industries fell behind the pace elsewhere. Almost anything involving experimental physics, such as mining with its need for pumps and ventilators, soon became uneconomic, for Galileo was the father of experimental physics and neither he nor his scientific method could be taught. Even the ancient silk and wool industries of Florence died when men in other cities developed better processes of dyeing and dressing.

The first turn for the better in Tuscany, and in this respect in Italy, came in 1723 with the accession of Gian Gastone following his father's fifty-three-year reign, the longest and most disastrous for Tuscany of any Medici. The new duke had a different attitude toward education. He restored controversial professors to their chairs, permitted scientific and philosophical works to be published and allowed solemn honors to be rendered to Galileo in Santa Croce. The Jesuits and monks were aghast. They denounced the University of Pisa as a nest of all the most dangerous heresies. On the other side, one of Gian Gastone's ministers observed: "One sole obstacle, the University of Pisa, prevented Tuscany from being reduced to that state of ignorance in which nearly all the rest of Italy has been suffocated." Plainly there were Italians eager to be up with their times and to profit by the extraordinary energy of the British and French by sharing in their ideas and discoveries.

These penetrated Italy in various forms and through various channels. The simplest and most direct way, of course, was by book, and although learned books, whether on political theory or applied science, were often banned by both Church and State, they generally were available to those who had contacts abroad and knew what they were seeking. But for those who were not aware of their ignorance, some stimulation was necessary, and this was apt to require some contact with men who had the new and different ideas.

One group of such men were the English aristocrats on their Grand Tours, and they brought with them not only the ideas but also an organization through which they could circulate them. English Freemasonry had been reorganized in 1717, and in 1733, with Gian Gastone's blessing, the Duke of Middlesex had founded a Lodge at Florence. Soon thereafter there were other Lodges at Milan, Verona, Vicenza, Venice and Naples, all with

Italian members. The meetings were primarily social, and the conversation probably turned more often on techniques of scientific farming than on political theory. The movement, however, was secret and Protestant in origin, and it was condemned twice by the Church and suppressed twice by the government at Naples. Nevertheless, the Lodges continued to exist and for almost fifty years formed a conduit through which new ideas of the age circulated on the peninsula.

Another, less organized but more pervasive because less restricted to the nobility, was formed by the interest of many priests and laymen in the Jansenist movement. The Jansenists were Catholics who wanted to reform the Church by returning it to the virtues of its early days. They wanted a greater simplicity of ritual and organization, a stricter morality among members, universal study of the scriptures, less frequent communion and a greater reliance on private judgment when it conflicted with the authority of Rome. They hated the Jesuits who, in turn, hated them, and each worked to destroy the other. But even though Pope Clement XI, in 1713, had condemned all the principal Jansenist ideas, the authority of Rome was too weak in France and even in Tuscany to insure that Jansenist ideas were not taught in seminaries or approved by some bishops. In France, for example, a Jansenist weekly periodical appeared regularly from 1728 to 1793.

Aside from their religious views, the significance of the Jansenists and their sympathizers lay in their readiness to think for themselves and to hold an opinion against authority. They were the kind of persons willing to examine a new idea and, if adopting it, to suffer for it. And because they attacked the hierarchy of the Church, they had a following among the lower clergy of the northern Italian cities, many of whom felt that the Jesuits and "Cathedral clergy" were constantly preferred by Rome and unduly better paid. When, therefore, Diderot's *Encyclopédie* began to appear in 1751, among its readers in Italy probably the majority were men with Masonic or Jansenist ties, if only because it was the summation of French thought and because the Jesuits tried to block its publication.

The *Encyclopédie* was intended by its editor, Denis Diderot, to offer an alphabetical classification of the whole field of contemporary knowledge. As such, it has been called "the acme of the age of reason" and "a monument in the history of European thought." Among its contributors, who eventually numbered almost fifty, were such men as Montesquieu, Voltaire, Jean-Jacques Rousseau and Anne-Robert-Jacques Turgot. Although they and their fellows did not directly attack the old ideas and institutions of the time, they undermined them just as effectively by implication and by citing factual evidence. The spirit of the articles was rationalistic: everything had an explanation and nothing need be taken on authority. The *Encyclopédie* was, in fact, as revolutionary as its enemies protested.

It was also successful. Each of the seventeen volumes of text and eleven of excellent plates was widely distributed and copied, and by 1780 at least seven pirated editions had been published, two of them in Italy, at Lucca and Livorno. No educated Italian could be altogether unaware of the new ideas spread abroad through the *Encyclopédie* nor unaware that most of them had their origin in France or England.

By comparison, Austria, where the Habsburgs favored the Jesuits, was intellectually dull and, particularly in the sciences, even backward. Generations of Italians would go to Vienna for their military and political honors, for Vienna increasingly became the seat of operative power in Italy. But for their ideas, whether on political or economic systems or even on methods of agriculture, they would go to Paris or London. The fact had a great influence on the Risorgimento, for it meant that the more intellectually adventurous Italians, those most open to the new ideas of the age, would tend always to be opposed to Austrian power and influence in Italy.

# PART I

PART I

# CHAPTER 4

Feudalism in Italy; in Naples, Savoy and Venice. Carlo Gozzi. Lucca. Genoa and its republican legacy to the Risorgimento. The position of the Church. The renaissance in Naples.

THE NEW IDEAS of the eighteenth century penetrated Italy slowly and un-evenly. The conditions of life on the peninsula differed greatly, north from south, or even in the more politically fragmented north between the neighboring republics, duchies and kingdoms. It was a difference not merely of the relative wealth of the state and its people; the role and position of the aristocracy, of the Church and of the middle and lower classes varied.

In the south Carlo di Borbone, known later as Carlo III, struggled in his Two Sicilies to lead depressed, feudal kingdoms out of a dark age. His royal authority extended little beyond Naples, Palermo and the other large coastal cities. Inland, life was still entirely feudal in its organization, and power was shared by the local barons and bandits. In 1734, the year in which Carlo started for Naples, that kingdom was reckoned to have 2769 cities, towns or villages, most of them huddles of ten or twenty houses and without connecting roads. All but fifty were under feudal government, the baron dispensing justice in his own seignorial court, collecting taxes in the form of feudal dues and enjoying a *Jus feminarum,* a *Jus stercoris* (manure) and a *Jus aquae pluviae* (rain water). The first could be commuted for a money payment, but the serfs, who lived like animals, seldom had a coin. In many of the villages only the baron's employees lived in the houses; all the serfs lived in huts or caves. Casanova, with his Venetian background, on coming south to be a bishop's secretary in one of the larger towns, was so appalled at the brutality of the people that he promptly left, urging the bishop to go with him. But for the peasants there was no escape from their poverty.

Carlo attempted to extend his royal laws to protect the peasants, to persuade the barons that as the peasants prospered so would they, and to stamp out the bandits that destroyed anything constructive done by anyone. But it was very slow work. He tried to attract the barons to Naples, to

relieve the peasants of their presence, but at the court the barons felt
ignorant and out of place and most retreated quickly to their mountain
strongholds. He issued an edict permitting the peasants to sell their produce
in the open market and not only to their feudal lords, but it was a brave
peasant who tried it under the eye of his lord. He extended the right of
appeal from the baronial to the royal courts, but few peasants had the wit
to understand an appeal, the money to afford one, or the ability to survive
the reprisals of an outraged baron. Carlo, also by edict, abolished a number of degrading personal services owed by peasants to their lords and
limited the number of armed retainers a baron could maintain. But by
1789, after fifty-five years of reform, only an additional 150 villages in the
Kingdom of Naples had emerged from feudalism. In Sicily progress was
even slower.

The situation was the same or worse on the island of Sardinia, an island
few ever visited. But on the mainland part of the Kingdom of Sardinia, the
part which was the Duchy of Savoy, the relationships between the king-
duke, his barons and the peasants had developed quite differently.

The House of Savoy over the centuries had demonstrated skill in ruling
its small duchy and, above all, in preserving it against the greed of far
more powerful neighbors. The people of all classes rewarded the House
with a loyalty and obedience famous in Europe. Perhaps they recognized
that as a small community on the crossroads of the Alps they would certainly be trampled if they did not hang together under one man.

As a result, Carlo Emanuele III and his forebears ruled their mountain
kingdom as benevolent patriarchs, supported by the nobility rather than
opposed by it. The king's word, therefore, was the law of the land, and the
only armed bands roaming the hills were troops of the king's army. At
Turin the king met with and knew personally all his nobles, gossiped about
their marriages and funerals, and sometimes granted and sometimes refused them permission to sell their fiefs, to leave their jobs at court or even
to travel outside the country. Some nobles found these feudal ties irksome,
but most, apparently, liked them. They formed the accepted way of life.

The new ideas of the century, therefore, which did not reach the barons
on the islands or in the mountains behind Naples, reached Turin, and were
rejected. The people of all classes there were content to continue with their
military tradition and proverbial piety to the exclusion of anything else. To
outsiders they seemed happy but dangerously self-satisfied and provincial.

In the Republics of Venice, Genoa and Lucca there were still feudal
ties but generally so transformed by years of commercial habit that they
were no longer personal to a lord. Rather, they had become almost state
laws of title and descent for violation of which fines were paid to quasi
government bodies. Carlo Gozzi, the Venetian playwright who wrote such

fantasies as *Turandot* and *The Love of Three Oranges,* has a passage in his *Useless Memoirs* which shows the change:

> About two hundred years ago, the father of my grandfather purchased some six hundred acres of land, together with buildings, in Friuli, about five miles from Pordenone. Many of the fields are meadows and are held by feudal tenure. Any heir, on inheriting the meadows, has a duty to renew the feudal investiture, and the renewal costs some ducats.
>
> On this point the officials of the Camera de' Feudi at Udine are extremely vigilant. If an heir, on his father's death, is slow in bringing the ducats to renew the investiture and in swearing homage, the officials without fail confiscate the meadow's hay.
>
> That happened to me after my father's death. A few months negligence cost me many lire more than the usual cost of renewing investiture.
>
> Probably from a similar old parchment originates my family's title of *Conte,* used in public acts and in the addresses of letters. If a man did not wish to concede me this title, I would not care; but I would care very much indeed if he withheld the hay from my meadows.[1]

This sort of feudalism was very different from that in Naples or Turin. The words were the same but their meanings were different. In the Republic of Venice investiture was no longer a public act of homage to a superior lord with personal rights and duties toward him acknowledged; it had become a trip to an office with money for a fee.

But still, even in Venice many of the trappings of the older age remained. Despite Gozzi's statement, his family's position and its right to the title of *conte* were important to him, and he is careful to start his memoirs with a detailed account of his pedigree. Yet at the same time he recognizes that the pedigree is worth less than hay and explains that he gives it only so that those who wish to poke fun at him "may have something to quiz." His ambivalent attitude, joking yet regretful, was typical of Venice in the eighteenth century.

The city was no longer rich, although many rich foreigners came to it for amusement. Its beauty and gaiety were proverbial, and when, in 1789, one of the last doges had the bad taste to die at the start of the Carnival Season, the sad news and the official mourning it would have caused were withheld till Lent. Venice was a city in which form and reality, fantasy and fact, finally had become completely separated.

Every year at the Feast of the Ascension the doge, surrounded by all his senators, would board his ship of state, the top-heavy, gilded, unsafe *Bucintoro,* and be pulled to the entrance of the Lagoon where he would cast his ring into the sea in token of the city's dominion over it. In fact, anything more than coastal trade in the Adriatic or Aegean was almost entirely in British bottoms.

Nevertheless, Venice continued to exert its peculiar fascination on Europeans and to offer them a special atmosphere of civilization. In addition to its medieval and Renaissance glories it presented a unique link with the classical past. Its doges, like the popes, stretched in unbroken succession back to Roman days; its councilors, sitting in state in their purple robes, represented, like the Curia at Rome, an organization inherited intact from classical antiquity; and Venice alone, of all the Roman communities, had never been conquered by the barbarians. Now even in its decline, as artists it had Canaletto and Tiepolo; its music was second only to that of Naples, and in performance, as opposed to composition, may have been better; it was the only city in Italy to support a tradition of legitimate theater, having as resident playwrights both Goldoni and Gozzi; and it was the center of Italy's printing and publishing both of books and music. With its host of visitors each year it was the most cosmopolitan city in Italy, and the new ideas of the time were discussed freely and without distorting passion.

Much of the republic's weakness lay in its political rigidity. The Venetian constitution had been set in 1297 when, by fiat, a patrician class had been created out of the leading commercial families. Thereafter only a patrician could vote in the council, be a senator or doge or hold any of the higher offices in the government. The number of patricians was very small and almost never enlarged. It included almost none of the leading families on the Venetian mainland, for they and their towns had not been absorbed into the republic until the fifteenth century, long after the decisive year of 1297. Yet with the decline of Venice's trade these mainland towns, such as Padua, Verona, Vicenza, Udine, Brescia and Bergamo, contained or manufactured the real wealth of the republic. Their fields in the Po valley were fertile, and they had thriving silk and cotton industries. The doge might better have thrown his ring at the land.

The Venetians knew it, if only because the mainlanders bluntly told them. Even so, the Venetian patricians could not bring themselves to make any changes. They loved their city as it was and had been, and if the reality of its glory was gone, then they would cling ever tighter to the form of it. But the tensions such an attitude created for the majority of the aristocracy were enormous.

There was never enough money. In Gozzi's family, where he was sixth of eleven children, his mother cheated the others to help the eldest. She was a Tiepolo, one of the oldest families in Venice, and she had extravagant ambitions for her firstborn son. To aid him and his five children she fraudulently sold lands which were entailed for the benefit of all her sons, and then she sold the evidence, the old deeds, to a pork butcher for wrapping paper. Only because a servant warned Gozzi was he able, by hurrying to the butcher, to repurchase the deeds before they were coiled around sausage rolls. Thereafter he spent eighteen years in the law courts unraveling the sales.

The fraudulent sales were, perhaps, unusual, but much of what else was done by Gozzi's mother was repeated in many patrician families struggling to make ends meet. To save expense the younger children often were left totally uneducated, and all younger sons were discouraged from marriage. At least one daughter usually was hidden in a convent, and dowries promised others were not paid in full. One son-in-law finally sued Gozzi's mother.

Gozzi himself indulged in some of the fantasy. For twenty-five years he wrote plays which made a troupe of actors rich while he refused to take a penny for his work. He claimed this gave him greater freedom to write what he wished, but there was also behind his reluctance the tradition, backed by old laws, that a member of the class of *cittadini originari*, a class only slightly less noble than "patrician," did not work at trades. When Gozzi wrote a play, he enjoyed reading it at a salon, posing as a patron of the arts, an amateur of the theater. The play was generally full of topical allusions, social references and, sometimes, slander. Doing it for money would have spoiled it; yet the reality of his life required him to pocket every ducat he could earn.

Finally, in a society declining from greater days, one in which money is short and the parade of it important, the public life will be corrupted by graft. In Venice at the end of the eighteenth century almost any patrician could be doge, if he paid enough; and the city earned a reputation for corruption. But the reputation was only partly justified, for only the patrician class was deeply involved. The middle class, artisans, lawyers and small merchants, had no vote in the Council, held no great positions and were largely unaffected by the traffic in bribes. In the last years of the republic these people watched the parade on the Piazza San Marco, if not with contempt, at least without any desire to have any part of it. In their dress and customs they refused to follow the lead of the patricians, and some of the younger nobles even chose to dress like the middle class and to consort with them. In Venice the social revolution came first: the patrician class began to disappear even before the republic fell.

The position of the aristocrats in the other republics, Lucca and Genoa, was far less artificial than in Venice. In tiny Lucca, whose land area was too small to support a landed aristocracy, the patricians had always engaged in trade, and the position of anyone in the community, whether momentarily up or down, reflected some real merit or achievement, generally success in business. In fact, the aristocracy of Lucca in its life and attitudes had already merged with the middle class.

The state was run by a Grand Council on business lines. There were government loans without interest to farmers and merchants in difficulties; there was a price-fixing system based on partial nationalization and lavish welfare programs to aid widows, orphans and the disabled. Every inch of the soil was tilled and by the latest scientific methods. The people of all classes were prosperous and contented, and there was no crime. Lucca had little to fear or to learn from the new ideas of the time.

Still, most Italians preferred Venice. The Lucchesi produced no art, no music, no literature; the life of the spirit, for all of their churches, was a dried, forced flower. They had an institution called the *discolato,* a kind of state-run inquisition which met every two months and inquired into all reports of blasphemy, debauchery or irreligion. A Neapolitan count, Giuseppe Gorani, observed: "Frankness and gaiety, the very cornerstones of society, are unknown at Lucca, where people spend their time spying on one another. The Lucchesi call themselves free, and there is no nation more enslaved than they." Their prosperity was envied, but they were judged to have missed the good life.

The political and social traditions of the Republic of Genoa were midway between those of Venice and Lucca. The patrician class entered business, at least the financial end, and they kept the profits. Indeed, they were reported to be stingy about spending them. The English Lady Miller observed tartly: "The present families inhabit the palaces as their grandfathers and great-grandfathers left them; and until the velvet and damask will no longer stick together, they have no notion of new furnishing." But still the palaces in town and the villas outside of it were beautiful, handsomely furnished and with good art on the walls. Their tradition, however, condemned all ostentation in clothing, and the men always wore black as also did the women after the first year of marriage.

As in Venice, the nobility of Genoa kept all the political power for itself. Only nobles could serve on the Grand or Little Council or hold any of the higher offices. But unlike Venice it was relatively easy for an ambitious man to ennoble his family by money or services rendered the republic. In the eighteenth century, for example, the Cambiaso family rose from nothing, bought its way into the *Libro d'Oro,* the Golden Book which recorded the nobility, and then supplied the republic with two doges.

A reason for this difference in tradition between the two cities may be that the Venetians were asked to share the government with men from other cities, men they considered to be foreigners, whereas the Genovesi, whatever social qualms they may have felt, never doubted the loyalty of the new men. All Genovesi were famous for their scrappy loyalty to the city, *Genova la superba,* and to the republican form of government.

In the next century one of the most important strains of the Risorgimento was the desire, in uniting Italy, to make it a republic. Men of many cities contributed to this dream, but particularly those of Venice and Genoa. But even the Venetians did not match the continued energy and sacrifice with which the Genovesi supported it. Mazzini, the prophet of the dream, was born and grew up in Genoa; it was the spiritual home of Garibaldi, who was born farther along the coast at Nice; and it was from Genoa that Garibaldi and his Thousand sailed, one dark night, to conquer Sicily and Naples. The city's traditions and the loyalty of its people to them was a power in Italian history.

The position of the Church varied as widely in each of the Italian states as did the social organization, and in all of them, even including the Papal States, its reformation was one of the objects of men excited by the century's new ideas. At all times and in every state there were individual priests, generally with Jansenist ideas, who joined the reformers, but understandably the Church as a whole refused to consider its position to be unduly privileged and actively resisted change.

The problem at its simplest was one of real estate and taxes. It was reckoned that in the Kingdom of Naples the Church, by ancient conquest and gift, had come to own about one-third of all the land and in the city of Naples about one-half. Even in the days of the Spanish there had been so many churches in Naples that the laity had petitioned the viceroy not to permit the clergy to build more. And on the value of these holdings or on any form of income derived from them the Church paid no tax of any kind.

In return for this privileged position, besides preaching the word of God, the Church ran hospitals, foundling homes, poorhouses, schools and in its convents and monasteries offered a contemplative life for those who wanted it. It also lent its support to "begging" orders which owned no land and lived on charity.

The proportion of the population in the Church was large, estimated in the Kingdom of Naples to be one out of forty and, of course, heavily concentrated in the cities, where it may have been closer to one out of ten. For a population of well under five million the Church provided twenty-one archbishops, one hundred sixty-five bishops and abbots, fifty thousand priests and an even larger number of monks and nuns. And for this army of mixed clergy it provided its own system of judicial courts in which were tried all cases involving a priest or nun or one of the Church's institutions.

Excluding Rome and the Papal States as a special case, Naples was one extreme of the Church's position. At the other was Venice which, for many years, had insisted that the clergy be subject to the ordinary courts and that no church or religious institution could be endowed without the state's consent. Venice, because of its extremely limited land area, had early recognized its vital interest in not allowing too much of its land to pass off the tax rolls, and, because of its commerce, wanted money free for use rather than tied up in corporate holdings. But Venice was almost more of an exception than an extreme. In most of the states, particularly in the Kingdom of Sardinia and in Tuscany under the Grand Duke Cosimo, the Church's position was as privileged as it was in Naples.

In all of them there arose an anticlerical party, sometimes led and sometimes opposed by the reigning king or duke. In Naples, Carlo, who was personally devout, constantly pointed out to the local clergy and, by ambassador, to the pope at Rome that the enormous number of religious holidays interfered with work, that the clergy often used its aura of sanctity to smuggle goods through customs and that, in general, the Church's excessive numbers, its ever-increasing property and immunity from taxation and its separate jurisdiction were obvious causes of economic hardship and political unrest.

The result, after negotiation, was a concordat with Pope Benedict XIV by which the clergy was to be liable for half the amount of taxation paid by the laity, although with a long list of exemptions. Further, the ratio of clergy to laity was fixed at one to a hundred, although the new proportion was obviously for the future; present monks and nuns were not declared excess and defrocked. At the end of nearly half a century the proportion was down to about one in eighty, a real accomplishment and one achieved with the consent of the Church.

But many areas of disagreement among Church, State and people remained. When a cardinal archbishop attempted to reintroduce the Inquisition to Naples, a large deputation of the people surrounded the king's carriage in the street near the Carmine Church. On learning their fears Carlo left the carriage and entered the church. There, in sight and hearing of the crowd, he knelt before the altar, drew his sword and swore as a knight, not as a king, that there would never be an Inquisition in Naples. And he kept his word.

Still, Carlo and his people did not always unite against the Church. When he encouraged the Jews to settle in Naples, the Church and the people, aroused by bigots and jealous merchants, made common cause against him. A Jesuit Father even assured Carlo that he would never have a son so long as the Jews remained, and, in the end, Carlo gave in.

Church and people likewise looked with suspicion on the reforms put through at the University in Naples which, during Carlo's reign, had a true renaissance. The curriculum was brought up to date; superfluous lectures in jurisprudence and scholastic theology were dropped and replaced with others on botany, chemistry, political economy, astronomy and experimental physics. Many of the scholars were priests, and the most distinguished was an abbate, Antonio Genovesi. He was the first man to lecture at a European university on political economy, and, like Galileo, deliberately aimed his courses at the average citizen by lecturing in Italian.

In his courses on Montesquieu and the theory of the state he expounded such new ideas as that the state had a duty to educate its people and that science should permeate all classes of people through courses on applied science, for "the state needs men, not pedants." He recommended an equitable distribution of land, an end to feudal laws, advanced medical practices and a commerce and industry left free to develop itself so long as it did not run counter to the general welfare of the state. This was in direct opposition to mercantilism, the general economic theory of the time, and the conservatives in Naples chattered their disapproval.

His interest in the new ideas, the "liberalism" of the times, led him into some of the first direct expressions of nationalism. Thus, the best cure for Italy's commerce and industry, plagued by overregulation, lay in unity for "common Mother Italy." And he recognized and stressed the importance of language in creating a large community of people, a nation.

Genovesi was not the first Neapolitan to have these views. His teacher, Giambattista Vico, 1668–1744, had approached many of them and with greater originality. In his book, *Scienza Nuova,* published in 1725, Vico had written the first history of man since pagan times to be based on a secular philosophy, and in it he had foreshadowed the concept of social evolution which is basic to modern minds. But Vico had been so far ahead of his time that, though he had taught at the University of Naples, he had remained relatively unknown. Genovesi, on the other hand, was a brilliant lecturer, and it has been estimated that he influenced directly some thirty thousand students.

Nor was he the only great intellectual in Naples at the time. In the field of law there was Gaetano Filangieri and in economics, Ferdinando Galiani, and though Carlo III was not himself intellectually inclined, he supported these men against their conservative detractors and even sent Galiani to Paris as his representative. The intellectuals, on their part, responded to the king first with respect and then with a patriotic affection.

Doubtless Carlo understood only half of what they talked about, for his great interest, other than government, was hunting, in which he indulged every afternoon. But he felt no animosity toward men with different tastes, and he had an ability to make out of them something for himself. He did not like opera, for example, but he saw that his subjects did, and he built them one of the largest and most beautiful opera houses in Europe, the

San Carlo. The Neapolitans were delighted, and Carlo had adorned both the city and his reign with something beautiful and permanent.

He had much the same attitude toward the University. He was by nature an autocrat and did not like disputations. Further, he was not about to reform himself into a constitutional monarch according to Montesquieu. But he saw that out of all the talk, the trial and error, there often came some application useful to government or commerce, and he took care to make good appointments and to see the University was well housed. Under him Naples became the first city in Italy for music and clear thinking, and, in spite of the great poverty of the poorest classes, it could claim, because of its sense of purpose and progress, to be the happiest. It had, in fact, a renaissance or, as the next century would call it, a risorgimento. But the terms on which Carlo and his people achieved it were those of the early eighteenth century. Carlo thought of himself not only as a king, but, in his most solemn moments, as a knight with a strict code of service and honor. Both he and his people conceived of patriotism as loyalty to the king's person, not to a particular city or land; language and cultural background, so important in the next century, were irrelevant to the concept. In the coming years many men of the Risorgimento would argue that only on a different set of terms, republican terms, could all men achieve dignity and happiness. The argument had less appeal to Neapolitans than to other Italians partly because of their experience of what had been achieved under Carlo. In less fortunate times in the future, that was the period to which, in memory, Neapolitans longingly returned.

# CHAPTER 5

Parma's renaissance and its collapse. Carlo III of The Two Sicilies leaves for Spain. Ferdinando and Maria Carolina. The decline of the renaissance at Naples.

BESIDES NAPLES, Parma, too, had a small renaissance under Carlo's younger brother, Filippo di Borbone. The little duchy had suffered during the various wars, and Carlo, when he had taken the Farnese treasures to Naples, had stripped it of its chief glories. During the period of the Austrian occupation, 1736–49, a rapacious governor had further depressed it in wealth and spirit till, in the end, it had reached a state of squalid misery and destitution. The ducal palaces, empty of furnishings, were deserted and decaying; the nobles were in retreat at their country villas, and in the city, under the exactions of war, trade had almost stopped.

Under their new duke, however, the Parmigiani made a startling recovery. Filippo contributed little to it personally, being interested largely in his clothes, his family and the court functions. He brought with him, however, a large subsidy from France and Spain, both of which wanted to build a strong Bourbon state between the Habsburg duchies of Milan and Tuscany. He also brought with him a number of French administrative assistants, all imbued with the latest ideas of efficiency, and he put in as his chief minister another Frenchman, Guillaume du Tillot, who enjoyed government and was eager to demonstrate what enlightened ideas could do. Du Tillot saw that both industry and agriculture were suffering from unemployment, underproduction and poor techniques, and he attacked on all three fronts at once. He pushed the development of mulberry plantations whose fruits were edible and whose leaves could be used as a food for silkworms. He offered free land to new luxury industries that might use silk, and he imported artisans from France and Switzerland to teach the new methods of working the material. He also introduced the potato, which was just beginning to spread through Europe.

He had the same problem as Carlo III in Naples of the Church holding too much land; and it was more acute, perhaps, in Parma because there

37

was less land. Backed by Filippo he published an edict forbidding the gift or sale, in fee, of any land or money to the Church as well as some restrictions on transfers already made. The pope at once threatened excommunication and renewed his claim to the duchy as part of the Papal States. Filippo and Du Tillot replied by expelling the Jesuits and applying their property to school and hospitals.

The action in Parma followed similar action in Portugal, France, Spain and The Two Sicilies. In each, elaborate accusations were made against the Jesuits and probably believed by many people, although today most of the accusations seem very unlikely. In Italy, at least, the action was entirely political, although to say so begs the question of defining what is a purely political or spiritual act. But no Italian prince or government ever seriously challenged the validity of the Church's message or of its dogma; the challenge was always to the political and social power the Church wielded in the community. Whereas in England, under Henry VIII, this was cut down in one cataclysmic generation, in Italy, at least until the Risorgimento, it was done by a constant nibbling.

To match its material gains under Filippo, Parma also had an artistic renaissance. Again the duke's personal contribution was small, confined almost entirely to enjoyment of the works of the others, but he did, at least, welcome the artists, musicians and philosophers and with his pensions and support made them comfortable. The result was that for about ten or fifteen years Parma was, as it claimed to be, "The Athens of Italy."

Very little survives of all the excitement except perhaps for the work of the duke's printer, Giambattista Bodoni. He produced magnificent books with flourishing title pages and luxurious margins and designed a "modern" typeface which is still used. The court poet, Carlo Frugoni, needs a large anthology for any of his poems to be included, and the court musician, Tommaso Traetta, who started a reform of opera, is well known only to scholars, although in his day he was thought to be the equal of Gluck.

Filippo's success with the duchy, however, was somewhat artificial. Although the Parmigiani responded, even eagerly, the impetus came mostly from the imported Frenchmen, and there was some reaction against them. A shopkeeper, "a stout, good-looking woman," told Casanova that the new fashions were "a bad mixture of French freedom and Spanish haughtiness" and a dressmaker, thinking back to the last Farnese, complained of the high-toned seriousness of it all: "Can such manners suit us? Here we laugh willingly and heartily! Oh! The good Duke Antonio (God rest his soul!) was certainly as great a prince as Duke Filippo, but he did not hide himself from his subjects when he was pleased, and he would sometimes laugh so heartily that he could be heard in the streets."

Given sufficient time the new ideas might have taken root and developed into a strong, local tradition able to withstand setbacks, but the cost of the reforms was high. Filippo and his Duchess Louise, Louis XV's daughter, refused to consider any economies in their court functions, and many of the reforms took time to pay back their costs. The mulberry trees grew slowly, and a new registry of lands, started by Du Tillot to make taxation more efficient, was not completed, what with the opposition of the nobility and clergy and also the Napoleonic wars, until 1830. Still, the financial difficulties might have been managed by loans or a cut here and delay there if the court had continued to be interested.

But Filippo died suddenly in 1765 of smallpox, leaving a fourteen-year-old son, Ferdinando, who had been educated to be a philosopher-king. He had been stuffed with the most enlightened maxims, the most liberal culture, the most extensive smatterings of the arts, the classics and the sciences, and it all meant nothing to him. He had a religious nature and wanted to be a bell ringer. In a *Storia della mia Vita*, which he wrote at nineteen, he described how since the age of ten he had wanted to be a Dominican and how at thirteen he had painted the Fifteen Mysteries of the Rosary on the wall of his study and had arranged the furniture to represent a private oratory, the tables and chairs being the altars and empty inkstands, the bells. When he became duke, he could gratify this passion more authentically, and often in the evening he would trot round from the palace to the Church of San Pietro Martire to ring the Angelus.

At nineteen Ferdinando married Maria Amalia, the sixth daughter of Maria Theresa. Du Tillot, who represented the Bourbon interests in Parma, would have preferred a marriage with an Italian princess, and the fact that he was unable to arrange one was evidence of his declining influence. The Habsburg match, as it turned out, was a disaster for Parma. Maria Amalia was already twenty-three and, in the words of Bernini, the Parmigian historian, "No less eccentric than the other daughter of Maria Theresa." He lists her faults, starting with the worst: "ugly, cunning, shifty, intriguing, dominating, vindictive, sensual, careless of manners, wasteful, loving parties." Even Maria Theresa soon had nothing good to say of her daughter.

Dominating by nature and older than her husband Maria Amalia ruled the court and the country. Du Tillot and the other Frenchmen were dismissed and replaced by Austrians who were both less competent and less enlightened. The good works were allowed to die for lack of attention, the Jesuits were invited back, the Inquisition re-established and all the artists dispersed. The Athens of Italy was no more, and the duchy sank into the backwaters of Italian life. Each year, because of Ferdinando, the role of the clergy increased and because of Maria Amalia, the role of the Austrians; each year the division between the court and the country became greater. By the end of the century the government was detested, and no Parmigiano would have spoken of his duke or duchess with the affection a simple dressmaker had once felt for the fat and laughing Duke Antonio.

At the other end of the peninsula the Kingdom of The Two Sicilies had a similar setback, although less severe and more gradual. Carlo's father, Philip V of Spain, had had two sons by his first wife. The eldest had predeceased Philip, but the second had succeeded him and reigned as Ferdinand VI. In 1759 Ferdinand died childless, and Carlo di Borbone of Naples became Carlos III, King of Spain. The succession was a blow the Neapolitans had foreseen but had hoped would be delayed for at least another ten years when Carlo's sons would be grown. He himself was only forty-three and, in his battles with the barons and the Church, growing stronger.

There was never any question that he would go to Madrid, however much he had come to like his Neapolitans. Nor was there any question of merging the kingdoms. On this point Carlo felt his father's decision to separate them was sacred. In preparing to leave he was, characteristically, scrupulously honest, turning over as state property all the crown jewels and even including a ring it had been arranged for him to find in the excavations at Pompeii. On the other hand, his idea of personal property included a porcelain factory which he had started at Capodimonte and now shipped entire to Spain.

Carlo planned to leave behind him as King of The Two Sicilies his third son, Ferdinando, who was only eight years old. His eldest boy he was forced to declare publicly an imbecile and excluded from the line of succession. His second son he planned to take with him as heir to the Spanish throne.

On his last day in Naples, while a Spanish fleet waited for him in the harbor, Carlo met with members of his Council of State and deputies from the cities of Naples, Palermo and Messina. To them he formally announced his intention to abdicate in favor of the eight-year-old Ferdinando. The prime minister, Tanucci, slowly read through the act of abdication and both Carlo and Ferdinando signed. Carlo then gave his son a sword, the same sword which as a young man he had brought to Italy and which, years before, Louis XIV had given to his grandson, Philippe de Bourbon, to take to Spain. In handing it to Ferdinando, Carlo urged him to use it to defend his religion, his person and his subjects. Then the city deputies spoke. They of course said nothing uncomplimentary about the little prince, but their regret at Carlo's departure and their agitation over the uncertainty of the future after the progress of the past was so evident and pathetic that the queen burst into tears and Carlo was visibly shaken. Finally the ordeal was over, and the royal party embarked. Ten days later they landed at Barcelona.

At Madrid the queen mother, Elisabetta Farnese, had come out of retirement to act as temporary regent until her son's arrival. She was now old, fat and almost blind but still strong-willed. When she was carried in a litter into the king's apartments to meet her son for the first time in twenty-eight years, she made the effort to rise in order to welcome him as King of Spain. Both wept as they embraced. She was proud of Carlo, and she had cause to be. He was probably the best Bourbon king of his century; best in what he accomplished and best in his sense of mission. He quite sincerely believed it was a king's duty to make his kingdom flourish and to devote all his attention to the welfare of his subjects, and he did both.

As Ferdinando was only eight, Carlo, in effect, continued to rule Naples. Through Tanucci, the able minister he had selected and trained, he set the policies and even, by a constant flow of letters and memoranda, directed their execution. Ferdinando, as he grew, exhibited no interest in government and was happy to leave everything to Tanucci. In order to save himself trouble he even gave the minister a facsimile stamp of his signature.

Ferdinando as a boy, by all reports, was bright and boisterous and with signs of a natural intelligence. Among his brothers and sisters he was generally the leader, and his father had sometimes referred to him as "the lawyer." Unfortunately, over the years almost nothing was done to develop these talents or to train his mind. His tutor, a Neapolitan noble selected by Carlo, seems to have felt that physical health was sufficient for a king, and he provided much roughhousing, outdoor play and hunting. This was the fashion in which many of the Neapolitan nobles educated their sons. They considered learning, for it was not recognized as an ability to think clearly, to be an eccentricity, necessary only for priests and merchants. Tanucci had a high respect for learning, but he seems to have been engrossed in his work and eager not to be bothered. There was also a tradition of Spanish etiquette at the court which tended to isolate the young king from his noble contemporaries and to surround him with circles of ignorant servants, grooms and hunting guides. From them he learned democratic manners and the slangy, Neapolitan dialect, both of which made him very popular with his people.

But foreign visitors, especially the English, were appalled at his lack of education. They admired his capacity for enjoying life and people but found in him no balancing sense of responsibility. Mrs. Piozzi, Samuel Johnson's friend, wrote of Ferdinando as a grown man: "He rides and rows, hunts the wild boar, and catches fish in the bay, and sells it in the market—as dear as he can, too—but gives away the money they pay him for it, and that directly; so that no suspicion of meanness, or of anything worse than a little rough merriment, can ever be attached to his truly honest, open, undesigning character." But giving away fish is not governing.

As long as Ferdinando was young, his father in Madrid was able to provide the needed sense of responsibility. But plainly the arrangement could not go on for long: Carlo himself might die, Ferdinando might develop a streak of perverse independence, or some third person or party might seize control by dominating Ferdinando. It was this last, after sixteen years of domination by Carlo, that finally occurred, and Carlo himself, as with Ferdinando's faulty education, was partly responsible for it.

On his abdication Carlo had attempted to bolster his son's international position by settling, once and for all, the Habsburg claim to The Two Sicilies. Maria Theresa, occupied with other problems, had never seriously pushed it, and perhaps she felt her father had waived it. But the feudal barons and clergy opposed to Carlo's policies, searching always for support, tended to coalesce into a pro-Austrian party. Carlo hoped to undercut them and any resurgence of Habsburg interest in the kingdom by a treaty with Maria Theresa guaranteeing his son's succession. In return he offered to Tuscany, where one of her sons had succeeded her husband, the two Tuscan seaports known as the Presidii which were still held by Spain. The treaty was thoroughly sensible, removing a thorn for a thorn, and out of it arose the desire on both sides to cement it by a marriage of Carlo's Bourbon son with one of Maria Theresa's Habsburg daughters.

The negotiations proceeded leisurely while the children aged. At first, although unofficially, Ferdinando was engaged to Joanna, Maria Theresa's fourth daughter. But Joanna died of smallpox, so that he then was engaged, this time formally, to Maria Josepha, the fifth daughter. But she too died of smallpox, and Ferdinando was then given the choice of Maria Amalia or Maria Carolina. He chose the latter, who was younger than he, and the rejected and aging Maria Amalia soon after married Duke Ferdinando of Parma.

Maria Theresa's supply of daughters was large; she had, in all, eight, of whom four died before marriage. The others she used to further the aims of the House of Habsburg. At the time of Josepha's engagement to Ferdinando, Maria Theresa, having heard of the young king's untutored ways, had written: "I look upon poor Josepha as a sacrifice to politics. If only she fulfills her duty to God and her husband and attends to the welfare of her soul, I shall be content even if she is not happy."

Her letters to Maria Carolina, who had left for Naples, included such sensible remarks as "Do not always be talking about our country or drawing comparisons between our customs and theirs" and such politically dubious ones as "In your heart and in the uprightness of your mind be a

German; in all that is unimportant, though in nothing that is wrong, you must appear to be Neapolitan." Such advice and training when combined with the constant example of their mother inclined all of Maria Theresa's daughters to be politically minded and, given the chance, strong-willed.

Maria Carolina arrived in Naples eager to dominate her husband and to play a part in political life. She achieved the first almost at once; Ferdinando had neither her intellect nor her interest in politics. But an active part in political life took longer. Under the terms of the marriage contract she could not attend meetings of the State Council until she had borne Ferdinando a son, and the first two children were daughters. But a son finally appeared in 1775. Within a year Maria Carolina had forced Ferdinando to dismiss Tanucci and to appoint in his place a former ambassador to Vienna. Thereafter the queen's support was the key to success at court, and the kingdom broke its traditional alliance with Bourbon Spain and substituted for it one with Habsburg Vienna. In Spain the sixty-year-old Carlo was furious, but from Madrid he could do nothing. He had given The Two Sicilies almost forty-four years of enlightened government. His rule was over.

Maria Carolina's rule that now began was not all bad; she brought youth and gaiety to a court made drab by the elderly Tanucci and she had some intelligence, more at least than either of her sisters in Parma and France. The new alignment with Vienna was not unreasonable, particularly as it brought with it friendlier relations with Britain, whose fleet controlled the Mediterranean. Clearly The Two Sicilies, with a long coastline and almost every town or industry of any importance on it, had to give special attention to Britain. And internally Maria Carolina inclined to be on the side of reform. She saw her eldest brother Joseph, who had succeeded Maria Theresa, instituting radical reforms in Vienna, and she admired him extravagantly.

But much of the good she might have accomplished was stillborn because of the defects of her personality and the inevitable results of trying to rule from her position. She was positive, sharp-tongued and dominated Ferdinando by obvious pressures. One time they were closeted together for more than twenty-four hours. When he went in, he thought one way; when he came out, another. He was particularly susceptible to a gloved arm and by pulling on long white gloves and smoothing them down her bare arms, she could persuade him to agree to almost anything. But her methods were not always peaceful. In a letter to his father he described his domestic life: "In the evening she became a fury. She jumped at me like a dog and even bit my hand, of which I still bear the scar." Earlier she had screamed at him, "For at least a year, whether you die or burst, I refuse to be pregnant." And later that evening she screamed at her spinster ladies-in-waiting "like an eagle."

Her scenes and nagging naturally aroused sympathy for him, but his plain refusal to rule her was evidence of his refusal to rule his kingdom. His inaction created the political vacuum which someone had to fill, and others as well as Maria Carolina thought there could be no one better than the queen. But she was generally blamed for whatever went wrong and seldom given credit for a success.

She brought many Austrians to the court and a number of Tuscans into the administration. She kept as her minister for most of her reign a political adventurer named John Acton, an Englishman born and raised in France. He was good at building up the army and navy but otherwise not brilliant; and to the burden of being a foreign queen she added, unnecessarily, that of supporting a foreigner as her minister. He was also a bachelor, handsome and constantly in the palace, and there were rumors that he was her lover. It may have been so, for her conduct, in spite of seventeen children borne to Ferdinando, was not above suspicion.

Her activity and the inactivity of the king ultimately weakened the monarchy and the health of the kingdom. Where Carlo had offered straightforward and consistent autocratic government, Maria Carolina offered one of devious, backstairs influence. Where Carlo's government, by its nature, tended to reform abuses; hers tended to create them. In the last year of Tanucci's ministry she had supported the Freemasons against both Tanucci and Ferdinando, and when some self-confessed Freemasons were arrested, she succeeded in freeing them by discrediting the arresting officer. She considered her success a victory for liberalism, which in the context of the times it may have been, but she seems never to have considered what such a victory and others like it did to the morale of the government's servants or to the administration of justice. Under her and Ferdinando the kingdom gradually lost its sense of progress, and the people began to drift into more and more secret organizations, like Freemasonry, rather than attending open, public lectures. In Sicily, where Ferdinando had never bothered to set foot, the Spanish tradition continued strong, and the Sicilians thought again of their old independence. At the University of Naples, in which neither Ferdinando nor Maria Carolina took an interest, the excitement supported by Carlo began to dwindle into routine. Throughout the kingdom some intangible sense of purpose, nurtured by Carlo, began to weaken. Naples became more like Venice, a wonderful city for tourists, a place where rich nobles gave fabulous parties, but not, somehow, a place where men lived vigorous, constructive lives. Maria Carolina may have ruled, but Ferdinando set the tone. Between the two of them, the luster of one of Italy's brightest cities began to fade.

# CHAPTER 6

Maria Theresa and the Habsburg family in Italy. The family's concept of itself. Changes in the concept. The Duchy of Milan. The spirit of reform. *Il Caffè*. Habsburg reforms in Milan and their consequences.

WITH THE EMERGENCE of Maria Carolina as the dominant voice in Naples, the Habsburg family controlled directly the Duchies of Milan and Tuscany, indirectly the Duchy of Parma and the Kingdom of The Two Sicilies and, further, the Duchy of Modena whose duke admired the family extravagantly. In fact, he was delighted to leave his own duchy in order to live in Milan and to serve there as Maria Theresa's governor. Seventy years after the War of the Spanish Succession, on Maria Theresa's death in 1780, her children controlled more of Italy than their grandfather, Charles VI, had won by the treaties ending the war.

It was a remarkable achievement and seemed, at least to the Habsburgs and to many Italians, to give the peninsula a unity of outlook that would in time give it strength. But the concept of the Habsburg family was changing, and in a way that not only changed its own view of itself but that of the Italians as well.

The Habsburg holdings had never had a common name such as "France" or "England." They were simply "the lands of the House of Habsburg" or "the lands of the Holy Roman Emperor." The lands themselves were not bound together by either geography or nationality. There were holdings such as the Austrian Netherlands, Tuscany or Milan entirely surrounded by other countries and peoples. Most ruling families had gradually become identified with their lands or people, but the Habsburgs had not. Vienna, their capital, was a German city, but the Habsburgs and their court even in the eighteenth century generally spoke Italian or, increasingly, French; the court poet, Pietro Metastasio, wrote in Italian, and all the court music was Italian. The Habsburgs did not think of themselves as a German dynasty but as Europe's First Family with estates in every corner of the continent. The lands were expected to produce rents that

ITALY IN 1780, AT THE DEATH OF MARIA THERESA

1. Kingdom of Sardinia,
   Vittorio Amedeo III

2. Republic of Genoa

3. Duchy of Milan, Joseph II, Maria
   Theresa's eldest son and
   Holy Roman Emperor.

4. Duchy of Parma, Ferdinando and
   Maria Amalia, Maria Theresa's
   daughter.

5. Republic of Lucca

6. Duchy of Modena, Ercole III
   whose only child is married to
   Ferdinand, Maria Theresa's son.

7. Republic of Venice

8. Papal States

9. Grand Duchy of Tuscany,
   Leopold I, Maria Theresa's son.

10. Kingdom of the Two Sicilies,
    Ferdinando and Maria Carolina,
    Maria Theresa's daughter.

would allow the Habsburgs as landlords to cut a great figure in Europe. Hence their constant effort by treaty, marriage or conquest to acquire richer lands, to increase the return on their holdings. Their centuries-old argument with the Bourbons was, at least on their side, as much social as political.

This concept of the Habsburgs began to change, at least visibly, when in 1713 Charles VI, to permit a daughter to succeed him, promulgated the Pragmatic Sanction. He had just witnessed the division of the Habsburg holdings, known for convenience as the Spanish Empire, and he wished to avoid a similar partition of his holdings on his death. So, while still living, he named Maria Theresa as his successor, defined exactly what she was to inherit, and asked the foreign powers as well as the lesser ones within his holdings to agree to it. In doing so, perhaps without realizing it, he took a long step toward the creation of a Habsburg monarchy and empire as both were understood in the nineteenth century. No longer would the Habsburg holdings be divisible among members of the family; no longer would they be merely a collection of provinces, duchies and kingdoms, unrelated except in having the same family as landlord. In future they were to be indivisible and to form one large holding in which each part would, of necessity, bear a closer relation to the others.

The concept, while it solved the problem of succession, caused Maria Theresa other, new difficulties, most spectacularly in Hungary. The nobles there saw no conflict in asserting their loyalty to her as their queen while, in refusing to give up their exemption from taxation, they asserted their lack of relation to other parts of her empire. In a less spectacular fashion the concept gradually cost her descendants the allegiance of the Duchy of Milan, which both she and her father had planned to make the rock to which to tie their other Italian holdings.

The nobles in the duchy had a strong tradition of service with Habsburgs. Under Charles, one had been a field marshal and two, viceroys at Naples. But perhaps the most notable career was that of Conte Belgiojoso. After serving in the army he had become, under Maria Theresa, ambassador first to Sweden and then to London. Under her son, Joseph II, he was vice-governor in the Netherlands. With the appointments also went affection, for he was one of Joseph's most trusted friends.

Such careers or relationships with the Habsburgs were often feudal in origin, many of the oldest Milanese families tracing their lands back to some original fief granted by some early Habsburg emperor. And although in the duchy there was almost no feudal relationship left between peasant and lord, there was considerable between lord and emperor. Thus in 1768 when a Trivulzio died without issue some of his land which he held as a fief reverted to Maria Theresa, his overlord, rather than to another branch of his family. Or, more domestically, when in 1743 a Borromeo wished to marry a suitable lady of whom his mother disapproved, he appealed to his overlord, Maria Theresa, who brusquely ordered the mother not to interfere.

Beside the feudal nobility there was a patrician class in the city of Milan. It was just as splendid and sometimes as ancient as the old nobility and the two intermarried constantly. Any noble could be called to Imperial service but only a patrician could hold civic office in Milan. Both groups owned huge estates which they farmed with care and skill. The peasants were almost everywhere freed from feudal obligations and many lived as tenant farmers on the great estates. Both the feudal nobles and patricians engaged in trade, and many were immensely wealthy. One Milanese on visiting Versailles reported that it compared poorly to the town house of the Litta family in Milan.

The noble class was not large, numbering in the duchy only about sixty-five hundred or one percent of the population. But it owned nearly half the land and controlled all the administrative posts in local government, both in the city of Milan and outside. Maria Theresa, toward the end of her reign, and even more her son, Joseph II, collided with the nobles first over finance and then, partly as a result, over the organization of the local government. What happened was typical of what was happening in other Italian and foreign states wherever monarchs, responding to the new ideas of the century, attempted to give enlightened government.

Under Charles and Maria Theresa the duchy was represented in Vienna by a rather grand Council of Italy in which the emperor, meeting with his lords from Milan, decided on a policy. This was relayed to the governor in Milan who was assisted by a consultive council, composed entirely of nobles. Below this there were more councils, senates and magistracies, also composed entirely of nobles. Between all the councils there was no connection at all, no hierarchy of administration, no central source of power. Many of the councils were centuries old, able to claim all sorts of privileges and precedents, and they mixed legislative, executive and judicial functions in a magnificent jumble. The members could seldom be dismissed for insubordination, for almost all had received at some time from some emperor a patent giving him the right to sit on such and such a council.

The result was that the emperor at the Council of Italy in Vienna could say, "Raise the taxes," and his noble advisors, on hearing him, would nod in agreement, absolutely confident that back in the duchy the taxes could never be collected. The moment the new program was announced, and even in the announcement it was often diluted, the nobles would file petitions with the local council claiming privilege, question the council's jurisdiction or take appeals to other councils. There was no end to the delaying tactics, and no additional money for the emperor.

Not all nobles were against the emperor. Those in the army wanted more money to support the military, those in the diplomatic service perhaps saw a wider picture, and many in business saw that the labyrinth of councils and magistracies was a drag on trade. These argued for reform in the interests of public prosperity, which they conceived in larger terms than did most Milanesi, and between 1760 and 1780, drawing heavily on French and British political and economic ideas, they conducted in salons, cafés and literary sheets a propaganda campaign for reform.

The most famous of their efforts, and one which had an influence throughout the peninsula, was a journal entitled *Il Caffè*. The name was intended to suggest an imaginary coffeehouse where the customers, under the guidance of an old sailor, discussed the ideas of the day, subjecting many of the older ones to a merciless criticism. The founder was Pietro Verri, a noble who had served as Maria Theresa's chamberlain and who knew her family intimately. With him he associated his younger brother, Alessandro, and a young marchese, Cesare Beccaria, who was both lazy and unstable but a brilliant writer.

The journal appeared every ten days for almost exactly two years, June 1764 to May 1766, and then stopped as the three men began to pursue separate interests. But in the meantime educated Italians in every state had read learned and witty articles on such subjects as agricultural methods, smallpox inoculations, the ridiculousness of titles, the civil law and the Italian language. None of these was intended to undermine the sovereignty of the Habsburgs, and for a time, indeed, they had just the opposite effect, stimulating both the rulers and the ruled to the need for reform, and from about 1760 to 1780 the Milanesi under Maria Theresa had an extremely happy, prosperous and progressive quarter-century.

Nevertheless, in the long run, the articles contributed to the antagonism developing between the Habsburgs and their subjects. Reforms cost money, and the Milanesi assumed that they would continue to have a voice in raising the money by taxation and then in spending it. They did not see that Maria Theresa and her son Joseph II, who succeeded her, had no intention of sharing their sovereignty with any class of subjects. Indeed, the new concept which the Habsburgs were developing of themselves and of their lands, of a unified holding, required greater, not less control, particularly of finance.

The first step in this direction of reform, at least from the Habsburg's point of view, was taken by Maria Theresa. She created a new council to deal with finance, and she put a Tuscan, not a Milanese, in charge of it. He developed his own bureaucracy, so that soon the empress had a royal official in every ward and county. These men owed allegiance only to her. At the same time she expanded the local councils responsible for apportioning the tax burdens within each ward or county to include all landowners, not merely the nobility. For the first time the empress had local allies in her struggle with the nobles, and gradually more taxes were collected. But there were some hard feelings. When Giuseppe Parini, the great Milanese poet and satirist, was asked to write a eulogy on Maria Theresa after her death in 1780, he withdrew, in best poetic fashion, to the country. After a long stay he finally emerged with the poem unwritten, saying: "I cannot find any satisfactory idea round which to compose a eulogy of the Empress. She was only generous: and giving away the property of others is not a virtue."

Her son Joseph was even more unpopular, for he expanded the independent bureaucracy his mother had created to gather taxes into every phase of his government. Even under Maria Theresa the old Council of Italy had been abolished and Milanese affairs transferred to a simple department of the Imperial Chancery. Under Joseph, one by one, the local councils were abolished and a centralized administration substituted, one that owed allegiance only to the emperor. Nowhere in its hierarchy were there representatives of the nobles or of any other class of Milanesi. Even the bureaucrats themselves were largely Viennese or Tuscan, and for convenience in talking among themselves, with their headquarters in Vienna, they slowly made the language of government German. The government of the duchy was enlightened, according to the ideas of the time; but its servants were increasingly foreigners using a foreign language, and in its concentration of power in the emperor it was absolutely autocratic. "I am the Emperor of the German *Reich*," said Joseph; "therefore all the other states which I possess are provinces of it."

Joseph, in effect, created a modern state in his duchy. What feudal ties remained between peasant, lord and emperor he broke, transforming former feudal subjects of the nobility into individual citizens of his state. For the first time the legal sovereignty of the emperor began to have a meaning for the middle class and peasants.

But Joseph's concept of a modern state was not the goal toward which the liberals of the nobility, such as the Verri and Beccaria, had hoped by their enlightened interest and reforms to guide the duchy, and after Maria Theresa's death they became more and more silent. For them, eighteenth-century liberalism by itself was a failure. Something more was needed.

The nobles, in their struggles against Joseph's reforms, had raised a cry that they were defending the rights and independence of the duchy against government by foreigners. They did not direct the claim to the middle class or peasants as neither group had any political power to lend, and both would have rejected the claim in any event as merely a class slogan. But the cry of "Home Rule," although ineffective, had been raised and never thereafter ceased to echo. In it were the seeds of national feeling.

To the cry of "Home Rule" liberal aristocrats, disappointed in the outcome of the reforms, began to add that of *"Statuto,"* a written constitution. The American Revolution had impressed them, and they saw in a written constitution the best defense against the encroachments of royal power. Both cries in part were born of the Habsburg's new concept of their monarchy and empire, and both posed for them problems which succeeding emperors were never able to solve. Of their difficulty, in part, was born the political movement which, combining liberalism and nationalism, was the Risorgimento.

# CHAPTER 7

The unpolitical temper of the eighteenth-century in Italy. Metastasio. Alfieri. His plays. His *Vita* and *Della tirannide*. The new spirit.

THE NOBILITY of Milan collapsed before the reforming Habsburgs with
remarkably little struggle and for reasons that often applied in varying degrees to the political life of the other Italian states. The larger blocs of
power, France, Spain and Austria, dwarfed the smaller Italian states and
pulled out of them many of their ablest men. France's Cardinal Mazarin
was born a Sicilian and became a Frenchman simply because in France he
had greater scope for his talents. Cardinal Alberoni and Elisabetta Farnese
both conducted Italian careers from Madrid, and in the Duchy of Milan
one of the nobility's natural leaders, Conte Belgiojoso, during the struggle
over reform, was away serving the Habsburgs in Sweden, England and the
Austrian Netherlands. This continual dispersal of Italian talent ended only
after the effects of the French Revolution and Napoleon had recast European society into a national rather than cosmopolitan mold.

Also the occupation of large parts of Italy, first by Spain and then by
Austria, had dulled the spirits of all classes of people. For the nobility of
Milan the Spanish, with their interest in protocol and etiquette, had set up
an organization, the Heraldic Tribunal, which the Austrian Habsburgs
continued. It determined such matters as the number of tassels on the
horses, the kind of uniforms for the children's nurses, the lengths of the
trains on the dresses, the use of footstools in church, the number of torches
to be carried before a coach and the kind of engraved invitations for wed-
dings or funerals. After several hundred years of this the Milanesi were, as
their historian Cantù remarked, "used and trained to the bit."

The Habsburgs, in fact, whether Spanish or Austrian, made every
effort to discourage the Milanesi from an active interest in government,
which was not difficult, for the Milanesi were, by nature and habit, commercial rather than political, and this traditional emphasis of their character proved a distraction to them rather than an aid in their struggle with
the Habsburgs. Their attention was concentrated on new developments in

agriculture and business, which they expected to change, and not on the structure of the government which many felt was sacred and immutable. Men born after the French Revolution have difficulty imagining the acceptance men born before gave to the idea of a king or emperor supported by a nobility. When news of the fall of the Bastille and the actions of the National Assembly reached the French peasants, they did not at first light bonfires, dance and rejoice at the fall of the feudal regime. Instead, a sense of confused terror filled their hearts: the *grande peur*. They deserted their villages, hid in caves and forests, gathered into bands and armed themselves against a danger which, in their overheated imaginations, was the more fearful for being undefined. Only later, when their panic had subsided, did they begin to riot and burn châteaux. The nobility of Milan were infinitely more sophisticated than the French peasants, but many of them shared the belief that the old systems of government would go on forever. They did not see, in time to unite and act effectively, that Joseph's reforms were effecting a revolution.

Further, in Italy in general it was an unpolitical age. Younger sons might stress the new political ideas, but for most men the interesting developments were in the arts, in agriculture or in the new mechanical applications of science. A great deal of energy, perhaps too much, also went into the graces of living. Maria Theresa's court poet, Metastasio, caught the spirit of the time with a long poem entitled *La Libertà* in which liberty, rhymed fifty different ways, is freedom from a woman. He manages by the sheer felicity of his lines to keep the limited subject alive for thirteen stanzas, and even such a distant and different poet as Thomas Gray considered him a great lyric poet.

In the succeeding century Italians felt Metastasio and his generation were trivial, but in their criticism they often overlooked the strength and civilization concealed behind the graces of the time. One night at the theater in Milan, during the occupation by the French Revolutionary army, the performance was stopped by Milanese radicals who got up and shouted, *"Viva la Repubblica!* death to tyrants!"* At which an old man rose up in his box and with a great effort made his voice thunder in reply, *"Viva la Repubblica!* Death to no one!"* It was Parini, the satirist poet. The new age may have been, as it claimed, more courageous, more politically astute; it was certainly more brutal.

The spirit entered Italian life through a noble playwright, Conte Vittorio Amedeo Alfieri, who brought to the aristocratic graces of his time a strange, new intensity of feeling and violence. Being in Paris after the mob had sacked the Tuileries and the king had been imprisoned, he attempted to leave and take with him his mistress, who was his wife in all but name, their five servants in livery and two carriages loaded with possessions. At the gate for Calais the guardsmen were about to let them pass when a mob suddenly surrounded them shrieking, "Stone them!", "Burn their carriages!" and "They're rich aristocrats! Take them to the Hôtel de Ville!"

Then, as Alfieri describes it in his *Vita:* "I immediately sprang out of my carriage into the midst of this rabble and, fortified by my seven passports, began to argue, vociferate, and storm like themselves, knowing by experience that this was the only means to succeed with Frenchmen. The passports were perused one after another by those among them who could read. Furious, and beside myself, I was hardly aware of the terrible danger which threatened us. I tore my passport three times from their hands, exclaiming aloud:

" 'Look, listen! Alfieri is my name! I am an Italian, not a Frenchman. Look at me! Look at my description! Tall, thin, pale, red hair, that's me! I've got a perfectly good passport, all in order. We want to pass this barrier and by God we shall!' "

After an uncertain half hour the force of his personality, continually exerted, overpowered the mob, and he was allowed to proceed. About two weeks later most of those who had been taken to the Hôtel de Ville and transferred to a prison while being investigated were murdered in the September Massacres.

Alfieri at the time of this incident was forty-three with most of his best writing behind him although not his *Vita* which he had just begun and worked at intermittently until his death in 1803. During his life he was most famous for his tragedies, which were written and played in the style of French classical drama. In almost all of them a hero rebels against tyranny. This was the theme that stirred him most, and he returned to it again and again. It reflected both the unconscious cast of his personality and his conscious political aim, which was personal and political liberty for all. When he looked at Italy, as he wrote in his *Vita,* he "was ashamed of being an Italian," for the country was "wholly degraded from her rank as a nation and the Italians divided, weak and enslaved." He dedicated his two plays about Brutus, *Bruto primo* and *Bruto secondo,* to George Washington and to the Italian People of the Future. The political message, reenforced by a vibrant, personal voice, was clear.

Today the tragedies, even in Italy, are seldom performed; the style and subjects are out of fashion, and they make hard reading. Most men can reach the essence of Alfieri, the man and his thought, more easily through his *Vita* and the political tract on tyranny, *Della tirannide.*

The title of the *Vita* is hard to translate for the book is not the usual "Life" or "Memoir." Alfieri wrote it to explain how he, an ignorant, idle aristocrat raised in the world of Metastasio, could have written such great and emotionally charged works as the tragedies or *Della tirannide.* He viewed his life, like St. Augustine, as turning on a crisis before which it was wasted and without purpose and after which it had meaning. His *Vita* is the study of a personality, a self-portrait painted, as later research has shown, in true colors although painted for a special purpose.

As a result Alfieri leaves out much that others might have put in. The mistress who made the last twenty-five years of his life extremely happy was the Countess of Albany, the wife and later the widow of Bonnie Prince Charlie, the Young Pretender. As such she was considered by some to be the uncrowned Queen of England. Alfieri had many meetings with her husband, one of the most romantic figures in the Stuart line, and any ordinary writer, with an eye on the British reading public, would have included several scenes about him. Not Alfieri; he dismisses Charles Edward Stuart in half a sentence as "old, peevish and drunken" and hurries on to things more relevant to his purpose. Even the good countess is pushed severely to the background and allowed to intrude only occasionally.

On the other hand, Alfieri includes how as a child he stole, how he puffed his vanity buying English horses, how he had fits of avarice, how he contracted venereal disease and how he struck his servant. All these have the purpose of emphasizing the change which he accomplished in himself by a prolonged act of will.

He was born in 1749 at Asti in Piedmont, a subject of the King of Sardinia. His father died before he was a year old and his mother soon remarried. At nine he went off to the Military Academy at Turin where he spent eight miserable years. They were miserable at the time because he made few friends, was nicknamed "Rotten Carcass" because of his skin diseases, and was bullied by the servant in charge of him. They were miserable in retrospect because he realized that he had been taught almost nothing. The school was run by fledgling priests of peasant background who were generally more interested in the life of the town or their own studies at the University than in the education of their pupils. The languages used were French and Latin, and Alfieri became completely at home in the first while understanding very little in the second, although Latin was the language in which most of the lectures were delivered. Italian, which the Piemontesi scorned as merely the Tuscan dialect, was scarcely spoken in Turin, and later when Alfieri began to write his plays, he had to learn it as a foreign language.

At seventeen he was able to leave the school. An uncle had died a few years earlier while serving the king as viceroy in Sardinia, and Alfieri might have had a career at court if he'd wished. But he already had his inheritance, was young and dissatisfied with everything and decided to travel. And in traveling, almost inadvertently, he began to educate himself.

He was impressed by the freedom and prosperity he saw in Denmark,

Holland and England and was enraged by the despotism of Frederick the Great in Prussia. Pondering what he saw, he read many political works, particularly Montesquieu. At the various courts he sometimes met ambassadors from the states in Italy who were cultivated men and who urged him to talk Italian and to read, incredibly for the first time, Dante, Petrarch, Boccaccio, Tasso and Machiavelli. But Alfieri is careful, in recounting his life abroad, to make plain that he was by no means a reformed character. He describes in detail all his emotions during an affair in London with a titled and married lady, Penelope Ligonier. His conduct caused himself to be wounded in a duel and the lady to be divorced by her husband. Then, having ruined her reputation, he threw her over because his noble sensibilities were outraged by her revelation that she had previously responded to the advances of a groom. So he heaped abuse on her and departed, swearing never to see her again. But he returned in an hour and spent the rest of the day with her, which he felt was disgraceful.

One of the most attractive qualities of the *Vita* is Alfieri's self-confidence, possibly arising from a sense of security in his class or from his accomplishments as a writer. But, whatever the cause, he never writes a sentence calculated to win the reader's sympathy or approval; he cares nothing about either.

On returning, finally, to Turin, Alfieri could think of nothing to do except to buy a large house and to entertain. His brother-in-law urged him to seek some diplomatic post from the king, but Alfieri was so sarcastic about the institution of monarchy and its servants that the brother-in-law, who was a Lord of the Bedchamber, never mentioned the subject again. In the midst of this life of dissipation Alfieri again fell in love, this time with a lady whom he recognized from the first to be unworthy. It was in breaking loose from this affair that he passed through his crisis and emerged a man with a purpose.

The crisis, which had been building for two years, seems to have started with a bad night in the lady's box at the opera, an entertainment Alfieri disliked. Once home he determined to free himself and, knowing well his irresolute nature, took steps to insure success. He cut off his hair because "no one but peasants and sailors appeared in public with short hair." After his hair grew back, if he felt a fit of lust coming on, he had his servant tie him in a chair, but in such a way that the ropes were concealed, his hands were left free, and he could still receive guests. During these months, spent almost entirely indoors, he read constantly and began to scribble verses. Gradually he became obsessed with the idea of glory, literary glory, and his first play, *Cleopatra,* was a success.

As some men have a spiritual conversion which transforms their lives, Alfieri had an artistic conversion. After *Cleopatra,* in fairly swift order, he wrote ten tragedies which were performed in Italy and published in Siena in 1783 and also an essay on tyranny, *Della tirannide,* which was published later in Baden, although in Italian. It was an extraordinary accomplishment for a man who, at the start, could neither speak nor write Italian correctly and, although twenty-seven, had, like any schoolboy, to study grammar and spelling.

Because of his writing Alfieri determined to quit the Kingdom of Sardinia forever. The king, Vittorio Amedeo III, required any book written by one of his subjects to be submitted in manuscript to his censors, regardless of whether it was to be published in his kingdom or outside it. Further, as part of the censorship law, subjects were forbidden to leave the kingdom without the king's express, written authority. Alfieri feared that if he wrote a play or a tract attacking the institution of monarchy, not only would the work not be published but he himself thereafter would be imprisoned in Piedmont.

So, before publishing anything, he applied to the king for permission to leave permanently. He also needed the king's permission to transfer his property to his sister, for her thereafter to pay him an annuity, and again for her to pay him a capital sum which he planned to invest in a French annuity. The paternalistic, feudal organization of life in Piedmont seemed to Alfieri an outrageous interference in his personal affairs. As a noble he even needed the king's permission to marry. By the end of a year, however, he succeeded in satisfying the king that all he wished was for the king's good as well as his own, and he left his home in Piedmont forever, living thereafter mostly in Florence.

It was probably well that he did. His *Della tirannide* is a direct attack on monarchy, which he equates, however benevolent, with tyranny. He urges as the best form of government, as the only nontyrannous form, a republic, of which he considers the sublime example to be the Roman Republic before Caesar corrupted it with Imperial ambitions. He owes many of his ideas to Machiavelli's *Discorsi* and *Il principe* and even more to Montesquieu's *De l'Esprit des lois.* But where Montesquieu's guiding muse was reason, Alfieri's is righteous indignation. "Death to the tyrants!" he cries and, where necessary, by assassination and popular revolt.

Though his ideas are not very original, they are important in Italian history on two counts: first, expressed as they were in Italian and in part put on the stage, they were the form in which most Italians absorbed the new political ideas of their time; and second, arising from the first, the ideas, as impressed with Alfieri's personality, were a direct inspiration to the men who in the next century made the Risorgimento.

Tyranny, for Alfieri, occurs when "he who is charged with creating laws can execute them." The definition includes enlightened despots like

Joseph II, for to Alfieri enlightenment was not a saving grace. It also includes a legislative tyranny such as England had for a time under Cromwell. Good government for Alfieri therefore must separate the executive and legislative powers, and in Europe he can find such a separation only in England. Yet even there he sees a threat to liberty in the hereditary nobility. A republic would be better, although not with universal suffrage. When Alfieri talks of the people "I only mean that mass of citizens and peasants of more or less moderate circumstances, who possess private resources or trades, and have wives, children and relatives: but I never include that more numerous but much less worthy class of indigents of the lowest populace." Almost a hundred years later in a united Italy the right to vote was dependent on a property qualification such as this.

What Alfieri said of the Church likewise continued to echo down through the years. Machiavelli in his *Discorsi* had blamed the Church for teaching Italians, through the bad example of the Papal Court, how to be wicked and irreligious; and further, "by the Church our country is kept divided. For no country was ever united or prosperous which did not yield obedience to some one prince or commonwealth, as has been the case with France or Spain. And the Church is the sole cause why Italy stands on a different footing, and is subject to no one king or commonwealth."

To this political attack of Machiavelli, Alfieri also added several on religious grounds to explain why, in his opinion, it was "almost impossible for a Catholic state either to make itself truly free or to remain so if it remains Catholic." He then discusses one by one "the six rings of the sacred chain" which support tyranny. These are the pope, the Inquisition, purgatory, confession, marriage as indissoluble sacrament, and the celibacy of priests. The tract promptly went on the Index, but nevertheless it was read.

Still, in Alfieri the ideas are less important than the tone. He begins *Della tirannide* with a dedication to Liberty. He is the first Italian author to have such a dedication, and he makes of it a call to action. "Thy burning sparks, O Liberty, have not been entirely quenched in all modern hearts." He ends with a "Protest": ". . . A fierce god, a god unknown, has been ever at my back, scourging me on since my earliest years, which now in maturity I contemplate fearlessly. And the fervent turmoil of my free spirit can never find peace or truce unless I pen harsh pages for the destruction of tyrants."

As a writer, with his turbulent vocabulary, his emphasis in his tragedies on the heroic elements of man's nature, and in his unknown and harassing *daemon,* he comes as close as any Italian to sharing fully in the romantic revival which was beginning to dominate European literature. He introduced its new tone of violence and intense feeling into Italian literature and from there into Italian life. It was said that he found the age Metastasian and left it Alfierian; the age, not just the literature.

Once on his travels Alfieri had been given the chance in Vienna to meet Metastasio at the Habsburg Court, and he had rejected it. "I would never," he said later, "have consented to contract friendship or become familiar with a muse hired out or sold to the despotic authority which I so vehemently detested." And indeed two men for whom liberty had such different connotations would hardly have understood each other. But still, if they had met, Metastasio, less passionate, less earnest and a bit more clever, might have won the exchange, inquiring softly if the crisis in Alfieri's life had not involved winning his freedom from a woman.

# CHAPTER 8

The decline of faith. Suppression of the Jesuits. Pius VI. The Papal
States. Religious reforms of Joseph II, of the French Revolution.
The French deputies and the Papacy.

IN HIS ATTACK on the Church Alfieri pushed into open hostility an attitude
of skepticism held by many educated Italians. They followed, in their
daily lives, the forms of the Church, such as marriage, mass or confession,
but often with little belief in the substance. Nurtured on a generation of
writers led by Voltaire, they had come to believe that much of the
Church's dogma was superstition and that the Church itself was merely a
selfish party maintaining itself by unjustified privileges. The peasants, the
nobility of Piedmont and, perhaps, of Sicily continued devout and believing, but elsewhere Alfieri found an audience for such an argument as:
"Pagan religion must have been, and in fact was, quite favorable to freedom . . . but the Catholic religion is almost incompatible with freedom."
His audience might not be convinced, but it was willing to listen.

This decline of faith was reflected in the decline of the pope's role as
the acknowledged, universal mediator among Christian people. In 1494
the pope, by drawing a line on a map, had divided the newly discovered
continent of South America between two Catholic powers, Spain and
Portugal, and his division had been incorporated in a treaty which both
parties observed. But by 1700 when two Catholic powers, France and
Austria, fell to fighting over the division of the Spanish Empire, neither
considered arbitration by the pope; and toward the end of that century the
papal secretary of state could observe sadly, "There was a time when the
voice of the Roman Pontiff was heard, respected and obeyed; now . . . it
is scarcely ever listened to and never has any effect."

Men might argue the cause of the decline, but the fact of it was beyond
dispute for it was constantly on display. In 1773 Pope Clement XIV gave
in to pressure from the Catholic powers and suppressed the Jesuits. The
General of the Society was imprisoned in the Castel Sant' Angelo and died
there; the buildings of the order were generally transferred to other reli-

gious orders and the Jesuits themselves either released into secular life or allowed to join the secular clergy. Only in Prussia and Russia, countries with non-Catholic sovereigns, did the Society continue to exist.

The suppression, even in Italy, caused no protests among the people. The Jesuits, who had worked largely with the educated classes or in foreign missions, were not greatly loved by the peasants, and for simple people the larger issue of the spiritual independence of the Church was concealed by the fact that it was the pope himself who had suppressed the Society. The issue was further confused by the obvious pleasure of the members of the other orders of the Church, many of whom were jealous of the Jesuits. But for any thinking man the Church, by submitting to the pressure of the states, had suffered an obvious defeat.

It suffered another, just as plain, nine years later when Clement's successor, Pope Pius VI, went to Vienna in an effort to persuade Joseph II to rescind some of his reforms. Joseph was reorganizing the Church in his various kingdoms and duchies so that it would be controlled by the state. Besides the usual demand of sovereigns to nominate bishops, to give state employment to non-Catholics and to censor Papal bulls and briefs, Joseph planned to have the seminaries run by the state, to cut the international ties of the religious orders, to suppress some orders and to combine others, to rearrange dioceses and parishes, to fix the number of masses to be said, to make marriage a civil contract, and to give a state Court of Ecclesiastical Commission jurisdiction over the behavior of the clergy and the administration of Church property. The program was, in fact, a reformation of the Church, undertaken without Papal support and threatening, if successful, to make the Papacy unnecessary in Habsburg lands.

The pope's journey, in one sense, was a success. Along his route thousands turned out to watch him pass and to receive his blessing. In Vienna there were receptions, orations and pleasant but inconclusive conversations with Joseph. From Vienna, Pius continued on to Munich, Augsburg and then back to Italy via Trento and Venice. It was a triumphal tour, but in form not reality. Of his main purpose he accomplished nothing; the course of Joseph's reforms continued as before. And symbolically the journey to Vienna was the reversal of another, more famous journey to Canossa, a small town in the Apennines. There in 1077 a Holy Roman Emperor, seeking to have the ban of excommunication against him withdrawn, is said to have stood three days barefoot in the snow before being admitted to the pope's presence.

Joseph's position as Duke of Milan and also of Mantua brought the reforms into the Po valley, and within a year of the pope's trip to Vienna, Joseph had further persuaded Pius to sign an agreement by which Joseph, as duke, acquired the right to nominate all the bishops, abbots and heads of other religious institutions. The language of the agreement implied that the right of nomination was the pope's, either to give away or, at some later date, to resume. But Joseph had won the practical power of naming his men to the positions.

In Tuscany, Grand Duke Leopoldo I, who was Joseph's younger brother, followed a similar course of reform. He was aided by a bishop with Jansenist ideas, and together they hoped, by giving more power over the local Church to the state and by resisting the "encroachments" of Rome, to restore to the Church in Tuscany the simplicity and purity of an earlier time. The Papacy, they felt, had sacrificed the virtues of the early Church for an inappropriate pomp and wrongful political power. Accordingly, in best Jansenist fashion, they denounced Rome as "Babylon," denounced the Jesuits' Veneration of the Sacred Heart of Jesus as "cardiolatry," and began to burn relics which they felt were dubious and encouraged superstition. They also began to remove the side altars from the churches and to have the mass said in Italian.

The simpler Tuscans were stunned by it all, and when those in the hills near Prato heard that their favorite relic, a girdle supposed to have been worn by the Blessed Virgin, was to be taken from its chapel in the cathedral and the altar itself to be removed, they revolted. On a Sunday evening in the spring of 1787, while ringing all the bells they could lay hand on, they burst into the cathedral, wrecked the bishop's throne, burnt his new-fangled missals, brevaries and prayerbooks and then moved on to destroy his palace.

Leopoldo, without changing his mind about the need for reform, recognized that his people were wholeheartedly against the new practices and withdrew them. In fact, all but a few of his bishops were also against them, most preferring to be controlled by a lax Papacy at a distance rather than by an interested state close by. But it was the peasants rather than the pope who defended the traditional forms of the faith, and it was the duke and the emperor rather than the pope who attempted to make reforms. The facts confirmed, even for persons of opposing views, the need for some sort of reform at Rome.

The pope, Pius VI, was in spirit the last of the Renaissance popes, exhibiting in his long reign, 1775–99, many of their qualities, good and bad. He was by birth and temperament an aristocrat, highly cultured and worldly. His greatest interest was classical antiquity, particularly that of Rome, and first as treasurer under Clement XIV and then in his own right he created the Museo Pio-Clementino, which is now the antiquities section of the Vatican Museum. He also built the sacristy at St. Peter's, opened the Vatican Library to scholars and re-erected three Egyptian obelisks brought to Rome by the Caesars. Under him the city had an artistic renaissance.

Artists, writers and scholars from all nations came to study in Rome or simply to enjoy its cultivated and cosmopolitan society. When they left, they took away with them the start of a classical revival which they spread throughout Europe. In painting, most famous perhaps was the Frenchman, David; in sculpture, the Italian, Canova; and in archaeology and scholarship, the German, Winckelmann. Among the writers were Goethe and, of more direct importance to Italians, Alfieri, whose plays yearn for the civic virtues of ancient Rome.

These were not in evidence either under Pius or his predecessor, Clement. When the latter died, rumors at once sprang up that he had been poisoned by the Jesuits for suppressing their Society. It seems more likely that in attempting to cure a skin disease he took too much mercury internally and so poisoned himself. But it says little for the morals of churchmen of the time that his successor, Pius VI, and the French ambassador to Rome, the intelligent Cardinal de Bernis, both seem to have thought the Jesuits were responsible. Nor was it to the Papacy's credit that on Clement's death both his confessor and his official in charge of provisioning the city had to flee the Papal States. It is proven that the Spanish ambassador had bribed the confessor to procure the suppression of the Jesuits, and the provisioner had either been so inept or so greedy in his graft that the city on several occasions had almost starved and riots had been directed against the pope personally.

Pius was no better than Clement. He was handsome, vain, notorious for his bad language and for his ignorance of Catholic dogma. Like Clement he was constantly criticized for spending too much of his time and the Church's money on art rather than religion, and, far less rewarding for the Church, he was a nepotist. On one nephew he conferred a cardinal's hat, and on another, Duke Braschi, he showered Church lands and money. This nephew's wife, the Principessa Braschi, was said by scandalmongers to be the pope's mistress and, by some, to be at the same time his illegitimate daughter. Whether true or not, his conduct was not beyond suspicion and set a tone of sexual laxity in Roman life and the Church. There was a saying in the city that if a man wanted to go to a brothel in Rome he had to go in the daytime, for at night they were full of priests.

A more famous Roman proverb, one continuing through the centuries, is "Faith is made here and believed elsewhere." By the end of the eighteenth century, however, both its parts were ceasing to be true. The condition of the Papacy was only partly responsible; the questioning attitude of the time also upset many who, in an Age of Faith, might have been content not to question. Simple people, like the peasants of Prato, still believed fervently, even violently, but many of the educated suffered a real loss in faith. Symptoms of it were the attacks of writers like Alfieri, the political pressures put on the Papacy by the foreign ambassadors, and the attempts by various sovereigns to conduct reforms on their own. Many men, including dedicated churchmen, began to wonder if the Church would not do better without the Papacy.

This spiritual disarray of the Papacy had a political counterpart in the government of the Papal States. These were a random assemblage of provinces broken sharply in two parts by the Apennine mountains. The southern portion faced west and south, forming the coast of the Tyrrhenian Sea with easy communication to the Kingdoms of Naples, Sicily, France and Spain. With its chief city, Rome, being the seat of the Papacy, the traditions of this part were autocratic, conservative and entirely agricultural.

The northern part, on the other hand, faced the Po and Adriatic Sea. It communicated easily with Venice and Milan, and its traditions were republican, liberal and as much commercial as agricultural. The chief city was Bologna, larger than Rome, with an excellent university and musical academy, and as secular in its outlook as Rome was clerical. Further, Bologna was rich and Rome chronically bankrupt. The Bolognesi were unkind enough to say, on every occasion, that laymen knew better than priests how to govern.

There was some truth in this even though the countryside around Bologna was far richer than that around Rome. The Bolognesi, when they had become part of the Papal States, had reserved rights and immunities and were almost completely self-governing. The pope, for example, had no part in the city's finances, policing or provisioning. In other Papal districts north of the Apennines where the pope's representative, a cardinal-legate, had more power, there was less prosperity and less freedom. In some of these Legations, so called from the cardinal-legates, there was poverty, censorship and discontent. Inevitably the Legations, rich Bologna and those less fortunate, looked on Rome with distrust and were eager to separate from it if the opportunity offered. Rome, on the other hand, tried to bind these richer cities to her with ever tighter control. This conflict made the Papal States the most unstable political unit on the peninsula.

In contrast to Bologna the poverty of Rome was striking, particularly when set off by the pomp and splendor of a Papal ceremony. The population over the centuries had shrunk from more than a million to a mere 165,000, and these occupied only about a third of the area enclosed by the old Aurelian and more recent Papal Walls. The city had space for gorgeous vistas ending in magnificent ruins, and the rich were able, within the city walls, to surround their villas with enormous gardens. The city had an extraordinary beauty; yet its emptiness was a reproach to its rulers. There was no commerce of any kind except tourism, and there was as much violence and begging in the streets as in Naples. The Jews every night were locked in a ghetto and said to be more wretched and despised than in any other city in Europe. For all of its surface glitter it was a depressed city.

Other cities in the southern and Roman part of the Papal States were no better. Perugia, Orvieto and Urbino were shadows of their medieval selves and only the churches and monasteries showed any sign of wealth. "The cities of the Papal States," said Goethe, "seem to stand only because the earth is unwilling to swallow them up." Even good farmland lay desolate.

Pius, like other popes, attempted reforms and improvements, most notably draining some of the marshes near Rome to reduce the malaria and increase the amount of arable land. The scheme was only partially realized, and even its good effects were tarnished when it became known that his nephew, Duke Braschi, who was building a large palazzo in Rome, had received concessions on the reclaimed land. In much the same way the pope's attempts at governmental reform in the Papal States were undermined by a reluctant clergy who could see only that the Church was already in a privileged position and that reform would threaten it.

In fact, the Church's position and its role, both in the Papal States and elsewhere, had become thoroughly confused. In France, where the Church was the First Estate of the Realm, it not only owned one fifth of all the land and was itself exempt from paying taxes, but it had also the right to levy a tax, the "tithe," on other landowners. Such wealth and power made the bishops and abbots who controlled it independent not only of the king but of the pope as well. Contemporaries complained that the bishops and abbots had become administrators of provinces rather than of the sacraments. In Germany there were twenty-two prince-bishops and a number of ecclesiastical electors, each combining in his person temporal and spiritual power over his domain.

With these examples before them the pope and clergy in the Papal States saw no merit in the wish of some of their cities and laymen that the temporal power be shared. Nor did they see any reason why they as prince-pontiff and cardinal-legate could not be successful administrators. But there were some important differences between a pope and a bishop in France or Germany. The pope almost invariably came to the office when he was old and his energies waning. The probability of his early death and the fact he was often a compromise candidate prevented him from building within his clergy any personal party that he could use as an instrument of reform. His real power was limited. Further, being pope, he dealt with ecclesiastical matters over the world and the problems of the Papal States were often last on his agenda and handled for him by his least competent cardinals or bishops. And, most important, experience seemed to show, as the Bolognesi insisted, that a priest was rarely a good political administrator. If the pope or priest was genuinely religious, he was apt, by nature and training, to be unable to handle the problems of a commercial city such as the Papal port of Ancona. If he were not religious, then as pope he was apt to embroil the Church in political problems which interested him, and as priest he was apt to use his position for his own ends or, perhaps, merely be eager to get to Rome and cut a figure in society. In either event the prosperity of the community suffered.

Pius fussed at the edges of the problem. He changed a man here, made a ruling there but never considered the problem as a whole. Like his predecessors he saw Bologna, with its privileges, immunities and lay administration, not as an example of success to be followed in other Papal cities but as an unwanted exception to be squashed into conformity at the first opportunity. In the Papal States, so the argument went, the Papacy could not share power with laymen if its spiritual independence was to be secured. A difficulty with the argument, of course, was that the threat to spiritual independence came not from Bologna but from Vienna and, as the French Revolution began, Paris.

From Vienna, Joseph had extended his reforms into all parts of his holdings and encountered increasing opposition. His efforts to force a centralized administration on a variety of provinces that had always thought of themselves as independent kingdoms and duchies in a Habsburg federation offended all classes. The nobilities objected to the loss of privileges and political power involved in the rule of equal treatment before the law and in the extension to others of the rights and duties of citizenship. The lowest classes, simple and often bigoted, objected to the religious reforms. In the outlying provinces such as the Austrian Netherlands and Hungary the opposition to the Church reforms blended with a patriotic movement in favor of national privileges; for once, people, clergy and nobility joined forces. The result surprised everyone. In the Austrian Netherlands the combined classes, meaning only to protest, found they had conducted a revolution and hastily formed a "United States of Belgium." As in Tuscany the people were more vigorous than the pope in defending the faith.

Joseph talked of sending an army to discipline his subjects, but he was at war with Turkey and had no troops to spare. And further, about the same time and for the same reasons, the Hungarians broke out into civil disorder. Joseph was able to calm them only by renouncing almost all of his reforms. He was already ill, but the loss of family holdings and, harder, the renunciation of a lifetime of idealism and hard work undoubtedly contributed to his early death in February 1790. As he had no children, his brother, Leopoldo I of Tuscany, succeeded as Emperor Leopold II.

Churchmen everywhere were pleased, for Leopoldo had shown that he was more moderate than his brother. But any rejoicing was spoiled by the news from Paris where the National Assembly had begun to show itself more reforming than Joseph and more dangerous in that it included among its members representatives of the nobility and clergy. Where Joseph, an autocrat, had failed, it was possible that a representative assembly might succeed.

Most Italians watched the start of the French Revolution with a detached interest. In the calling of the States General and the oratory of the first months they heard only the whirrings of an ancient feudal mechanism, not the voice of the future. The fall of the Bastille excited them, and Alfieri, who was in Paris, wrote an ode on it. But the crisis seemed a purely French one which Louis XVI would handle either by concessions or, as seemed more likely, by repression. In the winter in which Joseph died, however, the Assembly began to pass a number of laws, many on Church affairs, which started a flow of refugees into Italy. Thereafter for Italians, and particularly for the pope, the Revolution became the sole and exhausting object of attention.

Louis XVI had called the States General because the monarchy, which was still absolute and therefore France, was bankrupt. He and his ministers had tried to put through reforms but these had been blocked primarily by the clergy and nobility, both of whom were unwilling to give up their feudal privileges, particularly their tax exemptions. In spite of the Bastille the lower classes, the third estate, were far more opposed to the clergy and nobility than to the king; in fact, they were opposed to the king largely because they feared he would give in to the clergy and nobility, restore to them all their feudal privileges and pay for it by even more crushing taxes on the third estate. As soon as it became clear in the States General that the third estate would have a majority of the votes, it looked to the king as its ally against the hated, privileged classes. This was, in fact, the traditional alliance in the development of France, and it was Louis' tragedy that he could not bring himself to continue it.

The States General, dominated by the third estate, turned itself into the National Assembly and set about destroying, not the monarchy, but the feudal privileges of the nobility and clergy. In a series of laws the deputies abolished the titles of nobility and along with them what they symbolized: inequality before the law, restriction of army, Church and court positions to the nobility and the exemptions from taxation. This concept of equality, before the law, in taxation and opportunity, was extended into the heart of the noble's family: the rights of primogeniture and male succession in feudal inheritance were abolished. In future children of either sex and regardless of age would share equally. The nobility, in short, was to disappear as class and become part of the people.

Many of the nobles fled to Germany or to Italy, chattering to one and all about the wrongs they had suffered and hoping to organize a counter-revolution with foreign assistance. But of even greater interest to Italians than the treatment of the nobility in France was that of the Church, for the Assembly's religious laws sent as *émigrés* into Italy priests of every class. Naturally their fate as well as that of those remaining in France was the preoccupation of the pope, and it was from such *émigré* priests that many of the lower classes in the Italian states received their only idea of what the deputies in France were trying to do.

The deputies wanted to reorganize the Church along lines, as it turned out, similar to those of Joseph. Their approach, however, was different because in assuming the legislative functions of the absolute monarchy they had also necessarily assumed responsibility for the state's imminent bankruptcy. The situation was desperate. The king, earlier, had been forced to suspend payment on the public debt, and the Assembly, with anarchy spreading in the country, could find no way to resume it. There was only one way out, a way often followed by Christian governments when in really serious straits: to lay hands on the property of the Church. The first religious bill passed in the Assembly declared all the Church's property at the nation's disposal.

No logically satisfactory argument could be made in support of the bill, and there was, perhaps, no justice in it. Nevertheless, the deputies passed it, largely because the financial situation was truly desperate and because throughout the country most men were angry at the Church. They considered that it had grown wealthy over the years at the expense of others, and they were emotionally prepared to despoil it for the common good. Even those who might ordinarily be expected to defend it were against it. The peasants had just lost a bitter dispute over the extension of tithes from the traditional crops, such as oats, rye, barley and wheat, to include new and experimental crops such as roots, potatoes and millet. Even more significantly the parish priests were against it. They lived close to starvation because the bishops, who lived in great luxury, took such a large part of the tithe. When the priests united to demand reform, their bishops persuaded the king to make it illegal for parish priests to hold meetings without the permission of their spiritual superiors. In desperation the parish priests turned to the National Assembly to reform the Church. Some of them were deputies to the Assembly, and their views carried weight. The parish priests, they said, were ready to have the Church lands sold and to receive their salaries from the State because the salaries could not be worse and might very well be better.

So the Assembly in a series of laws abolished the tithe, confiscated the Church lands and pledged itself to provide for the expenses of the Church including the salaries of the clergy. But obviously if some money from the sale of lands was to be available for the debts of the State, then the expenses of the Church would have to be reduced, and it was here that the Assembly began to repeat the reforms Joseph had attempted. The religious orders were abolished, and dispossessed monks and nuns fled into Germany and Italy. The dioceses were rearranged to make them more nearly equal in size and number of parishioners, and the salaries of all the clergy were readjusted. These reforms distributed the money in more reasonable proportions and reduced the total expenditure by half.

The confiscation of Church property and the closing of the monasteries affected many interests and caused much unrest, but as long as the parish priests supported the bills, the Assembly carried the country, as opposed to all individuals, along with it. But, like Joseph, once started on a course of reform the Assembly went further and further. In a succession of bills it introduced great changes into the structure of the Church's hierarchy and discipline. Henceforth a parish priest was to be nominated by the electors of his district, and a bishop by the electors of his department. The pope was to have no control, not even a veto, of the nominations. He was simply to be notified "as visible head of the Universal Church, in witness of the unity of the faith."

No one who was not noble cared about the nobility, but all sorts of men who were not priests cared about religion and were appalled at the effect of the laws. The priest and bishop were to be nominated by the electors in their district and department, and among the electors, by law, were Protestants, Jews and freethinkers. It was ludicrous; what if non-Catholics were in the majority? Even worse was the effect on Church discipline. How could the bishop remove a priest who was preaching bad doctrine? How could the pope discipline a bishop?

The Assembly wanted to prevent the pope, as a foreign power closely allied with conservative interests, from interfering in France's internal affairs; it wanted, by destroying the bishop's power over the parish priest, to prevent him from building up another quasifeudal organization. But its laws also upset the stability of doctrinal observance, put the unity of the faith at the whim of each district's electorate and made of the pope merely an address for unimportant letters.

Many Frenchmen were profoundly upset and looked to the pope for guidance. But Pius made no public statements. He may have moved slowly because of his age, which was now seventy-three; because he feared the Assembly might seize the two Papal domains in the south of France, Avignon and the Comtat Venaissin; or because he feared, by direct action, to cause a schism in France. As population then was distributed, France contained one third of the world's Catholics, a very high portion to risk losing into a separate, national church.

But the conflict was not to be avoided. In January 1791 the Assembly insisted that its clerical deputies swear to uphold the Civil Constitution of the Clergy, as the laws were called, or resign their livings and be liable to arrest if they performed priestly functions. The galleries were packed and outside the Assembly an excited crowd cried, "Death to those who refuse the oath!" The Bishop of Agen rose to declare, with the perfect manners of an aristocrat, that "he had no regrets for office or for wealth; but he would grieve at the loss of his colleagues' esteem, which he hoped to deserve, and he therefore begged the Assembly to accept the expression of his sorrow at being unable to take the oath required of him." One of his parish priests was called next, and the man replied that "he took pride in following his bishop's example, as the deacon Laurance had followed Pope Sixtus, his pastor, to his death." In the end, of forty-nine bishops, two took the oath, and of the parish priests, about a third. The proportions remained the same among the clergy throughout the country.

The resolute attitude of the French clergy forced Pius to take a stand, and in March 1791 he made a public pronouncement condemning the various bills, known as the Civil Constitution of the Clergy, as schismatic and heretical. The following month he suspended all those priests who had taken the oath and did not retract within forty days.

Thereafter in France there were two Churches, one of "nonjuring" priests and another of those who had taken the oath. The former held the allegiance of the faithful and appeared as defenders of the Catholic faith. The Assembly, growing more radical as its conservative deputies were driven out, persecuted the "nonjurors," and many died for their cause. In the next decade about thirty-five thousand fled the country of whom about five thousand found their way to the Papal States. Of those who remained in France most were forced to hide and if found were imprisoned, guillotined or deported to French Guiana.

The seven bishops and the clergy who did take the oath formed the nucleus of the Constitutional Church. Gradually over the decade it expanded itself by hurried ordinations to thirty thousand, but its moral influence was never as great as that of the "nonjuring" Church.

In the eyes of the Assembly the two Churches made the pope, regardless of his intent, an enemy of France. In retaliation it seized Avignon and the Comtat Venaissin, much to the joy of their inhabitants, and it cast angry mutterings toward Rome. In the years to come the leaders of the

Revolution would be unable to heal the division between the two Churches, and when they burst into Italy with their armies, one of their purposes would be to force the pope to come to some sort of accommodation with them.

# CHAPTER 9

The French Revolution. Its four periods. The principle of monarchy. The rejection of feudalism. The Directory. The Consulate.

THE FRENCH REVOLUTION had a great effect on the Risorgimento, both
directly, as Napoleon led French armies into Italy and introduced the new
ideas at gunpoint, and also indirectly, as an inspiration to Italian patriots
to think and act for themselves. But the Revolution, even in France, was
not a single cataclysm. If considered to start with the summons of the
States General in 1789 and to end with Napoleon's declaration of a French
Empire in 1804, it passed through four periods, each quite different from
the others and with a different effect in Italy. The first of these periods,
although spotted with violence and ending in war, was essentially a period
of peace and of domestic reform within France, a period in which most
Italians, except for the heads of states, the priests and the poets like
Alfieri, took little interest. Yet it was in this period that most of the lasting
gains of the Revolution, later exported to Italy, were won.

The period continued, roughly, from May 1789 to August 1792 or
throughout the lives of the National and Legislative Assemblies. In both
the deputies gave almost their whole attention to reforming the government
and social organization of France. Their concern was with themselves, not
others, and the fact that at the end of the three-year period they were at
war with almost every monarch in Europe, including most in Italy, was not
the choice of the French deputies but of the foreign monarchs.

These were alarmed by the principles of the Revolution which the
deputies, amid the greatest excitement in August 1789, had summed up in
a Declaration of Human Rights. The Declaration is a resounding statement in seventeen short paragraphs of all of eighteenth-century revolutionary thought. "Men are born free," it begins, "and remain free and equal in
their rights." The succeeding sentence, "Social distinctions can only be
based on the requirements of the common good," gives both the source and
the meaning of the first: the deputies were exasperated with feudal privilege and preparing to abolish it.

The monarchs, however, cared nothing about feudal privilege. In his Duchy of Milan, Joseph had himself effectively abolished it. What upset the monarchs were the principles embodied in the phrases "The law is the expression of the general will" and "The principle of all sovereignty is vested in the nation." No Habsburg or Bourbon believed this. For each of them all sovereignty was vested in the king, not the nation, and the law was the expression of the king's will, not "the general will." To admit to something less, even in France, was to subvert the principle of monarchy. Gradually the monarchs passed from intrigue against the deputies to war. The leader of this first coalition against the new France was the head of the House of Habsburg, Francis II, who in 1792 succeeded his father, Leopold, as Holy Roman Emperor. He carried along with him Maria Carolina and Ferdinando in Naples, his brother Ferdinando III of Tuscany and also Vittorio Amedeo III of Sardinia. The republics in Italy, not being involved with the principle of monarchy, remained neutral. Outside of Italy the monarchs in Spain, Holland, England and Prussia also joined Francis II.

The coalition was a mistake of policy. The deputies had adopted as an article of the country's constitution that the French nation would never wage a war of conquest, and they were observing it, even to the extent of refusing to absorb the Papal city of Avignon whose citizens had voted for union with France. Further, in their constitution they had given Louis XVI, as king, a place as the chief executive. The position was similar to that of the President of the United States but was to be held for life and to be hereditary. The deputies as yet did not seriously consider the idea of a republic; in fact, the first publication to urge a republic in more than theoretic terms did not appear until the period was almost half over. But this experiment in constitutional monarchy failed. The deputies were too idealistic, the king too weak and foolish, and the country too disrupted by the clerical issue and the collapse of the old administrative system. Principally, however, it failed because the king's intrigues with the foreign monarchs caused his subjects to imagine spies everywhere, to suspect every moment that an invasion by foreign armies was about to begin and to put their trust, bit by bit, in the more violent and immoderate deputies. Finally in August 1792, while the foreign monarchs talked of destroying Paris, the constitution was overthrown. The Paris mob stormed the Tuileries, the king became a prisoner, and elections were ordered for a National Convention which, everyone understood, would proclaim France a republic. It was at this point that Alfieri, although a republican, was so alarmed and disgusted by the mob violence that he left Paris.

In their constitutional adventure the deputies failed. They and their subordinates throughout the country, after centuries of having no share in the government, could not suddenly improvise the necessary experience.

Reading Montesquieu on the separation of powers or Rousseau on the general will could not teach them how to control a section of Paris or to administer an illiterate, rural community. But in the legal and social side of their work they succeeded, even brilliantly, and made the important and permanent gains of the Revolution.

Their work had both a negative and a positive aspect, the former being the destruction of what remained of medieval feudalism, lay and ecclesiastical. This was done, in part, by the deputies passing their bills and, perhaps in still greater part, by the people in town and country refusing any longer to render feudal rights to those who claimed them. This revolt was the sudden end of years of slow change and probably flared into its scattered violence only because of the opposition of the clergy and nobility to reforms by the monarchy. The two estates, refusing to modify their privileges in any way, forced the government into a lengthy crisis in which it seemed, for a number of years, as though the advances already achieved toward a freer society, socially and commercially, might be wiped out.

The positive side of this rejection of feudalism was the skill with which the deputies, many of whom were lawyers, brought into being a new system of law to support the more fluid society which was evolving. One key to understanding the difference between the old and new is in the conception men held of property and wealth. Most men at the time equated wealth, which was the chance to "better their lot," with feudal privilege, and so their demands for economic equality of opportunity tended to be stated in political terms: abolish feudal dues, tithes, services and so on. Even before the Revolution the commercial class, the richer peasants and the intellectuals wanted property to exist in something like its modern, capitalist sense as something marketable, divisible, accessible to women as well as to men and in forms other than land. Under feudalism, property was almost exclusively land together with the rights and duties that went with it. It was apt to belong in common either to the family or to a collective religious body, was subject to entail or to the bond of mortmain and could be neither transferred nor divided up. The system of law in existence before the Revolution supported these medieval concepts. The rich peasant often could not piece together a larger farm or the merchant buy an estate in the country without taking on the many duties, some personal, owed by the landholder to the feudal overlord. Business was hampered because wealth, being land, had no mobility.

To provide a framework for the freer society that was evolving the deputies went back to the principles of Roman law which had been formulated for a commercial rather than agricultural community and in a time when property had mobility. They did their work well, and in spite of the difficulties the country suffered during this first period of the Revolution, for all but the dispossessed few it was a time of tremendous excitement and hope. Men worked harder at their farms or business because suddenly expansion and greater rewards seemed possible. At the same time, as privilege was abolished, they had a new sense of dignity. When the Assembly, in April 1792, declared that war was necessary against Austria and Prussia in order to protect the gains of the Revolution, peasants and middle-class men by the thousands volunteered to fight. They felt, many for the first time, that they had a real stake in society, and they formed a national army, very different in temper from the small, professional armies of the eighteenth century that were sent against them. The Frenchmen were ill-trained and ill-equipped but they had morale, and when they defeated the Prussians at Valmy and the Austrians at Jemappes, they had secured their revolution and they knew it. Others knew it too. Goethe, who, as adviser to the Grand Duke of Weimar, was at the battle of Valmy, observed to his companions, "Here and now, a new era begins in the history of the world."

The emergence of this new organization of society together with its supporting law, later rewritten as the Civil or Napoleonic Code, was the greatest accomplishment of the French in their Revolution, even greater than substituting for the principle of monarchy the idea that all men should have a share in their government. On the latter the French were often to compromise, but from their new social organization, largely formed in this first period, they never retreated. It is what gave force and meaning to the rhetoric of the Revolution, phrases such as "Men are born free." The phrases were exciting but vague, whereas the new relations between people and property in daily life were real. This was the part of the Revolution that continuously shone from France into the other countries of Europe no matter how hard their governments tried to block it out or how much the French themselves seemed to threaten its glow with the awful excesses of later periods in the Revolution. It was the part that no French politician, general or Bourbon king restored by foreign armies ever undid and those who were statesmen never tried. It was the part Frenchmen, taken at their best, wished to carry to other peoples they considered less fortunate than themselves and the part liberals in other countries wished to import. In every Italian city, but particularly in the north, there was from this time on a revolutionary party that looked toward Paris for example and guidance.

The second period of the French Revolution, from September 1792 to August 1795, was that of the National Convention, which succeeded the Assemblies. At its first meeting the deputies declared that "the monarchy be abolished in France" and proclaimed a republic. Thus France became the first European country to attempt to govern itself without a king and hereditary ruling class, replacing them by a political assembly which was, at least in theory, a mandatory body of the whole population exercising a universal suffrage. The experiment, like that of a constitutional monarchy, was a failure; the convention became a legislative tyranny. The deputies made fine high-flown speeches, but gradually the more radical of them, by means of tightly organized clubs and committees, seized the power, excluded from the convention those deputies who opposed them, and ruled France according to the whims of the few. It was during this second period that the king was executed, Reason was proclaimed a God in the Cathedral of Notre Dame, the names of the months were changed and the week made ten days instead of seven. It was also the period of the Reign of Terror in Paris and of civil war throughout the country. Of the eighty-three departments throughout the country, sixty-seven rose against the government in Paris.

Most of the wilder deeds and laws of this second period were later repealed or regretted and had, in the end, little effect in France or elsewhere. People in other countries who wanted to maintain the old organization of society spoke with smug horror of the mob and violence; revolutionaries attempted to explain or belittle what had happened; and journalists, in advance of novelists, playwrights and composers, seized on the opportunities for rattling good stories. But few Frenchmen or foreigners changed their political sympathies because of the Reign of Terror. It was like an eclipse of the sun, startling, even terrifying and watched by all, but soon over and almost immediately discussed as a curious phenomenon not likely to reoccur for many years. The period as a whole added little to the accomplishments of the first, and the issues that kept revolutionary France and her neighbors in a desultory war were still the issues of the first: the structure of society and the principle of monarchy.

In the third period, which was of tremendous importance to Italians, the French exploded over the Rhine and Alps, carrying their Revolution with them, and by enormous and continuous confiscations on the foreign people tried to force them to pay for their liberation. Inevitably, many who at first welcomed the French soon hated and accused them of using the ideals of the Revolution merely to extend French domination and influence across Europe, even as the monarchy had always tried to do.

The period began or at least took its name, "The Directory," from yet another constitution, this one adopted in August 1795 by the National Convention. This time the deputies attempted to combine the better parts of a republic and a monarchy. There were two legislative chambers, a lower to originate laws and a higher one to pass on them, and an executive committee of five men, the Directory, to administer them. The deputies, in view of the inadequacies of the National Convention, this time gave the executive real power so that the Directory was almost a constitutional monarch by committee. Its members were chosen by the deputies, but as only one member came up for election each year, the committee had an identity that continued. It stayed in power, often in opposition to the deputies and increasingly overshadowed by the military, until Napoleon, in November 1799, assisted in a *coup d'état* that made him First Consul of a reorganized government.

This fourth period, generally called "the Consulate," was as important to Italians as the previous one. During it, the executive power of France, which had been exercised first by assemblies and then by a committee, finally was concentrated in one man, and the period ended, badly in the opinion of many, when five years later, on 2 December 1804, Napoleon had himself crowned emperor. Nevertheless, during the Consulate, many of the previous gains of the Revolution were consolidated. The enormous changes in law, for example, finally appeared as the Civil Code, in a form much easier to export than a mass of legislative bills and proclamations. The fight with the Church in France was resolved by a concordat, many parts of which easily could be applied elsewhere. And, finally, during this period Napoleon had the power to rearrange frontiers and governments as he, personally, saw fit. He had always had a special interest in Italy, and during this period he was able to indulge it. Much, if not most, of the permanent good he was able to do for Italians was accomplished in this last period of the Revolution.

# CHAPTER 10

The war in Italy. Napoleon. Political settlements and difficulties. Tolentino. To Vienna. Preliminaries of Leoben. Collapse of Venice. Gozzi. Foscolo. Cisalpine Republic. Campoformio. Effects of the war in Italy.

NAPOLEON MADE the start of his reputation in what came to be known as the First Italian Campaign, the extraordinary climax of a five-year war in the first years of which almost nothing happened. For Italians the war began in the months before Valmy, 20 September 1792, when Vittorio Amedeo III of Sardinia joined his fellow monarchs in the coalition against France. He probably expected, in the tradition of his family, to conquer a city or two in France and then at a peace conference to give them up for a city or two in the Po valley, perhaps Milan or Pavia, while the Habsburg emperor was compensated for the loss of these with something elsewhere. It was not an unreasonable plan. The part of France bordering the mainland provinces of Sardinia was more royalist than republican; Louis XVI's brother, the Comte d'Artois, was in Turin urging the expedition and giving it the spirit of a crusade, and the chief fighting would be in the north along the Rhine where the Prussian and Austrian armies were in camp.

But the plan, typically eighteenth-century in its view of war as a kind of chess game in which the monarchs swapped towns and forts like pieces, was not vigorously pursued. Vittorio Amedeo was old, not very able, and the French moved faster than he, occupying most of Nice and Savoy, the two Sardinian provinces on the French side of the Alps. The war settled into what seemed to be a stalemate. The French tried to invade the island of Sardinia and were beaten off, and the coalition forces, Sardinian, Neapolitan, Spanish and British, were unable to hold Toulon, which they captured in August and lost in December of 1793.

The siege of Toulon, the French trying to retake their city, has a historical interest greater than its significance in the war. At Toulon, Nelson, already an admiral, was in command of the British fleet, and Napoleon, first a lieutenant and then a captain, had a corps of the French artillery. It was as close as the two men came, in their long wars, to being directly opposed. Toulon, also, was important in Napoleon's career. After it, in recognition of his service there, he was promoted to brigadier general, which meant his future commands would be of armies rather than corps.

He was still at this time spelling his family name in the Corsican or Italian style, with a "u": Buonaparte. Corsica had become a dependency of France only in 1768, the year before Napoleon was born on the island. The Republic of Genoa, which had never been able to control the Corsicans, had finally sold its rights over their island to Louis XV, who wanted it only to keep the British out of its harbors. It was a wild land and unproductive, except for its timber, and its people were proud, poor and much given to banditry. They spoke a dialect of Italian and their political traditions were republican. Before Genoa, they had been under the medieval Republic of Pisa, and Pisa and Genoa were, at fifty and a hundred miles, the closest mainland ports. Napoleon spoke Italian before he spoke French, and his mother and elder brother, Joseph, had been born citizens of Genoa. Although Napoleon received most of his education on military scholarships in France, Joseph, who was then the head of the family, earned his degree in Law at the University of Pisa.

This Italian tradition of the Buonapartes was important. Because of it, in the years to come, many Italians thought of Napoleon as one of them, one who in typically Italian fashion had merely gone to a bigger, more powerful country to make his career. They were quicker to praise his virtues and to excuse his faults than they otherwise might have been, and readier to accept his Italian-speaking brothers and sisters as their rulers. On Napoleon's side, it was a reason why as a general, although wholly loyal to France, the command he sought from the Directory was that of the Army of Italy.

By the winter of 1795–96 the war in the Alps had all but ceased. The French still held most of Nice and Savoy, but their army was ill-clothed, ill-fed and ill-equipped; there was even talk of withdrawing it. Vittorio Amedeo's troops were in better condition and with promised Austrian and Neapolitan reinforcements might soon be able to mount a serious attack. To forestall it the Directory, reminding Vittorio Amedeo of his family's traditional and successful policy of changing sides in the wars between France and Austria, offered him the Duchy of Milan in return for Nice and Savoy. Without any hesitation Vittorio Amedeo refused the offer, although, as it turned out, he might better have accepted it. But Savoy was the seat of his family, the offer came not from a fellow monarch but a regicide and republican regime, and, most important, the French did not possess Milan to give away and seemed unlikely ever to obtain it.

The winter was the last in which eighteenth-century Italy enjoyed itself. At Venice, where the Teatro La Fenice had recently opened, everyone was again mad for opera, and the whole town was divided between the partisans of the soprano Luisa Todi and the castrato Marchesi. Each side circulated scurrilous poems about its favorite's rival, but the lady's friends triumphed and with a sensational coup: they had the opposition's poems suppressed by the Blasphemy Tribunal.

In Genoa life was, as always, less gay than in Venice, and the war was nearer. Both sides had, in fact, repeatedly violated the republic's neutrality by marching armies across corners of its land. The Genovesi complained but did nothing and were delighted with the opportunities to sell supplies, particularly to the French who were their traditional allies against the tricky House of Savoy. They saw no reason why, just because France had become a republic, they should trust Vittorio Amedeo.

The Habsburg viceroy in Milan, a younger brother of Francis II, also sold supplies to the French even though Milan, as a Habsburg duchy, was at war with France. And in Tuscany the grand duke, another brother of Francis II, had followed Spain's lead and made a separate peace with France. Now he refused to be anything but neutral and enjoyed posing as a mediator between Paris and Vienna. But in Naples, Habsburg family loyalty was still strong. Maria Carolina grieved for her sister, Marie Antoinette, and had sworn to avenge her. She urged her nephew, the Emperor Francis, who was also her son-in-law, to fight harder, and she urged her reluctant husband, Ferdinando, to send Neapolitan troops to the front in Piedmont and ships to the blockade of the French Mediterranean ports. She had never been popular in Naples and now, when she saw politics entirely in terms of her family, she grew even less so. The kingdom was not rich, and it badly needed the proceeds of its traditional trade with France. There was hardly any trade with Austria and no obvious benefits for Naples in an Austrian victory. So, even in Naples, where Ferdinando's father, Carlo III, seemed to have established the dynasty so firmly, there was a revolutionary party meeting secretly in clubs, arguing over reforms and talking wildly of a Neapolitan republic. But the number of revolutionaries was tiny and drawn almost entirely from the middle and upper class of Naples. The countryside was fervently loyal, and everywhere in Italy the French Revolution seemed to be still a domestic crisis in France and one that would be contained there.

Then in March 1796 Napoleon arrived in Nice to take command of the French Army of Italy. He was twenty-six years old and, although a distinguished professional soldier, his appointment by the Directory was partly an act of political favoritism. France had several generals who, at the time, were more distinguished, more experienced and, if youth were a criterion, almost as young. But Napoleon had spent the winter in the political salons of Paris and had married, just a few weeks before the appointment, Joséphine de Beauharnais, the ex-mistress of a powerful member of the Directory. Gossip said the appointment was a wedding present and unmerited; Napoleon was perhaps therefore all the more determined to make something glorious of the opportunity.

The Directory hoped to impose a peace on the Emperor Francis II in Vienna itself by a campaign north of the Alps in which one army approached the city down the valley of the Danube and another, farther to the north, down the valley of the Main. The generals were Moreau and Jourdon. In Italy the Directory wanted Napoleon to pay for the war by confiscating whatever could profitably be taken and perhaps, as a third column, to push on through the Venetian Alps toward Vienna. But on this purpose the Directory wavered. The Alps were rugged, and Italy was rich; collecting wealth was probably the first purpose of the Army of Italy and defeating Francis in the field better left to the armies in the north.

This was also how Francis understood the plan. He put his best general, his brother Charles, and the greater part of his troops in the north. His Italian army he planned to reinforce when he could; as it turned out, generally with troops that were tired and too few. Part of Napoleon's success, at least at the start, was the poor quality of his opposition. But when every explanation of his success has been recorded there still remains, unexplained, the element of his genius, as a commander in the field, as a political force and as the creator of a legend. All were consciously applied to turn what was supposed to be merely the third area of the war into the first, and thereby to advance the man who had done it.

He arrived in Nice at the end of March and was appalled at the condition of the men. Years later, when using his memoirs to amplify the legend of himself, he wrote: "The picture of the army which General Scherer laid before me, was even worse than anything I had been able to conceive. . . . The state of affairs daily grew worse; there was not a moment to be lost; the army could no longer subsist where it was; it was indispensably requisite either to advance or to fall back. I gave orders to advance . . ."

He reviewed the troops and told them: "Soldiers, you are naked and ill-fed; the government owes you much and can give you nothing. The patience and courage you have shown in the midst of these rocks is admirable, but they gain you no renown, no glory results to you from your endurance. It is my intention to lead you into the most fertile plains in the world. Rich provinces and great cities will be in your power; there you will find honor, glory and wealth. Soldiers of Italy, will you be wanting in courage or perseverance?"

It was glorious rhetoric; but it was also, for the first time in the idealistic republican armies, an appeal to greed. Nevertheless, by means of more like it he was able, after an early skirmish in the mountains, to march his barefoot troops past Austrian supply wagons loaded with shoes in order to continue the pursuit. By the end of April, just a month after taking command, he had crossed the Alps behind Genoa, defeated the Sardinian army in several battles and forced Vittorio Amedeo from the war. The peace treaty with Sardinia, signed by the Directory in Paris, was very favorable to France, giving it control of all the Alpine passes, all of Nice and Savoy outright and rights in the rest of the country. The Sardinian militia was disbanded, the regular army retired to garrisons and much of its artillery and stores turned over to the French.

Napoleon, meanwhile, had crossed the Po at Piacenza, south and east of Milan, so that he threatened the supply lines of the Habsburg army, which then had to withdraw toward its base at Mantua. It was a brilliant maneuver as it forced the Habsburg generals to abandon most of the rich Duchy of Milan to the hungry, ill-equipped French. But it was possible only by violating the neutrality of the Duchy of Parma. First Genoa, then Parma and later Venice: each time the neutrality of one was ignored, it was a further demonstration of the artificiality of state boundaries in the north of Italy. No commander in any of the Wars of the Austrian, Polish or Spanish Succession had observed them, and neither did Napoleon nor any of the Habsburg generals.

Napoleon's orders from the Directory were explicit: "His dominions [the Duke of Parma's] should furnish us with what we need as well as help in cash." Neutrality was to be merely a day to day sufferance, to be bought in goods and cash. The possessions and peoples of actual enemies were to be even more roughly treated: "The Milanesi in particular should not be spared; you should levy contributions in cash on the spot, while the first terror caused by the approach of our arms is effective."

Traveling with Napoleon's armies were civilian agents of the Directory who handled the confiscations. They kept accounts according to whether the money or goods came from churches, pawnbroking establishments or public funds. The pawnbrokers were the safe-deposit vaults of the time, and the nobility kept much of their cash, jewelry and other precious articles with them. Many noble and merchant families were ruined by the confiscations, and it is a reason why their opposition to Napoleon was so feeble: their wealth was their power, and without it they were merely individuals, often having to struggle to feed and clothe themselves.

These organized and public confiscations together with the many unorganized and private thefts of individual French soldiers turned many Italians against the French. Less than two weeks after Napoleon made a triumphal entry into Milan, Pavia, the second city in the duchy, rose in a revolt against him. Thousands of peasants, led often by their landlords and priests, invaded the streets waving sticks and scythes, threatened and killed the local republicans and penned the French garrison in the castle. The next day, when the garrison capitulated, the leaders of the revolt began to discuss a march on Milan. But while they talked, Napoleon marched on Pavia, stormed it, and, after taking it, turned his soldiers loose on it. He also imposed a heavy fine, sent two hundred citizens to France as hostages and had the Town Council shot. Soon after, for the same cause, he gave identical treatment to Tortona, a city in the Sardinian province of Piedmont. The Milanesi and Piemontesi were impressed, and Italians of the neighboring, neutral states, such as Parma, Modena or even Venice and Genoa, were made highly nervous. It was plain to all that the only opposition with a chance of success was the Habsburg army. As had happened so many times before, France and Austria were to fight in the Po valley for the control of Italy.

The key to victory was the great fortress at Mantua, impregnable, strategically located and a superb base of supplies for whichever side held it. In June, almost immediately after his entry into Milan, Napoleon began his siege of Mantua, and thereafter the war in the Po valley turned almost entirely on Habsburg efforts to relieve the city.

The first attempt was in July under General Würmser who, although defeated, broke through the siege long enough to revictual the city and increase its garrison. In a second attempt, in September, Würmser was again defeated and, with his retreat to Austria cut off, he could save himself only by breaking through the siege lines into the city. But Mantua needed the siege lines broken, not more men within it to share its dwindling supplies.

In each campaign Napoleon defeated a numerically superior army by quick marches and concentration of his forces. He marched his men so fast, often days ahead of their food and supplies, that he was able, again and again, to attack and defeat the various columns of the Habsburg army before they could unite. His opponents, in trying to keep up, gasped in astonishment: "The French do not march, but run." Contemporary witnesses, including Napoleon, confirm that his soldiers throughout the campaign fought in a state of exultation: they were whipping the traditional enemy of France who was also a monarch while they were republicans, they were bringing liberty and a new life to his subjects, and they were making themselves rich with endless pilfering. And, of course, with each victory, in spite of the casualties, the morale of his army improved. It was during this summer that his men began to call him "The Little Corporal," granting him an affection they never withdrew no matter how much he abused it.

His energy that summer of 1796 was extraordinary. Not only did he defeat Würmser in two difficult campaigns, but he negotiated settlements with people he had "liberated," such as the Milanesi; with people who, quite independently, had revolted against their rulers, such as the citizens of Reggio against the Duke of Modena; with cities where he had helped or instigated revolts, such as the Papal cities of Bologna and Ferrara; and with the sovereigns themselves, such as the pope over the fate of his two legations or with the ambassadors of Venice over the fate of Verona, a Venetian city he had occupied and continued to hold. All of these representatives and diplomats saw him playing the role of the great man: in a tent about to dash into battle, or hot and dusty after a victory, or in a moment snatched from a triumphal entry into Milan or Pavia, Brescia or Verona. But always, everywhere, victorious. Small wonder they began to think of him, depending on their point of view, as a God, the new Alexander, or as the Devil Incarnate.

The third attempt to relieve Mantua began in November. Once again Francis sent two armies toward the city, one from the Tirol down the valley of the Adige and the other from Gorizia north of Trieste, both marching across neutral, Venetian territory. The first skirmishes went in their favor, and at the news all those who supported the established regime took heart and began again to show their colors. This time, it seemed, the armies would join at Mantua, break the siege and then march on to Milan, rolling the French back as far as Turin or even across the Alps. But Napoleon, as before, managed to keep the columns apart and defeat them separately, the one from Gorizia in a brilliant victory at Arcola.

The result, however, was not decisive, and Arcola was followed by a truce of two months during which both sides prepared for a final battle. This took place, on 14 January 1797, at Rivoli, and was decisive. The Habsburg army, defeated on the field and relentlessly pursued, fled into the Venetian Alps, and three weeks later Mantua, starving and without hope of relief, capitulated. Rivoli and its consequence, the fall of Mantua, was the greatest success the armies of the French Republic had achieved. In Paris the deputies congratulated the Directory, and the crowds shouted *"Vive Bonaparte!"*

The military victory left Napoleon supreme in Italy, and neutrals, enemies and friends alike waited to see what he planned for them. In his political dealings he could be soft, as he seemed to want to be with Genoa and Parma, a republic and a duchy; or hard, as he was with Venice and the Papacy, a republic and an elective monarchy. There seemed little reason or consistency, which only increased the terror of those who knew they were subject to his whim. The poor Duke of Modena, Ercole Rinaldo d'Este, had his entire state simply declared forfeit on the ground that he had revictualed the Austrians at Mantua. As he fled for the safety of Venice, with as much treasure as he could carry, Italy's last link with the great days of the Renaissance parted. The duchy became a republic on the French model and soon thereafter joined with the Legations of Bologna and Ferrara, which had revolted against the pope, to form the Cispadane Republic.

To Italian republicans Napoleon, the general of a modern republic, recalled the ancient glories of a republican Rome, and Latin models and phrases were very much in the air. Little republics were to rise and fall all over Italy, generally with some Latin tag for identification. The names have a pattern which assumes Rome to be the center of all that matters and therefore the point from which everything is judged. Starting from Rome, then, certain words can be combined with mountain ranges, rivers or any other natural boundary to describe an area. These are "Cis," meaning "this side of"; "trans," meaning "across"; and "sub," "at the foot of." "Cispadane," therefore, means "this side of the Po," for "padana" is the adjectival form of Po. Briefly also there would be a "Transpadane" Republic, being Milan which, starting from Rome, was across the river. Later both would be combined into a "Cisalpine" Republic, and the Kingdom of Sardinia became, for a time, the "Subalpine" Republic. Even at the time men found the names confusing or even comic. The Spanish ambassador at Rome wrote a colleague about the Cisalpine Republic: "Do see if you can get this *Alpine* name changed, for I do not like it. It seems to belong to the nomenclature of zoology: *mus alpinus.*" But the revolutionaries took their classical mantle very seriously.

The political settlements required of Napoleon after Rivoli were beset with difficulties which he could not altogether solve. Yet the defeat of Austria and withdrawal of all its forces left a vacuum which had to be filled with some sort of governmental structure if chaos and anarchy were to be avoided. The crux of the difficulties was that Napoleon, his men and the Directory had several purposes in Italy, some of which conflicted. Many in the army, even generals, were idealistic and had fought, in some part, to bring the benefits of the French Revolution to the Italians. At Bologna, for example, with Napoleon's approval, French agents had helped the local republicans to secede from the Papal States and declare themselves a free city with a republican form of government. But at the same time Napoleon, following the orders of the Directory, levied a contribution of two million livres on the city, took an additional 1,200,000 livres from its public funds and 800,000 livres from the pawnbrokers, and carried off property valued at two million livres. Just when the new republic needed all its resources to establish itself, it was thrown to the verge of bankruptcy and, inevitably, onto the supporting mercies of the French army. Napoleon also took most of its artillery and muskets, with the result that if he withdrew his troops from the city, the Papal troops would be able to retake it without opposition and, as their generals threatened, execute all the local republicans as traitors. Plainly the establishment of republics in this fashion was a trap for the French and, if they withdrew, certain death for the Italians who had helped them.

In other ways, as both the Directory and Napoleon perceived, establishing republics in Italy might be less useful to France than to leave the established governments in power. New republics, as the French well knew, were unstable; the deputies were much given to oratory and little to government; the people were apt, for a time, to be confused by the new system of law and social organization. If Napoleon was to lead his army to Vienna, and the thought was still very much in his mind, he did not want to leave chaos in his rear.

A more cynical reason for not establishing republics arose from the failure of the Directory's two-pronged campaign north of the Alps. The Emperor Francis' brother, Archduke Charles, had defeated one of the French armies and forced it and the other to retire behind the Rhine. He could not, however, win back the Austrian Netherlands, modern Belgium, and Francis began to indicate that he would let France keep the Netherlands if he could have something in return, something in Germany or, perhaps, in Italy. And that something, the Directory realized, could be more easily absorbed by the Habsburg system if its government was a single man, a monarch, rather than an assembly of excited deputies.

Because of these conflicts in principles there was no uniformity to French policy in the north of Italy. The Duke of Parma was supported in his duchy while the Duke of Modena was deprived of his. In the Republic of Genoa, an oligarchy, the ruling class was supported; in the Republic of Venice, it was subtly undermined. Individual cities threw out the local garrison, declared themselves free, and then might or might not join with their neighbors in a federation. Much depended on the energy and skill of the local republicans and the support given them by the French, which varied with the political views of the commander and the military requirements of the moment. Meanwhile, republicans everywhere, aided by French revolutionary agents, propagandized their neighbors, sent petitions to Napoleon, and called conventions to which they were elected deputies and at which they drafted constitutions on the French model. In all the confusion the towns, in effect, governed themselves as best they could, and the only real power was the French army.

Gradually a Transpadane and a Cispadane Republic emerged. The former was composed of the Duchies of Milan and Mantua north of the Po, and the latter of the Duchy of Modena and the Papal Legations of Bologna and Ferrara. In the Congress at Reggio which created the Cispadane Republic the deputies adopted for their flag a tricolor of red, white and green, the flag of the Italian Republic today. By following the French flag in form the deputies proclaimed their republicanism while substituting a traditional Italian color, green, for the French blue. A few months earlier a regiment of volunteers, on leaving Milan to fight under Napoleon, had used a tricolor with green as its regimental colors, but the Congress at Reggio seems to have been the first governmental body in Italy to adopt it.

The revolt of the Legations had already brought Napoleon into open war with the pope, but the latter's few troops were no match for the French army and after some skirmishing there had been an armistice. Under its terms Napoleon had agreed to hold his fire, and poor Pius VI had agreed to send an ambassador to Paris to "obtain from the Directory a conclusive peace"; to close his ports to enemies of the French Republic; to give up the citadel and port of Ancona with all its artillery to the French army; to allow passage of French troops through his States on demand; to pay an indemnity of twenty-one million French livres of which 15,500,000 was to be in cash; and to send one hundred pictures, busts, vases or statues and five hundred manuscripts to Paris. These were to be "at the choice of the commissioners who will be sent to Rome."

The Directory was still plagued with the problem of two Churches in France, of which the larger and more influential was composed of the "nonjuring" priests, and was determined to humble Pius into withdrawing his opposition to its State-controlled Church. After the battle of Rivoli, as soon as it became clear that Mantua would fall, the directors ordered Napoleon to attack the pope again. A letter to him shows what they hoped to achieve:

CITIZEN GENERAL,
    In considering the obstacles that stand in the way of the consolidation of the French Constitution, the Executive Directory has come to the conclusion that the Roman religion is the one of which the enemies of freedom can, for a long time to come, make the most dangerous use. You are too intelligent, Citizen General, not to have realized, just as we have, that the Roman religion will always be an irreconcilable enemy of the Republic, firstly, by its very essence and, secondly, because its ministers and votaries will never forgive the Revolution for attacking its wealth and the influence of its ministers, as well as combating the beliefs and habits of its followers. We shall no doubt find means at home to destroy its influence gradually, either by legislative means or by institutions which will efface the old views by substituting new ones more in keeping with things as they are, with reason and with ethics. It is the task of the Government to discover these means. There is one thing, however, probably no less essential for attaining this end, and that is the destruction if possible of the centre of the unity of the Roman Church; it is for you, who have so

far shown that you possess not only the qualities of a great general but those also of an enlightened statesman, to carry out this object, if you consider it practicable.

"The Executive Directory therefore asks you to do everything possible . . . to destroy the Papal government, either by subjecting Rome to another Power or, and this would be even better, by setting up an internal government which would render the present government of priests worthless and hateful. By this means the Pope and Sacred College would realise that the Apostolic See could never hold sway in Rome and would be forced to look for asylum elsewhere, where at least they would have no temporal power.[2]

The decision of what course to follow was left to Napoleon as the man in the field, but the Directory's aims were not secret. The more radical revolutionaries, both in France and Italy, talked openly of the Papacy coming to an end. Most of them imagined that after the death of Pius, who was seventy-nine, a new pope simply would not be elected. There would be no convocation of cardinals, and the bishops thereafter, as in France, would be appointed by the various states.

Exactly a week after Rivoli, on 21 January 1797, Napoleon declared war on the pope. Again there was only token opposition, and four weeks later at Tolentino, a small town in the mountains behind Ancona, he dictated his terms to a delegation of cardinals which also included the pope's nephew, Duke Braschi. The pope was to recognize the previous cession to France of Avignon and the Comtat Venaissin; he was to give up his claims to his Legations, Bologna, Ravenna and Ferrara; he was to pay double the indemnity previously agreed to in the armistice and to hand over more works of art. Considering that no one could stop Napoleon from marching into Rome and setting up any sort of government he wished, it perhaps was a generous settlement. He explained in a letter to the Directory: "It is my opinion that, deprived of Bologna, Ferrara and Romagna (Ravenna), as well as the 30 millions that we are taking, Rome cannot continue to exist; this ancient machine will fall to pieces without outside help." He also added that, rather than go to Rome himself, he thought he should stay with the army until there was a general peace with Austria. He still had very much in mind pushing on to Vienna, particularly as he knew the Directory was organizing still another two-pronged campaign north of the Alps. If the pope was one pillar of the old way of life, the Habsburg emperor was another and, being more difficult to knock down, would confer even greater glory on the general who did it.

The peace terms of Tolentino, even though they left the pope on his throne and with a state to govern, were humiliating and nearly disastrous for him. He was held up before the world and his subjects, for the second time in a year, as a prince who could offer his subjects no protection of any sort, a prince who, in order to save the trappings of his life, sent the wealth of his country out of his country. In fact, the papacy was close to being bankrupt. Even as it tried to feed and employ thousands of refugee priests, it was forced to give up the only profitable lands and towns it owned and all its spare cash. In the place of hard coin it had begun to issue paper currency which every week depreciated in value. Even its works of art, some of which it tried to sell, brought in less than expected as hundreds of stolen masterpieces came on the market. In the Papal cities outside of Rome the Papal government was already disintegrating, and Napoleon's view that it might soon collapse of itself in Rome as well was reasonable.

The Directory accepted his arguments, even though the terms were considerably less severe than its letter had suggested or the situation made possible. It was the first time on an important and public issue that Napoleon did not follow, even slavishly, the Directory's orders or suggestions. The balance of power between him, the republic's most successful general, and the civilian heads of the government was shifting.

Judging by his later career and some of his actions in Italy during this first Italian campaign, Napoleon's approach to the problems arising from the republic's rift with the Church was more practical and less doctrinaire than that of the Directory or of the deputies in Paris. In writing to the Directory about the politics of the Cispadane Republic he explained that there were "three parties: (1) those who support the old form of government; (2) the partisans of a somewhat aristocratic constitution; (3) the partisans of the French form of constitution—in other words of a complete democracy. The first I repress, the second I support, and the third I moderate. . . . I support the second and moderate the third because the second party consists of wealthy landowners and priests who, ultimately, would win over the mass of the people which it is essential should be rallied round the French party. The latter is composed of young people, writers and men who, as in France and everywhere else, only wish to change the government and only love freedom in order to effect a revolution."

Napoleon, although himself a young person, had a strong conservative streak and an excellent eye for the realities of a situation. His genius as a political leader in his first decade of power, which began with this campaign in Italy, lay in his ability to make the revolutionary ideas effective by giving them a conservative base. In Italy he correctly gauged the ultimate power of the big landlords and of the local priests, and he tried not to push them too hard or too fast. Perhaps he had pondered the history of the religious reforms which Duke Leopoldo, the emperor's father, had tried to introduce into Tuscany and which had ended in the debacle at Prato. Napoleon wanted the Legations for his Cispadane Republic because geography and economic interest made them part of the Po valley, and he wanted to control the Papal ports, such as Ancona, for military reasons. But, unlike the Directory, he did not want to humiliate the pope merely out of republican spite or to destroy the Papacy altogether because of some abstract republican principle. He could see that such a course would exasperate not only the Romans but also the underground Catholic opposition in France, Belgium and, particularly, northern Italy which he was trying hard to reconcile to a new form of government and social organization.

After Tolentino, Napoleon refused to return to Milan where the local republicans were eagerly awaiting him. They needed his approval to hold their primary assemblies, the first step in changing the duchy from a state under military occupation, however benevolent, into an independent republic. But both Napoleon and the Directory were anxious to slow the Revolution in the north of Italy until a conclusive peace had been reached with Francis in Vienna. This seemed the key to future developments in the Po valley, and Napoleon stayed in Mantua, pleading that he had to devote all his energies to preparing the army for its march on Vienna.

Such was the speed of his preparations that by the third week in March, only a month after he had been dictating peace terms in Tolentino, he and the main column of his army had reached Gorizia on the Isonzo river and had entered the Habsburg Duchy of Carniola. On today's map the bulk of this ancient duchy is in Yugoslavia and corresponds roughly to the region of Slovenia which centers on the town of Ljubljana. But as Napoleon advanced, a serious disturbance broke out behind him. In two cities of the Venetian Republic, Bergamo and Brescia, the local republicans, aided by French officers, succeeded in expelling the doge's representatives and declared the cities independent. Both were close to Milan, and the republicans hoped to join their cities with the democratic republic they thought they saw forming there. But the peasants in the Alpine foothills and some of the other towns were solidly pro-Venetian, and for several weeks it seemed likely that rough, local skirmishing was going to flare into a revolutionary civil war such as had nearly destroyed France.

Napoleon saw his supply lines threatened by, as he chose to view it, a deceitful Venetian government. He sent a young aide-de-camp to Venice with a brutal message for the Senate, and the young man, following Napoleon's intent if not actual orders, insisted the senators interrupt their Easter Day celebrations to listen to it. But it was Napoleon who was deceitful, for, at the same time that he wrote a letter to the doge threatening Venice with war if it did not re-establish order on the mainland, he published a proclamation "to the people of the mainland of the Venetian Republic" in which he denounced the Senate as "a small number of men who, since the age of barbarism, have clung to power." He promised: "The Venetian Senate may rule you by right of conquest, but I will release you." The senators were thoroughly cowed, and the Venetian government in all its branches finally reached a state of total ineffectiveness. On the mainland and even in Venice itself French revolutionaries, both in and out of the army, worked actively to undermine what little was left of Venetian authority and aimed at replacing the ancient oligarchy with a democratic type of republic on the French model. On the mainland each town began to rule itself, and Napoleon, although he could not spare a man, detached a regiment from his army and sent it back to re-enforce the garrisons he had left along his route.

He continued on into the Alps with his army spread out in a long line, running through the valleys from west to east and pointing like an arrow at the Semmering Pass only seventy miles from Vienna. His troops were now in some of the oldest of the Habsburg possessions, the County of Tirol, the Duchy of Carinthia, and at Neumarkt were penetrating into the Duchy of Styria. In Vienna the public was seized with panic and expected to see him before the walls in another week. Francis sought an armistice, to which Napoleon agreed, and negotiations began for a general peace.

Napoleon's position looked more brilliant than it was. The other French armies that were to form the northern half of the pincer on Vienna had never started, and it seemed to the world as if Napoleon, unaided, had brought down the Habsburg emperor. But the emperor was not down. His army had not been defeated and Napoleon's was too small and too far from its base of supplies to take Vienna alone. Further, as Napoleon admitted in letters to the Directory and to the Habsburg representatives who could see it for themselves, he could not even hold his army where it was for more than a week or two. The people of the valleys and mountainsides were hostile and their farms, in early spring, too poor to provision a large army. He was, in fact, under even more pressure than Francis to negotiate a treaty quickly, and in doing so he often made decisions on his own, not waiting for instructions from Paris and sometimes not even waiting for the emperor's representatives to hear from Vienna.

He succeeded in reaching a conclusion in ten days, partly by the force of his personality and partly by the terms he offered and accepted. These were embodied in "the preliminaries of Leoben," so called from the small town where the meetings took place and because they were to be amplified later by a more formal treaty. This followed six months later, 18 April– 17 October 1797, and likewise was named after the town near which it was drawn up, Campoformio, a tiny village on the Venetian mainland.

The preliminaries of Leoben contained nine open articles and eleven that were secret. The gist of these last became, in six months' time, open articles in the Treaty of Campoformio. From the day they became known men have argued whether by them Napoleon accomplished for the people of Italy a great good or inflicted on them a terrible harm.

The open articles were about what most men had expected and what the republicans had feared. There were to be further discussions about the principalities along the Rhine, but the Austrian Netherlands were to go to France and, in return, France was to evacuate all Habsburg holdings on both sides of the Alps. For the Milanesi it meant that they would again be subjects of the emperor. Undoubtedly the majority were delighted. The French, after a year of arrogance, confiscations and anarchy, had won to their support very few others than Napoleon's "young people, writers and men who only wish to change the government." But still for all those who had actively worked to establish a republic in the Duchy of Milan the restoration of the emperor as their duke would certainly mean exile.

But black as the future must have seemed for them, it was not without hope. The preliminaries left many ends loose, suggesting a great deal of negotiating remained to be done. Such matters, for example, as the future of the Cispadane Republic. Preliminaries were, after all, only a start, and between the start and the finish there might be many changes. So the republicans in Milan worked even harder than before, believing that their best hope for protection lay in bringing their Transpadane Republic to life.

The French, too, continued their revolutionary activities, particularly against the Republic of Venice which still desperately tried to convince Napoleon of its good will. But the Republic now was no more than the city on the lagoon, and on 3 May Napoleon, with a great show of indignation, declared war against it. The Grand Council begged for an armistice to have time to do anything Napoleon wished, and this he granted, extending it from day to day so that his revolutionary agents and sympathizers in the city could spark a spontaneous revolution. But on every occasion when the agents cried *"Viva la libertà!"*, the Venetians answered *"Viva San Marco!"* and resolutely refused to revolt.

The end finally came, amid confusion and mistake, at a meeting of the Grand Council on 12 May 1797, just five hundred years after the council had founded the republic by creating a patrician class of its members and thereafter restricting office in the state to them and their descendants. Now, on this final day of the republic's existence, the council listened to the last doge, Lodovico Manin, urge its patrician members to dissolve their caste and to abandon their sovereignty to a provisional government. A man was speaking against the motion when suddenly outside the windows on the piazza there was a volley of musket fire. It was a Venetian regiment from Dalmatia on its way home and firing a last salute to the city. But inside everyone supposed it was the revolution and panicked. "Men of venerable age, the gravest senators, presidents of the council of forty, leaped from seat to seat amid the convulsion of terror and the starts of despair." During the commotion the vote was taken: 512 in favor of dissolution, 20 against and 5 abstentions. "Take this," said the doge, removing his cap of office and handing it to a servant, "it will not be needed any more."

Council members, meanwhile, rushed down the staircase and out of the building. Some threw off their gowns of office as they ran, others shouted revolutionary slogans, hoping to save themselves from the mob that was not there. When the people gathered, attracted by the noise, they thought the council had stood firm, and they rejoiced. They carried the sacred images out of the cathedral and looked for patricians to lead them; they could find none. They went to the doge's house, but he was not there. Then, gradually, as they realized what had happened, they turned on French sympathizers, burning republican emblems and breaking into the French legation, which they sacked.

Then in the coming weeks, with the aid of French agents and the support of the French army, local republicans set about creating a democratic republic of the city. On orders from Napoleon they burned the *Libro d'Oro,* the register of the patrician class, and planted a tree of liberty in the center of the Piazza San Marco. They addressed each other as "Cittadino" instead of "Signor" and destroyed feudal emblems and liveries. They argued over the details of the government, planned the dissolution of monasteries and convents and, after a lengthy discussion, changed the symbol of Venice from the Lion of St. Mark to a Madonna-like figure tamely labeled the "Municipality of Venice" and placed between two sentinels, "Liberty" and "Equality." Most Venetians expressed their anger at such actions in the only way they could, and each new act or proposal of the government produced a harvest of satiric poems and cartoons: under democracy the city had left to govern only itself, so Our Lady of the Municipality was an appropriate symbol; under democracy even simple goodness was threatened, so it was right that Our Lady should have two guards; or what an incontrovertible advance in civilization from a Lion, the king of beasts, to a captive Lady guarded by two French sentinels! But there was no joking, only tears, as they watched the French remove the four horses from the porch of the basilica and the Lion of St. Mark from his column in the Piazzetta in order to send them all to Paris.

The playwright Gozzi, just finishing his *Useless Memoirs,* had an aristocrat's distaste for the vulgar, earnest and often threatening republicans, and he refused to write more than a few sentences on what he saw:

The howlings of the dreamers, screaming *Liberty, Equality, Fraternity*, deafened us; and those of us who were still awake were forced to pretend to dream in order to defend our honor, our property and our lives. . . . I always feared and predicted the terrible consequences of a revolutionary and intoxicating doctrine sown freely in our century over the heads of men and women alike. Yet all the warnings proved to be useless, just as these *Memoirs* will be—as useless as a doctor's prescriptions for a man whose lungs are rotten.[3]

He was only fifty-seven, but he was firmly and forever of the old way of life. He lived on into the nineteenth century, until 1806, and saw many interesting events, but he refused to partake of them or even comment on them: "Let us leave to serious and candid historians the task of relating what we are sure, if we live, to see." For him, and for many others in northern Italy, life ended in 1797 when the French, under a general of genius, burst over the Alps and descended, like the Goths of old, on an older, weaker civilization.

Not all Venetians felt as did Gozzi, and one who greeted the new republic with joy and returned to Venice to hold office under it was Ugo Foscolo, a nineteen-year-old playwright who was to develop into one of Italy's great poets. His life was to be unhappy, and like many of the time, to be tortured by conflicting loyalties. But in the summer of 1797 his conflicts seemed to be resolving rather than increasing. Shortly after the start of the year he had been forced to flee Venice because of his radical, democratic opinions; now he returned, with honor, to work for his city and his political ideals, both of which he loved.

His background was different from Gozzi's and yet equally Venetian and, in many ways, typical of those who supported the new republic. His father had been a doctor working in the Venetian outposts of the Adriatic, the last signs of the republic's vanished empire. By the year of Foscolo's birth, 1778, these included only the Ionian Isles off Greece, of which Corfu was the chief; a long strip of the Dalmatian coast which included such cities as Zara and Spalato (today, Split); and most of the Istrian peninsula. Foscolo was born on Zante, the southernmost of the Ionian islands, and one of his famous and most lovely sonnets celebrates it. When he was six, his father was appointed head of a hospital in Spalato, and the family moved there. But then after four years his father died, and his mother took him and his brother back to Venice. Life there was hard. Like many Venetians in the last century of the republic, they found themselves without connections, without money and without any representation in the government or even the possibility of qualifying for any of the small government positions that often, in those times, had the effect of pensions. Yet they were a family with aspirations, the widow and children of an educated, professional man who had spent much of his life serving the republic in out-of-the-way places.

Foscolo educated himself largely by reading and found his friends among other young writers and political idealists. He was one of a group of Venetian republicans who kept in touch with similar groups in other cities, all of whom discussed every twist and turn of the French Revolution and hoped to produce something like it in their various Italian states.

His first literary success was a tragedy in Alfieri's style and which, with characteristic frankness, he dedicated to Alfieri. In the next century Foscolo, both for his life and his poetry, would be the favorite poet of Garibaldi; the strain of republican idealism among these men, passing from generation to generation, is clear and strong. The tragedy, *Tieste,* had ten performances, enough to bring Foscolo to the attention of the government and, although he might not have been imprisoned, he felt he should leave Venice. He went to Bologna, which was then the capital of the Cispadane Republic, and took a commission in a cavalry regiment, he also wrote an ode, *To Bonaparte, the Liberator,* which, unlike the hundreds of others being scribbled daily, was read by a great number of persons, including the Liberator himself.

For republicans like Foscolo, during the summer of 1797, there seemed no limit to Napoleon's glory, no possible spot on his radiance. After the Great Man had first destroyed Venice and then made peace with its new government, he moved his headquarters to Mombello, near Milan, where he dispensed orders, so it seemed to the faithful, like a God. A young French diplomat, Trouvé, on his way to Naples, stopped to present himself and later wrote to a friend:

> As I saluted in his person the glory of Republican France, I was overcome by emotion and admiration. He lives in a great house which belongs to M. Crivelli, with a vast view as far as the Alps, whose snowy peaks are still discernible, though it is actually very hot here. The appearance of the General-in-Chief is very imposing. Although he is affable and cheerful, his officers never fail to approach him with respect, since he is severe and does not allow familiarity. With him are his wife, his sister and a young brother, and he seems like the father of a family, whom everyone reveres. With all this, he is not yet twenty-eight, if one can believe his wife, who ought to know. After your testimony, I already had a high opinion of his political qualities. From his conversation I have realized that he is indeed a statesman. I cannot speak too highly of the kindly way in which he has received me.[4]

Italian republicans were even more dazzled by Napoleon's presence than was Trouvé, for they were less aware of the Directory behind him and had no experience of the trappings of power, the comings and goings of generals, ambassadors and beautiful ladies. The more sophisticated of them sensed that the Napoleonic legend had begun, that he was consciously developing a cult of himself. But he did it so well, he was so able, so cultivated and powerful and at the same time so young and charming that all criticism, all disbelief dissolved, for the moment, in admiration. The simpler ones went away with a vision no later harsh realities could quite dispel.

And still the revolutions went on. In May in Genoa, the republicans revolted in the name of the people against the oligarchy. But the people rose to defend the doge, and the republicans appealed to Napoleon for help. He could not refuse, particularly as the angry Genovesi had sacked every house owned by a Frenchman, killed several men who were French subjects and thrown several hundreds more into jail. But no troops were needed. Napoleon had merely to summon the doge to come, with clerical aides, to Mombello and receive a new and more democratic form of government. Thus on 6 June 1797 was born the Ligurian Republic. Within a month the two most famous republics in Europe, Venice and Genoa, each lost their independence, and became dependent states of France, for no one doubted for a moment that if the French army withdrew, the republican minorities in each city would be overwhelmed by a combination of the nobility or patricians, the peasants and city poor, and those of all classes who might be influenced by the Church.

Napoleon, meanwhile, continued negotiations with the Habsburg representatives for the final treaty which was to incorporate the preliminaries of Leoben and provide peace not only along the Rhine but also the Po. By the preliminaries France was to evacuate all Habsburg territories, which meant, among others, the Duchies of Milan and Mantua. The Emperor Francis, however, was indignant at the fashion in which Napoleon was surrounding the duchies with democratic republics and demanded the restoration to Venice of its old government. His representative at Mombello complained to a colleague: "Until the Emperor comes to Italy and assumes the power which the preliminaries accord to him, everything will be in disorder in Italy. The French are digging themselves in, the country is decaying, evil and confusion increase daily." It was true. With the constant shifting and changing of governments, authority had broken down. Brigandage and vandalism had increased greatly; business, except for provisioning the army, was almost at a halt, and everyone was dissatisfied with the inflationary paper money with which the French paid for the provisions. Two weeks later the emperor's representative wrote again: "Italy is going to ruin. Each day a government falls; each day democracy extends and is consolidated. If the Pope dies, his state will be another prize for the

French, and another cause of disorder, to the ruin of the Catholic religion and the political system of Italy."

Republicans naturally were delighted with all that Napoleon was doing, and on 29 June he pleased many of them even more by announcing the formation of a "Cisalpine Republic." This was to be made up of the Duchies of Milan and Mantua and the Cispadane Republic. In Vienna the government was outraged, and feelings even among the republicans in Italy were mixed. Those in Milan were beside themselves with joy, seeing in the action a promise by the French not to desert them. But those in Bologna, the capital of the Cispadane Republic, were not sure they wished to be merged with their ancient rivals, the Milanesi. Which city now would be the capital, Milan or Bologna? And if the Cispadane Republic was to be merged, then why not also the Venetian Republic? If there were good economic and geographic reasons for unifying the republics in the Po valley, why did not the reasons apply even more strongly to the republic which controlled the river's many mouths?

Napoleon did nothing to answer the question, which disquieted some republicans. For the first time they could not understand or imagine reasons for his actions. Then, presumably in retaliation for the creation of the Cisalpine Republic on his territories, the emperor seized the strip of the Dalmatian coast and that part of the Istrian peninsula which belonged to the Venetian Republic, Napoleon's creation. The Venetians looked to Napoleon for help. He had, in a year of crossing their territory and warring on them, commandeered almost all their arms and cannon. But he would do no more than protest, and the question of what Napoleon really intended for northern Italy was raised again in yet another form.

The answer finally came on 17 October 1797 with the signing and proclamation of the Treaty of Campoformio. As in the preliminaries of Leoben, the Austrian Netherlands would go to France, but thereafter the new treaty almost exactly reversed the public provisions of the old, and, in view of Napoleon's actions over the summer, no one was left with the slightest doubt that he had in essence agreed to the new provisions in secret articles signed at Leoben. By the Treaty of Campoformio the Emperor Francis renounced to the Cisalpine Republic all his rights to the Duchies of Milan and Mantua and confirmed to it the Duchy of Modena, the three Legations and that part of the Venetian Republic west of the Adige river, a long strip which included the three important cities of Bergamo, Brescia and Peschiera. In return the emperor was to have all the rest of the Venetion mainland, Venice itself, the Istrian peninsula and the Dalmatian coast. By a seeming irrelevancy the Ionian islands were to go to France.

Just as the Habsburg emperor, Charles VI, in the War of the Spanish Succession had won the Duchy of Milan by fighting the French in the Po valley, so now his great-grandson, Francis II, was able to exchange the duchy for the even larger Republic of Venice by fighting the French in the Po valley. And just as in 1713 the wishes of the Milanesi had not been considered in the peace settlement after the Spanish War, so now, in 1797, any wishes the Venetians may have had were ignored. The result, however, was not as happy. Venice was not Milan, and between 1713 and 1797 the feelings of men had changed.

Venetians of every sort of political persuasion were stunned. They simply could not believe that after a thousand years of independence they were to be handed over to a Habsburg, to be ruled, like some minor fief, by a viceroy. The shock was worst for the republicans, men like Foscolo, who suddenly found themselves stripped of their self-respect and revealed as fools, fools of the worst sort, men who had been tricked into inflaming their fellows into vain quarrels about aristocracy and democracy, into starting a civil war in their country which had cost it both its wealth and independence. Desperately the Municipality of Venice sent ambassadors to the Directory and to Napoleon begging that the city be allowed to defend itself. Napoleon imprisoned those sent to him, and those going to Paris arrived too late to have any effect. Meanwhile a French commissioner, sent by Napoleon, came as a grave-robber to the republic. He dismantled most of the ships that were left and sent the remainder to Toulon with spare parts, cannon, paintings or anything else movable that he could claim. He even scraped the gilding off the doge's old ship of state, the *Bucintoro,* and then burned the hulk. By winter the Austrians were in command, and Foscolo and most other republicans had fled. The patrician class, deprived of the salaries from positions in the government, had collapsed. Those with productive country estates on the mainland retreated to them, and the rest struggled against poverty. Lorenzo da Ponte, Mozart's librettist, came to Venice in 1798 and went to the Piazza San Marco, but all was changed: "My reader may judge my surprise and grief when in all that vast space, where in happy times nothing is to be seen but a great concourse of gay and happy people, I now saw on every side only melancholy, silence, solitude, and desolation. There were but seven people there when I entered the square."

The betrayal of Venice at Campoformio shocked other north Italians almost as much as it did the Venetians. The French had entered Italy claiming that the war they brought was different from those in the past, that it was not fought to rearrange dynasties on the peninsula, but to bring a new and better way of life to the various peoples there. But no republicans in Italy, whether of Milan or Genoa or any other city, could see any Liberty in the fate of the Venetians or any Fraternity in the betrayal of one republican by another. Even Frenchmen, in the army and in Paris, were shocked, for in many the strain of revolutionary idealism was still strong. After Campoformio, Napoleon's reputation, at least in Italy, was soiled. He never shone again in such a sunburst of glory as he had at Mombello during the summer. Republicans in Italy continued to worship him, but without trust and only as a man of extraordinary ability and power who might be useful to them. Napoleon's deal with Francis cost him his innocence and the Italians their illusions.

Because of later research it is clearer today than it was to contemporaries that Napoleon's march toward Vienna was not the brilliant campaign he persuaded the world to believe it was. His letters to the Directory show him concerned about his extended position and willing to make large concessions to Francis in order to extricate himself with honor. This meant, if the campaign was to have a purpose, some sort of treaty. The letters from the Directory to him show that it was appalled at the generous terms he offered and, during the negotiations at Campoformio, it even ordered him to resume the war rather than allow the Habsburgs into Venice. Napoleon disobeyed, and the Directory, not daring to repudiate publicly its most successful and popular general, accepted the treaty.

But, as the Directory had warned Napoleon and as most Italians grasped at once, it was a bad treaty. Far from insuring peace, it insured war, and on terms that would be more favorable to the emperor. In taking Venice for Milan, Francis plainly had made an excellent exchange, even counting the Austrian Netherlands as part of the cost. The Venetian Republic joined directly with the Alpine duchies of the Habsburgs and could be more effectively integrated with their other holdings, along the lines of Joseph's reforms, than ever the isolated Netherlands or Milan might have been. Further, Francis now controlled the length of the Adige river which, coming down from the Brenner Pass, led directly into the heart of the Po valley. He had, in his defeat, obtained a stronger position in northern Italy than the Habsburgs had ever before achieved.

Victorious France, on the other hand, was committed by the treaty to support a weak position. It had no direct land communication with the Cisalpine Republic at Milan and, at least in theory, was dependent on the friendship of Sardinia and Genoa for access to it. The Sardinians and Genovesi at once began to tremble for what shreds were left of their independence.

It had also undertaken to support a revolutionary form of government and social organization in a former duchy where the majority of the people preferred the old ways. Given a chance to vote, however the franchise might be limited, it was almost certain that a majority would vote the republicans out of office and then change the form of government to something aristocratic rather than democratic. To prevent this the Directory advised Napoleon to appoint republicans to the important posts rather than to risk elections. But some of the most able republicans refused to serve on such terms, and the government was weak and suspect.

In fact it was based in Paris, and it faced, just across the Adige river, a government opposite in form and principle, which was based in Vienna. Always before in northern Italy, even when a monarch had ruled in France as well as Austria, the two governments had kept a buffer state, Sardinia, between them. But now Napoleon had set them face to face. Every Venetian who fled "the tyranny" at Venice would go to Milan, as did Foscolo, and plead for help for those he had left behind, and disaffected Milanesi would cross the border into Venice equally full of pleas. Few in Italy believed that the Treaty of Campoformio was any more than an armistice.

This was the bad in the treaty, and it was apparent from the start. The good appeared very much more slowly. Meanwhile Napoleon, who had transformed the states of northern Italy, returned to Paris and began, in January 1798, to inspect Channel ports and fortifications with an eye to invading England which was still at war with France. He left behind in Italy an unstable situation, a group of generals less able than himself to cope with it, and an exhausted and often bewildered people. By toppling so many governments Napoleon had revealed how flimsy their structures were. By impoverishing and undermining the ruling classes he had made impossible any return to the eighteenth-century forms of life and government. The patricians in Venice, for example, had ceased to exist as a class, and even if the Habsburg viceroy could be expelled, the city could not again become an oligarchy. Napoleon in his first Italian campaign had carried the French Revolution into Italy and driven it deep into Italian life. No matter what the future held, life for the northern Italians could never be the same.

# CHAPTER 11

18th Fructidor (4 September 1797). Revolution in Rome. Pius expelled. Loot of Rome. Revolution to Naples. Nelson. Battle of the Nile. Neapolitan invasion of Rome. Disaster. Flight to Palermo. France's position in Italy.

ALTHOUGH NAPOLEON had introduced the doctrines of the Revolution, together with its chaos, into all the states of the Po valley, except the small Duchy of Parma, he had not yet crossed the Apennines into central Italy. Twice in threatening the pope over the Legations, he had started troops up into the mountains, but each time he had won the terms he wanted without crossing them. The Directory had wanted to press on, to destroy the Papacy and to establish a republic at Rome, but as long as fighting continued in the Po valley, Napoleon had always had an obvious and valid reason for not putting any part of his small army across such a difficult barrier. The Directory, however, did not forget its plans for the pope and Rome, and after Campoformio it returned to them.

It was an even more revolutionary Directory than before because it had, in a *coup d'état,* expelled its two more conservative members. During the summer of 1797 the Royalist and Catholic parties in France had gained support among the people and threatened, through orderly elections, to win control of the legislative chambers and of the Directory itself. The revolutionaries who had won for the people the right to vote, were now as a result about to be voted out of office. They thought it intolerable. The people, they argued, must be protected from themselves. Liberty, the right to vote, could be used for any purpose except, by voting for a return of the monarchy, to abolish the right to vote. And to prevent such an occurrence the Directory arrested fifty-four deputies of the opposition and one of the conservative Directors. The other escaped. The prisoners were deported to Guiana, severe laws were passed against political clubs and censorship imposed on the newspapers. All opposition was silenced or forced into exile. France had, in the name of Liberty and Democracy, a dictatorship of revolutionaries.

101

The armies, both those on the Rhine and the Po, supported the *coup,* which is known from its date on the revolutionary calendar as 18th Fructidor (4 September). The soldiers, away from wife, priest and home, were more revolutionary than the civilians in France and less aware of the Directory's failures as a government. On the anniversary of Bastille Day, which the people of Paris greeted without enthusiasm, the soldiers passed vehement resolutions expressing their confidence in the Directory and their hatred for the Catholic and Royalist opposition. Napoleon, in writing to the Directory, urged it to act and promised, "If you need force, call on the armies." He even sent one of his more revolutionary generals to Paris to aid in the *coup.* One result was that, after it, he stood very well with the new Directory, was given command of the army that was to invade England and left Italy in November 1797. The invasion, in the end, was deemed impossible, and in its place Napoleon took an army to Egypt, an expedition he wanted to undertake but one which was of no military use to France. The penalty for the Directory of relying on its generals for political support was that the generals began to determine its decisions.

Still another result of 18th Fructidor was that the new Directory, alarmed by the show of Catholic strength in France, was inclined for the moment to do nothing about the Papacy, or at least nothing open. It was unhappily aware, as one of its envoys had written to Napoleon in December 1796: "We have failed in our religious revolution. The French are once more Roman Catholic, and we have perhaps even reached the point where we need the Pope himself to ensure that our revolution is supported by the priests, and hence by the countryside which they have got once more in their power. Had we destroyed the Pope three years ago, we could thereby have regenerated Europe; to lay him low today would surely be to alienate for ever from our government a mass of Frenchmen who are faithful to the Pope."

But the soldiers in Italy were not among the Frenchmen faithful to the pope, and they and Italians from the Cisalpine Republic gradually forced the Directory into action. The Italian republicans, with the connivance or open aid of the French troops and political agents accompanying them, revolutionized first one town and then another inside the northern and western borders of the Papal States. Each town declared itself an independent republic or tried to join the Cisalpine Republic to the north or a new republic to the west which had declared itself in existence at Ancona. The confusion was immense, and in an effort to sort some order from it the Directory sent three generals to Rome. Their purpose was vague, and their presence, which excited local republicans to uprisings, only compounded the confusion.

Then an incident occurred. One of the generals was shot in a riot before the French embassy. The French ambassador, Joseph Bonaparte, withdrew to Tuscany, and the Directory gave secret orders to General Berthier to lead the French army over the mountains to Rome. Once there, Berthier was to force the pope to flee and to organize a Roman Republic. The orders were secret, so that if the plan went awry, the Directory could deny any knowledge of it and publicly reprove its obedient general. But it hoped that French interference would appear to the world as a spontaneous revolution of Roman republicans.

Starting from Ancona, Berthier and his army marched in eleven days across the mountains to the walls of Rome. During that time the Romans, led by their priests, exhausted themselves in prayer. As couriers brought news each day of the French advance, the city gradually slipped into religious hysteria. In every church priests lamented, choirs intoned and relics were exposed and closed and carried in procession from one church to the next. For eight days in St. Peter's the faithful appealed for the city's safety to the image of Santa Maria di Campitelli that supposedly had stopped the plague in 1656. Then it and the chains St. Peter was said to have been wearing when he saw Christ on the Appian Way were taken in solemn procession to Santa Maria Maggiore where they were exposed again and then on to San Giovanni in Laterano and finally back whence they had started, the Chiesa Nuova. Every day cardinals said mass, bells were rung and incense burned. Immense, stupified crowds stood or knelt for hours at a stretch. All work stopped, and the Papal government all but ceased to function. There was a rumor, spread from every pulpit, that the King of Naples would defend the city, but no Neapolitan troops appeared. "The Pope," observed the Spanish ambassador, "is insensible and does nothing but vegetate."

Finally, on 11 February 1798, Berthier entered the city without opposition, and his troops occupied the Castel Sant'Angelo and disarmed what was left of the Papal army. Then the French waited for the Romans to depose the pope in a republican revolution. But nothing happened. "I have found in this country," Berthier wrote to Napoleon, "nothing but the profoundest consternation and not a glimmer of the spirit of liberty; only one single patriot has come to see me." So Berthier had to order a revolution made. French soldiers and civilians circulated petitions calling on the French to assist in establishing a republic, and a few days later a rally of patriots was held in the ancient Forum. A tree of liberty was planted, there were speeches beginning "O Romans" and an *Act of the Sovereign People* was adopted. Then a provisional government was formed, and Berthier, with an olive wreath on his head, rode in state to the Capitol to give the new government his blessing.

There was, however, one point of disagreement. Under the *Act of the*

*Sovereign People* the Romans, while deposing the pope from his temporal power, had specified that he should retain his spiritual authority and be provided with buildings and moneys suitable to his position. Religion was Rome's only industry, and even republicans recognized that without it the city could not exist. But Berthier knew that, to the Directory in Paris, the pope was both the symbol and source of the continuing resistance in France of the "nonjuring" priests; and he knew that, in Rome, the pope's presence would sooner or later, even if only at his death, lead to a reaction in his favor. So he ordered Pius to leave within three days. It was a brutal thing to do. Pius was eighty, his legs were partially paralyzed, and to be jounced in a coach might well kill him. At very least it would be a torture. He refused and then agreed; the French, after all, could put him in a coach and order the driver to start.

At daybreak on the third day, with only two priests and a doctor, Pius started for Siena in neutral Tuscany. The Papacy in effect had ceased to exist. The pope no longer had any administrative or spiritual control of church affairs, the cardinals were dispersed and each bishop, in whatever country he served, was left to run his diocese as he saw fit. The Directory might well hope that after several years of such disorganization the bishops would have come to like their independence, and the Papacy thereafter would never be reconstructed.

Immediately after the pope left Rome, the civilian agents of the Directory arrived. Fourteen of them led by Haller, probably the man most hated by Italians of all states and classes, put the city to the sack. It was one of the greatest exercises in looting of modern times, and the most complete Rome had experienced since the days of the Vandals or the Habsburg sack of Rome in 1527. It began with Haller and his men making an inventory of everything in the Vatican and Quirinal palaces. When these were ready, a number of French businessmen, chiefly from Marseille and Lyon, who had financed Napoleon's crossing of the Alps, were invited to take their pick of the contents of both palaces, naming their own prices. As soon as these worthy men were taken care of, Haller packed almost everything of value and sent it to Paris. Furniture, plate, sacred ornaments, chasubles, ciboriums and even the best Papal carriages were carted off. Long lines of specially strong wagons, often painted red and drawn by oxen, started north with the loot among which were the Apollo Belvedere, the Laocoön and the busts of Junius and Marcus Brutus from the Capitol. The cases with the statues and paintings rested on rollers. The larger pictures had been taken off their stretchers and packed one above the other with padding between and then rolled on cylinders supported at the ends. Finally, the cases were tarred on the outside and then covered with a wax cloth as protection against the damp.

Behind the larger wagons went smaller ones with tools and spare parts. Mechanics and soldiers accompanied the convoys to protect them and to keep them moving. Even the famous *Propaganda Fide,* the best language school in Europe, was shipped *in toto:* presses, type, printers, teachers and students. Rome, the capital of the ancient world and the glory of its successor, the center of the civilized world for a thousand years, was to be superseded by Paris and the French Republic.

Besides the contents of the palaces every church in Rome was stripped of its gold and silver, and even the grave of San Filippo Neri was opened because he had been put in a silver coffin. St. Peter's alone produced four thousand pounds of silver and seventy of gold. Private wealth of every kind was plundered in the same fashion. The Borghese family, who had a fine stable of sixty horses, were left with only two old nags, and an eyewitness reported of the Villa Albani, in which a cardinal had assembled a collection of ancient sculptures: "Every statue, every bust, every column, every chimney-piece, every bit of marble of decorative value or practical use was torn from its place and either sent to Paris or taken there by the commissioners as presents for the members of the Directory." The loot from this villa alone filled 290 packing cases.

Not all the French in Rome approved of the looting. Many of the junior officers, meeting in the Pantheon to protest the arrears in their pay, drew up a statement for Berthier in which they demanded "the restoration of all property confiscated under various pretexts in the houses and churches of foreign neutral powers and that all buildings shall be restored to the state they were in before our troops moved in. Apart from our pay, we insist on the chastisement of the robberies committed by high-ranking monsters, corrupt and degenerate officials who wallow day and night in luxury and dissipation." And the next day they met again to issue a proclamation to the Romans in which they stated, "We came to give you freedom, not to plunder you of all you possess." They had no power to enforce their views, but there is no reason to doubt the sincerity of them. There is plenty of evidence that many individual Frenchmen including some generals were aghast at the behavior in Italy of their government and countrymen.

The Roman Republic was almost wholly corrupt and ineffective. The atmosphere of plunder never lifted, for after the commissioners and dealers in art came others, including Romans, who speculated on the paper money, on the tax collections or on the grain supply. With the Church and the rich being despoiled the number of unemployed rose steadily, and as convents and monasteries were closed, dispossessed nuns and monks were added to the number. Tourism and religion supported Rome, and one was interrupted and the other driven by the government, as a matter of principle, out of the city. Not only were there republican festivals at which bonfires were made of cardinals' hats, patents of nobility or anything else suggesting the old order, but even within the bare churches religious services were interrupted and sometimes prevented. The great majority of the Romans were offended and, as they came closer to starving, came to hate the French and the republic.

Outside the city the republican government had no authority at all. At the start sympathizers, in at least some of the towns, staged rallies such as the one at Velletri where a child dressed as a cherub, representing the new age, took the *Libro d'Oro* of the city from a very antique gentleman, representing time past. After a pretty, little speech the child tore out the pages which listed the nobility "and threw them into a brazier standing on an altar; while the patriots' applause rang out, and the little French garrison stood motionless in the square." But whatever enthusiasm there was soon turned into hatred of the French and the republicans. The country people were religious and enraged at the suppression of convents, the plundering of churches and persecution of priests. They lived in small towns of which they were inordinately proud, and the government ruled, with enormous consequences in administration, that no community of less than ten thousand souls was any longer a town. They were poor, and the government, in an effort to solve the crises at Rome, raised the taxes, and at the same time to save money it stopped work on some Papal projects such as draining the Pontine marshes. By the summer of 1798 revolt threatened everywhere and broke out in a number of towns, particularly in the south near the Neapolitan border. The French army succeeded in putting down the insurrections, but only with difficulty. Fighting in the hills and mountains around Rome was very different from fighting in the flat, open Po valley.

The next extension of French power in Italy, the conquest of Naples, was technically not of the Directory's choosing. Yet, by occupying the Papal States, it had produced a situation in which war at some time was almost inevitable. It had, by creating at Rome a republic hostile to the Bourbon monarchy at Naples, pinched off The Two Sicilies from trade with its nearest neighbor. It had, by plundering Rome and humiliating the pope, offended the highly emotional religious feelings of most Neapolitans and Sicilians, and it had, by failing to win the support of the peasants and townspeople to the south of Rome, created a border problem. Romans, noble or peasant, who did not like the republican regime often fled south of the border, rested and then returned, sometimes with active support, to renew their disagreement with the government. In such a situation the virtues needed, in both Paris and Naples, were patience, humor and emotional control, the very virtues lacked by both the Directory and Maria Carolina, still the dominant voice in the government at Naples.

The Directory's doctrinaire and provocative attitude appeared, for example, in the envoys it sent to Naples. One was Trouvé, who had so admired Napoleon at Mombello. For him republican principles came before common politeness and he refused, when presented, to kiss the king's hand or to stand when the king and queen entered the theater, and he demanded a biography of Louis XVI be banned because the author had described the National Convention, which ordered Louis' execution, as "regicide." In Trouvé's successor the Directory did no better, for it sent out the man who had announced the death sentence to Louis. Maria Carolina wrote to a friend: "You may easily imagine that I have no ardent desire to see this representative whose former embassy is ever before my eyes. But since it is a question of duty, I am ready to drain the chalice however bitter." But constantly having to do her duty clouded her eye with irritation so that she failed to see clearly what were the political and military realities of the moment.

She was eager to strike at the regicides who had killed her sister and brother-in-law, and she scolded the Emperor Francis in Vienna, who was both her nephew and son-in-law, for not renewing the war against France. There was much talk at the time that the Treaty of Campoformio was impossible, and she echoed it all without seeing that Francis needed a year or two of peace in which to reorganize his armies and finances; he, after all, had not looted the wealth of Italy. In her arguments at home she was seconded by a group of cardinals who had taken refuge at Naples and who spent their time urging Ferdinando to return them in state to Rome. And beside the voices of the cardinals there were those of the English colony at Naples which was led by the British minister, Sir William Hamilton. His young wife, Emma, had become one of the queen's best friends, and the friendship of the Hamiltons gave the British admiral, Nelson, when he came into port, the queen's ear.

Britain, after the Treaty of Campoformio, was the only state of the first coalition still at war with France. Ferdinando had withdrawn The Two Sicilies in October 1796, in the midst of Napoleon's campaign in the Po valley. By the terms of the treaty all Neapolitan and Sicilian ports were to be closed to belligerent shipping, which meant that Nelson could no longer rewater and reprovision his ships at these ports. It was a severe blow, and after eighteen months of handicap Britain responded by ordering its captains to regard as hostile any Mediterranean port which refused to let British ships reprovision. "Nominally neutral but never in our feelings," Maria Carolina had written Lady Hamilton after the treaty with France was announced. "We shall give proof of this on every available opportunity." And one proof of it was that Nelson was given, in June 1798, an informal order in the king's name authorizing all port governors of The Two Sicilies to give the British admiral supplies and assistance, *sub rosa*. It was an order which bound Naples to Britain and made its contribution, however small, to a major defeat for the Directory.

Napoleon, on his return to Paris after Campoformio, had organized an army for the invasion of Britain, and when this had not proved feasible, he had persuaded the Directory that he could take Egypt, loot the wealth of the Middle East and then march on to Bombay, taking from Britain her richest colonies and giving them to France. It was an ill-conceived plan, born of Napoleon's restless imagination. Two months after coming to Paris from Italy he had told his secretary: "I do not wish to remain here; there is nothing to do. They will not listen to anything. Everything wears out here. My glory is threadbare. This little Europe is too small a field. Great celebrity can be won only in the East." The glamor of the idea, himself as the new Alexander carrying civilization to the East, had obscured for him the significance of British sea power.

At first, however, he was favored by fortune. A terrible storm scattered Nelson's patrols along the French riviera, and Napoleon was able to sail from Toulon, with his entire expedition, undetected. The first news of him, which Nelson heard only three weeks later, was that the French had taken Malta, an island still controlled by the medieval Knights of St. John and over which Ferdinando claimed a vague suzerainty.

Guessing that Napoleon was aiming for Egypt, Nelson set off in pursuit. He still had not yet recovered his frigates, which had been scattered by the storm, and for lack of them on a foggy night he missed the French fleet by only a hair, arriving at Alexandria before it. Finding no ships, nor even hearing of any, he immediately sailed off to search the southern shore of Crete. The next day Napoleon arrived at Alexandria, disembarked his army and easily took the city from the astonished Mameluke governor.

Nelson, meanwhile, running short of water and food, put in at Siracusa on the eastern shore of Sicily. Producing his *sub rosa* order from Ferdinando he was able to rewater and provision and start back at once for Egypt. Without the order he would have had either to take what he needed by force or return to Minorca or Gibraltar.

This time, as he approached Alexandria, he saw the French tricolor over the city and beyond it to the east, in Aboukir Bay, thirteen French men-of-war at anchor. He saw that the French had moored in a line close to the shore but leaving enough room for their ships to swing at anchor without grounding, and he suspected, as proved true, that the shoreside guns were not ready for firing. Accordingly, he sailed straight up, split his fleet, sailing half between the shore and the French ships and anchoring them opposite the first six French vessels. These he also attacked from the seaside, concentrating all his fire power on half the French fleet, his favorite tactic. The battle began at half after six in the evening, and by seven it was dark, the only light being the flash of the guns and then, later, fire.

By dawn the victory was complete. Of the thirteen French men-of-war, nine were taken, two burned, and two, accompanied by frigates, of which Nelson still had none, escaped to sea. "Were I to die this moment," he wrote in his dispatches to the Admiralty, *"want of frigates* would be found stamped on my heart!" But the consequences of the victory were great enough without the destruction of every last French ship.

In London, Vienna and Naples the battle of the Nile was recognized at once as the greatest victory of the war. Not only was the Directory's Mediterranean fleet destroyed, but its best general and finest army were marooned in Egypt with no immediate possibility of escape. Maria Carolina was delirious with joy. According to Lady Hamilton, "She wept, she kissed her husband, her children, walked frantically about the room, burst into tears again, and again kissed and embraced every person near her, exclaiming, 'Oh, brave Nelson! Oh God! bless and protect our brave deliverer! Oh Nelson! Nelson! What do we not owe you! Oh conqueror-savior of Italy!' "

Three weeks later Nelson sailed into the bay of Naples and received a tumultuous welcome. All efforts of the king, court and people to preserve a show of neutrality broke down. As the *Vanguard* dropped anchor, every little boat or barge in Naples started from shore. Singers caroled joyful but vague versions of "Rule Britannia" and everyone, with each bobbing wave, shouted *"Evviva!"* The British envoy, Hamilton, was the first alongside and saluted with thirteen guns. He and then Lady Hamilton were hoisted aboard by a chair slung from the main yardarm, and Nelson in a letter to his wife, Fanny, described the scene: "Up flew her Ladyship, and exclaiming, 'Oh God, is it possible?' she fell into my arm more dead than alive. Tears, however, soon set matters to rights." The conquering hero, though not yet aware of it, had just been conquered.

After the Hamiltons there came the king, alone, for Maria Carolina was ill. He was greeted with twenty-one guns, and a lavish breakfast was served the guests. Later when Nelson went ashore, fishermen released hundreds of caged birds as he passed, and in the evening the British embassy with three thousand lamps blazed Nelson's name across the bay. It was an occasion no one there ever forgot, and it was all repeated with improvements a week later, for Nelson's fortieth birthday.

Throughout the summer, Ferdinando had been impressed by the urgings of the Marchese di Gallo to remain neutral, but now with Nelson's voice added to those already urging him to march on Rome, he began to waver. Gallo had recently returned from Vienna where he had been Ferdinando's ambassador and where also the Emperor Francis, disregarding national origins in a manner typical of the eighteenth century and of the Habsburgs, had used him to negotiate with Napoleon the preliminaries of Leoben and the Treaty of Campoformio. Gallo, more than any other Neapolitan, had had the opportunity to assess the relative strengths and weaknesses of the emperor and the French army. But now his voice of caution was drowned by the chorus calling for war.

Ferdinando's first move, on 21 November, was to publish a proclamation, one which so mixed reality and illusion that it caused some hilarity even at the time. He began by declaring that he wished to remain friends with France but was outraged by the seizure of Malta, which he claimed belonged to the Kingdom of Sicily. He protested that he would not suffer the Papal States to be invaded, belonging as they did to a former ally and to the head of the Church; and he announced that his army was marching into Roman territory to return it "to its legitimate sovereign." He therefore invited—and here the laughter broke out—all armed forces to withdraw from the Roman territory, on pain of having war declared on them.

To back up this warlike stand Ferdinando in the six weeks previous had expanded his army by forced levies from fifteen thousand to fifty thousand. To his regular officer corps he had added Swedish mercenaries, several princes from the German states and, as commander-in-chief, an Austrian, General Mack. Maria Carolina had hoped that the emperor would follow Ferdinando's example and declare war, but Francis refused, at least until the following spring at the earliest, to do more than to furnish a general. The sudden arrival of so many new officers into important posts naturally caused confusion; Mack, for example, could not speak Italian. It also caused resentment among the Neapolitan officers, and they became even more demoralized when Mack quickly demonstrated his total lack of ability. In war games outside of Naples he allowed himself to be surrounded and lost the battle to "the enemy." A good émigré general, Roger de Damas, who had been brought into the army nine months earlier, observed sadly: "Three quarters of the troops were only peasants in uniform who, never having been drilled, hesitated during firing exercises and barely satisfied the requirements for a simple review."

Such was the army Ferdinando planned to send against one of the best disciplined, most experienced and enthusiastic armies Europe had seen in more than a century. Just at the last, in a moment either of wisdom or fear, he hesitated. But Nelson berated him so to his face that he

*Carlo III di Borbone, while King of The Two Sicilies, by Francesco Liani*

*Maria Carolina, by Landini*

*Ferdinando I,*
*by Gennaro Maldarelli*

*Pius VII, by Sir Thomas Lawrence*

*Vittorio Alfieri*

*Ugo Foscolo, by Antonio Fabre*

Giacomo Leopardi

CASA DEL MANZONI, MILANO

*Alessandro Manzoni, in 1848, a drawing done "in two rainy hours" by his stepson Stefano Stampa*

*Giuseppe Mazzini in 1857 or 1858, a photograph circulated by the Sardinian police*

Carlo Alberto

Leopoldo II

Ferdinando II

From a popular print of 1848

*Daniele Manin*

*Pio Nono*

*Massimo d'Azeglio, by Francesco Hayez*

*Francesco II of The Two Sicilies*

*Cardinal Antonelli*

*Camillo Cavour, a photograph taken at the Congress of Paris, 1856*

*Bettino Ricasoli*

*Giorgio Pallavicino*

*Giuseppe La Farina*

*Giuseppe Cesare Abba*

*Giuseppe Verdi in 1853*

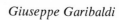
*Giuseppe Garibaldi*

*In Naples in 1860*

*In his old age*

*Vittorio Emanuele II*

*Pio Nono as "the Prisoner in the Vatican"*

gave in and ordered the campaign to proceed. On the third day's march the van met the French, not yet acknowledged to be the enemy. The Neapolitans, as they had been ordered, asked the French to withdraw, which the French did. Their general, Jean Championnet, planned to evacuate Rome except for a garrison of four hundred in the Castel Sant'-Angelo, and then when the Neapolitan columns were scattered through the Roman territories, to fall on them. He had no illusions about the identity of the enemy.

His plan worked brilliantly. General Mack rushed on into Rome, on 29 November, with his army straggled out behind him. Artillery, food, ammunition were all days behind. It had rained continually, the weapons were rusted and the men footsore and hungry. Instead of reorganizing the army Mack sent it out in columns to occupy villages and towns on all sides of Rome; he still assured the men they would never be attacked by the French. For a week the French stayed in the mountains, watching where each column went, noting its number, its artillery and possible support. For the same week Ferdinando stayed in Rome, celebrating himself as he had Nelson. Churches were reopened, bells rung, trees of liberty cut down and the pope invited back, although Ferdinando sometimes talked of annexing the Roman territories to Naples. Then Championnet began his attacks.

Each hour, it seemed, another defeated, demoralized column staggered back into Rome, often preceded by its officers. Two of the German princes, being wounded, simply abandoned their troops. Mack, although his army still outnumbered the French, ordered a retreat, and the first troops left Rome by the southern gates even as more troops arrived at the north and west with news of more defeats. The retreat soon became a rout. Ferdinando left hastily in a carriage and in such great fear of being captured that he is supposed, in order to conceal himself, to have exchanged uniforms with his aide. Mack was unable to keep any sort of organization, and soon each man thought for himself. Many of the peasants, on being ordered off the roads by officers fleeing in carriages, threw down their muskets and disappeared into the hills. Others, led by Damas and the Neapolitan Duke of Roccaromano, fought well and at a stream or a castle delayed the French for hours or even days. Damas, in his *Mémoires,* blames the collapse of the army on the ignorance, incapacity and even treachery of the commanding officers. Certainly the Swiss mercenary general, Tschudy, surrendered the impregnable fortress at Gaeta for no obvious military reason, and some of the Neapolitan officers seem to have had revolutionary sympathies and had suppressed dispatches.

Two weeks after starting from Naples, Ferdinando was back and wondering, in panic, if he should continue on to Palermo. His fear was real enough, and shared by most around him. But even it could not shake him free of all illusions. Now, from Naples, he issued a proclamation, antedated as though he were in Rome, declaring war on France: "While I am in the capital of the Christian world to reestablish the Holy Church, the French, with whom I have done everything to live in peace, are threatening to enter the Abruzzo [his most northern province]. I shall hasten with a mighty army to exterminate them; but in the meantime let the people arm, let them succour the Faith, let them defend their King and father who risks his life, ready to sacrifice it in order to preserve the altars, possessions, domestic honor and freedom of his subjects."

The country people responded magnificently. They were, like high-landers in many lands, illiterate, hardy and clannish, and they took poorly to discipline. But skulking around their mountains and valleys they were formidable, and the French found their easy victory was il-lusory as the provinces they supposedly had conquered rose in anger around them. The peasants, often led by their feudal overlords or priests, burnt bridges, destroyed supplies and even recaptured towns, generally killing all republican sympathizers. They even, unlike the demoralized army which could only flee or give up, made furious and unexpected stands against French troops. "A singular campaign, indeed," wrote one French general, "while huts that no soldier would have dared to defend, resisted till extermination, the best-armed places opened their gates as if at the wave of a wand."

Meanwhile, as the French drew nearer Naples, the panic at the court grew greater. Ferdinando in his fear imagined treachery everywhere and seemed uncertain what to do. Maria Carolina, however, never doubted: the Bourbons of Naples were not to be caught, imprisoned and executed by republican revolutionaries as had the Bourbons of France. Every day she packed clothes and valuables, sending them by night to Lady Hamil-ton, who then gave them to Nelson's seamen. They, in turn, stowed them aboard the British men-of-war against the day the royal family might leave for Palermo.

In the king's eyes Nelson was still the man of the hour, although he, more even than the Hamiltons, the prime minister John Acton or Maria Carolina, had influenced Ferdinando to declare war. Nelson had arrived from the battle of the Nile in an aura of glory; he had seemed to speak with the tongue of victory and with all the power and wisdom of Britain. But in fact he had not. The Foreign Secretary in London, throughout the same period, had insistently urged the Neapolitan ambassador to keep his country neutral until the Emperor Francis could be persuaded to renew the war. Nelson, so glorious at sea, stumbled badly on land. He had advised a secondary power, The Two Sicilies, to measure strength on a sudden against the greatest military power in Europe, and disaster had followed. Although a sensitive man, Nelson felt no responsibility for his bad advice. *"Down, down with the French!"* was the motto he once had suggested "ought to be written in the council-room of every country in the world." And to down the French he would use any tool at hand. If one proved unsuited for the job, then he would discard it with a curse. Nelson's comments on the Neapolitans, whose lives and country were being overturned partly because of his own bad judgment, were unpleasant and unfair. The Neapolitans, for their part, thought that the little group of influential English had ruthlessly sacrificed Naples to advance British interests.

Ferdinando, however, continued to rely on Nelson who, along with Maria Carolina, Acton and the Hamiltons, now urged him to take the royal family to Palermo with as much of their treasure as possible. Naples was not to be looted as Rome had been, and pictures, statues, the city's public funds and bank reserves were all quietly packed and stowed aboard either the *Vanguard* or a fleet of merchantmen anchored far out in the bay. Then on the night of 21 December the royal family, escorted by Nelson, left the palace by a secret passage and were rowed to the *Vanguard*. The next morning Naples awoke to find itself deserted by its king and faced with a royal proclamation stating that he had gone to Sicily to raise reenforcements for the army.

Unfortunately the weather was bad; the fleet could not leave; and each day it remained in the bay something more was revealed of the flight's planning that wounded Neapolitan sensibilities. The fault seems to have been an unhappy combination of Bourbon, Habsburg and British insensitivity. No member of the royal family, for example, would sail on a Neapolitan man-of-war, nor was any of the treasure stowed aboard one. The Neapolitan commodore, Caracciolo, who was a good sailor, was treated as though he were either incompetent or untrustworthy and simply ordered to follow along.

British subjects in Naples and French *émigrés* had boarded the ships about the same time as the royal family, but few Neapolitans had known of the flight. Now many of the nobility rowed out with hastily packed possessions and asked to be taken aboard, which they were. But they thanked the bad weather for their safety, not their king or his English friends. Then a cardinal, the municipal councilors and magistrates came out to plead for an audience with Ferdinando. Acton dismissed all but the cardinal who, admitted to the king's presence, begged him to remain. But Ferdinando would not. Historians wrangle over whether Ferdinando or Acton stated that he, Ferdinando, would return only when his subjects by their acts should have proved their loyalty. One contemporary Neapolitan, Carlo de Nicola, believing it was Ferdinando, wrote in his diary: "That a prince who is idolized by the entire nation should have been heard so to speak will lead posterity to believe that the King's trust in the Neapolitans has been ill-requited, and yet it is most certain that each one of us is devoted to him and would lay down his life for him. . . . he is betrayed by those nearest to him, the English have sacrificed him, and the desire for vengeance that animated his wife has ruined her and us."

So the king sailed away from his capital city. He had shipped his hunting dogs and guns with him, and the first night out he talked with Hamilton and his principal gamekeeper about the chances in Sicily for woodcock: "This wind will bring them—it is just the season, and we shall have rare sport."

The provisional government he had left behind in Naples signed an armistice with the French. By its terms the fortress of Capua was ceded as well as all Neapolitan territory north of a line drawn across the peninsula. In addition the Neapolitans were to pay an indemnity of ten million francs within two weeks, which was quite impossible as Ferdinando had taken all the money with him. In no time the provisional government had lost control over the city, and the lowest class, the *lazzaroni,* had begun to riot. When the French, unable to collect the indemnity, finally marched in, they were met by the highly excited *lazzaroni* who defended the city, street by street, for three days. The fighting was like that in the mountains: narrow, winding streets and subterranean passages made it difficult for the French to clear an area; the *lazzaroni* were constantly fading away only to burst out again in the rear. But General Championnet finally succeeded in turning the people's attention to looting the royal palace and those of some of the departed nobles, and by the end of January 1799 he had control of all the city's strong points and was able to impose order.

There were few genuine republicans among the Neapolitans and, as at Rome, the French had to create a spontaneous revolution and impose a republic on a people who plainly did not want one. So the Parthenopean Republic was born, by fraud and force, taking its name from the Greek city, Parthenope, which had occupied the site before a Neapolis (Napoli, in Italian), a new city, had replaced the old. Royalist wits, to show their classical learning was great as that of the republicans, pointed out that the city, Parthenope, had been named after one of the Sirens who had lured men to their destruction. But the republicans refused to be dismayed. With tremendous enthusiasm and idealism they set about destroying the feudal basis of society, abolishing primogeniture, discussing ways of redistributing the land and planning to suppress the religious orders and corporations. In the evening they went to performances of Alfieri's tragedies and philosophized about civic virtue.

Republics on the French model now stretched the length of Italy, the Cisalpine, the Roman and the Parthenopean. Besides these Genoa had been turned into the Ligurian Republic, and even more recently what independence had been left to the mainland provinces of Sardinia had been revoked by the French and a Subalpine Republic made of them. Like the Bourbons, Carlo Emanuele IV, who had succeeded his father as King of Sardinia, had been forced to retreat to the island half of his kingdom. Even little Lucca, in a desperate effort to keep its independence, had declared itself a revolutionized republic; the patricians had renounced all titles of nobility and special privileges and any man of property now could sit in their Senate. The Duchies of Parma and Tuscany retained a show of independence and the old forms of government, but in both every wish of France was quickly granted. Only in Venice, Sardinia and Sicily was French influence not supreme. After a century of France and Austria, Bourbon and Habsburg, fighting for dominance in Italy, it seemed for a moment as if a new, revitalized France, without the Bourbons, had finally won.

# CHAPTER 12

Ferdinando and Maria Carolina in Palermo. Ruffo's campaign in Calabria. The capture of Naples. Nelson. Caracciolo. Bourbon cruelty. The decline of Naples under Ferdinando.

FERDINANDO, deprived of his Kingdom of Naples, set about enjoying his Kingdom of Sicily which, at forty-eight, he was seeing for the first time. He fitted out a villa in the country for shooting and another by the sea for fishing; and when forced to remain in Palermo, he spent his evenings at parties or the theater. He fussed over the internal government of Sicily and talked of recovering Naples. But he left the doing of it almost entirely to others and, except for an occasional twist of temper, seemed perfectly happy. "The King, God bless him, is a philosopher," wrote Nelson, "but the Queen feels sensibly all that has happened."

After thirty years of marriage and seventeen children the difference in their temperaments was dividing them. Maria Carolina as much as Nelson was the very heart of opposition to France, and the king's inactivity, in the face of his appalling defeat, exasperated her. She felt the collapse of the army and loss of the capital city as a personal humiliation and was determined to recapture Naples, if possible, at once. Her spirit endeared her to Nelson but not to the king. He forgot that others had urged the same policy and blamed her alone for the incompetent General Mack and the disastrous war. He no longer trusted her judgment, and her suggestions, intrigue and activity, supported as always by tears and tirades, now only irritated him. More and more he stayed away from her, meeting his ministers at his villas.

Those around the court were quick to notice, and she might have lost all her influence over policy and appointments except that she still had Nelson's ear, and the king, more than ever, relied on Nelson. But it was a tortuous line, leading through Lady Hamilton, and although Nelson began in Palermo to live with the Hamiltons and to share the expenses of their palazzo, there were still times when he put to sea; and then the line was broken. In addition Maria Carolina still had Acton, the minister she had appointed and supported for twenty years, but he was now over sixty and less active; his influence with the king was decreasing, and because of the divided court she had less opportunity to see him. And he, too, was evidently a little tired of her, for he sometimes used ill-health as a pretext for avoiding an interview. Her power from this time began to decline, but as long as Nelson and the Hamiltons remained at court, she had a voice in affairs.

The king's return to Naples came sooner, perhaps, than even Maria Carolina had dared to hope but for reasons and in a fashion which had little to do with his efforts or hers to reorganize the Neapolitan army and navy. To the north, Britain had finally succeeded in forming a second coalition against France. Beside Britain there were Austria, Turkey and, appearing with troops for the first time in the heart of Europe, Russia. On 15 March 1799 a Habsburg army, operating from bases in the Veneto, crossed the Adige river into the Cisalpine Republic and by the end of April allied troops had taken Milan. At once French generals in Rome, Naples and other cities and forts south of the Po began to consider routes of retreat, and the bulk of the French army in and around Naples started north. It was enough to have one French army marooned in Egypt without another isolated in southern Italy. But even before the fall of Milan, mountaineers in the boot of Italy, led by a cardinal in purple on a white horse, had started a campaign to retake Naples which was proving surprisingly successful.

The cardinal, Fabrizio Ruffo, had followed Ferdinando and Maria Carolina to Palermo but had remained with them only four days. During that time he persuaded them he could save the foot of Italy, Calabria, from the republicans and perhaps also make a start on recovering Naples. He asked for money, guns and unlimited authority, and Ferdinando granted him all three. But the royal treasurer refused the money on the ground that the funds were already committed elsewhere, and the generals were so disinclined to release guns to a man they considered an amateur that Ruffo left Sicily without having received one. The king, however, held nothing back; he signed a decree authorizing Ruffo to act on the mainland as the king's vicar and *alter ego*.

On 7 February Ruffo crossed the Straits and landed in Calabria. He had with him only eight companions and a banner bearing the royal arms on one side, the cross on the other and inscribed *in hoc signo vinces*. He had, however, several unusual assets in his person. It was said at the time that even the most miserable peasant in Calabria had a crucifix on one side of his bed and a gun on the other; and Cardinal Ruffo was uniquely the man to appeal to both sides of peasant nature.

He was a member of one of the great feudal families of southern

Italy, a family which owned or controlled almost the entire province of Calabria and which, by marriage into the Roman aristocracy and service to the Church, had stretched its power northwards over half of Italy. Typically, Ruffo's mother had been a Colonna of Rome and one of his uncles an influential cardinal. His father had been the Duke of Baranello and Ruffo and his brothers held a variety of titles, castles, hunting lodges and villas scattered throughout southern Italy. Attached to each in varying degrees of feudal service were scores of peasants whose first loyalty was to their overlord, and from them Ruffo could recruit the core of an army and bind it to him with a strong feudal and personal loyalty. When he landed in Calabria, he went at once to the country house of a brother and hoisted his banner from the balcony. There was no need to test the loyalty of the peasants who gathered or to prove his right to be their leader.

In appealing to the other side of their nature he could exert the full glamor and power of his position as cardinal, a prince of the Church. His uncle who had been a cardinal had sponsored the young priest who later became Pius VI, and Pius in turn had sponsored Ruffo, making him Treasurer of the Papal States, a post which included the ministry of war. Ruffo had done well but had been forced to leave Rome in 1791 somewhat under a cloud; some said that his attempts at reform were unpopular, and others, that he had been too greedy in feathering his nest. But in leaving he retained the pope's good will, for it was then that Pius made him a cardinal, although Ruffo was not in orders. But this check in Ruffo's career at Rome, although possibly a reason he was eager to do something dramatic for the Church and thereby to rehabilitate himself, meant nothing to the country people and priests of Calabria. They saw in him only one who had been exceptionally close to the pope and who therefore spoke with all the pope's authority. When Ruffo raised his flag at his brother's house, he at the same time sent an encyclical letter to all the local bishops and priests, urging them to preach a crusade against the infidel republicans. Within a month he had an army of seventeen thousand.

He called it the Christian Army of the Holy Faith, and the men fighting in it or even merely sympathetic with its aims were known as *Sanfedisti* or "Holy Faith-ers." They were a mixed group, including every kind of ecclesiastic, some rich landowners and many artisans from the towns and peasants from the mountains and fields. There were also men, as Ruffo described them, "of no good intention and stability." Others, more bluntly, called them "assassins and thieves, thirsty for plunder, vengeance and blood."

To feed the army Ruffo imposed forced loans, payable in cash or kind, on the estates of landowners living in French-occupied territory, and to show his impartiality he again started with the estate of a brother. But many landowners, monasteries and towns voluntarily contributed food, money or guns, and a deputation from one town typically offered Ruffo a letter of loyalty to the king, ten thousand ducats and eleven fine horses for himself. The sight of the white-haired cardinal on a beautiful Arab, followed by his staff and banner, excited the Calabrians tremendously. Every man of them loved first, shooting, and then horses, and had been raised on epic stories of Christian warriors fighting the Saracens. The cardinal and his crusade were childhood fantasy become real.

Ruffo consciously fostered this image of himself in the interests of discipline. The only hold he had on the men was his personal magnetism, and he did everything possible to increase it. He worked in his cardinal's robes and generally rode a white horse to show them off; he constantly walked among the men, sat with them, ate their food and allowed them in his presence to talk only of *guapperie,* a Calabrian term for deeds of valor. But his control of them was slight at best and disappeared almost entirely whenever fighting began.

As his army approached the town of Cotrone, every man in the neighborhood who had a gun joined it, so that, as Ruffo's secretary later wrote, "they increased like a torrent in flood." Looking out from the town walls the Cotronesi were aghast. The ranks of ragged, half-naked but excited peasants were a mile deep, and the republicans who had captured the town's government and reenforced its little garrison with thirty-two French noncommissioned officers were able to argue that the town would be sacked whether it defended itself or not. Therefore better to fight. So they rejected the cardinal's terms, and after a long night's siege the town was taken. Undoubtedly in the sack that followed many more townfolk were murdered for being rich than revolutionary, and even historians with a Bourbon bias admit that it was a sack from which the town "never recovered."

Ruffo was appalled by the slaughter and, in his role as general, horrified to see seven-eighths of his army, staggering under its plunder, head for the hills and home. For most of the peasants a few valleys made up their entire world, and Naples was a dim and distant place where the king reigned, like God in Heaven. So that as Ruffo advanced up the peninsula, he had constantly to recruit his army anew and begin again with discipline.

But in spite of all his efforts the campaign continued to be bloody, with frightful atrocities on both sides. Ruffo always offered the towns in which republicans had gathered good terms; he left escape routes open and in private messages urged that they be used. But the republicans frequently behaved as if they had lost their senses. At Altamura, before retreating up the road to Naples, which Ruffo had obligingly left open, they shot forty-eight royalist prisoners, chained in couples, and pushed them, dead and dying, into a vault of a cemetery. The next day the Cardinal's men lifted the blood-stained slab and discovered among the dead several who were still gasping for breath. Three ultimately survived. But a republican sympathizer from the town, even as he was talking to Ruffo, was shot dead by a relative of one of the many who had died. Avenging family honor was something even a cardinal's presence could not slow.

But still, the people of Altamura fared better than those of Cotrone and in part because of Ruffo. Having fought till their ammunition was exhausted, the leaders of the town, as opposed to the republicans, determined to evacuate their people. During the night the men made a sortie to the front, shouting and clashing iron spoons and pans, while the women and children went out the open road at the back and dispersed in the hills. Among them was the composer Mercadante, then a boy of four. Ruffo's men the next morning poured into the empty city and sacked it. Ruffo soon proclaimed a general pardon and invited the inhabitants back to their plundered homes. Gradually they drifted in, preserved in life if not in property.

By the end of May, Ruffo was at the outskirts of Naples. A squadron of British ships blockaded the bay, and small detachments of Turkish and Russian troops, symbols of the second coalition, were cooperating with Ruffo on shore. The Parthenopean Republic had dwindled to the city of Naples and a few strongholds to the north of it. Its forces were few and desperate.

The French army, except for a garrison left in one of the forts of Naples, had long since retreated north, and although its departure had left the city and Republic almost defenseless, even the republicans had been half-glad to see it go. The Directory had tried to squeeze money out of Naples just as they had at Rome. On the heels of the army had come a Civil Commissioner who had confiscated every form of royal property including the deer in the palace parks and the antiquities from Pompeii and Herculaneum. He had put the commission's seal on the property of all banks, convents, monasteries and absentee landlords, even of foreigners whose countries were at peace with France; it had appeared on the mint, on the customs and even on the saltworks at Barletta. Nothing was spared that produced income, and all income was to go to France; or to the Civil Commissioner, for he had also imposed a special war tax payable to himself alone.

The French general, Championnet, who believed in the ideals for which he had fought and who wanted the new republic born of them to succeed, protested to the Directory. Even more, he expelled the commissioner and his henchmen from Neapolitan territory. But the Directory, which refused to recognize the Parthenopean Republic, preferring to treat Naples as a conquered province, supported the commissioner. Championnet was recalled to France and court-martialed for insubordination.

Deserted by the French, the Neapolitan republicans drew together, although even the city's imminent capture could not stop the flow of their rhetoric. The Legislative Council continued to debate the abolition of fiefs just as if it, and not Ruffo, controlled Calabria, and at night for inspiration the legislators went to the Patriotic Theater to hear Alfieri's *Timoleone*. But what power the government still had now shifted to the men controlling the forts and gunboats. The most famous of these was Commodore Caracciolo. He had returned to Naples, with the king's permission, to protect his property which the republic was threatening to seize and once there, after some hesitation, he had agreed to command its gunboats. To explain his change of allegiance he published a proclamation in which he accused the English surrounding the king of misleading and betraying him and "of sacrificing every right to their own interest." Now as Ruffo approached the city along the southern shore of the bay, Caracciolo fought a fine series of delaying actions for the republic.

The closer Ruffo approached to Naples the more orders, counter-orders and letters of advice he received from Ferdinando in Palermo. First, he was to await the arrival of Nelson who was to take supreme command. Then he was told that Nelson had instead sailed off to intercept a French fleet coming to the republic's aid, and he was ordered, unless he had already taken the city, to withdraw to an impregnable position outside it. The order was one he probably could not have executed at any time, given the sort of irregular army he commanded, but now it was plainly too late. He already held one of the city's four forts, the republicans were concentrating in the other three, and fighting and pillaging had broken out in all sections of Naples. If the city was to be preserved from total destruction by riot, fire and anarchy, he had to proceed to gain control of it.

Even so, for almost a week, despite all of Ruffo's efforts to stop them, his men and the *lazzaroni* indulged in an orgy of murder and plunder. Most people of any substance fled from the city or sought safety inside the forts, for as Ruffo wrote to Acton, it was the possibility of plunder that generally preceded an accusation of republicanism. And the accusation once whispered, an assault by the mob generally followed. The lucky ones were taken before Ruffo, who even so lamented: "They must have massacred or shot at least fifty in my presence without my being able to prevent it, and wounded at least two hundred whom they dragged here naked." He was able, however, to preserve several thousand by imprisoning them in the warehouses by the shore. There they suffered agonies of hunger and thirst, were robbed and terrified by the guards, but they did survive. The less lucky, several thousand more, were shot in the streets or market places, many having been tortured first. Ladies were forced to pose naked as Liberty or were minutely examined to discover if they were tattooed with its sign, and many were pelted with filth before being shot. After death their heads were sometimes used as soccer balls and their flesh cooked and eaten.

In an effort to end the carnage quickly and to free his better disciplined soldiers for police work, Ruffo offered good terms to those still in the three forts. In doing so he consciously ignored the intent of his sovereigns to punish vigorously. Ever since leaving Calabria he had received letters from his king and queen such as one in which Maria Carolina had written: "Rebellious Naples and her ungrateful citizens shall make no conditions: order must be restored to that monstrous city with rewarding the faithful and chastising the wicked as an example." Ruffo, of course, did not reply that she had fled with her cash and jewels while most of the ungrateful citizens, remaining in their city, had fought the French and lost everything. But he did complain to Acton: "What is the use of punishing; indeed, how is it possible to punish so many persons without an indelible imputation of cruelty?"

Ferdinando was as eager to punish as Maria Carolina, although more unctuous: "As a Christian I pardon everybody, but as he whom God appointed, I must be a strict avenger of the offences committed against Him, and of the injury done to the state and so many poor unfortunates." But to Ruffo a policy of forgiveness was morally right, in the long run politically wise and for the moment, in view of the chaos in Naples, expedient. He offered the commanders of the forts, as well as persons who had taken refuge in them, the honors of war and the right to remain in Naples if they chose or to embark for Toulon. Under these terms a man like Caracciolo, who was thought to be in one of the forts, was free to go to France.

The terms were agreed upon and signed by the commanders of the forts, by Ruffo and by those in command of the Russian, Turkish and British detachments cooperating with him. The last signature, that of Captain Foote who commanded the British squadron, was received on 23 June and, under the terms, those going to Toulon were to embark on the twenty-fifth. Those electing to remain in Naples, meanwhile, dispersed quietly in the city. Then late on the twenty-fourth Nelson, with the Hamiltons aboard, sailed into the bay with eighteen men-of-war and, on hearing of the agreement, repudiated it.

He had no order from the king to do so, for neither he nor the king had known of the capitulation or its terms. Nor had he at this time any order putting him in command of Ruffo who was still, in the Kingdom of Naples, the king's vicar-general and *alter ego*. But what Nelson did have was a fleet that could pulverize the city and through which no transport ships could sail to Toulon. He had also the certain knowledge that both Ferdinando and Maria Carolina wished the republicans forced to surrender without conditions and thereafter punished and that they had both repeatedly stated as much to Ruffo.

First Nelson summoned Captain Foote and, on being shown a copy of the capitulation agreement, told him that he "had been imposed upon by that worthless fellow, Cardinal Ruffo, who was endeavoring to form a party hostile to the interests of his Sovereign." Captain Foote, however, described what the situation in Naples was, and had been, and urged Nelson to honor the agreement. Nelson then ordered Foote to take the fastest ship and sail to Palermo for orders.

The next day Ruffo and the commanding officers of the Russian and Turkish forces each visited Nelson on his flagship, the *Foudroyant,* and tried to persuade him to allow the agreement to operate. But Nelson threatened, if he saw the garrisons and people in the forts embarking, either to keep them prisoners in their ships or, if that proved too difficult, to blow the ships and the people in them, out of the water. Nelson spoke no Italian and very poor French, so that at these conferences one or the other of the Hamiltons generally acted as his interpreter. When Ruffo went out to the *Foudroyant* a second time, Nelson merely handed him a memorandum to the effect that upon his arrival at Naples he had discovered an agreement with rebels which he considered should not be executed without the king's approval.

On ship as well as on shore, therefore, everyone, nervous and angry, awaited Foote's return. Yet neither side ceased to act. On shore, Ruffo, in an effort to make good on as much of his agreement as he could, suggested to the Neapolitans in the forts that, whether soldier or civilian, they disperse within the city and take their chances of being discovered later and brought to trial. But the republicans suspected a trap and refused. On the *Foudroyant,* Lady Hamilton saw one of the leaders of the *lazzaroni* and, in an effort to undermine Ruffo ashore, arranged for the man to be furnished with guns. As a result he and his men were able to ignore Ruffo's edict that nonbelligerent citizens were not to be molested, and there was more murder and looting and even pitched battles between Ruffo's troops, struggling to keep order, and gangs of the *lazzaroni*.

Then, before Foote's return from Palermo, the stalemate between Ruffo and Nelson resolved although in a fashion that has ever since kept historians arguing over whose faith was bad. Ruffo received from Hamilton a letter stating that Nelson was "resolved to do nothing which could break the armistice," and also, from two of Nelson's captains, a written statement on Nelson's behalf that he would not oppose the embarkation of the Neapolitan soldiers and civilians in the forts. Ruffo, the other commanders on shore and those in the forts took these letters to mean that Nelson had changed his mind. Ruffo celebrated the event with a service in the Church of the Carmine at which he presided as a prince of the Church, and he also wrote a note of thanks to Hamilton and Nelson. Hamilton replied: "I can assure Your Eminence that Lord Nelson congratulates himself upon his decision not to interrupt the operations of Your Eminence, but to assist you with all his power to conclude the affair which Your Eminence has conducted so well hitherto in the very critical circumstances in which Your Eminence has been placed."

So the Neapolitan republicans embarked, the forts were occupied by the royalist forces, and then Nelson refused to let the transports sail. Soon thereafter Foote sailed into the bay with letters from the king and queen. The capitulation was repudiated; nothing but unconditional surrender was acceptable, and Nelson began to transfer leading republicans from the transports to the brigs of his British ships.

Maria Carolina set the tone for their treatment in a letter to Lady Hamilton: "Finally, dear Milady, I recommend Lord Nelson to treat Naples as if it were a rebellious city in Ireland which had behaved in such a manner. We must have no regard for numbers: several thousands of villains less will make France the poorer, and we shall be better off. They deserve to be dropped in Africa or the Crimea. To throw them into France would be a charity. They ought to be branded so that nobody could be deceived by them. Thus I recommend to you, dear Milady, the greatest firmness, force, vigor and rigor."

And so they were treated, not as men and women who had surrendered on conditions agreed upon or even as prisoners of war but as common criminals, and their treatment left scars of hatred running through Neapolitan society which even the passage of time could never entirely heal.

Historians have never agreed on the extent to which Nelson was personally responsible for the deception. Some have put the entire blame on Hamilton, and a few have even suggested that Ruffo was so eager to resolve the stalemate that he read into the messages what was not there. But it seems likely that, at very least, Nelson was a willing accomplice. He was, although on shipboard, anxiously watching the shore, and two of the forts were on the shore directly before him. If he did not himself see the soldiers and civilians evacuating the forts and going out to their ships, it is absolutely incredible that his lookouts did not report the movement to him. Yet at the time or later he never seems to have questioned what was happening or why, although it was the movement he had alerted his entire fleet to prevent; and after the movement was accomplished, he never suggested he was surprised by it. Neapolitans of every political persuasion have never doubted that in this instance Nelson acted dishonorably.

Unfortunately for his reputation, in the succeeding days he was at the center of still one more incident which although not so serious was in some ways even more sensational. One of Caracciolo's servants, in order to gain a reward, betrayed his master, and at 9 A.M. on 29 June Caracciolo, still in peasant disguise, was brought aboard the *Foudroyant*. Nelson had letters from both the king and queen urging him to punish Caracciolo above all others, and the tone and sentiment of these letters reenforced his own ideas of the need for naval justice to be swift. He immediately convened a court-martial on the *Foudroyant,* appointing as its members five Neapolitan officers and as its president a Count Thurn, an Austrian in the royal service. At ten the trial began, and by noon Caracciolo had been found guilty of treason and condemned to death by hanging. There was no question of his guilt. Many witnesses testified that they had seen him, while in command of the republic's gunboats, order his men to fire on his former ship, the *Minerva*. But no witnesses for the defense were heard, his plea for another trial was denied, as was also his request that he be shot rather than hanged. Under Neapolitan custom at the time the nobility, if executed, were beheaded or at least shot; hanging was for common criminals, and Caracciolo, as a commodore and a prince, felt the disgrace of it keenly. But his request to be shot was rejected by Nelson personally and at five in the afternoon Caracciolo was hanged from the foreyard of the *Minerva* and left hanging till sunset when his body was cut loose and allowed to drop into the sea. It was then retrieved, carried far out in the bay, and sunk with heavy shot tied to its legs.

The execution, which was plainly visible from the shore, made a tremendous impression on the Neapolitans. They were not used to swift, public justice, particularly not when it involved a member of one of the city's greatest families. They conceived of justice in more personal terms, something direct between the king and his subject or, on a lower level, of a vendetta. They did not see in Nelson's actions an example of impartial British justice or even of Neapolitan justice, for the king was miles away and knew nothing about the trial which, in any event, was on a British ship. They saw only a personal vendetta pursued by a British admiral against a distinguished Neapolitan, a vendetta masquerading as justice. Once again, regardless of political persuasion, most Neapolitans felt that Nelson had acted dishonorably.

Historians have argued the rights and wrongs of his swift justice. He was, by letters from Palermo, empowered to arrest even Ruffo so that he was unquestionably the supreme commander of all royalist forces at Naples, and a strong argument can be made that all his actions were legal and truly reflected the king's intent. Yet Neapolitans at the time and others since have wondered why Caracciolo alone of the rebels was not preserved to be tried by the civilian and military courts the king later appointed for that purpose; why no witnesses were heard in his defense, however futile; and why he was denied an appeal, even if only to his Sovereign for mercy.

But the incident did not end even with the unfortunate man's execution. Shortly thereafter Ferdinando came to visit his rebellious city of Naples, and for four weeks he lived aboard the *Foudroyant,* occasionally fishing or shooting seafowl but never once setting foot on shore. Cardinal Ruffo went out to plead with him to observe the terms of the capitulation, but Ferdinando, with the support of Nelson and the Hamiltons, was adamant.

Then one day a fisherman reported that Caracciolo had risen from the bottom of the sea and was swimming back to Naples. Soon thereafter the body appeared, upright in the water, still clothed and recognizable, and moving slowly toward the *Foudroyant* and the king. Ferdinando, as superstitious as any of his subjects was aghast. "What does he want?" he murmured. "Christian burial, Sire," answered a chaplain, and Ferdinando, with a shudder, ordered it done. The body was towed to Santa Lucia and buried in the Church of Santa Maria la Catena. Later Ferdinando tried to pretend that the dead man had come to ask his pardon, but many Neapolitans saw in the grisly episode a reproof by the good God in Heaven of Ferdinando and Nelson.

But they, if they were bothered by it at all, quickly recovered, and when news came of the surrender of the last republican strongholds, at Gaeta and Capua, they planned to celebrate the recovery of the whole kingdom which coincided, most opportunely, with the first anniversary of the battle of the Nile. A grand illumination of the British and Neapolitan fleets was planned for the evening of 1 August, and on that night the king dined with Nelson, drank his health and had a royal salute of twenty-one guns fired in his honor. Then, as Nelson described it in a letter to his wife, Fanny: "A large Vessel was fitted out like a Roman galley; on its oars were fixed lamps, and in the centre was erected a rostral column with my name; at the stern were elevated two angels supporting my picture. In short, my dear Fanny, the beauty of the whole is beyond my powers of description. More than 2000 variegated lamps were suspended round the Vessel. An orchestra was fitted up, and filled with the very best musicians and singers. The piece of music was in a great measure to celebrate my praise, describing their previous distress. *But Nelson came, the invincible Nelson, and they were preserved and again made happy.* This must not make you think me vain; no, far, very far from it. I relate it more from gratitude than vanity."

Then later, when Nelson returned with the king to Palermo, there were more festivities, this time honoring the Hamiltons as well. Life-size wax images of the famous three were enshrined in a Temple of Fame over which the goddess appeared blowing a trumpet. Maria Carolina gave Lady Hamilton a diamond necklace as well as a miniature of herself and two coachloads of dresses to replace those left behind in the flight from Naples. Ferdinando did as much for Sir William Hamilton, and Nelson he made Duke of Bronte, a Sicilian duchy with lands and rents attached to the title. He also gave him the family sword, the one Louis XIV had first given to his grandson Philippe de Bourbon and which Philippe had given to Carlo III and Carlo to Ferdinando. Hardly anything Ferdinando could have given to Nelson would better have symbolized Ferdinando's abdication of his duty to govern his own kingdoms.

In all the festivities Ruffo was always slighted. He received honors and awards but always less, and of all the persons at court only Maria Carolina had any sense of what Ruffo had accomplished. For the king and courtiers who followed his lead, it was all Nelson. Ruffo's title and position of Vicar-General was abolished, and he was given the high-sounding but inactive position of Lieutenant and Captain-General of the Realm. His army was partly absorbed into a new and reorganized Neapolitan army, but the greater part simply dispersed and went home. For most of his men the great adventure was over.

It was for Ruffo, too. He quickly saw that he had no support at court, was even suspect and soon retired altogether from political life. With him went much that the monarchy could have used to advantage. His proposed policy of leniency was almost immediately proved right. On Ferdinando's orders a scaffold and a gallows, for nobility and common folk, were set up in the market place of Naples and remained there for ten months while special courts tried republican prisoners. Estimates of the number executed vary widely, and there can be no certainty as court records were later destroyed as part of an amnesty. A conservative count by the pro-Bourbon historian, Harold Acton, suggests that: "Of 8000 political prisoners 105 were condemned to death, six of whom were reprieved, 222 were condemned to life imprisonment, 322 to shorter terms,

288 to deportation and 67 to exile, from which many returned: a total of 1004." The balance were set free after being held for various terms in prison.

But however few or many were executed, the number was great enough so that the contemporary De Nicola wrote in his diary: "The execution of prisoners of state has become a matter of such indifference, that it no longer makes any impression: it does not serve as an example to the people, nor has the ignominy that used to belong to this punishment any part in the present executions."

Even worse, Ferdinando's policy made heroes and martyrs of the monarchy's enemies at a time when the great majority of his subjects were prepared to despise them. The leaders, a tiny minority of the country, were unquestionably traitors, men and women who were prepared to call in a foreign army to impose on their neighbors a form of government which their neighbors most emphatically did not want. Yet Neapolitans as a whole disapproved when Ferdinando allowed a young man, somewhere between sixteen and twenty years old, to be executed for breaking the head off a statue of Carlo, the king's father. And they admired extravagantly a nobleman like Ettore Carafa who, on going to the block, insisted on lying on his back with his eyes unbandaged so that no one could say he had flinched in the face of death. Even Ferdinando, when he was told of it, used the Calabrian term for valor and observed with approval: "He played the *guappo* to the end."

In a few months the imputation of cruelty, which Ruffo had feared, attached itself to the monarchy, and even the pasage of a hundred years could not wipe it away. It was a burden the monarchy carried to its fall in 1861.

There were also lost opportunities, harder to gauge, but just as real. Ferdinando and his ministers did nothing with the spirit and excitement Ruffo had stirred among the people south of Naples. The crusade had taken men out of their valleys, exposed them to new sights and ideas, and awoken in them, or put in them, the new idea that they were all Neapolitans driving the foreigners out of their country. The idea was tightly entwined with that of Christians driving out infidels and as such reflected the close involvement of Church and State throughout the kingdom, particularly in the country provinces. But Ruffo's campaign had added something new; there was a feeling, a fact say some historians, that the campaign was a people's war against foreign invaders, a war springing from the anger of the people rather than from the policy of a court. In this sense it was the same kind of national war, in reaction to the French, that ultimately would defeat Napoleon in Spain and Germany.

This feeling might have been harnessed by Ferdinando to support the monarchy, particularly in its efforts to spread the king's power and law as opposed to that of the local baron. But Ferdinando did nothing with it. In his two kingdoms he knew only Palermo and Naples and seemed not to care for the rest. In fact, he reinstituted a number of taxes which he had allowed Ruffo to abolish, so that the king's return to Naples for the great mass of the people south of the city meant hard times again. Feudalism continued just as before, although perhaps with a little more peasant unrest; and localism, always an Italian vice, became even worse as poverty-stricken survivors in towns and valleys brooded over property lost and relatives killed.

In Naples itself all the forward momentum gathered under Carlo came to a halt. The decline in Neapolitan music was typical of what happened throughout Neapolitan life, in the arts, in the professions and at the university. The city's two most famous composers were Cimarosa and Paisiello, both of whom have operas still performed. Cimarosa, although *maestro di cappella* to the king, had refused to go to Palermo and, staying in Naples, had written odes and cantatas for the republic. He was imprisoned, released at the request of the Habsburg emperor, and soon after died in Venice. Paisiello, who had also remained at Naples, slowly worked his way back into royal favor only to be sent by the king, at Napoleon's request, to Paris. Meanwhile at a lower level the city's music schools, the most famous in Italy, struggled to find new pupils and teachers to replace those lost in the confusion of the times. But, largely, they failed, and the successors of Cimarosa and Paisiello were not of their caliber. After the Napoleonic wars were over, it became clear that the lead in Italian music had shifted to Milan where the authorities gave the art and its practitioners more active and intelligent support than did Ferdinando in Naples.

In similar fashion the glory of the University of Naples also departed, symbolically with the deportation of Vicenzo Cuoco, who had studied under men who had studied under Genovesi and Vico. But Cuoco had supported the republicans actively and was forced into exile. He took refuge in Milan and there, reflecting on his studies and experiences, wrote his *Saggio Storico,* or *Historical Essay on the Neapolitan Revolution of 1799.* It was published in 1801, and influenced many whose thoughts, like his, had been shaken by the turbulent events through which they had lived. In it Cuoco looked forward to Italy's gradual reunification; in effect, he took the legacy of Vico, Genovesi, Verri and Alfieri and shaped it into a political system. His emphasis was on man, and he predicated that a nation, like a man, had an individuality and a right to self-government and that language was a nation's expression of its history, customs and philosophy. These views, perhaps now for the first time consciously expressed as a political program, became the philosophic core of the Risorgimento, and it was a tragedy for Naples and its people that they could be expressed by a Neapolitan only in exile.

Ferdinando was not personally responsible for all the unhappy results in Naples of the Napoleonic Wars, but for the first disaster, which divided and impoverished his kingdom, he certainly was. And although he reigned, with interruptions, until 1825, he had neither the inclination nor ability to repair the damage, much less to continue building along the lines his father had started.

Under Ferdinando, Naples, which at the start of his reign, in 1759, had been one of the most brilliant and important cities of Europe, gradually slipped into relative unimportance, even in Italy. In the coming century, throughout the period of the Risorgimento, it continued to be the largest city on the peninsula and the Kingdom of The Two Sicilies to be the richest, in an absolute sense, of all the Italian states. Yet the great ideas and men of the Risorgimento were born in other states, and the majority of men who actively supported or opposed those ideas did battle for them in other cities. The most vital part of Italian life in the nineteenth century had moved elsewhere, with consequences for Naples and Italy which continue today.

# CHAPTER 13

Death of Pius VI at Valence. Napoleon returns from Egypt. 18 and 19 Brumaire (9 and 10 November 1799) First Consul. Conclave at Venice. Pius VII and his Christmas homily. Marengo.

AS THE FRENCH GAVE ground before the Austrians and Russians in the Po valley, their armies to the south hastened northward, bringing with them republicans who dared not stay behind and an occasional prisoner who might prove useful. The most distinguished of these was the pope, Pius VI, who had been expelled from Rome by the French in February 1798 and imprisoned, though lightly, in Siena. Six months later the Directory had ordered him moved to Florence, where he was more closely confined. In name, Tuscany was still neutral, but in fact Grand Duke Ferdinando III had no independence and did whatever the Directory suggested. Pius, now eighty-one and his legs wholly paralyzed, was kept in the Certosa outside the city, was allowed only an occasional visitor and was denied even his nephew, Duke Braschi, as an attendant.

But in another six months the French were evacuating Florence, and the Directory ordered Citizen Pope, as it called him, to be moved across the Apennines to Bologna. The coach trip nearly killed the old man, but when he asked to be allowed to die in Rome, he was told "one can die anywhere." From Bologna he was moved again, to Parma, into Piedmont, then over the Alps to Briançon. The Directory planned to take him to Paris or at least to Lyon, but by Valence it was plain that he could be dragged no further. In an old fortress converted into a civic center, the Hôtel du Gouvernement, in a bed from which he could see the Rhône and the mountains, on 29 August 1799 Pius died. He had been pope for twenty-four years and six months, the longest pontificate since the traditional twenty-five years of Saint Peter.

In Valence the town officials, with an ear tuned to smart republican talk in Paris, announced the death of the last pope and refused him any honors. The local clergy were all members of that Constitutional Church which Pius had condemned as schismatic and heretical, and they refused

131

to bury him. On the other side, the few Roman priests who had followed Pius to Valence were adamant that he should not be buried from a "Constitutional" cathedral or even in schismatic soil. They insisted the body be returned to Rome and interred with full honors. But those who had the power to make arrangements lacked the interest, and day after day the pope's body lay in its coffin, without Christian burial.

A week before the pope died Napoleon, abandoning his army in Egypt, had set sail secretly for France. A reason which he loudly proclaimed, after he was safely away, was that France had need of him, that a corrupt and ignorant government, the Directory, had squandered its position in Italy and seemed unable even to keep the enemy from its borders. Another, which he did not trumpet so loudly, was his feeling that in Egypt he could no longer advance himself, whereas in France, under a tottering government, he could. So one morning the splendid soldiers who for his sake, under strange and tropical skies, had faced hunger and thirst, wounds and death, suddenly found themselves deserted, and even General Jean Baptiste Kléber, who was left in command, only learned of his appointment by letter, too late to protest. Napoleon's Egyptian romance, which had begun in a blaze of glory, ended in a conspirator's flight.

Twice he was in sight of Nelson's patrols, but each time he was able to slip by and, on 9 October, landed on the riviera at Fréjus. The Directory was uncertain how to receive him, whether to court-martial him for leaving his post in the face of the enemy or to share in his popularity by embracing him as a hero. In the end it tried to ignore him, relying on time to fade his glory. But most Frenchmen had been dazzled by the glamor of the pyramids; they had never questioned the purpose of the expedition or the rhetoric of his bulletins, which had constantly exaggerated the numbers of the enemy and, at Acre, had even turned a defeat into victory. They had contrasted the recent defeats in Italy with the memory of his victories and felt that he was the man for France. They greeted the news of his return with wild enthusiasm, and his journey north to Paris became a triumph. When he reached Valence, he discovered in the Hôtel du Gouvernement a forlorn group of Italian priests huddled in a corner. Inducing them to talk he learned that they were watching over the body of Pius VI which, sealed in a coffin, was still in the Hôtel, unburied and unhonored.

"*C'est trop fort!*" he exclaimed. "It is too much!"

Proceeding on to Paris he organized with the Abbé Sieyès, a Director, the *coup d'état* of 18 and 19 Brumaire (9 and 10 November 1799), days famous for Napoleon's rise to civil power. Their coup involved both fraud and, as it turned out, violence, and finally, as between themselves, deception of Sieyès by Napoleon.

The fraud lay in the protest of the conspirators, at every step, that they intended to preserve a republican form of government. Republicanism was still the strongest political force in the country. It was the creed of some of the best generals, such as Moreau and of at least two of the five Directors; it was the creed of the great majority of the legislative assembly, the Council of Five Hundred, and of the great majority of the people of Paris. Any *coup d'état,* therefore, which seemed to put in issue a republican form of government, was likely to fail, for the vast majority of active political minds in France considered the issue to have been settled, once and for all, with the abolition of the monarchy and its supporting feudal regime. Napoleon and Sieyès, therefore, talked always of a republican form of government, though Napoleon at least, from the start, seems to have aimed at personal rule.

The violence became necessary when the deputies of the council, meeting at St. Cloud, silenced Napoleon as he tried to address them, with cries of "Death to the tyrant!" and "Outlaw him!" With such cries only five years earlier the deputies of the National Convention finally had turned on Robespierre and sent him to the guillotine. Napoleon lost his nerve, stammered and, half-fainting, was carried from the hall by his bodyguard.

Outside, his brother, Lucien, who happened at the time to be president of the council, persuaded a company of soldiers that a few madmen with daggers were terrorizing the council and requested the soldiers to restore order. The soldiers at first were skeptical, but finally, with drums rolling and bayonets fixed, they charged the meeting hall, and the deputies inside, fearing they were to be killed in their seats, rushed for the doorways, leaped from the windows, and in running away through the park left their red togas caught in the shrubbery.

A few hours later a subdued council of some fifty selected members voted to establish a provisional government with Sieyès, Roger-Ducos and Napoleon as consuls. Immediately Napoleon's supporters began distributing broadsheets and proclamations in which he appeared to be the hero of the day. He had taken the precaution to print them in advance and without consulting Sieyès.

The Revolution, the broadsheets announced, was over. Now its benefits would be secured. All Frenchmen must unite, regardless of political opinions, to support a government which would lead France back to victory, prosperity, law and order.

The new constitution was published a month later, and accepted by the nation in a plebiscite. It made a show of retaining a republican form of government, but in fact power was enormously concentrated in Napoleon's hands. In deference to the vogue of regarding ancient Rome as the source of all political virtue, the highest executive officers were called consuls, and Napoleon was named First Consul with a term of ten years. The other two consuls were ciphers and deliberately chosen as such. There was a Tribunate to debate bills but not to pass them, a Legislative Body to pass bills but not debate them and a Senate to safeguard the constitution. The most important body, which had Napoleon as its president, was the Council of State, a committee of experts which drafted laws. Out of it would come the Civil Code, which was later renamed *Code Napoleón*. But the best evidence of the transformation in the government lay in those offices which had formerly been filled by elections. Henceforth they were to be filled by appointment, of Napoleon.

During the first year there were public objections, chiefly by idealistic and outspoken republicans. But on Christmas Eve, 1800, as Napoleon was driving to the Opéra, some men attempted to explode an "infernal machine" or bomb near his carriage. He was unhurt, but others were killed and wounded. Napoleon thereupon seized the opportunity to purge France of his republican critics. He forced through the government an extraordinary measure: one hundred and thirty well-known republicans, who were for the occasion called terrorists, were proscribed without any legal process and either interned or deported to Guiana where they gradually died. A few days after the decree the true culprits were found. They were royalists, and they were tried, found guilty and guillotined. But the republicans who had been deported were not set free.

The incident of the "infernal machine" did not occur, however, until a year after the constitution had been announced, and by then Napoleon had started to negotiate a settlement with the Church, had the Civil Code drafted and about to be published and had defeated Austria both in Italy and in Germany. Further he had made plain that he intended to welcome into his service any man who would be loyal to him, whether previously royalist or republican; that he intended to advance a man for his talents rather than for reasons of class; and, perhaps most important of all, that he intended to confirm the redistribution of land which had taken place in the last ten years. No peasant or merchant would be required to transfer back to a re-established Church or returned *émigré* any fields or forests, whatever the price paid or means by which they were obtained. For that alone most Frenchmen were willing to allow him some excesses, and both before and after the incident the great majority of them expressed their approval of his actions in plebiscites. Some, very few, sensed in the denial of justice the beginning of tyranny.

One of the problems to which Napoleon gave immediate attention on becoming First Consul was that of his relations with the Church. By January 1800 the Austrians and Russians had pushed the French from every corner of Italy except Genoa, where a French army still held the city and the riviera leading to France. Napoleon hoped to reconquer Italy in the spring, and he would succeed more easily, he knew, if he could pose as a friend of religion and the Church. Similarly in France, if he could reconcile to his regime the priests who had remained true to Rome, he would not only be strengthened but the royalists would lose an army of agents. And the time was peculiarly ripe for some conciliatory action, if he could devise it, for the Sacred College of Cardinals, which was in conclave at Venice and supposedly dominated by the Habsburg emperor, was showing signs of independence by refusing to elect the emperor's candidate.

The conclave was at Venice because Pius VI, fearing a schismatic conclave in France might elect an antipope, with confusion resulting among the faithful, had stipulated some time before his death that the valid conclave would be the one attended by the largest group of cardinals meeting together in the territory of a Catholic ruler. And he had also stated that the arrangements for the conclave were to be made by the dean of the Sacred College. This man, Cardinal Albani, had been at Venice when Pius died and had summoned his brethren there, to the Benedictine monastery on the island of San Giorgio directly opposite the doge's palace.

Some cardinals grumbled at the choice of Venice. Rome had been evacuated by the French, and although a Neapolitan army now occupied it, it seemed unlikely that Ferdinando would exercise more pressure there than the Emperor Francis might in Venice. But none questioned that Albani was meeting the conditions laid down by Pius, and thirty-five cardinals during October and November 1799 slowly made their way to Venice. Among them was Ruffo, who used the conclave as an excuse to leave Naples. But all three French cardinals resident in France refused the summons, and the conclave was overwhelmingly Italian; in fact the only non-Italians were one French cardinal who represented the Bourbon pretender, Louis XVIII, two from Spain, one each from Savoy and Austria, and the Cardinal of York, brother of "Bonnie Prince Charlie" and last of the English House of Stuart. Revolutionary France was unrepresented, and as the conclave sat through January, February and into March, Napoleon had no direct way to make known his friendly intentions.

He did what he could. The officials at Valence were ordered, to their astonishment, to pay "homage" to the dead pope, and on a scale unheard of in their small city. Pius was to be placed in a coffin covered with a black cloth embroidered in gold. It was to be drawn on a "classical" hearse by eight horses suitably adorned, and the four presidents of the administrative and judicial authorities were to walk beside it. To avoid any conflict between "constitutional" and "nonjuring" clergy the ceremony was to be purely civil; the religious ceremony should await the return of the body to Rome. And six hundred copies of the Order of Burial were to be published.

One of them, Napoleon was sure, would find its way from Valence to Venice.

There the conclave, unable to reach a decision, was falling into disrepute. Even the cardinals were beginning to despair. The winter was cold, the island was frequently covered with snow, and the monastery had only one fireplace. Around it the princes of the Church huddled, complaining of the drafts, the damp and the constant chill in their bones; several took to voting from their beds. The stalemate had developed out of the fear of the majority that the victorious Habsburg emperor intended to dominate Italy through a revived Duchy of Milan greatly enlarged by the addition of the former Venetian Republic and the Papal Legations. The "Austrian" party, as it was openly called, controlled about twelve of the twenty-four votes needed, but it could not increase the number unless it could guarantee that the emperor would return to the new pope all his former territories, specifically the Legations. But it was just this that Francis refused to do, although he paid most of the expenses of the conclave. Like Napoleon he saw that the Po valley, because of its geography, was a natural unit, and he wanted to make it so politically and economically. He was willing to return to the King of Sardinia the province of Piedmont at the head of the river, for with Nice and Savoy it made an excellent buffer state between himself and France. But between himself and a militarily weak Rome he needed no buffer, and he would not give up rich Bologna, Ravenna and Ferrara.

Two men, neither of whom had a vote, finally broke the stalemate. One was the secretary of the conclave, Ercole Consalvi, a monsignor forty-three years old who was to become one of the most brilliant cardinals of his day. The other, Monsignor Despuig, was the envoy of the Spanish king who, with the Church being so poor after the indemnities and looting at Rome, had paid for the nine-day ceremony in San Marco which both honored the late pope and formally opened the conclave. The candidate of the two monsignors was the Cardinal-Archbishop of Imola, Luigi Barnaba Chiaramonti, a small, quiet man with a dry sense of humor and a nervous temperament which betrayed itself in occasional flashes of excitement, either of anger or enthusiasm. Like every other possible candidate he had already been voted on once and had failed respectably with twelve votes. In his favor had been the presumption that, as he was both a native and a bishop of towns in the Legations, he would not gladly see them pass from the Church to the Habsburgs. He was also an aristocrat which still seemed both natural and important for the head of a Church which had to deal with emperors and kings.

Against him had been his age, only fifty-eight, and his swift advancement under Pius VI: the cardinals were tired of the Braschi family and their protégés. And there was another matter which later historians have been surprised did not count more heavily against him: he could, in terms of the time, be accused of sacrificing the Church's interests in order to conciliate French and Italian revolutionaries. His diocese had been in the Cisalpine Republic and he had, for example, agreed to style himself "Citizen-Cardinal" and, in the interests of equality, to remove the baldachino from over his bishop's throne. But these were small things, although other bishops suffered for refusing them, compared to Chiaramonti's Christmas homily of 1797.

The occasion arose because the Cisalpine Republic had ordered the bishops within its domain, as a test of loyalty, to declare to the faithful that the laws of the Republic were founded on the principles of the Gospel and in no way contrary to the teachings of the Church. At least one bishop refused outright and was forced to flee; Chiaramonti's response was both more subtle and more startling. In his homily he said nothing at all about the revolutionary laws, many of which involved the abolition of tithes, the secularization of monasteries and civil marriage. He did, however, state flatly that a democratic form of government and the Gospel were compatible: "The form of democratic government adopted among us, most beloved brethren, is not in opposition to the maxims we are setting forth, nor is it repugnant to the Gospel."

But then he went on to say that of all forms of government the democratic had the greatest need of the Church and its teaching. The citizen of a democracy, because of the greater liberty and personal responsibility given him, had an even greater need of spiritual grace and guidance than the more passive subject of a monarch: "A quite ordinary virtue will perhaps suffice to guarantee the continuance and prosperity of other forms of government. Ours demands something more. Strive to attain to the full height of virtue and you will be true democrats. Fulfill faithfully the precepts of the Gospel and you will be the joy of the Republic."

Chiaramonti, in short, had tried to reconcile the Church with the Revolution, and almost everyone found in his effort something unsatisfactory. The republicans disliked his emphasis on the need of a Church in democracy, and churchmen were aghast at the suggestion that "the full height of virtue" involved democracy. Since the great days of Louis XIV the Church had consciously supported monarchies as the God-given form of government. The pope himself was both a spiritual and a temporal monarch, and the Church in its organization and in its claim to authority and obedience had nothing of democracy in it. Even forty years later Chiaramonti's first biographer would insist that the homily was the "work of other hands."

But at the conclave probably most of the cardinals were satisfied that it had been forced from Chiaramonti to save the Church at Imola; situations varied, and not all men were in a position like Ruffo to lead armies. Besides, the major problem facing any new pope would not be Napoleon and revolutionary France but the Habsburgs, against whose autocracy a slight tendency to liberalism would hardly be a weakness. So, on 14 March 1800, Chiaramonti, after considerable intrigue, was unanimously elected pope and, in honor of his patron and predecessor, who had suffered for the faith, he took the name Pius VII. A tailor had worked all the previous night to shorten and tighten the white soutane which would replace his Benedictine black one, but nothing could be done about his slippers. Consalvi months before, to keep expenses down, had laid in only two pairs of different sizes, and both were too large for the frail Chiaramonti. So as pope he went through his first ceremony, the kissing of his feet, with his two very small ones inserted into large white slippers carefully stuffed with cotton wool.

His difficulties with the Emperor Francis began at once. Venetian officials, after consulting Vienna, refused to have the new pope crowned in the Basilica of San Marco. Behind the refusal lay the problem of the Legations. During his coronation Pius, as a temporal sovereign, would swear to defend the traditional domains of the Papacy, and these were now wholly occupied by others, the Neapolitans in Rome and to the south, and the Habsburg armies in the Legations and to the east. If Pius made such an oath in a basilica under Habsburg protection, then was it not reasonable that Francis should help Pius to accomplish it, at least by withdrawing his armies? So the coronation took place in the monastic church on the island of San Giorgio. A few Venetians managed to crowd onto the little piazza facing the canal, more saw what they could from gondolas, and others from the main islands peered across the water with telescopes.

Francis wanted a Habsburg subject for the Papal secretary of state and suggested a Venetian cardinal, but Pius, who wanted a man of undivided loyalty, avoided the issue on the ground that, as he had no state, he had no need of a secretary for it. Instead he appointed Consalvi to the post of secretary to the pope. Next, a journey to Vienna was proposed so that Francis and Pius could discuss affairs of state, and Francis offered to pay all the expenses. But Pius, knowing his predecessor's failure at Vienna, declined; he preferred, he said, to make his first official journey his return to Rome. Then came a special envoy, Marchese Ghislieri, to demand outright for Francis the three Legations and, when that was refused, to offer Ravenna for Bologna and Ferrara. Again and again Pius refused, but all the advantages were not with him. Two months after his election he was still on the island, a prisoner.

For ten weeks, until the end of May, Francis refused to make any arrangements for Pius to leave for Rome. Then, with Napoleon preparing to cross the Alps, the good will of the Church in Italy seemed too valuable to sacrifice. Pius was told he could go but not by land, not through the Legations; Francis wanted no demonstrations in favor of the pope. Instead, Pius with only four cardinals, the Marchese Ghislieri and a few secretaries and servants was to sail from Venice to Pesaro, well down the coast, and then proceed to Rome by road. Even an embarkation in Venice was avoided. Pius was taken in a gondola to Malamocco, on the Lido, where the ship was moored. She was small and in bad shape: shipping water, without cooking facilities and with an inexperienced crew. The voyage, which should have taken twenty-four hours, took twelve days, and although there is no evidence to support the rumor, many people at the time believed that Ghislieri was commissioned to do away with the pope.

Shortly after the party landed and was started toward Rome, it heard that Napoleon had crossed the Alps at the Great St. Bernard Pass and soon after, on 14 June 1800, defeated the main Habsburg army at Marengo. When Ghislieri, at Foligno, formally returned to Pius the part of the Papal States between Rome and Pesaro, but not the Legations, the gesture was empty, for the Habsburg troops were already retreating to the north. The French by the terms of the armistice after Marengo occupied all of northern Italy west of the Mincio river; the area included all of the Duchy of Milan and parts of the old Venetian Republic. By July when Pius made his formal entry into Rome, it seemed likely that Napoleon and not Francis would be the man with whom the Church in Italy would have to deal.

# CHAPTER 14

Napoleon in Italy. The Concordat. The Cisalpine Republic. Napoleon's despotism. The Civil Code. He becomes Emperor. Pius VII goes to Paris. Francis becomes Emperor Franz of Austria. Napoleon's reforms in Italy.

THE ARMISTICE following Marengo lasted only five months, until November 1800, and then in a series of battles, of which the most important was won by Moreau at Hohenlinden, the French under Napoleon as First Consul defeated the Habsburg armies in Germany as well as Italy. The campaigns, north and south, broke up the second coalition against revolutionary France. The Tsar, in a fit of pique, had already recalled his troops to Russia; now, in February 1801, Francis II agreed to Napoleon's terms in the Treaty of Lunéville and the following month Ferdinando for The Two Sicilies signed the Treaty of Florence. Britain alone was left, and it soon began negotiations which, in March 1802, produced the Treaty of Amiens. Europe had peace for the first time in ten years, and tourists from Britain and even from America hurried to the continent.

In the opinion of most Frenchmen, Napoleon had justified his *coup d'état* and made a brilliant start as Consul. The various treaties re-established France's position as it had been after Campoformio, and where there were changes, they were to the benefit of France. North of the Alps, Napoleon had again put the frontier on the Rhine by acquiring the Austrian Netherlands and all the small German states to the west of the river. At the river's delta Holland again became the Batavian Republic just as, at its source, Switzerland again became the Helvetian Republic.

In Italy, two of the Alpine provinces of the Kingdom of Sardinia, Nice and Savoy, were incorporated directly into France, and the third, Piedmont, was forced to support a military occupation, which put a French army permanently in the Po valley. Genoa again became the Ligurian Republic. In Parma, the bell-ringing duke, now doddering, was allowed to remain, but a French administrator governed from his side. Tuscany was renamed the Kingdom of Etruria, and the Habsburg grand duke forced to retire to Vienna. In his place the Duke of Parma's son, Luigi, who had married an Infanta of Spain, was made king. This curious bit of make-believe was, on Spain's part, a last vestige of Elisabetta Farnese's aggressive Italian policy and, on Napoleon's part, a sop to Spain for the forced return of the Louisiana territory. As in Parma, however, French administrators effectively ran the new kingdom in French interests, and five years later when Napoleon wanted the farce to end, he was able to annex Tuscany to France merely by proclamation.

Most important he revived the Cisalpine Republic, granting to it as before the Papal Legations. What was left of the Papal States was to be respected pending a concordat with the pope, Pius VII, but the Adriatic port of Ancona was to have a French garrison: Napoleon still had his eye on adventures in the East. Pius objected but could do nothing, and Napoleon talked always of the need for a concordat. At Naples, Ferdinando also had to agree to support French garrisons in provinces along the Adriatic coast, and further he had to declare an amnesty allowing republican exiles to return to Naples, to pay indemnities to France and to hand over three of his warships. In all of Italy the only areas free of direct French influence were the island Kingdoms of Sicily and Sardinia and the Habsburg province of Veneto. And until his downfall in 1814 Napoleon's grip on the peninsula was never shaken but steadily grew firmer and harsher till he eventually lost the allegiance of almost every kind of Italian.

His actions in Italy, as in France, were a strange mixture of profound thought and opportunism, of understanding and obtuseness, of deceit and candor; of good and evil, both morally and politically. But the good was often not what he had expected or intended, and the ill effects of many of his actions, as he could not imagine himself ever to be evil or even merely wrong, often took him by surprise. Thus, although he set about undermining the Cisalpine Republic from the moment he revived it, still it became the prototype of a unified, independent and national Italian state that he seems to have originally hoped it would be. Similarly, although he swiftly concluded a concordat with the pope, a concordat which governed relations between Church and State in France for more than a hundred years, he was able from his exile on St. Helena to say: "The Concordat was my worst mistake." For within six years after signing it he transformed Pius VII into the symbol of righteous opposition to him by attempting to violate it. And though there was a political gain for all of Italy out of the experience of the Cisalpine Republic and spiritual gain out of the opposition to Napoleon of the pope, yet there was loss, too, for the very intensity of their experiences under Napoleon tended later to keep Italian republicans and churchmen in opposition to each other longer and more fiercely than might otherwise have happened.

The negotiations leading up to the concordat, which both Napoleon and Pius signed in the summer of 1801, went remarkably quickly considering the difficulties involved, and the speed of them is the best evidence of how much both sides, after ten years of religious chaos and persecution in France, wanted some sort of settlement. In 1790 the Assembly had disestablished the Roman Church and in its place had established the new "Constitutional" Church, but then in 1794 the Directory, with an empty treasury and eager to stop the salaries paid to priests, had disestablished the "Constitutional" Church. Thereafter in France, until the concordat, Church and State were separate: all sects of any kind, including Protestants, atheists and Jews, were free to make their way as best they could with none favored by aid from the State. It was the solution France reached in 1905 when it abrogated the concordat and again disestablished the Roman Church, and it was the solution which, a hundred years earlier, most republicans favored because they conceived of liberty as necessarily anticlerical.

Napoleon himself had no spiritual beliefs, and many of the Catholic ideas irritated him. He thought it absurd that, when the State was about to execute a criminal, the Church should give the man absolution and promise him paradise; or that a theological prejudice should obstruct a clear hygienic improvement such as cremation. He saw in religion not the mystery of the incarnation but an aid to social order: "It attaches to heaven an idea of equality which prevents the rich man from being massacred by the poor." In the State's position of neutrality among competing sects he did not see freedom of worship but merely a lot of spiritual forces allowed to run loose and dissipate themselves. He had an orderly mind and a military background, and he itched to discipline those forces to his purpose: "The people," he said, "must have a religion, and that religion must be in the hands of the Government." So in order to reunite altar and throne in France for his own benefit, he opened negotiations with the pope. His policy was popular, in spite of republican opposition, because it soothed the Catholic tradition of the country and reflected the deep-rooted idea of governmental omnipotence, which was the legacy of the monarchy to the Revolution.

The pope, on his side, was eager to resolve the schism between the Roman and "Constitutional" Church and hopeful of regaining the Church's confiscated property or, failing in that, of placing the priests on the payroll of the State. He had also a problem of lack of priests which every year grew more acute and could not be solved without some sort of settlement with the State. Few priests had been ordained since the start of the Revolution in 1790 and even four years after the concordat, in 1806, it was reckoned that one out of six parishes lacked a priest and that a quarter of the priests serving were over sixty years old. So that although the negotiations were long, bitter and tangled, they did proceed and in July 1801 the concordat was signed.

Napoleon, however, did not announce it as the law of France until a week before the following Easter, in April 1802. He may have wanted the emotional pull of Easter among the faithful to override republican objections, for these continued to be strong, both in the representative bodies of the government and in the army. He ordered all the generals in Paris to attend a Te Deum sung after the ratification of the concordat and one, according to the French historian François Mignet, said to Napoleon: "Pretty monkish mummery! Only those million men were absent who died to overthrow what you are setting up again." But throughout most of the country the concordat was greeted with genuine joy.

By its terms Catholicism was declared to be the religion of the majority of the French people, which it plainly was; Napoleon had refused to go further and declare it the religion of the State. He had also refused to restore to the Church its old property or to endow it with any new. Either, he feared, would allow it again to become a separate estate within the State, and a restoration of old lands would have meant arousing the estimated 1,200,000 Frenchmen who now held some piece of *émigré* or Church lands. He did bind the State, however, to pay salaries to all the secular clergy, bishops and parish priests, although not to monks or students. Bishops were to be appointed by the State but invested with their spiritual authority by the pope, a provision requiring Church and State to work in unison. Over it, in a very few years, Napoleon and Pius came to blows.

But the Papacy's disenchantment with Napoleon began at once. At the same time that Napoleon promulgated the concordat, he announced a series of Organic Articles designed to police the Church. Pius and the Italian cardinals at Rome had understood that these would be a few rules for open-air services and church parades, but they went much further. The State was to decide the number of students who might be ordained each year, to supervise the seminaries as it did the civil schools, to sanction Church councils as it did those of civil bodies. The Church was forbidden by law to acquire landed property, and the cathedrals and churches were declared to be merely at the disposition of the bishops. A Minister of Cults was empowered to watch every aspect of the Church's teaching and administration, and the curé in each village was expected to support the State's policy from the pulpit. In return Napoleon seemed to offer very little; in particular, he made no move to return the Legations.

Republicans, both in Italy and in France, shared the Church's swift disillusionment with Napoleon. He drew up a constitution for the revived

Cisalpine Republic, which the republicans in Milan accepted eagerly and in a first flush of enthusiasm sent a deputation to Paris begging him to appoint their chief officials. He graciously consented and agreed to meet a commission of 450 members at Lyon early in 1802. There a new constitution was adopted, Napoleon arranged for himself to be elected President of the Republic and then changed its name from Cisalpine to the Italian Republic. The new name at once aroused hopes among republicans that he had a design for unifying Italy and, for fear of it, aroused protests from both the pope at Rome and Ferdinando at Naples.

But the republicans, as they soon discovered, might better have protested, for the constitution was designed to be unworkable. "I know more," observed Napoleon, "in my little finger than is known by all the heads in Italy put together." And he arranged for the voting power of the new Italian Republic to be divided among three bodies: a Consulta di Possidenti or Council of Property Owners which was to meet in Milan, a Consulta di Dotti or Council of Learned Men which was to meet in Bologna, and a Consulta di Commercianti or Council of Merchants which was to meet in Brescia. The members of these bodies were to be elected for life, to meet at least once in two years for a period not exceeding fifteen days, to submit to a body of twenty-five men, the Censura, a list of candidates for the legislature and the judiciary. The Censura was to make the final selection at Cremona. Napoleon could claim that he had bowed to the strong streak of municipal pride in Italian life by dividing the bodies among four rival cities. Actually he had made it almost impossible for the government to function and constructed it in such a way that no posts were truly elective; he did not trust the Italian republicans to support him. "It is the soldier," he said, "who founds a republic, and it is the soldier who maintains it." He appointed the first legislature of the new Italian Republic and thereafter never permitted the cumbersome system of appointment and election to provide a new one. Some years later when the Legislature dared to protest some items in his program, notably the large sums of revenue allocated for the support of French troops, he declared: "I have adjourned the legislative body. When these legislators have a king to themselves he may be amused at these games of prisoners' base, but as I have no time, and as they are all passions and faction, I shall not summon them again." So much for political liberty in the Italian Republic.

Napoleon's actions in Italy generally reflected similar actions in France. In August 1802, over republican opposition, he had himself declared Consul for life with the right to choose his successor. It was now that his Christian name, like royalty, began to be used officially. What powers remained in the various legislative bodies, the Tribunate and the Legislature, were whittled away. First he made the Senate, in violation of the constitution which it was supposed to safeguard, expel for the safety of the State all opposition members of the Tribunate and Legislature. Then five months later a new constitution was proposed and accepted which greatly increased the Consul's power.

Earlier he had sent the most republican regiments of the army out of the country to fight in San Domingo, where they were almost entirely destroyed by yellow fever. Later he put the distinguished and popular general, Moreau, on trial for treason, allegedly for aiding a plot to restore the Bourbons. The jury acquitted Moreau, whom historians, too, have declared innocent, but Napoleon insisted on a second trial. This time the court, put under extreme pressure, brought back an equivocal verdict with a sentence of two years' imprisonment. Napoleon, however, with a great show of clemency commuted the sentence to exile in America.

He was more brutal in the example, arising from the same plot, which he gave to the royalists. He knew that the conspirators expected a Bourbon prince to appear in Paris to lead them, but which prince he did not know. The police suspected the Duc d'Enghien, a young man who was staying at a hunting lodge in Baden, close to the French border, and Napoleon ordered his arrest, his trial and his death. The Duc was kidnapped in Baden, brought in the following six days into France and taken to the castle at Vincennes, near Paris. With six days in which to examine the Duc's papers the police and Napoleon knew, even before the Duc's arrival at Vincennes, that they had the wrong man. Yet he was put on trial the evening he arrived and at half past two the following morning, with the ink still wet on his sentence, he was taken out into the moat, shot and thrown into a grave prepared before the trial had ended. Earlier in the evening in Paris, speaking of the Bourbons and their supporters, Napoleon had said: "These people wish to slay the Revolution in my person; it is my duty to defend and avenge it. We have left behind the age of etiquette. I have shed blood. It was my duty. I shall shed more perhaps in future."

In its immediate goal the act was effective: no Bourbon prince ever afterward attempted to plot Napoleon's murder, and most Frenchmen, with only Napoleon's controlled press to read, believed the accusations against the Duc. But not all. Chateaubriand, who was to become the most powerful French writer of his time, quit Napoleon's service because of it and gradually turned into his implacable enemy. Outside France no one believed the accusations for a moment, and hostile governments and critics made a cause of it. Eventually many of those Frenchmen who had at first believed began to doubt, and the Duc's ghost, year after year, haunted Napoleon's regime, charging it with an act of gangsterism which most men found repellent.

As was typical of Napoleon, in the same week that he spotted his reputation with the murder of the Duc d'Enghien, he added to it by passing
into law the Civil Code which registered and perpetuated many of the
social improvements introduced into Europe by the French Revolution.
It was founded on the principles of toleration, equity, the sanctity of
private property and the binding value of family life. It was not a code for
all time: it gave far greater power to the father of a family than do most
modern codes, and in its treatment of married women it was less liberal
than the prerevolutionary French laws. As for master and servant, in
Article 1781 it stated flatly: "The master's word is taken: as to the rate
of wages; the payment of the salary of the previous year; and the advances
on the salary of the current year."

But if it was not perfect, it still had enormous virtues. It was in one
small volume, all of it, and in a language most men could read and understand. No longer was the law something produced out of a musty document, or written in a strange, antique language, or different in each town or
something to which many men could claim exception by reason of birth
or position. And in recognizing civil marriage and divorce it freed thousands from a double tyranny exercised by Church and society. The
Church fought the code in every community to which French arms tried
to extend it, and not because of the provisions on master and servant. The
loss of power for the Church, in the sense that a sacrament is power exercised, lay in the provisions for civil marriage and divorce. These meant
that a man and woman could unite, live, die and raise a family, all with
the official blessing of the State, and therefore to at least some extent of
the community, without ever paying even lip service to the Church. Of
course in rural communities everywhere and particularly in Italy there
was no immediate change in the old ways, but the possibility of an enormous change had been opened.

Two months after the code became law in France, in May 1804, Napoleon had one of his supporters in the Tribunate propose that he be
declared Emperor and the office be made hereditary in the Bonaparte
family. One sincere republican, Lazare Carnot, the former Director who
had organized Napoleon's armies for him, voted against the proposal. It
was a courageous gesture, for Carnot knew that he made it in a vacuum
and that it could not stir any support. Napoleon as early as 1800 had suppressed sixty out of seventy-three existing newspapers and put the chief
of police in charge of censorship. No news unfavorable to Napoleon was
reported. Two weeks later, on 18 May 1804, Napoleon was proclaimed
Emperor of the French when the Senate approved the proposal. Later a
plebiscite recorded 3,572,329 votes in favor and 2569 against. As before,
the vote was taken on open registers; in the villages long lists of names

were written in the same hand and in Paris only sixty-six dared to vote against. Some twenty-six million did not bother to vote at all.

As long as Napoleon remained merely First Consul, Citizen Bonaparte elected for a ten-year term, and as long as the Tribunate retained some power, the republican dream of parliamentary government for France might still have been realized. The forms were there, capable of being inspired with life by a man who believed in them. But Napoleon in his journey from First Consul to Emperor, deliberately crushed even the possibility of it. Parliamentary government implies the responsibility of ministers to a popularly elected chamber, freedom of speech and adequate guarantees for personal liberty. Under Napoleon these conditions ceased to exist, either in France or in the neighboring republics with which he surrounded it.

His imperial coronation at Notre Dame was a masterpiece of theatrical statecraft. He delayed it until 2 December 1804 by which time his supporters, who had now become his court, were gorgeously arrayed with new uniforms, new titles and a new point of view about themselves. His brother Joseph had become the Grand Elector; his brother-in-law Joachim Murat, the Grand Admiral; and his sisters, nagging him at a family dinner for more and better titles for themselves, had forced him to remark in a rage: "They talk as if I had robbed them of their shares of the patrimony of our late father, the King."

As the day approached, the preparations for the coronation at Notre Dame harked back, not to the Bourbons who had been merely kings and crowned at Reims, but to Charlemagne, "our illustrious predecessor," as Napoleon called him. The new regime was careful to present itself as a step forward into a new and mystic world of grandeur, not a return to something tried and found wanting. Following the example of Charlemagne, Napoleon wished to be crowned by the pope, but with a difference: Charlemagne had gone to Rome; Napoleon, more imperious, brusquely invited the pope to Paris. If Pius VI could journey to Vienna to confer with a Habsburg, then Pius VII could come to Paris to crown a Napoleon and show that he was the Father of the French as well as of the Austrians.

Such a request had no precedent, and most of the cardinals at Rome considered it preposterous. But Pius, who still hoped to come to terms with the men and doctrines of the Revolution, decided to go. He hoped by discussions with Napoleon to strengthen the Church's position in France, perhaps by obtaining a revision of the police regulations which Napoleon had imposed on the Church; or to strengthen its position in Italy by persuading Napoleon to return the Legations to the Papal States. In any event, crowning and anointing the emperor, he felt, would be a reminder to all of Europe of the Church's primal position in the organ-ization of society.

So, on All Souls' Day, after saying mass in St. Peter's, Pius started for Paris. He was accompanied by six cardinals and more than a hundred secretaries and attendants in a caravan of coaches. He followed the same route over which, six and a half years earlier, Pius VI had been hurried to his death, and he wondered often if he had decided wisely, if he was not, in fact, already a prisoner. In Rome and elsewhere, he knew, many considered he had sacrificed his spiritual integrity merely to save his temporal throne.

Shortly after he arrived in Paris, he was informed that in the cere-mony he would merely bless the crown; thereafter Napoleon would take it and, putting it on his own head, crown himself. Even the traditional coronation service had been rewritten in order to reduce the role of the Church. Still, Pius remained. He was determined not to be put off or even give the appearance of it. When he went to an official dinner and was seated below the Archbishop of Paris, he merely smiled. He used every opportunity to demonstrate his affection for France and the French and to erase the impression that, with regard to the Revolution, Rome was irreconcilable. To some extent he succeeded. Crowds followed him when he went out, had rosaries blessed by him and received communion from him. Thousands saw in him a simple, kind priest and not a tyrant; so much so that Napoleon soon wished him out of Paris, and the journals and papers, on order, began to understate the size and response of the crowds. But when, four months later, Pius returned to Rome, he had none of the concessions he had hoped to obtain, and the general opinion both inside the Church and out was that he had been outsmarted.

All of these actions of Napoleon, the concordat, the Civil Code, the Duc d'Enghien and the coronation, had their counterparts in Italy, re-flections through his Italian administration of what he had already done in France. Soon after his coronation in Notre Dame, Napoleon declared that it was absurd for him to be Emperor of the French and merely Presi-dent of an Italian republic, and the solution he suggested, which perforce the Italians accepted, was for the Italian Republic to become the King-dom of Italy with himself as king. His stepson, Eugène de Beauharnais, would act as viceroy. Another coronation, therefore, was announced, to take place in the Duomo in Milan, and Napoleon asked the pope to of-ficiate as before, to bless the iron crown of Lombardy which he, Napo-leon, then would place on his own head.

Pius refused. Besides any wounded feelings he may have had from his first experience with Napoleon at a coronation, he had special reasons for avoiding this particular one in Milan, reasons similar to those for which the Emperor Francis had refused to allow Pius to have his coronation in the Venetian Basilica of San Marco. The reasons were three: the Legations. If Pius went to Milan, or so he reasoned, then that part of him that was a temporal prince of Italy would seem to condone Napoleon's inclusion of the Legations into the new kingdom. And this, Pius would never do; he had not yielded to Francis, and he would not yield to Napoleon. So on 26 May 1805, in the Duomo at Milan, Napoleon crowned himself King of Italy with merely a cardinal in attendance.

The pope's refusal to go to Milan did not win him any new friends in Italy. Those churchmen who felt he had already sacrificed too much of his spiritual independence by agreeing to the concordat and by going to Paris, thought it perverse: a demonstration that Pius, the man, confused the relative importance of his spiritual and temporal roles. Republicans, however disillusioned they were with Napoleon, saw merely an old truth made plain: that the Church as an institution, regardless of the liberality of any individual pope, would never agree to any political changes in Italy that did not increase its own temporal power. And, of course, any good will that Pius, by his journey to Paris, may have stored with Napoleon drained swiftly away. Pius, in attempting to find some middle ground between the opposing forces, became increasingly isolated.

For Napoleon the Italian coronation was a long step toward a new war with Francis. Under the Treaty of Lunéville, which had ended the campaigns of the second coalition in Italy, Napoleon had guaranteed the existence of the Cisalpine Republic as a buffer state between Francis in Venice and Napoleon who had military rights in Piedmont. Instead Napoleon by degrees had turned it into a Kingdom of Italy in which the king ruled not from Milan but from Paris. Eight months earlier he had also violated the treaty by incorporating the province of Piedmont directly into France, and then, the week after the coronation, in order to gain the port of Genoa and its fifteen thousand sailors he incorporated the Ligurian Republic. Britain, made nervous by Napoleon's continued expansion, had already resumed the war against him, and in August 1805 Francis and Tsar Alexander joined it in the third coalition.

Mercifully for Italians the campaigns of this war, with the exception of a long and bloody war in Calabria, were all fought outside of Italy. At sea they ended with the British victory at Trafalgar and the death of Nelson; on land, with the battles of Ulm, where General Mack of Neapolitan fame was badly defeated, and of Austerlitz, often described as Napoleon's most perfect battle. In it he anticipated every move of his enemies, concealed every one of his own and lost only eight thousand men to the enemies' thirty-seven thousand. The battle was fought on the first anniversary of his coronation at Notre Dame, and by it he was able to offer the French people a victory such as Louis XIV, in a long life and born to the throne, had never been able to win. Napoleon was only thirty-five and in ten years had risen from subaltern to emperor. Friends and enemies alike were dazzled.

They were also stunned by the magnitude of the changes his rise to power had worked. In Germany in 1803 he had reduced the number of tiny principalities, palatinates, bishoprics and imperial cities from 250 to 39 and as one result had secured a Protestant majority in the Diet. These changes threatened the hold of the Catholic Habsburgs on the position of Holy Roman Emperor, and in 1804 Francis, following the proclamation of Napoleon as Emperor of the French and seeking to insure for himself some symbol of unity for his complex holdings, had declared himself to be "Emperor of Austria." In 1713, almost a hundred years earlier, the Pragmatic Sanction had defined the lands of the House of Habsburg which Maria Theresa was to inherit and now finally, for the first time, they acquired a common name: they became, whether in Germany, Italy, Poland or Hungary, the "Austrian Empire."

The change was more than just in name. With the loss of the Austrian Netherlands and some of his holdings in Germany, Francis no longer had any isolated lands and never attempted again to have any, even after Waterloo. Under the bludgeonings of Napoleon and with the centralization of power that war always involves, the German-speaking core of the Habsburgs and of their civil service centered on Vienna became more pronounced. Francis, in a style typical of the older tradition of the Habsburgs, had not been born in Vienna or even in Austria but, as the son of the Grand Duke of Tuscany, in Florence. Italian was his first language, and he did not see Vienna until he was sixteen. This was never again true of a Habsburg emperor. From 1790 until after Waterloo in 1815 travel was almost impossible, and an entire generation of the family grew up in Vienna, knowing little else. The experience helped to change them from the most cosmopolitan family in Europe into a local, Austrian dynasty.

The change was gradual, but after Austerlitz, Francis took a significant step toward realizing it. By the treaties following the battle Napoleon abolished what was left in Germany of the Holy Roman Empire and substituted for it a Confederation of the Rhine from which the Habsburgs were excluded. Francis, in reply, then abdicated the empty title and became thereby the last of the Holy Roman Emperors. It was a title his family had held, with only one break at the start of Maria Theresa's reign, from 1438 until 1806. Thereafter the family's highest title and the one generally used was Emperor of Austria, and Francis was known more familiarly by most of his subjects as "Kaiser Franz." (To reflect this change from Holy Roman to Austrian Emperor, the German form of his name will be used hereafter.)

The treaty of Pressburg or Bratislava which Napoleon imposed on the Emperor Franz after Austerlitz made a tremendous change in Italy, for by it Napoleon excluded Austria from the peninsula altogether. All of Veneto, Venice and its mainland, also Istria (but not Trieste) and Dalmatia now were merged into his Kingdom of Italy which became thereby the largest, most populous and richest of the Italian states. And on the day the treaty was signed, 26 December 1805, Napoleon publicly declared that the dynasty of Naples, which had aided the third coalition, "has ceased to reign: its existence is incompatible with the peace of Europe and the honor of my crown." Maria Carolina once again had persuaded Ferdinando to join with those fighting France, and although Neapolitan troops at the time had not yet fired a shot, Napoleon, referring to their queen, promised to "hurl from the throne that criminal woman who has so shamelessly violated everything that is held sacred by men." The following January she and Ferdinando, faced with an overwhelming French army, retreated to Palermo. From there, with the help of the British navy, they continued to hold Sicily while the French occupied all of the mainland. The Neapolitan diarist, De Nicola, observed: "This is the second time in eight years that Carolina of Austria and Ferdinando di Borbone have fled: may God help them to return and recover the Kingdom as they did before, but without so much terror and bloodshed."

Neapolitans, perhaps remembering the carnage at the previous arrival of the French, this time offered no opposition. Napoleon installed his elder brother Joseph as king and called him Giuseppe-Napoleone. Two years later, when Napoleon moved Joseph to Spain, he installed Joachim Murat as Gioacchino-Napoleone. Of the two, Murat made the greater impression on the Neapolitans. He was far more colorful, and he held the throne longer, 1808–15. But neither of them nor any other relatives whom Napoleon set up in kingdoms elsewhere were kings in any ordinary sense. All of them remained French subjects, retained their positions as dignitaries of France and commanded their French troops only as French generals. Orders came from Paris, and the kings were expected to execute them. When his brother Louis as King of Holland showed signs of independent thought, Napoleon marched an army into Holland and threw Louis out. At Naples, both Joseph and Murat were viceroys rather than true kings, and both resented the fact.

It was now, in the nine years between 1805 and 1814, that what good Napoleon did in Italy was largely achieved. Politically, he organized the peninsula into three large units: the Kingdom of Italy with himself as king and Eugène de Beauharnais as viceroy in Milan; the Kingdom of Naples with first Joseph and then Murat as nominal kings; and then all the rest, including eventually Parma, Tuscany and even the Papal States, he incorporated directly into France. Parma, for example, became the Department of the Taro, taking its name from a small tributary of the Po.

From the start this organization had an air of impermanence about it. At Naples, Joseph was out and Murat in; at Parma, French was declared the official language but each year an Imperial decree was required to permit the use of Italian; at Genoa, a proud tradition of independence and republicanism was squashed; in Piedmont, Nice and Savoy, an extremely popular, native dynasty was dethroned but allowed to exist in nearby Sardinia; finally, at Rome, preparations were started to move the Papacy, bag and baggage, to Paris. Italians of whatever region or political allegiance simply did not believe such arrangements would last.

The one exception was the Kingdom of Italy in which many Venetians, Milanesi and Bolognesi frankly preferred Napoleon, for all his despotism, to the Austrians or the pope. There alone some strong political forces worked to support what he had created. Under him the Po valley became a single economic unit, and trade prospered, although high prices and taxes caused constant grumbling. Milan, his capital city, became the center of finance for the valley, clearly first among itself, Venice and Bologna, and at the same time it also became the cultural and intellectual capital not only of the valley but of the entire peninsula, a position it has never since lost. It was from Milan that Napoleon conducted an economic and social revolution which, unlike its political counterpart, did achieve something permanent in Italian life. But the further it traveled from the Po valley the fewer years it had to work and the less of permanence it achieved. Nine years in the Kingdom of Naples was too short a period for the new French system of administration and the Civil Code to shake the feudal organization of life in remote areas like Calabria.

In the north, however, and even in Rome and Naples, many persons were eager for reform and therefore inclined to accept it when it came. In 1764 Cesare Beccaria, who with the brothers Verri had published the journal *Il Caffè,* also had published a small book on penal law, *Dei delitti e delle pene* or *Of Crimes and Punishments,* which had created a sensation throughout Europe. The opening sentences had become famous as a description of the state of law in general and of the need for its reform. Beccaria, personally a mild, shy man, had written in a tone of outrage and scorn:

> A few remains of laws of an ancient people who once had been conquerors, compiled by order of a prince who ruled in Constantinople twelve centuries ago, then mixed with Lombard customs and gathered up in cumbersome tomes by obscure commentators each

with his own interpretation—such make up the traditional body of
opinion that in the greater part of Europe today passes for law. . . .
These laws, this debris of barbarous times, are examined in this book
in so far as they bear on criminal procedure.[5]

Beccaria had thereafter limited himself to criminal law, but his general
statement included civil law, "debris of barbarous times," and many educated Italians agreed with him. In the old Duchy of Milan both Maria
Theresa and Joseph II had made piecemeal reforms as had also Filippo di
Borbone in Parma. But in Beccaria's eyes and in those which he had taught
to see, nothing of the old system was worth preserving. Yet a general
reform in eighteenth-century Italy had been impossible because of the
multitude of small states each going about it differently and because of the
law's association with ancient Roman law. It needed a revolution to unite
the people of the many states and to break the tradition of centuries, and
this Napoleon in his person supplied. In France the Revolution had been
a movement of many men working out a new system of social organization. In Italy the Revolution was one man, Napoleon, who embodied much
of the new system and who imposed it on the Italian people. But they, for
their part, were not altogether unprepared for it nor altogether unwilling
to accept it.

In decree after decree, always with the force of the French armies in
the background, Napoleon changed the basis of life in Italy. Feudal laws,
particularly those on inheritance, were abolished; restrictive laws against
the Jews and the use of torture were abolished; the civil and criminal
jurisdictions were divided; open trials were introduced and lawyers argued
their pleadings in court instead of submitting them in writing; the court
systems were reorganized, and finally came the Civil Code, permitting
civil marriage and divorce and before which all men were equal, regardless
of position or birth.

Administrative divisions everywhere were redrawn on a logical rather
than historical basis. In the former Duchy of Parma, for example, the
ancient rivalry between Parma and Piacenza over which was to be the
administrative center of the area was firmly resolved in favor of Parma.
Everywhere new systems of bookkeeping were introduced, and clerks and
accountants were closely watched.

In this area of administrative detail Napoleon was at his best and
probably continues to be the greatest administrator the world has ever
known. Once when at camp at Boulogne, for example, he wrote the minister of the Public Treasury at Paris: "In column 22 of your account . . ."
and then went on to point out by referring to a number of entries, that the
minister was paying annuities to more than twenty-six hundred persons

over eighty-five. And he ordered an immediate check to discover who actually was receiving the money.

He had an extraordinary eye for detail and an equally extraordinary capacity to assimilate technical information in any branch of government. He needed little sleep and worked sometimes eighteen hours at a stretch. No clerk, however insignificant, was ever quite sure that tomorrow Napoleon himself would not read his report, and under Napoleon's sharp eye and tongue the clerks and administrators everywhere trembled, and worked. When he visited Parma in 1805 he himself went over the administrator's financial accounts and, afterward, had the man removed. The French administrations in Italy served as schools of modern government for the Italians, who had been used for centuries to slow and secretive despotisms. Chateaubriand, who disliked Napoleon, still could remark with admiration: "We brought to Rome the germ of administration"; and Stendhal reported in 1818 that if you met an intelligent elderly man in the streets of Milan, it was safe to assume he had served in the French administration.

As Napoleon's Italian coronation had followed his French one so, too, his policy toward the Church in Italy followed that of the concordat in France. By a series of decrees issued from Milan at the time of his coronation there he reorganized the entire ecclesiastical structure in northern Italy without any reference to Rome at all. Parish lines were redrawn and many parishes eliminated as surplus; religious orders had their regulations reformed or were wholly suppressed, in which case annuities were sometimes given to members suddenly thrust out in the world; and, under the Civil Code, provisions for civil marriage and divorce were introduced with the possibility of family life passing from the Church's control. Pius protested, again and again, and Napoleon sometimes answered and sometimes did not. But he never retracted any of his actions. He refused to return the Legations and, in fact, soon had incorporated all of the Papal States except Rome itself either directly into France or into the Kingdom of Italy. He expressed his attitude in a letter to his half-uncle, Cardinal Fesch, who represented him at Rome:

"The Pope has written to me, under date 13th November [1805], a quite ridiculous and lunatic letter. . . . For the Pope's purposes, I am Charlemagne. Like Charlemagne, I join the crown of France with the crown of the Lombards. My Empire, like Charlemagne's, marches with the East. I therefore expect the Pope to accommodate his conduct to my requirements. If he behaves well, I shall make no outward changes: if not, I shall reduce him to the status of Bishop of Rome. . . ."

The disagreement was a direct conflict between two ways of life, between two powers in society each of which wanted to mold and direct the course of Italian civil life. But it had taken an emperor of Napoleon's stature and ability to match, on the State's behalf, the power of a long-established Church. Under Napoleon for the first time since the Lombard invasions the three great obstacles to Italian unity were simultaneously broken: the Papacy's hold on the center of the peninsula, the foreign dynasties and the obstinate spirit of locality. For the first time since then the whole peninsula was governed on a single plan with a common system of law and administration, and in that experience the foundations of a modern, united Italy were laid. The obstacles were broken and the experience lasted for only a moment in history, for after Napoleon's fall in 1814, much of his work was undone. But that moment was long enough for many Italians, particularly those in the Po valley, to see what might be achieved.

# CHAPTER 15

Opposition in Italy to Napoleonic regimes. By the peasants in Calabria. By Foscolo and the republicans in the Kingdom of Italy.
"Dei Sepolcri." By the Pope at Rome. His kidnapping and imprisonment.

THE NAPOLEONIC REGIMES in Italy, for all the benefits they may have
imposed, seldom won more than a sullen obedience from the majority of
their subjects. The Church and many of the nobility were against the
reforms themselves; the republicans, while applauding the reforms, began
to balk at the increasing despotism of the governments imposing them;
and the great mass of peasants and poorer townspeople constantly protested against the taxes, particularly against the conscription or "blood
tax" which took the young men out of the economy and life of the family
for years at a time.

The conscription law was ruthlessly enforced, for Napoleon not only
used up millions of men but he believed in conscription as a method of
indoctrinating the people with a respect for authority. Aside from what
obedience the conscript learned in the army, parents were sometimes imprisoned as hostages for sons refusing to serve and whole villages were
punished for the desertion of a single conscript. And further to infuriate
the peasants the law, at least in their eyes, was a denial of the much
trumpeted doctrine of equality, for a man of property could always buy an
exemption and even a man of art, such as the composer Rossini, was
sometimes excused by a whimsical general or administrator. Over the conscription law sullen obedience frequently flared into open revolt.

Each year, in spite of the penalties, some peasants in the Po valley fled
to the Apennines or Alps to join bands of others who had also refused to
serve. When caught, they were shot; but catching them was not easy, for
they had the sympathy of the people, and Napoleon's viceroy, Eugène,
had always to keep some troops chasing them. The most difficult years for
Eugène were 1809–11 when peasant unrest in parts of the Kingdom of
Italy threatened to become general because of a continuous rise in prices
and the imposition of a new tax on the grinding of grain, probably the most

difficult of all taxes for a peasant to evade. Eugène kept control but only by establishing courts-martial in rural centers and by executing the leaders of the discontented and, where he could not catch them, by executing their relatives.

In the south the peasant unrest was far greater and merged into the small war waged by the Bourbons from Sicily to recover the Kingdom of Naples. For several years, 1806–09, the Bourbon forces with the aid of the British navy captured and held islands off the coast, made landings on the mainland and supported with money and officers a guerrilla war in Calabria and the mountains running north between Naples and Rome. Napoleon constantly urged his brother Joseph to make some bloody examples of men and villages, and when an important Bourbon leader, Marchese di Rodio, was finally cornered and captured, Joseph did so. He refused to treat the Marchese as a prisoner of war but ordered a military commission to try him on charges of rebellion and incitement to insurrection. On these charges the commission acquitted him, so Joseph appointed another commission which understood what was expected of it and which condemned Rodio to death. But the example was not effective. The Bourbons were given a martyr to exploit, the Calabrian sense of honor exalted Rodio and not Joseph, and even a French staff officer who was present, Paul-Louis Courier, wrote back to France: "His death is looked upon here as a murder and as a mean revenge. . . . Everyone is horrified, perhaps the French even more than the Neapolitans. He was shot from behind like a traitor, a felon, a rebel to his *legitimate* sovereign. . . . Assuredly, sir, this does not belong to the time and century in which we are living."

The mountain war was even more horrible than the campaign under Ruffo in 1799, for it continued year after year and without any of the restraints of humanity that Ruffo, however slightly, had succeeded in imposing. The peasants, ground down by taxes, hating the conscription and having used up their small reserves against starvation, began to live by war. "Better a bull for two years than a cow for a hundred," was an expression of the time and, when they could not rob and kill the enemy, they turned on themselves. In another of his letters the French officer Courier described the kind of war it became:

> After having sacked without knowing why the pretty town of Co-
> rigliano, we came . . . to Cassano, along a small river or "torrent"
> that they still call the *Sibari,* though it no longer flows through Sybaris
> but only through some orange groves. The Swiss battalion marched at
> the head, its uniforms in tatters like all the rest and commanded by
> Muller, for Clavel had been killed at Santa Eufemia. The people of
> Cassano, seeing this red company, mistook us for the English: this has
> often happened. They come out to meet us, embrace us and congratu-

late us on having beaten those rascally Frenchmen, those robbers, those men the Pope has excommunicated. They did not flatter us, to be sure, on this occasion. They told us of our follies and said even worse of us than we deserved. Each cursed the soldiers of *Maestro Peppe* (Master Joe); each boasted of having killed a few. With their pantomime, joining the gesture to the word: "I stabbed six of them; I shot ten." One said he had killed Verdier; another had killed myself . . .

You see how they recommended themselves and settled their affairs. Thus we received all their confidences, and they only recognized us when we fired at them point-blank. Many of them were killed. Fifty-two were taken and shot that evening on the square of Cassano. But a feature of party rage worth noting is that they were despatched by their compatriots, by the Calabrians, our friends, the good Calabrians of Joseph, who asked as a favor to be employed in this butchery. They had no difficulty in obtaining this boon, for we were tired of the massacre at Corigliano . . .

The scene at Marcellinara was of the same kind. We were mistaken for Englishmen, and as such welcomed in the town . . .[6]

The war did not end until 1811, long after Napoleon had transferred Joseph to Spain and installed Murat in his place. In its horrors and in the manner in which a whole people rose to fight the French it was similar to the people's war in Spain which Napoleon was to find he could not win. The fact that the Calabrians sometimes slaughtered each other rather than the French should not obscure the fact that for four years they tied up an army of fifty thousand Frenchmen and killed fifteen thousand, almost twice as many as died at Austerlitz. For a simple, primitive people it was, purely in terms of war, a creditable performance.

For Napoleon it should have been an omen that his despotism was giving birth to a new kind of war, one in which the people rather than their king or government were his opponents and, consequently, one which he could not win by a single, brilliant victory. In the following years in Spain, in Germany and in Russia, he always sought another Austerlitz, and always in vain. He did more, perhaps, than any other man to instill in the peoples of Europe feelings of nationality, the bond of common language and culture against the foreigner, against the invading French and himself; but he was too involved with himself to understand the feelings of others or even to make sensible allowance for them. By the time the last Calabrian had been either shot or beaten into obedience, Napoleon's bulletins and letters show him becoming both more imperious and, as a direct consequence of increasing impatience and refusal to hear any advice, less intelligent about the problems facing him.

True republican opposition to Napoleon was possible only in the

Kingdom of Italy, for elsewhere it tended to be absorbed in support for the absent king or duke or for the harassed Church. It was intellectual opposition, for it was faced all the time with the difficulty of having to approve of what Napoleon was doing while disapproving of his method of doing it. But it was neither weakly stated nor without effect, for its chief spokesman was Foscolo who, after Alfieri's death in 1803, had become the outstanding poet in Italy.

Foscolo's career was an expression of his love of liberty, which as a republican he presumed was necessarily antimonarchic and anticleric, and of his vision of Italy, united and independent; with him, the two were so closely identified that they were often one. As a nineteen-year-old refugee from the old Venice of the oligarchy he dated a letter to a friend in the first Cisalpine Republic: *"2 Maggio, Anno I della Libertà Italiana, 1797."* And in Milan and nearby cities during the following year he had made speeches in which he spoke of the Cisalpine Republic as merely a beginning to the freeing and uniting of all Italy. Once he was so carried away that he ended up shouting: *"Viva la repubblica dell'universo!"*

But he was not all youth and hyperbole. He had reflective moments in which he recognized that among the Venetians, Milanesi and others proud of their native cities "we are now only a little Italian"; and he often talked and wrote of the need for a national renaissance. In an article for the Milanese *Monitore italiano* he forecast accurately that the main forces working against a republic were: "the omnipotence of the priests, the ambitions of great men, the avarice of government officials, attachment to old ways, (and) the poverty of the people." He emphasized the last with a citation from Plutarch: "An imbalance between rich and poor is the oldest and most fatal ailment of a republic." It is an ailment that plagues the Italian Republic today.

Foscolo also backed up his ideas by fighting for them. He believed that arms and literature would free Italy and that he should engage in both. So at the time of the second coalition, when the Austrian and Russian armies drove the French out of Italy, Foscolo fought first for the Cisalpine Republic and, when that was extinguished, for the French in their defense of Genoa. In both campaigns he was wounded and, for a brief period after the fall of Genoa, he was a prisoner. But then Napoleon at Marengo reversed the situation in Italy, and Foscolo was able to return to Milan.

He was greeted as a hero not only for his military exploits but for his novel *Ultime Lettere di Jacopo Ortis* or *The Last Letters of Jacopo Ortis,* which everyone had been reading. It is a romance, proceeding by a series of letters, in which an Italian patriot from Venice suffers for politics and love and finally commits suicide. In the first sentence of the first letter Napoleon's Treaty of Campoformio is referred to with anger and shame, and republicans everywhere knew that Foscolo, at least, did not intend to excuse the First Consul for his sins against Italy.

Each step that Napoleon took toward emperor and each step taken thereafter to strangle Italian independence and initiative angered Foscolo more. Yet he approved of the Civil Code, the suppression of monasteries and even of the conscription, for he believed that for Italians to be free they had to learn to fight. He himself rejoined the Cisapline army as a staff officer to General Pina, whose regiments were attached to the French army at Boulogne. From time to time he appeared on leave in Paris or Milan, but most often he returned to Florence where he was famous for his gambling and his appearances at the salon of Alfieri's mistress, the Countess of Albany.

After Alfieri's death in 1803, the countess in the twenty years remaining to her succeeded in establishing her salon as the most important in Italy. She perhaps was aided by her claim, as Bonnie Prince Charlie's widow, to be the rightful Queen of England, Scotland, France and Ireland, and undoubtedly gawkers were titillated by the servants in Stuart livery and the silver tea services emblazoned with the British royal arms. But in addition she was evidently an excellent hostess and correspondent, and the Swiss historian Sismondi wrote of her with genuine admiration, *"La grande lanterne magique passe tout par votre salon"* or, roughly, that she had made the Casa Alfieri the wall against which all the brilliant figures of the time were projected as though by a magic lantern. And chief among these, at this time, was Foscolo.

He was Alfieri's heir in the Italian world of letters, and with the blessing of the countess and her salon as a forum from which to project his republican ideas he was able to make a strong impression. To a few he seemed merely a rather seedy soldier who scribbled verses, but to the great majority, particularly to the young and impressionable, he seemed the personification of the romantic poet who was also a man of action.

In 1807 he published the poem generally considered his masterpiece, "Dei Sepolcri" or "On Tombs." Napoleon, who by then was emperor, had decreed that because of overcrowding and the danger of disease no more persons in the Kingdom of Italy were to be buried in the vaults inside the churches. With this as a starting point, "Yet a new law today sets graves beyond the pitying glances and to the dead denies their name," Foscolo quickly built around it a short, lyric poem of only 295 verses which in its evocation of the history and culture of Italy and ancient Greece seemed more like an epic. It was also, like many great works in Greek literature, didactic. Foscolo, while seeming only to talk of tombs, succeeded imaginatively in calling out of them the great men of the past and in setting them to fight again the battles of their time. The poem was much more subtly and profoundly anti-Napoleon than merely a protest against one of his decrees. Garibaldi, for example, whose favorite poet was Foscolo, thought the last four lines awoke in Italians more love of Italy and willingness to die for it than any other "cry of the poet":

> *E tu onore di pianti, Ettore, avrai*
> *ove fia santo e lagrimato il sangue*
> *per la patria versato, e finchè il Sole*
> *risplenderà su sciagure umane.*

> (And you, Hector, will be honored in tears
> wherever they deem holy and lament blood
> shed for one's country, and so long as
> the Sun shines upon human sorrows.)

The essence of the poem is Foscolo's tragic view of life, which is suggested by the fact that having worked his way through a discussion of specific men in Italian culture, he ends in the Homeric world of fantasy with Hector, the noble and yet defeated. This, he suggests, is man's lot in life, yet how noble. And this view of life, hopeless but magnificent, is reflected in the poem's tension between the specific and the fantastic and, even more, in its sense of agitation easing itself in the calm of contemplation. The tone of the poem became the dominant tone of the Risorgimento. Again and again Italians would act in a manner that seemed to say: We know our acts will probably achieve nothing except to cause us to die, yet we must do them if we are to be men.

The section of the poem in which Foscolo calls a symbolic roll of the great men in Italian culture had an immediate extraliterary effect that has lessened in time. In it Foscolo imagined himself in Santa Croce in Florence and wrote (in literal translation):

The tombs of brave men, O Pindemonte [the unimportant young man to whom the poem is technically addressed], fire the strong spirit to great deeds and make the earth that holds them beautiful and holy to the pilgrim. When I saw the monument where lies the body of that great man who, even as he strengthened the sceptre of rulers, took leaves from their laurel, and revealed to peoples with what tears and blood it runs [Machiavelli]; and the ark of him who in Rome raised a new Olympus to the Deities [Michelangelo]; and of him who saw more worlds turning under the ethereal canopy, and the Sun, motionless, lighting them [Galileo], whence he first cleared the ways of the firmament for the Englishman who there stretched so great a wing [Newton]; I cried out, you blessed one [the city of Florence], for your happy breezes stirring with life, and for the streams that Apennine pours down to you from her crests! The moon, glad with your air, clothes your hills, that are rejoicing for the wine-harvest, with clearest light, and the clustering valleys peopled with houses and olive groves send up a thousand flowering incenses: and you first, Florence, heard the song that lightened the anger of the fugitive Ghibelline [Dante], and you gave parents and speech to that soft lip of Calliope [Petrarch] who, adorning Love, naked in Greece and naked in Rome, with a veil of the whitest, restored her to the lap of Heavenly Venus: but more blessed because you keep, gathered in one temple, Italian glories, that are unique perhaps, since the ill-contested Alps and the changing omnipotence of human fate have spoiled you of arms and possessions and altars and native land and everything, except memory. So when hope of glory comes to shine upon daring minds and upon Italy, from these shall we draw auguries. And to these marble tombs Vittorio [Alfieri] came often for inspiration. Angry with his country's gods, he would wander silently where the Arno is most barren, and look longingly at the fields and the sky; and when no living sight softened his cares, here the austere man rested; and on his face there was the pallor of death and hope. He lives eternally with these great: and his bones tremble with love for his country.

At the time the poem was published, Italians noted, with amusement or anger, that Foscolo had chosen to reminisce in Santa Croce rather than, say, in St. Peter's; that he had chosen to celebrate Machiavelli, Alfieri, Galileo and even Newton without mentioning any pope or even a churchman; and that he had named no Italian prince at all. Men recognized that he had called a republican roll in which republican ideas were plainly implicit: a united Italy, with an end of the Church's temporal power; an emphasis on science, with an end of the Church's control of education; and a republican state, with an end of the kings and dukes. This extraliterary effect, of course, has no bearing on the poem's existence today as a work of literature, but at the time it was both a sign and a seed of the strength of the republican tradition in Italian life.

The year after the poem appeared several Academies of Literature honored Foscolo with degrees and membership, and more important he asked for and was granted the Chair of Eloquence, which today would be called of Literature, at the University of Pavia. While he was preparing his opening lecture, the post, along with its counterparts at the Universities of Padua and Bologna, was abolished by order of the viceroy. The object was not so much to silence Foscolo as an individual as, by making the Italian curriculum conform to the educational system Napoleon was establishing in France, to prevent the kind of independent thinking and individual development that such liberal arts chairs seemed to foster. In France, Napoleon was reorganizing secondary education on more classical, military and utilitarian lines. After the *lycée* abler students were to continue in professional training schools. He was uninterested in and even disapproved of individual development. As for the arts, he wrote once: "People complain that we have no literature: it is the fault of the Minister of the Interior."

Even without the post Foscolo went ahead with his lectures, and in January 1809 before the faculty, many of the leading men in the kingdom and some four hundred students, he read a paper on "The Origin and Function of Literature." Again his ideas of Italy, liberty and republicanism are inseparable: "The virtues, the misfortunes and the faults of great men cannot be written in academies or monasteries." He urged a literature that would be not of the courts, not of the Church nor of private Academies of Learned Men, but of the people. "O my fellow-citizens! How meagre is the consolation of being upright and cultured unless it preserves our country from the ignorant and vile." And then, using the word in a triple sense of visit, study and know, he cried, "Visitate l'Italia!"

The students applauded frantically. The faculty, more decorously, suggested that Napoleon might be persuaded to award him the Legion of Honor if he would publish the lecture with a preface in praise of the emperor "that is customary on these occasions." But Foscolo replied that "a distinction is even greater if it merits a decoration without having it." Again the students approved.

After the lecture Foscolo gave a series of classes in which he explained and enlarged on his points, and then later he gave a second formal lecture on "The Origins and Limits of Justice." From the classrooms and lecture hall where they had listened to Foscolo, many students went out to be in the first rank of conspirators, martyrs and exiles of the Risorgimento.

Sooner or later, it was evident, the viceroy would have to silence Foscolo, and the Milanesi waited with interest for the occasion. It came on the night of 9 December 1811 with the presentation of his play *Ajax* at La Scala. The play is not a great work and important only because after the première it was banned. It expressed patriotic sentiments, and many people saw in the character of Agamemnon, portrayed as a tyrant, a picture of Napoleon. Foscolo had powerful patrons in Milan, but even so he found it opportune to leave the city. He could not visit the Countess of Albany in Florence, for Napoleon, angered by the focus her salon had given to discontent with his Italian regime, had ordered her to live in Paris for a year. So Foscolo went first to Venice, where he visited his mother for three months, and then on to Bologna and later to Florence. But he had made his point, often enough and in a sufficient number of ways for it to have sunk into the Italian consciousness. Thereafter there would always be Italians, many not even republicans, who shared Foscolo's view of Napoleon in Italy.

Clerical opposition to Napoleon centered inevitably on Rome and on the pope, who had the position to make his protests audible, even if not effective. Cardinals and bishops either flocked around Napoleon out of admiration or fear, or else they were apt to be in prison or in exile. As for parish priests, if they were in Calabria, they were actually fighting Napoleon, and if they were elsewhere they were entirely at the mercy of the State. When a nun near Bergamo had visions and a priest alleged that she had received the stigmata and proclaimed her a saint, the chief of police promptly arrested them and put them in dungeons. The viceroy, who feared that a nun who was a saint might cause the people to question Napoleon's policy toward the Church, approved the arrest, sentenced the two to six months each in prison and deprived the priest of his living. There was no formal inquiry or public trial. No witness was heard for the defense, nor was anyone consulted other than the chief of police and the Minister of the Public Workshop. Presumably the neighbors wondered where the priest and nun had gone, and presumably those two decided after six months in prison that the political climate was unfavorable for saints. But the incident was not allowed to become known, much less a cause, and sainthood, which to most men seems peculiarly a matter for the Church to investigate and pronounce upon, was treated as a matter wholly for the State.

The pope's difficulties with Napoleon increased rapidly after his return to Rome from the Imperial coronation. Not only did Napoleon refuse to return the Legations or to give up the Adriatic port of Ancona but under his pose as Charlemagne he now claimed to be the pope's feudal lord and, if Pius VII failed in his feudal duties, to have a right to all the Papal States. Pius, of course, denied that a thousand years earlier Pope Leo III had received the lands from Charlemagne in fief and pointed out that a thousand years of sovereignty was better title than any other monarch in Europe could show. Napoleon's claim was amusingly pert, but it concealed, as Pius only now began to realize, a threat of naked force.

Napoleon wanted to close the Papal ports to British and allied shipping, and to do this he tried to force the pope into his Imperial confederation. Pius refused: "We are the Vicar of a God of peace, which means peace toward all, without distinction between Catholics and heretics . . . Only the necessity of withstanding hostile aggression, or defending religion in danger, has given Our predecessors a just reason for abandoning a pacific policy." Napoleon, who had protested previously that "Your Holiness means well, but he is surrounded by men who do not," now occupied the ports.

To conciliate Napoleon, Pius accepted the resignation of his Secretary of State, Consalvi, who was one of the men Napoleon disliked. At the same time he told Napoleon's ambassador: "Repeat to him that We do not wish to make any bargain, that We wish to remain independent because We are sovereign, that if he takes violent action against Us, We shall protest in the face of Europe, and that we shall use the temporal and the spiritual means which God has placed in Our hands." It was a plain threat of excommunication.

Napoleon once remarked that it was necessary to treat the pope "as though he had an army of 200,000 men," and now for eighteen months he hesitated. Part of his claim to be a legitimate emperor was that this very pope had anointed him, and in Spain, Poland, Italy and France excommunication would shake that claim seriously. But Napoleon wanted to control the coastline as well as the ports and in November 1807 he occupied the Papal provinces on the Adriatic coast and united them to the Kingdom of Italy. Against the provinces on the west coast, those with Rome at their center, he proceeded more cautiously. He occupied them, including Rome, but left the pope's political authority in Rome technically untouched.

The occupation created an impossible situation. There was no question this time of any native republican enthusiasm. The people rallied to Pius, and he in the interests of peace kept them from attacking the small French garrison. The French for their part, knowing they were few among many, walked carefully and politely. One of their generals observed: "The Pope ruled by moving his finger far more effectively than we with our bayonets." Yet Pius was a prisoner. Napoleon had ordered all cardinals who were subjects of the French Empire or its dependent states to leave Rome, so that Pius had less than ten left to support him. The Papal printing presses were closed down, the mail was slowed and intercepted, messengers were arrested and even the Papal guards were gradually disarmed so that the pope's authority soon stretched no farther than the Palazzo del Quirinale unless his orders could be smuggled out. Yet he said to the French ambassador: "You may tell them at Paris that they may hack me in pieces, that they may skin me alive, but I always shall say NO to any suggestion that I should adhere to a system of confederation."

If Pius had doubts over his course, he never wavered publicly. Always he maintained a steadfast refusal to negotiate, insisting that for the Church to insure its spiritual independence it must also have political independence; if not in its entire traditional domain then, at very least, in Rome, its port, and the countryside immediately around them.

In later years, when a secular Italian government controlled all the pope's former territory, the ports would be closed to shipping hostile to the secular government although not hostile to the Church, and most men and the Church accepted this as reasonable. But in the days of Pius VII drawing the line between temporal and spiritual in such a place was new, and Pius was not old-fashioned in rejecting it, although there were French laymen and even cardinals who accused him of caring more for his "petty duchy" than the spiritual interests of the Church. These men and Napoleon, however, had pushed the line a great deal further into the generally accepted domain of the spirit than merely the Papal ports. In France, the Church, led by its French cardinals and supported by a number of Italian cardinals who clustered like moths around Napoleon, had introduced a catechism into the Sunday Schools in which typical Questions and Answers were:

Q: What are the duties of Christians toward the princes who govern them, and what, in particular, are our duties toward Napoleon I, our Emperor?

A: Christians owe to the princes who govern them, and we, in particular, owe to Napoleon I, our Emperor, love, respect, obedience, loyalty, military service, and the taxes ordered for the preservation and defense of the Empire and his throne; we also owe him fervent prayers for his safety and for the spiritual and temporal prosperity of the State.

Q: Are there special reasons why we should have a particular loyalty to Napoleon I, our Emperor?

A: Yes there are; for God raised him up in difficult times to reestablish the public practice of the holy religion of our ancestors, and to protect it. He restored and preserved public order by his deep and active wisdom; he defends the state by the strength of his arm; he has become the Lord's Anointed by the consecration he received from the Sovereign Pontiff, the head of the Church Universal.

Q: What ought one to think of those who fail in their duty toward our Emperor?

A: According to the Apostle Saint Paul they are resisting the order established by God Himself and making themselves worthy of eternal damnation.

And there were more Questions and Answers, often with more of what was owed to Napoleon than to God. Pius and the Church at Rome never approved this catechism. Plainly, if Pius accepted Napoleon's plan that the pope be merely Bishop of Rome, then Emperor Franz would have a similar catechism for Austrian children, the Bourbons for Neapolitan children, and the one, true Faith would dissolve into a number of national churches each at the service of its state. Pius never doubted that it was his duty as pope to prevent such a dissolution of the Church, and although the issue between himself and Napoleon was, on its surface, temporal, directly underneath was the spiritual issue.

The pope, through his Secretary of State, smuggled orders out to the clergy in his Adiatic provinces not to take the oath of allegiance to the

Kingdom of Italy into which Napoleon had put them. As a result, the French general in Rome arrested the Cardinal-Secretary and imprisoned him. Pius, in defiance, then appointed as Secretary a cardinal, Bartolomeo Pacca, who was considered to be the toughest cardinal in the Curia. In the circumstances he was the right man for the job: he was short, thick-set, physically strong and without any doubts at all; he had never believed in the policy of coming to terms with revolutionary France; and he boiled with indignation over Napoleon's treatment of the Church. He was a natural foil for the more frail, gentle Pius who, with his nervous temperament, tended to become flushed at any excitement or even, sometimes, physically ill.

The French soon wished to be rid of Pacca, and an incident in the summer of 1808 seemed to give them their chance. The French general, S. A. F. Miollis, had tried to organize a system of volunteer civic guards in Rome and other Papal cities, but Pacca, on the pope's orders, had managed to placard the walls of the various towns urging the citizens not to enroll. So Miollis sent some officers to the Palazzo del Quirinale to arrest Pacca and remove him from Rome. Pacca had time to get word to the pope, who was in another part of the building, and before the arresting officers could hustle Pacca out, Pius appeared in the room. Pacca later wrote that then, for the first time in his life, he saw a man's hair literally "standing on end" with indignation. Controlling himself, Pius informed the officers that he would no longer suffer such outrages as this, that he understood the French hoped by them to make it impossible for him to exercise his authority, spiritual or temporal, and that he therefore commanded the cardinal to follow him into his private chambers and be his companion "in prison." And if General Miollis intended still to seize Cardinal Pacca he would have to do so in the pope's presence and in his private chambers, and he would have to suffer the consequences for such an outrageous act before the judgment of Europe. Turning on his heel and with Pacca at his side the pope left the room. Two great gilded doors closed behind him and were bolted shut. As the two men passed through the palace, seventeen doors in all slammed and locked between Pius and General Miollis. Back in the pope's apartments Pacca set about notifying the ambassadors of the great powers of what had happened.

For the moment Napoleon did nothing, consoling himself with the arrest and exile from Rome of various lesser Church officials. Throughout the winter of 1808–09 he was at war in Spain and southern Italy and in the spring, for the fourth time, he went to war with the Emperor of Austria. In all three countries the people were increasingly aroused against him, and he did not wish to appear before them as an excommunicated emperor. Pius, reduced now from the former extent of the Papal States to merely a few rooms, had left to play only the card of excommunication, and he waited for the best moment.

Napoleon's campaign against Austria went well but not decisively. He captured Vienna and installed himself in the Habsburg palace at Schönbrunn, but the Austrian army was undefeated and, led by the Archduke Karl, had won some minor victories. Still he was in the enemy's capital and confident. On 17 May 1809 he decreed that what was left of the Papal States was to become part of his empire. Rome was to be a "Free Imperial City" and the pope was to be allowed to remain as Bishop of Rome, in possession of his palaces and of a suitable revenue, but holding no temporal power. The decree expressed Napoleon's thesis, now fully developed, that Rome was a fief of Charlemagne which he, as Charlemagne's heir, could revoke. And on 10 June the Papal flag over Sant' Angelo was lowered, and the French tricolor raised in its place. Neapolitan troops sent by Murat and French troops reenforced by a regiment of cavalry from Florence policed the streets. Yet before nightfall on the walls of each of the three great basilicas, Saint Peter's, S. Giovanni in Laterano and Santa Maria Maggiore there mysteriously appeared two proclamations. One called on the Romans not to support the new regime; the other was a bull of excommunication against Napoleon.

Napoleon's police did everything in their power to prevent word of the excommunication from spreading, but it was an impossible job: too many people were too interested in using it against him and thousands of copies of the pope's bull soon appeared in Spain, Austria, Belgium, Poland and even in the more Catholic parts of France. News of it reached Napoleon two weeks before the battle of Wagram when he still had not won his Austrian campaign. He wrote at once to Murat, who, although in Naples, had Neapolitan troops at Rome and was technically in command of all troops in the city: "The Pope is a raving madman who must be shut up. Arrest Cardinal Pacca and the other adherents of the Pope." This letter, taken alone, would seem to support Napoleon's claim of later years that he had never intended and did not order the pope's arrest.

But the day before he had learned of the excommunication, he had written General Miollis in Rome in broader language: "You should arrest, even in the Pope's establishment, all those who plot against public order and the safety of the army." And at the same time he had written to Murat at Naples in greater detail: ". . . matters at Rome must be dealt with brusquely; no resistance can be tolerated. . . . If, contrary to the spirit of the Gospel, the Pope preaches revolt, and uses the immunity of the Quirinal to print circulars, he must be arrested. There is no more time for discussion. Philip the Fair arrested Boniface, and Charles V kept Clement VII for long in prison; and they had done much less to deserve it."

But Miollis, the general in day-to-day command at Rome, had received the less explicit of the two letters, the one without the clear historical examples. After the bull of excommunication he was quite prepared to break into the Palazzo del Quirinale to arrest Pacca, but he hesitated at arresting the pope. His aide, General Radet, did not; to him Napoleon's intent was clear and, in view of Miollis's hesitation, he saw a chance to make his name. Miollis would not give Radet a written order but he did agree orally that if Pius refused to renounce his temporal sovereignty then Radet could arrest him and remove him to the Certosa outside Florence, the same one in which the Directory had imprisoned Pius VI eleven years earlier.

Radet divided his troops into two groups, one to scale the walls of the palazzo by ladder and to enter through the roof, and the other, as a reserve group, to surround the building. The assault started in the early hours of the morning, shortly after two. The night was hot and still, and the men worked quietly. Then a ladder broke, dropping Radet and several others to the ground in a heap. None was injured, but the noise alerted those inside the palazzo which was soon ablaze with lights. Some French, however, succeeded in climbing in through the roof and opened the doors for the others.

The Swiss Guards were under orders not to resist French soldiers and did not. But some doors were bolted and had to be hacked open, orders were shouted, and some mirrors and vases were smashed. As a result there was considerable time lost, noise and confusion. Eventually Radet found himself at the entrance to the Hall of Audience, where inside he saw the pope with Pacca and four other cardinals sitting at a table, waiting. They were dressed, for there had been plenty of time, in their robes of office, the cardinals in red and the pope, in the center, in white. Radet, hatchet in hand, hot and perspiring, hesitated. Later he was to say "in the road, on the roofs, mounting the stairs with the Swiss, it all seemed splendid. But when I saw the Pope, at that same moment, I saw myself once more at my first Communion."

Then, in agreement with an account by Pacca, Pius, who had seen the general hesitate, asked softly:

"And why have you come?"

"Most Holy Father, to repeat, in the name of the French Government, to your Holiness, the proposition that he should renounce his temporal power."

"We cannot yield what does not belong to us. The temporal power belongs to the Church."

"Then I am under orders to take you away."

"Assuredly, my son, those orders will not bring divine blessings upon you." 9

But Radet could not turn back; indeed, if he was to have the pope out of Rome before the city woke, he had to hurry on. So within three quarters of an hour, shortly after 4 A.M., he had Pius and Pacca, still dressed in their robes, in a coach and started for Florence. Pius, ordered to collect quickly what he might need for a journey, for neither he nor Pacca knew where they were to be taken, took with him his ciborium, containing the Blessed Sacrament, his breviary and his rosary. It did not occur to him to pack any money, tobacco, clean linen or even an extra pair of shoes.

When Napoleon heard of the kidnapping, he was angry or pretended to be. To the chief of police in Paris he wrote: "It is a piece of utter folly. Cardinal Pacca should have been arrested and the Pope left peacefully at Rome. But there is no way to remedying the matter; what is done is done . . . if he stops being so foolish I should not be opposed to his being taken back to Rome." To a number of others, almost as if trying to spread his innocence on the record, he wrote similar thoughts. And to Miollis, perhaps forgetting the broad terms in which he had previously written, he now insisted: "I ordered that Cardinal Pacca should be arrested and not the Pope"; and, he added, "An operation of such importance ought not to have been carried out without my being warned in advance and without my naming the place to which he should be taken."

Napoleon's last point leads to the best evidence that perhaps truly he had not intended to abduct the pope, for the operation, after the actual arrest, was bungled. Radet made the pope travel all the first day, in the steaming July of central Italy, in a closed coach. By the next morning Pius, who was sixty-six and never a good traveler, was vomiting and had dysentery. So Radet laid over for the day at Radicofani and left the next night at eleven. He drove the horses hard, fearing an attempt at rescue by the peasants who were beginning to line the road. Near Poggibonsi an axle broke, and the coach overturned. When the party finally arrived at Florence, less than two days after starting, the pope, haggard and obviously suffering, was already half a martyr in the eyes of all who had seen him.

At Florence he was allowed barely four hours of sleep before he was started on again. The French officials in Tuscany thought him "a very embarrassing present" and were eager to pass him on to others. His face, according to Pacca, was green with exhaustion, and at Florence the two men were separated. Pacca was sent directly to the Fenestrelle prison in the mountains of Savoy; Pius was taken first around the city of Genoa into Piedmont, then over the Alps to Grenoble whence, on Napoleon's order, he was returned via the Rhône valley and riviera to Savona, which is near Genoa, and installed in a small, bishop's palace. Although a prisoner, his trip down the Rhône valley and along the riviera had become a triumphal procession, and the fact of the pope's imprisonment hurt Napoleon as much as the bull of excommunication. Whatever Napoleon may have intended before the pope's arrest, after it he did not remove Miollis or Radet from their posts, nor, in spite of what he suggested in his letters, did he show any inclination to return the pope to Rome. In fact in the following six months he moved everything he could of Papal government to Paris: all the cardinals except a single ancient, all the heads of the religious orders, chief officers of the congregations and departments of state and the entire archives at the Vatican Palace. Paris became the seat of the Church, and Rome was proclaimed, in place of being a "free imperial city," the "Second City of the Empire" and incorporated into France. General Miollis appointed Duke Braschi to be the mayor, and the Civil Code was introduced. All the monks, priests and bishops who followed Pius' proclamation and refused to swear allegiance to the new government were exiled or imprisoned, and clerical opposition in the city, while continuing often to be a cause of personal suffering, ceased to be an effective political force.

By the winter of 1811–12 Napoleon's regime in Italy, in whatever form it assumed locally, was well established. But even those who approved of it, who could see the benefits in the new roads, the new laws and the new system of administration, were increasingly unhappy with it. Even rabid anticlerics, when faced with the pope's imprisonment, were forced to admit that the regime was a tyranny, more complete than Italy had known in hundreds of years.

# CHAPTER 16

Wagram. The Treaty of Schönbrunn. Metternich. Marie Louise.
The black cardinals. Napoleon and Pius. The Pope returns to Rome.

WITH THE BATTLE of Wagram on 5–6 July 1809, Napoleon closed his fourth campaign against the Austrian House of Habsburg. The battle was a victory, but not like Austerlitz. Napoleon's army of 182,000 was almost half again as large as the combined Austrian armies led by two archdukes, yet his losses were considerably greater. His best troops were tied up in Spain, and their absence was significant. After the first day's exceptionally bloody fighting his right wing nearly collapsed in panic when Austrian patrols appeared on its flank, and although the situation was saved, he could not pursue the Austrian armies as they retreated. He held the field and Vienna, but he was not in a position to dictate.

The Austrians, through their minister of foreign affairs, offered to negotiate, and Napoleon agreed to listen. The Austrian minister was Klemens von Metternich, a German from the Rhineland, who had entered the service of the Habsburgs in 1801 and was just beginning his forty years of power as their chief minister. Considering the military situation after Wagram the terms Metternich agreed to in the Treaty of Schönbrunn were extraordinarily harsh. On the Adriatic, Austria lost its port of Trieste, as well as most of its ancient Duchies of Carniola and Carinthia which lay behind Trieste. It also lost most of its Kingdom of Croatia. All these lands Napoleon combined with Istria and Dalmatia, which he detached from the Kingdom of Italy, to form a large, eastern Adriatic state which he called "The Illyrian Provinces" and incorporated directly into France.

In the Alps, for the third time in four years Austria gave up the County of Tirol to France's ally, Bavaria. Twice a peasant leader, Andreas Hofer, had led a revolt against the Bavarians, defeated them and returned the strongly Habsburg County to its "good Kaiser Franz." But now Metternich again let it go. His policy can only be understood in terms of a note he wrote to Franz after Wagram: "From the day we make peace we

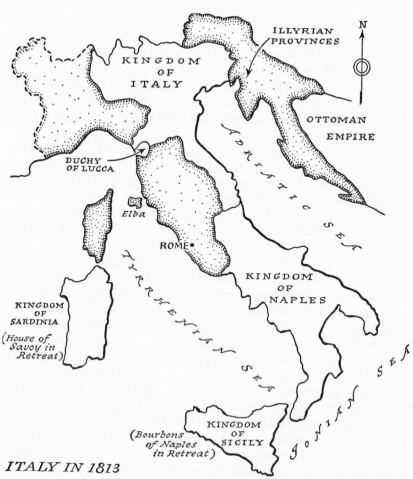

**ITALY IN 1813**

*Jagged borders* ▬▬▬ *show extent of the French Empire under Napoleon who was also King of Italy....His brother-in-law, Joachim Murat was King of Naples and his sister, Elisa, was Duchess of Lucca.*

must confine our system entirely to maneuver, evasion and compliance. In this way alone can we hope possibly to maintain our existence until the day of general deliverance. We have only one expedient; we must reserve our power for better times."

Metternich knew that Napoleon, even if never defeated, must at least someday die, and he gauged, quite correctly, that Napoleon's arbitrary political schemes would not survive his defeat or death. Two years before Wagram, Metternich had already observed: "It is curious that Napoleon, while tormenting and modifying incessantly the relations of all the European states, has not yet taken a single step which will tend to assure the permanence of his successes."

For Metternich the treaty was merely a truce. Basing his policy on the idea that for Napoleon, the supreme egoist, the demonstration of power was more important than the permanence of anything achieved by it, Metternich was willing to let "The Illyrian Provinces" go. Austria would easily pick them up again in the confusion following Napoleon's death or defeat. Habsburg experience showed that in contemporary Europe isolated holdings, such as Belgium had been for Austria and as The Illyrian Provinces would be for France, were always the first to gravitate toward a nearer center of power. So, if Napoleon wanted to talk grandly of his outpost to the east, to gesture into being a new state with odd boundaries and to invent a new name for the historical record, Metternich was willing to let him; meanwhile Austria would wait, with its armies intact, for better times.

Such a policy, when it involved giving up the intensely loyal County of Tirol, offended many. But Metternich at least did not require more of the people than he did of their Emperor Franz. He knew that Napoleon wanted an heir and was ready to divorce Joséphine, who was unable to provide one, and he also knew that Tsar Alexander had recently refused an overture from Napoleon for one of the tsar's sisters. It seems probable that Metternich was the first to suggest that Napoleon marry a Habsburg archduchess, but wherever the idea originated, he adopted it and persuaded Franz to offer his nineteen-year-old daughter, Marie Louise. Napoleon was pleased. The girl was pretty, came from a fertile family and was more or less descended from Charlemagne. The Habsburgs were more doubtful: there was, first of all, Napoleon's lack of background, and his appalling family, then the scandal of his divorce from Joséphine, and finally his hostility to the Habsburgs. And even Maria Theresa had not married her daughters to men of state against whom she was actively working and hoping would die. At Palermo the girl's grandmother, Maria Carolina, from the depths of her adversity wailed of "the infamy of this alliance."

But the marriage took place, first by proxy in Vienna with an archduke acting for Napoleon and then again on 2 April 1810 in the Salon Carré of the Louvre. Napoleon, who had gone to meet Marie Louise at Compiègne, had already consummated the marriage before the second ceremony and was delighted and even half in love with his bride, as was she with him.

The marriage in the Louvre, which was then called the Musée Napoléon, was probably the greatest spectacle in the history of the palace. The ceremony included a bridal procession throughout the entire length of the Grande Galerie with massed spectators lining the way. On the walls was the best of the art that Napoleon and the revolutionary armies had looted from the Netherlands, Germany and Italy. In the wedding party were marshals of France, cardinals in scarlet robes and a number of kings and queens. In the center of all was the self-made emperor with the eldest daughter of the first family of Europe as his bride. At the wedding banquet Metternich, representing Emperor Franz, raised his glass "To the King of Rome!", the title Napoleon had chosen for his prospective son because it was reminiscent of the heir apparent's title in the defunct Holy Roman Empire: King of the Romans. Even the Habsburgs seemed now to acknowledge him as the new Charlemagne.

The occasion had just the combination of history and splashy grandeur that appealed to Napoleon, and yet he was not pleased. Thirteen cardinals had refused to attend the marriage and half a row of prominent stalls had been empty. Napoleon made no attempt to conceal his anger; he muttered audibly: "The fools! I see what they want! To protest against the legitimacy of my blood, to ruin my dynasty! The fools!"

The thirteen, led by Consalvi, had protested on behalf of the pope, who was still a prisoner at Savona and had not been consulted about the divorce. Napoleon had obtained it simply by ordering a Parisian ecclesiastical court to grant it. He handled the cardinals by summoning them to an audience, making them wait two hours in a busy antechamber and then sending a servant to turn them out into the street. In Consalvi's words: "It is easier to imagine than to describe this expulsion of thirteen cardinals in full ceremonial dress, an expulsion carried out in so public a place, in front of everybody, and with such ignominy." They were driven through antechambers, reception rooms and the great hall until they reached the street, where, their carriages not having been ordered, they had to walk home. Further Napoleon deprived them of their pensions and their right to wear scarlet robes and exiled them to provincial cities in France. Because they could not wear their scarlet robes but dressed as ordinary priests they became popularly known as "the black cardinals."

The fate of these men compounded Napoleon's disagreement with the pope, who refused to withdraw the bull of excommunication, continued to demand to be returned to Rome and, most important, refused to invest with spiritual authority the new bishops Napoleon wanted to appoint to vacancies in France. This last became the crucial point, for Napoleon could not ignore it. With French troops occupying Rome, the pope's protests hardly affected the reality of Napoleon's power in the city. But when the Archbishop of Paris died in 1808 and no one was able to succeed with the pope's blessing, the vacancy continued day after day in the center of the city's religious life, making it difficult for the Church there to function and reminding the people that Napoleon was excommunicated and the pope his prisoner. And in addition to Paris there were twenty-six other vacant sees.

The pope's right to invest new bishops with their spiritual authority was guaranteed by the concordat which Napoleon, who had taken credit for it as a great triumph, was loathe to abrogate. Yet each time Napoleon suggested solutions to their disagreements the pope replied that in considering them he must have the advice of the "counsellors of his choice," Pacca and the black cardinals. But their advice was just what Napoleon was determined to prevent Pius from having.

In his effort to force the pope to some sort of agreement Napoleon gradually increased the severity of the imprisonment. Pius was deprived of servants, of writing paper, of exercise and of visitors, except for cardinals and bishops who supported Napoleon and were sent to Savona to assure him that far from preserving the spiritual authority of the Church he was destroying it through pride and eccentricity. There is even evidence that on one occasion, in May 1811, Pius may have been induced to agree to the proposals of three visiting bishops through having been drugged with morphine in the guise of sedatives. If so, he had at least signed nothing and was able the next day to repudiate the agreement.

The following month Napoleon tried to circumvent the pope by convening a council of bishops in Paris. He made much of the council's authority as a body of French bishops "attached to the soil by all the ties of blood" and stated that Pius VII "had shown nothing but indifference for the true interests of religion." But the bishops, even without Pacca and the black cardinals in their midst, resented Napoleon's interference. They said bluntly that they disliked his treatment of the pope, and they swore an oath of "true obedience to the supreme Roman Pontiff." And they refused to discuss the investiture question further without the pope's permission, in writing.

Napoleon's oppression was beginning to create its own opposition, but he was incapable any longer of changing course. He dissolved the council, put its leaders in jail and then reconvened the more timid bishops. But even these, although they agreed with Napoleon's proposals, insisted that their approval was subject to the approval of the pope. So once again a delegation of red cardinals and bishops went to Savona.

This time Pius indirectly submitted to what he understood was the opinion of a majority of the bishops of the Church convened in a council. The delegation styled itself "deputies from the Paris Council," but it is doubtful how much of the history of the Paris Council Pius knew. He had been imprisoned for more than two years without any disinterested source of news. He could see that neither Pacca nor Consalvi ever came to visit him, whereas in each delegation the members were more than ever toadies of Napoleon. But much more than this he probably did not know. Napoleon had persuaded the rump council to approve a plan whereby the metropolitans, the heads of ecclesiastical provinces, should be empowered to invest bishops with their spiritual authority if the pope had failed to invest them six months after Napoleon had nominated them. Pius now capitulated and approved this proposal.

But he did so in his own way. He refused to recognize any authority in the Paris Council, which had been summoned without his consent, and he therefore refused to approve any decisions reached by the council. Instead he wrote a "Brief to the Bishops of the Empire" in which he granted the essential point but made it clear that the Roman Church, as opposed to the French or Spanish Church, was "mother and mistress of the other Churches."

The delegates were delighted and so filled the palazzo at Savona with their rejoicings over the prospect of peace between Church and State that even Pius began to believe in it. But Napoleon angrily rejected the Brief, and through his Minister of Cults he forbade the delegates at Savona to accept it. He was angry over the phrase "mother and mistress of the other Churches," angry that Pius denied official status and authority to the Paris Council, and angry that Pius had worded the brief so that the new method of investiture did not apply to the former Papal States. And he insisted that he would not restore the pope to his former freedom and position until the bishops already nominated had been invested with their spiritual authority by the pope.

What, the bishops wondered, did Napoleon expect of Pius? Some years later, on St. Helena, Napoleon stated that he had hoped to separate Church and State completely, and the words he used to describe that hope suggest how he could have rejected the pope's Brief: "I was in a position to exalt the Pope beyond all bounds and to surround him with such pomp and ceremony that he would have ceased to regret the loss of his temporal power. I would have made an idol of him. . . . Paris would have become the capital of Christendom, and I would have become the master of the religious as well as the political world. . . . My Church councils would have been representative of all Christendom, and the Popes would have been mere chairmen. I would have opened and closed these assemblies, approved and made public their decisions, as did Constantine and Charlemagne."

As early as 1807 Talleyrand had wondered if Napoleon were still sane, and these words with the concept of the pope as an idol suggest, at least, that for Napoleon the gap between what he imagined was possible and the reality of it was steadily widening. It is not conceivable that Pius VII or any successor or substitute, elected by the cardinals, would have agreed to such a plan. Yet Napoleon, even though the wild words were spoken later, acted at the time as though they described the immediate object of the pope's imprisonment. In February 1812 he suggested to the pope by letter: "Since the Pope finds himself unable to distinguish what is dogmatic, and thus essential to religion, from what is temporal, and thus subject to change, why does he not resign?" But Pius refused, and the sees continued vacant.

During the spring and summer Napoleon started his campaign into Russia. From Dresden he ordered the pope moved secretly to Fontainebleau. He was to be taken through Turin, Chambéry and Lyon, at night, and he was to travel in the black robes of a plain priest. At Savona no one could find any black shoes that fit Pius' small feet, so they inked over his white slippers.

The coach ride over the Alps almost killed him. As usual for him in a coach, after the first day his digestion ceased to function and this time, also, his urinary system broke down, so that although always feeling the need he was unable to relieve himself except by a few drops at a time ejected with the greatest pain. When the coach arrived at the top of Mont Cenis Pass, he had a high fever, and the monks at the hostel thought he was dying. The captain in command appealed to Turin for permission to delay, but orders came back that secrecy was to be maintained and the journey continued. Pius had earlier threatened to throw himself from the coach if forced to continue, but now he was too weak to stand. A litter was slung within the coach, and a local doctor agreed to accompany him to Fontainebleau. The passage through Lyon was taken at a gallop, and the doctor has left a description of it: "The uneven paving of the streets, together with the speed at which the horses were driven, made the carriage shake abominably. I was obliged with one hand to hold the Holy Father's head, to save it from being violently shaken, and with the other I held his stomach. When we had passed through, and after the horses had slackened their pace, His Holiness asked me if the rushing was over. I assured him that it was, and then the Holy Father murmured these remarkable words, which will always remain engraved on my mind: 'May God pardon him since, for my part, I have already pardoned him!' "

At Fontainebleau, Pius slowly recovered. He was allowed visitors but none of his own choice and he again had no disinterested source of news. Finally, in January 1813, after three and a half years of confinement, he learned that the emperor himself was coming to see him. Napoleon by then had lost his Russian campaign and for the second time in his career had left a defeated army in a hostile country while he returned to Paris. Once there he found himself surrounded with problems, many of which seemed to lead back to his unsettled business with the pope. In France as well as abroad Catholics were restless and resentful of his treatment of Pius. The Poles refused to enlist in his armies and conscripts complained of being made to fight a heretic's war. The sees were vacant, and the Church while moved from Rome was not yet established in Paris. On his return from Egypt he had soothed Catholic feelings by announcing a concordat; perhaps on his return from Russia he could soothe them again with a new concordat.

He sent down to Fontainebleau before him a delegation of red cardinals and French bishops to urge a new series of proposals to Pius. These included, beside the usual question of investiture, demands that the Papacy be established in Paris; that two-thirds of the cardinals be appointed by "the Catholic sovereigns," a euphemism for Napoleon; and that the black cardinals be condemned for their behavior. Pius refused, but he cannot have avoided being shaken by the number of cardinals and bishops who urged that he accept. Then came Napoleon.

For six days the two men were closeted alone in the Papal apartments at Fontainebleau, Church and State face to face. There is no record of what was said or done, and neither man in later life talked much of it. Pius, in some offhand remarks made later, did reveal enough to suggest that Napoleon attempted, by alternating violence with persuasion, either to frighten or to bewilder his seventy-one-year-old opponent into signing an agreement. Pius always insisted that he had not been physically assaulted, but he also told how Napoleon had grabbed him by the front of his soutane and pushed him around the room. And there seem to have been moments when he expected to be struck. There is also a story that Napoleon in his fury smashed a set of Sèvres china on the floor. In the end Napoleon called in the red cardinals to add their arguments and finally Pius signed a short paper, which Napoleon agreed to treat as confidential, and on which ten proposals were listed as the basis for a new concordat.

The pope, as he had already done in his brief, agreed that the metropolitans might invest bishops with their spiritual authority if the pope had not done so, within six months after their nomination. The other nine points were defeats for Napoleon. In sum, the pope was recognzed as temporal sovereign of Rome and, as a sign of it, had special rights of nominating and investing bishops in the Papal State; there was no mention of moving the Papacy to Paris. All the cardinals in prison or exile were to be released and restored to the pope, and there was no mention of punishment.

Pius considered that he had signed no more than a memorandum on which discussions for a new concordat would be based. But Napoleon, violating his agreement to keep the memorandum confidential, published it as the new concordat and presented it to the Senate for ratification as a treaty signed by the pope. And, making a show of observing its terms, he released Pacca and the black cardinals from prison and exile. Most Frenchmen, knowing only what Napoleon wished them to know, rejoiced that the conflict between Church and State was finally resolved.

Pacca, when he reached Fontainebleau, found Pius "bent, pale, emaciated, with his eyes sunk deep into his head, and motionless as though he were dazed. He greeted me, and said distantly that he had not expected me so soon. When I told him that I had made haste, so as to have the joy of placing myself at his feet and bearing witness to my admiration for the heroic constancy with which he had suffered so long and grievous an imprisonment, he was filled with distress and replied in these precise words: 'But, in the end, I was defiled. Those cardinals . . . they dragged me to the table and made me sign.' "

Surrounded again by cardinals he trusted, Pius wrote to Napoleon insisting that there was no concordat and repudiating the memorandum on the ground that it was extorted from him when he was a prisoner and deprived of his councilors. Most Frenchmen knew nothing of his efforts to deny the new concordat but were unhappily aware that he was still a prisoner. On the other hand they saw the cardinals were released. But then the issue was swallowed up for everyone by the military disasters that began to overtake Napoleon.

In August 1813 Austria joined the allies, consisting of Russia, Britain and Prussia; and in October, after a series of engagements around Dresden, Napoleon fought the continental powers at the battle of Leipzig and lost. He was heavily outnumbered and thrown into a disastrous retreat in which he lost thousands of men by death and desertion. He was forced back to the Rhine and from Spain another defeated French army retreated in disorder into southern France. The empire began to disintegrate, and Austrian troops started into The Illyrian Provinces. At the end of December, when Napoleon refused to accept a peace which would have left France with a frontier on the Rhine and Belgium, the allies began their invasion of France. As they advanced toward Paris, Napoleon ordered the pope returned for safer keeping to Savona.

In Italy the situation grew increasingly confused. At Milan the viceroy, Eugène, remained faithful to Napoleon and fought to keep the Austrians out of the Kingdom of Italy. But Murat in Naples, deserting Napoleon, drove the French from Rome and led an army north to join the Austrians against Eugène. For his help Murat was guaranteed his throne at Naples by Austria, and in his rear the British fleet prevented the Bourbons in Sicily from attacking him. Eugène fought well, but when his four French divisions were recalled to France, he was left in a hopeless position, and soon the Austrians and Murat had occupied the entire kingdom. Unaware of the changing situation Napoleon, meanwhile, had ordered the pope to be transferred to Parma as a step toward restoring him to Rome and toward embarrassing Murat, who had occupied the city and was planning to annex it and Ancona to his kingdom. But when Pius and his guards reached the outskirts of Parma, they found themselves surrounded by Austrian troops. After nearly five years as Napoleon's prisoner Pius VII finally was free.

From Parma, Pius traveled slowly on to Rome. His journey was a triumph. No head of state had suffered more from Napoleon nor resisted his tyranny with greater patience and dignity. Even anticlerical Italians admired him as a man, and for the faithful he represented both the triumph of Christian goodness over sinful pride and the victory of an Italian prince over a foreign invader. As a result his personal prestige was enormous, and it extended all over Europe. It procured for him immediately, through Austrian intervention, the evacuation from Rome of Murat's troops. Later, at the Congress of Vienna, it would retrieve for the Papacy the balance of the Papal States.

He entered Rome on 24 May 1814. Pacca was at his side in the coach, but Consalvi was in Paris representing the pope to the allies. Young nobles of Rome drew the Papal coach down the Corso; their virgin sisters, dressed in white, waved palms from the balconies; and cheering Romans jammed the side streets and squares. As in 1800, on his arrival from Venice, he did not go first to the Palazzo del Quirinale, the seat of his temporal government, but to St. Peter's, to give thanks for his deliverance and to ask guidance for the future. And for many men his return to St. Peter's was a triumphant vindication of the primacy in life of spiritual over temporal values, of the Church, if need be, over the State.

# CHAPTER 17

Franz regains Milan and Venice. Genoa given to Sardinia. Congress of Vienna. Form of the treaty. Napoleon's Hundred Days. Murat's attempt to make a united Italy. Maria Carolina exiled. Her death. Ferdinando restored to Naples. The Habsburg settlement of Italy.

THE SERIES OF TREATIES that reconstructed Europe after the Napoleonic wars are generally known as the treaties of the Congress of Vienna, although several preceded the congress and others, even after the congress opened, were not signed in Vienna. The first, which the allies signed with Napoleon at Fontainebleau, gave him the island of Elba, a large allowance to be paid by France and the right to keep the title of emperor. The second, signed in Paris, restored the Bourbons to the French throne in the person of Louis XVIII, the last king's brother. In this treaty, known as the First Peace of Paris, France renounced all her claims to Holland, Belgium, Germany, Italy, Switzerland and Malta, and some important decisions on the fate of these countries were adopted and included.

For Italians two of the decisions then made and adopted by the four allies as well as the new France were of crucial importance. First, Emperor Franz of Austria successfully reclaimed his Habsburg Duchies of Milan and Mantua and also the Veneto, Venice and its mainland on the peninsula, which he had received under the Treaty of Campoformio. Austrian troops already occupied the areas, and their presence together with the swift award of the land and peoples to Austria prevented, as they were designed to do, a rising of Italian republicans to continue the Napoleonic Kingdom of Italy as an independent republic. Foscolo and a number of lawyers and generals conspired to start such a movement, planning to make use of the Italian divisions of Eugène's army, some forty-five thousand men. But the Austrians, able to work openly, were also able to work faster. They gave one general a high post in Moravia, they replaced most of the junior officers and particularly the colonels of regiments with Austrians, and they stationed the regiments on the edges of the kingdom, separate from each other and difficult for the conspirators to get at. Mean-

182

while Austrian troops were posted at the center of affairs, in all the big cities and forts, and the conspiracy soon collapsed.

In the other decision made promptly in Paris the allies gave the entire former Republic of Genoa to the King of Sardinia. Once again, Italians of every political persuasion noted bitterly, the House of Savoy had detached another leaf of the artichoke and digested it with the general approval of Europe. The Genovesi were openly furious. For centuries their traditional enemy had been the House of Savoy and now they, with their strong republican tradition, were made to become the subjects of a king they hated. In the next forty years the tension this forced transfer introduced into the Kingdom of Sardinia almost wrecked it. Not until the 1850s, when Sardinia's king and prime minister, Vittorio Emanuele II and Cavour, openly embarked on a policy of unifying northern Italy, did the Genovesi become even partially reconciled.

The transfer was more the result of the wishes of the allies than of any energetic action on the part of the King of Sardinia. At the start of the revolutionary wars, in 1792, Vittorio Amedeo III had fought with the first coalition and as a result had lost Nice and Savoy to France and been forced to allow the French to occupy a number of forts in Piedmont. His son, Carlo Emanuele IV, had been more interested in his relations with God than with either the French or his own people, and under him Piedmont was lost to France and the kingdom reduced to the island of Sardinia. Shortly afterwards, in 1802, Carlo Emanuele abdicated in favor of his brother and retired to a monastery in Rome where many years later he died.

His brother, Vittorio Emanuele I, was hardly more energetic or competent as a king, although under him the dynasty recovered Piedmont, Nice and Savoy and added Genoa. The allies, perhaps, remembered the services and sufferings of the kingdom which had, after all, the oldest dynasty in Europe; and the wars had been fought, at least at their start, for the principle of monarchy. But a more powerful reason, perhaps, for the allies was their desire to re-establish a buffer state in Italy between France and Austria extending the line of such states that Switzerland, Holland, Bavaria and other German states formed to the north. None of the four allies was a republic, and none had any interest in reviving the Republic of Genoa. Transferring the former republic to Sardinia was a way of resolving the rivalry between the two neighbors in favor of the monarchy.

The transfer, like those in the past to Sardinia, increased the distrust with which most Italians regarded the House of Savoy and, at the same time, further tipped the interest of that House, whose lands straddled the Alps, away from France and toward Italy. With every Genovese taken into the king's service, with the acquisition of the riviera, the sailors, the merchant marine and the navy of Genoa, the attention of the government at Turin turned increasingly toward its Italian subjects, who now were a strong majority in the kingdom. The small, alpine farms of the French-speaking Savoyards were less rewarding to the government than the larger farms in the Po valley or the commercial enterprises of the Genovesi, and in the coming years the Savoyards, while continuing to be fervently loyal to their king, felt increasingly out of sympathy with the Italian aims of his government.

The issues not decided at Paris, such as the fate of the Legations, were postponed for Vienna under Article XXXII of the Paris treaty: "All the powers engaged on either side in the present war shall within the space of two months send plenipotentiaries to Vienna for the purpose of regulating in General Congress the arrangements which are to complete the present treaty." And every power or even would-be power sent a representative and sometimes whole camps of diplomats and their families. The Kingdom of Naples was even represented twice, with a delegation from Murat and another from Ferdinando. The pope sent Consalvi for the Papal States, and all the displaced dukes, even if only relying on the favor of some great power, had a recognized spokesman for their interest.

Technically the Congress of Vienna, as a meeting of the whole body of plenipotentiaries, never came into existence. When the number of representatives and the consequent clash of tongues became evident, the idea was discarded as unworkable. A committee of the great powers examined the credentials of the representatives, set a date for the congress to open and then postponed the date indefinitely. Meanwhile the representatives of the minor powers enjoyed the theater parties, balls and court functions that Emperor Franz provided, and the work of the congress was done in committees of the five great powers: Britain, France, Austria, Prussia and Russia. Few seriously challenged the system for, in the eyes of most men, Europe was still the governments of the states rather than the peoples governed. Yet the powers meeting in Vienna had a sense that, besides the states, the peoples of Europe were exhausted with the wars and looked to the congress to provide the next generation with a European settlement that would prevent any renewal of the upheaval and sufferings of the previous twenty-five years.

The form of the treaty which finally emerged from the congress was unusual and reflected the sense of mission with which the powers approached their work. In the past a congress, such as the meetings at Utrecht after the War of the Spanish Succession, produced a number of treaties each of which carried the signatures of only those parties who had an interest in the issue the particular treaty resolved. But at Vienna the many separate treaties, at the end of the congress in June 1815, were incorporated by reference into one great document which every power had to sign if it was to claim the benefit of any part of it. Further, by signing, each power undertook to guarantee the whole and not just those articles in which it had an interest. No reservations could be written in, and every power eventually did sign except the Ottoman Empire and the Papacy. The sultan was angered by Tsar Alexander's efforts to establish Russian influence in the Black Sea and Balkans, and the pope adopted the position that the Church should not undertake to guarantee any particular political order. The pope's position struck many diplomats as inconsistent and self-serving for under the treaty the Papacy recovered its three Legations and expected the other temporal powers to guarantee the settlement.

But the pope's refusal to sign was not significant and was hardly noticed except by the diplomats at Vienna, for in the same month, June 1815, all of Europe was waiting to see if Napoleon would win or lose the battle which was eventually fought at Waterloo. Louis XVIII had failed, apparently out of spite, to pay the allowance guaranteed to Napoleon by the Treaty of Fontainebleau, and Napoleon had used the arrears as an excuse to leave Elba. Evading British naval patrols for the third crucial time in his career, he had landed in southern France and once in Paris had promised to provide France with liberal institutions and a parliamentary form of government. His "Hundred Days," however, were never more than a personal adventure and, in the opinion of most historians, without a chance of success. The result for France, after his defeat at Waterloo, was the Second Peace of Paris, which was far harsher than the First. France now was forced to give up strips of its frontier to the Kingdom of the Netherlands and a part of Savoy, left to it before, was returned to Sardinia. All the works of art taken in the revolutionary and Napoleonic campaigns were to be returned, an indemnity to be paid and an army of occupation to be supported for five years. Even in France, Napoleon was thought to have put his personal glory before the good of the country, and the great majority of the people saw him exiled to St. Helena without regret. The legend of the glorious Napoleon was still in the future.

In Italy, Murat had a personal adventure similar to Napoleon's and one which also ended in exile. During the winter of 1814–15 Murat had begun to fear, with justice, that the congress planned to replace Ferdinando on the throne at Naples. Knowing of Napoleon's escape from Elba and expecting that Austria's attention and troops would be diverted to events in France, Murat marched north with a Neapolitan army and from Rimini on 30 March 1815 proclaimed to Italians of every state: "From the Alps to the Sicilian straits I hear a single cry: the independence of Italy . . . Eighty thousand Italians of the States of Naples are marching under command of their King, and they have sworn not to ask for rest until after the liberation of Italy!"

Except at Bologna, where a group of four hundred of Eugène's army responded to Murat's appeal, Italians in the Po valley hesitated, waiting to see what Murat could do. The Austrians had fifty thousand troops in the valley, and although many were dispersed in forts and at bridgeheads along the Po, they numbered in all nearly twice as many as Murat's army. At first Murat and his Neapolitans won a succession of small battles in the Legations, south of the Po, but never the overwhelming victory he needed to rally the hesitant. If he could have crossed the Po and reached Milan, he might have succeeded, but he was never able to cross the river. Gradually the Austrians took the offensive and pushed him back toward Ancona, while the British talked of invading his rear in Calabria. Finally, at the battle of Tolentino in May, he was clearly defeated and, after retreating with the army toward Naples, fled to Corsica. Undoubtedly many north Italians were sorry he had failed but delighted they had done nothing to help him.

The result of Murat's campaign was that Ferdinando, with the blessings of the congress, recovered his Kingdom of Naples. Maria Carolina, however, did not live to see it. In their last years in Sicily she and Ferdinando had suffered greater humiliations than ever before. The British representative, Lord William Bentinck, had swiftly built a party of Sicilians which, with British money and backing, dominated the court. Bentinck himself was an ambitious opportunist with little political judgment and perhaps not even wholly sane. Ultimately he was repudiated by his government, but meanwhile he ruled by constantly threatening a British occupation of the island. He forced Ferdinando to abdicate in favor of his son and to exile his queen. Ferdinando reluctantly signed the order for her departure, "advising as a friend, begging as a husband and commanding as a King."

Maria Carolina protested the right of the British government to force her to part from her husband and family, but Bentinck at the moment was all-powerful. She was sixty years old and to reach Vienna, the only place where she could go, she had to travel by boat to Constantinople and then overland through southern Poland. As she approached Vienna, her nephew and former son-in-law, Emperor Franz, forbade her to enter the city and, in the Habsburg formula of exile, ordered her to stay at least six miles distant from the place where the court resides. "But I shall go nevertheless," she remarked. "Yes I shall go; and I shall see if they drive the last daughter of Maria Theresa from Schönbrunn." And they did not dare.

She lived quietly at Hetzendorf, right next to the court, and followed political events with interest. She rejoiced in Napoleon's abdication at Fontainebleau but regretted that Marie Louise had not followed him to

Elba. She felt that her granddaughter should glory in the marriage, and if the powers opposed her reunion with Napoleon on Elba, then Marie Louise should tie her bedsheets to her window and escape in disguise. "That," said Maria Carolina, "is what I should do in her place; for when one is married it is for life."

Yet she was kind to Marie Louise, and the two refugees in Vienna comforted each other. She took an interest, too, in Marie Louise's son by Napoleon, the little "King of Rome," although at his birth she had exclaimed, "Only this calamity was held in reserve: to become the Devil's grandmother." She died in September 1814, before Napoleon's escape from Elba and Murat's Italian campaign, and she died unregretted by her husband, by her relatives in Vienna who were still supporting Murat, or by the people either of Naples or Vienna. In a different time, under different circumstances she might have succeeded in becoming a beloved queen; she had started her role with intelligence and energy. But those of her contemporaries who found qualities in her to admire felt that her character, neither good nor bad to start with, had been warped by marriage to a king who was incapable of governing. Both her friends and enemies made the same observation.

Within two months of her death, even before his mourning was officially ended, Ferdinando had married his mistress, a happy, pleasant widow whom he entitled the Duchess of Floridia. And in the following spring, in the week of Waterloo, he returned to Naples. In his triumphal entry marched Austrian, British and Sicilian troops, and the crowds greeted him warmly. In the same week in Vienna his ambassador signed a treaty of alliance with Austria by which Ferdinando was to provide Austria with twenty-five thousand troops for the defense of Italy and to accept an Austrian commander-in-chief. In a secret clause he was also bound "to admit no change in the government of his kingdom that could not harmonize with ancient monarchical institutions or with the principles adopted by His Imperial and Apostolic Majesty [Franz] for the internal administration of his Italian provinces." It was Maria Carolina's policy exactly; she would have rejoiced at the extension of Habsburg power down the peninsula. Meanwhile Ferdinando, the Bourbon, rejoiced in once again shooting over the familiar fields and mountains around Naples.

Austria's influence at Naples was by a separate treaty, but elsewhere in the peninsula her power rested on the settlements of the Congress of Vienna. The great powers, in ordering Europe, compensated Austria for the release of her Netherlands and Swabian lands in Germany by giving her most of Italy as either an outright possession or a sphere of influence. Spain and France were the two powers that traditionally had an interest in Italy opposed to Austria, but France, as the defeated power, had little to say about the disposition of the Italian states and Spain, much to its indignation, was declared to be no longer a great power and was excluded from the discussions. Neither Prussia nor Russia had an interest in Italy, and Britain, wanting only ports for its fleet, was content with Malta and the Ionian Islands. As a result Austria had almost a free hand in reorganizing the peninsula.

Metternich and Franz, recognizing that Napoleon's Kingdom of Italy had some virtues, followed its design, at least in part. The former Habsburg Duchies of Milan and Mantua were combined with Venice and its mainland (see map, p. 189) into a Kingdom of Lombardo-Veneto of which Emperor Franz was to be the king. Presumably, like Napoleon, he would eventually come to Milan to be crowned in the Duomo with the iron crown of Lombardy and then, on his return to Vienna, would leave behind a viceroy, probably an Austrian archduke. In a similar fashion Metternich and Franz followed Napoleon's design for The Illyrian Provinces and reorganized them into a Habsburg Kingdom of Illyria.

The new Kingdom of Lombardo-Veneto included all the area of its Napoleonic predecessor that lay north of the Po, which thus formed its southern boundary. The area south of the river, the Legations, was returned by the congress to the Papal States, which was a diplomatic triumph for Consalvi, who had represented the pope at Vienna. But in a letter to Pacca he ascribed his success entirely to "the immense personal reputation of the Holy Father, and the view that is held of his sanctity and character." The effect of Napoleon and his works appeared in many different forms in the decisions of the congress.

In the smaller states Metternich was able to insure Habsburg influence both by restoring or establishing Austrian archdukes on the ducal thrones and by military rights secured thereafter by treaty with them. In Tuscany the emperor's brother, Grand Duke Ferdinando III, was restored. Parma was given to the emperor's daughter, Marie Louise, as compensation for giving up Napoleon and France; and Modena was given to the emperor's first cousin, Francesco IV, whose father had been titular duke by virtue of marrying the last surviving D'Este.

Only in the former Republic of Lucca did Metternich not place a close relative of the emperor. There the widow of the last Duke of Parma, who was acting as regent for her son, became the Duchess of Lucca. Her brother was King of Spain, but Spain's power had fallen so low that all of its influence continually exerted at Vienna could not return the king's sister to Parma. She had to be satisfied with tiny Lucca and the reversion of Parma after Marie Louise's death.

The settlement of Italy imposed on Italians by the Congress of Vienna was not simply a restoration of power and spheres of influence as they had

ITALY in 1815,
AFTER THE CONGRESS OF VIENNA

*Emperor Franz of Austria was King of Lombardo-Veneto and also of Illyria; and his relatives ruled in Parma, Modena and Tuscany. Lucca became part of Tuscany in 1847.*

been before the French Revolution and the Napoleonic wars. Not only was France completely excluded from the peninsula, and Austria's grip thereby greatly strengthened; but the three republics of Genoa, Venice and Lucca were not revived, and the only form of government permitted on the peninsula, as a matter of Austrian policy, was one that harmonized with "monarchical institutions." The single exception was the Republic of San Marino, perched on the Adriatic slopes of the Apennines and surrounded by the Papal States. With an area of thirty-eight square miles it had, and still has, the distinction of being the smallest republic in the world and, also, of being the only state in Italy which Napoleon left undisturbed. The forced disappearance of the larger republics, however, took out of Italian political and civil life a traditional and popular form of government, and for the many Italians who missed it the sense of being dominated by a foreign power was greatly increased.

Even for those who favored the monarchical form of government, the settlement was a new order, not a return to the past. A hundred years earlier, after the War of the Spanish Succession, native dynasties had ruled in Sardinia, Parma, Modena and Tuscany. Now as the Habsburgs returned after years of exile in Vienna or, like Marie Louise, set foot in Italy for the first time, they appeared to their subjects rather more as Austrian archdukes and less as local branches of the Habsburg family. A native dynasty ruled in Sardinia, and another, more native than foreign, had established itself at Naples; but at Parma, Modena and Tuscany the rulers came from Vienna at the head of Austrian troops, the same troops against which many Italians, conscripted into Napoleon's armies, had fought.

For the nobility the sense of foreign domination was increased as a result of the extinction, ten years earlier, of the Holy Roman Empire. The concept of an empire which, like the Papacy, had its roots in Roman times, meant a great deal to many Italians, and its end, like that of the equally ancient Republic of Venice, was a real shock. An Austrian Empire was something quite different, something in which Italians had far less of a part to play. This was particularly true for the Milanesi. When Franz had abdicated his position as Holy Roman Emperor without naming a successor or allowing the election of one, he had brushed away the last feudal ties with his Italian subjects. The relationship between Maria Theresa and her Milanese nobles was warmer and more personal than any relationship her grandson Franz achieved with any Italian. No Milanese had a career under Franz such as many had achieved under Maria Theresa or even under Joseph II. When in the coming years other Europeans would remark with regret and astonishment that the Milanesi seemed unable to live peacefully under the Austrians, as they once had done in the past, the Milanesi would often reply with exasperation and justice that both they and the Austrians now were different.

But even though many Italians for many reasons disliked the settlement imposed on them, the chance of any effective protest ended with the collapse of Murat's adventure and the failure of the republicans to control the remnants of Eugène's Italian army. Thereafter the dissatisfied had no one to represent them at the Congress and no power with which to assert themselves outside it. They were reduced to individual muttering and, in the case of Foscolo, an individual gesture which stood as a symbol for the many less famous who could not themselves afford to make it. He refused to take the oath of allegiance required by the Emperor Franz and went into exile, living the balance of his life, until 1827, in England.

Many ridiculed his self-imposed exile, among them his old friend the Countess of Albany. He had written to her to explain his motives, and she replied in a way that showed she believed the assertions of his enemies, that he had acted out of cowardice, meanness and a desire to be conspicuous. In his reply to her he wrote with a strain of idealism and hope for Italy which, in the years to come, his gesture helped to keep alive:

> To have hated the tyranny with which Bonaparte was oppressing Italy does not imply that I must love the domination of the House of Austria. The difference for me was that I hoped that Bonaparte's frenzied ambition might bring about, if not the independence of Italy, at least such great-hearted deeds as might raise the Italians; whereas the regular government of Austria precludes all such hopes. I should be mad and infamous if I desired more war and tumult for Italy, when it needs peace; but I should be madder still and more infamous if, having despised to serve the foreigner who has fallen, I should accept to serve the foreigner who has succeeded. . . . But if your accusation of inconstancy is unjust, your accusation that I want to *"passer pour original"* is actually offensive and mocking.[10]

Yet for the moment, as Foscolo recognized, what Italy needed even more than independence was peace, and in the terms of the time the settlement imposed on Italy by the congress, in spite of the emphasis on monarchy, was not unreasonable. Even Napoleon had been unable to organize Europe except on the basis of a royal family, kings, queens and an emperor. Within the memory of living men no republic on the French model had offered a stable, viable government. The plenipotentiaries who met in Vienna were men with their roots in the eighteenth century and who had survived a generation of upheaval and suffering; almost inevitably, in trying to reconstruct a peaceful Europe, they thought in terms of their childhood. But so, too, did the millions of peasants and townfolk who also had suffered and survived. Most Italians, exhausted by their experience of domination by the French, were prepared to accept the Austrians, if not with joy, at least with hope. And at Rome, Naples and Turin there was much genuine satisfaction at the return of popular, native rulers.

# PART II

PART II

# CHAPTER 18

Reactionary government at Rome and Turin. Naples, Murat and the Carbonaro revolution. Ferdinando calls in Austria. Revolution at Turin. Lombardo-Veneto. Franz's personality. Metternich's philosophy. Carbonaro trials. Pellico and Confalonieri.

THE GOVERNMENTS which the returning monarchs established in their Italian states in 1815 were as varied as the rulers' personalities, but two of the more important, those at Rome and Turin, were severely reactionary. Pius VII sent Consalvi to represent him at the Congress of Vienna, and he put Pacca in charge of the administration at Rome. But Pacca, once so brilliantly right, was now the wrong man for the job. The only good he and most other cardinals could see in the French administration was its principle of centralizing the government's administrative power in the bureaucracy at Rome. This they kept; everything else they set about to erase.

Every man, priest or layman, who worked for Church or State and who had supported the French regime was to be fired from his job. For priests the issue was the nature of the oath of allegiance sworn to the French regime. Lists were prepared of those who had offended, and many were immediately dismissed; the fates of some, generally the least important, were left to the discretion of their bishops. For laymen the issue was even more clear cut: a clerical administration was to replace a secular one, and laymen, as fast as they could be replaced, were barred from office.

The various French legal codes, civil, criminal and commercial were repealed, and the previous confusion of conflicting courts and codes revived. The Index was reinstituted; sales or secularization of Church property were traced and revoked; distinguished professors were discharged from the universities; the Jews were forced again to live in a ghetto and to be locked in at night; and laws on the uniformity of weights and measures, street lighting and vaccination were repealed. Everything that could be done was done to re-establish Papal rule as it had been a quarter of a century earlier, before the French had brought their Revolution into Italy. The pope's experience with Napoleon seemed to have drained from him every drop of the spirit of compromise which he had shown in 1797 when, as Archbishop of Imola, he had attempted in his Christmas homily to reconcile the Church and the Revolution.

His policy, however, caused Consalvi difficulties at Vienna where the diplomats questioned the wisdom of it, and Metternich, before returning the Legations to the pope, laid down conditions: the existing secular administration of them was to be maintained, a general amnesty was to be granted to all who had supported the Napoleonic regime, the public debts of that regime were to be honored, and title to Church property that had been sold or secularized was to be protected.

Consalvi and perhaps one or two others at Rome saw the mutual advantage in Metternich's policy. Like the forced transfer of Genoa to the Kingdom of Sardinia, the return of Bologna and the other Legations to the Papal States was highly unpopular with the people affected, and only the threat of Austrian intervention from across the Po kept them from open revolt. A reactionary policy such as Pacca had instituted at Rome would inflame the region. Then, if Austrian troops moved in, they might refuse to move out, and Rome would lose the Legations altogether. Pius, on Consalvi's advice, accepted the conditions, but the cardinals at Rome and most of those sent out to administer the region worked over the years to subvert them, and largely succeeded.

The pope's reactionary government soon caused resentment, and the first attempt at revolt occurred in 1817 at Macerata, near Ancona, and had as its aim the abolition of priestly rule. It was a complete failure. Most of the conspirators failed to appear at the appointed place, and those who did fired a few shots and then dispersed. But the plot had been betrayed, and large numbers were arrested and tried by a court of priests with a cardinal as president. Of the accused, after waiting eighteen months in prison, ten were sentenced to death and twenty to the galleys for periods of five years or more. The sentences of death were later commuted to life in prison. The severity of the sentences, so out of proportion to the wholly ineffective crime, far from deterring others, merely convinced them that a government by priests was a government without mercy or sense; and conspiracies, most of which never matured into action, flourished.

The pope's immense prestige as the man in the Church who had resisted Napoleon to the end concealed for most Europeans the effects of his reactionary government, and the incident at Macerata hardly was noticed. Europe, after its experience with Napoleon, was having a religious revival and one in which the Roman Church was voluntarily, even eagerly, granted the position which Pius in answering Napoleon had claimed for it: "mother and mistress of the other Churches."

A gifted writer who served as one of the first philosophers of this movement was a Savoyard diplomat, Joseph de Maistre, who in 1819 published a book on the Papacy, *Du Pape,* in which he stressed the necessity of having an absolute monarch both within the Church and the State, and further he proposed that where the two came into conflict the Church should prevail. Both, he argued, should be supported by a ruling class, separated from other classes by privilege and authority, and he viewed the French Revolution as a punishment by God on the French aristocrats for their impiety in adopting the rationalistic thought of the eighteenth century.

Though few laymen or even priests were prepared to follow De Maistre to all his conclusions, the great majority were quite ready to believe that the interests of religion were best served by exalting Rome and giving the pope unquestioned obedience. In France the movement was called "ultramontanism" or "beyond the mountains," meaning Rome. In this favorable atmosphere Pius encouraged the revival of the older religious orders. In France, for example, the number of houses of contemplative orders had fallen from fifteen hundred before the Revolution to thirty at the time of Napoleon's abdication. Pius now was able to reverse the trend, to establish new orders and, most important, on 7 August 1814 to revive the Society of Jesus. The Emperor Franz II refused to readmit the Jesuits into his Austrian Empire, but in the Latin countries they were welcomed back.

At Turin, Vittorio Emanuele I allowed them to resume control of the educational system and encouraged them to set the tone of his court. He was an elderly gentleman who had passed most of the Napoleonic period in Sardinia, and once back in Turin he was as determined as Pius in Rome to restore the substance of the old regime as well as its shadow. He began by calling for the Court Almanac of 1798 and reappointing those still alive to their old positions. He re-established feudal dues and restored the judicial immunities of the clergy as well as the minor privileges of the nobility. All the old paternalistic restrictions which had so infuriated Alfieri were revived: whoever wished to read a foreign newspaper had to have a special permit from the king; students at the University had to attend mass regularly and to confess once a month; and the professors had periodically to present certificates that they had performed the prescribed religious rites. The Napoleonic codes, which had simplified life, were replaced by a confusing mixture of Roman law, canon law, royal decree and precedent, and as a final uncertainty the king had the right to review and change all decisions of the courts.

He was so violently anti-French that he dismissed all clerks who wrote the letter "R" in the French manner, although French was the language of the court and aristocracy. He even forbade lawful traffic to use the new road built by the French over Mont Cenis, and as a result it became a smugglers' highway. At first many of the Piemontesi were inclined to be amused, but soon they began to protest, and the king was forced to make some concessions. But not enough to satisfy the more liberal Piemontesi or the republican Genovesi. As part of the French Empire they had been subject to taxes, confiscation, conscription and exile, but they had also been stirred by the new ideas and institutions of the times, and many, sent in Napoleon's service out of Piedmont and Genoa, had seen more of the contemporary world than had the king. These openly grumbled at the reconstruction of the kingdom in such an antique fashion, and they were not simple, unsophisticated men like those involved in the incident at Macerata. They included in their number many army officers, who were aristocrats, most of the emerging middle class in Turin and Genoa and even, it was rumored, a prince of the House of Savoy.

Yet the first serious attempt to upset the settlement imposed by the Congress of Vienna occurred neither in the Papal States nor in Sardinia, nor even in the Kingdom of Lombardo-Veneto where dissatisfaction with Austria was increasing, but in the Kingdom of Naples where the restoration had been relatively mild. Ferdinando had returned to his capital in 1815 intending to root out every trace of Murat and the French administration. But first on his agenda each day was his hunting, and he left the work of the restoration to his minister, Luigi Medici. The problem was how, after an interregnum of ten years, to replace the new laws and institutions by the old with the least confusion, and Medici's solution was to leave as much as possible of the new without drawing attention to it. The result was an administration that was tolerant but drifting; one that gave an appearance of government but little of its substance. Problems that demanded action, such as the brigandage in the provinces, were merely discussed, and only one, the problem of Murat's claim to the throne, provided its own solution.

Murat had left Corsica in September 1815, ostensibly for Trieste and a sanctuary in Austria offered by Metternich. Instead, dressed in his most gorgeous uniform and with a few followers he had landed on the coast of Calabria near the tiny port of Pizzo (see map, p. 583). In the town square his followers had raised a cheer for King Gioacchino, but the people had fled. Starting down the coast for Monteleone, a traditionally pro-French town, he had stopped to buy a horse, and a mob had gathered, its mood clearly against him. Murat and his men retreated, but at the water's edge, as they tried to launch a fishing boat, the mob attacked. In the scuffle Murat was almost torn to pieces. One woman struck him in the face, screaming, "You talk of liberty, but you had four of my sons shot!" Another tore out a handful of his mustache, and in the end he was saved by the local police which had put him and his men under arrest. On Ferdinando's order he was promptly tried by a military court, which found him guilty of inciting a civil war and of appearing in arms against the legitimate king. The sentence was death by a firing squad. The charges were so clearly true that the sentence was accepted by almost everyone as just, and the threat of Murat was removed by his execution, on 13 October 1815, without his becoming a martyr.

But the other problems facing Ferdinando did not resolve themselves so easily. The most serious was the growth of a secret society whose members were known as the Carbonari or Charcoal-burners. The society, which to some extent succeeded to the place in Italian life previously held by Freemasonry, was organized by *vendite,* or "shops," for the ostensible sale of charcoal, and the society had "shops" or clubs in every state in Italy. The aims and membership of the clubs, however, varied so, from state to state, that they had little cohesion or cumulative power except regionally. In the north most of the members were professional men, lawyers, doctors, professors and journalists; in the south the members were less sophisticated. If they were professional men, the majority came from the smaller towns in the provinces, and there were many more small businessmen and officeholders. In the south there was also an element of sociability in membership; the meetings had a ritual, like Masonry, and after the political discussions, couched in vague and confusing rhetoric, there was much good-fellowship. In the north the meetings were more purely political, the clubs' aims better articulated, and the membership smaller and more conspiratorial. Generally speaking, however, where the Freemasons of eighteenth-century Italy had been in their attitudes relatively atheistic or Protestant, pro-French, and cosmopolitan or non-nationalist, the Carbonari of the early nineteenth century were relatively Catholic, anti-French and nationalistic.

North and south the members were the dissatisfied, men who wanted some change in the government under which they lived: a constitution, abolition of priestly rule or more self-government. In the Kingdom of Naples the provincial militias were a particularly fertile ground for such clubs. The militias were formed mostly of men from the small towns with the aim of suppressing the bandits and robber barons, for the brigandage, by the close of the Napoleonic wars, had become in the south a terrible problem. Business sometimes stopped altogether while small towns with difficulty held off the bandits. The clubs which formed in the militias or deliberately penetrated them were generally composed of small property-owners, town clerks and officials who were exasperated with conditions. Sometimes they blamed the bandits, sometimes the local baron and sometimes the distant government. They wanted peace and freedom to go about their business, and those on governmental salaries wanted better pay. They thought, or their leaders told them, that if they could have a constitution with the king as a constitutional monarch and have a parliamentary government to which they could send representatives to state their troubles, then conditions would improve. Their program, which for most of them hardly existed in greater detail, was thus a faint echo of the ideas of the French Revolution.

Ferdinando and his ministers, not unnaturally, considered the movement to be revolutionary, but they wholly underestimated the numbers involved and did nothing, except that for a time they supported another secret sect whose members were known as the Calderari, or the Braziers. The aim of these was to defend religion and the monarchy and to oppose any ideas or institutions left over from the French regime. They were, however, relatively unimportant, whereas the Carbonari continued to spread, and their number in the year 1820 has been variously estimated at anywhere from three hundred thousand to one million. If the higher figure is close to correct, then, as the kingdom's male population was about three million, every third or fourth man was a Carbonaro; and even at the lower figure the ratio is one out of ten, a phenomenal ratio for a secret society. But even when prelates and magistrates from the provinces came to Naples in person to protest the government's inaction, Ferdinando and his ministers continued to do nothing. Meanwhile the Carbonari began to penetrate the army.

Finally, on 2 July 1820, on news of a revolution in Spain, they persuaded General Guglielmo Pepe, who was not himself a Carbonaro, to lead them; and four days later, simply by declaring themselves, they had accomplished a bloodless revolution. Everywhere Ferdinando looked for support, to the army, to the provincial militia and even to the people, the Carbonari were in control. They demanded a constitution and parliamentary government, and Ferdinando had no choice but to grant them.

In celebration, on 9 July, the Carbonari made a triumphal entry into Naples. First came some detachments of the regular army, then the more ragged troops of the provincial militias and finally, on foot and without order, the civilian Carbonari. They marched by districts, wearing their native costumes, carrying banners to identify their club or district and wearing emblems to show their rank in the society. General Pepe led them and at his side was the Carbonaro Grand Master who was a priest. He was dressed in a cassock but carried arms and was covered with the symbols of the secret society. For the men from the provinces the procession was perhaps the most glorious event of their lives. For Ferdinando it was one of the most exasperating. He had already taken to his bed, announcing that as he was now in his seventieth year, his infirmities no longer permitted him to sustain the weight of government, and he appointed his eldest son, Francesco, to act for him as vicar-general.

The most important question facing the new constitutional monarchy was its relations with Austria, and the answer became clear within the month. Metternich, relying on the secret treaty, refused to recognize the ambassadors sent to him, and in a private conversation with a Neapolitan he said: "The present revolution at Naples is the work of a subversive sect; it is the product of surprise and violence. The sanction given by other Courts to such a revolution would help to spread its germs in other countries which are still free from them. The first duty and the first interest of foreign powers is therefore to smother it in its cradle."

In pursuit of this policy Metternich called a Congress of the great powers to meet at Troppau in October 1820, the same month in which the first parliament assembled at Naples. At Troppau, Metternich, with the approval of Russia and Prussia, drew up a Protocol according to which Austria had the right to interfere at Naples in order to preserve the general peace. Britain, however, refused to join with the others. At an earlier congress, at Aix-la-Chapelle in 1818, the British ministers had disapproved in a memorandum of the idea that the force of the great powers "was collectively to be prostituted to the support of established power without any consideration of the extent to which it is abused." The language was strong: prostituted, *any* consideration, abused; and although the memorandum was not specifically aimed at Austria's policy in Italy, yet by marking the end of the anti-Napoleonic alliance of Britain and Austria, it also marked the start of a new Italian policy for Britain. Negatively, that policy would merely be one of non-interference; on occasion, more positively, it would try to offer a middle way between the republicanism inherited by Italians from revolutionary France and the despotism of Austria. And with the Bourbons restored in France, Britain became for Italians of republican leanings the most sympathetic country in Europe. For almost twenty years it was the chief refuge of the steady stream of men who followed Foscolo into exile.

At Troppau, however, Metternich was not distressed by Britain's attitude. He had received a letter from Ferdinando in which the king expressed his desire to leave his kingdom and to win back his absolute power with the help of the Austrian army. To this end Metternich arranged for the Emperor of Austria, the Tsar and the King of Prussia to write letters inviting Ferdinando to confer with them at Laibach or Ljubljana, the capital of the Kingdom of Illyria, and on receiving the invitations Ferdinando at once requested permission from the parliament to leave his kingdom. In his message explaining his reasons he wrote: "I am resolved to sacrifice my every inclination to perform a duty that may avert the curse of war from subjects." With reluctance the parliament gave him permission to go.

The parliament was not proving itself an effective government. A revolution in Sicily, centering on Palermo, had been put down but only after the Neapolitan general in command was relieved and the terms he had granted were repudiated. And the Neapolitan gift of oratory often delayed the deputies from attending to serious business. The British representative reported, "The members occupy themselves with anything except what really demands attention. They had a long debate last week, which was pushed to a division, whether God was, or was not, the Legislator of the Universe. The question was decided in favor of the Deity by a small majority."

Such reports, when circulated, seemed to justify Metternich's policy, and from Laibach Ferdinando wrote back to his son Francesco, the vicar-general, that he had been unable to convince the great powers not to intervene. On the same day the Russian, Austrian and Prussian ministers advised Francesco that an Austrian army, with Russians in reserve, was already approaching the kingdom. Its intent was to restore the absolute monarchy, and depending on the attitude of the people it would enter the kingdom as a friend or a foe. Francesco, as he was duty bound, notified the parliament, and the deputies declared for war. Francesco's position was extremely difficult. He himself seems to have favored an amended constitution, and he was plainly distressed by his father's dependence on Austria. But the deputies made him honorary commander-in-chief, although he, like almost everyone else, predicted a swift Neapolitan defeat.

The army only five years earlier under Murat had been defeated by the Austrians, and since then it had deteriorated. A number of the best officers, being pronouncedly pro-Murat, had been relieved, and the discipline had been undermined by the infiltration of the Carbonari. The rate of desertion was high, the training and equipment poor and the issues, with Ferdinando at Laibach and Francesco at Naples, anything but clear.

The result, as expected, was an easy victory for Austria. The parliament dissolved with a protest; the leading deputies went into hiding or exile, and General Pepe left for London. Both Francesco and the British envoy were liberal in dispensing passports and helpful in arranging transportation. Francesco was mild by nature, and the envoy, remembering Nelson's role at Naples in 1799, was anxious to clear "the stain of blood upon our character here."

In the same week early in March 1821 that the constitutional government at Naples was put down by the Austrian army, a revolution with a constitution for its aim broke out in Turin, Alessandria and other cities of Piedmont on the mainland of the Kingdom of Sardinia. The occasion was the departure of the Austrian army from neighboring Lombardo-Veneto for the march on Naples. The revolutionists in Piedmont were army officers, and the Carbonari, which joined the cause a few days later, were less important than in the south. About half the Sardinian army backed the revolution and demanded a constitution. As at Naples, the revolutionists assumed that the king, Vittorio Emanuele I, would remain as a constitutional monarch.

The great powers, still at Laibach, acted as they had with Naples: they sent an ultimatum to the king threatening an armed invasion if he granted a constitution. The choice facing Vittorio Emanuele was whether to refuse a constitution and fight a civil war or to grant a constitution and fight a foreign war. The decision was too much for him. He abdicated in favor of his brother, Carlo Felice, who happened at that moment to be in Modena. As regent until his brother's return he appointed his twenty-two-year-old cousin, Carlo Alberto, who was, although a member of the cadet branch of the family, the heir to the throne after Carlo Felice.

The king's sudden and unforeseen abdication completely dislocated the revolution, for Carlo Felice was known to be more reactionary and rigid than his brother and quite incapable of being a constitutional monarch. Carlo Alberto, on the other hand, was considered liberal. Yet his decision in the end, for which many never forgave him, was to obey the new king's command to go into exile in Tuscany. Meanwhile, in April, the revolution collapsed. Austrian troops at Carlo Felice's request scattered what little opposition remained, and the Austrian general occupied Alessandria, sending the keys of the rebellious city not to Carlo Felice but to the Emperor Franz.

Both revolutions, aiming at forms of constitutional monarchy, were put down by an Austrian army and an absolute monarch was firmly fixed on the throne. Of the seventy-year-old King of Naples, Metternich observed: "This is the third time I am putting King Ferdinando on his feet, and he has the bad habit of tumbling. In 1821 he still imagines that the throne is an easy chair in which to sprawl and fall asleep."

The restoration at Naples was mild compared to 1799 but still vengeful enough to cause the Austrian minister there constantly to protest. Ferdinando and his Minister of Police favored public whippings for the Carbonari, and for a time anyone caught with a symbol of the sect about him was taken at once into the street and whipped. Many others were arrested, put in jail but not brought to trial. The amnesty was drawn so narrowly that, on Austrian insistence, it was redrafted. The ministers of the great powers complained that the government was so arbitrary that it tended "toward measures more qualified to ruin than to promote the King's interest."

In Sardinia Carlo Felice, perhaps by design, delayed returning to

Turin for six months and although lists of offenders were drawn up, most were discovered by September to have left the country and there was much less harassment of individuals than in Naples. The aristocracy in Piedmont, however, was shaken by its experience of schism. Many of the families had at least one of its men in exile, and those at home, perhaps as a result, had a period of political inactivity. Carlo Felice, whose reign lasted ten years, was never thereafter troubled by his aristocracy, but the Carbonari movement, which was dominated by the republican Genovesi, continued to sputter underground. Metternich, however, kept an army of twelve thousand Austrians at Alessandria. In and around Naples he had an army of forty thousand. The final effect of the two revolutions was to introduce Austrian armies of occupation into the last states of Italy that could claim any real independence. Even the pope as a result of the unrest following the incident at Macerata was forced now to admit and support an Austrian garrison, and in the Kingdom of Lombardo-Veneto, where Austrian troops were by right of the kingdom being part of the Austrian Empire, there were garrisons in every city of any size.

In that kingdom, where Metternich and Franz ruled directly rather than through a subordinate monarch, their policy for Italy was most clearly seen. In 1815 the double title with the establishment of an administration at both Milan and Venice seemed to assure that the traditions and needs of each half of the kingdom would be recognized. The promise of a viceroy and belief that Franz would come to Milan for a coronation seemed to assure that the kingdom would have some independence and not be submerged under the German elements of the empire. Napoleon's concordat and most of the civil code were kept. Feudal ties were not restored, nor were the privileges of the nobility. Peasants were supported against the great landlords, and an archbishop was installed in the see of Milan, an Austrian named Gaisruck, who was opposed to the contemplative orders and the Jesuits and tried in their place to develop a corps of educated parish priests. Franz seemed to want to develop his kingdom along modern lines and, as he was the legitimate sovereign of the Milanesi, he started with strong support. Yet by 1820 he had already lost the allegiance of many aristocrats and of almost all the professional people of the towns. Much of the reason lay in his personality and the philosophy of his minister, Metternich.

Franz had succeeded to the Habsburg titles and lands in 1792 when he was only twenty-four. He had not been well educated, and he had no interest in either science or art. Compared to his uncle, Joseph II, he was dull, perhaps even stupid. But he was more stable and patient than his brilliant uncle, and these were virtues he needed to endure the hurricane of Napoleon. Besides these, his chief virtues were a certain shrewdness about people, a sense of duty and his industry. He worked hard at his job, but he conceived of it as daily routine: if he worked so many hours a day, then the job was well done. He seldom grasped the greater issues which transcended years. Metternich once compared his method of working at a problem to the narrow penetration of a gimlet.

He had a great sense of the House of Habsburg, and he interpreted his role as head of it to mean that all the business of governing its lands should be centered in himself. He disliked to delegate authority, distrusted able subordinates and with the exception of Metternich seldom supported them for long. Metternich could state with truth: "I have governed Europe sometimes, Austria never." But it was slow government Franz offered and one that was constantly upset by his personal interference.

Further as head of the House of Habsburg, he had ideas, which he had held from his youth, about his relations with others. "Peoples? What does that mean? I only know subjects." And when a man was recommended to him as a good patriot, he asked, "But is he a patriot for me?" The question could be understood in terms of Habsburg history, but the attitude it represented was archaic in a world in which feudalism was dying and nationalism already born.

By nature and experience Franz distrusted new men with new ideas. After twenty-five years of revolutionary France and Napoleon, his chief aim as emperor was to achieve stability for his house and empire and his chief fear was revolution. Given his slow, methodical nature his government inevitably was one of laws and punishments designed to prevent change and to keep adventurous spirits in check. And Metternich's philosophy of government and society reenforced these aims and fears of the emperor.

For Metternich the most important experience of his life occurred when, as a young man, he saw the men and ideas of the French Revolution arrive in the Rhineland. He had seen old governments swept away as if by an avalanche, he had seen excited people commit atrocities in the street, and he had seen the new, idealistic governments turn quickly into tyrannies. Like many who had grown up in those days he heard in the word Liberty the click of the guillotine. He had escaped from the Rhineland to Vienna and had matured believing that only by a monarchy could a government impose order on life. It was the common ground on which the stolid Franz and the more mercurial Metternich never failed to meet.

For both men the great periods of their lives was facing and, in the end, defeating Napoleon. Everything thereafter was a decline. Metternich felt it acutely and recognized that the opposition to Napoleon had used up the best in him. Thereafter Franz ruled until 1835 and Metternich until 1848, but under them Austrian policy and government gradually became notorious for its "immobility" and the empire, because of its size and impenetrability, was sometimes called by western Europeans "the China of Europe."

Metternich, being more intellectually inclined than Franz, rationalized his ideas of government and social organization into a number of principles which he discussed in his voluminous memoirs. He believed in a balance between extremes that extended into every part of life. At the end of the eighteenth century, so Metternich reasoned, France had upset the balance and dragged Europe after it to an extreme of anarchy. Austria's mission was to right the balance by reintroducing order into European government and society. Anarchy, for Metternich, was the idea of popular sovereignty let loose in Europe by republican France; order was the monarchy or absolutism of Austria, Prussia and Russia. Austria's mission in Italy, therefore, was to exclude France and its idea of popular sovereignty and thereby to give Italy and Europe a period of stability. Metternich was not a great thinker, and he seems to have been able to believe sincerely in the universal rightness of his ideas; many Italians, of course, dismissed them as self-serving.

But the idea of a balance in life was merely Metternich's general theory; more specifically he claimed to have isolated the class of men who were upsetting the balance. It was not the aristocracy, which had nothing to gain by an upheaval such as the French Revolution, and it was not the lower class, peasants and laborers, who wanted only a decent living and some surety for the morrow. It was the middle class: the financiers, civil servants, men of letters, lawyers, doctors, educators and journalists. These men, according to Metternich, were presumptuous, and their presumption was a result of the tremendous advances made during the Renaissance, a time when human experience had outstripped human wisdom. These men wanted to examine the order of society for themselves and not to accept it on faith. They acted on their private judgments rather than on those handed down by tradition and authority. Laws had little meaning for these men because they had not shared in drafting them. They had triumphed in the Revolution because the monarchy in France had been weak and frivolous. Now it was necessary for the monarchies to stand firm, to maintain authority and to conserve the existing order. Stability did not imply immobility, but improvements were best imposed on society from above, by properly constituted authority, not by mobs in the street.

What was missing in Metternich's philosophy and, in a different way, in Franz's personality was a vitality of spirit, a passion or great-heartedness that could embrace with sympathy all men, the good with bad, or in one man both the good and the bad. It was not to be denied that the French Revolution in Paris and other cities had run through the most terrible excesses and ended in tyranny, or that the chief principle of the Revolution was the sovereignty of the people in direct exercise of power, the freeing of men from the rule of kings and priests. Unquestionably it was a dangerous principle, but it could not be suppressed, as Franz and Metternich were to discover, because it is part of the psychological makeup of man: the desire to belong to the group and to play a part in its organization. To deny it, in a man who feels its urge, is to emasculate him.

When the Austrian army entered Naples, nineteen deputies of the parliament that had just been closed by force of arms issued a hopeless protest, which, from the point of view of their own safety, was very ill-advised. Yet they felt impelled to it: "We protest against the violation of the right of the people, we intend to preserve without faltering the rights of the nation and of the King . . ." But in Metternich's eyes they presumed too much to claim political rights for the people or to put any that the nation might have on an equal basis with those of the king.

Carbonarism which had flourished in Naples and to a lesser extent in Piedmont also flourished in the Kingdom of Lombardo-Veneto. There the dissatisfied were exactly those members of the middle class whom Metternich so distrusted and who were alienated by the policy Franz adopted toward his Italian kingdom. He would not be crowned at Milan, and, unlike Napoleon, he would not entitle himself King of Italy for fear of offending the other monarchs on the peninsula. He did not even appoint a viceroy until 1818, by which time it was evident that he expected to treat Lombardia and the Veneto merely as provinces of his Austrian Empire. Nearly all the civil servants and office holders of the French regime were dismissed and replaced with Slavs or Austrians, the language of the government was German, and decisions of any importance were referred to Vienna. In the Italian regiments raised by conscription the officers were Slav or Austrian as were also the judges in court and most of the higher police officials. Under Napoleon all these posts had been held by Italians. Further, Franz imposed such restrictions on business that the governor of the city of Milan wrote to Metternich that the country was being suffocated. A Milanese, for example, was not allowed to sell his product in Venice if it competed with one from Austria or Bohemia. Napoleon's economic policies had not always favored Italy, but he had created on the peninsula larger areas of unhampered trade. Franz reduced them.

Almost every order he issued was calculated to irritate self-respecting Italians, particularly the educated classes. Lawyers were no longer allowed to plead orally in open court but only in written statements submitted privately to the judge. No daily newspapers might appear except the official gazette. Learned and literary magazines flourished but were examined by Austrian censors before being printed or brought into the country. Modern history could not be taught at the universities, and Italians were forbidden to read such varied authors as Machiavelli, Rabelais and Bentham. If a man wanted to travel he had to apply, ultimately, to a minister in Vienna for permission, and the minister, in time, consulted the chief of police in the town where the applicant lived. If nothing ill was reported of the applicant, after about a year he might be allowed to start on his journey.

What Franz and Metternich created, whether it was their intent or not, was a state dominated by police and censorship. In reaction their subjects joined secret societies and began to conspire, particularly the middle class of professional and business men and also many of the more liberal and adventurous of the aristocracy. Inevitably the police tried to penetrate the societies and to find pretexts for arresting those they suspected of treason without being able to prove it.

They were greatly aided when, a month after the Carbonaro revolution in Naples, Franz promulgated a new law for his Italian subjects banning secret societies. By its terms the penalty for anyone conspiring, provoking or taking part in a political revolution was death; the penalty for failing to try to prevent such a revolution was very hard labor for life; and the penalty for those who failed to denounce anyone whom they knew to be guilty of any of the prohibited activities was hard labor for life. By August 1820, when the law became effective, the offense of failure to denounce put most suspects in the power of the police, for by then most Italians living in the towns of Lombardo-Veneto had at least one friend in a secret society. And the tempo of arrests increased.

There had been arrests and trials before the new law but generally of men singly. Now the Austrians in one trial of more than thirty men, all from a district south of Padua known as Polesine, condemned thirteen to death and the rest to various terms of hard labor. The trial and sentences caused a sensation, even after the emperor in his mercy commuted all the death sentences to hard labor. But as in many political trials there had been accusations of betrayal and extorted confessions that kept the shock and bitterness alive. Undoubtedly some of the accusations were put out by the police in the hope of gaining more information, for they supposed, as did their superiors in Vienna, that the movement was better organized than it was. Neither Franz nor Metternich could believe that treason could spring up spontaneously in so many towns, for they did not understand the general discontent of which it was a symptom.

Even before the mass trial had reached its conclusion, police in Milan had begun a series of arrests that would lead eventually to two important men, Silvio Pellico and Conte Federico Confalonieri. Pellico was the first to be arrested, in October 1820. He was a playwright and a journalist and the year before had edited a biweekly which he, Confalonieri and others had started. The paper, *Il Conciliatore,* had been a forum for the Italian Romantic writers, but it had also been much more, for to be a Romantic in Italy in 1819 was also to be a liberal and a patriot. The paper had been founded, for example, to oppose a monthly put out by Italian classicists who had the support and financial backing of the Austrian authorities. Into the literary articles and arguments Pellico consciously had mixed political propaganda, for which he had been reprimanded by the police and threatened with expulsion from the kingdom. Soon thereafter he and his friends had stopped the magazine, and he had joined the Carbonari. But at the time of his arrest, although a conspirator of very short standing, he was already a marked man with the police.

Pellico's importance in the history of the Risorgimento lies in the book he wrote about his prison experiences, *Le mie prigioni* or *My Prisons.* It appeared in 1832, two years after he was released and, being in several different ways an excellent book, was read by many Italians and others in Europe. In almost all of them it aroused a sympathy for the Italian patriots, and for Franz and Metternich it was a major defeat.

From Milan, Pellico was transferred by the police through a number of prisons to those beside the Doge's Palace in Venice. From these, one day, he was led out with his friend Pietro Maroncelli to hear their sentences published:

. . . The leader of the policemen now came forward and put handcuffs on us. Then we followed him, accompanied by the other policemen.

Down the superb Staircase of the Giants we went, remembering the Doge Marino Faliero who was beheaded there, passed through the great door leading from the palace courtyard into the Piazzetta, then turned left towards the lagoon. In the middle of the Piazzetta there was a wooden platform which we were to be taken up. From the Staircase of the Giants to the platform were drawn up two files of German soldiers. We passed between them.

On climbing the platform we looked around, and in the faces of the immense crowd below us we saw terror. At various points farther away other armed soldiers had been drawn up. Cannons with matches already burning were said to be everywhere.

In that Piazzetta, in September 1820, a month before my arrest, a beggar had said to me:

"This is an unlucky place!"

I remembered that beggar now and thought: "Who knows if he is among these thousands of spectators, and perhaps recognizes me?"

The German captain shouted for us to turn, face the palazzo and look up. We obeyed and saw on the loggia above us a lawyer of the

Curia with a paper in his hands. It was the sentence. He read it out in a loud voice.

There was a deep hush until he came to the words, *Condemned to death*. Then arose a universal murmur of compassion. A new hush followed in order to hear the rest of the sentence. And again the murmur rose at the words, *Condemned to hard labor; Maroncelli for twenty years, Pellico for fifteen years.*

The captain signaled for us to get down. We cast a last glance round the Piazzetta and descended. Into the courtyard we went again, climbed the great staircase, returned to the room from which we had been led into the Piazzetta. There our handcuffs were removed, and we were taken back to San Michele.[11]

Not long after they had arrested Pellico the police in Milan also picked up a much less important man, Gaetano Castiglia. They hoped to prove through him some connection between the Carbonari in Milan and those in Piedmont who had taken part in the abortive revolution there. They suspected, with justice, that the still unidentified Carbonaro leaders in Milan had tried to persuade the young Prince Carlo Alberto to lead his Sardinian troops into Lombardia, to drive the Austrians out and to unite Lombardia to the Kingdom of Sardinia under a constitutional monarchy. Such had been the plan but Carlo Alberto had rejected it, and the Carbonaro uprising planned for Milan had been cancelled.

The police had little evidence against Castiglia, and he probably would have been released had not a friend attempted to save him. One day, to the great surprise of the police, the Marchese Giorgio Pallavicino, a man far more important than Castiglia, suddenly appeared before the Inquisitorial Commission at Milan and announced: "Castiglia is innocent. He knew nothing about the dispatches [to Carbonari in Piedmont]. I took them myself." Pallavicino's impulsive, generous act proved fatal. The chief commissioner, Salvotti, who had been angling for minnows, suddenly found himself in the way to land larger fish, and under a skillful interrogation the courageous but inexperienced Pallavicino revealed more than he had intended. Sensing that he had gone too far and ruined not only himself but his friends he tried to feign madness. But Salvotti was not impressed. "Give him some chicken feed," he said sarcastically, when Pallavicino, flapping his arms and insisting that he was a bird, was brought before the tribunal.

From Pallavicino the trail led to one of the real leaders in Milan of the Carbonari, Conte Federico Confalonieri. Besides his connection with Pellico on *Il Conciliatore*, Confalonieri was famous in northern Italy for introducing the spinning jenny which started the area's cotton industry and for building the first steamboat to navigate the Po. Pellico had been arrested, in fact, soon after a trip on the boat between Pavia and Venice undertaken to spread Carbonaro propaganda.

Confalonieri was convicted of conspiring to start a political revolution for which, according to the law, the penalty was death. But his wife, the Contessa Teresa, hoping to intercede for him, bounced and jigged across the Alps as fast as horse could pull carriage in order to plead with the Emperor Franz. The trip generally took five or six days. Metternich was opposed to having the emperor see her, but after several days her friends succeeded in arranging an interview. To the contessa's pleas Franz replied: "Madam, as a special mark of my good will toward yourself, I inform you that a courier has already been dispatched with a sentence of death for your husband. If you wish to see your husband alive, I advise you to quit Vienna immediately." The poor woman then re-entered her carriage and attempted to overtake the courier in a race over the Alps back to Milan.

Happily the courier's carriage broke down, and the contessa passed him. Then a second courier arrived in Milan before the first with orders to the commission countermanding the death sentence but without advising what punishment should be imposed. So the contessa's brother hastened to Vienna with a petition from many of the leading Milanesi. In the end Confalonieri was sentenced to life imprisonment in Spielberg, the Austrian political prison in Bohemia to which Pellico had finally been sent.

Both men had been condemned to death and then had their sentences reduced. Yet in the case of Confalorieri, Franz's bureaucratic cruelty deprived him at once of any gratitude for his mercy. Teresa Confalonieri continued to live in Milan, and a whole generation of Milanesi were brought up on her story. When Pellico's book appeared with its horrifying account of Spielberg, Confalonieri was still in the prison; men and children imagined each day how he must be suffering, now, this moment. And it was not just Confalonieri, Pallavicino and Pellico, although they were the most famous. There were more mass trials, and although Franz and Metternich succeeded in stamping out Carbonarism in Lombardo-Veneto, they lost, because of their methods, the allegiance of an ever larger number of their subjects.

# CHAPTER 19

Mazzini's family and youth. Leopardi. His patriotic poems. Censorship. Manzoni's novel. Its importance for the development of a national language.

THE DEFEATS the secret societies suffered in 1821 did not end their existence in either the north or the south or cause their members to lose faith in their hopes and ideals. In the Kingdom of The Two Sicilies, after all, the Carbonari had successfully conducted a bloodless revolution and established a constitutional government which had survived for eight months. It had been strong enough to maintain order and even, in Sicily, to put down a revolt. It had failed only to defeat Austria, in 1821 the most powerful state in Europe. To the members of secret societies, both north and south, the performance of the Carbonari at Naples was highly creditable and an example less of defeat than of what could be accomplished. And in spite of persecution the secret societies in all the Italian states continued to find new members.

They were aided everywhere by the presence of Austrian troops which almost all Italians of whatever political persuasion found offensive. In the Kingdom of The Two Sicilies, for example, the Austrian army of occupation cost the kingdom a fifth of its annual revenue, and even civil servants were forced to take a ten per cent cut in salary to support it. Monarchists as well as constitutionalists, therefore, were eager to see it go. But the monarchists as opposed to the constitutionalists were allied with Austria and held responsible by all for the presence of the Austrian armies. And the monarchists in all states except possibly Tuscany offered a government of censorship and repression. The young and the generous-hearted of all ages continually moved in sympathy toward the opposition.

At Genoa one Sunday in April 1821 Giuseppi Mazzini, then a boy of fifteen, was walking along a street near the harbor with his mother and a friend of the family when:

> . . . A man of strong and rough countenance, dark, bearded and with
> a piercing look which I never have forgotten, suddenly came up and
> stopped us. He held out in his hands a white handkerchief and uttered

212

only the words: *for the proscribed of Italy.* My mother and our friend put some money into the handkerchief; and he went off to start again with others. . . . That day was the first in which there took shape confusedly in my mind, I will not say a thought of Fatherland and of Liberty, but a thought that one *could* and therefore one should struggle for the liberty of the Fatherland.[12]

Mazzini wrote this description forty years after the meeting took place, by which time he had become one of the leaders of the Risorgimento. Yet amid all the myriad impressions of his life as a revolutionary the memory of this meeting had never faded, and he proclaimed it to be the start of his political life. Soon after it, in 1821 he took his first public political action: when the Carbonari joined with parts of the army in demanding a constitution for the Kingdom of Sardinia, he demonstrated with other students in favor of the revolutionaries. Six years later a friend at the University of Genoa enrolled him in a Carbonaro society which had the code name of *Speranza* or *Hope.*

Political action came naturally to Mazzini. His father, who was a doctor and professor at the University, had been a republican in 1797, when the French had first entered Italy. He had held office under the Ligurian Republic and had fought against the Austrians when, in the months before Marengo, they had besieged Genoa. At that time he had known Foscolo and other famous republicans who had gathered to defend the city as the last post of republicanism in Italy. All had been discouraged by the lack of stability in the small Italian republics which Napoleon and the Directory had created, and at night when the fighting was slack, they discussed Italy's need to be unified before freedom there could survive. The year of the siege was the most stimulating of his father's life, and Mazzini grew up hearing stories of it, even though later his father gradually became disillusioned with republicanism and ceased to be active politically. By the time Mazzini was grown, his father had no sympathy for revolutionaries, and although he tried always to do his duty by his son, his distress and disapproval were evident.

Mazzini's mother, however, never lost her faith in the republican cause or in her son's role as its prophet. In her Catholicism she was strongly Jansenist and would have in the house only priests of similar persuasion, and undoubtedly much of Mazzini's austerity, sense of destiny and messianic zeal originated in her Jansenist teaching and attitude. When Paganini, the great violinist and a Genovese, returned to the city to unveil a bust of himself, she wrote to her son in exile: "I am unable to conceive how even a great player can be worthy of a statue while he is still alive. What in the world has he ever done for the good of humanity?" Part of Mazzini's fascination and a great part of his power was that he always worked entirely for the good of humanity, as he conceived it, and never for himself.

For his education his mother was not content with the standard curriculum or even with consulting her husband who, as a professor, might conceivably have had some ideas. Instead, she consulted first a friend in the army and then, dissatisfied, started a correspondence with a distinguished friend of Foscolo, Giacomo Breganze, a man she had known in Genoa during the months of the siege. Breganze's advice was not unusual in any way except that he made a point of recommending music, and as a result Mazzini in later life, when its pressures sometimes became very great, could ease his spirit by playing a guitar.

At his schools, the Royal College of Genoa and then the University, he studied the usual subjects including the language, history and literature of France, Rome and Italy, the last two from a Genovese point of view: Italy was great in the days of her medieval republics, Genoa, Venice, Florence and Pisa; and Rome, great as a republic, declined as an empire. The hero was Brutus, the man who had struck down the tyrant, and the fact that Dante had placed him in the deepest circle of Inferno, next to Judas, was ignored. The age and literature was increasingly romantic, exalting self-expression and idealism, however ineffective, over order and authority.

Mazzini, who was born in republican Genoa, raised on Foscolo and blessed with a mother of almost frightening moral intensity, represents an extreme of the liberalism of the times. His active role in the Risorgimento seems inevitable. At another extreme, an example of the power of liberal ideas to penetrate even the thickest walls, is Giacomo Leopardi, one of Italy's greatest poets. He too had a mother of extraordinary moral intensity, but in his case the liberal ideas were entirely his own, for there was nothing in his family or life to give him the faintest suspicion of them. Yet he, too, became in his own way an important figure of the Risorgimento.

He wrote of himself: "I was born of a noble family in an ignoble Italian town." His father was a Conte, and the town was Recanati in the Papal States. It sits high on the eastern slopes of the Apennines and is midway between the Adriatic and the larger town of Macerata where, in 1817, the Carbonari staged their first, feeble revolt. To anyone but Leopardi its setting might have seemed beautiful, a blue sky, a hillside covered with grape and olive and, in the distance, the sparkling sea. In the town itself the streets were dark and narrow but cool in summer and protected in winter. In Leopardi's time they were dominated by the churches and the palazzi of some forty noble families. But life for most of the town's aristocracy was restricted and provincial; and in the Palazzo Leopardi, particularly so.

Leopardi's father was a weak, ineffectual man who in his single moment of independence had married against his mother's advice. The step was disastrous and, as he wrote in his autobiography, "I have suffered a terrible punishment." His wife, the Contessa Adelaida, was a woman of strong character, interested in her position in the town and the state of her soul. The Conte lost considerable money attempting to introduce new methods of agriculture on his farms, and thereafter the Contessa ran both the house and the business. She did not dismiss a coachman, a lackey or any one of the three priests the family maintained. She economized by denying money and opportunities to her children and husband. The Conte was even reduced on occasion to stealing his own grain and selling it privately in order to raise pocket money.

In her religion she was haunted by a terror of sin. A prayer found among her papers asked, "Thou, O God, art the first father of my children. Grant that they may die rather than be a cause of offense to Thee." And of her eleven children, seven died at an early age and the eldest, the poet, was a hunchback. He wrote of her:

> I once knew intimately a mother who was not all superstitious but very staunch and exact in Christian belief and the exercises of religion. This lady not only used not to sympathize with parents who had lost their children but envied them deeply and sincerely, for the children had flown to paradise escaping the dangers of life and the parents were freed from the trouble of rearing them. Whenever she found herself in danger of losing her own children, as often she did, she would not pray to God to let them die, because her religion did not permit it, but in her heart she rejoiced . . . and if it happened that one of them died, the day of death was for her a day of joy, and she could not understand how her husband could be so foolish as to mourn. . . .
> She used to consider physical beauty a true misfortune, and seeing her children grow up ugly or deformed, she thanked God for it, not out of strength in adversity but out of desire fulfilled. She used in no way to help them to conceal their defects but rather because of their defects urged them from their earliest years to renounce life altogether. . . .
> She never missed an occasion of pointing out to them how ill-favored they were and dwelt with a ruthless and ferocious frankness on the humiliations to which their physical defects would expose them. . . .
> And all this she did in order to free them from the curse of original sin.[13]

Yet of all her children who survived into maturity only this one, the hunchbacked Giacomo, escaped from her domination into a larger life. He bore terrible emotional scars and never achieved happiness, but he did escape and through literature.

He had been educated entirely within the palazzo, which he was never allowed to leave unattended. The two family priests had taught him to read and had started him on Latin. Another priest, who had fled from France in the Revolution, introduced him to the language and literature of France. He was extremely precocious, and by the time he was ten, he had learned everything the priests could teach him. Thereafter he was allowed to read in the family library, which, with fourteen thousand volumes, was exceptionally good, and he perfected himself in Greek, Latin, Hebrew, French and Italian. Winter and summer for seven years he lived in the library. He so used up his eyes that in later years he had frequent periods when he could not read, and from hunching over the books he developed a severe curvature of the spine.

From books he learned of love, and when an elderly cousin brought a comparatively young wife to spend three nights at the palazzo, Leopardi fell madly in love with her. He suffered agonies, he kept a journal, and after much self-analysis he concluded, "I have experienced one of those attachments without which no man can be great." His attachment was to love in general rather than to the lady in question, and therefore false and passing; but his ambition to be great was very real and lasting.

From his library in 1817 when he was nineteen years old, he sent a translation of the second book of the *Aeneid* to various scholars and poets. All were impressed, but only one, Pietro Giordani, did more than politely acknowledge the translation. He was a liberal and a poet, who had lost his post at the University of Bologna on the restoration of the Papal government, and he took the trouble to write a friendly note. At once Leopardi unloosed on him all his troubles, hopes and fears. A deluge of letters went out from the library at Recanati, and Giordani, who was a busy, middle-aged man, was appalled at the confidences he received. But he was also moved by the young man's misery and eagerness, and he promised to visit Recanati and talk with Leopardi. After a long delay he made good his word and arrived at the town's inn.

For the first time in his life Leopardi left the palazzo alone, and almost immediately he ran into his father. He was allowed to go on only because the Conte assumed that Giordani, who had once studied in a seminary and was an Abbate, could not possibly be a liberal. And for five days Leopardi met with Giordani at the inn and went for walks and rides with him into the country. At the end of the visit Leopardi was a conscious liberal. Before it, he had already recognized that he was more deeply moved by Homer, Vergil and Ariosto than by histories of the Church or by discussions of philosophy or law. But he had wept over Hector and Andromache without transferring his feelings for them to the separated and defeated in his own country. For such a transference to take place, from literature to life, he needed to meet someone for whom literature was not vicarious experience but life itself. Giordani had supported Napoleon with his poetry and lost his post because of it. He was, in his minor way, Foscolo going into exile or Alfieri leaving Piedmont. Miraculously he had agreed to visit Leopardi and, having come, proved sympathetic. The visit, though short, was long enough for a man of Leopardi's sensitivity; thereafter, whenever he returned to the library, amid the thousands of old books there beat the heart of a contemporary man.

It was inconceivable that Leopardi, when he found his voice, would sound anything like Foscolo or Alfieri. What emerged from his pen were a series of prose essays, perfect in form and style, and thirty-four lyric poems written between 1818 and his death in 1837. It is on these that his continuing fame rests, for Italians have never stopped reading them. They were published originally either singly or in small groups, but even before his death they were collectively known as the *Canti* or *Songs*.

Their subject matter is often close to that of Foscolo, but the tone is different. Leopardi, because of his misfortunes and perhaps because he never experienced the joys of active life, is harsher and more despairing. He speaks more directly than Foscolo, often in the first person, and in place of classical allusions he is apt to use examples from recent Italian history, examples in which many of his readers might have been personally involved. And belonging to a later generation than Foscolo, one which never had to choose between republicanism supported by France and despotism by Austria, he is able to castigate both sides for what they have done to Italy and to call on Italians to save themselves. Yet his debt to Foscolo, in style and subject matter, is clear. As Foscolo had his *Dei Sepolcri* on Santa Croce in Florence, Leopardi too has an ode involving Santa Croce, *Sopra il monumento di Dante che si preparava in Firenze* or *On Dante's Monument which is suggested for Florence.*

The curious title refers to a manifesto issued in July 1818 in which a number of Florentine citizens lamented that a stranger coming to Florence would not find a monument to Dante anywhere in the city. Knowing that Ravenna would never give up his bones, they proposed a cenotaph be erected "in Santa Croce, alongside the tombs of Michelangelo, Machiavelli and Galileo." The project was accomplished in 1829, but shortly after the manifesto appeared Leopardi used it and the discussion it caused to lament the decadence of modern Italy.

He grieves for the country, urges the people to honor the illustrious dead so that "sleepy and sick-minded sons" will be inspired and, speaking directly to Dante, tells of the latest catastrophe Italy has suffered.

> O blessed you whom fate
> Did not condemn to live amidst such shame;
> Who did not see the wives
> Of Italy in barbarous soldiers' arms;

> Nor yet the hostile spear and foreign rage
> Despoil and ravage towns, lay waste the fields;
> Nor yet the works divine,
> Fruit of Italian genius, dragged away
> To wretched slavery beyond the Alps,
> The sorry way impeded by the press of carts;
> Nor yet the harsh commands and the proud reign;
> You did not hear the wicked insult of that
> Name of Liberty which mocked at us
> Amongst the sound of chains and crack of whips.
> Who does not grieve? What suffering is left?
> What did they leave untouched?
> What temple, altar or misdeed done?

And then once again, in the last strophe, he speaks directly to the Italian people:

> Have we for ever perished? and our scorn
> Is that now limitless?
> I while I live will go exclaiming still:
> Turn to your ancestors, O broken race;
> Look on the ruins here,
> The marbles, temples, pictures and the books;
> Think of that ground on which you tread; and if
> The light of such examples cannot wake
> You up, arise, depart.
> This nurse and school of lofty minds is not
> Fit place for usage that is so corrupt:
> Better it is for her
> To be widowed and lone than cowards' home.[14]

The tone is more impassioned, the words are hotter than in Foscolo: "sleepy and sick-minded," "corrupt," and "cowards." Leopardi worked in classic forms, but his tone is romantic. In another ode, *To Angelo Mai,* he allows true greatness among modern Italian poets only to Alfieri, who "first went down alone to the arena, and none followed him, for sloth and ugly silence press on us."

He attacked the French in *On Dante's Monument,* but in his very first ode, entitled simply *All'Italia* or *To Italy,* he attacked the Austrians. The time of the poem is firmly in the present, 1818.

> I see the walls and arches, O my Italy,
> The columns and the images, the lone
> Towers of our ancestors,
> But this I do not see,
> The glorious laurel and the swords they bore,
> In ancient times. Now you, become unarmed,

Show bare your forehead, and bare too your breast.
Alas, how many wounds,
What bruises, and what blood! how I see you,
Most beautiful! I ask both of the sky
And world:—Tell me, tell me;
Who brought her to this state?—and this is worse,
That both her arms are bound about with chains;
So that with loosened locks and without veil
She sits upon the ground disconsolate,
Neglected hides her face
Between her knees, and weeps.
Weep, for you have good cause, my Italy,
Born always to exceed,
When fortune smiles, and also when it frowns.[15]

No English translation can capture fully the quiver and sudden emphases of Italian poetry. The virtues of the languages are too unalike. The short words of Italian, dominated by open vowel sounds, can build a kind of sonority that, outside of nonsense verse, English cannot achieve. When men first read these poems or, better, heard them recited, they were often so moved by the combination of rhythm, sound and sense that they burst into tears, just as they might on hearing some incredibly lovely operatic aria. In Italian the first sentence of *All'Italia* is:

O patria mia, vedo le mura e gli archi
E le colonne e i simulacri e l'erme
Torri degli avi nostri,
Ma la gloria non vedo,
Non vedo il lauro e il ferro ond'eran carchi
I nostri padri antichi.

It is almost impossible to exaggerate the importance to Italians of their literature and even of their operatic music at this period in their history. Denied any chance to participate in the government of their states, forbidden to gather, either publicly or privately, in any groups of any size for any political purpose, forbidden to read foreign newspapers or to have any of their own, they turned increasingly to the arts in which they could express their ideas by allusion. As Stendhal observed of them: "If you are dealing with a race which is at once dissatisfied and witty, everything soon becomes an 'allusion.' "

Censors in the various states made the same observation and began to insist on changes in almost anything submitted to them. Leopardi's *All'Italia,* published at Rome in 1819, probably would not have been approved there fifteen years later and certainly would not have been approved at any time in Emperor Franz's Kingdom of Lombardo-Veneto.

The most liberal state was Tuscany, under one of Franz's younger brothers, Leopold, and a number of Leopardi's friends in Florence subscribed sufficient money in 1831 to publish all his *Canti* to that date. But outside of Tuscany the best hope of an artist to have his work published as he wanted it often lay in the laziness and confusion of purpose which the censors sometimes exhibited or in the chance of finding in another state another censor who would approve it. Thus Rossini was able to produce his opera *William Tell,* in which the anti-Habsburg allusion was perfectly clear, in Lucca and Florence but not in Milan or Venice.

The censorship, however, continually got tighter as Franz, the Pope and the various other monarchs on the peninsula grew increasingly nervous over the allusions which always seemed to conceal a threat of revolution or, at least, of riot and disorder. Rossini's opera and Leopardi's odes exalted patriotism and at the same time were good art, but Franz cared for neither art nor patriotism. He had announced in 1819, on a brief visit to the University of Pavia, "I want faithful subjects, not enlightened citizens." So, in Milan, after scarcely a year of publication, Confalonieri and Pellico were forced to give up their literary journal *Il Conciliatore.* At Genoa, in 1828, Mazzini acquired control of a commercial paper, *L'Indicatore Genovese,* and turned it into literary journal, but as he explained:

> The literary controversy turned itself into political controversy; it was only necessary to change some words to perceive it. There were skirmishes, scuffles between the shock troops on the frontiers of both sides. For us the independence in fact of Literature was nothing if not the first step toward another independence. . . . The government ended by perceiving and being irritated by this tendency. And when, at the end of the first year, we announced cheerfully to the readers that the journal would be enlarged, a governmental veto extinguished it.[16]

Mazzini, however, was not silenced. He had a friend in Tuscany who published a literary journal at Livorno, *L'Indicatore Livornese,* and he was soon writing regularly for that. But another writer who favored classical styles and forms challenged Mazzini to define what he meant by Romanticism, and Mazzini's answer was an essay in which he stated directly: "the authority which struck down in Italy *Il Conciliatore* and persecuted the young writers of that journal understood better than anybody else the true meaning of that word." Romanticism and revolution were publicly joined, for Confalonieri and Pellico had been convicted of treason.

Mazzini's attack on Austria was too direct for even the tolerant Grand Duke Leopoldo II, who was after all a Habsburg, and two months later he suppressed the journal. Three years later, on the insistence of Franz and Metternich, he suppressed the last and probably the best liberal journal in Italy, *L'Antologia.* It had, from 1821 until 1833, published articles of widely differing views by many of the most original minds of the day. It had, by attracting men to Florence, helped to make the city one of the intellectual centers of Italy. Now, its suppression at the insistence of Metternich proclaimed that Tuscany, like the other duchies, was ruled from Vienna and that the Habsburg emperor intended, if possible, to silence every voice of independent criticism on the peninsula. More than ever, Italians in order to communicate with each other, were reduced to joining secret societies and relying on allusions.

Literature, however, had still another contribution to make to the spirit of the Risorgimento in the impetus it gave to the development of a *national* Italian language. And the work which above all others made this contribution was Alessandro Manzoni's novel *I Promessi Sposi* or *The Betrothed*. It is the great Italian novel and has been described as representing for Italians all of Scott, Dickens and Thackeray rolled into one and infused with the spirit of Tolstoy. But because of the conditions in Italy in 1827, when it was first published, it had then, and increasingly each year thereafter, an extraliterary effect. This was partly because of its language.

In 1827 there was no *national* Italian language; the basis of what ultimately became it was still only a dialect, the Tuscan, spoken in and around Florence. It was, and is, called the *lingua del sì*. Elsewhere than Florence each region or even town had its own dialect, and not only did the accents vary but also the words for common objects such as windows or a carriage. A Neapolitan could not understand a Venetian unless they had in common at least a smattering of another language or dialect, usually Tuscan which was descended from the language of Dante.

The court or official languages of the various Italian states at the time were French in the Kingdoms of Sardinia and The Two Sicilies, Latin in the Papal States, and German in the Austrian dependencies of Parma, Tuscany, Modena and Lombardo-Veneto. And what was spoken at court often had no relation to what was used at home. Manzoni and his family spoke either French or a Milanese dialect, never German. Foscolo, a Venetian born on Zante, spoke first an Ionian dialect, then a Venetian and third, Italian. At Genoa and Nice the families of Mazzini and Garibaldi spoke a Ligurian dialect and, on occasion, French. Garibaldi, all his life, spoke Italian badly. For him, as for most Italians of the nineteenth century, it was a third or even fourth language. Peasants and simple townfolk, of course, spoke only their local dialect.

The dialects tended to keep the people of Italy divided and hostile. Since the days of Dante poets and statesmen had talked and written of "Italy" and "Italians," but the people had felt themselves to be Venetians, Piemontesi or Tuscans. Metternich's remark, "Italy is a geographical expression," stated a common idea but one which, by the beginning of the nineteenth century, was no longer true. The Italians were beginning to feel themselves to be a nation, and in their movement for unity and independence the development of a common language from the Tuscan dialect had a strong cohesive effect. Conversely, the political movement affected the development of the language. Of Italian words in common use today about half entered the languag as the men of the Risorgimento succeeded in unifying the country. To this development Manzoni contributed greatly by using his novel to bring the language and grammar of the Tuscan dialect, as he knew it, up to date.

When Manzoni, along with most educated Italians, had decided that of all the dialects the Tuscan was the richest and the most beautiful, he had only just begun on the problem of writing a popular novel in it. There was, for example, no authoritative dictionary. Probably the best was the *Vocabulario della Crusca,* which had been compiled by the academy of that name. The dictionary consisted almost entirely of words culled from the works of Tuscan writers of the fourteenth to sixteenth century. It was, therefore, dated and had almost no words for any concrete object or thought that had come within the province of literature since the sixteenth century. However excellent a dictionary it might be for poets writing epics of chivalry and courtly love, for novelists writing in the nineteenth century it was hopelessly inadequate.

To this was added the problem of flowery construction. Throughout the eighteenth century in Italy academies had flourished which had attempted to foster the arts and graces of life and also to preserve and purify the language. But one result had been to create yet another dialect, literary talk. It perhaps was pure, capable of subtleties, power and refinement; it certainly was involved, and no one, not even writers and educated aristocrats, consistently talked it. The great mass of Italians, the peasants and middle class, did not talk it at all. Writers of all sorts, literary and political, despaired over this; language was a barrier, not a bridge to communication.

Manzoni's novel was the first to break down the barrier. It succeeded, in its early editions, by using a happy mixture of literary talk for the descriptive passages with Milanese dialect for the dialogue. The vocabulary was a mixture of Lombard, Tuscan, French and Latin with made-up words he derived from one or the other by analogy or extension. The style was simple and straightforward. The story is of war, famine and plague and is subtitled "A Tale of XVII Century Milan." Manzoni wove into his tale, which was based in part on contemporary documents, many strands of which one at least was sure to appeal to every Italian: there was the irresponsibility of the governing classes, the simple honesty of the peasants who were its heroes, the beginnings of the Milanese silk industry, the adaptability of human nature to disaster, and finally, throughout, a devastating indictment of evil.

The form of the novel helped its popularity. Poetry, with its careful and sometimes contorted constructions, always requires close attention and even skill in reading to release its rewards. Leopardi had consciously tried to make his odes simple and popular, but even so the vocabulary of them was not that of daily speech. And Foscolo in his *The Last Letters of Jacopo Ortis* had still encased his prose tale in the form of letters. But Manzoni, with the fantastically popular novels of Walter Scott as examples, broke through into the form of the modern novel. Academicians might argue that Cervantes had merely been rediscovered, but for most Italians the form was new, very easy to read and therefore, being also an excellent novel, very popular. Manzoni reached a far larger audience than Leopardi, Foscolo or even Alfieri.

The novel sped through edition after edition until the definitive one Manzoni issued in 1840 after revising much of the language. He had visited Florence in 1827 and become convinced that the Tuscan dialect was the best for all of Italy. Thereafter in each edition he substituted more and more Tuscanisms, which gave rise to the quip that he had "washed his linen in the Arno." This referred to Emilia Luti, a Florentine governess, who besides teaching his children and doing a little family laundry became the oracle for testing words and phrases. But besides words Manzoni fixed whole ways of constructing sentences in the popular mind. The book became almost a primer and dictionary of the emerging Italian language, and from the first schools used it as such. Childish, piping voices recited the famous passages, as in other lands their counterparts do Homer, Racine or Shakespeare. Today children in the Italian government schools begin to study *I Promessi Sposi* at nine. In the 1830s when they first began to do so the fact had tremendous political significance. Without it or something like it the ultimate unification of Italy might not have been possible.

# CHAPTER 20

Francesco I of The Two Sicilies. Ferdinando II and his saintly
Queen. His character. Carlo Alberto. Mazzini's Open Letter. Papal
rule at Ravenna. The Sanfedisti. The problem of Temporal Power.
The Carbonaro revolution of 1831.

FOR ITALIANS of liberal leanings, whether in government, law or religion,
the twenty-five years after 1820 were increasingly discouraging. Nothing
the liberals attempted seemed to succeed, and the years themselves seemed
to produce no changes. Metternich continued in power at Vienna, and Emperor Franz, when he died in 1835, was succeeded by his son Ferdinand I,
who was almost an imbecile and quite incapable of governing. Metternich
was merely more powerful than ever and his policies more rigid.

In Italy, new popes and princes succeeded the old, but the policies of
their governments continued unchanged. At Rome, Pius VII died in 1823
and was succeeded by Leo XII, who was thought to be dying even as he
was elected. He survived for six years, but he had no solutions to the problems facing him. He disliked Consalvi and preferred, in place of him, some
of the most rigid of the Roman cardinals, men who admired Pacca but
who generally lacked his experience and abilities. They formed a faction
within the Church and were known as the *zelanti*. Their primary concern
was with the hierarchy of power at Rome and the government of the Papal
States; others, French, Swiss and German ecclesiastics, led the Church in
spiritual and scholastic matters. Leo was followed in 1829 by Pius VIII,
who survived only twenty months and who was, in turn, followed in 1831
by Gregory XVI, a Camaldolese monk. He was a theologian and philosopher, more obviously suited to the spiritual than to the temporal duties of
the throne. Like Leo, he favored the *zelanti* and had no doubts about the
ability of his priests to govern effectively, to balance a budget, to dispense
justice or to administer a city.

At Naples, Ferdinando I died in 1825, a few days before his seventy-
fifth birthday and after a reign of sixty-six years. So turbulent had been the
last third of it that most men found it hard to grasp that he had reigned in

peace for thirty years before the Bastille fell and for forty before a French revolutionary army had arrived at Naples. He was, at his death, the last of the eighteenth-century monarchs.

His son, Francesco I, was a mild man, middle-aged, domestic and, in comparison to his parents, who had dominated him, weak-willed. He had once had liberal tendencies but, as he explained to one of his ministers:

> There was a time when I thought that a partial sacrifice of the rights of the Crown in favor of national representation might have a beneficial influence on the development of our internal resources, efficient methods of administration, and the prosperity of the State in general, while diminishing the sovereign's burden of responsibility. In this illusion about the possibility of obtaining such desirable results I was completely sincere, but I was undeceived in 1820, when by my late father's wish I was placed at the head of the constitutional regime. I then became convinced that a Constitution . . . was only the first step towards democracy and anarchy, and I am firmly resolved not to take a road which must lead to the most fatal consequences.[17]

The government he offered, however, was not a good alternative. As a contemporary Neapolitan observed, Francesco and his ministers dispensed favors instead of administering justice, and they all, including the king, expected to be paid for them. Francesco's valet became one of the most important men in the kingdom, controlling even the appointment of an archbishop or of an administrator of a province. Francesco's attitude was: "A man who has paid for a job will try hard not to lose it and will therefore remain loyal." But when at every level of the government officials began to charge for the performance of their ordinary duties, the government quickly lost the respect of the people and, with it, the ability to lead them.

Fortunately for The Two Sicilies, in 1830, after a reign of only five years, Francesco died and was succeeded by his son, Ferdinando II, who at twenty was of age and did not require a regent. He was hearty and stout, with dark hair, dark eyes and an upturned nose. He sat a horse well, rising at the trot in the English fashion, and he had at all times a surprising dignity of manner for a young man.

Ferdinando had been born in 1810 and, therefore, had lived almost all his years after the Congress of Vienna. The events of 1799, the Parthenopean Republic, Nelson and even Napoleon were not part of his personal experience, and he could heal wounds which older men, who still felt the passions that caused them, could not. He reinstated in the army many officers who had been dismissed on suspicion of favoring Murat or republican doctrines. He granted an amnesty to almost all of the exiles of the Carbonaro revolution of 1820, and he employed liberals in his government. But he would not consider a constitution: "I would leave the crown and abandon Naples rather than subscribe to a constitution: in the backward state of civilization in this country its only result would be to encourage excesses and disorders, plunging us into a sea of woes."

The reasoning was unpopular with liberals because it was difficult to prove wrong, and even worse they were forced to admit that Ferdinando was attempting to provide good government of an alternative form even at the risk of unpopularity. Attacking the graft which had flourished under his father, he fired the valet, dismissed a number of ministers and dropped his prosecution of a former minister of war only when the man produced documents proving the late king's connivance. In an effort to balance the budget he gave up royal game preserves, cut his own allowance, stopped most of the private allowances granted by his father and halved those granted by his grandfather. He reduced certain taxes, including one on flour, and also cut the salaries of a number of officials. He held public audiences without court ceremonial, and he made tours of the provinces to find out for himself what the conditions were. His tutor had disapproved of dominating ministers, such as Acton, and had instilled Ferdinando with a distrust of them. As far as possible, Ferdinando tried to be his own minister in every department. His rule was autocratic but vigorous, and men of all parties watched to see if his interest would lag after the novelty of his position had worn off or if he was really one of those rare kings with a calling for the job.

In 1831 he married a princess of Savoy and, typically, he had conducted the marriage negotiations himself, never once consulting his minister for foreign affairs. The princess, Maria Cristina, had been raised in an intensely religious atmosphere and, left to herself, would have become a nun. But her relatives persuaded her that Christian duty could be as well performed at court as in a convent, and she did, in fact, raise the moral tone of the Neapolitan court and set an example of piety before the people. Yet she was not altogether popular, although Neapolitans greatly admired her Christian virtues and began to think of her, even in her lifetime, as a saint. But her northern piety was more inward than theirs, more modest and austere. Many of her acts of charity she did in secret, so that even the recipients of them did not know their benefactor. Neapolitans, however, liked things done with more of a swagger: Ferdinando handing a half-smoked cigar to a beggar. They admired Maria Cristina but without the warmth of enthusiasm.

She died in January 1836, two weeks after bearing Ferdinando a son, Francesco, who later was to be the last King of The Two Sicilies. Ferdinando was overcome with grief. At times of emotional stress he suffered from epilepsy, and now for a short while he was unable to walk and had fits of black depression. His mood was not helped by having his brother nearest in age, Carlo, Prince of Capua, elope with an Irish girl, Penelope Smyth. Ferdinando's sense of family position was very great, and in a furious scene with Carlo, just before Maria Cristina died, he had forbidden the marriage.

In his relations with his brothers there are clues to Ferdinando's character. Carlo's disobedience was clear, and his insistence that Ferdinando should elevate Penelope and their children into the royal line was outrageous. Nothing in the subsequent actions and behavior of the two lovers was impressive except their loyalty to each other. They dragged around Europe, from spa to spa, complaining about their ill-treatment, constantly in debt and used by Ferdinando's enemies, on occasion, to embarrass him. Until Ferdinando's death in 1859 Carlo and Penelope were a problem to him, and he would have done better to reach some sort of settlement, however right he was in his position. But then Ferdinando said once, "I may break, but I do not bend."

His relations with his next brother, Leopoldo, were almost as bad but in a different fashion. As soon as he had succeeded to the throne, he had sent Leopoldo, whose title was Conte di Siracusa, to be his viceroy in Sicily. Leopoldo was both attractive and able, probably the ablest member of the family; he was also liberal, and by a combination of his qualities he began to have a personal success with the Sicilians, with whom the Bourbons were not always popular. Ferdinando at once grew nervous and removed Leopoldo in what amounted to disgrace, dispatching a frigate to take him off the island and then sending him on a tour of Europe. The brothers remained friendly, even affectionate, but Ferdinando never again used Leopoldo in state affairs, nor would he ever consider any of the advice Leopoldo had to offer. The advice may have been self-serving, as some Bourbon historians claim, but in hindsight it was good advice, and the Neapolitan dynasty suffered because Ferdinando would not make use of it or of the man capable of thinking it out.

Ferdinando's first marriage had been popular with his people partly because he had married an Italian princess. But for his second wife he went to Vienna and in 1837 married Maria Theresa, a daughter of the Archduke Karl who had fought Napoleon. Her position at Naples was bound to be difficult: she followed an Italian queen who was not only a saint but the mother of the heir apparent. She would inevitably appear more foreign, less worthy and, as she produced children and planned for them, scheming. To some extent she avoided the snares by having her chief interests and virtues domestic. She had none of the ambition or ability that sixty years earlier Maria Carolina had brought to Naples. She favored Austria and the Church and, as a result, was a member of the court or conservative party as opposed to the liberals. But the fact had no political significance, for Ferdinando was the head of the party and, unlike his grandfather, intended to rule the kingdom himself. The liberals in Naples, however, regretted that he had gone to Vienna for a wife; it seemed yet another sign of an increasing conservatism.

Northwards, at Turin, Carlo Alberto had succeeded his cousin, Carlo Felice, on the Sardinian throne in April 1831, only five months after Ferdinando had become King of The Two Sicilies. The two kings, who, except for the pope, were the only native monarchs in Italy, could hardly have been more different. Where Ferdinando was plump, hearty, self-assertive and enjoyed being king, Carlo Alberto was thin, ascetic, hesitant and tortured by his position. He had been raised in the same religious atmosphere that had produced Ferdinando's saintly wife, but where Ferdi-nando was able only to accept and admire Maria Cristina, Carlo Alberto could follow and understand every shade of her feelings, for he shared them. The House of Savoy had always been famous for its piety, and in recent years the streak of it seemed to have grown even stronger. Of Vit-torio Amedeo III's three sons, all of whom succeeded him, the first, Carlo Emanuele IV, had abdicated in 1802 in order to retire to a monastery, and he died a Jesuit; the second, Vittorio Emanuele I, had re-established the Church in his kingdom in all its medieval glory and privilege and, during the constitutional revolution of 1821, had abdicated; and the third, Carlo Felice, who had shown little interest in governing, had allowed the army to deteriorate and the Church to dominate the court and the kingdom. Meanwhile the ladies of the family, of whom Maria Cristina was only the most notable, did many good works and, compared to most European royalty of the time, set a remarkable example of Christian living.

The sense of altar and throne, of divine right and knightly duty that surrounded Carlo Alberto, when he came to the throne in his thirty-third year, was very strong. But it was not necessarily a strength to him. It also contained ideas such as that political actions can be offensive to God, that the next world is more important than this and that saving the king's soul can be more important than doing the king's duty, and these ideas could lead to agonies of self-doubt, hesitation and abdication in moments of crisis.

For Carlo Alberto such moments had begun in 1821 during the consti-tutional revolution. In the few weeks that he had been regent, before Carlo Felice had agreed to take the throne, he had followed his liberal leanings and granted a constitution. But then when Carlo Felice repudiated it and ordered him to retire to Tuscany, he had decided, after much soul-searching, to obey. His aide-de-camp, the Marchese di Collegno, was so horrified at his decision that, on being told of it, he slapped Carlo Alberto in the face, broke his sword at the prince's feet and went into exile.

For the rest of his life Carlo Alberto was plagued by his equivocal behavior in 1821; the liberals considered him a traitor, and the conservatives a dangerous revolutionary. He was quoted as saying that he lived in fear "between the daggers of the Carbonari and the chocolate of the Jesuits." Carlo Felice, who had no son, brooded over his cousin's behavior and consulted with Metternich about the possibility of denying the succession to Carlo Alberto in favor of his infant son, Vittorio Emanuele. Nothing came of the plan except that Carlo Alberto was forced to subscribe an oath that, on his accession, he would maintain the existing, absolute form of monarchy and, as a consequence, never grant a constitution.

The issue was put to him publicly in the first month after he became king. Mazzini, signing himself merely "an Italian," published an Open Letter to him which was secretly distributed throughout Genoa, Piedmont and all the neighboring states. In Tuscany it sold freely on the streets.

Mazzini began by excusing Carlo Alberto for his defection in the revolution of 1821, explaining that it was common knowledge that he was not then his own master and that in the following years he had been forced to conceal his liberal leanings. But to these, Mazzini now appealed, urging the king to grant a democratic constitution and to recognize "the right, power and sovereignty of the nation." By "nation" Mazzini meant all of Italy, for he went on to assure the king that his mission was to unite all the Italian states in the struggle for independence. He need not fear Austria, France or any of the Italian Princes, for the people would assist him. Mazzini ended:

> SIRE! I have spoken to you the truth. The free men of Italy await your answer in your deeds. Whatsoever that answer may be, rest assured that posterity will proclaim in you—THE FIRST MAN AMONG MEN, OR THE LAST OF THE ITALIAN TYRANTS.— Choose! [18]

Carlo Alberto chose absolutism and, after determining that Mazzini was the author of the Open Letter, banished him from the Kingdom of Sardinia. In spite of Mazzini's insistence, Carlo Alberto had no choice. In the spring of 1831 the unification of Italy and constitutionalism were particularly dangerous issues as Austria had just put down a Carbonaro revolution that had started in February at Bologna and then spread throughout the other Legations into the Duchies of Modena and Parma. To have granted a constitution at Turin after a revolution with that aim had failed at Bologna was merely to invite the Austrian armies to cross the Ticino, as they had the Po, and to occupy Piedmont and Genoa, as they had Parma, Modena and more than half of the Papal States. An Austrian archduke might even be sent to replace Carlo Alberto at Turin and the House of Savoy forced to retire once again to the island of Sardinia. Mazzini's Open Letter was probably not intended and certainly was not taken by most of its readers as a realistic political program. But it was excellent propaganda for a united Italy and, being signed by "an Italian," stirred in its readers a sense of common nationality.

Even better propaganda was the Carbonaro revolution, though it failed, for it focused the attention of Europe, peoples as well as governments, on the shortcomings of the Papacy as a secular government. By 1831 these had become so great at Bologna, Ravenna and the other Legations that the Carbonari were able to turn them into a European problem. Immediately after the revolt was put down, the ambassadors to Rome of Austria, Prussia, Russia, France and observers from Britain and Sardinia conferred and then offered a memorandum of advice to the pope on how to reform his administration. The memorandum stressed the need to allow laymen to have some part in the government, either by appointment or by allowing municipal and provincial councils to be elected by the people. It recommended some sort of central council to control finance in a more responsible fashion, and it recommended that the pope restore the civic rights which Bologna, for example, had enjoyed by agreement with the popes from 1447 until the arrival of Napoleon and which the popes after Napoleon had refused to restore. The advice, as might be expected, was neither welcomed nor followed and, although all of it was relevant, it skirted the most emotional issue which underlay the more academic points about finance and municipal charters. This was the Papacy's use of police spies and bullies to keep order.

Leo XII, who had succeeded Pius VII and retired Consalvi, had appointed as cardinal legate at Ravenna a *zelante*, Agostino Rivarola, who was determined to stamp out Carbonarism. He took up his post in June 1825 and by the end of August, with the information given him by informers and by means of an emergency court with himself as president employing special powers, he had sentenced seven men to death, fifty-four to forced labor, six to life imprisonment, fifty-three to various terms of imprisonment, two to exile, 129 to police supervision in the first degree and 157 to police supervision in the second degree. Ravenna had at the time a population of about eight thousand and in this one trial 408 men, or about one in twenty, received sentences. Assuming that each man represented a family of five persons, not unreasonable in Italy, every fourth family in the town was directly involved in that one trial. And the effects of it did not end there, for an attempt to assassinate Rivarola killed the wrong man; Leo sent another priest, a monsignor, with a special commission to the city and more men were sentenced to death and hanged. Their bodies, denied Christian burial, were left on the gallows to rot.

As long as Ravenna was part of the Papal States, it never thereafter had a normal city life. Almost without exception all of the upper and middle classes, the aristocrats, business and professional laymen, worked steadily to undermine the government and join their city in some sort of union with others that would be free of the Papacy. To this aim the peasants were largely indifferent or opposed, but the priests, with the aid of a few office holders and gangs enrolled from the poorer and criminal classes, fought back. And Ravenna's history in the civic warfare that developed differed from that of its neighbors only in that it was the most bloody and tragic.

The gangs which the priests employed claimed to be the heirs of those who had fought with Cardinal Ruffo and others against the republicans of the previous generation. They called themselves "Sanfedisti" and organized themselves in bands of about a hundred each, with two bands in a small city like Ravenna. They were unpaid and without uniforms or barracks, but the advantages of serving the Sanfedisti and the dangers of using them to support the government soon became apparent.

They were often stronger than the police, and when they indulged in violence, which was frequent, they were not prosecuted. On the rare occasions on which they might be, they were frequently gotten off with little or no sentence by friends who were in the administration. Often in the larger towns they were able to keep their identities secret, so that even the priests did not know, beyond the man with whom they talked, whom they were employing or the source of information used to lay charges against the citizens. Yet the Sanfedisti were supported and used by the Church, and even those bishops and cardinals who disliked them seemed unable to imagine any way of governing without them.

It was in this area of creative political thinking that the Church's failure, in the forty years following, was to be complete and self-destructive. In 1832 the British aristocracy faced with riots and a threat of revolution by the other classes, was able, by the Reform Bill, to transform its privileged and aristocratic form of parliamentary government into one that represented more of the nation. And in France in 1830, when the Bourbon Charles X illegally suspended the nation's Charter, there were statesmen and leaders of all classes who, in repudiating him, were able to imagine a government with a wider base among the people and to form one under the more liberal Louis Philippe of the House of Orléans. But at Rome and in the Legations there was seemingly no group or movement among the priests, young or old, capable of thinking out an alternative form of government for the pope to use in place of repression, censorship and the Sanfedisti.

Admittedly the problem was difficult. By 1830 most of the Carbonari in the Adriatic provinces of the Papal States wanted to cut all ties with Rome and to join their cities either to some other state or to create a new one. They remembered the fifteen years spent under Napoleonic rule, mostly as part of the Kingdom of Italy, as happier and more prosperous, and the government then, with its good laws and economic freedom, had been secular. Even if Leo XII had been willing to grant a constitution, to reform the legal system and to permit some degree of self-government, he might not have been able to calm Carbonaro agitation.

But Leo and the *zelanti* cardinals were never willing to consider such a program. To have done so they would have had to think through, in nineteenth-century terms, the purpose of their temporal power and then to create some new forms for it. The old forms, as the memorandum of the ambassadors and the incidents of the Carbonari should have made them aware, were no longer tenable.

The traditional theory of the temporal power was both practical and mystical with the two inextricably intertwined. In the middle ages in order for the pope to be able to exercise his spiritual power (the appointment of cardinals, excommunication, etc.) with any degree of independence he had needed a fortified city, Rome, an army of his own and also some land in which to maneuver it, the Papal States. These last also provided the necessary agricultural area to support the city. But only with the walled city, the army and the surrounding countryside could the pope prevent the emperors of the world from kidnapping his person and dictating his decisions. Leo had to go back no further than Napoleon and Pius VII to offer an example within the memory of most men.

But liberals used the same example to demonstrate the obsolescence of the idea. Against the size of the armies that the great powers now put in the field, neither the Papacy nor any other small Italian state could maintain territorial integrity. No need, they argued, to go back to Napoleon; in the last ten years Austrian armies had violated Papal neutrality by marching to and from Naples and had put garrisons into Papal cities and then delayed in withdrawing them. In fact, the independence of the Papacy rested on the good will and balance between the forces of the great powers; therefore it could afford to allow self-government or even independence to its Legations.

The mystical side of the traditional theory was that the Papal States were literally a gift of God to his Church, the Patrimony of St. Peter. There is no reason to doubt that Pius VII and his successors believed it. To them as seeming evidence of it was the fact that the Papal States were the most ancient sovereignty in Europe. It was therefore the duty of any pope to defend every inch of his Patrimony; how could a pope alienate a gift from God?

Again the liberals were able to embarrass the Church with a recent example. In 1797 Pius VI had signed the Treaty of Tolentino with Napoleon by which the Papacy had voluntarily given up the Legations. And centuries before, in 1545, Pope Paul III had created the Duchy of Parma for his illegitimate son by carving it out of the Papal States. The idea of God's gift, so attractive and full of meaning for priests, struck liberals as merely a clever party slogan for influencing the illiterate and uneducated. The liberals would constantly accuse the Church of manipulating spiritual doctrines and dogma for political ends.

The change of regime in Paris in July 1830 inspired liberals everywhere and particularly in Italy where France had a tradition of fostering liberal ideas. Now after fifteen years of increasing absolutism under the Bourbons, France seemed once again to turn towards a more liberal form of government. Although the barricades in Paris had been manned by workmen, the movement was quickly dominated by the respectable middle class. Property was safe. Louis Philippe was known as the *bourgeois* king and, before assuming the throne, he transferred his fortune not to the public treasury, like a king who was the State, but to his family, like a businessman who mistrusts his venture. The nobility in disgust retired to their châteaux or town houses in a kind of second emigration, only this time psychological rather than physical, and the clerics, who had been growing increasingly arrogant, were chastened. It was the first break in the European settlement of the Congress of Vienna.

It was followed, a month later, by a Belgian revolution in which liberals allied with clerics separated Catholic Belgium from Protestant Holland and formed an independent, constitutional monarchy. This time Austria, Prussia and Russia were eager to reimpose the original settlement, but Great Britain and the new, more liberal France cooperated to support the Belgians and finally persuaded the absolutist powers to accept the new state. Liberals in Italy saw in it the perfect example for themselves.

They were most active in their secret societies in the Duchy of Modena and in the Legations. For the first time their aims, although confused, included the union of separate states under a single ruler. They hoped to combine Parma, Modena and the Legations, and as much more of the Papal States as opportunity might offer, into a constitutional Kingdom of Central Italy under the Habsburg Duke of Modena, Francesco IV. The idea and the effort, although not yet national, was becoming so, and some liberals talked and wrote of their plans to unite all of Italy into "one single, free and independent State."

The greatest obstacle in the planning was persuading most liberals to accept Francesco as their future king. Both in Italy and among the exiles in Paris, where much of the planning was done, he was the most hated and distrusted of all the monarchs in Italy. He had agreed, however, to accept the position and plainly his presence as king would incline Austria not to interfere. Further to deter Austria the liberals in Paris had conversations with Louis Philippe's ministers who promised that France would oppose any armed intervention by Austria in states that did not belong to it.

The revolution was set for February 1831 when all the cardinal-legates were at Rome in conclave to elect the successor to Pius VIII, who, following Leo XII, had reigned for only eight months. It began badly. On the night of 2 February, as the leaders gathered in Modena to make their final arrangements, Duke Francesco betrayed them, surrounded the meeting place with troops and took them all prisoner. Then he retired with them across the Po to the Austrian fortress at Mantua. Apparently he had not lost his nerve but had intended to betray them from the start.

The revolution, however, continued with surprising success and very little bloodshed. The Parmigiani forced their duchess, Marie Louise, to flee from Parma, and all the Legations and Papal cities except for Rome and a few on the Roman side of the Apennines declared themselves free. Delegates from all the cities met in Bologna and proclaimed the United Italian Provinces. A provisional government was formed of distinguished lawyers, professors and aristocrats and it made every effort to demonstrate to Britain, France and Austria that it was stable and conservative.

But Central Italy was not Belgium. This time there were Habsburg princes displaced, an Austrian army only a few miles away, and a newly elected pope, Gregory XVI, who called for it to re-establish the old order. In France, Louis Philippe broke his word, changed his ministers and refused to warn Austria against intervention. From the garrisons in Lombardo-Veneto the Austrian troops crossed the Po into the United Provinces, and in two months the revolution was over. Hundreds more Italians went into exile and along with wild-eyed conspirators were many distinguished men whose departures were a real loss for Italian life.

Once again government was imposed by force and kept in power by censorship and the Sanfedisti. Liberals despaired. Nothing succeeded. A liberal of the next generation lamented that his father had been forced "to pass the greater part of his life in that stagnant pool in which Italy lay between 1815 and 1848." Many felt as he did.

# CHAPTER 21

Mazzini in exile. His influence. La Giovine Italia. The invasion of
Savoy. Garibaldi at Genoa. Mazzini in London.

MAZZINI TOOK NO PART in the February 1831 revolutions at Parma, Modena and the Papal States, although Carbonari from all over Italy and
even a number of foreigners hurried to fight the Austrians and to serve
under the provisional government at Bologna. But in the week the revolutions began, Mazzini had only just been released from prison and, closely
watched by the police, was leaving Genoa to begin his life in exile.

He had been arrested on 13 November 1830, along with six others of
his lodge, on information given the Governor of Genoa by one of their
leaders, a man who seems to have had a genuine change of heart about his
Carbonaro activities, for the betrayal was not for money or position. The
arrest took place at Dr. Mazzini's door where the police had been waiting
since six in the morning. Mazzini tried to pass himself off as a patient calling on his father, and although he failed in that, he was able to conceal
evidence of conspiring against the state, so that the police were able to find
only a pistol and some gunpowder. During the subsequent interrogations
Mazzini denied everything, and the prosecution began to languish. The
police, meanwhile, had transferred him to a prison at Savona and sent the
testimony and evidence they had collected to Turin where a commission
undertook to examine it and make a report to the king, Carlo Felice.

The commissioners, perhaps because of Carbonaro influence in the
government, recommended that all seven prisoners be set free for lack of
reliable evidence that any one of them was a Carbonaro. The Minister of
the Interior concurred but recommended that Mazzini and one other be
forbidden to live at Genoa. Finally Carlo Felice, in an order signed on 28
January 1831, went still further and forbade him to live anywhere on the
coast. Mazzini, however, preferred voluntary exile in France to life in an
inland city of Piedmont; in France, he reasoned, he would have greater
freedom for his revolutionary activities. So, as the Carbonari began their

revolutions at Modena and Bologna, he started in a coach with his uncle for Paris.

His ten weeks of prison at Savona were a crucial period in his life. In the days of enforced idleness he thought out some basic ideas toward which he had already been groping and which he continued to develop, although not always consistently, for the rest of his life. He was disgusted with the Carbonari. He felt their aims were both too vague and too limited, their actions too few and ineffective; particularly he disapproved of their attempts to get help from France, "preaching the French initiative" he called it. And when in the first weeks of his exile France under Louis Philippe betrayed the Carbonari and made no move to prevent the Austrians from crossing the Po, he was more than ever convinced that he was right. He would start a new secret society which would take action itself and not put its trust in France. This was to be one of the important differences between La Giovine Italia or Young Italy, which he founded in the summer of 1831, and the Carbonaro societies which continued to exist.

Another was to be his constant emphasis on social as well as political change. Where the Carbonari talked of winning political rights, Mazzini would talk of regenerating Italians. His particular plans for achieving social change are generally confused and in action were always put second to the political needs of the moment. But they had an effect because of the fervor with which he surrounded them. Where a true socialist talked of abolishing poverty by readjusting the production and distribution of wealth, Mazzini would talk of destroying the spirit of egoism and self-interest which, in his opinion, was the cause of all social evils, including poverty. Time has changed the details of the political and social problems for which he sought a solution, and his programs have dated. But the nature of the problems has not changed, and the moral teaching with which he attacked them is still inspiring.

For Mazzini the value and meaning of a man's life lay in his obedience to Duty, and Duty required him to act. It was not enough for a man to save his soul or to live in such a way that he did not harm others. Duty required him "to translate every thought of good, come what may, into action. The moral man cannot be sundered from the practical or political man." He held up self-sacrifice as the only virtue and preached a solidarity of all classes and countries in the fight "for the victory of good over evil." His ideas are often undefined and even fantastic yet, as Gaetano Salvemini pointed out in discussing them, so are those in the Lord's Prayer:

Who is this Father of ours who is in Heaven? What is his Kingdom? And what the trespasses that we forgive? Nevertheless, not one of us who has learnt this prayer in childhood can think of it without feeling a fervent desire for righteousness, for love, for peace, or without the conviction that its Author, though not a philosopher, was a very wonderful character. It is a prayer that does not present a sequence of ideas, but raises a host of feelings.[19]

Mazzini, as he grew older, raised such feelings in almost all men who met him and in most who read his articles, particularly in the young and eager. The dedication of his life, its activity and anguish, was impressive. For him his political action was always secondary to his religious purpose, and although all but a disciple or two put the political action first, most men recognized that much of his power over them lay in his ability to stir their deepest feelings of what was right and good.

In the long run it was this ability to touch the best in human beings that spread Mazzini's name and influence far beyond Italy. An American social worker, Jane Addams, described in a book of reminiscences how one morning in 1872, when she was only eleven and living on a farm in Illinois, she had entered her father's room:

> He was sitting by the fire, with a newspaper in his hand, looking very solemn, and upon my eager enquiry what had happened, he told me that Joseph Mazzini was dead. I had never even heard Mazzini's name, and after being told about him I was inclined to grow argumentative, asserting that my father did not know him, that he was not an American, and that I could not understand why we should be expected to feel badly about him. It is impossible to recall the conversation, with the complete breakdown of my cheap arguments, but in the end I obtained that which I have ever regarded as a valuable possession, a sense of the genuine relationship which may exist between men who share large hopes and like desires, even if they differ in nationality, language and creed: that these things count for absolutely nothing between groups of men who are trying to abolish slavery in America or to throw off Habsburg oppression in Italy. At any rate I was heartily ashamed of my meager notion of patriotism, and I came out of the room exhilarated with the consciousness that impersonal and international relations are actual facts and not mere phrases.[20]

On his journey to Paris, Mazzini got no further than Lyon. There he met a number of revolutionaries who were going to Corsica and thence to Italy to fight for the provisional government at Bologna. He joined them, concealing his decision from his uncle and leaving behind only a short note of affection that explained nothing. On Corsica a band of some two thousand men had collected, but they had no money for passage to Italy. They applied to the provisional government at Bologna, but it, too, lacked money and, as it still hoped for aid from France, was reluctant to assist revolutionaries on a French island. Mazzini later referred to the men at Bologna as "that inept government which trusted only in diplomacy and shrank from arms." The experience only re-enforced his belief that Italians needed a new and more vigorous secret society.

He organized it in the spring and summer of 1831 at Marseille, but before then, and perhaps the last thing he did for the Carbonari, he wrote his Open Letter to the new King of Sardinia, Carlo Alberto. As a result, by royal decree, he was banished from the kingdom; his voluntary exile was now involuntary. He did not care. He had good friends in Genoa to act as his agents, and most of the leading revolutionaries were, like himself, exiles and in France.

At Marseille, he gathered round him a small band of devoted disciples, mostly men from Modena who had fled on the collapse of their revolution. To them he added a group of personal followers in Genoa, Livorno and other ports along the Ligurian coast as well as a number of sailors who served as a postal service connecting them all. Such was the nucleus of La Giovine Italia, or Young Italy, which at its start would enroll men only if they were under forty. Mazzini, who was himself twenty-six, considered men over forty to be too old to be regenerated, too inclined to temporize and, because they remembered the achievements in Italy of Napoleon, too inclined to look to France for aid. Later he relented and made exceptions for those old men who were "young in spirit."

At its start La Giovine Italia was very much like any Carbonaro Society. Each member chose a code name for himself from one of the warrior families of the Middle Ages and was responsible for arming himself with a dagger, a rifle and fifty cartridges. There was an entrance fee and monthly dues, a secret hand signal and a greeting: "What is the time?" With the response, "Time for the struggle." They called themselves "Brother" as the Carbonari called each other "Good Cousin" and, like the Carbonari, they tried to infiltrate into positions of responsibility.

The aims of La Giovine Italia were a united and independent Italy with its capital at Rome and a republican form of government, none of which was original with Mazzini. What he contributed was the sense of mission with which he preached them and with which he tried to inspire the members. Young Italians were to think of Italy's mission in the world, to show the way to a better future with social justice for all. On the way to it they would unite and free their country as they regenerated themselves by their self-sacrifice and struggle.

The society spread its aims and became known through its journal, *La Giovine Italia,* which it published in Marseille as often as Mazzini could collect articles for it and money to pay the publisher Six numbers were issued in all, three in 1832, two in 1833 and one in 1834. But they averaged more than two hundred pages an issue, although most of the articles were written by Mazzini himself. The few other contributors, considering the journal was banned in all the Italian states, wrote under pseudonyms. The single exception was the great historian Sismondi, who lived in Geneva, and who, as the price Mazzini paid for snaring such a luminary, was allowed to urge a federation of Italian states rather than a unified republic.

Such open propaganda was another difference between La Giovine Italia and the Carbonaro societies. The Carbonari leaders considered it unwise to talk so conclusively about a republic for fear of scaring the moderates; to talk of Rome as the capital was merely to raise the hopelessly complicated problem of the Papacy and to lose support among the devout and priests; and to talk of unifying all of Italy was to lose the possibility of playing off one prince against another. The Carbonaro oath which Mazzini had taken, and about which he complained, contained not "a syllable which gave a hint as to federation or unity, as to republic or monarchy. Just war against the government, no more."

Each society found certain obvious advantages in its policy. In retrospect the Carbonari certainly achieved more at the time. Their revolutions were better conducted and at least at Naples in 1820 and Bologna in 1831 came close to success. Mazzini, on the other hand, with his educational policy of open discussion, may have laid the more important foundation for ultimate success.

The distribution of the journal in Italy involved Mazzini and his colleagues in all the arts of smuggling: false addresses, trunks with false bottoms, and crates of fish or pumice stone with false centers. There were frequently disasters, and the police of the various states were often well informed about the society's activities and future plans. But the journals were passed from hand to hand and read; young men, particularly in the universities, were enrolled and older men, lawyers, doctors and even some priests, debated the doctrines and the question of which society to support. One that caused Mazzini particular trouble was *I Veri Italiani* or "The True Italians" which had much the same aims as Mazzini's society and was strong in Piedmont and Tuscany.

His plan for La Giovine Italia was to have uprisings in the extremities of the peninsula, Naples and Piedmont, with the central states joining later in the general upheaval. He hoped after an initial success that all the societies would join him and, as the provinces freed themselves, that they would send two deputies to a Central Junta which he described as a "sort of Committee of Public Safety." His description may have been ill chosen, for it tended to remind the Carbonari of the French Revolution at the time of Robespierre and, perhaps, to increase their distrust of him.

He talked of fifty or sixty thousand rising at the signal, and in an article in the fifth issue of *La Giovine Italia* he discussed the kind of tactics to be

used. He imagined a defensive war from the mountains such as the Calabrians and Spanish had used against the French. And he added:

> Not war alone, but we must prepare in every way for the resurrec-
> tion and emancipation of the people, the only principal foundation
> we recognize for free states. Even if the regular armies are sufficient
> to defeat us, we must forever agitate with words and facts for the
> holy war, the *war of the people*. . . . We are attempting a revolution
> of the *people,* not of factions of the military and civil aristocracies.[21]

But the lesson of the Bologna revolution seemed to be that, although
the middle class was prepared to fight, the peasants and the rich were not.
When others pointed this out, Mazzini insisted that under him the mass of
the people would rise. And then the rich would not hesitate to help with
their money. But there were many who doubted, and in an effort to win
allies in the other secret societies he had to agree to have a professional
soldier to lead the revolution in Piedmont and to have help, if possible,
from France.

Planning it all was perhaps the happiest period in his life. As he wrote
later:

> Without an office, without assistance, immersed the whole day and
> part of the night in work, writing articles and letters, interviewing
> travellers, enrolling sailors, folding up pieces of paper, doing up par-
> cels, alternating between intellectual and manual work . . . we lived
> as true equals and brothers, with only one thought, only one hope,
> devoted only to one spiritual ideal; loved and admired by the foreign
> republicans for our tenacity of purpose and capacity for uninterrupted
> work; often—since we spent our money on all this—we were in ex-
> treme poverty, yet we were cheerful as could be, and smiling with the
> smile of faith in the future. Those years between 1831 and 1833
> were two years of young life, pure and joyful in their devotion, as I
> would wish it for the coming generation.[22]

By the spring of 1833 he was ready and had begun on the last and
most dangerous step of preparation, the infiltration of the Sardinian army
at Genoa, Alessandria and the mountain forts in Savoy. His agents were
having considerable success when one night two soldiers who were in the
conspiracy had a fight over a girl. In the course of pushing, shoving and
calling each other names, one accused the other of having told the girl
more about the conspiracy than he should have. The police uncovered
enough of the story to scare the conspirators so that they and several others
turned king's evidence and revealed everything they knew, which was
enough, in turn, to scare the government.

For the first time Carlo Alberto and his ministers paid serious attention to Mazzini and his agents. The police and military arrested all the leaders and sent them before special military commissions for trial. Twelve men were found guilty and executed, and two more committed suicide. One of these was Mazzini's best friend, Jacopo Ruffini, and for the rest of his life Mazzini agonized over the possibility, which he thought to be true, that Ruffini, deliberately misled by the police, had died believing that Mazzini had betrayed him. The number of men shot was small, but many more scrambled for safety by turning king's evidence and were disciplined in other ways. And the penetration of the Sardinian army, with the aim of controlling the kingdom's chief arsenals, was brought to a complete stop.

The various trials in Piedmont and at Genoa showed conclusively that Mazzini was the head of the conspiracy and was directing it from Marseille. He had already been exiled. Now the military court at Alessandria condemned him to death, *in absentia,* and the sentence was to be "read and published, loud and clear" before his father's house in Genoa and to be preceded by a flourish of trumpets.

Carlo Alberto also put pressure on Louis Philippe to end Mazzini's asylum at Marseille, and under increasing police pressure there the group around Mazzini began to break up. He himself, at this moment of crisis, disappeared for more than a week, and to this day no one knows where he went. It seems likely he was with the lady he loved, the mother of his only child, a boy who died not long after. He seems also to have had a nervous breakdown over the destruction of his work and the suicide of his friend Ruffini, and the lady presumably nursed him through it. In any event he reappeared in July 1833 at Geneva, more tense and overwrought, and gradually his disciples and agents gathered around him there.

He was determined not to let the disaster in Piedmont and Genoa hold up the revolution. Whereas he had planned on having the lead come from the north, now he looked to the south, Naples. But week after week letters came to him without any news of a revolt, and day after day he sat in his room in the Hôtel de la Navigation at Geneva writing to the leaders in the south, urging them to take action, to give the lead. In May they had written they were ready, why in August could they not begin? The answer was, just as in Piedmont, a series of arrests had crippled the leadership and given second thoughts to most of the members. To the men in Naples the situation there seemed hopeless, particularly without the possibility of a successful rising in Piedmont at the same time.

But the longer the delay the more Mazzini insisted on immediate action and on the widest possible scale. After working for three years to start the revolution, he refused to consider whether the moment for it might not have passed. He became desperate. He hired a man to assassinate Carlo Alberto, with the murder to be the signal for the uprising. But the man merely lurked around Turin for several weeks and then departed without even an attempt. And still another project came to nothing.

One remained: a two-pronged attack on Piedmont—from the north, by land starting from Geneva and progressing through Savoy, and from the south, by sea starting from Marseille and taking Genoa. Then the garrison at Alessandria, in the center, would rise, and Carlo Alberto, with his retreat cut off in both directions, would be forced to capitulate. This was the original plan of the year before, but since the purge of the army and the loss of the best leaders at Genoa and Alessandria, it had far less chance of success. Nevertheless, at Geneva, Italian patriots, republicans of all nationalities and professional freedom fighters began to gather and the date was set for 12 November.

The day came and passed, however, and the professional soldier who was supposed to lead them did not appear. He was General Gerolamo Ramorino, the man who the secret societies in Piedmont, particularly the Veri Italiani, had insisted, should lead the expedition. He had been trained in French military schools, fought at Wagram and in the Russian campaign and been awarded the Cross of the Legion of Honor. After Napoleon's fall he had become a professional revolutionary soldier and fought both in Portugal and Poland. By the terms of his contract he was supposed to arrive at Geneva with a thousand armed men, many of whom would be Italian exiles. They were to make up about half the initial force which once into Savoy would swell many times over with Savoyards. But November passed into December and still he did not come.

Meanwhile among the faithful at Geneva a terrible row broke out over what should go on the flag. Some wanted *Dio e Popolo, God and the People,* which was one of the mottoes of La Giovine Italia. But it seemed rather vague for a call to arms. Others suggested *Unity, Independence, Liberty,* the specific aims of the society and of the expedition. But Mazzini, always more than merely political, was horrified. There must be *Equality,* too.

> Liberty is little, is nothing, if it is not the necessary means for founding Equality, for reconstituting a People. —Liberty is the *critical* part only. Liberty, by itself, is Protestantism in religion. Liberty by itself is Romanticism in literature. Liberty is a negation—of itself it constructs nothing.

And, having stunned the opposition with that, he moved on to still grander concepts, *Humanity:*

> We shall be invading with the Poles, the French, etc. To all these patriots from other countries who have come to die with us and for us have we no word to offer? Should we not show that on our banner

there is something upon which they can seize for themselves? If we put *Liberty, Equality, Humanity,* on one side, and *Unity* on the other, we say everything—everything.[23]

It was the sort of argument in which Mazzini was invincible, and in the end the flag had *Liberty, Equality, Humanity* on one side, and, as a concession, *Independence* as well as *Unity* on the other. But still Ramorino did not come, and December passed into January.

By now almost everyone around the shores of the Lake of Geneva knew all about the expedition, and spies had long since reported all its plans in detail to Metternich and to Carlo Alberto. Metternich, in turn, officially informed the Swiss cantons and asked that the revolutionaries be expelled. The Swiss were inclined to be tolerant, but they could not ignore the fact that their hotels were filled with revolutionaries preparing to invade a friendly neighbor. So the men were expelled, first from the Cantons of Fribourg and Berne and then, on 27 January 1834, from the Canton of Vaud, at least officially; unofficially the local prefects and police allowed them a few days to make arrangements to leave. Plainly if the invasion was to take place, it must start immediately, or the men would have to disband. The leaders at Geneva, even without Ramorino, decided to go ahead. The next day, 30 January, the general arrived and took command, but he arrived without men and without arms.

The Poles and the Germans, 160 in all and the most experienced soldiers in the force, were gathered around Nyon, a small town in the Canton of Vaud on the north shore of the lake. They mobilized in the town, which was friendly to them, and sent a detachment for their rifles and heavy coats which were hidden in the woods. Unfortunately the gendarmes of Vaud had already found the coats and taken them, but spirits were high, and the men enjoyed remarking significantly that the rifles were the important thing. Another detachment, sent up the lake toward Rolle, also came back empty-handed. The gendarmes at Rolle, an unfriendly town, had found their boat and confiscated it. A boat large enough to take them all was hard to find, and for three hours they marched up and down the shore of the lake, looking. In the end they commandeered two smaller boats, one of which was filled with planks and had to be unloaded. The process was noisy, and soon all the Swiss within earshot had gathered on the shore to watch them embark. Finally, more than six hours behind schedule, they pushed out onto the Lake of Geneva, preparing to cross it in two open boats on the last night in January and without coats.

The next morning they arrived off Geneva in broad daylight. The obvious plan was to stay afloat and out of sight until dark and then land on the south shore and march secretly to the point of assembly. But they had no bread, and besides, another ten hours in the boats would have congealed even the warmest revolutionary blood. So, hiding their rifles in the bottom of the boats, they landed at Geneva and were instantly arrested by gendarmes.

A few hours later they were released and permitted to re-embark, still with their rifles, provided they left the shores of the Canton of Geneva and did not attempt to return. They could hardly argue about the condition, although the Canton was the only one on the south shore and therefore the one in which they must land if they were to join the main body of the expedition. They rowed out, conscious that the gendarmes were following them by telescope, and wherever they turned in to land, there was a small detachment of soldiers, having arrived comfortably by horse or carriage, to oppose the landing.

Finally from Coppet, on the north shore close to Nyon, they sent a message to Ramorino. They could do no more. They were stranded in their open boats, their oars and sails had been taken from them, and they were surrounded by hostile craft. They had suffered, fought and lost a naval engagement of sorts, and for them the invasion of Savoy was over.

For the other half of the expedition the invasion was just beginning and under most discouraging circumstances. Without the men Ramorino should have brought and without the Poles and the Germans, the entire force now numbered only about 225 men. The nearest Sardinian outpost which they had to take, St. Julien, had just been re-enforced to 500 men, and an attack on it was no longer possible. Instead Ramorino marched the men to Annemasse, a small town on the border, where they disarmed the customs officials and burned their uniforms as a sign that Carlo Alberto's government was at an end. Then they planted a Tree of Liberty, and one of them read a revolutionary proclamation which Mazzini had written and dated from St. Julien as though the fort had been captured. It was a fine Sunday afternoon, and many Swiss had come out to see what was happening. They all knew St. Julien had not been taken, and as the Tree was planted, they joked about winter being a poor season for transplanting. And when the orator ended the proclamation with a ringing "aux armes!", which Mazzini had intended to electrify the crowd and start a stampede to enlist, no one moved. The invasion was obviously a complete failure, and faced with certain disaster Ramorino that night held a council of war which voted to end it. The few men still remaining disappeared into the scenery as tourists, and the leaders began to explain in letters and memoirs that it was all someone else's fault.

So much went wrong that historians have always disagreed in apportioning the blame among the chief actors. Clearly the delay of almost three months was disastrous, but behind the delay who was at fault? At the time many believed that Ramorino had accepted a bribe, either from Austria or Switzerland, to subvert the expedition, and certainly he did very little to make a success of it. But the charge has never been proved. On the other hand, throughout the delay Mazzini, rather surprisingly, urged all the other lieutenants to wait for the General, although, as the others attempted to persuade him, any commitment he had made to the Veri Italiani had long since been superseded. A reason for Mazzini's behavior may have been that he was confident that he would be Ramorino's political advisor, and he could not be sure of the same position with a substitute. And further, he knew that the others were so suspicious of him that they would never agree to let him lead the expedition. Therefore he supported Ramorino throughout the delay even after he knew the general would bring no men or arms with him.

None of this appears in Mazzini's official defense, *Young Italy's Letter to General Ramorino,* but it comes out in his private letters. The picture that emerges from them is of a power vacuum. Mazzini, in assemblying the contingents for the expedition, Poles, Germans, Italians and French, with all the subdivisions among them, had been forced to abdicate first place. Yet, as the others feared, he was ambitious, and he would neither put another strong man in it nor, out of it himself, cease intriguing to influence decisions. As a result the leadership was ineffective, and the decisions fell between stools.

The invasion of Savoy was only the northern half of the revolution Mazzini had planned, but the southern half, the rising in Genoa, had not even a beginning. The week before the date set, 11 February, the police, who had thoroughly infiltrated the conspiracy, began to make their arrests. Then came the news, printed in all the papers, of the failure in Savoy, and in Genoa not a revolutionary stirred.

The interest in what did or did not take place in Genoa lies almost entirely in the fact that Giuseppe Garibaldi, then a twenty-six-year-old sailor from Nice, was one of the conspirators. He had enrolled in La Giovine Italia sometime in 1833 and was full of enthusiasm for Italy, free, united and a republic. Tradition declares that Mazzini personally administered the society's oath at Marseille and that this first meeting between the two was momentous. But alas for tradition. The dates do not work out well, and almost certainly the man who administered the oath was not Mazzini.

As a new and untried member of the society Garibaldi's role in the projected uprising was small. In December he had entered the Sardinian navy to serve part of his compulsory military service and had been posted to the frigate *Euridice,* stationed at Genoa. He and a friend were to subvert the crew and, if possible, to capture the ship. Apparently he was so open and enthusiastic at his job that the police in little more than a month had fastened a spy on him. Even years later, however, he still insisted, "My propaganda on the *Euridice* was crowned with success."

On 4 February he was suddenly transferred to the flagship *Des Geneys,* a change he considered ominous, and he and his friend managed to get shore leave the next day, perhaps on the pretext of being sick. Later the friend was arrested, but Garibaldi succeeded in escaping. He afterward gave several versions of what happened, all of them mentioning women and disguises. He evidently had a good time, talked far too openly about the revolution and simply was lucky where his friend was not. But even in his luck he was a deserter with a record of treason, and he fled into France, not stopping until he reached Marseille. There, while reading in a paper about military trials at Genoa, he saw his name in print for the first time as a traitor sentenced, *in absentia,* to death.

For almost a year he served under an assumed name on French ships in the Mediterranean until in the autumn of 1835 he sailed to South America. He stayed there until 1848, making such a reputation for himself as a fighter that when he returned to Italy he was already a hero.

The complete failure of Mazzini's revolution shattered La Giovine Italia as a political instrument forever. One more issue of the journal appeared, and Mazzini continued thereafter with his writing, distributing it, when necessary, through secret channels. But he never again was in the position of political leader of the lodges. In the coming years these reorganized themselves as Democrats, Monarchists, Republicans or even Mazzinians. Most of them paid homage to him for at least some of their ideas, but very few followed his lead politically.

He became more than ever the soul or prophet of the cause. He preached year after year that Italy must become "one, free, independent and republican," which had from the start been the aims of La Giovine Italia. The cumulative educational effect was enormous. He kept the air forever agitated with the idea of Italy, so that thousands of men in arguing whether it should be a republic, a constitutional monarchy or some sort of federation suddenly realized that they had begun to assume that it would be one, free and independent.

The Swiss permitted him to stay in their country, half in hiding and frequently moving, until 1837 when the pressure from the great powers, particularly France, forced the Cantons to expel him. Great Britain was almost the only European country from which he was not already banished or which, like Austria and the German states, would not admit him. South America or the United States he never considered. All his interests were

European, and if he could not be at the center of them, then next best was England, which was at least close to them. Like Garibaldi he did not see Italy again until the fantastic year of 1848, when all of Europe seemed to boil over with revolutions.

# CHAPTER 22

The Bandiera brothers. Garibaldi in Brazil. Anita. In Montevideo
and the Italian Legion. The "red shirt." The Manifesto of Rimini.
Massimo d'Azeglio. His journey through the Papal States and his
interview with Carlo Alberto. The election of a liberal Pope.

AFTER THE FAILURE of Mazzini's revolution, both north and south where
it had not started at all, the secret societies never again attempted a general revolution in any of the Italian states. From time to time individual
men or even towns exploded into violence, but as much out of frustration
as in the hope of changing the form of government or of creating a new,
larger Italian state. Everywhere, except in the Papal Legations and some
of the Neapolitan provinces, the governments were able to control the
unrest with their ordinary police force. In the Legations, however, Gregory
XVI had still to rely on the Sanfedisti, over whom he tried to increase his
control, and in 1837, in the province of Abruzzi, Ferdinando had to use
soldiers to restore order in a town where the liberals had disarmed the
local garrison and proclaimed the Carbonaro constitution of 1820. But the
revolt, which had no real plan for its survival, was as much a result of a
cholera epidemic which had caused religious riots as of any organized
political movement and Ferdinando, in the mildness of his reaction to it,
seemed to recognize as much.

One attempted revolution which failed and yet captured the imagination of Italians, and even of Europeans, was that of Emilio and Attilio
Bandiera, two brothers from Venice who organized an expedition to
Calabria. Their father was an admiral in the Austrian navy which, unlike
the army, was not only manned but officered by Italians, mostly Venetians
or Dalmatians whose fathers had been Venetians. The city was the chief
base, arsenal and training station of the force, and through its Naval
Academy every officer passed, receiving not only a technical but a scientific
and liberal education. The school's faculty fostered in the young midship-
men a love for the history and tradition, not of the Austrian land empire,
but of the old Republics of Venice, Genoa and Pisa, of seagoing Italy, and

248

many of the graduates while being loyal to their service were also ardent Italian patriots.

The Bandiera brothers, however, were unusual in that they were also great admirers of Mazzini and in 1842 had started among their fellow ensigns a branch of La Giovine Italia. Most Venetians at the time were not interested in a unified and republican Italy but were thinking in terms of a revival of their old republic, or of home rule under Austria, or of a federation with other Italian states. Yet the Bandiera brothers had some success. They called their branch *Esperia,* an old and highly poetic name for Italy; they collected monthly dues for an insurrection fund, and they corresponded with Mazzini in London. But even so their idealism was not satisfied, and in 1844 with another ensign, Domenico Moro, they deserted the navy, picked up eighteen other idealists on the island of Corfu and then landed in Calabria near Cotrone. It was evening, and as they stepped ashore in an olive grove, the brothers knelt to kiss the earth, exclaiming, "This is our fatherland! Thou hast given us life. We spend it for Thee!"

They intended only to die, and two days later as they marched along a road approaching the town of Cosenza, they met a mob of peasants, townsfolk and police who had come out to meet them. There were cries of *"Viva Ferdinando!"* and *"A morte!"*, and the mob opened fire. The brothers and Moro attempted to persuade the crowd that they were, in fact, come to free the country, but the time for talk had passed, and the little band was forced in self-defense to return the fire. A few succeeded in escaping into the hills but later gave themselves up. The others, bleeding and beaten, were taken to Cosenza where a month later, on 25 July 1844, nine of them, including Moro and the Bandiera brothers, were executed. They went to their deaths singing an operatic chorus by the Neapolitan composer Mercadante, "He who dies for his country has lived long enough," and their last words were *"Viva l'Italia!"*

The theatricality of the expedition carried the facts of it around Italy, Europe and even to the Americas, to every place where Italians were in exile. Italy was a nation because Venetians had gone to Calabria to free men they insisted were fellow Italians. And the message was re-enforced by the social position of the brothers. Their father was not a Venetian patrician of the old class as his title of Baron came from the Austrians, but such close distinctions in Venice, and increasingly elsewhere, were disappearing. What mattered was that upper-class officers had been imbued with Mazzini's ideals. Not only had Venetians died for Calabrians but aristocrats had died for the people. All the Conservatives and even moderates who argued that such expansions of allegiance would take years to accomplish were suddenly faced with an example achieved within a few years, one of which Mazzini was undeniably the chief cause.

His influence as a prophet and propagandist continued to be strong, even from London. Almost every Italian who went there visited him; many, many more corresponded with him, some openly and others in secret; and he continued to write essays, pamphlets and even founded a journal, *L'Apostolato Repubblicano* or, freely, *The Republican Advocate*.

Through the journal and pamphlets of excerpts from it he broadcast among Italians in Italy the exploits of Garibaldi and his Italian Legion in South America. The accounts were often as much fiction as fact. Mazzini tried, by presenting Garibaldi as a handsome, virile hero fighting always for the underdog, to instill in Italians of all classes a sense of nationality, a pride in national achievement and a sympathy for the forces of reform. In doing so he exaggerated some minor and meaningless scuffles on the pampas into battles of epic significance, but the myth he created about Garibaldi was false only in the political significance he attached to all his hero's actions. The actions themselves, the facts of Garibaldi's thirteen years in South America, as they became better known, often exceeded the myth and were important later as the background and preparation for his actions in Italy.

When Garibaldi landed at Rio de Janeiro, an exile under sentence of death, he was still the enthusiastic, open revolutionary he had been at Genoa. He began at once to write to Mazzini, and he published an attack on Carlo Alberto in the local paper. With other exiles he started a trading company with a fleet of three small boats named *Mazzini, La Giovine Italia* and *La Giovine Europa*. From the boats, and even over the house in which he and his friends met, he flew the republican tricolor of Italy, and the Sardinian minister at Rio de Janeiro sent regular reports to Turin on all his activities.

The trading company was not a success, and when the most southern of Brazil's enormous provinces, Rio Grande do Sul, attempted to secede from the Brazilian monarchy and to establish itself as an independent republic, Garibaldi was delighted to put himself and his ship, the *Mazzini,* at its service. The Brazilians, not unnaturally, considered him merely a buccaneer, but he had letters of marque from the insurgent government, and he considered that he was a true warrior for liberty, freedom and humanity.

His first prize was an Austrian brig carrying a cargo of Brazilian coffee. In his *Memorie* he recalls with pride how he freed five Negro slaves and refused a man's diamonds as the price of good treatment. At the end of his life he could justly claim that he had fought only for his ideals and never for personal gain.

Later, in a battle with two Paraguayan gunboats, he was, in his words, "mortally wounded" by a bullet that entered his neck under one ear and buried itself under the other. Along with everyone else on the ship he was sure he was going to die and, quoting Foscolo's *Dei Sepolcri,* he asked to be buried on land with "a stone to mark my bones from the infinite number sown by death on land and sea."

Almost immediately thereafter he fell into the hands of an Argentine dictator who gave him a good doctor and a prison in which to convalesce for six months. Then, his strength regained, he escaped, was recaptured and brought back almost sixty miles on a horse with his arms bound so that the mosquitoes made of his bare face and hands "one continuous sore." Taken before the local commandant, he was struck in the face with a whip for refusing to reveal his accomplice and then was strung by his wrists from a beam for more than two hours. When the officer returned to torment him, Garibaldi spat in the man's face. But by the time he was cut down, he was unconscious. Later when his torturer fell into his hands, he astonished his South American followers by refusing to see the man and by ordering him to be set free on the spot.

Sometime later, again operating as a navy, he was shipwrecked when his vessel, heavily overladen with arms and stores, capsized in a storm. He was up the mast at the time, looking for a harbor, and so was thrown clear, and he was able, by his famous powers of swimming, to reach the shore. But every other Italian aboard, among them several of his best friends, was drowned. He was then thirty-two and discovered that he could not shake off the sense of loss, and when he was at sea again, it led directly to a crucial episode in his life.

> With the loss of Luigi, Edoardo and the others of my country-men I was left in a state of desperate isolation. I seemed to be alone in the world. Of all the friends who had brought a touch of home to those distant regions not one remained . . . I needed a human being to love me, and instantly! To have a friend near me; without one, life would be intolerable.
>
> Although not old, I knew enough of men to know how hard it is to find a true friend.
>
> A woman! Yes, a woman! Since I had always considered them the most perfect of creatures! And, as the saying goes, it is infinitely easier to find a loving heart among them. . . .
>
> By chance I cast my eye toward the houses of Barra—as they call a moderately high hill on the south side of the entrance to the lagoon, where there are a few simple and picturesque houses. —There, with the aid of a telescope which I usually had with me on deck, I spied a young woman. I ordered that I be rowed ashore in the direction in which I had seen her. I landed, and, making for the houses where I expected to find the object of my excursion, I began to think I could not possibly find her. Then I met a man of the town whose acquaint-

ance I had made soon after our arrival. He invited me to take coffee in his house. We entered; and the first person who met my eye was the woman who had attracted me ashore. It was Anita! . . . We both remained transfixed and silent, gazing on one another like two people who meet not for the first time and seek in each other's face something to start a memory.

I greeted her finally and said: *Tu devi esser mia* (You must be mine). I could speak but little Portuguese, and I uttered the arrogant words in Italian. Still, I was magnetic in my insolence. I had formed a tie, pronounced a decree that death alone could break! . . .[24]

She went with him. Garibaldi already was famous in Brazil, and she must have known instantly who he was. He was not physically dominating, being only five feet six and a half inches, but everyone who knew him, after he had been commanding men in South America for several years, remarked on his extraordinary power of personal attraction and dominion over others. His head and features resembled those of a lion, and the noble effect was accentuated by his reddish-blond hair which he wore long, like a mane, and in a full beard. His expression was quiet and grave, and his smile did not disturb it. But his eyes, which were blue or light brown, men did not agree, were "small and piercing," "full of smouldering fire" and, like the sea, appeared to grow darker as his emotions were stirred, so that when he was excited, they "became intensely black."

His voice seemed equally mysterious and magnetic. It was "calm and deliberate," "melodious and penetrating" yet "low and veiled" and, most important, "tremulous with inner emotion." Men seemed to respond to it instinctively, often far more than they realized. He could, with a few words of encouragement, make an exhausted soldier feel fresh, or, speaking from a balcony, hold a crowd silent and breathless with excitement. Often after the event was over men found it hard to believe that it had taken place.

Anita, who was eighteen at the time, had been born in Brazil of Portuguese parents although she may have had some Indian blood. She had black hair, dark eyes and a strong though not beautiful face. According to a British naval officer, who met her a few years later, she had the natural dignity and manners of a lady of old Spain. She was also an excellent horsewoman so that he considered "seeing her on a curvetting animal by the side of her husband . . . was a sight to be remembered." Because of her extraordinary physical stamina she was later constantly referred to as an Amazon, but no one who saw her with Garibaldi ever described her as larger than he, and her dresses, which survive in museums, indicate that she was shorter and, while strong, well proportioned.

Their life together lasted for only ten years and closed in tragedy among the marshes of Ravenna, becoming a legend of romance and a part of Italian history. Years after her death, as he wrote of their first meeting, the tragedy of their parting welled up again, and the broken, exclamatory phrases are as he wrote them in a continuous passage of passion and self-reproach:

> I had formed a tie, pronounced a decree, which death alone could break! . . . I had come upon a forbidden treasure, but yet a treasure of great price!!!
> If there was guilt, it was mine alone. And . . . there was guilt! Yes! . . . two hearts were joined in an infinite love, but an innocent existence was shattered! . . . She is dead! I am wretched! and he is avenged. . . . Yes! avenged! I, I knew the great wrong I had done, on the day when, still hoping to call her back to life, I clasped the hand of a corpse: and I was weeping the tears of desperation! It was I; I sinned greatly but I sinned alone.[25]

When this passage of his *Memorie* first appeared, Garibaldi's friends and admirers tried hard to deny the inferences which could be drawn from it. The traditional story, which his children believed and which he would neither confirm nor deny, was that Anita's father had betrothed her to a man she did not love, a man very rich and old, and when the father refused to consider any other suitor for her, Garibaldi had carried her off. Later, when they reached Montevideo, they were formally married by a Catholic priest. But all his life his enemies charged that he was not married to Anita, or, if he was, that the marriage was bigamous. And his mother, who was very pious, apparently would never let them live together in her house although she would take in the children or either one of them alone. Finally, in 1932, a historian found and published the record of Anita's marriage to a fisherman in 1835, four years before she met Garibaldi, and the entry shows her father as already dead. So, in fact, Garibaldi seems to have accepted the fisherman's hospitality and then stolen his host's wife. As an atheist Garibaldi did not care if, by Church standards, his marriage was bigamous or his children illegitimate, but for the injury to the fisherman, even after the passage of many years, he was unable to excuse himself.

Their life together almost ended in the first fortnight. The Brazilian navy had surrounded the three ships in Garibaldi's fleet and, as Anita fought by his side, a cannonball knocked her and two men to the deck. Before he could reach her, she was already up, miraculously uninjured, although the two men were dead. Thereafter their life was a continuous campaign but increasingly on shore. "She looked upon battles as a pleasure, and the hardships of camp life as a pastime; so that however things might turn out, the future smiled on us, and the vast American deserts which unrolled themselves before our gaze seemed all the more delightful and beautiful for their wildness."

One time she was captured by the Brazilian troops, but he was not. Escaping from her drunken guards she obtained a high-spirited horse from a peasant and, swimming rivers in flood, crossing the desert without food and galloping through hostile pickets, she managed after four days to rejoin him.

But eventually he decided that the cause against Brazil had been lost, or, at least, that he owed more than a life of such hardship to his wife and infant son, Menotti, whom he had named after the leader of the Carbonaro revolution of 1831, and he took them to Montevideo, the capital of the Republic of Uruguay. There he tried without much success to earn a living as a shipbroker and schoolteacher. But he was soon engaged again in fighting.

Across the Rio de la Plata a dictator had seized power at Buenos Aires and was threatening the independence of Uruguay. The situation was complicated by the personal ambitions of the local politicians, but for Garibaldi it was a clear case of a small republic being threatened by a larger, aggressive neighbor, and when he was offered command of the Uruguayan navy, he accepted. But the fighting went against him, and by the spring of 1843 there was nothing left of the navy and the republic itself had shrunk to the city of Montevideo.

The city, however, did not plan to give up. Most of its population of thirty thousand were foreigners, political exiles from France and Italy, men who were used to fighting and who had no place else to go. It also had more than five thousand slaves to whom it offered freedom if they would fight. This cramped but genuine gesture was presented to the world as the abolition of slavery, making Uruguay the first state in the Americas to adopt such a policy and concentrating the sympathetic attention of all the reformers in Europe on Montevideo. It was at this time, for example, that Mazzini began to make a hero of Garibaldi.

From the Italians in the city Garibaldi, at the government's request, formed an Italian Legion which at times numbered several thousand and at others, when the situation was less severe, dwindled to a few hundred. It was the prototype of all his volunteer forces later in Italy. He promised the men no rewards; they were not to be soldiers of fortune but men fighting for a principle. And for Garibaldi, at least, the principle was not entirely in Montevideo. His letters reveal that he never lost sight of the revolution that some day would come to Italy and that he considered everything done in South America to be in preparation for it. The flag he gave the Legion at Montevideo, for example, was black with a volcano in the center, and intended as a symbol of Italy mourning with fire in its heart.

The men of the Legion at Montevideo were also the first to wear the famous "red shirt" which later in Italy became the symbol of Garibaldi and his volunteer forces. The uniform seems to have originated in the most prosaic fashion. Apparently a merchant in Montevideo had bought a large supply of red woolen shirts, intending them for the men working in the slaughter and salting houses of Buenos Aires. They were woolen because the work was largely outdoors or in unheated buildings and red in order to conceal, as far as possible, traces of the bloody work. But because of the war the merchant was unable to ship them and, in desperation, offered them to the city at a very low price. And the city, after conferring with Garibaldi, agreed to take them. Red as a uniform for battle has a certain disadvantage, but Garibaldi, working with volunteer forces, always cared more for morale than the niceties of camouflage.

In its first battle the Legion disgraced itself, but gradually, in the fighting around the city in 1843, it did better, until finally, at the battle of Sant'Antonio, in February 1846, it defeated a much larger force by a combination of extraordinary courage and discipline. That battle had an importance which even Mazzini could not exaggerate, and thereafter Garibaldi and his men were hailed as the saviors of the Republic of Uruguay not only in Montevideo but throughout Europe and, of course, particularly in Italy.

There, in spite of the obvious futility of such expeditions as that of the Bandiera brothers, the example of Garibaldi and his Legion was exciting the more adventurous or, in the opinion of many moderates, the more irresponsible men in the secret societies to agitate for some general action. This was particularly true in the Papal States where the problem of the Sanfedisti, now called Centurioni, continued to grow worse. The Pope, Gregory XVI, and most of his cardinals still could imagine no response to the unrest except more and stiffer repression. After a series of small uprisings in 1843 they set up a military commission which traveled from town to town sentencing all men against whom it could sustain a charge. The Archbishop of Imola, who was to succeed Gregory as pope, wrote to the cardinal in charge of all the Legations protesting that in his jurisdiction the Centurioni were undisciplined and often criminal, that the Commissioner of Police was "one of those Papalini who are fanatics to the point of folly, and would like to see fifteen people hanged every hour," and that at least twenty thousand of his citizens were under sentence for political reasons. At nearby Forlí, the cardinal-legate was so disgusted by the martial law that he refused to let the commission sit in his jurisdiction. But these two were exceptions. At Ravenna in September 1845 the commission condemned thirty-six men to the Papal galleys, still in existence at Civitavecchia, and thirty-one more to police supervision. Without doubt

Gregory was the most hated pope within memory and, as he was over eighty, liberals of all shades eagerly awaited his death.

The division between the more moderate of the liberals and those who wanted immediate action was both increasing and important; and, shortly after the trials at Ravenna and toward the end of September 1845, an uprising at Rimini gave dramatic evidence of it. The men of action rose, captured the town and held it for three days and then were forced to flee. The moderates, meanwhile, had decided that the rising was premature, doomed to fail, and instead of supporting it had issued from Tuscany a "Manifesto of Rimini" in which they recounted the cruelty and inefficiency of the Papal government and stated the reforms without which no peace or compromise could be reached. Probably in the long run the manifesto, by arousing European opinion against the Papacy, did more good for the cause of Italian unity and independence, but the men of action, on the other hand, had freed a number of political prisoners and for these, at least, freedom lay in action, not words. But an increasing majority of men saw little profit in such isolated uprisings.

Everyone suspected, and the moderates feared, that the death of Gregory would be the signal for a general uprising throughout the Legations. The moderates argued that, just as at Gregory's election in 1831, the new pope, whoever he might be, would then call in the Austrian army and thereafter any chance of victory or reforms would be lost. To press their point and to prevent what they predicted would be a certain tragedy they started an agent going from town to town to urge moderation and delay.

The man they chose to represent them was the most unlikely man they could find and yet trust. He was the Marchese Massimo d'Azeglio, a younger son of one of the most distinguished families in Piedmont. His father had expected him, as was customary for younger sons, to enter the army, but d'Azeglio, after trying it for several years, had announced that he preferred to go to Rome to study painting. The shock to the family was great, for at the time painting was not a career an aristocrat followed, either in Turin or Rome. His father did not quite forbid him to go, but he tried to discourage him by giving him a very small allowance. D'Azeglio, however, was not deterred. He merely increased the family's alarm by announcing further that he hoped to add to the allowance, before long, by selling some of his pictures, and thus putting the family in trade. But for the first few years in Rome he lived in great poverty and saw no one in society except a contessa with whom he was in love. Whenever he sold a picture, he bought a horse, for like his countryman Alfieri, he was a passionate horseman. But he seldom could afford to keep one for long.

After ten years in Rome and some success as a painter, still a bachelor and only thirty, he returned to Turin, but he found life there unbearably provincial and soon moved to Milan, where he married Manzoni's daughter and began to write historical romances. Never in his life had he either secretly or openly played a part in politics, which was a reason the moderates chose him. But he also had a well-known name, charming and democratic manners, and a life of such obvious independence and integrity that men instinctively trusted him.

He started out from Rome in September 1845, the month of the trials at Ravenna and the uprising at Rimini, and he traveled with his paintbox prominently displayed and, to avoid any possibility of a spy, without a servant. He went from town to town in the Papal States, in each town being given the name of a man in the next, the man whose job it was to pass on all news, journals or people. He was never to ask for this man directly but to loiter around the town until the man presented himself. The circuit was called the *trafila* or, figuratively, "the succession," and the police never succeeded in breaking it.

D'Azeglio's assignment was twofold. First, he was to persuade the liberals not to attempt isolated revolts, and this, after Rimini and the Bandiera brothers, he found relatively easy. The majority of men in the secret societies were already disenchanted with Mazzini's calls for immediate action.

But the second part of his assignment he found difficult. He was to persuade them to put their trust in Carlo Alberto of Sardinia. Everywhere the idea was greeted with distrust or even derision: if Carlo Alberto had ever been liberal, he had long since forgotten it. Since coming to the throne, in 1831, he had refused to grant a constitution; he would have no liberals in his government or even at court; he had hounded the revolutionaries from his country, was married to an Austrian and bound to Metternich.

D'Azeglio himself believed most of these charges, yet he understood and argued the reasoning behind the moderates' position. First of all it was not altogether true that Carlo Alberto was bound to Metternich. He had, after coming to the throne, forced the recall of two Austrian ambassadors for undue interference in the country. He had reorganized his finances and strengthened his army, so that the kingdom was more independent of Austria than it had been for many years. And for what purpose? Every Italian knew that for a hundred and fifty years the House of Savoy had coveted the city and Duchy of Milan, Lombardia, and in this Carlo Alberto was no different from his forebears. Yet he could not have it without an army strong enough to defeat the Austrians, any more than the secret societies could achieve their aims without, ultimately, facing and defeating the Austrians. Therefore, to gain an army, they must make common cause with Carlo Alberto, the only prince in Italy who had an army strong enough to do the job. Ask a thief to become an honest man, d'Azeglio would argue, and you will have little chance of success, but ask him to help you in a robbery, in stealing the iron crown of Lombardy, and you will probably have a faithful ally. It was a potent argument and converted many.

At the end of his journey d'Azeglio, quite on his own, went to Turin and requested a private audience with Carlo Alberto. The request, which was not unusual after a journey, was immediately granted, and one morning soon after at 6 A.M., for the king regularly rose before dawn, d'Azeglio, his heart pounding, was ushered into a small room in the Palazzo Reale. The king, tall and pale, was standing by the window. Near him were two gilt chairs, their seats covered in green and white silk in a floral pattern which, whenever d'Azeglio was to see it again, would always remind him of this meeting.

Carlo Alberto was famous for the severity of his expression and manner which wholly concealed his thoughts, yet on this occasion his first words of welcome and inquiry were so unaffected and sympathetic that d'Azeglio had to remind himself, "Massimo, be on your guard." The conversation soon turned to d'Azeglio's journey through the Papal States, and he spoke out directly, describing how eagerly Gregory's death was awaited, how likely the provinces were to erupt in yet another futile rebellion, and how eager were the greater part of the liberals, including most of their leaders, to make common cause with Carlo Alberto against the Austrians. In that moment he offered Carlo Alberto the leadership of the movement in Central Italy for unity and independence.

He expected to hear in reply colorless, ambiguous words of sympathy, but Carlo Alberto, looking steadily at him, said quietly:

> Let your gentlemen know that they must remain quiet and make no move, there being for the moment nothing that can be done; but let them be sure that, when the moment comes, my life, the lives of my sons, my sword, my resources, my army, all will be spent in the Italian cause.[26]

The words and their import so startled d'Azeglio that for an appreciable moment, he realized with embarrassment, the king saw his surprise. But then, recovering himself and wanting to make sure he had not misunderstood, he said, "I am to tell these men . . ." and he repeated the words exactly. Carlo Alberto nodded, confirming the message and d'Azeglio's right and duty to transmit it.

The audience was over, and as d'Azeglio prepared to leave, the king embraced him, but in a manner so cold and formal that once again d'Azeglio was uncertain. So that when he wrote an account of the audience in code for the *trafila,* an account which he knew would reach every liberal leader in Central Italy, he added after the king's message, "These are his words, but God alone knows his heart."

D'Azeglio's interests now became wholly political, and in place of historical romances he began to write political pamphlets urging the moderate point of view. The first, *Degli ultimi casi di Romagna* or *On the recent events in Romagna,* was based on what he had seen and heard of Papal government in the region of Romagna, the area in which were the Legations. He took as his text the uprising at Rimini and began by lamenting the wastefulness of it. He pointed out that it had harmed the patriotic cause by rousing dissensions and crueler repression at home while convincing foreigners that Italians were a violent, fickle people, unworthy of sympathy and incapable of self-control. But then he went on to point out, in sober tone and detail, the reasons for it: the chaos of the Papal legal system, the 'multiple autocracy' of the Legates, the lack of an annual budget or publication of the state accounts, the refusal to build railways, the high custom dues whose collection was farmed out, the irresponsibility of the Centurioni, the insolence of the Swiss mercenaries, the frightfulness of the prisons, the summary jurisdiction of the extraordinary commissions, the lack of education, the interference with what education there was and the censorship.

The pamphlet, which was printed at Florence, was short, easy to read and easy to pass on surreptitiously, which was important as it was almost immediately banned in most of the Italian states. Yet it was read all over Italy, and elsewhere in Europe it convinced many that Mazzini, who was somewhat unfairly thought of as merely the advocate of assassination, was not the only type of Italian reformer. It caused such a stir that the Grand Duke Leopoldo, who seemed to be growing more autocratic as he grew older, expelled d'Azeglio from Tuscany, which only increased the demand for the pamphlet and caused the Florentines to honor its author with a farewell banquet. So d'Azeglio returned to Turin, almost the only city left in Italy where he could settle, but now that he had become an open reformer, he was not welcome at Carlo Alberto's court.

Then on 1 June 1846 Pope Gregory, who had become almost a recluse, died, and the secret societies, undoubtedly influenced by d'Azeglio and the moderates, did not rise. After nine days of mourning the cardinals assembled in the Palazzo del Quirinale in a conclave. The windows and doors were sealed with plaster, and the balloting began.

The election went swiftly; to avoid, said some, the possibility of a rising when the cardinal-legates were in Rome, or, said others, to avoid the arrival of Cardinal Gaisruck from Milan with orders from Metternich. The best-known candidate was Cardinal Lambruschini, Gregory's Secretary of State. But by the fourth ballot, when Gaisruck was only at Florence, an almost unknown cardinal, Giovanni Mastai-Ferretti, the Archbishop of Imola, had been elected. Apparently the division in the Conclave had been between the foreign and the local cardinals, the latter being those who wished to assert the spiritual and temporal independence of the Papal States against the great Catholic governments, particularly Vienna. Both groups were equally authoritarian in their ideas for ruling the Papal States. In fact, historians today think it unlikely that Metternich had given any firm instructions to Gaisruck. It seems more likely that he believed the condition of the Papal States, being one of repressed discontent, meant that any pope, short of giving up his temporal power altogether, would inevitably have to rely on Austrian arms. And the price of the Austrian army was Austrian influence. What Metternich seems to have feared most was the election of a religious zealot who in pursuing some minor point about convents might lose sight of the political realities of the Italian peninsula.

At first so little was known about the new pope that liberals hardly knew whether to rejoice or despair. He was comparatively young, born in 1792 and only fifty-four, and this was considered hopeful; he had lived all his life after the French Revolution. On the other hand, taking the name Pius to honor Pius VII, imprisoned by Napoleon, was ominous. But from Imola, a small city near Bologna, began to come reports that Pius IX, or Pio Nono, as Italians called him, was a good administrator, merciful and, above all, liberal. Then a month and a day after his election, on 17 July 1846, he astonished Rome and, as the news spread, Metternich and the whole of Europe by granting an amnesty, on an oath of allegiance, to all those who had taken part in the Carbonaro revolution of 1831 or who had since been convicted of activity against the state.

The political effect of this act was enormous, far greater undoubtedly than Pio Nono had expected. He probably viewed his amnesty as an act of local mercy affecting only the citizens of his state. But as news of it spread he became, whether he liked it or not, the symbol and leader of reform for almost all groups of the disgruntled. Everywhere in Italy his name was stitched on banners and scratched on walls. At Florence, at performances of Verdi's opera *Ernani* the audience changed the words of a chorus in praise of the long-dead Emperor "Carlo Quinto" in order to sing "glory and honor to Pio Nono." At Rome, huge crowds gathered night after night before the Palazzo del Quirinale to receive his blessing. He was the most popular pope in memory, and throughout the summer everything he did or proposed increased his popularity. He talked of lighting the streets of Rome with gas, of building railways and of improving agriculture. Everywhere liberals of all shades hailed him as a progressive pope who would lead the Papacy, at long last, out of the middle ages.

His political position in Italy at the time was particularly powerful. He was, of course, the ruler of a large state straddling the center of the peninsula. But in addition he was, by virtue of being pope, the natural leader of Italians in every state who felt themselves in some vague fashion to be the heirs of the Guelf party of the middle ages. Such vague historical feelings among Italians can be very powerful, and appeals to the memory of imperial Rome, or of ducal Florence, or of republican Venice often have stirred Italians to political action.

In Pio Nono's case, in 1846, the historical association that was stirred was the struggle between Guelfs and Ghibellines that had dominated medieval Italy from, roughly, 1250 to 1409. Speaking generally, the Ghibellines had sought order out of chaos in Italy by supporting the Holy Roman Emperor even at the cost of suppressing some Italian independence and self-government, while Guelfs, in struggling to subordinate the emperor to the pope, often thereby had fought to preserve the independence of Italian states. The issues, however, were very much more complicated, and even such a fervent Italian patriot as Dante had been a Ghibelline, in part because, as Machiavelli later complained, the popes again and again had invited foreign armies into Italy to do their fighting for them. Nevertheless, in the broadest sense, during the middle ages the Papacy had stood for the idea of Italian individuality and independence against German domination, and as Pio Nono began his reforms, it began to do so again.

This idea had been tremendously stimulated by one of the important books of the Risorgimento, Vincenzo Gioberti's *Il Primato* or, more fully, *On the Moral and Civil Primacy of the Italians,* which was published in Brussels in 1843. Gioberti, who had been born in Turin in 1801, was a priest, but not in any conventional sense; primarily he was a political philosopher and, on occasion, an active politician. Partly under the influence of Mazzini, the freedom of Italy had become the ruling motive of his life and shortly after Carlo Alberto had succeeded to the throne, in 1831, Gioberti had been banished from the kingdom on suspicion of political intrigue. He had gone to Brussels, where he had taught philosophy, and eventually wrote *Il Primato,* which he dedicated to one who had suffered for Italy, Silvio Pellico.

In it, Gioberti, building on the ideas of Vico, Genovesi and Cuoco, argued that an Italian race already existed, united in blood, religion and language, and that its natural leader was the pope. He proposed that the various states of Italy, in order to achieve independence from foreign interference, federate under the pope as president. The book was banned in most of the Italian states, but it was read everywhere, and because of it many Italians outside the Papal States looked to the Papacy for political leadership.

The question remained, however, of where a pope could find an army without once again inviting foreigners into Italy to do his fighting for him, and a solution to this ancient problem was suggested in yet another book, *Delle speranze d'Italia,* or *On the Hope of Italy,* published in 1844 with, significantly, a dedication to Gioberti. Its author was Cesare Balbo, like Gioberti a Torinese, and Balbo suggested that, in time, if Austrian interest turned more and more to the Balkans, as seemed likely, the Sardinian army, a native Italian army, would be able to do the job. He agreed with Gioberti that a federal state was the goal of any drive for Italian unity because the various peoples of Italy were so distinct that they needed different forms of government. But as a loyal subject of Carlo Alberto, he envisaged his king, rather than the pope, as the leader of any future confederation. Most Italians outside of Sardinia, however, mistrusting the House of Savoy, favored the pope; particularly after Pio Nono opened his reign with such liberal reforms.

The combination of Gioberti's and Balbo's ideas, into what later historians are apt to call the neo-Guelf movement, had an obvious appeal for many. Most importantly, perhaps, by associating resistance of Austria with the Church it made revolution seem respectable, and talk of it, of war against the Austrians and of Italy for the Italians greatly increased.

Strong republicans like Mazzini were against the idea of papal leadership, but others more moderate saw that it might succeed just where Mazzini always failed, in the countryside and among the priests. The peasants, because of their poverty and consequent illiteracy, were almost entirely nonpolitical. The literacy rate among the peasants of the Papal States at this time, for example, was two per cent. As a result political theorists, like Mazzini or d'Azeglio, had to confine their proselytizing to the towns, and the popular revolts within the towns often failed because the countryside, generally guided by the parish priest, refused to support them. But Gioberti's idea not only had an appeal for priests; it could also be easily explained to simple minds: the pope-president a father to the various governments. It had a double chance to win the support of the peasants. If it could also win the support of Pio Nono, then for the first time, many Italians reasoned, all levels of lay society and the clergy would be united behind a political theory, thus making it practical. Then Austria might be expelled, and an economic revolution started that would be bloodless.

The Church was generally thought to be against the idea, for it might mean sharing the rule of the Papal States with some sort of congress of all the states, which in turn might lead to interference with the Church's spiritual role. But as Pio Nono followed his amnesty with still other liberal measures, the possibility that he really intended to reorganize the Papal government created tremendous excitement. Every action he took was instantly reported and then discussed by everyone. In March 1847 he moved toward lifting the censorship by permitting the publication of newspapers and journals under the supervision of a body of lay censors, and in June he moved toward admitting laymen into the government by creating a Consulta, an advisory body of laymen under the presidency of a cardinal. Even Mazzini was carried away with enthusiasm for the new pope and from London wrote him an Open Letter full of turgid phrases about faith and social ideals, and from Montevideo Garibaldi wrote privately, offering himself and his Legion to further the good work. At Rome huge crowds gathered to follow him wherever he went and to cheer endlessly under his balcony until he would come out and bless them. On the first anniversary of the amnesty beacons burned up and down the peninsula, and the Te Deum was sung in churches. Bernini in his *Storia di Parma* tells of talking with peasants who remembered almost nothing of the entire Risorgimento except the excitement over the election of a liberal pope, Pio Nono. The future, as always, was obscure, but whereas it had been black with defeat and despair, it now was bright with hope.

# CHAPTER 23

*Effects of Pio Nono's reforms. Manin and the Venetians. Milan. Catholic tradition in the Po valley. Carlo Alberto's reforms. Cavour. His politics, his farming, his unpopularity. His newspaper. Death of Marie Louise in Parma. Metternich's opposition to reform.*

PIO NONO'S REFORMS at Rome soon caused repercussions elsewhere in Italy. In neighboring Tuscany the liberals, on seeing newspapers and journals starting up in Rome, by a mixture of threats and flattery not unlike what the Romans used to pressure Pio Nono, forced the Grand Duke Leopoldo to a similar concession, and at Florence and Pisa papers soon appeared which, for the first time in years, discussed political questions. Even their names were provocative, the *Alba* or *Dawn* in Florence and, more boldly, *L'Italia* at Pisa, and their policies were to begin at once demanding further concessions from the government.

At Modena the repercussions moved the new Duke, Francesco V, who had succeeded his father in 1846, in the other direction. The duchy was already entirely controlled by Austria in its policies, but Francis now asked for and received a garrison of Austrian troops, which brought the Austrian army closer to Florence and Rome. Some time before it had already crossed the Po in force when Metternich had ordered it to occupy the Papal city of Ferrara, where Austria technically had rights only for a small garrison. The occupation touched off a storm: Pio Nono protested to the great powers, Carlo Alberto offered his army to the pope for the defense of the Papal States, and the journalists used their new freedom to shriek of aggression. Finally, after six months of diplomatic warfare, Metternich was forced to withdraw the troops, but those in Modena stayed.

In Lombardo-Veneto, where Austria governed in its own right, events proceeded more slowly. Venice, after all, was nearly as close to Vienna as it was to Rome or Turin, and Milan was the headquarters of the Austrian army in Italy. Even so the Venetians, led by a lawyer, Daniele Manin, began to agitate for a form of home rule and never missed an opportunity to show how Austria had failed to keep its promises for better rights of trade and, one made in 1815 when Napoleon escaped from Elba, to allow partial self-government.

When Richard Cobden, who had a European reputation as the advocate of Free Trade, visited Venice, Manin and others organized a banquet in his honor despite the disapproval of the Austrians, who were protectionist in their theories of trade. Naturally in the speeches following the dinner there were cheerful references to the success in Britain of Cobden's Anti-Corn Law League, and he was hailed as the victor of a struggle in which a people had peacefully coerced its government. The banquet, indoors and on the island of Giudecca, was relatively private; but the subsequent procession of gondolas by moonlight up the Grand Canal, although "sufficiently romantic," as Cobden confessed, "to excite poetical emotions even in the mind of a political economist," was understood by all, Venetians, Austrians and even Cobden, to be just the sort of open, public demonstration for political liberty that the Austrians were determined to prohibit.

Next Manin arranged for the ninth Congress of Italian scientists, men generally learned rather than specialists, to meet in Venice. Each year the men had gathered in a different city and at the eighth Congress, which had met in Genoa, they had shown a tendency to discuss Italy's political problems. As a result the Austrian government was inclined to prohibit a Congress in Venice but finally, hoping by a concession to cool "the hot-heads," agreed to it. So in September 1847 more than eight hundred men of learning from all over Italy held their inaugural meeting in the Sala del Maggior Consiglio of the Doge's Palace, looked down upon by some of the glories of Italian art celebrating the military victories of the old Venetian Republic.

By order of the police, and there was a police observer at every meeting, the subjects of "moral and political science" were forbidden, but the delegates easily found ways to introduce them. In the discussions of geography one of the speakers constantly quoted Pio Nono, always to rapturous applause, though to cry *Viva Pio Nono!* was then punished as sedition in Austrian territory. And in a meeting of the Agricultural section the delegates lingered with pleasure on a discussion of a potato disease, its cause and possible cure, for in Italy, at the time, the words for *Germans* and *potatoes* were used as equivalents. But, as the police rightly feared, such public witticisms were merely the froth of the serious and private discussions which took place between the sessions.

After a fortnight the Congress came to an end and, although the delegates departed, they left behind, as if in the canals, a current of excitement which gradually flowed to every part of the city and was felt to some extent by every Venetian, scientist or illiterate. Fifty years earlier, Napoleon and the treaty of Campoformio had stunned Venice, stripping it of its independence, of its possessions on land and sea on which much of its economy depended and, most of all, of its dignity. The blow had hastened the social revolution already begun, and the patrician class, which in theory should have provided the leadership to surmount the disaster, had instead been unable to sustain itself at all and, merging into the middle class, had passed out of existence. As a result Venice had become perhaps the most democratic city in Italy, far more so than Naples, Rome, Turin or even Milan where the patrician class because of its own abilities and lingering feudal ties to Vienna still had some claim to position and right of leadership. But in Venice, a middle-class lawyer such as Manin, a man without a title, physically slight, often ill, and needing glasses, could become the acknowledged leader of the city. Men far more nobly born served him apparently without resentment, or without feeling any insurmountable differences because of class.

The Venetians had needed fifty years to complete this peaceful revolution while at the same time re-establishing their life on a reduced scale and a new economic basis. And they had accomplished it under a foreign occupation that denied them almost all positions of power together with the education and training such positions give to their holders. During all of the period, as if deliberately convalescing, the city and its people had stayed to one side of the movements that were agitating the rest of Italy. But now, in the autumn of 1847, caught up in the national excitement caused by the election of a liberal pope, the Venetians swiftly joined the common movement.

At the Teatro la Fenice, during performances of Verdi's opera *Macbeth,* whenever the tenors singing Malcolm and Macduff started a passage beginning *la patria tradita,* "Our country betrayed, invites us to weep; brothers, let us hasten to save the oppressed," the audience would grow restive and at the last note would rise to its feet in a single sweep, shrieking, sobbing and throwing red and green bouquets onto the stage. When the police prohibited bouquets in Italian colors, the audience the next night tossed bouquets in Austrian colors, yellow and black, just for the pleasure of seeing the singers tread on them.

The British consul-general reported that in only two months the sentiment of the city had gone from passive tranquillity to open agitation. Venetians no longer would be seen with Austrians, sit in cafés where they were present or admit them to their houses. The few who did or were suspected of favoring the government had their names written up on walls as traitors to their country.

Such popular demonstrations had begun almost a year earlier in Milan and had soon grown violent. One of the first, in December 1846, occurred at the funeral of Conte Confalonieri, who, after fifteen years in the prison of Spielberg, had been released by the Emperor Ferdinand but forbidden to return to Milan or even Italy. Another took place when a new archbishop, an Italian, arrived in the city to succeed the deceased Cardinal Gaisruck, an Austrian. Even after the archbishop's arrival the demonstrations continued into the next day as columns of young men surged through the city singing operatic choruses and hymns to Pio Nono. Finally some police, losing their self-control, attacked a crowd, and one man was killed and nine or ten wounded. Thereafter almost any pretext served for a demonstration. One day word got about: "Everyone to the Porta Romana in homage to Pio Nono and his reforms," and the corso to the gate was jammed with men and women of all classes of the city, until some new idea took hold. The police, backed by an Austrian garrison of fifteen thousand, were constantly less patient and casualties increased.

The appeal of Pio Nono, the liberal pope, was particularly great in the lower two-thirds of the Po valley where Venice and Milan had developed a Catholic tradition different from that of Rome, Naples or even Turin. The Venetians and Milanesi always had been less feudal and more commercial than the Romani or Torinesi and partly as a result they viewed the absolute monarchies, which tended to be protectionist in their trade, as enemies. Further, they were apt to consider the rather rigid, ceremonial Catholicism that developed around the monarchies, supported enthusiastically by the great feudal lords and by the Jesuits, as a hostile tradition, and they, while professing to be just as good Catholics as the others, developed one that was less autocratic. It appears clearly in Manzoni's novel, *I Promessi Sposi,* in which true Christianity is presented as simple faith and goodness of heart rather than as pomp, ritual and dogma, and the best representatives of it, both priests and laymen, are generally shown defending the poor and middle class against proud and powerful oppressors. The Milanesi and Venetians, imbued with this tradition, saw nothing unnatural in associating Catholicism with the liberal views of their times. For them Pio Nono's reforms were not an incredible deviation from the true and necessary tradition of the Papacy, as they were for Metternich, Ferdinando in Naples and even, to some extent Carlo Alberto, but an advance of the Church's real interests. And in Milan or Venice when a crowd gathered in a street or piazza to sing hymns to Pio Nono it always contained many priests. The fact infuriated the Austrians, for the open support of the priests gave the demonstrations throughout Lombardo-Veneto a strength and unity which they generally did not achieve in Piedmont or the south of Italy. In those areas Pio Nono's liberalism tended to throw the priests into confusion and because of it to leave many laymen uncertain.

In Piedmont the sense of uncertainty was compounded further by Carlo Alberto's apparent inability to make up his mind. He seemed always to be about to put himself at the head of the liberal movement and then, for some inner reason, to draw back. In October 1847 he dismissed his reactionary minister, Solaro della Margarita, and began to grant some substantial reforms, such as a relatively free press under lay censorship, the abolition of some special courts and a communal law by which members of the provincial and communal councils were eligible for election to the Council of State. But then in November on a trip to Genoa, where the Genovesi in gratitude gave him an extraordinary reception, he seemed to intend deliberately to repudiate them by attending mass at the Church of the Jesuits. Thereafter the crowds always added to their cheers, "Down with the Jesuits." A popular nickname for Carlo Alberto was Il Re Tentenna or King See-Saw, and years later in a famous poem, *Il Piemonte,* Giosué Carducci called him "the Italian Hamlet."

The reforms in Piedmont, as the Kingdom of Sardinia was called increasingly often, gave to a man who was to have an extremely important role in the unification of Italy his first opportunity. He was, to give him his full name, Camillo Benso di Cavour, but he himself generally omitted the middle name and the "di" from his signature. To add to the confusion, like all aristocrats in Turin, he spoke a Piemontese dialect to the uneducated and French among his family and friends, so that he grew up as Camille; and all his life his thoughts flowed most easily in French. But as he reached manhood, like Alfieri, he set out to Italianize himself, and he soon became proficient in the language, talking and writing in a simple, direct style capable of great precision but lacking any literary flourish and sometimes, even, good syntax.

Like Massimo d'Azeglio he was a younger son and tried first to make a career in the army. He had a brilliant mind for figures and might have made a good engineer or a superb administrator, becoming like Carnot an "organizer of victory," except that his real interest was political science, the theory and practice of government, particularly as it was being practiced in Piedmont. On these subjects he had, for a Piemontese aristocrat, very liberal views which, with all the enthusiasm of youth, he expressed openly and ably. His interest, however, was fatal to his military career. After a sojourn in 1830 in Genoa, where he had talked too much and too freely with the Genovesi aristocrats, most of whom were ardent republicans, he was ordered by King Carlo Felice to the fortress of Bard, a billet equivalent to arrest. And when, a few months later, Carlo Alberto came to the throne and showed no sign of liberalizing the government, Cavour, with his father's approval, resigned his commission.

His father's approval was necessary for, as a second son, Cavour had no money of his own and without his officer's pay would be entirely dependent on his father and, when his father died, on his elder brother. He came home aged twenty-one, with no visible career before him and in circumstances which, considering the Carbonaro revolution of 1831 had failed only eight months earlier, suggested that he had been guilty of treason. In fact he had not been, for he had always refused to join any secret society and had consistently argued that social and political reform, in order to be permanent, must come by growth and not by revolution. But both his father and elder brother were extremely conservative, and for them to have welcomed home such a radical black-sheep, as he must have seemed to them, says much about the quality of affection within the family.

The origin of his liberalism is more difficult to uncover than that of most Risorgimento leaders. At no moment in his life did a book, a man or an event seem to influence him decisively. Nevertheless one obvious influence in his early life remained constant and attractive to him and plainly did much to form his attitudes. His mother was Swiss and Protestant, a descendant of Huguenot refugees, and her family at Geneva was both more intellectually inclined and more liberal than that of the average aristocrat in Piedmont. There were frequent trips to Geneva and visits to Turin by his mother's relatives, and, as Cavour's earliest letters reveal, these always stimulated him. For many years he felt as much, if not more, at home in Geneva as in Turin.

As he grew up, he read everything remotely touching on government and was able to turn it all into arguments to support the liberal views he seems to have held from earliest childhood. He was not a republican and despised revolutionaries; what he admired was the English parliamentary system. Yet much of what he wrote, while compatible with advocating a parliament and constitutional monarchy, sounds more radical and certainly must have done so to his contemporaries who were used to hearing the same sort of opinions from Mazzini. To one of his Swiss uncles in Geneva he wrote:

Italians need to be regenerated; their morals, utterly corrupted under the ignoble domination of Spanish and Austrians, have regained a little vigor under the French regime; the ardent youth sigh for a national life; but to break utterly with the past, to be born again into a better state, great efforts are necessary; sacrifices of all kinds must put new strength into the Italian character. An Italian war would be a sure pledge that we are going to become a nation, that we are going to rise from the mud in which we have floundered for so many centuries.[27]

Some years later and more rhetorically he answered a lady who had urged him to abandon Piedmont, where his life was cramped and wasted, and to live instead in Paris:

No, Madame. I cannot leave my family or my country. Sacred duties interpose and keep me at the side of a father and mother who have never given me the least cause for complaint. No, Madame, I will never plunge a dagger into the hearts of my parents. . . . And why, Madame, abandon my country? To come to France to seek a literary reputation? . . . What good could I do for humanity out of my country? What influence could I exercise to help my unfortunate fellows, strangers and proscribed, in a country where egotism occupies all the principal social positions? What do they do at Paris all that mass of foreigners whose ill fortune or own wish has thrown them far from their native soil? . . . Which of them has been able to make a great career, to impose an influence on society? Not one. . . .

The political troubles which have desolated Italy have forced its most noble offspring to flee from her. . . . Not one alone has realized the brilliant hopes he had conceived. . . . No, no, it is not by fleeing one's country when she is unfortunate that one can reach a glorious end. Woe to him who abandons in scorn the land that bore him, who renounces his brothers as unworthy of him! As for myself, I have decided never to separate my fate from that of the Piemontesi. Though I be fortunate or unfortunate, my country shall have my whole life— I will never be untrue to her, not even were I sure of finding elsewhere a brilliant career.[28]

He burned with ambition, and one of his aunts may have revealed a clue to his emotional character when she remarked of him that "the idea of being a younger son dominates him; he can't submit to it, and it torments his life." Cavour, who himself reported the remark, considered it a ridiculous explanation of his Liberalism.

But several years after he resigned his commission he wrote in his diary:

All is over for me, politically speaking. I have aged so fast in a few years without acquiring a single new talent or acquaintance, that it would be ridiculous for me to cherish still the illusion of greatness and glory which flattered my years of youth. I must make a virtue of necessity and resign myself to be all my life only an honest and peaceable bourgeois of Turin. Ah! if I were English, by this time I should already be something, and my name would no longer be wholly unknown.[29]

Perhaps he saw in the English way of life and parliamentary system, or even in Swiss life and government, a chance for younger sons that was denied to them in Piedmont. There, after 1815, a feudal system, censorship and government by royal favor had been reimposed, and he found himself a second son in a country where primogeniture was the rule, an aristocrat in a society which allowed a gentleman to be only a soldier, a priest or a diplomat, three careers for which his liberal views entirely disqualified him. He had too much energy to do nothing and, unlike d'Azeglio, he had no skill in any art. In England he might have gone into business or, better still, into Parliament. His Aunt Henriette may have spoken more truth than he realized. The strength with which he clung to his liberal ideas for the reorganization of government and society and the force with which he presented them may have had an emotional basis in a desire to make life better for himself.

The arrangement he came to with his father was that he would take charge of one of the family's holdings at Grinzane, a village about forty miles from Turin. He was warned that the land was poor and that he would scarcely be able to keep a servant or a horse, but he went anyway: he would at least be working and independent, or almost so. And in the winters his father, who did not intend the farm to be a punishment, made it possible for him to visit Geneva and always welcomed him at the palazzo in Turin. But for a man of Cavour's temperament and interests the farm was a kind of exile.

To everyone's surprise, however, he made the farm pay and within three years he was managing the family's much larger estates at Leri, about twenty-five miles northeast of Turin, and steadily adding to them. Farming at Piedmont at the time was still backward. The peasants were superstitious, refusing to plow if the moon was in a certain quarter, and the landlords were often absent in Turin and knew very little about agriculture. Cavour, however, brought to it all the resources of an active mind and benefits of a landlord present and working. He introduced new kinds of chemical fertilizer and farm machinery, improved the strain of cattle, grew better rice, beets, corn and silk and devised new ways of financing and marketing them. He made farming a commercial enterprise and in the course of doing so made himself and his family rich. The Milanesi landlords had begun the process almost two centuries earlier, but Cavour now surpassed them and by the fifteenth year, 1832–47, that he had worked his farms, they were famous the length of the Po valley.

He broke his long periods in the country as often as he could by travel, arguing politics in Geneva, Paris and London while at the same time examining the latest agricultural improvements in each country. In the very first years he conducted an affair with a contessa from Genoa who was four years his senior, a republican and, judging from her rather hysterical correspondence, unstable, which may have been the reason they did not marry; she seems, however, to have been the only woman who even briefly captured his heart. But he was a good conversationalist, liked salons and had a number of feminine acquaintances in Geneva and Paris. Generally after a trip he would return to Piedmont, settle down at Leri and begin to write articles on such subjects as banking, railroads, poor laws, agriculture or education. Most, because of the censorship in Piedmont, were published in Swiss or French journals, and he developed a better reputation outside of Piedmont than he enjoyed within it, where he was still out of favor with the court for being too liberal and with the republicans and secret societies for being too conservative.

Barred from any direct role in government he busied himself, where he was allowed, on the fringe of it. He was one of the organizers of a steamboat company on Lago Maggiore and of the Banks of Turin and of Genoa. With three others he had founded an Infant Asylum Society, a system of elementary schools and hostels for the poor in Piedmont, although Carlo Alberto's prime minister, della Margarita, had opposed the project on the ground that to educate the children of the poor would make them neither good Christians nor good subjects. Cavour also had founded a Whist Club at Turin, which the government watched nervously for fear that between hands the players might talk politics. And, most important, he founded an Agrarian Association to encourage better farming and ranching. In a short time it had more than three thousand members and forty-one branches. It held cattle shows, an annual convention to which the branches elected and sent delegates, and published a journal. Both the government and the Radicals, as a group of extreme liberals was called, saw that Cavour had created an agricultural party that was developing all the organization and apparatus of a political party, and both wanted to control it. The Radicals moved first, successfully forcing Cavour out only in turn to be forced out by the government which took the nomination of the presidents and vice-presidents into its own hands.

The Radicals could force Cavour out because he was not popular. Mean-spirited men envied his wealth, were irritated by his ability and, being capable of it themselves, suspected that he had spied for his father, the Vicario, the minister in charge of internal security. The Radicals even suggested that he had contributed to a famine by cornering the grain market, and the aristocratic conservatives, of course, were easily persuaded that with his liberal opinions he had betrayed his class. His unpopularity was great enough so that the directors of the Infant Asylum Society, with regret, asked him to resign as treasurer lest his odium fall on the society and its work.

But by then Pio Nono had been elected and, although Cavour had retreated once again to his farms at Leri, Carlo Alberto's first reforms soon drew him back again to Turin. He saw in the new press law the opportunity to found a newspaper, and he had several meetings with men who might organize and support it. His friend, Michelangelo Castelli, later described one of these in which Cavour's unpopularity still played a part:

I had been invited by Conte Cavour to take part in the editorial management. Meetings of the principal subscribers and shareholders were held at Cavour's house, when, in one of these reunions, after long and complicated discussions, I noticed that all those present had gone out, one after the other, and no one remained except Cavour and [Cesare] Balbo. Not knowing what to make of such a desertion, while the two leaders were trying with much heat to understand the fact, and were protesting, each to the other, that even alone they would publish the paper, I had, so to speak, mechanically approached the door, when Cavour came hurrying towards me, and grasping my hand with much emotion said, "Even you abandon me? Stay, I will prove to you that I do not deserve the reputation they have given me." I returned, stirred to the bottom of my soul, and from that day to the last moment of his life I did not quit him.[30]

But Castelli was unusual. Most men, even in Cavour's great days in the future, would have reservations about him. He was an aristocrat but, unlike Massimo d'Azeglio, he was neither tall nor good-looking, nor did he hunt or ride, the aristocratic sports. He was short, stout, with blue-gray eyes which, behind glasses, seemed rather vague until he pursed his lids to concentrate on the speaker; then they made men uneasy. His success in business jarred the nobility and irritated the democrats who, nevertheless, accused him of having inherited his wealth and profited from his position as a noble. Somehow he lacked the charm to draw men to him. Even Vittorio Emanuele II, whom he assisted to be the first King of Italy, was never altogether at ease with him and sometimes seemed even not to trust him, a fact that for Cavour and the new kingdom had political importance.

The first issue of the newspaper, of which Cavour and Balbo continued to be the moving spirits, appeared on 15 December 1847 under a name which later seemed immensely prophetic, *Il Risorgimento*. But to contemporaries, of course, the name seemed no more prophetic than the more common *L'Italia* and far less provocative. Similarly the policies of the paper, compared to Mazzini's program of a unified Italy under a republican government, were mild: the independence of all Italian states; some reduction in their number, presumably by Piedmont absorbing some of the smaller ones in the Po valley; a league of Italian princes and a program of steady and orderly reform. But in conservative Piedmont to have any newspaper appear with a claim to being independent of the government was considered a great and dangerous step toward freedom, and it agitated men to argue the wisdom of it and to exclaim on the swiftness of the change and the uncertainty of the future.

Two days later, however, Marie Louise, the Duchess of Parma, died, and her death turned men's thoughts back to the certain past, to the days when the Emperor Franz had given his eldest daughter, a Habsburg arch-duchess, to the upstart Napoleon. She had remarried twice since then and become a frumpy, middle-aged duchess of no importance politically or even socially. But for most men she would always have some shreds of glamor simply because she had married Napoleon, lived with him at the height of his power and borne his only legitimate son. Metternich had controlled her government in Parma and Austrian troops had been stationed there, but she had been personally mild and, in a small way, a patroness of the arts. The Parmigiani, as they had watched the Modenesi suffer under Duke Francesco IV, "the Butcher," had known they were lucky and had remained relatively quiet. But Marie Louise had hardly been loved. Although she had lived the greater part of her life in Parma, to the end she had remained an Austrian archduchess, and her body was taken back to Vienna to be buried in the Capuchin vaults with other Habsburgs.

Her death brought the past into the present for a number of Italians with a rude jolt. Under the Italian settlement of the Congress of Vienna, on the death of Marie Louise the Duchy of Parma was to revert to the old Bourbon-Parma line which had been making do in the meantime with the tiny Duchy of Lucca. So now from Lucca came Carlo Ludovico, the great-great-grandson of Elisabetta Farnese, but the generations had left far more Bourbon and Habsburg blood in his veins, than Farnese. He was a middle-aged playboy whose only desire was to live the life of a "dandy." The English word had become Italian slang at the time, and the phrase "la vita di dandy" was understood by everyone to mean a good income, good clothes, a title, if possible, and a life filled with making arrangements to go from one watering place to the next.

The Parmigiani regarded their new duke, Carlo II, first with suspicion and then with outrage when the terms of a secret treaty became known. In 1844, even before Marie Louise had died, Carlo had contracted to cede Guastalla and eight other towns in the west of the duchy together with two in the mountains to the south to Duke Francesco IV of Modena. In return Carlo was to receive an annuity of seven hundred thousand francs. His old Duchy of Lucca, under the treaties of Vienna, passed to Grand Duke Leopoldo of Tuscanny, much to the relief of the Lucchesi. But the ceded towns of Parma, with their citizens priced and sold, protested and demonstrated against the transfer as much as they dared. Carlo, meanwhile, appointed an English jockey as his prime minister, signed new treaties with Austria and asked that the Austrian garrisons in Parma, like those in Modena, be re-enforced.

Everywhere that Metternich could exercise power directly he confronted the liberal agitation with more troops. In Lombardo-Veneto he gradually increased the army from thirty-six thousand to seventy thousand

and announced firmly on every occasion: "The Emperor is determined not to lose his Italian territories." But Ferdinand, the emperor, was close to being an imbecile, and everyone understood that the policy was entirely Metternich's. He was now seventy-four, continuously in power for forty years and still convinced that his theories on the nature of liberty and sovereignty were eternal truths.

In the states where he had to be more indirect, he continually sent the rulers personal and diplomatic letters in which he carefully mixed advice, flattery and warnings that often came close to threats. At Naples he had no difficulty. Ferdinando had grown steadily more autocratic, cursed the "wretched little priest" who was causing so much trouble and prohibited cheers for him, for Italy, or for a Customs League which Pio Nono had publicly favored for all the Italian states. But elsewhere Metternich's advice was noted and ignored. He warned the pope that a theocracy such as the Papal States could not share power, for it could not rely on the principle of authority in matters of the Church and relinquish it in matters of the State. But Pio Nono continued with reforms and announced the reorganization of the government of the city of Rome. And to Leopold of Tuscany Metternich wrote: "The cry of Italian nationality is but a blind; the cause into which the schemers would draw the rulers of Italy is the cause of the Republic; listen to them and you throw away your crown," and he went on to warn that there was no difference between constitutional monarchists such as d'Azeglio or Cavour and "the real Radicals—Mazzini and his crew." But Leopoldo dared not refuse the demand of his people for reforms, and he even, for the first time in his twenty-three years as grand duke, began to wear a Tuscan rather than an Austrian uniform.

Metternich summarized his view of the situation in the famous sentence he included in a circular letter to the diplomats of Europe. "Italy," he stated, "is a geographical expression." The contemptuous remark infuriated Italians, which Metternich no doubt had intended and which probably increased his satisfaction with it. But if it had ever been true, far back in the days of Metternich's youth, it was true no longer. Men and events such as Alfieri, the French Revolution, Napoleon and Mazzini had worked a change to which Metternich was blind, and his blindness opposed to the frantic enthusiasm of the reformers insured some sort of a collision. As 1847 closed, Italians everywhere could feel it coming, and in distant Uruguay Garibaldi, ever one with a nose for a fight, started his wife and children home for Nice and prepared, with as many of his Legion as he could bring, to follow soon after.

# CHAPTER 24

The year 1848. Communications. Tobacco Riots in Milan. *I Lutti di Lombardia*. Manin arrested in Venice. The effect on Venetians. Revolution in Palermo. The Genovesi and the Jesuits. The *Benedite* of Pio Nono. Carlo Alberto grants a constitution. The parade in Turin.

No ONE has ever numbered the revolutions which broke out in Europe in 1848, "the mad and holy year." If those in the small German states, the Italian states and the various provinces and kingdoms of the Austrian Empire are counted separately, there must have been over fifty. In almost every city of a hundred thousand or more within the triangle of Paris, Warsaw and Palermo the people suddenly demanded reforms and generally won them, sometimes peacefully and sometimes by force. Almost everywhere they asked for a free press and a constitution, or, if one existed, an extension of the franchise, but beyond these their aims were often conflicting, and in some instances the revolutionaries of one city were soon enlisting to fight against those of another.

The confusion of issues and events, as one revolution succeeded another, was very great and some of it was caused simply by the slow communications of the time. In 1848 the telegraph had been invented but was not yet in general use; news still traveled fastest by diplomatic courier on horseback and a few days slower by private letter in a mail coach. In Italy railroads were just beginning to appear, but most of them ran only a few miles, typically from a large city to its suburb. The longest was from Venice to Vicenza. No line yet crossed a mountain range either within the peninsula or connecting it to the rest of Europe. A letter from Milan to Paris took at least five days, from Venice to London eleven or twelve, and first reports, of course, were seldom accurate.

The slowness of communication caused most of the revolutions to take place in an isolation which today is scarcely credible. The Venetians and Milanesi, for example, began revolutions against the Austrians on successive days and yet, as their newspapers show, at least four and probably five days passed before either city learned of what the other was doing.

276

One effect of such isolation was tragic: cities almost everywhere failed to cooperate, and much that was gained was held for only a few weeks or months while the old order righted itself and returned with arms. The very spontaneity of the revolutions, however, was a striking demonstration of the peoples' frustrations. Suddenly everywhere the pot boiled over; and the fact that the slow communications made it inconceivable that Mazzini or any central committee was directing the upheaval only added to the sense of general excitement. But the lack of direction and common purpose also increased the confusion. From one city to the next, as revolution and counterrevolution succeeded each other, for months at a time in 1848 no one could be sure what government or group was in power, and in Italy the expression *"che quarantotto"* or "a regular forty-eight" is used still to mean "Good Lord, what a confusing mess!"

The first of the year's extraordinary events began in Milan on New Year's Day. The liberals there had organized a Tobacco Party inspired directly by the Boston Tea Party of the American Revolution. Tobacco in Milan was an Austrian monopoly and a rich source of income for the State. On New Year's Day the liberals, with posters, urged the Milanesi not to smoke and pointed out that an old ordinance, never repealed, forbade anyone to smoke in the streets. The protest was generally taken up and the few, mostly Austrians, who continued to smoke in public were scolded and hissed as lawbreakers. In reply the Austrians, particularly the soldiers and noncommissioned officers, began to parade along the Corso in groups, puffing ostentatiously. Soon scuffling began as the Milanesi tried to knock the cigars from the soldiers' mouths, and toward the end of the day the mayor, in trying to separate some men, was struck in the face, arrested and taken to the police station.

The protest might have ended on this comic mistake except that both the Milanesi and the soldiers, who were mostly Croats and Hungarians, felt that their honor was involved and were determined not to give in. Two days later occurred the incident which d'Azeglio soon after described for all Italians in a sensational pamphlet which gave its name to the incident, *I Lutti di Lombardia* or "The Mournings of Lombardy."

According to most Milanesi historians the Austrian officers supplied their soldiers with cigars, primed them with brandy and sent them out into the streets to provoke a riot; presumably their aim was, by means of a bloody incident, to cow the Milanesi and to break the antismoking campaign. Austrian historians, however, have insisted that the soldiers did not start out with any such intent, that they bought their own liquor and cigars, as any man in the city was free to do, and that they gathered in large groups only when the crowds began to menace them. But even an Austrian later admitted that as early as midday the soldiers "paraded the streets in batches of ten or twelve with cigars in their mouths, and some with a lit cigar at each corner of their mouths, and blew smoke into the faces of the agitators, and drew their weapons at those who interfered." Eventually someone, undoubtedly a Milanese, threw a stone, and the soldiers, claiming to act in self-defense, attacked the unarmed people with swords and bayonets. They evidently struck around them indiscriminately and in some cases pursued people into their houses and stabbed them there. They wounded seriously about sixty, among them a woman and a four-year-old girl, and they killed five, including a man seventy-four years old, who was known to be pro-Austrian, and also the cook of the special envoy Metternich had sent to aid the Austrian viceroy. Field Marshal Radetzky, who commanded the Austrian army in Italy, promptly confined his men to their barracks for five days, and the viceroy and his assistants, while not apologizing for the incident, did talk of it with regret, both privately and in a public proclamation. But the Milanesi were not to be soothed with soft words. D'Azeglio's pamphlet, which inflamed Italians everywhere, put a river of blood between them and the Austrians. Its first paragraph was repeated so often it became almost a chant of hate:

> A great iniquity has been committed in Milan.
> An iniquity, the greatest that could be conceived by a human mind; taking the lives of men who are unarmed; therefore it is *cowardice;* of men attacked unaware; therefore it is *treachery;* of men neither indicted nor condemned by law; therefore it is *oppression,* and oppression carried out by obscure assassins against men who could not get at their slayers, and therefore could not possibly have tried to provoke them; of men who on the contrary were deliberately provoked so that a cry from them, an exclamation or a whistle-call might be made a pretext for their death. Therefore—to sum up—*cowardice, treachery, oppression,* and *fraud.*[31]

The Austrians at first tried to handle the Milanesi by dividing them. The poor were told that the rich would always desert them; the middle class, that disorder would disrupt trade; and every effort was made with dinners, honors and private talks to persuade the aristocracy that its interest lay with Austria. From Vienna Metternich, misunderstanding the new spirit which was uniting the Milanesi, wrote to his minister in the city: "We have bored them. A people which wants *panem et circenses* does not want to be bored. It wants to be governed with a strong hand—and amused." But the formula, if it had ever been apt, no longer applied. The Milanesi of all classes stuck together, and d'Azeglio in his pamphlet thundered both in explanation and triumph, "We are a nation!—*siamo NAZIONE! NAZIONE! NAZIONE!*"

The people carried busts of Pio Nono through the streets in pious but political processions, and gave each other medals with *Viva Pio Nono!* on one side and *Viva l'Italia!* on the other. There were nights when, mysteriously, no one went to the theatre, others at La Scala when all the ladies wore the colors of Savoy, white and blue, or when all the men had white cravats and yellow gloves, the colors of the Pope. Finally on 22 February the Austrians put the city under martial law, and it became treason to wear certain colors or badges, to sing certain songs, to applaud or to hiss certain passages at the theatres. A special Commission was established to deal with cases of treason, of disturbing public order or of offenses against the peace. Trials were to begin immediately after the offense and be completed within fourteen days. Those found guilty were to be liable to the death sentence without any right of appeal or recommendation to mercy.

In the weeks after the *Lutti di Lombardia* the Milanesi were encouraged to remain united against the Austrians by the news that slowly came to them of what was happening in other Italian cities. In Venice on 8 January Manin, working always through legally irreproachable channels, presented the Austrians with a detailed demand for Home Rule. He began by recapitulating the promises made by Emperor Franz in 1815, in the days before Waterloo, and, pointing out that they had never been honored, turned them into a sixteen-point charter for Home Rule. The chief points were a separate government for Lombardo-Veneto dependent on the emperor alone and not subject to the Viennese bureaucracy; the army and navy to be entirely Italian, men and officers; a separate financial system and membership in a Customs union of all the Italian States; open and oral pleadings in the courts; abolition of censorship and of arbitrary police action; and permission to have a civic guard, by which he meant a police force in the usual, modern sense of one whose primary job was to keep order in the cities as opposed to spying for the government.

A few other courageous Venetians publicly supported him and pointed out that some of his demands such as the open pleading in the courts and the Italian character of the administration and the armed forces had been facts under the Napoleonic regime in North Italy. But the Austrians were not about to imitate Napoleon in this respect, and the government arrested Manin on the charge of stirring up and inflaming the public mind.

He was taken secretly to the Prison, on the Riva degli Schiavoni and connected to the Doge's Palace by the Bridge of Sighs. His room, for he was not yet a convict, was on the second-floor corner, with one window facing the Doge's Palace and two looking over the Riva to the Lagoon. The windows, since lengthened, were small and high, but by standing on a table and then pulling himself up on the window stanchions he could see out. After the Venetians discovered where he was, they came daily by the thousands to march along the Riva, taking off their hats and bowing to the windows, and once he heard a child's voice cry, *"Viva Manin!"*

His trial was delayed until early in March and then, like all others, was behind closed doors and without a jury. His defense was that his actions and statements were legal and aimed at restoring public order by securing the redress of grievances. The judge acquitted him, but the Austrian in charge of the police had warned the judiciary, on the day after Manin's arrest, that, convicted or not, he would remain in prison. And so he did.

The Venetians were indignant and, like the Milanesi, began as never before to unite against the Austrians. Leading citizens wrote to the government, protesting. Manin's fellow lawyers took charge of his legal practice and conducted it on behalf of his family. The municipal administration forebade the carnival festivities, proclaimed a time of patriotic mourning and sent a contribution from the money saved to the families of the Milanesi who had died in the tobacco riots. And even the poorest people joined as best they could in the protest.

One of the oldest, most colorful and often deadly rivalries in Venice was between the Nicolotti and Castellani, two factions representing roughly the landward and seaward sides of the city. In the great days of the Republic the Nicolotti with black sashes at their waists and the Castellani with red had met each year at some unfenced bridge, fought and dumped each other into the canal until one group or the other had triumphed by crossing the bridge and invading the other's territory. The fights, which the oligarchy had permitted, had been rough and had often produced fatalities. They were now forbidden, but the factional passions were still strong, and on occasion men would still kill for the color of a sash.

But after Manin's arrest the leaders of the factions put aside their ancient feud to unite against the Austrians. One morning at dawn, at the Santa Maria della Salute at the entrance to the Grand Canal, the leaders and lieutenants of both the Nicolotti and the Castellani gathered for mass. In pairs they took their sashes, wove red and black together and laid them on the altar steps. At the end of the service they raised their hands, swore a silent oath of fraternity against the Austrians and then disappeared quietly back to their districts. The police were mystified by the event and were even more bewildered in the following weeks to see black-sash men wearing red and vice versa. Even to Venetians the men would simply say that it was a sacrifice for *"La Patria."*

The spirit was new in Venice and, as at Milan, Metternich and the Austrians as a whole misjudged it. Manin was not released, and no concessions were granted on his sixteen points. And at Venice, again as at Milan, the tension between the people and the Austrians steadily increased.

The first successful revolution of 1848 occurred, however, not in northern Italy where the Austrian army was strongest, but in Palermo where the Sicilians demanded and, after sixteen days of fitful fighting in the streets, won a constitution from Ferdinando of Naples. The Kingdom of The Two Sicilies had never, in fact, become the single kingdom its name implied. The first Bourbon king, Elisabetta Farnese's son Carlo, had tried at the start of his reign in 1734 to cement the two halves by visiting Messina and, as was in the kingdom's historical tradition, by going to the cathedral in Palermo to be anointed and crowned. But Carlo's descendants had abandoned his policy. They remained always at Naples, except when forced by revolutions to leave, and they constantly preferred their Neapolitan subjects and institutions over those of Sicily. As a result, all Sicilians of every class shared one great enthusiasm, to free their island from the hated Neapolitans.

There was not even common cause between the liberals in the two kingdoms; in fact, their goals and traditions were different. In Sicily the liberals wanted to restore the "Constitution of 1812," a constitution worked out for them by the British envoy, Lord William Bentinck, in the period when the island was the chief British base in the Mediterranean against Napoleon. To the extent that the Sicilians had a liberal tradition apart from the desire to be free of Naples it was a British tradition. Most Sicilian liberals were not republicans; they were willing to have Ferdinando as a constitutional monarch so long as the constitution provided a strong House of Lords, as in contemporary Britain, and a separate administration of Sicilian affairs. In Naples, on the other hand, the tradition was French and more republican; the liberals there worked to restore the "Constitution of 1820," the Carbonaro constitution. Neither group forgot that the Neapolitan liberals, in their few months in power in 1820, had repudiated a promise of a separate administration for Sicily and sent an army to the island to quell the Sicilian liberals. Both groups worked against Ferdinando; but they could not work together.

The actual fighting of the Sicilian revolution took place almost entirely in Palermo, the capital city. The countryside took part mostly by showing itself ready to be actively hostile if given the slightest opportunity: troops entering or leaving Palermo were sniped at from behind walls and individual Neapolitans, particularly police officers, were killed. In Palermo the liberals posted a proclamation on 10 January stating that the revolution would begin on the king's birthday, two days later. Crowds filled the city for the birthday parade and also to see what would happen. For a long time nothing did, and then suddenly from within the crowd a young man began to shout *"All'armi!"* At the same time in the central Piazza Vigliena (now Quattro Canti) two priests raised their crucifixes and called the people to arms in the name of God, and in the Piazza Fiera Vecchia (now

Piazza della Rivoluzione), the center of the oldest quarter of Palermo, a young lawyer gave the signal. A few men and boys responded with cries of *"Viva Pio Nono!"* and *"Viva l'Italia!"*, but in general the response was so poor that most Palermitani shut themselves in their houses and waited for the Neapolitan troops to capture the rebels.

But instead the church bells continued to clang a call to arms, the tiny bands of patriots gradually grew larger and they were able, by slipping rapidly through houses and down side streets, to harass the Neapolitan patrols without themselves being captured. They did not, on that first day, even attempt to defend a barricade, but they refused to grow discouraged or to disband, and during the first night they established their headquarters in the Piazza Fiera Vecchia. In the center of the piazza is one of the oldest fountains in Palermo and the small statue adorning it became the symbol of the revolution. It is of an old man feeding a snake at his breast and, throughout the ages, the Palermitani had taken it to represent their city feeding its foreign conquerors.

For the next few days the revolutionaries survived, it would seem, only because the Neapolitans in Palermo had difficulty agreeing on the action to take and restricted themselves, mostly, to a defensive shuffling of troops. Apparently the extraordinary proclamation, announcing the revolution two days in advance, caused them to overestimate greatly the number and organization of the revolutionaries. The indecision of the Neapolitans, however, was fatal for them. The Palermitani, on seeing it, joined the revolutionaries in ever greater numbers. Each day they gathered more and better weapons, forced more of the Neapolitans into isolated strongholds and eventually even captured some of these. Finally, on 29 January, Ferdinando in an effort to hold Sicily for his crown promised to grant a constitution to each of his kingdoms; for the Neapolitan liberals, on learning of what was happening in Palermo, had begun to agitate almost as violently as the Sicilians. There was, of course, a lag in time between the promise, the drafting and the acceptance of the constitution, but meanwhile Neapolitan troops were withdrawn from every city of Sicily except Messina, and the Sicilians considered themselves, though still under Ferdinando, to be free of the Neapolitans.

The success of the Sicilians depended, perhaps more than they realized, on the diplomatic shuffling at Naples. Ferdinando, when his troops in Palermo had been hard pressed, had appealed to Metternich for Austrian aid under the secret treaty of 1815 which his grandfather had signed. By its terms Ferdinando I had bound himself never to grant a constitution and, in return, Austria had undertaken to defend the absolute monarchy in Naples. But now when Ferdinando II, uncertain of the loyalty of his own troops over the issue of a constitution, applied to the Emperor Ferdinand for Austrian troops, Metternich after some consideration refused them. He gave as reasons the unrest in northern Italy, the danger of some move by Carlo Alberto and, most important, the fact that the liberal Papal government would no longer allow Austrian troops to march across its territory. In 1821, after the Carbonaro revolution in Naples, he had sent an Austrian army south to re-establish Ferdinando I on his throne as an absolute monarch, but in 1848 he could not. Italy was less supine and Austria relatively weaker. Liberals elsewhere on the peninsula sensed it, without knowing any of the details of the diplomacy at Naples, and they increased their agitation in their own states for further reforms.

In the Kingdom of Sardinia the issue of a constitution arose out of the hatred of the Genovesi for the Jesuits. Early in January a crowd of some four thousand had gathered before the Jesuit College and were prevented from sacking it only when some trusted citizens promised to lay before the king a petition for the expulsion of the Jesuits and for the formation of a civic guard. Some weeks later the deputation, with a petition of twenty thousand signatures, arrived in Turin, were refused an audience by Carlo Alberto and were ordered back to Genoa. Their curt dismissal aroused sympathy for them, and a group of liberal Piemontesi, including most of the journalists and among them Cavour, met to agree on a policy which might reconcile the Genovesi with the government. The more radical journalists immediately advocated that all the persons and newspapers represented at the meeting adopt the Genovese petition as their own and support it publicly. Cavour, however, to the surprise of everyone present, suggested that they press for even more. He argued the advantages of liberal institutions and of the need of both the kingdom and the king for some sort of consulting body which would continue, though its members changed, and which would represent the intelligent public opinion of the country. "I propose," he concluded, with a reference to the liberals' efforts to win a constitution in 1821, "that we demand the Constitution."

After several more meetings he persuaded most of the men to his policy. Leading liberals in Turin began to talk of the need for a constitution and Cavour, of course, advocated it in his paper, *Il Risorgimento*. The radical journalists, however, furious that Cavour and not themselves had made the suggestion and got the credit for it, started on an oblique campaign against a constitution which immediately turned into a personal attack on Cavour. He was known to favor the English parliamentary system which, so they said, operated entirely in favor of the aristocracy. He was himself, therefore, untrustworthy and an enemy of the people. Others, or perhaps the same men, circulated a report that the meetings had been held to organize a rebellion. In answer to this Cavour and his supporters drew up an account of their meetings to give the king which, lacking any official intermediary, they sent him through the ordinary mail. Carlo Alberto read it without comment, but, through his censors, he prohibited any publication of it in the newspapers.

The last thing Carlo Alberto wanted was a constitution. In his mind the struggle against Austria was a project quite separate from the liberal program of a constitution and parliamentary institutions. In fact, in the circumstances of 1848, he considered the two to be mutually destructive. With his eye on the Austrian war which he felt sure would come, he observed "for war you require soldiers, not lawyers." To tackle the Austrian army he wanted a united country, not one divided into political parties; he wanted unquestioning support, not parliamentary debates on his actions and policies. To Roberto d'Azeglio, Massimo's eldest brother who was supporting Cavour, he remarked, "Remember, Marchese, I want the freedom of Italy just as you do, and for that very reason I will never grant a constitution."

But for most liberals, particularly those in northern Italy, the struggle against Austria was inseparable from the struggle for liberal institutions. Many confused the two and misinterpreted the significance of events. They assumed that because the Sicilians were prepared to fight for a constitution, they would also fight to drive the Austrians out of Italy. It was dangerous reasoning, but in the excitement of the times many liberals accepted it. They brushed aside Carlo Alberto's fears about the difficulties of making a constitution work in time of war as merely the factional arguments of an absolute monarch. If Ferdinando in Naples could be pressured into granting a constitution, then, reasoned the Genovesi and Piemontesi liberals, Carlo Alberto could also be persuaded, particularly at a time when there was a militant, liberal pope in Rome and the Milanesi and Venetians were at fighting pitch against the Austrians. In their clamor, which rose quickly, was the threat that if Carlo Alberto was not to disqualify himself as the leader in the struggle against Austria, he must also lead the struggle for liberal institutions. He had a mystic belief in his destiny as the national leader and almost none at all in the liberal institutions being forced on him as the corollary of that position. But the pressure increased daily and finally, on the advice of his ministers, he announced on 9 February that he would grant his people a constitution with parliamentary institutions. Their excitement and gratitude were enormous; never had Carlo Alberto been so popular and never, as the liberals had argued, had the kingdom seemed so united.

The excitement in Piedmont and Genoa grew greater, if possible, as news came that Grand Duke Leopoldo, similarly coerced, had promised the Tuscans a constitution; and from Rome that Pio Nono had published a *Motu Proprio* containing the phrase *Benedite Gran Dio l'Italia!* or "O

Lord God, bless Italy!" The phrase passed through Italy like an electric shock, causing a sensation as great as his amnesty eighteen months earlier. Many saw in it an acknowledgment that Italy must be united and free, for how else could "Italy" exist and also be blessed? Some even saw in it a secret blessing on a war against Austria.

It occurred in a part of the *Motu Proprio* in which Pio Nono had talked of the significance for Italy of the Catholic religion.

A great gift from heaven is this: one of the many gifts which he has bestowed on Italy; that a bare three million of our subjects [the population of the Papal States] possesses two hundred million brothers of every nation and every tongue. This fact in other times, during the destruction of the whole Roman world, was the salvation of Rome. Because of it, the ruin of Italy was never complete. And this will always be her protection so long as at her center stands the Apostolic See.

　　Therefore, O Lord God, bless Italy and preserve for her this most precious gift of all—her faith! Bless her with the benediction for which Thy Vicar with his head bowed to the earth is humbly entreating Thee. Bless her with the benediction. . . .[32]

And on the following day the pope had appeared on the balcony of the Palazzo del Quirinale to acknowledge the gratitude of the people for the great *Motu Proprio* and had again bestowed his blessings on Italy. Liberals saw in him their banner and in Carlo Alberto their sword against Austria. And in their constitutions and new parliamentary institutions they saw all the necessary essentials for their political freedom. The princes in Naples, Piedmont and Tuscany had promised constitutions and Pio Nono, who had already created a consulting body of laymen, was expected to grant one at any moment. Then the larger part of Italy, stretching from the Alps to Sicily, would have free institutions, almost certainly a customs' union and probably a defensive league. At Naples, Ferdinando had already sworn to uphold his constitution in a ceremony of great solemnity in the Church of San Francesco and before the grandees of his kingdom. And at Turin, Carlo Alberto and his ministers were drafting a *Statuto* or constitution that would provide for a Senate, whose members, appointed by the king, would hold office for life, and for a Chamber of Deputies, to be elected by duly qualified voters. The length of the peninsula there was constant rejoicing, particularly among the moderates, for the reform everywhere except in Sicily had been achieved by peaceful means.

In Piedmont, with royal approval, a parade was scheduled for 27 February in which anyone who wished could march to celebrate the granting of the Statuto. The parade was necessary, perhaps, because, as Roberto d'Azeglio's wife had exclaimed: "We have already cheered all we could cheer, and sung likewise, and our voices are frightfully hoarse. I do not know what will be invented to manifest our joy."

At dawn on the appointed day subjects of Carlo Alberto from every part of his kingdom began to gather at the Piazza d'Armi, a large, open parade ground. In all, some fifty thousand men marched in a procession that took five hours to pass before the king. They marched ten abreast in platoons of two files each with each platoon commanded by a captain. Every city of Piedmont was represented, every guild, profession and division of laborers and peasants. Most of them sang, as they marched, a new patriotic hymn, *"Fratelli d'Italia"* or *"Brothers of Italy,"* which had recently been written by a Genovese, Goffredo Mameli. The *Statuto* they were celebrating was to become in 1861 the constitution of the Kingdom of Italy, and the hymn, when Italy became a republic in 1946, the country's national anthem.

In the procession vestiges of the eighteenth century and feudal Piedmont mingled with clothes, attitudes and even professions that had only recently come into being. There were men in buckled shoes, knee breeches and their hair in queues following others in the modern and more monotonous trousers and frock coat. Many, particularly those from the country villages, wore the traditional coats or colors of their trade or province and marched as guilds or villages. Squeezed between the platoons of wine-keg carriers and those of the woodcarvers, a marshal had placed the thin file of journalists, a profession so new that no one knew where it belonged. "We are no better than so many dogs," joked Cavour with his colleagues.

Far in front of them was a great car, drawn by caparisoned oxen, which carried warriors in armor, trumpeters, a hermit and a bell, symbols of medieval Savoy, and from its tall mast streamers hung to the ground. The Genovesi had a delegation with banners and symbols of their old republic and six hundred Waldenses marched as a group reminding those who saw them of the days of religious persecution in the middle ages. A somber group, proud but few, carried a flag with the dates of Carbonaro history, 1821–1831–1833. They were the exiles of the revolutions in those years whom Carlo Alberto had recently allowed to return. Another group, which the crowds watched in silence, were the exiles of Lombardo-Veneto, all dressed in black in mourning for their countries.

Roberto d'Azeglio led the parade. First, out of the Piazza d'Armi, winding down to the Po and then across it for a Te Deum before the Church of Gran Madre di Dio, erected in 1818 to commemorate the return of Vittorio Emanuele I after Napoleon's defeat. From there d'Azeglio led the marchers up the wide Via Po to the Piazza Castello. In the arcades along the way no one could move, so great was the crowd, and at every window and balcony were cheering people. The walls and balconies were festooned with banners, the red, white and green of Italy and the blue and white of Savoy. In the Piazza Castello, Carlo Alberto flanked by his two sons, Vittorio Emanuele and Ferdinando, reviewed the marchers from horseback. In the entire excited throng only Carlo Alberto seemed out of place, withdrawn and alone. Men remarked on it. His face, as always, concealed his thoughts; no one could say whether he approved or disapproved. For five hours he sat his horse immobile, like a statue. When the last marcher had passed, he retired into the Palazzo Reale, and the city continued its celebrations. Some of the people had already heard that, three days before, there had been a revolution in Paris, that Louis Philippe had left the throne and that, probably, a republic would be declared. Republicans, of course, drank to that; but the great majority were content with their own *Statuto*.

# CHAPTER 25

The revolution in Paris and the Second Republic. The students in Vienna. Manin, the Arsenal and the Venetian Republic. The "Cinque Giornate" of Milan.

THE REVOLUTION in Paris which toppled the constitutional monarchy of Louis Philippe occurred almost as if by accident and had a result far out of proportion to its cause. Opposition to the king had been mounting gradually, aggravated in 1847 by a business recession, poor crops and a financial scandal implicating two ex-ministers. Most governments, however, survive such problems, and certainly Louis Philippe and his people expected his to do so. More serious was the constant agitation, largely by republicans and social radicals, to broaden the franchise. It was limited by a property qualification which allowed the right to vote only to 170,000 men out of a total population of 35.8 million, or to about one man in a hundred. Republican and radical orators accused the government of favoring big business, and it, in turn, denied the opposition leaders the right to speak at public meetings. So instead they spoke between the courses at enormous, subscription banquets, and the oratory was generally warmer than the soup and veal. But even this problem had an obvious and easy solution: the government at any moment could divide the opposition by making a show of reform and extending the franchise slightly.

The crisis arose out of one of the banquets which the opposition leaders had scheduled to be held in Paris on 22 February 1848. The guest list included a hundred deputies from the opposition, not all republicans but all advocates of reform of one sort or another. The government first forbade the banquet, then authorized it, then forbade it again while suggesting weakly that perhaps the courts should decide. In Paris the people grew restive, as much over their general grievances as over the banquet, but the banquet provided a focus. On the twenty-second, students and workers gathered in the streets and began to clash with the police. There was an incident: soldiers fired on a crowd and citizens threw up barricades. Louis Philippe went out to review the National Guard, but the troops, instead of shouting "Long live the King!", cried "Hurrah for Reform!" And Louis Philippe decided in the interest of peace in the country to retire to England. His decision may have saved France from a civil war; it certainly saved the citizens of Paris from being slaughtered by the regular army, but it caught the moderates, republicans, and radicals, who had been pressing for reforms, completely by surprise, and they were not ready. In the confusion the republicans managed to seize control and to declare the Second Republic. In France, according to the poets and orators such as Victor Hugo and Alphonse de Lamartine, the fountain of liberty had begun again to flow.

The effect elsewhere of the news that France was again a republic can hardly be realized today. In Rome one enthusiast is said to have died of joy. For centuries France had been the most populous country in Europe, and in 1848, except for Russia, it still outstripped every great power by five million or more. For centuries, too, France had been the most militaristic power in Europe, and in 1848 the armies of all the other powers and the navy of Britain existed primarily for protection against France. In the generation between the Congress of Vienna and 1848, for example, the only war for which strategists planned was a French war. Another reason for this was that, on the continent at least, all the other great powers were absolute monarchies, and France was the source of revolution, of the doctrine of popular sovereignty, and just as the armies of the absolute monarchs looked steadily west to France so, too, did the revolutionists in every country. Republicans and monarchists alike, when they heard that France was again a republic, assumed that sooner or later the years of the Directory would come again and that France, by war, would attempt to spread its ideas about liberty and the rights of man.

The French republicans were aware of this heritage and of the expectations it aroused in France and elsewhere. But they were also aware of their weakness. Their political position was precarious and a large part of the French army was in Algeria. If war should come, they had barely enough troops to defend themselves without attempting to revolutionize the rest of Europe.

The poet and historian Lamartine was in charge of foreign affairs and on 4 March he published a long "Manifesto to the Powers" in which he tried both to satisfy the expectations of the revolutionaries and to soothe the fears of the monarchies. First he announced that France repudiated the treaties of 1815, and then, that France would continue to recognize them: "The treaties of 1815 have no legal existence in the eyes of the French Republic; nevertheless the territorial provisions of these treaties are a fact which the Republic admits as a basis and starting point in its relations with other nations."

It was a tepid manifesto, and even before issuing it Lamartine had assured the British ambassador and, by private message, the Duke of Wellington that the republic wanted to keep the peace. But Lamartine, no matter how hard he tried, could not drain all meaning out of words. With the manifesto a great power repudiated the legal basis of the settlements of 1815. Some of their sanctity was stripped away, and it was easier for men to think of new settlements for Europe.

The Paris revolution made no change in the course of events in Italy, although it did, by encouraging the republicans, give a sharper tone to them. Louis Philippe's government had been a constitutional monarchy based on a limited franchise, and in Italy the princes were only just starting to give their people this kind of government which in Paris the people had already repudiated. Doubtless the princes were relieved that they had already promised constitutions to their people and, perhaps, thereby avoided Louis Philippe's fate; but doubtless, too, they saw with alarm how far the road to reform now stretched. For in Paris both the moderates, who wanted political reforms, and the radicals, who wanted experimental social legislation as well, were agreed on one basic principle—that of universal manhood suffrage. They were determined to try it, even though such an experiment was almost unprecedented in Europe, and even though more than a third of the prospective voters were illiterate. France, for all of Lamartine's protestations, was still the source of radical ideas which inspired men elsewhere to talk and to agitate and sometimes to act.

The Italians at the moment, however, were too taken up with their new institutions, which were just coming into being, to do more than talk of the news from France, but the students and workers in Vienna, who had no new institutions, were excited by it to act. As in Paris the crisis developed out of a number of incidents, in themselves unimportant, till finally, on 13 March, students and workers gathered in the streets, clashed with the police and, surging toward the Hofburg Palace, were fired on by the emperor's guard. In the next two days the revolutionaries, largely the students, forced Ferdinand I and his ministers to allow them to form a national guard and thereby to have arms, to abolish the censorship and to promise a constitution. Metternich, after forty years of power, quit his office or was forced from it and, borrowing money from his friends, for the Habsburgs would lend him none, left the city secretly in a common cab for exile in England.

In Vienna the students and workers thought they were copying the latest ideas and examples from Paris. But conditions in the two cities were so different that the revolutions they produced were also different. As has been frequently observed, Vienna was two or three revolutions behind Paris.

Even physically the city was more like the Paris of 1789 than of 1848. It still had its walls and moat, and a wide, green slope separated it from its suburbs. At night the city gates were closed and locked, and at any disturbance they were locked during the day. Unlike Paris, almost all the workers lived in the suburbs outside the city, while the students, middle class and nobility lived within.

This physical division between classes was also spiritual, and to a degree the classes in Paris had never experienced. When Baron Doblhoff, a Viennese noble, began to invite members of the middle class to his house, he was immediately put under police surveillance. The University taught the sons of peasants and of the middle class but not of the aristocracy; young nobles were either tutored at home or attended a school for training diplomats and army officers, the Theresanium, which required, for admission, that a boy be a baron or better. The classes grew up knowing almost nothing about each other and, because of a censorship severer than any Paris had ever known, unable to learn much even by reading. So severe was the censorship that fewer books were published in Austria than in any other region of western Europe and anything imported, a book, a paper or even an advertisement had first to be approved by the censor and then, if its subject concerned the army, the Church or the State, to undergo a second scrutiny by the appropriate ministry or institution.

Even travel was discouraged for all except the aristocracy. When one student requested permission from the police to return home for vacation by a slightly longer route than he had taken coming to Vienna, he was rebuffed and asked: "Do you think the Empire is a dovecote where everyone can fly around as he pleases?" The restrictions kept the classes in such ignorance of each other that in their relations they alternated between arrogance and terror. To the middle class and nobility within the city the workers, dirty and illiterate, squatting in their hovels in the suburbs, were contemptible; they were also terrifying.

The only group in Vienna which crossed the class lines to any extent was the students at the University. There, at least, the sons of the middle class, workers and peasants mingled and learned something about each other. At the same time, largely through smuggled books and pamphlets, they learned about the new ideas and relations between classes in other countries. They visited the workers in their suburbs and saw their misery; but also, living within the city, they saw the middle class at home and at work and were in touch with those who were discontented, the industrialists cramped by the endless restrictions, the lawyers and doctors, harassed by the police, and the booksellers, would-be journalists and other intellectuals who resented the censorship. The students, including with them many of their professors, were, in fact, the only group in Vienna that could hold the confidence of more than one class, and the only group that had any leaders ready to take command.

They formed an Academic Legion which patrolled the city to keep order, and they remained united with the workers for whom they developed an almost paternal affection. But as the weeks and months were to pass, it would become clear that the students, in fact, were accomplishing very little. Vienna was not the empire as Paris was France. The students in Vienna controlled only one city and in the countryside they had no direct support. The Emperor Ferdinand, kind, gentle and incompetent, promised anything they asked, but as they had no thought of abolishing the monarchy, the court continued to exist, and the court controlled the army which, unlike the troops in Paris, never for a moment wavered in its loyalty to the Habsburgs. But these facts and their consequences would only become clear in the future. In the meantime first reports of the revolution traveled quickly to Italy. Men heard first with disbelief and then with joy or fear of Metternich's fall, of the students outfacing the army, of the free press and the promise of a constitution. To Italian patriots and liberals in the Habsburg Kingdom of Lombardo-Veneto the revolution in Vienna, in the heart of the empire, gave the opportunity and therefore the signal for immediate revolt.

On the afternoon of the third day after the students in Vienna began their revolt, rumors of it reached Venice and by evening an excited crowd jammed the Piazza San Marco. But they could learn nothing definite, and neither could the Austrian governor, an Hungarian named Palffy, whose residence and offices were in the Procuratie Nuove on the south side of the piazza. This building, put up shortly after the battle of Lepanto, today houses the city's Museo del Risorgimento.

Early the next morning the crowd gathered on the Riva degli Schiavoni, in front of Manin's prison, to await the postal steamer from Trieste. At nine it entered the lagoon through the Porto di Lido and, as soon as it was sighted, a swarm of gondolas raced out to meet it. As they went alongside, a French merchant, well known in the city, leaned over the rail and shouted that the revolution had triumphed in Vienna; Metternich was gone and constitutional government promised. As evidence he waved over the side the blackened frame and canvas of a portrait of Metternich while shouting that a mob in Trieste had burned it the night before. Back to the Riva sped the gondolas, the men all crying the news, and the crowd, as it heard, made a rush for the piazza and the governor's window. With a roar that reverberated through the city they called for Manin's release: *Fuori Manin, fuori!* From all over the city, as fast as men could run or row, they came to jam into the piazza, into the piazzetta where Pellico had been sentenced, along the Riva and the Molo and even on the roofs around the governor's residence, and behind his window the governor listened.

His position was extremely difficult. He had no idea what the new Liberal government in Vienna might want done and, being without telegraph, he could not find out. He was himself a man of peace as was also his aide. Neither wished to go down in history as the Goth who had destroyed Venice, and their natural inclinations toward a compromise of some sort were seconded by the governor's wife who had been hissed out of the piazza the night before and, after an hour of the crowd's steady roar, was close to hysterics. More important, as Palffy no doubt now regretted and his wife undoubtedly pointed out, he had done nothing to surround himself with troops he could trust. The navy was at Pola and the non-Italian soldiers, four thousand Croats, were in their barracks on the far side of the Grand Canal. Except for a few servants and aides, he and his wife were alone with a mob.

After waiting as long as he dared, Palffy pulled open the French windows and, not knowing whether he would be allowed to speak or, perhaps, be shot, he stepped up to the balustrade which ran the length of the building. There for an hour, he argued with the crowd. He had, he said, no authority to release Manin, and when that defense had been shouted down, he promised to send to Vienna at once to obtain Manin's release. But all attempts at delay or compromise were rejected and finally, after the mayor of the city insisted it was the only way to avoid violence, Palffy gave in and ordered Manin's release. But already a small group of Venetians, led by Manin's son, had begun to break into the jail, and Manin was freed as much by popular action as on Austrian order. Like a careful lawyer, however, he insisted that his jailer sign a release before he would leave the prison.

Once outside several men hoisted him onto their shoulders and, with a large Venetian clearing the way before, he was carried through the tumult to a spot directly beneath Palffy's window. In the next minute Manin undoubtedly could have released the mob with a word, killed the governor and started the revolt against Austria. But he chose not to do so and instead merely said simply:

> Citizens, friends. I do not know by what sequence of events I am taken from the silence of my prison and carried here in triumph. What I suspect from the expression of your faces and from your excitement is that the feelings of patriotism and of nationality have made great progress. I rejoice at that, profoundly, and thank you in the name of our country. But let us not forget that true liberty cannot exist where it does not have order, and so we must make ourselves jealous guardians of order to show that we are worthy of liberty.

At this point Palffy, from his window, bowed and smiled his approval, but he was too soon, for Manin finished by saying:

Nevertheless there are certain moments and circumstances in which insurrection becomes a right and a duty.[33]

The crowd cheered; Palffy stepped back from the window, slamming it shut, and Manin, accompanied by the crowd, was carried off to his house and family in the center of the city.

In later years Manin remained convinced that his decision to delay a revolt was wise, and historians generally have agreed with him. The Venetians had no arms with which to face the four thousand Croats and although they were united in wanting Manin to be freed and in their hatred of the Austrians, many of them still thought in terms of freedom within the empire, of some sort of constitutional government and home rule. But Manin, who had led the movement, no longer believed in it. He had concluded, while in prison, that the Habsburgs would never keep their promises or even, as in his wrongful imprisonment, observe their own laws; the time for a compromise was past and the time for insurrection come. But he suspected, correctly, that in reaching this conclusion he had outstripped the other Venetian leaders. An immediate revolt would have split leaders and people and given the Austrians, who had the arms, an overwhelming advantage.

Once back in his home, however, Manin began to plan a revolution to be accomplished within the week. The key to it was to be the formation of a Civic Guard, Venetians with arms, which would assist the police to keep order. They would also, of course, form the nucleus of an army to oppose the Croats. And for just this reason Palffy at first refused to consider the idea. But his desire to avoid bloodshed undermined his position. Whenever he brought the Croats into the piazza, there were scuffles with Venetians who refused to obey the Austrian police officers, and Manin was able to argue that the crowd would obey only a Civic Guard of fellow Venetians. When the mayor and his entire council as well as the patriarch of the city backed Manin's plea, Palffy finally gave in and authorized a guard of two hundred men which would take its orders from the Austrian police.

Manin promptly enrolled two thousand, and when the police commissioner furiously accused him of planning a revolt, he insisted he was acting to maintain order, and if obstacles were put in his way, he would join the mob and lead the insurrection they all feared. The Austrians dared not return him to prison nor even to oppose him, and the guard continued to enroll members. Its uniform consisted merely of a white sash across the breast, and its weapons, of a few muskets and pistols and many spears and two-handed swords from private collections. Its commander was Angelo

Mangaldo, a Napoleonic veteran, who was famous both for surviving the retreat from Moscow and for losing to Byron in a swimming match from the Lido to the city. But no one doubted that the great majority of the guard, in any conflict of command, would obey Manin.

For four days after Manin's release on 17 March the city continued in a state of uneasy truce with the guard constantly expanding in number and importance as it demonstrated its ability to keep order. On the evening of 18 March the Trieste steamer, making a special trip, brought news that Emperor Ferdinand had agreed in principle to a constitutional government for Lombardo-Veneto, and that night, at the Teatro la Fenice, the audience applauded Palffy, who was present, and cheered the names of Manin, Pio Nono and the Emperor Ferdinand. It was a night of genuine good will between Austrians and Venetians, but Manin remained unconvinced and continued laying plans to seize the Arsenal on 22 March.

The Arsenal at Venice, which is still in use, is not a castle or a warehouse but, as the word originally specified, a dockyard; and it is as much the heart of Venice as the Piazza San Marco or the Doge's Palace. It has always been, as far back as Venetian history records, in the same spot on the eastern point of the city and very early was surrounded by a high wall of red brick which still stands and is kept in repair. Inside are the dockyards in which the Venetians used to build a galley a day. The main entrance, which is some distance back from the Riva, consists of a canal for ships and immediately to the left of it a gate for naval personnel and dockhands. The gate, as it is today, dates from 1460 and is embellished in the Renaissance style with a group of classical gods and four stone lions brought later as trophies from the Piraeus. Looking down on them, in bas-relief above the gate, is the winged lion of Venice. The canal, which cuts into the city from the south, passes through it for several hundred yards and then, after making a slight turn to conceal the Arsenal's entrance from anyone on the lagoon, enters the yard between two brick towers. Beyond, in the docks, the fighting ships of Venice, for centuries, were built, laid up and repaired, and from between the towers and out the canal went the oared galleys, crews and sailing ships that sacked Constantinople, defeated Genoa and defended the Mediterranean against the Turks. This canal together with its gate for pedestrians was, until the early nineteenth century, the only entrance to the Arsenal. Then, under Napoleon's regime, a second passage for ships only, one which opened directly into the lagoon, was cut through the east wall, and beside the Porta Nuova, as the new entrance was called, a brick tower was built.

Manin and everyone else in Venice, including Palffy, considered the Arsenal the key to the city; whoever held it could turn its cannon on any part of the city and force a government to terms. Inside were also stacks of muskets, cutlasses, cannon and ships to patrol the lagoons. Further, there were the two or three thousand Arsenalotti, as the dockhands were called, who were the only sizable groups of Venetians outside the Austrian navy who were trained in the maintenance and repair of the weapons. Control of the workmen was almost as important as control of the guns.

The Arsenalotti were fiercely patriotic. For centuries they had been the elite of Venetian workers and peculiarly aware of the city's glory, and conversely now, more than most, they were aware of Austrian power in the city. Particularly they hated the two Austrians who ran the dockyards, Martini and Marinovich. The first, the commandant, was a cipher, but Marinovich, his aide, was the most strong-willed Austrian in the city, perhaps the only one capable of holding the Venetians down. He was an excellent naval administrator but hard and tactless. When he discovered that the Arsenalotti, as they had for centuries, were taking from the yards for their own use anything from grain to firewood, he lined them up each evening and had them searched by Croat soldiers. For the last man searched the process added an hour on to the working day, and for all it was an infuriating and daily humiliation. And when he reduced their wages, he at the same time raised his own. They frankly hated him and, after news came of the revolt in Vienna, some talked of murdering him.

On the morning of 22 March all the different strands of murder, mutiny, bluff and planned revolt suddenly wound together into eight hours of confusion from which Manin and others tried to rescue order and freedom. The day began with many Arsenalotti gathering in a threatening crowd below Marinovich's office in the Lion Gate. He had escaped a similar mob the night before only with the help of the Civic Guard, but he was fearless and, against advice, had insisted on returning to work the next morning. The Arsenal contained a garrison of several hundred Croats, and a detachment of these was guarding the gate and Marinovich while stoically enduring the taunts of the Venetians. Martini, the commandant, thinking to appease the crowd ordered this detachment to retire to its garrison without considering that he thus left Marinovich unprotected. But the Arsenalotti realized it and rushed the gate at the same time that one of Manin's agents and a Venetian naval officer, in an effort to save Marinovich's life, hurried him out the back and into a covered gondola with four oars. Their hope was to reach the Porta Nuova and the open lagoon before the mob of Arsenalotti, running around by the docks, could cut them off. The gondoliers rowed furiously, and they reached the passage out before the Arsenalotti, but the water-gate was locked, and the custodian with the key had been seized by the Arsenalotti on his way to work. The only hope remaining was the brick tower, and inside it Marinovich went up the ladder-stairs from platform to platform while the others stayed below to defend him against the mob. They were brushed aside in an instant, and the excited, maddened workmen burst into the tower and started pulling and shoving their way up. Before they reached the top, they shouted to Marinovich to come down, and he asked, "Do you want me dead or alive?" "Alive," they replied. He descended the ladder-steps and handed them his sword. Even as he did, one of them ran him through with an iron tool. The men went mad. He was dragged by his feet down the 180 steps, still alive, and at the bottom was thrown into a shed where a few moments later he died.

Just as news of the students' revolt in Vienna had been the signal for the first phase of a revolution in Venice, so word of the murder of Marinovich, as it passed through the city, was the signal for the second. Some Venetians rejoiced, others were horrified, but all instantly knew that after the murder of such a prominent officer either revolution or reaction must follow.

Manin started at once for the Arsenal, calling on all members of the Civic Guard whom he passed to follow him. By the time he arrived at the Lion Gate he had collected about a hundred, and more, who had arrived ahead of him, were standing outside it. A few had already entered and were helping the officers who had sent for Manin to calm the Arsenalotti. Fortunately for Manin, news of the murder had paralyzed command in the Arsenal. The Croats remained uneasily in their interior garrison, awaiting an order, and Martini, who should have given it, sat in his office, white with terror. Outside, other Austrian officers had sent for troops, but when these arrived at the Lion Gate, they turned out to be Italian conscripts who refused to fire on the Civic Guard which denied them entrance and instead disarmed their Austrian officers. Manin, meanwhile, had toured the inside of the Arsenal and bullied Martini into giving him the keys to the armory where the muskets and swords were kept. But even with arms he dared not attack the Croats who, besides their garrison, still controlled another armory in which cannon and ammunition were stored. The best he could do was leave an officer of the Civic Guard with a few men and a cannon trained on a gate from which the Croats would have to emerge. The officer, who spoke Croatian, talked to the Croats for almost ten hours, mixing his talk with flattery, jokes and threats, until finally, late in the evening, they were persuaded to give up their arms.

As Manin came out of the Arsenal, he stopped on the top step of the Lion Gate and there before a crowd of Arsenalotti, Civic Guard and mutinied soldiers he raised a cry not heard in Venice for fifty-one years, *Viva San Marco!,* and the men roared back their approval. Perhaps nothing indicates better the extraordinary position and power which Manin had among the Venetians than what happened next. In the middle of the afternoon with a revolution under way he went into a nearby tavern to rest for an hour. Physically, he was a weak man and exhausted, but also he wanted word of the capture of the Arsenal to circulate through the city, strengthening the hearts of Venetians and causing fear in those of the Austrians. When he emerged at the end of the hour, the crowd of men was still intact, patiently waiting, and no one had tried to take his place as its leader. Putting himself at its head and raising an immense tricolor flag with the red cap of the republic on the staff he led it along the Riva degli Schiavoni into the great piazza.

There his co-conspirators had been at work and were awaiting him. Palffy had ordered four cannon to be set up before the basilica, to be loaded and aimed down the length of the piazza. One blast and, as everyone recognized, the piazza would be littered with the dead and dying. But again, although the officers in charge were Austrian, the troops were Italian, and Manin's colleagues had suborned them. When a group of the Civic Guard marched up and announced that it was to take charge of the battery, the troops already there disarmed their Austrian officers and re-positioned the cannon to fire into Palffy's window.

Inside the governor's office the mayor and his associates, independent of Manin's movement, were trying to persuade Palffy to transfer all his authority to them. While not actually opposed to Manin or his movement, they had less faith than he in the discipline of the people and hoped for an abdication of power by the Austrians rather than a seizure of it by the Venetians. But in the midst of the discussions a tremendous roar went up outside the window, announcing Manin's arrival in the piazza.

He was short and someone pulled out a table for him to stand on. He had in one hand the tricolor banner and in the other a drawn sword. He was sickly looking, with glasses, and dressed in a plain black frock coat, but he had lightning, they said, behind his spectacles and thunder in his voice.

> We are free, and we can glory doubly in being so, because we achieved it without shedding a drop of blood, either of ours or of our brothers; for I call all men brothers. But it is not enough to have thrown over the old government; we must also raise up the new. And the best form for us, I think, is a republic. It will remind us of past glories made better by modern liberties. In doing this we do not intend to separate ourselves from our fellow Italians, but rather we shall form one of those centers which, bit by bit, must serve to fuse all of Italy into one. Therefore, *Viva la repubblica! Viva la libertà! Viva San Marco!* [34]

Later that evening Palffy capitulated and agreed that the Austrians and all their troops would withdraw to Trieste, and for a few hours the city was ruled by a provisional government set up by the mayor. But the next day, 23 March, every Venetian who could squeeze into the piazza or see into it from a window or a roof was present to elect Manin the first president of the republic. First there was a solemn service in the basilica, and then the patriarch, coming outside, blessed the flags on the three tall poles before the church where for centuries had flown the banners of the captured Kingdoms of Cyprus, Crete and the Peloponnesus. On this day, in the center was the tricolor of the new republic and on either side banners of its fellow republics of the United States and France. Then Mengaldo, the commander of the Civic Guard, read out Manin's name, and the sovereign people of Venice, in full assembly and by acclamation, elected Manin to be president of the republic.

Their act was not simply a return to the past. The new republic was different from the old. Sovereignty was no longer in a patrician class but in all the people. One of the doctrines which French revolutionaries had carried into Italy fifty years before, the one which above all others Metternich had opposed, the democratic Venetians now adopted so easily and confidently that they hardly recognized the magnitude of the innovation.

News of the students' revolts in Vienna had reached Venice on 16 March; it reached Milan the next day, again first in the form of rumors. Throughout the evening in the most intense excitement men gathered in the streets and cafés to discuss the latest reports and to debate their action on the morrow. And in the end the course of their revolution was so different from that of the Venetians, though each in its way was extremely honorable, that a comparison raises in the most dramatic fashion one of history's great imponderables: the importance in the shaping of an event of the conditions surrounding it and, even more, of the personalities of the men involved.

In Milan there was no single leader, such as Manin, with the power to bring an entire city to support his policy. Instead there were two groups: one of young republicans who wished to throw out the Austrians and to proclaim a republic as the first step in freeing and uniting all of Italy; and the other of more conservative and aristocratic citizens who, while eager enough to be rid of the Austrians, wanted to merge the province of Lombardia into the Kingdom of Sardinia, hoping thereby not only to gain the protection of Carlo Alberto's army but also to avoid the perils of an untried and perhaps radical republican government. The leader of this group was the mayor of the city, Conte Gabrio Casati, whose sister Teresa had been the wife of the Carbonaro martyr, Confalonieri. The man who emerged, after a few days, as the leader of the republicans was Carlo Cattaneo, a well-known and respected professor at the University.

Cattaneo, however, was a republican with a difference. Unlike Mazzini he feared that unity for Italy, whether under a king or a republican assembly, was impossible because of the differences in law, language and custom of the various Italian peoples, and he favored, instead, a confederation of the existing Italian states. This federalist doctrine would divide him from many republicans after the fighting was over and, during it, would give him a double reason for opposing any merger of Lombardia with the Kingdom of Sardinia.

On the Austrian side, against Casati and Cattaneo, were Graf O'Donell, an Irishman in the service of the Habsburgs, who represented Austrian civil rule in Milan, and, representing the military, Field Marshal Graf Radetzky, the commander-in-chief of all the Austrian troops in Italy. O'Donell was an average man; Radetzky, an extraordinary one. Like Marinovich in Venice, he was a superb military administrator, but he had also the ability to make his men love him. He had passed his entire life in the Habsburg army, surviving seventeen campaigns, seven wounds and nine horses shot under him, and in 1813, as the Habsburg chief of staff, he had contributed to Napoleon's defeat at Leipzig. He was now eighty-one, still in splendid physical condition, a hard worker, a bold horseman and the father of a two-year-old illegitimate child. With his jovial face, white hair and handlebar mustache, he was, to men and officers alike, "Vater Radetzky" and the model of a professional soldier. Under him any revolution in Milan was certain to be bloody. His motto, often quoted, was said to be: "Three days of bloodshed secure thirty years of peace."

The revolution known as "Le Cinque Giornate" or "The Five Days," so glorious in the history of Milan, began on the morning of 18 March. The Austrian vice-governor, O'Donell, in an effort to minimize the demonstrations which he knew were forming, posted notices that Emperor Ferdinand was conceding representative government. At the same time he drafted a message to Radetzky, who had his headquarters in the Castello Sforzesco on the northwest edge of the city, asking for troops to occupy all its principal points. But before sending the message he consulted with the mayor, Casati, who advised against it on the ground that, as the Tobacco Riots had demonstrated, the appearance of troops would incite disorder. O'Donell was persuaded and substituted a message to Radetzky not to interfere with the demonstrations unless specifically asked. So the morning passed with the Milanesi, stimulated by the young republicans, gathering into a huge crowd in the Piazza del Duomo, and O'Donell and his staff, in the Palazzo del Governo on the east side of the city, growing increasingly nervous.

Shortly after noon the crowd, led by young republicans, left the piazza and surged toward the Broletto or City Hall, where it began to shout for the mayor and various reforms such as a free press and a Civic Guard.

The demonstration was far larger and more violent than any Casati had anticipated, and he was soon forced to choose between putting himself at its head and having some control over it or losing control of it altogether. He chose to lead it, and soon he and a tricolor flag were at the head of a demonstration of fifteen or twenty thousand Milanesi marching in ranks on the Palazzo del Governo to demand reforms. Church bells rang, women on the balconies and from windows waved their handkerchiefs and those men were not already in the streets rushed out to join the marchers. A few openly carried guns. Before the palazzo the Croat sentries challenged the leading ranks and, when they refused to halt, fired. The sentries were immediately killed, and their deaths turned the demonstration into a mob. The people broke into the palazzo and began to sack it. All the repressed indignation of the Tobacco Riots and a month of martial law broke out, and men smashed and shattered windows, mirrors and furniture merely to satiate their fury. Casati and a few others tried to stop the destruction and to reimpose some order, but in vain. Like a tide leaving debris in its wake, the mob flowed from room to room until it reached the Council Chamber where only one Austrian remained, O'Donell. Only hours earlier, on Casati's advice, he had not surrounded himself with troops. Now the two men, according to another present, "looked at each other with mutual uncertainty." O'Donell murmured, "Oh, Signor Conte!", and "Casati's answer . . . a sigh."

Then after much shouting and bullying, in which Casati took no part, a group of young republican leaders forced O'Donell to agree to a threefold decree by which a Civic Guard was to be authorized, police authority was to be transferred from the viceroy to the mayor and the existing police were to be disarmed. They took him to a window in order that the huge crowd in the street below could see him sign the decree. As he did so, he shouted out, "This signature is obtained under pressure." No one cared.

Thereafter O'Donell was Casati's prisoner, and Austrian civil authority in Milan was at an end. The military authority remained, and the Milanesi and Radetzky simultaneously went to war. Austrian soldiers appeared in the streets so fast that Casati was unable even to return to the Broletto and had to set up his headquarters in a private house.

The odds in a revolution greatly favored Radetzky. He had inside the city's walls a garrison of about twelve thousand men and thirty field guns and outside, the entire Austrian army in Italy. To oppose Radetzky the Milanesi had the city's population of 156,000, no trained soldiers and only about 650 firearms. Yet, united in their hatred of the Austrians, they did not hesitate.

Barricades began to go up at once. The city then had fewer open areas than today. The piazzas in front of both the Duomo and La Scala were

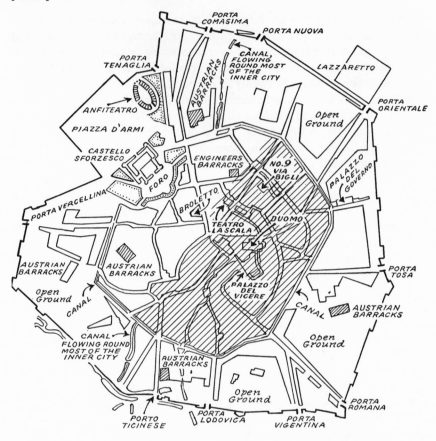

**MILAN** during the Cinque Giornate, 18-22 March 1848.
////////The lined area represents what the Milanesi
////////, controlled by the third day.

No.9 Via Bigli is where Carlo Cattaneo established
"The Central Committee of the Insurrection" on
the second day.

partially filled with houses; there was no gallery or street running directly from the Duomo to La Scala and no street like today's Via Dante running from the Castello to the Duomo at the center of the city. And most of the streets were only six or eight feet wide with tall buildings on either side. Soldiers trapped in such canyons with barricades before and behind would have a difficult time escaping.

The first day, 18 March, the barricades were not very successful, and every Austrian unit succeeded in reaching its post. But the Milanesi quickly learned how to make the barricades stronger, and on 19 March some seven hundred went up; at the end of the Cinque Giornate there were nearly seventeen hundred, in what was still a small city. In one stretch of a hundred yards there were five. Cesare Cantù, who published one of the first reports of the fighting, described how they differed from street to street and reflected the social conditions of the various parts of the city.

> In the rich quarters they used carriages, expensive furniture, elegant sofas, beds, mirrors; in the business quarters, barrels, bales of cloth, pumps, packing cases; in the poor quarters, the lowly broom, hen coops, small tables, anvils, benches; near the churches, pews, pulpits, confessionals; near the seminaries, straw pallets and mattresses that the clergy themselves piled up; near the schools, desks and benches; near the theaters, machinery, thrones, crowns, sham trees and sham giants; at the post office and under the archives, bastions of stamped paper and documents; wherever possible trees or shrubs were felled across the openings; here you will see models of statues and even funeral monuments; there, pitchforks, the pillory and equipment of the executioner; then the whole was completed with faggots, shutters, doors, paving stones, beer bottles and dirt.[35]

One of the most famous of all, built by seminarians, was about three yards high and built entirely of granite slabs from the sidewalk. It could resist any small-arms fire and, except for a continuous pounding, was impervious to the field guns.

At first the Milanesi had nothing but bottles, tiles and paving stones to throw down on the Croats. But two aristocrats with collections of weapons, many of them priceless, offered them to fighting men, and soon ancient fowling pieces, decorated swords and even halberts appeared on the barricades. Others, meanwhile, dug up caches of arms and ammunition saved for when this day should finally come, and chemists began, with remarkable success, to make gunpowder. Occasionally, but rarely, some arms and munitions would be captured.

By the end of the second day Radetzky was having trouble holding the center of the city. He had sent a detachment of Tyrolean sharpshooters to the roof of the Duomo and, firing between the Gothic pinnacles, they had greatly interfered with movements of the Milanesi below. But he was unable to keep them supplied with food and ammunition, and after about twenty-four hours on the roof they had to come down and fight their way back to the Castello. Thereafter from the hand of a statue of the Madonna at the top of the Duomo there fluttered a little tricolor flag. And another detachment of Austrians, in trying to clear a street, took the first two barricades easily, the third with difficulty and was repulsed at the fourth by a continuous hail of paving stones. At this point it had to retire for fresh troops and ammunition with nothing of real purpose accomplished, for what were three barricades out of 1700?

So during the end of the second day Radetzky evacuated the center of the city. "The nature of these people," he wrote to his daughter, "has been transformed as if by the touch of a magic wand; fanaticism has invaded all ages, all classes and both sexes." But he was still confident that he could quell the revolt. He held the Castello, various barracks in the city and, most important, the walls and gates, so that no food had entered the city in forty-eight hours. He knew that soon the Milanesi would begin to starve.

They feared it, too, and redoubled their efforts to win quickly, attacking and capturing the Austrian barracks one at a time. At the Genio or Engineers' Barracks they succeeded with the help of an old man, a cripple named Pasquale Sottocornola, who had first thrown some resin on the wooden doors and then, with a torch of burning straw had hopped and skipped a second time across the open street to ignite them. But even so the city was not opened to the outside.

On the fourth day the foreign consuls who were still in the city tried to arrange for an armistice, and Radetzky agreed to it. Casati and many of the more conservative Milanesi favored it, if only to allow time for Carlo Alberto to mobilize his army and come to the city's aid. A messenger had been sent to Turin on the first day, but he had not yet returned. Cattaneo and his young republicans, however, whose headquarters can still be seen at No. 9 on Via Bigli, refused any kind of terms and went ahead with their plans to capture one of the gates. Fortunately, the potential division between conservatives and republicans was smoothed over when one of Carlo Alberto's aides, who had spent eighteen hours trying to get through the Austrian cordon around the city without being arrested, finally succeeded and reported that Carlo Alberto would come if given some sort of public invitation or excuse for crossing the border. Casati then printed a proclamation and attached copies to hundreds of balloons which were released to float high over the walls and out. "The city of Milan, in order to complete its victory and to drive the common enemy of Italy beyond the Alps forever, asks for the aid of all Italian peoples and princes and especially that of neighboring and warlike Piedmont."

The republicans disliked the specific appeal to Carlo Alberto, and Cattaneo snapped at Casati's supporters, "Can't you bear to be your own masters even for once in your lives?" In his proclamations to the fighters on the barricades he stressed constantly the Mazzinian ideal of Italy and its people rather than its princes and, in the circumstances, his hostility to the House of Savoy was particularly noticeable.

But the knowledge that Carlo Alberto would come and the sight of the proclamations Casati posted in anticipation welcoming the Piemontesi undoubtedly cheered many faint hearts and strengthened all for a final effort to break through Radetzky's hold on the gates and walls. After testing the defense at several of the gates the decision fell on the Porta Tosa on the east side of the city. The attack was led by a young man, Luciano Manara, who came from a well-known family and who had distinguished himself in the fighting. He was aided by a former professor of military science in the Napoleonic regime who designed moving barricades of large rollers formed of fagots bound with ropes. All the city's artillery, two tiny cannon and three large flintlock guns, were concentrated against the gate, and the best sharpshooters were put in the building and streets close to it. The attack started in the early evening. Manara and his men advanced in two columns and finally succeeded in reaching the gate and setting it afire. Then it was retaken by the Austrians, who tried to douse the flames; then again by the Milanesi who rekindled them. Finally the Austrians retired onto the walls, firing laterally into the crowd that poured excitedly into the street. Houses near the gate were now afire and flames crackled into the sky. The excitement of the scene was intensified by the shouts of victory, yells of defiance and moaning of the wounded, and soon by the light of the burning gate the Milanesi could see the road beyond it, leading out to the open country. They had burst through the cordon.

That night Radetzky decided to abandon the city and retreat with all his men into the Quadrilateral, a strong area bounded at its corners by the four fortress-cities of Peschiera, Mantua, Verona and Legnago. The reports he had from Venice and almost every other city of any size in the Po valley were all bad. Some of the cities had risen and thrown out their small Austrian garrisons, and in his rear Carlo Alberto was about to cross the Ticino river and lead his army to Milan. And in Vienna the emperor's government seemed tottering and perhaps had already fallen. If he retreated, he could gather his scattered forces and fight another day; if he remained, he might be defeated piecemeal. So he retreated, and in good order. A week later, on 2 April, he established his headquarters in Verona, and in the course of his Order of the Day he said to his men, "It is I, not you, who have retired before the enemy. *You* have not been defeated and you will not be."

The Milanesi, however, in their jubilation considered him defeated, or almost so. They were justifiably proud. The Cinque Giornate still rank in history as one of the most successful instances of street-fighting. They had succeeded because every man, woman and child of them, whether rich or poor, priest or politician, royalist or republican, had determined, once the fighting began, to drive the Austrians out or die. The humiliation of being a subject people had eaten into every heart, and perhaps what meant most to them was the remark of one of Radetzky's officers who had come on the third day with an offer of truce. As he had left the Milanese headquarters on the Via Bigli, with the offer refused, he had said, *"Addio brava e valorosa gente."*—"Farewell, brave and valiant people." "And this," observed Cattaneo, "was the first time for thirty-four years that we heard one of our oppressors pay this well-deserved tribute to our people."

# CHAPTER 26

Sardinia declares war. *L'Italia farà da sè*. Pastrengo. Carlo Alberto. Political confusion. The Allocution. The problems facing the Papacy. The Sardinian army. Carlo Alberto's military and political decisions. The battle of Custoza. Carlo Alberto in Milan. The armistice.

CARLO ALBERTO declared war against Austria on 24 March, the day after Radetzky abandoned Milan, and the next day troops of the Sardinian army began to cross the Ticino river into Lombardia. In his proclamation to the peoples of Lombardo-Veneto the king declared: "We will support your just desires, trusting in the aid of that God who is visibly with us, of that God who has given Pio IX to Italy, of that God who, with such marvelous impulses, enables Italy to work out her own salvation." The final phrase, *pose l'Italia in grado di fare da sè,* was one he had used on occasion before in various forms, and in Turin was generally shortened to *L'Italia farà da sè,* or "Italy will make itself." Now, as the proclamation was read and studied all over Italy, the phrase in its shortened form became the popular expression of Italian hopes in 1848.

In it was all the pride of Italian patriots everywhere at the success of the Milanesi and Venetians in expelling the Austrians unaided, and also, of course, the suggestion that Italians of other cities would soon do as well. But the phrase was more than a war cry or even a summation of an emerging sense of nationality and unity; it was also a statement of policy for the future. Italians of all political persuasions remembered that with the French revolutionary armies had come not only freedom but tyranny, and many now hoped that if Italy could free itself without French aid, it might avoid French tyranny. *L'Italia farà da sè,* therefore, proposed a policy on which men who were usually opposed could agree. Carlo Alberto, the other princes and monarchists throughout the peninsula, despite Lamartine's soft-spoken manifesto, suspected the intentions of the French republicans; Mazzini and his followers had always preached that Italians must regenerate themselves and not look to France for help; and Pio Nono and the Church equated a republican France with an anticlerical France. All these and their supporters now found, or thought they found, a policy in common and felt more united than ever before.

In every state the people urged and even forced their princes to follow Carlo Alberto's lead. The grand duke, Leopoldo II, although a Habsburg, issued a stirring proclamation in which he reminded Tuscans that the holy cause of Italian independence would be decided on the fields of Lombardia. Ferdinando in Naples, who since January had been a constitutional king, proclaimed that "it is the duty of every prince and people in the peninsula to hasten to take part in the struggle." Pio Nono did not declare war, but he allowed recruiting of a volunteer force to defend his borders, and he sent a papal legate to Carlo Alberto's headquarters in the field, a fact which, when it became known, created a sensation. Duke Carlo II of Parma, forced by his people to form a provisional government, proclaimed his state to be under the protection of Carlo Alberto "who might regard it as one of the other Italian states which were cooperating in the great work of the independence of Italy." And the Modenesi, abandoned by Duke Francesco V who chose to retreat with the Austrians, formed a provisional government which recruited a regiment to represent Modena with Carlo Alberto's army. As one Italian state after another began to mobilize its troops and to recruit volunteers, the possibility of success without aid, of defeating Radetzky in the field and of forcing concessions from Vienna, seemed both real and imminent, particularly as the first reports from the front were of victories.

The first battle was fought on 8 April at Goito, near Mantua, for control of a bridge across the Mincio river. By one of history's extraordinary coincidences the young artillery lieutenant, Celestino Corte, who ordered the first round of artillery fired in this first battle of the Risorgimento was, twenty-two years later at the taking of Rome in 1870, the general who ordered the last rounds fired in the last battle. Also at Goito the corps of Bersaglieri, founded in 1836 and famous for its maneuvers on the double and for its cock-feather plumes, fought its first battle and founded its reputation for valor.

News of the victory at Goito increased, if it were possible, the excitement among Italians everywhere. But "crossing the Mincio" sounded to nonmilitary ears more important than it was. The river, which was the boundary between Lombardia and the Veneto, was also the western edge of the Quadrilateral and crossing it suggested to excited Italians that Radetzky's defenses were shaken. But Peschiera and Mantua, the fortified cities at either end of the Mincio line, had not been captured and both could withstand a siege for months.

More important than the Mincio was the Adige river which, flowing through Verona and Legnago, formed the eastern edge of the Quadrilateral.

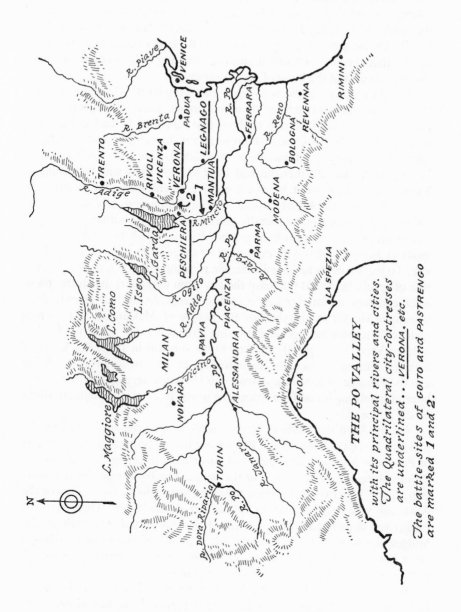

N

THE PO VALLEY

with its principal rivers and cities.
The Quadrilateral city-fortresses
are underlined...VERONA, etc.

The battle-sites of GOITO and PASTRENGO
are marked 1 and 2.

The Mincio was merely the outlet for Lago di Garda and, starting at Peschiera, was relatively short. The Adige, on the other hand, rose miles to the north and its valley led directly to the Brenner Pass, which at 4490 feet was the lowest across the Alps. As long as Radetzky controlled this valley, the traditional route for German invaders entering Italy, he could maintain his army forever in the heart of the Po valley.

For the moment he did not wish to risk a big battle. He had lost nearly twenty thousand of his seventy thousand troops, mostly through the desertion of Italian conscripts, and of those that remained he had to keep half in the garrisons of the Quadrilateral forts; for the field, he had an army of only about twenty-five thousand with which to face the Sardinian army of sixty thousand. Further, he had little idea of what was happening in Vienna or of how soon he might receive re-enforcements, whereas he suspected that Carlo Alberto would soon have thousands of volunteers and unlimited supplies from a friendly countryside. So he withdrew from the line of the Mincio to a position nearer Verona, which he made his headquarters and protected with every sort of defense his engineers could devise. To the Veronesi he issued a laconic proclamation that, on the slightest sign of revolt, he would bombard the city from every fort and turret on its walls and turn its interior into a rubbish heap. As he had already done something similar in slaughtering the people of Melegnano and burning their town to prevent a general uprising along his route of retreat, and as holding Verona was plainly the key to his survival in Italy, the Veronesi believed him and reluctantly remained quiet. Meanwhile, Carlo Alberto and the Piemontesi tested the defenses and began a siege of Peschiera in the hope of capturing it and then being able to cut Radetzky's communications up the Adige valley.

On 30 April the battle of Pastrengo developed out of clashes on the previous two days between the Piemontesi troops protecting the besiegers of Peschiera from a flank attack and Austrians protecting their communications along the western bank of the Adige. The battle once joined, however, Carlo Alberto put fourteen thousand men into it, too many for the Austrians who were forced to retreat across the river. Thereafter the Piemontesi controlled the west bank of the Adige and, although all the bridges had been destroyed, presumably soon would cross and cut Radetzky's line to Austria. Pastrengo, in which volunteers from Parma took part, was an important victory for the Italian forces.

It was also rewarding for Carlo Alberto personally. He and his escort had ridden into an ambush of some forty Austrian riflemen, and under the first shock of the firing a number of his escort's horses had bolted, carrying the men away from the king. He, however, had drawn his sword and with those who were left had charged and routed the Austrians, causing some of his own troops who had seen the small engagement from a neighboring hill to break out into loud cheers.

This first month of the war was probably one of the happiest in the king's life. His own troops responded warmly to his presence, for the loyalties of the feudal age still had some meaning in many parts of Piedmont and Savoy, and the men from those provinces fought better when he or one of his sons were with them. For a king like Carlo Alberto who had a strong sense of position the fact was gratifying. But even more so, because projected on a wider stage, was the fact of proving himself to Italians generally. He, as well as they, had never forgotten the equivocal part he had played in the liberal movement of 1821. Now, after years of holding himself in, even of deceit, he was risking, as he had promised d'Azeglio he would, his life, his sword, his army and his dynasty for the Italian cause. Both his sons, Vittorio Emanuele and Ferdinando, were showing themselves to be courageous and good leaders, and the House of Savoy, for which he cared passionately, was publicly earning the right to be the first family of Italy. He had always believed that he was born to free and unite Italy at the cost of his own life and now the moment of his destiny seemed to have come. He and the sons who would succeed him were ready for it and, although he continued to be solitary and impassive, he was visibly happy.

But the better the military side of the war seemed to go, the worse seemed the political confusion behind the lines. And to this the vagueness of *L'Italia farà da sè* contributed. Above the noise of the military bands and cheering crowds, as the volunteers marched off to train and to fight, there was the sound of argument, bitter and divisive, among the political leaders of the various states and towns. And everywhere, although in different guise, the same fundamental question arose: after the Austrians were driven out, what sort of political community would emerge in northern Italy?

Carlo Alberto, of course, had assumed, in entering the war, that he would emerge as king of some new and larger Italian kingdom, and to show that he had a larger purpose in mind than the mere expansion of his Kingdom of Sardinia he had stated in his proclamation to the people of Lombardo-Veneto: "In order still better to show by outward signs the sentiment of Italian union, it is our will that our troops entering the territory of Lombardo-Veneto bear the shield of Savoy superimposed on the tricolor Italian flag." It was something to give up the traditional blue and white of Savoy for Italian red, white and green, but his gesture was not altogether successful. Many continued to be suspicious of the House of Savoy, and when on the battlefields the Piemontesi troops cried, as they had for centuries, "Sempre avanti Savoja," "Always forward Savoy," the cry did not reassure those others about to die that their sacrifice was, after all, for a united Italy, not merely for an expanding Savoy.

The activities of the republicans, on the other hand, did nothing to reassure Carlo Alberto and the Piemontesi that they were not being used merely as a cat's paw to pull republican chestnuts out of the Austrian fire. The declaration of a republic at Venice, from the Piemontese point of view, was unfortunate but, considering the city's history and the fact that the declaration occurred before Sardinia had declared war on Austria, it could at least be understood. Far less easy to understand and more like a betrayal was the reluctance of the Milanesi to declare their city, and with it the province of Lombardia, annexed to the Kingdom of Sardinia.

But the republicans in Milan at the moment were very strong. They had taken the lead in the street-fighting and distinguished themselves; they could talk of merger, sooner or later, with the Venetian Republic and, in spite of Lamartine's manifesto, of aid from France. Mazzini had arrived in the city within days after the Austrians had left and had immediately founded a newspaper, *Italia del popolo,* and a political club. If he was against aid from France, he was even more against handing Lombardia over to Carlo Alberto. And along with Mazzini hundreds of exiles, mostly republicans, returned to the city in state of intense excitement and hoping now, at last, to transform their ideas into an Italy, united, free and republican.

The republicans, however, could not achieve any unity even among themselves. Some, led by Mazzini, were unitarians; they wanted an Italy of a single state with a single parliament. Others, led by Cattaneo, who had directed the street-fighting, were federalists and wanted a United States of Italy. The division between the two factions became increasingly bitter. Together they were strong enough for a time to prevent the provisional government of Milan voting to merge the city and Lombardia into the Kingdom of Sardinia, but separately neither had the strength to force a declaration of the kind of republic it favored.

And further, the choice was not merely between those favoring immediate fusion with Sardinia, probably the majority, and the republicans, the noisy, powerful minority. There was also the priest Gioberti with his plan for a federation of Italian states under the pope as president. He had begun a tour of chief cities in northern Italy and everywhere was drawing enormous crowds. Clearly many north Italians wanted to hold up any decisions until Gioberti could confer with Pio Nono and declare what could be arranged. But to Carlo Alberto and the Piemontesi, who were in the war partly at the request of the Milanesi and who had already cleared Lombardia of all Austrian troops, the political maneuvering and indecision was infuriating. It was also dangerous. If the war was to be won, it had to be won quickly, before Radetzky received supplies and re-enforcements. But speed required a unity of purpose, unity to strengthen the fainthearted, to bind the weak together and to take advantage of the heroism of the brave. But of unity there was none, and the possibility of achieving it greatly lessened in the last days of April when Pio Nono, the liberal pope, dramatically parted company with the liberal movement.

He did so at Rome on 29 April in an allocution addressed to the cardinals in consistory. His words, however, were addressed to Catholics everywhere and were immediately published, read, analyzed and discussed all over Europe. They made the Austrians jubilant, and most Italians, depending on their religious and political convictions, saddened, infuriated, embarrassed or simply strengthened in the republican prejudice that there was no help for Italy in the Papacy.

The issue, once again, was the conflict between the pope's spiritual and temporal power, raised by the war in the most dramatic fashion. The immediate question was whether Pio Nono, as one of the princes of Italy, would accede to his people's wish and join the other princes in a war on Austria. And behind that lay the general question of what sort of a political community would emerge in northern Italy and, depending on the answer, what would happen to the Legations?

The immediate question, whether to declare war on Austria, came to a head in the last weeks of April when the pope's army of seven thousand regulars and about nine thousand volunteers was kidnapped by its officers and led into the war. The officers were, in several instances, Piemontesi lent to Pio Nono by Carlo Alberto or, where not, were at least men in sympathy with the military tradition of Piedmont and eager to fight the Austrians. The pope's orders, approved by his cabinet under the new constitution, had been for the army to march to the state's northern border on the Po, to defend it if attacked and to await further orders. But long before reaching the Po many of the men and officers talked of crossing it to join the fighting; others, however, insisted that the pope must first declare war so that if they were captured, they could not be shot as bandits.

To excite these waverers the commanding general, a Piemontese named Giovanni Durando, issued a number of stirring orders of the day of which one, written by Massimo d'Azeglio, appeared on 5 April and had an enormous effect. The language was passionate and the meaning, extreme. Pio Nono was portrayed as ordering and blessing a holy war against the Austrians who are "the enemies of God and of Italy." It even implied that he would excommunicate the Austrians, for "such a war is not merely national but highly Christian." And in his final paragraph, d'Azeglio, speaking through Durando and deliberately confusing the temporal and spiritual powers of the pope just as the republicans accused the pope of doing, turned the war into a crusade:

> Soldiers! It is only right and I have made it an order that while march-ing to this war we should all be adorned with the cross of Christ. All those who belong to the Corps of Operations will wear it on their breasts, in form similar to that which they will see on mine. With it and in it we shall be conquerors—as were our fathers. Let our war-cry be: *God wills it!* [36]

D'Azeglio was smugly pleased with his Order of the Day, particularly when a few weeks later the Papal troops, including an excellent Swiss Bri-gade, crossed the river and joined the war. But with a little more patience and a little less eloquence he and Durando might have won the small army for Carlo Alberto on terms which would not have required Pio Nono to repudiate them. Pio Nono, for example, was perfectly willing to have his subjects fight under Carlo Alberto as "volunteers," but no pope, however liberal or patriotic, could allow others to preach a crusade in his name and threaten excommunication of the entire Austrian army. Even forty years earlier under greater provocation Pius VII had excommunicated only Napoleon, an individual, not his army. Pio Nono's answer to the world, made with an eye to preserving the unity of the Church and of preventing an Austrian schism, formed the central part of his allocution:

> Although some persons now desire that We, together with the other peoples and Princes of Italy, make war against the Austrians, We deem it proper to disclose clearly in this solemn meeting of ours, that it is wholly foreign to Our intentions, since We, however, unworthy, exer-cise on earth the functions of Him who is the author of peace and lover of concord, and according to the office of Our Supreme Aposto-late, We seek after and embrace all races, peoples and nations with an equal devotion of paternal love.[37]

It is hard today to imagine what else Pio Nono might have said or done. As one of his lay ministers, Marco Minghetti, observed, "This case drew forth the very breath of his Catholic soul." Yet such was the warlike fever of the time that in Rome demonstrations in his favor stopped at once, and overnight he passed from the most popular pope within memory to the most despised. The fear that friends or relatives at the front would, if captured, be shot as bandits provided much of the emotion which lay under the Romans' anger, but there was also the more abstract question: how could Pio Nono claim to be an important Prince of Italy with a large state and many subjects and yet claim that he did not have the right to declare war against the common enemy? It was a question that the simplest Roman could ask and which Pio Nono, when asked, had the greatest difficulty answering. When delegates from the governments of Venice, Milan and Sicily came to the Palazzo del Quirinale to urge Pio Nono to reconsider and declare war, he was reduced to exclaiming in the greatest frustration: "I am more Italian than you are, but you *will* not make the distinction in me between the Italian and the Pontiff."

They would not, perhaps because it did not suit them, and neither would he, perhaps for much the same reason. Four days after the allocution Pio Nono wrote a private, autograph letter to Emperor Ferdinand in which he said:

> Thus We trust that the nation (Austria) itself, worthily proud of its nationality, will not stake its honor in sanguinary attempts against the Italian nation, but will rather find its honor in nobly recognizing the latter as a sister, as both are Our daughters and very dear to Our heart, agreeing to occupy each its natural boundaries on honorable terms, and with the Lord's blessing.[38]

Ferdinand referred the letter to his ministers with the remark: "Austria possesses her Italian provinces by virtue of the same treaties which have reconstituted the temporal power of the pope." In Habsburg eyes the Papal States had no more "divine right" to be than any other petty duchy re-established by the treaties of Vienna, and the remark expressed exactly the theory of Austrian policy in Italy, adherence to the treaties. It cut through the fuzzy good intentions of the pope and showed that Ferdinand, like Metternich, had thought harder about the problem of Italy than had Pio Nono.

Short of something as wide as the English Channel there are no natural boundaries; only boundaries which are observed or violated as the neighbors consider in their interest. Both the Papacy and the Habsburg's Austrian Empire were based on ideas supposedly transcending differences of language, culture or climate. Neither could allow its north Italian subjects to form or join an independent state on a national basis with "natural" boundaries without by implication conceding the same right to all its other restive subjects and so preparing to pass out of existence.

For the Habsburgs there was not only the principle of the old Holy Roman Empire binding diverse nations together, there was also the very practical problem that the Italian provinces, the Kingdom of Lombardo-Veneto, while containing only one-sixth of the population of the Austrian Empire, provided one-third of its wealth. This, Austria was not prepared to give up. In the same way, by far the richest part of the Papal States, the area from Pesaro to Bologna, was north of the Apennines, a "natural" boundary, and in the Po valley. The loss of it would mean not only a severe blow to the Papal finances but, most probably, increased dependence on some outside power for whatever remained of the Papal States.

This was what Metternich had meant when he had said that a liberal pope was not a possibility. Liberalism in Italy, whether championed by a constitutional monarchist or a republican, had come to mean, at very least in northern Italy, some form of Italian unity, whether by conquest or merger. A pope could be liberal only if he was prepared to have his temporal power greatly reduced if not actually extinguished. No pope had yet been prepared to go that far, and Pio Nono by his allocution declared to the world that he was not.

It is probable also that Pio Nono, like his predecessors, believed that the Papal States were literally a gift of God to his Church, the Patrimony of St. Peter, and that to alienate any part of them would be a sin. He had been educated and surrounded all his life by priests who believed it, and except for a trip to Chile with a cardinal in 1823 he had never been outside of central Italy. In spite of his exalted position he was a simple man, and one Italian historian, Ernesto Masi, in speaking of his mind stated harshly that it was "the mind of the poor country curate." More moderately, one of his ministers who was also a historian, Luigi Carlo Farini, wrote of him and his feelings about the Papal States:

> Though a kindly man and a benevolent prince, as a Pontiff Pio IX was strictly uncompromising. His soul was not only pious but mystic. He referred everything to God, and he respected and venerated his own person as the Vicar of God. He believed that he must guard jealously the temporal sovereignty of the Church because he regarded it as indispensable to the custody and apostolate of the faith.[39]

As a liberal pope, therefore, Pio Nono might introduce court reform, better housing or start a program of public works, but he could not allow his subjects any real political power, for they might use it to merge the Papal States into some larger secular community. After 15 March, when he had granted a constitution and some real political power to his subjects, the vision of such a sacrilege began to haunt him.

In the first part of the allocution he had traced the history of the reform movement from its earliest days and spoke of how in the time of Pius VII, during the Congress of Vienna, the great powers had urged reforms on the Papacy and then how later, after the revolutions of 1831, their ambassadors at Rome had submitted a memorandum to Gregory XVI urging him to allow a consulting assembly to meet at Rome, to allow more self-government in the other Papal cities, to set up provincial councils and to allow laymen to serve in the government. All these things Pio Nono had done and now recited with approval, but significantly he said nothing about the constitution. To the politically minded of his lay subjects the implication was clear: he did not consider it a proper reform and presumably would work either to restrict it by amendments and qualifications or to repeal it altogether. And they were strengthened in this belief by the last part of the allocution in which he denied any part in a proposal to make Italy a united republic under his presidency and urged all Italians, not merely his own subjects, to reject such ideas and to continue loyal to their princes. In sum, the allocution was not only a refusal on the pope's part to declare war, it seemed also to be an appeal to Italians of other states to give up the war for independence and unity and to accept the settlement of the Congress of Vienna, improved as it might be by reforms and methods that stopped short of war.

It was not a popular message, and the many who disliked it at once identified Pio Nono with another pope, Celestine V, who in 1294 had resigned his office and, in a famous line, was characterized by Dante as the one "who from cowardice made the great refusal," *il gran rifiuto*. Dante's word for cowardice was *viltà* and implies the littleness of soul or meanness of nature by which a man refuses his calling and fails his destiny. With the allocution, *"il gran rifiuto"* to the liberals, Pio Nono lost completely and forever his position as moral leader of the Risorgimento.

If the Papacy had been a purely local church, like the Church of England, Pio Nono, given time, might have been able to work out some sort of imaginative adjustment to an emerging national state in Italy. But its success as a world church in the minds of men over the centuries hindered any such adjustment. The pope, as Pio Nono stated, was the father of all Christians and all his children were citizens of the Holy City. There all had a right to come, all were equally loved and made welcome, and all could share equally in the spiritual refreshments of their eternal home on earth. In a divided, harassed world it was a powerful idea. Catholics from all over the world were ready to come to Rome in order to fight the Italians to preserve it. Rome, in the opinion of most Catholics in 1848, was not an Italian city.

Nor were the Romans considered to be like other Italians. As late as 1866 John Henry Newman, later made a cardinal by Pio Nono's successor, could say of the Romans in a sermon: ". . . but, if once they were joined to the Kingdom of Italy, they would at length find what it is to attain temporal greatness. The words of Samuel to the Israelites would be fulfilled in them to the letter. Heavy taxes would be laid on them; their children would be torn from them for the army; and they would incur the other penalties of an ambition which prefers to have a share in a political adventure to being at the head of Catholic citizenship. . . ." Many Romans, however, did not see why they should not be allowed to choose for themselves between Catholic and Italian citizenship, and an increasing number, when given a chance, stated their preference for the latter. By 1870 a majority of Catholics around the world were prepared to have Rome become an Italian city. In 1848 they probably were not, and even if Pio Nono had himself wished to make such an adjustment, possibly his cardinals and the Catholic faithful would have prevented it.

The Romans, however, were so angry over the allocution that, in the three days immediately after it appeared, they conducted what amounted to a revolution although it was neither called nor recognized as such. Yet, in fact, the power structure of the Papal States was radically altered. First, Pio Nono's lay ministers all resigned on the ground that they were a war ministry and could not remain in office without a war policy; next, Pio Nono discovered that he could persuade no one else to form a ministry unless he made some important concessions; and, finally, he made those concessions. They were that the war policy be continued, even without a declaration of war; that the direction of foreign affairs be given to a layman; and that henceforth there be two foreign ministers, one for lay and one for ecclesiastical matters. The last was the most important and the clue to the new minister's policy. He was Conte Terenzio Mamiani della Rovere, a revolutionary who had gone into exile after 1831 and returned only after the amnesty of 1846. He was able and personally fond of the pope, and his plan was to split temporal from spiritual affairs so that the pope as a constitutional prince with little or no power could continue the war, as his ministers dictated, even as the pope as the Supreme Pontiff deplored the war, as his conscience dictated. The plan presupposed, however, that Pio Nono would permanently abdicate his control of the temporal affairs.

At the same time other changes, some formal and some more amorphous, took place at a lower level. The political clubs began to have a greater importance, and the Civic Guard, about nine or ten thousand armed men, began in first one instance and then another to work with the clubs, so that Mamiani governed as much through the clubs as through the regular administration. The Civic Guard, for example, occupied and controlled the city gates, the Castel Sant'Angelo, the powder magazines and the prisons. Gradually over the next three months Pio Nono lost control of his capital city and became more and more isolated.

Meanwhile in the Po valley the war began to go less well. There were many reasons for it, but not of the sort enthusiastic Italians could grasp easily. They saw only Carlo Alberto's numerical superiority and looked for a final victory in May or June. But the Sardinian army had been mobilized with great speed and immediately marched into what was then a foreign country. Many of the men had crossed the Ticino river without full equipment, and the supply corps, suffering itself from sudden expansion, only caught up slowly. And even after it had, still only one man in seven was in any sense a professional soldier. Most were men, registered

by annual class under the Sardinian conscription law, who had been selected by lot, trained for fourteen months and then discharged subject to
recall. Many had not been on active duty for five or six years. In Radetzky's
army, on the other hand, the shortest possible term of service was eight
years and most of the men were career soldiers, thorough professionals.

The same disparity of experience existed between the two officer corps.
In the Sardinian army most of the officers were aristocrats, and for most of
these war was an avocation for which they had received little or no training. Against them was the best officer corps in Europe, recruited from the
military-minded of every nationality, serving for life and with the further
advantage of having maneuvered in the summers over the area in which the
engagements were fought. Among the soldiers courage and enthusiasm
could sometimes make up for lack of training, but among the officers,
where technical knowledge and experience were needed, it could not.

And at the very highest level, Carlo Alberto was not Radetzky's equal.
In the field the king's speculative spirit, the brooding indecision for which
men likened him to Hamlet, was a serious fault. Opportunities were lost
while the king reflected; little victories were seldom exploited into larger
ones, and the primary aim of the war, the destruction of Radetzky's army,
was often lost in the careful weighing, pro and con, of each tactical movement.

Yet throughout May the Italian prospects, on balance, still seemed
good. The allocution, although it added greatly to the political confusion
behind the lines, had little effect on the men who were actually fighting,
and the Papal troops simply transferred their allegiance to Carlo Alberto
and became part of the Sardinian army. In Vienna a fresh revolt had
broken out, and the emperor and his court had fled to Innsbruck. Through
Great Britain Ferdinand offered Lombardia to Sardinia and a form of
home rule to Venice in return for peace. But Carlo Alberto's ministers in
Turin refused to accept these or any other terms as long as there remained
a single Austrian soldier in Italy, and most men still assumed that a complete victory, driving every Austrian out of Italy, was still possible. And
at the end of the month, as if in evidence of it, the Austrian garrison in
one of the Quadrilateral forts, Peschiera, finally surrendered.

Politically, Carlo Alberto was committed, by every sort of public
proclamation and act, to attempt to drive every Austrian out of Italy, and
it is doubtful if his dynasty could have survived, even in Piedmont, betraying that cause. Certainly it could never thereafter have become the ruling
family of a united Italy. But privately he would have liked to accept
Ferdinand's offer, and most of his staff were of the same mind. In a letter
to one of his generals he observed that to ask for more than Lombardia
and the Duchies of Parma and Modena, which could probably be had in

addition, "is rashness, in fact, folly. It is risking the loss, the ruin forever of the Italian cause." Then, characteristically, he added, "But if they want me to risk everything, I have my military honor to the fore, and I will go forward until a bullet enables me to finish with joy a life of ill-chances, entirely consecrated and sacrificed to my country." Where Pio Nono, the banner of the liberal movement, had chosen with great reluctance to leave it when it involved him in a war and seemed to be carrying him further than he wished to go, Carlo Alberto, its sword, with equal reluctance elected to stay with it.

But to those like Carlo Alberto who were actually fighting, the chance of a complete victory, such as the ministers in Turin or the people of Milan and Venice wanted, was plainly decreasing. For one thing the allocution had thrown many priests into a state of confusion and with them, the peasants. The Piemontesi troops had noticed at once, as they had followed Radetzky from Milan to Verona, that while the people in towns had always greeted them with tremendous enthusiasm, the peasants had been apathetic or even hostile, on one occasion even flooding a field to prevent troops from bivouacking. The older peasants remembered the misery and economic depression of the Po valley during the Napoleonic wars and held Carlo Alberto responsible for bringing back bad times; and the younger men, some of whom had spent eight years as conscripts in the Habsburg armies, had a tremendous, almost religious respect for Austrian power. The "Tedesco" was for them the master of masters, and in their cottages a legend was current that the family of the emperor was descended from close relatives of the Madonna. They did not doubt that Radetzky would win the war, and they not only refused to fight him, but, after the allocution, increasingly gave him supplies and information.

Even more important, toward the end of the month an Austrian army of sixteen thousand with food and supplies succeeded in reaching Radetzky at Verona. Executing just the sort of disciplined maneuver at which the Austrian army excelled, it had started in the middle of April from north of Trieste and in six weeks had outmarched and outfought the Papal army as well as several lesser groups of volunteers to cover the 150 miles to Verona intact. Typically, in one engagement several thousand Roman volunteers held up well under twelve hours of artillery and musket fire and then, while retreating, began to go to pieces. The ranks broke up, the men accused their generals of betraying them and some, in disgust, started back for Rome.

What Carlo Alberto needed, as he and his army well knew, was not more volunteers but more trained troops to offset those Radetzky had gained. At the start of the war Carlo Alberto, with his policy of *L'Italia farà da sè,* had hoped that Ferdinando of Naples, who had the only other

Italian army of any size, would send forty thousand troops north. And in Naples the liberal ministry with its increased power under the new constitution compelled Ferdinando to declare war on Austria and to promise the troops. But the Po valley was far from Naples, Ferdinando saw nothing in the war for himself, and the liberals were soon embroiled in their own constitutional problems and the need to reconquer Sicily. By 15 May only fourteen thousand troops under General Pepe, who had led the Carbonaro revolution of 1820, had reached the border of Lombardia, where they had halted while awaiting further orders to cross the Po and join the war. But on that day, in Naples, an extremely confused revolution broke out. Extreme republicans, apparently trying to imitate the Milanesi, set up barricades in the streets and disobeying the orders of their own liberal ministers, refused to take them down or to disperse. They had, in the words of most eyewitnesses, simply "gone mad." Opposed to them was the king's army, and when the republicans shot two royal guards, the street-fighting began. At the end of the day the army was completely victorious, the republicans were fleeing for the country and the incompetent liberal ministry had resigned. Ferdinando was again the government, and one of his first acts was to order the fourteen thousand troops under General Pepe to return to Naples. All but two thousand did, and those General Pepe persuaded to follow him across the Po and to fight for Italy.

For Carlo Alberto the loss of forty thousand or even fourteen thousand trained troops was a major disaster, and the official withdrawal of Naples from the war, following Pio Nono's allocution, made a mockery of *L'Italia farà da sè*. Politically, however, there was a gain in each as the hopes of those actively engaged in the war, whether clerical, republican or monarchist, were forced to concentrate on Sardinia and the House of Savoy. The Duchies of Parma and Modena had voted earlier in May to fuse with Sardinia; now in June Milan and Lombardia did likewise, and, finally, in the first week of July the Venetians in their Assembly agreed to end their republic and to join the others. A new Kingdom of Alta Italia, or of Upper Italy, was proclaimed with Carlo Alberto as its king, and he sent representatives to each of the former capital cities to take over the government. But even now the unity was more apparent than real. None of the difficult political questions had been decided, such as whether Milan or Turin would be the new kingdom's capital, or what powers the king and parliament should have, or what form the constitution should take. All of these, over which men still argued passionately, were merely postponed to a constituent assembly scheduled for the first day of November.

But long before then, before July was over, Radetzky had won the war. Re-enforced and with men and supplies beginning to come in regularly from Austria he was soon in a position to attack Carlo Alberto directly, and in a four-day battle, 22–25 July, known as the battle of Custoza, he defeated the Italians decisively (see map, p. 495).

For a time the issue was not clear, and as late as the third day a Piemontese counterattack, in which both the king's sons distinguished themselves, seemed about to turn defeat into victory. But by then the superior training and staff work of the Austrians was beginning to count heavily. On the Sardinian side rations and orders often arrived hours late and some men fought continuously, often without water and in ninety-degree heat, while others, because of the confusion, never fought at all. Radetzky, on the other hand, had arranged his reserves so that on the fourth day all the units of his attacking force had rested for at least one day and some were fighting for the first time. Before them the exhausted Italians began to give way.

Thereafter each day Radetzky grew stronger as the Austrians, conscious that at last they were winning, pressed hard after the Sardinian army. At each river after the Mincio, at the Oglio and at the Adda, Carlo Alberto planned to halt and form a defensive line, but the Austrians were always too close and his own men too tired. His staff advised him to retreat through Piacenza and Pavia, both south of Milan, where strong fortifications behind the Po would protect his army, cover Piedmont, and force Radetzky into a long siege, and from a purely military point of view Carlo Alberto agreed with them. But both chivalry and politics, he knew, required that he not desert Milan without a struggle of some sort that would win it terms from Radetzky. So, on the afternoon of 3 August the first Piemontesi troops, worn out and dispirited, began to camp within sight of the city walls. The next morning the first Austrians arrived and, attacking at once, were fought off with difficulty.

Inside the city a fearful hysteria had gradually gripped the people. Giovanni Visconti Venosta, who was there throughout the period, described in his *Memoirs of Youth* how, over the weeks as more and more bad news had come:

> . . . There gradually welled up a vague feeling of discontent. Accusations were made and suspicions cast on one and all. Political discussions daily became more bitter.
>
> Our imaginations, which had become inebriated by so many successes, recalled suddenly to reality, searched for explanations of our reverses in the strangest notions. People began to speak of treason, and to seek for traitors and spies.
>
> Then there arose a disorder of the spirit, a morbid excitement, a strange disposition to deny facts and to accept the suggestions of fancy; in some there began a strange agitation of public opinion which aggravated our disasters, and left long and sorrowful consequences.

A principal cause of suspicion arose out of the rumor that the government and Carlo Alberto had entered upon negotiations for terms of peace which, if accepted, would limit our demands to the Mincio. The facts were different, but the suspicion continued.[40]

Into the very heart of this city, to the Palazzo Greppi on the east side of the Piazza della Scala, Carlo Alberto now moved his headquarters. After the day's fighting outside the Porta Romana he met with his staff in a Council of War to determine what could be done. The determining facts were that the Piemontese artillery ammunition column was on the road to Pavia, that all the musket cartridges available had already been issued, and that there was only enough food for three days. The city itself had little more to offer. A Committee of Defense, composed almost entirely of republicans, had made a brave show of proclamations for defense but, in fact, the Milanesi had accomplished very little except once again to raise hundreds of barricades. This time, however, Radetzky had not twelve thousand but sixty thousand troops and five or six times the number of guns, and the council accordingly voted unanimously to ask for an armistice. Two officers left at once for Austrian headquarters, and by six the next morning temporary terms had been agreed on, preparatory to a more formal armistice, and there remained only the need to explain the terms to the excited and suspicious Milanesi.

The job, which was recognized as difficult, was undertaken by General Bava, who summoned the municipal officers, the Committee of Defense and general staff of the Civic Guard to the Palazzo Greppi and began to expound to them the situation of the army and of the city. At first all went well, but then two of the younger men, members of the Committee of Defense, began to protest and, quickly losing all control, began to shout *"Tradimento"* or "Treason." They rushed from the room and out into the piazza where a large crowd was already gathered and started it shouting abuse at the balcony: *"Tradimento"* and "Death to Carlo Alberto." Bava realized with horror that the king was in the center of the city, cut off from his troops by hundreds of barricades and protected only by a few staff officers.

The crowd quickly turned into a howling mob. It smashed all the Piemontesi carriages, threatened to hold the king prisoner or to kill him and shouted Bava down when he tried to reason with it. Some of them broke into the palazzo and succeeded in penetrating to the king's room. Cantù, the historian, was there and heard them tell Carlo Alberto that his life was in danger.

He received them with the impassiveness of a statue, without a movement of his body or a wrinkle of his brow. And with that hollow voice of his, soft and slow, and by the gestures of his long and flesh-less hands, he intimated to them to remain calm; and to go; that in a few minutes he would send them an answer.[41]

The Milanesi, that day, like the Neapolitans two months earlier, seem temporarily to have gone mad. Earlier in the day, Cantù recorded, a man was shot as a spy simply because he had a musket and cartridges; later Cantù saw a man galloping his horse up and down the streets without saddle or bridle and shrieking *"Tradimento"* to no one in particular. And before the Palazzo Greppi the crowd grew steadily louder and more furious.

Two members of the former provisional government talked with the king and told him that he must either fight or probably be murdered: they could not protect him. Carlo Alberto pointed out the lack of munitions and reminded them that their own mayor had approved the idea of an armistice. But they insisted the Milanesi were burning to fight, and in the end Carlo Alberto agreed to cancel the armistice. When the crowd heard this, it burst into wild cheering, but not a man of it left to face the Austrians; they all thought it more important to keep watch on the king.

Only Bava left, after being badly mauled by the crowd who took a long time to understand that he was leaving to take command of the army. He had suggested to the king that he lead a regiment back into the city to clear the square, but Carlo Alberto had forbidden it on the ground that it would probably start a purposeless civil war in that, long before the troops could take the barricades and reach the square, he and his staff would be dead. Better to keep their word and start fighting.

But, unknown to the little group in the palazzo, the mayor, backed by many of the more sensible citizens, was able to get to Radetzky and to continue the temporary armistice. Inside the palazzo they waited, hour after hour, for the bombardment to begin and listened to the roaring of the crowd. Carlo Alberto had developed a fever and lay down, but at one time the people were so demanding in their shouts for him that Cantù asked him to go out on the balcony.

A sigh more than any other mark of impatience, revealed his state of suffering. He put on his military tunic and buckled his belt, and then stumbled out and grasped hold of the balcony: I was at his side. He began to speak, but his voice gave out; so I asked him to tell me what he wanted to say. But the howling of the people prevented my understanding what he said, even at the trifling distance which sepa-rated his very tall figure from my short one. At that moment a bullet whistled just between us, and, raising his hand with a gesture of com-passion, he stumbled back into his room.[42]

For a short time he talked with Cantù, seeming to feel the need to explain his actions over the past months, but then his eyes filled with tears and he threw himself again on the bed. And Cantù, overcome with pity, left the room.

The mayor, returning from his meeting with Radetzky, managed to make his way back into the palazzo by about nine in the evening and went out on the balcony to announce his news. An officer held a lantern so that the crowd could see the mayor's face and recognize him, but even so he was greeted by shots. In his agitation he could only get out the phrase "I am your mayor" and the single word "capitulation." It was enough for the crowd, which continued the sporadic shooting and began now to collect fuel and gunpowder to blow up the palazzo and actually succeeded in setting the wooden doors on fire.

Before they managed to break in, however, the commanding officer of the Bersaglieri, who had slipped out a back window of the palazzo undetected, led back his men, without becoming involved in a fight, and the moment they appeared in the piazza, the mob faded away and howled from down the side streets. Carlo Alberto then walked away from the palazzo and rejoined his army.

The next morning at 2 A.M. he stood at the Porta Vercellina and watched his army, now scarcely twenty-five thousand men, pour in confusion out of the city. He was the last to leave except for the division under his son, Ferdinando, which remained behind to turn over the city to Radetzky.

The terms of the temporary armistice were a suspension of fighting for three days; the Piemontesi to retire behind the Ticino river within forty-eight hours; the Milanesi to receive generous treatment and all those wishing to leave to do so within twenty-four hours. It is estimated that somewhere between sixty and ninety thousand left the city, going to Piedmont, Switzerland or just simply into the country.

A few days later, on 9 August, a more comprehensive agreement extended the armistice for an additional six weeks. Known as the Salasco armistice, after Carlo Alberto's chief of staff who signed it, it further provided that the Piemontesi were to evacuate Venice, the Duchies of Parma and Modena and to surrender Peschiera. Less than two months before, Carlo Alberto had refused to accept the duchies and Lombardia at the sacrifice of Venice. Now the day after the armistice was signed he issued a proclamation to the people of the defunct Kingdom of Alta Italia in which, after briefly summarizing the campaign, he found it necessary to say:

I am not unaware of the accusations with which some people wish to stain my name; but God and my conscience are witness to the integrity of my intentions. I leave it to impartial history to be their judge.[43]

But he was a proud man and he would not linger on his private grief. The proclamation ends with the ringing assertion: "The cause of Italian independence is not lost."

# CHAPTER 27

The armistice in Venice. Manin as dictator. Military occupation of
Lombardia. Garibaldi in the Alps. His judgment of Carlo Alberto.
The armistice in Piedmont. Republican revolution in Rome. The
murder of Rossi. The Pope flees. Reaction in Naples. Leopoldo flees
from Tuscany. The new Habsburg Emperor, Franz Josef. Barricades in Paris. Louis Napoleon elected Prince-President. The armistice ends. Novara. Vittorio Emanuele becomes King.

THE SALASCO ARMISTICE of 9 August 1848, which halted the war between
Sardinia and Austria, effectively put an end to Carlo Alberto's Kingdom of
Alta Italia, although, in the confusion of the times, an important part of it
was only just coming into being. On 7 August, two days after his retreat
from Milan, his representatives, knowing nothing certain even of the temporary armistices, arrived in Venice to replace its provisional government
and officially proclaimed Carlo Alberto sovereign of the city, its lagoons
and mainland.

This royal government lasted only five days and ended almost in a civil
war. As rumors of the armistice reached the city, the Venetians, who had
never been enthusiastic for fusion with Sardinia and who feared that the
armistice was another treaty of Campoformio sacrificing them to the Austrians, gathered in the piazza throughout the evening, shouting abuse at
Carlo Alberto and demanding that his commissioners resign. At issue, or
so the Venetians thought, was control of Fort Malghera, on the mainland,
which guarded the railway bridge to Venice and which the Austrians had
begun to bombard the day before. The Venetians suspected that the terms
of the armistice would require the commissioners to surrender the fort,
and this they were determined to prevent. The commissioners, on their side,
knew no more of the terms of the armistice than did the crowd and said as
much at the same window of the Procuratie Nuove from which the Austrian governor five months earlier had attempted to reason with the Venetians; at the same time, however, the commissioners made it plain that they
would not resign their posts without orders from their king. To break the

impasse some extreme, Mazzinian republicans, mostly Lombardi who hoped to form a new, democratic government, entered the building and, in effect, made prisoners of the commissioners. This act in turn caused the commanding officer of the Piemontese garrison, some three thousand troops, to contemplate a rescue by using the men to clear the piazza.

Into the center of this explosive situation came Manin, whom the crowd had begun to demand, and who offered himself as a peaceful solution. At that moment he was peculiarly well suited to do so. Five weeks earlier, as president of the republic, he had asked all republicans to put aside their party feelings and, in order to provide Venice with an ally, to vote for fusion with Sardinia. Without his speech the plan for fusion might well not have carried the Assembly, and the speech was greatly admired at the time by conservatives and republicans alike as the act of a statesman. But it might have counted strongly against him now, after the collapse of Sardinia, except that he had thereafter declined to serve in the royal ministry on the ground that he owed some sacrifice to his republican faith. And he had retired from public life, except that he was seen as a private in the Civic Guard doing sentry duty in the piazzetta. In the five weeks since his retirement his popularity with Venetians of all classes increased. All admired his simplicity and self-denial, and the conservatives, who had feared him as a demagogue, came now to believe that he wished to serve Venice before himself or his republican faith. That night of 11 August, as he entered the Procuratie Nuove, he had, perhaps as much as any Venetian has ever had, the confidence of all his fellow citizens.

He talked for a few minutes with the Mazzinian republicans, probably the only men in Venice who were not delighted to see him, with some Venetian members of the government who were there and with the royal commissioners. Then he stepped to the window. At the sight of his short, stout figure and familiar, bespectacled face the crowd burst into cheers and then on his motion quickly fell silent. He announced that the two commissioners, without formally resigning, had agreed to cease all acts of government. "The day after tomorrow," he declared, "the deputies will meet and elect a new government. For the next forty-eight hours I will govern." *Governo io*. The Venetians shouted their approval, and when he was able again to make himself heard, he told them to disperse, for he and his aides "must have silence and calm to provide for the needs of the country." And soon, such was the people's confidence in him, the piazza was silent and empty.

Two days later the Assembly revived the Republic of San Marco and, in an act important to Manin's sense of legal fitness, ratified his assumption of power at a moment of public peril. It voted, further, to continue his dictatorship but, at his request, associated with him an admiral and a colonel to represent the armed forces, for although the Austrians were not yet in a position to press their attacks, Venice, while still open to the sea, was already isolated from the mainland. But the Triumvirate, in fact, was a dictatorship of one, Manin.

Nowhere else in the former Kingdom of Alta Italia did the armistice affect life so little or was the change from one form of government to another accomplished so smoothly. In the Duchies of Parma and Modena, Austrian troops re-entered in the names of Duke Carlo and Francesco V, and the people began to endure a military occupation with restrictive laws, arbitrary arrests, special taxes and arrogant soldiers. Soon many of the former volunteers and patriot leaders, not daring to remain, had crossed the borders into Piedmont, Tuscany or the Papal States.

On the Venetian mainland there was also a military occupation but, on the whole, not too severe, for several of the most important cities, such as Verona, had never thrown off Austrian control and were guilty only of sullen obedience. With Venice itself still free and fighting, the Austrian officers were inclined to seek cooperation rather than vengeance. But in Lombardia, and especially in Milan, the armistice, which left Radetzky in possession and control, was the start of a bloody repression.

Soon after the armistice had been signed, Emperor Ferdinand had issued a proclamation in which he promised the subjects of his Kingdom of Lombardo-Veneto "full pardon for the part they may have taken in the political occurrences of the present year, commanding that there shall not be practiced against them any inquisition or punishment, except in respect to those considerations necessary for the confirmation of public employees." He had also promised a constitution "corresponding not less to their respective nationality and to the needs of the country, than to their union with the Austrian Empire."

The words, however, meant nothing. Radetzky ruled by martial law, exactly as he saw fit. He ordered any Italian who was found with a weapon, even a knife, to be shot, and shootings were frequent. To finance his occupation he relied, in addition to taxes, on individual fines. He made a list of 189 prominent Milanesi, most of whom had held office under the provisional government but some of whom were merely rich, and fined them altogether the enormous sum of twenty million francs. Those who were able to produce cash were sometimes able to settle for smaller amounts than they had been assigned, but the others had all their property sequestered and were financially wiped out. In the countryside the occupation was equally harsh. Officers and men were nervous, irritable and inclined to be vindictive; a frequent punishment for an offending Italian was a public whipping. The soldiers were billeted in the larger houses and encouraged to live off the countryside. When caught by a peasant, stealing fruit or a chicken, they would shrug and say, "Pio Nono pays."

In Milan itself most of the palazzi, the public gardens and the parade ground were commandeered for military hospitals, barracks and bivouac areas. Croat soldiers were everywhere, and on good days they would set up their mess kettles out of doors, in the portico or yard of some palazzo, and heat their meals over pieces of broken furniture. The city was squalid, depressed and, except for the soldiers, seemed empty. Thousands of Milanesi had left, and most did not return for several months. Even when they did, like those who had remained, they stayed indoors, or, when out, walked about hastily as if ashamed. Gatherings of any size were forbidden and even the University and schools were kept closed; students were allowed to meet privately in groups that did not exceed ten. Nearly every day the military government had a new *"Notificazione"* setting forth yet another prohibition or requirement.

The people lived on illusions: that the Venetians were winning, that the French were coming or the English about to intervene; and particularly did they feed on the idea that they had been betrayed, that Carlo Alberto had quit the war with his army intact. In this idea they were encouraged by the propaganda of the republicans. Immediately after the armistice Mazzini had proclaimed, "The royal war is finished; now begins the war of the people," and it seemed to be true. At Venice, where there was a republic, the war continued; and in the Alps, in the mountain villages around Lago Maggiore, troops of the provisional government of Milan, led by Garibaldi, continued to fight.

He had left Montevideo and after a nine-week voyage had landed on 22 June at Nice, the city in which he had been born and in which Anita and his children were awaiting him. The people gave him a rapturous welcome. The Ligurian coast from Nice to Genoa and down to Livorno was one of the most republican sections of Italy, and Mazzini and Garibaldi, leaders of republican thought and action, were both native sons and heroes. Garibaldi was still under a sentence of death for treason for his part in Mazzini's attempted revolution of 1834, but the welcome he received at Nice and later at Genoa persuaded officials to ignore the fact.

After a week with his family Garibaldi had gone to Carlo Alberto's headquarters in the field and offered himself and the sixty men of his Legion who had returned with him to the Italian cause. There was no question of his enlisting as a private; he expected, and so did republicans everywhere, that he would be given a position of command. It is not clear whether he ever met with Carlo Alberto or merely with some lesser officials, but in any event he was referred, with his feelings rather wounded, to the Minister of War at Turin who suggested that he offer himself and his men to Venice. The Piemontesi in positions of power were enthusiastic monarchists, and they considered Garibaldi to be a radical republican; and further, those of them who were professional soldiers were inclined to dismiss him as an amateur with an inflated reputation.

Rejected twice by the Piemontesi, Garibaldi had then offered his services to the provisional government of Milan which, perhaps because Mazzini was in the city and able to exert pressure, accepted them, but with reluctance. It allowed him to recruit but refused to supply him with arms or uniforms, except for some white linen jackets left behind by the Austrians. These, Garibaldi and his men fashioned into a sort of blouse, so that the regiment, as one of its members observed, looked like an army of cooks.

Because of the delays he was unable to accomplish anything before the armistice and, at the first reports of it, he wrote quickly to Milan that it had nothing to do with him or his men: "The Italian war against Austria will continue." But in the next few days, as he and his men learned more about the armistice, most of the men deserted and he issued a public protest. It was a wholly republican proclamation, addressed to all Italians, starting with Mazzini's slogan *Dio e Popolo,* God and the People, and containing an attack on Carlo Alberto which became famous:

> I cannot force myself to accept the humiliating conditions agreed upon by the King of Sardinia with the hated foreigner who oppresses my country. If the King of Sardinia has a crown which he preserves by force of arms and cowardice, I and my companions do not wish to preserve our lives with infamy.[44]

His word for cowardice, like Dante's, was *viltà;* he granted nothing to Carlo Alberto, not even good intentions. He ended with a promise to continue "the holy war, the war of Italian independence."

He succeeded in doing so for about three weeks, during which the Milanesi deluded themselves into believing that he might dash from the mountains and retake the city or, at very least, that he might maintain a guerrilla warfare until either the French came, or Carlo Alberto rearmed, or the Venetians forced the Austrians to terms. He won two startling victories with a force of about five hundred against an Austrian army of five thousand, but soon he was forced to retreat into Switzerland and disband. The campaign was hardly more than his personal protest against the Austrians, but coming after the armistice it held everyone's attention and served to solidify his enormous reputation. Many who had doubted were now convinced that, given the opportunity, he could do as well in Italy as he had in Uruguay.

In Turin, just as in Venice and Milan, the armistice and collapse of the new kingdom produced a strong reaction against Carlo Alberto, but in Piedmont and Savoy, and to a lesser extent in Genoa, he had the majority

to defend him. His subjects were more aware than the Milanesi and Venetians of the cost of the war in men and money and even in institutions. The
politicians in Turin, for example, were acutely aware that after Lombardia's entrance into the kingdom, Carlo Alberto had put the mayor of Milan,
Conte Casati, at the head of his ministry. The gesture was hardly noticed
in Milan, as the bad news from Custoza had obscured it, but in Turin it
was considered a tremendous concession to unity. The Piemontesi did not
hesitate, when refugees from Lombardia talked of Carlo Alberto's deserting the common cause, to accuse the Lombardi of being too slow to make
the cause common.

The antagonism between cities and localities, always a stumbling block
to Italian unity, threatened now to grow even worse as those who had lost
the war began to turn on each other. Fortunately other facts and emotions
counteracted the tendency to recrimination. The refugees, at least, could
see for themselves that the army was truly defeated and not, as the republicans insisted, still intact. Carlo Alberto had led back into Piedmont only
some twenty-five thousand men, about half of those he had led out. Not all
the rest were casualties; many, on the retreat, had become separated from
their regiment or had deserted and started for home on their own. In one
regiment only six hundred out of twenty-seven hundred remained, and no
regiment had its full quota of men and guns. Further, as the refugees were
constantly reminded, the Piemontesi had taxed themselves hard for the war
and, providing more than three quarters of the combined Italian force,
they had suffered more than three quarters of the casualties. It was not the
fashion then to conceal grief and, as most families had lost at least one
relative, there were signs of it everywhere.

In Cavour's family, for example, his brother's son, the family heir, had
been killed in a battle near Mantua. Cavour had been particularly fond of
his nephew Augusto and, just as he had publicly urged the war in his newspaper, he had privately written his nephew exhorting him to do his duty.
Augusto had been carrying the letter when killed, and it had been returned
to Cavour. His friend Castelli, who knew that behind Cavour's reserve
were deep emotions, hurried over to comfort him and found him on the
floor, weeping desperately. Later Cavour put his nephew's blood-stained
uniform in a glass case and kept it in his bedroom. Such grief, in the customs of the time, was not extravagant and, repeated many times over in
the length of the Po valley, tended to bind all its peoples together.

In Rome the people's reaction to the armistice was particularly strong.
The republicans, as elsewhere, were angry at Carlo Alberto, but at Rome
they were even more bitter against Pio Nono. And after the armistice they
were joined by thousands of soldiers, mostly volunteers, who returned to
the city, guns in hand, convinced that Pio Nono had betrayed them. These

*reduci* or "returning ones" infected the city with an air of violence and swung the reality of power in its government even further from the regular channels of Papal administration into the meetings and organization of the republican clubs.

Even the new institutions and forms of government under the liberal constitution granted by the pope in March did not stop this trend. In the spring they had emerged with a hue of unreality about them which suggested they had died before coming to life. In the first election, both in Rome and outside, less than a third of the electorate had bothered to vote. At the opening of the first Parliament, despite the Italians' love of an occasion, only forty-nine out of one hundred deputies had appeared: not even a quorum.

During this period the pope's lay minister, Mamiani, had continued his experiment of trying to create a new form of Papal government by separating the spiritual and temporal power, but without success. Foreign governments, whether at home or in Rome, preferred to deal directly with one of the pope's cardinals rather than with one of Mamiani's clerks; the cardinal represented a world church, the clerk, merely a small Italian state. Further, at Rome the government offices, courts and police were almost entirely staffed by priests, and any division between spiritual and temporal duties and offices meant depriving some priests of their jobs and power. Naturally these men interpreted the allocution as an indirect order to drag their feet and hinder reform. In despair in July Mamiani had resigned.

Pio Nono replaced him with another layman ex-revolutionary, Conte Edoardo Fabbri, who had been imprisoned and exiled under Gregory XVI and who was therefore popular with the liberals and republicans. But Fabbri quickly became disgusted with the demagogues and, like Mamiani, was unable to control the clubs and *reduci* or to stop the drift in state affairs toward chaos. After six weeks he resigned, and Pio Nono then appointed Conte Pellegrino Rossi, the fourth ex-revolutionary he had appointed since granting the constitution.

But unlike the other three, Rossi, an arrogant, strong man, but a brilliant administrator, was unpopular not only with the conservatives but also with the republicans. He offended the latter by being contemptuous of demagogues, reserved and cold in his manner, and he offended the former, many of whom were priests, by his reputation for free-thinking and his Protestant wife. His policy was not to divide the spiritual and temporal power but to reform the traditional Papal government, men and offices, to make it more efficient and honest, and he intended to begin by restoring order in the streets, quelling the unruly crowds and disarming private citizens. His actions at once aroused the clubs and *reduci* against him, and their anger was increased by his insistence that any renewal of the war was hopeless and by his efforts to unite the Italian states in a loose, defensive federation under the pope as president. They were, at that time, enthusiastically supporting the Mazzinian idea of a Constitutent Assembly to meet in Rome which would unite Italy in a single state, by vote of the people, and end the armistice by declaring national war on Austria. The Assembly would also, they hoped, take the lead in the war away from Carlo Alberto and block the expansion of the House of Savoy. In Tuscany extreme republicans had captured the government and forced Grand Duke Leopoldo to agree to the plan, so that in one state it had official backing. Rossi, however, was a realist and, with Pio Nono's views on record in the allocution, treated the republican ideas as products of demented minds. Soon, like Mamiani, he found himself without any friends, other than the pope. By sheer force of character he sustained himself until 15 November when, like Caesar in March, he ignored warnings, started for the Chamber of Deputies in the Palazzo della Cancelleria and was stabbed as he started up the steps.

The murder was excellently done. As Rossi's carriage pulled under the portico, some fifty or sixty *reduci* formed two lines from the left-hand carriage door to the steps leading up to the Council Chamber. The carriage door opened and Rossi, a tall figure in a dark blue overcoat, stepped out and was followed by Righetti, another minister. After the two of them had taken four or five steps amid shouts of *"Abasso Rossi!"*, "Down with Rossi!", the lines on either side closed in front of them. Then they opened to let Rossi walk forward and then immediately closed again, so that he was separated from Righetti. He moved ahead alone, ignoring the shouts, and reached the broad, stone staircase. As he was placing his foot on the second step, someone to his right struck him lightly, so that he turned his head quickly to that side, exposing the carotid artery on the left of his neck. At the same instant another man to the front slashed the left side of his throat and neck with a hunting knife. A great fountain of blood jumped out, for the artery had been cut, and Rossi collapsed on the steps. Immediately all who were in the conspiracy raised their daggers and cloaks to conceal the murderer and hurried off with him unidentified.

Righetti, Rossi's servant and a few of the innocent bystanders carried Rossi upstairs and laid him on a sofa. He survived about twenty-five minutes, groaning but unable to speak. Nearby in the Chamber, although the deputies knew that he had been stabbed and was dying, knew that the pope's chief minister and the man whose address they were waiting to hear had been murdered on their doorstep, still they continued with their business, and when they adjourned, it was for lack of a quorum.

The murder of Rossi left Pio Nono in an impossible position. The clubs, which were now dominated by extreme republicans, demonstrated in the streets and demanded a government which would declare war and merge itself into an Italian state. Pio Nono would never agree to such a program and yet, under the constitution he had granted, he was required to appoint ministers acceptable to the Chamber. But he could find no one who would even try to form a ministry, not even among the most radical leaders. Politically he was isolated; spiritually, as the ambassadors of the Catholic powers came to the Quirinale to stay by his side, he was supported.

On the afternoon of 16 November a crowd of six thousand, many with guns, began a demonstration before the palazzo, and when Pio Nono refused to give in to their demands, they began firing. In defending themselves the Swiss Guards returned the fire; inside the palazzo, a shot coming through a window killed a bishop. Toward evening the crowd brought up a field gun, and then Pio Nono, refusing the offer of the Swiss to fight until dead, gave in. Making a formal protest before all the ambassadors, he agreed to the ministers proposed by the crowd and agreed that the question of war and a national state be discussed by the Parliament. The crowd and Pio Nono took this to mean that the ministers would declare war and also change the form of government by calling a Constituent Assembly of all Italians to meet at Rome. The next day, at the crowd's demand, the Swiss Guard was replaced with the Civic Guard, now wholly republican, and Pio Nono was a prisoner.

Metternich, driven from power himself, could at least draw cold comfort from having predicted it all. Earlier in the year, still in power, he had written to Count Lützow, his ambassador at Rome: ". . . many realities will have lifted from them the veils with which they are still covered. . . . The veil is liberalism; it will disappear in Italy, as in every other country, before radicalism in action." Of course, it was not true of "every other country." England had radically but peacefully reformed its government in 1832, and Metternich in 1848 was enjoying the benefits of it. But to Pio Nono, the liberal pope, a prisoner in the center of a historical event which daily appeared more likely to repeat the Terror of the French Revolution, Metternich's words and philosophy must have glowed with the peculiar brilliance of a truth perceived only in hindsight.

His escape was well arranged. He was allowed to see the foreign ambassadors and those from the great Catholic countries were constantly with him. On 24 November the French ambassador had a private audience with him. Through the door the Civic Guard could hear the Frenchman's voice droning on and on. Meanwhile the pope, dressed as a simple priest, followed his valet through a secret passage, down to a courtyard where a carriage was waiting. He left Rome by the Lateran gate accompanied by the Bavarian ambassador. They were challenged and passed. The pope carried with him the Blessed Sacrament in the same ciborium which Pius VII used when taken by Napoleon into France.

They traveled in a Berlin carriage to Gaeta, a seaport town across the border of the Kingdom of The Two Sicilies. There others joined them, and the party, with ludicrous attempts to remain incognito, put up at the "Giardinetto," a second-class hotel. The townspeople after a moment of stunned astonishment set themselves out to make the pope comfortable and a source of income. Papal couriers galloped to King Ferdinando in Naples to ask for his hospitality, and within days the king himself came and put a royal palace at the pope's disposal. The various ambassadors, secretaries, cardinals and staffs of all kind found what quarters they could. Pio Nono at once made it plain that he had no intention of returning to Rome on conditions, and everyone prepared to spend the winter. The Gaetans were delighted.

The Romans were not. The simplest people, at least, were disturbed. Although most of them could not read the bulletins the pope's adherents posted, their leaders could not conceal from them that the pope had fled voluntarily. The people were quite prepared to bully him and even perhaps to be bullied in return. But, after fourteen centuries of the Papacy, in their way they loved the pope, and his voluntary departure left a void which all the republican oratory could not fill. For the moderates the pope's departure was a disaster. No day-to-day cooperation was possible with a government miles away at Gaeta, and that part of the clerical government that remained in Rome was likewise immobilized. The extreme republicans were left in control of the city and government.

The republican revolution at Rome greatly increased the excitement of all the republicans, north and south, but particularly those in Tuscany, Genoa and the Po valley. At the same time it hardened the forces opposed to it as men increasingly, sometimes with despair, chose sides. From Gaeta, Pio Nono made it plain by his actions and proclamations that he was finished with his attempt to develop liberal institutions for the Papal States, that he intended to make his temporal power an international question and hoped to persuade the Catholic powers to replace him on his throne as an absolute monarch. Others who also thought this the best solution to the problem of government in central Italy began to gather at Gaeta, and Pio Nono was soon surrounded by men whom the liberals called reactionary.

Farther south, at Naples, Ferdinando moved steadily in the same direction. The day of the barricades, 15 May, had taught him that his army was loyal and that the liberal revolution, looked full in the face, was not so very formidable. Till then it had seemed irresistible, as it swept from capital to capital, toppling governments. But he had taken action against it and by doing so had won the applause of much of Europe. His new prestige had flattered him and increased his pride and sense of power. Although he had not abolished the constitution, he had begun to rule without it, dismissing the national guard, postponing the opening of Parliament and censoring the press. And he had turned his attention entirely to subduing his dis- orderly Kingdom of Naples and regaining his lost Kingdom of Sicily. In the south, the war for Italian independence in the Po valley was almost forgot- ten except by ardent patriots who were also, generally, the republicans who were not only out of favor but in exile or hiding.

In Tuscany, however, the extreme republicans, following the revolution at Rome and by much the same methods, came more and more into power, until finally on 7 February 1849 Grand Duke Leopoldo, like Pio Nono, fled. He had agreed to a Constituent Assembly at Rome, which would settle on the form of government for central Italy, but he had then begun to have second thoughts. He knew that Pio Nono had already condemned the idea, and he had a letter from Radetzky promising him thirty thousand troops as soon as the Austrian army had "subdued the demagogues of Piedmont." Why, reasoned Leopoldo, should he risk a Constituent Assem- bly that almost certainly would turn Tuscany into a republic? So one day when he was at Siena, he pretended he was merely going out in his carriage for an afternoon's drive and, much to everyone's astonishment, he never returned. He had driven on to the small Tuscan seaport of Santo Stefano, whence after two weeks of nervous negotiation he joined Pio Nono at Gaeta.

In Piedmont the demagogues to whom Radetzky referred included men of all classes, but they were not all republicans and many were unen- thusiastic about the course of events at Florence and Rome. Carlo Alberto and the monarchists were distressed at the number of republics that were emerging, Venice, Rome and Tuscany. With the advent of each one the republicans in Milan grew more insistent that Lombardia become either an independent republic or merged with the others. The Sardinian army feared that the Constituent Assembly, if it declared a national war on Austria, would insist on having Garibaldi in command. Others felt that the republican movement in central Italy was spoiling any chance of a settle- ment in the Po valley. Gioberti, who had become the prime minister in Turin, was so anxious to prevent Pio Nono from calling a foreign army into Italy, or Leopoldo from calling an Austrian army into Tuscany that he offered them Piemontesi troops to re-establish them on their thrones. When rumors of his offer reached the ears of the deputies, even though the duke and the pope had already refused it, there was a tremendous outcry in the Chamber. Gioberti defended it, insisting that the republicans at Florence and Rome, far from being heroes of liberty, were adventurers and reckless men who did not represent the patriotic majority of Italians and who simply were spreading discord and terror. He perhaps had the majority of the people with him but certainly not the majority of the deputies and ministers, and he was forced to resign. He was succeeded by General Chiodo, and the appointment of a military officer as well as the retention in the ministry of others who favored a renewal of the war suggested that Carlo Alberto would soon renounce the armistice.

All efforts to negotiate a peace continually came to nothing, largely because neither side really wanted it. Sardinia had its eager republicans and its king and army smarting for revenge, and Austria had in Radetzky, a general who was confident that, given time, he could recover for the Habsburgs all their former lands. His opinion was respected in Vienna because he presented it strongly and because, in this year of constant revolt and betrayal, he was wholeheartedly loyal, even to the point of being disloyal in order to further Habsburg interests. When, early in the fighting, Ferdinand had ordered Radetzky to negotiate on the basis of ceding Lombardia to Sardinia, Radetzky had refused and sent an officer to Ferdinand to explain how with twenty-five thousand more troops he would certainly win. Meanwhile he kept on fighting. In the same spirit now, in spite of all the negotiations for peace, he continued to prepare for war.

He was soon backed in this course by yet another revolution in Vienna, in early October 1848, which caused the court and Emperor Ferdinand to flee the city once again, this time to the fortress at Olmütz. But on this occasion an Austrian army under a conservative general, Windischgrätz, promptly retook the city and placed it under martial law. Like Radetzky, Windischgrätz was a strong man prepared to act on his own, and he recommended as the new prime minister his brother-in-law, Felix zu Schwarzenberg, who had served in the Austrian diplomatic corps and in Lombardia with Radetzky. Schwarzenberg was younger than the other two but like them his aim was the restoration of an absolute monarchy in Vienna by means of the army. Like them he believed in force, even in violence. Ideas were nothing, force everything. And he wanted a new emperor so that he could start his work unbound by any of Ferdinand's promises.

As Ferdinand I had no children, his heir was his younger brother, Karl, who was forty-six. But Karl was almost as weak and incompetent as Ferdinand, and Schwarzenberg wanted to pass over Karl to his elder son, Franz Josef, who had just become eighteen and was ideal for Schwarzenberg's purpose. Franz Josef was vigorous, handsome and military-minded; he was also inexperienced and young enough to be easily dominated. He had fought briefly with Radetzky in Lombardia and shown courage, and in the ups and downs of the court in revolutionary Vienna he had avoided any political promises and entanglements. His mother, the Archduchess

Sophie, who of all the court had the strongest will, was more eager to have her son than her husband the emperor, and so, too, were most of the diplomats. The only persons who might possibly object to the succession of Franz Josef were the emperor and his heir, Ferdinand and Karl, and Schwarzenberg was prepared to bully them into agreement.

So, on 2 December 1848, in the archbishop's palace at Olmütz, the court, the ministers, Windischgrätz and Schwarzenberg assembled in a large semicircle before Emperor Ferdinand who, dutifully reading the paper handed to him, abdicated his titles and position on the ground of ill health. Schwarzenberg then read a statement by Karl renouncing the throne on the ground that in such turbulent times a younger man was needed. Then all gave homage to Franz Josef, and his reign began. It was to last sixty-eight years, from 1848 to 1916.

The sudden change of emperor was obviously a fact of great importance for all Habsburg subjects in whatever land. For Italians the emergence of a strong man such as Schwarzenberg seemed ominous. Confusion in Vienna was an advantage to them, and under Schwarzenberg it seemed likely to end. They foresaw that he would back Radetzky in a harsh military occupation and refuse any political concessions. But at the same time the forced succession of Franz Josef created problems of its own, some of which were an obvious advantage to the Italians. At the beginning of the year the Hungarians, who had been extorting political concessions from Ferdinand, in return had been extravagantly loyal in voting men and money to re-enforce the Austrian army in Italy. But now, led by Kossuth, they too foresaw that Schwarzenberg and Franz Josef intended to repudiate the pledges made by Ferdinand, and they refused to recognize the abdication as legal. Four months later, in April 1849, they were to declare Hungary an independent country and the House of Habsburg dethroned. Meanwhile desultory fighting between Hungary and Croatia flared into a full-scale civil war between Hungary and Austria, and Italians were delighted. In Piedmont the pressure on Carlo Alberto to break the armistice increased.

This time, the wiser heads insisted, there could be no question of *L'Italia farà da sè*. Sardinia, for all the republican oratory up and down the peninsula, would probably have to fight alone and must look for an ally outside of Italy. The only possibility was France, a republic, which was bitter for Carlo Alberto. Even worse, France would undoubtedly demand some sort of price for assistance, and the price would almost certainly be the provinces of Nice and Savoy. After the battle of Marengo in 1800 Napoleon, as First Consul, had incorporated them directly into France, and it was not until after Waterloo in 1815 that the Congress of Vienna had required the last part of them to be returned. For many

Frenchmen the two provinces were a symbol of their humiliation at the Congress. But even so Carlo Alberto brought himself to agree to negotiate with France for help.

The Second Republic, however, had grown even more cautious than in the days of Lamartine's Manifesto. Somewhat like Vienna, Paris had suffered what was almost a second revolution. What had happened was that once again as in 1830 the workers of Paris saw, or thought they saw, the fruits of their revolution being plucked, this time by the liberal republicans, for the benefit of the middle class. The workers were interested in socialistic programs such as the right to work, and although the constitution of the Second Republic promised such rights, they did not seem about to be realized. So the workers began to riot; first in March, then in April, and finally in June they took to the barricades, for the second time that year. The fighting was bloody. The Archbishop of Paris was killed trying to utter a message of peace. The government, with a controlling majority of republicans, voted dictatorial powers to a general of the Algerian campaign, Louis E. Cavaignac, a fellow republican but of the old Roman type, high-minded and austere. Within three days he had quelled the revolt, and throughout the summer and autumn thousands of workers were deported without trial. Cavaignac ever after was called "The Butcher of June."

The episode was not one on which republicans anywhere liked to dwell. In France it probably made most men nervous and therefore more conservative, and it probably also played some part in the election for president in December. To everyone's astonishment Napoleon's nephew, Prince Louis Napoleon, defeated the nearest candidate, General Cavaignac, almost five to one. The general, an earnest man, refused to shake hands with the winner. No one quite knew what to make of the election. Louis Napoleon was not well known in France, and it is possible that he won because of it. The other candidates were all stamped with failures: Lamartine had shown that the republicans could not govern without calling in a dictator, Cavaignac; the people were tired of the middle-of-the-road Orleanists under Louis Philippe and disgusted with the reactionary legitimists. There was left only Louis Napoleon and some candidates from the socialist and radical parties. The election is important in French history because, by giving Louis Napoleon the presidency, it gave him the position from which he could, and in four years did by a *coup d'état,* make himself emperor of the French. His election at this particular moment excited Italian republicans greatly. They were stirred not only by the magic of his name but by the memory of his fighting for their cause at Bologna in the Carbonaro revolution of 1831, and they hoped to persuade him to do so again. But in the winter of 1849 he was still at the start of his career, an ambitious, ambiguous man, styling himself prince-president and wearing the uniform of a general in the National Guard. It was too soon for an Italian adventure backing liberalism, and he rejected all suggestions of French intervention in the Po valley, whether from the republicans of Venice or central Italy or from the constitutional monarchists at Turin.

Besides the French army, however, the Piemontesi also sought a French general, for the army staff had persuaded Carlo Alberto that his poor leadership had been a prime cause of their defeat. If they fought again, he must not command, and even to this Carlo Alberto agreed. But two French marshals in turn refused, and the staff had to settle for a Pole, Wojciech Chrzanowski, who had distinguished himself in the Polish insurrection of 1831. It also hired as a division commander, General Ramorino, who in 1834 had led Mazzini's expedition into Savoy.

On paper the king and staff, in the seven months of the armistice from August through February, had put together an army of 117,000 with 156 field cannon and 2000 siege guns. Its effective strength, however, was probably closer to eighty thousand men, and opposed to it Radetzky had an army of about seventy-five thousand, not including the additional forty thousand he would have to leave as garrisons in the towns. Supposing that the Hungarian civil war would prevent Radetzky being re-enforced, that Venice would make a special effort in Radetzky's rear and that several towns would rise, or at least sabotage his communications, the odds seemed to favor the Piemontesi. Even so, some of Carlo Alberto's generals urged him not to end the armistice. They pointed out that the disparities between the two armies in training and experience was even greater than before. The replacements in the Sardinian ranks were middle-aged men, and the Polish generals, if not actually distrusted, did not inspire loyalty. But Carlo Alberto neither wanted nor was able to continue the armistice. The relentless insinuations against his good faith had seared his spirit, the cost of the armed truce was ruining his country and as a constitutional King he could not withstand the pressure for war from his ministers and the Chamber of Deputies. Even the conservatives, whose numbers had increased in proportion to the rhetoric of the republicans, wanted it. Cavour, who at first had been opposed to a renewal of the war, on 8 March wrote a friend:

> I tell you that I desire it as a means of making an end. If we have one success, I suspect peace will be concluded. If we lose, the King will abdicate, we shall pay the expenses of the war, and all will be over. Of the alternatives, either will cost us less than to remain in the condition we are in.[45]

And, on 12 March, Carlo Alberto proclaimed the armistice ended and prepared, in accordance with its terms, to resume the war on the eighth day thereafter. The cabinet addressed a note to the European powers giving reasons for renewing the war: although the armistice had been purely military, Austria had set about re-establishing her political regime in Lombardia and the Veneto, ruling by martial law, extorting tribute from the inhabitants, and bringing back her vassal princes to the duchies. In short it had refused to negotiate a political settlement for northern Italy and had, instead, imposed one. Franz Josef and Schwarzenberg, on their side, blamed the abortive negotiations on Carlo Alberto's insincerity and the renewal of war on his ambition. The war began again on 20 March 1849.

Chrzanowski assumed that Radetzky would retreat toward the Quadrilateral, and to catch the Austrian troops before they could get behind the defenses of Mantua and Verona he had massed five-sixths of his army, fifty thousand men, near Novara, where a bridge crossed the Ticino and a road led directly to Milan. The rest of the army he spread along the river southwards to Pavia. On the morning of 20 March Chrzanowski ordered his divisions near Novara to cross the river and enter Lombardia. A few Austrians had been seen on the far bank, but they had soon disappeared, and there seemed to be no defense of the bridge prepared. At noon, with the sun high, banners up and bayonets drawn the Duke of Genoa's division was ready. Carlo Alberto put himself at their head and was first across the river. There was no opposition. From peasants they learned that Radetzky had withdrawn his troops toward Pavia.

The old man, now eighty-three, had not behaved as expected. Far from retreating, he had watched Chrzanowski mass the great majority of his army to the north, and then had himself headed for the south. He had out-maneuvered Ramorino, trapping him and his six thousand men on the wrong side of the Po, and had put his whole army across the Ticino into Piedmont and had started for Turin. Hastily Chrzanowski called his troops to the north back across the river, and the battle that developed on 23 March was fought not in Lombardia but in Piedmont, near Novara, and with the Austrian army between Chrzanowski and Turin.

Although for a time the Piemontesi seemed to be holding and even winning, in the end they collapsed and retreated in disorder to the walls of Novara. The defeat was complete, and Carlo Alberto at last ordered a white flag raised and sent an officer to seek terms. Meanwhile he stayed on the city walls hoping that some sniper's bullet would reach him.

Later that night he gathered with his staff and sons in the Palazzo Bellini in the town. The terms offered by Radetzky were crushing, and Carlo Alberto refused to agree to them. Then, after asking each officer in turn if there was no hope of renewing the battle, he observed quietly:

> For eighteen years until this moment, I have done everything possible
> to advance the interests of my people. And I grieve to see my hopes
> shattered, not so much for myself as for my country. I have not been

able to find death on the field of battle, as I would have wished it. Perhaps my person now is the only obstacle to winning from the enemy a fair treaty. And as there is no way of continuing to fight, I now abdicate the throne in favor of my son Vittorio Emanuele, in the hope that a new king may be able to obtain more honorable terms and procure for the country an advantageous peace. Here now [pointing to Vittorio Emanuele] is your king.[46]

Then, after an hour alone with his sons, he left the town in a carriage and, posing as the Comte de Barge, passed through the Austrian lines and started for Oporto, a large town in Portugal. There, four months later, he died, broken in spirit but consoled by his religion. He had failed in what he had set out to do, and for many years his countrymen judged him very harshly.

But on the night of his father's abdication the new king, Vittorio Emanuele II, reportedly said to one of his officers, Ottavio Vimercati, "I shall preserve intact the institutions my father has given. I shall hold high and firm the tricolor flag, symbol of that Italian nationality which today has been beaten, but which will one day triumph. This triumph will be henceforth the aim of all my efforts." Where his father had failed, he succeeded; and in that success Italians slowly came to see that Carlo Alberto had played a difficult and necessary role with honor.

The morning after the abdication, on 24 March, Vittorio Emanuele sought a personal interview with Radetzky. It seems to have been a wise act. Radetzky apparently hated the father for a perjurer but pitied and even liked the son. The two men, followed by their staffs, met in a field near the village of Vignale, and after the old marshal had been helped from his horse and had embraced the young king, the two men walked off a bit to confer alone. Radetzky's terms were, in essence, that Sardinia should return to the position and frontiers given it under the treaties of 1815. It was to recall its fleet from Venice, to disband its Lombard regiments, and to give up all claims to the territories of the Kingdom of Alta Italia, even to the Duchies of Parma and Modena. Further, it was to admit an Austrian garrison into its fortress city of Alessandria, to pay the costs of this occupation and also to pay a general indemnity for the costs of the war.

The terms were harsh but, considering that Sardinia twice had attacked Austria, not unreasonable. The House of Savoy kept its throne and, by reason of its kingdom forming a buffer between France and Austria, its independence. Despite the fact that both the king's mother and wife were Austrian archduchesses, Radetzky did not try to force Sardinia into the position of a dependent kingdom in the Habsburg family system, nor, despite the legend, did he ask Vittorio Emanuele to abolish the constitution and return to autocratic rule.

Vittorio Emanuele agreed to the terms; he could do nothing else. Renewing the war was out of the question. The defeat at Novara had knocked Sardinia out of the war for national independence, and with it the constitutional monarchists wherever in Italy. The defeat was more than just a battle lost. The small kingdom, after two campaigns, a long armistice and with indemnities to pay, was ruined financially and torn apart politically. After all the loss, toil and trouble in only one respect did some of its people feel they were better off than they had been in 1847: they now had a constitution and a king who had come to power under it and who might, therefore, feel it his duty to preserve it.

# CHAPTER 28

Republicans at Florence and Rome. Guerrazzi. The Grand Duke returns. Verdi and *La Battaglia di Legnano*. The Roman Republic proclaimed. The French support the Pope. Mazzini, Garibaldi and the defense of the Roman Republic. Manara's Bersaglieri Lombardi. Garibaldi's retreat from Rome. San Marino. Death of Anita. Garibaldi's escape.

DURING THE SAME MONTHS in which the constitutional monarchists of Piedmont were preparing to fight the Austrians a second time, the republicans of the peninsula, from their three centers of Rome, Florence and Venice, were continuing with their own efforts to free and unite Italy. For the Venetians, who had been fighting the Austrians continuously since March 1848, the war simply went on.

Throughout the winter they controlled the full length of the lagoon and made effective sorties onto the mainland, often taking and holding villages for a week at a time while they collected supplies. The Sardinian defeat at Novara, however, affected them immediately, for by the terms of the treaty following it Vittorio Emanuele was required to withdraw his fleet from the Adriatic, and then the Austrians could blockade Venice by sea as well as land. Thereafter, the Venetians were isolated from the rest of Italy and left to fashion their fate alone.

The republicans at Rome and Florence, however, were neighbors, and they talked not only of cooperation but of merger as the first step toward a free, united and republican Italy. They naturally counted Venice as ready to join them, and when a republican revolt broke out in Genoa, they saw it as the first of a series of revolts by the people which would lead to a national rising against the Austrians. Mazzini, who was at Rome, immediately proclaimed "the monarchical principle is condemned; may God and the People, who do not betray, triumph!" Republicans imagined a new state stretching from Genoa to Venice and down to Rome. But Vittorio Emanuele's Bersaglieri put down the Genovesi, the Venetians remained cut off and even the merger between Rome and Florence was put to one side, largely because of the provincialism of the Tuscan leaders. In the end

345

events overtook the two republics of central Italy separately, reaching a final determination first in Florence.

There, the most important leader was Francesco Domenico Guerrazzi, a violent, strong man with a gift for oratory. He was a native of Livorno, a lawyer and journalist who, in 1829, had published articles by Mazzini. As a young man he had been imprisoned several times for his activities in La Giovine Italia, and in one term of prison he had written a famous novel *L'Assedio di Firenze, The Siege of Florence.* After the news of Novara reached Florence, the republican deputies in the Tuscan Assembly, realizing that Radetzky soon would be free to send troops into the country, voted a state of emergency and made Guerrazzi dictator of the Republic. They were following the same political course as the Venetians and for the same reason, but Guerrazzi and Manin, in some important respects, were very different.

When young, Guerrazzi had been poor and unknown, and although in time he became rich and famous, the memories of his harsh youth stayed with him. They may have accounted for his hard, arrogant personality in middle age with its streak of bitterness. Many men, because of his genuine talents, followed and obeyed him, but few seem to have liked him. Of all the leaders of the Risorgimento, he was the least loved. And he was ambitious. He liked power, almost as if the exercise of it soothed the rancor of his youth. His unpopularity and his desire for power both influenced the course of events in Florence.

After Guerrazzi became dictator, he was opposed both in the Assembly and outside it, by three groups: the conservatives or reactionaries who wanted to restore the Grand Duke Leopoldo as an absolute monarch; the liberals who wanted to invite Leopoldo to return as a constitutional monarch and, in avoiding a restoration by Austria, to preserve the constitution; and the extreme republicans who wanted to merge with the Romans and, by calling on all the people, somehow to defeat the Austrians. All but the most extreme republican visionaries, however, could see the flaws in any program relying on a mass uprising. The peasants to a man, especially since the allocution, were loyal to Leopoldo and, led by their priests, had already demonstrated several times in his favor. In the towns loyalties were more evenly divided. At Livorno, a turbulent, democratic seaport, and at Pisa, the seat of the University, the majorities were ardently republican, but elsewhere they favored Leopoldo's return, if possible on conditions. In every man's mind loomed the fact of Radetzky's army and the impossibility of the Tuscan Republic's improvising an army to defeat it when Sardinia, with its regular army, could not.

Guerrazzi himself believed that the military odds against Austria were overpowering and that Leopoldo would have to be invited back. But, typically, he refused to make common cause with the liberals and tried to keep all the strings of intrigue in his own hand, so that Leopoldo would be grateful to him alone. But a riot between a troop of volunteers from Livorno and a Florentine mob tripped him. The riot grew out of the general unpopularity of the Livornesi in Florence and, more specifically, of their habit in the previous week of ordering wine and then, having drunk it, refusing to pay. Trouble seemed inevitable, and Guerrazzi ordered the Livornesi to be transferred to another post. As they were marching to the railroad station, some Florentines fired on them, and, in a flash, harsh words and sullen looks turned into a real battle. The Livornesi retreated into the Piazza di Santa Maria Novella where nineteen men were killed, and many, many more wounded. Guerrazzi, galloping his horse into the center of it and, followed by some of the National Guard, managed to separate the two sides and immediately hurried the surviving Livornesi out of the city.

But that evening the Florentine mob, inflamed against all Livornesi including Guerrazzi, began to demonstrate against him. In the hills around the city beacon fires began to glow, and peasants shouting *"Viva Leopoldo"* came down into the city. The next morning, 12 April 1849, outside the Palazzo Vecchio an enormous crowd demonstrated for Leopoldo, and there were shouts of "Death for Guerrazzi." Inside, the city government of Florence was supplanting the Tuscan Assembly as the government of the state. The "Municipio" announced in a proclamation that because of the disorder in the country it was taking over the government, and, in the guise of preserving Guerrazzi from the mob, it made him a prisoner. Because of his unpopularity, no one objected. It was the sort of *coup d'état* that could not have been struck against Manin, Mazzini or even Carlo Alberto.

Then the Municipio, adding some well-known liberals to its administration and calling itself a Governing Commission, began to rule in Leopoldo's name and sent an embassy to Gaeta to invite him to return, but as a constitutional monarch. They begged him to spare his country and people the disaster of an invasion and himself the unpleasant fact of basing his rule on foreign arms. Leopoldo made a polite but meaningless reply and remained at Gaeta. The commission sent another deputation to him, and this time Leopoldo, still not stirring, wrote in reply: "The Tuscans may rest assured that I shall strive to seek the means best suited to heal them of the calamities they have suffered and to restore the constitutional government in such wise that the renewal of past disorders may not be feared." His meaning was as obscure as any oracle from Delphi, but it soon became all too clear. An Austrian army invaded the state and proclaimed it was acting in response to the grand duke's appeal. The Livornesi held out for two days, but the other towns capitulated at once. On 26 May twelve thousand Austrian troops paraded into Florence, and more were to come. Soon thereafter Leopoldo returned, using his Austrian title, wearing an Austrian uniform and surrounded by Austrian advisors. The people watched unhappily as he turned more and more to reaction, suppressing the Assembly, reintroducting censorship of the press and, finally, abolishing the constitution altogether. They were aware that in their cautious compromise, in the subterfuge by which Guerrazzi was upset, and even in Guerrazzi's personal ambitions there was little to respect. Somehow events and personalities had combined in a way to produce very little. As two of the liberals who had played a part in Guerrazzi's overthrow and imprisonment later humbly observed: "If the events of 12 April must have this conclusion, it were better that they had never been brought about."

At Rome, however, events and personalities combined to produce a very different result. After Pio Nono had fled, the republicans attempted to rule through the Chamber of Deputies, but soon the disturbances in the city and even in the Chamber itself grew so great that they dissolved the Chamber and ruled through a committee of three; and the committee promptly announced that a Constituent Assembly, elected as in the Republics of France and Venice by universal suffrage, would meet in Rome on 5 February to devise a new form of government for the Papal States.

Meanwhile the excitement within the city daily grew more intense as many genuine republicans, along with many others who were merely seeking excitement, flocked into Rome for what they were sure would be the opening of a new, historic era. Inspired by Mazzini, they foresaw a "Third Rome" of the people rising out of the ruins and remains of the classical and Catholic cities. They met in cafés and talked eagerly of the rights of man or, referring more generally to the French Revolution, of "the principles of '89." At night many went to the Teatro Argentina where Verdi, an ardent republican, was conducting the first performances of his new opera, *La Battaglia di Legnano,* or *The Battle of Legnano.*

The opera houses at this time were one of the meeting places of Italian life. Intermissions were long, food and drink were generally available and sometimes gambling; men went to the opera for entertainment and also to talk business and politics. In many of his previous operas Verdi had managed, in spite of Austrian censorship, to include at least one chorus about "la patria" or one which, by allusion, referred to it, and patriotic Italians of every state had taken these up as national hymns. In a country where so many men were illiterate those great, swinging choruses with their patriotic sentiments were an important influence.

Now for Rome, where there was no censorship, Verdi had composed an opera turning entirely and openly on "la patria," for *La Battalia di*

*Legnano* celebrated the defeat, in 1176, of Frederick Barbarossa, Holy Roman Emperor and German King, by the cities of the Lombard League. The allusion was perfectly clear, and the première produced a "furore." Probably under the circumstances any opera would have succeeded that waved a flag and allowed the chorus to sing of "la patria." But *La Battaglia di Legnano* did more. In the finale of its third act the hero, locked in a tower room, hears the sound of trumpets as his friends march off to fight Barbarossa. To join them and save his honor he leaps from the window into the moat. The music is stirring: the man's agitation is contrasted with the sounds of the distant march. At one of the early performances a soldier in the gallery was so carried away by it all that, tearing off his coat, he, too, leaped from the gallery and landed sprawling in the orchestra. No one seems to have been injured.

The impresario repeated the opera as often as the singers' voices would allow, and generally at each performance the entire fourth act was repeated. Its finale was built around the line *"Chi muore per la patria alma sì rea non ha"* or "He who dies for his country does not have a guilty soul." Four and a half years earlier the Bandiera brothers had gone to their death in Calabria singing such a chorus by the Neapolitan, Mercadante. Now in Rome as Verdi's chorus was repeated the entire audience would sing it, and, as they called him endlessly onto the stage, he became a symbol of the patriotic movement. He had a solitary, prickly temperament and hated publicity, so that he soon left. But the excitement continued. At every performance the audience wore republican cockades, threw streamers at the stage, draped banners from the balcony and sang along with the chorus.

Meanwhile with equal excitement the people cast their votes for representatives to the Constituent Assembly. In Rome the political clubs organized swarms of speakers to harangue the crowds, extolling the dignity of man in governing himself and accusing the priests of depriving many of their right to vote by refusing to open the baptismal registers. The balloting itself lasted three days, and each night the ballot boxes were paraded through the streets with torches and brass bands. The result was a triumph for the extreme republicans, or so they claimed. Garibaldi, for example, who was recruiting a new Italian Legion in the Legations, was elected in four districts, which suggested that his vigorous republican views were generally supported. But as the clerical party quickly pointed out, only a small per cent of those eligible had voted. From Gaeta, Pio Nono had condemned the election and forbidden Catholics to vote, and the effectivness of the ban was an indication of the depth of his support. At Rome only twenty-three thousand of an estimated sixty thousand voted; in the countryside the proportion was even smaller. Many, out of simplicity or humor, voted for Pio Nono; others, for the General of the Jesuits; and there was even a bloc for St. Peter. Pio Nono's ban, however, effectively gave the election to the extremists, and when the Assembly gathered in the Palazzo della Cancelleria it was strongly republican.

There, at two in the morning on 9 February 1849, after a long debate, the Assembly voted that the Papacy was at an end and that the new form of government for the Papal States would be that of a republic, based on a constitution and with the capital at Rome. Nearly forty years earlier Napoleon had cut through the extremely complicated problem of the temporal power of the pope by attempting to make the Church with its spiritual power the servant of the State; now the Roman Assembly attempted to solve the problem simply by voting it out of existence. In the future, priests, cardinals and the pope himself, if he chose to return to Rome, would be citizens like all other men, each with one vote. At the same time the Assembly voted that the pope "shall have all the guarantees necessary to secure his independence in the exercise of his spiritual powers." But to mark the end of the temporal power some 140 members of the Assembly gathered in the morning at the Campidoglio, or Capitol, and, after the Roman Republic was proclaimed, watched the yellow and white flag of the Papacy hauled down and the tricolor flag of republican Italy hoisted.

News of the Assembly's action was not the sort to which men remained indifferent. Republicans, naturally, exulted; others felt the occasion was infamous. From Gaeta, Pio Nono issued a formal appeal to four Catholic powers, France, Spain, Austria and Naples, to intervene with arms and restore him to power.

Foreign diplomats and Italians noted at once that Pio Nono, while including Naples, had omitted Sardinia from the appeal; even though Sardinia, during Gioberti's ministry a few months earlier, had offered its army to replace the pope on his throne. The omission was interpreted everywhere as a rebuke to Carlo Alberto and his ministers for their adherence to their constitution and the Italian cause, and it must have been so intended for no effort was made to correct an otherwise important misinterpretation of Papal policy. The pope's stand, so wholeheartedly with the cause of reaction, ended the last hope that the Papacy and those wanting a united Italy and liberal institutions might find some middle ground. A head-on collision seemed assured, almost certainly at Rome.

The sympathy of Europe as a whole was with the pope. No government recognized the new Roman Republic; not France which was itself a republic, nor Britain where feeling against the Papacy was generally strong. Queen Victoria in fact broke a long historic silence by writing a personal letter of sympathy to Pio Nono, the first such letter from an English sovereign to a pope since the time of Elizabeth I. Among the people everywhere the devout, as might be expected, were outraged and talked of a crusade to re-establish the pope amid the holy places of Rome. Others, perhaps less idealistically, worried about the shift in power and prestige throughout Europe that would accompany the survival and success of a Roman Republic. At very least some sort of United Republic of Central Italy would develop, with the Tuscan Republic and perhaps Parma and Modena merged into it. There was also the problem of where the pope would go. Wits suggested St. Helena. France actually offered Avignon, but Pio Nono refused it. Only in Rome with the great powers at arm's length did there seem to be security both for the Papacy and the great powers. Practical politicians joined the devout in insisting that the pope must return to Rome.

Besides the devout and the practical there was also in every country, even in republican France, a large part of society that feared what it rather vaguely called radicalism. It viewed the Roman Republic with alarm as bearing the seeds of another Reign of Terror. To these people the Romans, by attacking the pope, already showed signs of running amok with power and soon would be packing their betters off to the guillotine. No one's property or person would then be safe. Italian exiles might talk of Italian unity and independence, but in fact at Rome the mob was in control. For these persons there were no great issues involved in Rome. Restoring the pope was simply part of a police action necessary to keep order in Europe.

Throughout February little happened. The great powers moved slowly. Both Spain and Naples were too weak to restore the pope alone, and France and Austria were suspicious of each other. The republicans hoped that France, as a fellow republic, would recognize the new state and by diplomacy prevent Austria from intervening. It seemed not impossible. In the Po valley the armistice was still in effect and the battle of Novara in the future. To his front Radetzky had Carlo Alberto rearming; to his rear, Venice still fighting; and even farther to the rear, a civil war in Hungary. Austria hardly seemed likely, with so many troubles of its own and a new and inexperienced emperor, to start on a crusade for the pope.

One of the first acts of the new republic was to confer honorary citizenship on Mazzini and invite him to Rome. He was then at Florence, helping Guerrazzi to set up the Tuscan Republic, but, being unable to dominate Guerrazzi or even to persuade him to merge the Tuscan with the Roman Republic, he decided to leave, and early in March, he arrived in Rome. His presence, his sad, long face and severe black clothes, raised the tone of the government. Before a man whose life had been dedicated to an ideal without regard for self, the smaller, noisier men fell silent. When the news of Novara reached Rome, the Assembly proclaimed a dictatorship of Mazzini and two others with the title of "Triumvirs." But of the three, Mazzini was the first and absolute. Not by force of character but by its refinement. For eleven years he had endured the poverty and loneliness of exile in London, sustained only by his vision of Italy as a republic, independent and united. He had not returned into the Italian sun from the London fogs in order to soil the vision with excesses. "Here in Rome," he told the Assembly, "we may not be moral mediocrities." And they believed it because he had said it and somehow thereby it became not only possible but true.

But the future of the republic looked increasingly black. Novara was as much a disaster for the Romans as for the Piemontesi, for with peace assured in the Po valley Radetzky would be free to use his troops elsewhere. And with the possibility of Austria's extending its military control down to Rome, the French began to think that they must have a hand in Italian affairs. From Gaeta the French ambassador urged Louis Napoleon, the new president of the French Republic, to restore the pope. As a military operation it would be easy, it would have the sympathy of Europe, and it would re-establish French arms and influence in Italy, whence they had been almost entirely excluded since 1815. The plan appealed to Louis Napoleon and his ministers for all those reasons and also because inside France the conservative and clerical parties were fast outnumbering the republicans. Perhaps out of fear of the radicals and socialists who had fought General Cavaignac in the Paris streets many moderate republicans were joining the parties that claimed to represent order, and in the election in May 1849 the moderate republicans in the Assembly shrank from five hundred to eighty while the conservatists, monarchists and clericals, won a majority. The Second Republic of France, as Louis Napoleon and his ministers realized, was fast becoming a republic without any republicans.

A difficulty, however, in sending an expedition to restore the pope was that Article V of the French constitution declared that the republic "respects foreign nationalities, as she means to have her own respected; that she undertakes no war for the purpose of conquest, and never employs her forces against the liberty of any people whatsoever." Republican deputies in Paris again and again asked the ministers the purpose of the expedition which they were asked to authorize. "Is the restoration of the Pope what you want? Have the courage to say so; come out of the clouds; rend the veil!" But the ministers would never answer directly. They spoke vaguely of a force for observation or to keep the peace, of the importance of balancing Austria's influence and of protecting France's interests in Italy; and in the end, without any clear statement of the expedition's purpose, the deputies authorized it by a vote of 325 to 283.

The force consisted of about ten thousand troops under General Oudinot, and before they embarked at Toulon, Oudinot read them a manifesto which implied they were going to Rome as friends of the Roman Republic. His orders were vague; he was to re-establish "a regular order of

things on a basis conformable to the interests and rights of the population."
He was specifically forbidden, however, to recognize the Roman Republic.
Nevertheless when his transports arrived at Civitavecchia, the port of
Rome, he asked to be allowed to land his troops whom he hoped "would be
welcomed and lodged as was becoming allies called by such friendly intentions." The Mayor of Civitavecchia hesitated but was eventually persuaded,
and on 24 April the French troops landed shouting, *"Vive la République!"*
and *"Vive l'Italie!"*

Oudinot's real purpose, however, soon became apparent. He seized
six thousand muskets which the Romans had bought in France, disarmed
the local battalion and seized the town's only printing press. For a few days
he tried to present himself as a disinterested archangel bringing peace to a
distressed country, but within a week of landing he was marching on Rome
and proclaiming that the leaders of the republic were "outlaws of all nations who oppress this country after having lost the cause of liberty in
their own." The Romans had no troops to oppose his advance, but they
tacked to posts and trees along his way copies of Article V of the French
constitution.

Oudinot's charge, that the Roman Republic was led and supported by
foreigners to the Papal States and imposed on the pope's subjects against
their will, was the chief ground on which those who moved to suppress the
republic justified their actions. And it posed the very issue which the defense of the Roman Republic, now about to begin, would decide: whether
Rome was to be a Catholic city, an extension of the Papacy, or an Italian
city, the capital of a nation.

The Constituent Assembly, which had proclaimed the Roman Republic, consisted of two hundred members, of whom 193 were citizens of the
Papal States, and of the three Triumvirs elected after Novara to serve as
dictators two were former subjects of the pope. But the third and most
important, Mazzini, was from Genoa; and from the same city came General
Giuseppe Avezzana, the Minister of War, and Goffredo Mameli, the young
poet whose hymn *Fratelli d'Italia* was *La Marseillaise* of the Risorgimento.
Garibaldi was from Nice, which like Genoa was on the Ligurian coast, and
his two chief lieutenants, Nino Bixio and Giacomo Medici, were both
Genovesi. Unquestionably the ancient and continuing republican tradition
of Genoa contributed a great deal to the defense of the Roman Republic.
Garibaldi's men, on the other hand, the thirteen hundred of an Italian
Legion he brought to Rome, were almost all from the Romagna, where he
had recruited them, and were former subjects of the pope.

Another group of volunteers, however, almost as large and equally
important, came entirely from without the Papal States. These were about
950 men from Lombardia known as the Bersaglieri Lombardi, trained

troops under the command of Luciano Manara who had led the fighting in the Milanese streets during the Cinque Giornate. These men, exiles from Lombardia during the armistice in the Po valley, had enlisted in Carlo Alberto's army in order to continue the fight against Austria. After Novara they could not return to their homes where they would be shot by the Austrians or at very least publicly flogged, nor, under the terms of the treaty, could Vittorio Emanuele permit them to remain in Piedmont. Some had disbanded, but two battalions of them had elected to go to Rome. Most of them were not republicans and had little enthusiasm for the Republic. But by April it had been plain that Rome would soon be besieged either by Neapolitan troops or those of Austria or France, and as the men's purpose was to fight for Italian independence, they had voted to go to Rome where they would soon be able to do it.

There is no question that the men from Liguria, Lombardia and the Romagna dominated the defense of the Roman Republic, particularly after Bologna fell to the Austrians early in May and the republic, shortly thereafter, had shrunk to the city of Rome. But at least half of the most active defenders were Romagnuoli, citizens of the former Papal Legations and when other contingents of Papal troops, National Guard and volunteers are added to them, the foreigners deplored by Oudinot and Pio Nono were never more than a fourth of the men fighting. And all but a very few of these were Italians. Whether they were foreigners in Rome was one of the issues they fought to decide.

The fighting began on 30 April when Oudinot arrived outside the city walls and believing, as he had sneered at Civitavecchia, "Italians do not fight," ordered an immediate attack. He refused even to wait for siege guns or scaling ladders, but by the end of the day his men were retreating toward Civitavecchia. Garibaldi wanted to pursue them, but Mazzini, who still had hopes of persuading the French to support the republic against the Austrians, called him back.

To Garibaldi this failure to follow up the initial victory was a disastrous mistake, one for which he never forgave Mazzini. The two men were already uneasy with each other, for Mazzini, deep in his republican heart, had disapproved of Garibaldi's offer the previous year to fight for Carlo Alberto. But an easy relation between the two was probably never possible, for Garibaldi could not imagine permitting a political need or end to influence a military decision, whereas Mazzini not only could but often did. And after this quarrel on the first day of fighting, the two men often disagreed openly and bitterly.

Back in the city Garibaldi continued to recruit volunteers, and, as in South America, his extraordinary presence seemed to draw men to him. G. M. Trevelyan in *Garibaldi's Defense of the Roman Republic* quotes a young Italian who had gone to Rome to study art and who went down to a piazza one day, hoping merely to catch a glimpse of Garibaldi:

> I had no idea of enlisting. I was a young artist; I only went out of curiosity—but oh! I shall never forget that day when I saw him on his beautiful white horse in the market-place, with his noble aspect, his calm, kind face, his high smooth forehead, his light hair and beard—everyone said the same. He reminded us of nothing so much as of our Saviour's head in the galleries. I could not resist him. I left my studio. I went after him; thousands did likewise. He only had to show himself. We all worshipped him; we could not help it.[47]

The volunteers Garibaldi gathered were a scraggly lot: artists, students, the poor and soldiers of fortune, and the sight of them at first discouraged the professional soldiers in Manara's Bersaglieri Lombardi. There were too many cockades, clanking swords, wild uniforms and belts bulging with daggers. It was all too much like a bad opera, with the irregular troops lounging in the cafés; Garibaldi's staff officers, some in red shirts, galloping hither and yon; and everyone breaking out from time to time in cheers or a chorus from Verdi. For the Lombardi the disorder unpleasantly recalled the atmosphere in Milan just before the Austrians retook the city.

But then there was an alarm: the French were approaching. And as Emilio Dandolo, the historian of Manara's brigade, described it:

> The fantastic costumes were lost sight of, and every one who wore the national colors grasped in his hand the weapon which was to defend them. We passed the night in the Piazza San Pietro enchanted with the spectacle, and happy to find ourselves in the midst of soldiers, and of a confident and resolute people. We realized that Rome was capable of offering a notable resistance, and we then thanked Heaven that, in the midst of the shame and calamities of Italy, a field had been opened to us, in which we might show that our hard fate had been undeserved.[48]

Pio Nono understood neither the quality nor the diversity of the men arrayed against him. He did not see that Manara's Bersaglieri Lombardi, known in Rome as "The Aristocratic Corps," were mostly monarchists looking to Sardinia to free Lombardia and yet were able for a concept of "Italia" to make common cause with Mazzini and his democratic republicans. Nor could he foresee the clarity with which the quality of these men, monarchists and republicans, would put the question of Rome's future before the world. The defenders acted out their roles, as Garibaldi described it, "in the greatest theatre in the world, the Eternal City," and the world watched and judged.

There was never any doubt, even in Mazzini's mind, of the military

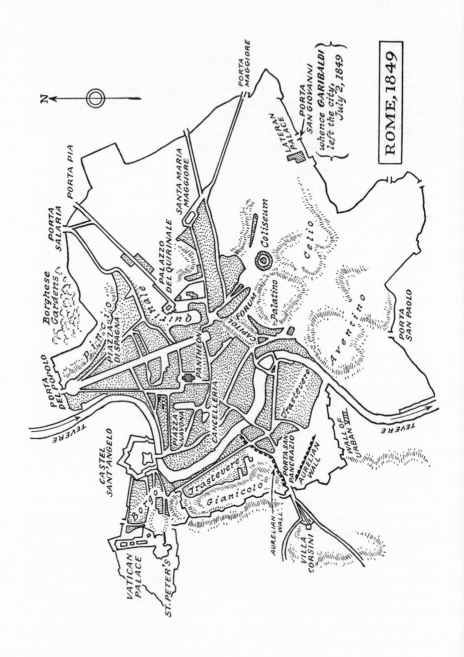

N

ROME, 1849

PORTA MAGGIORE

LATERAN PALACE

PORTA SAN GIOVANNI
{ *whence GARIBALDI
left the city, July 2, 1849* }

PORTA PIA

PORTA SALARIA

SANTA MARIA MAGGIORE

*Celio*

*Borghese Gardens*

PALAZZO DEL QUIRINALE

Coliseum

*Quirinale*

PORTA DEL POPOLO

*Pincio*

PIAZZA DI SPAGNA

PANTHEON

FORUM

*Palatino*

*Capitol*

*Aventino*

PORTA SAN PAOLO

TEVERE

PIAZZA NAVONA

CANCELLERIA

*Trastevere*

WALL OF URBAN VIII

TEVERE

CASTEL SANT'ANGELO

*Trastevere*

*Gianicolo*

PORTA SAN PANCRAZIO

AURELIAN WALL

AURELIAN WALL

*Borgo*

VATICAN PALACE

ST. PETER'S

VILLA CORSINI

outcome. France, the fellow republic, could not allow its army to be defeated. It sent reinforcements until thirty thousand French troops ringed the city. At that time Rome was still small and entirely enclosed by its Aurelian and medieval walls. Outside there were only a few villas and a convent; even the area inside was still not entirely built up.

The French strategy during the siege of Rome, which began in the first week of June, was to capture the Gianicolo, the high hill to the west from which they would be able to command the city. Breaking through the walls elsewhere would simply lead to street-fighting at which the French would be at a disadvantage. Most of the fighting, therefore, took place along the ridge of the Gianicolo, particularly outside the Porta San Pancrazio where a slight rise in the grounds outside the gate gave the French an advantage for their artillery. One time an Italian military band went to the wall and played *La Marseillaise,* but the French guns were not turned to cabbages by the irony of it.

The fighting was very bloody and often hand to hand. Garibaldi's direction of the defense was brilliant in the heroism he inspired but on perhaps the most important day of all it was unsuccessful and even inept. The occasion arose out of the cancellation of an armistice which both sides were observing. Oudinot had written to Pietro Roselli, the Roman commander-in-chief, that he was renouncing the armistice and had closed with the sentence: "I am deferring the attack upon the place [*de la place*] until Monday morning." On Sunday morning, however, he attacked and captured the Roman outposts on the high ground immediately outside the Porta San Pancrazio; and ever since argument has swirled over the meaning and intent of Oudinot's language: Did *"de la place"* include within it not only the city and its walls but also its first line of defense immediately outside it? Most historians have convicted Oudinot of deliberate bad faith; at the same time, they have convicted the Roman leaders, considering Oudinot's record of ambiguous behavior, of a foolish trust in his words and of a failure to take reasonable precautions for the city's defense.

Garibaldi's part in the affair began only when, at three in the morning, an aide burst into his room shouting the news of the French attack. All over the city, bells began to ring and drums to beat. The people rushed into the piazzas and, in their excitement and eagerness to help, interfered with the movements of troops up to the walls. By the time Garibaldi was able to study the situation for himself, the French had taken the Villa Corsini, a four-story house atop a small hill which sloped gently for about five hundred yards down to the Porta San Pancrazio. In just a few moments Garibaldi had decided that the villa with its high ground, where the Memorial Arch now stands, must be retaken. And no historian disagrees with that decision; the argument begins over his method for achieving it.

The Villa Corsini was almost perfectly situated for defense. The contours of its hill had caused, in ancient times, the road coming out of the Porta San Pancrazio to divide and pass around the hill on either side, so that the villa grounds pointed like a spearhead at the Porta San Pancrazio and the only entrance to them, because the roads had sunk and the grounds had high boundary walls, was through a gate at the tip of the spearhead, about halfway between the Porta and the villa. Through this gate the Italians would have to move to attack "like sand running through the narrows of an hour-glass." It was a point on which the defenders could concentrate all their fire.

Once inside the gate the Italians would be no better protected for the drive, which ran straight up to the villa, was flanked by high box hedges and at its end across the front of the villa was a low wall lined with orange trees in large, masonry pots, perfect for snipers. And even at the villa itself its design aided its defense, for its only entrance was through its third story which had to be reached by a large, double staircase. Yet so impregnable to Garibaldi seemed the villa's moats of sunken roads and boundary walls along its flanks that he determined to order a frontal attack, through the gate, up the drive and staircase.

For the whole of the morning frontal attacks were launched, repulsed and repeated. The volunteers responded to Garibaldi's commands with extraordinary courage. Once or twice they reached the steps and even penetrated the building, but Garibaldi never had re-enforcements enough to back them up, and they were driven out by the French counterattack. Later in the day about four hundred of the Bersaglieri tried under Manara. They had to halt before the steps, but those still alive knelt in the drive and fired at the French in the windows. Manara stood with them but when he saw the impossibility of anything but death for them all, he ordered the bugler to blow retreat.

The uselessness of the Italian bravery, the treachery of the French and the importance of the objective was enough to make men weep and it may, for a time, have made Garibaldi mad. Dandolo wrote later how, after the Bersaglieri under Manara had failed:

> In that moment of ineffable pain, Garibaldi approached, saying: "I shall require twenty resolute men and an officer for a difficult undertaking." I rushed forward and saluted, eager to escape finally from a state of inaction and to suffocate in danger the anguish which threatened to drive me mad.
> "Go," said Garibaldi to me, "with twenty of your bravest men, and take Villa Corsini at the point of the bayonet."
> Involuntarily I remained transfixed with astonishment—with twenty men to hurry forward to attack a position which two of our com-

panies and the whole of Garibaldi's Legion, after unheard of exertions, had failed in carrying! [49]

But they went, through the gate, up the drive, and by the time they had reached the steps the twenty-one were twelve. The men looked at Dandolo. They were "silent, ready for any effort." But he refused to waste them further, and ordered a retreat. On the way back six more were shot and two more, including Dandolo, wounded.

Dandolo later wrote that on this day Garibaldi had shown himself "incapable" of handling large bodies of men as opposed to the small guerrilla units with which he was so effective. Others since have questioned his use of artillery and even his judgment in not attempting a flank attack. And on all points something can be said in his defense. But all of them agree on his ability to inspire courage and further agree that, though the Villa Corsini was not retaken, the brave blood spilled in the attempt was not, ultimately, spilled in vain. The sacrifice of the hundreds who died there, in the drive or on the villa's steps, became part of the supporting legend of the Risorgimento.

After the French took the Villa Corsini on 3 June the fall of Rome became only a matter of days, except that Garibaldi and his men, by their continuing heroism, managed to extend the days into a few weeks. Mameli, the poet, was killed and so, too, was Manara. Dandolo, with some other Bersaglieri, carried Manara, their leader, to a hospital in the city, where:

> After having partaken of the Sacrament, he did not speak for some time. Then once again he commended his sons to my care. "Bring them up," he said, "in the love of religion, and of their country." He begged me to carry his remains into Lombardia, together with those of my brother. Seeing that I wept, he asked, "Does it grieve you so much that I die?" And, when my suffocating sobs prevented my replying, he added, in an undertone, but with the holiest expression of resignation: "It grieves me also." . . .
>
> . . . A short time before he died he took off a ring, which he held very dear, placed it himself on my finger, and then drawing me close to him, said, *"Saluterò tuo fratello per te, n'è vero?"* "I will embrace your brother for you." [50]

In Rome, for a time, the intensity of opera and reality of life had joined, and Dandolo put both into his history of the Bersaglieri Lombardi and of the siege. The book was published in Turin the following autumn and made a tremendous impression on Italians of every state. Dandolo intended it to be a memorial to his friends who had died; he did not want their sacrifice to be in vain, or to be forgotten. But the book was much more: passed from hand to hand it became over the years a stunning and continuing defeat for the Papacy.

Even in Rome, as the siege continued, the Papacy gradually lost the sympathy of many of the people traditionally most loyal to it. As the French cannonballs fell in the city, mostly in the slums of the Trastevere at the foot of the Gianicolo, the people there nicknamed them after the pope. *"Ecco un Pio Nono,"* "Here comes a Pio Nono," they would call to each other. They would ask why it was wrong for the pope to fight the Austrians but not wrong for him to call in the French to fight his own people; and the deep reservoir of affection which the poor people of Rome had always had for their "Papa" began to drain away.

Meanwhile as the fighting went into its second month the world continued to have its attention held on the question of Rome. In an allocution issued in April the pope had asked: "Who does not know that the city of Rome, the principal seat of the Church, has now become, alas, a forest of roaring beasts, overflowing with men of every nation, apostates, or heretics, or leaders of communism and socialism?"

But all sorts of men who had stayed in the city, men not republicans, nor even Italians, but foreign consuls, artists, priests, French prisoners and even a French negotiator trying to arrange a peace, wrote to their governments, newspapers and friends at home that the charges were simply not true. There was no Reign of Terror, no mass confiscation of property or persecution of priests. Five cardinals remained in the city throughout the siege, unmolested, and church services continued. Mazzini himself remained simple and democratic. He slept and worked in a small room in the Quirinale, and anyone could speak with him, workman or official. At night he ate either in a cheap restaurant or had a supper of bread and raisins in his room. Sometimes, when left alone, he would sing to his guitar.

His social program had been published in April before the allocution, and had been equally simple:

> No war of classes, no hostility to existing wealth, no wanton or unjust violation of the rights of property; but a constant disposition to ameliorate the material condition of the classes least favored by fortune.[51]

It was a program that the pope himself could have adopted, and by May, or before the siege proper began, the Romans and the foreign observers recognized that it was not the issue. The Romans, as opposed to Mazzini and the doctrinaire republicans, were willing, even eager, to have the pope return if he would give laymen some voice in the government. But it was just this which the pope in the balance of his "roaring beast" allocution showed he was unwilling to do. He openly condemned the proposition that the Church would benefit from the loss of the temporal power and made it clear that he would make no concessions in order to return to Rome. No concessions meant a restoration of ecclesiastical government just as it had been under Gregory XVI, and the threat of this kept the Roman people and the doctrinaire republicans united.

In the end, of course, the pope had no need to make concessions. The strength of the French army was overpowering, and on 30 June, after fighting for two months, the Roman Republic capitulated. Three days later the French entered the city. In the interim Garibaldi had retreated into the mountains, but Mazzini had elected to remain in the city, walking about the streets as a private citizen. The French dared not arrest him for fear of arousing the Romans, but after a few days Mazzini, too, departed, to return eventually to England. At the end of the month a Papal Commission of three cardinals arrived to take over the government and finally, in April 1850, the pope himself returned.

It had been a curious fight: Pio Nono, personally a genial man, a little stout and dressing usually in white and gold against Mazzini, sad, gaunt, and always in black; and around Mazzini like an angry fly, dashing back and forth, Garibaldi in his red shirt.

The defense of the Roman Republic caught the imagination of Italy, and therein lay Mazzini's ultimate victory. By the quality of the men he had enlisted to fight and die for Rome he had made the city seem glorious again. Not the old Rome of classical times or even Papal Rome with its churches and basilicas but a new Rome of modern Italians, a "Third Rome." In the future when Piemontesi or Lombardi, Venetians, Tuscans or even Neapolitans read Dandolo's book and then talked of a united Italy, they talked increasingly of its capital, of necessity, being at Rome. Such was the victory Mazzini fashioned out of the defeat of the Roman Republic. Like himself it was mystical and prophetic.

From the defeat at Rome, Garibaldi also fashioned a victory, and it was, like himself, a brilliant improvisation. It was the retreat from Rome, and it, too, captured the imagination of Italy.

Although it was plain that the Roman Republic was finished, Garibaldi could not bring himself to capitulate to foreigners on Italian soil. He planned to continue the fight from the mountains or failing in that to join Manin and the Venetians at Venice which the Austrians had not yet re-taken. Neither plan was feasible, but Garibaldi had not the sort of mind that calculated close chances. To carry on the war from the mountains meant relying on an aroused and friendly peasantry, but in the past it had never been either and almost certainly would not become so after the defeat at Rome. To get to Venice required reaching the Adriatic, which in turn meant that Garibaldi must lead his army through the heart of some thirty thousand French troops, twelve thousand Neapolitans, six thousand Spaniards, fifteen thousand Austrians and two thousand Tuscans, all eager to catch him. Even so, some four thousand men followed Garibaldi out of

Rome the night before the French entered. With him went his wife, Anita.

It soon was apparent that the peasantry would not support the little army with recruits, food or money, and Garibaldi's first plan of continuing the fight from the hills was abandoned almost at once. The discipline of his army was excellent. He requisitioned food from the peasants but always paid for it, and he shot any of his men caught thieving. He succeeded by feints and forced marches in losing himself in the mountains although at times Austrian armies were only miles away. The number of desertions, however, was very high. The marching was exhausting and many of the men undoubtedly started with the idea of continuing only as far as their own village. The army soon numbered only two thousand.

In the first weeks he escaped the French, Spaniards and Neapolitans to the south and east of Rome and reached the Tuscan hills. Austrian armies from bases in Tuscany and the Adriatic shore probed into the mountains to find them. There were some great disappointments. At Arezzo the nervous citizens refused to admit the army to the town, and Garibaldi, although urged by his troops, refused to attack. Inside the town the liberals attempted a revolution but were suppressed. That night, as the army retreated, the rear guard was attacked by Austrians, and many of the stragglers and wounded were hunted down by the peasants led by priests and friars. But from other towns little deputations of patriots talked with him, told him the lay of the land and then ever afterwards cherished the memories of Garibaldi at their town well, on his horse coming down the road, and above all what he had said. Outside of Città di Castello he told them: "This time things have gone badly, but the blood shed at Rome will be productive, and I hope that in ten years at most Italy will be free." In fact it was eleven years, and then as Vittorio Emanuele's troops marched down the same road the people could not stop laughing and crying as they reminded themselves again and again of how it had been in 1849 and of what Garibaldi had said. As a military action the retreat from Rome was meaningless; as a piece of political propaganda it was brilliantly successful.

After Arezzo even Garibaldi could see that far from being an opposing army they were in fact fugitives. With some peasants helpful and others not and the towns also divided, there was plainly no possibility of sustaining himself and his men in the mountains through a winter, even if they could survive that long. Equally it was clear that with the armies the Austrians were massing on the Adriatic plain he could not break out of the mountains, commandeer the necessary boats, and embark for Venice before the Austrians would surround him. And if by some miracle he could embark his army, there were still the Austrian gunboats patrolling

N

MOUTHS
of
THE PO

BOLOGNA

RAVENNA

BY BOAT

FILIGARE

CESENATICO

RIMINI

PRATO

SAN
MARINO

FIRENZE

R. Arno

EMPOLI

R. Tiber

URBINO

VOLTERRA

AREZZO

CITTÀ DI CASTELLO

SIENA

L. Trasmene

R. Tiber

ASSISI

S. MARIA

CALA MARTINA

ORVIETO

TODI

SPOLETO

R. Tiber

TERNI

RIETI

T  Y  R  R  H  E  N  I  A  N

GARIBALDI'S
RETREAT FROM ROME
3 July to 3 August
ESCAPE FROM THE AUSTRIANS
3 August to 2 September
1849

ROME

TIVOLI

S  E  A

the coast which could easily overtake any vessels he might be able to pick up.

To save his men, therefore, he headed for the tiny Republic of San Marino, perched on the farthest range of mountains and looking over the plain to the Adriatic. He was aided in reaching it by the bungling of the Austrian leaders and their fear of him. His whole army seldom came in view at any one spot, and the peasants and townspeople, who saw only parts of it, invariably reported that it was larger and better armed than it was. Garibaldi by reputation became a devil in a red shirt rising out of the ground where he was least expected. His system of scouts, which he adapted to the mountains from his experience on the pampas in Uruguay, aided him in this. In the month that he was in the Apennines he developed a cavalry that, although informal and operating almost entirely in single units, was probably the best in Europe at gathering information.

He reached San Marino with a final dash on the last day of July. The Sammarinesi, who had been watching nervously from their high towers, could see three Austrian armies converging on him. Garibaldi told the town leaders that he and his men came to them now as refugees and would lay down their arms in the Republic. "Welcome to the refugee," was the reply. "General, this hospitable land receives you."

For most of his fifteen hundred men San Marino was the end. Throughout the summer the Sammarinesi argued with the Austrians about the terms of surrender which in principle were that the men would give up their arms and then be free to go home. But there were no guarantees, and some were imprisoned, others flogged; the majority, however, were either passed or slipped safely through the Austrian lines. To each the Sammarinesi gave a sum of money and some civilian clothes.

Garibaldi, obsessed with the idea of never surrendering to foreigners on Italian soil and probably quite correctly assuming that no terms for safe conduct home would include him, did not even stay the night in San Marino. With a guide, two hundred and fifty devoted men, mostly his staff officers, and his wife, who was six months pregnant and ill, he pushed on for Venice. Keeping to the mountains, marching almost entirely at night and without lights, some of the men inevitably lost touch with the column and were left behind. One of these was a Swiss, Gustav von Hoffstetter, who had been with Garibaldi from the beginning in Rome. Back in Zurich he wrote a factual account of the siege and the retreat which was published in both German and Italian in 1851. Like Dandolo's history it was effective propaganda for the patriotic cause.

At the village of Gatteo, the guide, after leading Garibaldi and his men north across a little river called the Rubicon, left them to return to San Marino. Garibaldi now was in the Romagna, a fiercely patriotic area where everyone great and small would help him. He headed for the little town of Cesenatico on the coast where he might get boats. The fishermen, dragged out of bed in the dead of night, understandably were not enthusiastic about seeing their livelihood sail off to Venice and worked slowly and sulkily, but they did work, and an hour before the Austrians entered the town, the flotilla was under way.

The boats were poorly provisioned, particularly with water, and everyone suffered from thirst. His wife, Anita, was now seriously ill, in pain and feverish. In his *Memorie* Garibaldi describes the sail:

> We continued all the rest of the day along the Italian coast of the Adriatic, keeping a certain distance offshore, and with a favorable wind. Night, when it came, was very beautiful. The moon was full, and I saw rise, with a sense of distress, the sailor's companion on which I had gazed many times with reverent adoration! Lovely, as I had never seen it; but for us, unfortunately, too lovely! The moon for us was fatal that night!
>
> East of the point of Goro lay the Austrian squadron. . . .[52]

In the naval battle that followed at night and on a stormy sea most of the ships were captured, largely because the fishermen pressed into service refused to sail or fight. But Garibaldi was an experienced sailor and his boat and a few others managed to beach on a deserted section of the coast. The whole countryside had been aroused by the noise of the naval cannon, and there was no longer any possibility of reaching Venice as a group or even singly. On the beach they separated, and each man plunged into the underbrush of the marshy coast to save himself as best he could. Most succeeded in disappearing; others were caught and shot. Garibaldi was last off the beach as Anita no longer could walk, and he had to carry her. Fortunately the man who saw them first, Nino Bonnet, was a leading citizen and also a patriot. Two of his younger brothers had fought and one had died under Garibaldi at Rome.

While Bonnet arranged an escape through the patriotic underground, the same *trafila* which three years earlier had passed d'Azeglio from town to town, he hid Garibaldi in a succession of peasant farms near the lagoons and pine forests of Ravenna. In one of them, a dairy farm near Mandriole, Anita died in Garibaldi's arms as he carried her upstairs. As the Austrians were expected momentarily and the corpse if found would betray them all, the peasants, promising to bury it at once, pushed the stunned man on to the next haven. Days later, in yet another farm, he was hid in a room from which he could hear the gangs of farm laborers at their dinner. They talked of his miraculous disappearance, of how no one knew where he was, of how his wife, so hastily buried in shallow sand, had been dug up and chewed on by animals. At that the door swung open and the wretched man stood revealed before them, his lips moving noiselessly. He was immediately pushed back, and the door shut. All had seen him, but the Austrians did not learn his hiding place.

Bonnet's plan was to move Garibaldi along the *trafila* until he was across the Apennines and on the west coast of Italy where there would be an open sea and a better chance of escape. At night he was passed from one farm to the next. An important link in the chain was the parish priest of Modigliana. Another was a girl who distracted some Austrian soldiers as Garibaldi huddled in the shadows of the room. Still another was an old man who stared so long at Garibaldi's letter of introduction which mysteriously did not identify its subject that finally Garibaldi blurted out the truth. Calmly the old man replied: "Courage, General, all will come right again." With so many persons necessarily in a plot involving such a famous man, it is extraordinary that not one betrayed him.

Finally he was at the sea at Cala Martina, a wild and hidden spot on the Tuscan shore. It was the morning of the second day in September, a month after the naval battle and two since he had marched out of Rome. The sight of the open sea so excited him that he took off his shoes and socks and splashed childishly in the water. Soon a fishing boat appeared and turned into the shore. He embraced the men who had led him to the water's edge and stepped aboard. As the boat pushed off from shore, as the space of water between him and the land he loved grew wider and the men who had saved him smaller, he cried out in a voice they never forgot, *"Viva l'Italia!"*

# CHAPTER 29

The siege of Venice. Manin and resistance at any cost. The assault on Malghera. The railway bridge. The bombardment. Cholera. The failure of the fleet and surrender. Manin's departure. The end of the liberal movements of 1848–49. The settlement of Italy.

WITH THE FALL of Rome the republican movement in Italy was crushed except for Venice, where the Venetians still maintained their Republic of San Marco despite the Austrian blockade. And, except for the Kingdom of Sardinia, where the constitution survived, the more general movement for liberal institutions, which included in it many who were not republicans, was equally crushed. At Naples, Ferdinando II had recaptured his wayward Kingdom of Sicily by force and, although the constitution was still in being, he ruled increasingly without it. The French and Austrians together occupied the Papal States, and Pio Nono had announced that he intended to abolish all his liberal reforms. Grand Duke Leopoldo had returned to Tuscany at the head of an Austrian army of occupation, and Austrian arms ruled in Parma, Modena, Lombardia and the Venetian mainland. There was even an Austrian garrison in the fortress of Alessandria in Piedmont. At Turin, however, Vittorio Emanuele and his ministers governed through constitutional channels, and at Venice, the city which for a hundred years had been the symbol of decadence, the people continued to fight for their republic.

But the Sardinian defeat at Novara, by releasing Austrian troops for Radetzky to use elsewhere, was the beginning of the end for the Venetians just as it had been for the republicans at Florence and Novara. Soon after news of the battle reached Venice, the representatives of the people, elected on a basis of manhood suffrage and secret ballot, assembled in the great Council Chamber of the Doge's Palace, the Sala del Maggior Consiglio; the same room in which, only a year and a half before, the Scientific Congress had met and, because of the censorship, been forced to discuss the Austrian governments in Italy in terms of potatoes. Now as free men and self-governing the Venetians listened to Manin describe the situation

367

facing them. Neither the Tuscan nor Roman Republics had yet fallen and although no help could be expected from them, there was always a chance that France or England might intervene, diplomatically or with arms, and impose some general European settlement. Or the situation in Hungary might cause the emperor to make concessions. Manin painted a grim, truthful picture, almost without hope. But even so, when he asked the Assembly if it wished to resist the Austrians, every man cried yes, "Sì." Whatever the cost? "Sì." And then without a dissenting voice they passed a decree:

> Venezia resisterà all'Austriaco ad ogni costo. A tale scopo il Presidente Manin è investito di poteri illimitati.[53]

> Venice will resist Austria at all costs. For that purpose President Manin is invested with unlimited powers.

The resolution, so simple that anyone could understand it, was immediately published throughout the republic and was received soberly but with immense satisfaction. The Venetians after a hundred years of being scorned as decadent, after the humiliation of being betrayed and bartered by Napoleon at Campoformio and after having earned a reputation of being the most docile of the Habsburgs' Italian subjects, had felt themselves again a people ready to act in shaping their destiny. They were almost certain, they knew, to lose, as certain as had been the Trojans when the Greeks had surrounded Troy. But their own poet, Foscolo, in his *Dei Sepolcri,* had given pride of place and feeling, above all others, to Hector, who had defended his city and died for it, and now, much in Hector's spirit, the Venetians looked across the lagoon to the Austrian guns on the mainland and thought it better to fight and fail than not to fight at all.

The resolution needed no rhetoric to support it, for it was the result of genuine feeling common to Venetians of every class, and to commemorate that feeling, years later, the Venetians inscribed the resolution with its date, 2 April 1849, on a modest, bronze plaque which they placed on the east wall of the Sala del Maggior Consiglio. There, amid the historical paintings of the great days of the old Venetian Republic, it reminds the Venetians of today of another stirring moment in their history.

The republic which had determined to continue fighting, though the military odds were fast increasing against it, was more than just the city of Venice. It included the entire lagoon, ninety miles in circumference, and a total population of 200,000 living on several hundred islands. Chief among these, of course, was Venice itself, built on some 120 small islands and with a population of about 125,000; after it in size came Chioggia, at the southern end of the lagoon, with 50,000; and the balance was distributed among the larger islands such as Murano and the Lido. Spotted along the waterways connecting the islands in the shallow lagoon were nearly sixty forts with combined garrisons of nearly eighteen thousand men. The most important of these were the Forte di Brondolo, with which Chioggia defended Venice from the south, and the Forte di Malghera at the mainland end of the railway bridge to Venice. It was there that Radetzky decided to concentrate his forces.

On 4 May he began an assault on Malghera during which, in a few hours, some seven thousand projectiles, cannonballs and shells, were shot into the fort. It was, perhaps, the heaviest barrage in military history till that time, and Radetzky expected it to demoralize the inexperienced Venetians and cause them to surrender. He had even asked three archdukes to be on hand for the event. But at the end of the day more Austrian than Venetian guns were out of commission, the archdukes had left, disappointed, and Radetzky was forced to admit that he had underestimated the Venetians.

In fact, although most of the garrison were Venetians, the officer in command, Colonel Girolamo Ulloa, was a Neapolitan, one of the two thousand persuaded by General Pepe to cross the Po and fight for "Italia" when Ferdinando had ordered his army to return to Naples. Later many of the two thousand had also returned to their homes, but a number of officers had remained at Venice with Pepe and were to be of the greatest importance in the fighting. The Austrians had deliberately excluded all Venetians from the technical branches of the army, so that almost the only officers in Venice with any training or experience in engineering or the use of artillery were the Neapolitans.

Even though Radetzky's assault had failed, he called on the republic the next day to surrender. He offered no terms beyond a general pardon and permission, for those who wished, to emigrate. There was no mention of any rights of self-government or any other of the sixteen points which Manin had demanded of the Austrians eighteen months earlier. What Radetzky offered, or so the Venetians felt, was a return to the bondage against which they had revolted, and they refused. They still clung to the hope that, if they could only hold out, international events and diplomacy would eventually work in their favor.

The siege of Malghera continued for three weeks, at the end of which some sixty thousand projectiles had been shot into the fort and one man in six, or about four hundred, killed. Even at night, it was estimated, explosive shells often fell at the rate of one a minute. Ulloa led sorties out and, by cutting dikes, flooded the plain, but even though for a time the Austrians worked waist-deep in water, they succeeded in building artillery emplacements still closer to the fort and on 24 May the Austrian guns opened fire on it from close range. The Venetians replied, charge for charge, but around them their earthen breastworks were disintegrating into the plain and their stone walls crumbling. The Austrians estimated that on 25 May alone they fired fifteen thousand shells into Malghera.

Plainly the fort could not hold out forever, and the Austrians were known to be massing men for an assault on the morning of 27 May. So, rather than lose the garrison, Manin ordered the fort to be evacuated, and, on the night of 26–27 May, Ulloa led his men out in the greatest secrecy. A few, mostly the wounded, were taken directly to Venice in small boats. The majority, however, had to leave by the railroad bridge where discovery by the Austrians meant certain death or capture, for the Austrians would be able to rake the exposed bridge with their artillery. Ulloa put fuses on his cannon so that the pieces continued firing for three hours after the men had left, which was time enough for them to retire along the bridge and to prepare the next line of defense.

The bridge which now became the area of fighting was very much as it is today except that there was then no automobile road beside the railway. It was thirty feet wide and consisted of 222 arches spanning two and a fifth miles of open water. Every two-fifths of a mile there was a "station," a small, square bastion on which repair crews used to keep their equipment and building materials. There were five of these in all, and the Venetians retreated to the third, which was the largest, and turned it into a fort, although it was so small it could hold only seven guns and two mortars. And then, with every man safely out of Malghera, they blew up nineteen arches of the bridge between themselves and the mainland.

Just to the east of this third "station," which the Venetians now called the Batteria di San Antonio, was the tiny island battery of San Secondo, so that the Venetians had, in effect, a long pole pointing at the Austrians at the end of which were two pistols. But as artillery then had not the power to fire the two and a fifth miles into Venice, the Venetians felt perfectly safe. Food and ammunition, they recognized, would ultimately be greater problems than the number of casualties. Meanwhile their morale remained so high that a sentry refused to accept an Austrian dispatch addressed curtly to "Lawyer Manin."

For a month the Austrians bombarded the two batteries without accomplishing anything. Although they often could silence the Venetian guns by day, always during the night the damage would be repaired, broken walls filled with new bags of earth, damaged guns replaced and ammunition replenished. Then the next morning the cannonading would begin again.

In desperation the Austrians tried an attack on the Forte di Brondolo at Chioggia, but it was even stronger than Malghera, and they soon gave it up. Then they tried to take advantage of the prevailing onshore breeze and tied explosives to balloons which they released from a frigate anchored off the Lido. But the fuses were uncertain and the wind perverse. Most of the bombs exploded over the lagoon or dropped into it unfired, and a few caused the frigate alarm by blowing back toward it.

Although the city, shielded by its lagoon, was impregnable, it was beginning to starve. By the middle of July the people were living almost entirely on bread, corn and an occasional fish. When a raid on the mainland brought back a hundred oxen, a performance at the opera of *William Tell* was stopped in order to spread the news. And even wine was reserved for the sick and convalescent.

In June there had been a food riot, but Manin had convinced the people that the government did not have secret hoards of food, and in July he issued ration cards. They were good for two weeks, but no family could buy more than a day's supply at a time. And then on 10 July the city received more bad news. Bottles came drifting across the lagoon into which the Austrians had put bulletins of the fall of Rome and of the defeats which Austrian and Russian armies were inflicting on the Hungarians. While the republicans at Rome had held out, the Venetians had felt some companionship in their struggle. Now they were alone and, with the bad news from Hungary, assistance from outside was fast disappearing.

To pay for their war they consumed the city's wealth accumulated over the centuries. Enormous forced loans were imposed on the rich and cheerfully paid. In addition many donated jewels, plate and other valuables to the government to be converted into cash. General Pepe gave a portrait of Cesare Borgia which he and others incorrectly attributed to Leonardo da Vinci, and most of the public buildings were mortgaged, even the Doge's Palace.

Then suddenly during the night of 29 July cannonballs began to fall on the western two-thirds of the city, from the railroad station almost to the Piazza San Marco. The people poured out into the streets, less in dismay than astonishment. The city had never been bombarded. They believed that it never could be. Yet even as they realized their centuries-old invulnerability was crumbling, was over forever, they were enthralled by the beauty of the artillery display which was ending it. From the mainland near Malghera heated cannonballs soared in vast, red arcs toward the city, and at immense heights shells whose fuses were too short exploded in showers of powder and iron particles. The Austrians, in an effort to carry the war into the city, were firing toward it at an elevation of forty-five degrees. To do so they had been forced to dismount their cannon and set them on timber cradles with the breeches sunk in the soft soil near Malghera.

Not all the ballistic problems were solved in a night. At the start the guns tended to upset with almost every firing, the fuses on the shells almost invariably burned too fast, and the heated cannonballs generally fell short because, as the Austrians now discovered, they created a greater resistance in the air than the unheated. But even so, though the distance from Malghera to the city was about three and a half miles, a greater distance than artillery had ever shot before, the Austrians in the next three weeks were able to fire some twenty-five thousand projectiles into the city. And the Venetians were unable to reply, for their powder, mostly homemade, was so weak that they could fire only a mile.

The bombardment, however, caused relatively little damage. Most of the balls, by the time they reached the city, were merely falling of their own weight, and one, for example, dropped through the roof of the British consulate and, passing between the consul's legs as he lay on his back in bed, merely bruised him slightly. In all, only seven persons seem to have been killed and thirty injured. Even the damage to property was small. Because the red-hot balls and shells generally fell short, into the lagoon, there were few fires with which the citizens' fire patrols could not cope, and only one building, a church, seems to have burned.

But in another way the bombardment accomplished all that the Austrians wished. By forcing two-thirds of the population to leave their homes and camp with their neighbors in the eastern sections of the city it greatly increased the chance of an epidemic. Even though many of the refugees were quickly passed on to other islands, sanitary conditions, never easy at best to maintain in Venice, deteriorated, and soon cholera was killing the overcrowded and underfed Venetians far more effectively than the Austrians. In one week in August fifteen hundred persons died of it, which was six hundred more than all of those killed in the fighting, for once the Venetians had retreated from Malghera to the center of the railway bridge, the Austrians could not get at them.

The only hope of defeating the cholera lay in breaking the Austrian naval blockade and bringing in quantities of fresh food and water or wine. It was, in fact, the one hope for continuing to resist the Austrians, for the city's supplies of even the most diluted forms of grain were almost exhausted. But the Venetian navy, in spite of the city's long association with the sea, was now the weakest part of its defense. At the very start of the revolt many of the Venetian officers and men had been trapped and beguiled by their Austrian colleagues into remaining at their posts in Pola and Trieste, many of the others who had been at Venice had been taken by Manin and the government off their ships to serve as soldiers in forts around the lagoon, and in the period before Novara it had seemed unnecessary to build up the Venetian navy for the Sardinian navy was keeping the Austrians blockaded in Trieste. But even after Novara, Manin had been slow to reorganize and enlarge what navy there was, the one fault with which historians charge him. The small force felt its neglect and its morale was poor; it was, perhaps, the only group in Venice not caught up in the spirit of the city's endeavor.

Twice in August, Manin ordered the fleet to sail out and attack the Austrians, at any cost, but each time it returned without having fought. Its admiral could report, correctly, that his ships were outnumbered and outgunned, but still: not to fight was an Austrian victory. What was needed was a leader like Garibaldi, who would raise morale and attempt the impossible; and rumors that he was about to arrive kept circulating through the city. But by this time he had already failed in his effort to reach Venice and was hiding in the farms and forests of Romagna.

After the navy's second retreat before the Austrian blockade, Manin and the Assembly agreed that continued resistance would accomplish nothing. And on 23 August the republic capitulated. Its heroic defense did not even win it any political concessions. The Austrians merely promised, in writing, not to punish any individual, soldier or civilian, for his part in the Venetian revolt with the exception of forty men who were "to remove themselves from Venice and all the states of Imperial Austria." Number seven on the list was "Manin Daniele, lawyer."

His position in the hearts of his fellow citizens, however, was unique. The French consul had offered a steamer to take "the forty" and their families to France, and most, including Manin, accepted. He resigned his position as dictator and turned his unlimited powers back to the Assembly which voted him a small gift of money, for while serving as president and dictator he had refused to draw any salary. Then as a private citizen he walked to his house overlooking the Campo San Paterniano, today the Campo Manin, and began to pack what few belongings he and his family could take with them.

Outside his house at daybreak on 28 August, in the small campo where his statue now stands, the Venetians gathered and stood silently, looking up at his windows. From that house, eighteen months earlier, the Austrians had secretly taken Manin to prison; and, as one of the first achievements of their revolt, the Venetians had openly carried him back to it, on their shoulders. From it he had started for the Arsenal. Now as he was about to leave it and his city for the last time, the people stood quietly outside, expressing their grief and their love by silence. One man, however, spoke, as much to himself as to anyone in particular, and behind the window Manin heard the disembodied voice and forever afterward in exile it was for him the voice of Venice:

Quà sta el nostro buon padre, poveretto! Ha gia tanto sofferto per me. Dio le benedissa!

Here is our good father, unfortunate man. He has already suffered so much for me. May God bless him! [54]

Silently they escorted him and his family to the Riva, where they watched him go out in a gondola to board the French steamer. At six it weighed anchor and started down the channel to the Porto di Lido. In a few short minutes, as it rounded the eastern end of the city by the public gardens, it was out of sight and Manin and all the other Venetian leaders of any ability were gone. In future the list of the forty proscribed by the Austrians was to be the new *libro d'oro* of Venice, and to be related to one of them was also to share a bit in his glory.

Later that morning in the Piazza San Marco, the Austrians hoisted their yellow and black flags on the poles before the basilica, and in the afternoon they held a review of troops, shouting the commands in German.

Two days later Radetzky came from Verona to make a triumphal entry down the Grand Canal. All the palazzi, by military order, were decked with flags, but scarcely a Venetian was seen behind a window and not a sound was heard. In "perfect silence," according to the British consul, the gondolas carried the field marshal and his staff the length of the canal. At the Piazzetta they disembarked and entered the basilica where a Te Deum was sung, and the patriarch officiated, speaking with joy of the restoration of peace and order. As Radetzky emerged from the service a young priest rushed to his side, knelt and kissed his hand. In Venice, Church and State were again united, and the aspirations of the people to be free and self-governing were defeated.

With the surrender of the Venetians on 23 August 1849, the liberal and often revolutionary movements of 1848 came finally to an end, for ten days earlier the Hungarians, too, had surrendered to Franz Josef. The first revolt, in January 1848 in Palermo, had seemed to forecast a new settlement for Europe on a more democratic, constitutional basis, one that would incorporate, perhaps in diluted form, some of the principles of the French Revolution, nationality, the rights of man, some separation of Church and State, and popular sovereignty. But with the fall of Venice, eighteen months later, everywhere, even in France, the principle of government by force rather than consent was more apparent and seemingly more powerful than before. The only exception was the small Kingdom of Sardinia where a new constitution survived, but Sardinia was neither prosperous nor happy because of it. The kingdom's double defeat by the Austrians had shaken its dynasty, ruined its finances and exhausted its people.

Like most men who have been defeated those Italians who had fought and lost consoled themselves with the belief that at least they had learned from their mistakes, and certainly for most of them the defeats of 1848–49 did narrow and clarify the political issues before them. The events of the eighteen-month period conclusively ended any program for federation under the Papacy. They suggested that local reforms, state by state, must be supported by a national effort or fail. They established that none of the Italian princes, with the possible exception of Vittorio Emanuele II, would support reform or a drive for unity, and they showed that Italy could not make itself in despite of Austria without the active help of France or England. Other issues still remained to be decided, notably whether a free and united Italy should be a republic or a constitutional monarchy, but after 1848–49 these remaining issues were fewer and in better focus.

And further, those who had fought and lost, if they could have seen beyond their defeat, might have noted another positive gain with which to console themselves. They had, for the first time in generations, been leaders in the mainstream of European events. In all of Europe there was no greater hero than Garibaldi, no more important political thinker than Mazzini. No other people had harnessed barehanded courage better than the Milanesi or shown greater civic stamina than the Venetians. They had demonstrated beyond cavil that Italians were not decadent and Italy not merely a "geographical expression." They had moved their fight for unity and independence close to the center of European affairs where it could neither be concealed nor dismissed.

Austria, by force and with the reluctant assent of England and France, had been able to reimpose on Italy the settlement of the Congress of Vienna, but now the great majority of politically minded Italians did not consider that settlement reasonable, and an increasing number of other Europeans agreed with them. This time the Habsburg emperor was not the successor of a tyrannous Napoleon but was himself the tyranny. There was no hope of making the Imperial system function except by force. As the archdukes, viceroys and ambassadors reappeared, they were greeted in silence and treated as enemies. The national movement in Italy to which so many men had contributed, even Pio Nono, recant as he might, had changed the feelings and attitudes of the people. Though Franz Josef and his generals might refuse to see it, more than the passage of years separated the men and conditions of 1815 from those of 1849. Another Italian upheaval was almost inevitable, and grimly, bitterly Italians in exile and in Italy set about preparing for the day when the battle might be renewed.

# PART III

PART III

# CHAPTER 30

Changes in life and attitudes after 1848. King *Bomba*. His increasing autocracy. Vittorio Emanuele. His liberalism. The Proclamation of Moncalieri. The Siccardi Laws. Cavour's speech. Santa Rosa's death. Cavour enters the ministry.

As THE PEOPLE of Italy's towns and cities tried to pick up their lives, after the revolutionary upheavals of 1848–49, most of them found their way of life noticeably different. For those who were forced into exile, were impoverished by fines, or who had lost husbands or sons in the fighting the cause of the change was obvious and the effect of it often overpowering. But for the others, less obviously touched by events, the change was equally real. For the eighteen-month period from the Cinque Giornate to the fall of Venice had ended an era. The period had been one in which gradual changes had accelerated until they seemed to make a visible line of demarcation after which everything was different: domestic habits, civic life, custom and thought. It was less true for the Neapolitans than for any others and hardly true at all for the peasants, wherever they were, but for the people of most towns, the traditional leaders of Italian life, the change was noticeable, even dramatic.

In Milan, for example, the last personal and feudal ties between the great patrician families and the Habsburgs were broken. Those Milanesi who still felt some loyalty to the emperor, and there were some, packed their belongings and moved to Vienna. Life for them in Milan had become impossible; anti-Austrian feeling was no longer a question of policy or party, to be debated in drawing rooms, it was now universal in all classes within the city, and those who did not share it were ostracized.

Even in Tuscany the Florentine aristocracy, traditionally less fierce than the Milanesi, soon had established a social boycott of Leopoldo and his Austrians, and when a few of the ladies broke it to attend a ball at the Palazzo Pitti in honor of Radetzky, they were publicly compared to the city's harlots, to the advantage of the latter. The moderates throughout Tuscany did not forgive the grand duke for spurning their invitation to

379

return as a constitutional monarch. Leopoldo, once the only Habsburg in Italy with a claim to being loved by his subjects, could now have regained their favor only by dismissing the Austrian army of occupation and by changing his form of government from an absolute to a constitutional monarchy. But, as a Habsburg who had elected to stay within the family's Imperial system, he could do neither. And where before 1848 strong anti-Austrian feeling had been confined almost entirely to extremists in the Po valley, it now crossed the Apennines and reached almost to Rome.

One result of this feeling, another change from before 1848, was the extinction in all the Habsburg Italian states of any agitation for reform. The political end to which all liberal leaders north of Rome now aimed was, first of all, to drive the Austrians out of Italy. There were no longer any movements for home rule, such as Manin once had led in Venice, for a free press and liberal institutions or for representation in Vienna, the army or the local administrations. When in March 1854 a British minister suggested in Parliament that the Italians, instead of revolting against the Austrians, would do better to work for reform, Manin, speaking for most Italians, replied in a Paris newspaper, *La Presse:*

> We do not ask of Austria that she be humane and liberal in Italy— which, after all, would be impossible for her even if she desired; we ask her to get out. We have no concern with her humanity and her liberalism; we wish to be masters in our own house.[55]

The declaration was clear and accepted by most Europeans as final. It was useless now to talk of the Habsburgs' feudal right to the Duchy of Milan; the concept no longer had meaning. It was futile to talk, as men had before 1848, of Austria's right by treaty to Venice or Parma; Italians of the present refused to be bound by the treaties of a previous generation, treaties in which even their grandfathers had not been consulted. Austria held its Italian provinces by force, and only by force.

In the social life of the people, as well as in their political ideals, the cost of the war in property damage, taxes and Austrian fines had also hastened changes, particularly in the two Austrian provinces of Lombardia and the Veneto. Before 1848 no Milanese lady went out in a carriage drawn by a single horse or went on foot unless she was followed by a domestic in livery. After 1848, however, one-horse carriages became common, and footmen who followed in livery, rare. Manzoni, the novelist, for a time even had to give up his carriage altogether in order to pay the Austrian fine. Under the pressure of bad times the distinctions between the patrician and middle class rapidly began to disappear. And at Turin, where many of the noble Milanesi were living as impoverished refugees, the blurring of class distinctions was increased by the new Chamber of Deputies in which men of both classes sat as equals. As political parties developed, in order for the members to plan strategy and speeches, they even began to meet regularly outside the chamber.

And in the Kingdom of Sardinia, at least, the government hastened the mixing of classes by fostering the development of trade and industry. As banks grew larger, railroads longer and the first factories were built, the land and rents held by a family counted for less in determining its position in the kingdom. Cavour's activities, ranging from a chemical fertilizer plant to a newspaper, were typical of the new era that was emerging, and they brought him into contact with a far larger spread of his fellow men than was usual for an aristocrat. Conversely, the wealth and power resulting from successful enterprises began to thrust some of the middle class into the aristocracy. This intermingling had been going on for centuries in the commercial Republic of Genoa which, since 1815, had been part of the Sardinian kingdom, but was new in the feudal, landed province of Piedmont which surrounded Turin and provided most of the families of the court.

All of these changes existed but were less marked in the Kingdom of Naples. Its fields and towns had not been trampled and burned by the advance and retreat of armies, and its life, particularly in the provinces, was more agricultural, poor and feudally organized. Except in the larger towns on the coast, there was almost no trade of any kind. Naples, however, had suffered from other difficulties which had left behind them, perhaps, even greater tensions than the defeats suffered in the north. Ferdinando II, for example, had recovered his Kingdom of Sicily only after bombarding Messina so relentlessly for five days in September 1848 that he was ever after known as King *Bomba*. About a third of the city had been totally destroyed, and even after it had surrendered, parts of it continued to burn for another three days, despite efforts to put out the fires.

The fighting had been savage, and each side accused the other of brutalities. The Neapolitans are supposed to have raped and then mutilated the Sicilian women as well as bayoneted babies and the sick and wounded. The Sicilians, for their part, are said to have roasted the flesh of at least sixty wounded prisoners, hawked human offal in the streets, eaten human tongue in sandwiches and worn Neapolitan ears as rosettes in their buttonholes.

Immediately after the siege, France and England had imposed an armistice, and Ferdinando, certain that he could recapture the entire island, waited impatiently until he could do so with the blessings of the great powers. Meanwhile many Neapolitans and even some Englishmen asked if the Sicilians had a right to revolt which the Irish lacked, or whether General Cavaignac had won his title, "Butcher of June," by treating the people of Paris gently. The Sicilians, for their part, did almost nothing to prepare for the battle that was sure to come. Their kingdom had never known conscription and their traditions held soldiering in contempt. A popular maxim was "better a swine than a soldier," and a few Polish officers imported to create an army could not do it. After the Sardinian defeat at Novara, as the other powers began to lose interest in Italy, Ferdinando was able to proceed. The Sicilians fought but were easily defeated, and by May 1849 Ferdinando had recovered the entire kingdom.

He proclaimed an amnesty which included all but forty-three of the revolutionary leaders and ruled, for the time being, through his general, Carlo Filangieri, who was wise and firm. Filangieri soon had the king's authority re-established throughout the island, and Sicily ceased to dominate the attention of the government in Naples. But among Sicilians the memory of their momentary independence and the bitterness of its abolition did not altogether disappear, and the Bourbon dynasty in Naples, for the balance of its reign, was faced with the possibility and sometimes with the fact of small revolts on the island. Eleven years later, when Garibaldi toppled the dynasty, he began his campaign there.

Even on the mainland kingdom, however, Ferdinando did not achieve the peace he wished nor win the support of all his people. After the fighting in Naples, on the barricades of 15 May 1848, many of the liberals who supported the constitution had fled to Calabria, where they made the inland town of Cosenza their headquarters. From there they issued bulletins accusing Ferdinando of betraying the constitution and urging the proscription of the Bourbon dynasty. The Church, the peasants and his army were loyal to Ferdinando, and he had little difficulty mopping up the opposition even though the Sicilians, not yet reconquered, sent over a small expeditionary force to help the liberals. But even with Calabria quieted Ferdinando could not be sure of peace in Naples. There were frequent *fracassi* or small, anarchic riots often arising as much out of poverty and unemployment as political ideals, but inasmuch as they brought the people into conflict with the police they had an antigovernment tone and were exploited by the liberals. In his personal life Ferdinando withdrew, more and more, to his palace at Caserta, twenty miles outside the city; in his government he relied, more and more, on the police and he ignored Parliament, collecting taxes without reference to it, rejecting its addresses and keeping his ministers from its meetings. Finally in March 1850 he dissolved it and his constitutional venture was over.

He had already replaced the Italian tricolor flag, which the liberal Parliament had adopted, with the kingdom's traditional flag of Bourbon lilies on a white field. He recalled the Jesuits and persuaded Pio Nono, who had not yet returned to Rome, to come to Naples from Gaeta and to bless the population from the royal palace. The ceremony, he hoped, would lend an air of divine right to his position as absolute monarch. At very least the highest representatives of Church and State, both of whom had renounced their liberal concessions, would be seen standing together. In anticipation of the ceremony's effect on his people, he exclaimed, "Today the throne of Carlo III has been placed on a pedestal of granite." And the scene was effective. At noon, after a booming salute of guns and a flourish of trumpets, a hundred thousand Neapolitans fell to their knees in the Piazza del Palazzo Reale (today the Piazza del Plebiscito) as the pope, serene and stately, in white and gold, appeared on the balcony of the Palazzo Reale surrounded by the king and royal family.

But Ferdinando, somewhat like Metternich in the Po valley a generation earlier, misgauged the forces which gave rise to the liberal and republican movements within his kingdom. Putting some men in prison, defeating others in Calabria and then suspending the constitution did not cure the kingdom of the disease of liberalism; it merely caused certain symptoms of it to disappear. Others remained, notably a new, secret Society of Italian Unity, whose aim was "to liberate Italy from the internal tyranny of princes and from every foreign power, to reunite her and make her strong and independent."

Since the early days of the French Revolution a sizable minority of the subjects of the Bourbons of Naples had agitated and conspired for a voice in the government of the state. In the sixty years since 1790 the minority had succeeded once, with French aid, in establishing a republic and twice, unaided, in forcing a constitution on the king. Within the minority a new generation several times had replaced the old as individuals were exiled, imprisoned or merely died of old age, but always the minority existed, agitating for liberal institutions which would give them some part in the government. Ferdinando, rather than turning back to absolutism and relying on authoritarians, whether in the police, the church or the army, might have been wiser to come to some sort of terms with the ideas and desires of this minority. At least this is what the House of Savoy did under Carlo Alberto and Vittorio Emanuele II, and it is a fact that after 1848–49, the Kingdom of Sardinia, although smaller in size and population and with less absolute wealth than the Bourbon kingdom and perhaps even with less claim to be Italian, became the undisputed leader in Italian affairs while Ferdinando and his people, their time and attention almost wholly taken up with their local antagonisms, became increasingly isolated.

Historians used to present Vittorio Emanuele, who was twenty-eight when he succeeded his father, as a convinced liberal from the first day of his reign, a king who sincerely believed that the constitution he had sworn to uphold was the best form of government for his kingdom. More recent historians have modified this portrait, for the publication over the last twenty years of the king's private remarks and letters to the pope and various ambassadors of the Papacy have revealed another side to him. He once told the Papal nuncio in Turin, for example, that he would like to rule more autocratically but that he did not dare, even though he "held the constitutional system to be the worst possible" and awaited "the opportunity to bring about its downfall." His actions in office, however, suggest that he was speaking in a moment of anger at the constitutionalists or perhaps exaggerating his feelings for the benefit of the nuncio who favored an absolute monarchy. But in any event Vittorio Emanuele II was a proud member of the oldest dynasty in Europe, and no doubt he would have preferred to rule autocratically. Historians now present him as convinced, from the first day of his reign, that any attempt to do so would cost him his throne. French influence was strong in Turin, and he had before him the fates of Charles X and Louis Philippe in France. He recognized that among his own people the Genovesi were not only constitutionalists but republicans and that his aristocracy included among its most competent members such men as Cavour and Roberto and Massimo d'Azeglio, all of whom were convinced constitutionalists. Further he was ambitious for his House, and he seems to have understood from the first that, if he was to achieve a greater role in Italian affairs for himself and his heirs, he could do so only as the leader of the liberals and republicans, for most other Italians, those supporting the pope, the emperor or Ferdinando, were content to leave Italy as it was, divided into small states and dominated by a foreign power. Therefore, less as a matter of personal belief than of political policy, in the opinion of the more modern historians, Vittorio Emanuele, from the first day of his reign, seemingly was prepared to abide by his oath and to act like a constitutional monarch.

Even so, in the first summer of his reign, he became involved, on the advice of his ministers, in several unconstitutional actions which infuriated the more radical members of the Chamber of Deputies but greatly strengthened the confidence of the majority of the people in their new and untried king. The events arose out of the peace treaty with Austria which Vittorio Emanuele had signed, with his ministers' approval, early in August. By its terms the kingdom was to pay Austria an indemnity for the war of seventy-five million francs, an enormous sum, and to accept as its frontiers those set out by the treaties of the Congress of Vienna in 1815.

For the treaty to become the law of the kingdom, the Parliament, in both houses, had to ratify it. The upper house, the Senate, was composed of men appointed by the king for life and could be expected to rally to him; but the lower house, the Chamber of Deputies, was an elected body, and even though the right to vote for it, or to be elected to it, depended on property or intellectual qualifications, many of its members were openly hostile to the king and his ministers. The President of the Chamber, for example, was the Marchese Ernesto Pareto, a Genovese and an ardent supporter of Mazzini. He could be expected to support those who would argue that the treaty, by its silence on the subject, abandoned those Italian subjects of Franz Josef who had taken refuge in Piedmont. He would support those who would argue that the monarchy had deserted the national cause; that the king could not sign away the peoples of Parma, Modena, Lombardia and the Veneto, who had voted to join their states to Sardinia in a Kingdom of Alta Italia; and that, in any event, the king had no right to sign a treaty before submitting it to Parliament.

The points were highly flammable and the debates on them, heated. Because the constitutional system was so new, only thirty months old and many of those passed in a state of war, there were no precedents for handling a peace treaty, and some of the deputies recognized no limits on what they said or implied. The king and his prime minister, Massimo d'Azeglio, were accused of having a secret agreement with Austria to do away with the constitutional system, and the Minister of the Interior was forced to resign over the innuendo that he planned, on the king's behalf, to bayonet the deputies out of the Chamber, like Napoleon at St. Cloud. Against such rhetoric the moderates could not marshal a majority. But as Cavour pleaded: "Even if the present ministry did not exist and there were another chosen, we should be equally forced to recognize this fatal law and to accept the treaty." Austria had defeated Sardinia and no amount of patriotic rhetoric could alter the fact.

After two months of the debate d'Azeglio dissolved the Chamber. He was convinced that the deputies did not represent the will of the country, which had been exhausted by the war and was eager for peace. He advised the king to appeal to his people to elect a more reasonable Chamber. The king's appeal, known as the Proclamation of Moncalieri, after the royal château from which he issued it, stated the constitutional impasse and asked the voters to elect a Chamber that would approve the treaty. In the course of the proclamation he stated bluntly:

> If the country, if the Electors, deny me their cooperation, not upon me will fall the responsibility of the future; and, in the disorder that may arise, they must lay the blame not upon me but upon themselves.[56]

It was an appeal for a "King's party" such as the Hanoverian kings in Britain had used a hundred years earlier, and by the generally accepted ideas of constitutional law in the middle of the nineteenth century it was an unconstitutional act. The radical deputies were outraged and took their wrath to the hustings, but "Gianduja," the typical figure of Piedmont, celebrated for his common sense, judged that there was no possible alternative to the treaty and sided with his king. When the new Chamber assembled, it offered the king and his ministers a solid two-thirds majority, and the treaty quickly was approved.

The kingdom thus passed its first constitutional crisis safely, but more because of the people's ancient loyalty to the House of Savoy than because of their attachment to the constitutional system. They also trusted d'Azeglio. The king's choice of him for prime minister had been wise. Liberals and even republicans respected him for his pamphlets and because he had been wounded fighting the Austrians, and the conservative aristocrats felt he was one of them and would never betray the country. His presence gave the ministry a guarantee of character, and the constitution survived in part because both Vittorio Emanuele and d'Azeglio were, in fact, men of their word and did not attempt to turn a necessary exception to constitutional action into the rule.

A story, reported as true by two contemporary historians, had d'Azeglio saying to the king in an early interview: "There have been so few honest kings in history that it would be really fine to begin the series." "Am I to play the honest king?" Vittorio Emanuele asked, laughing. "Your Majesty has sworn faith to the *Statuto* and has had regard for Italy and not for Piedmont. Let us continue in this way to hold for certain that in this world king and humble citizen have only one word, and that they ought to abide by that." "Well," rejoined the king, "this seems an easy thing to me." And the nickname which his people gave him in these years was *Il Re galantuomo* or "King Honest-Fellow."

With the peace treaty approved the ministry was able to take up internal questions which, because of the war, had been put off. Unfortunately, the most important of these involved the relations between Church and State, so that the country was almost immediately plunged into a second highly emotional quarrel.

The Church's position in Sardinia was medieval in its numbers, splendor and power. The House of Savoy had always been known for its piety and, on its return to power after Napoleon's downfall in 1814, it had lavished every sort of benefit on the Church. By 1841 Sardinia had become the example of a perfectly governed state as Rome conceived it. The Jesuits controlled the lower education; the bishops, the universities. Church censorship controlled the publication of books and papers as well as their importation. Church courts had jurisdiction of any suit involving its interest, and offenses against religion such as sacrilege or absence from church were part of the State's penal code. Power might technically reside in the king, but the Church exercised much of it.

When in 1847 Carlo Alberto had granted his people a constitution in response to the swell of liberalism to which Pio Nono himself had contributed, and when in 1849 Vittorio Emanuele, in response to the same pressures, had sworn to uphold the constitution, some of the king's power thereby given away was certain, someday, to be turned against the Church; for reducing the Church's power and position in the kingdom was one of the chief aims of the liberals. And action in Parliament against the Church was doubly certain because the right to vote under the constitution was extremely limited. Carlo Alberto had not intended to share his power with the simplest peasant and had granted the right to vote for representatives to only about two per cent of the male population. Parliamentary democracy in Sardinia and later in Italy started with the aristocrats and professional classes and only gradually enfranchised all men. As a result the Church was unable to bring its enormous influence over the peasants to bear on the Parliament, and although it had bishops, priests and other friends representing it in the Chamber and the Senate, it was faced with a majority which, while insisting it had no desire to interfere in the Church's spiritual affairs, was anxious to reform its temporal relations with the State.

The *Statuto* or constitution which Carlo Alberto had granted had been based on French models and, harking back to the Declaration of Rights of the French Revolution, had declared that all citizens, aristocrat or peasant, priest or layman, were to be equal before the law. The Church, however, had denied the right of the State to bring ecclesiastics, persons in orders, within the jurisdiction of the State's courts. It had insisted on continuing its own system of courts in which it judged not only what it considered to be purely religious causes, such as divorce, but also any cause in which an ecclesiastic was involved. It had also insisted on continuing a right of asylum in its churches so that the State, on occasion, was balked in its pursuit and prosecution of criminals, lay or clerical.

From the moment Carlo Alberto had granted the constitution, the government at Turin had sought to reach some agreement with the pope about the ecclesiastical courts, and it had sent, roughly at six-month intervals, three different representatives to negotiate a new concordat. The first had seen the pope at Rome; the second, at Gaeta, and the third, at Naples; but none had been able to reach any agreement. Historians, liberal and clerical, divide sharply on whom to place the blame, on the ministers in Turin or on the pope and the man who would be his Secretary of State for the next quarter century, Cardinal Giacomo Antonelli. The division is one in which an examination of the facts does not clearly fault one side or the other: the right or wrong of the issue depends almost entirely on the historian's point of view about a people's right to make a revolution, to change the way their life is organized. In the Kingdom of Sardinia the

House of Savoy, its ministers and its people, ranging from the strongly anticlerical Genovesi to the strongly clerical Savoyards, with much uncertainty and internal argument were conducting a revolution, peaceful, but still, a revolution. They were attempting to reorganize the life of their kingdom along what they considered to be more modern and better lines. Squarely in their path was the Church, organized along lines that many of them thought medieval and no longer suited to their needs. Liberals of the time talked of the sovereign rights of the people and pointed to the fact that in France and Austria the Church had accepted such reforms many years earlier. Clerical supporters talked of the sanctity of law and pointed to a Concordat the Church had negotiated with Sardinia as recently as 1841. Further, they argued, the fact that the revolutionists in Paris and Joseph II in Vienna had forced the Church to accept changes in its law and structure did not mean those changes were for the better; the Christian way of life had suffered. Liberal and clerical historians have echoed the arguments ever since.

As long as the kingdom had the constitution, however, the ministry was under a duty to make the country's laws conform to it, and if the ministers could not reach an agreement with the pope then, sooner or later, they would proceed without one. And toward the end of February 1850 Count Giuseppe Siccardi, the Minister of Grace and Justice, introduced a bill to abolish the ecclesiastical courts. It was the first of a series of bills, known collectively as the Siccardi Laws, designed to reduce the power and position of the Church throughout the kingdom.

Besides the bill on the courts the ministry introduced bills to do away with the right of asylum, to limit the number of holy days that must be observed, to require approval by the State of acquisition of land by the Church. The debates in the Senate and the Chamber showed how divided opinion was, and several distinguished constitutionalists opposed the bills on the ground that such reforms, while correct in principle were premature, that they would cause bitterness and even riots throughout the kingdom, that negotiations with the pope must continue and that the consent of the pope must be obtained.

Several men spoke in reply and one of them, Angelo Brofferio, a criminal lawyer, had no difficulty showing the bad effects of a double system of laws, courts and punishments, or that the popes themselves had not hesitated to breach treaties which had conflicted with their temporal interests and that, under international law, a state had a right to abrogate a treaty harmful to its vital interests. On the second day Cavour spoke and, in supporting the bills, made his first great speech.

His parliamentary career until then had been intermittent and relatively unsuccessful. In the first election after Carlo Alberto had granted the constitution, Cavour had stood for the Chamber in four districts and been defeated in all four. Then in a supplementary election he had been elected in a district of Turin, been defeated in a general election, and finally, in July 1849, elected again. He was still unpopular, even suspect. Brofferio, who had a criminal lawyer's love of rhetoric, later described Cavour's person and style at the start of his parliamentary career.

> Against him were his bulky person, his vulgar aspect, his ignoble gestures, his unpleasant voice. Of letters he had no trace; of the arts he was ignorant; of all philosophy, devoid; no ray of poetry flashed in his soul; the scantiest instruction; words stumbled from his lips in French structures; so numerous were his blunders in Italian that to put him in accord with the language would have seemed to everybody an impossible task.[57]

The portrait is too harsh, and perhaps because Brofferio later was often defeated by Cavour in debate. Many others, however, testify to Cavour's matter-of-fact style and his difficulties with Italian. His great virtue in debate was clarity of thought; no matter how complicated the subject he could organize his ideas and examples, so that the entire Chamber could follow them. In so doing he complimented his colleagues on their ability to follow his arguments and to use their reason; they responded with their attention and often with their votes. But as a person he continued for most of them to be, somehow, *antipatico*.

In speaking for the Siccardi Laws, Cavour had his first chance to address the Chamber on a major issue which was still undecided, and he immediately put the debate on the highest level. The issue, he argued, was not one of party or special interest but a national problem of the greatest difficulty. He admitted at once his incompetence to deal with the legal and ecclesiastical aspects and spoke instead on the question of timeliness. He urged that the time to make major reforms was in a period of peace, that this particular reform had already been held up once by war and that, if postponed now, it might be held up again in the future by the possibility of "stormy times" ahead. He reviewed the history of the negotiations with the pope and saw no hope of persuading the Papacy, in its present mood of reaction, to come to an agreement. Then he drew a picture of what the kingdom would probably face if this first, major reform was postponed. Those liberals who had agitated for a constitution would feel that it had failed and would turn more and more to extremists; those conservatives who had opposed the constitution would be overjoyed and work harder than ever to undermine it or have it abolished. A far more revolutionary situation would develop and one in which the extremists, as in the French revolution, would crush the moderates. He asked the Chamber which country alone in Europe had escaped the horrors of revolution in the last hundred years? Not France, or Germany or Austria, but England. And because she had anticipated the desperate struggles by reform. Citing the Catholic Emancipation Act, the Reform Bill and the Corn Laws in Britain, he argued that there the reforms, made in time, had not weakened but strengthened authority. And he ended by urging the Chamber to follow the British example:

> Proceed steadfastly down the road of reform and do not be put off by declarations that the reforms are inopportune: do not fear to weaken the power of the constitutional throne which is entrusted to your care, for rather you will strengthen it so that even if the revolutionary tempest should rise against it, it will not only resist that tempest, but drawing to itself all the living forces of Italy, will lead our nation to those high destinies to which it is called.[58]

The speech raised a storm of applause and in a single morning established Cavour as one of the most important men in the Chamber. It also decided the issue for many and when the bill on the eccesiastical courts was put to the vote it passed both houses with good majorities, the Chamber by 130 to 27 and the Senate by 58 to 29.

Probably, too, a majority of the people in the kingdom approved. The excitement over the reforms had been very great, greater even than when Carlo Alberto had started his second campaign against the Austrians or when, after Novara, the Austrians had seemed about to invade the country.

But the excitement did not end with the passage of the bills. The Archbishop of Turin, Luigi Fransoni, issued a pastoral letter to his priests forbidding them to obey the new laws. The government, after failing to persuade Fransoni to change his stand, had him arrested and tried, and the Court of Appeal sentenced him to a month in prison and to pay a small fine. Two other archbishops with sees on the island of Sardinia followed Fransoni's example and also went to jail. Pio Nono, meanwhile, withdrew the Papal nuncio from Turin and demanded the release of the "persecuted" Fransoni. Some Catholics considered Fransoni a martyr and subscribed to a gift for him, other Catholics subscribed to erect an obelisk to commemorate the liberation of the kingdom from ecclesiastical tyranny.

The excitement had only just begun to burn itself out when Fransoni by yet another act caused it to flare again. As Pietro di Santa Rosa, the Minister of Agriculture, lay dying, a priest, on the archbishop's order, refused to grant him absolution unless he acknowledged the sinfulness of the Siccardi Laws and repented of his part in their passage. "My God!" the dying man exclaimed. "They require of me, things to which my conscience cannot bend: I have four children—they shall not inherit a dishonored name from their father." And he died unshriven. Then Fransoni gave instructions that his body should be denied Christian burial.

When the fact became known, a sense of outrage swept the city. The Torinesi gathered in angry crowds that threatened at any moment to turn into mobs. The government quickly sent the Servite Orders, to which the priest belonged, out of the city; the archbishop had already fled. Two cabinet ministers visited him in his country retreat and, after argument, persuaded him to withdraw this prohibition. Thousands attended the funeral and turned it into an impressive demonstration of support for the laws. The incidents of Santa Rosa's death, however, greatly embittered the struggle between clerical and liberal supporters and, to the distress of many moderates, made any agreement with the pope even less likely.

It also led directly to Cavour's appointment to the ministry, though not immediately. Santa Rosa died in August and within the month the Minister of War, La Marmora, was urging d'Azeglio to appoint Cavour to Santa Rosa's post. But d'Azeglio was reluctant. He recognized Cavour's ability and at the same time, perhaps, resented it: "He would turn the Ministry topsy-turvy in a month." La Marmora, however, persisted, and d'Azeglio finally agreed to propose Cavour to the king. Vittorio Emanuele then balked. He wanted "a more sympathetic name." He did not know Cavour well, but perhaps he shared his father's distrust of a man who had left the army, made lots of money and was a highly articulate liberal. But again La Marmora persisted, and plainly Cavour's power in the Chamber was growing too great to ignore; the king and ministers had either to accept him or to face an opposition led by him. In the end the king agreed. But "I warn you," he said to d'Azeglio, "this man who enters the ministry by the little back door will soon turn you all out." Nevertheless, in October 1850 Cavour became Minister of Commerce and Agriculture, and his presence in the ministry guaranteed the movement for reforms would continue.

# CHAPTER 31

Franz Josef's character. Radetzky's attitude. Austrian occupation of Lombardo-Veneto. Mazzini's National Italian Committee. Contessa Maffei's salon. *Crepuscolo*. The lesser Habsburgs. Pio Nono and the hierarchy for Britain. Ferdinando and Poerio. Gladstone's *Letters to Lord Aberdeen*. Ferdinando's character and its effect on his Kingdom. Pio Nono's government. Its failings. His relations with his people and with the rest of Europe.

ACROSS THE TICINO RIVER from Piedmont, in Lombardia, life was very different, harsh and repressed. The people, once again subjects of the emperor, were allowed no political freedoms of any sort. The Habsburg emperors, first Ferdinand and then Franz Josef, had sustained their House with its many different holdings by military force, and now Franz Josef, with Schwarzenberg to guide him, made his army the basis of his rule. Lombardia and the Veneto were kept under martial law and became simply the Italian provinces of the Austrian Empire. For the first time in their history the Habsburg holdings became a truly unitary empire. Everything was ordered from Vienna and in German. Under the revolutionary pressures of 1848–49 the centralization of administration started years earlier by Joseph II now reached one of the conclusions implicit in its beginnings, although perhaps not exactly the one at which Joseph II would have aimed.

For although Franz Josef, on his succession to the family throne, had added the "Josef" to his name in memory of his reforming great-great-uncle, he was a very different sort of man, far more like his grandfather, the Emperor Franz. Unlike Joseph II he distrusted ideas or brilliance of any sort; like Franz, he favored routine, a bureaucracy in which he made the decisions. And, unlike either of his ancestors, he was a militarist, always appearing in uniform, constantly attending maneuvers of his armies and, on occasion, himself taking command. His sense of position was great. When an elderly and distinguished general allowed himself a variation on Franz Josef's orders during maneuvers, the young emperor snapped, "I command to be obeyed!" and sent the man back to repeat the maneuver as ordered.

This attitude, perhaps springing from the uncertain start of his reign in a revolutionary period, showed itself in a number of ways. The pictures he hung, for example, on the walls of his audience chamber were mostly of the repression of the Viennese revolution of 1848. Even Schwarzenberg, in describing Franz Josef to Metternich, who was living in retirement, wrote:

> His intelligence is acute, his diligence in affairs astonishing, especially for one of his age. He works hard for at least ten hours a day, and nobody knows better than I how many ministerial proposals he sends back to be revised. His bearing is full of dignity, his behavior to all exceedingly polite, though a little dry. Men of sentiment—and many people in Vienna lay claim to kindliness—say that he has not much heart.[59]

Franz Josef's character, in both its virtues and defects, was re-enforced by that of Radetzky, who commanded the military occupation of Lombardia and the Veneto, so that between Vienna and Verona there was never any disagreement over the policy to be pursued. In November 1849, after the fall of Venice, Radetzky wrote to his daughter: "These Italians have never loved nor will they love the Germans; but persuaded that they cannot liberate themselves by force, they have surrendered and we are avenged and that suffices." As a policy such an attitude, which refused to consider the underlying reasons for the revolutions, merely insured more bitterness, more conspiracy and a constant series of incidents.

One of the first occurred in Milan on 18 August 1849, Franz Josef's birthday. On that day a glovemaker, presumably to stimulate sales, decorated her window with the Austrian eagle. Instead, the decoration gathered a hostile, patriotic crowd that hissed and hooted while Austrian officers in a café opposite applauded. Eventually soldiers dispersed the crowd, but for taking part in such a political demonstration fifteen men were flogged by soldiers and also two women, one of whom was a seventeen-year-old girl from Florence who had "laughed during the transaction." By Radetzky's order the city government was forced to make a gift of thirty thousand lire to the glovemaker and to pay for the cost of the rods used in the floggings and for the services of the soldiers detailed to deliver the blows.

No wounds were healed by such a policy; the people, more than ever solidified in opposition. They expressed their resentment as best they could and succeeded frequently in making the Austrians look ridiculous. At Pavia, for example, where the citizens had organized a boycott of the theatre, the Austrian commander hysterically ordered the theatre to keep open and declared, "If anybody by criminal political obstinacy should persist in not frequenting the theatre, such conduct should be regarded as the silent demonstration of a criminal disposition which merited to be sought out and punished." The policy designed to suppress all political acts succeeded only in making every act, even staying quietly at home, political and criminal.

Many Italians, however, did more than merely avoid those theatres and cafés which the Austrians frequented. Soon after the fall of Venice committees began to form secretly in the towns of Lombardia and the Veneto with only the vague purpose of maintaining relations with each other and preparing for some unknown, concerted action some day in the future. In London, Mazzini organized a National Italian Committee which issued a proclamation asking the people to subscribe a loan of ten million lire by buying bonds on which six per cent interest would be paid. The purpose of the loan, according to the bonds' coupons, was "Directed only to the hastening of The Independence and Unity of Italy."

The proclamation seemed at the time to be of the greatest importance, although the people were impoverished and subscribed little. But offering the bonds gave the local committees something positive to do and made their members feel part of a larger movement. Once again Mazzini became the nominal head of a large conspiratorial organization. At the committee meetings the political discussions generally followed the lines of his thought, advocating an Italy united and republican. His slogans *Dio e il popolo,* "God and the people," *pensiero ed azione,* "Thought and action," were again the watchwords of those eager to act, and his patriotism and suffering, their inspiration. Gradually, with Mazzini's blessing, the committee at Mantua emerged as the most important, and beginning in November 1850 it became the Central Committee to which the others reported.

Not all Italians, of course, were members of secret committees, and others organized thought and action against the Austrians in their own fashions. One who was important was a lady, the Contessa Clara Maffei, who ran a salon in Milan. She had come to the city from Bergamo in 1834 to marry Andrea Maffei, a gentleman poet who was sixteen years her senior. The marriage was not a success and in 1846 she and Maffei separated, in sorrow as much as anger, and he continued to be welcome in her house on the Via Bigli. By then she had been "at home" in the evenings to her friends for ten years and had developed a recognized circle, a salon which continued, except for short periods when wars with the Austrians forced her from the city, for fifty years.

The Contessa Maffei's salon was, in many respects, the successor to the Countess of Albany's salon in Florence in the first quarter of the century, except that it was far less pretentious. The Contessa Maffei was a simple, almost middle-class lady without any of the beauty, distinction or even arrogance generally associated with a great hostess. Her charm lay in her gentle manners and in her open and enthusiastic affection for people. Her friends used to joke that she had "an especial predilection for—all."

While she had been married to Maffei, he had brought to their house most of the leading writers of the day and also had introduced her to Verdi, for whom he wrote the libretto of *I Masnadieri*. She in turn, many years later, introduced Verdi to Manzoni, in whose memory Verdi composed his *Requiem*. Verdi was not often in Milan after 1846, but his correspondence with the contessa from then until her death in 1886 is an extraordinary record of art and politics during the period. After she had separated from Maffei, she acknowledged a liaison with Carlo Tenca, who was then the editor of the literary periodical *Rivista Europea*, and their relationship lasted until his death in 1883; and Tenca, like Maffei, continued to introduce her to many important artists of the time.

Her special interest, however, was the fate of Italy, and after 1848 it became the dominant topic at her evenings. She was herself a follower of Mazzini in her hopes for Italy, but she was not a doctrinaire republican, and one of her best friends and a frequent guest at her salon was Conte Cesare Giulini, an important supporter of the House of Savoy. He had been a member of the Provisional Government of Milan after the Cinque Giornate, and he continued to argue ably in favor of uniting Italy under a constitutional monarchy. At the contessa's salon ideas were exchanged, not imposed.

The public counterpart of the salon was a weekly journal which Tenca founded in 1850 and called *Crepuscolo* or "Twilight," a title suggesting the dark times of the Austrian occupation. He had, as an editorial problem, the fact that the Austrians, who had always relied on censorship to stifle ideas, would not allow any critical discussion of their actions or policies. And the penalty for transgression could be death. In Venice, in 1851, a man was hanged for smuggling books into Italy from Switzerland.

Tenca's solution to the problem was to publish in each issue a review of the political events of other countries but never to mention anything that happened in Austria or its Italian provinces. This silence, which could hardly be judged criminal, was complete and was adopted by Italians as a continuing protest against Austrian rule.

The larger part of the journal each week carried articles on nonpolitical subjects, art and literary criticism, natural science, hygiene, law and economics, and most of the authors were frequent guests at the contessa's salon. Tenca was a strong editor and the journal, from the start, had a style which was serious yet hopeful; its patriotic aim, though never expressed, was evident, and it quickly became the leading journal of the Po valley.

In accordance with his rule Tenca did not mention Franz Josef's first visit to Lombardia after the wars of 1848–49. The emperor came, in September 1851, not to Milan, but to the heaths of Somma where the Austrian army was holding maneuvers. The Austrians asked the town council of Somma to prepare some festivities, but the councilmen protested that the bad times made any extraordinary expenditures impossible, and the town of Como did nothing on the ground that its councilmen were absent. The maneuvers went badly. By some bungled order the troops got out of hand and ransacked the emperor's tents and kitchen, and he left in anger. Throughout his visit he had stayed with his army and, as the Milanesi noticed, he left without having spoken a word of kindness or of peace. The division between the emperor and his people constantly deepened.

The lesser Habsburgs in Modena and Tuscany and the Bourbon Duke of Parma did little better with their people. The Bourbon, Carlo III, had attained his throne when his father, "the dandy," decided that a life of leisure was better even than being a reigning duke and had abdicated, at the start of the Novara campaign in March 1849. The Austrians, making a show of abiding by the treaties of 1815, had supported the supposedly independent Bourbon line in Parma. But, as everyone recognized, the duchy, since the days of Marie Louise, had been a part of the Habsburg system. The new duke was a young man interested in ladies and military reviews; he was personally attractive, although a trifle arrogant. The Parmigiani considered themselves lucky to be no worse off and looked forward to the day when they again could vote to merge themselves into the Kingdom of Sardinia. Even before 1848, unlike the Milanesi, they had realized that their small duchy could not retain a separate identity with even a show of independence. The businessmen and prosperous farmers wanted to be part of a larger area of trade, to share in a common system of weights and measures, coinage and customs. Like the Lucchesi, who had seen their small republic merged into Tuscany without regret, the Parmigiani were fully prepared to become members of a larger unit, to become, if not Italians, at least Sardinians. Carlo III they considered a nonentity, a pawn to be used or sacrificed for the greater end.

Both the Modenesi and the Tuscans were less happy with their dukes, especially the Modenesi. Francesco V continued the repressive rule of his father and soon had his jails filled with political prisoners and his towns swarming with informers. The majority of his people felt nothing in common with him or his Bavarian duchess and, except for a few in his small army, they were eager to be rid of him. Like the Parmigiani they were ready to merge their separate state into a larger one, provided it was Italian. The Parmigiani being neighbors of Sardinia tended to favor unifying under the House of Savoy; the Modenesi being closer to Bologna and the Veneto, under a republic.

For the Tuscans the case was not so clear cut. Leopoldo II had once been popular and Tuscany a greater duchy than either Parma or Modena. Memories of its former independence and glory lingered, yet no one could imagine an alternative to Leopoldo that might succeed except some sort of merger into a larger Italian state. And Leopoldo, a kind, bumbling man of fifty-five, who might with luck have regained some of his popularity, seemed determined to deny himself the chance. He wore the Austrian uniform, he made a trip to Vienna, he ordered the memorials to Tuscans who had died fighting Austria in 1848 to be taken off the church walls, and he prohibited memorial services. When, despite his prohibition, a memorial service was held in Santa Croce in the spring of 1851, his police fired into the crowd. Meanwhile he continued to keep ten thousand Austrian troops in the country, which was expensive, and in 1852 he formally abolished the constitution. More and more, because of his reactionary policies, he was compared to King *Bomba* in Naples and contrasted unfavorably with *Il Re Galantuomo* in Turin. And the contrast inclined many Tuscans, for the first time, to look north, to Turin, for leadership in Italy rather than south, to Rome or to Naples.

Ferdinando's failings at Naples were only partially realized, even in Italy, until suddenly in the summer of 1851 they were put before all of Europe by a curious stroke of chance, the result of an English father's belief that a trip to Naples might help his daughter's eyesight. The father was William Ewart Gladstone, the Conservative member of Parliament for Oxford University, and in August 1850 he, his wife and his child set out for Naples, expecting to spend several months there. Gladstone, who was only forty, was already an important figure in government circles. He was an outstanding speaker in the House, had served in two cabinet posts under Sir Robert Peel and plainly soon would be in the cabinet again. Personally, he was tall, good-looking and capable of immense moral indignation.

The Gladstones arrived in Naples in September to discover that everyone's attention was wholly taken up with the trial of forty-two men accused, at the least, of distributing seditious literature and, at the most, of attempting to kill the king with a bomb. As the crowds had gathered the previous year to receive Pio Nono's blessing, a bomb had exploded, causing some dismay but no damage or panic. Ferdinando's police, in their investigation of it, had uncovered the secret, political sect, calling itself the Society of Italian Unity. The relation of the accused to the sect was one of the questions at issue in the trial. But neither the police investigation, which had relied on informers and had become, in a year, a tangle of forgeries, perjuries, denunciations, confessions and retractions, nor the trial itself, which lasted from June 1850 through the following January, could make the answer clear.

Most of the accused were relatively unimportant men, but one, Carlo Poerio, was a distinguished, famous liberal who had served as the king's Minister of Education in the period when Ferdinando had ruled by the constitution. Poerio's presence in the dock gave the entire trial an air of political persecution.

There was no question about Poerio's liberalism: throughout his life he and his family had consistently opposed Bourbon absolutism. His father had supported Murat and been exiled twice; his cousin had fought the Austrians in 1848, and his brother had followed General Pepe to Venice and died in the siege. Poerio himself, on three occasions, had been imprisoned for his politics, and now he and many other Neapolitans believed that Ferdinando was simply attempting to remove a difficult man from the political scene. To a lesser extent the same was true of a number of the other defendants.

Throughout the trial Poerio conducted himself with great dignity and considerable rhetorical skill, and the British colony in Naples, as if to make amends for its support of the Bourbons in times past, now made Poerio's cause its own. When Gladstone arrived, its members immediately swept him up in their enthusiasm, taking him to the trial, introducing him to leading Neapolitan liberals and urging him, somehow, to use his influence for the cause of right and justice.

Gladstone was appalled at what he saw and heard. He attended the trial and after Poerio had been sentenced to twenty-four years in irons, he visited him in prison at Nisida, an island in the bay of Naples. At first he he could not recognize the man. Poerio's features were changed by exhaustion and sickness and round the waist of his convict's red jacket was a leather strap attached to two chains. One was fastened to his ankle, the other to another convict. They were never undone, for any purpose, and the cell was filthy.

Gladstone returned to England "boiling and seething with indignation," convinced that Poerio and others of the defendants were guilty only of being true to the constitution, a political stand he would have maintained if in their place. He was determined to bring the terrible things he had seen and heard to the attention of Europe. He proposed to write an open letter to the Earl of Aberdeen, who was soon to be Britain's prime minister, and in July 1851 appeared *Two Letters to the Earl of Aberdeen on the State Prosecutions of the Neapolitan Government*.

The British government sent copies of the *Letters* to all its ministers and consuls abroad, so that they had every appearance of government backing, and throughout Europe they caused a sensation, particularly in

France and Britain. Whatever may have been the right and wrong of each defendant's case, Gladstone's condemnation of the methods of trial and conditions of imprisonment at Naples was total. What he had seen and heard had stirred him deeply:

> It is not mere imperfection, not corruption in low quarters, not occasional severity that I am about to describe, it is incessant, systematic, deliberate violation of the law by the Power appointed to watch over and maintain it. It is such violation of human and written law as this, carried on for the purpose of violating every other law unwritten and eternal, human and divine; it is the wholesale persecution of virtue when united with intelligence, operating upon such a scale that entire classes may be with truth said to be its object, so that the government is in bitter and cruel, as well as utterly illegal, hostility to whatever in the nation lives and moves, and forms the mainspring of practical progress and improvement. . . . The governing power, which teaches of itself that it is the image of God upon earth, is clothed, in the view of the overwhelming majority of the thinking public, with all the vices for its attributes. I have seen and heard the strong and too true expression used, *"È la negazione di Dio eretta a sistema di governo"*— "It is the negation of God erected into a system of government." [60]

Gladstone's accusation was wrong in some details: Ferdinando's government, for example, was not opposed to "practical progress and improvement." Partly because of the king's interest, his state had been the first in Italy to have a railroad, an iron suspension bridge, an electric telegraph and a lenticular lighthouse, and its merchant marine, which could claim the first steamship launched in the Mediterranean, had greatly expanded. Yet the accusation was true enough in general to obscure its errors in details, and throughout Europe most men took it as wholly true. In the battle for public opinion Ferdinando had suffered a tremendous defeat. Instead of gradually shedding his nickname, *Bomba,* he had added to it, as a description of his government, "the negation of God."

He responded to the accusation and the outcry it caused in a fashion that was increasingly characteristic of him. He simply ignored it, insisting that he knew what was best ror his people, and he allowed his director of police to institute a new series of trials in which more than three hundred more men were condemned for politically motivated acts, many being sentenced to eighteen years in irons. Although he was only forty-two, he behaved increasingly like an old man, rigid, eccentric and fearful. Under the pressures of his reign the confidence with which he had started twenty-one years earlier had disappeared. A Bourbon historian, Harold Acton, has suggested that the director of police had "gained a sinister influence over the King by keeping his dread of conspiracy alive." And a contemporary, Carlo Troya, who had been the king's prime minister under the constitution but who escaped prosecution now because of ill health and his family's influence, observed to an Englishman:

> Among the exiles, and, to a certain degree among the prisoners, may be reckoned the King, for he has taken refuge within the palace walls of Caserta, and ventures to Naples only from time to time to attend some ceremony when he can be surrounded by 40,000 troops. He does not shed blood, and therefore thinks himself the most merciful sovereign in Europe, while thousands have died, and thousands are slowly dying, in his prisons. No passion is so cruel as fear.[61]

His fear, however, was not a personal cowardice but an eccentric distrust of people. He had decided that beards were a badge of liberalism, and when in 1852 he made a tour of his provinces, officials who were meeting their king for the first time were often dismayed to hear as his first words, "Go away and remove that beard." And at the small town of Catanzaro when he arrived shortly after noon, several hours before he was expected, he immediately assumed that the deserted streets were the sign of a plot, whereas actually the townspeople, in preparation for the great event of his arrival, were merely taking their siesta early. The visit was not a success.

He disappointed the Calabrian nobles by refusing to accept their hospitality, although even tourists at the time were often passed on from one great estate to the next. Ferdinando, however, traveled with his own kitchen and stayed either with the local officials or in religious houses. His manners were gracious or brusque, often depending on his view of the other man's loyalty. When the judges of the criminal court at Cosenza came to pay him their respects, because the court had recently acquitted a man accused of subversive activities he greeted the president of it by saying, "I am dissatisfied with you." The man bowed in silence, retired to doff his robes and returned in frock coat to offer his resignation. Ferdinando accepted it and granted the man a pension. But the fact remained that Ferdinando, as an absolute monarch, had removed a judge from office because he did not like a decision of the man's court. It was just the sort of arbitrary government that turned many of his subjects into liberals.

Ferdinando's character, as it was developing, tended to isolate him from his people. He was at ease only with the officers of his army and members of the Church, the two piers on which he based his government. And partly because of his character his kingdom, too, was becoming increasingly isolated, absorbed with internal problems that it seemed unable to resolve: Sicilians against Neapolitans and liberals against the government. Carlo Troya observed sadly to an Englishman: "Naples is no longer a part of Europe. We are cut off from information as to all that is passing in the rest of the world, Italy included, except what we collect from your newspapers. So few persons read English that the government lets them in." As a result of this isolation, the Risorgimento, in the next eight years, would develop almost entirely in the north of Italy, which was to be a misfortune both for the Kingdom of The Two Sicilies and for Italy. And Rome, too, although to a lesser extent, shared in this misfortune as the pope, like Ferdinando, grew more isolated, both from his own people and the rest of Italy.

Pio Nono had returned to his city in April 1850 and taken up his residence in the Vatican rather than in the Palazzo del Quirinale, from which he had made his escape two years before. The change was a sign of a new relation with his people. The Quirinale, which had been the chief residence in Rome of the popes for almost two hundred years, was on higher ground and healthier, especially in the summer, but it was also in the center of the city and easier for a mob of Romans to surround. The Vatican, on the other hand, was across the Tiber, backed up against the city walls and was connected by an underground passage to the Castel Sant'Angelo. No one, not even the Romans, denied the justice of his reasons for the move, yet it marked a kind of spiritual withdrawal from the people of his city. He had been popular and liberal, and his reforms had ended in anarchy and murder. Now he was more absolute and also more distant.

He surrounded himself almost exclusively with men of the Church and among them tended to favor the Jesuits, so that over the next quarter century the Society and its journal published at Rome, *La Civiltà Cattolica,* had an increasingly important voice in Church affairs. He followed foreign affairs closely but relied so much for the details on his Secretary of State, Cardinal Antonelli, that the cardinal, in the opinion of many, was the power behind the throne. He busied himself more with the spiritual affairs of the Church, and perhaps his happiest moment as pope came on 8 December 1854 when, in St. Peter's, he proclaimed the Dogma of the Immaculate Conception of the Blessed Virgin Mary: that the Virgin Mary at the moment of her conception, which was in the normal, human manner, was miraculously exempted from the taint of original sin. To commemorate the proclamation he erected a tall column topped by a statue of the Virgin which still stands in the Piazza di Spagna. Ten years later to the day, a significant one in Pio Nono's reign, he issued his most famous encyclical, *Quanta cura,* to which he appended the controversial Syllabus of Errors. And finally as the culmination of his interest in Church affairs and of his career he called into being, on 8 December 1869, the first Vatican Council, which was the first general council of the Church since the Council of Trent in 1545.

Yet at the same time he continued to be the head of an Italian state and responsible for the civil government of his people. While he had been visiting Ferdinando in Naples, he had issued a *Motu proprio* in which he had outlined the sort of government he would form on his return to Rome· it was to be an absolute monarchy. At Gaeta, the French ambassador had urged him to promise to restore the constitution which he had previously granted and to pardon in a general amnesty all those who had served in the revolutionary government. Pio Nono did neither. His amnesty excluded so many that most men considered it to be less an amnesty than a proscription, and the furthest he would go toward any sort of parliament was a Consultative Assembly which could advise but not order. He gave his subjects just what he had promised, an absolute monarchy with some recognized channels for petition. D'Azeglio once remarked that Liberty was like a high-spirited horse, inspiring some to try to ride and confirming others in their desire to walk. Pio Nono had tried to ride, been thrown and declined to mount again.

Because he was pope as well as prince his monarchy was a theocracy, although he did not require a man to be a priest to serve in the government. Antonelli, though a cardinal, was only in minor orders and could not officiate at mass; and at the lower levels most of the jobs now were held by laymen. This was a real though not significant change from Papal government in the past, for as much as any priest, a layman who was serving in the government was bound by interest and inclination to the clerical point of view. The government offered no way for opposition to be both peaceful and influential.

The quality of this government which Pio Nono now offered his people is a subject on which historians, clerical and liberal, have always sharply divided. Republican historians describe it as a hideous tyranny of incompetent, unctuous priests, and republican speakers used to tour the Protestant countries giving lurid descriptions of conditions in the pope's prisons. Antonelli, whose career was almost entirely devoted to preserving the pope's temporal power, was also one of their chief targets, and they described him as a sort of horrible animal and accused him of every vice, particularly nepotism, sensuality and robbing the Church. Even the German historian, Ferdinand Gregorovius, in describing Antonelli's appearance remarked on his prominent jaw: "a jaw that is thousands of years old and belonged to the creatures of the mud who devoured, devoured, devoured." A British historian, E. L. Woodward, writing much later, described him as "the son of a robber family" and "the perfect type of a low political adventurer," and Italian historians who are hostile to him almost choke with rage. Though the descriptions surely are overdrawn, it is fact that Antonelli, when he died, left a large fortune to his family, that one of his illegitimate children went to court over it, and that the evidence produced in the suit reflected no credit on him. He was, however, an able diplomat, and Pio Nono, perhaps remembering that Antonelli had stayed by his side when the mob was assaulting the Quirinale, never would replace him.

But even disregarding the republicans and protestants as prejudiced against the Papal government, Catholic moderates, too, found little good to say of it. Luigi Carlo Farini, a former minister of the pope and a historian, a man who had been bitterly opposed to Mazzini and the Roman Republic, wrote to Gladstone in England in December 1852:

> The Government, as in time past, is purely clerical, for the Cardinal Secretary of State is the only real Minister; Cardinals and Prelates prevail, if not in number, at any rate in authority, in the Council of State and in the Consulta of Finance; Cardinals and Prelates govern the Provinces; the clergy alone have the administration of all that relates to instruction, charity, diplomacy, justice, censorship, and the police. The finances are ruined; commerce and traffic at the very poorest; smuggling has again sprung up; all the immunities, all the jurisdiction of the clergy are restored. Taxes and rates are imposed in abundance, without rule or measure. There is neither public nor private safety; no moral authority, no real army, no railroads, no telegraphs. Studies are neglected; there is not a breath of liberty, not a hope of tranquil life; two foreign armies; a permanent state of siege, atrocious acts of revenge, factions raging, universal discontent; such is the Papal Government at the present day.[62]

On the other side, the Comte de Rayneval, the French envoy at Rome, reported in May 1856 to the Minister for Foreign Affairs in Paris:

> . . . In short, that there is not a single detail of interest to the well-being, either moral or material, of the population which has escaped the attention of the government, or which has not been treated in a favorable manner. . . . Are we then to be told that the pontifical government is a model—that it has no weaknesses or imperfections? Certainly not; but its weaknesses and imperfections are of the same kind as are met with in all governments . . . the pontifical government is a government of Romans, acting after the Roman fashion. . . . It likes alterations and accommodations. It is deficient in energy, in activity, in taking the initiative, in firmness, as is the case with the nation itself. . . . There is, in truth, misery here as elsewhere, but it is infinitely less heavy than in less favoured climates. Mere necessities are obtained cheaply. Private charity is largely exercised. Establishments of public charity are numerous and effective. . . . Important ameliorations have been introduced into the administration of hospitals and prisons. Some of these prisons should be visited, that the visitor may admire—the term is not too strong—the persevering charity of the Holy Father.[63]

And pious, clerical historians have presented life in the Papal States as idyllic.

The truth seems to be that if a man was either in the Church or could live without drawing a political breath, and many could, then he found life pleasurable or at least bearable. But if he could not, then it was hateful. And certain facts or events were likely to determine his point of view. In the Legations, for example, a number of conspirators were arrested for conspiring against the Pope, and, although they were Papal subjects and should have been tried in Papal courts, Pio Nono turned them over to the Austrian army which he had called in to restore him and did not thereafter ask to withdraw. Three of the conspirators were shot, and the rest imprisoned. Their fate, however, was less important than the spectacle of the Papal government handing its judicial functions over to the Austrians. This tended to keep the Legations, as they had been for generations, solidly anti-Papal.

Others were depressed by the continuing obscurantism of the Church at Rome. The best Catholic scholars, in or out of orders, were generally French or German, certainly never Roman. Perhaps the greatest scholar of the day, Dr. Ignaz von Döllinger, complained bitterly that there were more books on religious questions published in Germany, England or North America in one year than in Italy during half a century. The monasteries had completely lost their scholastic tradition; and in the schools and universities, even though Galileo's *Dialogue* had finally been taken off the Index in 1835, science still had only the smallest place in the curricula; even a modern language was a rarity and modern history was often prohibited. An American educator, Dr. Samuel Gridley Howe, stated bluntly, "There is not a school in Rome which must not be considered as a beacon to warn rather than a light to guide the inquirer."

Visitors often met this obscurantism first at the customs, and in 1853 a young Milanese, Giovanni Visconti Venosta, who was making his first trip to Rome, was astonished to have his copies of Machiavelli and Molière confiscated as he landed at Civitavecchia. He was traveling with his brother, and as they were both members of the Contessa Maffei's salon and ardent republicans, they visited all the places hallowed by the defense of Rome, the Porta San Pancrazio, the walls, and the Villa Corsini. When they saw French soldiers patrolling the city, they silently cursed Louis Napoleon for responding to the pope's appeal to restore him to his temporal power. When they saw the pope himself in a carriage, however, they were impressed by "his delicate smile of goodness" and his "aureole of peace and sanctity." But what impressed them most was the disrespect with which the Romans treated their priests. In Milan where the priests had fought with the patriots, they were highly regarded, but in Rome the two men were shocked "to hear people swearing at the priests." And, Visconti Venosta exclaimed in astonishment, "What was not said of the priestly Roman government!" In the Legations and even in Rome, Pio Nono's government was more isolated from its subjects than before and was failing once again to earn their respect.

At the same time it was also becoming more isolated from some of the other European governments and even from their people. Not only was the saga of the defense of Rome and the awkward fact of two foreign armies of occupation having an effect on people's sympathies, but Pio Nono became embroiled with both Great Britain and Holland on an issue which, although it seemed relatively small, yet had an important aftereffect.

His troubles came to a head first with Britain in September 1850 when, by a Bull of Restoration, he abolished the long-standing regime of apostolic vicariates in England and established a regular diocesan hierarchy such as had not existed since before the Reformation. At the same time he made an English Catholic, Nicholas Wiseman, a cardinal and appointed him to the newly created post of Archbishop of Westminster.

The title, the place-name so peculiarly rich in Anglican connotations, and the fact that there had been no such cardinal in England since Wolsey raised a sudden storm of popular protest. Wiseman contributed to it with some foolish and unnecessary language: ". . . Till today all who have known what was proposed have been under strict secrecy. . . ." Pio Nono was burned in effigy, the British prime minister forced to complain of "Papal Aggression," and Parliament passed some minor antihierarchy laws which were never enforced.

Pio Nono wisely took a long time to appoint his bishops, and the storm subsided, but not altogether. Everything Pio Nono had done had been in accordance with British law and had been discussed as early as 1847 with British statesmen, and probably could have been accomplished then without rousing any opposition. But three years later, Garibaldi and Mazzini had made heroes of themselves at Rome, and he had abandoned his liberal reforms and had stirred the French army into action in Europe. In England, popular feeling turned strongly against him, and general indignation against the Papacy began to re-enforce the more specialized enthusiasm for the Risorgimento. This was to be reflected in the country's policy: whereas in 1848 the British government had supported Pio Nono, in 1859 it would not.

Two and a half years later, Pio Nono issued a similar Bull of Restoration for Holland, and again there was popular outcry, known as the "April Agitation," which even toppled the Dutch cabinet. Again, one of the chief points of complaint was that he had made the city of Utrecht, particularly famous in Protestant tradition, the seat of the new archbishop.

Protestants thought him singularly lacking in imagination or even deliberately provocative. From a purely political point of view the acts were unfortunately timed, as they cost Pio Nono important political support in a period when he needed it. From a spiritual point of view they were a suitable outward symbol of what amounted to a Catholic spiritual revival throughout Europe, even in Protestant countries.

Yet for many, Catholics as well as Protestants, the pope's temporal failures heavily outweighed any spiritual gains he achieved for the Church. Visconti Venosta concluded his account of the trip he and his brother had made with an extraordinary statement for a Milanese whose first aim in life was to drive the Austrians out of Italy:

> After having traveled through the States of the Church and the Kingdom of Naples, it must be confessed that we experienced a sense of relief in returning to Lombardia, despite the state of siege and the hardships of martial law. We felt that we lived in a country that was socially less retrograde and under a government that was less stupidly tyrannical. The Austrian government had always been, in political matters, pedantically absolute; and we were living in a period of violent reaction; yet it was a civil government of the nineteenth century. But the Papal and the Neapolitan governments were still in part of another age and rightly judged to be among the worst of the civilized world.[64]

After the publication of Gladstone's *Letters,* Europeans as well as Italians were beginning to believe it.

# CHAPTER 32

Cavour and Sardinia's economic revolution. Louis Napoleon's *coup d'état* and reactions to it. Increasing pressure on Sardinia. The *Connubio*. Cavour resigns from d'Azeglio's ministry. His trip abroad. The Civil Marriage bill. Cavour becomes Prime Minister. Napoleon proclaims the Second Empire.

THE CONTRAST among the three Italian states with a claim to independence, Sardinia, The Two Sicilies and the Papal States, continued steadily to increase and in more than just the political freedoms enjoyed by their peoples. Shortly after Vittorio Emanuele II and d'Azeglio had invited Cavour to enter the ministry as Minister of Agriculture and Commerce, they added to his duties those of the Minister of the Navy and, still later, those of the Minister of Finance. From this triple position Cavour launched an economic revolution to accompany the legal and political revolutions already transforming the kingdom.

He acted for the ministry and with the approval of the king, and the ultimate success of the revolution was the work of hundreds, even thousands of ordinary men who became excited about the new methods and opportunities for trade and industry and who, by taking advantage of them, made the revolution. Yet Cavour dominated it in a way that no single man had dominated the legal and political revolutions, and because of the reputation he made for himself in economic affairs he was able, in time, to dominate the kingdom's political life to an extent he probably could not otherwise have achieved.

His first and perhaps most dramatic act was to propose, by a series of treaties, that the kingdom abandon its traditional protectionist system of trade in favor of a freer system which Cavour argued was bringing prosperity to others, particularly to Great Britain. In quick succession he negotiated commercial treaties with France, Belgium, Great Britain, Holland, Switzerland and the German Customs Union. His object in all of them was to reduce the import duties as low as was compatible with the protection of the best home industries and thus to stimulate production by competition. Both industry and trade in the kingdom were cramped by old methods and machines and were as often hindered as helped by special privileges, tariffs and taxes going back many years. Most of these Cavour wished to sweep away as the debris of an economic age that was past. He wanted to transform Sardinia from a simple, mountain kingdom guarding Alpine passes into a complex center of trade and industry with ports on the Mediterranean and railway lines into Europe. In his hopes and plans he was the spiritual descendant of such eighteenth-century liberal thinkers as Genovesi, Beccaria and Montesquieu.

Negotiating the treaties, however, was far easier than persuading the Chamber and Senate to ratify them. Most men, at first, could not imagine abandoning the tried and true protectionist theory of trade, not necessarily because of some special privilege they held, but because all their associations, instincts and traditions were bound up with it. The Genovesi, because of their commercial background, were inclined to be enthusiastic, but the landowners in Piedmont and Savoy were very uncertain. For centuries there had been the lord and the peasant, the land and the rent, the produce and the protected market, and sometimes a small home industry. Now suddenly all that was threatened, for French wine, for example, would be allowed into the kingdom at a price people could pay.

Cavour was uniquely fitted to argue the case for the treaties. He was perhaps the only man in the kingdom with practical experience in farming, banking and manufacturing; one of the few who had read extensively on the theories of economics and again perhaps the only one who had studied the theories as applied elsewhere, on his trips to Switzerland, France and Great Britain. His success in his own farming and business ventures was widely known and envied. When he spoke in the Chamber or Senate on business and theories of trade, many of his listeners were prepared to accept his views as proven. He had practiced what he was preaching, and he had grown rich. The fact was a persuasive argument.

Even so, if he had presented the entire program at one time, he probably could not have persuaded the Parliament to accept it; the change would have been too great. But he was pragmatic rather than doctrinaire in his approach. He took up each treaty separately, often recommended a reduced protection in some form when it was advantageous and was always ready, in person, with facts and figures, to answer any question. His way was slow and personally exhausting; in the six-month session ending in July 1851 he must have answered hundreds of questions from the floor, and he spoke at length about tariffs fifty-two times. At the end of the session, however, he had persuaded the deputies and senators to ratify the treaties and to start the kingdom on a road which in fact led to a great expansion of trade and, in a few years, to a remarkable prosperity for a country which had recently been defeated.

The treaties, however, were only the external side of the economic revolution which included such internal programs as the improvement of roads and bridges; the construction of a network of railways to connect all the kingdom's chief cities, particularly Genoa and Turin; the expansion of credit facilities at the banks; the transfer of the naval arsenal from Genoa to La Spezia and the expansion of the commercial facilities at Genoa to make it the greatest port on the Mediterranean. To pay for these improvements Cavour, as Minister of Finance, proposed to increase the taxes greatly, to float a small loan within the kingdom and to negotiate a large one with the House of Hambro in London. Again he was successful in persuading the Parliament to accept his program. The people, too, were evidently persuaded, for they oversubscribed the internal loan by double the amount. The kingdom buzzed with activity, and most of its people, like the Neapolitans a hundred years earlier under Carlo III, had a conscious feeling of progress.

Both the treaties and the business activity within the kingdom had an external political effect which Cavour had predicted and made use of in arguing for them. British interest and support, he knew, would follow British money and goods into the kingdom. As Montesquieu had observed, "two nations who traffic with each other become reciprocally dependent." And in urging the treaty with France, Cavour had talked openly of the great importance to Sardinia of French support and friendship. His listeners understood, as he intended them to do, that the commercial treaty with France might well lead to a military alliance with France aimed at Austria.

Yet even though France was the kingdom's traditional ally against Austria, and even though men's feelings throughout the kingdom ran high against Austria, still their feelings about France at this time were mixed. Republicans and constitutional monarchists alike were perplexed, both about what was happening in France and about the actions and ambitions of its president, Louis Napoleon. Republicans wanted to rejoice that the first nation of Europe, in the glorious year of 1848, had again become a republic, yet they were faced with the fact that the Second Republic, led by Louis Napoleon, had been quick to restore the pope to Rome and to extinguish the Roman Republic. The constitutional monarchists, while prepared to rejoice at that, were uneasy that Louis Napoleon recently had asked the French Assembly to restore the right to vote to every Frenchman without property or educational qualification, a right the French monarchists had only just succeeded in limiting. The Sardinian monarchists remembered that Louis Napoleon had fought near Bologna with the Carbonari in 1831, and they feared that, in spite of his actions at Rome, he was a radical republican at heart with a desire to spread his beliefs.

The uncertainties of neither were eased by the political situation developing within France. During the autumn of 1851, barely six months after the Sardinian Parliament had ratified the commercial treaty, the Second Republic, which had never been strong, limped to a halt. In the Assembly at Paris neither the republicans nor the monarchists were numerous enough to govern alone, yet neither would consider a compromise. As the months passed without any solution to the stalemate, the possibility of a civil war in France increased alarmingly.

The circumstance was ideal for an ambitious man who could lead the country safely out of its dilemma, and Louis Napoleon had a program: he wished to restore Bonapartism to France with himself in the leading role, to be Emperor of the French with the blessing of the people. But he was blocked by a provision of the constitution which provided that the president could not succeed himself in office, and a bill to amend the provision had already failed in the Assembly to win the necessary three-fourths majority. His position was similar to that of his uncle, the first Napoleon, who had been blocked from a legal ascent to power, on his return from Egypt, by a constitutional provision of the First Republic, one prohibiting a man under forty from becoming a Director. Like his uncle, Louis Napoleon preferred power to legality, and he planned a *coup d'état*. He proposed to elevate himself to emperor by two steps, the first to carry him into a position of power without the name of emperor, similar to his uncle's position of First Consul, and then second to add the name and trappings of emperor to the accomplished fact.

He laid his plans carefully, removing from command all generals who were ardent republicans and ingratiating himself with those he promoted. At the same time he ingratiated himself with rank-and-file republicans, as well as with the three million Frenchmen who had lost their right to vote, by continuing to press for universal, male suffrage. And the monarchists aided him once again by defeating his suffrage bill in the Assembly. Four weeks later, during the night of 1–2 December 1851, Louis Napoleon, with his close councilors around him, opened a bundle of papers which he had marked "Rubicon" and gave last instructions. All drumheads in the National Guard were stove in so that an alarm could not be sounded, and even bell ropes in the churches were cut. Nearly seventy leaders in the Assembly and a number of generals were arrested in their beds. A presidential proclamation was printed and posted about Paris. It urged the army and the people to remain calm and to obey their president. It declared the Assembly dissolved and universal suffrage restored. It promised to submit

the acts of the president to the people for approval or rejection by plebiscite, and it proposed a new constitution.

The few republicans remaining at large, among them Victor Hugo,
attempted to arouse Parisians to defend the republic. But the city was
apathetic. A few barricades went up, and a few idealists were killed, but
the soldiers easily cleared the streets. On the third day a bloody incident
occurred: nervous soldiers fired into a crowd mostly of women and children. This roused the city, but by then it was too late. Hugo went into
exile in Brussels and many others fled to England. The incident marred the
myth that Napoleon wished to create: that the *coup* was bloodless; and
from outside of France republicans, and particularly Hugo, never let the
world forget that Louis Napoleon came to power by stepping over the
bodies of Frenchmen he had killed.

Three weeks later he submitted his *coup d'état* to the country in the
form of a new constitution which was approved by a vote of 7,440,000 to
646,000. It provided for a president who was to hold office, like the First
Consul, for ten years. The president was to have all the legislative and
executive power of the government and to be advised by a Council of
State, an élite of technicians of the sort who, with the first Napoleon's
active participation, had drafted the Civil Code. There was to be a Senate
to bring together "the most illustrious personages in France"; that is, those
who had helped Louis Napoleon. And there was to be a Legislative Assembly, elected by universal suffrage and with no powers at all. Louis Napoleon, technically, was still only president, but he moved at once from the
modest Élysée into the Tuileries Palace. He was emperor in all but name.

For republicans everywhere the *coup d'état* confirmed their fears and
Louis Napoleon, who had now extinguished two republics, became the
hated "man of 2 December." Monarchists, or at least those who favored
absolutism, felt differently. "He is perfectly right," Franz Josef declared
when he heard the news. "The man who holds the reins of government in
his hands must also be able to take responsibility. Irresponsible sovereignty
is, for me, a phrase without meaning." And on 31 December 1851 he
formally abolished the constitution which he had been ignoring and published a Patent which proclaimed that Austria henceforth would be governed by the emperor alone with an Imperial Council to advise him. Thus
he wiped away the very last vestige of liberalism forced on his family by
the revolutions of 1848 and became in theory the absolute monarch he was
already in practice. Both he and absolutists elsewhere felt that his dynasty
had thereby gained prestige.

But in Sardinia, Louis Napoleon's *coup d'état,* although it resolved the
feelings about him of the republicans, made those of the constitutional
monarchists only more uncertain. They were delighted to have the threat

of a revolutionary republic in France removed, and they hoped that the country would no longer give asylum to the more extreme republican exiles. Yet at the same time the emasculation of the Second Republic left Sardinia as one of the few states in Europe with a parliament which had some power, and the likelihood of that parliament's survival seemed increasingly poor. Louis Napoleon soon asked that criticism of him in the republican papers of Sardinia be curbed and that certain French exiles be expelled. Franz Josef and the King of Prussia, through an intermediary, suggested bluntly to Vittorio Emanuele that he renounce the constitution and join the circle of absolutists. Within the kingdom the reactionary party, containing many conservative aristocrats, clerics and peasants, gathered strength with the argument that Sardinia, pressed between two large absolutist states, could no longer afford its liberal experiments. The king stood by the constitution, but the situation was serious, and he consulted with his ministers.

A result of their deliberations was a bill for a new press law, a concession to Louis Napoleon. In future, legal suits against the press for libels on foreign governments or monarchs would be tried before judges and not submitted to juries, which had consistently refused to convict. The bill made no change in the handling of suits involving internal affairs. The reactionaries supported the bill and even suggested that the time had come to restrict further the right to vote, which was already limited. The liberals, on the other hand, attacked the bill as a step toward reaction and a concession to foreign pressure. The bill eventually was passed, but in its passage an event took place of even greater importance, an alignment of parties within the Parliament, which was the result of a kind of personal *coup d'état* by Cavour.

In the debates over the commercial treaties Cavour had become, in effect, the ministry's representative in Parliament. D'Azeglio, often unable to stand because of the wound in his thigh and disliking debates anyway, concerned himself almost entirely with foreign affairs and appeared in the Chamber as little as possible. The other ministers, except for Cavour, followed d'Azeglio's example, so that Cavour, far more than the others, was aware of the difficulties of trying to govern through a parliament without the support of a government party. With each bill he presented for the ministry he had almost to start afresh persuading individual deputies and senators to support it, for he had no working majority on which to rely.

At the time the deputies in the Chamber divided roughly into four groups: an Extreme Right, a Right Center, a Left Center and an Extreme Left. The Extreme Right, the reactionaries, was loyal to the House of Savoy but against its liberal and Italian policies. The Extreme Left, mostly republicans, was strongly liberal and Italian but the degree of its loyalty to the king was hit off in d'Azeglio's mot: *Viva Vittorio, il re provvisorio,* "The provisional king." The Right Center was the group to which both Cavour and d'Azeglio belonged, liberal aristocrats, loyal to the king and sympathetic to the idea of "making Italy" although many of its members tended to think of "Italy" in terms of Carlo Alberto's short-lived Kingdom of Alta Italia which, with the exception of Genoa, had been restricted to the Po valley. The Left Center was more middle-class in its members, more radical in its liberalism and tended, like the republicans, to think in terms of uniting all of Italy, although unlike the republicans, into a single kingdom. The differences between the two Center groups were not great, and together they could have provided a majority for a ministry. But emotions kept them so divided that most men could not imagine an agreement between them. The leader of the Left Center was Urbano Rattazzi, a lawyer and brilliant speaker with democratic manners and a perfect mastery of Italian; but he was also the man who, as minister under Carlo Alberto, had hastened the kingdom to the disaster of Novara. The military, perhaps unfairly, held him partly responsible for the kingdom's defeat; as did Vittorio Emanuele, for the forced abdication of his father. The king is supposed to have said soon after his accession that he would never have Rattazzi as a minister. Most aristocrats tended to share the king's antipathy both on political and personal grounds. D'Azeglio, for example, who had known poverty as an art student, disapproved of the leisurely pace at which Rattazzi seemed to pay off his financial debts. Even Cavour had little liking for him as a person or politician.

Yet, in January 1852, Cavour began meeting secretly with Rattazzi in order to reach some agreement on joint action in the Chamber. He felt that with the reactionaries growing stronger within the kingdom and its liberal institutions threatened by both France and Austria the ministry must devise some sort of control over the Chamber's decisions. Because their real differences were not great the two men were able quickly to settle on a general program: to support the monarchy, the *Statuto,* the kingdom's independence, and civil progress and reform within it. Rattazzi was to offer the ministry the support of his group during the debates on the new press law and Cavour in accepting it was to make a definite break with the Extreme Right to which, on individual bills in the past, he had frequently looked for support.

The debate began on 3 February and, in the course of the first day's speeches, Rattazzi made his offer to support the ministry, and in a speech the following day Cavour accepted the offer. The exchange caused an immense sensation, both because of the fact of it and because Cavour had not consulted d'Azeglio or his fellow ministers in making the agreement.

D'Azeglio was angry but, as he wrote later, "I acted like the general who, disobeyed by his troop, nevertheless put himself at its head to hide the sedition from the enemy." By all the accepted rules of ministerial behavior Cavour's action was dishonorable, the act of an untrustworthy man. Those who had distrusted his character in the past now felt their suspicions confirmed.

The next day one of the leaders of the Extreme Right expressed his astonishment that the ministry had affected a *divorzio* with one group while at the same time contracting a *connubio,* a marriage, with another. And the term *Connubio* has been used ever since to describe this critical transformation in Sardinian politics.

Purely as a political act the *Connubio* was a masterly stroke, replacing emotion and weakness in the government of the country with common sense and strength. And the furor it created at the time may be evidence, as some historians have suggested, that it could not have been achieved openly. Cavour, in defending it before the Chamber three years later, said:

> . . . I declare from the roof-tops that there is no other act, in my already unfortunately somewhat long political life, which I recall with greater satisfaction. . . . In my opinion, Gentlemen, it was not only opportune but necessary, indispensable in order to construct a great liberal party that would include all persons who, however much they might differ on secondary questions, were nevertheless in agreement on the great principles of progress and liberty. And I believe—I am forced to say it—that with the *Connubio* I performed a service to our country, because by it a barrier was raised sufficiently high so that Reaction can never overcome it.[65]

Three years after the event many men could see some truth in what Cavour claimed for the *Connubio,* but in the weeks immediately after it emotions were still too strong, and Cavour and his fellow ministers clashed over it constantly. In March the ministry nominated Carlo Boncompagni for election as vice-president of the Chamber, but Cavour, deserting his colleagues, supported Rattazzi, who won. A month later when the president of the Chamber died, Cavour did his utmost to persuade the ministry to support Rattazzi for the post, but d'Azeglio and the others would not hear of it. Again all the ministers but Cavour and one other supported Boncompagni, but Rattazzi was elected. D'Azeglio thereupon tried to resign, but the king would not allow it and instead Cavour resigned. He was still a deputy and for a few weeks he took his seat in the Chamber, but his presence obviously embarrassed the ministry and he decided to take a trip abroad.

Before departing he went, as etiquette required, to take leave of the king, who observed bluntly that he would not recall Cavour to the ministry for a long time. And when Cavour attempted to persuade the king that Rattazzi and his followers had modified their ideas and were loyal subjects, Vittorio Emanuele listened impatiently and then broke in: "Signor Conte, you have an income of 150,000 livres and whatever happens it is all one to you, but understand, I do not intend to end as my father did."

Cavour, by his actions, had publicly indicated that he thought d'Azeglio's ministry was no longer up to its job, and the king and his ministers were glad to see him go. Yet d'Azeglio refused to hold any rancor and ordered the Sardinian ambassadors in London and Paris to treat Cavour with special courtesy. "He is a man who can help the country," d'Azeglio wrote to the ambassador in London. In a common patriotism the two men were able to overcome many differences.

On his tour, over which he dawdled four months, Cavour went to London, Edinburgh, to which he lost his heart, and Paris. In each city he talked to the men in power and to the men likely to be in power. To his disappointment he found that the only Sardinian statesman whose name was well known was d'Azeglio. "To him alone," Cavour wrote a friend, "they attribute all the good that has been done in Piedmont. You will say that this is a mistake, an injustice, perhaps: but there it is, and one cannot rectify it without doing harm to the reputation of our country."

He did not sulk, however; he looked forward to the future. He visited docks, arsenals and factories, and spent an evening in the London slums with the chief of police. When he discovered in Paris that Rattazzi was generally thought to be a wild demagogue, he summoned Rattazzi to Paris, arranged for the two of them to have dinner and a private audience with Louis Napoleon and was able thereafter in a letter to quote the president as saying: "I am delighted to have met M. Rattazzi. A quarter of an hour's conversation was sufficient to destroy the erroneous opinion I had been led to conceive of him: I was told he was a hothead: I have found him very reasonable."

Cavour's interviews in Paris convinced him that secreted in Louis Napoleon's ambition was the key to Sardinian policy with regard to Austria. "We shall be either aided or sacrificed," he wrote, "according to whether it suits L. N. to oppose or be friendly with Austria." And like most men he could not conceive of a Napoleon who would accept for long the settlements of the Congress of Vienna. "It is upon France, above all, that our destiny depends. Whether we like it or not we must be her partner in the great game that sooner or later must be played in Europe." He was opposed equally, therefore, to Mazzini's policy of making Italy by an uprising of the people or to Carlo Alberto's policy of *L'Italia farà da sè* led by a king. And although he talked much with republicans such as Manin in Paris, he did not with Mazzini in London.

He returned to Turin in October when the country was in a furor over the fate of a civil marriage bill permitting persons to marry without the Church's sacrament. D'Azeglio's ministry had introduced the bill to the Chamber where in July it had passed by ninety-four to thirty-five. But then the reactionaries, with all the assistance the Papacy could give them, attacked the bill in the Senate, and the ministry did not dare bring it to a vote. A defeat on such a major issue of reform would require the ministry's resignation, and a victory needed just the sort of party organization which Cavour alone had been able to provide. He had delayed his return, with care, until the crisis was full-blown.

Almost everything conceivable had gone wrong, from the ministry's point of view, in its handling of the civil marriage issue. Some months after the passage of the Siccardi Laws abolishing the separate ecclesiastical court system d'Azeglio had again started a succession of envoys to Rome in an effort to reach a new concordat with the Church. At least one of the envoys was not as skillful in discussion as Cardinal Antonelli and revealed how eager the ministry was to reach an agreement, which only encouraged Antonelli to adopt a hard line. In essence, Sardinia was to return the Church to its position before 1848 and, further, to guarantee that there would be no changes in the future. But the ministry could not repeal laws which it had proposed after the Parliament had approved them, nor could it bind itself or its successor for the future. Negotiations languished, and d'Azeglio, who was ill much of the time, introduced the civil marriage bill to the Chamber which passed it.

At once accusations and counter-accusations flew back and forth between Rome and Turin. The king, who was personally devout and genuinely upset at the tangle of negotiations, thereupon wrote Pio Nono a personal, autograph letter, with his ministers' approval, protesting his devotion to the pope as a Catholic and assuring him that the ministry had no intention of interfering with the Church's spiritual affairs. It was a simple letter, and the king intended it to be private and conciliatory, although he allowed his ministers to add a postscript to it in which they pointed out that the proposed law had long since been adopted by France, Austria, Belgium and a number of other Catholic states. Pio Nono, in his reply, stated flatly, "Among Christians, conjugal union is only legitimate in the marriage sacrament, outside of which there is simply concubinage." And further, he added, the Papacy had never approved of the laws adopted by the states cited by the king's ministers. The reply left no room for negotiation, and Antonelli re-enforced its uncompromising stand by publishing the king's letter. At once throughout the kingdom liberals of all shades began to lament that the king was back-sliding while the devout and reactionaries, including his mother, wife and most of the court, implored him not to disobey the pope.

Vittorio Emanuele might have, as a friend declared, "the piety of brigand," tinged with superstition and self-interest, but he was genuinely upset by his family's agitation and by the pope's public reproof. And on 21 October at a meeting with his ministers he declared to them that he would never consent to a law which "might displease the Pope."

For d'Azeglio it marked the end of a trying year: the clash with Cavour, the pain and exhaustion of a wound reopening and, finally, the miscarriage of the civil marriage bill. He had publicly pledged himself to support the new law, and he would not go back on his word. "The hour of dying," he said to his colleagues, "comes at one time or another for all, but the hour of dishonoring one's self ought never to come." Rather than withdraw the bill, the ministry resigned; and d'Azeglio advised the king to send for Cavour. "The other one," d'Azeglio wrote to a friend, "whom you know, is diabolically active, fit in body and soul, and then, he enjoys it so much!" D'Azeglio, an artist and aristocrat, had never been able to make out what there was to enjoy in politics.

The king summoned Cavour and asked him to form a ministry on condition that no further ecclesiastical legislation should be taken up until an agreement had been reached with the pope. Cavour refused to accept the condition. "I am sure of the King's loyalty," he wrote a friend. "The astuteness of the priests and d'Azeglio's feebleness have led him astray; he misunderstands the state of the country. As soon as facts have disabused him, he will send the clerical party to the devil before its time."

So the king, perhaps glad to be free of Cavour, sent for the distinguished Cesare Balbo who had been the leader of the first ministry under the constitution. But Balbo pointed out that there was no group left out of which to form a ministry except the Extreme Right, and as he read over the list of possible ministers, each more reactionary than the last, the king's common sense conquered all his other emotions. "Enough, enough," he said to Balbo, and he sent again for Cavour. The country already had been more than a week without any ministry, and the people's sense of the crisis was growing.

This time the king imposed no conditions, and Cavour for his part, while refusing to withdraw the civil marriage bill, agreed not to make its defeat a cause for resignation and, further, agreed to reopen negotiations with the Papacy. He did not agree, however, if negotiations failed, not to introduce legislation affecting the Church. But on another point he compromised for the king. He persuaded his colleague Rattazzi, for the time being, to continue as president of the Chamber and not to insist on a post in the ministry. So each of them gave up something. Rattazzi's sacrifice also allowed Cavour to construct his ministry exactly as it had been under d'Azeglio except for the change of its leader. Cavour took this way of stating to the kingdom that, as d'Azeglio had fallen on a bill which Cavour was for and not against, the new ministry would continue the policy of the old.

So on 4 November 1852 the *gran ministero* or Great Ministry, as it came to be called, started its work, stronger because of the *Connubio* than its predecessor and, in its strength, more determinedly liberal. Yet on its first important issue, the defense of the civil marriage bill in the Senate, it was defeated. On the first ballot, after several days of debate, the vote was tied, thirty-eight to thirty-eight: then the president of the Senate cast his vote against it, and the ministry withdrew the bill. The exreme republicans immediately accused the ministry of betraying the liberal cause, and the reactionaries loudly proclaimed that at last the liberal cause was defeated. But of greater significance in the bill's history was the large majority by which it passed the Chamber and the single vote by which it failed in the Senate. Ten years earlier the bill could not have been imagined in Sardinia nor did a Parliament exist to consider it. Whether a single bill failed or passed, opinion in the kingdom was moving steadily in the liberal direction.

France, on the other hand, was not. On 2 December 1852 Louis Napoleon, acceding to the wishes of his people expressed in another plebiscite, proclaimed the empire with the office and title of emperor to be hereditary. The day was the anniversary of his own *coup d'état,* and of the first Napoleon's battle of Austerlitz in 1805 and coronation in 1804.

He took as his title Napoleon III, because Marie Louise's infant son had been acclaimed Emperor Napoleon II on 23 June 1815, following his father's abdication after Waterloo. The reign, which had never properly started, had been immediately cut short by the entry of the allied powers into Paris. But reference to it in 1852 perhaps made Louis Napoleon's reign seem more legitimate in pretending to resume a broken tradition rather than starting a new one.

He had no coronation, but in January 1853 he married an aristocratic Spaniard, Eugénie de Montijo, who, although not royal, was very well born and stunningly beautiful. He was forty-four, famous for his ladies, and yet it was said with some reason to be a love match. The ceremony took place in Notre Dame, and as the emperor believed in a show for the people, it was a gorgeous spectacle of matching horses and colorful uniforms. The Second Empire, almost everyone agreed, was at least more entertaining than the drab frock coats of the Second Republic.

It was also, to most men, more threatening. Napoleon insisted he would keep France out of war. *"L'Empire, c'est la paix,"* he proclaimed in a speech at Bordeaux. Yet no one altogether believed him, neither Frenchmen nor foreigners. The settlement of the Congress of Vienna was a challenge that a restored Napoleonic empire could not ignore. Many more than just Cavour believed that sooner or later the emperor would want some glory for himself and some land for France, such as Belgium and a frontier on the Rhine, Savoy or Nice. Yet somehow, Cavour insisted, Sardinia was to be "a partner" to France, though the kingdom and the empire were unequal in their size and population and even in their theories of government. "Liberty," intoned Napoleon, as he opened the French Assembly in 1853, "has never been able to build a lasting political structure; when time has consolidated the edifice, Liberty crowns it." Cavour, however, believed the opposite, that Liberty insured a lasting political structure. Britain had not had a violent change of government since the end of the seventeenth century; the United States since the end of the eighteenth. But in France, where Liberty had frequently been sacrificed, within the memory of living men eight governments had met a violent end: in 1792, 1799, 1814, twice in 1815, in 1830, 1848 and now in 1851. The problem which Cavour pondered was how to make use of France against Austria, a traditional end of Sardinian policy, without the kingdom either being absorbed by France, as happened in the era of the first Napoleon, or being forced to sacrifice its liberal institutions. Napoleon III, like Franz Josef, might object to an example of liberty on his borders.

# CHAPTER 33

Mazzini's committees and the trials at Mantua. Mazzini's rising in Milan, 6 February 1853. The sequestration decree. Sardinia's response. The character of Franz Josef and Count Buol. Sardinia as "Piedmont."

THE NEW SARDINIAN MINISTRY with Cavour at its head caused less excitement in Lombardia and the Veneto than either the proclamation of the Second Empire under Napoleon or the underground activities of Mazzini's supporters. As Cavour himself had discovered, outside of Sardinia, even in neighboring Lombardia, neither he nor his work were well known. D'Azeglio had lived in Milan, had married Manzoni's daughter, and had written his pamphlet, *I Lutti di Lombardia*, about the Austrian brutalities in the city during the Tobacco riots; and he had received his wound fighting the Austrians outside the Venetian city of Vicenza. To both the Milanesi and Venetians he was a popular, unequivocal figure, and they heard of his resignation with regret. Cavour, on the other hand, was not only less well known, but he was, even for those who knew of him, something of a political enigma. He was an aristocrat but liked by neither the king nor the court. Yet he was not, like Alfieri, a republican, but a constitutional monarchist. Many in the Po valley were both liberal and monarchist, but they thought in terms of creating a new kingdom of Alta Italia, not of expanding an old one of the House of Savoy. After Cavour had met Manin in Paris, he had remarked that he found Manin's sentiments "rather too Venetian." The Lombardi and Venetians, in turn, feared that Cavour's sentiments might prove to be "too Piemontese."

Speculation about Napoleon, however, was even greater. When the first news of his *coup d'état* had reached the Po valley, it had caused tremendous excitement, particularly in Milan. Republicans, of course, had raged and talked angrily of the new tyrant; and even the plebiscite endorsing the empire was dismissed as merely a passing infidelity of universal suffrage. But there were many others, survivors of the first Napoleon's armies and civil administrations, on whom the fascination of the First Empire was still strong. If, after the first flush of excitement, they could

420

not foresee clearly the new Napoleon crossing the Alps to create another Kingdom of Italy, at least they were confident that a Napoleonic France was bound to affect Europe, perhaps by war with Austria, and they watched with hope every move that Napoleon made.

The attention of the Austrians, on the other hand, was fixed for the moment almost entirely on the republicans in Italy, on the members of Mazzini's secret committees. Throughout 1851 the police had succeeded in arresting a number of men distributing Mazzinian leaflets and proclamations about Italian unity and independence, but even though they had shot several of those arrested, they were unable either to put an end to the committees or to find out more about them. Then one day in December, near the Swiss border, the police arrested a merchant on the suspicion that he was a counterfeiter. But they found in his pencil case, instead of false bank notes, a subscription bond of Mazzini's National Italian Loan. Threatened with execution the merchant named the man who had given him the bond and then that man, similarly threatened, named a priest, Don Enrico Tazzoli, who was a professor at the seminary at Mantua. Arresting the professor, the police found among his papers a small book with hundreds of entries in code. They suspected that they had stumbled on an important member of Mazzini's network in the Po valley, but for the moment, until they could break the code, they could not be sure, for Tazzoli, no matter how threatened, refused to talk.

The more important republicans, however, knew that the priest was, in fact, their leader, and as rumors began to circulate about the book, they suspected rightly that it was a list of all who had either contributed or received money for the National Loan. In republican circles, therefore, the trial and examination of Tazzoli and the others arrested with him became the supreme subject of conversation.

Throughout 1852 the police continued to make arrests, and one of the men taken was a member of the Contessa Maffei's salon. Arrested in Milan, he was sent to Mantua to face the special military tribunal which Radetzky had appointed to conduct the trials. Another Milanese, doubting his ability to resist the tribunal's examination, hanged himself in prison in Milan, for the Mantua tribunal had developed a reputation for brutality. Others lived constantly prepared to flee, or avoided their homes or quietly crossed the borders into Switzerland or Piedmont. By the end of the summer with one hundred and ten men on trial in Mantua and many more held in prisons elsewhere, no one doubted any longer that the Austrians had pierced the code, and without exception the prisoners and their friends believed that Luigi Castellazzo, the secretary of the Central Committee, had broken down under torture and, in return for a promise of his own freedom, had revealed the key to it.

Castellazzo was, besides Tazzoli, the only man in Italy who knew the key, a system of numbers for letters based on the Lord's prayer in Latin and the first three lines of Canto IV of the *Inferno,* and some months after Tazzoli and four others had been convicted of treason and hanged, Castellazzo was indeed set free. The question of his part in the death of his friends agitated republican political life thereafter for thirty years.

Castellazzo consistently protested his innocence, and he fought bravely under Garibaldi in 1859, 1860 and 1866. His fellow soldiers, in a court of honor he had requested in an effort to clear his name, declared that such a good soldier and patriot could not have betrayed his comrades in 1852. But most men still believed otherwise. So when in 1884 he was elected to the Chamber of Deputies of the Kingdom of Italy and one of the deputies refused to sit in the Chamber with him, he requested and received a vote of confidence in his innocence. Yet many still felt that party politics rather than evidence had been tested. The Austrian interrogator in 1852 had repeatedly stated "Castellazzo has confessed everything," and had used him on occasion to confront the other prisoners and at the end had set him free, although he was the secretary of the most important of the secret committees.

Finally, in the years after Castellazzo's death, the Director of the Archives at Mantua made an extended study of the question and turned up much new evidence. On the basis of it historians have concluded that, whatever the virtues of Castellazzo's later life, in 1852 he did betray his fellow conspirators. He did not reveal the code, for experts in Vienna had already broken it. But faced with the fact that it was broken, he had decided to reveal all he knew in return for his own safety and freedom, and his additional revelations were the cause of further arrests, trial and condemnations to death.

In all, of the hundred and ten men prosecuted for treason forty-one were condemned to death, of whom thirty-one had their sentences commuted to imprisonment. The other ten were taken outside the city to Fort Belfiore and executed. Soon, all over Italy, they were known as "the martyrs of Belfiore." The rest of the prisoners, with the exception of one who died during the trials and another who was handed over to the Duke of Modena, received prison terms. The Austrians had reason to be pleased with their work. They had uncovered a widespread conspiracy and effectively scotched it; in fact, Mazzini's network of committees in the Po valley never regained its strength.

Yet, like Emperor Franz and Metternich with the Carbonaro trials thirty years earlier, Franz Josef and Radetzky made less of their success than they might have, for they too confused the symptom with the disease, behaving as though eradicating a conspiracy was to end the desires of a people to be a nation. Part of Mazzini's appeal undoubtedly was to wild-eyed, anarchic men who enjoyed lurking in the streets in order to throw a bomb or to stab a solitary soldier, but it was not all of Mazzini's appeal any more than it had been all of the Carbonari's. Of those executed at Mantua along with some simpler men there had been an aristocrat, two priests, a doctor and a lawyer's clerk. All of them, regardless of class or training, had responded to Mazzini's ideal of a united, independent Italy and had felt themselves, in working to achieve it, to be Italians. Yet neither Franz Josef nor Radetzky would consider any concession to this Italian spirit.

The issue, however, was not clear, for just as the trials were drawing to a close, Mazzini staged an uprising in Milan, on 6 February 1853, which exhibited all the worst evils of his conspiratorial method and seemed to justify those who argued that he and his conspiracies should be met by stronger police action rather than a change in Austrian policy.

Mazzini, who was undoubtedly made desperate by the collapse of his committees, hoped to start another Cinque Giornate in Milan which, in turn, would start a general revolt in the Po valley. Many of his most responsible followers, however, advised against it, pointing out that their leaders were in hiding or on trial at Mantua, that the city still had not recovered its vitality after the disasters of 1848–49, and that neither Sardinia nor France was ready to fight Austria. When Mazzini refused to listen to them, most of them withdrew from the project, and he had to recruit new leaders and send in agents from outside, and these men, in turn, were forced to recruit their troops of conspirators almost entirely from the lowest class. It was an unlucky start.

Mazzini provided money, proceeds of the National Loan, and models from which stilettos and bombs could be manufactured. He also promised that some Hungarian troops stationed in the city would join the revolt and that a Hungarian general would come from London to lead it. His chief agent in the city, a Roman, enrolled five thousand conspirators, at least by report, and then divided them into companies of several hundreds each. These in turn he assigned variously to attack the Castello, which had a garrison of twelve thousand Austrians, the Palazzo di Corte, several barracks and the fort at the Porta Tosa. Remarkably, the Austrians learned nothing of the plans.

As the appointed day approached, some of the leading republicans in the city sent two emissaries to Mazzini, who had arrived in Switzerland, to urge him to cancel the rising. But a blizzard swept down from the Alps, blocked the roads, and the men were unable to get through. Mazzini, meanwhile, prepared a proclamation for the rising which began: "The mission of the National Committee is finished; yours begins. The last word which today your brothers send to you is insurrection. . . ."

The day came, and the hour of four in the afternoon when the revolution was to start, and nothing happened. Or almost nothing. Instead of four hundred men only thirty turned up to take the Castello with its garrison of twelve thousand, and their leader, after waiting a time, dismissed them. At the Palazzo di Corte, instead of four hundred, ten or twelve appeared, and one seized some guns from a stack by a sentinel; a few shots were exchanged. Near the hospital a sort of half-barricade went up and quickly came down. No Hungarian troops joined the revolt. Most Milanesi, learning that some trouble was afoot, quickly shut their shops and homes, and except for Austrian patrols the streets were soon deserted. Mazzini's uprising, as ineffective as his expedition into Savoy in 1834, was over.

Unfortunately, in the course of it, ten Austrian soldiers were killed or wounded, several of them by stabbings in otherwise quiet streets. Most Milanesi were both disgusted at the methods of the revolt and dismayed at the probable results of it. A group of leading citizens quickly formed a committee to wait on the Austrian commandant, General Gyulai, and it expressed the surprise and displeasure of the greater part of the citizens and begged the commandant not to hold the city responsible. It was the first break in the city's refusal to deal or even talk with the Austrians, and many deplored it, although condemning Mazzini for the revolt.

The commandant seemed to recognize the opportunity to improve relations. He praised the committee for its action, urged the more responsible classes to break away from the revolutionaries and issued a series of mild orders which reassured the city that the actions of a few would not be held against the many. But two days later all was changed as violent, almost hysterical orders came from Radetzky in Verona and were followed by others from Franz Josef in Vienna. The brutality which they had been accused of using at Mantua and their lack of imagination about the issues involved were now applied against the Milanesi with such force that their actions became a European issue.

The city was declared to be in a state of siege. No one was allowed to enter or leave without a permit, and for a month Milan was closed to the world. Meanwhile a number of men were arrested from whom six were chosen, indicted, condemned and hanged for their part in the revolt. In the next few days ten more were hanged. Not long after, at least four were shown to be innocent. One was simply a sick man who had gone into the street to buy some milk; another was a lame man who had been arrested because of his cane.

A ten o'clock curfew was set and every citizen given an identity card without which he was liable to arrest. The people were allowed out of doors only in couples and no more than two could stand together in the streets, which were patrolled by troops. Landlords were required to keep lights burning in front of their houses in case the gas pipes should be cut, and all the military posts and sentinel boxes were surrounded by iron railings. Hundreds of arrests were made, and although the Austrians succeeded in capturing a number of the conspirators, many innocent men were kept in prison for weeks before the cases against them could be heard and dismissed. And finally, by Imperial decree, the city was obligated to support the wounded soldiers for the rest of their lives, to support the families of those who had died and to assume the cost of extra pay given to the garrison on account of the revolt.

But the Austrian government was not content with punishing the actual conspirators, either in Milan or Mantua, or even with punishing the entire city of Milan. Within a week after the revolt Franz Josef, through his Minister for Foreign Affairs, Count Ferdinand Buol-Schauenstein, had issued a decree sequestrating or confiscating all the real and personal property of all political exiles from his two Italian provinces. Franz Josef saw no reason why a Venetian living in Turin on an income drawn from a farm or a business in the Veneto should be able to contribute to Mazzini's conspiracies, and one way to stop it was to confiscate the income at its source.

In spite of its general language the decree was aimed primarily at the Kingdom of Sardinia for that was where the exiles had gathered. The American consul in Turin, writing the day before the decree was published, estimated that there were in the kingdom more than one hundred thousand refugees from Lombardia and the Veneto of which about twenty thousand were in Turin. Some had crossed the border without passports and were living abroad without Austrian permission; some, by taking advantage of certain amnesties, had secured that permission, and still others, also with Austrian permission, had renounced their allegiance to the emperor and become subjects of the King of Sardinia. Austria, in its treaty with Sardinia, had explicitly agreed to respect the property rights of the last two groups, and the sequestration decree broke the treaty.

The outcry over the decree in Turin was immediate and loud. Not only were most of the exiles affected, many losing all their income, but most Sardinians felt, as Cavour observed to d'Azeglio, that Austria's real motive was "to discredit our government, to degrade it in the eyes of Italy and of Europe." Yet he refused to be hurried into reprisals. "As you can well believe," he added, "we have no intention of risking a third war of redemption: the time of follies is passed."

Instead, Cavour reaped what advantage he could from the illegality of Austria's action. He asked in a series of notes if Austria intended to enforce the decree against the subjects of Sardinia, if it had considered proceeding against the exiles individually on the basis of evidence of conspiracy, and if it had considered that the decree violated its own civil code as well as international law. To all of which Count Buol replied, in effect, that Austria was an empire of forty million persons and Sardinia a kingdom of only four million and that Austria, therefore, would do as it pleased.

Cavour drew up a memorandum reviewing the issue and, presenting it first to Buol, sent copies to all the other governments of Europe. Then he formally severed relations with Austria by withdrawing the Sardinian ambassador from Vienna. Sardinia could not force Austria to withdraw the decree, but it had stood firm and done what little it could with dignity and steady purpose. In the eyes of most European diplomats and ministers Austria, forever referring to its rights under the treaties of Vienna, had lost the exchange. At the start of the trials at Mantua, other states in Europe had accepted Austria as the necessary policeman of Italy, one imposing law and order on an unruly people. But at the end of the trials, which Radetzky formally closed five weeks after the sequestration decree, Austria had itself become a troublemaker in Italy, and in a fashion which most states judged to be unnecessarily provocative.

Austria's defeat in public opinion was partly the result of Buol's personality, which was to have a part in shaping a number of events in the coming year. Schwarzenberg had died suddenly in April 1852, and Franz Josef, in accordance with his absolutist tendency, had become his own prime minister and divided Schwarzenberg's duties among several men; and he had appointed Buol, who at the time was ambassador to Britain, to be his Minister of Foreign Affairs. Buol, like Schwarzenberg who had recommended him, was a man of violence. While he had been in London, the British Foreign Secretary had reproved him for his bullying language and his "coarse and insolent manner." But where Schwarzenberg had contrived generally to make his violence effective, so that it was a force, Buol's more often degenerated into bluster and lost for him what he was striving to gain.

This streak of violence, a sympathy for the forceful solution to a problem, was a characteristic of Franz Josef's government which Buol, perhaps, carried to an extreme. But others, including the emperor, shared it, and also a weakness which seemed to accompany it: an inability to know when to stop, to recognize the moment in which a policy, pushed too far, becomes self-defeating. Radetzky's punishment of Milan, considering the ineffectiveness of the revolt, was so extreme that it reunited the Milanesi against the Austrians at the very moment they were beginning, for the first time, to divide. Franz Josef commuted many of the death sentences at Mantua at the very moment when his agents sent bills to several mothers for the cord used to hang their sons, and most Italians, on hearing of the two actions, were convinced, not that the emperor was merciful but that his Imperial State was barbaric. If Buol had sequestrated the estates of individual exiles, presenting evidence that they were trying to undermine Austrian government in the Po valley, he would have had the sympathy of Europe, for there was no question that many of the exiles in Sardinia were devoting all their time and wealth to that end. Probably the other states, most significantly France and Great Britain, would have put pressure on Sardinia to expel the worst offenders or at least to curtail their actions, and Sardinia could not have resisted the pressure. But by insisting on a blanket confiscation and by defending it in offensive language he ended by losing the sympathy of Europe for his country. Cavour, on the other hand, although starting with a weak case and a weak kingdom to back it, won the sympathy of Europe for Sardinia and, on his first foreign issue, impressed the governments of other states as a reasonable man.

Sardinia's stand against Austria improved its relations with all but the most extreme republicans, particularly after Cavour introduced a bill, which Parliament passed enthusiastically, granting pensions to the exiles impoverished by the sequestration decree. The act, which was generous for a small kingdom financially pressed, drew no distinctions among exiles because of their political beliefs, and many republicans in spite of their prejudices, began to think of Sardinia as the leader in a common cause against Austria. After the sequestration decree, even men without much interest in politics began to sense the value of a diplomatic corps to present a cause to Europe and to look to Sardinia to represent them.

This change in attitude was very gradual, but a symptom of it was the increasing number of men who referred to the Kingdom of Sardinia as "Piedmont." Even the diplomats, in speaking informally, now sometimes used the name of the province to denote the kingdom, perhaps because most of the men around the king were Piemontesi as opposed to Savoyards or Genovesi, or perhaps because Turin, the seat of the government, was in Piedmont. But whatever the balance of the reasons the informal term reflected the fact that the House of Savoy, in spite of its French background and tradition, had finally anchored itself on the Italian side of the Alps. Symbolically, although French was still the common language of the provinces of Savoy and Nice and of polite society and the court, the Parliament debated in Italian, the king governed in it and, by royal decree in 1852, it, and not French, replaced Latin as the official language of all the universities in the kingdom. Perhaps, in the shades of Santa Croce, Alfieri smiled. In his day the Tuscan dialect or, as he called it, "the real Italian," had been "frowned on" in Turin.

# CHAPTER 34

The Crimean War begins. Cavour's vision of its effects in Europe.
Franz Josef and Nicholas. Duke of Parma assassinated. The Law
on the Convents. The State's position. The Church's position. The
constitutional crisis. D'Azeglio's letter to the King. The bill passes.
Its significance.

IN THE NEXT TWO YEARS, 1854 and 1855, two issues, one foreign and the
other internal, began to dominate the political life of Sardinia; and as the
Sardinian Parliament was the only forum in Italy in which the issues could
be debated freely, Italian patriots of other states watched and listened
eagerly, increasingly certain that their fate was somehow involved in events
in Sardinia. The first issue to arise although the last to reach a conclusion,
was the war in Crimea and Sardinia's part, if any, in it; the second was
another round in the Parliament's efforts to reorganize life in Sardinia with
a smaller, less powerful role in its civil side for the Church. In the debates
on both issues, and even in the creation of the first, Cavour took a leading
part, a role made difficult for him by the fact that his supporters on the first
were his opponents on the second. Sometimes within a week, or even
within a day, he would be in and out of favor with the king, or able and
then not able to count on Rattazzi's support in the Chamber. The fact he
could survive as prime minister in such circumstances, while at the same
time accomplishing more than most men had imagined to be possible,
greatly increased their respect for him, even if not their liking. It was in
these years and for his handling of these issues, particularly Sardinia's role
in the Crimean War, that many men began to feel a kind of awe for him, to
conceive of him as a "man of destiny" who must be followed even though
his ways were often crooked and unclear.

The Crimean War officially began with a Russian declaration of war
on Turkey delivered on 1 November 1853. The war was the ninth in 180
years between the two countries and might have been relatively unimportant, at least in Europe, except for one fact: for the first time in its history
the Ottoman Empire, the scourge of Christian Europe, had reason to

believe that it would have the armed support of a Christian power, either of Great Britain or of France, or possibly of both.

It had the interest and moral support of Britain, even at the start of the war, because the Ottoman Empire, by reason of its geographical position, was custodian of a treaty controlling the strait between the Mediterranean and Black Seas. In 1840–41, because of the empire's dwindling power, the strait for the first time had been treated as a European problem and, by a treaty signed by most of the great powers, had been closed to warships of all nations and free passage for their merchant ships assured. But when the Russians, at the end of the first month of the war, succeeded in destroying a large part of the Turkish fleet at Sinope, suddenly it seemed possible or even likely that the Russian fleet would close the strait and turn the Black Sea, an enormous area of trade, into a Russian preserve. After Sinope, the government in Britain began to consider seriously whether it should send troops and ships to aid the Sultan.

France, although not a signatory of the treaty, had benefited by it and like Britain, was disturbed by Russia's success at Sinope. And it had an additional reason to support the sultan against the tsar because of a dispute between some Greek Orthodox and Roman Catholic monks in Jerusalem over who should have custody of the holy places. Since the time of the Crusades, France had been the protector of Catholics in the Holy Land, and with the clerical party in France growing stronger Napoleon had taken up the issue. Undoubtedly he saw in it a chance to reassert France's position in the eastern Mediterranean, to stir memories of the time when the first Napoleon had carried French arms and culture into Egypt and Syria and, perhaps in a similar fashion, to attach some eastern color and glory to his own regime.

But the tsar, Nicholas I, was not inclined to back down. Orthodox pilgrims to the Holy Land had been increasing until they outnumbered the Catholic by a hundred to one, and, with Mohammedans in Constantinople, the Orthodox looked to the tsar, as the heir of Byzantium, to protect them. Pilgrims and monks periodically rioted in Jerusalem, Napoleon and Nicholas protested, and the sultan attempted to placate first one and then the other with privileges for his sect. As the war started, Napoleon and many Frenchmen were inclined to support the sultan, if only to punish the tsar, and the government soon was considering an expedition to the East in alliance with Great Britain.

Cavour watched the war begin, saw that Great Britain and France would probably be drawn into it as allies, and sensed that in the ensuing shifts of power and interests Sardinia, and through it Italy, might profit at Austria's expense. He recognized that an alliance between Great Britain and France, constant opponents for the last two hundred years, would be, as he called it when it came about, "the greatest fact in modern history." He hoped that Austria, which had survived its Hungarian revolution in 1849 only because of Russia's help in the form of an army of two hundred thousand men, would feel it had to side with Russia now, either out of gratitude or a desire to absorb some of the sultan's Balkan provinces. But even if it did not, he wanted Sardinia to associate itself with Britain and France. In January 1854, more than two months before the two countries announced an alliance or declared war on Russia, Cavour one day asked the king: "Does it not seem to Your Majesty that we ought to find a way to take part in the war that the Western Powers are about to declare on Russia?" To which Vittorio Emanuele replied, "Certainly, and if I cannot go myself I will send my brother!"

Cavour's question was the result of careful thought; the king's quick answer, more likely, sprang from his character. He was young, vigorous and himself a good soldier; he was proud of his army, which he had helped to reform after its defeat at Novara, and he knew it needed battle experience. Perhaps also he remembered that when he had communicated his father's death to the heads of other states, the only one who had not replied was the tsar.

A few weeks later Cavour went to Genoa for the official opening of the railroad that pierced the Ligurian Alps and connected Turin and Genoa. The line, which was one of Cavour's pet projects, reduced the journey between the two cities from one of several days and nights to a single day, and on the first through trip Cavour rode in the cab of the locomotive. But while in Genoa he told a Milanese exile, Conte Toffetti, who was a close friend of the British minister to Sardinia, Sir James Hudson, that both he and the king were eager to send a contingent of troops to the East in alliance with Great Britain. Thereafter, in London, the possibility of using part of the Sardinian army to bolster Britain's small standing army, should Britain declare war on Russia, was constantly discussed.

But when Cavour sounded out his fellow ministers on the idea of participating in the war in the East, he found all but one angrily against him; and as the idea gradually became public, the ministers' objections resounded everywhere: There was no reason to fight Russia, Austria was the enemy; with an Austrian army in Lombardia it was foolish to send any Sardinian soldier out of the kingdom; the raising of the Austrian sequestrations was a more pressing problem and should be solved first; it would be too expensive for the kingdom, already financially pressed; and, finally, a suggestion by Cavour that Britain might help Sardinia financially in return for fifteen thousand troops was rejected by the army as humiliating. The Minister of War was outraged and officers, when they heard of it, threatened to resign. Republicans, and even such men as Rattazzi, accused

Cavour of wanting to betray the Italian cause for a few baubles of glory for the House of Savoy. As Britain and France declared war against Russia on 31 March 1854 and on 10 April proclaimed their formal alliance, with an invitation to others to join it, the king and Cavour stood alone in support of their idea. Yet neither dropped it, and the others in the ministry and army were forced constantly to consider it a possibility.

Negotiations continued with France and England, but slowly and even aimlessly, for the ministers of those powers were far more interested in securing Austria as an ally than Sardinia. Franz Josef, however, seemed unable to make up his mind. He himself dealt directly with Nicholas, two absolute monarchs deciding peace or war for millions of their subjects by personal letters. Nicholas was proud, moody and self-righteous, and Franz Josef, who owed the preservation of his throne to Nicholas, was polite, distant and censorious. Nicholas saw his cause as "almost a crusade, in which Russia defends Christianity while France and England are guilty of the infamy of fighting for the Crescent." Franz Josef, however, argued for peace and the *status quo*. Undoubtedly he feared that a Russian victory might threaten his own position in the Balkans, but he did not say so directly to Nicholas. Instead he warned that Russian advances against the Turkish provinces around the mouth of the Danube might cause "a new flare-up of revolutionary activity in Europe and new upheavals of incalculable outcome." The House of Habsburg had survived the upheavals of 1848–49 with the greatest difficulty, and no hope of gain at the Sultan's expense could induce Franz Josef to risk a repetition of those years.

But Nicholas, who had not experienced 1848–49 and who had little trouble handling his revolutionaries, interpreted Franz Josef's remarks, apparently, as an appeal for help should revolutionary troubles again beset the Habsburgs. All the greater was his indignation, therefore, when Franz Josef finally spoke out unequivocally, stating that not only would Austria not help Russia in the war, it would only remain neutral if Nicholas would not go further into Ottoman territory and cross the Danube, or "should military developments compel you to cross it, you will not depart in the least degree from your previous declarations, according to which you seek no territorial gains, no interference between the relations of the Sultan and his subjects, no rights that do not proceed from your old treaties with the Ottoman Empire."

Nicholas in his life had never heard such direct language, and it sounded particularly offensive from a man whose family's fortune was based on fighting the Turks, a man he considered to be his protégé. Besides, Nicholas was quite sincere. Had not all the great heads of state in the past carried Christianity to the heathen by the sword? "Are you truly to make the Turk's cause your own?" he asked in astonished disbelief. "Emperor Apostolical, does your conscience permit it?"

Franz Josef's subjects asked the same question and put into it a little less of religion and more of realism. The alliance between Austria and Russia had defeated Napoleon, had secured the treaties of Vienna, had secured the eastern frontier of the Habsburg empire and, by posing a threat to Prussia, had secured the northern frontier. What, the emperor's subjects asked each other, could he put in its place? Almost everyone else in his government, except Buol who favored an alliance with the West, thought Franz Josef had made a dreadful mistake. High-ranking army officers are said to have wept when they realized they would not fight beside their Russian fellows.

But Franz Josef stood his ground, both against Nicholas and his own people, and the break with Russia was complete, beyond healing. When Nicholas died in March 1855, killed, as everyone said, by Austrian ingratitude, his son, Alexander II, answered Franz Josef's letter of condolence in unmistakable terms:

> You will readily understand the effect of the political events of this last year on his heart—they broke it—when instead of finding in you a faithful friend and ally, on whom he relied and whom he loved as his own son, he saw you follow a political course which brought you ever closer to our enemies and which will still bring us inevitably, if that course does not change, to a fratricidal war, for which you will be accountable to God.[66]

The break with Russia was to be of immense importance in the later history of the Habsburg empire and, like the alliance of France and England, was a readjustment of power certain to drain from the settlements of the Congress of Vienna much of the force which had supported them. Yet more immediately for Cavour and Vittorio Emanuele it was a setback, for it encouraged France and Britain to believe that Austria would join them, and it increased the opposition of many in Sardinia to any participation in the war. An expedition to the East which might fight the Austrians was conceivable but one that might fight the Russians with Austria as a friendly ally was out of the question. Yet neither the king nor Cavour would give up the idea. Cavour kept in touch with the British minister, and the king told the French ambassador, "Only Cavour and I count. If it is necessary to change the ministers, I will change them." He thought Franz Josef, in the end, would not join the alliance, and he added, "When our soldiers have once mixed with yours, I shall laugh at Austria. And after all, we must do something. If we do not go to the East, we shall be hurried along by all those revolutionary screechers to commit some blunder in Italy."

The screechers had already hurried Sardinia into a blunder at Novara and, led by Mazzini, had produced another in Milan. Now in March 1854 they produced still another, this time in Parma.

The event arose out of an announcement by Parma's Duke Carlo III that he intended to lead his army of six thousand to the war in the East; and to pay for the expedition he proposed to levy on his subjects a large, forced loan. The protest from the Parmigiani was immediate and unanimous, both by official petitions and by angry squibs on the wall. The duke, however, ignored all warnings and one Sunday afternoon, 26 March, started on a stroll through the city of Parma accompanied only by an orderly. On the way back to the palazzo he stopped to watch a ballerina lean out a window and, as he gazed up with admiration, an assassin stabbed him. Twenty-four hours later he was dead, and his wife, Luisa Maria di Borbone, thereupon became regent on behalf of their infant son, Roberto.

Mazzini was not responsible for the murder, but the fact hardly mattered. Italians as well as Austrians blamed him or, at least, his doctrines and adherents for a useless crime, and the Austrians delighted in presenting it to the world as typically "Italian" and the reason why Austria's presence was necessary in Italy. Throughout the summer Franz Josef avoided coming to any agreement with France and Britain, protesting that he could not take troops from Italy to send to the East. He pointed to the conspiracies, such as the one exposed by the trials at Mantua, to the murder of a head of state, as at Parma, and to the constant threat of an invasion of Lombardia by Sardinia, such as had already happened twice. Finally in December he signed an evasive treaty with France and Britain in which he agreed to make war on Russia only if Russia attacked the sultan's provinces on the Danube. But by then the war was being fought on Russian territory, in the Crimea. Inevitably the two western allies, disappointed in Austria, even angry with it, began to listen with greater interest to the proposals of Cavour and the king.

Just at this moment, however, when Cavour and the king might well have been pleased with each other for supporting an unpopular policy to the threshold of success, they were, in fact, split and angry with each other over the second issue dominating Sardinian politics: the question of whether the State, through the Parliament, could reform its corporation and property laws to the detriment of the Church. In particular, the ministry had introduced into Parliament a bill, known either as the Rattazzi bill or the Law on the Convents, which proposed to abolish all the religious orders except those devoted to preaching, nursing or teaching; to forbid the organization of any new orders except by special permission of the State; to suppress, with certain exceptions, the chapters of the collegiate churches and the simple benefices; to use the revenues of these suppressed chapters and benefices to pay pensions to the ecclesiastics whose orders and chapters had been suppressed; and to restrict the salaries of the bishops and to use the money thereby saved to raise the salaries of the most poorly paid priests. In short, the ministry with its bill asked Parliament to reduce the number of ecclesiastics, to confiscate Church property and, by its power of taxation, indirectly to set Church salaries.

The bill was the result of a report by a commission appointed by Parliament to make a census of the clergy and an inventory of the Church's resources throughout the kingdom. Even though some two hundred cloisters on the mainland had not responded to the questions, the report showed that simply as a percentage of the population the number of priests, monks and nuns in Sardinia was extraordinary. In a country of 4,916,084 persons there were 23,000 ecclesiastics of every kind; about 1 priest, monk or nun to every 214 inhabitants, while in Belgium the ratio was 1 to 500 and in Austria, 1 to 610. In the United States in 1962 the ratio of priests, exclusive of monks and nuns, to Catholic laymen was about 1 to 775. In 1854 Sardinia had 41 bishops and archbishops, and Belgium with a population of 4½ million had 6. In the United States in 1962 there were 234 (including 5 cardinals) for a Catholic population of about 42,875,000; the various ratios were Sardinia, 1 to 121,000; Belgium, 1 to 750,000; and the United States, 1 to 183,000. Many laymen felt the numbers were a social evil, allowing too many men to escape the duties of citizenship, particularly taxation and conscription. They referred to the contemplative orders as "the useless orders" and in deploring the begging orders spoke of "able-bodied idleness" which they felt was wholly out of place in a poor country.

The wealth of the Church was even more extraordinary. Its estimated income from lands and endowments, wholly apart from what it received in fees, collections, or subsidies was about one-thirteenth of the national revenue. And the individual income of the hierarchy was on the same scale. A table prepared by A. J. Whyte for his book on Cavour shows the relative amounts:

| | |
|---|---|
| The Archbishop of Turin | 100,000 lire |
| The Bishops (average) | 30,000 |
| Cabinet Ministers | 15,000 |
| Chief Justice on the highest court | 12,000 |
| The Director of the National Bank | 10,000 |
| The Counsellors of State | 8,000 |
| Vice-Admiral | 8,000 |

| Intendant General | |
|---|---|
| (highest Civil Servant) | 7,500 |
| Rear-Admiral | 7,200 |

The archbishop's salary was twice that of the Archbishop of Paris and almost as large as those of all the Belgian bishops combined. Meanwhile many parochial priests in Piedmont were paid almost nothing. The bill proposed to reduce the salaries of the archbishops to 18,000 and the bishops to 12,000, and to use the balance to pay the poorer priests.

While the commission had been gathering its facts, Cavour, true to his promise to the king, had reopened negotiations with the pope in the hope of reforming the Church's position in Sardinia by agreement with the Church. Many men, of course, hoped that the Church would reform itself and argued that, in time, Pio Nono would return to his liberalism. But, as before, negotiations failed. This time, however, the king, who was most anxious to end the religious quarrel, immediately thereafter sent a personal delegation of three bishops to see the pope, but he did so without the ministry's approval. His act, going behind his ministers' backs, was unconstitutional and, if successful, might have destroyed the parliamentary system in Sardinia by aligning the king with the reactionaries against the more numerous constitutional monarchists and republicans.

Cavour, however, cut the danger short by introducing the bill to Parliament. The pope promptly protested against this new "horrible and incredible assault of the subalpine government," and the three bishops wrote in a letter to the king: "The law is based on principles that the Church can never admit and always rejected. It presupposes that the State can suppress at its will religious communities and that it is master of the possessions of the Church. No compromise is possible on such principles." Vittorio Emanuele was mortified at his scolding by the pope and the bishops and angry at Cavour for exposing him to it; at the same time he was rejoicing with Cavour that negotiations with France and Britain were beginning to ripen into a treaty of alliance.

But the religious issue gave the king no peace. After he received another reproof from the Archbishop of Genoa, he wrote to La Marmora, his Minister of War and the only minister with whom he felt at ease:

> I see clearly that the affair is becoming serious, and the person who is going to bear all the brunt of it is I; for, so far as the rest of you are concerned, when you are in a fix, I know well what you do; and I am left in the soup.
>
> My mother and wife do nothing but tell me that they are dying of shame for me; you can understand what pleasure that gives me; now they will hear the rest. From what Rattazzi said, I thought that the

affair would not present such grave difficulties and that there was a
semi-accord with the bishops and with Rome; but it is quite different.
In a word, I do what I can. We shall see where it comes out.[67]

The pressure put on the king by his womenfolk and clerics to be
obedient to the Holy Father was repeated in many households throughout
the kingdom. The ministry on Cavour's insistence, had laid the bill before
the Parliament as a financial measure, on the ground that because the government contributed almost a million lire a year to support the poorer
clergy, it had the right to rearrange the salaries more equably. Cavour had
hoped, by talking finance, to keep emotions out of the public and parliamentary debates, but everyone immediately recognized that the bill involved more than facts and figures and was an attempt by the State to
reduce the Church as a political opponent to one of manageable size. In
spite of Cavour's maneuver, men and women argued the pros and cons on
this ground, and throughout the kingdom the arguments waxed furious.

The ministry presented the bill to the Parliament on 28 November
1854, and in the six weeks before it came up for debate both sides circulated petitions and protests which thousands signed. And when the debate
in the Chamber began, on 9 January 1855, the first speaker against it,
symbolic of the division in the country, was Cavour's elder brother.

In the first few days a number of speakers treated the questions of law
and the need for reform in quiet, effective speeches. Then, in the other
tradition of Italian speaking, Brofferio, the greatest republican orator, rose
and, although bitterly opposed to Cavour on the Crimean issue, defended
the religious bill in a tremendous swell of rhetoric. He went back to the
Donation of Constantine, a gift from a State, which had been the source
of all the Church's wealth, and he argued that what the State had given
out, it could take back. He traced the iniquities of the Church through
the ages: its greed, its persecutions and its love of calling foreign armies
into Italy, two of which at the moment were occupying the Papal States.
He talked of the *Index:* "Chemistry was proscribed, anatomy was proscribed" and, after a long list, he insisted that "If the Inquisition had succeeded in destroying all the works it has proscribed, what, today, would
be the inheritance of the human intellect? —Emptiness, ignorance and
darkness." And finally, after complaining that the bill did not go far
enough, he concluded:

There are 490 convents in the State. Does the ministry propose to me
to suppress them all? I will give it my vote with great exultation. Does
it wish to suppress only half of them? I resign myself and vote for the
abolition of 245 convents. Does it ask me to suppress 100? I vote for
100. Will it suppress 10? I vote for 10. Will it suppress one? I vote for

the suppression of a single convent. Will it abolish one priest? I vote for the abolition of one priest. In politics, to refuse an atom of good because you cannot get more, is, in my eyes, a great error. Let the ministry begin; for if it begins in good faith, then in spite of everything it begins in order to end, and not to remain stuck in the middle of the road as it has with the law of civil marriage. Therefore, I vote for this law; but I declare that I vote for it awaiting better times, better men, and better laws.[68]

Brofferio's position was an extreme, but he shared it with many republicans, including such a popular leader as Garibaldi. His closing words, that he was awaiting better times, men and laws, was notice to the king and Cavour, perhaps even a threat, that the republicans would not support them if they did not push the liberal cause. But unknown to Brofferio on the very day that he was supporting the king and Cavour in the Chamber, they were signing the preliminary papers of alliance with France and Britain in the palazzo, and Brofferio previously had described any expedition to the East as "economically reckless, militarily a folly, politically a crime." Since most republicans shared this view, their support in the Chamber on the religious issue was still uncertain.

The Conte Solaro della Margarita answered Brofferio's speech for the Church and in much the same style. For eighteen years he had been Carlo Alberto's minister in the days before the *Statuto,* and he looked back to that time as a golden era. He asked the deputies simply: were they Catholics or were they not? To endorse a policy not approved by the Church was to cease, *ipso facto,* to be a Catholic. His reasoning might be too simple, but it was clear; and clear and simple were the old minister's faith and fears. "Oh may it please God," he exclaimed, "whose avenging arm still holds the chastisement of man, to spare from any ill this our dear country! But if upon us should fall any of those calamities that form the human lot, how many will say, and perchance with truth: This unjust law has been the cause, we have provoked the anger of Heaven!"

Early the next morning the king's mother died; Maria Teresa, the widow of Carlo Alberto. Her life had been a tragedy, torn twice in two. As an Austrian archduchess she had seen her husband lose his throne fighting the Austrians, and she had found her consolation watching over a convent which, as she died, her son's government was about to abolish as "useless." The morning of her death, 12 January, the Chamber adjourned its debates for ten days of mourning.

But in the streets and cafés the debate went on, and to it was added another: first by rumors, and then by confirmation of them, that Sardinia would send an army to the East and receive a loan to finance it from Great Britain. The treaty, of course, had to be approved by the Parliament, but there was no question that it had been signed, as one of the ministers had resigned in protest. Army officers insisted that they would not fight as mercenaries and the most radical republicans circulated protests among the troops urging them to refuse to fight "except for the unity of Italy and for the peoples that aspire to avenge their nationality."

On 22 January the Chamber reconvened to continue its debate on the convents, but its session began with an announcement of what most men already knew: that, on 20 January, the Queen, Maria Adelaide, had died. She had given birth earlier in the month to a son, her sixth child and the king's namesake, and had contracted puerperal fever. The Chamber, of course, adjourned, and a deep wave of sympathy swept the country for its doubly afflicted king. But the government had to continue, and four days later Cavour presented the Chamber with a treaty that would send fifteen thousand troops to the Crimea and accept a loan from Great Britain of £2,000,000 at three per cent payable after the war. Brofferio declared the treaty "neither just, rational, useful nor necessary," and republican newspapers came out strongly against it.

Meanwhile the public and parliamentary debates on the religious issue continued, and at Rome, in a secret consistory, Pio Nono pronounced and published an allocution against the proposed law, declaring it "repugnant to national, divine and social law" and "absolutely null and void." At the consistory various documents were circulated setting forth the premises of the Church's position and published by the pope as his justification for opposing the bill. Cavour also circulated them as his reason for supporting the bill. Some of the premises were:

The Church is a superior order to Civil Society.

A State cannot be given or receive a Constitution that has the effect of subjecting the persons and goods of ecclesiastics to all the laws of the State. Equality of Law cannot be applied to ecclesiastical persons and property.

The State cannot permit the public exercise of non-Catholic religions. The erection of a Protestant Church, permitted in Turin and Genoa, was a memorable outrage against the Catholic Church.

A State cannot pass a law to regulate the civil status of its members without first putting itself in accord with the Holy Father.

The liberty of the Press is not reconcilable with the Catholic religion in a Catholic State.

The State has no right to require that the provisions of Rome, outside matters of faith, are subject to royal approval before becoming effective.

Bishops and clergy that refuse obedience to the Civil Law (as that relating to the abolition of the Foro Ecclesiastico) and that urge resistance to such law, do their duty.[69]

With such premises, as the bishops had written to the king, no compromise was possible, and the deputies and senators in Turin and the people throughout the kingdom realized that one side, Church or State, would have to be victorious. It was no longer possible to evade the issue: the collision of principles and power was head-on.

Caught between Church and State, and almost crushed in their collision, was Vittorio Emanuele, kept prisoner between the two by his sense of duty to each. The pope had written him a personal letter of condolence on hearing of the queen's death, and he assured the king that there was nothing personal in the allocution. Vittorio Emanuele replied, in his forthright way, that the allocution had been a mistake: it had only inflamed anticlerical passions in the kingdom. And in a postscript, on a separate slip of paper, he added:

> Your Holiness should know that it is I who prevented the Civil Marriage Bill from reaching a vote in the Senate, that it is I who will now do what is possible to prevent a vote on the Law of the convents. Perhaps within a few days this Ministry of Cavour's will collapse, and I shall nominate one from the right, and make it a condition, *sine qua non,* that it brings me as soon as possible to a complete adjustment with Rome. (Do me the kindness of helping me.) I for my part have always done what I could. (Those words to Piedmont have not helped us in this, I fear lest they have ruined everything for me.) I shall take care that the law does not pass, but help me, as well, Holy Father.

> Please burn this piece of paper.[70]

Meanwhile the debates on the treaty of alliance continued, and except for Cavour, his fellow ministers and one or two other members of the Chamber no one supported it, at least not with any enthusiasm; the republicans attacked it strongly, predicting that it would interfere with overseas trade, delay the economic development of the country, and of course, align Sardinia with Austria, which was unthinkable.

In reply a general, Giacomo Durando, made a speech which had a great effect and was one of the rare occasions in which someone stated Cavour's position almost more clearly than Cavour himself. Durando's closing sentence was: "Remember, that in a war of this magnitude, if, when Europe opens her arms to you, you repulse her; if you remain inactive, if you proclaim a policy of neutrality, in which nobody will believe, you may perhaps live politically, but your sons or their sons will die unhonored at the foot of the Alps and with them will be buried the last hopes of Italy."

But the chief burden of the defense was carried by Cavour who made several long speeches and many short ones in response to questions. He could not say that he hoped by the expedition to win a seat at the peace conference which would follow the war and there to challenge Austria, and he was forced to rather general remarks on the merits of "glory" and "valor" which would show the world that not all Italians were skulking assassins. His main point, in fact, was an attack on Mazzini and his methods which "far from helping Italy, have been one of the greatest calamities that have afflicted this beautiful part of Europe." To repair the damage done by the revolutionaries Sardinia must "prove to Europe that Italy has enough civilized judgment to govern herself in orderly fashion" and "that her military worth is equal to that of her ancestors." As for neutrality, he reminded the Chamber of the fate of Venice at Campoformio after it had remained neutral in a European war.

After six days of debate, on 10 February 1855, the Chamber voted and ratified the treaty, 101 to 60; and later it passed the Senate, 63 to 27. Neither vote carried much enthusiasm, nor was there a great deal of it in the countryside. In a kingdom where only one in three or four could read, a war in the Crimea was remote and incomprehensible; the people agreed to it with misgivings and only because the king and his ministers were so eager for it. Even d'Azeglio, who had supported it in the Senate, considered it "no very gay thing."

Republicans, and particularly those who were not Sardinian subjects, were disheartened or even outraged by the treaty. Manin, in Paris, could see no good in it, and Guerrazzi in Tuscany called it "the last disillusion given to the Italians by the monarchies whether limited or not." Mazzini, as might be expected after Cavour's speech, went further. He published an open letter to Cavour in which he rejoiced that Vittorio Emanuele's government had at last stated publicly "We are with Austria," and he published an address to the Sardinian army urging the men to desert. Others, however, saw the treaty very differently. Both the pope and Ferdinando in Naples were upset at an alliance between France and Sardinia, and a Prussian diplomat remarked "This is a pistol shot in Austria's ear." Meanwhile, within Sardinia, officers and men of the army gathered enthusiasm for the expedition as they made their preparations to embark, although saddened by the death in February of the man who was to have been their commander, the king's brother, Ferdinando.

This third death in his family had all but broken the king. He had outbursts of grief which he almost could not control, and the country began to fear that he might collapse under the pressures of his grief and his office.

The liberals feared that for peace of soul he would give in to the clerics, and the clerics, that for peace of office he would give in to the liberals.

In the Chamber, Cavour spoke at length on the bill twice, acknowledging the service to society which the monastic orders had rendered in the middle ages but pointing out also that those same services, in arts, sciences, industry and agriculture, were performed better now by uncloistered men and women. He cited a study of the Swiss cantons which showed that the prosperity of each was in an inverse ratio to the number of begging friars it supported. And he compared the prosperity and progress of Spain, Naples and the Papal States, each with many monks and nuns, to that of Britain, France or Prussia, each with few.

In the public debate, d'Azeglio answered the pope's allocution and the premises underlying it with a public letter. He described his experiences in trying to negotiate with Rome; he regretted that he had found the Roman Curia, not a gathering of pious, holy men, but a gathering which had become a political sect, men who judged everything by the Church's political interest and who had lost touch with reality. To every offer of compromise and reform he stated that Rome replied: "No, no, and forever no! Let the State dash to its ruin, let it be torn by parties and by tumults, does that matter to us? No!" And he continued with a statement of fact to illustrate his criticism of Papal methods.

> For many centuries the Court of Rome has had the governing of some three million subjects. It exercises over them with unrestricted power the two authorities, spiritual and temporal. Of these subjects, what has it made? It has wrought so that it required four armies to restore the Papal Court to power, and it requires, and always will require, two foreign armies to keep it there.[71]

Finally, on 2 March, the Chamber voted and passed the bill, 116–36, and Cavour promptly brought it up for debate in the Senate. The majority in the Chamber was far larger than the government usually could command, but it did not necessarily insure an easy passage for the bill in the Senate, for there the Church was stronger. The uncertainty and agitation continued. The distressed king sighed to General Durando, who was leaving for the Crimea, "You are fortunate, General, in going to fight the Russians; while I must stay here to fight monks and nuns." His battle was not to be without its own excitement, however, for in the midst of the debate in the Senate, he precipitated a constitutional crisis which caused Cavour's ministry to resign and put angry crowds into the street.

In April, the Sardinian bishops, believing that the vote in the Senate was likely to go against the Church, wrote the king a letter with the following offer:

As the principal object of the proposed law, according to the literal expressions of the Minister of Finance in his report on the Bill, is to find the means of meeting the charge of 928,412 lire provided by the Government for the support of the parochial clergy, the undersigned, duly authorized, declare that, if the law is at once withdrawn, the episcopate consents that the said sum shall be raised out of the ecclesiastical resources on the mainland and guarantees the consent of the Court of Rome for the same.[72]

The offer, which liberal historians have sometimes called "The Bishops' bribe," in fact had been cleared with Rome and carried the pope's blessing. Vittorio Emanuele was overjoyed. He at last had a way to reconcile his conflicting duties, to carry out the wishes of his dead family as well as his duty toward the living. He summoned Cavour and gave him the "very gratifying news." Cavour was anything but gratified, particularly as he had to admit that his insistence on treating the bill as a financial measure had opened the door to the bishops' offer and helped to obscure for the king the real issue of Church and State. He tried to explain this to the king and, failing, agreed to submit the bishops' proposal to the Senate two days hence.

The next day he made a long speech in the Senate which he brought to a close with a note of warning about clerical reaction undermining the principles of liberty and progress. He cited examples from history and pointed out how the Stuarts in England and, more recently, the Bourbons in France had lost their thrones. Everyone understood that he was conveying a warning to the House of Savoy. The following day the bishops presented their proposal to the Senate, and Cavour adjourned the meeting so that the ministry could consider it.

That evening the ministers met and unanimously decided that they could not accept the proposal. To give the king complete freedom in forming a new ministry, they all resigned.

But the king could not persuade anyone to form a ministry. The clerical party on the Extreme Right could not command a majority in the Senate, much less in the Chamber, and no liberal leader would consider withdrawing the bill after it had passed the Chamber by such a large majority. The court was conservative and clerical, and it put all the pressure it could on the king, forcing from him finally a cry of despair. "They tell me that God has punished me: that he has taken my mother, my wife and my brother because I have consented to these laws; they threaten me with still worse; but do they not know that a sovereign who would win happiness hereafter must try to make his people on this earth happy?"

As day after day passed without a new ministry formed, Vittorio Emanuele's subjects showed their displeasure with him. Huge, silent

crowds gathered in the Piazza Castello within yards of the Palazzo Reale.
"One of these days," the king said impatiently to his valet, "I'll make an
end of these demonstrations." To which the valet is supposed to have replied with all the familiarity of a trusted servant, "And if they make an end
of Us?" But the king was not willing yet to yield. Even the ambassador at
Paris was summoned in the hope that he could form a ministry, but he
could not.

The king sent a servant out into the sullen crowd, and the man, on
returning, hesitated to speak out. "But, Sire, I have heard something
shocking." "Never mind, tell it." "They say," ventured the servant, "that
your Majesty is a great scoundrel." Vittorio Emanuele exploded with a
coarse word and brought his fist down onto the table. He ordered troops
out to disperse the crowd, and they succeeded without any incident. But
when battalions of the National Guard were called on to cheer the king,
they remained silent.

For two days d'Azeglio had called at the palazzo to see the king and
both times had been turned away, his request for an interview refused. He
cared enough for the king and country, however, to risk a violent personal
breach with the king by sending him a letter generally and inaccurately
known since as the "Spagna" letter. The inaccuracy has arisen because of
an early misreading of "Spain" for "Sparta" in the opening sentence.

Majesty,
In Sparta it was forbidden to touch the King under pain of death. It
happened to one King that his clothes caught fire: no one would risk
touching him and he burnt to death. But I, though I should risk my
head or altogether lose your favour, would think myself the meanest
of men if at a time like this I did not direct to you a word in writing
since Your Majesty has denied me the chance to speak to him.

Majesty, believe an old and loyal servant who in serving you
thought of nothing save your welfare, reputation, and the good of
your country. I say this to you, with tears in my eyes and kneeling at
your feet: *Do not go further on the road you have taken.* There is still
time. Go back to the former way.—An intrigue of friars has succeeded in one day in destroying all the work of your reign, in upsetting the country, and in weakening the constitution and obscuring the
honour of your reputation. *There is not a moment to lose.* . . .

Piedmont tolerates much, but to be placed once more under the
yoke of the priesthood—by heavens, NO!

Look at the intrigues of the Spanish friars against their queen to
make her sign a shameful concordat, and to what end these have led
her!

Such intrigues ruined James Stuart, Charles X, and many others.
. . . Amedeo II resisted Rome for thirty years and won. Let Your

Majesty stand firm and you will win likewise.

Do not be angry with me. My action is the action of an honest man, a faithful subject and true friend.[73]

The letter had an effect. But kings do not like to be reproved, and although Vittorio Emanuele and d'Azeglio continued to have cordial relations, on the whole d'Azeglio's political influence with the king ended with his letter.

Vittorio Emanuele was a simple, elemental man, not unlike his mountain peasants. His manners, by Paris standards, were rough, his speech abrupt, and his heart unsophisticated. He was proud, pious and, again like his peasants, shrewd and inclined toward common sense. As the crisis, on 2 May, entered its seventh day, he saw that he was courting disaster both for himself and his country to continue it. He sent a message to the clerical party giving them until three in the afternoon to form a ministry. If they did not, "I shall recall the *bestia neria,*" the bugbear, Cavour. Three o'clock came, and the clericals had no ministry. He sent for Cavour.

The next day the Senate resumed its debate, but even now the king's personal tragedy was not over. On 17 May his five-month-old son, Vittorio Emanuele, died. Five days later the Senate passed the bill as amended, fifty-three to forty-two. The chief purpose of the amendment was to spare an order of nuns which neither preached, nursed nor taught but which had been the favorite of the king's mother. Cavour had not been in favor of even this concession and had been persuaded to it by Rattazzi. It is doubtful if Cavour, for all his great qualities, could imagine what the king had suffered over the religious issue.

The Chamber quickly passed the amended bill, ninety-five to twenty-three, and the king signed it. Soon thereafter the pope excommunicated him and his ministers.

The "Law on the Convents" was as important in the history of the Risorgimento as any of the battles. By it Sardinia with its king's approval undertook to become a secular state. The law which accomplished this did not attempt to deny a man the right, if he so wished, to live a life of contemplation and prayer, to wear distinctive clothing or even to associate himself with others in the same pursuit. It did, however, deny him the right to receive special privileges for doing it, unless he was either teaching, nursing or preaching. Except in those socially useful categories, he and his fellows would not have the right to hold land in perpetuity, to hold it free of taxation, to be free of taxation personally or to avoid conscription, without the permission of the State. In this he became like the other citizens of the State, artists, engineers or lawyers who band together in associations.

The step was taken slowly, and each side was given a chance to air its arguments either in Parliament, the papers or private conversation. The bill was first presented in November 1854 and not finally passed until the following May. Unquestionably within that time the majority of the Sardinian people became convinced of its necessity if their kingdom was to become a modern state. Everywhere Italians compared Sardinia's recovery after 1848–49 with the continued depression and military occupation of the Papal States, and the discrepancy each year became greater. Sardinia set the pattern for Italy not only in military leadership but in its political and economic development. With each year and each development it became increasingly the inevitable leader of the movement for Italian unity and independence.

# CHAPTER 35

The Crimean expedition. The battle of Tchernaja. Manin's letter: "If not, no!" Vittorio Emanuele's visit to Paris and London. The Congress of Paris. Cavour's maneuvering. Lord Clarendon's speech. Cavour's success.

THE EXPEDITION to the Crimea was slower in coming to an issue than the Law on the Convents. Throughout the spring of 1855, as the debates on the religious bill came to an end and the bill became law, the people in all parts of the kingdom, constantly stirred by republican orators and newspapers, continued to question the reasons for the expedition and to wonder in what way it could ever justify its cost. Cavour, the king and their few enthusiastic supporters hoped for a battle in which Sardinian troops might play a glorious part; a defeat, or even a series of bureaucratic slights by the British or French might cause the people to demand the return of the expedition.

For weeks there was no news and then only that the British never tired of admiring the organization and neatness of the Sardinian camp which was brightened throughout with little gardens. Then came news of cholera. More than twelve hundred men died of it, including the commanding general's brother, Alessandro La Marmora, who had founded the Bersaglieri. Finally, on 17 August, the Minister of War in Turin received word of a battle at Tchernaja. Fifty thousand Russians had attacked the allied lines, and in the fighting a Sardinian general and thirteen others had been killed and 170 men wounded. But the Russians had been repulsed, and the Sardinian army had fought well. As the news spread, the people's pride in their men absorbed their doubts about the expedition and a sudden enthusiasm for the army, Cavour and the king surged through the kingdom. Novara was no longer the most recent battle in memory or history.

Such a reaction might be expected in Turin, but it was repeated in other cities of northern Italy and even in Paris where there were not only many Italian exiles but also, that summer, many Italians visiting the first Paris Exposition, a project of the industrially minded emperor. Typically, the most popular Italian exhibits were Verdi's *Les Vêpres Siciliennes* at the Opéra and a statue, *Spartacus,* by a Piemontese, Vincenzo Vela. Both glorified efforts by Italians of the past to free themselves of a tyranny.

When news of the battle reached Paris, late in the evening of 16 August, the Italians in the city were swept together in an extraordinary, emotional upheaval. General Pélissier, the French commander had closed his communiqué with the words, "Les Sardes se sont vaillamment battus," and as newspapers distributed handsheets with the entire communiqué, everyone read it. It was summer, the evening was pleasant, and thousands of French and Italians poured out into the streets to celebrate. Householders illuminated their windows, hung out flags of Britain, France and Sardinia and cheered any Italian they saw. Huge crowds milled along the boulevards, cheering *"Vive la France!," "Vive l'Angleterre!,"* and equally loud and often *"Vive les Sardes!,"* or even *"Vive l'Italie!"* For most Italians in the city, whether republican or monarchists, the experience of being both popular and respected was rare and intoxicating. They sought each other out, cheered, wept and felt, and even continued to feel in the days thereafter, that a new era for Italy had dawned.

Three weeks later, on 8 September, Sevastapol capitulated in a battle in which the Sardinian troops had no part. Cavour and the king were disappointed, but the less important Tchernaja continued to serve their purpose, particularly as the Austrians, allied by treaty with both Russia and the Western powers, had not fought in any engagements.

After Tchernaja, a rapid change began in the opinions of many Italian republicans, both in Paris and in northern Italy. They talked less of Napoleon as "the man of 2 December" and more of him as an ally who might be useful in Italy as well as in the Crimea. And they talked more of Cavour as a statesman to be followed and of Sardinia as the core around which Italy should be constructed.

In the last weeks of September, Manin, who was by prestige and activity the leader of the republican exiles in Paris, wrote an open letter to the House of Savoy which he had published in the London *Times,* the Paris *Siècle* and the Turin *Diritto.* In it he stated:

> . . . The Republican Party, so bitterly calumniated, again performs an act of abnegation and sacrifice for the national cause.
>
> Convinced that before all else Italy must be made, that this is the question everywhere to be put first, it says to the House of Savoy: "Make Italy, and I am with you! If not, no!"
>
> It says to the constitutionalists: "Plan to make Italy, not to enlarge Piedmont; be Italians and not municipalists, and I am with you! If not, no!"
>
> . . . I, a republican, plant this unifying standard. If all who want Italy to exist gather around and defend it, then *"Italy will be."* [74]

And he went on with pride to declare that the republican party was the truly national party and also to add, with sorrow, that its day was past. He had come to think that independence and unity were more important in the making of Italy than the form of its government, and that the best hope for independence and unity lay in the constitutional monarchy of Sardinia. Yet his offer of support was conditional, and his "If not, no!" became a slogan used by republicans both as a defense for not changing their allegiance at once and as a challenge to the monarchists to prove their good faith.

At first, however, Manin's letter won him neither popularity nor support. The more fervent disciples of Mazzini considered it a betrayal of true republicanism, and many monarchists saw in it more of a threat than an act of political self-sacrifice. They remembered that Mazzini, in 1831, had made a similar offer of support to Carlo Alberto and in 1848, when Carlo Alberto had tried to free and unite northern Italy, Mazzini's republicans had not been helpful. Probably Vittorio Emanuele reflected the opinion of most of his supporters when he thanked a friend of Manin for the letter and, in the same breath, referred to it as an "ultimatum." Yet in the coming year Manin's letter was to be of the greatest importance, for by it he provided the words and concepts with which moderate republicans and constitutional monarchists could draw together.

Sardinia's participation in the war naturally tended to draw it closer to France and Britain, and Cavour, who was eager to exploit the trend, suggested that Vittorio Emanuele should pay a visit of state to Paris and London to meet Napoleon and Queen Victoria. All three monarchs were delighted with the idea, and the trip was planned for November and December, when winter would have slowed the war to a standstill. As Cavour was apt to do whenever he wanted to present Sardinia as highly respectable and antirevolutionary, he put forward d'Azeglio as the man to accompany the king, while he himself proposed to remain in Turin. But neither Vittorio Emanuele nor d'Azeglio would hear of it and, in the end, the three went together.

They made an exceptional team, and the visits were highly successful. The king was an attractive representative of the oldest dynasty in Europe and honest enough to be interested and enthusiastic about what he saw. His blunt speech and rough manners frequently made his staff nervous and startled a number of ladies, but as it turned out, he offended no one. By way of contrast d'Azeglio, who had combined painting, patriotism and the office of prime minister, could provide as much charm and cultivation as the most sophisticated might require. And finally there was Cavour, with his extraordinary intellect and memory, who was prepared to discuss any European problem in the greatest detail.

Yet, even though Napoleon had asked in a private interview what he could do for Italy, Cavour was disappointed in the visits. In neither Britain nor France had he been able to extract any assurance from the men in power that Sardinia, for its part in the war, would receive any territorial compensation in Italy, or even that Sardinia, in the congress of powers that probably would follow the war, would be allowed to sit at the conference table as an equal. And he desperately wanted something positive to offer the Sardinian people as a reward for their sacrifices.

The two points assumed immediate importance in January 1856 when the tsar accepted Franz Josef's offer to act as a mediator and peace became assured. In France, the news was received with enthusiasm, particularly as Napoleon succeeded in making Paris the seat of the congress, a sign that France rather than Austria had the lead in European affairs. In Britain, though the people were pleased, the government was wary, fearing a betrayal by France at the conference table; and in Sardinia, the news caused consternation: peace had come too soon. Liberals had been hoping that as Russia began to lose the war, Austria would be forced to go to its aid and then would become the enemy. Or they had hoped, at least, for several more battles such as Tchernaja to cement Sardinia's hold on its allies. But at the first mention of a congress, liberals of all the Italian states began to despair. What good had ever come to Italy from a congress? Particularly from one in which Austria had a voice?

Cavour, to everyone's surprise, insisted that he would not represent Sardinia at the congress, and he persuaded the ministry instead to appoint d'Azeglio. The best explanation of this odd maneuver is that Cavour could see no benefit for Sardinia in the congress and rather than risk his own political future by associating it with a failure, he preferred to have d'Azeglio, who had less to lose, risk his. D'Azeglio agreed, but on one condition, that the Sardinian representative should sit as an equal with those of the great powers. Cavour knew that this condition had been explicitly refused: to please Austria, Britain and France had already agreed that Sardinia would be invited to share only in those sittings of the congress which affected her interests. Cavour deliberately misled d'Azeglio on this point, but at the last moment d'Azeglio, growing suspicious, insisted on seeing all the diplomatic notes about the congress. In reading them, he discovered the true situation and, in a violent fit of anger, refused to go. After Cavour's deception had been exposed, he hardly could recommend someone else for the thankless job, so in February he himself left for Paris fully believing that a policy for which he was largely responsible was about to come to a bad end with himself as its chief victim.

Though Cavour was often pessimistic about the distant scene, his nature, in its essence, was optimistic, as his faith in liberty and progress implies. And further, being a practical man, he generally grew more optimistic the more immediate the problem became. By the time he had arrived in Paris, the congress with all its difficulties had excited him to the point where he was viewing it as an opportunity for Sardinia rather than as a certain defeat, and he set about to make the most of it with astonishing energy and skill.

His first task, to win for Sardinia an equal voice at the conference table, was accomplished for him largely by others. Against his position were precedent and all the influence Austria presently could exert. At the Congress of Vienna all the important decisions had been made by a Committee of Five composed exclusively of the great powers, France, Britain, Russia, Austria and Prussia. It was the pattern to which most diplomats felt the Congress of Paris should conform. Further, as Count Buol was quick to point out for Austria, with the rights of a first-class power also went duties, and Sardinia, perhaps, was too small and poor to assume these. If, for example, the congress should decide to have an international patrol of the lower Danube, could Sardinia keep a flotilla in the Black Sea? And anyway, what was Sardinia's interest in the Danube or the Black Sea? And the diplomats who had already arrived in Paris to set up the congress admitted the justice of the points.

The British and French, however, were beginning to have some second thoughts about the position of their ally. The British representative, Lord Clarendon, pointed out that Sardinia had joined the alliance without requiring any pledges of Britain and France, and he, at least, felt it unfair now for them to begin to set conditions against it. The French foreign minister, Count Alexander Walewski, however, was inclined to be pro-Austrian on most points, and he was to preside at the congress. Fortunately for Cavour, when he arrived in Paris, he found that Napoleon had overruled his minister, and Sardinia apparently, for the decision was never formally declared, was to sit as an equal. Clarendon remarked to him, "You have too much tact to take part in matters that do not concern you at all. You will assist at their discussion and think of something else. But," he added quickly, "in truth I cannot imagine what the question would be that did not interest you." So Sardinia was to be present at all the meetings and in principle, at least, to have an equal voice in all discussions. But what its position and voice would be in fact still remained to be seen.

The Congress officially opened on 25 February, 1856, at the Ministry of Foreign Affairs, and the sittings were generally in the afternoons, three or four times a week and usually from one to five o'clock. Walewski presided, and to avoid any jealousy the delegates were seated in alphabetical order of country starting with Buol for Austria on Walewski's right and ending with the Turks on his left. Next to them sat Cavour and the Sardinian ambassador to France, a modest and efficient man, the Marchese Salvatore Villamarina. In all, there were twenty-four sittings from the first on 25 February to the last on 16 April.

Cavour's aim, as he sat at the table, generally silent, was to turn the discussion from the Danube and the Black Sea to Italy. But his chance of doing so was extremely slim. The problems of Italy were outside the purpose and scope of the congress, and the delegates had no instructions to deal with them and no desire to do so. They were far too thorny and too likely to open fresh wounds rather than to heal old ones. How could France question Austria's occupation of the Legations when it occupied Rome? Or how could a congress at which a majority of the delegates were Protestant, Moslem and Russian Orthodox undertake to solve the question of the pope's temporal power? Yet Cavour's aim, and every delegate at the table knew it, was to raise the question of Italy, to impeach Austria before the assembled states of Eurpoe and to suggest that as long as Austria was allowed to tyrannize Italy so long would there be an Italian problem to disturb the peace of Europe.

Even before the first sitting Cavour had extracted a promise from Clarendon to speak on the Italian question—if it was raised. Clarendon and his staff were inclined to be sympathetic with Cavour's aim. They had all been inflamed by Gladstone's *Letters* on the Bourbon government at Naples; they tended to be strongly anti-papal, particularly since Pio Nono had abandoned his liberalism and had reintroduced a Catholic hierarchy into England; and they approved of Sardinia's parliamentary government as much as they disapproved of Franz Josef's absolutism, particularly as the latter resulted in arbitrary, illegal actions such as the sequestration decree. But Clarendon's first concern was Britain's interests in the Black Sea, and then, perhaps, its relations with Austria, its traditional ally on the continent or its relations with France, its traditional enemy. Italy was an afterthought. Yet Clarendon would speak on it, if someone else raised it.

The obvious person to do this was Walewski, but here Cavour ran into difficulty. Walewski, who was the illegitimate son of the first Napoleon by a Polish countess, had very different feelings about Italy from those of his first cousin, the emperor. Walewski had not fought in a Carbonaro revolution nor experienced Papal government and an Austrian occupation, and he was not about to say a word against either the Papacy or Austria.

Fortunately for Cavour, most of the delegates disliked Walewski personally, considered him incompetent to run the congress and attempted, sooner or later, to go over him directly to the emperor. This pleased Napoleon, for he became, as he probably had always intended to be, the real moderator of the congress. For Cavour he established a direct line of communication through his physician, Henri Conneau, and even after the congress ended the two men continued to use Dr. Conneau as a go-between whenever they wished to bypass Walewski.

But even though Napoleon was sympathetic to Italy and its problems, Cavour could not persuade him to order Walewski to place it on the agenda, and largely for a reason beyond Cavour's power to modify. The empress was about to give birth, and the Imperial couple wanted the pope to be godfather to their child. Napoleon, while he was sending to Rome to ask Pio Nono for this favor, would not allow the Papal government to be attacked in Paris. It was just the mixture of politics, religion and paternal pride to exasperate an unsentimental man like Cavour, and he despaired in a report to the ministry in Turin, "The mania for conciliating the Pope and having him for a godfather has spoiled everything."

Even so he tried to keep Italy in Napoleon's mind. He saw him periodically and each time suggested another solution to some Italian problem: what to do about the Austrian occupation of Bologna, or of Ferrara, or about the Habsburg Duke of Modena or the Regent Duchess of Parma. Most of the suggestions were impractical, yet they served a purpose. Even as the emperor waited in an antechamber for his child to be born, he was heard muttering, "Certainly something must be done for Italy." And Cavour kept adding new facts and reasons why the Italian problems must be discussed. He asked one of the pope's former liberal ministers, Marco Minghetti, to bring to Paris a memorial signed by distinguished men on conditions in the Romagna, and after Minghetti arrived with it, he had him draw up a history of Papal reforms and failures in the Legations and also a proposal for secularizing their government. He submitted both papers to Napoleon and also to Clarendon whom also he wished to keep excited about conditions in Italy. To this end he wrote a series of letters to the Sardinian minister in London which were really aimed for the ear of Lord Palmerston, and he constantly urged the minister to "échauffez Palmerston," to "Heat up Palmerston," the Prime Minister, just as he was attempting to heat up Clarendon, the Foreign Secretary.

No opportunity was dismissed as too small. In Turin, Cavour never bothered with society or tried to make himself agreeable, even to the king. In Paris, as he wrote the minister in London, he even had made up to Lady Holland's dog with such success that he got it to put its large paws on his new coat! And when the Marchioness of Ely arrived to represent Queen Victoria at the birth of the Imperial child, Cavour was one of the first to call on her. And in making himself agreeable he made himself well liked, which Buol, on the other hand, did not. He had arrived in Paris prepared to dispense order and charm like Metternich in 1815, but the role eluded him.

Count Orlov, the Russian delegate, observed one day to Cavour in a voice that was meant to be heard, "Count Buol talks exactly as if Austria had taken Sevastopol," and another time he observed to Walewski, knowing that his remark would be repeated: "We've been tearing away at each other like the honest bulldogs we are. Now we have to work together to make sure that this mongrel Austria gains nothing from our quarrel." One of the facts that emerged as the meetings continued was a new cordial relation between France and Russia, former enemies, and it made both Britain and Austria nervous, tending to bring them together, a corollary which displeased Cavour.

On 16 March the Empress Eugénie gave birth to a boy, the Prince Imperial, and for almost a week the sittings were suspended while Napoleon gave himself up to an orgy of parental pride. The birth was announced by a salute of a hundred and one guns, and the baptism was splendid and solemn with the pope present by proxy as the boy's godfather. The emperor, however, had not forgotten Italy. A few days later he promised Cavour that the Italian question would be discussed, but he insisted on a condition: the peace treaty must be signed first. Meanwhile, Clarendon, Cavour and the emperor continued to consider every possible way in which some Italian state might be added to Sardinia, or the Legations freed of the Austrian occupation or the pope or Ferdinando compelled to improve their governments.

On 30 March 1856 the treaty ending the Crimean War was signed, and then finally, eight days later, Walewski raised the question of Italy. He began by remarking that, although the purpose of the congress had been achieved, his government thought the powers should discuss informally some of the problems which might disturb the peace they had just concluded. He spoke first of the situation in Greece. Then he referred to the Austrian and French occupations of parts of the Papal States, which he hoped soon would be ended, and wondered if perhaps the congress should advise certain of the Italian princes to be less repressive in their governments. And finally he discussed the press laws of Belgium, which allowed libels to be published on neighboring governments and rulers. He closed with some pleasant generalities about the accomplishments of the congress.

Clarendon spoke next. "He charged," wrote one of the Sardinian aides present, "like Lucan at Balaclava." He had listened to Cavour for almost ten weeks; he had checked his facts with his own consular agents in Turin and Rome, both of whom he had summoned to Paris; he was absolutely sure of the truth of what he was going to say and of the conclusions he was going to draw from it. He made the briefest mention of Greece and Belgium and then started on Italy. He began with the Romagna, the Legations. The Austrian occupation, he said, was becoming permanent. After eight years it showed no sign of ceasing. He recognized that Austrian troops could not be withdrawn at once because without them the Papal government would collapse. That government, he stated flatly, was the worst in the world and must reform itself from top to bottom. He described its worst features in detail, the arbitrary exercise of power, the military brutality, which was as much Austrian as Papal, and the corrupt administration which degraded the people subject to it. Passing on to The Two Sicilies he said much the same of Ferdinando's government. "There can be no peace without justice, and the King of Naples must be forced to amnesty his political prisoners." He believed it the duty of the congress, he concluded, to compel Ferdinando to heed its warnings. Then Clarendon sat, and Buol rose for Austria.

He was both astonished and distressed that at a congress called to make peace between the allies and Russia a subject outside that purpose should have been introduced. His emperor, Franz Josef, had not instructed him to discuss the subject, and he would not. Buol was plainly very angry, but he made his stand on a point which he, and everyone else, knew was logically correct. He did not need to do more, and the delegates all recognized that the congress would not act on Clarendon's speech. Yet Walewski, as procedure required, went round the table asking a delegate of each country to speak to the question. Baron Manteuffel for Prussia made a few generalities and complained of the abnormal situation in one of the Swiss Cantons, and Count Orlov for Russia refused to speak for lack of instructions. Next was Cavour for Sardinia.

He rose to speak for Italy. For the first time in a congress of European powers a man, whom others recognized as an Italian, was to speak on behalf of an Italy which, although still undefined, was already plainly more than the "geographical expression" which Metternich had called it only nine years earlier.

Cavour evidently decided that he could not cap Clarendon's speech in vigor and indignation, for he spoke quietly and unemotionally. He acknowledged the correctness of Buol's position but then went on to confirm all of Clarendon's charges. He described Austria through its military occupation and political influence as "actual mistress of the larger part of Italy" and a constant threat to Sardinia. "For this reason I demand that the opinion of the delegates of France and of Great Britain, as well as my formal protest, be inserted in the protocol."

To have a summary of the remarks on Italy published in the official report of the congress was about as much, Cavour knew, as he could hope to achieve. And to achieve even this required another week of wrangling, with Buol objecting to every sentence and almost every word proposed. The report, when it appeared, read weakly and suggested neither the importance nor the passion of what had been said.

Had Cavour achieved anything at the Congress of Paris? Opinions differed, and at the start most men, particularly those in Italy, were inclined to think he had not. In spite of Clarendon's speech and Napoleon's support, the congress took no action or even discussed any. Italy was left as it was, and Sardinia received no visible benefits for its sacrifices in the Crimea. When the protocol of the congress was published, it reported only four of Cavour's speeches, and his quoted remarks were tame. Republican newspapers and orators were sarcastic and bitter. Others struggled to sound pleased when they were obviously disappointed.

Cavour, perhaps fortunately, did not return to Turin at once. Napoleon had said, "Go to London, come to a thorough understanding with Palmerston, and see me on your return." And, in London, Cavour had immediately discovered that although many shared Clarendon's views on Italy, none shared his passion. Britain, government and people, was not prepared to do anything practical to support Sardinia. The best hope for it and for Italy, Cavour again believed, lay in Napoleon's ambition.

In the two weeks his trip had required, however, opinions about the congress and Cavour's role in it had already begun to change. Some of those who had been in Paris had returned to Turin and were reporting that the published accounts gave no picture of what had actually occurred and many more had written to friends describing how Cavour was "the *lion* of the occasion" and had won not only a great personal victory but a great victory for Italy. So that when he arrived in the city without, as he said, "even the tiniest duchy in his pocket," he was welcomed, although not effusively.

The next day, when he entered the Chamber of Deputies, he was cheered, and a few days later as he made his report to the deputies on the congress, he was applauded. But his speech was dull, for he could not put into it his private conversations with Napoleon, and he was left with rather vague and repetitious statements about what had occurred with an occasional hint that the only solution to Italian problems was war against Austria with the aid of France.

> With regard to the Italian question there are not, it is true, any grand and positive results. Nevertheless we have gained, in my opinion, two things: first, the unnatural and unhappy condition of Italy has been denounced to Europe not, as formerly, by demagogues [the Secretary here recorded laughter in the Chamber], not by excited revolutionaries or passionate journalists, and not by men of faction, but by representatives of the foremost powers of Europe, by statesmen who stand at the head of their governments, by illustrious men who are accustomed to consult the voice of reason rather than to follow the impulses of the heart.

This is the first fact and one I consider to be of the greatest use.

The second is that these same powers have declared it to be necessary, not alone in the interests of Italy but rather in the interests of Europe, to apply to the ills of Italy some remedy. I cannot believe that the views put forward, the considered judgments of nations such as France and Italy will remain sterile for long.[75]

He was attacked both from the Right and the Left. Solaro della Margarita, for the conservative, clerical party expressed horror that the representative of Catholic Sardinia should have joined the British delegate, an heretical Protestant, in attacking the Holy Father's government. And for the republicans Brofferio delivered an oratorical outburst. He treated with scorn the claim that at the congress for the first time Italy had received a hearing, as if Dante, Machiavelli or Alfieri had never spoken for Italy. "No, no!" he cried, "Italian Liberty will never arise out of diplomatic meetings! No, the independence of Italy will never be the gift either of Prussia or of Russia or of France or of England; Italy will shake off the slumber of the tomb when the Italians awake her!" At this indirect reference to Foscolo's *Dei Sepolcri* many in the galleries burst into applause and by implication repudiated an alliance with a Napoleon.

But as the weeks passed, the sense that, in fact, Cavour had achieved a great deal began to gain rapidly. Liberals in all the Italian states sent him testimonials of their gratitude. Tuscans presented him with a bust of himself by Vela on which was inscribed a line from Dante, x *Inferno* 92, "Colui che la difese a viso aperto," or, roughly, "The one man who defended her openly." And Roman and Neapolitan liberals sent him medals struck in his honor. In Vienna, an aged Metternich, whose Italian system Cavour was undermining, observed sadly, "There is now in Europe only one statesman and, unhappily, he is against us: this man is Cavour." The expedition to Crimea and the Congress of Paris made Cavour not only an Italian but a European figure. And that in itself, Italians began to realize, was a great gain for Italy.

# CHAPTER 36

Significance of Cavour's success. Manin's letters. Franz Josef starts
a policy of conciliation. His tour of Lombardia and the Veneto.
Mazzini's expedition to Sapri. Pisacane. La Farina, Manin, Pallavicino and the *Società Nazionale Italiana*.

SOME EFFECTS of the Congress of Paris began to appear almost at once
and confirmed for reflective Italians the belief that at it Cavour, in fact, had
achieved something of value. Manin, who was living in Paris and who knew
many of the French officials and journalists, in the month after the Congress closed wrote a series of letters on it which he had published in *Il
Diritto,* a Turin newspaper, and which from there were picked up and
widely reprinted. In them he concluded that the House of Savoy's claim to
the support of the Italian national party, by which he meant the republicans who wanted to unify Italy, had increased greatly because it had
spoken out for Italy and embarrassed Austria and thereby increased its
own prestige and moral influence. He predicted that Vittorio Emanuele II
and his government would go on from this first step and to support them
in their next was the best "present practical application" of the principle
of independence and unification for Italy.

Eight months earlier Manin, in a self-appointed role, had spoken for
the republican party and said to the House of Savoy: "Make Italy, and I
am with you! If not, no!" The present series of letters showed that in his
opinion, at least, Vittorio Emanuele was continuing to meet the conditions
of that offer.

But as with the previous letter these later ones at first did not win
Manin either popularity or support. He was promptly accused by the more
ardent republicans of abandoning the idea of a popular revolution and of
allowing initiative only to those in power, monarchists. Manin, whose belief in republicanism was profound, hotly denied the charge but not in a
way to convince those who questioned him. He insisted on the need for
agitation but then defined it not as insurrection but as the preparation for
insurrection. It was to provide "a healthy exercise, that reveals, educates,

457

reinvigorates the intellectual and moral forces of the future combatants."
He warned against untimely risings that accomplished nothing, and in line
with his lifelong belief in the necessity of French aid for any national revolt
to succeed, he insisted that a clash with the French troops at Rome must
be prevented "at any cost."

To men who hoped to conduct a social as well as a political revolution
and by it to regenerate Italians as well as to make Italy, Manin sounded
old and defeated. Where was the man who had led the popular revolution
in Venice, proclaimed the Republic of San Marco, and for six months
sustained it against the Austrians, "at any cost"? Now he was recommending caution and mental exercise.

The monarchists, on their side, continued to consider him an uncon-
verted republican and to distrust him. During the congress, Cavour had
met several times with Manin and then had written of him to the ministry
in Turin: "He is still somewhat Utopian. He has not abandoned the idea
of a war frankly popular; he believes in the efficacy of the press in stormy
times; he desires the unity of Italy and other trifles; but nevertheless, if the
practical issue should arise, all this might be made use of." Cavour, like
most monarchists, did not believe that "the people" could free or unite
Italy, and he hoped to achieve a political revolution with a minimum of
social change. But, unlike most monarchists, he was quite ready to make
use of the people or social change, if "the practical issue" arose. But
meanwhile neither he nor any other important monarchist either publicly
or privately welcomed Manin's support.

In the midst of the discussion of his letters Manin excited still another
debate by a letter which appeared first in the London *Times* and in which
he attacked the use of political assassination as a weapon to free Italy.
This time he aroused even moderate republicans against him. He had
hoped by the letter to persuade public opinion in Britain, and wherever
else the letter might be reprinted, that all Italian revolutionaries were not
assassins, such as the man who had stabbed the Duke of Parma; and he
had hoped to isolate from the leadership of the republican party Mazzini,
who had the reputation, however undeserved, of advocating assassination.
As such the letter was a public attack on Mazzini, particularly as it appeared first in the leading newspaper of London, where Mazzini was in
exile and well known.

Many Italians, however, took it as a slur on Italians in general. Political assassination, the "theory of the dagger," was the bitterest charge that
foreigners and monarchists of all kinds laid against the revolutionaries, and
to have it repeated by one revolutionary against another seemed to suggest
that Italians had in fact used it as a weapon, that the national cause itself

was not holy and pure but a back-alley fight, bloody in principle as well as practice.

Most Italians, however, felt they could distinguish between assassination and revolution, and when Mazzini answered with a letter reminding Manin that his position, both in Venice and Paris, was the result of revolution and accusing him of unclear thinking, most men felt that Mazzini had the better of the argument and also had exhibited the greater dignity. Manin's friends in Paris told him bluntly to stop writing letters to the press, and in a private letter to a friend in Turin he sadly recalled a Venetian proverb: "If everyone says you are drunk, go to bed." And he left Mazzini's letter unanswered.

These years of exile were hard for Manin. They undoubtedly are hard for any exile, but Manin, perhaps, had an unusual number of misfortunes to bear. He was a family man, and his wife had died in 1849, on the journey from Venice to Paris; later, in 1854, his daughter, too, had died. He refused to accept aid from others on the ground, correctly taken as he showed, that he could support himself, his son and daughter by giving lessons in Italian; but of his skill as a lawyer he could make no use. Further, he was by nature melancholic and partly, it seems, as a result of continual ill health. "The act of living," he said once, "in a healthy body, ought to be in itself a pleasure. In me, since infancy, it has always been an effort and a penance. I have always felt tired." He longed continually for rest and sometimes even for death. Yet for much of his life he had sustained long periods of action but always, apparently, by an exhausting effort of will. After his daughter's death he almost gave up. "I cannot do wrong," he said, in the sense of repudiating life, "because I have a natural horror of it; because I am born so. But where is the merit? Where is the law? What is the object of this world?" And then, having turned once again to face the world and having tried to do something constructive in it, he was told by his friends that he had not only disgraced himself but damaged the cause for which he had gone into exile.

Yet, however great Manin's personal discouragement in these weeks, in the months following he began to sense that his letters, perhaps with the exception of the one attacking Mazzini, had been constructive, that many men's opinions were gradually shifting in the direction to which he had pointed.

The change had begun even before his letters, and an example of it was the shift in feeling toward Mazzini which the Milanesi had exhibited during the weeks before and after his uprising in February 1853. Even before it had proved a failure, they had tried to stop it; and after it many Milanesi republicans had begun to think of uniting Italy under the House of Savoy. Inevitably, after the defeats of 1848–49, patriots of all political persuasions had begun to consider new ways and combinations to achieve their goals, and Manin, by writing directly on these shifting beliefs and attitudes, had accelerated the changes. A symptom of his influence, a private one, occurred during the summer in a letter Garibaldi wrote to the Marchese Giorgio Pallavicino, who served as Manin's lieutenant in Turin: "I must tell you in two words therefore, that I am with you, with Manin, and with all the good Italians whom you mention."

Garibaldi, who had returned from his years in America and recently bought a farm on Caprera, a tiny island off the northeast coast of Sardinia, was eager to fight again and, like many others, was looking for new leadership and allies. From Mazzini he had learned to love a united and republican Italy which did not yet exist, and to believe that the people would support a revolution to achieve it. But their failure to support him on his retreat from Rome had shaken his faith in them, and he still blamed Mazzini directly for the defeat at Rome. In view of these experiences, he now was ready, like Manin to sacrifice the form of Italy's government to achieve the country's independence and unity. So he wrote his letter, asking Pallavicino to "admit me to your ranks and tell me when we ought to do something."

He wrote as if an organized, national party existed, which it did not, but Manin and Pallavicino, by September 1856, were beginning to have some success in trying to create one. Pallavicino was a Lombard exile, rich and famous for having been imprisoned in Spielberg for his part in Confalonieri's conspiracy of 1821. He was presently a deputy in the Sardinian Chamber where he was relatively ineffectual, but he had a real flair for using newspapers to create public opinion, and by September he and Manin had access to about thirty papers in Italy, and as many in other countries of Europe, which would print their letters and articles. At the same time they were themselves reprinting the articles, often several at a time, in pamphlets on which they put a heading in capital letters *Partito Nazionale Italiano,* or *National Italian Party.* Below this they placed two subheadings, *Indipendenza* to the left and *Unificazione* to the right. They distributed the pamphlets in every Italian state, for there was to be no compromise on the unification of Italy, and Pallavicino paid for everything. Garibaldi was not alone in thinking that there was more of an organization than just two men, and in a sense he was right. A sympathetic audience existed which might soon be turned into a national party.

Manin's efforts in the summer after the congress to lead a majority of republicans into a new course of action was aided in August by Cavour who, acting quite independently, asked Garibaldi to come to Turin for an interview. Like Manin, Cavour was anxious to isolate Mazzini, and he knew by report that Garibaldi, who expressed his opinions freely, had developed his anger at Mazzini in Rome into a substantial grudge and, further, that Garibaldi was reported to admire Vittorio Emanuele as a robust, fighting king. No details of the interview have come down and probably not much in detail was stated. No doubt Cavour flattered Garibaldi but not altogether insincerely. He admired him as a man and as a power, and if "the practical issue" of a war against Austria should arise, which Cavour undoubtedly assured Garibaldi he was working to bring about, then he wanted the republican general, the greatest popular leader in Italy, to be actively on his side. In return he could offer Garibaldi's volunteers, in whatever form they might arise, the assistance of the Sardinian army and navy. And Garibaldi returned to Caprera more than ever inclined to act not with Mazzini and the extreme republicans, but with Manin or Cavour. Significantly, in October, when there was a small, Mazzinian uprising in Sicily which Ferdinando's army easily put down, Brofferio promptly argued that the Sardinian government should have supported it. Garibaldi, on the other hand, made no public statements.

In this same summer after the Congress the Austrians, too, began to change their policy in Lombardia and the Veneto, for just as much as Manin or any Italian, Buol and Franz Josef had been impressed by what Cavour had done to them in Paris. Soon there were rumors in Milan and Venice that the Austrian emperor planned a tour of his chief Italian cities and, in the course of it, might end the military government and inaugurate a new regime. The first positive notice of it was a circular addressed to the aristocrats in the various cities, asking them to declare whether they desired to take part in the festivities of the Imperial tour, so that they might receive invitations.

The circular was a stone thrown into a hornet's nest: no one talked of anything else for several weeks, but as almost no one replied to it, the Austrians were forced to send out another and to follow it up with personal visits. Most of the nobility, however, refused to accept any invitations, and of the exceptions most were men who held public office and felt their presence was required at some function. The Milanesi went even further than the social boycott and collected money publicly to erect a statue in Turin in which a Piemontese soldier would defend the Italian flag.

The Contessa Maffei's salon was as usual at the center of resistance, and its members through their social and business contacts attempted to make sure, as the emperor's visit drew closer, that no one wavered in his resolution either through fear or hope of favor. Several weeks before Franz Josef was due to arrive, the police banished from the city a number of the better known patriots, among them Emilio Dandolo, the historian of the Lombardi Bersaglieri at Rome. They also summoned Carlo Tenca, the editor of *Crepuscolo,* and ordered him to publish an account of the emperor's visit. Tenca replied that, as it was the journal's policy not to discuss the internal affairs of Austria, he saw no reason to mention it. When he was summoned a second time, he again refused.

Franz Josef started his tour with Venice. He was still young, only twenty-six, and, in his uniform, expectionally handsome. At his side was his even younger wife, Elizabeth of Bavaria, who was one of the most beautiful women of Europe. In ordinary times they might have proved irresistible, but in the winter of 1856–57, in their progress through northern Italy, they could not melt the Italians, not even when the emperor announced the repeal of the sequestration decree or an amnesty for political prisoners which included those convicted by the trials at Mantua. In every city the Imperial couple visited, they were met with signs of hate, and to continue the progress to the end required courage. In Venice, at the receptions in the Procuriate Nuove, the Austrian staff was not large enough to make the rooms look filled, and nothing could stop the sound of hissing outside as an occasional Venetian passed through the crowd to reach the palazzo. And whenever the Imperial couple went out, though the piazza might be filled, they were watched by the crowd in silence; no one ever cheered.

At Padua, on the other hand, the people did. The mayor was in the first carriage and, as he was popular, he was greeted with shouts and cries of good will. Standing up he mouthed, "No, no," and pointing back to the third carriage, where the emperor was, he asked them to cheer for that. With instant wit the crowd complied by cheering the third carriage, *"Viva la terza carrozza."*

Milan was the worst, if only because Buol and Franz Josef, perhaps foolishly, hoped for the most from it. The Austrian Habsburgs had been connected with the city longer than with any other in Italy, a hundred years longer than with Venice. Families in Vienna and Milan had intermarried, and both Maria Theresa and Joseph II had been popular with many in the city and accepted by all as the rightful Dukes of Milan. There were men and women of all classes who could remember those times, and Franz Josef hoped with his visit to stir those memories. It seemed not impossible; in 1835 the city had turned itself out for a week of festivities to celebrate the coronation in the Duomo of Franz Josef's predecessor, Ferdinand I.

But in spite of all the efforts of the police the emperor's entrance into the city was chilling. The tacit agreement among the Milanesi was that there should be no decorations along the streets through which the emperor would pass and that the blinds should be closed. The police succeeded in forcing some householders to open their blinds and to hang out rugs, but most of the way from the Porta Orientale to the Piazza del Duomo, Franz Josef and Elizabeth drove through a shuttered city with only a few people, almost entirely of the lowest class, on the street. When some boys, excited by the horses and carriages, began to cheer, they were hissed into silence by their elders. The nobility and business leaders set the tone and form of resistance, but their lead was followed generally by all classes in the city. Opposition to the Austrians was one point on which Mazzini and the monarchists agreed, and at this time most of his followers were among the lower classes.

During that first day news arrived that the City Council of Turin had accepted as a gift from the Milanesi the statue to honor the Sardinian army, and photographs of the statue soon appeared all over Milan, in the suites and even on the desks of Austrian officials. A few days later a reception was held at which the leading Milanesi were to be presented to the emperor. The great majority of the nobility, however, did not attend, and at a gala evening for the emperor at La Scala, many, having agreed to come, sent their servants to fill their boxes. By the time Franz Josef returned to Vienna, he had been snubbed from Venice to Milan and told, as effectively as a repressed people could speak out, that it was not reverence for the Imperial family that kept them within the empire but force, only force.

He had also, quite by accident, become embroiled in a diplomatic struggle with Sardinia. The police of Milan, in preparing for his visit, had arrested and expelled from the city as undesirable a foreigner who had turned out to be a member of the Sardinian Senate. Cavour and Vittorio Emanuele were undoubtedly looking for just such an incident. Besides their political opposition to Austria, the king had a personal grudge against the emperor because Franz Josef had omitted to send him, as was proper between royalty, any expressions of sympathy on the deaths in his family. So he had taken the expulsion of the Senator as a personal insult, had refused to nominate a delegate to represent him in Milan, and, as much as the Milanesi, had ignored the emperor's visit.

It was the moment for Buol to talk softly. With the lifting of the sequestration decree, the freeing of political prisoners and the promise of a more liberal government in Austria's Italian provinces he had pleased Britain and most Frenchmen even if not, perhaps, Napoleon. And if Buol could have brought himself to apologize for the mistake of the police, which was so obviously a mistake, he might have won back for Austria much of the sympathy which Cavour had won for Sardinia at the Congress of Paris. But an apology was beyond Buol, and instead he sent an angry note to Cavour in which he cited as deliberately provocative acts by Sardinia the anti-Austrian articles in the newspapers, the acceptance of the statue from the Milanesi, the refortification of Alessandria, which was within Sardinia's borders, and the acceptance of contributions from other than Sardinians to buy cannons for the fort. Buol's points, perhaps, had merit, but the bullying style in which he couched and delivered them had not. Cavour replied correctly but without offering any satisfaction, and Buol thereupon recalled his chargé d'affaires from Turin. So that in spite of all his concessions on behalf of Austria, particularly lifting the troublesome sequestration decree, Buol ended rather than restored diplomatic relations between the countries. In London, Lord Clarendon observed "Buol has committed *une grosse bêtise,* and Cavour must be very grateful to him for having so thoroughly played into his hands."

In other ways, too, Buol and Franz Josef tended to dilute the effects of their new policy of conciliation. The emperor announced that the military rule of the two provinces was ended and that he would send his brother, Archduke Maximilian, to Milan as his viceroy. But soon thereafter he also announced that he had given the Palazzo Reale, in the heart of Milan, to Radetzky, as a place for his retirement. The general was now ninety-one and would not live forever, yet many wondered why Franz Josef, if he wanted truly to make a fresh start, should send Radetzky again to Milan. Even pettier and yet at the same time more important was the blow aimed at the *Crepuscolo.* Tenca, the editor, had stuck to his policy and not printed any news of the emperor's journey; now his permission to print an article even on foreign political news was withdrawn, and the only political journal allowed in the provinces was the *Gazzetta Ufficiale.* The Milanesi observed the change of policy with interest but remained skeptical. It seemed likely that the emperor did not contemplate giving any real freedom or self-government to his subjects.

Patriots, monarchist or republican, and in whatever state in Italy wanted the new Austrian policy in Italy to fail. It was as true of patriots in Florence or Bologna as in Milan or Venice, and in their efforts to keep a united front against the Austrians, they more and more looked to Cavour in Turin for leadership and support. The only group which would not, although as anxious as any to subvert Austria's efforts to please, was the Extreme Left, the followers of Mazzini.

Unlike the majority of Italians, they had been alarmed rather than pleased by what Cavour had achieved at the Congress of Paris. They disliked him for making a constitutional monarchy successful at home and abroad, disapproved of his efforts to create an alliance with France, and suspected that he wanted only to expand Sardinia into a Kingdom of Alta Italia, to digest another leaf of the artichoke rather than to merge all the states of Italy, including Sardinia, into one. This last was a fear which all republicans, even the most moderate, shared. It kept many from joining Manin and Pallavicino and, conversely, kept many in sympathy, if not in action, with Mazzini. Even Pallavicino often had doubts. "More than Mazzini," he wrote to Manin, "I fear Camillo Cavour." And Manin had replied with an answer profoundly wise in its analysis of Cavour's character. "I think Cavour too intelligent and too ambitious to deny himself to the Italian undertaking when public opinion imperiously asks it." But very few republicans could find continuous comfort in such tenuous reasoning.

The Mazzinians most emphatically could not. They continued to believe in a popular revolution sweeping the length of Italy, and they continued to plan for it. They were aware that Manin and Pallavicino were shaking the loyalty of many of their adherents, and they were eager to win back the doubters and at the same time, by forestalling Cavour, to insure a republican Italy. They had, also, another reason for action which partly determined the course of their planning. At the time Italians of all parties were immensely excited over rumors that Napoleon secretly was preparing to support Murat's son in an attempt to drive the Bourbons from Naples. By the hindsight of history it is clear that Napoleon never did more than consider the idea as a remote possibility, but just because the idea seemed so historic, a Murat and French influence again in Naples, many Italians were inclined to believe it. And many republicans were inclined, further, to believe that Cavour perhaps had made a deal with Napoleon whereby for help in expanding Sardinia in northern Italy, Sardinia would give France and Murat a free hand in southern Italy and both, as a sop to Catholic feeling, would guarantee the pope's inviolability in a reduced Papal State in the center. The neatness of the theory convinced many of its truth, and to forestall the Muratists the Mazzinians planned one of their risings for Naples.

Some of their followers there were enthusiastic; others not. There had been the small Mazzinian uprising in Sicily in November 1856, and then the following month, quite independent of Mazzini, a soldier had tried to assassinate King Ferdinando at a review by lunging at him with a bayonet. But the king had only been wounded slightly. Some Mazzinians interpreted the failure of these efforts as evidence of disorganized, random plotting by individuals; but others insisted that the country was seething with revolution and ready to rise on signal in concerted action. Mazzini believed the enthusiasts, if only because he was himself eager to act. But Garibaldi, when approached, would have no part of an expedition to Naples. He would not send men to their death to "make the rabble laugh."

In his place, the expedition was led by a Neapolitan duke, Carlo Pisacane, who with twenty-two men on 25 June 1857, boarded a steamer at Genoa as passengers for Tunis. Once out of sight of land, they seized the ship and forced the captain to head it for Naples. Twelve of the men were Sardinian citizens and had left behind them in Genoa a signed statement of their motives for the expedition:

> Our conscience tells us: so long as twenty millions of Italians are slaves we have no right to be free unless we devote our lives to the

emancipation of all. Our small fatherland of Genoa and Piedmont is not sufficient! . . . Therefore we depart. . . . We are compelled by a selfish and cowardly government to fly through the darkness like smugglers. . . . The province in which we hope to plant the Italian banner is inhabited by good but ignorant people who will probably be made to believe that we are bandits or pirates come for plunder. Perhaps we shall be received like the Bandiera brothers. So be it! Poor people, we have only our lives to give to Italy and we offer them with all our hearts.[76]

The organization of the expedition, however, did not match its fervor. A boat with arms and more men, which was to rendezvous with the steamer, lost its bearings and returned to Genoa. Mazzini, who was in the city in hiding, passed two distracted days uncertain whether Pisacane was proceeding and not knowing whether to confirm or countermand his instructions to his agents in Naples. Then the steamship line announced that, for reasons unknown, the *Cagliari* had not put into port in Sardinia, and Mazzini surmised correctly that the expedition was still on. Fortunately for Pisacane and his men, the steamer had been carrying a small cargo of arms.

They landed first at Ponza, an island prison about thirty-nine miles from Gaeta and, after freeing more than a thousand prisoners, mostly common criminals, added about 325 of them to their band. While they were refueling the ship, however, they foolishly allowed a priest to escape from the island in a small boat, and he carried news of the expedition to Ferdinando, who was at Gaeta. At once army posts up and down the coast were alerted to watch for it, even before Mazzini got word of it to his agents.

From Ponza the men steamed past Naples and landed in the evening of 28 June at Sapri, a small village of about two thousand persons on the Gulf of Policastro. The village was a short way inland, sheltered by two hills, and the beach was deserted except for two telegraph employees whom Pisacane arrested. At Sapri itself most of the villagers had fled. The next morning at the next village the reception was much the same. Pisacane and his men had been told that the countryside was seething with patriots, but with the exception of an occasional peasant who cheered, *"Viva Murat!"* and one old man who actually joined them, no one cheered for Italy, or hung out a flag, or opened a house to them. Among the men who had joined the expedition at Ponza, desertions became frequent.

Pisacane himself had not expected anything better. Before starting he had been to Naples to check the arrangements and had returned to Genoa convinced that an expedition had almost no chance of success. Yet even so he had wanted to continue it, and he had led his small band in signing a statement: "If we fall, do not weep for us. We say with the Bandiera brothers: Our death will be more useful to the Italian cause than a sterile life prolonged." So the reception at Sapri and the other villages did not deter them, and they started north for Naples.

They soon met a detachment of the army and were defeated in a battle outside the village of Padula. Some died in the battle, but many more were killed in the village itself when, in trying to escape, they ran down a blind alley where the local police and villagers butchered them. Pisacane and perhaps sixty others got away, into the hills. But the next morning, having been led or perhaps deliberately misled by a peasant to the village of Sanza, they were attacked by its people as "Anointers," persons who supposedly passed through the countryside putting poison in the wells. The village priests, with icons of St. Anthony and St. Sabino, led out their people who were armed, except for an occasional gun, with scythes and staves and pitchforks. Pisacane gave orders not to fire and started to reason with the peasants. He was almost immediately shot, and rather than wait to be cut to pieces, he used his pistol on himself. Several others followed his example but nearly thirty were hacked and stabbed to death before a detachment of the army arrived and stopped the slaughter. The survivors, about half the group, were bandaged and forwarded to Salerno for trial where they were condemned to prison.

The expedition in its immediate purpose was a failure, yet in the next few years, as Pisacane may have foreseen, its tragedy, and even nobility, provided the emotional basis on which some new ideas entered some Italian minds. Pisacane was a political philosopher, and he left behind him, as his political testament, a four-volume work, *Historical, Political and Military Essays on Italy,* which began to be published the following year. These revealed him to be, perhaps, the first Italian socialist. He conceived of the drive for independence and unity in economic rather than political terms. He predicted that the commercial and industrial revolution, "this vaunted progress," merely would make the rich even richer and the peasants poorer. Only by easing the economic discontent of the peasants, he argued, could Italy become a nation. This emphasis on the peasants, on the differences between classes, and on the distribution of wealth were almost all new ideas to the men of the Risorgimento. And although such ideas would continue for many years to have little influence, nevertheless, because of the drama of Pisacane's expedition to Sapri, they continued to resound in the minds of some.

The Neapolitan venture, however, was only a part of Mazzini's plan for sparking a national revolution. He also had groups organized to capture the ports of Livorno and Genoa, both of which then would serve as staging areas to support the capture of Naples. The attempt at Livorno was over in a few hours. At four points in the city Mazzini's men rose, killed a soldier or two and then were dispersed or arrested by army squads which began to patrol the city. At Genoa, a man partially betrayed the plans for the revolution to city officials and at the same time warned Mazzini that his plans were known. So Mazzini, when he saw the guards being doubled around the Palazzo Ducale, canceled the rising. But unfortunately the countermanding orders failed to reach one group in time, and by suborning some soldiers it captured and held for a few hours a small fort.

In the next few weeks, as the full extent of Mazzini's projected revolution became known, almost all Italians repudiated his actions. Even the Genovesi were for the most part shocked and even angered that in the political circumstances of the time, in June 1857, more than a year after the Congress of Paris, Mazzini still could be thinking in terms of a rising against Vittorio Emanuele and Cavour. But though the Genovesi repudiated Mazzini's actions, they would not repudiate Mazzini, the man. He had been in and out of Genoa since early May, and now he stayed on in the city until 8 August. He hid, mostly in the palazzo of the Marchese Ernesto Pareto, but he often went out in disguises, and his whereabouts must have been known to many. Still, though the police arrested more than a hundred persons, no one betrayed him.

The fact infuriated Cavour. The projected rising was embarrassment enough. He had been assuring France and Britain that his form of liberalism made revolutionary activity in Sardinia unnecessary or even impossible and that it would be found only where tyrannous governments made men desperate. And to be unable to arrest Mazzini, week after week, when all of Europe knew he was in Genoa, was to appear incompetent. But even though he borrowed Napoleon's best Paris detective, he was never able to announce Mazzini's arrest. The best he could do was to argue that the uprising's complete failure in Genoa was evidence that the revolutionaries had no following in the liberal Kingdom of Sardinia. But it was an argument that held just as true for Ferdinando's illiberal Kingdom of Naples.

In the autumn, however, the voters in Sardinia repudiated Mazzini at the polls. In a general election the Extreme Left was all but wiped out, and the reactionaries, particularly the clerical party, gained, even in Genoa. The center groups with Cavour at their head kept their sizable lead only in Piedmont, and though they still had a working majority in both the Chamber and the Senate, it was reduced.

The republicans further repudiated Mazzini and his policies by turning more to Manin and Pallavicino and their program of independence and unity for Italy under the House of Savoy. And these two men, for their part, moved further toward turning their *Partito Nazionale Italiano,* which was still only pamphlets with a steady readership, into a true political party. The final steps, publishing a credo and asking for signatures and dues, caused Manin doubts. He feared that the "unifying standard" he had planted, around which men of all parties might gather openly, would become just another secret society. He still thought in terms of propaganda and education, of binding together through reason all those who loved Italy. Pallavicino, on the other hand, was more eager to bind together only those who agreed on certain principles and, through an organization, to make of their agreement a weapon for exercising political power.

Manin, however, was not wholly against Pallavicino's idea, only hesitant. And he was persuaded, in the end, not only by Pallavicino but perhaps even more by the energy and activity of another man who had joined their group, Giuseppe La Farina, a Sicilian who edited a newspaper in Turin. La Farina was most anxious to organize, and circumstances and his own abilities worked in his favor.

Manin was in Paris, sick and, as it turned out dying, and Pallavicino had a year of ill health in Turin; so that throughout 1857 La Farina, more and more, made the decisions. Perhaps because he was a Sicilian he had been particularly upset by the possibility of Napoleon putting Murat in Naples, and he had published numerous articles and pamphlets, including those by Manin and Pallavicino, against it. He had also asked for an interview with Cavour and had been granted it, at 6 A.M. At that hour in the Palazzo Cavour the two men had discussed Sardinia's position with regard to Murat and then, more generally, its role in Italy. Cavour, who wanted even more than Manin to lead republicans to support the monarchy, had listened to La Farina's plans for a national party and had urged him to "Go ahead and prosper," and then had added, "but if you fail, or if I am questioned on your account in the Chamber or by the needs of diplomacy, I shall be forced to deny you like Peter." And thereafter La Farina often saw Cavour, always before dawn and always entering by a secret staircase which took him directly up to Cavour's study.

La Farina's contact with Cavour did not make him Cavour's man in all things, but it may have influenced his concept of what Manin's national party should be. With Manin the fact that republican support for the government was conditional, the "If not, no!" was always stated. With La Farina that fact was more muted. He conceived of the party as more of a government party than a republican party; it was to be a way of organizing people in support of the government. "The revolution," he once wrote to Pallavicino, "is not in those people who read, who write and who argue politics" but in the broader class that as yet lacked the ability "to think for itself." He wanted to organize that broader class and then to tell it what to think. "The prestige of authority, of organization, of force, is worth much more for them than a good reason." To Pallavicino, caught between the two views, Manin had the greater faith in the people, but La Farina understood them better.

Manin gradually gave in to the pressure from Turin, and the three men composed a credo which they would ask their readers to sign. It stated that the *Partito Nazionale Italiano* would subordinate every issue of political form and local interest to the "great principle" of independence and unity; that it would support the House of Savoy "so long as" that House was for Italy "in all the extension of the reasonable and the possible"; that it would support any ministry in Sardinia that favored Italy; and that it believed popular support and action would be necessary for Italy to be unified.

At first, Pallavicino and La Farina were unable to persuade anyone to sign. Manin himself was still hesitant, and other republican leaders, particularly those in Genoa, were loath to bind themselves, however loosely, to support the monarchy. Then, from Caprera, Garibaldi sent back his copy of the credo, signed. He did not know he was only the third member to join the party or that his act saved and insured its growth. Probably, with his exuberant nature, he had not even considered all the political niceties which deterred his friends in Genoa.

Thereafter Pallavicino and La Farina sent out a new batch of letters, adding a preface to the credo which bound members to pay fifty centesimi a month as dues to cover printing costs. And to avoid any confusion with Mazzini's followers who called themselves "the national party," La Farina changed the name to *Società Nazionale Italiana* or The Italian National Society.

Manin died on 22 September 1857, but before then he had signed a membership blank in the new society and had given it his blessing. It was, he had recognized, La Farina's organization rather than his own, but for Venice and for Italy he had already sacrificed too much to balk from vanity at this last compromise. He died, a friend reported, confident that Italy would be made free and united. Doubtless he was sorry not to live to see it, but doubtless, too, his weary body greeted death as a friend.

The *Società,* like Manin's letters from which it grew, like Franz Josef's new policy for his Italian provinces and Mazzini's attempts to start a national revolution, was another symptom of Cavour's success both in Sardinia and abroad, at the Congress of Paris. In spite of Mazzini's efforts and the equivocal results in the recent general election, Cavour was stronger in Sardinia and in the rest of Italy than ever before. As he continued the liberal and national trend in Sardinia's government, many who had doubted were converted, and the base of his support noticeably broadened. So much anyone could see; a few others knew also that he was in contact with Garibaldi, La Farina and the civic leaders of almost all the Italian cities north of Rome. Abroad he had the sympathy of Britain, which had been reinvigorated by Buol's diplomatic blundering, and, even more important, he had the sympathy of Napoleon, which he hoped somehow to extend into active support with arms. Diplomatic relations with Austria were now completely severed, and the two countries, facing each other across the narrow Ticino river, were in a strange state of neither peace nor war. By the close of 1857 most Italians in the Po valley were certain that war, not peace, would be the resolution. The only uncertainties, which men debated, were when? and with or without France?

# CHAPTER 37

Orsini attempts to assassinate Napoleon III. His trial. His letters. Cavour and Vittorio Emanuele resist pressure from France. Mazzini's attack on Cavour. The meeting at Plombières. Clotilde. Napoleon's greeting to the Austrian Ambassador. The King's speech: *il grido di dolore*. Efforts for peace. Verdi's name and Dandolo's funeral. Napoleon hesitates. Cavour's collapse and victory. Austria declares war.

IN DECEMBER 1857 Napoleon, through his embassy in Turin, began secretly to distribute throughout Lombardia and the Veneto a "Medal of St. Helena," which he awarded all soldiers, whether French or not, who had fought under Napoleon I; to officers he gave the medal of the Legion of Honor. As he hoped, the medals stirred memories of battles fought against the Austrians. Old men reminisced of Bonaparte, often with tears in their eyes, and young and old who heard them as often transferred the emotion to Napoleon III. In their fancy they saw the new Napoleon coming over the Alps into Italy and driving the Austrians out. Cavour's hope for a popular alliance was repeated in many a patriotic heart, and a secret excitement swept the Po valley. Sardinia was eager for war, and the emperor seemed willing.

Then on the evening of 14 January 1858, as Napoleon and the empress were on their way to a performance of Rossini's *William Tell* at the Opéra in Paris, an assassin tried to blow up their carriage. Three bombs exploded, more than 150 persons among the cavalry guard and the spectators along the way were killed or wounded, and yet, in the center of the explosion, Napoleon and Eugénie escaped unharmed. A fourth bomb which had landed directly beneath their carriage had not exploded. They succeeded in appearing calm and went on to the Opéra, taking their seats in the Imperial box just in time to hear the famous conspirators' chorus in which the Swiss patriots bind themselves with an oath to free the cantons of the Habsburgs.

In Turin, when Cavour first heard that assassins had attempted to kill the emperor, he exclaimed, "I hope to God they are not Italians!" The good relations between Sardinia and the emperor had survived the shock of Mazzini's attempted revolutions, but they might not survive another shock of that kind. Napoleon, as a former conspirator who had founded his power on a bloody *coup d'état,* was determined to have no conspiracies in France or even in neighboring states, unless, of course, he was one of the conspirators. But the Paris police almost at once disappointed Cavour. In less than twenty-four hours they had arrested the bomb-throwers, and their names were Orsini, Pieri, Gomez and di Rudio.

The leader and only one of importance was Felice Orsini, a Romagnuolo, born at Medola in the Papal States. He was thirty-nine and from his youth he had been filled with a determination to help Italy. His father, a conte, had died in 1831, fighting in the ranks which the emperor, as a young Carbonaro leader, had commanded. He himself had been a follower of Mazzini and had served the Roman Republic with distinction at Ancona. After the defeat of the republic he had again turned to conspiracy. He had been arrested by the Austrians, sent to the prisons in Mantua to be tried and had made a remarkable escape. Thereafter he had lived in England where he had supported himself by lecturing on the evils of the Papal government and by recounting his Italian experiences. But in England he had broken with Mazzini, whom he had found dictatorial and obsessed with the idea of exposing ten or twenty men to be shot in hopeless revolutions, and had decided, as he was to state later at his trial in Paris, "that only one man was able to relieve my country from occupation by the foreigner, and that this man was Napoleon III who is omnipotent in Europe. But all his past convinced me that he would not do what he alone could do. I confess freely, therefore, that I considered him an obstacle. And then I said to myself that we must get rid of him."

Before the trial began, as Cavour had feared, Napoleon lashed out at home and abroad at the persons and states he felt were in any way assisting or harboring conspirators. He put France under martial law, dividing the country into five departments with a marshal of the army at the head of each, and he replaced the Minister of the Interior with a general. Then despite some protests in the almost powerless legislature he pushed through a new law against suspected persons and two thousand men were arrested. Eventually, in spite of Orsini's confession, four hundred of these were deported, and the new Minister of the Interior, General Espinasse, observed: "The essential is not to allow those who are deported to be seen again." Not only Napoleon but also the men who had mounted to power with him were determined that no one should unseat them.

Abroad, Napoleon attempted the same military bullying, principally against Belgium, Britain and Sardinia, three states with relatively free press laws and in which French and Italian exiles had collected. In Turin, the French ambassador, on instructions from Walewski in Paris, called on Cavour and demanded that the Mazzinian journal in Genoa, *L'Italia del Popolo,* be suppressed, that Mazzini and all his works be disapproved, that various persons be expelled from the country, and that the law making it a crime to write critically of foreign heads of state be amended and strengthened.

Lord Clarendon, for Britain, could listen to such demands, murmur a few generalities and then neglect to reply. Cavour could not. Sardinia was not only less powerful; it also had an immediate need for a French alliance. Yet his reply to Walewski was a firm refusal:

> Carlo Alberto died at Oporto rather than bend his head before Austria. The young King will go and die in America, or fall, not once but a hundred times, at the foot of our Alps, before soiling the untarnished honor of his noble race; and we, his ministers will follow him. We are enemies of revolution, we hold assassination and those who preach it in as great horror as you; but we are Liberals, because we believe that liberty alone will save Italy, and Liberals we shall remain; if we must lose your precious friendship and fall into isolation, at least we will fall flag in hand and with our honor intact.[77]

Nevertheless, he started doing everything that Napoleon asked. He harried *L'Italia del Popolo* with fines and confiscations, forced some refugees to leave the country, and when a jury refused to convict an editor for publishing an article excusing regicide, he proposed a new law with severer penalties and a revised jury system.

While Cavour was doing this, Vittorio Emanuele sent an aide to Paris to congratulate the emperor on his escape. During the interview Napoleon spoke out harshly. He protested his friendship for Sardinia but added, "If nothing is done there, if you cannot find means to muzzle the press, to protect morality and religion, if you have no police, well, my friendship will cool, and I shall be forced to close an alliance with Austria." And, the aide reported to the king, the emperor ended with the words "read the papers and see the addresses that I have received from the army. I have had to suppress the strongest of them. I have only to raise a finger, and my army, and the whole of France will march enchanted to whatever spot I point out as the home of the assassins."

The menacing tone ruffled the king's pride and, with Cavour's approval, he wrote back a letter for the aide to read to the emperor. In it he covered Napoleon's points about the press, the refugees and the police in much the same fashion as Cavour had already done, but his final remarks were entirely his own:

*If the words which you send me are the Emperor's own words,* tell
him, in the terms you think best, that this is not the way to treat a
faithful ally; that I have never suffered insults from anyone; that I
pursue the path of honor always without stain, and that as to this
honor I hold myself responsible only to God and to my people; that
for 850 years my family has held its head high, and that nobody
shall compel me to lower it; and that in spite of all this, I desire nothing else than to be his friend.[78]

As the aide finished the letter, Napoleon exclaimed, "That is what it
means to have courage! Your King is a brave man—I like his reply."

During these weeks, hindsight can see, Napoleon was making up his
mind to attack Austria in Italy. He had many reasons for the decision: a
small but influential group of Frenchmen sincerely believed that only by
making peace possible in Italy was peace possible in Europe; others thought
the dynasty needed some more glamour and, perhaps, adjustments along
the country's frontiers to solidify its hold on the people; and the army was
eager to fight, to win medals and glory. A successful war in the Po valley,
with Sardinia as an ally, might win for Napoleon and France a new frontier
on the Alps, by Sardinia's cession of its French-speaking province of Savoy,
and the destruction of the treaties of Vienna by the substitution of French
for Austrian influence on the Italian peninsula.

Some historians, such as Arthur J. Whyte, think Vittorio Emanuele's
letter was "the deciding factor" in Napoleon's decision. Whyte cites as
evidence of it Napoleon's words to the king's aide, Enrico della Rocca, as
he was about to return to Turin: "Assure your King that in case of war
with Austria I will come and fight beside my faithful ally, and tell Cavour
to put himself in direct communication with me, we shall certainly understand one another."

But it seems likely that Napoleon reached his decision earlier. For by
12 February, when he heard della Rocca read the king's letter, he already
had determined to use Orsini's trial, which began on 25 February, as a
forum to arouse public feeling for a war in Italy against Austria. And in
preparation for the trial he already had sent his prefect of police to interview Orsini and to persuade him that Napoleon was, in fact, the best
friend Italy had. The outcome of this interview was that Orsini completely
reversed his thinking and stated so in a letter from Mazas Prison dated 11
February, or the day before the king's letter reached Napoleon.

In his letter Orsini wrote: "Remember that the Italians, among whom
was my father, shed their blood with joy for Napoleon the Great, wherever
he chose to lead them; remember that they were faithful to him until his
downfall; remember that the tranquillity of Europe and that of your
Majesty will be a chimera until Italy shall be independent. . . . Free my

country, and the benedictions of twenty-five millions of citizens will follow you through posterity." This trumpet call to action Napoleon allowed to be read at the trial and to be published—perhaps because he had in the meantime received Vittorio Emanuele's letter or perhaps because of a plan previously decided upon. Historians have always found Napoleon III an enigma. Even his first cousin, Princess Mathilde, an intelligent woman who knew him well, once remarked, "How I wish I could break his head to find out what goes on inside!"

By the end of the trial Orsini was a hero and quite obviously with the emperor's approval. Fashionable ladies had sighed over his black hair, his gestures, his passion and his noble air of resignation. His letter had been read and caused a sensation; and his lawyer, again obviously with the emperor's approval, had intimated that Orsini, the Italian patriot, had merely wanted to advance an Italian policy which Napoleon I and Napoleon III both favored. The fact that he had attempted to assassinate the emperor was treated, until the last moment, as almost irrelevant. Then the jury returned a verdict of guilty, and at La Roquette Prison on 13 March he was guillotined.

Even then the propaganda did not cease. Just before his execution Orsini had written another letter condemning political assassination and at the same time full of patriotic phrases pointing to Austria as the troublemaker in Italy. Napoleon wanted this published in the Sardinian papers, and Cavour, not divining the extent to which Napoleon was prepared to offend Austria, insisted on confirmation by the emperor. Back came the letter with a heading approved, and perhaps even written, by Napoleon: "The Italian patriots may rest assured that it is not by crimes condemned by all civilized societies that they will be enabled to obtain their just desires; to conspire against the life of the only foreign sovereign who nourishes feelings of sympathy for their misfortunes, and who alone can yet do something for the welfare of unhappy Italy, is to plot against their own country." And on 31 March, 1858, the letter appeared in the *Gazzetta Piemontese*. Vittorio Emanuele's comment was: "The Orsini letter is a good thing. We used to say dead men tell no tales; but everything changes. What times we live in!"

The following month Cavour brought before the Chamber the bill to increase punishments for those conspiring to kill a foreign head of state and to reform the jury system in order to improve the possibility of convictions under the statute. The debate transcended the particular issue; every speaker, at some point, left it to discuss the Kingdom's relations with France and Austria. The sum of their remarks was a vote of confidence in Cavour. In January under pressure from the Right, which had accused Rattazzi of negligence or worse in not preventing Mazzini's activities in

Genoa, Cavour had accepted Rattazzi's resignation from the ministry; the *Connubio* was formally at an end. But the debates on the new press law showed that Cavour's personal ascendancy was now enough to provide a safe majority in the Chamber. Many of the speakers were confused about the trend of events and asked in various ways to be enlightened. But this was just what Cavour could not do. He could not say directly what sort of an alliance he hoped to negotiate with Napoleon, what price he would pay for it or when a war with Austria might make it operative. He could not, partly because he didn't yet know himself and partly because, as he remarked, "While diplomacy can prepare events, it cannot complete them. To do that one does not require the Minister of Foreign Affairs—but one of his colleagues. The honorable member will excuse me if I go no further." And with this the Chamber was satisfied because it had confidence in the prime minister.

The extreme republicans, of course, were irate at anything that cut down the freedom of the press, and from London Mazzini attacked Cavour in a letter, of pamphlet length, which he published in *L'Italia del Popolo* at Genoa. In it, all his anger and frustration came out hissing hot and wasted itself in a personal attack. "Though earlier I did not like you, now I abhor you. Till now you were an enemy merely; now you are basely, indecently an enemy." He concluded:

> Between us and you, Sir, runs an abyss. Our two programs from their very roots divide. Why will you not, as we do, admit it? Why must you persist in deceiving Italy and Europe as to your intent?
>
> We represent Italy: you, the aged, covetous, faint-hearted ambition of the House of Savoy.
>
> We desire above all National Unity: you seek only to increase the royal domain in the north of Italy. You are against Unity, because you have given up hope of ruling or dominating it.
>
> We believe in the initiative of the people of Italy: you fear it, and study how to hold it off. You work for your desired expansion relying on diplomacy and the consent of European governments. Each *rising* for you, therefore, is a risk, and you deny the Nation the opportunity to rise and make itself.
>
> We wish the country, when once it is free, to choose the form of government to rule over it: you deny sovereignty to the people and insist they agree to a monarchy before aiding their undertakings.
>
> We seek our allies among peoples who have with us a common interest, common griefs and struggles: you seek allies among our oppressors, among the powers deliberately and necessarily opposed to our Unity. . . .
>
> We adore one faith: THE NATIONAL FAITH; one principle: THE POPULAR REPUBLICAN PRINCIPLE;—one policy: the fer-

vent and continuous expression with words and deeds of Italian *rights:* you bow your knee to force, to the treaties of 1815, to despotism, to anything whatever so long as it is smiled on by the *big bullies.* You have no trace of morality or of faith. . . .[79]

Some of what he charged perhaps was true; certainly it was all deeply felt. But after the revolt in Milan, the trials at Mantua, the expedition to Sapri, and the debacles at Livorno and Genoa, it was all too late. Manin and Garibaldi had insisted that there was another way with a better chance of success and had led most of his followers into the *Società Nazionale Italiana.* Mazzini now was isolated, he who, in the opinion of most men, had worked hardest and longest for Italy, and for the least reward. Now that Italy, perhaps, would be made free and united, he would be left out of it. He was a man of ideas, and although he often had been disappointed by men he seldom, if ever, hated them. But now he hated Cavour and for the ideas Cavour represented.

Cavour, for the same reason, hated Mazzini. Years before Cavour had written to a friend "in politics there is nothing so absurd as rancour," and he had given evidence of his belief in the principle by using men of all parties on missions for Sardinia. But Mazzini, whom he had never met, he hated personally; he would admit no good in him at all, and he pursued him with rancour. On various pretexts he succeeded in closing down *L'Italia del Popolo,* he harried more of Mazzini's followers out of Genoa, and he had Mazzini, in absentia, condemned to death. Unquestionably he did these things in part because he wanted to strike at Mazzini the man as well as, in order to please Napoleon, to curb Mazzini the conspirator.

His actions, nevertheless, did please Napoleon, and in May the emperor proposed that the king's eldest daughter, Clotilde, be married to Prince Jérôme Napoléon, who was the emperor's first cousin and known as Prince Napoléon or, informally, as "Plon-Plon." The emperor had suggested the marriage the previous autumn and had been put off politely on the ground that the princess could only marry an heir to a throne. But now the emperor coupled the proposal with two others which the king and Cavour could not ignore: that France and Sardinia have an alliance for war against Austria, and that they plan the formation of a Kingdom of Upper Italy, presumably to incorporate all of Carlo Alberto's short-lived Kingdom of Alta Italia.

Through Napoleon's physician, Dr. Conneau, Cavour expressed his government's interest in the proposals, and a secret meeting was planned between Cavour and the emperor. Cavour would go in July to Geneva for a short vacation and from there would join the emperor at some spot in France, and on 20 July, traveling as Giuseppe Benso, he met the emperor at a small spa in the Vosges called Plombières.

He passed the day with Napoleon, mostly closeted in the emperor's suite at the hotel, but in the late afternoon the two men went for a drive in the emperor's phaeton. Napoleon handled the pair of horses, Cavour sat beside him, and following at a distance, well out of hearing, came a single groom. For another three hours, as they drove through the valleys and forests of the Vosges, the men continued their talk. At the day's end Cavour wrote a short account of it to the king and two days later, a longer one. These are the only direct sources for what was said.

Napoleon opened the discussion by stating that he had decided to support Sardinia in a war against Austria, provided that a nonrevolutionary cause could be found, one that would win the sympathy of French public opinion and of the other powers. The cause had to be nonrevolutionary, without a tinge of such Mazzinian ideas as popular revolt, social change or, even, of Italian unity. Austria was to be driven from the peninsula, but thereafter the peninsula was to be divided into four kingdoms: Upper Italy, under Vittorio Emanuele, was to include all the Po valley and the Legations down to Ancona; Central Italy, under the Duchess of Parma, was to include Tuscany and most of the mountainous backbone of the Papal States: the pope would have a reduced Papal State and the Bourbons, The Two Sicilies. The four kingdoms would form a confederation under the pope as president and have a constitution similar to the German Confederation.

A federation of Italian states was a concept which most Italians, Cavour included, had discarded after 1848–49 as unworkable. How could liberal Sardinia, which was conducting a revolution in its civil life against the Church, yoke itself into a federation of which the Papal State was an equal member and the pope the permanent president? But for the moment Cavour did not argue. Republican historians have cited his acceptance of such a crippled program for Italy as evidence of the narrow limits of his own planning for it; others have argued that, as a representative of the weaker state which could do nothing without the alliance, he hardly could begin the discussions with an attack on the fundamentals of Napoleon's program. Certainly, as he listened, Cavour must have thought of the many opportunities for change before the program could be realized and counted on taking advantage of them. His genius was for using opportunities.

The incident to start the war was a problem. Napoleon insisted that it be one to satisfy public opinion in France, and Austria's actions and policy in Italy, though often illegal under the treaties of 1815, were not enough. After Cavour had offered a number of suggestions, they agreed that the inhabitants of Massa and Carrara, two unruly towns in the Duchy of Modena that were close to the border of Genoa, should appeal to Vittorio Emanuele to annex their towns to Sardinia. The king would address a threatening note to the Duke of Modena who, relying on Austria, probably would reply in kind. Then Vittorio Emanuele would occupy Modena, and the war would begin. Given the heavy-handed diplomacy that Buol and Franz Josef practiced, such a result seemed probable.

As the price for French aid in the war, two hundred thousand men with guns, Napoleon demanded the provinces of Savoy and Nice. Both had been part of France from 1795 to 1814, and Savoy, at least, was French in language, culture and political desires. Nice was not; its language and feelings, although frenchified, were primarily Ligurian, and Cavour protested that its transfer to France would violate the principle of nationality for which the war was to be fought. Napoleon, Cavour reported, stroked his moustache several times, and the question of Nice was left open. The transfer of Savoy, however, with much moaning by Cavour about its being the cradle of the king's family, was conceded.

It was an extraordinary concession, even granting that Vittorio Emanuele was ambitious and desired to be king of a larger Italian state than Sardinia. His ability to let Savoy go, albeit for a price, showed imagination and also, because the Savoyards were bitterly opposed to his Italian policy, common sense. Franz Josef could neither work out nor even imagine any way in which he might benefit by letting go of his Italian provinces.

During the afternoon drive Napoleon raised the question of a marriage between the king's daughter, Clotilde, and Prince Napoléon. On this subject Cavour had exact instructions from the king: unless Napoleon insisted on the marriage as a condition to the alliance, Cavour was not to agree to it. Beside any question of family pride, Vittorio Emanuele was anxious for his daughter. The Principessa Clotilde was only fifteen and Prince Napoléon was thirty-six, older, even, than her father. He was also a republican, an atheist, quarrelsome and with a reputation for free living, not an ideal match for a young and sheltered Catholic princess. Napoleon stressed his cousin's abilities, which were real, and his loyalty to his friends, for which he had suffered a little, but at the end of the drive the question was left open. Cavour, however, in his letters to the king, stressed the importance of the marriage to the rest of the plan. The emperor was eager for it and, if balked in it, might withdraw from the military side of the alliance.

Rumors of the meeting began to circulate at once, for members of Napoleon's staff knew Cavour by sight, and even as the two men had been talking, Napoleon had received a wire from Walewski in Paris which warned that Cavour was somewhere in the neighborhood. In the days after the meeting, therefore, neither man attempted to deny the fact of it, and newspapers, at least outside of France, speculated on what might be the results of it. But the articles never passed beyond speculation, for the principals and the few others who knew something of what had been agreed never broke their silence.

By the first of August Cavour was back in Turin and starting to prepare the kingdom for a war which in his own mind he planned to begin in the spring of 1859, or in about nine months. He set the Minister of War, La Marmora, to work increasing the army up to one hundred thousand men and collecting in arsenals the necessary guns and ammunition. He met in the early mornings with La Farina to plan for the National Society to cause the petitions from Massa and Carrara for annexation to Sardinia to be the inevitable result of unrest in the towns. He also planned with La Farina to enroll through the National Society as many young men as possible from the other states of Italy to fight as volunteers for the national cause. And in October he summoned Garibaldi from Caprera and offered him command of the volunteers, who would form a part of the regular army, and Garibaldi accepted, with enthusiasm.

As far as Cavour was able, he kept his various lieutenants apart and ignorant of what the others were doing. Aside from the general need for secrecy he had certain specific problems. The regular army had no use for volunteers or for Garibaldi. It was strongly monarchist and therefore disapproved of republicans, and as a professional army it scorned volunteers. Cavour, however, considered it impolitic if not impossible to conduct a successful war in the Po valley for the nationalist cause without the republicans. He might be able to isolate Mazzini, but he could not ignore Garibaldi, La Farina and the influence of Manin. Therefore, hoping to harness their power to his end, he planned to work with them and to present La Marmora with a volunteer corps in being.

Another reason for secrecy, however, was that he was violating his unwritten agreement with Napoleon to have a nonrevolutionary war. The volunteers and Garibaldi would bring with them all those tinges of Mazzini that Napoleon was anxious to avoid. They would want to unify all of Italy, to make one state of it instead of Napoleon's four; they would insist on Rome as the new state's capital, and they would treat Pio Nono insensitively, to say the least. As journalists were beginning to tell all the world, on Caprera Garibaldi was calling his two ugliest donkeys "Pio Nono" and "Antonelli."

Nevertheless Cavour went ahead with the volunteers, and probably, given his pragmatic nature, not out of any desire or intent to create a unified Kingdom of Italy with its capital at Rome. He had told La Farina at their first meeting that while he believed this was the ideal solution to the problems of Italy, he also believed that at the present time it could not be realized. More likely, Cavour had decided that he had a greater chance of success in persuading Napoleon, one man, why he had to include the republicans in his preparations than in persuading the republicans that the good of Italy required that he exclude them. Brofferio was still a persuasive speaker in the Chamber, and Garibaldi, the most popular national figure.

With regard to Clotilde, however, he worked hard for Napoleon. When her father had first put the proposal before her, she had burst into tears and refused. Later, as she had come to understand what was at stake, she had consented but on condition that she be allowed to meet Plon-Plon before the contract was signed in order to be sure he was not actually repulsive to her. From the start Cavour's attitude on the marriage was unyielding. He wrote the king a long and merciless summary of the unhappy marriages forced on the princesses of Savoy in previous generations, and he pointed out that in the other ruling houses of Europe no more suitable matches were possible. He observed to La Marmora that he hoped no considerations of "rancid aristocracy" would prevent the marriage.

Cavour's attitude toward the fate of Clotilde has struck many as unnaturally cold-blooded, a repetition of his attitude a year earlier when the king apparently, for the facts are obscure, proposed that he marry his mistress, the daughter of a corporal. Cavour's response had been to present the king with evidence, gathered by detectives, that the lady, on occasion, preferred others to the king. In both instances, Clotilde and her father, Cavour felt that only a marriage of political advantage could be considered. If soldiers were to sacrifice themselves for Italy on the battlefield, then Vittorio Emanuele or Clotilde could not do less with their lives. Cavour's attitude, as his biographer W. R. Thayer points out, "must be judged historically." At the time in Latin Europe "no bourgeois above the grade of grocer expected his daughter to choose her husband"; much less did royalty marry for love, king or princess.

The preparations for war could not be concealed forever, and by December the diplomats of every state knew that France and Sardinia were arming, as was also Austria. By then, too, Cavour was making little effort to pretend to the contrary and even told an English diplomat Odo Russell, who was on his way to Rome, that there would be war in the spring. Russell remarked that Austria had only to adopt a policy of delay in order to exhaust Sardinia's resources; the small kingdom could not support a huge, inactive army for long. And if Sardinia started the war, Austria would have the sympathy and support of Europe. To which Cavour replied, "But I shall force her to declare war on us." And when pressed for the date, he said "about the first fortnight in May." Russell, disbelieving, noted the conversation and date in his diary.

As the war became more certain, Napoleon's role became more difficult. Cavour had a united, eager kingdom behind him, Napoleon had not. Against him and led by the empress was the clerical party of France,

Catholic conservatives who feared that any change in Italy could only be to the detriment of the pope's temporal power and to that they were wholly opposed. Many of his most intimate supporters, men who had organized his *coup d'état* warned that the dynasty would not survive a failure, and war was always risky. Business men, large and small were enjoying the country's prosperity and disinclined to risk their share of it on a quixotic adventure in Italy. Others questioned the benefit to France in a new larger and stronger kingdom on its southern border. Was there not strength for France in Italy's weakness? Many thought so.

Cavour had hoped to pay some of the expenses of the war by a loan raised in Paris and guaranteed by the French government. But the House of Rothschild refused him, and the emperor was having so much difficulty with his own loans that he could be of no help. In the end Cavour successfully floated the loan entirely within the Kingdom of Sardinia.

Each week a new difficulty arose. The tsar, who at one moment had talked of keeping Prussia neutral and even of putting troops in the field against Austria, decided that he could not do so without revisions in the treaties which had ended the Crimean War. And in order to accomplish these he suggested putting off the war in Italy for a year or two. Cavour had little difficulty convincing Napoleon that such a delay was impossible.

Then at a reception for the Diplomatic Corps in the Tuileries Palace on New Year's Day, 1859, Napoleon said to the Austrian ambassador, "I regret that the relations between us are so bad; nevertheless tell your Sovereign that my personal feelings for him have not changed." The words, which were probably innocently intended, were widely interpreted as the prelude to a declaration of war. The Paris stock market plunged. The new telegraph systems carried the words over Europe within twenty-four hours. Napoleon went out of his way the next day to chat pleasantly with the Austrian ambassador, but so keyed up had men become with foreboding or hope that ordinary words and actions no longer carried ordinary meanings. The impression of imminent war remained.

A week later at Turin, on 10 January, it was greatly increased by the king's speech from the throne as he opened a new session of the Parliament. Cavour had drafted the speech and, on a sudden thought, had sent it to Napoleon for approval. Napoleon, protesting that the final paragraph was too strong, had rewritten it and, to Cavour's astonishment, had made it even stronger. Then Cavour, who still mistrusted his Italian grammar, had used a friend to turn Napoleon's French phrases into Italian before giving the speech to the king, who further improved on the improvements by changing a phrase, "cries of suffering," to a singular "cry of suffering" which, in its context, carried a greater sense of unity in pain. Out of these many hands emerged one of the most famous speeches in the history of modern Italy.

The king delivered it to the two houses of Parliament from the throne in the Senate Chamber in the Palazzo Madama. His voice was clear and strong, and his final words were:

> Encouraged by the experience of the past we resolutely go forward to meet the eventualities of the future. This future will be happy, with our policy based on justice, love of liberty and of country. Our country, though small in territory, won credit in the councils of Europe because it is great through the ideas it represents, the sympathies that it inspires. This condition is not without dangers. For while we respect the treaties, we are not insensible to the cry of suffering [*il grido di dolore*] which is raised towards us from so many parts of Italy. Strong through concord, trusting in our good right, prudent and resolute, we await the decrees of Divine Providence.[80]

*Il grido di dolore*. The king, standing before the throne, looked calmly but boldly at the throng of senators, deputies and guests crowded into the room before him. Many of the exiles among them were openly weeping. Some republicans began to sing Mameli's hymn and monarchists joined them and led the cheering. From the Senate Chamber to all of Italy went out Sardinia's answer to the cry of grief. The extent of Cavour's agreements with Napoleon were still secret, but d'Azeglio probably spoke for most men when he wrote Cavour, "Today it is no longer a question of discussing your policy, but of making it succeed." And the flow of volunteers into Piedmont to join the army began to increase.

Six days later Prince Napoléon arrived in Turin. He brought with him a treaty for the king's signature which represented six months of negotiations by Cavour and Napoleon following their meeting at Plombières. In its most important terms it followed those already agreed on except that two undecided issues were now resolved in favor of France. Nice as well as Savoy were to be ceded, and Clotilde was to marry the prince. And on 30 January 1859, in the royal chapel of the Palazzo Reale, the two were married. Thereupon the king signed the treaty.

The couple left the next day for Genoa where, although the match was generally unpopular in Italy, they were greeted ecstatically by the crowds. The Genovesi, usually so hostile to the House of Savoy, cheered Vittorio Emanuele as King of Italy; they cheered for independence, unity and war; and they cheered Clotilde personally. As she sailed out of the harbor for France, she knew that, for better or worse, her sacrifice for Italy had been noted.

"The first act of the drama closes," Cavour wrote to his ambassador in Paris. He finally had the alliance in writing, and although it was still to remain secret, its existence and the fact that it would someday be published with Napoleon's signature on it, gave Cavour, for the first time, some hold on Napoleon.

The marriage, Napoleon's remark to the Austrian ambassador and the king's speech from the throne excited European diplomats and the British in particular to press for peace. In Vienna, Buol was blunt: "If you wish to preach peace to prevent war, address yourselves with firmness to France and Piedmont. We are not meditating war: we shall not be the aggressors." Then he added, "We can never come to an understanding with France, because we do not recognize her as an Italian power and because she sympathizes and protects the cause of nationalities; we support that of Sovereigns, Governments and established order." Metternich and Emperor Franz in 1815 had ignored the problems of nationality and now, even after the events of 1848–49, Buol and Franz Josef were prepared to continue to ignore them.

The British were equally prepared to ignore the cause of nationality and to treat Italy as though it were still a "geographical expression." The Liberal party, of which Palmerston and Gladstone were leaders, was out of office, and the Tories, as well as Queen Victoria and Prince Albert, favored Austria and the established order. At the same time they feared an expanding, militaristic France. The mass of the people, however, favored Sardinia because they were strongly against the pope and because Sardinia seemed, by confused thinking, to be leading a liberal-Protestant cause in Italy. One British M.P., when asked by French friends what the English wanted, replied with perception: "We want, first, that the Austrians should beat you French thoroughly; next, we want that the Italians should be free; and then we want them to be very grateful to us for doing nothing towards it." And British efforts for peace, starting with such confused premises, won no concessions from anyone. France and Sardinia continued to arm, and Austria, to bring re-enforcements into Lombardia.

Italian patriots of other states made demonstrations in support of Sardinia whenever they had an opportunity. Verdi, already a symbol of patriotic aspiration, now became even more so. Repressed Italians in all the cities suddenly realized that his name was an acrostic for *Vittorio Emanuele Re d'Italia,* King of Italy, and *Viva V.E.R.D.I.!* was scratched on walls and shouted in the streets. At Rome, where he was preparing the première of his opera *Un Ballo in Maschera,* if a crowd saw him, he would be stopped, surrounded and cheered. And in Lombardia and the Veneto the audiences, at the end of one of his operas, often would turn to the boxes containing Austrians and roar *Viva Verdi!* while shaking their fists in the air.

At Milan the patriots also made a demonstration out of the funeral of Emilio Dandolo, who had died of tuberculosis, peacefully in his bed. But his white, emaciated features had become for the Milanesi a symbol of resistance to Austria. He had fought at the Engineers' Barracks in the Cinque Giornate; as one of Manara's Bersaglieri he had defended Rome against the pope and the French in 1849; and as historian of that battalion he had published a moving account of its heroism. After the book's publication in Turin he had been a man marked by the Austrians. When he had gone to the Crimea as an officer accredited to the Sardinian staff, the Austrian government had forced him to return under threats of a trial and sequestration of his property for unlawful emigration. Later when Franz Josef visited Milan, Dandolo had been banished from the city until the emperor had left. He had made no secret of his hope to live long enough to fight again with the Bersaglieri against Austria, and he had died regretting it had been denied him.

The funeral took place on the morning of 22 February, and the bier was carried to the church of San Babila. During the service the crowd, for which there was no room in the small church, began to increase in the piazza until it filled the neighboring streets, dense, silent and imposing. The police ordered the people to disperse, and when they would not, an officer went into the church and ordered the procession to the cemetery to be suspended. When the order became known, the crowd, still refusing to move, began to protest. In the sacristy the family tried to convince the officer that it would be less dangerous to allow the procession to go on. After a long time, when the crowd had not decreased, he agreed, and the bier, carried upon the bearers' shoulders moved toward the church door. There a friend nailed to the top of the coffin a crown of flowers which Dandolo's mother had made of red and white camellias interspersed with green leaves, the Italian colors.

Scarcely had the bier with the tricolored crown appeared when a cry rose from the crowd that, as it resounded round the piazza and down the streets, became a prolonged roar, frantic and terrible.

The bier was carried on the shoulders of friends who relieved each other from time to time. Beside them walked a Barnabite priest and behind a squadron of the surviving officers and soldiers of the Manara Battalion, some of whom were cripples. The crowd pressed in so close, the bier could scarcely proceed. At each step as the tricolored crown tilted, dipped and righted, it seemed to start the roar again, and soon the procession of grief had become one of triumph.

The police and guards had disappeared, unable to face such a crowd. But at the cemetery, troops guarded the gates and walls, and only the bier and a few of the family and friends were allowed to enter.

The funeral was hailed in northern Italy as a decisive moral defeat for the Austrians, and they themselves compounded its effect by attempting to arrest the men connected with it, those who had spoken at the grave, the pallbearers, and even Dandolo's Negro valet who could barely speak the Milanese dialect. Most of the men, in spite of the increased number of Hussars patrolling the Ticino river, managed to cross into Piedmont where Cavour and the most distinguished generals and statesmen promptly organized a memorial service for Dandolo.

Cavour was now eager to provoke Austria into a declaration of war. By the terms of the secret treaty, France would come to Sardinia's aid in a war with Austria only if Austria was the aggressor, and Cavour had the responsibility of fulfilling this last condition. Without it the treaty did not come into force.

Cavour continued openly to prepare Sardinia for war. He mobilized its army on the frontier, called up its reserves and continued to enlist volunteers into both the regular army and a special volunteer corps which he was forming. By the middle of March more than twenty thousand volunteers had entered the kingdom, registered at the bureaus in Turin and gone off to camps where the government went through the form of interning them as political refugees. But generally in a few weeks they had disappeared into army camps and had begun training. They came from every Italian state but mostly from those in the Po valley or from Tuscany. Those from Lombardia or the Veneto were Austrian subjects and included among them deserters from the Austrian army. The fact that Sardinia was able to recruit so many volunteers from the other Italian states was a judgment on condition in them, and although Austria had the right by treaty to demand the return of its subjects, as Cavour hoped it would, it did not. Instead it, too, called up men for service, doubled its garrisons on the frontier and passed war bills.

Then in March, to Cavour's dismay, Napoleon began to show signs of wanting to postpone the war. But the king and Cavour had passed the last point at which they could change their policy. As the king wrote bluntly to Napoleon, if France deserted Sardinia now, the defeat for the kingdom would be worse than that of Novara. Like his father, he would have to abdicate.

Napoleon was having difficulties rather than doubts over his policy. He was disturbed by the number of Frenchmen who were either against him or, at best, uninterested. He was discouraged and even angry that his plan for an Italian confederation, which he had expounded in a pamphlet he had caused to be written, had not stirred up any interest among Italian patriots. And he feared he was losing the good will of Britain. More than anything else he feared an alliance between Britain and Austria which might be the start of a coalition against him. So when in March Russia suggested a congress to settle the Italian problem, he had shown interest, hoping that Austria would refuse to attend or make such unreasonable demands that it would put itself in the wrong.

At the first rumors of a congress Cavour had wired his ambassador in Paris: "Oppose Congress with all your force." Meanwhile the five great powers once again began to argue whether Sardinia should be allowed to sit as an equal. Austria placed as conditions to accepting an invitation to a congress: that no territorial changes be made in Italy; that other Italian states but not Sardinia should be included as the other states were the ones to be reformed; and that Sardinia should disarm before the congress. Back and forth across Europe fluttered diplomatic notes and memorandums, while Cavour, protesting to Napoleon, grew more and more anxious. Finally he went to Paris, but he was allowed only one private interview with the emperor. At the second Napoleon kept Walewski present.

Cavour could do little more than recite the reasons which before had persuaded Napoleon to do something for Italy, to apply some pressure gently by talk of someday publishing the treaty if Napoleon backed out, and to state publicly on every occasion that Sardinia would not disarm and that war was inevitable because Austria's repressive rule in Italy made it so. Just before he left Paris he wrote a memorandum for the emperor in which he went through the various points which the congress had raised: disarmament, Sardinia's right to attend, and policies to be followed at the congress. With it he sent a personal letter, very different in tone. He asked the emperor not to let down his ally. Vittorio Emanuele, for his part, had done all he had been asked. A policy of peace would ruin Italy: the patriots would cry they had been betrayed; the army would be used to keep order instead of fighting the Austrians; Mazzini would again become the hope of the people and the Austrians be justified in their repressions. And in an Italy dominated by either Mazzini or the Habsburgs there was no benefit for France.

On his return to Turin, Cavour continued to prepare for war, as in Vienna and Paris did Franz Josef and Napoleon. In all three states the pressure for war mounted as the generals made more and more dispositions for it, and gradually the power in each shifted into the hands of the military men. The diplomats, however, did not cease their efforts for peace. Austria still insisted that Sardinia must disarm before any congress, and although Prussia and Britain were ready to support Austria's demand, Napoleon as yet was not. To the Austrians his refusal to coerce the little kingdom was further evidence that the real enemy, as in centuries past, was France; the real war was over whether France or Austria should dominate Italy. To the Austrians the national cause of the Italian patriots was irrelevant, a matter still for the police. Austrian army officers talked of Turin as only the first stop on the road to Paris.

The last effort of the diplomats reached its climax on 18 April. During the previous days Cavour, supported still by Napoleon, had refused pleas from Britain, Prussia and Russia to disarm unless guaranteed a voice equal to Austria's at the congress. And this, Austria still refused. But now Britain shifted the main object of its pressure from Cavour to Napoleon and proposed that France join with it in a demand on Sardinia to agree to a general disarmament before the congress, while at the same time both would pledge to support Sardinia's right at the congress to an equal voice. The British diplomats, led by Lord Henry Cowley, reasoned that Napoleon had no ground to refuse to join in such demand and that Cavour, faced with it, would be forced to agree. Then Austria would stand alone in its refusal to compromise.

Throughout 18 April, as Cavour in Turin hoped every moment to hear that Austria, finally exasperated beyond bearing, had declared war, Cowley, Walewski and the Austrian ambassador were arguing with Napoleon in Paris. And by the end of the day they had convinced him that, with Britain promising to support Sardinia's right to an equal voice in the congress, he could not, for the good of his dynasty and the peace of Europe, refuse to join with Britain in a demand that Sardinia disarm on these terms. Walewski hastened out to telegraph his embassy in Turin.

At 1 A.M. on 19 April the first secretary of the embassy staff in Turin ran with a telegram to the Palazzo Cavour. The porter showed the man upstairs, and Cavour received him in his bedroom. There, half-dressed and sitting on his small, iron bed, Cavour read Walewski's telegram. "There is nothing for me to do now," he said to the secretary, "but to blow out my brains." At 8 A.M. he wired back to Paris: "Since France joins England in demanding Sardinia to disarm in advance, the king's government, although foreseeing that this measure may have grievous consequences for Italy, declares itself disposed to submit."

After he had sent the telegram, Cavour shut himself in his bedroom and seems to have had a sort of nervous collapse. He refused to see anyone, not even Farini who was one of his most trusted supporters. He began to burn papers, and his servants feared he was preparing to kill himself. Farini, after being turned away, hurried to find Michelangelo Castelli, the man for whom Cavour had the greatest affection, the man who, years before, had stayed once to listen to Cavour when others, pointedly, had left. Castelli ran to the palazzo and was met by the butler who begged him to do something, and Castelli ran on up the stairs and burst into the room. Cavour was sitting in a chair surrounded by torn-up papers; others were burning in the hearth. Castelli said that he knew no one was to enter and that was why he had come. Cavour stared at him in silence. Then Castelli said, "Must I believe that Cavour will desert the field before the battle; that he will abandon us all?" And, unhinged by excitement and his great affection for the man, he burst into tears. Cavour rose, embraced him convulsively, and began pacing around the room in a state of great agitation. Then he stopped opposite Castelli and said slowly: "Be easy; we will face everything, and always all of us together." Castelli went out to reassure the household and friends.

But at the very moment Cavour thought he had lost the diplomatic game, he was winning it. On the evening of the same day, 19 April, a courier left Vienna with an ultimatum from Austria to Sardinia: consent within three days to disarm or face the consequences. While the courier traveled by post and rail, stopping in Lombardia to alert the Austrian commander in Italy, General Graf Gyulai, Buol rejected the British proposal. The nineteenth and twentieth of April had been terrible days for Cavour, but on the twenty-first his ordeal ended: he received news through the British embassy at Turin that Austria had refused Britain's proposal and was sending an ultimatum, an aggressive act. The secret treaty with France would come into effect. As d'Azeglio observed, for Sardinia to have agreed to disarm at the very moment Austria refused "has been one of those pieces of gambler's luck that happen only once in a century. Whether we are prepared or not, the moral victory is ours and more than half our enemies have become our friends, seeing us now as victims and not as provokers." And he added, "It has been a terrifying bit of navigation, a shoal every moment: but one does not go to to heaven in a carriage."

At Vienna, in a full ministerial council, Franz Josef had once again chosen a forcible solution to his problem. Buol so misread the situation that to the end he argued that Prussia and England would fight with Austria against France. The military advisors argued that France only was stalling for time to prepare and that Austria ought to invade Sardinia, destroy its small army and then from Turin declare itself ready to negotiate in a congress, whenever and how the powers desire. These were arguments that appealed to Franz Josef, who intended to lead his army in the field personally. And all at the council were exasperated by Sardinia, such a small kingdom to stand up to the Austrian Empire.

The ultimatum arrived in Turin on 23 April as Cavour was requesting the Chamber of Deputies to grant plenary powers to the king for the defense of the country. "And who," he asked, "can be a better guardian of our liberties? Who more worthy of this proof of the nation's trust? He, whose name, throughout ten years of reign, has been synonymous with loyalty and honor. He, who now, as always holds high and firm the tricolor of Italy: he who at this moment prepares himself to fight for liberty and independence!" During the frantic applause Cavour received a note: "They are here; I have seen them," and he left the Chamber to meet the messengers of Austria bearing the ultimatum. He had three days in which to answer it, three days during which French troops began to march into Sardinia, and when he rejected it on 26 April, the war officially began, about one week earlier than the date Cavour had predicted to Odo Russell in the previous December that he would force Austria to a declaration of war.

Never, perhaps, has a statesman worked for war with such persistence and grim determination as Cavour. Is he admirable? Was Clotilde, whose marriage was unhappy, sacrificed for Italy or for her father's ambition? Liberal historians are apt to avoid such questions or to answer them by insisting that by 1856 the House of Habsburg had shown itself incapable of creating any solution to the problems of Italy, that the Congress of Paris had shown conclusively that diplomacy had no solution for them and that the war therefore was justified. Such a conclusion, of course, assumes that patriots have some right to be patriots, that men must be allowed to choose their own form of government and that the basic group to make that choice is a nation of persons who share a cultural identity. Many men do not believe these premises. Cavour, however, as an heir of the French Revolution believed them, yet even he was not blind to the conflict between his personal and his public morality. He once observed, "If we did the things for ourselves that we do for the state, we'd be great scoundrels indeed." But is such a division of morality merely a self-serving excuse or an honest justification? Men do not agree on an answer.

# CHAPTER 38

Gyulai's slow advance. Metternich and Ferdinando of Naples die. Napoleon's war. Magenta. Proclamation of Milan. Revolution in Tuscany. Italian patriots cheer Napoleon but turn to Cavour. Papal forces retake Perugia. Garibaldi and the *Cacciatori delle Alpi*. Solferino. Peace of Villafranca. Cavour and the King. Napoleon returns to France. Cavour resigns.

AT THE START of the war Sardinia's position was perilous. It was a small kingdom with its best natural defense, the Alps, between it and its ally, and relatively open ground between it and its enemy. Its army, including volunteers totaled about sixty thousand, and across the Ticino river Austria had massed more than one hundred thousand, not counting reserves in the garrisons of Lombardia, the Veneto, the duchies and the Legations. Most observers in Europe, including the French and Sardinian general staffs, assumed that the Austrians would cross the Ticino, drive for Turin and probably capture the city before French troops could debouch from the Alps and join in its defense. So sure were the young Austrian officers of taking Turin that many had letters addressed to them there; while within the city Cavour talked privately of transferring the government to Genoa.

But to everyone's astonishment the Austrian commander-in-chief, General Ferenc Gyulai, started late and, once started, moved slowly. The Austrians had delivered their ultimatum on 23 April and the next day, even before Cavour's reply, Napoleon had started French troops for the Alpine passes in Savoy. On 26 April Cavour rejected the ultimatum, but not until the thirtieth did Gyuali start the main part of his army across the Ticino. And three days later, although only slightly opposed, he had advanced only twenty miles, hardly a third of the way to Turin. Meanwhile French troops, through Genoa and Savoy, were arriving in Piedmont at a rate of eight or ten thousand a day. A week later, still lightly opposed, Gyulai had advanced to within fifteen miles of Turin, but then he began to withdraw, apparently suspecting a trap or unnerved by the combined Sardinian and French force building up on his southern flank. He retreated back to the

Ticino, deploying his army along it, and there waited for the allies to attack. Then, after several weeks more of reconnaissance, skirmish and a small battle at Palestro, he withdrew his men across the river because, as he wired to Franz Josef, he "regarded it as his first duty to maintain the strength of the army for further operations."

His action, or lack of it, largely determined the course of the war: the fighting thereafter would be on Austrian territory, on the plains of Lombardia rather than in the foothills of Piedmont; the battles would be between armies which, for the time, were of enormous size, for each side soon had about two hundred thousand men in the field; and, most important, the allies, once across the river, could immediately pose as "liberators" and, in the event of a stalemate somewhere in Lombardia, would have Austrian territory with which to bargain.

Military historians without exception have condemned Gyulai for wasting advantages, and most have seen in his caution a result of the kind of army Franz Josef, who was his own war minister, had created. The emperor, of course, wanted a magnificent, fighting army, but he had no military experience himself, and he was not inclined by temperament to listen to those who had. Gyulai was a modest, workaday professional who, in his own opinion, was unfit for high command, but he did not question the emperor. Three of Gyulai's five corps commanders, reflecting Franz Josef's emphasis on social position, bore famous Austrian names, Schwarzenberg, Liechtenstein and Stadion. The men were brave, but none was experienced or proved outstanding. The only corps commander to distinguish himself was a Hungarian named Benedek, a Protestant and a member of the middle class. But Franz Josef had done little to seek out and advance such men. He had created a parade-ground army; told to fight, it nervously assumed a defensive position.

On 6 May, in the month that Gyulai was advancing and retreating, Metternich died in Vienna. His death had no political significance; he was wholly retired, eighty-six and inclined to bore anyone who would listen with stories about himself and the first Napoleon. His death, however, was well timed to mark the end of an epoch. He had served the Habsburgs for almost half a century and one of his chief accomplishments had been to keep France out of the Italian peninsula; now, for the first time since 1814, a French army was back in the Po valley.

Two weeks later on 22 May, while the war was still without a battle, Ferdinando II of Naples, King "Bomba," died after a long illness. Early in the winter he had caught a cold which gradually had congested his lungs, and the wound in his thigh, caused by the soldier's attempt to assassinate him, had become infected. He was only forty-nine and might have been expected to recover. The queen, however, at the start had selected a doctor on the basis of politics rather than skill, and Ferdinando had alternated between doing too much and too little, declining often into a fatalism in which he believed he was a victim of the "evil eye" and beyond the help of doctors. He had come to the throne at twenty with health, hope and vigor, but the experiences of his reign had drained all from him. He died at forty-nine an old man, worn out in mind and body and, in his palace at Caserta, shut off from the world, physically and spiritually.

His death, however, unlike that of Metternich, offered the possibility of a change in political alignments, and liberals and patriots in all the Italian states looked hopefully to the new king, Francesco II, whose mother, Ferdinando's first wife, had been the saintly Maria Cristina of Savoy. Cavour quickly sent an envoy to urge an alliance against Austria and reforms leading to a revival of the constitution of 1848, and, equally, quickly, Franz Josef sent one to urge continued neutrality and autocracy. In purely dynastic terms Franz Josef had the advantage for, in January, Francesco had married the Empress of Austria's younger sister and his stepmother, the widowed queen, was a Habsburg. On Cavour's side, actively urging an alliance with Sardinia, were two of Francesco's uncles, but neither had much influence at court. For the time being, at least, Francesco seemed unlikely to do anything sudden or different. He was twenty-three, shy, religious and strongly attached to the memory of his father, and he continued his father's policy of neutrality.

Meanwhile, as May ended, the war in the north suddenly came alive. Napoleon had landed in Genoa on the twelfth, announcing that he had come "to free Italy from the Alps to the Adriatic" and two days later, at Alessandria, had taken command of the allied armies. To his French troops he proclaimed:

> Soldiers! I have just put myself at your head to lead you to the combat. We are going to second the struggle of a people reclaiming its independence and to rescue it from foreign oppression. This is a holy cause, which has the sympathy of the civilized world.
>
> I do not need to stimulate your ardor: every day's march will remind you of a victory . . . in passing Marengo, Lodi, Castiglione, Arcola, Rivoli, you will be marching on another Sacred Way, surrounded by glorious memories. . . .
>
> Already from one end of France to the other resound words of happy augury: "The new Army of Italy will be worthy of her elder sister!" [81]

The war was the first in which a government subjected its own people to propaganda in the modern style. The spread of telegraph wires now made it possible for events abroad to be reported home in hours rather than days or weeks and, further, as quickly to be re-reported out again to

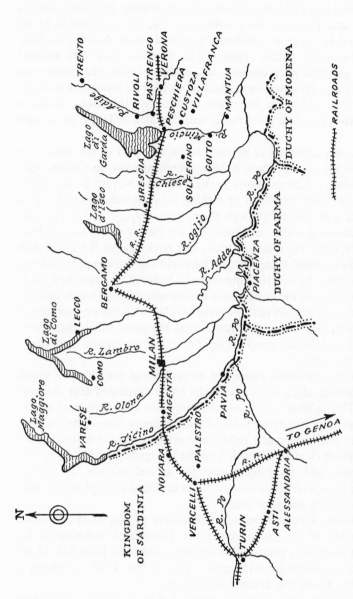

THE CAMPAIGN OF 1859 IN THE PO VALLEY —

Note... The river Mincio is the boundary between Lombardia and the Veneto. The fortified parts of both Peschiera and Mantua are on the west bank of the river and in Lombardia.

RAILROADS

the people. Napoleon, whose rule in theory was based on the will of the people expressed in a plebiscite, never forgot that many in France, clerics, conservatives and peasants, were uninterested in or even hostile to his Italian war, and he attempted deliberately with his bulletins from the front to mould a favorable public opinion. The bulletins rang with military rhetoric: the generals were dashing, the soldiers, brave; the nation was amassing glory and again was embarked on its historic mission of carrying liberty to others. And in the first week of June as Napoleon executed a daring maneuver, fought a great battle and liberated Milan, it all seemed to be true.

The maneuver consisted of moving the greater part of his army from Alessandria in the south, where it had assembled close to Genoa, right across the Austrian forward posts to Vercelli and Novara in the north, whence he could strike for Milan by turning the Austrian lines rather than by battling his way directly through them. (See map, p. 495.) The plan was daring because it offered the Austrians the chance to cut him off from Genoa or even from Turin and to press him back against the Swiss Alps from which, Switzerland being neutral, he could not draw supplies. It was imaginative because he saw the potential of a railroad as a new weapon in war and made effective use of its power to concentrate large forces quickly. And it suceeded, at least in part, because Gyulai, who lacked such daring and imagination, had convinced himself that the main attack must come from the south and did not grasp the significance of the reports he began to receive from the north.

There, as the Austrians attempted to probe and the allies to screen Napoleon's movements, a small but crucial battle developed near the town of Palestro. The fighting was hard, continued for two days, and on the allied side was done largely by units of the Sardinian army. Their victory was complete: left, center and right the Austrians were defeated. In the final charge which cleared the field, Vittorio Emanuele, carried away with excitement, rode with his subjects and for several minutes, in the last flicker among European heads of state of the medieval concept of a warrior king, actually fought alongside them.

After Palestro, Gyulai, who was still unsure of Napoleon's purpose, withdrew the last of his troops across the Ticino and, ordering all the bridges to be destroyed, prepared to defend Lombardia from behind the river. His sappers, however, did a careless job, and the French, arriving at the river's edge, found two bridges still intact.

At that moment, early in the morning of 4 June, Napoleon still was expecting to be attacked, if at all, on the Sardinian side of the Ticino, and he deployed the main part of his army with reserves in depth between Novara and the river. He himself with about thirty thousand men crossed and started by several roads toward the village of Magenta, which he intended to secure as his bridgehead in Lombardia. The day was hot and sunny, and he expected to have an easy advance. By noon, however, he realized that, far from clearing out a few sharpshooters and reconnaissance patrols, he and his men had stumbled into a heavy concentration of Austrian troops.

It was not the battle Napoleon had sought. Both he and his men knew that if ever the Austrians could get behind them and destroy even one of the bridges, then much of the French van would be trapped and either shot down at leisure or forced to surrender. The Austrians, too, realized the opportunity, and the skirmishing quickly flared into a major battle with both sides calling up reenforcements as fast as possible.

The land between Magenta and the river, although flat, was criss-crossed with irrigation canals and farm lanes which were lined on either side with heavy scrub growth. Even in the fields the crops were already taller than a man so that often the soldiers could see only a yard or two before them. Maneuvers in any large sense were impossible, and the battle developed as a multitude of separate, small fights for a canal bridge, a cemetery, a crossroads or a farmhouse. On neither side could the generals contribute much direction to the fighting, and Napoleon, although he stayed with his troops, passed an agonizing six hours unable to do anything except to rely on the valor of his men and to hope that their reenforcements would appear before those of the Austrians. And finally, late in the afternoon, the French Second Corps under General Maurice MacMahon began to arrive in force, and by eight in the evening it had captured Magenta and the Austrians had begun to disengage, retreating in good order.

No one at that hour considered the battle over. Neither Gyulai nor Napoleon had been able to engage more than a third of his men, about fifty thousand apiece, and both looked forward to fighting on the morrow with even greater numbers of wholly fresh troops. But during the night Gyulai became convinced that the odds had turned against him. He had fewer fresh troops than Napoleon, many of his men who had already fought were demoralized and he was short on supplies. He drew back farther and began a slow, orderly retreat to the Mincio river, where he would be based on the forts of the Quadrilateral.

Napoleon claimed a great victory and, in the fashion of the first Napoleon, made General MacMahon a marshal and awarded him the title of Duke of Magenta. Three days later, on 8 June, he made a triumphal entry into Milan with Vittorio Emanuele at his side and, again reminiscent of his uncle, was hailed as the "Liberator of Italy."

In a proclamation he published that day he stated to the Milanesi and by implication to many others:

Your welcome shows that you have understood me. I do not come among you with a preconceived system to dispossess the sovereigns or to impose my will on you; my army will busy itself with only two things, to fight your enemies and to maintain internal order. It will oppose no obstacles to the free manifestation of your legitimate desires.[82]

And in the balance of the proclamation he urged the Milanesi to put their trust in Vittorio Emanuele and to enlist in his army: "Be today all soldiers, to be tomorrow the free citizens of a great country."

The Milanesi were ecstatic in their enthusiasm for Napoleon, and patriots everywhere were inclined to accept his words at face value and to hail him as a truly disinterested liberator. Even republicans, though they retained their suspicions, could not deny that he had forced the Austrians back to the Mincio and in little more than a month had liberated most of Lombardia.

In fact, however, neither the military nor the political scene was as clear and hopeful as the cheering crowds wanted to believe. Napoleon had not pursued Gyulai because his own supply lines, like those of the Austrians, were breaking down. The reason lay partly in corruption and inefficiency and also simply in the size of the army. The first Napoleon had campaigned in the Po valley with thirty thousand men; Napoleon III's army, including the Sardinians, numbered more than two hundred thousand, and as the Austrians had torn up the only railroad in Lombardia, the men had to be supplied, just as in the days of the first Napoleon, by horse and wagon. As a result whole regiments were often close to starving, and men by the thousands, weakened by wounds or hunger, came down with malaria, dysentery and other camp diseases. The Austrians were as badly off, but Gyulai, unharassed by any pursuit, had been able to reorganize his men, so that the Austrian army still existed and now, based on the Quadrilateral forts, was probably stronger than before.

Politically, Napoleon and Cavour were already at odds and over a problem in which the people of several Italian states were directly involved. Both men had assumed, even as far back as their meeting at Plombières, that as their allied armies advanced down the Po valley, the Duke of Modena and the Regent Duchess of Parma would retire with the Austrians into the Quadrilateral and that the two abandoned duchies would be joined in some fashion with the Kingdom of Sardinia.

Neither, however, had foreseen that on 27 April, before a shot in the war had been fired, the townfolk of Tuscany would be able to conduct a revolution in which not a pane of glass was broken and which yet would be so unequivocal that the Grand Duke Leopoldo II would be forced to leave with his family for Mantua. The last Austrian garrison in Tuscany had been withdrawn the previous year, and now, as the war with Austria seemed about to begin, Leopoldo awoke one morning to discover, after a few hours, that the only orders he could give which would be obeyed were orders for his own departure. The revolution was sparked by the liberals and republicans of Florence, but their colleagues in the duchy's other large towns, Pisa, Lucca, Livorno, Arezzo and Siena, gave it such complete support that Leopold had nowhere to go but out of the duchy. The day after he rolled away in his carriage, still before the fighting began, a provisional government in Florence offered Vittorio Emanuele the dictatorship of Tuscany for the duration of the war with the understanding that a final political settlement would follow the peace.

The offer was just the sort of unexpected opportunity that Cavour had expected the war to produce and of which he hoped to take advantage. Obviously, if Vittorio Emanuele could rule in Tuscany for the duration of the war, he might well be able to continue to rule there after its end. Equally, the offer was just the sort of alarming, revolutionary change which Napoleon had hoped to exclude from his war in Italy. He was on record, privately at Plombières and publicly thereafter through pamphlets, as favoring a Kingdom of Central Italy, ostensibly to act as a buffer between Sardinia and the Papal States but perhaps also to be a sphere of French influence in Italy. Without Tuscany such a kingdom was impossible.

Cavour and Napoleon met in Piedmont to discuss the offer and as a result of their meeting Vittorio Emanuele refused the position and power of dictator but did accept command of any Tuscan troops which might be raised and undertook to protect the duchy during the war. It was an uneasy compromise. Cavour sent a representative of the king to Florence, but the man had very little power, and the Tuscans continued to govern themselves. Meanwhile Cavour and Vittorio Emanuele saw the first fruits of the war withheld from them, and Napoleon was reminded, or perhaps discovered for the first time, that Cavour's aims in the Italian war were both more ambitious and more purely Italian than his own.

The problem arose again, after Magenta, as Gyulai ordered his Austrian garrisons south of the Po, in the Duchy of Modena and the Papal States, to withdraw into the Quadrilateral, north of the river. In all the towns of Parma, Modena, the Legations and south to Ancona, the people rose, tore down the ducal or Papal arms and installed provisional governments. This area, south of the Po and reaching into the hill towns of Central Italy, was where La Farina's *Società Nazionale Italiana* was strongest, and with impressive unanimity the provisional governments of each town or district offered a dictatorship to Vittorio Emanuele and asked for union with Sardinia. The members of the *Società* were organized and ready with their program: Italy, united and independent, under the House of Savoy.

Perhaps because Napoleon had not been in Italy since the days of the Carbonaro revolution of 1831, he had misgauged the aims and organization of the Italians of 1859. The first Napoleon in Italy had been not only the military victor but also the political arbiter, receiving deputations, handing out constitutions and supporting this group while squashing that. Napoleon III had imagined himself in the same role, but it was denied to him. The Italian patriots of 1859 knew what constitution they wanted, what assembly they wanted to sit in, what men they wanted for their king and minister. And in the weeks after Magenta, Napoleon discovered to his surprise and irritation, that although the Italians would cheer him as their liberator, they would send their deputations to Vittorio Emanuele and Cavour.

He had no real objection, however, to citizens of Parma and Modena offering themselves and their cities to Sardinia, even if he would have preferred to have had the offer pass through him. The end was, at least, one he was fighting to achieve. But similar offers from the citizens of the Papal States entangled him at once in one of the great Italian problems: the temporal power. What was to be done with the Papal States, particularly with the Legations? The first Napoleon, backed by a highly anticlerical, republican France, simply had wrested them from the pope and joined them to the North Italian state he was forming. But Napoleon III was backed by a different France. Many of his strongest supporters were devout Catholics, and he had promised them, in leaving Paris: "We are not going to Italy to foment disorder, nor to disturb the power of the Holy Father, whom we restored to his throne, but to shield him from that foreign pressure which weighs on all the Peninsula." And again, as in Tuscany, he forced Cavour and Vittorio Emanuele to accept less than what was offered to them, and the people were left for the moment to govern themselves.

Napoleon's logic did not endear him to the people of the Legations and of the other towns of the Papal States which had revolted, however peacefully, against the pope. They had hoped for some French troops to help in their defense, but Napoleon pointedly kept his men out of Papal territory. And further, as commander-in-chief of the allied armies, he kept out Sardinian troops as well. Cardinal Antonelli quickly took advantage of the opportunity offered and sent three thousand Swiss Guards to retake Perugia. After a short fight the Swiss took the city and, on entering, sacked it.

The looting and killing were medieval in their ferocity and from a purely military view a success. The hill towns of Umbria and those on the Adriatic side of the Apennines south of the Legations, in an area known as the Marches, quietly resumed their allegiance to the pope. But diplomatically and even in a religious sense the retaking of Perugia was a defeat

for the Papacy. Many Europeans were shocked at the barbarity of it and
shocked again when Pio Nono ordered a special medal struck for the soldiers and promoted the officer in charge to general. As in 1849, the Pope
seemed able to sustain his temporal power only by besieging and killing
his own subjects.

After the sacking of Perugia, Cavour, disregarding Napoleon's wishes,
sent d'Azeglio and a troop of eleven thousand volunteers, not Sardinian
regulars, to Bologna. D'Azeglio's orders were vague, even self-contradic-
tory. No political decisions affecting the future were to be considered, and
he was to remember that Sardinia was at peace with the Papacy. Yet he
was also "to resist and expel any Papal invasion to reconquer" the cities of
Romagna, which included all the Legations. Perhaps in part because of
Cavour's action, Antonelli did not attempt to reconquer the Romagna but
kept his troops at all points south of its border.

On one political question, however, Napoleon, Vittorio Emanuele and
even Cavour found themselves in agreement: on the need to hide Garibaldi's light under a bushel. Cavour, with an eye on Italian public feeling
and over the opposition of Napoleon and of most of the high-ranking
Sardinian officers, had created for Garibaldi a volunteer corps of about
thirty-five hundred which was known as *Cacciatori delle Alpi,* or *Hunters
of the Alps,* and Vittorio Emanuele on 9 May had given him orders "to
operate on Lago Maggiore on the Austrian right flank in any way he considers advisable."

Garibaldi had started out immediately and on 16 May in the foothills
of the Alps, two weeks ahead of the main army, he and his men had
crossed the Ticino and begun fighting in Lombardia. Even before then
Cavour had ordered him to put himself under another general's command,
but Garibaldi had decided instead to push ahead. In this campaign he
fought as a Sardinian general, wearing a regular army uniform instead of
his red shirt and gray poncho, but for some weeks his uniform was almost
his only acknowledgment that he was part of the Sardinian chain of
command.

His aim was to cut Austrian supply lines coming down from the Alpine
passes, and he fought like a whirlwind, back and forth, and always appearing where he was least expected. Because of the way the war developed
his exploits ultimately proved to have no military value, but at the time
they had a strong political effect in that they provided Italian patriots with
an Italian hero. Giovanni Visconti Venosta, who acted as Cavour's agent
in organizing the Lombard towns Garibaldi liberated, describes how "the
General," as everyone now called him, would enter a town:

> . . . like the head of a new religion followed by a crowd of fa-
> natics. No less than the men, the women were enthusiastic for him

and brought their babies for him to bless and even to baptize.

To these crowds that thronged him, Garibaldi would speak with that beautiful voice of his which was part of the fascination he exerted. "Make arms of every scythe and ax," he would say to the crowds on the streets or in the squares. "Come! He who stays at home is a coward. I promise you weariness, hardship and battles. But we will conquer or die."

They were never joyful words, but when they were heard the enthusiasm rose to its highest. It was a delirium. The crowd broke up, deeply moved, talking of what the general had said. Many had tears in their eyes.[83]

Such scenes had too much revolutionary fervor and republican sentiment for Napoleon, Vittorio Emanuele and Cavour, and Garibaldi was ordered to the Valtellina, to guard the upper valley of the Adda river which led to passes into Austria. Mazzini, always suspicious of French aid, had warned him: "You will be shut up in some corner of the Tyrol or Valtellina, while the French Emperor does exactly what he wants without any possible intervention on your part." Some military reasons can be cited in support of the order, such as the difficulties of supplying an army which, with volunteers, had swelled to twelve thousand men, but most historians have agreed that the essential reason was political. Garibaldi always thought so, and he was inclined to blame Cavour, the civilian politician, rather than Napoleon or Vittorio Emanuele.

Four days after the *Cacciatori* were sent to the Valtellina, on 24 June, the allied armies under Napoleon fought the Austrians, now commanded by Franz Josef himself, at Solferino, a small village on the Lombard side of the Mincio river. Franz Josef, determined to retake his province of Lombardia, had led his men out of the Quadrilateral, crossed the river and offered to fight the great battle which Gyulai had avoided. Its general plan was simple: Napoleon strove to pierce the Austrian center by capturing Solferino, and the Austrians tried to crush the French right wing and to roll it back on its center. The fighting ranged over an enormous area, almost sixty square miles, and almost three hundred thousand men were engaged. In size and numbers Solferino was far greater than Waterloo and except for Leipzig, where the allies of 1813 had finally defeated Napoleon I, was perhaps the greatest battle Europe had seen. It was also one of the bloodiest, and both Napoleon and Franz Josef were profoundly shaken by the numbers of the dead and the agonies of the wounded. So, too, was a young Swiss tourist, Henri Dunant, who was caught between the armies as the battle began and, after it, stayed on to help with the wounded. Two years later he published an account of what he had seen at Solferino, and it led directly to the founding of the Red Cross.

As at Magenta, the fighting by itself was not altogether decisive, but during the night Franz Josef started to retreat behind the Mincio, and Napoleon the next day claimed a victory. But he did not pursue, and the two armies with the river between them, set about reorganizing their regiments. Franz Josef had lost a battle and retreated, but his army still existed, more than a hundred thousand strong, still in control of the Quadrilateral forts and still holding all of the Veneto. If Napoleon was to redeem his pledge "to free Italy from the Alps to the Adriatic," the war was only half-won.

Napoleon, however, was having second thoughts, as were others, in Paris. On the eve of Solferino he and Vittorio Emanuele rode out together to inspect their positions, and when they were beyond hearing of all except the Sardinian chief of staff, Napoleon read aloud a letter from the Empress Eugénie in which she urged him to bring the war to an end. She marshaled an impressive order of reasons, among them the doubts of many in France as to the value of the war, the dangerous political and religious problems it was producing in Italy, and above all the fact that Prussia was mobilizing additional army corps. Vittorio Emanuele listened in silence and when Napoleon finished, made no comment. But he must have wondered if this was Napoleon's way of announcing peace.

The next day, however, the battle was fought and proved a victory for the allies. The day after, Cavour, summoned by the king, arrived at Sardinian headquarters. He had an interview with Napoleon and soon after returned to Turin. No record exists of this interview, but from Cavour's actions and letters following it, he came away apparently convinced that the emperor did not intend to make peace, hardly an unreasonable conclusion when Napoleon was just announcing a great victory.

Napoleon, however, did mean to make peace, and at once. Through his ambassador in London he tried to arrange for Britain to propose an armistice and peace which would unite Parma and Lombardia to Sardinia while placing Modena and the Veneto under an Austrian archduke and returning Leopoldo to Tuscany. Palmerston, the British prime minister, declined to foster such a scheme: "It would obviously fall short of the wishes and expectations of Italy; and if we made it, we should be accused of having interposed and stopped the allied armies in their career of victory, and having betrayed and disappointed the Italians at the moment when their prospects were brightest."

The reasoning was so obviously true that Napoleon did not look for another cat's paw but on 6 July sent an aide directly to Franz Josef to ask for an armistice. Throughout his negotiations with Britain and the start of those with Franz Josef, he acted secretly, violating Article 6 of his treaty with Sardinia "not to receive any overture or proposition tending to the cessation of hostilities without having previously deliberated in common." Vittorio Emanuele did not learn definitely that an armistice was being considered until the seventh; and Cavour not until the eighth, hours after representatives of the three monarchs had met in the village of Villafranca and signed an armistice to expire on 16 August. The next morning the French government's paper, *Moniteur,* announced the terms, and that evening Cavour left for Sardinian headquarters at the front.

The armistice astonished Europeans and, as Palmerston had foreseen, alarmed and angered Italians, who immediately suspected that a peace treaty was being negotiated. At Sardinian headquarters Cavour had an unpleasant interview with the king. His comments, as Vittorio Emanuele explained what he knew of Napoleon's reasons for the armistice, were caustic and perhaps tinged with personal rancor. The tempers of both were shortened by anxiety over the course of events, and Cavour, further, could complain with justice that once the war had begun, the king and his staff had not kept him properly informed. Apparently the king, who always enjoyed the company of military men, had delighted in being free of Cavour's strong personality and had condoned a tendency among members of his staff to feel themselves superior to the civilian minister and to conduct the war without reference to him. On occasion Cavour first heard of developments at the front by letter from Prince Napoléon or even by reading of them in the *Moniteur.*

The next morning, 11 July, Napoleon rode to Villafranca where he had asked Franz Josef to meet him in order that they might negotiate personally the preliminaries of a peace treaty. Neither Cavour nor even Vittorio Emanuele was invited. The meeting of the two emperors was carefully staged for pomp and a painter's eye. Both Imperial Guards were in full dress uniform with guidons, clanking swords and spurs. At the moment of actual meeting, the emperors cantered forward graciously to greet each other and then rode together to the farm house where they would settle the fate of Italy. While they conferred upstairs in a small room, their staffs mingled together in a colorful parade below and a French and an Austrian sentry, in contrasting uniforms, guarded the farm house door. No Italian soldier or statesman of any rank or position was present.

The meeting lasted about an hour and that night copies of the preliminaries which had been signed by Franz Josef were delivered to Napoleon. He summoned Vittorio Emanuele, explained the terms to the bitter but self-controlled king, and then left it up to the latter to explain the terms to Cavour. Throughout the entire period that Cavour was at the front Napoleon refused to see him, even with others present, and the most reasonable explanation is that he feared the force of Cavour's arguments and of his anger.

The king, with the terms of the preliminaries, rode back to his own headquarters at the Villa Melchiorri and arrived there shortly before midnight. He immediately sent for Cavour and Costantino Nigra, the Sardinian ambassador to France, asking them to join him in his study. The night was hot and steamy, and the king sat in his shirt sleeves, bare elbows propped on the table. His face, which was always ruddy, was fiery red in the heat, and he puffed at a cigar. Cavour stood to his left and Nigra before him. At the king's command, Nigra handed Cavour the preliminaries. In brief they were:

(1) The Emperors of Austria and France will favor the creation of an Italian Confederation with the Pope as President.
(2) The Emperor of Austria cedes to the Emperor of France all his rights to Lombardia, except for the fortresses of Mantua and Peschiera. [See note, map, p. 495.] The Emperor of France will transfer this territory to the King of Sardinia. The Veneto will remain with the Emperor of Austria and be a state in the Confederation.
(3) The Grand Duke of Tuscany and the Duke of Modena will return to their states proclaiming a general amnesty.
(4) The two Emperors will ask the Pope to make reforms in his government.

Franz Josef's position had been that he would not give up anything not actually won from him and so, beside the Veneto, he kept the Quadrilateral intact with two of its fortresses on the Lombard bank of the Mincio river. He would not give up Tuscany or Modena as they were not his personal possessions and, further, as head of his family he had to support his relatives' claims to them. About Parma he would make no agreement, as the duchy was a Bourbon possession and therefore not his to dispose.

Cavour read the terms and burst out in furious protest. For this they were to give up Nice and Savoy? For a little half Kingdom of Northern Italy which stopped at the Mincio? Where was the kingdom which was to stretch from the Alps to the Adriatic? The Venetians were to continue under Austria, the people of the Legations to be returned to the pope, the Tuscans to Leopoldo and the Modenesi to the hated Francesco; and Austria was to control a confederation with votes in council and troops garrisoned in the Veneto and the dependent duchies. Not one condition essential to Italian independence had been achievd. Austria, as before, would dominate the entire peninsula and, because of the treaty, with a new show of legality. He urged the king to reject such terms, to save his honor by fighting on alone, to abdicate if necessary. When the king tried to reason with him, Cavour swept all reasons aside in a great rush of words. After twenty-four hours of waiting impotently while he suspected his country and honor were being betrayed, he lost control of himself. He grew sarcastic, even insolent in his efforts to persuade the king not to agree to Napoleon's terms, and when he realized that he could not shake the king's resolve to do so, he announced that he, at any rate, would have no part in such a treaty. He offered his resignation, which the king accepted. The interview was ended.

Throughout it, Vittorio Emanuele held himself in with remarkable control. He was just as betrayed by Napoleon as was Cavour, and could with justice argue that Cavour, not he, had created the alliance which had led to such a shameful end. "Ah, for you gentlemen," he said to Cavour that night, "things always come right, for you settle them by resignation. I am the one who cannot get out of a difficulty so nicely. I cannot offer my resignation. I cannot desert the cause. We work all right until there comes a difficulty, then I am left alone to face the music. I am the one who is responsible before history and the country."

The next morning another interview took place at which Prince Napoléon and La Marmora also were present. The king, perhaps influenced by the heat of Cavour's passion, explained to the prince his repugnance to the preliminaries, and the prince undertook to persuade the emperor to insist to Franz Josef that force should not be used to restore the refugee dukes to their thrones. This concession was not included in the preliminaries as they were signed. In fact, however, it was part of them because Napoleon made plain to Franz Josef that the French army would not stand by idle while the Austrians marched into Modena or Tuscany. The dukes would have to be restored peacefully, probably as the result of a European congress. This fact was to be of the greatest importance in the months to come. And the king won another concession. When he signed the preliminaries, he was allowed to add before his signature: *pour ce qui me concerne,* "for what concerns me." The meaning of the phrase was not defined, but because of it in the future the king and his ministers were able to argue that he was not under any duty to help create an Italian confederation or to return the dukes to their thrones.

The news of Villafranca stunned Italians of every state north of Rome. As Napoleon started on his return for Paris, the Milanesi, who had good reason to think of him as their liberator, gave him an ovation, but at Turin, when he appeared with Vittorio Emanuele, the crowd cheered only for the king, and the shopkeepers filled their windows with pictures of Orsini. A delegation arrived from Parma to protest the armistice, and no one doubted what were the feelings of Venetians. The news of Cavour's resignation only increased the sense of shock and anger.

At Turin, Napoleon justified the treaty on military grounds and told Vittorio Emanuele, "Your government will pay me the expenses of the war and we will say no more of Nice and Savoy." And in a cold interview with

Cavour he promised to plead the Italian cause at a congress which would meet to write the preliminaries into a final and more conclusive treaty. But to a citizen of Bologna who urged him to permit the Legations and the duchies, including Tuscany, to join Sardinia, he replied: "If annexation should cross the Apennines, unity would be accomplished, and I will not have unity, I will have independence only. Unity would stir up for me dangers in France itself, on account of the Roman Question; and France would not be pleased to see rise beside her a great nation that might diminish her preponderance." Napoleon's Italian war was carrying him further than he wished to go, and back in Paris, alluding perhaps to this new Italian threat as well as to the more obvious Prussian one, he explained to his own people, "To serve Italian independence I made war, against the wish of Europe; as soon as the fate of my country seemed to be imperilled I made peace."

Most historians, in the years since Villafranca, have judged Napoleon justified, in the interests of France and of his dynasty, in stopping the war. Sentiment among the governments of Europe, particularly in Britain and Prussia, was rising against him, and another victory over Austria, if it caused a coalition against France, would have been as disastrous as a defeat. And further, attacking the Austrians in the Quadrilateral would have been expensive in men and money and would have required weeks or, more probably, months to achieve a victory. As it was, in less than eight weeks, having gone to Italy and wrested Lombardia from Austria, he was back in Paris as a magnanimous victor with peace assured.

Yet he was followed out of Italy by cries of rage and hatred. He had promised "to free Italy from the Alps to the Adriatic," and he had stopped at the Mincio. Because he had started, patriots everywhere had revealed themselves, the people of Perugia had seen their town sacked and friends killed, and several thousand men in the Sardinian army had died. Now suddenly Napoleon, deciding he had had enough, wanted to stop; the old order was to be restored and life to go on as before. But how could it? And how had he decided to stop? Like a sneak, making his own terms with the enemy and then imposing them on his ally.

The patriots of Foscolo's time had a weakness for the first Napoleon and were willing to forgive him much, perhaps even Campoformio, because he brought into Italy ideas of liberty and equality which they found exciting and needed. Italian historians have continued to share this weakness, for much the same reason. But Napoleon III had no new ideas to bring to Italy, and the patriots of 1859 spared him nothing in their anger; and here, too, most Italian historians have followed contemporary opinion, perhaps unfairly. For however great the shock of Villafranca to Italians, it was also a shock to Franz Josef. Napoleon had come into the Po valley and done what the Italians could never have done by themselves: he had hit the Austrian army so hard that he had cracked the thick crust of Austrian power which covered the peninsula and smothered every effort of the Italians to free themselves. As a result of that blow, Lombardia was to join Sardinia, and probably, too, the Duchy of Parma; and the crack in Austrian power remained to be exploited.

But in the weeks after Villafranca the Italian patriots could not see what had been accomplished; they saw only what had been promised and then withdrawn. On Cavour's return to Turin he spoke with bitter irony of Napoleon: "He would have given up Milan, Turin. *He was tired! The weather was hot!*" And in an interview with Kossuth, the Hungarian patriot, and Pierre Pietri, Napoleon's prefect of police and confidant, he broke out passionately:

> I say to you—and I say it to Monsieur which is as if I were talking to his Emperor—this peace will never be made! This treaty will never be executed! If necessary, I will take Solaro della Margarita by one hand, and Mazzini by the other. I will turn conspirator! I will become a revolutionist! But this treaty shall not be carried out. No, a thousand times no! Never, never! [84]

He had no plan. He was only one man and going out of office. Nevertheless, in that moment, he spoke for many.

# CHAPTER 39

Italian resistance to the terms of Villafranca. Ricasoli. Tuscany and Emilia offer to unite with Sardinia. Murder of Anviti. Garibaldi and the Papal States. Treaty of Zurich. Napoleon's maneuvers toward a Congress. His pamphlet *Le Pape et le Congrès*. The Congress postponed. Plebiscites in Tuscany and Emilia. What the votes represented. Plebiscites in Nice and Savoy. Garibaldi's anger. Cavour's defense of his actions. Italian attitude toward Napoleon.

IN THE CONFUSION immediately after the sudden peace of Villafranca, Vittorio Emanuele required several days to form a new ministry, and Cavour had almost a week in which to influence the attitude of many toward the treaty. To the man he had appointed royal commissioner to represent the king at Parma he wrote, "Parma must be annexed to Sardinia. Prepare the oath and act with the utmost energy. I am resigning." He urged the royal commissioner at Modena, Carlo Luigi Farini, to "increase the army," and Farini replied, "If the Duke, relying on conventions about which I know nothing should make any attempt to return, I shall treat him as an enemy of the King and country. . . . I will allow no one to drive me out, though it costs me my life." To which Cavour replied, "The Minister is dead, the friend grasps your hand and applauds the decision you have taken."

Without exception Italian patriots were outraged by the terms of Villafranca and others who had power, besides Cavour and Farini, immediately set about exercising it to prevent the treaty's execution. At Florence the Minister of the Interior, Bettino Ricasoli, on hearing of Villafranca, sat down, wrote his will and, in his own rough expression, "spat upon his life." To a colleague he announced in a phrase what the provisional government's policy now must be: "We must put ourselves at the head of the agitation." In the Romagna, d'Azeglio chose to treat Cavour's order to remove himself and his volunteer troops from the province as an order solely for appearance, to soothe Napoleon.

I believed that the King would not have wished to dishonour himself and me, leaving those provinces to anarchy, and I *disobeyed*. Instead of moving my forces to Turin I sent nine thousand men to the frontier of Romagna to defend those who had trusted me against the Swiss Guard of Perugia. I invested all my powers in Colonel di Fallicon, my chief of staff, and I left everyone at his post and the government in absolute control. Thus there was no disorder; and on the fifth day I arrived in Turin to tell the King he could send me before a Court-martial. The King said I had done the best thing possible; and it turns out that the order had been a misunderstanding. In this way time will be given to the Romagnuoli to organize and to act for themselves.[85]

With the king and Cavour prepared to undermine the preliminaries whenever possible, local leaders were inclined to do likewise, particularly after word came down from Turin that Napoleon would not let Austria restore the refugee dukes or legates by force. In the Romagna the people used the time and protection d'Azeglio gave them to elect Conte Leonato Cipriani their governor-general, and he adopted Farini's attitude that he would submit to no one. At Modena, Farini, on receiving his official recall to Turin, resigned his commission as the king's representative and was immediately elected by the Modenesi to be their dictator. At Parma the royal commissioner, on his recall, entrusted the government to a group of patriots who then ruled not in the king's name but "in the name of the people." Cavour and the minister who would succeed him could claim that Sardinia, by recalling its troops and commissioners, had acted to accomplish the aims of the treaty. The fact that the people of the duchies and the Legations refused to do the same was not a failure on Sardinia's part but a judgment on the terms of the treaty.

The new ministry took office on 19 July 1859 with General La Marmora as its president; with Rattazzi, who became its guiding spirit, as Minister of the Interior; and with Giuseppe Dabormida, an honorable, patriotic but cautious gentleman, as its Minister of Foreign Affairs. Cavour retired to his farms at Leri but soon left to visit friends in Switzerland. His purpose was twofold: to give himself a vacation and to give the new ministry a chance to start its work free of his presence. He did not return to Piedmont until the last day of August, and then he again retired to Leri.

The immediate question before the new ministry was the peace treaty which would incorporate the preliminaries and settle the problems they raised, and to this end representatives of France, Austria and Sardinia gathered in Zurich in early August and began meetings. Their efforts, however, were constantly undermined by events in Italy, particularly in Tuscany, and by the absence from Zurich of some of the most important parties. The three powers represented could not create a Confederation of Italian States with the pope as president without the participation of the pope or without the blessing of the other European powers. The Treaty of Zurich, therefore, which the delegates finally signed on 10 November, did little more than confirm the preliminaries and form, in turn, the basis for a congress of European powers which was to meet in Paris in January. Meanwhile, however, the situation in Italy continued to develop in a way that threatened to make an important part of the preliminaries impossible to execute.

In Tuscany, a man with a most unusual personality, particularly among the practical-minded Tuscans, had begun to dominate the provisional government. He was Bettino Ricasoli, the Minister of the Interior, and he was not a great deal more competent than some of his colleagues or even more hard-working. He was, however, more certain than they that the Italian states, including Tuscany, must become one Kingdom of Italy under Vittorio Emanuele, and he was equally certain he understood exactly what Tuscany's role should be in that process. This certainty was re-enforced by his personality and, at a time when many men were full of doubts, gave him an extraordinary power. Unlike Farini, Ricasoli never was elected dictator; he simply dominated first his colleagues and then all of Tuscany by his will.

His spirit was essentially puritan. He lived austerely, judged himself harshly by his own standards and communed directly with his God, for "between me and God no one can enter." His own interior life was not only his greatest pleasure but his greatest concern, and he made summaries of his reading in history and philosophy to help him make his life more principled and worthy; for life was a serious business. Every evening he asked himself: "Have I lied to myself in thought, in action?" And his proudest boast at the end of his political career was that he had never deviated from his principles and his program by so much as a hair. His contemporaries, as they came to know him, often referred to him as "the Iron Baron" and compared him to Oliver Cromwell, seeing in each the same intellectual limitations and moral grandeur, the same sincerity and self-deception, narrowness of understanding and depth of character. Like Cromwell, too, he came to political power suddenly, after his fortieth year and with his ideas and character formed beyond alteration. Men who had to deal with Ricasoli frequently lost their tempers, exasperated beyond bearing by his self-assurance, his autocratic tone and his inflexibility.

Before 1859 he had not played a large part in the government of the duchy, although as an aristocrat and large landowner he might have. But in 1848–49 he had been the only important Tuscan to look to Turin rather than to Rome for a solution to the problems of central Italy, and the ancient distrust of Tuscans for the House of Savoy had attached to him and kept him from power. And for Grand Duke Leopoldo's government he had been both too liberal and too uncompromising. When in 1847 one of the duke's ministers had asked for his views on the duchy's problems, Ricasoli had opened his remarks by stating firmly, "The honest man must speak the truth," and then had lectured the minister at length on the government's shortcomings. His advice was neither followed nor sought again, and although he was one of the moderate liberals who had ousted Guerrazzi in 1849 and had recalled Leopoldo, he was not used thereafter in the grand duke's government. Most of the following ten years he had spent either traveling or in his castle at Brolio, near Siena, where he had occupied himself with his land and his peasants, determined to improve both.

His family was the oldest in Tuscany, the only one to retain the medieval title of barone, and it had controlled, since some time before the eleventh century, the Chianti hills between Siena and Florence. Much of the best Chianti wine is still produced on the Ricasoli estates. Until 1777 the Master of Brolio, as the head of the family was known locally, had ruled his lands as a feudal lord, making and executing his own laws. And although the legal basis for this had passed, much of its paternalistic spirit continued. Ricasoli took a careful interest in his farms and posted bulletins for the peasants: "The Master notifies the peasants that this is the time to put lime on his corn. Lime is a secure protection against the Fox. . . . Anyone who has his corn *foxed* in the coming year, if he has not taken lime, will pay the penalty."

But beside scolding his peasants Ricasoli also tried to educate them, for he believed that much of the backwardness of the Tuscan peasantry sprang from lack of education. He was aware, and unhappily so, that in 1838, the year he had assumed control at Brolio, only about one child in sixty-nine in Tuscany attended school as against one in twelve in Lombardia and the Veneto. So he started schools wherever he could, and his wife and daughter held classes for children and on Sundays he himself tried to teach the adults. Mostly he read them parables from the Bible which he then explained in simple words, teaching his peasants not only about finding the lost sheep or being the careful sower but also about God. For education, he believed, should not only improve a man's farming but also his relation to God. And always as a premise to his thought or act was the certainty that what he believed or wished was right. As he once explained to the peasants, "It is a happy thing to know that my will ought to be your will, since that which I will is to do you good in every way."

The more sophisticated Tuscans were alternately amused and infuriated as Ricasoli carried this premise into his work in the government. Yet at the same time they were awed by the strength it generated. Shortly after the news of Villafranca the provisional government decreed an Assembly to meet in Florence with representatives elected by the people, and Ricasoli as Minister of the Interior ran the elections and also the Assembly. His success in both made him the first man in the government.

He considered organizing a government party to be immoral, no better than winning votes by bribes or threats. But as a believer in education he felt it not only fair on the government's part but its duty to try to "illuminate" the people. In a circular he explained to them that "the government, faithful executor of the will of the country, has left to the press in these difficult times liberty to help, and not to harm, the national cause." By national cause he meant union with Sardinia to form a new Kingdom of Italy, and no one who advocated anything else, not even independence for Tuscany, could publish a pamphlet or even an article in a newspaper. Further, some restrictions on who could vote were either strengthened or weakened to favor the national cause, and a tax on dogs, which was very unpopular with the peasants, was repealed. The result was an Assembly which on 16 August 1859, in the Sala dei Cinquecento of the Palazzo Vecchio, resolved that the Habsburg-Lorraine dynasty had fallen and would not be received back. Four days later, in a second resolution, it asserted "the firm intention of Tuscany to make part of a strong Italian kingdom under the constitutional sceptre of Vittorio Emanuele."

Both resolutions passed unanimously, although three deputies who were opposed to the second stayed away in order not to spoil the unanimity of the vote. Without doubt the deposal of the dynasty represented the will of the leading classes, the townfolk. After 1849 they had increasingly turned against Leopoldo, and they would not consider his son Ferdinando as an alternative, for Ferdinando had fought for the Austrians at Solferino. A majority of the peasants, on the other hand, were probably still loyal to Leopoldo, their "father," but under the election law many of them had not qualified to vote.

Whether the second resolution represented the will of a majority even of just the townfolk is a more difficult question. Many Tuscans felt that joining their duchy to Sardinia was like mixing cream with milk. In their eyes Tuscany was the most cultured and most Italian of all the Italian states, whereas Sardinia was the least. Some, given a free choice, would have preferred independence under a minor prince, provided he was not a Habsburg. Others believed that, as such a solution was the likely fate for the duchy, the Assembly certainly should ask for something that, diplomatically speaking, was more: union with Sardinia. This idea was much discussed at the time, and unquestionably many who voted for Ricasoli's second resolution did so only because they thought it might be useful in bargaining with Napoleon.

Nevertheless the unanimous vote is impressive and evidence of the extent to which the thinking of many Tuscans had changed. In 1848–49 Ricasoli, unable to interest them in union with Sardinia, had been isolated politically. Ten years later with the same program he was able, peacefully, to become virtual dictator of the duchy.

Some of the sources of his power in 1859 are perfectly clear. Within the government and on its edge were a number of able men who had come to share his conviction and were prepared to support him at least until Tuscany's fate was decided. They in turn were supported in each of the duchy's cities by a majority of the nobility and of the lawyers and professors. Often these were organized into active groups, holding meetings, distributing pamphlets and in direct touch with members of the government at Turin as well as with their leaders at Florence. Further, in Florence, the crucial city for controlling Tuscany, the politically minded workers and small shopkeepers had an exceptional leader in a baker named Giuseppe Dolfi. He was a Mazzinian, but following Garibaldi's lead he had joined the *Società Nazionale Italiana* in 1857 and had become convinced that unity and independence under Vittorio Emanuele was the best hope for Tuscany and for Italy. He was humorous, shrewd, eloquent and proud of his people; he was also responsible. He worked closely with Ricasoli and shared the minister's belief that the national cause should be achieved without strife, and in his own fashion and sphere Dolfi, as much as Ricasoli, set the peaceful tone of the Florentine revolution and of Ricasoli's government after Villafranca.

Ricasoli was delighted with the Assembly's work and after it had legalized the provisional government by yet another unanimous vote, he prorogued it and sent a deputation to Turin to offer Tuscany to Vittorio Emanuele. But what seemed so clear, right and inevitable to Ricasoli seemed only highly inopportune to the Sardinian ministers. Napoleon, on being consulted, forbade the king to accept the offer: unity was not to cross the Apennines. The Treaty of Zurich had not yet been signed and Lombardia, with more than a hundred thousand French soldiers in it, had not yet been joined to Sardinia. The king, his ministers argued, could not accept the offer, yet how, as the leader of the Italian cause, could he refuse it? They came to wish the resolution had never been passed and hoped the deputation would leave Turin with the offer unstated. But Ricasoli was adamant, and in the end the king gave the Tuscans an audience, promised to support the wishes of their people before Europe, but said nothing about union. Privately, however, he left no doubt that he longed for it.

His ministers' embarrassment did not end with the departure of the

Tuscans. A few days later a deputation sent by Farini and representing Parma as well as Modena arrived with another offer of union. The Parmigiani had taken the first step toward it in August when they had voted to unite with Modena and had elected Farini their dictator. Now the people of the two duchies were eager to take the next step. But again Napoleon was not ready for it, and Vittorio Emanuele had to refuse.

Neither Farini nor Ricasoli, however, would be stopped in their movements toward union. If Vittorio Emanuele would not accept sovereignty, they could take other steps, such as adopting the Sardinian system of currency, of weights and measures, of customs and postal arrangements. Ricasoli went even further. He simply pretended that Vittorio Emanuele had accepted. He announced that Tuscany and Sardinia were now one state and that Tuscany's act had meant "not vassalage of provinces, but constitution of the nation." He had a Te Deum sung in the church of the Santissima Annunziata, the city was illuminated and a huge transparency of Vittorio Emanuele lit up and surrounded by banners; and at the same time he had the government redeem for the poor all the blankets they had pawned during the summer. Some of his colleagues wondered if the pretense of union was wise or even moral, but the people seemed willing to be deceived and before long Ricasoli himself was deceived. He spoke of union as an "accomplished fact." He put the cross of Savoy on the tricolor banner, put up the arms of Savoy in public places and, after 29 September, headed all public documents "In the Reign of His Majesty . . .", *"Regnando S.M. Vittorio Emanuele."* When the ministry in Turin anxiously warned him that Tuscany might have to take back the grand duke, he replied, "Tell General La Marmora that I have torn his letter into a thousand pieces."

Farini's tactics were more devious, perhaps because his position was more difficult. On the last day of October, Cipriani had resigned as leader of the Romagna, and the Romagnuoli immediately had joined their province to Parma and Modena under Farini as dictator. The new, enlarged state was known as Emilia, and because it included Papal territory it was entangled in the question of the pope's temporal power. Farini hoped to strengthen his position by uniting with Tuscany, but Ricasoli continually refused because he did not want to entangle Tuscany in the Papal question and because, further, he believed that to create a single, large state in central Italy was simply to invite Napoleon to put a prince over it. Tuscany and Emilia, Ricasoli insisted, should pursue courses "identical but distinct."

The Assemblies in both, therefore, in November voted that Prince Eugenio di Carignano, a member of the House of Savoy, accept the post of regent over each of them. Again Napoleon objected and Vittorio Emanuele, although he received the deputations, refused. Nevertheless, though the ritual of offer and refusal was repeated, the situation was changing.

Each month that Tuscany and Emilia sustained itself free and in good order while at the same time inching toward union with Sardinia, the sentiment among the European powers to permit that union grew stronger. This was particularly true in Britain, where a Liberal ministry led by Palmerston and Lord John Russell had come to power. Their policy was "Italy for the Italians," both from sympathy for a people struggling for independence and also from a desire to keep France out of Italy. And they were outspoken in opposing the use of force to restore the dukes. Napoleon was very sensitive to British opinion, and partially as a result of it the Treaty of Zurich, although for the most part repeating the preliminaries of Villafranca, subtly changed the position of the dukes. It did not stipulate their return to their duchies but merely reserved their rights till the future of Italy was settled at a congress.

The Tuscans and Emilians took this as a victory and after 10 November, when the treaty was signed, many who had believed that in the end the dukes would return now began to think that union with Sardinia was a real possibility. The sentiment for it within the former duchies, therefore, also increased.

The greatest threat to it most men realized was disorder. If the people of the Legations began attacking priests or the Tuscans moved to liberate the Perugians, then the Austrians or the French or the two together would cross the Po or the Apennines and occupy the country. The troops would stay for six, seven or more years just as they had after 1848–49, and any possibility of union with Sardinia or even of modified independence under some prince would disappear.

And in October an incident occurred. Conte Luigi Anviti who had been the favorite of Duke Carlo III of Parma and perhaps the most hated man in the former duchy was seen boarding a train going from Bologna to Piacenza, and the fact of his presence was telegraphed ahead to Parma. When the train arrived there, a crowd was waiting. Men swarmed onto the cars, dragged Anviti from his seat and, pulling him out to the platform, tore him to pieces.

The murder created a sensation in Italy and outside it. Depending on men's sentiments, they argued that to prevent anarchy union must be accomplished, and quickly, or that the Austrians or French must occupy the duchies. Fortunately for those in favor of union the great powers admonished but did not act, perhaps because the crowd's anger had been directed at Anviti personally rather than at a class of persons or of property.

A few weeks later another incident, potentially much more dangerous, was averted. Emilia and Tuscany had a Defensive League with a force of about twenty-five thousand men, and second in command of it was Garibaldi. Over him was Manfredo Fanti, a Modenese, who had risen to the rank of general in the Sardinian army. Both men wanted to use their little army to attack the Papal States and liberate the towns of Umbria and the Marches. General Fanti soon saw the dangers in such a program, but Garibaldi did not. He was surrounded by republicans who, taking their lead from Mazzini, who was in hiding in Dolfi's house in Florence, constantly urged him to carry the revolution farther, to Perugia, to Ancona and even to Rome. From Florence, Mazzini warned that "the revolution that stops in one place is lost," and Garibaldi actually started his advance. Farini and Fanti, however, with the aid of Vittorio Emanuele, stopped him. The king sent for him and presumably succeeded in convincing him that the drive for unity could not go further against Napoleon's wishes, not while the French army was still in Lombardia, the Austrian in the Veneto, and the fate of Emilia and Tuscany still undecided.

Immediately after the interview Garibaldi gave up his command and retired to his home on Caprera. On the way he published a manifesto praising the king and promising to serve him when the right moment came but scorning "the miserable, vulpine policy" of his ministers. When Mazzini, whom Ricasoli had expelled from Tuscany, heard of Garibaldi's surrender, he wrote, "The man is weak beyond expression; and the King, by subscribing himself 'your friend' or patting his shoulder, will do anything with him." In this instance, however, most patriots were thankful.

Though the invasion of the Papal States had been stopped before it crossed the border, the fact of it emphasized to Napoleon, to Italians of all States and to others in Europe how precarious was the situation in Italy. The Treaty of Zurich had just been signed and yet the Papal border still was undefined and the political future of some seven million Italians still was uncertain. Plainly, too, if Vittorio Emanuele was prevented much longer from pursuing the national cause of independence and unity, the provisional allegiance of the republicans, which Cavour and the *Società Nazionale Italiana* had won for the king, was likely to be withdrawn. The treaty on its face was no more than a step toward an Italian settlement which still had to be negotiated, and on 21 November formal notes, issued by the ministries in Paris and Vienna, invited all the interested powers to a congress which was to meet in Paris on 19 January. Its purpose would be to learn of the decisions embodied in the Treaty of Zurich and "to take into consideration the pacification of Central Italy."

Napoleon, however, was already in doubt about what a congress might accomplish. His agents reported to him that they could discover no sentiment in either Emilia or Tuscany for a return of the dukes or an accession of a Napoleonic prince, and his plan for a Confederation of Italian States pleased only the pope and the Austrians. And what he wanted most for himself out of his Italian war, the provinces of Nice and Savoy, a congress seemed unlikely to give him. Extending the French frontier from the foot of the Alps into the midst of the range would add eight hundred thousand persons to France, strengthen its defenses greatly and confer the most permanent kind of glory on his dynasty. But Britain, always suspicious of Napoleonic ambitions, would never support the transfer of the provinces and would use a congress as a forum to oppose it. And Sardinia, which had the provinces to cede and which had been promised northern Italy "from the Alps to the Adriatic" in return for them, would never let them go for less.

Even before the Treaty of Zurich had been signed, therefore, he had begun to think of other ways to achieve what he wanted and, impressed by the firmness of Ricasoli and Farini, had considered uniting Tuscany and Emilia to Sardinia in return for Nice and Savoy. But it was not an idea he could pursue at a congress. It required him to break his word to Austria to restore the dukes and to create an Italian confederation, and it required him, somehow, in order to release the Romagna, to untie the knot of the pope's temporal power. And further, when he gave the barest hint of the idea to the British, through diplomatic channels, he was rebuffed. Palmerston replied that to filch Savoy from Sardinia was to lower the purpose of the war from generosity to self-seeking.

Nor was a hint of the plan much better received by the king and his ministers at Turin, for they still thought in terms of a kingdom of northern Italy "from the Alps to the Adriatic," one which would include the Veneto. They did not grasp the changes in the political situation in Italy or Europe as quickly as Napoleon, who was causing most of them, and they lacked the ability, so strong in Cavour, constantly to provide the emperor with alternatives and half-solutions which might lead to something advantageous. The ministers, too, even if not the king, lacked the political strength to face the Italian people with a program to give up Nice and Savoy. Cavour was needed, and both from abroad and at home the pressure on the king to recall him increased.

Napoleon, meanwhile, continued to prepare for the congress while privately pursuing his other plan which, after Britain's rebuff, he felt could be accomplished best without Britain's knowledge, by a secret treaty with Sardinia rather than through the congress. As a first step toward it, and as if preparing for the congress, he proposed that the British Foreign Office ask Austria to abandon the return of the dukes, because of changed circumstances since the days of Villafranca, and to acquiesce in the union of Emilia and Tuscany to Sardinia. This proposal, without any mention of Nice and Savoy, had the backing, as far as Austria could see, of France, Britain and, of course, of Sardinia. And on 8 December Count Rechberg, who had succeeded Buol as Franz Josef's Foreign Minister, agreed to it with the proviso that the powers put an end to Sardinia's intrigues in Italy.

Such an answer, if it had come from a strong state, might have meant nothing at all, but the war, although apparently inconclusive, had been a genuine defeat for Franz Josef. His autocracy had proved unsuccessful in Italy, and its defeat there had shaken it severely at home. After Solferino the discontent in his empire began to rise ominously. The Hungarians, as always, wanted a special position in the empire; the middle class wanted some voice in its rule, and, as a result of the war, its treasury was almost empty and its position in the German Confederation about to be challenged by Prussia. In the next ten years Franz Josef would need all his skill and attention to bolster himself at home, and Napoleon and the British ministers already suspected that this would be so. They did not discount Austria as a power in Italy, for it still held all the Veneto, including the Quadrilateral forts, and if Napoleon withdrew, then unquestionably Franz Josef would advance again into central Italy, installing Habsburg archdukes and garrisoning Papal towns. But they began to behave as if they accepted Rechberg's answer as true, treating Austria's pronouncements on the Italian situation as bluff and bluster designed to give Franz Josef the appearance of honoring his commitments to the dukes and to the pope even as he withdrew from them.

This diplomatic exchange succeeded for Napoleon's purpose in loosening Austria's claims to Emilia and Tuscany, and two weeks later he proceeded with a plan to loosen the Papal claim to the Romagna. On 22 December at Paris appeared a pamphlet entitled *Le Pape et le Congrès*, "The Pope and the Congress," which proposed a new policy for the pope with regard to his temporal power. The author remained anonymous but professed to be a "sincere Catholic."

He began by asserting unequivocally that the pope should have temporal power. Both Catholic doctrine and political reason required it, for otherwise "he would be French, Austrian, Spanish or Italian, and the title of his nationality would deprive him of the character of his universal office." But he ended by arguing that, as the spiritual and temporal power often came into conflict, the spiritual power could be served best if the temporal power was reduced to a minimum, such as the city of Rome or, at most, the city and the area surrounding it which was known as "The Patrimony of St. Peter." The congress which was soon to convene, the sincere Catholic concluded, if only it would adopt such a plan, could bring peace to Italy and, at the same time, strength to the Papacy.

The pamphlet, which of course enraged the Papacy's supporters, was only one of several to appear in December, and its central idea was neither original nor unusual. D'Azeglio, for example, a few days earlier had published a pamphlet, also in Paris, entitled *La Politique et le droit chré-tien,* in which he reviewed the origin and history of the temporal power and asked, "If instead of having to fight against three million subjects who reject him as their temporal prince, the August head of the Church reigned in majestic calm in a Rome become a free city, what other guarantee would one need to find for the independence of the Spiritual power?" But even though d'Azeglio's pamphlet was the first to appear and was widely read, the other, *Le Pape et le Congrès,* caused the greater stir, for everyone in Europe, except for Pio Nono and the Church at Rome, at once assumed from the style, and correctly, that Napoleon himself was the author of it or, at least, its spiritual father.

The failure of the pope, Antonelli and others in the Curia at once to penetrate the authorship of the pamphlet, as did everyone else in Rome, was evidence of how little they understood the realities of their position in Italy, or in Europe. Pio Nono, for example, in accepting the invitation to the congress, to which he had been asked as a temporal prince, had claimed that his envoy should take precedence over all others, and the claim had been rejected on the ground that his position as a spiritual leader in Europe did not entitle him, as a very minor temporal prince, to any extraor-dinary precedence. And when Napoleon, in the months after Solferino, kept urging the pope to reform his government along the lines recom-mended to him and his predecessor in 1849 and 1831, Pio Nono and Antonelli always refused to act until after the Legations had been returned to them; although in irritating Napoleon they were alienating the man most able to help them. And now Pio Nono, after pronouncing the pamphlet "a monument of hypocrisy," assured the French general in command at Rome that Napoleon would condemn the principles the pamphlet set forth.

The failure of the Papacy for more than a hundred years to imagine any solution either to the problems of its States, or to the problem of its dependence on foreign powers to police them, seemed to have resulted, finally, in an inability even to understand what was happening. Pio Nono and the hierarchy in Rome were dumbfounded when, barely three weeks after the pamphlet had appeared, Napoleon wrote directly to him stating that, in his opinion, the best solution to the Italian problem was for the pope to give up the Legations. "If the Holy Father, for the peace of Europe, will renounce his claim to these provinces, which for fifty years have embarrassed his government, and, in exchange, demand from the Powers a guarantee for the remainder, I do not doubt the immediate return of order." Summaries of the letter, presumably released by Napoleon, appeared in Italian papers within three days after the pope received it.

Pio Nono, feeling betrayed and insulted, immediately announced that he would not send a representative to the congress. And Franz Josef, dissatisfied by Napoleon's reply to his demand that France at the congress would neither propose nor support the opinions of the pamphlet, also withdrew, so that in a circular to the powers on 3 January 1860 Napoleon announced that the congress was indefinitely postponed.

"So much the better," exclaimed Ricasoli and also every other Italian patriot, for none wished to trust the national cause to a congress. But Napoleon, too, though he lamented publicly, privately was delighted, for the indefinite postponement left him free to pursue his goal of a separate treaty with Sardinia for the cession of Nice and Savoy. And further, Austria's withdrawal from the congress seemed more evidence that although Franz Josef would protest a settlement in central Italy which did not restore the dukes or which deprived the pope of the Romagna, he would do nothing to upset it, and the reception of the pamphlet in France had indicated that, in spite of the many furious replies written to it by clerics, most laymen cared little about the Pope's temporal power, or at least not in its extensions beyond the bounds of Rome. The prospect, therefore, of a separate treaty permitting Emilia and Tuscany to unite with Sardinia, for a price of Nice and Savoy, seemed to improve steadily, and on the day after Napoleon had announced the postponement of the congress he improved it further by retiring Walewski as his Foreign Minister and substituting Edouard Thouvenel, who was known to be more anticlerical and anti-Austrian. The change was interpreted by most Europeans as a step on Napoleon's part toward Britain's policy of "Italy for the Italians," and the Italian patriots, in particular, were pleased. Cavour, in discussing the significance of the emperor's actions, wrote to a Swiss friend, "As to Italy, I am convinced that the restorations will not take place, the Temporal Power of the Pope is destroyed, and that in a very short time the principle of unity will triumph from the Alps to Sicily."

The substitution of "Sicily" for "the Adriatic" was neither a slip on Cavour's part nor a thought unique to him. Many north Italians who had never done so before were beginning to think seriously of unifying the entire peninsula. The Veneto, for the moment, was lost, but if Tuscany were gained and unity crossed the Apennines, then, as Napoleon had observed, it might continue on to Naples and Sicily. This had always been Mazzini's goal, but as long as the Papal States had cut across the peninsula, separating north from south, the majority of patriots had thought it an idle dream. But now, for the first time in hundreds of years, the leading Catholic power instead of supporting the Pope's temporal power was opposing it and was talking of a Papal States shrunk to "Rome surrounded by a garden": the girdle which for years had kept the north and south of Italy apart at last might be removed. The pamphlet and Napoleon's letter were as great a victory for the Italian national cause as the defeat of the Austrians at

Magenta and Solferino, and in a way this victory was even more striking for it caused a more dramatic change in Italian thinking and, ultimately, in the country's future.

Soon after Napoleon postponed the congress and changed his Foreign Minister, La Marmora's ministry at Turin resigned and the king summoned Cavour. Their interview, the first of any length since their bitter debate in July, was stiff but satisfactory, and on 21 January 1860 Cavour resumed office, keeping for himself the ministries of Foreign Affairs, Marine, and Interior and filling the balance of them with relatively undistinguished men. "You know our policy," he wrote to d'Azeglio on the day he took office, "liberal conservatives at home; *italianissimi* to the extreme limits of possibility abroad." And with a sympathetic government in Britain as well as in France these were greater than ever before.

His recall was a source of great joy to Italian patriots and in many towns they celebrated by illuminating the town halls and having an evening *festa*. Some republicans, however, among them Garibaldi, who had intrigued against his return, were disappointed, and La Marmora and Dabormida, both of whom considered themselves his supporters, felt that he held at too low a value their efforts to carry on his policies. They acknowledged his greatness and confessed that he had not intrigued to return to office, yet both had been wounded by his manner toward them. Though his popularity soared with those who did not know him, he continued for most of those with whom he worked to be a difficult, strange person, *un uomo antipatico*.

The immediate job before him was the union of Emilia and Tuscany to Sardinia and the cession of Nice and Savoy to France. Both he and Vittorio Emanuele, independently, seemed to have become convinced that one could not be achieved without the other. As early as 17 January, four days before Cavour took office, Garibaldi had sent an officer to Vittorio Emanuele to ask if Nice, as rumored, was to be ceded to France. The king was to "answer me at once by telegraph Yes or No!" Vittorio Emanuele, after he had recovered from the peremptory tone of the request, had replied, "Very well, Yes! but tell the General that not only Nice but Savoy as well! And that if I can reconcile myself to lose the cradle of my family and my race, he can do the same." The king's firmness on this point was to be a source of strength to Cavour in the coming months as Napoleon continued to maneuver to gain Nice and Savoy without letting unity cross the Apennines to Tuscany.

In his first week in office Cavour set forth in a diplomatic circular his program for northern and central Italy. Without any equivocation he recommended: No restorations in any of the States, union of them all with Sardinia, and union to be carried out by the Italians. It was a stronger program and more firmly stated than any put forward by La Marmora's ministry, and soon it was seconded indirectly by a French dispatch to the Austrian Foreign Minister in which Napoleon, citing the failure of the powers to convene in a congress to consider the terms of Villafranca, politely informed Franz Josef that he would no longer be bound by them. Cavour's principles were supported further when Britain put forward a four-point program similar to his but requiring the various Italian states to elect new assemblies to vote on the question of union. Napoleon then took up the British program, accepting its general principles but suggesting the votes should be by plebiscites rather than by assemblies. Cavour and the British agreed to the change. No one doubted how the assemblies or the people would vote.

While these proposals went back and forth the rumors that Nice and Savoy would be ceded to France constantly increased, particularly after a French journal, plainly with Napoleon's approval, published articles on the claims of France to the provinces. British envoys in Paris and Turin promptly demanded to know the truth of the rumors, and although in fact there was no treaty the possibility of one inclined the ministers in both cities to qualify their denials. Cavour, for example, ended his reply by adding, "the question of Savoy is in the hands of the good sense and feelings of the Savoyard people." Evidently he already had in mind the possibility of justifying the loss of Nice and Savoy by the same act of testing the people's will, a plebiscite, which might gain him Emilia and Tuscany. Britain's suspicions, understandably, were not lulled, and its ministers and envoys kept a steady pressure on Napoleon and Cavour to prevent any such cession.

But even now the diplomatic maneuverings were not at an end, for Napoleon, in an effort to get more for France while keeping the states in Italy small and divided, suddenly in February put forward a new proposal: Of Emilia, only Parma and Modena were to unite with Sardinia, while the Romagna was to remain a Papal State but be ruled by Vittorio Emanuele as the pope's vicar; Tuscany was to be an independent state under some prince; and Nice and Savoy were to pass to France. The heart of the program was the proposal for Tuscany, for no one believed that either the pope, Vittorio Emanuele or the Romagnuoli would accept the solution proposed for the Romagna. But if Tuscany could be kept separate, even if the prince were of the House of Savoy, then Vittorio Emanuele would be confined to the Po Valley, north of the Apennines; and if the prince were French, then France would be strengthened and pleased, and if a Habsburg, then Austria.

As the club with which to beat Cavour and Vittorio Emanuele into accepting the proposal Napoleon accompanied it with the threat that if it were not accepted, he would order the French army out of Lombardia and leave Sardinia alone to face Austria. In short, by declaring Italy free of French interest he would invite Austria to retake it, which in spite of Austria's internal weaknesses it certainly would do, for its Italian provinces had been its richest. Nor was that all of the threat: for as Nice and Savoy were to pass to France, the French troops on their return from Lombardia could occupy the two provinces.

Cavour first heard of this new proposal while he was in Milan with the king to celebrate the union of Lombardia to Sardinia. Thouvenel, the French Foreign Minister, had shown it in draft to the Sardinian and British ambassadors in Paris, and each had reported it to his government. Cavour's inclination was to reject it, even at the cost of a renewed war with Austria, for which he immediately ordered his ministers to prepare. To Ricasoli he wired, "the moment for energetic decisions approaches, but not yet arrived; count upon my devotion and, if necessary, even audacity." He had no doubts that Ricasoli would stand firm against any offers or threats Napoleon might make directly to the provisional government at Florence, but he was concerned that the British government, tired of the unending international crisis caused by Italian affairs, might decide to back the proposal, or some part of it, and join France and Austria in imposing a settlement on Italy.

Cavour's appointment with the French ambassador in Turin in which, he knew, the proposal would be put to him formally, as an ultimatum, was scheduled for the afternoon of 28 February. As the day began, he still had no knowledge of Britain's position, but during the morning Sir James Hudson, the British ambassador, asked for an audience and reported that Britain disapproved of every part of the French proposals as they were "subversive of the independence of Italy." During the afternoon, therefore, Cavour was able to listen calmly to the French ambassador, to suggest that the Tuscans and Emilians vote on their future in the French manner, by plebiscites, and then, after arguing politely for a few minutes, to astonish the man with a copy of the British dispatch. And the ambassador, faced with a situation very different from what he had expected, was forced to withdraw to ask his government for further instructions.

Britain's emphatic position, perhaps its greatest contribution to the Risorgimento, ended any further discussion of the proposal, and before Napoleon could put forward yet another, Cavour, Farini and Ricasoli, as if trying to follow his wishes, arranged for plebiscites in Emilia and Tuscany. When the French Foreign Minister protested to Cavour and asked for a delay in order to make another proposal, Cavour replied that Ricasoli and Farini had gone too far with proclamations to be stopped. And when the French agents at Florence officially warned Ricasoli that Napoleon disapproved of the haste and would not be bound by the vote, Ricasoli observed that the Tuscans, after waiting for ten months, were now going to act for themselves. Out of respect for the emperor they were going to have a plebiscite based on universal, manhood suffrage. The voting would be held on 11 and 12 March, and the results would be announced in the Piazza della Signoria at midnight on 15 March. Thus instructed, the agent withdrew to make his report to Paris.

The Tuscan patriots had never liked the idea of appealing to a vote of their whole people, and from the moment Cavour had put forward the idea, Ricasoli had been against it. He considered it a humiliation for Tuscany, which had already voted by its Assembly to unite with Sardinia, to be forced to do it again, and he was also unhappy at the prospect of peasants voting in any large numbers.

The Tuscan peasants, in general, were simpler people than their counterparts to the north, in the Po valley. They were less literate, less politically minded and more inclined to be led by their priests. Many still turned the soil with the plows of Vergil's time and threshed their corn with the hand flails of their Etruscan forebears. In the remoter districts they still believed in the evil eye, and when they thought they had found a witch, they would bake the old granny in an oven. Nationality and national independence were strange ideas to men who had never been outside their valley or off their hill, and even democracy, the right to cast a ballot in an urn, had little meaning. In 1799 the peasants of southern Tuscany had fought for the Virgin Mary against the French, and in 1849 they had rallied to Leopoldo, their *Babbo,* who was being mistreated by the townfolk.

For months the patriots had been trying to give the peasants the same enthusiasm for Italy and Italian independence which so stirred the people of the towns, but no one was sure how well the job had been done. Ricasoli and the patriots were not afraid of losing the vote. The question to be submitted to the people had been phrased in such a way that the grand duke was not a direct alternative: Do you prefer union with the constitutional monarchy of Sardinia, or a separate kingdom? But they did fear that peasant abstentions in large numbers or demonstrations for Leopoldo might disgrace the national cause by making it appear partial and partisan.

In the ten days before the voting, patriotic propaganda swelled to its climax. The local committees printed thousands of pamphlets and dedicated members rode out into the countryside to distribute them. Great ladies in Florence wrote directly to their peasants urging a vote for union; sample ballots, correctly marked, were distributed, and the press, every morning, poured forth exhortations for a heavy vote. As always with Ricasoli he attempted, in his fashion, to keep the plebiscite free and fair.

He appointed judges to oversee the voting, and he restored freedom of the press, though only six days before the vote. And in an official proclamation he reminded voters that they were under no restraints, responsible only to themselves and to God, though he ended by congratulating them on becoming, in a few days, Italians under Vittorio Emanuele.

He wanted no riots or even noisy demonstrations on the voting days: "It is not with the importunate cry nor with plebeian shouting that Italians are made. Nations are made by firm will, by discipline and by sacrifice." In this spirit the Tuscans were to join themselves to Sardinia to make Italy, and to insure it he gave instructions for the manner in which they were to vote:

> The bailiffs at the head of their own administrations, the most influential peasant proprietor at the head of the men of his parish, the most authoritative citizen at the head of the inhabitants of one street, one quarter, etc. . . . will order and lead his voters in a troop, in a file more or less numerous, but always disciplined and marching in good order, to the urns of the Nation. The Italian flag will be at the head. Each one will lay in the urn his paper, and then retire, and at a fixed point the troop will be dissolved with that quiet and dignity, which comes from the consciousness of having performed a high duty.[86]

On 11 March the voting began and continued through the next day. Of the 534,000 voters who had registered, 386,445 declared for union, and 14,925 for a separate kingdom. About five thousand ballots were declared void. And throughout the two-day period only one incident occurred to mar the perfect order which Ricasoli so earnestly desired. In the Chianti, some of his own peasants had tried to upset the urns.

In Emilia, as expected, the vote was even more one-sided. Of 526,258 voters registered, 426,006 had declared for union, and only 756 for separation. About 750 ballots were ruled void.

In each state the percentage of those eligible to vote who had done so was high and the majorities for union, overwhelming. In Emilia, composed of the Duchies of Parma and Modena and of the province of the Romagna, the vote unquestionably represented the will of all classes. The people of the Po valley, by 1860, felt themselves to be culturally one people, and they understood and desired the advantages of being one in their political and economic organization. Although many, perhaps, would have preferred to be organized as a republic, the great majority, in order to achieve unity, were prepared to accept and even to work actively for Vittorio Emanuele.

But just what the Tuscan vote represented has been disputed. It is clear from the arguments used by the Tuscan patriots in 1860 that their drive for unity was largely idealistic and cultural. Unlike their counterparts in the Po valley very few of them thought in economic terms: of the benefits to Tuscany of a larger market area or of new industrial enterprises backed by northern wealth. Such thoughts for most came as satisfactions after union. Equally clearly, the drive for unity was strongest in the towns, and the vote represented the majority will of all classes of townfolk, who by themselves probably formed a majority of the duchy. But what of the peasants? In Tuscany, for the first time on a large scale, the patriots attempted to implant feelings of nationality and democracy among peasants who knew or cared little about either. Some historians, pointing to the size and unanimity of the vote, have argued that the effort was successful; and others, that it was essentially fraudulent, that the upper and middle class used the peasant to further their drive for unity and independence without attempting to improve the peasant's lot. Some argue that the peasants weve given their first experience of democracy in being given a vote; others, that they were deprived of it by being marched to the urns. The argument continues, and it began at once. Only months after the plebiscite F. Dall'Ongara published a short biography of Ricasoli in which he spoke of the vote as a "spontaneous lyric song" of the Tuscans: "the spontaneous outburst of a need long suppressed, the manifestation of a latent principle sown by the words of patriots and confirmed by the exiles, the sufferings and the blood of the most generous." Opposite this passage Ricasoli noted in the margin of his copy, "Ricasoli believes it possible to doubt this assertion as too absolute." But "too absolute" by how much remains the question.

After the plebiscites Cavour, Farini and Ricasoli continued to push ahead toward union with elections, in accordance with the Sardinian *Statuto,* for the new Sardinian Parliament which would meet on 2 April. For the first time representatives from Tuscany, Parma, Modena, Lombardia and the Romagna would sit with those of Sardinia and legislate for a kingdom in Italy which in energy, population and wealth would dominate the rest of the peninsula.

The price for it, however, was Nice and Savoy, and Napoleon, unable to delay the plebiscites, now hurried to collect his fee. On 1 March he had told the French legislative bodies that "the transformation of northern Italy" required him "to reclaim the French slopes of the mountains," and although he insisted he did not intend to realize the claim by force, the speech created a sensation in Europe. The British, in particular, became anxious, although as Lord Clarendon observed, the British were "taking to ourselves credit for the arrangements agreeable to the Italians without our having made the smallest sacrifice or even being prepared to share with the Emperor the slightest responsibility." The general feeling, however, was of outrage and there was much talk, both in and out of Parliament, of French "aggression" and of the need to look for "other allies."

But this time Napoleon was not to be deterred. He demanded and on 12 March obtained Cavour's signature to a secret treaty ceding Nice and Savoy, and then, still not satisfied, he demanded and obtained it on 24 March to another which could be made public. In both instances Cavour had insisted that the transfer would be made only if the people of the two provinces voted for it and if the Sardinian Parliament approved it. But when Napoleon published the treaty the next day, he omitted any reference to the plebiscites, probably because he wanted the French people to believe that the provinces came to France as a result of his power rather than through a vote of their people.

On 2 April the king opened the Parliament with a joint session of the Senate and Chamber in the Palazzo Madama. He read a stirring address in which he thanked France for its generous aid, regretted the need to sacrifice Nice and Savoy and promised, though firm in his devotion to the Catholic religion and to the pope, to maintain every liberty for his people. At the reference to the pope the Assembly rose and applauded for several minutes, less because the words were moving than as a rebuke to Pio Nono who, three days earlier, had excommunicated all the leaders, including the king and Cavour, who had worked to unite the Romagna to Sardinia. To most of the men present the pope's action was a deliberate attempt to confuse his spiritual and temporal powers in order to advance an interest which was purely temporal.

Four days later Garibaldi, who had been elected a deputy both for Nice and Milan but who had chosen to sit for Nice in its moment of "danger," appeared in the Chamber and rose to interrogate the ministry about its cession. He was furious at the prospect of being "made a foreigner" in "Nizza," the town of his birth, and his anger was double because it was being sold "like a rag" to Napoleon, the "man of 2 December," who in France had betrayed the republican revolution of 1848 and in Italy had destroyed the Roman Republic of 1849. He blamed Cavour personally for it and he was encouraged in this by a group of republicans who hoped to use the issue, and Garibaldi, to force Cavour from office. So as he rose to speak, the other deputies stirred with excitement.

Cavour, however, was able to avoid a debate by pointing out that the officials and committees of the Chamber had not yet been appointed and that, until they were, any questions on any subjects were not only out of order but violated the constitution. Cavour was right, and although Garibaldi appealed the point, he was overruled and forced to postpone his questions for another week.

Cavour was most anxious, if possible, to hold off any debate on either

the need or constitutionality of the treaty of cession until after the plebiscites in the two provinces had been held, for he expected them to
strengthen his case by revealing in each an overwhelming majority for
union with France. But on 12 April Garibaldi was able to start again, and
in a short and restrained speech he questioned the constitutionality of the
treaty and asked that, until the Chamber had approved it, the plebiscites,
which were scheduled for 15 and 22 April, be postponed.

His argument was direct and had the virtue of being divisible: the
plebiscites could be postponed whether or not the deputies wished, at this
moment, to debate the constitutionality of the treaty. Cavour met it partly
by reason and partly by a display of political power. He replied that the
treaty was not an isolated fact but a step in the unification of Italy and that
the need for it could be debated better when more of the steps had been
completed. All he would say now was that he believed the cession to be
necessary and not unconstitutional. And although several speakers tried to
start a debate on the treaty, a majority of the Chamber supported Cavour.
The debate was postponed, and the plebiscites left as scheduled.

Three days later the people of Nice went to the polls, and of 30,486
who had registered 25,933 voted, 25,743 for annexation to France and
160 against it; 30 ballots were defective. A week later in the much larger
province of Savoy where the total registration was 135,449, 130,839 voted
of which 130,533 declared for annexation to France, 235 against it, and
71 cast defective ballots.

In Savoy, as in Emilia, the vote unquestionably represented the will of
all classes. The Savoyards by culture and geography were French. In the
Sardinian Parliament they had insisted usually on debating in French, as
the *Statuto* guaranteed them the right; they had protested every step of
the kingdom's expansion into Italy and, as the most extreme Catholics in
the kingdom, had opposed the liberal reforms which had brought it into
conflict with the Church. Chambéry, the capital of Savoy, was closer in
time by train to Paris than to Turin, and all the migrant workers of the
province went down the slopes into France rather than across the range
into Italy. For Italian monarchists the province had a strong emotional
appeal as the seat of the House of Savoy, but as long as Vittorio Emanuele
was prepared to let it go, no one else was inclined to make a cause of it.

Nice was different. The Nizzardi were as much Italian as French or,
more accurately, were Ligurians, a seacoast people who, more than a
thousand years before, had spread themselves along the coast between
Marseille and Genoa. Living by trade on the sea they had penetrated only
slightly into the mountains, and the fact that the Alps rose higher between
Nizza and Genoa than between it and Marseille meant very little to the
Nizzardi; by sea Genoa was close and the nearest large port. On the other

hand most of the Nizzardi had traded as much with French as Italian ports and perhaps more spoke French as a second language after their Ligurian dialect than spoke Italian. The House of Savoy had acquired the province in 1388, but at that time the Counts of Savoy had been neither French nor Italian but Provençal; and, within the memory of many, the province, under the first Napoleon, had been part of France. The only certainty about the plebiscite of 1860 was that its result did not represent truly the division of feeling among the people of Nice. Its conclusion, perhaps, was true, but its unanimity was false. French agents had been in the town before the voting openly urging annexation to France; perhaps secretly they had done more. Garibaldi thought so and because "Nizza" was his birthplace, unlike Vittorio Emanuele and Savoy, he would never let its loss be forgotten by Italians or forgiven to Cavour. His anger, possibly unjustified, put a wound in Italian political life which festered into the next century.

The debate on the cession of the two provinces, when it finally began on 25 May, was relatively tame, partly because Garibaldi by then was in Sicily, but also because by then all the deputies except for some of the most extreme republicans realized that, as Napoleon wanted the provinces, they could not prevent him from having them. Even before the plebiscites he had sent in agents and after them more agents and even soldiers. The provinces had been annexed before the debate began. Nevertheless Cavour had to defend his action in both the Chamber and the Senate, and his speeches, giving the reasons for his action, are basic documents in the history of the Risorgimento.

He did not equivocate. "On me and on my colleagues," he had said, "be all the obloquy of the act!" and he did not now try to shift the blame or to hide behind the king. He explained, speaking in effect to all of Europe, that his policy had always been based on liberty at home and nationality abroad, and he traced the development of it from 1850 up through the Treaty of Zurich and union of Sardinia and Lombardia. Applying the principles to Nice and Savoy he argued that by nationality they were French and by free choice had declared their desire to join France, and if nationality and liberty, the freedom to choose, were to apply to the states of central Italy, they could not be denied to two provinces of Sardinia. He did not minimize the loss but emphasized it by stressing what had been received in return for it, Lombardia, Emilia and Tuscany. The principle of nonintervention by European powers had been established and that of the pope's temporal power been questioned and found wanting. Referring to Napoleon's pamphlet and letter to the pope which had been published he said, "With this letter the Emperor, in my opinion, has acquired a title to the gratitude of the Italians not less than that which he obtained by the battle of Solferino. Because with that letter he put an end to the rule of the priests which is perhaps as harmful to Italy as the predominance of Austria." And finally he analyzed the basis of the emperor's support within France and argued that "to maintain the mass of the French people favorable to Italy, the cession of Nice and Savoy was a necessity." This argument, the deputies realized, looked to the future as well as to the past, for at the time Cavour made it, Garibaldi was fighting in Sicily to add it to Sardinia, and a benevolent France was vital to his effort.

In the end, with only 23 abstentions, the Chamber approved the treaty by a vote of 229 to 33, which was a larger majority than Cavour had expected, and later, in June, the Senate, too, approved it by a similar majority. Yet Cavour came out of the debate weakened, and he never altogether regained his power or, even with the people, his popularity. Nice and Savoy, but particularly Nice, remained a spot on his name. Simpler men, who would have been the first to admit themselves less competent than he, never quite believed that he could not have saved Nice, at least, if only he had tried a little harder or perhaps been a little less devious or a little less clever. They did not question his judgment that the loss of the two provinces was necessary, but the passion with which they condemned Napoleon for taking them was in itself a reproach, and one Cavour always felt.

For many Italians, Napoleon now became the villain of the Risorgimento, and even today Italian historians are apt to slight his services to Italy. Yet without him neither Austrian power nor Papal pretensions to temporal power would have been defeated. But his sudden stop at Villafranca which abandoned the Venetians, his devious and often high-handed diplomacy in the following months and finally his price of Nice and Savoy were sufficiently unattractive to obscure, by exaggeration, his contribution to what was accomplished. By April 1860, as Vittorio Emanuele opened a Sardinian Parliament that included deputies and senators from Tuscany, Parma, Modena, Lombardia and the Romagna, a larger and more viable state had been formed in northern and central Italy than had existed for a thousand years.

# CHAPTER 40

The Sicilian expedition. Mazzini's preparations. His letter of 2 March. The rising on 4 April at the Gancia Convent. Rosolino Pilo. Garibaldi decides to go. Cavour and Vittorio Emanuele. The stop at Talamone. The landing at Marsala. Abba's description of Sicily. Calatafimi. Republican misgivings. The taking of Palermo.

GARIBALDI'S EXPEDITION to Sicily, which led in six months to the unification of all of Italy, except for the Veneto and a province surrounding Rome, was not his work alone but the result of an extraordinary conjunction of all the various strains of Italian patriotism. Mazzini and his followers first had the idea, persuaded Garibaldi to adopt it and prepared the way for him. He, his personal followers and members of La Farina's *Società Nazionale Italiana* made up the greater part of the expeditionary force and insured, at the cost of some republican recruits, that its purpose would be to unite Italy under Vittorio Emanuele; and Cavour and the king, unable either to prevent or to control the expedition, gave it varying amounts of help and hindrance as it progressed. Even the ancient vice of Italian political life, the scorn of one region for another, aided it, for by 1860 Sicilians of every class so hated the Neapolitan army and police which ruled them that, after Garibaldi's first successes, they gave him the kind of general, popular support that no other patriotic expedition to the south had ever achieved. But even though other men and events contributed greatly to the success of the expedition, what Garibaldi contributed was so much greater and so unique that his contemporaries began at once to talk of it as if it were his personal adventure, his personal contribution to the unification of Italy. And historians, though careful to point out the role of others in it, have not talked of it differently. It is an instance in history in which a man, by taking action, made history conform, at least in part, to what he personally wished of it.

Mazzini first proposed a Sicilian expedition to Garibaldi in March 1854, when Garibaldi was in England on his way back from America to Italy. But Garibaldi had refused to consider an expedition, as he continually would refuse later, until the Sicilians were in open revolt. He thought of himself as a soldier, leading troops in the field, as he had done at Rome and in South America, not as a conspirator. And Mazzini thereafter had attempted to produce viable revolts in the south only to fail again and again, most notably with Pisacane's expedition in 1857. Yet in spite of the failures Mazzini continued to hold the threads of conspiracy in Sicily and Naples, and with the start of the war against Austria his followers in Sicily began again to plan a revolt.

This was not hard in Sicily where hatred of the Neapolitans was universal and where the idea of uniting with other Italian states had been gaining strength. In the years since 1848 the leaders of almost every class and political sect had concluded that the lesson of that year, in which nine months after a successful revolt the island had been reconquered by "Bomba," was that for Sicily to remain free after a revolt it must ally itself with some other state, preferably with Sardinia which had an army and a navy. Cavour's followers, of course, encouraged this idea, and Mazzini's were not wholly against it for, although it would make the island part of a constitutional monarchy rather than of a republic, it would be a large step toward the unification of all the Italian states. Accordingly, the Sicilian revolutionaries, feeling stronger and more united than in previous years, planned a revolt for October 1859 and invited Garibaldi, who was then with the Emilian army in central Italy, to come to Sicily and to lead it.

As before, he refused, but with a friendly letter urging them to "unite yourselves to our program—*Italia e Vittorio Emanuele*—indissolubly" and promising, by implication, to come if the revolt should prove successful. But except for a local rising outside of Palermo, which was easily put down, the revolt never took place, for the police got wind of the plot and arrested several of the leaders.

Nevertheless, the Sicilians remained in a state of active conspiracy, and the Mazzinians did not despair of Garibaldi, particularly as he seemed, at the time, to be unable to succeed in anything he undertook. In November he had resigned from the Emilian army, disgusted with the official timidity in Turin which had prevented him from attacking the Papal States, and then, deciding that Cavour's influence on the *Società Nazionale Italiana* was growing too great, he had resigned as its President. Soon thereafter he ostentatiously endorsed the *Liberi Comizi,* a rival society established by the republican orator, Angelo Brofferio, who was campaigning actively to keep Cavour from office, and when that society began to disintegrate, he announced an entirely new one of his own, *La Società della Nazione Armata,* whose stated purpose was to free all of Italy by force, plainly implying war on the Papal States.

But his purpose was too warlike for the diplomatic situation and within a week, at the king's request, he had dissolved the *Nazione Armata* and substituted for it a subscription for the purchase of "a million rifles." What use would be made of them was not stated, but because the fund was administered by a distinguished and conservative board of directors who were allowed to use the royal arsenals to store the rifles as they were purchased, the fund soon had an air about it of "rifles for defense," presumably in case of an attack by Austria. For a second time on the issue of uniting all of Italy, Garibaldi had been forced publicly to back down.

His actions confused and saddened his admirers. In the end few followed him out of the *Società Nazionale Italiana,* and many felt as his friend Giacomo Medici remarked: "Poor Garibaldi . . . he ruins himself in times of inaction; he talks too much, writes too much, and listens too much to those who know nothing." Yet he was not altogether without support for he did voice, however ineptly, a feeling of republicans that the monarchists were holding up the drive for unity and independence of all of Italy in order to be sure of Napoleon's blessing in crowning Vittorio Emanuele king of part of it.

Garibaldi's personal life, too, at this time was equally unhappy, both for his friends and himself. Against their advice he had insisted, in February, on marrying a girl who plainly did not love him. He was fifty-two and sometimes crippled by attacks of arthritis; she was seventeen. At the church door, after the ceremony, a stranger had thrust into his hand a letter which stated that the bride had married him only because her father had forced her to it and that she had spent the previous night in a younger man's arms. Garibaldi as a freethinker cared nothing about the girl's virginity, but the other charges bruised his vanity severely, and when the girl admitted them, he accused her in a violent scene of being a whore and left her forever.

Returning to his farm on Caprera, he brooded on his personal and patriotic disappointments, and when the issue of Nice came to the fore, he threw himself into it with passion. He consulted with deputations of Nizzardi, accepted election as their deputy and tried twice to argue on their behalf in the Chamber. But each time he was defeated by Cavour without being able even to reach the merits of the case, and his feeling that Cavour was the chief obstacle to the making of Italy increased to the point of becoming an obsession. He told the king, "Sire, if you wish, in six weeks you and I can make Italy. Rid yourself of this diplomat, who ties your hands, and then we will go forward." To which the king said nothing, and "That," Garibaldi later admitted to a friend in Genoa, "is what maddens me." And the more he thrashed around, angry and frustrated, the more certain were Mazzini's followers that in the end they would persuade him to lead an expedition to Sicily.

Partly with this expectation in mind, Mazzini, in the first week of March, wrote from London to his followers in Palermo:

> Brothers! it is necessary that I should tell you from time to time the true state of affairs. . . . I confess I no longer recognize in the Sicilians of today the men who flung down the challenge in '48. . . . First of all I repeat to you our declaration of two years ago: *It is no longer a question of Republic or Monarchy; it is a question of National Unity, of existence or non-existence.* . . . If Italy wishes to be a monarchy under the House of Savoy, let it be so. If, at the end, they choose to hail the King and Cavour as liberators or what not, let it be so. What we all will is that Italy shall be made; and if she is to be made, she must be made by her own inspiration and conscience, and not by giving a free hand, as to methods, to Cavour and the King, while we remain inert and wait. Wait for what? In good faith, can you believe that Cavour, the King and L. Napoleon will come to give you liberty? . . . Cavour has only a single aim—to add Venetia to the Monarchy, as was agreed at Plombières. L. Napoleon has only a single aim: to secure Savoy and maintain French supremacy in Italy. . . . Fixed in his single purpose, Cavour does not desire new complications. L. Napoleon fears them. Neither from one nor the other, therefore, can you expect salvation. . . . Garibaldi is bound to aid. . . . For heaven's sake, dare! You will be followed. But dare in the name of National Unity; it is the condition *sine qua non.* Dare: summon to power a little nucleus of energetic men; let their first acts speak of Italy, of the Nation; let them call on the Italians of the Centre and of the North. You will have them.[87]

When the letter was read at a secret meeting of his followers in Palermo, it made a tremendous impression. It followed by only a few weeks secret messages from La Farina, now president of the *Società* and considered Cavour's unofficial spokesman, to the effect that Sardinia, because of the European situation, could not help the Sicilians to free themselves but that if the Sicilians could accomplish this alone, then Sardinia would protect them against reconquest. And now Mazzini, in his letter, not only waived aside the usually divisive question of monarchy or republic, almost allying himself with Cavour, but he as much as promised that Garibaldi, the one man behind whom all Sicilians could unite, would come, if only they would rise. And soon after, the Committee of Palermo, as the revolutionary leaders called themselves, determined on the morning of 4 April for a rising.

The secret was not well kept, and when the morning came, detachments of the Neapolitan army, about twenty thousand strong in Palermo, were patrolling the streets. Nevertheless, about fifty revolutionaries, led by a plumber named Francesco Riso, attempted to rouse the city. Shortly after 5 A.M. they sallied from a warehouse in the old district, shouting *"Viva l'Italia!"* and *"Viva Vittorio Emanuele!"* and began to exchange shots with a patrol. Soon they were forced to retreat into a convent called the Gancia, where they rang the convent bell, first as an alarm, then as an appeal for aid, and in another hour the Neapolitans had brought up a cannon, blown in the convent door and either killed or captured all of them. Elsewhere in the city some aristocrats who had attempted to rouse the people were arrested and marched publicly off to prison. By 8 A.M. the revolution seemed at an end, another of Mazzini's failures.

It was not quite over, however. The committee's plan had called for *squadre,* gangs of peasants from the large towns in the mountains surrounding Palermo, to fight their way into the city, and though all had been defeated outside the city gates, a number of these *squadre* did not disband. Night after night they prowled around the outskirts of the city, moving in and out of the citrus groves on the *Conca d'oro* and shooting at the Neapolitan patrols or sometimes just into the air. Gradually the Neapolitans pushed them back, passed Monreale and Gibilrossa, into the high, hilly plateau of central Sicily. There, after a battle on 18 April, the last of the bands was about to dissolve when a man, Rosolino Pilo, whom everyone thought was in Genoa with Garibaldi, suddenly appeared and announced that "the General" definitely was coming.

Pilo was himself a Sicilian, of noble family, and famous for his part in the revolution of 1848. Thereafter he had gone in exile to England, had become a close friend of Mazzini and one of the important leaders of the revolutionary wing of the republican party. The peasants and their leaders, therefore, were inclined to believe him, and the message spread quickly throughout the island: Garibaldi is coming!

But it was not true. Pilo, who had come out from Genoa only to report on the revolution, was dismayed by its collapse and determined to keep it alive in order to force Garibaldi to come and lead it. The lie, he decided, and probably quite correctly, was the only way to do it. The *squadre* did not disband and Pilo, always insisting that Garibaldi was on his way, led them back toward Palermo.

Meanwhile, at Genoa, Garibaldi in conference with two Sicilians, Francesco Crispi, an agent for Mazzini, and Giuseppe La Masa, who was close to La Farina, went over and over the reports from Palermo and finally decided, to the great distress of the others, that "it would be madness to go." And although volunteers already were arriving in the city and trying to insist that he form them into an expedition, he would not be persuaded. Then on 29 April some messages, possibly invented by Crispi, arrived from the south, all to the same effect. The most important was from Pilo, outside of Palermo: "Tell the General that Sicily is in full revolt; urge him to collect as many young men as he can and for love of his country to come quickly to help these Sicilians who are ready for anything and who lack a great leader to guide them to battle."

Perhaps Garibaldi believed it; perhaps, after the defeats of the winter, he only wanted to believe it. But after reading Pilo's message and another, which confirmed it, from Mazzini's agent in Malta, he said, "Then let us start." If Napoleon was to be paid with Nice for uniting Italy then he, Garibaldi, would see to it that Italy was truly united, all of it: he would not be satisfied with any of Cavour's cautionary half loaves. And the next day, at a council of war with his staff, the decision to go was formally taken.

A week later, on the night of 5/6 May at Quarto, a suburb to the southeast of Genoa, he and some eleven hundred men, with as many old muskets on which even the bayonets did not always fit properly, embarked on two small steamers. Except for the taking of these, which was done that night without notice to the owners, who were later compensated, the preparation and embarkation of the expedition was an open secret. For weeks volunteers had been arriving at the railroad station, and now the flow of them increased; food was purchased, money collected and arms procured, mostly from the *Società Nazionale Italiana*. The men in the expedition, immortalized in Italian history as *I Mille* or "The Thousand," came mostly from the towns of northern Italy. The youngest was a boy not yet twelve, the oldest, a veteran of the campaigns of the first Napoleon; but the average age was young. With only a few exceptions all were civilians and dressed in their ordinary clothes. Bergamo sent the greatest number, 163; then Genoa, 154; and the towns of Parma and Pavia subscribed especially large sums to underwrite the expedition. Garibaldi's purpose, constantly announced, was to unite Italy under Vittorio Emanuele, but the complexion and background of the expedition was largely republican. The great majority of the men were lawyers, doctors, students, barbers, cobblers, tradesmen and artists, men who could read and who, like Garibaldi himself, had been stirred by Mazzini's patriotic idealism.

The place and time of the embarkation supposedly were secret, and the volunteers had been ordered to walk the three miles from Genoa to Quarto singly or in small groups, in the belief that their civilian clothes would keep them inconspicuous. But Genoa, the birthplace of Mazzini and foster home of Garibaldi, was wholly republican, and the road for almost its entire length was lined by the people of the city who stood uncovered and in silence as the men passed. Today at Quarto, at the top of the rocks from which the thousand stepped into the little boats to be rowed out to the steamers, there is a small marble column supporting a star.

Years later, thinking of that night, Garibaldi wrote in his *Memorie,*

"O night of the fifth of May, lit with the fire of a thousand lamps with which the Omnipotent has adorned the void! the Infinite! Beautiful, tranquil, solemn with that solemnity which swells the hearts of generous men when they go forth to free the slave. Such were The Thousand. . . ." Before embarking he had exclaimed to a friend: "At last, I shall find myself in my element—action put at the service of a great idea."

On the second day at sea he issued an Order of the Day and had it read aloud on both ships. Among the more fervent republicans it caused misgivings, for he proclaimed that their purpose was to unite Italy under the House of Savoy and that their cry, therefore, would be *Italia e Vittorio Emanuele*. On each ship the republicans met in groups and, after debating the point, most decided to continue with him. A few, however, planned to abandon the expedition on the first opportunity; for them Italy under a monarchy was not the Italy for which they had striven or were prepared to die.

The extent to which Cavour and Vittorio Emanuele backed the expedition or even looked the other way as it started has become, perhaps, the greatest point of argument in the history of the Risorgimento. Two British historians, for example, although both writing in the 1950s, can reach conclusions almost wholly opposed. In *The Struggle for Mastery in Europe, 1848–1918* A. J. P. Taylor, of Oxford, states, "Cavour did nothing to interfere with Garibaldi," and even writes of Cavour "launching Garibaldi," while D. Mack Smith, of Cambridge, in his article on Italy in *The New Cambridge Modern History, Vol. X, 1830–1870,* states that "Cavour did all he dared to stop him." Taylor's view, although stated in unusually extreme terms, is the older one, and most contemporary historians, with some reservations, now follow Mack Smith. Garibaldi, at the source of the controversy, had no doubts: in his *Memorie* he accuses Cavour of throwing "a net of insidious and miserable opposition over our expedition right to its very end."

The argument is more important than merely a disagreement over how men thought or behaved at a crucial period in the unification of Italy, for the view a historian adopts here is apt to color his view of the largest question of all: whether, in the most extreme terms, the Risorgimento was a success or failure. The older historians such as Trevelyan, Thayer or Croce wrote of it as a great political success: Italy was united and a constitutional government established. But today many historians pronounce that judgment too narrow and conclude that the Risorgimento, although politically a success, was socially and economically a failure: many Tuscans, Romans, Neapolitans and Sicilians did not feel themselves become Italians because of it, did not have their social or economic lot bettered by it and lost with their paternalistic governments, however corrupt, cer-

tain values which parliamentary government did not replace. Those who
incline toward this view are apt, like Garibaldi, to blame Cavour and the
monarchists for the failure, and many of the events to which they point for
support occurred during the Sicilian expedition and its extension, which
carried Garibaldi north of Naples. During those six months, they argue,
many opportunities to make the Risorgimento a social and economic success were not only lost but deliberately ignored, for a social or economic
revolution was not what Cavour, the Piemontesi and other monarchists
wanted.

A difficulty with the argument, however, is that the evidence of what
Cavour did or wanted to do about the expedition is extremely equivocal
and cannot be reduced to a consistent pattern. Much of it occurs in his
letters or statements, and what he wrote or said was influenced by what he
thought the other man wished to read or hear. To his ambassador in Paris,
who talked often with Napoleon, he protested that he was doing all he
could to prevent disorders in the Papal States and The Two Sicilies, and
to his ambassador at Naples he wrote of the possibility of starting a revolution there. He would not order d'Azeglio as governor of Milan to arm
the expedition with rifles from "The Million Rifles Fund," after d'Azeglio
had refused on the ground that it was deceitful to arm an expedition
against a state with which Sardinia was at peace; but he did authorize La
Farina to arm it with rifles from the *Società Nazionale Italiana*. To Garibaldi's fury these turned out to be rusty, smooth-bore muskets, almost
useless, but there is no evidence that Cavour knew this. In April he went
to Genoa personally to discourage Garibaldi from the expedition but was
refused an interview; so he arranged for others more acceptable to the
general to present his views, which, of course, were all cautionary: any
expedition to Nice or against the Papal States, both of which Garibaldi
then was contemplating, would offend Napoleon, and one to Sicily with a
hundred or even a thousand men was certain to be wiped out. A bloody
defeat or, even more, an astounding success would upset all of Europe
just as it was becoming reconciled to the union of Emilia and Tuscany to
Sardinia.

During all this period Cavour, in fact, could do little more than give
his opinion. In all the northern cities Garibaldi's prestige was immense,
and the people daily were growing more excited about an expedition to
the south. Cavour could not have arrested him or even, too obviously,
have impeded him: the repercussions in Parliament, to say nothing of in
the streets of Genoa or Bergamo, would have been terrifying; and worse,
they would have preceded the debates in Parliament on the cession of
Nice and Savoy. So that Cavour's position after all his hesitant steps forward and back seems that of an unwilling spectator. As he wrote to Rica-

soli of the expedition, "whether it prove a blessing or a disaster it was in any case inevitable." The republican ideal of uniting Italy by a rising of the people was too strong a strain in Italian political life to be suppressed at a time that seemed especially favorable to it.

Unlike Cavour, Vittorio Emanuele favored the expedition and in secret ways supported it. Garibaldi, in an interview, had laid all the plans before him and had requested a brigade of the army, and this the king, after consulting Cavour, refused on the ground that it would weaken the army's discipline and the kingdom's defense at a time when war with Austria was still possible. Nevertheless he encouraged one of his officers to join Garibaldi's staff, and he provided the vice-governor of Genoa with funds to pass on to a committee which was helping the volunteers with lodging, clothing and board, and his sympathetic interest encouraged Garibaldi to continue with the expedition while discouraging Cavour from preventing it. The king and Garibaldi felt they understood each other, and Garibaldi considered he had the king's private support which would become public with a successful campaign.

Early in the morning on 7 May, his second day at sea, Garibaldi put the steamers in to Talamone, a lonely Tuscan village with a small harbor, and remained there two days. He wanted to organize and drill his men for the landing in Sicily, which might be opposed, and he also wanted to rest them from the sea, for many, crammed together on the deck and unused to a ship's roll, had been terribly seasick. And here, much to Garibaldi's fury, several of the most uncompromising republicans left the expedition and, in Trevelyan's words, "walked off inland out of the page of history."

But besides the organization and health of his men Garibaldi had two reasons of even greater importance for stopping at Talamone. The expedition was under way with almost no ammunition, for in the darkness on the night of embarkation the ammunition boats had been deserted by their guides and had missed their rendezvous with the steamers. And further, he planned to launch from Tuscany an expedition against the Papal States. This was not to be a diversion; he intended it to be successful, and its object was to free Perugia and the Adriatic side of the Papal States and then to join with him, coming up from the south, in an attack on Rome.

He solved the problem of the ammunition by persuading the colonel in command of a small Sardinian garrison nearby to open the arsenal. Garibaldi wore his uniform of general in the Sardinian army, his aide who also had been a member of the army was displayed and the king's name used, again and again. In the end the colonel gave in, "Since you assure me that the undertaking has started under the auspices of the King," and though he was tried later by a court-martial for his action, he was acquitted.

For the expedition against the Papal States, Garibaldi made up a force of about 230 men, half of whom were Tuscans who had joined him at Talamone. He gave them some of his best rifles, which he could ill afford to lose, and put in command Callimico Zambianchi, a man of dubious ability. Then as Garibaldi re-embarked, Zambianchi started with his men for the border. About two weeks later he led them into the Papal States, and after a skirmish with some Papal troops, he led them out, into Tuscany, where Sardinian troops disarmed them. Most of the men later rejoined Garibaldi in Sicily. It was just the sort of attack on the Papal States which Cavour had tried to prevent. Fortunately for him, though not for Garibaldi, it was so weak and badly led that the Papal army was able to repulse it unaided, without involving or even alerting the French army stationed at Rome.

Garibaldi and The Thousand, meanwhile, now numbering 1089 in all, steamed on to Sicily and on the afternoon of 11 May landed at Marsala, a small port on the western end of the island. By chance, only the day before, a battalion of Neapolitan infantry had left the town to return to Palermo, and the expedition was able to land unopposed. Even so, it escaped annihilation by only a few minutes. Some ships of the Neapolitan navy, patrolling the coast, had sighted the two steamers, and the fastest of the warships reached the port as the men were disembarking. Inside the harbor's mole were five British merchant ships and outside of it two small British men-of-war. For a long time the Neapolitan captain, although expecting Garibaldi, held his fire, and the most probable reason seems to be that, on seeing the British warships, he assumed that Garibaldi's men, about one fifth of whom were in red shirts, were in fact British redcoats beginning a British invasion, a possibility which many Neapolitans at the time considered to be real. While this confusion was being cleared by a boat sent politely over to a British man-of-war to inquire, Garibaldi unloaded his men, five cannon and all his ammunition and hurried them down the long, exposed mole into the town. When the Neapolitan bombardment began, it wounded one man in the shoulder and a stray dog in the leg.

Even before the landing the great powers had begun protesting to Cavour at his government's part in the expedition, and though he denied complicity, none believed him. Garibaldi's cry was *Italia e Vittorio Emanuele,* his flag was the Italian tricolor adorned with the arms of the House of Savoy, and his position in Sicily, by his first proclamation at Marsala, was dictator in the name of Vittorio Emanuele; and the government at Turin neither repudiated nor confirmed the acts. Plainly, it was waiting, with no regard for principles, to see how events turned out. Fortunately for it and Garibaldi, neither Prussia, Austria nor Russia had warships near Sicily, and France and England, because of the cession of Nice and Savoy, were for the moment more nervous about each other than careful for the fate of the Bourbon king at Naples. So for the moment, too, Garibaldi and those in Genoa hoping to forward him men and supplies had only the Neapolitans to face.

The Sicily in which Garibaldi and his men had landed was a strange, exotic land to most northern Italians; few knew anything about it, and fewer still had visited it. To Giuseppe Cesare Abba, one of the writers among The Thousand, it was simply the island where huge almonds grew and which as a boy he had heard described as "a land burning in the midst of the sea."

Although Garibaldi's staff had ransacked the libraries and bookstores of Genoa for a good map of the island, they had failed to find one, and even at Marsala they could obtain maps only of the district around the town. A reason was that most of the island's trade was done by ship, and inland there were almost no roads at all. Between Palermo and Messina, the two most important cities, the only road became, for forty-two miles, a mule track. And from Marsala to Palermo there was only a single road or track that could take wheeled traffic, and as Garibaldi with his thousand men and five cannon planned to strike at once for Palermo, he had only one way to go.

As the men left Marsala, the morning after the landing, they stopped on the height over the town to gaze at the sea stretching off to Africa. Marsala had been a surprise to most of them, for it had a strong Arab influence and its women, supposedly Italian women, were veiled and kept indoors. Then they turned and started inland, marching by companies, with Garibaldi sometimes in the rear, sometimes in the lead, and the men cheering as he galloped back and forth. Later he walked at the head of the column, his red shirt tucked in gray trousers, his hat pulled low over his eyes and a silk neckerchief pulled up on his face against the sun. Behind him came his staff and in the midst of the 7th Company, composed mostly of students from the University of Pavia, the special banner of the expedition, a tricolor on one side of which was embroidered "To Giuseppe Garibaldi, from the Italian residents in Valparaiso, 1855," and on the other a figure of Italy as a woman with broken chains at her feet, standing over a trophy of cannons and rifles, worked in gold and silver.

For a time a noble of Marsala, a barone, followed them astride a donkey, but soon he turned back and then some time after, when they were about fourteen miles from Marsala, the road dwindled to a track winding off between vineyards. It was harder walking for the men and even the ponies pulling the cannon, which had been put in small carts painted with sacred scenes, had difficulty with the rough ground. Accord-

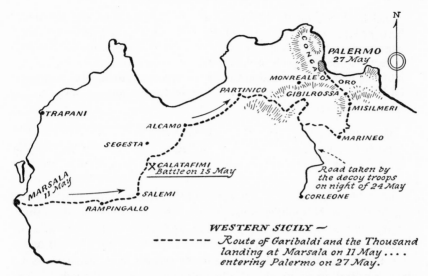

WESTERN SICILY —
------- *Route of Garibaldi and the Thousand*
*landing at Marsala on 11 May . . . .*
*entering Palermo on 27 May.*

ing to Abba, who was keeping a notebook of the expedition, their little
bells tinkled constantly with the effort.

The column had started at four in the morning, and after more than
eight hours of marching Garibaldi stopped the men for lunch beside a
farmhouse with a well. Bixio stood guard to prevent anyone from over-
drinking. Abba jotted in his notebook: "What joy in a bit of shade, what
flavor in the bit of bread they have issued us! And the General, seated at
the foot of an olive tree, himself eats bread and cheese, slicing it with his
own knife and chatting simply with those around. I look at him and have
a feeling of greatness of bygone days."

Later that evening he wrote of the afternoon:

Starting again, after a good hour's rest, we found ourselves going
through a vast, open country. No more vines or olive groves, but occasionally a small field of beans and then no more cultivation. The
sun poured down on us like a liquid as we entered an endless, undu-
lating, barren land where the grass grows and dies as in a cemetery.
And never a trickle of water, a brook, or even on the horizon the
glimpse of a village. "But we are in the Pampas!" exclaimed Pagani
who as a young man had been in South America.

These solitudes, these huge distances where the eye could find no
limit, sometimes were quickened by a shepherd's hut or by a herd of
horses running loose, almost wild in their freedom. On seeing us they
would gallop away, chased by their fear, and sometimes they would
stop, prancing gaily. In the afternoon, by the edge of our track, we
came upon an old shepherd. He was dressed in goat-skins and on his
proud and almost savage head he wore an enormous woolen cap. He

rested his hands on the shoulders of a young boy, who might have been fifteen, and he watched silently as we passed. When my company reached him, he called out to the captain in a loud voice and in dialect: "Raise the revolt in the capital." And he thrust the young boy into our midst. Then he dried his eye, turned his back, and started off into that deserted land. Far, far away on the horizon, we saw a hut which perhaps was his.[88]

That night they stopped in the protection of a feudal castle, the manor of Rampagallo, where about fifty Sicilians led by a local lord offered to join them. There, on a grassy slope, they stacked arms, ate their bread and quickly fell asleep.

On 15 May near Calatafimi, about a third of the way to Palermo, there was a battle. The Neapolitan governor had sent out a detachment of three thousand men with some heavy guns and, as Garibaldi came up, most of them were on a high, bare hill which overlooked the road. The hill had a name, the Pianto dei Romani or Tears of the Romans, because on its slopes, by local tradition, the Carthaginians once had defeated the Romans. It stood some distance from the town, and its slopes now were lined with terraces on which the peasants grew vines and grain or which they had abandoned to cactus and scraggly brush. As the battle developed, Garibaldi's men had to charge up the hill taking each terrace in turn. Their muskets were no match for the Neapolitan rifles, and their ammunition was so scarce that some men, at the beginning of the battle, had only ten bullets. For the Garibaldini, as they were beginning to be called, most of the fighting was with bayonets or bare hands, each terrace being taken with a separate charge and a confused fight of stabbing, fists and grappling. And by early afternoon they had not succeeded in pushing the Neapolitans from the top. They were exhausted, without food and, even more telling, without water. They were city men, students, lawyers and doctors, and unused to such violent physical effort under a noontime, southern sun. As they huddled close to the wall on the highest terrace they had taken, some began to wonder if they could force their bodies onward. Nino Bixio, the second in command and the bravest of the brave, taking everything into account, finally went to Garibaldi and said, "General, I think we should retreat." And Garibaldi turned on him with passion and said: *Qui si fa l'Italia o si muore.* "Here we make Italy—or die."

He was a superb guerrilla leader, a master of feint and retreat and of husbanding his resources, but he recognized that this first battle had to be won, for the morale of his men, for the destruction of that of the Neapolitans and to convince the Sicilians that he could win. About two hundred of these had joined him, following their semifeudal leaders into battle, but many more, Garibaldi knew, were in the hills. He could see them, about eight hundred in all, watching.

He moved to the highest terrace his men controlled and with Bixio and all his staff prepared for the final assault. About three hundred men were gathered there, crouched in the angle of the terrace which protected them from the fire of the Neapolitans above. Some of the men were near hysteria with exhaustion and kept asking, "What shall we do, General? What shall we do?" And he, quite calmly scrambling among them, in a voice which inspired them replied, "Italiani, here we must die."

Then, as he crouched to cross a gap in the terrace wall, a heavy stone thrown by a Neapolitan landed on his back, and suddenly he was shouting, *"Avanti!* Come on! They're throwing stones. They're out of ammunition." And he was clambering up the bank followed by his men. They ran stumbling up the hill, and many were wounded, for not all the Neapolitans were out of ammunition, but still they pressed on for they knew they must close with the enemy to win. When they reached the top the fighting was ferocious, a raging, shrieking madness which no man could remember exactly, and then after a time they had won, and the Neapolitans were running down the backside of the hill. Today, just at the brow of the hill, stands a simple monument and on it only the words: *Qui si fa l'Italia o si muore.*

There was no question of pursuit. Most of the men sank to the ground, among the dead and wounded, and only slowly recovered the strength to move about. Later, in the cool of the evening, from their hilltop they watched the Neapolitans filing back into Calatafimi. The next day the classically minded among them walked three miles out of their way to admire the lonely temple of Segesta, in its setting one of the loveliest of Greek temples.

The battle achieved for Garibaldi all that he had hoped. Though he had lost thirty men killed and about one hundred and fifty seriously wounded, among them Manin's son, he had succeeded in demoralizing the enemy while giving his own men the conviction that, whether they lived or died, they had a place in Italian history. And, most important, he had convinced the Sicilians that he was invincible. The next morning as he followed the retreating Neapolitans and entered the town of Alcamo, the people fell on their knees before him.

The north Italians, with their literate backgrounds, were aghast at the superstition and ignorance of the Sicilians and inclined to feel superior to them. Even Abba, who was generally sympathetic, could complain bluntly, "They don't know anything." But the northerners seem never to have reflected that their surprise at the Sicilians indicated, on their own part, an ignorance of the Italy they were trying to unite. Many of the inland Sicilians had no concept of "Italia"; some thought "la Talia" was a princess married to Garibaldi and that he was the warrior in one of their legends who comes to restore justice.

Garibaldi, more simple than his men, was not ashamed of the Sicilians nor did he feel superior to them. And, again more sophisticated than his men, he took political advantage from the Sicilians' feelings. Most of The Thousand as good republicans had a strong anticlerical bias which Garibaldi shared. But in Sicily, although he later expelled the Jesuits from the island, he saw that the parish priests were as poor as the peasants and more oppressed than oppressing, and on every opportunity he appeared in their churches, partook of their ceremonies and admitted them to his ranks. Doctrinaire republicans were scandalized.

The result was that in Sicily, unlike the north, the uprising that followed Garibaldi's success at Calatafimi and later at Palermo became genuinely popular. Everyone fought, even if only with paving stones or a nail stuck in a board. The Sicilians unquestionably fought not so much for "Italia" as merely to drive out the Neapolitans, their traditional enemies. Many probably fought only out of excitement and for the opportunity to steal a cow from the local Barone. But with their energies harnessed and directed to Garibaldi's purpose, the incredible result was that by 31 May, slightly more than three weeks after The Thousand had embarked at Quarto, Garibaldi had taken Palermo from twenty-four thousand Neapolitan troops supported by their navy.

The capture of Palermo against such odds, like the expedition itself, was an extraordinary conjunction of men and events in which every turn of fortune seemed to favor Garibaldi. In the week after Calatafimi he had arrived in the mountains behind the city but with only seven hundred and fifty of his men in condition to fight and of these, after several days of rain, many were barefoot and with their clothes in rags. In addition he had about three thousand Sicilians, enthusiastic but wholly undisciplined. Even if he doubled the number of Sicilians, which might have been possible, he still could not take the city by siege, and he planned, therefore, to slip into it and then calling on the Palermitani to rise, to drive the Neapolitans out by an insurrection.

Neapolitan patrols, meanwhile, probed into the mountains after him and in a series of engagements succeeded in killing Pilo and a number of Sicilians and forced Garibaldi and his men from the west of the city, from behind Monreale, to the east, to Misilmeri and the pass of Gibilrossa. While making this circuit Garibaldi, hoping to pull the main Neapolitan patrol of four thousand men away from the city, started his entire force south toward Corleone, as if retreating to the interior of the island. After two hours march he left the road with his able-bodied men and crossed the mountains by footpath to Misilmeri, leaving his wounded, his artillery and a small force of Sicilians to continue on as a decoy. He executed the maneuver so perfectly that some Sicilians, seeing him start for Corleone, had believed themselves betrayed, and the patrol, confident that it would soon catch him, chased the decoy halfway across the island before discovering its mistake and, as a result, missed the battle of Palermo. And chance added something more to Garibaldi's skill by including in the patrol the best battalion of the Neapolitan army and at least two men who were probably among its most able and aggressive officers. It is entirely possible that if these officers and their men in place of four thousand others had been in Palermo, Garibaldi would have been defeated.

Late on the evening of 26 May he led his men and about three thousand Sicilians over the pass of Gibilrossa and began to descend by a footpath to the *Conca d'oro,* the plain on which Palermo lies. By midnight, under a strong moon, they were hurrying along one of the main roads from the east through groves of olive, orange and lemon trees.

Within the city the Neapolitan viceroy, Ferdinando Lanza, a frail, deaf old man, had been so certain that Garibaldi was retreating to Corleone that even when he received reports that the general had been seen at Gibilrossa, he had refused to believe them or even to strengthen his outposts. As a result Garibaldi and his men, as they approached the city, were able to push back without much difficulty some Neapolitans stationed at a mill and then more who were at a bridge and to arrive at the eastern edge of the city at the Porta Termini, now the Porta Garibaldi, where they were stopped by a solid barricade of boards and paving stones.

Palermo, on the side from which the Garibaldini approached, was not a walled city with a gate, but the outer ring of houses was built wall to wall and the only way a large body of men could enter the city was through one of the main streets. So the barricade had to be faced.

The Sicilians for the moment lost heart and while Garibaldi tried to encourage them, men of The Thousand tore at the boards and paving stones. Several were hit, for the Neapolitans were able to keep up a cross fire at the barricade from the houses on either side and even a warship was able to fire its cannon across the front of it by aiming up a street that ran straight down to the harbor. Nevertheless just as Garibaldi came up with some of the Sicilians, Bixio and others succeeded in reducing the barricade to a height where they could scramble across it and following Garibaldi who was on a horse and shouting, *"Avanti! Avanti! Entrate nel centro!,"* "On! On! To the centre of the town," they poured into the street behind the barricade and headed for the Fiera Vecchia, now the Piazza Rivoluzione, the tiny market square of Palermo's oldest district and the place from which the revolution of 1848 had spread to the entire city. And to encourage the Sicilians, who were still inclined to hang back, to enter the town and to convince them that not every Neapolitan bullet killed or even wounded, a young Genovese, only seventeen, walked calmly through the Neapolitan cross fire to a spot before the barricade, planted a chair and, holding a tricolor flag over his head, sat down. By 4 A.M. on 27 May Garibaldi and all his men were inside the city and spreading out in small groups from the Fiera Vecchia to rouse the Palermitani.

At first they had little success. The people of the city doubted that Garibaldi was among them; they remembered too well the failure of the other revolts, of Francesco Riso's at the Gancia Convent only seven weeks earlier; and they had been searched so often for arms that they had none, and few men were inclined to venture into the streets unarmed. Yet gradually, as they heard the strange, northern accents or saw Garibaldi himself, they did come out and, to protect the center of the revolt, began to build barricades, and within four hours, partly because of General Lanza's actions, the entire city was committed with passion to the revolt.

Lanza, who had come out from Naples only a few weeks earlier, had announced from the first that if the Palermitani rose against him, he would bombard their city, and shortly after the Garibaldini broke into it and the first Palermitani appeared in the streets, he ordered the bombardment to begin. For several hours the forts within the city as well as the Neapolitan warships in its harbor threw shot and shell into it, while Neapolitan troops in several districts looted, burned and demolished whole sections of houses. A British admiral who was present reported later that "A whole district near the Palazzo Reale, about a thousand yards in length by a hundred yards in width, was a crushed mass of ruins, still smouldering in its ashes. Families had been burnt alive within the buildings and the atrocities committed by some miscreants of the Royal troops were frightful."

Yet for Garibaldi the bombardment was a double blessing for not only had it committed every man, woman and child in the city to his service but while it had continued, the Neapolitan troops had not been active, and he had been able to occupy most of the city, isolating the Neapolitans in their forts or the areas immediately around them. If Lanza had used his troops to isolate Garibaldi in the district around the Fiera Vecchia, while preserving order throughout the rest of the city, he might have been able to starve the Garibaldini into defeat within two days.

As it was, the street-fighting continued for three days, during which improvised barricades of carriages and furniture were replaced by ones of paving stones, and a Committee of Barricades constantly erected new ones so that the center of the city soon was protected by concentric lines of defense at the outer rim of which were the Neapolitan strongholds, the Palazzo Reale, the Mint, the Prison and the Castellamare. More *squadre* from the mountains came down into the city, and all fought bravely although, to the fury of their northern leaders, all the Sicilians were subject to sudden fits of lethargy or despair from which they could hardly be roused even to defend themselves. Then, mysteriously, the mood would pass and they would again be almost childishly eager to prove their heroism in battle. Garibaldi alone seemed never to grow angry with them, and for the simpler among them he became a personal hero to whom they offered gifts, little baskets of fruits or flowers which they left for him around the Piazza Pretoria where he sat in the open air and directed the fighting. As they saw him, day after day, walk as if charmed amidst the bursting shells, they said he was related to Santa Rosalia, the city's patron saint. For it was plain that a hero named *Garibaldi* must be descended from the saint's father, *Sinibaldi*.

After the third day of fighting, early in the morning of 30 May, Lanza sent a note to Garibaldi suggesting a truce and a conference aboard a British warship in the harbor. Garibaldi immediately agreed, for the truce rescued him, momentarily at least, from almost certain defeat. He had practically no ammunition left, and the Neapolitan troops which had pursued his decoy toward Corleone had returned and were at the moment entering the city in his rear. In fact they were stopped by the truce only after they had recaptured the Porta Termini and the Fiera Vecchia. If they had arrived the day before, or if Lanza had delayed his truce for even half a day, as some of his staff were urging, Garibaldi probably would have been forced to capitulate.

He went to the conference in his uniform of general in the Sardinian army, although he had no right to wear it and although only the previous night the captain of a Sardinian warship in the harbor had refused to give him any ammunition. Nevertheless the British marines, to the fury of the Neapolitan generals, saluted him with the same honors they gave to the representatives of the King of Naples. The conference resulted in a truce to last until noon the next day during which wounded were exchanged or transferred to ships, and the dead were buried, among them the Sicilian boy who had joined Abba's company on the first day's march out of Marsala. Both sides also used the time to prepare for further fighting. But Lanza, on reviewing the situation in the morning, countermanded his order of the evening before for a general attack and asked instead for an extension of the truce for another three days.

During this period he sent to Naples for advice, and Francesco II and his ministers, apparently fearing that to renew the fighting might involve them in difficulties with Britain and assuming that the situation must be desperate for Lanza to have asked twice for a truce, ordered him to evacuate the troops from the city. And on 7 June the Neapolitan soldiers, still twenty thousand strong and undefeated in any ordinary sense, marched out of the city to a temporary camping ground. The British admiral described it as "one of the most humiliating spectacles that could have been witnessed."

Two days later a ship from Genoa steamed into the harbor with guns and ammunition for Garibaldi and on 18 June a "second expedition" of twenty-five hundred volunteers, all well armed, landed to the west of the city. The next day twenty-four ships steamed out of the harbor carrying the Neapolitan army back to Naples.

Lanza's actions in defense of Palermo have struck most historians as well as most men who were there at the time as not only incredibly inept but even unreasonable: the latter in the sense that the true reasons for his actions may lie in such imponderables as the effect on him of his deafness; of his age, which was seventy-two; or of his relationship to his king, a Neapolitan, when he was himself a Sicilian and conscious that he was not fully trusted. There is no question that he was loyal, but he hardly could have served his king less well than he did, for in bombarding the city and then giving it up to inferior forces, he made Francesco's name odious and Garibaldi's even more glorious.

But men did not judge Garibaldi any less noble because of Lanza's weakness. All over Europe and in the Americas men and women, not necessarily Italians, reveled in the audacity of his expedition, in the stories of his personal courage and in the simplicity of his character. He soon was more than a famous Italian patriot; he became one of the greatest heroes of his world and century, the most "popular" in the sense of "of the people." In their eyes he stood for all that seemed best in the Risorgimento and in themselves. He could make heroes of ordinary men and turn dull, drab lives into romantic adventures, and they loved him for it. And instinctively, just like the Sicilians, they associated with him all their desires for social justice, for freedom and dignity. They were sure he was a good man and that his cause was just and without altogether realizing it they waited eagerly for him to get on with it. And he, administering Palermo from the small room he had taken for himself in the Palazzo Reale and without a care for the odds against him, was just as eager; first Naples, then Rome and finally Venice. *Italia e Vittorio Emanuele.*

# CHAPTER 41

Francesco's need for aid and his decision to appeal to France. Its significance. Vittorio Emanuele's letter to him. He revives the Constitution of 1848. Its effect on the Kingdom. Garibaldi's columns into the interior of Sicily. Abba's description of the march and of events at Bronte. The problem of annexation. Crispi and La Farina. La Farina deported. The battle of Milazzo. The Bourbon government disintegrating. Garibaldi reaches the Strait.

EVEN BEFORE THE GOVERNMENTS of Europe had learned of Garibaldi's landing at Marsala, they had begun to protest to Cavour, for they all assumed, like Palmerston in London, "that Garibaldi's Expedition has been planned, encouraged and assisted by the Government of Turin." The United States minister to Turin, for example, simply on what he had seen of the preparations for the expedition and judging from Cavour's lack of interference with them, concluded unequivocally in his report to Washington: "This is *undeclared war* of Sardinia against Naples." And to most diplomats the speed with which Garibaldi landed, captured Palermo and set up his dictatorial government, all in the name of Vittorio Emanuele II, was further evidence of it.

Yet Cavour, for reasons having nothing to do with Garibaldi or the expedition, had a relatively easy time with the protests while, at Naples, Francesco II and his ministers were unable to glean a benefit from them. The most strongly worded came from Tsar Alexander, Franz Josef and Wilhelm, Regent King of Prussia, all autocratic rulers eager to support Francesco as a fellow autocrat. They were against any revolution, even one conducted in the name of a monarch, if it encouraged the ideas of the French Revolution: that sovereignty resided in the people and that a sense of nationality was a basis for a state. Undermining their common aim, however, was the emerging antagonism between Franz Josef, a Habsburg, and Wilhelm of Prussia, a Hohenzollern, for leadership of the German Confederation; and, even more damaging, the full-blown antagonism of Tsar Alexander for Franz Josef because of Austria's failure to help Russia during the Crimean War. In 1849 Tsar Nicholas had put down the otherwise successful Hungarian revolution and freed Franz Josef to restore absolutism in Italy. But in 1860, as both Cavour and Francesco were aware, there was no possibility of such joint action, and there was even little chance that Franz Josef would act alone. He had been defeated at Solferino; France was still allied with Sardinia, and the Hungarians were restless in his rear. Prussia and Russia, for their part, were both far away, and neither had ships or interests in the Mediterranean. Cavour was able, therefore, to answer the strong protests in soft words rather than actions, regretting his inability to control a figure as popular as Garibaldi and stressing the hatred among Italians of all states for the Bourbon government at Naples. And Francesco and his ministers, on their side, were forced to conclude during the month of May that their kingdom's natural allies, of which one, Austria, was bound to it by close family ties and long tradition, would not come to its defense.

Francesco could look for aid, therefore, only to Britain or to France, the two states with fleets and interests in the Mediterranean but also the two countries least disposed to help him. Since the days of Gladstone's *Letters to Lord Aberdeen* British governments of whatever party had urged reforms on the kings at Naples, and with Palmerston and Lord John Russell in power Britain was certain to require Francesco, as a precondition to any aid, to grant an amnesty to political prisoners and to revive the constitution of 1848. The likelihood of help from Sardinia's ally, France, was hardly better. Napoleon was thought still to favor a Murat for the throne, and a strong tradition of hostility had existed between the Napoleonic and Bourbon dynasties since the days of the first Napoleon and Maria Carolina. On the other hand, the present Napoleon was known to dislike republican revolutionaries and to dislike the idea of a united Italy. Presumably, therefore, he would want to preserve the southern kingdom in some form, and after a series of meetings during the week in which Palermo was falling, Francesco and his ministers determined to ask Napoleon to guarantee the autonomy of the kingdom. "I put myself into the Emperor's hands," the king remarked sadly, and for the first time since the days before Maria Carolina the Bourbon king at Naples, in making such a remark, did not mean the Habsburg emperor in Vienna.

The break with tradition emphasized for all of Europe the change of power in Italy. After 150 years the Habsburg domination, which had started at the close of the War of the Spanish Succession, was over. The Kingdom of Sardinia, which had been founded in that war, had expanded to include almost half of Italy, and France was again in the peninsula. If the King of The Two Sicilies would not ally himself with Sardinia, then, even though as a Bourbon and a Habsburg he had a double reason to oppose a Napoleon, he was forced, if he wanted aid, to turn to France. Austria no longer could supply it.

Francesco needed aid, though his army numbered more than a hundred thousand and his navy was larger than that of Sardinia, because he could not be sure that his forces, even with the odds in their favor, could preserve his throne. The ranks of both were loyal, and the army, at least, was eager to fight. If it had been led in Sicily with average skill, Garibaldi probably never would have reached Palermo. But too many of the officers of all grades were old and inept. Like Lanza, again and again under the crash of events, the general officers would collapse into agitated inaction. The small middle class of the kingdom, which might have provided good officers, was against the king, and its members, for the most part, refused to enter his service. And the lesser military posts frequently were filled by petty noblemen of the worst sort: untrained, exclusive and contemptuous of their men. As a result in many regiments between officers and men there was not only little respect but sometimes actual distrust. Aid from France, by making the recovery of Sicily certain, would shore the army's morale before it began to crumble. And if the army gave way, then, Francesco knew he would never be able to count on the support of his people. Although probably a majority of them, too, were loyal, the Carbonaro revolution of 1821 and that of 1848 had shown how many millions of his subjects, particularly in Calabria, could be roused to demand some share in the government of the kingdom. Now, after the repressions of the last twelve years, there would be more.

Even within his family autocracy no longer had unanimous support. On 3 April, the day before the rising in Palermo which had ended at the Gancia Convent, Francesco's uncle, the Conte di Siracusa, had sent him a letter which had been circulated widely in copies and private printings. "The principle of Italian nationality," the conte had written, "having remained for centuries in the field of ideas, has now descended vigorously into that of action. To disregard this fact would be delirious blindness when we see others enduring it as an extreme necessity of the times." He went on to argue that Austria would not recover its position in Italy and that France and Britain each would prevent the other from succeeding to it. There was, therefore, only one protection against upset: to follow a national policy, identifying the kingdom with a free and independent Italy and forming an alliance with Sardinia. The idea may have been good and probably an increasing number of persons thought so, but at court it was not considered on its merits but on those of its author, and the conte was considered a libertine who all his life had been disloyal to his family.

Two weeks later Francesco received another semipublic letter on the same subject, this one from his cousin, the King of Sardinia. Vittorio

Emanuele wrote on Cavour's advice, and the letter since has been cited alternatively as evidence of their sincerity and of their hypocrisy, for the king wrote it on 15 April, 1860, several days after he had heard from Garibaldi of the latter's plan to invade Sicily but more than three weeks before Garibaldi set out or achieved his first success. The king wrote to his "dear cousin" of Naples:

> It would be useless for me to call Your Majesty's attention to the political facts of Italy now that the great victories of Magenta and Solferino have destroyed the influence which Austria used to wield over our country. The Italians can no longer be governed as they were thirty years ago. They have acquired a full consciousness of their rights and possess the wisdom and sufficient strength to defend them. Still further, public opinion has approved the principle that each nation has the incontestable right to govern itself as it believes best. Besides, with the destruction of the former omnipotence of Austria, it was natural that the people of central Italy should free themselves from the minor princes and try to form a nation unified and independent. *Thus we have arrived at a time in which Italy can be divided into two powerful states of the north and of the south,* which, if they adopt the same national policy, may uphold the great idea of our times—NATIONAL INDEPENDENCE. But in order to realize this conception, it is, I think, necessary that Your Majesty abandon the course you have held. If you repudiate my advice—which, believe me, is the result of my desire for your own good and that of your dynasty—if you repudiate my advice, the day may come in which I shall be placed in the terrible alternative of putting in jeopardy the most vital interests of my dynasty or of being the chief instrument of its ruin. *The principle of "Dualism," if it is well established and honestly followed, can be accepted by all Italians.* If you allow some months to pass without heeding my friendly suggestions, Your Majesty perhaps may experience the bitterness of those terrible words "too late"—as happened to a member of your family in 1830, at Paris.[89]

The reference was to the youngest brother of Louis XVI, Charles X, who had pursued a reactionary policy in the Restoration after Waterloo and, in the revolution of 1830, had been supplanted by his more liberal cousin, Louis Philippe. But whatever Vittorio Emanuele and Cavour may have intended by the reference, a friendly warning or a threat, Francesco and his ministers, deliberating on it in April before Garibaldi had started, chose to ignore it and with it the implied offer of an alliance. And any Italian prince of the previous two hundred years, whether Medici, Farnese, Bourbon or Habsburg, would have done the same. The House of Savoy, swallowing up the states of Italy one by one, was not to be trusted.

Yet early in June, after the evacuation of Palermo, Francesco's deputies to Napoleon, who were authorized to promise a constitution or almost any other reform in return for French support, heard the "terrible words" from the emperor: "It is too late. A month ago these concessions might have prevented everything. Today they are too late." He insisted that, as the liberator of northern Italy, he could not oppose in Sicily what seemed to be a continuation of the same movement. "The Italians are shrewd," he said, referring to the patriots of every party. "They perceive clearly that since I have shed the blood of my people for the cause of nationality, I can never fire a cannon against it. And this conviction, the key to the recent revolution, when Tuscany was annexed against my wishes and interests, will have the same effect in your case." He distinguished the case of Pio Nono at Rome, should it arise, for there religion was involved and French troops were already in the city as an army of occupation. The best he could do for the king at Naples was to advise him to adopt a program of home rule for Sicily under a prince of the House, a constitution for the Kingdom of Naples and an alliance with Sardinia. For Francesco and most of the members of his court the advice was very bitter.

Nevertheless, on 21 June he, his ministers and members of his family met in council and, in a debate in which his young queen voted for reform and his elderly Habsburg stepmother voted against it, resolved to adopt the emperor's entire program. Four days later Francesco announced to his subjects that Sicily would henceforth have a form of home rule under a prince of the House, that an alliance would be sought with Sardinia and that the constitution of 1848 was revived. The tricolor flag, symbol of Italian nationality, was hauled up on all the public buildings, ships and regimental flagstaffs and the Bourbon lilies on a white field hauled down. Political prisoners were released, exiles allowed to return, envoys left for Turin to seek an alliance, and, pending elections to a Parliament, a new and more liberal ministry was installed.

But just as the reactionaries at court had predicted, granting the constitution and the reforms that followed from it seemed only to weaken the monarchy further. The newspapers that sprang up debated the merits for Naples of Cavour and Mazzini as if Francesco already were deposed. The exiles and political prisoners recited the dynasty's shortcomings, and fervent monarchists, displaced by the appointments of the new constitutional ministry, left office angry at the king and disinclined to defend him. The soldiers disliked the new flag, which seemed to symbolize their humiliation in Sicily, and the officers began to wonder why they should fight Garibaldi at all if the king was going to grant a constitution, adopt a tricolor flag and seek an alliance with Sardinia. In the peasant towns between Naples and the Roman border, the most pious area of the kingdom, the constitution was considered to be an act against the Church; elsewhere it was considered a subterfuge that Francesco, like his ancestors, would revoke when danger passed. Then in Naples one day, while the new ministry was still making its appointments and forming a National Guard, riots broke out which were directed primarily against the police. The new ministry was reluctant to use the army to keep order, for that would have smacked too much of autocracy, and finally, in an effort to prevent the spread of anarchy, the new prefect of police, Don Liborio Romano, struck a bargain with the leaders of the *Camorra,* an organization of the Neapolitan underworld. In return for controlling the poor and criminal class of the city, the *Camorra* could fill positions of power within the police force itself. Most historians, in spite of the bargain's frightening legacy to the city, have judged it to have been necessary if Naples was to avoid a week of riot and terror such as revolutionary Paris had experienced in the September Massacres. Francesco, however, had not made the pact, and by it Don Liborio Romano replaced him as the ruler of the city. He became a minister whom Francesco could neither discharge nor control, and within a week after Francesco had granted the constitution, by the first of July, he had become a guest in the city, safe in his person but without any power. Naples now, as well as Palermo, was lost to him.

Perhaps if Francesco, on hearing of The Thousand landing at Marsala, had joined his army in Sicily and had led it to a victory over Garibaldi, he might have made himself and his form of government seem glamorous, efficient and inevitable. But though he could see the need for such action and talk of it, he could not do it. He was diffident, gentle and, for a monarch, pious to a fault. Before granting the constitution, an act of desperate remedy, he had insisted on receiving the pope's approval, and on another occasion he had telegraphed five times in one day for the pope's blessing. Such acts soon became public knowledge and communicated to others his political weakness and uncertainty, and by contrast it was Garibaldi who seemed glamorous, efficient and inevitable. To him in Palermo the eyes and hearts of most Neapolitans turned, some in hope, some in fear, but all in expectation. What Francesco did or tried to do was hardly noticed.

In Palermo, Garibaldi devoted the month of June to consolidating his military control over the island and to establishing his government. The first was easier. After Lanza evacuated Palermo, taking an army of twenty-four thousand with him back to Naples, the only Bourbon force of any size, about eighteen thousand men, was stationed at Messina; there were also three small garrisons at Milazzo, Siracusa and Augusta. All four points were seaports and if supplied and supported by the Neapolitan navy probably could resist any attack Garibaldi could mount against them. The rest of the island, however, was open to him at the slightest display of military power. Accordingly on 20 June, the day after Lanza and his troops steamed away from Palermo, he started a column of five hundred men, taken mostly from The Thousand, eastward across the center of the island to Catania. Five days later he started another of twelve hundred men under Bixio southward to Girgenti, now Agrigento, on to Licata where it embarked and sailed to Terranova whence it marched straight to Catania. A third and stronger column started down the north coast toward Messina.

The two columns going south and east had no opposition and, as the representatives of the men who had driven out the Neapolitans, were greeted in every town they entered as heroes, generally by brass bands which, in Abba's opinion, played execrably. But much of the time was taken up with marching from one village to the next, and they often sang as they marched. One time the Genovesi at the head of the column were in the middle of Mameli's hymn when they abruptly broke off, startling Abba in the rear with their sudden silence. But when he reached the spot where they had fallen silent, he understood. "It was the first view of Etna, far, far away, dark and enormous, casting its shadow over half of Sicily and the sea beyond, looming gigantic to eye and imagination."

Later he was impressed by mountains in another fashion and exclaimed in his notes: "Why have they made us march across mountains by tracks such that only by a miracle has no one lost his life?" But then he reflected:

> At least we have seen a lush countryside looking like a cup of gold. The cattle grazing in the meadows would scent our arrival and gaze with startled eyes at our endless column of red shirts. One bull chased two of our men who had dropped out of ranks, wandering off perhaps in search of water. We saw them running up a slope with the formidable horns of an angry animal only two paces behind them. One was able to scamper up a tree; the other continued to run along a bank where the bull would have caught him. But a cowherd came galloping up, bent so low that his head was almost on the horse's mane, and, lowering his pole, thrust it into the animal's flank like a lance. The bull fled bellowing, kicking up chips of turf and furiously lashing the air with his tail.[90]

But the expedition into the interior of the island was not always so delightfully bucolic. Garibaldi's success at Palermo and the arrival of the two columns in the interior towns, which generally was preceded by the departure of the Bourbon agents and chief supporters, was a revolution and was often accompanied by peasant unruliness in the form of land-squatting, rick-burning and cattle-slaughtering. Garibaldi was sympathetic to the problems of the peasants and, by his emotional response to them, often arrived at the same conclusions on how to solve them as the more intellectually inclined Carlo Pisacane had reached by reasoning. Garibaldi, for example, in his untheoretical fashion, seems always to have understood that the fundamental problems of Sicily, unlike Lombardia, were social and economic rather than political; and in some of his decrees, by reducing the price of salt, abolishing certain taxes on food and opening up recently enclosed pasture land, he attempted to attack those problems. But it was not always easy for him or for his lieutenants in the field to distinguish between true counterrevolutionary acts, lawless acts by honest, decent peasants expressing legitimate grievances, and lawless acts by criminals or others engaged in personal vendetta.

Sometimes the riots, confusion and bloodshed involved whole districts, and Abba, in one of his longer notes, describes how the revolution came to the north and west slopes of Etna. The worst trouble was at Bronte, the feudal estate which sixty years earlier the Bourbon king, Ferdinando I, had given to Nelson for his part in putting down the republican revolution in Naples. At Bronte "there had been divisions of property, burnings, vendettas, orgies to darken the sun, and, to cap all, cheers for Garibaldi." And the result was "houses burnt down with their people inside; people with their throats cut lying in the streets; pupils in seminaries killed at the feet of their old Rector." And when Bixio arrived with some troops, "one of the horde is tearing with his teeth at the breast of a dead girl."

Abba, his own emotions reflecting the confusion of right and wrong in what was happening, recounts how Bixio, by proclamations, judgments and executions, restored order in the villages around Etna, but he suspects with despair that neither the bloodshed nor the discipline will achieve any good. And he ends the note taking refuge in a republican indignation which he knew was righteous because he had learned it in school and because it involved finished history. "At the end of the last century the title Duke of Bronte was given to Nelson. And what title shall we give to Bixio? Not the one that belonged to the man who murdered Caracciolo!"

In Palermo, Garibaldi's problems were less bloody than those faced by Bixio in the interior, but they were equally confused and arose from the same fundamental question of how Sicilian life in the future should be organized, both politically and socially. The landing at Marsala with the cry *Italia e Vittorio Emanuele* and the subsequent decrees in the king's name had decided less than most men at first realized, for all the conditions on which the joining of the two kingdoms would be accomplished, as well as the timing of it, had been left uncertain. But once Garibaldi had taken the capital of the island and had established his control over its western half these questions became acute.

The one which at first absorbed all others was the one of timing: when would Garibaldi turn the island over to representatives of Vittorio Emanuele? The Sicilians had very mixed emotions about it. Some feared that Garibaldi and his chief political advisor, Crispi, if continued too long in their dictatorial power, might conduct by decree a radical social revolution. And some, of course, hoped for this. At the same time all recognized that once they and the island had been turned over to Vittorio Emanuele and the government at Turin, they would have no more chance of setting conditions on their allegiance, such as retaining their own legal system and some privileges of home rule. But again, the sooner the island kingdom was joined in some fashion to the greatly expanded Kingdom of Sardinia the less likely it was to be reconquered or handed by diplomats back to the Bourbons, for what if Garibaldi lost the next battle?

He, as everyone knew, was single-minded in his purpose to cross the Strait to the mainland, to liberate Naples and then, perhaps, to march on Rome. The Sicilians, although they did not say so loudly, cared little for this. They were content to let the Neapolitans, their former masters, suffer under the Bourbons for another hundred years. But to Garibaldi, Crispi and the volunteers this was the purpose of their expedition, and to achieve it they needed Sicily as a base which they controlled. They had no doubt that the moment Garibaldi turned the administration of the island over to the government in Turin, Cavour would begin to interfere and even perhaps, in the name of diplomacy, prevent them from crossing the Strait. They were, therefore, strongly in favor of continuing the dictatorship until they had achieved their military aims.

The dictatorship, however, placed Cavour and Vittorio Emanuele in an embarrassing position. Everything was done in the king's name, but he was never consulted. Before the world he was the one ultimately responsible for the island, but he had no share in its government, except for receiving an occasional message from Garibaldi. Understandably he and Cavour wanted a hand in the island's government and, while not unaware of the diplomatic problems that might arise, hoped to annex the island officially as soon as possible. Then, even if Garibaldi lost the next battle, Sicily might be saved for their new kingdom of free Italians. And as a step toward assuming a part in the government Cavour, in the first week of June, sent La Farina to Palermo as his representative.

To Cavour, who was still defending the cession of Nice and Savoy in the Senate, the appointment probably seemed conciliatory. La Farina was a Sicilian and president of the *Società Nazionale Italiana* which had assisted the expedition with arms and recruits. But to Crispi, the Mazzinians on the expedition and even to Garibaldi, La Farina was the man who had supplied them with rusty muskets, who had stopped Garibaldi from invading the Papal States the previous October, and who had perverted the *Società* into a tool of Cavour. When he landed in Palermo on 7 June, he was not welcome, and he quickly became the center of opposition to Garibaldi's dictatorial government. This opposed him most directly to Crispi, to whom Garibaldi had left the civil side of his government, for Garibaldi hated the daily round of political administration and concerned himself almost wholly with military matters, descending from them only occasionally to settle a wrangle between his civil subordinates.

Three days after his arrival La Farina wrote Cavour a report in which he stated that Garibaldi's government was incompetent and corrupt, was dominated by Mazzinian hotheads, was issuing an avalanche of ill-advised decrees on every phase of Sicilian life and was without any direction or control because Garibaldi, now that he was not fighting, was a hero out of his element and growing bored. He concluded, the Sicilians "want the immediate convocation of the Assembly to vote annexation and to order universal suffrage. The Government knows that it could not live a day if the Assembly were convened, and it opposes on the pretext that the hurried annexation would render the Naples undertaking impossible."

His conclusion that Garibaldi's government was unpopular and could not "live a day" if the Sicilians could express their will was wholly wrong. Garibaldi had the affection and trust of the Sicilians and again and again when he appealed to them, they supported him, even when they thought he was misguided. La Farina in his conclusion simply was believing what he wanted to believe.

His charges of corruption, ineptitude and radicalism, on the other hand, had some basis. Crispi was personally honest and while preparing the expedition to Sicily, although a Mazzinian, seems to have accepted once and for all Garibaldi's decision that it should be for *Italia e Vittorio Emanuele*. But, as was natural, he filled the government at Palermo with republicans, so that it had a radical cast which was reflected in its decrees. Further, as he had an entire, new government to construct and as many of the men he appointed had never held a government office, a good number turned out to be inept and among them some were corrupt. Incidents in the interior, such as that at Bronte, suggested that the government could not govern and others in Palermo, that offices were bought and sold, salaries drawn twice and profits made on the awarding of contracts. Undoubtedly some of it was true, as it probably is true of any revolutionary government during its first, confused months in office. La Farina, however, went to work as if it were wholly true, and as if the only way to save Sicily from a fate worse than Bourbons was to have Sardinia annex it as soon as possible.

He started a newspaper *L'Annessione*, "The Annexation." He printed notices urging immediate annexation which he posted throughout the city, and he organized street mobs to cry for annexation. One day Crispi, unable to get a mob to listen to him, left the balcony and walked into the midst of the angry crowd, shouting: "If you want to make a united nation, then leave it to the Dictator; but if all you want is your own freedom, we can go away and leave Sicily for good." His courage won the people over and they dispersed.

But still La Farina continued intriguing, and finally he succeeded in persuading the Civic Council of Palermo to register an official motion to the dictator in favor of immediate annexation. Garibaldi left his military affairs, his columns departing into the interior, his re-enforcements arriving and his plans for attacking Messina, to reply:

> . . . It was I who gave you the cry of *Italia e Vittorio Emanuele.* . . .
> It is now equally in my power by dictatorial act to proclaim annexa-
> tion; *but let us have this quite clear,* I came here to fight for Italy
> and not for Sicily alone. And if we do not free and unite the whole of
> Italy, we shall never achieve liberty in any single part of it.[91]

The council accepted this as an answer, and Garibaldi returned to his military preparations for clearing the last Neapolitans from the island. Nevertheless La Farina's political agitation was not without effect. The next day two important Sicilians resigned from the government, and Crispi announced that electoral rolls would be prepared for a vote by universal suffrage on the question of annexation. And a few days later Crispi himself resigned as Secretary of State to become secretary to the dictator, a position of almost equal power.

In accepting Crispi's resignation and in deciding to have a plebiscite on the question of annexation, Garibaldi retreated from his position before the council, but he saw nothing inconsistent in a dictator changing his personnel or policy as a result of public pressure, for he always conceived of his dictatorship as a government in which his ministers to some extent would reflect and represent popular feeling. Nevertheless he was growing tired of La Farina's troublemaking, which had created a major issue where there had been none, and he saw in it an effort by Cavour to interfere with his advance on Naples, for once Sicily was joined to the Kingdom of Sardinia, Cavour rather than himself would command the island.

Ten days later, therefore, he had La Farina arrested and deported, to-gether with two criminals, to Genoa. The government paper at Palermo announced, possibly in Crispi's words: "The three men thus deported were in Palermo conspiring against the government," and went on to say that the *Società Nazionale Italiana* was "reduced in means after Garibaldi had resigned its Presidency" and "a hindrance rather than a help to the cause for which we fought at Calatafimi and Palermo." Republican tempers in Palermo were boiling, and in Turin government officials at every level picked up La Farina's fury and indignation and accepted all his charges against Garibaldi's government as wholly true. Cavour even telegraphed the officials at Genoa that no more volunteers were to be allowed to sail, but then on reflection he waived the order and on 11 July 1860, the fifteenth expedition with men and arms departed for Sicily.

The truth or falsity of La Farina's charges, now repeated many times over in accusation and denial, became the stuff of Italian party politics for the next forty years. When in 1895 Crispi, as prime minister of Italy, unveiled the monument to Garibaldi on the Gianicolo, his speech revealed that his opinion of Cavour was still the one he had formed during this summer of 1860. And besides Crispi and excluding Cavour there were nine other future prime ministers who had a part in the struggle that now developed between monarchists and republicans to control the revolution which Garibaldi had launched with such startling success.

In its largest sense the struggle was over the means by which the Kingdom of Italy was to be made, whether by popular revolution of volunteers or by diplomacy and declared war of Sardinia in alliance with France. It was also a struggle over the end, whether the revolution should cross the Strait of Messina, proceed on past Naples and plant itself on the Campidoglio at Rome. For though the republicans, for the most part, had followed Manin and Garibaldi in accepting a kingdom in place of a republic, they were all still firm in their belief that the new Kingdom of Italy must have Rome as its capital. But in a more limited sense, in July, the struggle centered on the timing and conditions on which Sicily would join Sardinia.

Garibaldi had promised a plebescite on the question, and Crispi dutifully had set about registering the men of Sicily for a vote on 20 July. But he began at once to run into difficulties, for, typically, the local official at Floridia, a large town near Siracusa, reported:

> Despite all my efforts, out of nine thousand people I cannot make more than six hundred inscribe themselves. The reason for this unfortunate fact is the rumor that those who inscribe as electors will be chosen for conscription. Because of this current impression I summoned the clergy and arranged that they should give a sermon on the importance of voting. . . . What was my surprise when Mass began and still the priest made no attempt to mount the pulpit as he had promised. Seeing this, and still hoping for some result, one of the electoral commission stood up and began to speak. But his first words were taken wrongly, and the people took fright. Everyone in the church fled into the fields, and most of them heard no Mass that day.[92]

Again and again Crispi had to postpone the voting while advising the provincial governors on the island: "The program of the Dictator's government is this: slow, gradual annexation, as the opportunities become more or less easy, and in the meantime a *de facto* assimilation of Sicilian administration to the governmental system of Piedmont." Meanwhile, back in

Turin, La Farina was insisting that three hundred Sicilian towns, or most of the island, had petitioned for annexation. But very few of these petitions have ever been discovered, and there seems less reason to believe La Farina's statements about conditions in Sicily than to doubt the sincerity of Crispi's efforts to prepare for a vote as the opportunity became "more or less easy."

Ricasoli had managed a peaceful and dignified plebiscite in Tuscany which had impressed the European powers and influenced the fate of the Duchy, but Crispi in Sicily had a more difficult job. The peasants were poorer, more illiterate and, unlike those in Tuscany, had undergone a violent revolution which in some towns had destroyed fields and houses. Probably in the interior not one person in a hundred had the faintest conception of what was involved in immediate as opposed to delayed annexation. The peasants knew they were against conscription, and in the eastern part of the island they had a tradition that when in 1713 Vittorio Amedeo II of Savoy had come to the island before exchanging it for the Kingdom of Sardinia, his visit had been followed by terrible crop failures. Probably their passionate devotion to Garibaldi would overcome their fears of conscription and distrust of the House of Savoy, but no one could be certain.

In the large seacoast towns they understood the issues well enough, but the debate on alternative choices, which Ricasoli by his censorship had limited so severely, under Garibaldi's freedom became all too public. The newspapers bristled with arguments for and against annexation, immediate or delayed, by plebiscite or by vote of an assembly of representatives. Journals carried essays on the joining of England and Scotland to make Great Britain, on the effect annexation would have on trade, on the Church, on the legal system and on taxes. In Tuscany almost without exceptions the nobility and middle class had been in favor of union with Sardinia and had given a strong lead to the peasants. In Sicily, on the other hand, there was the confusion of too many voices crying too many different programs, and in Palermo there was the confusion of a capital city one-third in rubble.

Probably most Sicilians favored early annexation, for they had little interest in liberating Naples and feared a defeat for Garibaldi might be a disaster for them. But they wanted annexation on their own terms: perhaps preserving their own legal system, a separate church and certain rights of self-government, for they feared the strong centralization of the Sardinian government which they considered a French trait and unsuitable for them. Nevertheless they recognized that annexation could not precede the departure of the last Neapolitans, for neither an assembly could be elected nor a plebiscite held while Messina and other seaport towns were still held by the Bourbons, and with La Farina deported the pressure for immediate annexation lightened greatly.

Meanwhile Garibaldi's strongest column of soldiers, about two thousand men under Giacomo Medici, was proceeding down the north coast of the island and on 17 July began to skirmish with some three thousand Neapolitans sent out from Messina to support the garrison at Milazzo. The garrison, about one thousand men, held the castle of Milazzo, an ancient stronghold built on a narrow neck of land which stretched north almost four miles into the sea. The castle was situated only about a half mile from the mainland, but it sat on a rock precipice three hundred feet high and dominated the sea-level town at its foot which, with the protection of the palisade and spit of land had a good harbor and a road leading off to Messina, only fifteen miles away. As the Neapolitans and Garibaldini began to skirmish among the farms and villages on the mainland, the Sicilians fled not to the castle but into the hills of the interior, and for the next week the town and surrounding villages were almost completely deserted.

When Garibaldi realized from Medici's reports that a battle was shaping up against good Neapolitan troops, he immediately sent re-enforcements, about a thousand men of which nearly six hundred were Sicilians, mostly boys from the back streets of Palermo. Then he went down to the harbor, stopped from landing a force of one thousand volunteers which had just arrived and steamed with them under his own command down to Medici. On the way he was convoyed by a warship of the Sardinian navy. His departure from Palermo caused consternation, for the city was preparing the next day to celebrate his official birthday, 19 July, and many North Italians and Sicilians, when they heard where he had gone, threw up their posts, civil or military, and hastened by foot, carriage or boat to join him.

The battle was joined on 20 July. In numbers the Garibaldini had the advantage, for with the re-enforcements they totaled somewhere between four or five thousand whereas the Neapolitans were only three thousand, for the garrison in the castle did not come out to join the battle before the town. The Neapolitans, however, had cavalry, of which Garibaldi had none, and artillery, of which he only had two pieces which proved in the fighting to be useless. His men were a strange assortment. Perhaps half of them had some training and experience, but the thousand volunteers which had just arrived had never trained and hardly knew their officers. Several hundred had Enfield rifles with a sight they could not use, and some of the Sicilian boys were so small that they staggered under their guns.

The battle began badly for the Garibaldini when some Tuscan volunteers on the left flank were raked by the Neapolitan artillery and retreated in a mood that was close to panic. Garibaldi sent over one of his best generals, Enrico Cosenz, who was himself a Neapolitan, and he succeeded in reorganizing the troop. But during most of the morning there was no advance on the left. Elsewhere, however, enthusiasm with some skill seemed to be enough. Bit by bit the Neapolitans were pushed back through the olive groves and canebrake toward the town with its castle behind it.

Garibaldi attempted to be everywhere. When the Genovesi sharpshooters came up to their position, he was in the road ahead of them, under fire, but calmly showing them where to go. A group of men who were having trouble driving the Neapolitans away from a wall suddenly were aware that he had come up on horse, dismounted, and without a word or a look was leading them in a bayonet charge. And as one section of the young Sicilians went into the front line he called them "men" and kept repeating in a low voice, *"Avanti! Coraggio, uomini!"* A few days later in an improvised hospital one of them said proudly, "Our Colonel says that after the battle of Milazzo no one can say again that Sicilians never fight," and beside him lay a twelve-year-old whose leg had just been amputated.

Even on the left in the afternoon the battle went better. A small Neapolitan gunboat appeared, but its crew had deserted the Bourbon service and had come to help Garibaldi. He rowed out to it, showed it where to fire its guns, and the Neapolitans on shore were forced to retreat. By late in the afternoon, after a full day's fighting under the Sicilian sun, the Garibaldini were on the edge of the town and preparing to advance into it. To their amazement they discovered it was deserted. The Neapolitan troops had grown discouraged and, vastly overestimating the numbers against them, had withdrawn into the castle. The battle was over.

The victory, however, was not yet certain. The Neapolitans in the castle with their artillery and cavalry were still a force capable of defeating the Garibaldini, and before the latter could rest in the town they had captured they had to barricade all the streets leading to the castle, post guards and prepare for the counterattack which seemed certain sooner or later to come. At Messina, after all, there were fifteen thousand more Neapolitans who in a day could either march or sail to Milazzo, and, supposing they could trap Garibaldi between themselves and the castle, could almost certainly annihilate him.

But now, for the first time, the extent to which the Bourbon government was disintegrating began to become clear. The Neapolitans in the castle, being half a mile out to sea, could communicate easily by relays of semaphore with Messina or even with the points on the mainland. And the messages that went out soon revealed that water and food were low and that morale had collapsed completely. Without re-enforcement there would be no counterattack. Further, the continued dejection of all messages going out seemed to indicate that no message promising re-enforcements had come in.

Then on 23 July, without there having been any change in the position of the forces, some Neapolitan warships steamed into the little harbor, and for a time the Garibaldini feared that they would be bombarded and forced to retire. But on the contrary the ships had come from Naples with an envoy from the constitutional ministry to negotiate the capitulation of the garrison at Milazzo and of the one at Messina. All the Neapolitan troops were to be evacuated or neutralized. What had started at Marsala and Calatafimi had ended at Milazzo. In two and a half months Garibaldi had won all of Sicily.

At Naples, Francesco and some of his ministers had wanted to fight, to assume the offensive in Sicily and attempt to destroy Garibaldi in the field. But a majority of the constitutional ministry had determined to abandon Sicily or at least to hold on only to the garrisons at Messina and Milazzo while at the same time asking Britain and France, in return for this more peaceful course, to guarantee that Garibaldi would not be permitted to cross the Strait. Such a course, they argued, was also more likely to produce an alliance with Sardinia, for it would avoid any clash between the Neapolitan fleet and the Sardinian ships which often now were aiding the Garibaldini.

But the defensive policy had not been adopted firmly enough to prevent the Neapolitan general at Messina from sending out the force of three thousand toward Milazzo although it prevented him, or so he claimed, from re-enforcing his men after they were in trouble. And at Naples, when the news of Milazzo arrived, the ministry, as if it never had adopted the defensive policy, ordered troops sent direct from there to the garrison's aid, but the navy, led by the Conte d'Aquila, one of Francesco's uncles, refused to embark them. The ministry, faced with a mutiny, backed down and the relief for Milazzo returned to its barracks. Francesco's power steadily was dwindling and so, too, was the power of his ministers, for they were crippled by the dilemma of their position: because of Garibaldi, Francesco had revived the constitution and called them to power; but if they defeated Garibaldi, then Francesco probably would revoke the constitution and send them to prison, as in similar circumstances his father had done. This dilemma, in varying degree, faced everyone in the new constitutional government and tended to paralyze them. To take action, almost any action, was to make a political declaration, and many sought safety in doing nothing. For the ministers their best course, and probably some of them sincerely thought it the best course for Naples too, lay in abandoning Sicily to Garibaldi and Vittorio Emanuele and in seeking an alliance with France and

Sardinia which they might use if necessary to keep Francesco, as well as Garibaldi, in check.

Accordingly, at Milazzo on 25 July the Neapolitan troops in the castle marched down to the ships and boarded for Naples. They had been allowed to keep their arms and half their battery mules, but the rest of the mules and all the horses, together with the cannon and ammunition in the castle, were left behind. That afternoon, as Garibaldi's men were rounding up the horses which had been left running loose on the castle grounds, he got out his lasso and gave them a demonstration of roping, South American style.

Three days later at Messina, Giacomo Medici on Garibaldi's behalf signed a treaty which gave the town to the Garibaldini, provided for the complete suspension of hostilities, and withdrew the Neapolitans into the citadel where they would remain passive spectators of whatever action Garibaldi later might take.

So by the first of August he was on the Strait, convinced now that the Bourbon government at every level was collapsing and that he could reach Naples and even Rome.

# CHAPTER 42

The Strait of Messina. Garibaldi urged on by the King. Cavour's actions to stop Garibaldi. First attempt to cross fails. Bertani's volunteers. Cavour stops further re-enforcements. Origin of plan to invade the Papal States. Garibaldi's second attempt to cross succeeds. Collapse of the Neapolitan army in Calabria. Cavour clears his plan for the Papal States with Napoleon. Garibaldi decides against annexation for Sicily. Francesco abandons Naples. Garibaldi enters.

GOD, SAY THE SICILIANS, first made the world and then made the Strait of Messina to separate men from madmen. But the proverb alone does not specify on which side of the Strait the men are mad, and this the Sicilians determine by the mood of the moment and reveal in the tone of voice. In much the same way Italians of every state repeated the news that Garibaldi and his men had arrived at the Strait: the adventure was over; it was just beginning.

The Strait is more than merely a body of connecting water; it is one of the wonders of the Mediterranean which has always fascinated men. In the fifth century B.C. the Greek historian Thucydides wrote of it: "The Strait in question is the sea that lies between Rhegium (Reggio) and Messana (Messina), the place where Sicily is the closest to the Continent, and it is the so-called Charybdis through which Odysseus is said to have sailed. It naturally has been accounted dangerous because of its narrowness and its currents which are caused by the flow into it of the Tyrrhenian Sea." At its narrowest the Strait is two miles wide, and modern science has verified Thucydides' report that the Tyrrhenian Sea to the north flows steadily southward through it. The Tyrrhenian is both warmer and less dense, that is less salty, than the Ionian Sea to the south, and so on the surface the current is southward, but underneath, well below boat-level, the flow is northward. This convection, flowing at less than a knot, would not be serious except that the Strait is also one of the very few places in the Mediterranean where tides are felt, and in the narrow, shallow part of the Strait these can flow at as much as four knots, twice each lunar day northward and twice southward, first re-enforcing and then battling the current. But even with this the wonders and dangers of the Strait are not complete, for when the deep-water tidal currents of the Tyrrhenian or Ionian Sea strike the barrier shallows forming the Strait's bed, they are violently deflected upward, bringing with them from the depths squid and fish not seen anywhere else in the Mediterranean. And as the waters of varying temperature and density attempt to sink or rise, whirlpools form which can suck down a small boat. The location and number of these have changed with shifts in the sea bottom, but even today when they are less severe than formerly, the *Admiralty Pilot* warns small ships of three in particular which form always near the same place and continue for about thirty minutes before disappearing.

For Odysseus, in a small boat, superstitious and ignorant of tides, the terrors of the Strait were great, and even for Garibaldi, who was experienced in calculating wind and tide, the crossing of it posed special problems. He had only two small steamers and many of his men, perhaps the majority, would have to cross in small, open boats. To avoid the Neapolitan naval patrols and batteries on the opposite shore they would have to put out at night, without lights and making as little noise as possible. A miscalculation in tide or current or a delay in midpassage might scatter the small boats for miles along the Calabrian coast. And in addition to these obstacles of wind and water there were also the Neapolitan forts on the opposite shore, the Neapolitan navy patrolling the Strait and the possibility that at any moment Britain and France, impressed by the efforts of Francesco II and his constitutional ministers to introduce reforms, would order their warships to join the patrol.

Garibaldi, however, had no intention of allowing the difficulties of the Strait to stop him or of waiting for events to aid or, more likely, to hinder him. After his victory at Milazzo on 20 July 1860, he was convinced he could reach Rome and, because of two letters he had received from Vittorio Emanuele II, convinced that the king wished him to try. The letters came by courier and in the first, an official letter, the king wrote with Cavour's knowledge and guidance:

> You know that when you departed for Sicily your expedition did not have my approval. . . .
>
> To put an end to the war between Italians and Italians I counsel you to renounce the idea of crossing with your brave army to the Neapolitan mainland, provided that the King of Naples pledges himself to evacuate the entire island and to leave the Sicilians free to decide their own future. I reserve my full liberty of action, in the event of the King of Naples not wishing to accept this condition.[93]

By the time Garibaldi received the letter, on 27 July, Francesco had evacuated his troops from Milazzo and had agreed to evacuate or to neutralize those at Messina, so that Vittorio Emanuele's conditions were met and, if Garibaldi were truly his servant, his advice became an unequivocal order. Nevertheless Garibaldi immediately sat down and wrote a flowery response in which, while protesting his reverence for the king, he insisted that he must disobey: "As soon as I shall have fulfilled what I have undertaken, freeing the people from a hated yoke, I will lay down the sword at your feet and obey you for the rest of my life."

Cavour promptly published the exchange of letters as proof to Napoleon and the governments of Europe that the king was not supporting Garibaldi, could not control him and could not be held responsible for him. In Italy, Garibaldi's letter of disobedience thrilled all patriots, but the king's letter, while delighting republicans as evidence of his lack of interest in unifying the peninsula, only depressed his supporters. Where a year before in the Po valley Vittorio Emanuele had been a hero and a leader, now he seemed merely a bystander. Ricasoli, for example, believed the king simply had put himself in the wrong with national sentiment while knowing that his advice would be flouted. In letter after letter to Cavour, Ricasoli insisted that "Our real Garibaldi should be Vittorio Emanuele," and always he demanded action.

The king's private position, however, was very different from the one assumed on Cavour's advice in public. He had sent two letters to Garibaldi after Milazzo, or it seems likely that he sent two letters for there is some question whether the second was sent, or if sent was delivered, as it was found among the courier's papers years later with its seal unbroken. Possibly the king had instructed the courier to recite the message and to deliver the letter only if Garibaldi doubted the oral message, which was unlikely to happen. This second letter, in the king's hand, advised Garibaldi to disregard the first, official letter and to "reply that you are full of devotion and reverence for your King . . . but must reserve full freedom of action." And inclining most historians to believe that the king's message was delivered in some form is the fact that Garibaldi's reply to the official letter is almost a paraphrase of the king's secret urging. But in any event there is no question about the king's private position at this time, for only ten days later he sent another courier to Garibaldi, who now was with his army at Faro on the shore of the Strait, urging him orally to go on to Naples and "according to opportunity either occupying Umbria and the Marches with his troops, or allowing bands of volunteers to go." This was an invitation to Garibaldi not only to take Naples but to invade the Papal States, although not Rome. The king at this moment, secretly at least, was almost as much of a revolutionary as the republicans.

Cavour's position at this time, however, is much more obscure. There is no evidence that he knew of the king's secret letter or of the later message to Garibaldi, and to the extent that a pattern emerges from his actions throughout the summer, he would have disapproved of them and might have tried to stop them. Up to the beginning of July 1860 Cavour had not given his first attention to Garibaldi and events in the south; he had been concerned with the consolidation of the vastly enlarged Kingdom of Sardinia in the north, with elections throughout it of a new Parliament, with the final steps in the cession of Nice and Savoy and with his relations to Napoleon and the other European heads of state. But by the middle of June the cession of the two provinces was completed, and when, early in July, Garibaldi deported La Farina from Sicily, Cavour was put on notice that events in the south were slipping away from him. If he was to control them or even to influence them, he would have to assert himself.

Whether he saw the danger in Garibaldi more clearly than the king or merely imagined a danger where none existed is argued by historians. But in Cavour's eyes Garibaldi, for all his devotion to the king, was a republican who had surrounded himself with republicans who were not devoted to the king, who were even Mazzinians. He had won for their cause all of Sicily, had brought into being an army of twenty thousand volunteers and had excited patriots the length of the peninsula to hope that he would unite all of Italy. What had been a dream was already partly fact, and if Garibaldi took Naples, the republicans then would control half of Italy, won without a French alliance, without sacrificing anything comparable to Nice and Savoy and relying solely on the people to free themselves in just exactly the fashion Mazzini had always advocated. Such success would not only overshadow Vittorio Emanuele, it would undermine him. Republicanism had always been strong in the Po valley, in the Romagna, at Venice and even at Milan. If Garibaldi crossed the Strait and swept up the peninsula, his revolution might not stop at Naples or the Papal States. And if it swept on to Rome or into the Po valley, then, as had happened every other time republicanism had broken loose in Italy, the great powers would come to some agreement about restoring order in the peninsula, and every Italian state, whether republican or monarchist, would lose its independence.

Judging events from this point of view, Cavour was anxious for the sake of Vittorio Emanuele and the best interests, as he conceived them, of all Italians to stop Garibaldi on the Strait. But in July and August he had to act from a position of weakness, for, as the U.S. minister at Turin reported to Washington shortly after the battle at Milazzo, "Since the affair of Savoy and Nice, public opinion is no longer with Cavour, but it is with Garibaldi. Cavour cannot oppose him." Nevertheless, beginning in July,

Cavour set about to do so and to retrieve for himself and for his king the leadership in Italian affairs.

Partly because his nature was secretive and partly from necessity he worked in a devious fashion. After the victory at Milazzo and the surrender of Messina, for example, he wrote to Admiral Carlo di Persano, who had been using the Sardinian navy on occasion to aid the volunteers, "Please convey my warm and sincere thanks to General Garibaldi. . . . After so splendid a victory I do not see how he can be stopped from crossing to the Continent. . . . Garibaldi must do it. The work cannot stop half-done. The national flag raised in Sicily must be unfurled on the mainland and carried along the Adriatic coast until it floats over the Queen of the Sea."

But against such a letter, which seems to invite Garibaldi to unify all the peninsula including Venice, must be put Cavour's actions. Even before writing it he had sent agents to Naples to try to start a revolution there in conjunction with the known liberals such as the king's uncle, the Conte di Siracusa. He hoped that a revolutionary committee might take over the city and then ask Vittorio Emanuele for protection. The Sardinian army then would land on the plea of preserving lives and property, and Garibaldi would be forestalled.

In August, however, after several weeks of intrigue Cavour wrote in exasperation to Ricasoli: "We have given Naples everything necessary for a revolution, arms, money, soldiers, men of counsel and men of action. If after all of this the kingdom turns out to be so rotten as to be incapable of action, I do not know what to do; and we must resign ourselves to the triumph either of Garibaldi or of the reactionaries." But the conspiracy, although it sputtered on, never flamed into a revolution. The Sardinians never had been popular in Naples, and few Neapolitans saw any reason to risk a revolution for Cavour when Garibaldi, any day, would be across the Strait and driving the Bourbons away.

But if Cavour could not unseat the Bourbon dynasty, he at least could avoid rescuing it with an alliance, and this he did by setting conditions which Francesco and his ministers could not meet: Naples must cut every tie with Austria, must persuade the pope to adopt the nationalist cause, must give up Sicily and must come to some understanding with Garibaldi. But whatever Francesco and his ministers might promise to do about Austria or Sicily, they could not set the policies of Pio Nono or Garibaldi, and Cavour was able to waste weeks in talk while Francesco's government continued to lose power and effectiveness. This, though, was as much a gain for Garibaldi as Cavour, for in the mountains of Calabria and Basilicata, in the towns where there were no garrisons of Neapolitan troops, the power slipped into the hands of revolutionary committees, and these did not look with hope toward Cavour in Turin but to Garibaldi on the Strait.

And in an even more direct fashion the contradictions in Cavour's policy aided Garibaldi, for in order to preserve freedom for Sardinia to act in the south, Cavour worked to prevent France and Britain from aiding Naples to patrol the Strait. Napoleon was eager, as Garibaldi massed his army on the beaches of Faro, to isolate him and the revolution in Sicily and proposed an international patrol in the interests of peace in Europe. The details were worked out by the French and Neapolitans, and only British approval was needed. But the British were still nervous about Napoleon's ambitions in Italy and inclined increasingly to believe that the best hope for peace there, while at the same time excluding the French from the peninsula, lay in uniting all the Italian states under Vittorio Emanuele. Cavour through his ambassador and a special agent, Joseph Lacaita, played skillfully on this sympathy for Italy and fear of the French, and in the last week of July the British announced that they would have no part of an allied patrol. Napoleon thereupon also withdrew, not wanting to act in opposition to British policy or to be the only one to support the Bourbon dynasty. Garibaldi, who considered diplomacy a form of dishonesty, never appreciated what Cavour had accomplished, but Francesco, who had revived the constitution at Naples in order to obtain just this sort of aid and diplomatic backing, was fully aware that in the end he had received neither.

Garibaldi, meanwhile, was maturing a plan for crossing the Strait. Encamped around a lighthouse or "Faro," which gave its name to the beaches and a small village nearby, was his army of about twelve thousand men. Food and water were short, conditions unsanitary and many of the Sicilians, who had little interest in crossing the Strait, were beginning to wander off. Opposite Faro, on the Neapolitan shore, were two small forts, Torre Cavallo and Altifiumara, whose guns commanded the entrance to the Strait. On either side of them in the towns along the coast were sixteen thousand Neapolitan troops.

Garibaldi's plan was to send two hundred men across in the early night to capture one of the forts, Altifiumara, whose guns then could be used to force the Neapolitan warships out of the Strait, making it possible for the rest of the army to get across in the two steamers and hundreds of fishing boats. One of the volunteers, a Calabrian, had crossed in disguise a few days earlier and arranged for the fort's gate to be opened from the inside, so that if all went well the Strait could be crossed and the fort captured in three or perhaps four hours and the main part of the army be across by dawn or before the Neapolitan troops could mass to oppose the landing.

The night of 8/9 August was cloudy, and Garibaldi led the expedition

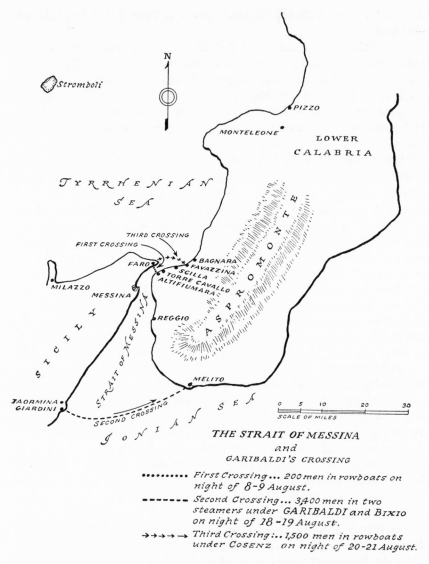

THE STRAIT OF MESSINA
and
GARIBALDI'S CROSSING

•••••••• First Crossing... 200 men in rowboats on
night of 8-9 August.

------- Second Crossing... 3,400 men in two
steamers under GARIBALDI and BIXIO
on night of 18-19 August.

→→→→→ Third Crossing:.. 1,500 men in rowboats
under COSENZ on night of 20-21 August.

of two hundred men in rowboats out into the main channel. Then he
turned back to wait with the rest of his men for a signal announcing that
the fort had been captured. The two hundred rowed on, passing in the dark
near several Neapolitan ships, and landed close to the fort. Its gate, however, was not opened to them. The alarm was given and after exchanging
some shots they retreated, in the only direction they could, up the mountain
behind the fort. For a time they followed the bed of a dry stream; later, still

in the dark, they dragged each other up the steepest places by the muzzles of their guns. By dawn they were several thousand feet up the mountain.

Although the expedition had not accomplished its purpose, it was not altogether a failure. The highland into which the men had climbed is a long ridge of mountains known collectively as "Aspromonte" or "harsh mountain," and at three thousand feet by night the men froze and by day, under the August sun, they broiled. But they were across the Strait, and every night they lit bonfires to show they were alive and to alarm the Neapolitan troops on the coast below them. Calabrian peasants, mountaineers in knee breeches with conical hats ornamented with streamers of black velvet, began to join them, and a revolutionary committee in Reggio sent a train of mules up to them with food. One night they even came down to the coast, captured Bagnara and held it for several hours. The Neapolitans never knew where they might strike next and were distracted from watching the Sicilian shore. The revolution was across the Strait, and in the provinces south of Naples the revolutionary committees grew bolder and the Neapolitan troops more disheartened.

In the north the excitement over Garibaldi continued strong. Throughout the summer patriots constantly quoted an Ode which Manzoni had written in 1821, the year of the Carbonaro revolutions, but which he had not dared to publish until the year of freedom in 1848: "Oh days of our country's ransom! Unhappy for ever shall be the man who shall hear of it from afar, from the lips of others, like some foreigner; who when he tells the story to his children must say with a sigh 'I was not there.' " And all through July volunteers had continued to arrive in Genoa and be organized by Garibaldi's staff there into expeditions to go to Sicily. In all, in the three months following the capture of Palermo about twenty thousand volunteers were shipped south from Genoa.

In the beginning most of these had been recruited by the *Società Nazionale Italiana* which then turned the men over to some of Garibaldi's staff officers who organized them and shipped with them to Sicily. But toward the end of July another and more radical group became increasingly important. This was the Committee of Aid organized by Dr. Agostino Bertani, who was more radical than Garibaldi and in his heart may never have accepted the need for *Italia* to be joined with *Vittorio Emanuele*. His activities during the first two weeks of August, the time when Garibaldi's two hundred men were crossing the Strait and retreating into the mountains, brought Cavour's increasing opposition to Garibaldi into the open.

During July, Bertani had collected six thousand volunteers whom he had held together as a unit instead of shipping them out in smaller groups. He had given them rifles and uniforms, had organized and drilled them and was planning to use them and two thousand more men he had collected in

Tuscany for an invasion of the Papal States. Mazzini, who was in hiding in Genoa, urged him on to this, and so did Garibaldi from Faro. Cavour, as always, opposed the plan and sent his Minister of the Interior, Farini, to negotiate with Bertani about the little army's destination. Cavour did not feel strong enough to disband the volunteers or to prevent them from joining Garibaldi but he did feel strong enough to deflect them from the Papal States. Farini told Bertani bluntly that the Sardinian army and navy would be used to prevent the army's leaving Genoa unless it went to Sicily, and to this Bertani finally agreed. The men sailed from Genoa on 10 and 11 August, and by the end of the week most of them were on the island and marching to join the volunteers at Faro.

Several days after they sailed, on 13 August, Farini issued a proclamation forbidding any more private recruiting of volunteers or launching of expeditions against friendly states. "Italy," he proclaimed in a phrase calculated to irritate the republicans, "must belong to the Italians and not to the sects." And to the surprise of the diplomats and the fury of the republicans, the government enforced it. Thereafter, except for the volunteers already recruited who finally were allowed to sail, Garibaldi's supply of men from the north was cut off.

The proclamation and the threat of force behind Farini's negotiation with Bertani are clues indicating that Cavour, sometime during the preceding weeks, had decided on a course of action to forestall Garibaldi and to reinstate the king as the leader of the nationalist cause. Historians, of course, have uncovered more clues, but even to contemporaries the proclamation seemed an unequivocal notice that the government at Turin now had a plan of its own which to some degree, at least, was opposed to that of Garibaldi.

The plan, which was not revealed for another four weeks, was that the Sardinian army, in force and led by the king, should invade Umbria and the Marches, the mountain and Adriatic provinces of the Papal States, and even perhaps to invade the Kingdom of Naples from the north, thus limiting Garibaldi to Sicily or, if he succeeded in crossing the Strait, to Sicily and the southern part of Naples.

The dangers in it were immense. The Sardinian army would have to invade the Papal States while leaving the Austrian army in the Veneto in its rear. An invasion of the Papal States would raise at once the question of the pope's temporal power, would antagonize to some extent all Catholic States and might strain to the breaking point Sardinia's alliance with France. And in starting the Sardinian army southward as the volunteers came northward, it risked a confrontation between two excited armies which Garibaldi and Vittorio Emanuele might not be able to control, even supposing both of them wanted to. Nevertheless, it was the plan Cavour had chosen or, he might have argued, which events had forced on him.

It seems to have been suggested to him first, at least in principle, in a letter which Prince Napoléon wrote him on 30 June, when Garibaldi was still in Palermo and had not yet won the battle of Milazzo.

> Italy is in a supreme crisis. She must emerge from it united under the sceptre of my father-in-law [Vittorio Emanuele] with her capital at Rome, or else she will slide back under the oppression of priests and Austrians, at Turin as well as at Naples and everywhere else. The die is cast. . . . *Daring alone* can save you today. Be strong. *Don't trust to yourself;* no illusions, no vanity; *you need* France and you can get her by means of the Emperor. So be completely open with him. No more *finesse;* that won Tuscany for you; it will not win Sicily, Naples and Rome. *Explain to him your views of the future,* not only your end but your means and your conduct. . . . Let France secretly be in accord with Italy, then everything can be accomplished. Without that you will have a disaster and Italy will have lost the best opportunity to regenerate itself, an opportunity that may not come again for centuries.[94]

To a great extent the letter foreshadowed Cavour's actions and he later acknowledged its influence on him, for when the invasion of the Papal States actually took place, he spoke of it as "the plan of Prince Napoléon." He seems to have decided on it sometime in July, perhaps after the battle of Milazzo when it became evident that Garibaldi had not only won all of Sicily but seemed likely also to win all of Naples. For on 1 August in an "ultra-confidential letter" to his ambassadors in London and Paris he talked of it as decided, and on that same day Farini in his talk with Bertani hinted that the government intended some action by arguing against an invasion of the Papal States by republican volunteers on the ground that "before many days our own bugles will be sounding." But to the world at large the proclamation forbidding any more volunteers to be recruited was the first hint of any action by the government and as for the moment nothing further happened, everyone's attention continued to focus on Garibaldi at Faro.

He now had devised another plan for crossing the Strait, quite different from the first, and to accomplish it had started his two steamers around the island. Then on the morning of 18 August he left the army at Faro and drove south in a carriage to Giardini, a small town on the coast at the foot of Taormina. Gathered there were the two steamers and Bixio with thirty-four hundred men. These were the two columns which had crossed the interior of the island and had joined in late July at Catania, even farther to the south. They had never been part of the army at Faro, and their presence in Giardini had not required any troop movements south from Faro, which might have alerted the Neapolitan on the opposite shore, nor had the Neapolitan naval patrol any reason to suppose that the two steamers, whose departure from Faro had been noted, had gone right around the island rather than merely to Palermo or Genoa.

When Garibaldi arrived at Giardini, in the afternoon, Bixio had most of the troops aboard one of the steamers, but the other had a leak which no one seemed able to find. Garibaldi, however, as an old seaman took the matter in hand, and to his great self-satisfaction succeeded in finding the hole and in calking it, at least well enough, with a homemade paste of straw and cow manure. And at ten that night both ships started for the coast of Calabria.

The sea at Giardini is not really part of the Strait. Messina is thirty miles to the north and the mainland at the closest is about twenty-four miles to the northeast; due east or south is open water, and Garibaldi steamed almost due east, heading for Melito on the southern shore of the mainland. Thus, although he made the crossing a voyage of almost thirty miles instead of a possible two, he avoided the tidal difficulties of the Strait and was able to land unopposed, for at Melito the coast was deserted. The nearest Neapolitan soldiers, a garrison of a thousand men, were fifteen miles to the north at Reggio.

The crossing was completed during the night, without sighting a Neapolitan warship. But the next afternoon several appeared and sank one of the steamers which had run aground; the other had already returned to Sicily. That night the first expedition to land in Calabria, the two hundred men with their Calabrian volunteers, appeared in the mountains behind Garibaldi and joined him the next day.

In spite of warnings from the war minister at Naples, General Galotti at Reggio did nothing to prepare for an attack by Garibaldi except to insist that Reggio could be attacked only from the sea. Galotti was another ancient general, like Lanza, and he did not even ask for re-enforcements though he knew his men were outnumbered and the townspeople disloyal. Nevertheless he left the gates and the walls to the townspeople who were formed into a National Guard, and placed his loyal troops in a potential trap, the large piazza before the cathedral. As a result when the attack came, close to midnight on 20/21 August, the gates were opened to Garibaldi and his men, and they were able to reach the center of the town before firing a shot.

Once the battle began, the Neapolitans fought well; but they were outnumbered, surrounded and at a disadvantage in the open piazza, and by dawn they had retreated into the castle. There they could have held out for weeks, for the castle was well provisioned, but a number of incidents the next day sapped their morale. When a relieving column of two thousand was seen approaching the town, the soldiers begged to be ordered out to catch Garibaldi between two fires, but Galotti refused to allow a sally. The men on the battlements, therefore, saw their relief approach and then retreat, and they felt themselves to be not only incompetently commanded but also deserted. Then when Garibaldi's sharpshooters on the mountainside, which rose up steeply behind the castle, began to pick off anyone appearing on the battlements, the Neapolitans lost heart and surrendered. Less than four days after Garibaldi had landed on the mainland he had captured Reggio, the chief city of Lower Calabria.

And while Garibaldi was taking Reggio and the sound of his action there had pulled the naval patrol southward, Enrico Cosenz at Faro in the late night led nearly fifteen hundred men in rowboats through the currents of ancient Charybdis, in a detour past a fort built on the rock of Scilla and landed them safely on the beach at Favazzina. They were soon attacked on one side by Neapolitan troops from Scilla and on the other, from Bagnara, but they succeeded in fighting their way through to Aspromonte and disappeared into the highlands. The next morning as the Neapolitan warships hastened back from Reggio, they could sink or capture only the empty rowboats which fishermen were taking back to Faro.

The news that Garibaldi himself was across the Strait followed so soon after by the fall of Reggio, the provincial capital of Lower Calabria, convinced all the simple people and many of the Neapolitan soldiers that he was invincible. The Calabrian peasants thought him touched with divinity, the brother, perhaps, of Jesus. "Il nostro secondo Gesù Cristo," they exclaimed. The soldiers, on the other hand, said he had sold himself, body and soul, to the devil. They said that his life was charmed and that his red shirt was a shield from which he shook out the bullets after the fight.

At Naples the more sophisticated believed that his movement, at least, was invincible, and signs of further disintegration within the government appeared almost daily. On 20 August, Don Liborio Romano, the prefect of police at Naples, presented the king with a memorandum in which he recommended that Francesco retire from the kingdom in order to spare his people "the horrors of civil war." Garibaldi, presumably, would remain in the kingdom. And four days later the Conte di Siracusa, who was now admittedly in Cavour's service and boasting that after the revolution he would be the only Bourbon prince allowed to live in Italy, published a letter to the king in which he urged Francesco to sacrifice the throne to the cause of nationality: "While there is yet time save our House from the curses of all Italy! Follow the noble example of our royal relative in Parma [the Regent Duchess], who released her subjects from their allegiance and made them arbiters of their own destiny." And in the provinces of Upper Calabria and Basilicata the revolutionary committees, dominated often by the great landlords, controlled the countryside and began to raise small armies like feudal levies.

Down in the toe of Italy, in Lower Calabria, Garibaldi and Cosenz, operating from two bases, kept the Neapolitan troops divided and quickly picked off the garrisons and forts along the coast one after another. In several instances there was no fighting at all. The Neapolitan officer in command would offer to surrender; his men would look sullen and be uncertain what to do and Garibaldi would ride toward them: "You as well as my companions," he would say in his extraordinary voice, "are the sons of Italy—remember that. You are at liberty. Whoever wishes to remain with us may apply to General Cosenz, your countryman, who has authority to enlist you. But whoever wishes may go home." Few enlisted; the great majority, confused and disconsolate, started walking home.

The Neapolitan common soldier was not famous for his sensitivity but the violence done to his sense of duty in these surrenders plainly was a traumatic experience for many of them. When some who had not sur- rendered recognized a general who had, passing through a town in civilian clothes, they rushed at him, shouting *Traditore!*, killed him, cut off his head and genitals, and killed and burned his horse. Very few, to Gari- baldi's distress, would ever join him, and many, after weeks of walking, reached their homes and then pushed on to rejoin their king and army. The collapse of the army was primarily in the officer corps.

Garibaldi's advance now became a race northward along the coast to cut off the retreat of those Neapolitan regiments, about twelve thousand men, which were still intact and hurrying back to Naples. And on 30 August he caught them between his own army and another of six thousand Calabrians which had been raised by two of the feudal leaders in Upper Calabria.

The Neapolitan position was difficult, although perhaps not impossible, but men and officers alike were too demoralized to fight. All around them the countryside was in arms and proclaiming Garibaldi its dictator, and now he had caught them on a mountain road where retreat was cut off by felled trees, ditches and an excited peasant army. Not a shot was fired. Without argument the soldiers stacked their rifles and gave up their cannon and horses. Then, listlessly, sullenly, line after line broke ranks and started walking home through the mountains.

While they were leaving, Garibaldi was handed a message from Don Liborio Romano in Naples stating that at the first sign of reaction on Francesco's part he would proclaim Garibaldi dictator of the kingdom. Nothing but distance now kept Garibaldi from Naples, and he started at once, leaving his army days behind him on the road. He wanted to forestall anarchy or civil war from breaking out in the city, and he wanted to fore-stall Cavour from snatching it from him and then preventing him from invading the Papal States.

Whatever timing Cavour may have intended for his plan of invading the Papal States with the Sardinian army, Garibaldi's success in crossing the Strait and in capturing Reggio and the forts along the coast road of Lower Calabria accelerated it. If Cavour was to prevent Garibaldi from striking for Rome and to preserve for Vittorio Emanuele the larger share of glory in the making of Italy, he needed to act before Garibaldi reached Naples or run the risk that on the fall of the Bourbon government Gari-baldi in a few days might be with an army on the border of the Papal States. Accordingly on 28 August, two days before the final collapse of the main Neapolitan army south of Naples, he sent Farini and General Enrico Cialdini to see Napoleon, who was at Chambéry, the capital of Savoy. Publicly, on behalf of Vittorio Emanuele, the two men were to welcome Napoleon to his new province; privately, they were to tell him of Cavour's plan and to explain the necessity for it.

The next day Cavour reported the meeting in a letter to his ambassador at Paris:

> Farini and Cialdini returned this morning from Chambéry. The Em-peror was perfect. Farini, following Conneau's advice, explained to him the plan we have adopted. Here it is in a few words:
>
> It is too late to prevent Garibaldi from reaching Naples and being proclaimed Dictator there. We must no longer fight on this ground; consequently I have written Persano to content himself with seizing the forts, collecting the Neapolitan fleet, and for the rest simply to do whatever Garibaldi wants.
>
> Not being able to forestall Garibaldi at Naples, we must stop him elsewhere. That will be in Umbria and the Marches. A revolutionary movement is about to break out there; immediately, in the name of the principles of order and humanity, Cialdini enters the Marches, and Fanti, Umbria; they throw Lamoricière [the Papal Commanding Gen-eral] into the sea and take Ancona, while declaring Rome inviolable.
>
> The Emperor approved everything. . . . He said that Diplomacy would utter shrieks but would let us go ahead; that he himself would be placed in a difficult position, but that he would put forward the idea of a congress. . . .[95]

At the close of the interview, according to tradition, Napoleon said to Cavour's envoys, *"Faites, mais faites vite,"* or "Do it, but do it quickly."

Undoubtedly, as Cavour's letter suggests, Farini stressed to Napoleon that the purpose of the invasion would be to preserve order and hu-manity, but when the invasion started, Cavour presented it to Italian patriots as a move to liberate fellow Italians from Papal tyranny and to continue the unification of Italy. This was the summer in which he remarked, "If we did the things for ourselves that we do for the state, we'd be great scoundrels indeed," and his policy and actions were never less straightforward than in these weeks. To achieve the independence and uni- fication of Italy on the terms he thought best he misled in varying degrees almost every person with whom he had dealings. He assured the Neapoli- tan diplomats that he wanted an alliance with Naples while he worked to avoid it and even to spark a revolution behind their backs. He assured the Austrian diplomats that he had no designs on the Veneto, while assuring Kossuth and the Hungarian patriots of the opposite. He assured Napoleon that he would do nothing without his consent, while protesting to the British that he was independent of France. He urged Garibaldi through Persano to cross the Strait and march to Venice, while hoping to stop him short of Rome, and to the Sardinian army and bureaucracy he talked always of "annexing" the other "provinces" of Italy, while to the patriots at large, in the other Italian states, he talked of Italians liberating them- selves and of making a new Kingdom of Italy. Some of the contradictions would plague the Italians for generations, but most of them Cavour was able to use to his advantage and, in the opinion of most historians, to the advantage of Italy. Trevelyan described the invasion of Umbria and the Marches, which ended the pope's temporal power as a major issue in Italian life, as "the crowning act of Cavour's life," and even the more anti- Cavourian Mack Smith called it his "finest and most typical achievement." Scholars and historians who favor Cavour are even more laudatory.

While Cavour was preparing his invasion, Garibaldi, traveling mostly in a small carriage, fast was approaching Naples and on 6 September entered Salerno, only thirty miles to the south of it. His nearest troops were two days behind him, and the main body of the army, coming along by forced marches, was considerably more. With him were only a few officers and a number of English hangers-on who had been able to afford their own carriages.

The journey had not been without danger, and during the week it required, two important decisions were reached, one military, the other, political. The military decision was made by the Neapolitans and affected the defense of Naples. Not all the Neapolitan troops south of the city as yet had surrendered, and Garibaldi often had avoided them by leaving the main road or, on one occasion, detouring past them by sea. In particular a large garrison at Salerno had seemed likely to block his way until it had been dislodged by a series of lying telegrams. His officers on arriving in Eboli had wired the Minister of War in Naples that certain regiments which in fact were still loyal had deserted to Garibaldi and that Garibaldi had five thousand men with him and was expecting momentarily to be

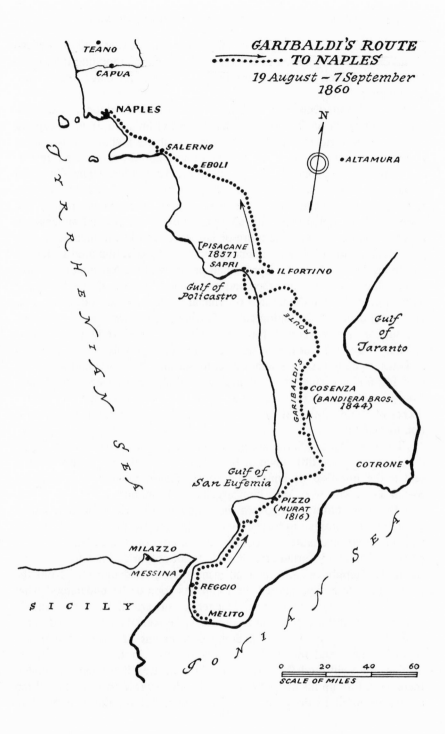

GARIBALDI'S ROUTE
TO NAPLES
19 August – 7 September
1860

N

TEANO

CAPUA

NAPLES

SALERNO

EBOLI

ALTAMURA

[PISACANE
1857]
SAPRI

IL FORTINO

Gulf of
Policastro

GARIBALDI'S ROUTE

Gulf
of
Taranto

COSENZA
(BANDIERA BROS.
1844)

COTRONE

Gulf of
San Eufemia

PIZZO
(MURAT
1816)

MILAZZO

MESSINA

REGGIO

MELITO

SICILY

TYRRHENIAN SEA

IONIAN SEA

0      20      40      60
SCALE OF MILES

joined by five thousand more. The minister in Naples was ready to believe it and ordered the garrison at Salerno to fall back, abandoning the mountain position which was the natural line on the south for defending Naples. (See map, p. 620.)

The political decision was Garibaldi's and involved once again the question of when Sicily should be joined to Sardinia. In July, to replace La Farina, Vittorio Emanuele had offered Garibaldi a choice of two men, and of them Garibaldi had selected Agostino Depretis, a moderate republican, and had appointed him pro-dictator. Thereafter, while Garibaldi concerned himself with crossing the Strait, Depretis and Crispi had worked together, not always amicably, to support Garibaldi with men, money and supplies while implementing his civil policy of "slow, gradual annexation, as the opportunities become more or less easy, and in the meantime a *de facto* assimilation of Sicilian administration to the governmental system of Piedmont." On 3 August, Depretis had proclaimed the Sardinian constitution the law of the land and then had proclaimed successively the Sardinian mercantile code, communal and provincial administrative codes, the military penal code and had adopted the Sardinian currency system, although it would be many years before the Sardinian "lire" fully replaced the Sicilian "onze." The next step seemed to Depretis, to Cavour and to many Sicilians, to be the island's annexation to Sardinia, which would substitute civil for military rule and stabilize Garibaldi's improvised government. Now that he was across the Strait, there seemed no reason to delay a decree of annexation, and Depretis sent a messenger to ask for authorization to make it.

The messenger, a Sardinian naval officer, caught up with Garibaldi on 4 September in the little town of Il Fortino, and in the town's tavern presented the question of annexation to Garibaldi. Generals Cosenz and Stefan Türr, who were with him, urged him to authorize it on condition that Depretis continue to govern the island as Vittorio Emanuele's lieutenant and to continue to forward men and money to the army, conditions which Depretis probably had assumed as a matter of course. Garibaldi was persuaded and had started dictating a letter of authorization when Bertani, the radical republican whose small army Cavour had deflected from the Papal States to Sicily, entered the room. As soon as he understood what was afoot, he began to protest: "General, you are abdicating." And in spite of all that Türr or Cosenz could say, he soon had persuaded Garibaldi not to rely on Cavour and the government in Turin to continue supplying men and money but to rely directly, in the best Mazzinian fashion, on Sicily and the provinces which he was liberating. Garibaldi, thereupon, tore up his first letter and in its place wrote to Depretis: "I am always disposed to do what you recommend, but on this one point of annexation . . . I prefer that all should be done simultaneously when we reach Rome."

The decision was to have bad consequences, and if Depretis had started the messenger only a week later, Garibaldi might have decided differently. For the very next day Cavour's Minister of War, General Fanti, went to join the Sardinian army in its autumn maneuvers, which were taking place on the northern border of the Papal States, and by the week's end Cavour's invasion of the Papal States had begun. But as Garibaldi sat in the tavern at Il Fortino, the invasion was still a secret plan, and Bertani was able to present Cavour as the man who twice had stopped an invasion of the Papal States, had stopped the recruitment of volunteers, had sent La Farina to Sicily, and who had bartered away Nice and Savoy to Louis Napoleon who had himself betrayed a republican revolution. However Cavour might have appeared to Garibaldi a week later, after the invasion of the Papal States had begun, on 4 September he was a man who opposed the unification of Italy, and the best way to defeat his intrigues was to delay annexation and to hurry on to Naples.

On 6 September as Garibaldi was entering Salerno, Francesco, his queen and the main part of his army were leaving Naples. The lying telegrams had convinced the king that the situation was worse than it was, and he had determined to withdraw to a stronger position to the north based on Gaeta, Capua and the Volturno river. He also was eager to spare Naples with its millions of civilians the death and destruction which three days of fighting had brought to Palermo. He was leaving behind him about six thousand men in the four great castles of the city, Nuovo, dell'Ovo, Sant'Elmo and Carmine, but he had instructed their commanding officers to remain neutral and not to shed blood. It is not clear what he intended if the garrisons were attacked; he seems to have thought of them as merely a force for peace and order until Garibaldi's troops could take over.

All of Naples knew he was going, for he had announced his departure with the reasons for it in a proclamation which had been posted in every part of the city. In the afternoon he summoned his ministers to bid him goodbye. Neither he nor they expected them to accompany him. He was going to Gaeta to conduct from that corner of his kingdom a purely military defense, and if he was successful both he and Don Liborio Romano expected him on his return to dismiss his powerful but disloyal minister. "Don Libo," he remarked as they parted, "look out for your head." Unperturbed, Romano replied, "Sire, I will do my best to keep it on my shoulders."

A few hours later Francesco II and Maria Sophia walked down from the Palazzo Reale to the dock at its foot and boarded a small gunboat. As it steamed out into the Bay of Naples, the captain signaled the rest of the fleet to follow, but not one ship stirred. Slowly through the crowded harbor, in full sight of the city, the Bourbon king sailed away before the onrush of a republican revolution, much as Ferdinando I and Maria Carolina had done in 1799. Francesco, however, unlike his predecessor, had scarcely had the chance to be a good king or a bad one. When he had come to the throne, in May 1859, the war in the Po valley was already begun and Napoleon was about to win the battle of Magenta. In the fifteen months thereafter, as one crisis had followed another, he had not proved himself to his people. Probably most of them who saw him go found their personal feelings, of hatred or affection, untouched. Like the scapegoat of old, he was being driven into the wilderness because of the sins of others, mostly of his own family.

As soon as the king's ship was well out in the Bay, Don Liborio Romano started two men south to Salerno to invite Garibaldi to enter Naples and to report that the mayor and the general in command of the city's National Guard would attend him to make plans for a suitable entry. The messengers traveled by railway, which at that time extended as far as Vietri, two miles north of Salerno, and arrived late on the night of 6 September; the mayor and general came early the next morning. At a conference with Garibaldi and his staff the mayor described his ideas for triumphal arches, speeches and a parade, the general talked of the Bourbon garrisons in the castles and of some loyal Bourbon companies in a troop train on the rail line, and Garibaldi's staff pointed out that the nearest volunteers, about fifteen hundred men, were still two days behind him. Their unanimous conclusion was that he should remain two or three more days in Salerno while his own men came up, the troop train was run north to Capua and the city made its arrangements and perhaps, somehow, neutralized the troops in the castles.

Garibaldi listened and disagreed. "Naples is in danger," he said. "We must go there today; we must go this minute." And he would hear no more discussion. He rose, the conference ended, and a telegram was sent to Don Liborio Romano announcing his arrival at noon.

At half past nine he left Salerno by carriage in a scene of wild enthusiasm. An English tourist, W. G. Clark, watching from a window saw a man who was cheering suddenly fall as if in a fit, and he asked his landlady if the man was drunk. " 'No,' she replied, 'it is joy. Ah,' in a tone of reproach, 'you English, who have always been free, cannot imagine the delight of deliverance.' And she made a gesture as if she were about to fly."

Clark was so impressed with the excitement that he hurried to Vietri and succeeded in squeezing himself onto Garibaldi's train. Scores of others had done the same, and by the time the train pulled out, it had men hanging out the windows, on all the platforms and on the roof. For the entire journey most of them sang over and over again

| | |
|---|---|
| Siamo Italiani | We are Italians, |
| Giovani freschi, | Strong young men, |
| Contro ai Tedeschi | Against the Austrians |
| Vogliam pugnar | We wish to fight |
| Viva l'Italia | Viva l'Italia |
| Viva l'Unione | Viva l'Unione |
| Viva Garibaldi | Viva Garibaldi |
| E la libertà | E la libertà |

For most of the journey Garibaldi sat silent, his face radiant with emotion. In the mayor's carriage they planned the triumphal procession, proposing to take it through the center of the city rather than along the waterfront in order to avoid the two castles of Carmine and Nuovo. And the troop train of Bourbon soldiers was simply shunted onto a siding and passed without incident.

As the train drew closer to Naples, it hardly could proceed for the track at each village was covered with people determined to see Garibaldi. Fishermen came up from the seaside, women brought down their babies, and priests and monks led flocks of school children and adults to see the great man. But finally, an hour and a half late, the train pulled into the Naples station.

A moderate and orderly crowd, the National Guard and Don Liborio Romano were there to greet him, and Romano began his speech of welcome. Many Neapolitans, perhaps fearing trouble with the garrisons in the castles or perhaps suspecting that Garibaldi himself would not come on the first train, had stayed home. But as soon as he stepped out on the platform, word that he truly had arrived flashed through the city, and a great multitude poured into the streets and converged on the station. It knocked aside the lines of National Guard, paid no heed to Don Liborio and took Garibaldi to itself. Don Liborio, his speech unfinished, was unable even to push his way to the carriage in which Garibaldi had taken refuge, nor could the mayor or the general of the National Guard. Even Cosenz who had been standing close to Garibaldi was whirled off in another direction and unable to work his way back. He had been an exile from Naples since 1848 and now he went off to see his mother. A few of Garibaldi's aides succeeded in getting into the carriage with him and so, too, did Bertani, but no officials or guards, and in his *Memorie* Garibaldi expresses a republican's joy that he, "a son of the people, *un figlio del popolo,*" should have had such a direct rapport with them.

The crowd, knowing nothing of the mayor's careful plans, started the carriage down to the waterfront, requiring it to pass directly under the guns of the Castel Carmine. As it approached, the soldiers could be seen peering out over their cannon. Garibaldi stood up, folded his arms and looked the men straight in the face. A few saluted and, mindful of their orders, none fired.

Then as the carriage turned into the waterfront, an enormous cry broke out. All of Naples seemed gathered in ships' rigging on one side or in the commercial buildings on the other. Garibaldi remained standing, his head uncovered and bowed. The carriage moved slowly. Hanging on to its rear was an artist who had improvised a large tricolor flag with the horse of Naples on one side and the lion of Venice on the other. The sun blazed down, and it seemed to Garibaldi's companions that his face visibly had tanned before they had reached the Castel Nuovo. Here again the gunners did not fire.

The end of the procession was the Palazzo Reale, the north side of which looks out on an enormous semicircular open space which then was called, after the church at its back, Largo San Francesco di Paola but today, the Piazza del Plebiscito. From an annex of the palace, then called the foresteria but now the prefettura, he addressed the crowd from a balcony, and though his exact words have been quoted differently, in essence all the versions are the same:

> You have a right to exult in this day in which ends the tyranny which has oppressed you and begins an era of liberty. And you are worthy of it, sons of Italy's most splendid jewel. I thank you for this welcome not only for myself but in the name of Italy which will be united with your help: and not only Italy but all of Europe should be grateful to you.[96]

Perhaps it was not his greatest speech, but he delivered it in his moving and resonant voice and as he stood before them, bareheaded and dressed in a spotted, sweat-stained red shirt and baggy, gray trousers, he was immensely appealing to them, and they felt as he did that he was "a son of the people." That night when they went to cheer him at the Palazzo d'Angri, an aide stepped on the balcony and laying his cheek on his hand indicated that Garibaldi was sleeping. *"Ah,"* murmured the crowd, *"egli dorme,"* and instantly fell silent, going off to other parts of the city to weep and shout and sing.

For three days the city gave itself over to wild celebration. All business stopped, and people seemed hardly to go to bed. W. G. Clark, the English tourist, wrote:

> The noise was indescribable. The hero's name was repeated in all manner of forms, as if it were a declinable noun—Garibaldi, Garibaldo,

Garibalda—nay it was metamorphosed into Garribar and Gallipot and Galliboard; at last the two first syllables were suppressed, and "Viva *Board*" was the favorite cry, the sound of the last syllable being prolonged to the utmost. You heard too, "Viva Vittorio Emanuele," and still more frequently, "Viva l'Italia unita" which at length was shortened into *una*, and when people got so hoarse that they could not articulate any longer, they held out the forefinger and shook it as they passed, indicative of their desire for unity. . . . Here and there an excited orator addressed the crowd about him in wild declamation; little bands of enthusiasts, headed sometimes by a priest and sometimes by a woman, went dancing through the streets and burst into the *cafés*, compelling all present to join in the popular cry. . . . When I was in the Café d'Europe a priest rushed in with frantic gestures, with eyes starting from his head, with a banner in one hand and a knife in the other, uttering horrible and inarticulate howlings. . . . An unfortunate man who did not cry "Viva Garibaldi!" when he was bidden was ripped open by another enthusiast and died on the spot.[97]

But in the midst of this civic frenzy which bordered on madness there were others in Naples who, as the British minister there reported, were "in the most gloomy and despairing humor, for it was understood that Garibaldi had thrown himself into the hands of the extreme party, and that he would not hear of annexation until 'both the Roman States and Venetia had been conquered.' "

Increasingly the more deliberative sections of the public, north or south, began to fear that Garibaldi himself might be touched with a little of the madness he inspired in others. Palermo and Naples were one thing, but in Rome there was the pope and the French, and in Venice, the Austrians. No one doubted Garibaldi's courage or his ability to persuade an army to follow him, but when, on 11 September, the Sardinian army invaded Umbria and the Marches many men heard of it with a sense of relief. They trusted Cavour to have weighed the chances of a European war in which all that had been gained might be lost, or, unlike Garibaldi, he would never have started.

# CHAPTER 43

Pio Nono's view of the invasion of the Papal States. His volunteer army. Its defeat at Castelfidardo. Garibaldi asks for Cavour's dismissal. Cavour's estimate of Garibaldi. The republican dream of Rome. The volunteers and the Bandiera Brothers at Cosenza. Garibaldi again postpones annexation of Sicily. Failure of his government at Naples. Mazzini, Pallavicino, Cavour, and the threat of civil war. Garibaldi's reception of the Sardinian army. Battle of the Volturno. Cavour declares Rome to be the capital. Annexation by plebiscite or assembly. Pallavicino asks Mazzini to leave Naples. The plebiscites and their significance. Garibaldi meets the King at Teano. Lord John Russell's dispatch. The regular army and the volunteers.

IN PREPARATION for Sardinia's invasion of the Papal States, Cavour first sent the army to maneuver close to the Papal border; then he sent the Minister of War, Manfredo Fanti, who was to be in command, to oversee the maneuvers. Two days later, on 7 September 1860, he sent Pio Nono an ultimatum citing certain unspecified massacres perpetrated by the Papal army and demanding that Pio Nono disband his foreign mercenaries "who suffocate in Italian blood every expression of the national will." The next day, by prearrangement with him through the *Società Nazionale Italiana,* revolutionary committees in a number of Papal cities in Umbria and the Marches succeeded with volunteers in forcing the Papal garrisons to surrender and then, as their first act of freedom, sent delegations to Vittorio Emanuele asking for immediate annexation to Sardinia. Then finally, on 11 September, as Cavour in Turin talked alternately of preserving order and of freeing oppressed Italians, the Sardinian army crossed the border, one column of it moving through the mountains of Umbria toward Spoleto and the other, down the Adriatic coast of the Marches toward Ancona.

To Pio Nono all of Cavour's reasons for the invasion were merely hypocrisies used to support a great sacrilege, the wresting from God's vicar of God's gift to the Church. Sardinia under Cavour had attacked the Church with the Siccardi Laws and the Law on the Convents, then under the protection of Napoleon III it had filched the Romagna, and now it was preparing to absorb Umbria and the Marches. To Pio Nono the foreign mercenaries of which Cavour complained were devout Catholics who had come from France, Austria, Belgium and Ireland to defend a Catholic idea, the Papal States, which had been accepted internationally for more than a thousand years; and the "national will" which wished to destroy that idea by annexing Papal provinces to Sardinia was merely Sardinian self-seeking created and supported by Sardinian gold.

On both points, in some measure, Pio Nono was right. The Papal army, which he had recruited hastily in the previous nine months, was as much a volunteer force imbued with an idea as Garibaldi's army, and the *Società*, to the extent it was responsible for the expressions of national will, had ceased to be an independent party supporting Cavour's policy in part and on conditions and had become a government party acting on his command. Yet more fundamentally, Pio Nono altogether missed the significance of what was happening in Italy. On 21 June, after the fall of Palermo, he gave an audience to Odo Russell, the British agent at Rome, and in the course of it he said:

> . . . The Papacy has had severer trials than the present one and the Pope knows how to suffer, to wait and to hope. The day will come when the Church will triumph again over her enemies. I fully understand now that we are in a crisis which must develop itself to the end. We cannot arrest its progress and the duty of the Pope is to wait, defend the rights of the Church and not give way to his enemies so long as it pleases God to send us these trials. The Italians are not a bad people but they are easily led astray by foreign agents who revolutionize the country for their own wicked purposes.[98]

Russell thereupon observed that such movements depended on the amount of confidence a people had in its government and institutions and that the task of Italian governments, therefore, was to establish such institutions as would inspire confidence in the governed for the government. He thought it unreasonable to suppose that Sardinian money and agents could produce a national movement of the size and intensity which presently was disturbing the Italian people. To which the Pope replied:

> . . . You are mistaken if you take the present crisis in Italy for a national one. What is being done now will all be undone again in time. Piedmont is an instrument in the hands of the Emperor Napoleon, who thinks it is his duty to carry out the ideas of his uncle. What his ultimate objects are I know not, but whatever he establishes will end with him as the Kingdom of his uncle ended with the Empire. The Grand Dukes or their heirs will return to their dominions and the rights of the Papacy are everlasting.[98]

On his election Pio Nono had taken the name Pio in memory of Pius VII, the pope whom the first Napoleon had imprisoned, and he tended now to cast himself and Napoleon III in the same roles. But the situations were not truly similar, and when the third Napoleon's empire ended in 1870, the dukes or their heirs did not return and the pope became a "prisoner" in the Vatican, to the extent he was one, because of the Italian national movement which he had misunderstood. When Russell tried to convince him that the movement was deeply rooted in Italy, had been nurtured by the tendency of Italian princes to call in foreign assistance against their subjects and had grown into a belief that the only way the Italian people could keep their independence was to unite under one sovereign, Pio Nono replied:

> *Figlio mio,* you speak in ignorance of past events. I tried to give national liberties to my subjects and they murdered my Minister [Pellegrino Rossi] and forced me to fly. The Grand Duke of Tuscany's government was universally admitted to be good and yet he was driven away. The Romagnoles are devoted to the Papacy, and yet a small and criminal minority was sufficient to terrorize even the better people into voting for annexation for Piedmont. As I said before, the Italians are not bad. See only how they attend the procession of the Holy Virgin in Rome. But they are timid and easily led astray. They can never govern themselves, they require a firm hand to guide and govern them. As to my Government it belongs to the Catholic world and not to Italy alone and those who serve it cease to have a nationality of their own. They serve God and Christianity. . . .[98]

In this spirit Pio Nono had prepared to meet the attack on his states which seemed sure to come, either from Cavour in the north or Garibaldi in the south. Twelve years earlier, in 1848, he had seemed the liberal pope for whom Italian patriots had longed, and his reforms, such as the amnesty, the press law and the constitution, had put him at the head of the national movement as it then was. Its destination, however, had been war with Austria, and with his allocution the pope had left the movement and, as he reminded Russell, soon thereafter had been forced from Rome. On his return in 1850 he had seemed so different, so illiberal, that some patriots had referred to him as a new pope: Pio Nono Secondo.

But during the ten years leading up to 1860 his approach to the problem of his temporal power suggests that in fact he never had changed; rather the patriots of 1848 had misunderstood him. He seems always to have conceived of the Papal government, spiritual and temporal, as a trust committed to him personally, which he was to discharge personally. He could be liberal in the exercise of his authority, which he had tried to be in 1848, but he could not introduce liberal institutions into his government, as he had discovered then, for they presupposed a sharing of his personal authority. They also presupposed, at least in temporal affairs, laymen in the government, the elevation of reason and compromise over the principle of authority and a preference for material over spiritual values.

Yet the desire for liberal institutions and a share in the government continued strong among many of his subjects, and whereas in 1848 it had forced him toward a war with Austria it now, coupled with the increasing desire for unity, was forcing him toward a war with his fellow Italians. He had been unable to imagine any solution to the problem of his temporal power except, as always before, to call in foreign soldiers, whether an army or volunteers, to repel invaders and to discipline his people. This failure of creative imagination, in which most of his hierarchy shared, isolated him and the Church more and more, and the Papacy as a temporal power began to have about it the air of a lost cause.

Of the volunteers who had answered his call, about fifteen thousand men, six thousand were professional soldiers from the Austrian army who had left their regiments with Franz Josef's approval, and the balance were a mixture of rowdies, idealists and true mercenaries, mostly Swiss. The tone of the army, however, was set by the great number of French nobles of the old aristocracy who came to serve as officers. Most of them including the army's commanding general, Christophe Lamoricière, were "legitimatists" in their French politics, men who wanted to dethrone Napoleon and to replace him with the Bourbon pretender. And often in the evenings at Rome they would go to the French garrisons or the embassy and cheer not for Napoleon but for "Henri V."

Cardinal Antonelli, who would have preferred diplomatic pressure on Sardinia to a volunteer army, constantly warned Pio Nono against alienating Napoleon, who already was prepared to defend Rome and, being on principle opposed to Italian unity, might do more. But the pope listened instead to Frédéric de Mérode, a Belgian soldier turned priest, whom he had made his Minister of War. De Mérode was an enthusiast, and he fascinated Pio Nono with the idea of the Church militant. Rome bustled with military activity: bugles sounded, soldiers drilled, bullet and powder factories were set up close to the Vatican, and in the barracks and cafés the volunteers talked fervently of their duty to die for the Holy Father. Pio Nono enjoyed it all, and he, de Mérode and the volunteers, convinced they were on a crusade, simply ignored the contradictions and dangers of his policy. Once the Sardinian invasion began, however, these immediately became apparent. (See map, p. 594.)

Cavour sent about half the Sardinian army, thirty-three thousand men, into the Papal States and kept the rest to face the Austrians in the Veneto.

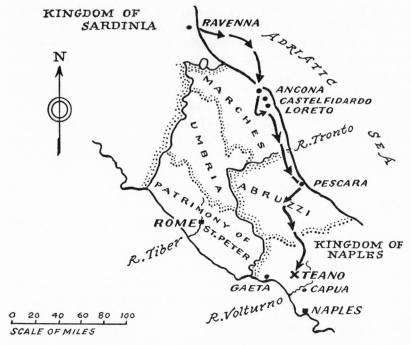

ROUTE OF VITTORIO EMANUELE ➤
TO MEET GARIBALDI,
2-26 October, 1860

As Lamoricière's volunteers numbered only thirteen thousand, they could
not win alone, and his strategy was to hold the mountain forts of Umbria
and the seaports of the Marches, particularly the large port of Ancona,
until either Napoleon or Franz Josef sent troops to the pope's aid. The
Sardinian strategy, on the other hand, was to take the forts and seaports,
to destroy Lamoricière's army and to occupy the two provinces, while
declaring Rome inviolable, all before the French or Austrians could act.
Cavour for ten years had worked to cement his alliance with Napoleon,
and if he almost had split it apart over Villafranca, he had tried hard to
patch it up since. He had cleared the plans for the invasion with Napoleon
on 28 August at Chambéry and a second time three days later, only a
week before he sent his ultimatum to the pope. Pio Nono, on the other
hand, had never acknowledged the value of Napoleon's services in returning him to Rome in 1850, had refused to make the reforms Napoleon then
had suggested, and in the last year had recruited an army in which many
of the officers were Napoleon's enemies. Further, he had permitted and
enjoyed the public insults these men had offered the French emperor.

When the invasion began on 11 September, Napoleon was embarking on a cruise in the Mediterranean, where, as it was before the days of radio, he could not be reached. And for twelve days he remained at sea.

During that time the two Sardinian columns moved swiftly southward, capturing the forts inland and on the coast, and on 17 September the column under General Cialdini succeeded by forced marches in placing itself between Ancona and the main army of volunteers under Lamoricière. Ancona, which was strongly fortified, was the traditional port of entry into the Papal States for Austrian troops, for which reason Lamoricière hoped to keep it open and Cialdini, to close it. The next morning, on 18 September, the two armies fought near the small town of Castelfidardo, close to the shrine of Loreto where many of the Papal volunteers, in the manner of medieval crusaders, spent the night in prayer.

The Sardinians numbered seventeen thousand, the volunteers only six thousand, and the Sardinians had the better equipment, so that the battle from the start was one-sided. But the volunteers fought well and many of them, heroically. Nevertheless, at the end of the day, they were defeated completely, and only Lamoricière and forty-five others on horseback succeeded in breaking through to Ancona.

The garrison there held out until 29 September, hoping each day that the Austrian fleet at Trieste would appear to support them. But instead the Sardinian fleet had appeared from Naples and with a bombardment had destroyed the weaker, seaward fortifications. With the fall of Ancona, which coincided almost exactly with Napoleon's return to Paris, the invasion was completed. Two provinces were torn from the Papal States, and the link of land taken by which the north and south of Italy could be united in a single, continuous kingdom.

Cavour, as Napoleon had advised, had pursued a policy of *"faites vite,"* for the war had lasted only two and a half weeks and was for its time an extremely quick and well-organized campaign. If the Austrians under Gyulai in May 1859 had moved as fast toward Turin at the start of the war in the Po valley, there might never have been a Magenta, a Solferino or a Castelfidardo.

The diplomatic outcry from Catholic countries was great, and the French government, while Napoleon was at sea, recalled its ambassador from Turin and sent four more regiments to Rome. But it would not do more without the emperor's orders, and with him obviously evading the issue and with Britain openly sympathetic with Sardinia, the other powers refused to act. Only Austria, conceivably, could have acted alone, and Cavour apparently had gauged correctly the internal troubles that would cause Franz Josef to hesitate; and quite possibly the total destruction of the Papal army at Castelfidardo, only a week after the campaign began, finally determined the Austrian emperor against intervention.

Pio Nono issued an allocution condemning the Sardinian and the French governments for their behavior, but in clerical circles in both France and Italy the emphasis of the indignation fell on Napoleon. For once Cavour's actions, although condemned as self-serving and hypocritical, were excused by comparison to Napoleon's evasion as relatively open and honest. Napoleon, however, was judged to have betrayed the pope. In fact, he followed the policy he had stated publicly, almost a year earlier, in his pamphlet *Le Pape et le Congrès*. His general at Rome required the Sardinian army to withdraw from several cities close to Rome which had been occupied, such as Civitavecchia, Viterbo and Orte, and the pope was guaranteed his independence in a coastal "garden," "The Patrimony of St. Peter," which was roughly one hundred miles long and forty wide with Rome at its center. Pio Nono considered leaving Rome to seek support by visiting the Catholic capitals of Europe but in the end decided to remain. The succeeding months were distressing for him, and he frequently was ill. Nevertheless, again listening to de Mérode rather than to Antonelli, he began to recruit another volunteer army, insisting that at any moment the French might withdraw and leave him alone to face either Vittorio Emanuele and the Sardinian army or Garibaldi and his volunteers.

The campaign had brought the Sardinian army to the northern border of the Kingdom of Naples, where Umbria and the Marches abut the Neapolitan province of Abruzzi. And even before Ancona fell, the revolutionary committees in Abruzzi had seized control of the province and had established a provisional government in the name of "Italy, Vittorio Emanuele and Garibaldi Dictator." It was not difficult. Francesco II was concentrating all his loyal troops at Capua.

Vittorio Emanuele's royal army, however, was near and Garibaldi's volunteers were two hundred miles to the south, held between Naples and Capua by Francesco and his army. So in the hope of averting a breakdown of government into anarchy and brigandage, the provisional government of Abruzzi petitioned Vittorio Emanuele to cross the Neapolitan border immediately and to annex the Kingdom of Naples to Sardinia. For the moment Vittorio Emanuele and Cavour did not respond, waiting to finish the campaign in the Papal States and to gauge the diplomatic reaction to it; an Austrian army, after all, was still in their rear in the Veneto. But for Garibaldi the petition from Abruzzi, and others like it which began to appear in Naples, immediately embroiled him in Naples in the same quarrel over annexation, when and how, which was plaguing him at Palermo.

In his eyes the question was artificial and kept alive only by those who opposed him for other reasons. When he had landed at Marsala in the name of Vittorio Emanuele he had buried forever the possibility of an independent, republican state in southern Italy. And in all his acts since then he had continued to show his loyalty to the king. On entering Naples he had proclaimed himself dictator in the king's name, and all his decrees thereafter bore the insignia of the House of Savoy. With his very first decree he had transferred command of the Neapolitan fleet to the Sardinian admiral, Persano, who had entered the bay with a flotilla of Sardinian ships, and the Neapolitan fleet was larger and stronger than that of Sardinia. After the Neapolitan garrisons of the city's castles, under an evacuation agreement, had marched off with hardly a man deserting to rejoin their king at Capua, he had put a company of Bersaglieri from Persano's ships into the garrisons. And in the civil government he had appointed moderates, had continued Don Liborio Romano in office and, at the end of his first week in Naples, had decreed the Sardinian constitution to be the new law of the land.

Yet in spite of such actions his relations with Cavour over the issue of annexation and even with the king were growing steadily worse. And, as he suspected, less because he wanted to delay annexation than because he continued to insist publicly that the goal of his campaign was Rome. On 8 September, the day after he had entered Naples, he talked privately of starting for Rome within three days, even though the Neapolitan army, forty thousand strong, was still before him and most of his own troops had not yet reached Naples. Two days later he repeated his plan to the British minister in the city and, speaking bitterly of Cavour's dependence on France and cession of Nice, insisted that Rome was an Italian city and that "neither the Emperor nor anyone else" had a right to keep him out of it. And on the same day he published a proclamation to the people of Palermo in which he spoke of "the vile persons who urge annexation today" and suggested that the Sicilians ask those "cowards" who had not fought on the barricades of Palermo if he would have been able to continue the fight for Italy and to liberate Naples if he had decreed annexation in the past months. He promised to decree it soon, but from Rome, from the balcony of the pope's Palazzo del Quirinale. There was no secret about Garibaldi's animosity for Cavour. Everyone, in the north and south of Italy, understood that the "vile persons" were Cavour and his supporters.

The day after this proclamation, on 11 September, Garibaldi wrote two letters to Vittorio Emanuele. In the first he requested that Pallavicino, who with Manin and La Farina had founded the *Società Nazionale Italiana,* be sent to Naples to serve under him as pro-dictator. And in the second he demanded that Cavour be dismissed:

Till now I have been silent about the shameless opposition I have suffered from Cavour, Farini, etc., but today when we approach the climax of the great Italian drama, I must implore your Majesty, for the good of the holy cause I serve, to dismiss those individuals.[99]

The king showed the letter to Cavour, who had a copy made to send to the Sardinian ambassador in Paris. Napoleon at the moment was on his Mediterranean cruise, but Cavour wanted the letter shown to Thouvenel, the Foreign Minister, as evidence of the necessity for the Sardinian invasion of Umbria and the Marches if Garibaldi was to be kept from attacking Rome. "I believe all commentary useless," he remarked to his ambassador and added, "The King has at once replied to Garibaldi in a calm and forceful tone."

Cavour, true to his principle that "in politics there is nothing so absurd as rancour," did not now grow angry personally with Garibaldi, value at any less his immense achievements in southern Italy or even cease to try to work compatibly with him. Early in the summer, in another letter to his ambassador in Paris, he had gauged the emotional source of many of Garibaldi's actions:

Garibaldi has a generous character and the instincts of a poet; but at the same time he has a primitive nature on which certain impressions leave an indelible imprint. The cession of Nice has wounded him deeply; in a sense he regards it as a personal injury, and he will never forgive us for it. His anger further is aggravated by the memory of his disagreements with Fanti and Farini in central Italy. In fact I believe he desires to overthrow the Government as much as to drive out the Austrians.[100]

During the summer, while Garibaldi was winning Sicily and Naples, Cavour wrote many letters expressing admiration of him. Some of these, such as those to Persano, who saw Garibaldi frequently, Cavour undoubtedly hoped would be shown or quoted to him and must be discounted as efforts to improve relations. But on 9 August, two weeks after the battle at Milazzo, he wrote to his ambassador in Paris who had no contact with Garibaldi and who had suggested that Cavour must act to recapture the leadership of the national movement:

To assemble Parliament and to deliver a great parliamentary battle would be very much to my taste. But I am persuaded that even though I should succeed in saving my prestige I should ruin Italy. Now, my dear Nigra, I tell you without emphasis that I would rather see my popularity disappear, my reputation lost, and yet see Italy made. To make Italy at this juncture, we must not set in opposition Vittorio Emanuele and Garibaldi.

Garibaldi has great moral influence; he enjoys an immense prestige not only in Italy but above all in Europe. You are wrong, in my
opinion, in saying that we are placed between Garibaldi and Europe.
If tomorrow I started a struggle with Garibaldi, it is possible that I
should have the majority of the old diplomats for me, but European
public opinion would be against me. And public opinion would be
right, because Garibaldi has rendered to Italy the greatest services
that man could render to her: He has given the Italians confidence
in themselves; he has proved to Europe that Italians know how to fight
and die on the field of battle to reconquer their own country. . . .

We must not enter the lists against Garibaldi except in two cases:
(1) if he wished to involve us in a war with France; (2) if he renounced his program, by proclaiming another political system than
that of the Monarchy under Vittorio Emanuele. So long as he is loyal
to his flag we must march in step with him.[101]

The letter, so intimately concerned with the making of Italy, is written
in French, the language in which Cavour as a Piemontese aristocrat still
thought most easily and clearly, and, although written in August, fore-
casts accurately the issues over which he and Garibaldi began to collide in
September. By then the problem before Cavour was how to stop Garibaldi
from marching on Rome, in order to avoid involving Napoleon, and how
to wrest from him political control of The Two Sicilies, in order to substitute parliamentary for dictatorial government. In short, Cavour had to
stop Garibaldi's advance while at the same time detaching half of Italy
from him and his republican volunteers and advisors, all without actually
fighting them. A civil war between Italians at the very moment they
achieved independence and unification was unthinkable. Yet by the middle
of September the possibility of it was in everyone's thoughts.

Disregarding the opinions of those who were actors in the events, most
historians of the Risorgimento have thought that an attack on Rome in
September 1860 by republican volunteers was a very bad idea. And among
the English and American historians only Mack Smith, in his *Cavour and
Garibaldi, 1860: a Study in Political Conflict,* has suggested that the idea
"had something to be said in its favor"; and even he argues only that it
was militarily a legitimate idea and politically not as dangerous as it has
been judged subsequently. Many persons at that time assumed that with
the invasion of Umbria and the Marches the pope's temporal power was at
an end, that he might die soon and a more liberal pope be elected, or that
he might leave Italy and Napoleon then would withdraw his army from
Rome. And Napoleon himself even stated privately that in such event he
assumed Vittorio Emanuele would occupy and annex the city. But it is
most unlikely that he would have allowed Garibaldi to take it. The heads

of states then all were terrified lest 1860 turn into another 1848 when revolutionaries had forced them all to flee; even as many patriots feared it would turn into another 1848 when, in spite of initial successes, in the end they had accomplished nothing. The disaster each group feared was different, but both saw an attack on Rome by Garibaldi and his volunteers as disaster's prelude. Napoleon, in defending the city, would have had wide support and been able to pose in a single action as both defending the faith and preserving the peace.

For Garibaldi, however, the taking of Rome and the proclamation from there of a united Italy would be the accomplishment of a lifetime's ambition, and he therefore was inclined to believe it was possible. He also believed passionately that it was necessary, for if the new Italy were not organized around Rome rather than Turin then the making of Italy in which Italians of every state had shared would seem to them, and to the rest of the world, to be no more than the conquest by Sardinia of the other Italian states. This fear haunted many republicans and drove them to talk constantly of Rome. But others who were not republicans also shared it. At Palermo the newspapers and people debated bluntly, "Are we to become *Italiani* or *Piemontesi?*" And the majority, although beginning to favor immediate annexation to Sardinia, wanted that act to be part of the formation of a new Kingdom of Italy. Vittorio Emanuele was to cease to be Vittorio Emanuele II of Sardinia and to become Vittorio Emanuele I of Italy. But the new title surely needed a new capital nearer the center of the new kingdom; then what of Rome? Even such a staunch monarchist as Ricasoli in Florence kept insisting by letter and telegram to Cavour that the king must not ignore the call of Rome but must go there directly.

The public opinion such counsel represented plainly was widely based and growing, and it soon influenced Cavour to the point where he was admitting privately that Rome would have to replace Turin as the capital of the new Italian kingdom. At the same time, of course, it also supported Garibaldi and the republicans in their belief that a march on Rome was both a necessity and possible.

Garibaldi's volunteers now numbered forty thousand, but of these perhaps only half were prepared to fight. With his entry into Naples the ranks had swollen with hangers-on, and many of the best men had been wounded earlier or transferred into administrative jobs. Nevertheless, a hard core of about twenty thousand remained of which about two thousand were Sicilians, and twenty-five hundred Calabrians, while most of the rest were from Tuscany, Genoa and the Po valley. These twenty thousand were loyal, enthusiastic and republican. On the march north to Naples, a number of regiments had met at Cosenza, the capital of Upper Calabria and near where the Bandiera brothers and seven other Venetians had been executed in 1844 for attempting to start a revolution in the name of Italy. (See map, p. 583.) At Cosenza the volunteers had visited the cathedral where the Venetians were buried under an unmarked slab and then had marched by regiments out to the spot where the nine men had died before a firing squad. After a commemorative parade Bixio had made an address which, in Abba's words, "set fire to the air": "Soldiers of the Italian revolution, soldiers of the European revolution; we who uncover our heads only before God, now bow them at the tomb of the Bandieras who are our Saints!" And in this spirit the best of the volunteers arrived in Naples and immediately marched out of the city to the north to take up a position before the Neapolitan army which, with Capua as a fortified bridgehead on the south bank, controlled everything north of the Volturno river. Many of the volunteers were in rags and some were without shoes, and the rainy season would begin in November; but by then they expected to be in Rome.

Meanwhile in their rear the demand for immediate annexation flared up again in both Palermo and Naples. Depretis, the pro-dictator of Sicily, had been dismayed by Garibaldi's decision in the tavern at Il Fortino to delay annexation, and he came now to Naples himself, determined either to persuade Garibaldi of the reasons for it or to resign. As he doubtless tried to explain, it was not just a question of helping or hindering Garibaldi in his effort to reach Rome. The Sicilians were suffering from the ills of transitional government: taxes were not paid, the new laws were neither enforced nor obeyed and trade languished. The Sicilians wanted peace and prosperity, and as they became convinced that a provisional government with its interest tied to an army on the mainland could not achieve either for them, their desire for annexation as a solution to their problems steadily increased. But Garibaldi was not persuaded. Instead, accepting Depretis' resignation, on 17 September he went himself to Palermo and installed a new pro-dictator, Antonio Mordini, whom he considered to be more opposed to Cavour and annexation.

As always the Palermitani greeted him with rapturous affection. Whatever they might think of his political decisions, they loved him personally as the hero who had freed them. To explain his position he published a proclamation and made many impromptu speeches to crowds in the city, all to the same effect: "At Rome, people of Palermo, we will proclaim the Italian kingdom. . . . At Palermo once they wished for annexation because I had not passed the Strait. At Naples now they wish for it because I may not pass the Volturno." Or more informally to a crowd: "You have had faith in me, and I thank you for it in the name of Italy. . . . I love Vittorio Emanuele. . . . I love him because he represents Italy. . . . He has no better friend than me." And then, referring to Cavour, "If I do not wish annexation, it is because I think it untimely. With it we give ourselves bound hand

and foot to diplomacy, which will hinder us . . . will stop this irresistible movement." He asked them again to have faith in him, and without hesitation they agreed. But none of the underlying problems of his government or of the island kingdom were solved, and the news from the front in the following week only increased the fears of the Sicilians and their desire to divorce themselves from his military adventure.

While he had been in Palermo, one of his generals had crossed the Volturno in force and had been thrown back with heavy losses; and everyone in Palermo and Naples as well as the men in both armies realized that the volunteers, for the first time in their campaign, were on the defensive. Francesco's position at Capua and along the Volturno was strong, the peasants and townspeople of the area were loyal to him, and his army, which was larger and better equipped than the volunteers, had shed its most inept and disloyal officers. Now it was prepared to fight, and if Francesco could reorganize its command, it might retake Naples within a few weeks or, if the morale of the volunteers cracked, within a few days. Capua, after all, was only eighteen miles north of Naples and connected to it by good roads crossing relatively flat country. (See map, p. 620.)

In Naples the realization of how close Francesco II was to retaking the city fanned the desire of many for immediate annexation, and Garibaldi had a harder time combatting it there than in Palermo. His government in Naples had alienated more persons and he had, in any event, less popular support. Like the Sicilians most Neapolitans, particularly in the lower classes, were enthusiastic about his person, but they were far less ready to put up with his provisional government or his political advisors such as Bertani or, later, Crispi. In Sicily he had driven out the Bourbon government; in Naples he had driven out merely the head of that government, or so the Neapolitans conceived. When Francesco had departed, his ministers had remained, expecting that their power or at least that of the constitutional government would continue. But on 22 September, after a fortnight of Garibaldi's dictatorial government, all the ministers he had appointed on his entry into the city resigned in a body, infuriated at being overruled and ignored by Bertani in his role as the dictator's secretary. And Bertani thereafter filled the offices with his own men.

The government he offered, however, continued to offend almost all Neapolitans in some fashion, largely by attempting too much too fast and by not paying enough attention to law and order. In the city, for example, he released ordinary criminals on the ground they were political prisoners, and the rate of crime rose sharply. In the countryside where Garibaldi's control was often slight, liberals who had suffered under the Bourbons revenged themselves on former Bourbon officials and supporters who, in turn, organized themselves into bands to fight back, and the government broke down. Bertani, however, was more interested in decreeing new laws than in enforcing old ones. Priests were fined and imprisoned for preaching against the decrees, all the property of the Jesuits was confiscated, as was the property of the bishops who were put on an allowance. An archbishop was exiled for refusing to sing a Te Deum, a pension was given to the mother of the soldier who had tried to assassinate Francesco's father, King *Bomba,* and fundamental changes were made in the principles of law, finance and administration, all merely by decree. Less controversial and dear to republicans were decrees on social reform and free education, but an attempt to abolish gambling served only to put everyone against the government.

The English tourist, Clark, observed in his diary:

> In three weeks I have seen the extinction of a popularity that seemed boundless. The people who were wild with delight at the arrival of Garibaldi would now be equally delighted to get rid of him. . . . His refusal to declare at once the annexation of Southern Italy to Northern has alienated the moderate party and generated suspicions of his intentions which his violent language on several occasions has tended to confirm. . . . A feeling has been created that he is dragging Naples on, not towards a peaceful union with the rest of Italy, but towards an abyss of anarchy and war. . . .[102]

The situation was not eased nor was anyone's fears over it allayed by the fact, which gradually became known, that Mazzini was in Naples. He had arrived on 17 September and although he did not push himself forward to join the men around Garibaldi, neither did he go into hiding. A stranger who met him one evening at a private party, where a number of Garibaldi's officers were present, described him as "an old man with a sweet voice saying wise and noble things." And an admirer, Giorgio Asproni, wrote to Angelo Brofferio in Turin: "Mazzini lives by himself, aloof from everything, a spectator of what is going on. Not only does he not put forward his republican ideas, but he restrains the haste of the more impatient, and preaches that it is imperative to subordinate every sentiment to unity. He has aged considerably and his face shows how much he has suffered." Then, reflecting the extraordinary impact of Mazzini's personality, he added, "I think this man has a gigantic spirit and an intellect above everyone's."

Mazzini's mood, apparently was one of melancholy resignation. His dream had been of an Italy different and better than the other states of Europe: a nation with a mission to be "the bearer to the Nations of the good news of an epoch of Justice and Love." This was to be achieved by the Italian people regenerating themselves through an internal social revolution in which every thought of good was to be translated into action so that the moral and political natures of the people became one as well as their different states and kingdoms. But now the goal of the revolution seemed to be merely to make an Italy like every other state, and the revolution within the people themselves had been pushed aside and forgotten.

He wrote to an old friend in England, Peter Taylor:

> . . . [Unity] you may consider as settled, and so far so good. The rest is all wrong. And as for myself, don't talk of either prosperity or consciousness of having done, etc. All that is chaff. The only real good thing would be to have unity atchieved [sic] quickly through Garibaldi, and one year, before dying, of Walham Green or Eastbourne, long silences, a few affectionate words to smooth the ways, plenty of seagulls, and sad dozing.[103]

The seagulls and dozing, however, were still many years off, for although Mazzini made no public statements, his mere presence in Naples was a fact of political importance. Most men recognized that he probably had little power himself, if only because he lacked an organization through which to exercise it. But almost everyone, including Cavour, assumed that his influence over Garibaldi would be great and that it would be directed towards establishing at Naples a successor to the Roman Republic of 1849. The Neapolitans who favored immediate annexation went through the streets shouting, "Death to Mazzini," and in Turin, Cavour toyed with a plot to have him kidnapped and imprisoned on a Sardinian warship until the crisis in Naples was resolved. Both the crowds and Cavour overestimated his influence on Garibaldi and also his desire to establish a republic at Naples. In fact, like Garibaldi he was ready to accept Vittorio Emanuele in return for unity. But they gauged correctly the radical cast of Mazzini's thought, for after he had been in Naples only a week, on 23 September, he wrote Garibaldi a private letter in which he urged him to offer Vittorio Emanuele immediate annexation in return for the dismissal of Cavour and immediate war with the Austrians for Venice.

The letter, demonstrably, had no influence on Garibaldi's actions, for he already had sent Pallavicino, who had only just arrived in Naples, back to the king in Turin with a letter of his own in which, for the second time, he demanded Cavour's dismissal. Pallavicino, who with Manin had helped to reconcile the republicans and monarchists in the years after 1848–49, was eager to repeat his role of peacemaker, and in some ways was well qualified for it. He was an aristocrat, a marchese, with easy entry to the court and supposedly was well liked by the king. With Garibaldi he stood well, for he, too, had resigned from the *Società* when La Farina began to dominate it, and, most important, he had voted against the cession of Nice. Finally, he was older than Cavour, Garibaldi, or the king, and as one of

Confalonieri's colleagues in 1821 he had been imprisoned by the Austrians in Spielberg for fourteen years and so held an honorable place among the first heroes of the Risorgimento. On the other hand, he was physically short and, in the opinion of many, too self-assertive and self-admiring. In any event, he had no success with either the king or Cavour.

The king's sense of royalty was outraged by Garibaldi's efforts to dictate a change of ministers, and his anger on the point was kept sharp, perhaps, by a growing envy of Garibaldi's exploits. When Pallavicino tried to pacify him by stressing the record of Garibaldi's loyalty, Vittorio Emanuele snapped, "Tell him to annex at once, or to retire." He sent an equally blunt reply to Garibaldi and prepared to leave immediately for Ancona to take command of his army. He wished to deal in person with Garibaldi and from a position of strength. Cavour explained to Prince Eugenio, whom he summoned to Turin to serve as regent in the king's absence, "it is this insolent ultimatum brought by this imbecile Pallavicino that has decided the King."

Unable to move the king, Pallavicino then had two interviews with Cavour and again was unsuccessful. Cavour was courteous and frank. In August, before he had called Parliament to meet and before Garibaldi had made their disagreements so public in his proclamations, he would have resigned for the sake of harmony. But now his resignation would put the wishes of a private citizen, Garibaldi, over the king and constitution. "If Garibaldi wants war," Cavour said, "I accept it. I feel myself strong enough to fight him." And when Pallavicino argued that if Garibaldi retired, then probably Mazzini and anarchy would rule in Naples, Cavour replied, "So much the better; we will then make an end of Mazzinianism." "But that would be civil war!" Pallavicino protested. "The responsibility for it," said Cavour, "will recoil on those who instigated it."

He spoke from a position of strength. The invasion of Umbria and the Marches was almost complete, the battle of Castelfidardo had been won, and public opinion in both north and south was increasingly with him while slipping from Garibaldi. In less than ten days Parliament would meet with deputies and senators eager to play a part in the making of Italy, which they could do through him and the king but not through Garibaldi. Cavour, therefore, was certain of their support, particularly with delegations from Umbria, the Marches, Sicily and Naples all submitting petitions for immediate annexation. In this particular forum, as both he and Pallavicino knew, he could put Garibaldi wholly in the wrong.

Pallavicino, on his return to Naples, reported in full to Garibaldi the positions of the king and Cavour and urged him to conciliate them; at the very least, by dissassociating himself from the extreme republicans, particularly from Bertani and Mazzini. But he found Garibaldi just as inflexible as the king and Cavour. Bertani, a few days earlier, had resigned under the pressure of the almost universal dissatisfaction with his government, but as his successor Garibaldi appointed Crispi, who had as strong a Mazzinian background and who, because of his fracas with La Farina in Sicily, was even more unpopular in Turin. And when Pallavicino urged that Mazzini, the symbol of all that the king and Cavour feared, be exiled from Naples, Garibaldi refused. He protested that Mazzini was harmless, that the monarchists invented crimes with which to charge him and that Italy must be a refuge for a man who had suffered so much to make it. So Pallavicino's efforts to bring the two great forces of the national movement into some kind of rapport ended in failure. And what the leaders knew, their followers sensed and the possibility of civil war seemed ever to grow greater.

Garibaldi, however, unlike Cavour, was absolutely unwilling to fight such a war. The idea of it was appalling to him, a denial of the brotherhood of Italians for which he had striven and was prepared to die. On 24 September, when Pallavicino was still in Turin, Garibaldi replied to one of his officers in Abruzzi who had requested instructions in case the Sardinian army invaded the Kingdom of Naples: "If the Piemontesi enter our territory, receive them like brothers." And three days later, after he had heard Pallavicino's report and mistakenly believed that the Sardinian army already had crossed the border, he issued an Order of the Day to his entire army: "Our brothers of the Italian army commanded by the brave General Cialdini are fighting the enemies of Italy and conquering. The army of Lamoricière has been defeated. . . . Our brave soldiers of the Northern army have passed the frontier and are on Neapolitan territory. We shall soon have the good fortune to press these victorious hands."

In fact, the Sardinian army had not crossed the border. It was still besieging Ancona and would not enter the Neapolitan kingdom for another two weeks. But the sentiment behind the order was unequivocal, and those who understood Garibaldi best saw the order as another act demonstrating his loyalty to the concept of *Italia e Vittorio Emanuele* and therefore one from which he probably never would retreat. The telegraph lines to the north at this time were broken so news of the order was some days in reaching Turin, but when Cavour learned of it, he fully realized the extent of his victory; the possibility of a civil war, of armed opposition to Vittorio Emanuele, had vanished or, at the very least, been minimized. By being prepared to set Italian patriots fighting each other, he had defeated Garibaldi without actually fighting him. But who then was the more civilized, Cavour, the aristocrat, or Garibaldi, the "figlio del popolo"?

On 2 October 1860 Parliament met in Turin, and Cavour's opening speech revealed the extent to which he felt the victory was his. He proposed, in a single-clause bill, that the king's ministers be empowered "to accept and confirm by Royal Decree the annexation to the State of those Provinces of Central and Southern Italy in which the people by direct and universal vote freely manifest their desire that their Provinces become an integral part of one Constitutional Monarchy." In other words, annexation would be quick, for it would be by royal decree, and it would be unconditional, for in the simple "yes" or "no" vote of a plebiscite, "the direct and universal vote," the former kingdoms and Papal provinces would be unable to set conditions. Cavour thus publicly vetoed in advance any plan the republicans might put forward demanding that the king proclaim a new Kingdom of Italy before annexation could be completed or requiring that it be accomplished by treaties, that is on conditions, between the king or Parliament of Sardinia and assemblies in the former kingdoms and provinces which their peoples had elected for the purpose. Particularly in Naples and Sicily, as Cavour well knew, the idea of annexation on conditions by a vote of an assembly, appealed to many.

At the same time, however, he disappointed some of the Sardinian deputies and senators by refusing in his bill to propose that the Sardinian Parliament merely proclaim the provinces annexed by its own vote, for, as he explained, that would be to deny to the peoples of Umbria, the Marches, Naples and Sicily the right to self-determination which had been exercised by the people of Parma, Modena, the Romagna and Tuscany. And it also, although he did not say so, would waste an opportunity to embarrass Napoleon into supporting annexation of the provinces, for if, on the principle of nationality, the provinces of Nice and Savoy were to be French by a vote of their peoples, then why should not the central and southern provinces of Italy be Italian by a similar vote?

His proposal cut through many difficult issues, such as whether the Sicilians could keep their own system of laws or whether the voting might be restricted by qualifications of property or of literacy, in favor of providing a quick and easy solution to the problem of annexation, and while introducing it he stressed the danger of continuing provisional governments and of the need, in order to impress Europe, of returning as soon as possible to constitutional government. He also stressed the need for a vote of confidence in the ministry because "one voice justly dear to the people has made plain to the Crown and the country its distrust of us." And on the very day Cavour was engaging Garibaldi in this figurative battle, Garibaldi in fact was fighting the largest and, in some respects, the most important battle of his campaign.

The battle of the Volturno, as the historians later called it, was a complicated series of engagements on 1 and 2 October in which the Neapolitan army, crossing the Volturno river in force, attempted to break

through Garibaldi's lines and to open a road to Naples. For both Francesco II and Garibaldi much turned on how decisively either could win it.
If Francesco could return to Naples, then he and not Vittorio Emanuele II
could pose before Europe as the king to contain the republican revolution.
Then, when Franz Josef, the tsar, and the King of Prussia met in Warsaw
three weeks hence, if Francesco, as a legitimate monarch who had just
recaptured his capital from revolutionaries, were to ask for aid, he almost
certainly would get it. For Garibaldi, of course, a decisive victory would
open the road to Rome.

As the battle developed, it was just the sort of large-scale defensive
action which Garibaldi's critics, who were eager to characterize him as
merely a guerrilla leader, had been insisting he could not win. Like all his
battles it involved bayonet charges with himself in the lead and words of
encouragement to tired soldiers, but it also involved a careful deployment
of men and reserves, communications over a wide front and staff work. In
all these areas Garibaldi and his officers proved themselves more able than
the Neapolitans, so that in spite of fewer men, about twenty thousand
against thirty thousand, and of poorer equipment, the volunteers held, lost
and recaptured their lines, and at the end of the second day of fighting, the
Neapolitan army retired into Capua and behind the Volturno.

For many years because of political reasons the battle would be
slighted by monarchist generals and historians, but in reality it was one of
Garibaldi's finest military ventures. In it he proved himself able to defend
as well as to attack and to control large forces of men, larger in fact than
the Sardinian army had been either at Castelfidardo or in the Crimea. But
still, though he had the victory, it was not in the fashion he wanted. One
day soon after the battle he received a letter from Mazzini which he
showed to an aide. "Read this," he said. "Mazzini urges me on to attack
Rome. . . . But I cannot advance on Rome leaving behind me 60,000 men
entrenched in Capua and Gaeta, who can march into Naples the moment
my back is turned." And the fact was plain to everyone. Strangely, in the
end, Rome had been secured from Garibaldi by Francesco and his Neapolitans rather than by Napoleon or Cavour.

Further, as Garibaldi recognized, the volunteers lacked the equipment
to besiege Capua or even to hold their lines throughout a cold, wet winter.
A professional army was needed, and on 4 October he wrote Vittorio
Emanuele a letter urging him to come to Naples in person either by sea or
with his army by land: "If I were informed in time, I would move forward
my right wing to meet you and would come in person to present my
homage and to receive your orders for the final operations." Meanwhile, as
Vittorio Emanuele proceeded to Ancona to take command of his army

and as Cavour opened the debate on the annexation bill in Parliament, the war along the Volturno settled into a stalemate.

In Turin, Cavour had just the success with Parliament that he had expected. Early in the session he wrote the king, "public opinion is ferociously anti-Garibaldian and insists that we end a system of government that so much dishonors Italy and the cause of liberty." The speeches on the annexation bill quickly revealed that it would pass almost unanimously, and on 11 October Cavour closed the debate with one of his great speeches in which he reviewed all the issues before the Italian people, including many that technically were not before Parliament.

He began by congratulating the Chamber that "with one splendid exception" it was unanimous in its desire to have immediate annexation of the central and southern provinces by royal decree in response to plebiscites, and he offered reasons to explain why immediate annexation was appropriate now whereas a year ago in the case of Emilia and Tuscany it had not been. Then he passed on to the question of the "one splendid exception" who opposed immediate annexation. He spoke fully and frankly of the difference of opinion that existed between the government and Garibaldi and explained why, after the disagreement became public, the ministry had decided to take it to Parliament as a matter not of personalities but of policies:

> In fact, Gentlemen, in coming to you openly to acquaint you with the existence of this dissension and in provoking a vote of the Chamber not on the conduct of General Garibaldi but on our policy, we shall obtain this result: if your vote is against us and a ministerial crisis follows, it will have been brought about in conformity with the best constitutional principles, in which case a change of ministry will not undermine those principles which I have stated but rather strengthen them. If, however, your vote is favorable to us, we trust that the fact will exercise a great influence on generous mind of General Garibaldi.[104]

His presentation of the issue was very fair. He never pled his own case or, with an emotional word, prejudiced that of Garibaldi. Every reference to the general was courteous and admiring. Scoffers may argue that, as Cavour knew in advance that the Chamber's judgment would be favorable to him, he found it easy to be fair and dispassionate, but such a view overlooks his genuine attachment, which was lifelong, to the parliamentary system.

From the issues of Garibaldi and annexation he moved on to Rome and Venice, two issues which were in the minds of all Europeans as well as Italians. They were the issues on which Garibaldi had stumbled in leading the national movement and on which Cavour, as he well knew, might stumble too, if he did not step carefully. Italian patriots felt strongly about Rome and Venice and so, too, in opposition did the pope, Franz Josef and other European heads of state. But the issues existed, and Cavour could ignore them only at the peril of losing control of them. He began:

> It is a serious thing for a responsible minister to declare his opinion on the great questions of the future. Nevertheless, I recognize that a statesman, to be worthy of the name, ought to have certain fixed points that serve, so to speak, as a polar star guiding his path, though reserving to himself the choice of means or the right to change them according to events, yet always keeping his eye fixed on the point at which he aims.
>
> During the last twelve years the polar star of King Vittorio Emanuele was the desire for national independence. What will be his polar star with regard to Rome? (Here the Secretary records a "movement of attention" in the Chamber.) Our star, Gentlemen, I declare it openly, is to make the Eternal City, on which twenty-five centuries have accumulated every type of glory, the splendid capital of the Italian Kingdom.[105]

It was an extraordinary statement for a minister of one state to make about a city in another, and Cavour probably would not have made it if he had felt that public opinion in Italy would have allowed him to avoid it. Even in Italy, he knew, it would offend many, Pio Nono and the clerical circles, conservative monarchists who felt the House of Savoy should remain in Piedmont and even to some extent ordinary citizens of Turin. And outside of Italy it would provoke devout Catholics to protest, would increase pressure on Napoleon to defend the Holy City, and would provide Franz Josef with an aggressive act of which to complain at Warsaw. Nevertheless in this speech he publicly subscribed the monarchists to the republican dream of Rome as the capital.

But in his next words he made plain that unlike the republicans, he would not use force to achieve it. He would rely on the growing acceptance in Europe of the liberal idea that liberty fosters true religious feeling.

> When this principle will be generally accepted, Gentlemen, . . . when it will have acquired strength in the minds of other peoples and is rooted in the heart of modern society, we do not hesitate to affirm that the great majority of enlightened and devout Catholics will recognize that the august bishop who stands at the head of our religion will be able to exercise the duties of his sublime office with greater freedom and independence, when guarded by the love of twenty-two million of Italians rather than when defended by twenty-five thousand bayonets.[106]

For most Italians, on reflection, it would be an unsatisfactory statement. The ardent patriots would miss the threat of force, and the less ardent and others would feel that the difficult problem of maintaining the freedom of the Church's spiritual power had been slighted. Since the days of the French Revolution the relations between Church and State in the various states of Europe had swung, often violently, from one extreme to the other, and every moment and method of balance in between had some adherents. Cavour in his thinking was working towards the concept generally expressed as "a Free Church in a Free State," but it is not a concept rooted in Latin tradition. He had developed his ideas, mostly before 1848, out of his contacts with political circles in Geneva, England and the relatively nonsectarian France of Louis Philippe. The kind of separation of Church and State he hinted at in his speech was unknown to most Italians and would puzzle them even later when he developed it more fully. For the moment, however, the great thing was, Rome to be the capital.

And from that he passed to Venice, which he treated in the same fashion. Unequivocally he stated that the Veneto and its chief city must be part of Italy, but equally firmly he ruled out fighting for it. Instead he would rely on a moral law similar to a physical one, that attraction is in proportion to the mass: "The stronger and more compact Italy becomes so much the more powerful and irresistible becomes the attraction it exercises over Venice. When this is recognized by France, England and Germany, Venice will join her Mother Country."

The statement, like the one on Rome, was strong or weak, depending on a man's convictions and prejudices. But for most of the deputies and senators, who were aware that Austria recently had been increasing its army in the Veneto, the blunt assertion that Venice must someday be Italian was strong enough; and Cavour ended his speech amid an ovation. Soon therafter the Chamber and Senate began to vote, and in a short time both by large majorities had passed the bill permitting immediate annexation by royal decree after a plebiscite, had declared their confidence in the ministry and unanimously had passed a resolution of thanks "to the heroic General Garibaldi who with warm and generous spirit had gone to the aid of the people of Sicily and Naples and who, in the name of Vittorio Emanuele, had won for Italians so great a portion of Italy."

Cavour's ability to make a policy and to rally men to it was seldom more effective than during this period, and following directly on his successful invasion of the Papal States it recaptured for him and the king the leadership of the national movement. By contrast, while he was in Turin preparing a parliamentary accolade for his chief opponents, proclaiming his carefully defined positions on Rome and Venice and debating the question of annexation to the exact conclusion he wanted, Garibaldi in Naples was caught in the center of an extremely bitter, public squabble among his political advisors which, for lack of Cavour's ability, he seemed unable to resolve.

At issue once again was the question of annexation, but this time in a different aspect. Garibaldi's letter to the king, after the battle of the Volturno, in which he had invited Vittorio Emanuele to come with his army to Naples, had determined finally that annexation would take place and probably soon, for the king could not come as a provisional monarch who might or might not be asked by the peoples of Sicily and Naples to succeed Francesco. And the point of the king's being asked to succeed was important. Carlo III di Borbone had founded the Bourbon dynasty in The Two Sicilies, 126 years earlier, simply by marching south from Parma and conquering the kingdoms, but the Risorgimento had nurtured the ideas of nationality and of sovereignty residing in the people to a point where these ideas, by demanding some expression, prevented anything so simple. The question of annexation which now plagued Garibaldi was whether the peoples of Sicily and Naples were to express their desire for the king and for union with the other Italian peoples by a simple plebiscite or through an assembly of representatives specially elected for the purpose.

It was the same question which Cavour in Turin was answering unequivocally with the introduction of his bill requiring a plebiscite. But at Naples Garibaldi's chief political advisor, Crispi, favored an assembly of representatives. His reasons and those of his supporters were mixed and ranged from the politically sound to the wholly partisan. Those that were sound all partook in some way of the general idea that the peoples of the two southern kingdoms, in their laws, customs and institutions were different from those of the north and in some respects, therefore, should be treated differently. An assembly was the place to work out these differences and to propose adjustments for them. More at the partisan end of the scale was the desire of republicans to keep control of almost half of Italy for as long as possible, to keep the volunteer army in being so long as possible and to make conditions, before annexation, about Rome, Venice and even about their own jobs and positions in the new government that would be formed.

Opposed to Crispi and those favoring an assembly was Pallavicino, the pro-dictator of Naples; and as Crispi was officially Secretary of State for the mainland and in fact Garibaldi's closest advisor, the disagreement that flared between him and Pallavicino was between the two most important men in Naples after Garibaldi himself. Pallavicino, of course, urged the same arguments as Cavour in Turin: a plebiscite, being quick, would make it possible for Italians of all states in just a few days to present themselves to Europe as a unified, national state. An assembly, on the other hand, might sit for months while Francesco, perhaps, improved his position or persuaded Franz Josef or Napoleon to intervene. France, after all, at the start of the invasion of the Papal States, had recalled its ambassador from Turin, so that not one of the continental European states was sympathetic to Italian unity. If in the face of such disapproval unity was to be achieved at all, it must be achieved quickly. And of course to anyone not a republican an assembly of revolutionaries was ominously reminiscent of 1848.

The argument, which pulled Garibaldi first one way and then the other, developed with peculiar bitterness partly because Pallavicino's use of the same arguments as Cavour made him seem to be Cavour's man, which he was not, and partly because one of his acts as pro-dictator turned many republicans against him. When he had returned from Turin and had found he could not persuade Garibaldi to conciliate Cavour and the king by disassociating himself from Mazzini, he had tried to achieve the same end a few days later by publishing, on 3 October, an appeal to Mazzini. *"Even not wishing it,"* he had proclaimed, *"you divide us.* Your presence in these parts creates embarrassments for the Government and perils for the nation. . . . Show yourself great by departing, and all decent persons will praise you for it."

Mazzini's followers and admirers quivered with indignation: that the man who had done more than any other for the unity of Italy, who had even sacrificed his republicanism for unity, should be charged with dividing the country and be asked to leave it, was simply not to be borne. Besides republicans, many who perhaps privately had been wishing that Mazzini would go now felt compelled to defend him, while others, particularly Neapolitans, because of the open letter felt the more free to wish him gone and to cry death to him in the streets.

Garibaldi for his part, on this point at least, was decisive. He asked Mazzini to come to see him and, according to Crispi, greeted him by saying: "I hope you will not quit Naples according to the advice given you. Pallavicino's letter is an aberration, and you must know well that I can neither distrust you, nor suppose that your presence in Naples can be a hindrance to the triumph of the national cause for which we both worked."

Mazzini, thus reassured, wrote a gentle and moving reply to Pallavicino, although not without some barbs for the politicians in Turin, and it was published on 6 October. The incident was closed, except that in the streets of Naples and in the circle around Garibaldi, which perforce included both Crispi and Pallavicino, the passion of it kept voices shrill and angry.

For the next seven days, either at Caserta or Naples, Garibaldi and his advisors met in councils all of which were dominated by the question of how to annex: by plebiscite or by assembly. The debates were heated and the arguments used were sometimes personal and even, perhaps, unscrupulous. Crispi and those favoring an assembly constantly reminded Garibaldi that Nice had been lost by a plebiscite which had not reflected truly the will of the people. Pallavicino, on the other hand, by a mistake which has never been explained satisfactorily, proclaimed publicly on 8 October that thirteen days later a plebiscite would be held on the statement: "The people wish Italy one and indivisible with Vittorio Emanuele as their Constitutional King and his legitimate descendants after him." But Garibaldi had not signed the decree or approved it. So the debates continued, although so far as the country knew the proclamation was still in force for it was not withdrawn or, for the moment, superseded. And in Palermo, Garibaldi's Sicilian government, on learning of what it supposed was a valid decree representing the dictator's final decision, canceled its plan for an assembly and instead prepared for a plebiscite.

Into the midst of this debate Vittorio Emanuele launched from Ancona a proclamation, "To the People of Southern Italy." Farini had written it for him, and it rehearsed, from a monarchist's point of view, the history of the national movement, starting with Carlo Alberto's abdication and ending with the king's invasion, which was about to begin, of the Neapolitan kingdom. In it the king promised the southerners: "I am not coming to impose my will on you, but to see that your will is respected." He referred to the Garibaldini as "a faction ready to sacrifice the national triumph to dreams of fanatical ambition," and promised that he "would never allow Italy to become the roost of cosmopolitan sects." And in his final sentence he stated, "I know that in Italy I am closing the era of revolutions." As he nowhere mentioned Rome or Venice, he presumably was prepared to close the national movement without including them, or so republicans immediately accused him of intending.

The proclamation preceded by two days Cavour's speech in Parliament on these issues and by comparison was tactless. The references to Garibaldi, with one exception, were derogatory, and the achievements of the volunteers were ignored. Even granting that the proclamation was addressed as much to the governments of Europe as to the people of southern Italy, its language was needlessly scornful and only increased the determination of the republicans in Naples to have an assembly in preference to a plebiscite in order to debate the terms of annexation.

Two days later, while Cavour was making his pronouncements on Rome and Venice and Parliament was passing its resolution of thanks to Garibaldi and its bill requiring plebiscites, Crispi, Pallavicino and others were again in council with Garibaldi at Caserta, still debating the question. This time, however, Pallavicino lost his temper and began to rage at

Crispi: "Without you Italy would be made already; with you she never will be." Crispi replied with self-control, irritating Pallavicino further, and then Garibaldi, in attempting to add to Crispi's defense, said: "I ought not, I cannot, I will not sacrifice my friends to the ill humor or caprices of anyone. Stay or go, Marchese, as you choose. If you stay, I shall be content; but if you want to go, I shall certainly not hold you back." And Pallavicino, exclaiming that Garibaldi never should have summoned him from Turin merely to ignore his advice, picked up his hat and left.

The Neapolitans, when they heard of it, were aghast, and they protested his resignation in petitions and by little, white cards on which they wrote *"sì," "*yes," to indicate how they wanted to vote—in a plebiscite. They wore the cards in their hats, pinned them to their coats, and nailed them to doors of houses and carriages. When Garibaldi came into Naples two days later, the city was in an uproar, and as he proceeded down the main street, the Toledo, it "snowed *sìs*" into his carriage, and he heard crowds cheering for himself and Pallavicino but crying death on Mazzini and Crispi.

He was impressed. He believed that a dictator should be responsive to the will of the people, and although the plans were drawn for calling an assembly, he had doubts about the decision, which now increased. With his head he seems to have been convinced that Vittorio Emanuele must come to Naples with speed and power, which meant a plebiscite; but with his heart he favored an assembly, for it meant more time and the possibility, however faint, of continuing the march to Rome or, at least, of not capitulating without conditions to the politicians in Turin, to Cavour.

Later that day, 13 October, still another council was held in the Palazzo d'Angri, Garibaldi's headquarters in Naples. Pallavicino was present and refused to take back his resignation unless the plans for an assembly were cancelled. Again he and Crispi began to wrangle, and as their voices grew louder, General Türr handed Garibaldi a petition signed by thousands of Neapolitans in favor of a plebiscite.

It was the tiny weight that finally decided the issue. As Garibaldi slowly turned its pages, those near him followed his gaze, waiting for his comment, and when he raised his eyes, they saw, from the sudden serenity in his face, that he had made his decision and made it irrevocably. "If this is the desire of the Neapolitan people," he said, "it must be satisfied." And turning to Pallavicino he added, *"Caro Giorgio,* we need you here still." A few hours later Crispi resigned.

The plebiscite was held on 21 October, the day Pallavicino previously had set for it, and on the proposition he previously had announced: "The people wish Italy one and indivisible with Vittorio Emanuele as their Constitutional King and his legitimate descendants after him." The vote, quickly counted, was: In Naples, 1,302,064 "yes"; and 10,312 "no." In Sicily, 432,053 "yes" and 667 "no." A similar plebiscite, held a few days later in Umbria and the Marches produced votes in favor of annexation of 99,628 against 380 and 133,072 against 1212.

The significance of these votes always has been questioned. Historians with a Papal or Bourbon bias naturally disparage them; liberal historians defend them. The voting was public and by urns, and anyone wishing to vote "no" had to drop his marker in a different urn from those voting "yes," all before the eyes of his neighbor. The military situation may also have intimidated some. In all the provinces except Sicily the voting took place in the presence of an army which to some of the voters, at least, was a hostile, foreign army. Indeed, in the Kingdom of Naples, because Vittorio Emanuele by then had crossed the border into Abruzzi, there were three separate armies. In Naples itself many did not register to vote for fear, if Francesco returned, of being charged later with treason, and of course in the large area he still controlled they did not vote at all. Even in Sicily, which was in a sense the freest of the provinces, the vote was small. In Palermo, for example, out of an estimated 250,000 men, only forty thousand registered and only thirty-six thousand voted. In some of the interior towns the men fled to the hills thinking that the polls, somehow, were an ambush leading to conscription, and in at least one town when they refused to vote for either Vittorio Emanuele or Francesco, *"sì"* or *"no,"* but wanted to vote for Don Peppino—Garibaldi—the officials persuaded them that they could do so by voting *"sì."*

Nevertheless, though the vote unquestionably exaggerated the number of persons who favored union, it probably was not untrue to majority opinion, for at that particular moment several points of view, some even conflicting, had joined to favor a vote for annexation. Cavour and most monarchists were sure that the southern Italians had voted for annexation to escape the dangers of Garibaldi's military adventures and the chaos of his government; while many others, like the Neapolitan diarist Pasquale Mancini, were equally sure that "if the people now accept union with Piedmont, it is because Garibaldi wished it." And to some extent both views were right. Further, Mazzini had urged his followers to vote for annexation as the best of a bad bargain, and undoubtedly many others who cared little for Cavour, Garibaldi or Mazzini voted *"sì"* merely because annexation seemed the quickest and best way to have peace. Once the possibility of an assembly was foreclosed and the voters were restricted to a simple "yes" or "no" on annexation, an enormous majority in favor of it was predictable, and Vittorio Emanuele was able to enter the Kingdom of Naples certain its people would call him to its throne.

He crossed the border, the Tronto river, on 15 October, before the voting but after Pallavicino's triumph over Crispi and after Cavour's speech on Rome and Venice. In the following ten days as the army with all its heavy guns slowly marched the two hundred miles toward Capua and its double meeting, with Francesco's Neapolitans and with Garibaldi's volunteers, each day seemed to have a new alarm and sometimes a new relief. For those with the army these consisted mostly of capturing brigands and Bourbon supporters and attempting to restore order in a countryside where politics and personal vendetta had become mixed. For Cavour in Turin, however, and for the king on the march there was the larger question of diplomatic reaction to the invasion and even more specifically of the meeting at Warsaw and what might come out of it.

When Cavour had notified Francesco's envoy at Turin, on 6 October, that Vittorio Emanuele intended to go to Naples with an army, he had described the project as an act of peace undertaken in response to many petitions for it from the peoples of The Two Sicilies. Francesco, he explained, had abdicated, or close to it, by abandoning his capital in a time of civil war. Government in the kingdom now was breaking down, and Garibaldi and his republican idealists were proving unable or unwilling to re-establish it. Vittorio Emanuele, therefore, was undertaking the task not only to restore peace to The Two Sicilies but to preserve it in the rest of Italy, and even in Europe.

Francesco, however, had called the project an invasion, promptly had asked his fellow monarchs again for aid, and in the following week Russia, Prussia and Spain all severed relations with Sardinia. The Prussian note criticized Sardinia for permitting the claims of nationality to override established rights, and the Spanish note insisted that Europe would never accept universal suffrage, a plebiscite, as the basis of a state. As France and Austria had already broken off relations only Britain remained friendly. And by a personal envoy to Sir James Hudson, the British minister at Turin, Vittorio Emanuele forwarded an appeal directly to Lord John Russell for Britain's "moral support," pointing out that his constitutional form of monarchy was unpopular among his fellow monarchs on the continent and asking if on his arrival in Naples he could be supported in some public fashion by the British representative there.

Meanwhile, as Franz Josef, Wilhelm of Prussia and the tsar started for their meeting in Warsaw, Cavour alternated between confidence and fear. On 20 October he was certain that Franz Josef, in spite of re-enforcing his army in the Veneto, did not plan to attack, although the opportunity for it improved daily as half the Sardinian army moved ever further southward. But the next day, because of rumored changes in the Austrian command and of concessions to the Hungarians, he was equally sure of the opposite and called up more reserves to the army.

He worried, too, over the meeting between the king and Garibaldi, for he was determined, if humanely possible, to present Europe and particularly the monarchs at Warsaw with an Italy in which the Italians as well as their states were united. His theme, to which he returned in letter after letter to the king or Farini, was: "No compromise with the Mazziniani; no weakness with the Garibaldini, but infinite consideration for their General." He regretted that the king was taking General Fanti with him to Naples as chief of staff, for he knew that Fanti and Garibaldi disliked each other intensely, both personally and professionally. And he wrote to Farini:

> If Garibaldi's army acclaims the King, it must be well treated. Here you have to struggle against military exactions and pedantries. Do not yield: a supreme reason of State demands it. Woe to us if we show ourselves unresponsive and ungrateful towards those who have shed their blood for Italy! Europe would condemn us. Throughout the country, a tremendous reaction in favor of the Garibaldini would set in.
>
> I have had on this point a very lively discussion with Fanti. He spoke of the army's exigencies. I replied that we were not in Spain, that among us the army obeys.[107]

He then discussed a method of absorbing the best of Garibaldi's men and officers into the new Italian army which would come soon into being and which also would have to absorb the best of Francesco's army. Fanti was willing to take the latter, as professional soldiers, but not Garibaldi's volunteers, all of whom, regardless of merit, he wished to dismiss with a gratuity. But, Cavour warned Farini:

> A cry of disapproval would be raised if the grades were kept for the Bourbon officers who ran away shamefully, and if the Garibaldini who whipped them were sent home.
>
> On this point I will not compromise. Rather than assume responsibility for an act of black ingratitude, I will go and bury myself at Leri.
>
> I despise ingrates so much that I do not feel angry at them, and I pardon their offenses. But by God! I could not bear the merited blot of having failed to recognize services like that of the conquest of a kingdom of nine millions of inhabitants.[108]

Cavour feared that Farini would be almost as rigid at Fanti, and when he read the king's proclamation "To the People of Southern Italy," he thought some of the phrases Farini had written about the Garibaldini were unnecessarily harsh. But he was not with the army and from a distance could not moderate the king's phrasing or the advice of his counselors.

The meeting between Vittorio Emanuele and Garibaldi and parts of their armies finally occurred on 26 October near Teano, a small town about ten miles north of Capua. Garibaldi, in order to meet the king, had crossed the Volturno and, keeping to the hills which ring the Capuan plain, had turned the end of the Neapolitan line and come in behind it. He had with him his staff and a few regiments, in one of which was Abba, whose mind was filled with historical parallels to the scene he was about to witness. Six hundred years earlier Charles of Anjou had won the crown of Naples at the battle of Benevento. But "today a man of the people as brave as . . . does it matter to say it? . . . a man of the people as generous as none can ever be again . . . who in the name of the people snatches that crown from the King of Naples and says to Vittorio Emanuele: 'It is yours!' "

Such an attitude, if expressed, would anger the Sardinian regulars, from king to common soldier, just as several of Farini's phrases in the king's proclamation had angered the volunteers. But Abba's historical parallels did not stop with Charles of Anjou. As he watched the van of the king's army march past, while Garibaldi and his staff waited by the side of the road for the king to come up, Abba saw "in my imagination the great dead Romans of the second civil war, Sulla and Sertorius, who met at this very spot." And then he wondered: "What elements are lacking to bring about another civil war?"

The question was in many minds that day, whether they were in Turin or Teano, for however much Garibaldi, Cavour and the king, each in his own way, were determined to make the meeting peaceful and a step toward the unification of Italy, the political animosity of the two armies and their military jealousy was the stuff which an angry word or hurt feeling might ignite into fighting. And nothing would give greater aid to Francesco or pleasure to the pope, to Franz Josef and perhaps even to Napoleon. Much depended on the example the king and Garibaldi could give.

From his camp in the hills, the night before their meeting, Garibaldi had sent a messenger ahead to announce his presence to the king and to offer his homage, and at dawn the next morning he led his staff to a point where he knew the king must pass, where two roads coming out of the hills behind Teano join to begin their descent to the plain. At their junction was a small tavern shaded by some poplars and in the open space before it, a little back from the road but in full view of all who might pass, Garibaldi and his staff dismounted and prepared to await the king.

The early morning was damp and overcast, and to keep the dew from his ears Garibaldi knotted his handkerchief into a skull cap and put it on under his "pork-pie" hat. He was wearing his gray poncho, and his staff was all in red shirts, stained and dirty. Elsewhere along the road and on

Vittorio Emanuele and
Garibaldi met here

TEANO

GAETA

CAPUA

CASERTA

R. Volturno

ROADS

NAPLES

Vesuvius

SARNO

Pompeii

Procida

Ischia

CASTELLAMMARE    SALERNO

VIETRI

SORRENTO

0    5    10    15    20
SCALE OF MILES

*ENVIRONS OF NAPLES, 1860*

RAILROADS

the hillsides beside it the volunteers watched and waited in their variety of
uniforms.

Soon the van of the Sardinian army appeared, and as it approached
the place where Garibaldi stood, its bands halted beside the road and
played the battalions by him. The men stared at him with interest, and
their commanding officers, as they had been ordered, gave him a salute;
some in open, friendly admiration, others in obvious dislike and distrust.
Two generals whom he knew and liked, however, Della Rocca and Cialdini, greeted him warmly. But whether the Sardinians were friendly or
hostile, neither Garibaldi, nor his staff, nor his men could mistake the
quality of their equipment, the good uniforms, the rifles and siege guns.

Then suddenly down the road came the strain of the Royal March and
cries of "The King! The King!" Garibaldi and his staff mounted and
moved forward to the edge of the road. A troop of carabinieri on horseback swept by, and then came Vittorio Emanuele on a piebald Arab and
in resplendent uniform. Behind him came a long train of staff, orderlies,

chamberlains and courtiers. Garibaldi had prepared his opening words carefully, and when he caught sight of the king he rode forward and, sweeping off his hat, cried out: *"Saluto il primo Re d'Italia,* I salute the first King of Italy," and behind him his men shouted *"Viva, il Re!"*

The king held out his hand:

| | |
|---|---|
| *Ah, caro Garibaldi, come state?* | Ah, dear Garibaldi, how are you? |
| *Bene, Maestà; e Lei?* | Well, Majesty; and you? |
| *Benone.* | Very well. |

For a short time the two men, on horseback, talked together in front of the tavern and then, side by side, they started down the road, followed by their staffs mixed altogether, pell-mell.

It is a scene painters and historians of the Risorgimento love to celebrate, full of color and significance; the union of Italy, north and south, monarchist and republican, red shirt and the cross of Savoy. The meeting at Villafranca of the two emperors, Napoleon and Franz Josef, had also been colorful and significant for Italy, but then no Italians had been present. At Teano, however, all the chief actors were Italian.

But before the cavalcade had proceeded very far, the staffs had sorted themselves; the red shirts to one side of the road, the Sardinians, in dark uniforms with their crosses and braid, to the other. The peasants from all around, on hearing the noise of the bands, had gathered by the roadside, and when they saw Garibaldi they broke into cheers. He reined in his horse, so that he fell behind the king and then pointing to him he shouted at the cheering peasants: "This is Vittorio Emanuele, the King, *your* King, the King of Italy. *Viva il Re!"*

But the peasants only stared at him and, after a moment's silence, broke out again, *"Viva, Viva, Galibardo!"*

The king spurred his horse into a gallop, forcing Garibaldi to gallop after him, and after they had left the peasants behind, they resumed their conversation. Exactly what was said is not known. The king is supposed to have spoken bluntly and said, "Your troops are tired; mine are fresh. It is my turn now." Garibaldi listened in silence.

After a while, at the bridge which crosses the stream before Teano, he saluted the king and, turning off to the left on a country lane, led his staff and men back through the hills toward the Volturno. At a little village they stopped for breakfast, a piece of bread, cheese and a glass of water. No one talked much. Alberto Mario, one of the staff, later wrote: "Garibaldi's face was full of melancholic sweetness. Never did I feel drawn to him with such tenderness." That evening in camp he was still silent, and no one disturbed him.

The next morning, apparently for the first time, he spoke of what was on his mind. He met Mario's wife, Jessie, who had crossed the Volturno to set up a field hospital north of the river. "My wounded," he said to her sharply, "are all south of the Volturno." Then wearily he added in a voice of infinite gentleness, "Jessie, they have sent us to the rear."

Shortly thereafter Della Rocca took over the siege of Capua, and Fanti and Cialdini began to drive the Bourbon troops north of the river back toward Gaeta and north to the Papal border. To avoid any possible friction over the change of command Garibaldi arranged, until the last of the volunteers had been withdrawn from the front, to have Della Rocca's orders to them appear to come from himself, and in gratitude Della Rocca paid him a visit at Caserta and the two men passed a pleasant hour together.

On 2 November, after a day of bombardment, Capua fell, and the garrison of ten thousand men became prisoners. The fortress that had stopped Garibaldi thus fell in a day before the Sardinian army, which undoubtedly increased the feeling among some of its officers, such as Fanti, that the volunteers were capable of very little. And during the next ten days more than seventeen thousand Bourbon troops were driven across the border into the Papal States, where they were interned, while the remainder of the army was shut up with Francesco in the fortress seaport of Gaeta.

At this point, however, Napoleon intervened by ordering the French fleet to interpose itself between the port and the Sardinian fleet which was moving into position to blockade it. His action surprised most of his contemporaries, for it seemed illogical after he had allowed Cavour and the king to dismember the Papal States and to invade the Kingdom of Naples. But perhaps, like breaking relations with Sardinia on the invasion of Umbria and the Marches, this, too, was a sop to the conservative Catholics of France who were eager to support the pope and Francesco, a legitimate monarch, against one who seemed scheming and irreligious. Or perhaps it was just a way of dramatizing to the rest of Europe his dissatisfaction with the extent to which the unification of Italy had gone. In any event, coming so soon after Villafranca, Napoleon's action at Gaeta fixed securely the low opinion in which he was held by most Italian patriots. He was the man who at Villafranca had abandoned the Veneto to Austria, who at Rome sustained the pope, and at Gaeta, the Bourbons. His very real services to the Risorgimento were obscured for patriots by the anger these names and events aroused; even as he was vilified, for different reasons, by the Austrians, the clerics and Bourbon supporters.

A few days later a British dispatch was published which rendered his action at Gaeta relatively unimportant and made Britain rather than France seem the best friend of the Italian national movement. The dispatch was Lord John Russell's answer to Vittorio Emanuele's plea for

Britain's "moral support" and had been forwarded to Hudson at Turin on 27 October:

> It appears that the late proceedings of the King of Sardinia have been strongly disapproved by several of the principal Courts of Europe. . . . Her Majesty's Government must admit that the Italians are the best judge of their own interests. . . . It is difficult to believe, after the astonishing events that we have seen, that the Pope and the King of the Two Sicilies possessed the love of their people. . . . Her Majesty's Government can see no sufficient ground for the severe censure with which Austria, France, Prussia and Russia have visited on the acts of the King of Sardinia. Her Majesty's Government will turn their eyes rather to the gratifying prospect of a people building up the edifice of their liberties, and consolidating the work of their independence.[109]

When Hudson read this to Cavour, he later reported to Russell, Cavour "shouted, rubbed his hands, jumped up, sat down again, then he began to think, and when he looked up, tears were standing in his eyes. Behind your dispatch he saw the Italy of his dreams, the Italy of his hopes, the Italy of his policy." And when the dispatch was published in the early days of November, Italian patriots of every opinion repeated Cavour's excitement, for they all understood instantly that after such blunt talk by Britain the powers at Warsaw might grumble, but they would not act; and Napoleon, who had acted at Gaeta, would go no further. A united Italian kingdom had been made which this time, unlike 1815 or 1849, the powers of Europe would allow to survive.

Historians coming later to the events of this week have been inclined to lower slightly the importance of the dispatch, for they suspect that, even without it, the powers at Warsaw were about to conclude that they would protest but not act. To some extent, too, historians have emphasized differently the reasons which gave rise to it, pointing out that Russell and Palmerston, the British prime minister, probably wrote it, as much to undercut France as to advance Italy, for the British were still extremely fearful of a Napoleonic France. If so, it succeeded brilliantly, for it not only supported a new, large, national state on France's border but it also obscured among the people of that state the fact that, while at times British governments had talked in favor of their national movement, Napoleon had led French soldiers into the Po valley to die for it.

Nevertheless, no historian questions the importance of the dispatch for contemporaries, for its impact was enormous. One of the Sardinian diplomats at Naples, Villamarina, valued it at "100,000 men." It tended, too, by giving such overwhelming approval to Vittorio Emanuele, to make Garibaldi's transfer of power to the king seem more inevitable and therefore, to all but the extremists, more right. The great majority of the volunteers, from the generals like Cosenz and Bixio down to the privates, were prepared and even eager to accept Vittorio Emanuele. From Marsala to Capua, after all, they had fought as Garibaldi had insisted, for *Italia e Vittorio Emanuele.*

Accordingly, on 6 November, behind the lines at Caserta, the volunteers assembled on order for a review by the king. It was to be their last review as an army. Thereafter most would return home, and some, though the program was still uncertain, would be absorbed into the Sardinian army. Garibaldi was to present his staff and officers, and the red shirts were to march past the man for whom they had won half of Italy. They were drawn up in line by regiments of their origin, Sicilian, Calabrian, Tuscan and Northerners, a strange, mixed group of men, oddly dressed but full of pride and courage. They waited. The appointed hour passed, and the king did not come. Nor did he ever come.

He sent no apology or explanation and never later offered one. He would not even write a proclamation thanking the men. Nor would his chief of staff, Fanti, sign such a document; someone lower down had to be found. The public incident, which was soon known all over Italy, was the first awful sign that Vittorio Emanuele was too small a man to act with wisdom the enlarged role Cavour and Garibaldi had prepared for him.

For the rest of his life Garibaldi blamed Cavour for the insult to his men, and most unfairly. The evidence is perfectly clear that Cavour had foreseen the possibility of such an incident and tried to guard against it. He had written Farini: "If Garibaldi's army acclaims the King, it must be treated well. . . . Woe to us if we show ourselves ungrateful to those who have shed their blood for Italy!" But his warnings went unheeded. Farini later wrote to Cavour, boasting that in taking over the civil government from Garibaldi he had never once spoken to Garibaldi or even seen him. Fanti and Farini were bad companions at this moment for the king, but the king, too, as Cavour knew from his experience during the campaign in the Po valley, grew more conscious of his royalty and autocratic, when surrounded for long by the military.

But if Cavour could see the jealousy of the regular army officers and that Vittorio Emanuele himself, perhaps, was not man enough to bear the blaze of Garibaldi's glory, Garibaldi could not. Blinded by his fury over the cession of Nice, he was prepared to blame for the insult to his men the very man who had tried to avert the disaster. For it was a disaster for the monarchy. Every volunteer who could walk had assembled for it, and each in his home town for the rest of his life would be a hero. In the years to come no child with an interest in his country's history would fail to read Abba's account of the review: "We waited. The King was due to come. . . ." And how in the end Garibaldi had reviewed the men himself, and "We knew this was the last hour of his command." When in 1946 the Italian people voted to depose the House of Savoy, they did so partly because of their collective memory of the inadequacies of the first King of Italy.

But Garibaldi would bear no grudge against the king, only against Cavour, Fanti and the politicians. The next day he sat beside the king in a carriage during Vittorio Emanuel's triumphal entry into Naples. And when the Kingdom of The Two Sicilies was formally annexed to Sardinia and Garibaldi resigned as dictator, he issued a letter calling on all Italians to rally behind the king in whom "every quarrel should disappear, every rancour be dissipated." In the same letter, however, he urged Italians to be ready in the spring to march against Rome and Venice.

The king offered Garibaldi various rewards for his service, all revealing how little he understood the man with whom he was dealing. Garibaldi did not care for a commission in the Sardinian army, to serve under Fanti; or to be Duke of Calatafimi with the right to call the king "Cousin"; or even to have a castle, a steamer, or a dowry for his daughter. He wanted to lead his men to Rome, but that was denied him; and he wanted, in order to keep the southern peoples free of the parliamentary politicians, to be the king's viceroy for The Two Sicilies, but that, too, was denied him. So in the end he embarked for Caprera as a private citizen, taking with him two horses which he named "Calatafimi" and "Milazzo," a portable bath he always carried on campaigns, and a few bags of food and seed for his farm.

On the way out to the ship which would take him home he boarded a British warship in order to say goodbye to his friend, Admiral Sir Rodney Mundy, and in the course of their conversation, he broke out vehemently, "I shall never rest satisfied till freedom from foreign rule has been won throughout all of the Italian kingdom. Rome and Venice are not French and Austrian cities. They are Italian cities. They belong to Italy alone." And he insisted he would be in the field again within five months. His last words to some republican friends, as they left him aboard ship to return to the quay, were *"Arriverderci sulla via di Roma,"* "Until we meet again on the way to Rome."

But if many, like Garibaldi, looked ahead, far more looked behind, and with amazement. In April 1859 only Sardinia, from a patriot's view, had been free, and eighteen months later only Rome and Venice were not free. The new Kingdom of Italy was yet to be proclaimed, but already it was made. At Manzoni's house in Milan one night, as Visconti Venosta and the other guests discussed the problems of annexation, of Gaeta, of Garibaldi and Cavour, and of the king, and talked themselves into a mood of despair, Manzoni rallied them by saying: "Within a few years, and perhaps within a few months, who will remember all these little woes which now occupy us so much? Only one thing will always be remembered; it will always be remembered that within these two years Italy was made!"

# PART IV

# CHAPTER 44

Failures of the King and Farini with the volunteers and southerners. The first Italian Parliament and the franchise upon which it was based. Francesco abandons Gaeta. Cavour's negotiations with the Papacy. The Pantaleone Memorandum. Pio Nono's Allocution and Cavour's speech on the Roman Question. Parliament resolves Rome to be the capital. Garibaldi attacks Cavour in the Chamber. Cavour's last speech. His death.

IN THE LARGEST SENSE Manzoni was right: in the two years of 1859 and 1860 Italy was made, and if a hundred years later it was a republic rather than a kingdom, that fact was less important than its existence as a nation, a community of peoples numerous and powerful enough to control, as much as any people can, its destiny. Other European peoples, such as the Poles or the Hungarians, did not achieve as much in the nineteenth century, and in the twentieth achieved it only periodically; and because of their failure, for whatever reasons, they led lives less rich and more full of suffering.

But to many Italians in the last months of 1860 their new united and national state seemed very strange indeed. With Cavour and Farini in control at Naples, Mazzini, who by Sardinian law was still under sentence of death, quietly departed once again for exile in England. In the new Italy which had been made there was, apparently, no place for him. And even for Garibaldi a place in it seemed uncertain. As Abba observed, in almost the final sentence of his *Notes:* "The General is leaving for Caprera, to live as on another planet." And he continued, "Here I feel a gale of discord blowing up. I look at my friends. This wind will catch us all and churn us about. . . ."

For if Italy could be made, it also could be unmade, and in the first months after Garibaldi's departure for Caprera almost everything the monarchists did in the south seemed designed to raise rather than to dissipate the storm which Abba feared. Cavour's appointments, without exception, were poor, even provocative. Besides keeping Fanti and Farini at Naples, where the volunteers were massed while waiting to go home or to

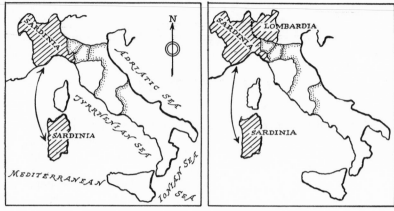

AT THE BEGINNING OF 1859 ⌐          AFTER JULY 1859 ⌐
*The unification of Italy, or the expansion of Sardinia, I*

be commissioned into the Sardinian army, he sent to Sicily as his royal commissioner, Marchese Massimo Montezemolo, who had been the governor of Nice at the time of its cession. The marchese was an honest man of average ability, but in the eyes of many he was a sort of Judas who had delivered Nice to Napoleon. But worse than Montezemolo, Cavour sent to Sicily as his aide La Farina, starting up once again all the animosities of the summer. And by midwinter La Farina was fleeing Palermo in peril of his life. Cavour can be excused for Fanti, for the king controlled assignments within the army, but for the other appointments he was responsible, and it is hard to find any reason for them except carelessness and, perhaps, arrogance. Each caused trouble.

At Naples, Farini had no sympathy for the people he was trying to rule and did nothing to make them feel welcome in the new Italy. In fact, privately, in a letter to Cavour, he excluded them. "The country here is not Italy but Africa, and the bedouin are the flower of civic virtue when compared to these people." Nor did he have more sympathy or tact for the volunteers, most of whom, like himself, came from the north. He forbade the singing anywhere of what was known as Garibaldi's Hymn, and in assuming Garibaldi's position as head of the civil government he ostentatiously made no mention of his predecessor. And neither did Montezemolo in Palermo, nor the deputations from Parliament which came out from Turin to congratulate the peoples of Naples and Sicily on the completion of their revolutions.

The king's example, too, continued to be bad. After offending the republicans by failing to review the volunteers at Caserta, he paid a visit of state to Palermo and insulted the Sicilians. When the Palermitani in

*AFTER MARCH 1860 ⌐*                      *AFTER OCTOBER 1860 ⌐*
*The unification of Italy, or the expansion of Sardinia, II*

their frantic and enthusiastic manner unhitched the horses and themselves dragged his carriage from the harbor to the cathedral and then surged alongside him into the building, he told the mayor to inform them that he was neither an operatic tenor nor a ballet dancer and wished the Sicilians to behave like men and not like beasts. And during the rest of his stay in the city he seldom appeared in public.

But as La Farina wrote Cavour: "Our southerners need to know the person *materially* and to see it, in order to love it. . . . Four or five promenades . . . would arouse greater sympathy for the King than four or five acts of civic or military virtue. . . .*Garibaldi showed himself lavishly.*" But Vittorio Emanuele II had not the knack of it. He did not like his new, southern subjects, and they quickly discerned it.

His attitude in its feeling of regional superiority was typically Italian. D'Azeglio once had remarked, "after making Italy we must make Italians." But to this aspect of unification the king contributed very little, and most of his Sardinian civil and military servants shared his attitude and followed his example. They behaved as much like conquerors as brothers, and educated southerners soon were making bitter jokes about "the latest invasion of barbarians."

The Sardinian form of government, particularly in its administration, was far more centralized than any of those it replaced, and to southerners it seemed too frenchified and rigid to suit their needs. The dominant class in the south was one of landowners, men tenacious of their privileges and traditions, and they were quick to resent the unsympathetic bureaucracy with which Farini and Montezemolo attempted to rule them. Even as far north as Tuscany, Ricasoli was sure, by the end of October, that only the speedy acquisition of Rome could make a community of peoples, a nation, of the united Italian states, for "otherwise the scandalous Piemontese bureaucracy will impel us to another revolution to get rid of a yoke which I find more antipathetic than the Austrian. They will not believe that we want to be Italians and have an Italian soul rather than be automatons on their model." By the end of the year the king's government in Naples and Sicily was more unpopular than ever Garibaldi's had been and was finding itself no more able than his to bring a quick peace and prosperity to an area in which the enormous social and economic problems had been aggravated by a revolution.

Cavour was aware of the failures, but as he wrote about a specific problem to the Minister of Works at Naples, "I am too far away and not sufficiently informed to give you advice as to what should be done." In principle, however, his solution was to have a session of Parliament as soon as possible, one to which the southerners would send representatives and by sharing in the government come to feel it was their own. Thirteen years experience of parliamentary government had convinced him that an honest and energetic ministry had nothing to fear from questions in the Chamber and that the country gained rather than lost when the questions were debated.

Many others, however, did not share his faith in the parliamentary system for handling the kind of problems the south presented. Not only was the general dissatisfaction there expressing itself more and more in open disorder, especially in brigandage, but Francesco II, the area's legitimate monarch, was still holding out at Gaeta and offering the disaffected an alternative government. Garibaldi, of course, advised a dictatorship, but so too did Ricasoli, who earlier had urged Cavour "to proclaim the dictatorship of the King." But Cavour distrusted dictatorships. As he explained to a friend, "I cannot betray my origin, deny the principles of all my life. I am the son of liberty, and to it I owe all that I am. If a veil is to be placed on its statue, it is not for me to do it." And in this spirit, against the advice of many, he announced that elections for Parliament would be held on 27 January.

The terms on which the elections were held are a measure of the distance between republicans and monarchists or, as many republicans put it, of how much Garibaldi had given up on their behalf when, in order to achieve unity, he had abdicated to Vittorio Emanuele. Most republicans thought of the right to vote in terms of universal (manhood) suffrage, as had been the rule in the plebiscites. And if they had won control of Italy in 1860, presumably, after a period of dictatorship, they would have instituted a relatively broad franchise. But Garibaldi had abdicated, and the conservative monarchists were in control. The right to vote in an election for Parliament, therefore, was determined by Sardinian law and was very restricted. Only men over twenty-five who were literate and also paid a fairly large amount in direct taxes could vote, and even in 1871, ten years after this first election, only about 530,000 out of twenty-seven million Italians of both sexes, or about 1.98 per cent, qualified. In that year almost 73 per cent of Italian men were disqualified for illiteracy, including the vast majority of all southerners outside of the larger towns.

The share in parliamentary government that Cavour offered to the southerners, therefore, was meaningless for most of them. The dominant class of landowners continued to dominate, the problems of the peasants and poorer townsfolk continued to be ignored, and many of the social and economic aspects of the Risorgimento were held in check for years. The first, modest extension of the franchise, for example, did not occur until 1882, almost a generation later, and even then only after the republicans under Depretis, finally had won control of Parliament. The monarchists, whether under Cavour or his successors, had no desire to create a new social order or to share power with the masses.

Historians recently have tended to stress this check to the social and economic aspects of the Risorgimento and to lament it, even at times writing of the Risorgimento as a revolution that failed. The older historians, on the other hand, emphasized the achievement of national independence and unity and the extension throughout the length of the peninsula of a parliamentary government which had proved itself able to function and which could reform itself peacefully as time and experience indicated the need. Neither view, of course, is right to the exclusion of the other. Without question much of value in the Risorgimento was lost when the conservative monarchists won control of it, but whether those values could have been preserved and realized under the republicans is a question history did not answer.

Three weeks after the elections, on 18 February 1861, representatives from all the former states or provinces of Italy, except for the Veneto and the area around Rome, met in Turin for what opened, technically, as the eighth session of the Sardinian Parliament. But as the Kingdom of Italy was proclaimed during it, it closed as the first session of the Italian Parliament; and with it most histories of modern Italy begin. Present as deputies and senators were men from the former Duchies of Parma, Modena and Tuscany, from the Kingdoms of Naples and Sicily, from the Legations of Romagna and from the Papal provinces of Umbria and the Marches.

For almost the first time in two years the peninsula was at peace and seemed likely to remain so. Though Garibaldi talked of taking Venice or Rome in the spring, Cavour was in control and in October had ruled out force as a means of obtaining them. Franz Josef, if not attacked, seemed content to remain in the Veneto; Pio Nono, with his volunteer army shattered, could not retake his provinces, and farther south, too, the fighting was concluded. In January, Napoleon III, under pressure from the British, had withdrawn his fleet from Gaeta, and on 14 February, after a month of blockade by the Sardinian fleet, Francesco II capitulated. Bidding his soldiers farewell in an emotional review, he boarded a corvette Napoleon had ordered to stand by and, under the French flag, sailed with his queen and a few courtiers through the Sardinian navy to exile at Rome. By the time the deputies and senators gathered in Turin, Francesco was a government in exile, protesting to the world from the Palazzo del Quirinale which the pope had lent him. From the Vatican, too, protests went out to the world, for Pio Nono, though not forced into exile, had lost three-fourths of his Papal States. Between them these two Italian princes at Rome claimed almost two-thirds of the Italy which the Parliament at Turin was preparing to confirm should be ruled by Vittorio Emanuele, by the will of the Italian people.

At the opening session the king greeted the members with a brief speech which perhaps reflected Cavour's influence, for after touching on the help given by France and Britain toward the making of Italy, the king also mentioned the help given by Garibaldi. And then, after praising the Sardinian army and navy for their part in the national movement, he called on the deputies and senators to devise sound laws to insure the political unity and independence of the new kingdom. Cavour, then, as the first order of business, presented a bill to proclaim Vittorio Emanuele the first King of Italy. No one doubted how Parliament would vote, but the bill was given all the usual consideration and debate. Some favored the title "King of the Italians" over "King of Italy," but Cavour convinced most men that only the latter was appropriate because it alone expressed the fact of *Italy,* the idea which so many men since Dante's time had striven to realize. On 17 March 1861 the bill was voted and passed unanimously. Thus a Kingdom of Italy, based on the sovereignty and common nationality of its people, formally came into being.

One fact which accompanied it irritated some. The king, to the confusion of many persons since, insisted on being counted Vittorio Emanuele *Second* rather than *First,* in order to keep his sequence in the line of Savoy. It was unimportant, perhaps, but James VI of Scotland had been willing to become James I of England, and Henri III of Navarre had become Henri IV of France. Vittorio Emanuele, many of his new subjects felt, should have been willing to do as much for Italy.

Three days after the proclamation of the Kingdom of Italy, Cavour and his fellow ministers resigned in a body in order to give the king a free hand in constructing the new kingdom's first ministry. The gesture was largely formal, and few seriously considered that anyone but Cavour should be the first prime minister of Italy. Vittorio Emanuele, however, had never felt at ease with him, and on occasion they had exchanged angry words, over the king's mistress and at Villafranca. The king now saw an opportunity to have a prime minister he might find more congenial, and he offered the post to Ricasoli. Cavour, he explained, was accused constantly of being "too Piemontese" in outlook and was hated by the republicans, whereas Ricasoli was a Tuscan and had the respect of all parties. If he would accept the post, then Europe would see, as the king put it, "that we have other men besides Cavour." But Ricasoli insisted that Cavour was indispensable, and the King was forced back to the man he did not like. Cavour formed his new ministry, however, to have a more national complexion, and its members came from Turin, Milan, Locarno, Florence, Bologna, Modena, Naples and Messina. Though in their native dialects some were unintelligible to others, they had Tuscan Italian in common and working together as a cabinet were a symbol of the nation's cultural as well as political unity.

The problems facing the ministry and the Parliament were enormous and pervaded every aspect of government. One of the most basic, and typical in its scope and ability to raise regional feeling, was the question of how the government was to be organized throughout the kingdom: by the recent territorial divisions of kingdom, duchy and province or by some new and perhaps more sensible division? And if a new administrative unit was adopted, should the French system of departments be copied or the ancient Roman system of regions? Finances, too, had to be reorganized and tax rates adjusted, always a sore point. The army had to be reorganized to include Neapolitan officers and men as well as some volunteers. Judicial systems had to be merged, tariffs abolished and railroads connected. As Cavour wrote to a friend in March, "My task is more laborious and thorny than in the past. To constitute Italy, to fuse together the diverse elements of which it is composed, to put North and South in harmony, offers as many difficulties as war with Austria and the struggle with Rome."

The latter, because of the confusion of the Church's spiritual and temporal power, was an especially thorny problem now made more difficult by the apparent need of both the new kingdom and the Church to have its capital in Rome. It was a problem Cavour was particularly eager, if possible, to resolve, for nothing would improve the prospects of the new kingdom, both at home and abroad, as much as an accord with the Church. And it was a problem on which he and Pio Nono had begun to negotiate secretly in November 1860 and which each, in characteristic fashion, brought to a head in March.

The basis of their negotiations was a memorandum prepared by two professors at Rome, one a distinguished priest and the other a doctor of medicine. They had discussed their ideas with Vicenzo Santucci, a cardinal known to be sympathetic to an accommodation between Church and State, and he had presented their memorandum to the pope, who, although not enthusiastic about it, at least had discussed it with Cardinal Antonelli and had authorized secret talks to begin.

The memorandum proposed in principle that the pope renounce his temporal power, including thereby his exclusive right to Rome, in return for the Church's complete freedom from interference by the State in all its spiritual affairs. Such freedom would be more than the Church ever had achieved in the past, even under the most favorable concordat, but philosophically for the Church, at least, the method suggested for achieving it was most unusual. Traditionally in the Catholic countries of Europe, Church and State to some degree were merged, and the special privileges of each in the other were defined by a concordat. The premise of the memorandum, however, was that freedom in spiritual affairs could be achieved best not by merger with special privilege but by the clearest possible distinction and separation between the spiritual and temporal powers. The idea was not new, for during the French Revolution, under the Directory, the Church in France had been "disestablished" in a similar fashion, but under circumstances most unfavorable to it and not for the purpose of benefiting it. Most churchmen, therefore, looked back on the period as one of weakness and hardship for the Church, and for a pope to consider such a separation, even under more favorable conditions, as a possible benefit to the Church was a sign of the extent to which even the Church's thinking about itself was changing.

Specifically, under the memorandum the Sardinian state would give up its right to nominate bishops, to supervise certain aspects of the Church's teaching and to prevent the publication and enforcement of Papal legislation and discipline in spiritual affairs. On its side, the Church would give up the Patrimony of St. Peter, including Rome, while preserving for the pope complete immunity from the State's law and all the prerogatives of sovereignty. The pope would continue to have his own diplomatic corps and to own the palaces, museums and monuments which presently were his, and he would receive an income from the State sufficient to support his court, the College of Cardinals, and the local bishops and clergy. Further, Rome would be an open city to which all the world would have free access.

By contemporary Sardinian and French standards what the memorandum offered the Church was generous; so much so that Napoleon III, when Cavour informed him of the propositions, was distressed by them, for his government's relations with the Church were still governed by the first Napoleon's concordat and Organic Articles which greatly favored the State. Nevertheless, just as the negotiations were advancing to an official footing, Pio Nono suddenly broke them off. The Sardinian representative coming from Turin was warned not to enter Rome, or he might not be allowed to leave it; the professor of medicine, Dr. Diomede Pantaleone, by whose name the memorandum sometimes is called, was given twenty-four hours to leave the city, and Cardinal Santucci was given such a dressing down by the pope that, supposedly because of it, he lost his mind and in fact shortly after died insane. Then on 18 March Pio Nono spoke out directly in an allocution to the hierarchy of the Church. He reminded the cardinals and bishops of all the wrongs which the Church had suffered because of Sardinia and, referring to the lost provinces, declared that he could never permit "the unjust aggressor to remain peacefully and honorably in possession of that which he had wrongfully seized"; for to do so would be to "establish the false principle that wrong-doing is justified by success." A pope, he insisted, "can in no wise consent to such a vandalic act of piracy without violating the basis of that moral discipline of which he is recognized to be, as it were, the prototype and exemplar." To some his position on the provinces seemed logical and his speech a clear statement of a basic principle; to others he seemed once again to have confused the preservation of the Papacy's temporal possessions, most of which it had acquired by conquest, with its spiritual task of preserving by teaching and example the souls of men.

A week later Cavour presented the other side of the Roman Question, as it was beginning to be called, in two speeches to Parliament delivered on 25 and 27 March 1861 which, taken together, form a single oration. In them he examined the problem from every side, insisting always that, as its solution was important not only to Italians but also to many millions of Catholics elsewhere, the solution must be not only politically beneficial for Italians but also morally beneficial for Catholicism in general. The new Italian government, he promised, would try "to solve the Roman problem by convincing the more responsible section of the Catholic community that the reunion of Rome with Italy would be in no way prejudicial to the independence of the Church."

He asserted again, as he had in October 1860, that Rome must be the capital of Italy. Only Rome was pre-eminent among Italian cities and could still the demands of regional pride and jealousy. It was not a question of climate or location or even of strategy, but of national sentiment. Only at Rome could the histories of the Italian cities and principalities become the history of the Italian nation.

Cavour rarely allowed anything of himself to appear in his speeches,

but in speaking of Rome as the capital he admitted that for him it would
be a grievous day when he had to leave Turin with its straight, formal
streets, for Rome and its splendid monuments, for which he was not artist
enough to care. And he called on Italy of the future, when firmly established at Rome, to remember the cradle of its liberties and the sacrifices
Turin had made for it.

But Italy could go to Rome, he continued, only in concert with France
and only if the great mass of Catholics understood that the move meant
not less but more freedom for the pope. Then he quoted part of the message the government intended to address to the pope:

> Holy Father, for you the temporal power no longer is a guarantee of
> independence. Renounce it, and we will give you that freedom which
> you vainly have sought for three centuries from all the great Catholic
> powers. You have tried to win some part of this freedom by concor-
> dats, to gain which, Holy Father, you have been forced in return to
> concede privileges and, even worse than privileges, to concede your
> spiritual weapons to those temporal powers which were granting you
> some small portion of freedom. But now, that which you have never
> been able to gain from those powers claiming to be your allies and
> your devoted children, we are prepared to offer you in full measure.
> We are ready to proclaim throughout Italy this great principle: A
> Free Church in a Free State.[110]

And he reminded his audience that the policy of the government, of the
political party in whose name he spoke, was:

> ... to introduce the system of liberty into all parts of society, religious
> and civil. We desire economic liberty; we desire administrative liberty;
> we desire full and absolute liberty of conscience. We desire all the
> political liberty compatible with the maintenance of public order.
> And then, as a necessary consequence of this order of things, we think
> it necessary to the harmony of the system which we seek to introduce
> that the principle of liberty should be applied to the relations between
> Church and State.[111]

As he ended, the deputies and senators gave him an ovation. Many of
them, perhaps, did not grasp his concept of a Free Church in a Free State,
but they recognized the sincerity of his belief in the principle of liberty
and understood fully the arguments about Rome. And they immediately
passed a resolution that Rome should be united to the new Kingdom of
Italy and be its Capital. In October, Cavour had said as much in a speech.
Now the Parliament of the new Kingdom of Italy had voted it. Never again
could *Roma capitale* be dismissed as the dream of revolutionists and poets.
From the parliamentary vote there could be no turning back.

Both the speeches and the resolution followed long enough after Pio

Nono's allocution for everyone to understand that they could not lead to any immediate solution to the problem of Rome. But by stating openly the government's position they influenced public opinion to favor it while at the same time warning Garibaldi and others inclined to forceful action that the government had a policy of peace which it intended to pursue. Similarly they warned foreign Catholics and their governments that as the temporal power made the pope an Italian prince, the Roman Question was an Italian question, to be settled by Italians. But at the end of March 1861, with both Church and State firmly and publicly in opposition, any settlement seemed a long way off.

Even today it is not absolutely clear what caused Pio Nono to end negotiations so suddenly and emotionally. From his point of view, of course, Sardinia was villainous, but as far as the negotiations had gone Cavour, apparently, had negotiated honestly and had good and obvious reasons for wanting to do so. Yet without warning and in the most abrupt fashion the talks were broken off.

Some of the speculations on the reason seem fantastic, and yet serious and intelligent persons at the time and later did not dismiss them as ridiculous. The most sensational involves the Society of Jesus. Since Pius VII had revived it in 1814, its influence at Rome had grown steadily and its members were devoted, even fanatically devoted, to the preservation of the temporal power. So much was visible to anyone, but many persons suspected something more. The historian Thayer reflects this when he wonders of Pio Nono's decision: "Had his Jesuit entourage intimidated him? Did he remember that Clement XIV, the last pope who had dared to resist the Company of Jesus, sickened mysteriously and died, of poison their enemies believed?" Thayer himself is disinclined to believe it, and so is the Contessa Martinengo Cesaresco. But, writing in 1898, she concluded, "However that be, the recollection of what befell Clement XIV is still a living force at Rome."

Less sensational and with some demonstrable basis is the speculation that the Sardinian government had not offered enough in bribes to insure approval by the Curia. That bribes were discussed is beyond doubt. The propositions, for example, included clauses to the effect that the Italian government should confirm all the contracts between the Papal government and the Antonelli family, should confer special honors on Antonelli's brothers and should give Antonelli himself three million lire.

A variant of this sort of corruption, which many were inclined to believe, was that a majority of the Curia had made it plain that they would never vote to give up the temporal power for fear that, if the Church became a truly international, spiritual organization, then Italian cardinals and bishops would have to share the offices, sinecures and bureaucracy of the Church with foreigners. Centuries earlier Dante had described Rome as the place where every day Christ is bought and sold, and undeniably since then the merchants with the chief profit from it were all Italians.

But even if the key to Antonelli's piety was in his purse, most historians have refused to believe that every churchman was equally corrupt and have searched for other, more honorable reasons to explain Pio Nono's sudden action. And the most probable is the extension into Umbria, the Marches and The Two Sicilies of Sardinia's Siccardi Laws and Law on the Convents. These laws, as they began to be enforced, constituted a second revolution. Not only did political control of vast areas pass to Sardinia but within the areas the position of the Church was upset and its influence greatly lessened. And the revolution was conducted harshly. A cardinal and a monsignore, for example, who refused—in obedience to Rome—to allow their clergy to sing a Te Deum to celebrate the anniversary of the Sardinian constitution were arrested and imprisoned. Ecclesiastical courts were abolished and convents lost their special privileges at law and were closed. The secular revolution which d'Azeglio and Cavour had conducted in Sardinia over a period of ten years, with each act debated first by Parliament, was conducted in central and southern Italy in just a few months and without the debates to prepare the clergy and people for it. Pio Nono was not prepared for it; and as a priest he was angered by it and felt, perhaps, that as pope he must oppose it.

For this haste Cavour has been blamed, both personally as well as in his role as a minister. In the autumn of 1860, for example, he wrote the royal commissioner of Umbria, "Put into force energetic measures against the friars. You have done well to occupy some of the convents. . . . Go on like that so as to heal the leprosy of monachism which infects the territories remaining under Roman domination." The language reflects his excitement at Sardinia's success, and like many of his fellow countrymen he ascribed much of it to the vigor which this secular revolution seemed to have injected into their kingdom. He, the commissioners and the lowest civil servants were eager to spread it and behaved with much the same mixture of missionary zeal and force as did the French armies of 1796–97 which had carried the republican doctrines of the French Revolution into Italy. Similarly, too, they stirred resentment and created their own opposition.

But should not Cavour, as a minister, have foreseen this and restrained his own enthusiasm as well as that of others? Many historians think so. E. E. Y. Hales in *Pio Nono,* for example, puts the full blame for the failure in negotiations on "the glaring contrast between Cavour's fair words and his government's ruthless actions," as does also Arturo Jemolo in *Chiesa e Stato in Italia negli ultimi cento anni.* And indeed, for Cavour not to have delayed the secular revolution, even granting that the republicans would have been angered by any delay, seems to have been a serious error of judgment.

On the other hand Pio Nono's behavior in the negotiations is sufficiently similar to his behavior in 1848–49 to suggest that some of the reason for the failure may lie in his character. For Pio Nono to have renounced the temporal power would have been a tremendous act, one requiring extraordinary imagination and courage. No formula of words existed whereby he could renounce it and indeed all the words, the oaths he had sworn, required him to preserve it. In 1848–49 he suddenly had reversed himself with an allocution and parted company with a movement that was taking him further than he wished to go, and so now, too, perhaps when he fully realized how far he was going to have to go he again lacked the imagination and the courage to continue. And in fairness to Pio Nono: only an exceptional man would have had them.

But whatever the reasons underlying the failure of the negotiations, the fact of it, in years to come, while a serious annoyance for the State, was to be a tragedy for the Church. Not until 1929, long after Rome had been taken from it, would the Church be able to bring itself officially to make an agreement with the Kingdom of Italy, and by then it had lost the allegiance of many Italians who had despaired of its ever taking a place in the modern world. In a sense this was the penalty the Church paid for its refusal, in the hundred years after 1815, either to reform itself or to come to terms with the forces and ideas that surrounded it. Italian republicans and monarchists, on the other hand, in that time changed their positions and even compromised their ideals, perhaps, but they did succeed by coming together, in making a united and independent Italy, which probably neither could have done alone.

The Roman Question with its inconclusive answer and the parliamentary resolution that Rome must be Italy's capital was the first great issue to come before the Parliament. The second, in which Garibaldi's anger with Cavour boiled over, was to test the Parliament severely and, to some extent, to prove its strength. The issue at its simplest was the fate of the volunteer army, but in a larger sense it represented an effort by the more extreme republicans to dominate the policy of the new kingdom and to win back control of the revolution.

Garibaldi had passed the winter on Caprera, working on his farm and also on the duties which his fame imposed on him. Every boat brought letters, persons and sometimes even deputations eager to praise him, to ask for a favor or to complain bitterly about what was happening on the mainland. Many of those who wrote only wanted a lock of hair or a nail clipping, and he almost always complied. A friend who helped him with the letters even began to send out chips of stone so that admirers might have something from the island. Some of the letters, however, were more important. Lord John Russell wrote, urging him "seriously to reconsider" his declaration that he would begin a war for Rome or Venice in the spring, since no "individual, however distinguished, has a right to determine for his country the momentous question of peace or war." But Garibaldi replied that, much as he hated war, it alone could finish the process of unification, and that he hoped for a victory in a few months.

More often the letters requested him to be the honorary president of some workers' organization, for he was the hero of the poor and humble everywhere. In a typical response he wrote to the "Workers of Parma": 'Yes! I am a son of the people and yours, and more proud of this than of any title on earth. Nevertheless, I accept gratefully the honorary presidency of your Society, and also a place at your side in the first and final battle of the redemption of the people."

These replies generally caused the greatest excitement wherever they were received, and, as they were almost invariably published in the local paper, Garibaldi often sought help in writing them to make sure he was using proper Italian and not lapsing into Ligurian dialect. As he explained to a friend, "I was born in a land where they do not speak Italian, and I have lived so long in countries where men have other languages on their lips. Be kind and send me a dictionary from Genoa in which the words are set out with an explanation of their proper use. It will help me. . . ."

But as the winter passed, he grew more and more angry. He had left Naples with a promise from the king that his volunteers would be preserved as a separate army. And at the time this had been Cavour's plan: to disband the greater part of the ranks with a gratuity; to constitute the remainder with their officers as a separate volunteer division of the army under the name *Cacciatori delle Alpi;* and to give a small number of volunteer officers commissions in the regular army. Garibaldi had understood, perhaps only by self-deception, that the volunteer *Cacciatori* would have, in fact, five divisions rather than one, and so would be a sizable army and a strong nucleus for attracting more volunteers for an attack on Rome or the Veneto. But on 11 November 1860, the day after Garibaldi departed from Naples, Fanti persuaded the king, and a few days later Cavour, that this was impossible. A permanent force of volunteers would arouse professional jealousy between it and the regular army, would give the republicans a weapon with which to blackmail the government and would constitute a standing threat to Austria and France. And on 16 November, while Fanti was in Turin conferring with Cavour, the government issued a decree announcing the disbandment of the volunteer army. Some privates and officers, to be selected by a military commission on which three of

Garibaldi's generals were to sit, would be taken into the regular army; the remainder would be discharged with the equivalent of six months pay and their expenses home.

The timing of the decision, so soon after he had left, and the personalities involved, Fanti conferring with Cavour, were enough to infuriate Garibaldi, but in addition, as the commission began to work, the regular army officers on it showed sympathy to the Bourbon officers and men and hostility and even scorn for the volunteers. Complaints began to pour in to Caprera, and by the end of March 1861, Garibaldi had determined to take his seat in Parliament, representing a district in Naples, and to put the issue of the volunteers, of Cavour and Fanti and of Rome and Venice before the country.

Early in April he arrived in Turin preceded by reports of wild words he had addressed at Caprera to a deputation of workers from Milan: "We have been badly treated. They [the ministry] have wished to create a dualism between the regular army and the volunteers . . . they have undone the work of unification started by us." And in a letter published in Bologna in which he accepted the honorary presidency of a workers' society there, he had written that the duties of every good Italian were:

> To make possible the completion of the country's redemption by unit-
> ing the means and preparing the men; and to pay no mind to the
> cowardly fears that inspire those who have dragged the country's
> honor in the mud, and who do not understand that the Italian nation,
> today rallied round the honest King (Il Re galantuomo), will con-
> front any enemy who may wish to lay hands on it.[112]

Two days later, on 10 April, Ricasoli rose in Parliament to express his disbelief that Garibaldi ever had uttered such words. Ricasoli's tone was sarcastic, but his purpose, serious: to warn Garibaldi and his supporters that the general must subordinate himself to the king and to Parliament. Garibaldi, it was true, had won Naples and Sicily for Italy, but Ricasoli, under difficult circumstances, had held Tuscany for it, and he was one of the few men in the country who could scold Garibaldi publicly and not be dismissed by him and his supporters as a lackey of Cavour. But Garibaldi's reply, consisting of two letters to the Chamber, merely protested his devotion to the king and otherwise continued his criticism of the government's policy in the south and its treatment of the volunteers. The king, meanwhile, attempting to prevent the storm which seemed about to break over the government, summoned Garibaldi to the Palazzo Reale and repeated his argument that if he could give up Savoy for Italy, Garibaldi could give up Nice. But for once even the king was without influence, and it became evident that Garibaldi intended to speak out, come what may, and constantly was being excited and urged to do so by the most extreme, Mazzinian republicans.

The occasion finally arrived on 18 April, and in anticipation most of the 443 deputies were present in the Chamber, and its galleries were filled. The debate scheduled for that day was the reorganization of the army, and both Cavour and Fanti, as Minister of War, were to be present to answer questions. The sitting began at half past one, without Garibaldi; but, shortly before two, the deputies heard such cheering in the street outside that they knew he was coming. He entered suddenly, not by the main entrance on the floor, but by a small door which opened onto the top row of seats on the left where most of the republicans sat. He was dressed in the garb he had made famous, the red shirt and gray poncho, and was accompanied by two deputies not in themselves important except that they were well known for their Mazzinian views.

His theatrical entrance, delayed, upstage and with the flash of red among the rows of black coats, caused a Frenchman present to describe him as "an old comedian," but to most of the deputies, regardless of party, he was a hero. They were genuinely moved by the sight of him and greeted him with cheers. For some minutes Rattazzi, who was president of the Chamber, attempted to call them to order, and when he finally succeeded, the clerk administered the oath and Garibaldi, as deputy for the first district of Naples, took a seat on the top row to the left, among the opponents of the government.

Because of the greater number of deputies gathered for this first Italian Parliament, the Chamber, instead of using its former hall in the Palazzo Carignano, was meeting in a temporary hall put up in the Palazzo's courtyard. In shape the new hall was like a small, covered Roman theatre: a semicircular well or stage with a straight wall at its back and rows of seats rising from the stage in expanding, semicircular arcs. The president and clerks sat on a high dais at the back of the stage along the straight wall; the ministers, at a long green-covered table at stage-level directly below them, and the deputies in the curved tiers of seats. Behind the last row of these was a small, cramped gallery for visitors, with a similar one in a balcony above it. But even though the hall was built to be larger, it was still, by modern standards, very small. There were only eleven rows of seats for deputies, and as these were stalls, without desks, the farthest row was only about forty feet from the ministers' table. Everyone, even those in the galleries, could see everyone else plainly.

When the debate on the army resumed, Ricasoli spoke, and perhaps only because Garibaldi's presence made everyone nervous, several of his remarks ruffled Fanti while others of them irritated the republicans. And Fanti, in replying to them and explaining why it was not always possible to commission an officer of the volunteers into the regular army at the rank he had held under Garibaldi, described some of Garibaldi's promotions as "fabulous" and "without measure," stating that to take such men into the army at their rank would be "to pronounce the dissolution of the regular army." Long before Fanti had finished, Garibaldi plainly was chafing to reply and, following a few short questions by Crispi and Bixio, he was recognized and, amid a general movement of attention, rose to speak.

He had a speech in hand, written out and perhaps, as many suspected, written for him by others, and after putting on his glasses he began to read it. But after the first few sentences he lost his place, failed to find it and put the speech aside. Looking up, he started directly on the subject that interested him most and thanked Ricasoli for raising the question, "vital to me," of the volunteers. He spoke fervently and the clear, vibrant quality of his voice, as always, moved those who heard him. He stood short, square-shouldered, browned by the sun and seemingly out of place in a closed hall filled with lawyers, clerks and diplomats. And yet, perhaps because of it, he radiated a simple dignity which was immensely appealing.

He agreed with Ricasoli that "Italy was made." He was sure of it because he had faith "in our brave army, and even more in the enthusiasm and generous spirit of a nation which had already given proof of its valor, without being a disciplined, professional army." And he repeated that Italy was made, adding "in spite of the obstacles that intriguing individuals wished to interpose." Speaking faster and more fervently, he insisted that he was not responsible for the "dualism" which existed instead of a national unity. Proposals of reconciliation had been made to him, it was true; but only in words, never in deeds. "But Italy knows I am a man of deeds, and the deeds offered have always been directly opposed to the words of reconciliation. I say now: Whenever this dualism might have harmed the great cause of my country I have yielded and I shall always yield." The deputies and those in the galleries here broke in with applause so that he had to wait for a moment. "But taking me just as an ordinary man," he continued, "I appeal to the conscience of these representatives of Italy to say whether I can offer my hand to the man who has made me a foreigner in Italy."

Cavour, maintaining his attitude of close attention, neither moved nor spoke, and the great majority of the deputies did not applaud. Some persons in the gallery, however, applauded so vigorously that Rattazzi threatened to expel them if they did not keep order, and this drew murmurs of *"Bravo"* and *"Bene"* from around the hall.

Garibaldi, however, was beyond noticing. "Italy is not split in two; it is whole. Because Garibaldi and his friends will always be with those who battle for it." And he charged Fanti with saying that the Sardinian army had invaded central Italy only to put down anarchy, implying that Fanti and others like him had not intended to make Italy. Fanti, unlike Cavour, did not remain silent, but rose to deny that he ever had said such a thing, and his protest raised loud cries of *"Sì!"* and *"No!"* from the deputies and galleries.

Rattazzi tried to smooth over the difficulty by suggesting that Fanti had said merely that there was a possibility of anarchy. But he had lost control of the debate. Garibaldi verbally swept him aside with the unequivocal assertion, "There was never even the slighest danger of anarchy," and then in a rush of words, growing angrier with each, he began to speak of the volunteer army. "Above all I should tell of its glorious deeds. The marvels it accomplished were dimmed only when the cold and hostile hand of this Ministry began to impose its evil effects." And as considerable noise and agitation broke out at this, he raised his voice to add vehemently, "When for love of concord, the horror of a civil war, provoked by this same Ministry . . ."

The rest was lost in cries of protest. Hundreds of deputies rose, calling "Order," "Order," and in the roar of sound neither Garibaldi nor even Rattazzi with his president's bell could make himself heard. The words of only one man rose partially above the hubbub and were heard distinctly by those near him. Cavour, his face fiery red with anger long held in, was on his feet, pounding the ministers' table: "It is not permitted to insult us like this! We protest! We have never had this intention. Signor Presidente, see that the government and representatives of the nation are respected! Establish order!" And Rattazzi continued to demand silence and to ring his bell.

But in the first lull Garibaldi insisted, "After thirty years of service to the country, I believe I have earned the right to tell the truth to the representatives of the people." Rattazzi without reproving him merely begged him to express his opinion in terms that would not offend the deputies or the ministers.

But again Cavour was on his feet. "He has said that we have provoked a civil war! This is very different from the expression of an opinion!"

This time Garibaldi thundered from the top row, making himself heard throughout the hall: *"Sì, una guerra fratricida!"* "A civil war!"

In an instant the aisles were filled with deputies rushing down them, to demand order, to accuse Cavour, to defend him. One even tried to strike him but was prevented and hustled from the hall. In the midst of the fracas an English journalist saw Crispi "bawling and gesticulating like a fanatic." Rattazzi rang and rang the bell, but the tumult continued; so he put on his hat, a sign the meeting was suspended, and retired from the hall.

Twenty minutes later he reopened the meeting. Most of the deputies were appalled at what had occurred and were determined that nothing like it should happen again. The debate resumed with Garibaldi sticking to his subject but in a lower key. He asked why, if the new Italian kingdom was willing to accept Naples and Sicily, it was not willing also to accept the army which had won them. Then, outlining "a plan for the nation," he asked the government to recruit and equip a volunteer army of half a million men for use, though he did not say so directly, in taking Rome and Venice, and for this larger army the original volunteer army should be regrouped as the nucleus. "I believe," he concluded, "that this is the only way of salvation for our country."

Fanti replied. He did not agree. Again cries began to come from the galleries, and again a considerable body of deputies called on Rattazzi to keep order. To their appeal he replied rather tartly that he alone, as president, had the duty to keep order. Whether, as many thought, he was part of a cabal using Garibaldi to upset Cavour in their own favor, on this day at least he was too weak a president for such a difficult meeting and, in his weakness, responsible for much of the disorder.

But just as the meeting seemed once again about to break up in a riot, Bixio, "the Second of The Thousand," got the floor and made an appeal for Italy and peace between parties. "I am one of those," he said, "who believe in the sanctity of the ideas which guided General Garibaldi in Italy,"—and he was interrupted by cries of "Bravo"—"but I belong also to those," he added, "who have faith in the patriotism of Signor Conte di Cavour"—and this, too, won applause. His appeal was noble and impassioned, and he concluded, "I would give my family and my person if I could see these men and those who, like Signor Rattazzi, have directed the Italian movement, grasp each other's hands."

Cavour rose instantly. His face was flushed and drawn, and he spoke carefully, plainly making an effort to control himself. He spoke of the origin in 1859 of the first volunteer corps, the *Cacciatori delle Alpi,* which he had created against the opposition of Napoleon and of the regular army and to command which he had summoned Garibaldi from Caprera, also against opposition. His part in this made him feel keenly the injustice of certain accusations made against him. Nevertheless, "In spite of that," he said, "I will be the first to accept the appeal made to me by General Bixio. For me, the first part of this meeting is as if it never happened."

Cheers greeted this remark, and everyone instinctively looked from Cavour to Garibaldi. According to a correspondent from the London *Times* who was in the gallery, Garibaldi's impulse was to go down and shake Cavour's hand, but he was "forcibly prevented" by the deputy beside him. No one else seems to have seen this, but everyone saw that Garibaldi remained seated and said nothing.

After a moment Cavour went on to explain why, in the ministry's opinion, it was impossible to continue the volunteer army in active service, stressing, in addition to all the problems it would create within the army, the likelihood that France or Austria might consider it an aggressive act, almost the equivalent of a declaration of war. Directly beneath the surface of the argument about the volunteers, as everyone knew, was the larger, more general argument between republicans and monarchists over the timing and method of winning Rome and the Veneto for Italy. If Garibaldi could not succeed in keeping the volunteers in existence, then he had no chance of marching on Rome or Venice in the spring. And in his reply, now, he would not concede the justice of any of Cavour's points or even utter a conciliatory word. He stood, like a fool or a hero, on his plan for the nation, only adding to it, although in less inflammatory language, new charges against Cavour.

Again Cavour rose, and in another attempt at conciliation, began by saying:

> I do not indeed flatter myself that I can bring about that concord to which the Honorable Deputy Bixio invited us. I know that between the Honorable General Garibaldi and myself exists a fact that creates an abyss between the two of us. [Here Garibaldi interrupted and requested Cavour to turn toward him, so that he could hear more easily, and Cavour, complying, repeated the sentence.]
>
> I believed that I performed a painful duty, the most painful of my life, in advising the King and in proposing to Parliament to approve the cession of Nice and Savoy to France.
>
> By the pain I felt, I can understand what General Garibaldi must have felt, and if he does not forgive me for this fact, I shall not hold it against him.[113]

To which Garibaldi replied evasively that he had not doubted that Cavour loved Italy and repeated his arguments for a large volunteer army. When the meeting adjourned, he had conceded nothing and had not uttered a single generous word.

For two more days the debate continued with neither side conceding its basic points. Garibaldi spoke continually and sometimes effectually, and Cavour with his usual clarity constantly restated his position. In the end, however, the Chamber supported Cavour by a vote of 190–79. "Thus," concluded Cavour's biographer, Thayer, in 1911, "was Garibaldi's policy overwhelmingly repudiated by the representatives of the nation to whom he had appealed."

Today some historians, at least, might argue that the Chamber, because of the narrow franchise on which it was based, was not truly representative of the nation and that the vote in its proportions reflected only the natural dominance of the monarchists in such a Chamber. This view has the strength, at least, of offering an explanation of the fact that Garibaldi's standing with the great mass of Italians was not greatly lowered, if at all, by his behavior in the Chamber. Most of them, particularly the 73 per cent who were illiterate, probably never learned or cared about what went on in Parliament, and for them Garibaldi continued to be the hero of the national movement. He seemed to stand for all that was best in the Risorgimento, all that was heroic, loyal and honest. Whereas Cavour, for all his skill and success, seemed to stand for what was double-faced, deceitful and merely diplomatic; for deals with Napoleon, lack of generosity to volunteers and a lesser love of Italy. And it was not simply the uneducated who thought so. There were others who felt that there was truth in Garibaldi's charges. If Cavour had not actually provoked civil war or perhaps not even threatened it, certainly he had flirted with it; and if to some Italians he had talked of liberating central and southern Italy, to others, to Napoleon and to Europe, he had talked of containing the revolution and of preventing anarchy; and in making Italy, he had made it in such a way that out of the sacrifice of others he had retained his own position of power, enormously expanded, while others as diverse as Francesco II di Borbone or Garibaldi had been forced from theirs or voluntarily abdicated.

Nevertheless, within the circle of those who had a share in Parliament, the military, the more prosperous townspeople and the monarchists, Garibaldi's behavior cost him much support. As Ricasoli wrote to a friend: "Who Garibaldi is, is shown in these last debates; but what whoever was absent could not see is the *expectation* of all honorable hearts, after Cavour's generous and chivalrous words, that Garibaldi would withdraw his resolution, and quitting his seat would go and grasp Cavour's hand."

General Cialdini felt even more strongly and sent the newspapers an open letter: "You are not the man that I thought, you are not the Garibaldi I loved. . . ." And after a list of complaints, including some that were trivial or false, he stated:

> General, you achieved a great and marvelous undertaking with your volunteers. You have reason to be proud of it, but you do wrong to exaggerate its true results.
>
> You were on the Volturno in the very worst condition when we arrived. Capua, Gaeta, Messina and Civitella, did not fall by your work, and 50,000 Bourbons were beaten, dispersed and made prisoners by us, not by you.

Therefore, to say that the Kingdom of The Two Sicilies was wholly liberated by your army is inexact. . . .[114]

Garibaldi wrote a letter in reply, countering Cialdini's charges with others of his own and ending with the challenge: "I, speaking in my own name only, and alone responsible for my words, await calmly a demand for satisfaction on account of them." Under the customs of the time a duel seemed inevitable, but in a few days their tempers had cooled and friends were able to effect a reconciliation.

On the same day, 25 April, the king arranged a meeting between Garibaldi and Cavour at the Palazzo Reale, and a reconciliation of sorts took place. Cavour described it to a friend as "courteous without being affectionate." After Garibaldi's public announcement that he would never shake Cavour's hand, Cavour kindly did not advance it; and later to Ricasoli who had asked what had happened about hands, he reported, "I never saw his hands at all; he held them under his Prophet's mantle all the time." But at least they had parted in a semblance of peace.

A few days later Garibaldi returned to Caprera, defeated, angry, unrepentant and yet, in his fashion, personally almost uninvolved. In spite of a month of the most extraordinary private and public tumult, which in most men would have kept heart and head throbbing with angry afterthoughts, he seemed able to drop at once into enjoying the sea and sky, his fields and his animals.

Cavour had no such respite. For him the reorganization of the army, with its episode with Garibaldi, was only a small part of the government's business. He was working on a similar reorganization of the navy, on the administrative units of the kingdom, on the extension of tariffs to the new provinces, and on a new approach to the problem of Rome, this time with Napoleon rather than with Pio Nono. Early in May, however, his colleagues began to notice signs of ill health and exhaustion. His complexion was either flushed or ashen; his face, drawn. He became more irritable and confessed to an old friend that he had not been well since the *maledetta* struggle with Garibaldi. He was troubled often by vomiting and could not sleep at night. Nevertheless he refused to take a vacation or work any less hard.

On 25 and 29 May he spoke on a question involving rewards and pensions for all patriots of whatever party who had fought to make Italy. It was a thorny question, for it involved the government's attitude toward men like Mazzini who were still under sentence of death. But he tried to treat it with good humor and a broad sense of justice, and his final words on it were:

It has been said that we must fuse all parties, at least on the foreign question; when the foreign question is finished we will discuss among ourselves; we will even fight each other. [Here the recording stenographer adds "Hilarity and cries of No! No!"] But first let us finish the foreign question.

Now, to reach this end no difference must be made between those who fought at Venice or at Rome; between those who fought at Rome or Bologna; between those who fought at Bologna or at Palermo.

This is the thought of concord which Deputy Bixio's resolution expresses—that is to say, that all those who fought, even if under a Republican banner, previous to 1859—because since then there has been no more fighting under this flag—have indeed deserved well of Italy. We support this declaration; and thereby, I believe we perform the greatest act of conciliation that is possible under existing circumstances.[115]

As circumstances turned out, these words of conciliation, of defining patriotism to include even Mazzini, were the last Cavour spoke to Parliament. He went home from the session feeling tired, and that night was troubled again with vomiting. The strain of it made him flushed, and fearing apoplexy he sent for his doctor. The two of them, unable to stop the stomach spasms, agreed on a bleeding, a remedy already going out of fashion but one in which Cavour, in other matters so in advance of his time, had faith. And twice the next day, Thursday, he was bled; and with apparent success for the spasms stopped.

Friday, against the doctor's advice, he held a cabinet meeting at his bedside, and worked with his secretary, but Saturday he had chills and fever, and when the doctor gave him quinine, he again was sick to his stomach. The next day he was bled twice and rested, weak but lucid. By evening, however, he was delirious, and his niece, the Contessa Alfieri, discovered that although his brow was hot and feverish, his left hand and arm were ice cold.

The exact nature of his illness has never been diagnosed, but the excessive bleeding, which continued with Cavour's full approval, probably made recovery impossible. The doctors, for there were now several, in desperation applied mustard plasters to his freezing limbs and bladders filled with ice to his burning head.

Turin was a small city, and its people knew Cavour by sight. They were used to seeing him every day take a walk along the arcades of the Via Po, down to the river and back. They called him "Papa Camillo" or, in joking reference to his love of English precedents, "Milord Risorgimento." Now when they heard he was seriously ill, they closed their shops and gathered silently in the streets around the Palazzo Cavour. He was under ban of excommunication for his part in taking the Romagna from

Pio Nono, and they remembered how the Church had persecuted Santa Rosa on his death bed for his part in passing the Siccardi Laws. A workman asked to see Cavour's friend Castelli, who was in the palazzo: "If the priests refuse," he said, "one word is enough and we will end it." But whatever he intended, it was not necessary, for Fra Giacomo, Cavour's parish priest, had promised to come when called.

For three days the vigil continued while the doctors applied the mustard plasters and bladders filled with ice. The king came by the private staircase, and Cavour, trying to sit up, began to speak rapidly of "the poor Neapolitans" who were not bad by nature but had been corrupted over the years by the Bourbons. He was often delirious, but his mind, whether lucid or wandering, returned again and again to Italy and its problems. But his voice gradually grew weaker, and one of the servants voiced everyone's fear: "When the Signor Conte stops talking, he will stop living."

Early Thursday morning, 6 June, his niece summoned Fra Giacomo. Cavour recognized his friend and supposedly murmured, "Friar, friar, a Free Church in a Free State!" For an hour after he had confessed and received communion, while his niece sat beside him, his pulse and mumbling lips showed signs of life. His last intelligible words were: "Italy is made—all is safe," and then sometime, not long after, heart, voice and mind all ceased to function.

The king wished to bury him at Superga, the basilica overlooking Turin, so that he would lie among the princes of Savoy; and the Florentines suggested that he lie among the great of Italy in Santa Croce. But in his last weeks Cavour had mentioned several times that, when he died, he wished to be buried among his family on their estate at Santena, south of Turin. And there in the family chapel he lies, his tomb no different from those of his parents, brother, aunts and uncles. Each bears only a name and the dates of birth and death. Close to him lies his beloved nephew, Augusto, who died in 1848 fighting the Austrians at Goito and whose bloodstained uniform Cavour ever after had kept in his bedroom. Within the family circle no distinction is drawn between the one who gave his life and the other, his life's work, to his country; and this was Cavour's wish. For behind all the policy, though many could not see it, was a man of heart as well as mind.

At the time of his death only Britain had recognized the new Kingdom of Italy, but it was not a neighbor or even a continental state, and Cavour with an eye on Austria had been negotiating with Napoleon for recognition by France. But Napoleon, on learning of his death, dropped all his conditions and granted recognition at once. "The driver," he said, "has fallen from the box; now we must see if the horses will bolt or go back to the stable." And at Rome, Pio Nono exclaimed, "Let us pray for Cavour—

God's mercy is infinite." And later, "He was a great patriot!" Nevertheless, Fra Giacomo was summoned to Rome and disciplined for administering communion to a person under a ban of excommunication. The Kingdom of Italy, however, awarded the friar a pension. Cavour's death neither altered nor settled the issues before the Italian people.

# CHAPTER 45

Italy's loss in Cavour's death. The division of allegiance between the government and a concept of Italy. Ricasoli as Prime Minister. The war in the south. Rattazzi succeeds Ricasoli. The Constitutional question. Garibaldi's tour of northern Italy. His technique of speaking. His speech at Marsala. He crosses the Strait. Aspromonte. The government's complicity.

THE LOSS to Italy in Cavour's death, when he was only fifty, was very great. None of his colleagues or successors had his breadth of vision or his diplomatic and parliamentary skills, and in the years ahead their lack of them would cost Italians some bitter and humiliating moments. As a result, the last stages of the Risorgimento, in Trevelyan's words, "were shorn of their meed of glory," and many patriots who had given their support conditionally to the constitutional monarchists half withdrew it and lapsed into chronic complaint and disillusion: a tragedy not simply for the monarchy, which had won control of the Risorgimento, but for Italy as a whole.

How many of the disappointments Cavour might have prevented is uncertain, of course, but if past success with similar problems is a criterion then possibly many of them. For the next ten years, for example, one of the strains in Italian history was to be the failure of Cavour's successors to gain anything for Italy from its alliance with France. Another was the king's attempt, with Cavour dead, to play a greater role in the government, a role which may not have been constitutional and which at least with regard to Garibaldi certainly was for the worse. And still another was the failure of successive ministries to come to grips with the basic economic facts of Italy, the country's poverty, particularly in the south, and the desperate situation of its peasants as the industrial revolution, which was just beginning in Italy, started to change the traditional way of life.

Diplomacy, parliamentary government and economics were all areas in which Cavour had proved his abilities, but even supposing he had been unable to offer anything positive on these problems, simply his presence in the government would have given it an authority and prestige it sorely needed. It was a misfortune for Italians that, as the Risorgimento developed, Garibaldi and Mazzini, its greatest soldier and its most effective propagandist, were both in varying degrees hostile to the government that dominated its final stages. And the misfortune was compounded when Cavour, the only man of similar stature among the constitutional monarchists, died just as their government started to establish itself throughout the length of Italy. It needed the glamor of his success and prestige to convince the doubting and disappointed that the true glory and spirit of the Risorgimento were also in Turin with the government as well as in London with Mazzini or on Caprera with Garibaldi. Without Cavour or any successor of his stature the government failed to win for itself in the new Kingdom of Italy the same kind of prestige and authority that it had won under him and d'Azeglio in the smaller Kingdom of Sardinia.

As a result, many Italians, perhaps unconsciously, began to divide their allegiance, even as do many today, giving it without reserve to a concept of *Italia* but withholding it in various lesser ways from the government. The composer Verdi, for example, gave an early and unusually public example of this in his *Inno delle Nazioni,* or "Hymn of Nations," which he composed for the London Exhibition of 1862. He had been invited to represent the Kingdom of Italy at the exhibition and he was at the time a deputy in the kingdom's Parliament, nevertheless in the climax of the cantata, where the soloist, chorus and orchestra entwine the national songs of Italy, France and Britain, Italy was represented not by the Royal March of the House of Savoy but by "Mameli's Hymn," a republican national song associated with Mazzini and the defense of the Roman Republic.

Verdi's love of *Italia, O patria mia,* is evident in his music, and he had been a republican most of his life, only supporting the monarchy after Manin, the Contessa Maffei and others had convinced him of the necessity of it. But in the years thereafter he had come to admire Cavour extravagantly and even, though believing himself unsuited for Parliament, had stood for the Chamber of Deputies because Cavour, who was eager to get such a national figure into the government, personally had urged it. Once there, although often sympathetic to republican positions, he generally had voted as had Cavour, explaining to a friend, "That way I can be absolutely certain of not making a mistake." But after Cavour's death, as the cantata revealed, his allegiance to the government was with his head rather than his heart, and with his head he prevented any performance of the cantata in Italy during his lifetime. But significantly neither the king himself nor any of the men he appointed to Cavour's position in the years to come captured Verdi's imagination as had Cavour or could inspire his formal allegiance to the government with any real enthusiasm or admiration. And their failure with him was repeated with many others.

Soon after Cavour's death the king appointed Bettino Ricasoli to be president of the Council or, as the post was beginning to be called, prime minister. As the former dictator of Tuscany he was known and respected throughout the country and had the start, at least, of a reputation outside of it, although as the man who had thwarted Napoleon's plan for a Kingdom of Central Italy he was not popular with Italy's chief ally. Nevertheless, he was the obvious choice, particularly as he was the acting leader of the majority in the Chamber of Deputies, was a good speaker and had a firm grasp of the problems before the country. And for these he offered no new solutions but set about trying to solve them within the policies he had inherited from Cavour.

Several months earlier Cavour had written the king that he planned to do nothing about Austria and the Veneto for two years, and similarly Ricasoli began by concentrating on Rome where at least he had an ally, however reluctant, in Napoleon and about which swirled the deep emotions involved in *Roma capitale* and Rome the capital of the Catholic world. Nothing would help Italy more than arriving at some solution of the Roman Question, and Ricasoli with the high sense of mission typical of him began by attempting to reopen negotiations directly with the pope.

He was rebuffed; and he was rebuffed again by Napoleon, who disliked his moral tone, in discussions over the evacuation from Rome of the French army. Nevertheless, the negotiations at Rome and Paris revealed that the situation was not without hope for the Italians. The Papacy's attitude, since Pio Nono's allocution in March, had hardened into a rigid stand: the seizure of three-fourths of the Papal States was an aggressive act, legally void, and the antireligious policy of the Italian Parliament in the occupied regions was an outrage. Until the lost provinces were returned, including even the Romagna, discussions were pointless. In sum, the Papacy's position was the same in 1861 as it had been in the days of the first Napoleon, and it denied the argument of Italian patriots that the conditions under which the provinces now had been taken were quite different and warranted a different policy on the part of the Papacy.

But Napoleon's attitude, although he had refused to commit himself to Ricasoli in any way, was well known from pamphlets and speeches that had his approval and was directed as much against the Papacy as to its defense. And in sum it was that the Papacy must reach some agreement with the Italian kingdom because France would not keep an army at Rome forever, and once the army was withdrawn the city would be taken either by the Italians or by Garibaldi and his republican volunteers. Therefore, though for the moment Ricasoli's efforts had failed, clearly, if the Italian government could keep Garibaldi in check for a few years, it might obtain Rome, as Cavour had insisted it must, with the consent of France.

An easy way to keep Garibaldi in check suddenly appeared in the summer when President Abraham Lincoln, who was in the midst of the United States civil war, offered him command of a corps in the Union Army of the North. Since Garibaldi's days in South America he had cared deeply about freeing slaves wherever they were, and he applied for and received Vittorio Emanuele's permission to go. But he insisted on two conditions from Lincoln: he was to be given supreme command of the Union Army, and slavery in the United States was formally to be abolished. At the time, however, Lincoln was not prepared to satisfy either condition, and in the end Garibaldi remained on Caprera, idle, complaining and a sure source of trouble for the government.

An allied but different kind of problem for the government, one which throughout the summer steadily grew worse, was the breakdown of government and the rise of brigandage in the former Kingdom of Naples. In a sense the Risorgimento was a succession of civil wars, against the Habsburg princes, the Bourbons and the pope, all of whom claimed with varying justice to be Italian rulers of traditional Italian states. And now, in the name of Francesco II, the longest and cruelest of these civil wars began to develop, particularly in the province of Abruzzi which had a long, common border with the Papacy's Patrimony of St. Peter.

Historians have argued the extent to which the fighting was truly a civil war. Croce, a Neapolitan in the liberal tradition, dismissed it in his *History of Europe in the Nineteenth Century* as merely "guerrilla warfare . . . which the legitimists and reactionaries tried to transfigure in European opinion and imagination into a civil war of conflicting ideas, a sort of second Vendée—a complete transformation of its substantial reality, which was that of military operations and police work against flagrant brigandage."

As Croce suggests, however, the war had both a reality and an image, and many persons who were not legitimists or reactionaries were inclined for months and even years to believe in the truth of the image, if only because most of what they heard or saw of the fighting was so reminiscent of the Calabrian civil war against the French under Joseph Napoleon or of Cardinal Ruffo's campaign in 1799 to retake Naples. Village priests preached against the excommunicated king, Vittorio Emanuele, the hierarchy passed messages from Francesco at Rome to his commanders in the field, and the Italian government replied with a harsh, antireligious policy, exiling bishops, closing monasteries and confiscating property. At Rome, Francesco and his government in exile enrolled soldiers who slipped back and forth across the Papal border, coined money with which to pay them and printed proclamations calling the Neapolitans to arms. Royalist agents in Spain enlisted a famous soldier, José Borjès; Francesco made him a general and authorized him to appropriate public funds in any Neapolitan town. And for three months Borjès marched the length and breadth of the former kingdom, apparently with the aid and support of the people.

At Turin the Italian government's embarrassment was increased when a senator who had asked d'Azeglio for his view of the war allowed the private reply to be published in a French newspaper. D'Azeglio had written:

> At Naples we have driven out its sovereign to establish a government based on universal suffrage. But we need sixty battalions to police the kingdom, and even these, it seems, are not sufficient; for it is notorious that between brigand and non-brigand no one can tell the difference.
>
> But someone will say: what of the vote of the people? I know nothing about the vote. But I do know that in the other provinces of Italy we don't need battalions of soldiers. Therefore at Naples there was some mistake, and it is necessary to change our actions and principles. We must ask the Neapolitans once again if they want us, yes or no. . . .[116]

The suggestion was appalling and could be dismissed as ridiculous, but not the truths leading up to it. D'Azeglio was living quietly in retirement and working on what is probably his finest painting, "Ulysses meeting Nausicaa," yet he was also a senator of Italy, a former prime minister of Sardinia, a famous pamphleteer and one of the few Italians with a European reputation. His remarks were publicized widely and many persons began again to debate the idea which Napoleon was thought still to favor: that Italy should be divided into two kingdoms, north and south. D'Azeglio himself, though privately, favored it, believing that the sections were too different in language, custom and literacy to be merged successfully under a single parliamentary government.

But it was an idea which few patriots shared, and in December 1861 Garibaldi paid a quick visit to Turin, and those in government circles noticed that he had a private interview with the king. The following month Ricasoli, apparently under pressure from the king, sent a senator to Caprera to say that the government was ready to cooperate with him. And then in February, despite a large majority in the Chamber, Ricasoli suddenly resigned, and in his place the king appointed Rattazzi, who was a Piemontese, more of a courtier and far less scrupulous. A disapproving deputy described the change to the Chamber as a royalist *coup d'état*, which it probably was.

The uncertainty which many felt over the king's action arose because the Sardinian *Statuto,* which had become the constitution of the Italian

Kingdom and would remain so until 1948, had been in effect only fourteen years, and the practices which were developing under it were only just beginning to become constitutional conventions which men felt must be observed by the king, his ministers and Parliament. The practices were often no more than Cavour's ideas of how the government should operate, but as he had dominated the government for the nine of the fourteen years, he had accustomed men to his practices almost to the point of accepting them as the only constitutional method of governing. And concealed within the method or practices, as Cavour had been aware, frequently were important rights regarding the source and exercise of power within the government. His steady emphasis on Parliament, for example, had shifted power away from the king toward the Chamber of Deputies, for the Senate was relatively unimportant. In 1848 the king's ministers were responsible only to the king, who could appoint or dismiss them without reference to Parliament, but by 1861, when Cavour died, he had developed the idea of the prime minister's responsibility to the majority of the Chamber to the point where he was as much the leader of a political majority whom the king had to accept as he was the king's minister whom the Chamber had to accept. The substitution of Rattazzi for Ricasoli reversed this trend, for Rattazzi was not a member of the majority coalition in the Chamber, and Ricasoli's resignation was plainly that of a proud man who had discovered the king intriguing behind his back. "They have made a game of my honesty, of my resolution, of my dignity," he lamented, as he withdrew to Brolio to "disinfect himself."

The *coup* succeeded, therefore, partly because of the deputies' uncertainty about its constitutionality and partly because Ricasoli, with his moral tone, had irritated many of them. He had made a point, for example, of not drawing his salary and of not using the free railroad tickets to which he was entitled, and in managing the coalition, which still was supporting him when he resigned, he had been inflexible and uncompromising. Many deputies, therefore, saw him retire with mixed feelings, suspecting that such a rigid puritan was temperamentally unsuited for parliamentary government and yet regretting the pressure which ousted him. The king, on the other hand, was delighted to see him go. Ricasoli had been far too much his own man. He had been censorious about the king's sensuality, had refused to wear the usual ministerial uniform on the ground that his ancestors had never worn anyone's livery, and had remarked publicly that his ancestry was longer and, by implication, better than the House of Savoy. For Ricasoli himself, his failure was a shock. He believed that "Faith in wise principles should create force to fight for them," and the fact that it so evidently had not left him puzzled. And for those outside the government it was distressing to see one of the most distinguished men in Parliament after Cavour forced out in such dubious circumstances.

The most immediate result of it, however, seemed to be the establishment of better relations between Garibaldi and the government. At Genoa, without any opposition from the government, he presided at a meeting of all the republican nationalist groups in Italy, an extraordinary gathering of the radical left from which only the most famous, Mazzini, was absent. Soon after, by express invitation of the government, he began a tour of cities in northern Italy as part of a government campaign to encourage rifle practice among the people. The tour was at government expense and he was surrounded by deputies and senators, entertained by members of the royal family, feted by mayors with public banquets, and in Milan stayed with the governor, the highest government official in the province. While there, on 21 March, he spoke to the people from the balcony of the Palazzo Municipale:

> Greetings to the people of the Cinque Giornate! Greetings to this generous people who showed others how to free themselves from the Austrian rabble! Greetings to this people among whom I count so many worthy companions at arms! Let *Roma e Venezia* be our cry: we wish to cleanse Italy of the dirt that still soils it! The people of Milan, I am sure, as always will be in the van, in the war to redeem our sister cities, Roma e Venezia! Greetings O people of the Cinque Giornate. Now I know that you will be not only of the five but of the twenty-five days! I recommend to you practice on the carbine! I recommend it to you even though I know that you handle well enough the bayonet! Greetings! Greetings! [117]

Even today it is not altogether clear just what Rattazzi and the king had expected of Garibaldi or how they planned to use him. But from the explanation Rattazzi later offered to the British minister, Sir James Hudson, they had hoped he would raise some volunteers, land on the Dalmatian coast, and either simply cause trouble for Franz Josef in the Balkans or, marching northward through the coastal cities which for centuries had been Venetian, attack Venice from the east. If he succeeded in taking it, well and good. If he failed, then he could be disowned as an impossible revolutionary. Garibaldi apparently accepted these conditions, and to insure success Rattazzi promised him a million lire.

But what neither Rattazzi nor the king, nor even Garibaldi himself seems to have expected was the almost hysterical reception he received in every town on his tour. His simple speeches aroused a furor of patriotism, which delighted him. The revolutionary spirit, he felt, far from dwindling among Italians after the creation of a united kingdom was growing stronger. He was convinced that, more than the ministers in Turin, or even the king, he from his tour knew what the country wanted and was prepared to do. At the end of April, in an unusual meeting with all his lieutenants, he proposed an expedition to Dalmatia with Venice as its goal.

Reportedly a majority opposed the plan. Many doubted the government's support and suspected that he would be sacrificed on a diversionary expedition, safely outside of Italy, while Rattazzi and the king acquired Venice later or even at the same time by some diplomatic deal with Napoleon. Their republican suspicions of "the man of 2 December" were still strong, and many were less impressed by the enthusiasm of the crowds than was Garibaldi. The meeting, in the end, adjourned without any definite decision.

The government, however, was growing alarmed. The crowds were bigger than it had anticipated, and far more enthusiastic. Responsible citizens, deputies and senators were beginning to question what was happening, Garibaldi was growing more and more open about the government's complicity, and Rattazzi supposed that at the meeting of Garibaldi and his lieutenants an invasion of Dalmatia had been agreed on. Although presumably this was what he and the king had intended, apparently it no longer seemed wise, and he ordered the arrest at Sarnico, on 15 May 1862, of one of Garibaldi's principal staff officers and a hundred volunteers. When some of these a few days later tried to escape from prison they were shot dead by the police.

Garibaldi was overwhelmed with anger and resentment. At a memorial service in Como, when the crowd interrupted him with cries of *Roma e Venezia* he broke down and, crumpling his hat convulsively, could only stammer, *"È una vergogna"* . . . "It's a shame" . . . "It's a shame."

He wrote a letter to Parliament protesting passionately that the government sent him from Caprera to prepare the next step in Italian unification and then had abandoned him. Despite the government's protestations to the contrary many persons believed him, and some deputies demanded an inquiry which the ministry avoided only by using all its own and all the king's influence. The volunteers still in prison were released without trial, the king and Rattazzi attempted to soothe Garibaldi with private assurances, and Rattazzi insisted publicly that the million lire had been intended "to encourage emigration." The sequence of events was left unresolved and unclear, and though many persons expected Rattazzi to resign or be dismissed by the king, he continued in office. Around the country, however, the affair at Sarnico had shaken the respect of many for the government, and the breach between it and republicans, which Cavour, Bixio and many others had sought to narrow, began again to widen.

After scarcely a month on Caprera, at the end of June, Garibaldi suddenly left for Sicily with a small staff of followers. "I am going towards the unknown," he announced portentously, and in fact he had told none of the men where he was taking them or why. Again began a sequence of events which convinced contemporaries, as the weeks passed, that he was backed by the government, if not at the start then soon after.

In his tour of the north Garibaldi had been impressed by his success as a public speaker and had begun to develop a technique for addressing large crowds. His voice always had been peculiarly affecting but he had used it without art, simply to express himself to individuals or deputations or soldiers. And in Parliament, in speeches requiring careful analysis and detail, he had not even been particularly effective. But in Milan and the other cities of the north he had begun to give short speeches with short sentences which could be interrupted and picked up again at almost every word. And now at Palermo he developed the style further, almost to the point where he and the crowd had a dialogue. He would say something, and the people would repeat it, or applaud or call out *"Sì!"* or *"No!"* "I greet you, people of Palermo; I greet you with my whole heart, because here is a people who deserve my affection, the fine people of Palermo." Delivered from a balcony, by a hero, to a people he had led to an extraordinary victory, such words could be extremely stirring. And as in the north, he began now to speak to huge crowds on every occasion and often from a balcony. On 29 June he told a deputation of students that he was tired of the idleness in which he was kept. The next day from the balcony of the Palazzo Municipale he told a large crowd that "the tyrant Napoleon is not our friend, no . . . !" that the pope was "a disease," and that "we shall go soon to Rome and Venice." Five days and many more speeches later he was saying bluntly, "Rome will be ours."

Between speeches he toured his battlefields, greeted always by frantic crowds, and on 19 July he arrived at Marsala. In the midst of his speech there when a voice cried out, *"O Roma o morte!"*, "Either Rome or death!" he picked it up, *"Sì. Roma o morte,"* and built much of the rest of the speech about it. The next day at mass in the cathedral, with the mayor, the City Council and seemingly the whole city packed in, the priest, a Garibaldino, preached on Rome and Venice and then called on Garibaldi to speak. He rose, raised his hand toward the altar and swore, *"Roma o morte,"* and in an instant everyone was on his feet repeating it. One of the most famous slogans of modern Italian history had been born and baptized and a particular sort of political movement started.

It is not clear at just what moment in this summer of 1862 Garibaldi decided to try a second march on Rome, starting from Sicily. Nor is it clear just when or to what extent the government decided to abet him in it. But it is clear, and was so even to contemporaries, that after the speech and oath at Marsala, Garibaldi began openly to raise a force of volunteers with the declared purpose of attacking Rome, and that the government, either out of fear or complicity, did nothing to hinder him beyond posting some proclamations against recruiting which the Sicilians quickly tore down. No one was punished or even warned, though at all times in the next six weeks the government had more than enough troops on the island to have stopped him.

Many Italians, seeing what was happening, could not believe that Rattazzi had learned nothing from his experience at Sarnico and expected the government, at any moment, to take a firm stand. It was in this period, for example, that Verdi forbade the performance of his *Inno delle Nazioni* in Italy because of the "imminent danger of civil war." On the other hand, many others, particularly in Sicily, were convinced by the government's action that this time Rattazzi and the king really intended to follow through in their support of Garibaldi.

On 20 August, Garibaldi led three thousand volunteers from Palermo and started for Catania, on the east coast of Sicily opposite Calabria. His force had fewer seasoned soldiers than The Thousand of two years before, and its general level of education was lower. Most of the volunteers were very young Sicilians, full of enthusiasm and caught up in the magic of Garibaldi's personality, but as an army, although three times more numerous than The Thousand, they probably were less able. Nevertheless, they reached Catania in three days, for nowhere on the march did the government troops oppose them, and those in Catania shut themselves up in their barracks and left the city to Garibaldi and the volunteers. Two naval officers, on receiving orders from Turin to "do anything the occasion warrants, but always keep in mind the good of your King and country," interpreted the order to mean that they were not to interfere, and they steamed their warships out of the harbor. Garibaldi, always acting in the name of *Italia e Vittorio Emanuele,* was able to seize two merchant ships, to stack and load his rifles openly on the docks and, having embarked his men, to cross unopposed to Calabria, landing once again near Melito.

Rattazzi, meanwhile, was suggesting to Napoleon III that Garibaldi could be stopped only if the Italian government was allowed to occupy Rome. It was a policy similar to Cavour's of two years before, but attempted without Cavour's touch and in circumstances that were very different. Rome was a far more explosive stake for which to gamble than Umbria and the Marches, and Garibaldi now was moving toward it not through the intermediate Kingdom of Naples but through the Kingdom of Italy, which Vittorio Emanuele and Rattazzi supposedly governed. The conservative Catholics of France clamored that the pope be protected, and Napoleon insisted that the Italian government act against the volunteers. So, too, did many Italians who were aghast at the example of a government conspiring against itself, and even Rattazzi and the king seem to have begun to have second thoughts. The Neapolitans already were involved in what the government denied was a civil war, but even where at the moment there was no actual fighting the people were being forced to live under martial law and restrictions with regard to the press and self-government as severe as any the Bourbons had imposed. Conceivably they might turn to Garibaldi as a third force, seeking peace through a separate state under him as dictator, and many in government circles doubted his loyalty under such circumstances. General La Marmora, for example, was convinced that Rome was merely a pretext for Garibaldi and that his real intention was "to undermine the monarchy and to destroy the army."

Accordingly, on orders from Turin, General Cialdini, who was in Naples, instructed a Colonel Emilio Pallavicino, who was in Lower Calabria, to make up a column of "six or seven battalions" of his Bersaglieri troops, to find Garibaldi and "to attack and destroy him if he offers battle."

Garibaldi knew nothing of this and apparently believed just what he told a deputation of citizens from Reggio Calabria who warned him of the government's hostility: "There won't be any civil war, because the government does not want it and makes these preparations only to convince the diplomats of Europe that there is no understanding between me and the King. La Marmora and his friends know nothing of it. . . ." And even after some of Pallavicino's men had fired from a distance at his rear guard, he apparently still believed that he had only to avoid a head-on collision with the regular army to be able to proceed. So he led his men on a long, forced march, high on Aspromonte, but at its end, either through ignorant or deceitful guides or through some failure in his own sense of direction, he had brought them back, hungry and exhausted, almost to the point where they had started. And late that afternoon, on 29 August, they saw the Bersaglieri below them, advancing up the mountain.

The volunteers held a strong position which they could defend easily, but Garibaldi, as always, would not consider firing on fellow Italians and ordered his men simply to hold their positions. Presumably he expected to explain to Pallavicino the nature of his understanding with the king. The Bersaglieri, however, as soon as they were within range, opened fire and some of Garibaldi's men on either wing began to reply. Immediately he had his trumpeter sound a "Cease Fire," sent messengers with the order to the wings, and himself stepped out in front of his lines, shouting to the men, *"Non fate fuoco!* Don't fire! Don't fire!"

Suddenly in sight of many he clutched at his left thigh and fell to the ground. A few of his men rushed forward, picked him up and, carrying him back through the lines, set him on the ground with his back against a tree. One of his officers started a cigar and handed it to him and a doctor examined his wounds. He had been hit twice, and there has never been any doubt that the bullets were fired by the Bersaglieri and with deliberate aim. The first bullet had entered his thigh but had done little harm; the second, which had entered his left foot and lodged under the ankle bone, gave him a wound that never completely cured. The doctor probed for the bullet but could not find it, and Garibaldi ordered him to amputate at once if necessary. The doctor, however, decided to wait.

Meanwhile the sporadic firing continued for a quarter of an hour and many of the volunteers, unable any longer to see Garibaldi, retreated into the pine woods behind them. Soon thereafter, without any flag of truce, an officer of the Bersaglieri galloped up and, without dismounting or saluting, ordered Garibaldi to surrender.

Garibaldi was indignant. "I have seen thirty years of warfare; thirty years, which is a good deal more than you. And I tell you men in charge of negotiations never present themselves like this." And he refused to talk further with the man and ordered his men to disarm him.

Colonel Pallavicino himself arrived shortly after and approaching Garibaldi, hat in hand, explained quietly that he was under orders to ask for unconditional surrender but that he would do everything he could to make the general comfortable. "I have to fulfill a very painful duty," he said.

That night, in a fifteen-hour march Garibaldi was carried in a sling down to Scilla on the coast and put aboard an Italian warship, taken to Spezia and imprisoned at Varignano on a charge of treason. Some of his volunteers who had deserted from the regular army to join him were shot without trial; the others soon were allowed to return home under an amnesty. Garibaldi was very bitter about the fate of the first, and about the amnesty he observed acidly, "You only give an amnesty to persons you consider guilty." He saw no guilt, except possibly in his failure to win his gamble. But the gamble, at least, had been urged by the king and Rattazzi, and their efforts to clean their hands of it, at the expense of others, disgusted him. For the first time his faith in the king was shaken.

The army, for its part, made much of its campaign on Aspromonte. Cialdini referred to the fifteen-minute exchange of shots, which had killed seven soldiers and five volunteers, as "a fierce combat." Pallavicino was promoted to general, and the Bersaglieri received seventy-six medals for valor.

But most Italians were disgusted by the affair. In the north though the great majority disapproved of Garibaldi, few outside of government or military circles felt any pride in the government's handling of him. And in the south, where the government was unpopular and sympathy for Garibaldi strong, royal proclamations were torn down and government officials hooted and hissed. Elsewhere in the world, but especially in England, sympathy was wholly on his side, making it almost impossible for the government to prosecute him or for him to learn anything from what had happened.

Telegrams, poems, cigars, books, presents of every sort were sent to him. More than twenty doctors from Italy and Europe came to examine his ankle, and finally, after he had endured almost three months of probings and dressings, a Tuscan succeeded in extracting the bullet. One of his most ardent, republican friends, Jessie White Mario, who held his hand during the operation, immediately noticed that the bullet, crushed against his ankle bone, had assumed "the perfect form of a cap of liberty."

In her *The Birth of Modern Italy* she describes how:

> It was a supreme moment of emotion when Zanetti held it up to view. Garibaldi embraced the surgeon, then all of us: the news spread— spread like magic and rejoicing was universal. Sheets and bandages, stained with the blood of the martyr of Aspromonte, were eagerly sought for, and torn to ribbons for distribution, to be treasured as sacred relics. Menotti, the General's son, kept the bullet, refusing to part with it, though an Englishman offered a fabulous sum for its possession.[118]

The government, in the end, dropped its charges and let Garibaldi return to Caprera. It could not prosecute "the martyr of Aspromonte" without explaining why it had not stopped him in Sicily, at the water's edge in Catania or even earlier in Palermo. Some of the more innocent members of the ministry were for holding a trial in any event, arguing that a rebel and traitor, even if he was Garibaldi, must not be set free uncondemned, without even a charge brought against him, and to avoid the dangers of a public trial with a jury the possibility was considered of one by a military tribunal. But the question was dropped and buried when the ministry was shown at one of its meetings a mysterious "piece of paper," a document of which perhaps not even Rattazzi had known before, for it was he who had suggested the trial by military tribunal. Just what the paper contained has never been revealed but presumably some sort of written evidence of an "understanding" between Garibaldi and the king. So Garibaldi returned to Caprera a free man, and for the second time in a year, as after Sarnico, the respect of many Italians for their government was undermined.

# CHAPTER 46

Rattazzi resigns. Farini. Minghetti. Resentment of Piedmont. The September convention and the move to Florence. The Turin riots. The Southern problem. The "Liberal Catholic" movement. Montalembert. Döllinger. The Syllabus of Errors. The Civil Marriage Bill. *Non expedit*. The problems prove the strength of the Risorgimento's basic ideas.

PERHAPS THE ONLY GOOD to come out of Aspromonte was the cruel one of Garibaldi's wound. Even after the bullet was extracted, his ankle and foot continued swollen and festered constantly as slivers of bone worked their way through the skin; and for all the next year, 1863, he was penned by the wound on Caprera. People by the hundreds continued to write and to visit him, and he received the visitors first from his bed, then from a wheelchair and finally on crutches. But even the most enthusiastic could see that it would be months before he could lead another expedition or, even supposing he wished it, could take his seat in the Chamber. And meanwhile the government, both king and Parliament, had a chance to grapple with the kingdom's problems without the distraction and intoxication which Garibaldi's presence seemed to provide.

Perhaps, too, another good from Aspromonte was the resignation, in December 1862, of Prime Minister Rattazzi, although it soon was offset by the king's appointment of Luigi Carlo Farini as his successor. Farini was a disciple of Cavour and had an honorable career in the Risorgimento; but at the time of his appointment he was not a party leader in Parliament, and he already had suffered a nervous breakdown and was beginning to show signs of insanity. His appointment, therefore, was interpreted by most men as another effort by the king and court party to dominate the ministers and thereby to avoid domination by Parliament. And again, as in the case of Rattazzi, the king succeeded in his tug-of-war with Parliament over the state's legislative power because the constitutional conventions were still uncertain and the party organization in the Chamber too embryonic for the deputies to assert themselves effectively.

But it soon became clear that Farini was not up to the strain of office.

His behavior became more and more erratic and finally, after he had threatened the king with a knife to force a declaration of war on Russia, he was persuaded to resign. Shortly after, he died.

His successor was Marco Minghetti, whose appointment, in March 1863, to some extent represented a concession by the king to men who favored Parliament over king and court and who resented the preponderance of Piemontesi in the army and the government. Minghetti was a Bolognese who had served as a Minister of Interior under Cavour and who was known to favor the development of strong regional governments within the kingdom rather than the centralization of all its power in the government at Turin. This and the fact that he favored moving the kingdom's capital, assuming Rome to be unavailable, either to Florence or to Naples, inclined many Piemontesi to regard him with suspicion while encouraging Italians from other provinces to support him. He was, therefore, more independent of the king than either Rattazzi or Farini, and he was also, by temperament more easygoing than Ricasoli. Both qualities helped to make him the first prime minister after Cavour to hold the office for more than a year.

The resentment other Italians felt for the Piemontesi continued to be strong, not only in the south where the fighting, whether civil war or brigandage, continued seemingly without end, but also in the north where Rattazzi had extended Sardinian law and administration into Lombardia, the Legations and the duchies faster than their people were prepared to believe was necessary.

Some of the resentment was unjustified in the sense that Parliament, with deputies and senators from all the former Italian states, itself had rejected a plan prepared by Minghetti and Cavour to divide the kingdom into six regional units based on "the old autonomous states of Italy"; and in place of this it had approved a plan to divide the kingdom into fifty-three provinces, each with a prefect responsible directly to the minister in Turin. This was centralization at its severest and followed the example of the first Napoleon, who in his passion for unity and efficient administration had replaced the regions of France with departments. Inevitably, however, it made the government at Turin seem to Italians elsewhere to be a distant and hostile bureaucracy, but the deputies and senators had feared this less than the divisive effects of regional governments. And although jealousy for their own power may have played a part in their decision, still the greater part was a desire to foster unity by establishing as fast as possible for all of Italy a single system of law, administration and trade.

But both the idea of such uniformity as well as the speed with which it was imposed caused resentment. Ricasoli lamented that the Piemontesi dominated the commissions studying how to merge local law and methods into those of the national government, and at Milan irritation over the process reached a point where the Lombardi and Piemontesi would not mix in society. At Bologna thirty-five professors at the University refused to swear allegiance to the new government and lost their posts, and everywhere people complained loudly, with a new word, of being "piedmontized."

Sometimes, too, the changes produced real hardship. Piedmont and Genoa were the provinces most advanced industrially, and as trade barriers between the former states were obliterated, the Piemontesi and Genovesi of all Italians had the greatest profit from the enlarged trade area. Elsewhere, in fact, many beginning industries failed, so that unification for some, instead of prosperity, brought economic disaster.

There was little the government could do about this, considering the limited scope of its powers, but other difficulties might have been avoided if only the king and bureaucracy in Turin had shown more tact and sympathy. The ducal palaces in Parma, for example, were filled with fine pictures, tapestries and furniture collected by the Bourbons and Marie Louise, and the palaces and their contents, upon unification, were transferred to the Italian Crown under a law which required the contents to be kept in place and eventually opened to the public. But beginning in 1862 and continuing for the next seven years the government bureau in charge of Crown property, under a succession of special laws, dispersed the collections and sold many of the pieces, despite protests and appeals by the Parmigiani to the king. By 1870, therefore, the Parmigiani had to begin by private subscription the difficult task of creating their own museums and buying back what they could of the furnishings. Understandably some of them asked aloud if Vittorio Emanuele was any better for Parma than Napoleon or Carlo di Borbone. The latter two, at least, though taking much of the art, had left something. Vittorio Emanuele left nothing. In 1872 the Palazzo di Colorno, stripped, literally, of everything, was turned into an asylum for the insane.

Long before then, however, the resentment of other Italians for the Piemontesi had grown to a point where Minghetti felt he safely could propose to Parliament that the capital be moved from Turin to some other city, even if not to Rome. Both Florence and Naples were more central and more Italian, and in the end Florence was chosen because the Minister of Education, a Sicilian, insisted that his fellow islanders would never abide any pre-eminence of Naples.

Minghetti announced the move on 17 September 1864 when he made public a convention he had negotiated with Napoleon by which France would withdraw its army from Rome within two years, provided Italy would guarantee to protect the Papal State from attack by anyone and provided Italy moved its capital within six months to Florence. This last provision Napoleon presented to the world as a pledge by Italy that it had abandoned any hope of Rome for its capital. Neither Minghetti nor the terms of the convention, however, stated so much exactly, and few Italians considered the move as anything more than a step toward Rome.

The announcement of the move pleased most Italians moderately but fell like a blow on the people of Turin. Minghetti had negotiated the convention so secretly that even the king had not heard of it until the negotiations were completed, and for four days after the announcement the Torinesi remained quiet, while property values in the city steadily dropped. Then suddenly, on 21 September, they began to protest, and their protests developed into such violent riots that the army had to be called in to restore order. It did so with astonishing severity. A Commission of Inquiry later reported that 197 persons had been killed and hundreds more, wounded. "The Austrians never did worse," d'Azeglio wrote to a friend. In his opinion the only persons to gain by the riots were the republicans, since for the first time in its history Turin had turned against the House of Savoy. Guests going to a state ball and even the king himself, it was said, had been hissed.

The king dismissed Minghetti by telegram, as if Parliament were irrelevant, and appointed an army general, La Marmora, to be prime minister. Nevertheless, partly out of fear of offending France, the convention was presented to Parliament and, although many republicans voted against it on the ground that it surrendered the national claims to Rome, it was approved. And within the six months, by March 1865, La Marmora most efficiently had installed the government at Florence.

In spite of the riots and of the republican reservations about Rome the move helped to unify the country by lessening the resentment against the Piemontesi. Now they, too, had given up something cherished for the creation of the new kingdom, and the argument that Italy was made not by the expansion of Sardinia but by the unification of all the former states gained force. Time cured more resentments particularly in the north where the beginnings of industry were changing the old way of life and providing men with new interests to which customs and traditions were not attached, and as the other European states recognized the kingdom many educated Italians who traveled or were in the government became accustomed to thinking of themselves as Italians, at least with regard to the rest of Europe, rather than as Tuscans, Neapolitans or Lombardi.

Nevertheless, after centuries of division, regional feeling in Italy remained strong, not necessarily an unhealthy thing, and it continues strong even today. When a commission in 1946 set about drafting a new constitution for the Republic of Italy, which in that year replaced the kingdom, it returned, in part, to the idea of federation urged in 1848 and the years following by Carlo Cattaneo. One of the major innovations of the new constitution was the division of the country into nineteen regions which could be granted various degrees of local autonomy. And under this provision Sicily, Sardinia, the Val d'Aosta and the region known as Trentino-Alto Adige all were granted extensive powers of self-government.

In the first years of the kingdom, however, the region which seemed most dissatisfied, the most likely to split off from the kingdom, centered on Naples. After London, Paris and St. Petersburg, Naples was the fourth largest city in Europe. It had been the capital of a kingdom which had been the largest and, in an absolute sense, the richest of all the former Italian states. Now after unification, it was no longer the seat of a government, of a court or even the chief naval base of the new, unified navy. The Neapolitans were hurt in their pride and also in their pocketbooks. The brigands who were causing so much trouble were often former Bourbon soldiers who could not find work, and their counterparts in the cities and towns were often former officeholders whose jobs had evaporated with the Bourbon court and government. To outsiders, and particularly to the Italian government, therefore, the turmoil in the south often seemed truly to aim at a Bourbon restoration.

A parliamentary Commission of Inquiry, however, had left Turin in January 1863 to study the causes of the civil war or brigandage on the spot and, in its report, came to a different conclusion, one which, negatively at least, offered the government some comfort. After a truly careful study the commissioners concluded, reflecting, consciously or not, many of Carlo Pisacane's ideas, that the causes underlying the fighting were economic rather than political. Brigandage was least, they noted, where relations between worker and employer were satisfactory, which generally meant least feudal. It was least therefore in the commercial cities, particularly the seaports, and least where agriculture was organized by a system known as *mezzadria* under which tenants, sharing the crops with the landlord, tilled the same farms each year and felt they had an interest in the land. Conversely it was worst where the workers were simply day laborers for the landlord, competing with each other for occasional work.

The commissioners reported:

> Wherever large estates are the rule, the proletariat is very numerous . . . and many people are at their wits' end to make a bare living. . . . The existence of a bandit has many attractions there for the poor laborer . . . and brigandage becomes a savage protest against centuries of injustice by men reduced to the utmost poverty. With such people there is an absolute lack of confidence in the law and the exercise of

justice. . . . Corruption in communal and provincial administration, justice not always honestly administered, and the hopeless inadequacy of the local police, are new and powerful contributions to the spread of brigandage. . . . The barons and their retainers have set the example of lawlessness, and now people have learned to reserve their greatest respect for men who have committed the worst crimes and atrocities.[119]

The fighting seemed caused, therefore, less by a man's preference for the Bourbons over the House of Savoy than by his inability to find work or by his inability, if he had an interest in some land, to produce enough food on it to avoid starvation. The commission, besides suggesting the need for more troops to quell the disorder, also urged Parliament to "extend education and see to a fairer distribution of land. Roads must be built, marshes reclaimed, public works begun, the forests looked after . . ."

But such a program of reclamation was larger than any government of the time was prepared to undertake, and indeed was beyond the imagination of most men. The building of roads, perhaps, was a government duty or prerogative, but forest conservation was hardly even a concept. Men could see that the Lombardi with their irrigation systems and special rights for anyone, rich or poor, to carry water across his neighbor's land, were reaping the benefit of one thousand years of work and experience in the use of water. But very few as yet could appreciate the extent to which the poor of southern Italy were struggling against the accumulated effects of two thousand years of deforestation: soil erosion, dessication, flooding, silting and malarial marshes. And the techniques for combating those effects on a scale of any size were still undiscovered.

The commissioners who had seen the country could also see the problems it posed, but very few deputies or senators had been south of Rome, and most of those who came from the south were themselves the great landlords who wanted only peace and not social change. Certainly they did not want anything so radical as the breaking up of the large estates. So Parliament, instead of attacking the basic causes of unrest in the south, attempted only to control their symptoms, voting to send more soldiers there and passing harsher laws to aid them: "The government shall be empowered to confine under house arrest for anything up to a year any vagabond or unemployed person, or anyone suspected of belonging to the *camorra* or of harboring brigands."

Soon almost half the national army, 120,000 men, were in Sicily and the Neapolitan provinces, and by 1865 the fighting was largely over. Those who at the start had fought for Francesco II had quit, convinced that the Bourbon cause, if it ever had existed, had degenerated into brigandage or local wars between towns, often over the use of communal land. Francesco himself seemed to acknowledge this although he continued to style himself "King of The Two Sicilies," to hold court in the Palazzo Farnese at Rome, and to protest to the diplomatic world whenever he had an occasion. But one by one the foreign diplomats withdrew from his court, as their governments recognized the Kingdom of Italy, and by the end of 1865 all but a few fanatical courtiers considered the Bourbon cause to be quite dead.

Thus within the Kingdom of Italy in the first years of its existence the north pacified the south by force and without curing or alleviating any of the south's basic problems. And nurtured by this force and failure the ancient problems of the south grew into Italy's problem of the south, *la Questione Meridionale,* which now involved more than it had in the past for it included new disillusions and hatreds. The fighting, whatever its political purpose, had opposed men who supposedly were fellow Italians; it had continued for five years, and it had been costly. More Italians on both sides died in this war than were killed in all the other wars of the Risorgimento put together.

Unification for many in the south meant only hard times, martial law and a death in the family. The survivors resented it, and their resentment continued from generation to generation. For many it grew even stronger as the industrial revolution toward the end of the century made the north richer even as the south grew poorer, and its people by the thousands in desperation began to leave for America. Each departure was a personal judgment on the north and Parliament for failing once again in different circumstances to help the south rather than merely to police it. But emigration was no answer to the problems, for the best and strongest left first and those that remained were lacking in leaders.

Yet a generation later the emigration ultimately provided the first real attack on the poverty and illiteracy of the south and in a way that Mazzini would have insisted was the best and the only way possible. In 1960 Luigi Einaudi, who served from 1948 to 1955 as the first president of the Republic of Italy, writing of Italy in 1910 and of the emigration, observed:

> The south was reborn through the efforts of the returning emigrants who brought back a modest sum of money from the United States, bought small farms from the great landlords and built little houses that they wanted to be clean and pretty, and having learned the hard way the handicap of illiteracy wanted their children to go to school and wanted good schools and competent teachers. The social and moral revolution was the work of the poor people themselves who had learned a new and better life in the American melting pot.[120]

After World War II the Italian government began seriously to attack the problem of the south, and on a scale no government in the nineteenth century could have supported. All the points first raised in the almost century-old parliamentary report now became government programs: to build roads, dams and schools, to reforest whole provinces and to break up the large estates. The government directed money into the south in huge amounts. Industry was lured there by special tax rates, foreign investments were encouraged and special schools for on-the-job training opened. Nothing so revolutionary had happened to the south since the barbarian invasions.

And the program continues. But whether it will succeed is still doubtful. Early in the 1960s a commission appointed by the European Parliament in Luxembourg arrived in Sicily to investigate the island's economic condition with regard to the feasibility of aid by the European Bank. The commissioners were all northern Europeans, and they were shocked by what they discovered. "Sicily," they reported, "reminds one of a gloomy picture in a gilded frame." Even after fifteen years of land reform, they observed, nine out of ten peasants who actually had obtained their fifteen acres under the law had received land so arid that they could not support themselves on it and had been forced back again to dependence on the landlord. "The unhealthy economic situation of the country," the commissioners concluded, "must be blamed on the persistence of feudalism."

In the interior and western third of Sicily feudalism of a sort, almost two hundred years after the French Revolution, is still a way of life. The nobility and Church, regardless of the law or government, are still in effect Estates with special powers and privileges, though these must often be exercised through the Mafia; and the great mass of Sicilians forming the Third Estate of the island still can be divided into the unemployed and the partially employed.

The situation still drives men to brigandage. In 1950 a Sicilian bandit, Giuliano, for a time became an international figure. Journalists reported his escapades as if he were a Robin Hood and recounted his death by treachery with rhapsodic detail. But Giuliano was no Robin Hood. His most famous escapade, planned at the request of landlords in the Mafia, involved shooting down peasants who had voted for land reform. Meanwhile poor Sicilians in despair over their hopeless lot emigrated by the thousands to northern Italy.

The problem of the south as it exists today may prove too difficult and expensive even for a twentieth-century government to resolve, and as it existed in the nineteenth century, it probably was too great for either the Bourbon or Italian government. Both tended to ignore it except as a problem for the police. Garibaldi, who had the trust of the southern people, sensed the magnitude of it, was eager to tackle it and, in his Mazzinian ideas about land reform and education, had a program for it. As a dictator he might have succeeded, supposing he could have kept his dictatorial powers for a substantial number of years, but even so it is doubtful, considering that a twentieth-century government with far greater power and technical knowledge is having such difficulty. But of course, as the Risorgimento developed, it was Garibaldi's decrees of social and economic reform which, more than anything else, cost him the opportunity even of trying.

So for decades the problem of the south remained unsolved and largely ignored, except that Parliament and northern Italians occasionally were puzzled by the fact that the Risorgimento, which seemed to be such a success in the north, evidently in some important respect had failed in the south. For even the rich and middle-class southerners complained that the south had given up more than the north for unification and had gained less from it. Naples, which had been a capital, was now only a provincial city and seemed depressed as a result, and in the countryside the possibility of peasant unrest, like the southern volcanos, Etna or Vesuvius, was always on the horizon, threatening to erupt and bury whole villages in fruitless violence.

Another problem which the men of the Risorgimento failed to resolve, but for quite different reasons, was the relations of their new kingdom with the Church. But this was a problem which the government could not ignore, for it affected all Italians of whatever political persuasion, rich and poor, northern and southern, clerical and anticlerical. Unlike the southern problems of soil erosion and malarial swamps, however, the men of the nineteenth century were as well equipped as their successors to resolve it, for Church-State relations is not a problem of technical knowledge or ability but of men, men of various opinions negotiating over how they want society to be organized. And in 1863 it seemed on a number of occasions that the Church was developing within itself a movement which might carry it toward a new concept of itself and of its relations with states and perhaps even with the Italian State.

One of these occasions was a Catholic Congress of Malines, Belgium, in the summer of 1863. The principal speaker was the Comte Charles de Montalembert, a leader in France of what was rather vaguely called the "Liberal Catholic" movement. He believed, as a general principle, that toleration, a free press and the disestablishment of the Church, or of any Church, was absolutely desirable in the modern world, a condition good for both the States and the Church, and he had agreed to go to the congress to give two speeches on "the future of modern society and of the Church."

He spoke first, on 20 August, about "a formula already famous: *a free Church in a free State,* which, though snatched from us [i.e. from Montalembert] and put into circulation by a very guilty man [Cavour] remains none the less the symbol of our convictions and our hopes. . . ." He pointed out that the ancient regime of absolute monarchies and Church privileges guaranteed by concordats "had its great and beautiful side: . . . (but) it is dead." In the new world which had come into being since the French Revolution a different method was needed, and he recommended with enthusiasm liberty of education, of association and of the press, ending as if speaking for the clericals to the anticlericals: "We accept, we invoke, the principles and liberties proclaimed in '89. . . . You made the revolution of 1789 without us and against us, but *for us,* God wishing it so in spite of you."

Montalembert was a famous man and his speech was widely read. In it he broadcast a strain of thinking which in Church history went back at least as far as 1797 when the Bishop of Imola, who was later to be Pius VII, had attempted to reconcile the Church with "the principles of '89" in a Christmas homily. The strain had never been strong and had all but disappeared under the bludgeonings of Napoleon and the reaction after 1815, but it had reappeared for a time in Pio Nono and might reappear again if it developed support within the Church rather than being imposed from without.

In Montalembert's second speech, on the following day, he took up the question of religious toleration. He pointed out that Protestant countries had often been more guilty than Catholic in using the State's power to suppress religious liberty, but as bad examples in Catholic countries he cited the revocation of the Edict of Nantes by Louis XIV and the policies pursued by the House of Savoy and the Bourbons after 1815 in Sardinia and The Two Sicilies. Of these latter he remarked: "Those Paradises of religious absolution have become the scandal and the despair of all Catholic hearts." He did not entirely approve, however, of the direction religious reform had taken in Sardinia. He made it clear that he considered Cavour's program offered merely "a despoiled Church in a despoiling State," and that the Papal State, with its mixture of temporal and spiritual power, was not only proper but necessary if religious freedom anywhere else was to be maintained.

Translated into the situation in Italy, Montalembert's views might mean that the Kingdom of Italy would have to forego Rome as its capital but receive in return, after negotiation, the Church's blessing and cooperation in the new secular organization of Italian life which had originated in the Kingdom of Sardinia. The congress, therefore, seemed hopeful to many, both in and out of Italy.

The following month there was another, equally significant congress at Munich in which the dominant figure was Ignaz Döllinger, a professor of theology and Church history at the University of Munich. The congress at Malines had concerned itself mainly with the relations of Church and

State; the one at Munich discussed the independent intellectual rights of history, reason and science, and their relations both with theology and with religious authority.

Döllinger himself was a Catholic and as a young man had been ordained, but his fame resulted from his work as a historian. In the 1840s and 50s he had published a massive work on the Reformation and a shorter one on Luther, both of which had caused excitement in the intellectual world because of their exposure of the selfish motives underlying the actions of the Protestant leaders. At Rome he had been regarded with favor. Döllinger, however, was less interested in favor than truth as he saw it, and in 1857 at Rome he had offended the hierarchy with a series of lectures in which he maintained that, while the temporal power was extremely important to the Church, it was unhistorical to regard it as inextricably part of the Papacy. To which he added his opinion that it was also unwise so to regard it in view of its probable collapse. As he continued to scold the Papacy as well as Protestants, he was plainly, by 1863, a man likely to come into conflict with Rome.

At the Munich congress he expatiated on the defects of Italian education and scholarship, which, considering his field was Church history and that most education in Italy was dominated by the Church, was a direct criticism of the Church's educational methods and purpose. This alone might not have been too serious, for the defects were recognized as facts by all but the most fanatical churchmen. He went on, however, to say that true theology depended on a proper understanding of history and of philosophy, by which he meant that except for the small area of belief covered by the Church's dogma, as opposed, say, to its opinions expressed by the books it put on the Index, a historian or theologian should follow his research to the conclusions to which his reason led him.

This, however, was directly opposed to the opinion dominant at Rome. The most influential Church journal there, one which had the full approval of Pio Nono, was *La Civiltà cattolica,* founded in 1850 by members of the Society of Jesus. Its leading political writer was a Jesuit, Father Taparelli, and almost nothing better indicates the smallness of the world in which the Risorgimento took place or the kind of division that it created in Italian life than the fact that Taparelli was Massimo d'Azeglio's brother. He was the second son in the family and the one their father had put into the Church even as he had tried to put d'Azeglio into the army. And the two men, although they hardly ever saw each other after childhood and although their opinions on almost every subject differed greatly, continued to be fond of each other.

Taparelli's views, which appeared in articles and later in a book, were based on a thesis exactly opposed to those put forward by Döllinger and

Montalembert. For Taparelli it was axiomatic that a man could not be guided by his reason, for reason alone might reach an incorrect conclusion, one opposed to the truth, which was taught by the Church. The foundation of human society, therefore, was authority, and liberty of education, of association and of the press could not operate without restrictions. To those who objected that the unalterable truths of religion could not be inculcated by force, Taparelli replied: "The man who ensnares the monster of error, like the man who muzzles a bear, does not claim to have converted the beast, but merely to have saved innocent men from its clutches." To save men, therefore, the Church, according to Taparelli, not only had the right to keep a check on moral opinion but also to have control of political and economic matters as well. Above all it must have control of education.

Expounding these views, throughout the 1850s Taparelli deplored almost everything that the Sardinians attempted to do in their kingdom, and the greater their success the more Pio Nono and the hierarchy seemed to make Taparelli's views their own. Consequently with regard to the congress at Malines, Pio Nono later wrote a private letter of condemnation to Montalembert, pointing out that the Church had condemned the Edict of Nantes, and with it the principle of toleration, and in an encyclical in 1832 had condemned such other freedoms as those of conscience and of the press. And with regard to the congress at Munich he wrote a public letter, a brief, to the local archbishop, hoping the congress would prove fruitful but regretting that such a meeting of theologians had been held without permission and pointing out that Catholic thought was bounded not only by the definitions of dogma but also by the more general authority of the Church expressed in the decisions of the hierarchy and their staffs at Rome, with particular regard to be paid to the decrees of the Index.

The letters were issued in February 1864 and caused consternation among liberal Catholics in every country. Montalembert fell silent; another congress at Munich being planned was canceled; and the British Catholic scholar John Acton announced that his *Home and Foreign Review* would cease publication because ". . . the conductors of this *Review* are unable to yield their assent to the opinions put forward in the Brief." Behind these actions was the fact, well known and considered typical of the Church, that Copernicus' *De Revolutionibus,* published in 1543, and Galileo's *Dialogue of the Two Greatest Systems of the World,* published in 1632, finally had been dropped from the Index only in 1835. To scholars in every field, therefore, but particularly to scientists, philosophers and historians, the Church's position, as expressed in the brief, condemned

Catholic education and thought to remain forever centuries behind the best contemporary thinking.

The pope's letters, however, proved to be only a preamble to something much greater. In December 1864 Pio Nono by an encyclical to his bishops announced a Jubilee Year in 1865, when a plenary indulgence might be gained, and he accompanied the encyclical, entitled *Quanta Cura,* with a Syllabus of Errors "in order that these Bishops may have before their eyes all the errors and pernicious doctrines which he has reprobated and condemned."

The syllabus caused a sensation wherever it penetrated, for it condemned as errors the premises on which the most liberal states of the time were founded. Eighty propositions were stated and condemned, among the earlier ones such things as Bible societies and such concepts as pantheism or communism; among the later propositions were such concepts as freedom of conscience and religious toleration (No. 77), freedom of discussion and the press (No. 79) and finally (No. 80) the idea that "The Roman Pontiff can and should reconcile and harmonize himself with progress, liberalism and recent civilization." To many Catholics and non-Catholics alike the syllabus seemed an incredibly reactionary attack on all that was best in the nineteenth century.

Italians more easily than others could see that its roots lay in the pope's experience with liberalism in Italy, in his own personal experience of it at Rome where he felt his introduction of liberal reforms only had led to the murder of his minister, Pellegrino Rossi, and in his larger experience of it in the rest of Italy, first in Sardinia and then more recently in Umbria, the Marches, Naples and Sicily. But though the roots of the condemnations might be in Italy, Pio Nono by his sweeping language applied them to all the world and for any time. Within the Church the syllabus greatly strengthened the authoritarian party and stopped the Liberal Catholic movement altogether. Among Catholic laymen and non-Catholics it stirred indignation and confusion.

Neither subsided when the Bishop of Orléans tried to explain that the pope had in mind the principles for "the perfect society" rather than those that might be expedient or even just for an existing, imperfect society. Many Europeans and Americans had come to believe that toleration and freedom of thought and press were ideal principles and the only ones on which a "perfect society" could exist. To these the syllabus proclaimed that the Church was not merely slow to move but altogether at a standstill, and their inclination to protest that the city of Rome must be preserved to it was lessened. Outside of the more authoritarian clerical and lay circles the syllabus was a major defeat for the Church in its battle with the Kingdom of Italy for public opinion. Yet the defeat did little to help the government to resolve its difficulties with the Church, for the syllabus was evidence to all Italians that while Pio Nono lived, and probably even for a generation or more after his death, there would be no accommodation within the kingdom between Church and State.

The syllabus and the fate of Rome, however, was not all that aggravated the hostility between the two. On 1 January 1866 a civil marriage bill, based on the Code Napoléon, became law in the State. Under it the State no longer recognized a marriage in the Church, though it did not forbid one or oppress one with regulations. A man and a woman could, if they wished, still be married by a priest, but now they had also to be married by a representative of the State, or they might be prosecuted for living together illegally. Over the years, in practice, most Italians continued to be married in a Church and then, while their friends gathered for the reception, rushed to the town hall to be married by a clerk. Nevertheless, there now was an alternative to marriage in Church, and the Church's grip on the social organization of the country thereby was loosened. (But see Appendix for law after 1929.)

In response to these pressures Pio Nono, on 27 February 1868, approved a decree, known as *Non expedit,* stating that it was "not expedient" for Catholics to take part in the elections of the kingdom. In their municipal governments they could take part, but in the national elections for the Chamber of Deputies they were to be neither "electors nor elected." In a diplomatic sense the Kingdom of Italy was not recognized; in a broader sense it was condemned, like the propositions of the syllabus.

The decree *Non expedit* stayed in full effect until 1904 and in partial effect until 1919, when the Church finally recognized officially that the ban had neither brought down the kingdom nor prevented the secular revolution of Italian life. Catholics who obeyed the decree met in congresses from time to time to debate the issues before the country, and, in accordance with Taparelli's views, the meetings always were attended by an observer from the Church who held a right of veto over subject matter and conclusions. But whatever wisdom and experience these congresses may have contained were largely lost to the country as a whole, and because of them the Chamber of Deputies for fifty years was more anticlerical than the country it represented, and the government was denied the abilities of many men, even in opposition. For both reasons the government was weaker than it might have been.

The decree also weakened the Church. Each national election produced a crisis of conscience for men of character and religion, and in the end many decided against the Church, concluding with regret that its position was unrealistic and self-defeating. Those that continued to abide by the decree in every city went into voluntary isolation, forming separate communities which boycotted schools and clubs, tried to be economically self-contained, and refused to cooperate in any way with persons or programs lacking the Church's approval. But such conduct struck many Italians as fanatical, and in the large industrial cities that were developing the great majority of the people grew up outside the Church.

These problems which the government could not resolve, the regional jealousies, the poverty and illiteracy of the south and, above all, the hostility of the Church, caused deep wounds in Italian life which even time did not heal, for they are still problems today, though perhaps to a smaller degree. To them must be added two more problems, less serious but significant, which also harassed the government year after year. One was the hostility of Garibaldi and Mazzini, which in its most extreme form induced many republicans to refuse to take the oath of allegiance to the king and so kept them from serving in the Chamber even when elected. The other was the failure of any Italian statesman, until the advent of Alcide de Gasperi in 1945, to develop a skill equal to Cavour's for parliamentary government. Every Italian was involved personally in one or more of these problems and had reason to be disappointed in the results of the Risorgimento.

Yet significantly the problems and the disappointments caused by them did not undermine the basic work of the patriots. The compromise worked out by Manin and accepted by others, a united Italy but under a king, proved sound for its time, and in spite of all the disappointments no one seriously suggested that any other solution be attempted. In this the Italians displayed a common sense which already had carried them safely through the struggle of Cavour and Garibaldi. Always they had refused to embrace one to the exclusion of the other. Even when the two men were most opposed, the Italian people insisted on supporting both, sending men and money to aid Garibaldi's expeditions to the south while insisting that Cavour continue as prime minister. In much the same way after unification the majority of them opposed the Church's political position for generations while at the same time insisting that they were good Catholics. Meanwhile no one seriously proposed a State Church, like the Church of England, or no church at all, such as the French revolutionaries had attempted. All of which, while testifying to the good sense of the Italian people, also testifies to the soundness of the most basic idea of the Risorgimento: that for Italy to be independent of foreign domination, whether Spanish, French or Austrian, it must, all of it, be united into one state. From the achievement of that sprang many of the problems which later distressed the country but from it also sprang the strength which caused the country to survive the problems.

# CHAPTER 47

Garibaldi's visit to England. The Galician scheme. The Prussian alliance and third war against Austria. Custoza. Lissa. The Veneto annexed. The failure of the Venetians to rise.

GARIBALDI'S WOUNDED FOOT kept him on Caprera, out of politics at least physically, until March 1864, when he suddenly departed for a visit to England. To a reporter for the London *Times* who interviewed him at Malta, and to anyone else who asked, he insisted that his purpose was only "to obtain the benefit of medical advice and to pay a debt of gratitude he considers he owes to the English people." And no one could deny he still needed the heavy cane on which he leaned or that the English people of all classes had showered him in his convalescence with gifts and invitations. In fact he, his son and even his staff traveled to England on a Peninsular and Orient steamer diverted to Caprera from its regular run by a director of the company who greatly admired him.

Yet the Italian government, which in the spring of 1864 was still in Turin, was sure he had a political purpose. Though his wound had restricted him to Caprera, he had never ceased after Aspromonte to rail against the government, declaring that Parliament was no place for an honest man, that the government was denying freedom of speech to some of his friends and imprisoning others, and that it was "preparing a nauseous reaction and spending the riches of Italy in hiring spies, police agents, priests and similar rabble."

Many Italians beside those in the government feared he would repeat such sentiments in England and, though loving Italy, discredit it. They remembered, too, his success in addressing crowds and feared an enthusiastic reception. The English were traditionally anti-Papal and anti-French: suppose Garibaldi began to address them as he had the Sicilians two years before, calling the pope "a vampire-priest" and Napoleon "a thief, a predatory monarch, a usurper." And further, Mazzini was in England: suppose the two met. Would they not inevitably plot some new revolution?

The British government had the same fears. Palmerston, the prime minister, made it plain to Garibaldi's sponsors, such as the Duke of

Sutherland, that the visit was to be private. The general was to be entertained, as far as possible, in their homes and be discouraged, on the ground of his health, from accepting invitations to testimonial dinners where "he would say foolish things and other people mischievous ones." Neither Garibaldi's feelings nor those of many English people coincided with British policy on the Polish question, the United States' civil war or the fate of the Danes in North Schleswig.

The visit began quietly, as most everyone hoped it would. Garibaldi arrived at Southampton in the rain, was greeted by an enthusiastic but small crowd and made a short speech of gratitude in English which was barely intelligible. Then he was driven off to stay at the mayor's house until he could leave the next day for the Isle of Wight. There he stayed for almost a week as the guest of a member of Parliament with his only public event a tour of the Portsmouth harbor and arsenal. Occasionally a friend called, and one of the first to come was Mazzini. But even though no one could understand what the two were talking about, as they conversed in their Ligurian dialect, they seemed harmless enough, like any two old men in a garden, talking of times past. Later he called on Tennyson, reciting for him Foscolo's "Dei Sepolcri," and Tennyson was enchanted: "He is more majestic than meek and his manners have a certain divine simplicity. . . ." Wherever Garibaldi went, he seemed to please, and always a crowd was waiting to greet him. By the end of the week, as he left Southampton by special train for London, it was evident that, whatever he or his sponsors may have intended or whatever the British or Italian governments may have hoped, his visit was going to be public and to have political overtones sufficiently strong to jar several governments in Europe.

His reception in London was stupendous, the greatest by far the city had ever seen. No other visitor, sovereign or soldier, had ever received such a welcome, and it irritated such diverse egos as Queen Victoria and Karl Marx, who thought it "a miserable spectacle of imbecility." Although nothing official had been planned, during the morning about half a million persons gathered along the streets from the station to the Duke of Sutherland's house where Garibaldi was to stay. When he arrived in the afternoon, his carriage took six hours to travel the three miles, while behind and before him marched trade union officials, radical politicians, members of friendly and temperance societies, members of the Working Men's Garibaldi Demonstration Committee and finally the duke's private fire brigade. It was, as the *Times* reported, "most emphatically a people's welcome, a working-men's reception from first to last."

One of the most remarkable things about it was its good order. The people clapped and shouted, laughed and cried, waved scarves and handkerchiefs of red and even sang Garibaldi's Hymn, yet there was no accident, no drunkenness; no pockets were picked or tempers lost. The fifteen hundred policemen the city had assigned to the demonstration could have done nothing in half a million people spread over three miles, yet nothing needed to be done. As Lord Clarendon wrote to Napoleon, trying to reassure him that the reception did not have the official blessing of the British government, it was a "grand" spectacle "because it was entirely the doing of the working classes who looked upon Garibaldi as a real hero because he had risen from their own rank of life . . . because he was poor. . . . The people kept order for themselves without police or soldiers. . . ." But for some, of course, that only increased the terror of Garibaldi's strength.

For two weeks the excitement continued. Society took him up. Ladies competed for his arm at functions, and when he smoked his cigar in the Duchess of Sutherland's boudoir, the Earl of Malmesbury gasped at the favor granted in "such a sacred spot." Meanwhile the duchess' servants started a profitable traffic in soapsuds from Garibaldi's basin. Through it all he behaved with a simple dignity everyone found charming.

He also had dinner with Palmerston and after an hour's private talk emerged red in the face. Palmerston reportedly urged that revolution in Rome or the Veneto should be delayed while Garibaldi argued that it was never too soon to break the chains of slaves. He had a more harmonious dinner, evidently, at the house of Alexander Herzen at which several of the most notorious European revolutionaries, including Mazzini, were present. At its end he rose to say:

> I am about to say something which I ought to have said long ago. We have among us a man who has rendered the greatest service to our country and to the cause of freedom. When I was young, with aspirations to do good, I sought for one able to act as the guide and counsellor of my youthful years. I sought for a guide as a man who is thirsty seeks out a spring of water. I found one. He alone watched while all around him slept, he alone kept and tended the secret flame. He has remained always my friend, always full of love for his country and of devotion to the cause of liberty. This man is Giuseppe Mazzini—my friend and teacher.[121]

Garibaldi had said many harsh things about Mazzini in the past and would again in the future, but in its essence this declaration was true. Queen Victoria, however, was not pleased when she read it in the newspapers and complained to her ministers that their object of keeping Garibaldi out of dangerous company had "hardly been obtained." Later, when Palmerston inquired about the necessity of the lunch or of the remarks after it, Garibaldi explained that "had he found Mazzini in prosperity, he would have avoided all misunderstanding by not seeing him; but finding him in adversity, he could not throw him aside." There was little Palmerston could say.

Nevertheless the British ministers, while admiring Garibaldi, were anxious for him to leave. No one objected to his visiting Eton and Windsor, inspecting model farms or laying a wreath on Foscolo's tomb at Chiswick, but his remarks on political subjects invariably were against some government's policy, and the French, Prussian, Belgian, Papal and Italian governments already had complained. Further, all the provincial cities wanted to repeat London's demonstration, and Garibaldi had accepted invitations for an appearance in almost fifty of them, with more invitations arriving each day.

So on behalf of the British government, Gladstone tried to persuade him to cut his tour from fifty cities to six. But both Garibaldi and the majority of the British people, when they learned of it, took this to mean that he had been asked, however politely, to leave the country, and among the people, the apparent discourtesy raised a storm of protest.

The government in fact had not meant so much. The decision to go, without visiting even the six cities, was made solely by Garibaldi and put down publicly to reasons of health. But there was more to it than that. He was bored with the festivities and beginning to realize that they would not lead to any support by the government for his ideas. And, further, two messengers had come from Vittorio Emanuele, first a colonel and then a full general, with the suggestion that he should take an expedition to Galicia and attack Austria in the rear. The chance to free the Veneto once more seemed closer in Italy than in England, and so he departed for Caprera on the Duke of Sutherland's yacht, bidding the English farewell with a gracious speech of admiration for their law and liberty.

His visit to England, though ending in failure, is one of the phenomena of European nineteenth-century history. When it is remembered that he went, not as the conqueror of Sicily but as the defeated of Aspromonte, against the wishes of his own government and without the backing of any other, his reception seems all the more astonishing. Plainly, he touched something very deep in persons of all classes, and particularly in the working class. Quite aside from whether his influence was good or bad, probably no other man in the century except for the first Napoleon had such a personal impact on the peoples and governments of Europe.

The reasons for this can hardly be separated from his character, for he was, as everyone remarked, a simple man. Rather than holding ideas he seemed to embody them. The Prince of Wales, in trying to explain Garibaldi to the disapproving Victoria, wrote, "he is so *uncharlatanlike,* if I may use such an expression . . . and though his undertakings have been certainly revolutionary, still, he is a patriot and did not seek for his aggrandisement." To this should be added only that, unlike Mazzini, who was equally selfless, he was a man of action, and most men find deeds easier to understand and more exciting than ideas. But, unquestionably, what fascinated men most was his return to Caprera, after conquering Naples and Sicily, with nothing for himself. Like some great bell, that act rang through Europe for half a century, startling men to attention and admiration. Even today, it continues to sound as an inspiration to many.

Soon after Garibaldi returned to Caprera from England, he received another message from the king, who again was intriguing behind the backs of his ministers, and in June, still using the Duke of Sutherland's yacht, he set off for Ischia, in the Bay of Naples. He had called a meeting of his lieutenants in order to lay the king's plan before them and had chosen Ischia for the rendezvous because its mud baths would be good for his arthritis, which the English trip seemed to have aggravated. His health, therefore, gave an obvious reason for going to Ischia.

His lieutenants, however, used his health to argue against the plan. They had no interest in a revolution in Galicia, outside of Italy and deep in the Austrian Empire, and they stressed the king's ambition to find a throne for his second son, a concern, perhaps, of the House of Savoy but not of Italy. To prevent anything coming of the scheme, someone gave its outline to the newspapers. The king promptly withdrew from it; Garibaldi fired his secretary, although it is not clear that the man was responsible for the leak, and the Galician plan was buried. Rome and the Veneto were still outside of Italy, and Garibaldi returned to Caprera, angry and complaining.

When in September 1864 Minghetti announced the convention with France whereby French troops in two years would be withdrawn from Rome in return for the Italian government's agreeing to protect the Papal State and to move its capital to Florence, Garibaldi exploded in a letter to the newspapers:

> Let the guilty who wish search for accomplices; it is natural. But don't look for me in the mud of the men who soil Italy with the Convention of 15 September. With Bonaparte there can be only one convention: to purify our country of his presence not in two years, but in two hours.[122]

But he had no program to offer, and he passed the next year, 1865, on Caprera, still inactive, angry and complaining. His views continued the same, but his expression of them grew sharper. He debated for a time going to Mexico to fight for Benito Juárez against the Emperor Maximilian, for that would be to fight for a people against a Habsburg and against Napoleon III who supported him, but in the end, the possibility of taking

Rome or Venice, however remote, kept him in Italy. Not seeing any immediate chance for either, however, he once again requested the king to appoint him dictator of Naples and Sicily. "The government is now more hated there than were the Bourbons," he wrote, "and the day war breaks out against Austria there will be a cataclysmic revolt against us all over the south." It was a mournful prophecy and, with its "against us," one of the few occasions on which he associated himself with the government.

In the spring of 1866, however, the chance to take the Veneto suddenly grew more likely when Italy and Prussia, where Bismarck was now the prime minister, signed a commercial treaty and also an offensive and defensive alliance whose object plainly was Austria. Under Bismarck, Prussia was starting on a course which in 1871 would unite twenty-five German states into a German Empire with the King of Prussia as emperor. Like the unification of Italy, that of Germany, if accomplished under Prussian leadership, could be achieved only at the expense of the Habsburg position in the German Confederation and therefore almost certainly would involve Prussia and Austria in a war. And for Italians such a war would offer the ideal opportunity for capturing the Veneto, for it would be a war in which Austria would have to divide its army between two fronts and also a war in which Italy would not incur any further obligation toward France. As far back as 1861, Cavour had foreseen the possibility of it and had sent General La Marmora to Berlin to congratulate King Wilhelm I on his accession, and in return the king had sent a special military mission to Turin. Now at a time when La Marmora himself had become prime minister, following the riots in Turin over the capital's removal to Florence, the seeds he had carried to Berlin five years earlier began to sprout.

The chief uncertainty in the situation was the attitude of Napoleon, and La Marmora steadfastly refused to commit Italy in any way without his approval. As long as a French army remained at Rome, Napoleon inevitably had a special place in Italian policy. But Bismarck, the prime actor in the negotiations, journeyed to Biarritz to have an interview with him and, after it, reported to La Marmora that France would be neutral in a war between Prussia and Austria and that Italy was free to suit itself, at its own risk. La Marmora, meanwhile, had been negotiating directly with Austria and had offered to buy the Veneto for a thousand million lire. At the time, however, Franz Josef and his ministers were confident of their position and rejected the offer without opening any other line of negotiation for the province, and in the end, on 8 April 1866, La Marmora and Bismarck signed a Prussian-Italian alliance.

Austria, not unnaturally, considered it an aggressive act, and the three countries immediately thereafter approached a state of war in much the same fashion that France, Sardinia and Austria had done in 1859. Austria accused Italy of strengthening its army in Lombardia and began to send re-enforcements into the Veneto. La Marmora then ordered a mobilization of the Italian army which brought still more Austrian troops into the Veneto. Napoleon suggested a congress, and Wilhelm of Prussia hesitated while Bismarck tried to force Austria to attack. Finally the Prussians ordered a partial mobilization. Meanwhile, in an effort to detach Italy from Prussia, Austria now offered it the Veneto in return for neutrality. Cavour conceivably might have found some way to accept this, but La Marmora stood by his treaty with Bismarck which included a clause forbidding a separate settlement. But beside the question of honor, La Marmora and his colleagues had other reasons for preferring a war: the "Venetia" which Austria offered was just the Veneto and did not include either Trieste or the region known as Trentino—Alto Adige (see map, p. 689); a huge sum of money had been spent on turning the small Sardinian army into a large Italian one, and a war would justify it, and further, everyone hoped to cap the national movement with a victory over Austria. Nothing, it was felt, would unify the country more.

The diplomacy leading up to these moves was complicated, involving besides the fate of the Veneto, the fate of North Schleswig, of Romania and of the German States on the Rhine. Nevertheless, the skill of both the Italian and Austrian diplomats, compared to that of Napoleon and Bismarck, seems very poor in that they arrived at a position in which Italy, after offering to buy the Veneto, could not accept it as a gift, and Austria, after refusing to sell it, insisted on giving it away. For after Italy refused to accept it, Austria by a secret treaty agreed to transfer it to Napoleon, in return for his neutrality in the expected war, to hold for Italy regardless of how the war turned out. This cast Napoleon in his favorite role as arbiter of Europe and would permit him at the war's end to appear to have done something for Italy as if in partial recompense for the abandonment of Venice at Villafranca. At the same time it cost him nothing, for he already had decided to be neutral, although the Austrians evidently were not sure of it. Bismarck, of course, did not care whether Austrian troops fought in the Veneto to preserve it or to give it away, so long as they fought.

Finally, as in 1859, Britain, France and Russia made a last effort to find some basis for peace, but Austria now more than ever was standing on pride and refused to consider any sort of settlement. On 16 June, therefore, Prussia declared war. Four days later Italy did likewise, and Ricasoli came out of retirement to be prime minister as La Marmora went to the front to take command of the Italian army.

For Italians it was the third war of independence against Austria within twenty years, and almost all the higher officers in the regular army, in-

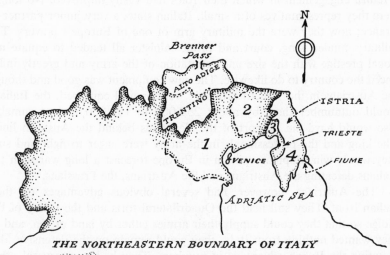

**N**

Brenner
Pass

ALTO ADIGE

TRENTINO

1

2

3

ISTRIA

VENICE

TRIESTE

4

FIUME

ADRIATIC SEA

### THE NORTHEASTERN BOUNDARY OF ITALY

*The line* ~~~~ *shows the boundary as it was from 1866 to 1919.
After World War I Italy acquired the Trentino - Alto Adige
region and the Istrian peninsula. It acquired Fiume in
1924. After World War II it lost Fiume and most of Istria,
except for Trieste and its connecting costal plain, to Yugoslavia.*

### NOTE ON VENICE AND THE VENETO...

*The term "the Veneto" as used in this book, means Venice,
the island city and its coastal plain, which includes,
roughly, the areas marked "1" and "2". This is the traditional
sense of the term, designating the Capital and Italian
mainland of the Republic of Venice and, later, the
Venetian part of the Habsburg Kingdom of Lombardo-
Veneto. It is the sense in which most writers and Italians
still use the term.*

*The Italian government, however, in dividing Italy in 1946
into nineteen regions, limited the region of Veneto to the
area marked "1". It designated "2" as part of Friuli —
Venezia Giulia, which also includes "3" of Trieste and its
connecting coastal plain. To add to the confusion some
writers and maps refer to the "TRE VENEZIA" or "THREE VENICES".
These are VENEZIA EUGANIA, roughly "1" or the government's
"Veneto"; VENEZIA TRIDENTINA, roughly the region of Trentino
—Alto Adige; and VENEZIA GIULIA, roughly "2", "3" and "4",
the last being the part of the Istrian peninsula ceded to
Yugoslavia.*

cluding the king, had fought in 1848–49 and 1859. For them the war was a return engagement in which their roles had vastly improved. No longer were they representatives of a small, Italian state, a very junior partner to France; now they were the military arm of one of Europe's powers. The military-minded king, court and prime minister all tended to equate national prestige with the size and reputation of the army and greatly influenced the country to do likewise. The new equipment was good and though the Austrians in the Veneto probably were as well equipped, the Italians would outnumber them by about 250,000 to 190,000 and presumably also would have the support of the Venetians behind the Austrian lines. The king and the professionals in the army were eager to fight and sure they would win. Popular opinion in Europe forecast a long war with the Italians defeating the Austrians and the Austrians, the Prussians.

The Austrians, however, had several obvious advantages on their Italian front. They still held the Quadrilateral forts and the valley of the Adige so that they could supply their armies either by land or sea, and as they wanted nothing from Italy, they could remain on the defensive, discounting the Italian advantage in numbers. They had, too, several other advantages which became clearer as soon as the fighting started.

The Italian army was divided into three parts and command of it was splintered into four. Farthest to the north, in the Alps, was Garibaldi and about twenty thousand volunteers aiming, as in 1859, to capture Trento and to close the valley of the Adige. La Marmora's control over him was slight. In the center, north of the Po, was La Marmora himself with the main army and also the king who fancied himself as a strategist and whose ideas could not be ignored. And finally, south of the Po with another large army was Cialdini who was jealous of La Marmora, disinclined to cooperate with him and who had succeeded in arranging the chain of command in such a way that La Marmora could not give him orders but could only invite him to alter his dispositions. It was a chain of command for which, in the case of Garibaldi, national politics was responsible and, for the rest, the traditions and jealousies of a small court which were wholly inappropriate for the government of a large state. And the first result of it was the failure of the Italian staff to evolve a sensible plan of attack. The three armies, each in its own time, pressed forward and established a long, straggling front before the Austrians who, secure in their fortresses, could choose where to concentrate their forces.

The first fighting occurred with La Marmora. On 24 June he led his men across the Mincio, believing that the main Austrian line of defense would be along the Adige with Peschiera and Mantua as outposts. (See map, p. 495.) But the Austrian commander, Archduke Albrecht, had entrenched himself on the high ground between Peschiera and Verona, and the Italians, as they approached the village of Custoza, where in 1848 the Austrians had defeated Carlo Alberto, suddenly found themselves in a serious fight, one in which the Austrians had the advantages of interior lines, high ground and prepared positions. The fighting lasted all day and was not a defeat or a victory for either side. The two armies, or parts of them, met, fought and disengaged with casualties being about equal. La Marmora, however, behaved as though the second battle of Custoza, as it soon was called, had been a tremendous defeat. The poor work of his intelligence corps had allowed Austrians in defensive positions to seem like a surprise attack in force, and when one Italian division gave way in something like a panic, running in disorder to retreat across a bridge, he apparently concluded that the whole army had collapsed and, leaving the front, galloped twenty miles to find reserves to cover the retreat. Meanwhile the various divisions fought on individually until evening when, under La Marmora's leadership, they began a retreat not to the Mincio but all the way back to the Oglio. What should have been treated as the indecisive engagement it was, became, as word of the retreat spread, a tremendous psychological defeat not only for the army but for the entire country.

The Austrians, however, made no attempt to invade Lombardia by following La Marmora across the Mincio, and when ten days later, on 3 July, the Prussians won the decisive victory of Sadowa, Archduke Albrecht and the bulk of his force were recalled to Austria. La Marmora meanwhile had resigned his command and been succeeded by Cialdini, who started the army forward once again and, bypassing the Quadrilateral forts, began to occupy the Venetian cities behind them, such as Padua and Vicenza. To the north, in the mountains around Lago di Garda, Garibaldi, wounded in the thigh, led his volunteers from a carriage and after some fighting, succeeded in clearing the two valleys leading into Trento. But his campaign, while creditable, was not very exciting and, as the high command of the regular army had intended, plainly was secondary. Patriots in and out of the government still hoped for a brilliant victory to erase the shock of Custoza, to justify the money spent on the army and to bring the Venetians into the kingdom in a way in which all Italians could take pride.

For a brief moment the navy seemed about to supply it. The first reports of an engagement with the Austrian fleet in the Adriatic implied a victory. The Italians on 20 July had been bombarding the fortifications on Lissa, an island which guards the entrance to Split or, as it then was called, Spalato, when the Austrian fleet suddenly had appeared from the north. The Italians, under Admiral Persano, had twelve ironclads and the Austrians under a Dane, Wilhelm von Tegethoff, only seven. Nevertheless, Tegethoff, as soon as he had heard that the Italian fleet was at sea, had hurried down from Trieste and knowing he had fewer ships, less armor and smaller guns, had given orders to use the ram if possible. With himself in the lead, on the *Ferdinand Max,* he smashed directly into the Italian line and, in the confusion that followed, rammed and sank the *Re d'Italia,* Persano's flagship. Another Italian ship, the *Palestro,* also was rammed and, after burning for a while, blew up. After an hour's fighting, the Italians withdrew, and the Austrians, who had not lost a ship, were left in control of the Dalmatian coast. Later, at Ancona, a third Italian ship, badly damaged in the fight, sank at its mooring.

The battle was the first in naval history between fleets of ironclads, and for Italians their defeat by an inferior force was particularly galling in that, despite the expensive armor, the ships had been sunk by the simple and ancient tactic of ramming. But even worse revelations were to follow. Persano, although with the superior force, had not wanted to put to sea at all and had done so only when peremptory orders coupled with the threat of removal had been placed in his hand personally by the Minister of the Marine. Even more strange, just before the engagement started he had left his flagship, the *Re d'Italia,* for another ship without informing the fleet of the change, so that when the flagship sank with more than four hundred men aboard, the rest of the fleet had assumed that the admiral had gone down with his ship. The discovery that he had not was a terrible shock, and he later was tried for incompetence and cowardice. Lissa, like Custoza, was a national disaster, the second within a month.

But even worse was to follow. Lissa had been fought on 20 July. Six days later Bismarck, violating the terms of his alliance with Italy, signed a preliminary peace with Austria without consulting his ally. Austria at once began to re-enforce its Italian front with all available troops and, by the first week in August, had almost three hundred thousand troops in the Veneto or on the way. For Italians the nightmare of being left alone to fight Austria had become a reality, and on 12 August the government agreed to an armistice.

By the final treaty which was signed in October 1866, Italy gained two things: recognition by Austria, which ended even formal claims of the Habsburg archdukes to their former duchies, and the Veneto. But the latter was received not from Austria but from France, or technically from Venetian representatives who had the freedom of their province from France, and the usual plebiscite was required before it could join the Italian kingdom. The vote was 647,246 to 69 for union, and when the result was announced officially to the king by a deputation from Venice, he said, "This is the finest day of my life; Italy is made," and then referring to Rome, "but it is not complete."

The patriots of every party, of course, were delighted to have the Veneto become part of Italy, but the king's rhetoric could not cancel their disappointment over how it had been accomplished or even over what had been accomplished. Trieste and Trento with their surrounding regions were still to be Austrian, leaving many Italians under Austrian rule and giving Italy an indefensible northeastern boundary, for the Austrians controlled the mountains which circled the Italian plains. The fate of these Italians and the placement of the boundary were to agitate Italian policy until after World War I, and the problem at its creation was aggravated still further by the fact that Garibaldi had been about to capture Trento when he was ordered to withdraw from the region as one of the conditions of the armistice. "I obey," he had replied to the order, but at the same time, at much greater length, he had issued a proclamation to the volunteers, regretting that Italy was to lose "the fruits of your labors" and, while praising them for what they had achieved, blaming the government for giving them poor clothing and "old smooth-bore rifles that were the joke of the enemy." His complaint had some truth in it and was made more galling for the king and regular army officers by the fact that his campaign, though minor, was the only one of the war to be well conducted. But his bitterness, often and loudly expressed, did nothing to heal the psychological wounds of the country.

But what wounded Garibaldi and the government alike was that the Venetians had not risen. Not one town had attempted to evict its Austrian garrison, and in the countryside not one peasant had volunteered to fight. The conclusion to which patriots were forced was that the Venetians, who had fought so gallantly in 1849, no longer cared whether they were to be free or Italian. In the mountains, to Garibaldi's indignation, they even had seemed to prefer Austrian rule. For fervent patriots the fact was puzzling and, particularly for the thousands of Venetians in exile, just as great a humiliation as Lissa or Custoza.

The reasons behind this failure to act are very obscure, lying perhaps in the stratum of psychology rather than of history, and most historians do not attempt to offer any explanation of it beyond noting that the peasants in Italy, of whatever region, seldom had concerned themselves with the movement for independence and unification. But the observation, while true, skirts the fact that in the past the Venetians of the towns and lagoons frequently had; and now they had not, at least not actively. Yet elsewhere in Italy the excitement among townspeople over the war was great, and something like fifty thousand men tried to volunteer to fight under Garibaldi.

Possibly a number of facts and strains combined to inhibit the Venetians. In 1849 they had lost their leaders, Manin and others of "the forty" who had led their revolution, and thereafter they produced no others of equal ability, partly because most Venetians who were also patriots sooner or later went to Turin, or volunteered to serve under Garibaldi, or in the Sardinian or Italian army. And this depression in men of ability had an economic counterpart in the region's wealth as the Austrians, as a matter of policy after 1849, deliberately favored Trieste over Venice. In the seventeen years between 1849 and 1866 the region, except for its agriculture, was relatively depressed. Then, too, as the war was manufactured by Bismarck rather than growing out of a series of incidents involving Venetians and Austrians, it became a reality for the Venetians suddenly and without any emotional preparation. As Austrian subjects they had not listened to speeches or martial music whose only purpose was to excite them to fight Austria. Further, they may have been influenced by a feeling, indefinable but evident also in Vienna, that the Veneto was bound to join Italy someday, somehow, and perhaps Venetians who felt this also wondered why, if union was inevitable, a man should die to achieve it. But whatever the reasons, the Venetians in 1866 did not stir to free themselves, and the fact inclined many, particularly those who had lost relatives at Lissa or Custoza, to wonder again if the Italians really wanted to be unified and independent.

Such thoughts were stimulated even further in September 1866, when Garibaldi's prophecy of a revolt in the south came true. Bands of disgruntled Sicilians gathered in the mountains around Palermo and then, as Garibaldi had shown them how to do, burst into the city and held it for six days. They were angry about the taxes, the conscription and the bureacracy in Turin, but they had no single leader or program and at various times followers of Mazzini, Garibaldi, the pope, the Bourbons and even Sicilian autonomists seemed to be the true leaders. Nevertheless, in spite of the confusion, the rebels created a provisional government in which some aristocrats served and which did not capitulate until Ricasoli sent a strong force of the regular army into the city. Even then the rebels did not capitulate unconditionally but negotiated a surrender through the French consul. Thereafter the government did not probe deeply into the revolt's causes, which therefore were neither remedied nor even understood, and dissatisfaction in the south continued to erupt from time to time in spates of violence.

In all, the year 1866, viewed one way, was a year of disaster for Italians; and yet their kingdom remained united and in its recognition by Austria and its acquisition of the Veneto even made itself stronger. And finally at the year's end, in December, the French army at Rome, in accordance with the September Convention, was withdrawn and the pope's Patrimony of St. Peter left by the convention's terms to the protection of the Italian kingdom. In the Biblical parlance of Rome: the wolves were put to guarding the fold.

# CHAPTER 48

Ricasoli's effort to negotiate the Roman Question. Garibaldi's election campaign. His preparations for a march on Rome. Mentana. The French back in Rome.

WITH THE VENETO UNITED to the Italian kingdom, Austria finally was excluded from all but the fringes of the peninsula, and with the departure of the French troops from Rome, so, too, was France, although only physically for the September Convention gave it a direct interest in the fate of Rome. Nevertheless, by the end of 1866, one of the chief aims of the Risorgimento, to drive the foreigners out of Italy, in large part had been achieved, and the Italians, more than at any time in the past three hundred years, were left alone to work out their problems. In spite of the disasters which had accompanied the war against Austria, most patriots were aware of how much had been accomplished.

The Roman Question remained and, in its new isolation, magnetized everyone's attention. The temporal power, the Papal State, now consisted of only a single province, the Patrimony of St. Peter, which contained about six hundred thousand persons, of whom nearly a third lived in or around Rome. Though the terms of the September Convention required the Italian government to protect this state from attack, they did not preclude a peaceful solution to the problems it posed or prevent extremists from attempting to impose a forceful one. And as the last French troops left the city men, according to their natures and prejudices, began to work on solutions of both sorts.

The first effort of significance was initiated by the government. Ricasoli, who had succeeded La Marmora as prime minister at the start of the war, was anxious to find a peaceful solution, and as soon as the peace treaty with Austria was signed, in October 1866, he put the Roman Question to the front of his program. As a religious man he was eager to resolve the kingdom's difficulties with the Church not only for the good of the kingdom but also, as he saw it, for the good of the Church. Like Cavour, he believed that a free Church in a free State would benefit both

Church and State, and although when prime minister five years earlier the Church had rebuffed him on this program, still he was determined now to try it again. Before the last French soldier had left Rome, therefore, Ricasoli's agent, Michelangelo Tonello, had arrived in the city to begin negotiations.

What he proposed on the government's behalf was again the complete separation of Church and State: the Church to give up its claim to temporal power, and the State its right to veto ecclesiastical nominations, known as the *exequatur,* and its right to forbid the publication of Papal bulls and encyclicals, the *placet.* At the time the negotiations began there were eighty-two sees in Italy without bishops because the State in its struggle with the Church had vetoed the nominations for them. In return for Rome, therefore, Ricasoli was offering the Church something substantial; in fact, more freedom within its spiritual domain than it enjoyed in any other Catholic country. But the question, of course, was whether the Church would see a benefit in what was offered, whether Pio Nono and the Roman cardinals could imagine the spiritual power separated from a temporal base. Antonelli, still Papal Secretary of State, told Odo Russell, the British agent at Rome, that if Signor Tonello "proposes to negotiate on the principle of the recognition of the Kingdom of Italy by us and of the sovereignty of Vittorio Emanuele over any other part of Italy than Piedmont, then it will be useless to proceed."

Nevertheless, negotiations did proceed, although slowly and not on the larger issues; after several weeks of talk agreement had been reached only on the appointment of fourteen of the eighty-two bishops. Meanwhile in Florence, where the government had to work more publicly and was also under pressure to produce something in order to frustrate the extremists, Ricasoli in January introduced a bill to the Chamber entitled "Freedom of the Church." It provided for the separation of Church and State, stipulating that the Church in its spiritual affairs should be governed exclusively by its canon law and denying the State any rights in the appointment of clergy or promulgation of bulls and encyclicals. The Church, however, as part of the continuing secularization of Italian life, would not be allowed to own real estate, and it would therefore have to sell off its lands, transferring a percentage of the proceeds to the State, which intended to assume many of the educational and charitable functions previously performed by religious orders. To the Church, of course, its holdings did not seem exorbitant, badly managed or socially unproductive, and the forced conversion appeared only as an unjustified confiscation. Nor was it mollified by being allowed to manage the sales. It threw all its influence against the bill.

It was joined, in an unusual alliance, by many republicans who thought the bill did not go far enough in stripping the Church of power and wealth, and even many moderates wondered if the government should abandon its few controls over the Church before the Church had shown some signs of self-reform or of accepting the principle of separation. For although Pio Nono had not yet decreed his *Non expedit,* whereby Catholics should not be "electors or elected" in the kingdom's government, he already had issued the Syllabus of Errors, with its condemnations of all the freedoms which constitutional monarchists and republicans alike had sought. With opposition from both sides the bill clearly would not pass, and Ricasoli, much distressed, persuaded the king to dissolve Parliament in the hope that a new Chamber would be more favorable.

The elections, which took place in March 1867, were fought with unusual bitterness, largely because of Garibaldi, who made a campaign from Florence northward to Venice, denouncing both the government and the Papacy. That he should have nothing good to say about Lissa and Custoza was to be expected, but he extended the blame for them to include not only the armed forces and the ministers but also all the deputies. He wanted a clean sweep of the Chamber, and no one was to be elected who had a good word for priests or the pope. The priests were "the murderers of liberty" and "satellites of the fallen dynasties"; the pope was "a filthy priest who had debased, trampled and disfigured Rome. Rome that is our capital, and we shall go there as a man returns to his own home!"

Garibaldi spoke from balconies and windows, always to huge crowds, and his language constantly grew more virulent. The Papacy had replaced the Bourbon government as "The Negation of God," and in place of Roman Catholicism there should be a "new religion of brotherhood, of love and peace, with God as the legislator and all men as his apostles and priests." He was sixty; his hair had grown white and thinned, and his face often showed the pain of his arthritis. Yet he had lost none of his magic with the common people, and although they probably paid little attention to his religious ideas, still they cheered him for them, occasionally brought him babies to baptize and encouraged him to think of himself as the prophet of a new religion of Christ which had no priests, altars or doctrine. Always, however, the main theme of his speeches was *"Roma capitale!",* and by the end of the campaign its realization had become for him almost an obsession.

For his immediate purpose, however, his campaign was a failure. The small electorate of the literate and well-to-do elected him to the Chamber as a matter of course, but it refused to return even one of the sixty other candidates he had recommended. For Ricasoli, too, the election was a failure, for the new Chamber proved as hostile as the old to the Church bill, and when it became plain that the bill would never pass, he resigned.

The king, just as he had five years earlier when Ricasoli resigned, appointed Urbano Rattazzi to succeed him.

The failure of the government to produce a peaceful solution to the Roman Question aggravated the excitement among republicans for one of force. Garibaldi continued to make pronouncements and to receive deputations on Caprera; Mazzini by letter from London urged on those who continued to look to him for leadership; men such as Crispi and Bertani, at the next level of command, began to assemble companies of volunteers near the Papal border, and in Rome revolutionary committees tried to organize the Roman people. The volunteer groups and committees were often temporary, confused and even conflicting, but their revolutionary aim was common and clear, and unless the government firmly suppressed those on the borders, some of them in time seemed certain to start an invasion of the Papal State in conjunction with an insurrection in Rome.

On the political aim of the movement Garibaldi and Mazzini partially disagreed. Mazzini wished to go to Rome and from the Campidoglio to proclaim Italy a republic, a continuation of the Roman Republic of 1849. After Lissa and Custoza, he was too disgusted with the monarchy to continue to support it, but Garibaldi wrote him: "I think we ruin the Roman affair by imposing a political program. Let the child be born; once born it will be baptized and we will baptize it. The urge today is to ruin the Papal Government. Let us both work together then to that end." Garibaldi's phrase "and we will baptize it" suggests that, after capturing Rome, he might be willing to proclaim Italy a republic, but not at the start of the expedition when he and his lieutenants were hoping to get arms and money from the government. Mazzini had to give way, for in these years Garibaldi's influence was much greater than his.

In June 1867, however, several events took place which seemed to indicate that the government intended to stand by the convention. A French general in Rome, at the request of Papal officers, inspected a corps of Frenchmen who, calling themselves the *Légion d'Antibes,* had volunteered to defend the Papal State. Unquestionably this action by a French general who retained his rank in the French regular army was a technical violation of the convention, for by recognizing the national character of the Legion it suggested the Legion was an extension of the French army. The Italian papers made a tremendous fuss of the incident; Rattazzi protested to the French government, which apologized, and, on his report to the Chamber, the deputies had a debate on the Roman Question. The conclusion to which Rattazzi led them was the one originally put forward by Cavour; that while Italy must eventually go to Rome, it must do so by peaceful means which, because of the convention, meant with the consent of France. The words used were unequivocal and were supported by deeds.

The army had confiscated a cache of arms near the Papal border and dispersed a company of volunteers while arresting seventy-two of them. The government, it seemed, was not going to be drawn into another Aspromonte.

Yet despite its words and deeds it could not dispel the belief, widely held among republicans, that when the moment came, it would either support the volunteers or occupy Rome itself on the plea of preserving order. Many of its deputies openly supported the volunteer movement and two of its most important permanent officials aided it secretly. These two men were the top career officers in the Departments of the Interior and of the Marine, the men from whom the prefects, subprefects, officials of the railway and telegraph systems, harbor and dockyard officials took their orders and received promotion or dismissal. The order that went out from the government, regardless of what Rattazzi said publicly, was that volunteers were to be carried free on the trains, helped across borders and given every assistance to reach and remain with a volunteer unit. Small wonder, then, that a volunteer, recruited perhaps by a deputy, carried free on a train or boat and aided by almost every official he met, was sure that the government's real intent was something quite different from what it professed to be. The Minister of War, General Genova di Revel, one of the few men in the government truly determined to stand by the convention, lamented: "Italy is made, but can this be called a State when it lacks a government superior to the individuals within it. Here is Garibaldi, a Deputy who will not take the oath, a citizen who gives no heed to the laws. We have reached a point when a private individual can do as he likes, can prepare a war against a neighboring state which the government has pledged itself to respect! Is this a government?" It was a question friends as well as enemies began to ask.

Early in September, Garibaldi suddenly departed for a congress in Geneva held by the International League of Peace and Liberty. He had been appointed honorary president of the congress, and he gave one of the principal speeches, telling the delegates that their aim should be, first, to destroy despotism everywhere; second, to abolish war; third, to introduce democracy as the only effective remedy against war. "The slave alone," he declared, "has the right to make war against a tyrant; it is the only instance in which war is permissible"; and his argument became specific as he went on to recommend that the Papacy should be brought formally to an end and in place of Roman Catholicism should be substituted "the religion of God—that is to say, the religion of truth and reason," by which he meant that the priests of revelation should give way to priests of science and free inquiry. His remarks, however, were not very well received. The delegates were not so sure as he that revelation must give way to science or that the pope was a tyrant and the Romans, slaves. Among themselves, at least, they argued the points, and when he left Geneva, on 11 September, he left behind him a buzz of controversy and indignation. Though he could not see it, the speech had been a blunder, the kind of blunder Cavour had been careful always to avoid. For by attacking the Church's spiritual side as well as its temporal power he inclined many Europeans, most significantly conservative Frenchmen, to defend the Papacy in its temporal power as well as its spiritual.

Back in Italy, Garibaldi hurried the volunteer movement on to a climax, forcing the government to take a stand. Rattazzi tried to persuade him to return to Caprera, but he refused. His actions and attitude, even the public could see, were more openly rebellious than in 1860 or 1862. His cry was no longer *"Italia e Vittorio Emanuele"* but *"Redimire l'Italia o morire,"* "Redeem Italy or die." Spurred on by Revel, Rattazzi finally agreed to arrest him, and on 24 September at Sinalunga, close to the Papal border, a company of soldiers surrounded the house in which he was sleeping and took him in custody.

The outcry was immediate and strong. Deputies protested that his deputy's immunity had been violated and, as he was taken north to Genoa, crowds gathered under his window wherever he was and shouted, "To Rome, to Rome." Through a visitor he passed a message out to the people: "The Romans have the rights of slaves, to rise against their tyrants: the priests. The Italians have the duty to help them. . . ." The government, however, persevered, and although it laid no charge against him, it returned him by force to Caprera and ordered nine naval ships to keep him there by a patrol of its coast.

Four days after the arrest the first band of volunteers crossed the Papal border and began to skirmish with detachments of the Papal army, the greater part of which, about fifteen thousand men, was concentrated in Rome. There, the revolutionary committees collected twelve thousand signatures on a petition to the mayor begging him to persuade the pope to call in the Italian army to maintain order. In the next two weeks more bands of volunteers crossed the border, but even though the committees in Rome were ready and eager to lead an insurrection, the Romans refused to rise.

The situation embarrassed both the republicans and the government, for without an insurrection in Rome all the talk of slaves and tyrants and of the need to occupy Rome to preserve order was exposed as empty rhetoric. Republicans and ministers alike appeared before Europe as troublemakers who lacked an honest grievance. In France, the pressure on Napoleon to do something, either to enforce the convention or, abandoning it, to preserve Rome for the pope, steadily mounted. In Italy, moderates and conservatives argued that the government should abide by the convention, but the extremists perhaps were more numerous and, aided by the newspapers, made more noise. The papers reported insurrections in the Papal State which Revel, at least, characterized as "All lies!" Crowds everywhere gathered to cheer for Garibaldi, and one in Florence even attacked Rattazzi's house. Volunteers continued to gather and cross the border and although most of the bands did little more than march around the less populated parts of the Papal State, reports of them kept up the excitement.

On 17 October, Revel proposed at a cabinet meeting that the Italian army march into Papal territory, arrest the volunteers and then withdraw, at the same time announcing that it would continue to recognize and to protect the Papal State. The king and Rattazzi had agreed to the plan that morning, but apparently in the cabinet meeting Rattazzi did not support it strongly and the other ministers, afraid of the public outcry if they tried to arrest the volunteers in Papal territory, refused to adopt it. Revel, the one strong man in the cabinet, thereupon resigned.

His resignation may have been just what Rattazzi and the king secretly wished to have, for although their actions in this period are obscure, plainly their intent, as before Aspromonte, was to use the volunteers to blackmail Napoleon into letting them have Rome. Crispi in his diary, for example, under 8 October, notes "Rattazzi enters the system," and most historians have taken this to confirm that by this date at the latest Rattazzi had admitted to the republicans that he hoped and was working for an insurrection at Rome.

But his plans, if ever well conceived, soon were shattered by events. On 14 October 1867 Garibaldi disappeared from Caprera, and three days later, on the very day that Revel resigned, Napoleon at Biarritz, despairing of the Italians to protect the Papal State, abandoned the convention and ordered a French army back to Rome. When news of these events reached Florence, Rattazzi and the king suddenly saw their dishonest scheme turn into an unmanageable monster. No longer would the Italian government, like some god, bring peace and order to the Italian peninsula, while at the same time planting its seat at Rome. Instead, the French and the volunteers under Garibaldi would fight, and if the government aided either, it would be cursed by half its people; and if it refused to aid either, it would be cursed by all its people and by the French as well.

Faced with such a prospect the king made his decision. He ordered Rattazzi to issue an order for Garibaldi's arrest. Rattazzi, however, could not bring himself to take any action at all, and on 19 October he resigned, leaving the country without a government. The next day Garibaldi appeared in Florence.

He was afterwards very proud of his escape from Caprera. He had tried first, on 8 October, simply by riding the mailboat through the patrol to Maddalena, the neighboring island, but he had been discovered and turned back. For his second attempt he made greater preparations. He had found a small, leaky boat, almost a canoe, which had long since been abandoned under a gum tree. With it he proposed to cross the open water to Maddalena; from there in a larger boat to cross to Sardinia and then from there to sail the hundred and fifty miles to Livorno in a small ship which his friends in Florence would have waiting. He darkened his hair and beard, calculated the hour after sunset when the moon would not yet have risen above Caprera's single mountain and left a friend to impersonate him on his terrace by wearing a poncho and walking with crutches. The night was stormy, and propelling his boat with only a paddle he succeeded in evading three warships and reached Maddalena. Six days later he was in Florence.

Rattazzi had resigned the day before, and the king was searching for someone who would form a ministry on a program of arresting Garibaldi. The search was to take eight days, and in the three days Garibaldi remained in Florence he had the freedom of the city, for no one dared oppose him in anything until the government's position became clear. He recruited volunteers, issued proclamations about "redeeming" Italy, and in an address before Santa Maria Novella borrowed a phrase from Nelson and intoned that "Italy expects every man to do his duty." On 23 October he left for the border near Terni, and two days later he and the main force of volunteers captured the Papal city of Monterotondo.

While he was reorganizing his forces there, the king issued a proclamation condemning the invasion and announced the appointment of Luigi Federico Menabrea to the position of prime minister. Menabrea, a Savoyard, was a general, a member of the king's household and a conservative in politics. He initiated a program of stopping the invasion, arresting Garibaldi, and cooperating with the French whose soldiers had begun to land at Civitavecchia.

Garibaldi's position, in spite of his victory at Monterotondo, was desperate. He had with him in his main force about ten thousand men; a band of about eight hundred was farther south, near Frosinone, and several smaller bands, almost wholly uncoordinated, were also across the border. All, in theory, were pressing on to Rome where they would support an insurrection by the Romans. But the Papal army and *Légion d'Antibes,* both concentrated at Rome, numbered fifteen thousand, a reason perhaps why there was never an insurrection, and to these now were to be added the Italian and French armies with their almost unlimited numbers and supplies.

N

MENTANA
*3 November, 1867*

The less dedicated volunteers decided that their cause was lost, and Garibaldi seemed to confirm their conclusion when, instead of leading them onto the Roman plain and racing for the city, he simply moved them farther to the south in the mountains near Tivoli. The men in large numbers began to drift away. In later years he was to blame Mazzini for this and claim that Mazzini's followers, disappointed in the decision not to head straight for Rome, had been the first to desert and had undermined the loyalty of the others. But there is no evidence of this, and the obvious explanation seems quite sufficient: the volunteers, expecting to fight only the Papal army, suddenly found themselves opposing also the French and Italian armies.

By 3 November his main force was only four thousand and a combined French and Papal force, which had come out from Rome to meet him, numbered nine thousand. They met near the village of Mentana. The volunteers were dispirited from the start. Among other reasons, the French had a new breech-loading rifle which fired twelve times a minute and could be loaded lying down, while many of the volunteers had muzzle-loading muskets or rifles which could be loaded only if standing. Though Garibaldi rode up and down before them, urging them to "Come die with me! Are you afraid to die with me?", not enough followed him in his charges to affect the battle. By evening the fight was over. Almost half of the volunteers, sixteen hundred, had been taken prisoner and four hundred more were killed or wounded. The rest, led by Garibaldi, retreated across the border into Italy.

Garibaldi believed that in his period of exile, after 1849, he had become a citizen of the United States, and he assumed that this foreign citizenship and his immunity as a deputy would prevent his arrest. He ordered a special train to take him to the coast and a steamship to stand by to take him to Caprera. But Menabrea intended to be firm. The police stopped the train, and when Garibaldi resisted arrest, they hauled him forcibly from his carriage and imprisoned him at Varignano.

He was wholly unrepentant, but to save the government embarrassment he offered "to voyage around the Mediterranean or the ocean" on an Italian warship and, "in case it doesn't suit me to remain aboard," to return to Varignano "to the same conditions in which I find myself today." The government did not dare to accept the offer. Public opinion was running strongly against it and considered it and the king as responsible as Garibaldi for the events which led up to Mentana. A trial or even self-exile, the government decided, was out of the question, and after keeping Garibaldi in prison for three weeks it returned him to Caprera without laying a charge against him.

For Garibaldi it was the third time he had started a march on Rome, and the third time the government, after encouraging him, had opposed him. Worst of all, this time he had been defeated by the armies of the pope and of Napoleon, the two men he most despised, and for the rest of his life he was bitter over the events of 1867. His language about the pope grew even more vitriolic, and in his proclamations and public letters from Caprera he accused both Mazzini and the government, indirectly but plainly, of treachery. Most Italians dismissed his accusations against Mazzini but accepted as true those against the government. His anger was a sore in Italian life for which there was no cure, partly because it expressed for many Italians their disappointment in events and in their government.

For the government Mentana was a worse disaster even than Lissa and Custoza, for in the Austrian war only the armed forces had performed badly. But Mentana revealed the entire government at fault. Menabrea, determined to counter the example of Garibaldi and to educate the Italians in the need for responsible government, published reports on how the trains had been put at the service of volunteers, how telegrams ordering arrests had been delayed and how eyes that should have seen and reported had been deliberately blinkered. The facts increased the national sense of shame but in being honestly faced were salutary. Rattazzi in self-defense made a three-day speech which was considered to be extraordinarily eloquent, but even though less was known then than now of his complicity, he was never again a power in the Chamber. The pill of truth, however, was not easily swallowed, and when the Chamber gave Menabrea a majority of only two, he resigned, was reappointed and, after reconstituting his ministry, continued in office. In the circumstances this was a victory for responsible government.

The worst result of Mentana, however, was beyond the power of the government to correct: it had brought the French back into the peninsula and in a fashion humiliating to Italians. When their army had crossed the border to pursue Garibaldi, the French general had ordered it to get out of the Papal State, and Menabrea, unwilling to fight France, had withdrawn it. Later in Paris during the debate in the French Chamber, which upheld Napoleon's actions, the chief minister, Eugène Rouher, had announced grandiloquently that the Italians should *never* get Rome: *"Jamais!"* The word infuriated Italian patriots, but they could do nothing. There was no longer even a convention between France and Italy: the French were present by invitation of the pope and by right of superior force. Mentana, for which Garibaldi and the government were perhaps equally responsible, by bringing back into the heart of Italy a major power, had undone one of the great achievements of the Risorgimento.

# CHAPTER 49

Results of Mentana. Religious events under Pio Nono. The Vatican Council in prospect. Manin's return to Venice. The Kingdom's economic problems. Its desire for a large army. Lanza replaces Menabrea. Franco-Prussian war. The ministry's plan for Rome. Its execution. Pio Nono's last act in a Papal Rome. Rome taken. The Romans don't rise. The plebiscite. The Law of Guarantees. *Roma capitale* realized. The Risorgimento ends. Was it a success?

FOR MOST ITALIANS the presence of the French at Mentana destroyed their last feelings of gratitude to Napoleon III for his services to Italy. Republicans in particular, hostile from the start of his career because he rose to power by destroying the French Second Republic, would remember only his intervention at Rome in 1849, his abandonment of Venice at Villafranca in 1859, his taking of Nice and Savoy in 1860, and his second intervention at Rome in 1867. They would forget or deliberately overlook his sympathy for the concept of an Italian national state, his diplomatic support of Sardinia against Austria throughout the 1850s, his fighting at its side against Austria in the Po valley in 1859 and, on Cavour's death, his quick and unconditioned recognition of the new Kingdom of Italy. Individuals, and Vittorio Emanuele II was one, would remember the good as well as the bad and be grateful for it, but throughout the country as a whole, after Mentana, Napoleon was damned, and today in Italy hardly a piazza, street or statue celebrates him.

For many Italians, Mentana also changed their attitude toward Garibaldi, or at least greatly sharpened it. Among the educated, particularly in the north, many had been willing to forgive him Aspromonte. It had been less serious in its consequences, and it had been the first error, or unsuccessful venture, after The Thousand. When he had called for volunteers in the Austrian war of 1866, many of the best of the young in Milan and other cities of the Po valley had rushed to serve under him. After Mentana such a response was inconceivable. Among the poor and simple, admiration for him as a hero continued to increase, but among the elec-

706

torate, the well-to-do and educated, though his service to Italy was acknowledged, he now was regarded as a troublemaker to be watched and isolated. In 1868 he flamboyantly resigned his position of deputy as a condemnation of the parliamentary form of the government, but the act also was an admission that he had lost his influence with the government and, except for a few of the more extreme deputies, had no friends in it. He was allowed freedom of speech for his proclamations and letters, but it is doubtful if he had freedom of movement. For almost three years he remained on Caprera, so closely watched by the government that he was perhaps a prisoner.

For Italians who supported the Church, however, Mentana, the abrogation of the September Convention and return of the French to Rome were joyful facts, and doubly so because of the conditions under which they had taken place. The refusal of the Romans to rise and the success of the Papal army increased the Church's confidence in its position, reenforced its claim before the world to be a functioning, sovereign state and weakened the pressure which Napoleon, as its protector, could impose on it to force a settlement with the Italian kingdom. In the month immediately after Mentana, in an effort to settle the Roman Question, he proposed a congress of European powers, Protestant as well as Catholic, to meet in Paris, and Pio Nono agreed to be represented. But as Odo Russell reported to the British government, directly after a conversation with Antonelli: "The only solution of the Roman Question his Holiness could admit was the unconditional restitution of the provinces and property of the Holy See, of which the Church had been robbed by the Piedmontese Government." The powers had many reasons for being reluctant to grapple with the problems Rome presented, and in the end the congress never met. But the Church's position of "unconditional restitution," representing either strength or stubbornness, had been broadcast.

Menabrea's response to it was to ignore the Roman Question as much as possible. Personally he was one of a minority of Italians who cared very little about Rome and who would have been happy to leave it to the Papacy. D'Azeglio, who had died early in 1866, had been the most important of these and in March 1861 had published a pamphlet, *Questioni Urgenti,* in which he had argued the unsuitability of Rome as the capital of Italy, both because of the problems it posed with the Church and because of the corruption of its people. The pamphlet had been a failure, selling only three thousand copies, and Cavour, then in the last months of his life, publicly had stigmatized its views as "futile." But after Mentana more Italians, including the king and many in the government, were willing to share D'Azeglio's view, even if only temporarily and out of disappointment, and Menabrea was able to concentrate the government's attention on the economic problems of the kingdom.

One point, however, was much discussed among patriots, at least privately: the refusal of the Romans to rise against the pope and exhibit a national sentiment. Coming so soon after the failure of the Venetians to rise against the Austrians, the inaction of the Romans was a disappointment that no amount of patriotic rhetoric could soothe. D'Azeglio's charge that the Roman people had suffered a corruption of character after centuries of priestly government was an ancient one and widely believed, but there were other, less hypothetical reasons which, when analyzed and discussed, contributed to a subtle change in the way patriots thought of Rome.

It was the Papal city in a way that Bologna, Ravenna, Ancona or other former Papal cities had never been. Almost every man in Rome worked for the Papal government whether directly as a priest or indirectly as, perhaps, a cardinal's coachman. Even men seemingly independent, such as innkeepers, made their livings out of the tourists and pilgrims and the Church's festivals, for outside of the affairs of the Church the city had almost no social or business activities. With the Papal State reduced to Rome and the single, relatively barren province around it, the concentration of cardinals, Papal soldiers and religious officials of all kinds had grown even greater and increased the feeling that the city's entire life was bound up with the Church. Aside from the possibility that union with the Italian kingdom might cause the pope once again to desert Rome, possibly, for Spain or Malta, with consequent massive unemployment, there was the certainty that union would mean a revolution in law and land tenure, conscription and higher taxes. As patriots both in Italy and the Papal State debated these reasons, they began increasingly to think it unreasonable to expect the Roman people to stage an insurrection and began to think more in terms of taking Rome, even without an insurrection, simply because the non-Roman Italians wanted it to be the capital of a united Italy. The change in thinking was slight, perhaps, but it tended to discourage patriots from supporting revolutionary committees, whether organized by followers of Mazzini or Garibaldi. Further, it inclined them, both inside the city and out, to look to the Italian army, at some future date and in some unforeseen circumstance, simply to take Rome from the Church by a display of overwhelming force. Meanwhile the unique quality of Rome's life continued and was emphasized by a succession of events which was scheduled to reach a climax with the Vatican Council of 1870.

The political events of Pio Nono's reign tend to obscure the religious events which were equally if not more important. As pope he was more of a priest than a diplomat or Renaissance prince, and throughout his reign, ultimately to be the longest of any pope to date, he had a constant interest in the dogma of the Church and in its organization and administration. One of the first of his important acts in this regard occurred on 8 December 1854 when he had defined the Dogma of the Immaculate Conception of the Blessed Virgin Mary. Then in 1862 he had invited all the bishops to attend the canonization of the twenty-six missionaries to Japan who had been killed in 1597, and four years later he had again invited all the bishops to Rome for the eighteenth centenary of the martyrdom of Saints Peter and Paul. It was on this occasion that he first publicly talked of his desire to convoke a council of the Church and revealed that much of the preliminary work for it already had been done.

Later he announced that the council would meet in Rome and would open on 8 December 1869, the anniversary of the proclamation of the Virgin's Immaculate Conception. Presumably the council would continue for at least two years and conclude with festivities in 1871 to celebrate the twenty-fifth anniversary of Pio Nono's election to the Papal throne. From a purely economic point of view what the council might mean to the Roman people could be gauged by the estimate of persons attending the much smaller and shorter meeting for the centenary of Saints Peter and Paul: 500 bishops, 20,000 priests and 130,000 other pilgrims.

From the first rumors of the council, reactions to it were mixed. Within the Church the "liberal-Catholics," already disheartened by the episodes with Montalembert and Döllinger, were against it, fearing further strictures on them and a strengthening of the Jesuits on whom Pio Nono seemed increasingly to rely. Conversely those, like the Jesuits, who favored a strong, authoritarian pope, with the authority administered by the hierarchy in Rome, looked forward to it as a way of increasing their strength and of achieving their aims. The governments of Europe generally were against it, fearing that the authoritarians within the Church wanted the council in order to make a dogma of the Syllabus of Errors, with its condemnations of the premises on which many of the states were founded. The Italian government feared in particular that a dogma would be made of the temporal power, inciting more Catholics to come to Rome to defend it and perhaps even to attempt to retake the provinces already lost. Though Mentana had stirred sympathy for the Church, the council, simply in prospect, canceled much of it.

Like the Church, the Kingdom of Italy had its reunions, canonization of martyrs and festivals, though of course on a very much smaller scale. After the Venetians had been united to the kingdom, the king paid a visit of state to Venice, which included speeches, salutes and, of course, a procession up the Grand Canal. Later the visit was commemorated by a plaque in the arcade of the Library and by a huge equestrian statue of the king on the Riva degli Schiavoni. The Venetians, however, remembering the course of the war which brought them into the kingdom, always have regarded the statue with a slight sense of irreverence.

A more meaningful celebration for them took place on 22 March 1868 when the body of Daniele Manin was brought back to the city. The date was carefully chosen, being the twentieth anniversary of the day on which Manin had left his home in the Campo San Paternian to capture the Arsenal and, that done, to proclaim the Republic of San Marco. "In doing this," he had explained on their behalf, "we do not intend to separate ourselves from our fellow Italians, but rather we shall form one of those centers which, bit by bit, must serve to fuse all of Italy into one." And so it had come about, but not before he and his fellow Venetians had suffered much.

The day of his return was clear and bright, and though the presence of a coffin made men solemn, it did not make them sad, for, more profoundly, the occasion was triumphant. The coffin was landed at the piazzetta as cannon saluted and the people waited quietly. Behind it formed a small group of men, Manin's only son, Giorgio, who had been wounded at Calatafimi, and survivors of "the forty." Then, following the coffin, all proceeded into San Marco for a service. Later Manin was entombed outside the north wall of the basilica in the little square of "the lions." Few men in Venice have been so honored, but then Venice, generally speaking, has been a corporate effort, and few men have made such an individual contribution to its history.

But events such as the king's visit to Venice or the return to it of Manin's body were the pomp and nostalgia of life, not its daily routine; and for most Italians as well as the government the chief issues of both 1868 and 1869 were economic: taxes, which fell hardest on the poor, and the deficits in the government's budget which were undermining its credit. By the end of 1866 the national deficit was more than 60 per cent of the total state expenditure, and to obtain the money the government was having to pay 8 per cent interest on its loans and to offer them at 70 per cent or less of their value.

Some of the government's expenses, such as the war with Austria, the policing of the south or the move from Turin to Florence, were extraordinary, and the government attempted to pay for them, at least in part, by the sale of Church property. After Ricasoli's failure to reach an agreement with the Church, Parliament in 1866, under the pressure of the war with Austria, passed a bill whereby ultimately 2382 monasteries and convents were suppressed, their twenty thousand inmates pensioned and their property confiscated and sold. The sales were handled by the government rather than the Church, as they would not have been under Ricasoli's bill, and the proceeds were less than expected. There was some profiteering, doubtless, but also the sudden availability of more than a million acres of land depressed the market. The sales were, however, an extraordinary method of meeting extraordinary expenses and did not touch the chief cause of the kingdom's financial problems, which was its desire to have a large, well-equipped army and navy.

The king, the court, the military and, probably, most of the deputies and government officials were eager to have Italy a great power; indeed, for most of them the idea was an integral part of becoming unified and independent. They could not imagine a united and free Italy, given the kingdom's population and size, being anything less than a great power; and as France, Prussia and Austria all had large armies and Britain a large navy, Italy must have forces equally splendid. To obtain them the government was prepared to spend annually more than a quarter, and sometimes more than a third, of the kingdom's revenue.

It was too much. The kingdom was poorer than the government realized, and with the advent of an industrial society, as it lacked coal, oil and iron, it would become, relative to the other powers, even poorer. Of course there were other reasons in favor of a large army and navy: they fostered unity, provided employment and were needed as a defense against Austria. There was some validity in all the reasons, but they did not justify the cost. Again and again in the years ahead fiscal reformers would attempt to set the kingdom's finances in better order by cutting back on the armed forces, but generally their battle was lost in Parliament.

The defeats would not have been so serious as they were if Parliament had been willing to reform the tax structure so that it raised more revenue out of the upper and middle class and less out of the poor peasants. A fact of the Risorgimento that soon became clear was that its greatest beneficiaries, the people of the towns, were unwilling to pay for it. The relatively rich who dominated Parliament put the greatest burden on the poor who had no vote. Italy had almost the lowest wages in Europe and almost the highest indirect taxes on food; consumption in almost all forms was taxed heavily but income and personal property only lightly. One of the great Sicilian landlords, the Duke of Gualtieri, as a senator argued against a progressive tax on income and property because:

> . . . if the origin and the extent of men's needs are attributable to their upbringing, to habits acquired in early childhood, to the fortune which they possess, to the environment in which they have always lived, as well as to heredity, it should be recognized that the wealthy classes have a much greater number of needs than the lower classes, with the result that the burden of the progressive tax, by depriving them of the means of satisfying certain of those needs, is likely to entail for most

of them sacrifices proportionately far greater than the classes less favoured by fortune will be called upon to bear.[123]

The duke's view was an extreme one, but it was shared in lesser degree by the majority of the deputies and, when coupled with their desire to keep the army large, forced even the most able ministers of finance, almost all of whom hoped to reduce the army, to meet the enormous deficits by raising taxes on consumption, typically on salt, tobacco and the grinding of wheat and corn. The grinding tax had been opposed bitterly in the Chamber by the republicans and had passed only by a vote of 182 to 164. When the collection of it began in January 1869, riots at once broke out, north and south, and within a fortnight 250 persons were dead, 1000 wounded and 4000 in prison. The latter were not all peasants. Among them were priests and newspaper editors who had thought the tax unfair.

Order was restored, and the tax continued to be collected. Nevertheless, the unbalanced budgets, the inequities of the tax burdens, and the spates of violence were to be a continuing problem for the government, and in November 1869 a particularly unhappy incident in their cycle forced Menabrea to resign. His ministry had farmed out the government's tobacco monopoly for a cash payment, and shares in the bank which put up the cash became a profitable investment. A republican deputy accused several of the ministers of speculating in them and even implied that members of the royal family had turned a profit. A few days later the deputy was found stabbed to death. Though no one considered Menabrea responsible, still the reputation of his ministry was ruined and he resigned.

Menabrea had been a relatively strong prime minister and had been appointed as such by the king to lead the kingdom out of the debacle of Mentana. But he had been also a senator, a general and a member of the king's household, and all were points which assumed some importance in the appointment of his successor, Giovanni Lanza, who at the time was president of the Chamber. The deputies and many of the electorate disliked, even disapproved of, having the head of the government a senator rather than a deputy, for a man became a senator by appointment of the king whereas a deputy was elected. The difference seemed to many to touch the heart of parliamentary government.

For much the same reason they distrusted generals, who, aside from any oath of office, already had sworn a military oath to obey the king and so were in a special way his servants. Vittorio Emanuele, who had had a military upbringing, was inclined in moments of crisis to turn to the army, and he had put generals at the head of the government after Villafranca in 1859, after the Turin riots in 1864 and after Mentana. But to the deputies a general as head of the government always suggested the possibility of a royal *coup d'état* supported by the army.

The danger seemed even stronger when the general, like Menabrea, was an intimate member of the court and, as he had done, appointed two other members of the king's household to the ministry. The propriety of it came directly in issue with the king's first conversation with Lanza. He offered the post of prime minister but only on condition that Lanza make up, in effect, a coalition government by including Menabrea and the other two men in the government. Lanza, who earlier had been elected president of the Chamber over Menabrea's candidate by a margin of forty votes, not only refused but even demanded the dismissal of the three men from their court posts as a condition of forming a new ministry. If they were to be active in politics, as they had been, then they could not also be active at court.

The king gave way, and Parliament through Lanza won an important round in its continuous bout with the king for control of the government. Royalist historians have praised Vittorio Emanuele for his understanding of the role of constitutional monarch in circumstances in which the limits of the role constantly were changing. Unquestionably on several occasions he gave up power gracefully and, except perhaps in his dealings with Garibaldi, never imperiled the development of the government along civilian, parliamentary lines. As perhaps befits a king, however, he gave way only before strength, when opposed by men like Cavour and Lanza. When he had a weak minister, like Rattazzi, he expanded his power. In a sense his defeat now by Lanza was the penance exacted for a misuse of his power in the events leading up to Mentana. Significantly after the resignation of Menabrea he never again appointed as prime minister a man who was either a senator, a general or a member of his court.

Lanza and his colleagues began by attacking the kingdom's debt and annual deficit. He pledged that all public monies would be spent "with the parsimony of a miser," and, after deciding with his Minister of Finance, Quintino Sella, that the country could not stand more taxation, he announced a budget bill in which the appropriations for the army and the navy, in Sella's words, were "cut to the bone." The outcry was immediate and loud, especially in the Senate where General Cialdini, who was considered to speak for the king, accused the ministry of endangering the national security.

Unfortunately for Lanza two events took place which made his job of persuasion even harder. On 8 December 1869 the Vatican Council opened with seven hundred bishops present, and though it requires special circumstances to make a meeting of bishops convey a sense of menace, for Italians those circumstances existed: they had seized three-fourths of the

Papal State and they were in the midst of a secular revolution in which they were confiscating and selling the Church's property. The last previous council, at Trent in 1545, had launched the Counter-Reformation. Suppose the pope and bishops now launched a Counter-Risorgimento? There were many who agreed with Lanza on the need for economy but who wondered if a better time for it would not be the following year when the council's actions were known.

The other event was a rising, early in the year, by Mazzini's followers. After the war with Austria and the annexation of the Veneto he had started yet another organization, the Universal Republican Alliance, whose aim was to annex Rome, the Trentino and Istria, and to make a republic of the Italian kingdom. "The Republic," he proclaimed, "is the word of order for all; Rome, the objective; insurrection and national war to the invader [France], the means." His language and purpose were the same as before, but now very few responded. In Genoa, Padua and Ravenna there were feeble risings, hardly more than demonstrations, and at Pavia, while arresting the conspirators, one soldier was killed and two wounded. Mazzini, for all his great reputation, was no longer a threat; merely an irritant. Yet for those, like General Cialdini, who opposed cuts in the army, the rising was another reason for opposing Lanza's budget bill.

Nevertheless, in spite of the opposition, the bill finally was passed. A majority of the deputies and senators was persuaded that a smaller, less expensive army and navy could serve adequately the needs of the kingdom. But before the economies could be affected, a third, quite unforeseen event took place which changed the situation completely and forced Lanza to enlarge the army by calling up reserves and to request additional sums from Parliament for the armed forces. The event was the start, on 19 July 1870, of the Franco-Prussian war.

Lanza, and indeed most Italians, had no doubt of what the government's policy should be: Italy should be neutral. Its financial condition was poor, and its army unprepared for a European war. Within the decade both France and Prussia had been active allies, and a choice between them was almost impossible, particularly as the issues of the war did not concern Italy. At stake, ostensibly, was the succession to the throne of Spain. In 1868 Queen Isabella II, whose policies and private life had been equally objectionable, had been forced out and a regency declared. For two years the Spaniards had cast about for a constitutional and liberal sovereign, and early in July their choice fell on Prince Leopold of Hohenzollern-Sigmaringen, a distant cousin of the King of Prussia. Many Frenchmen imagined the situation was similar to that which had led up to the War of the Spanish Succession. Then Bourbon France had been threatened by the possibility of a Habsburg on either side, in Vienna and in Madrid;

now it was a Hohenzollern, in Berlin and in Madrid. There was a great outcry, particularly in Paris, and Prince Leopold withdrew his candidacy. But many of the French were not satisfied. They had an idea that Prussia, after its victory over Austria in 1866, needed to be taught a lesson. The protests continued, and out of one of them, the visit of the French ambassador to the King of Prussia, Bismarck was able to fashion a telegram which suggested a falsehood, that the king had snubbed the ambassador. The telegram was published in the German newspapers, and the people of Paris, the French press, the *Corps Législatif* and all those militarists who courted glory cried out for war. Napoleon knew that rural and provincial France did not want war and that at the moment the Prussian army was considerably stronger than the French, but in the last few years he had aged and was suffering badly from an infection in his bladder and kidneys. He had not the will to resist the pressure and against his better judgment declared war.

With all this vanity, the real cause of the war, Italy plainly had nothing to do, and few Italians questioned the policy of neutrality. What concerned them was the fate of Rome.

The war from the start went badly for France, and on 2 August 1870 the Italian government received word from Paris that the French troops at Rome would be withdrawn and the September Convention revived. Lanza agreed to abide by its terms even though in doing so he made the Italian government once again the guardian of the Papal State. But he and his fellow ministers had a plan for taking Rome, as any ministry at this time must have had if it was to survive. Part of the plan, as always before, involved the use of secret service funds to finance a rising in Rome. Historical hindsight, however, can see that from the start the rising in Rome was secondary to an invasion of the Papal State by the Italian army in full force regardless of whether the rising took place. The invasion, in turn, was based on three premises: that the government could prevent any action in the field by volunteers; that before going to Rome it could win the consent of the Catholic governments of Europe; and that when it started for Rome it could do so in overwhelming force so that the Papal army would have to surrender before any blood was shed.

On the first premise the ministry was fortunate, for Garibaldi was already on Caprera, and the naval patrol could be intensified without the affront of an arrest, which would arouse the general's followers. Garibaldi, however, had no doubt about his condition, for he complained to his son-in-law that he was "a prisoner." The ministry was fortunate, too, with Mazzini, who had been corresponding with Bismarck about sending three thousand volunteers to fight for Prussia against Napoleon. The government discovered that he was in Palermo, arrested him and interned him at

Gaeta. The ministry had greater difficulty, however, with the republican deputies whom it could neither arrest nor silence. In the debate on the appropriation for the army one of them cried out: "If *you* will not go to Rome, at least let *us* go. This attitude of yours thwarts the revolution." Exactly such was the ministry's intent; but Lanza could not soften its effect by explaining publicly what else the ministry had in mind, and the debate was stormy. Nevertheless he succeeded in making it sufficiently plain that the government intended to go to Rome for the Chamber to support him by a vote of 214–152.

Strangely, it was the confidence of the king that for a time he lost. As appeals began to come from Paris for aid, Vittorio Emanuele, remembering all that Napoleon had done for Italy, grew exasperated with the policy of neutrality. Though Italy was poor, he argued, it could do something for an ally. He stated his view so strongly and so often that Lanza submitted his resignation, stating that he had "no longer the heart to remain at the head of the government after the repeated manifestations of the King's distrust and dissatisfaction." But Vittorio Emanuele saw his mistake and requested Lanza to continue in office.

On the second premise, winning the consent of Catholic Europe to the taking of Rome, Lanza began by circulating a memorandum to the governments of Europe in which he pointed out that the September Convention contained a clause to the effect that "in the case of extraordinary events both of the contracting parties would resume their freedom of action" and set forth the reasons why Italy should occupy Rome at once. The circular was well received; that is, no government protested. France plainly was losing the war, a new arrangement for Rome would be necessary, and the Italian proposal solved a number of difficulties. But certainly another reason that no government protested was that the Vatican Council on 18 July had proclaimed the dogma of the pope's Infallibility in matters of faith and morals and seemed likely soon to extend it further into the area of Church-State relations. At the moment most Catholic governments viewed the Papacy, in which the Jesuits once again seemed to be gaining control, with distrust.

Then suddenly, on 4 September, which was sooner certainly than Lanza or his fellow ministers had expected, an "extraordinary event" took place that freed Italy from any obligation to France under the convention. Napoleon III lost the battle of Sedan and was himself taken prisoner. The Empress Eugénie fled to England; the Second Empire came to an end, and two days later in Paris the Third Republic was declared. For republicans of every state of Europe it was the day for which they long had been waiting, the day to avenge "2 December" 1851 when Napoleon with a *coup d'état* had ended the Second Republic. For republicans, at least,

France was once again free and liberal, and would return from the parade of empire to the principles of '89 which it first had given to the world. The three thousand volunteers Mazzini had been collecting to aid Prussia changed course and departed to fight for France. Garibaldi, too, promptly wrote to the provisional republican government: *"Ce qui reste de moi est à votre service. Disposez."* "What is left of me is at your service. Make use of it."

The opportunity to take Rome was plain, and the excitement in non-Roman Italy very great. The prefects around the country reported to the ministry the possibility of revolution if the government did not act, and many republican deputies began to hint that they might abandon Parliament altogether. At Rome, at least among those directly connected with the Church, the mood was one of determination mixed with anger and despair. The council had adjourned and most of the bishops departed. The Papal army of about fifteen thousand men, mostly French and Swiss and reportedly without a single Italian or Roman, prepared its defenses and waited.

Lanza and his fellow ministers, however, were determined to stick to their plan and not to be hurried. On 7 September he sent out another memorandum to the powers, setting forth in detail the steps which the Italian government proposed to take to insure that the Church, while losing its temporal power, would retain its freedom in spiritual affairs. He even offered, because of the world-wide interest in the question, to make the conditions on which Rome would be occupied a matter of international agreement. But the powers by their answers showed they preferred to leave the problem to Italy. The governments of Spain, France and Austria were prepared by 1870 to have the temporal power end and to have Rome become an Italian city.

Lanza also had the king send an envoy to the pope asking him to agree to the annexation. Pio Nono refused. The king's letter, often quoted by clerical writers as a supreme example of hypocrisy began:

> Most Holy Father:
>     With the affection of a son, the faith of a Catholic, the loyalty of a king, the spirit of an Italian, I address myself, as before, to Your Holiness's heart. . . .[124]

Because of the Franco-Prussian war, the king continued, he felt a responsibility to keep order on the Italian peninsula. The danger of revolutionary disturbances had become greater. The envoy, therefore, was empowered to arrange with the pope for the Italian army to occupy all the forts and strategic places within the Papal State.

Pio Nono pointed out to the envoy that there were no disturbances within his state nor were there likely to be any. Garibaldi was penned on Caprera, and Mazzini was in prison at Gaeta. The Papal army was quite capable of handling any internal disturbances that might occur. As he talked, he grew more angry. The king and his ministers, he told the envoy, were "whited sepulchres and vipers." They would never have Rome. Then, with the charm for which he was famous, he called back the chastened envoy and, with a reference to the recent council, added with a smile "but that assurance is not infallible!"

At which Lanza, confident that he had the consent of the powers to act and with no volunteers in the field to confuse the issue, on 11 September ordered detachments of the Italian army, more than thirty thousand men with artillery, to cross the border and to start for Rome. Other detachments occupied the smaller Papal cities, and reserves moved up to positions on the border. The army deliberately moved slowly so that it would arrive at each strategic point or city with an overwhelming force.

Eight days later, on 19 September, Pio Nono made his last journey through Rome, going to San Giovanni in Laterano to review his army. Through the gate by the Church he had made his escape from the city after the murder of Rossi in 1848; now, once again about to lose control of Rome, he had elected to stay in the city. Before the troops assembled in his honor he stepped down from his carriage, an old man, seventy-eight and white-haired. Slowly, on his knees, holding the arm of an attendant, he ascended the *Scala Santa*. At the top he prayed aloud, turned and blessed the troops, and then, re-entering his carriage, drove back to the Vatican Palace. It was the last public act of a pope in Papal Rome.

The next morning at dawn the Italian army arrived before the walls of the city on the east, opposite the Porta Pia, and, after a short fight in which forty-nine Italian and nineteen Papal soldiers were killed, an armistice was agreed upon, and the Italians occupied all the city except San Giovanni in Laterano and St. Peter's and the Vatican Palace.

Thus, a fortnight after Sedan, Italy gained Rome, almost casually, and as in the case of the Veneto as a by-product of a Prussian victory. The patriots were surprised, even chagrined, at the manner in which it had been accomplished and in later years were inclined to join the Church's supporters in characterizing the manner as shoddy. This is one way of regarding what happened and, probably, the most common. Without doubt the event lacked glamor and, to the extent that the Italians based it on the need to restore order in the Papal State, it was hypocritical.

Another view of the event, however, stresses the preparatory actions of the government rather than the language with which it clothed them. It admires the ability of men in the government to learn from Aspromonte and Mentana how Rome must not be taken and to prepare for the event in such a way that it cost very few lives, did no damage to the city, and did not bring foreign powers back into Italy even to the extent of sharing in the government of Rome as an international city. Viewed this way, the taking of Rome still lacks glamor but was a solid achievement of a government mature enough to be realistic about what it was attempting to do and how to go about it.

There remains the problem of the hypocritical words: the restoring of law and order when there was no disorder. Doubtless, in retrospect, the government would seem more admirable if it had discarded the pretext and simply stated the premise on which it was preparing to act: for certain reasons of our own we must have Rome and are going to take it.

It did not, perhaps, because it was a government of its time, and the idea of an insurrection sparked by national sentiment was then very much in the air. In certain times and places the idea proved to be a myth; in others, very much a fact. But the language of the idea was the language most men spoke, and the government, though able to divorce its actions from the language, could not imagine the new words to suit its actions. In a sense it was a partial prisoner of words in a way that the pope seemed to be wholly a prisoner. Pio Nono could not imagine the Church retaining its spiritual freedom without its temporal power because, perhaps, he could not imagine the new formula of words necessary to express a new way that the Church might retain its spiritual freedom. He could only repeat the old formula over and over until finally almost only himself and the hierarchy at Rome believed it. Yet he lived long enough after the taking of Rome to see that, in fact, the Church did not need a Papal State to insure its spiritual freedom. If earlier he had been able to free himself from the tyranny of the old formula of words, he might have been able to reach a compromise with the State that would have benefited both.

Within two weeks after the occupation of Rome its citizens offered another example of the mystery of words and actions. On 2 October the Papal subjects voted in a plebiscite to join their state to the Kingdom of Italy. Out of 167,000 eligible voters, 133,000 voted for annexation and 1500 against. Considering the number of priests in Rome and considering that the vote was taken even within the Vatican, the protest was extraordinarily small. What did the vote mean? That within the Church many thought the temporal power should come to an end? Or that the Roman people, who had refused twice to lift a finger to bring about annexation, were delighted to have it forced on them? The plebiscite at Rome was the last in the unification of Italy and, in its meaning, the most impenetrable. The vote was not meaningless, for the Romans took the trouble in great numbers to vote, but it remains a question mark in history, an act from which historians have never been able, to the satisfaction of others, to extract a meaning. Pio Nono, meanwhile, announced from the Vatican that he was a prisoner, not because he was imprisoned but because as the rightful sovereign of Rome he could not move about the city when it was controlled by another without seeming to acquiesce in that control.

Many individual Catholics protested at his fate, and in some of the rural areas of Italy wild stories circulated of how he was being mistreated. But Lanza's preparatory work had been done well, and the Catholic states took no action beyond protesting formally that his spiritual independence must be preserved. Meanwhile at Florence the ministry prepared to submit to Parliament a bill which would guarantee the Church its freedom in spiritual affairs and govern its relations with the State.

This bill, which after parliamentary debate became law on 13 May 1871, was known as the Law of Guarantees, and it governed the relations between Italy and the Church until the Lateran Treaty of 1929 which, with regard to the temporal power at least, continued the same principles. The Law of Guarantees, however, was never a treaty. Successive popes refused to sign it or even discuss it, for they continuously maintained that the Italian government had no right to Rome and therefore no right to legislate about it. The government, however, observed its principles as did also foreign governments, and unofficially at least it gradually became the rule by which the Church with regard to the State lived its daily life.

The law was divided into two parts, the first of which related to the temporal power. By its terms the pope was deprived of all his sovereign rights over former Papal territory and allowed to keep possession, though not ownership, of only the Vatican and Lateran Palaces and of his villa at Castel Gandolfo outside of Rome. He was, however, to retain many of the privileges of sovereignty: the rights of precedence conceded him by Catholic princes, personal immunity from arrest, a diplomatic corps, a personal guard, and his own postal and telegraphic service. Cardinals and ambassadors were to be free to come and go, and cardinals, even if undergoing punishment for crimes against the State, were to be free to take part in conclaves. Lastly the government promised to pay him an annual allowance of 3,225,000 lire and agreed never to expel from Rome any priest whose work lay within the city.

This part of the Law of Guarantees gave form to the idea that the pope could be a prince without land, a spiritual sovereign without subjects in the temporal sense. The crux of the idea lay in the immunities which the State guaranteed, for it undertook not to act against the pope even if he declared State laws unlawful and incited men to disobey them or even to destroy the State. Such immunities had no precedent in the theory or practice of governments, and the conception of them and the imagination to see how they could be of use in this circumstance was one of the great achievements of the men of the Risorgimento, an achievement which even the Church, slowly and grudgingly, came to acknowledge.

The second part of the Law of Guarantees concerned the relations between Church and State and represented a partial attempt to separate them on the lines Cavour, Ricasoli and others had been suggesting. The State gave up all control over the promulgation of ecclesiastical laws and announcements and in general over the acts of ecclesiastical authorities. It abandoned its claim to nominate bishops in certain cases, ceased to require bishops to swear allegiance to the king on taking office, but retained the right to veto the Church's nominations in most cases.

Two days after the Law was promulgated, Pio Nono condemned it in an encyclical in which he insisted that only the restitution of the Papal State as it had existed before 1859 could guarantee the freedom and authority of the Church. When the government offered him the first installment of his allowance, he refused it. "I need money badly," he admitted, "but you, what do you bring me . . . ? A part of what you stole from me? Never will I accept it from you by way of reimbursement and you will obtain no signature which might seem to imply an acquiescence in or resignation to the Spoliation." He referred to the government, whenever he had occasion, as the "Subalpine" government lest the word "Italian" might suggest it stood for something more than an irreligious, thieving force; and after the day on which Rome was taken from the Church, 20 September 1870, he never emerged from the Vatican.

Not until after the Law of Guarantees had become the law of the land would Lanza transfer the government to Rome. Then on 30 June 1871 the move was made. The Senate was installed in the Palazzo Madama, formerly the Custom House, and the Chamber in the Palazzo Montecitorio. Both continue to meet in these halls. Two days later the king and his household moved into the Palazzo del Quirinale, which now that Italy is a republic is the residence of its president. On 27 November 1871 the king opened the first meeting at Rome of a Parliament representing an independent and united Italy. *Roma capitale* had been achieved.

With the destruction of the temporal power, the promulgation of the Law of Guarantees and the establishment of an Italian government at Rome the Risorgimento came to as much of a formal end as such a movement of men and ideas is likely to have. Though the taking of Rome from the Church was one of the Risorgimento's less exciting episodes, it was, nevertheless, its climax. Centuries earlier Machiavelli had reviled the temporal power as the greatest obstacle to national unity, and, even before him, Petrarch and Dante had lamented the damage it did to Italy. Not only did the Papal State lie across the peninsula from sea to sea, physically preventing union, but, to support itself there, again and again it had brought into Italy the foreign powers which dominated or rearranged the states to suit their own purposes. The eviction of the Austrians or of the French was perhaps the primary cause of the movement and its first objective, but most patriots soon came to believe with Machiavelli that no eviction could be permanent without the destruction of the temporal power.

The substitution for it, by the Law of Guarantees, of a new concept on which the Church should base itself, a concept which time has proved viable, was probably the greatest achievement of the Risorgimento. The eviction of the Austrians may have been a more difficult problem, in the sense that it required more force to resolve, but it was not so complicated diplomatically nor did it require such an imaginative solution. The first Napoleon had shown Italians how to clear Italy of the Austrians; he had not shown them how to resolve the problem of the Papal State. This they thought out for themselves and in doing so made their greatest contribution to peace not only on their own peninsula but in Europe generally.

Was the Risorgimento a success? The question hardly occurred to most historians writing before the first World War. And it may occur to historians now only because the problems the movement solved have disappeared, whereas those it failed to solve are still present. Even after the the advent of Benito Mussolini, whose rise is often used as an example of how the movement failed, Benedetto Croce in his *History of Europe in the Nineteenth Century,* wrote:

> If it were possible in political history to speak of masterpieces as we do in dealing with works of art, the process of Italy's independence, liberty, and unity would deserve to be called the masterpiece of the liberal-national movements of the nineteenth century: so admirably does it exhibit the combination of its various elements, respect for what is old and profound innovation, the wise prudence of the statesmen and the impetus of the revolutionaries and the volunteers, ardour and moderation; so flexible and coherent is the logical thread by which it developed and reached its goal. It was called the Risorgimento, just as men had spoken of a rebirth of Greece, recalling the glorious history that the same soil had witnessed; but it was in reality a birth, a *sorgimento,* and for the first time in the ages there was born an Italian state with all and with only its own people, and moulded by an ideal. Vittorio Emanuele II was right when he said, in his speech from the Throne on 2 April 1860, that Italy was no longer the Italy of the Romans or of the Middle Ages, but "the Italy of the Italians." [125]

This is an extreme, even though Croce is careful in his opening words to restrict himself to "political" history. At the other extreme is Alberto

Moravia, writing just thirty years later, in 1963, in an essay entitled "The 'Vulgarity' of Giuseppe Verdi":

> There is something petty, tired and provincial about the Italian nine-teenth century. It is a middle class century—only, unlike the French and English, the Italian middle class had no proper identity papers. It had never beheaded kings, or made a Reformation, or adored the goddess Reason; it was, and still is, a timid, cautious, narrow-minded middle class that cringed before the aristocracy and licked the boots of the clergy. True, urged on by the French Revolution and the Napoleonic wars, it made a supreme effort and managed to bring about the Risorgi-mento, but even the Risorgimento lacked men, made little impression on the masses, was full of humiliating contradictions, and was far behind the rest of Europe. A petty affair in all. And there is the question of proportion. Though in any other country the Risorgimento would have been an important upheaval, in Italy, given her grandiose past, it was a mean little enterprise. The men of the Risorgimento were provincial middle class and their mixture of nationalism and liberalism produced something very weak in alcoholic content. Their romantic intoxication was a prelude to the drunken orgy of rhetoric under Fascism, and the lower-middle-class camomile-infusion under the Christian Demo-crats.[126]

The fact that Moravia is a novelist rather than a historian must not of itself be used to discount his view. Revolutions do not belong exclusively to historians but to people of all kinds who are their heirs. Most men, however, would accuse Moravia of having both his facts and judgments wrong. If the men of the Risorgimento accomplished their revolution with less bloodshed and brutality than the Frenchmen of 1789, this surely is to their credit. Certainly they succeeded in establishing a more stable govern-ment than the French and without undergoing the iron rule of a Cromwell or a Napoleon. And, going further afield for examples, though enormous problems were left unsolved, notably those of the south, the country the men of the Risorgimento united did not fly apart within its first hundred years into brutal, civil war, as did the United States of America. But in arguing such points another book could be written, and it would be better if, between the extremes of Croce and Moravia, each man thought out his own position.

# EPILOGUE

# CHAPTER 50

The deaths or burials of Foscolo, Mazzini, Napoleon, Manzoni, Vittorio Emanuele, Pio Nono and Garibaldi.

THE LIVES of men and the movements in which they play a part do not always coincide exactly, and several of the chief actors in the Risorgimento lived on after the Italian government established itself at Rome. Readers may wish to know how the men, as well as the movement, came to an end.

The first to reach a state of peace, though he had long been dead, was Foscolo. In the same week of June 1871 that the government moved to Rome, his remains, brought from England to Florence, were solemnly reinterred in Santa Croce. There he joined Alfieri, Machiavelli and the other great Italians he had celebrated in "Dei Sepolcri." He was Garibaldi's favorite poet, and he had inspired Mazzini as a young man to plan a complete edition of his works. He had been the first Italian to go into exile because of Austrian rule in Italy, and his return, for many, marked the close of the era of protest and revolution.

Mazzini, the most famous exile after Foscolo, lived until 10 March 1872, ending his days in Pisa. The sentence of death against him had been rescinded in 1866, after the annexation of the Veneto, and following the seizure of Rome, during which he had been interned at Gaeta, he was released under a general amnesty. He was by then, as he realized, almost wholly out of touch with the political and social currents of Italian life, and his last years were saddened by the belief that his life's work, with all the suffering and sacrifice it had cost him and others, had been a failure. Never after Lissa and Custoza was he reconciled to the monarchy, and although a district in Messina elected him to the Chamber, he would not take his seat, for to do so would have required him to swear allegiance to the king. When he died, Parliament by a unanimous vote expressed the nation's sorrow, and a public funeral was held at Pisa. But the official world in Italy was anti-Mazzini, and the national mourning was muted. Later his body was taken to Genoa and interred at the Staglieno Cemetery. Today, in the old part of Genoa, the house in which he was born, the Casa Mazzini, contains the Istituto Mazziniano and a Museo del Risorgimento.

Garibaldi, at the time, seemed unable to make up his mind about Mazzini. He made a point of not attending the funeral at Pisa, although his presence would have made a much more important event of it. Yet later, when the body was returned to Genoa, he wired, "Let the flag of The Thousand be unfurled over the bier of the great Italian." It was the highest honor he could pay, and to no one else, ever, did he pay it. Nevertheless he was soon repeating his old complaints: that Mazzini had prevented victory at Rome in 1849, had interfered in Sicily in 1860, in the Veneto in 1866, and at Mentana in 1867. "One of the obstacles to Italian unification," he wrote, "certainly has been Mazzini." It was a point on which he could not be consistent.

For almost two generations, until almost all the actors of the movement had died, Mazzini's reputation, relative to those of Cavour, Garibaldi and the king, remained low. Since then it has risen in a positive and negative fashion: positively, for the sense of national identity and the desire for unity with which he inspired Italians, and negatively, in that he provided Cavour with the specter of revolution with which to frighten Napoleon III into supporting Sardinia against Austria.

Napoleon was the next to die, in January 1873, in exile in England while undergoing the third operation within a week to remove a stone from his bladder. Though he was over sixty-five, he was hoping to return to France and once again to replace a republic with an empire based on a plebiscite. The republicans at the time had been unable either to defeat the Prussians or to keep order in Paris and were losing the country's support. But the Man on Horseback must be able to sit a horse, and Napoleon in his eagerness to mount, probably hastened his own death. The republicans, meanwhile, rallied, and The Third Republic of France continued until World War II.

In Italy, four months after Napoleon, Alessandro Manzoni died. As a poet and novelist he was more of a symbol of the Risorgimento than an actor in it, and as he was eighty-nine at the time of his death, on 22 May 1873, his life had encompassed most of the movement's great events. He had been four years old when the Bastille fell. As a young schoolboy he had cut off his queue to show his sympathy for the republican army the first Napoleon was leading into eighteenth-century Italy. As a young man in Paris he had seen the celebrations when the same Napoleon, now an emperor, had married Marie Louise, a Habsburg archduchess. He had known Foscolo and had remained a republican until after 1848. Always he had refused the honors with which the Austrians in Milan had tried to lure him to their side, but in 1859 when Vittorio Emanuele II had entered the city, he had called on the king promptly to pay his respects and the following year had accepted the appointment of senator in what was about to become the first Italian Parliament.

These were quiet acts but not without influence. Manzoni was the honorary president of many literary societies and a public figure throughout the peninsula. One of his very last acts, in 1872, was to accept the freedom of Rome offered by the city's Town Council because to do so was "an acknowledgment of the constant aspiration of my long life for the independence and unity of Italy." At the time most priests were protesting the seizure of Rome, and after Manzoni died, the Catholic *Giornale degli Studiosi* published an attack on him as a bad Catholic for having insulted the pope by accepting the Roman gesture with such pleasure.

His funeral was made a state occasion, attended by princes of the blood royal, members of the ministry and the presidents of the Senate and the Chamber. All over Italy, even in the mountain towns of Calabria, streets and squares were named after him, but his greatest monument is Verdi's *Requiem,* composed to honor him and first performed on the first anniversary of his death.

He is buried in the cemetery at Milan, and his house, "No. 1" Via Morone, has become the center of Manzoni studies with exhibitions and rooms open to the public. The Via Morone together with the Via Bigli close by are among the few streets left in Milan which have not been widened or straightened and still can give an idea of how the Milanesi with their barricades were able to defeat the Austrians during the Cinque Giornate. On the Via Bigli, "No. 9" served as headquarters for the Milanesi during the uprising, and "No. 21" was the seat of the Contessa Maffei's salon in its most important years, 1850–59.

Manzoni was too shy to have a salon, but on the ground floor of the Casa del Manzoni, looking into the garden, is the study where he worked and received visitors. Two chairs flank the fire, inviting conversation. His favorite topics, and he was apt to lead the conversation, were the Italian language and, toward the end of his life, the French Revolution and its influence in Italy.

Vittorio Emanuele II, whose health was proverbial, died suddenly on 8 January 1878 from a fever. He was only fifty-eight, and his death was a surprise and a loss to the kingdom. Nine years earlier, when he had been ill, he had finally married morganatically the most important of his mistresses, which had removed one of the scandals dividing him from the Church. Now when the pope, still Pio Nono, heard that the king was dying, he sent a priest authorized to lift the ban of excommunication, and Vittorio Emanuele was able to receive the last sacrament and to die within the Church. Pio Nono further allowed him to have a public Catholic burial in the Pantheon provided that he was never referred to as the King of Italy during the liturgical prayers. When Umberto, Vittorio Emanuele's son, was proclaimed King of Italy, the Papal Secretary of State formally protested his right to sovereignty over Rome and the Papal States.

Vittorio Emanuele's reputation, conversely to that of Mazzini, among the latest generation of historians has declined to a point where he is no longer considered one of the three or four great leaders in the making of Italy. This does not seem to be merely a fashion of history, a reflex of the fact that Italy now is a republic, but the result of new knowledge of the past. In recent years, for example, many of the king's letters to Pio Nono have been published by Vatican scholars, and in them he appears less staunch in defense of the Sardinian constitution than previously presented and more ready, in serving his own ends, to go behind the backs of his ministers. Earlier historians made of him a courageous, bluff and thoroughly honest man, the last conquering hero in European royalty. Mack Smith, writing in 1959 with more facts available, describes him in *Italy* as a "puny and usually insignificant man, good-natured and shrewd, but superstitious and ill-educated, possessing a rough hewn and by no means despicable character but little of the luster and aureole of majesty."

Certainly he lacked the majesty to overawe the pope, the cardinals or even the great Roman families. He was always uncomfortable in Rome, and despite the tomb in the Pantheon and the enormous monument looking down on the Piazza Venezia, there is nothing of his spirit in the city. The House of Savoy comes alive in Turin, most attractively, and for one of its most illustrious members to be buried in the Pantheon at Rome rather than in the basilica of Superga overlooking Turin is an anomaly.

A month after the king, on 7 February 1878, Pio Nono died. He had been pope for thirty-one years, longer than any pope before or since, and six years longer than the traditional twenty-five assigned to St. Peter. For three days his body lay in St. Peter's, and the Romans filed past touching crosses and rosaries to his clothing. But the Romans are nothing if not changeable. Three years later, when his body was interred finally in the Church of San Lorenzo fuori le mura, they were displeased with the Church and, though the coffin was moved at night, they gathered to throw mud on it.

Of all the actors in the Risorgimento, the role of none, not even of Cavour, is more difficult to assess than that of Pio Nono. Under him the Papal State, at the time the oldest sovereignty in Europe, ceased to exist. Beyond the statement of the simple fact controversy rages. Every shade of opinion has been and continues to be put forth. Did he betray the national movement in 1848 or merely "come to his senses"? Was he wise or misguided to rely so exclusively on Antonelli and authoritarians within the

Church? Were there alternatives to the actions he did or did not take? A historian's answers to such questions depend on beliefs transcending the usual area of politics, on emotional responses to the concepts of authority and of freedom, and it may be that about Pio Nono no historical "truth" is possible without first obtaining an impossible unanimity in background and outlook of all who would judge him.

The last of the chief actors to die was Garibaldi. In 1870 he had gone to France to fight the Prussians, after Napoleon had fallen, and an international corps of volunteers had gathered under him. A French journalist had described him as "looking like a soldier with one foot in the grave," and because of his wound and his arthritis he could not walk and most of the time was carried about in a stretcher. Nevertheless, fighting with an army of five thousand in the Vosges, he hindered the Prussian movements and, to the fury of the French, was the only general on their side in the war who succeeded in capturing an enemy flag, and who was not defeated.

Thereafter, except for a rare visit to the mainland, he lived on Caprera, issuing blasts at the government in his letters to the papers and to workingmen's societies. Like Mazzini he was disappointed with what he had helped to create. Through his bitterness ran some strains of truth. He criticized, for example, the size of the army, the pursuit of prestige and, always, the neglect of the south. It used to be said of Garibaldi that he had the heart of a hero and the brains of an ox, but more recently, without making an intellectual of him, historians have been more inclined to allow that he had some basic ideas that were sound; among others, his belief that the south needed a dictator until its people were more educated to liberty and less in thrall to poverty and the landlords. On the other hand, his tirades against the priests, which grew more and more vitriolic as he grew older, soon became an obsession.

Finally in May 1882 when he was seventy-four, he had a bronchial catarrh which made it difficult for him to breathe and his family soon recognized that he was growing weaker steadily. Each day he had his bed pulled to the window so that he could see the birds and the sea, and on 2 June very quietly he died. By his bedside, and open, was a book of Foscolo's poems.

He always had wanted to be burned, not cremated, but actually burned in the open, like Shelley or one of Homer's heroes, and in his will he instructed his wife, a housekeeper whom he had married in order to legitimize their children, to prepare and light the pyre before she told any officials of his death. She was to use aromatic wood of aloes and myrtle, both native to Caprera, and she was to dress him in a red shirt. The ashes, after the fire, she was to bury in a crystal bottle beneath his favorite juniper tree. In an appendix to the will he warned her, "You will need plenty of wood."

She tried to do as he wished but was overruled by his elder children and the official world. Garibaldi alive had been an irritant; but dead and silent, his funeral offered an opportunity to heal old wounds and to confer honor on the living while paying homage to the dead. Besides, the officials argued, burning would offend people's religious sensibilities.

So, in the end, he was buried near his house with representatives standing by from the royal family, the government, the army and the diplomatic corps. But as if in protest, when his body was lowered into the earth, the sky darkened, a strong wind sprang up and in a flash the heavens opened and rain poured down; at the same moment the block of granite which was to be laid over his grave cracked and broke.

Garibaldi's spirit hovers in many places of Italy, for he was one of the few men of the Risorgimento to see all parts of it. He was a native of Nice and Genoa, had fought at Rome, escaped from the Austrians near Ravenna, led two campaigns in the Alps and walked over most of Sicily and Naples. But of all the places associated with him two have a special quality. One is the area around Ravenna. The farms and pinewoods in which the patriotic Romagnuoli hid him from the Austrians are still there, and so, too, is the farm in which his beloved Anita died. The intensity of his emotion seems to have penetrated the walls and trees, for on a hot August day the very air seems to quiver with it: under this tree, up those stairs, and, for the last time, in that room.

The other place, Calatafimi, has a different quality. Under the noonday Sicilian sun in May it is dead, or almost so. The sun beats down. There are no trees. The scraggly vegetation is green but lifeless; the air, breathless; the earth bakes. At the top of the hill, where the Neapolitans were, there is the single sentence carved in marble, an assertion of one man's will that changed history: "Here we make Italy—or die." *Qui si fa l'Italia o si muore.*

# APPENDIX

The Lateran Pacts do not fall within the story of the Risorgimento, yet something must be said of them in order to explain how the basis of relations between Church and State, established by the Law of Guarantees, became the basis with which persons today are familiar. Briefly:

Under the Law of Guarantees the pope was deprived of his temporal sovereignty but allowed to keep possession, though not ownership, of the Vatican and Lateran Palaces and the villa at Castel Gandolfo. He was, however, to retain many of the attributes of sovereignty: immunity from arrest, his own diplomatic corps, personal guard, post office, etc. . . . He was also offered an annual allowance of 3,225,000 lire, which Pio Nono and his successors refused.

This remained the situation until 1929 when Mussolini and the Secretary of State for Pius XI negotiated the Lateran Pacts.

These pacts consist of a treaty, a financial agreement and a concordat. Under the treaty the pope was given or returned his temporal power, actual sovereignty, over what is known as Vatican City, roughly the palace and St. Peter's; the villa at Castel Gandolfo; at Rome, the churches of San Giovanni in Laterano, Santa Maria Maggiore and San Paolo fuori le mura; at Assisi, San Francesco; at Loreto, Santa Casa; and at Padua, Sant'Antonio. And he was again given all the rights of immunity, personal guard, etc.

Under the financial agreement he received 750,000,000 lire ($37,-500,000) in cash and 1,000,000,000 lire ($50,000,000) in state bonds.

Under the concordat, crucifixes and religious education returned to the public or government schools, and the State agreed to give civil effect to Roman Catholic marriages.

In exchange, the pope agreed to recognize the Kingdom of Italy, to have a prayer said annually for the health of the king, to give the government a veto over the appointment of priests to certain positions in Italy, to rearrange dioceses to conform to Italian boundaries, to have bishops with Italian sees swear to support the Fascist government, and to forgive the present owners of previously confiscated Church property the sin of holding it.

Very strong emotions still swirl around these pacts which brought

733

neither to the Church nor to Mussolini the lasting renown and peace or victory each was seeking. Pius XI described Mussolini as "the man sent to us by Providence," but in making the Church one of the largest holders of state bonds he found he had given it a financial interest in supporting a dictator and government which many Catholics thought unchristian. Mussolini, for his part, basked in the pope's praise but soon discovered that on many points he was opposing the Church just as hard as his predecessors.

The point for this appendix, however, is that the concept of spiritual sovereignty without a temporal base was continued. The Papacy wanted and received the form of a sovereign state in the Vatican City, its scattered churches and villa. But it is no safer from interference by the Italian government because its title is recognized in a treaty rather than set forth by a Law. The real basis of its spiritual freedom is still the desire of the Italian government to have it free, regardless of whether that desire is based wholly on altruism or partly on fear.

# BIBLIOGRAPHICAL NOTES

These are limited to the longer quotations, those that are indented in the text. Thorough documentation of a history covering such a vast subject, so many revolutions, governments and generations of men, would have required a volume of notes out of all proportion to the length of the text. The notes that follow, while omitting much, will be sufficient to start a student toward the sources of a history of the Risorgimento. The general reader can skip them, or can search for a book in English on some aspect of the subject in the "Suggestions for Further Reading." Full bibliographies can be found at the end of each chapter of *Questioni di Storia del Risorgimento e dell'unità d'Italia* (Ed. E. Rota); Milan, Marzorati, 1951; and in the *Enciclopedia italiana*.

## PART I

1. GOZZI, CARLO. *Memorie inutili* (ed. Giuseppe Prezzolini). Bari, Laterza, 1910. 2 vols. Vol. 1, p. 26.
2. quoted by FERRERO, GUGLIELMO. *The Gamble, Bonaparte in Italy, 1796–1797* (trans. Bertha Pritchard and Lily Freeman). London, Bell, 1939; 1961. p. 153. Citing, Debidour *Recueil* 4 p. 787.
3. GOZZI. *Memorie inutili.* Above. Vol. 2, p. 245.
4. quoted by FERRERO. *The Gamble.* Above. p. 227.
5. BECCARIA, CESARE. *Opere* (ed. Sergio Romagnoli). Firenze, Sansoni, 1958. 2 vols. Vol. 1, p. 41. The opening sentences addressed "To the Reader."
6. COURIER, P. L. *Oeuvres.* Paris, Firmin Didot, 1861. p. 465. In a letter from Mileto dated 16 October 1806 to a Monsieur . . . , an artillery officer stationed at Naples.
7. FOSCOLO, UGO. *Opere edite e postume di Ugo Foscolo.* Firenze, Le Monnier, 1923. 9 vols. Vol. 9, p. 184.
8. FOSCOLO. Above. Vol. 9, p. 181.
9. This dialogue is from E. E. Y. Hales' *Napoleon and the Pope, The Story of Napoleon and Pius VII.* London, Eyre & Spottiswoode, 1962. p. 120. It is used here as the clearest and most vivid summary of what seems actually to have been said. Both Pacca and Radet left accounts of the confrontation, and these, agreeing completely on the substance of the exchange, vary slightly only on the words reported to have been used. See PACCA, BARTOLOMEO. *Memorie Storiche del Ministero de' due viaggi in Francia, e della prigionia nel forte di S. Carlo in Fenestrelle.* Roma,

Bourlie, 1830. 2nd edn. p. 65. At p. 445 as "Documento Numero I" is a letter from Radet to Pope Pius VII in which he attempts to answer those writers who had criticized his conduct. In it he gives an account of the kidnapping. The letter is dated 12 September 1814.

10. FOSCOLO. Above. Vol. 7, p. 122. The quotation is taken from what is thought to be a draft of a letter which may never have been sent, for another letter, written several months later, on 21 December 1815, implies that it is his first reply, after several months of silence, to the Countess' accusations. The draft, however, states very succinctly Foscolo's feelings, and these, for the remaining years of his life, he laid before the Italian people from his exile in England.

## PART II

11. PELLICO, SILVIO. *Le miei prigioni.* Milano, AMZ, 1960. p. 113 (in Chap. 53).

12. MAZZINI, GIUSEPPE. *Scritti editi ed inediti.* Milano, Daelli, 1861–1891. 18 vols. Vol. 1, p. 14. The account occurs in the first of the Autobiographical Notes written by Mazzini between 1861 and 1865 as editorial explanations to this first collected edition of his writings. This edition hereafter will be referred to as *Scritti Mazzini.*

A National Commission in 1905, the centenary of Mazzini's birth, began to publish a more complete edition: *Edizione Nazionale degli scritti di Giuseppe Mazzini.* Imola, Galeati, 1905. This was completed in 96 vols. Vol. 77 contained all the Autobiographical Notes which were also published as an independent volume: *Note Autobiografiche di Giuseppe Mazzini* (ed. Mario Menghini). Firenze, Le Monnier, 1944.

13. LEOPARDI, GIACOMO. *Zibaldone di Pensieri* (ed. Francesco Flora). Milan, Mondadori, 1937; 6th ed. 1961, p. 309. From the poet's notebook, *Zibaldone,* 1, 25 November 1820.

14. The translation is by John Humphreys Whitfield. *Leopardi's "Canti."* Napoli, Scalabrini, 1962. pp. 41, 45.

15. Whitfield. *Leopardi's "Canti."* Above. p. 27.

16. *Scritti Mazzini.* Above. Vol. 1, p. 20. In his first Autobiographical Note.

17. quoted by ACTON, HAROLD. *The Last Bourbons of Naples, 1825–1861.* London, Methuen, 1961. p. 41.

18. *Scritti Mazzini.* Above. Vol. 1, p. 81. Or in the later *Edizione Nazionale* of his works, Vol. 2, p. 17. The letter, really a pamphlet, though published at Marseille was written in Italian and smuggled into the Italian states. Mazzini later claimed that this was the only one of his political writings not to appear over his own name and gave as reasons that it was his first, when his name meant nothing, and that the views expressed were not truly his own, but those of many Italians which, by articulating, he hoped to prove ill-founded.

19. SALVEMINI, GAETANO. *Mazzini.* (trans. I. M. Rawson) London, Jonathan Cape, 1956. p. 104.

20. ADDAMS, JANE. *Twenty Years at Hull-House.* New York, Macmillan, 1920. p. 21.

21. quoted by PIERI, PIERO. *Storia militare del Risorgimento, Guerre e in-*

*surrezioni.* Torino, Einaudi, 1962; p. 131. Pieri devotes a section of a chapter to a discussion of the idea and of its sources.

22. *Scritti Mazzini.* Above. Vol. 1, p. 395. From an Autobiographical Note.
23. *Edizione Nazionale degli scritti di Giuseppe Mazzini* (See Note 12.) Vol. 9, p. 96. Letter to Luigi Amedeo Melegari, dated (Geneva), 2 (October 1833), and signed "Filippo Strozzi," Mazzini's code-name at the time.

    The greater part of the letter is translated into English in *Mazzini's Letters* (trans. A. Jervis). London, Dent (Everyman Library), 1930; p. 2.
24. GARIBALDI, GIUSEPPE. *Edizione Nazionale degli Scritti di Giuseppe Garibaldi.* 6 vols. Bologna, Cappelli, 1932–1937.

    Vol. I: *Le Memorie di Garibaldi in una delle redazioni anteriori alla definitiva del 1872* (memoirs in a version before the definitive one of 1872 in which he cut out some of the more poetic passages).

    Vol. II: *Le Memorie di Garibaldi nella redazione definitiva del 1872.*

    Vol. III: *I Mille.* (His autobiographical novel about the Thousand in Sicily.)

    Vol. IV: *Scritti e Discorsi politici e militari, 1838–1861.*

    Vol. V: *Scritti e Discorsi, ecc., 1862–1867.*

    Vol. VI: *Scritti e Discorsi, ecc., 1868–1882* (includes his Political Testament). Hereafter a reference to Garibaldi that reads simply *Memorie,* I, or *Scritti,* IV, refers to the volumes of this *Edizione Nazionale.*

    ———. On the meeting with Anita: *Memorie,* II, p. 77.
25. GARIBALDI. *Memorie,* II, p. 79.
26. D'AZEGLIO, MASSIMO. *I miei ricordi.* Milano, Rizzoli, 1956; p. 475.
27. BERTI, DOMENICO. *Il Conte di Cavour avanti il 1848.* Rome, Voghera, 1886. pp. 118–119. Letter to his uncle Sellon, dated 5 February 1831 and written in French.
28. CHIALA, LUIGI (ed.). *Lettere edite ed inedite di Camillo Cavour.* Torino, Roux, 1884–87. 6 vols. Vol. I, p. 287–90. Written in French while at Paris, dated only "mai 1835," addressed to Contessa Anastasia de Circourt.
29. BERTI, DOMENICO (ed.). *Diario inedito con Note autobiografiche del Conte di Cavour.* Roma, Voghera, 1888. Diary entry dated Jeudi, 31 Juillet (1834) and written in French: "Ah, si j'étais anglais."
30. CHIALA, LUIGI (ed.). *Ricordi di Michelangelo Castelli, 1847–75.* Torino, Roux, 1888. p. 112.
31. D'AZEGLIO, MASSIMO. *Scritti e discorsi politici di Massimo d'Azeglio* (ed. Marcus de Rubris). Firenze, La Nuova Italia, 1931. 3 vols. Vol. 1, p. 425. Documents in support of his assertions, such as a list of those killed or wounded with their addresses, ages, professions and types and severity of wounds, are in Vol. 3, p. 547. Most of these were published in the pamphlet as appendices to the text. The pamphlet was published first in Florence and soon after in Venice.

    Hereafter this edition of D'Azeglio's works will be referred to as *Scritti D'Azeglio.* Vol. 1, 1846–48; Vol. 2, 1848–52; Vol. 3, 1853–56. Note: *I miei ricordi* is not included.

32. FARINI, LUIGI CARLO. *Lo Stato Romano dal 1815 al 1850*. Firenze, Le Monnier, 3rd edn. 1853. 4 vols. Vol. 1, p. 337.

33. MARCHESI, VINCENZO. *Storia Documentata della Rivoluzione e della difesa di Venezia negli anni 1848–49 trattata da Fonti Italiane ed Austriache*. Venezia, Istituto Veneto di Arti Grafiche, 1916. p. 109.

34. MARCHESI. Above. p. 123.

35. CANTÙ, CESARE. *Le Cinque Giornate di Milano. Lettere Cinque*. Venezia, Milesi, 1848. The excerpt is from the third letter, which was entitled "L'Eroismo" and dedicated to General Guglielmo Pepe. Cantù was not in Milan during the fighting. He explains in the first letter that he entered the city on the night of 25 March.

36. FARINI. *Lo Stato Romano*. Above. Vol. 2, p. 55. Also *Scritti D'Azeglio*. Above. Vol. 1, p. 549. Dated Bologna, 5 April 1848.

37. FARINI. Above. Vol. 2, pp. 92–98.

38. quoted by HALES, E. E. Y. *Pio Nono, A Study in European politics and religion in the nineteenth century*. London, Eyre & Spottiswoode, 1954; p. 79.

39. FARINI. *Lo Stato Romano*. Above. Vol. 2, p. 59.

40. VISCONTI VENOSTA, GIOVANNI. *Ricordi di Gioventù, Cose redute o sapete, 1847–1860*. Milano, Cogliati, 1904. p. 138 (in Chap. 7).

41. CANTÙ, CESARE. *Della Indipendenza Italiana, Cronistoria*. Torino, Unione Tipografico, 1872–75. 3 vols. Vol. 2, p. 948. Some historians cite this work simply as *Cronistoria*.

42. CANTÙ. Above. Vol. 2, p. 956.

43. CAPPELLETTI, LICURGO. *Storia di Carlo Alberto e del Suo Regno*. Roma, Voghera, 1891; p. 588. Cappelletti publishes twenty-five documents of which this is No. 17.

44. GARIBALDI. Scritti, IV, p. 93.

45. quoted by THAYER, WILLIAM ROSCOE. *The Life and Times of Cavour*. Boston, Houghton Mifflin, 1911. 2 vols. Vol. 2, p. 102. Citing a letter to De la Rue dated 8 March 1849.

46. CAPPELLETTI. *Storia di Carlo Alberto*, etc. Above. p. 505. As might be expected of such a sudden act performed under such circumstances, those present vary slightly in reporting the words the king spoke, but all agree on the substance of what he said. Cf. Cantù, *Cronistoria*, above, Vol. II, p. 1015. Or for a discussion of the problem, cf. Niccolò Rodolico, *Carlo Alberto negli anni 1843–1849*, Firenze, Le Monnier, 1943; p. 563, fn. 51.

47. quoted by TREVELYAN, GEORGE MACAULAY. *Garibaldi's Defence of the Roman Republic (1848–9)*. London, Longmans, 1907; 1949. p. 119. Citing an unpublished source.

48. DANDOLO, EMILIO. *I Volontari ed i Bersaglieri Lombardi*. Milano, Albrighi, Segali, 1917. p. 153.

49. DANDOLO. Above. p. 192.

50. DANDOLO. Above. p. 218.

51. *Scritti Mazzini*. Above. Vol. 7, p. 17. In a declaration published 5 April 1849.

52. GARIBALDI. *Memorie*, II, p. 308.

53. One of the best accounts of the meeting of 2 April 1948 is in PLANAT DE LA FAYE, FEDERICA. *Documents et Pièces Authentiques laissés par*

*Daniel Manin*. Paris, Furne, 1860. 2 vols. Vol. II, p. 171. The account reads like a secretary's minutes and contains in a footnote Manin's words. It is followed by an account of the American consul, Edmond Flagg, who was present.

It is an anomaly of Venetian history that one of the first and best source books on this dramatic period should be in French, with all the documents translated. But as the Veneto was still Austrian, the French publisher was denied the obvious market and forced to search for profits out of French sales. The author in her preface wrote ". . . nous nous consolions par cette espérance que, lorsque Venise sera libre, ces documents seront publiés dans leur langue originale, et que notre travail aura servi à rendre leur publication plus facile et plus assurée." After Venice achieved its freedom and joined the Kingdom of Italy, the work was translated into Italian: *Documenti e scritti autentici di Daniele Manin*. Venezia, Antonelli, 1877.

54. MARCHESI, VINCENZO. *Storia Documentata*. Above. p. 495, fn. 30. In this account, the entire crowd says it.

## PART III

55. MAINERI, B. E. (ed.) *Daniele Manin e Giorgio Pallavicino, Epistolario Politico, 1855–1857, con Note e Documenti*. Milano, Bortolotti, 1878. Full text of letter published in *Presse,* 22 March 1854, given in Appendix, p. 324.

56. *Scritti D'Azeglio*. Above (See Note 31). Vol. 2, p. 195. Issued 20 November 1849. About half the proclamation is translated into English in Whyte, A. J. *The Political Life and Letters of Cavour, 1848–1861*. London, Oxford University Press, 1930, 1959. Appendix A.

57. BROFFERIO, ANGELO. *Storia del Parlamento Subalpino, Iniziatore dell'- unita Italiana*. Milan, Battezzati, 1869. 6 vols. Vol. 1, p. 146.

58. CAVOUR, CAMILLO. *Discorsi Parlamentari del Conte Camillo di Cavour*. Torino, Botta, 1863–72. 11 vols. Vol. 1, p. 409. Debate of 7 March 1850.
Hereafter referred to as *Discorsi Cavour*.

59. quoted by CRANKSHAW, EDWARD. *The Fall of the House of Habsburg*. New York, Viking, 1963. p. 51.

60. GLADSTONE, WILLIAM EWART. *Two Letters to the Earl of Aberdeen on the State Prosecutions of the Neapolitan Government*. New York, Nichols, 1851. p. 9. (From early in the first letter.)

61. SENIOR, WILLIAM NASSAU. *Journals Kept in France and Italy from 1848 to 1852 with a Sketch of the Revolution of 1848*. (ed. M. C. M. Simpson) 2 vols. London, King, 1871. Vol. 2, p. 5.

62. FARINI. *Lo Stato Romano*. Above. Vol. 4, p. 307. The letter to Gladstone, written from Turin on 20 December 1852, is printed as a sort of epilogue to the history.

63. MAGUIRE, JOHN FRANCIS. *Rome: Its Ruler and its Institutions*. New York, Sadlier, 1862; p. 445. The entire report, dated Rome, 14 May 1856, is translated into English and published, pp. 432–49, by Maguire in his Appendix.

64. VISCONTI VENOSTA. *Ricordi di Gioventù.* Above (see Note 40). p. 316 (in Chap. 12).

65. *Discorsi Cavour.* Above. Vol. 9, p. 114. Debate of 6 February 1855.

66. quoted by CRANKSHAW. *The Fall of the House of Habsburg.* Above. p. 127.

67. CAVOUR, CAMILLO. *Lettere edite ed inedite di Camillo Cavour* (ed. Luigi Chiala). Torino, Roux, 1884–87. 6 vols. Hereafter referred to as *Lettere Cavour.* Vol. 2, p. 76; written in French; undated, but written in Turin shortly after 26 November 1854.
   In the collection the volumes cover the following periods:
   Vol. 1, 1821–1852
       2, 1852–1858
       3, 1859–1860
       4, 1860–1861
       5, 1819–1856
       6, 1856–1861.

68. BROFFERIO, ANGELO. *Storia del Parlamento Subalpino.* Above. Vol. VI, p. 796.

69. BROFFERIO. Above. The entire text of the Church's statement is set out in Vol. 6, Appendix 2.

70. PIRRI, PIETRO. *Pio e Vittorio Emanuele II dal loro carteggio privato.* This is a very large work which appeared in three parts, in 1941, 1951 and 1961, in volumes of a magazine, *Miscellanea Historiae Pontificiae,* published at Rome by Pontificia Universita Gregoriana. Vittorio Emanuele's letter is at p. 157 of Vol. VIII of the magazine.
   The work includes far more than the title suggests. Considerable space is given to the pope's correspondence with other sovereigns, particularly Napoleon III, and to correspondence within the Church. Pirri is an Italian Jesuit historian working in the Vatican archives and he has presented and edited a large number of hitherto unpublished documents. Each of the three sections of his work consists of a text, a narrative history, followed by the documents to which he has referred. The sections with the volume number of the magazine are as follows:
   (1) La Laicizzazione dello Stato Sardo, 1848–1856. Text and Documents, Vol. VIII.
   (2) La Questione Romana, 1856–1864. Text, Vol. XVI; Documents, Vol. XVII.
   (3) La Questione Romana, 1864–1870. Text, Vol. XXIV; Documents, Vol. XXV.

71. *Scritti D'Azeglio.* Above (see Note 31). Vol. 3, p. 33; dated Turin, 12 February 1855.

72. quoted by WHYTE, A. J. *The Political Life and Letters of Cavour, 1848–1861.* London, Oxford University Press, 1930, 1959; p. 175. The background of the letter is given in detail, though not the letter itself, in Pirri (see Note 70), Vol. VIII.

73. *Scritti D'Azeglio.* Above. Vol. 3, p. 43; written in Italian and dated Turin, 29 April 1855.

74. MAINERI, B. E. (ed.) *Daniele Manin,* etc. Above (see Note 55). Full text of letter published in *Diritto,* 26 September 1855, given in Appendix, p. 333.

75. *Discorsi Cavour.* Above (see Note 58). Vol. 9, p. 457. Debate of 6 May 1855.

76. quoted by ACTON, HAROLD. *The Last Bourbons of Naples.* London, Methuen, 1961. p. 362.

77. quoted by WHYTE. *The Political Life and Letters of Cavour,* etc. Above. p. 246.

78. CAVOUR, CAMILLO. *Carteggi di Camillo Cavour* (ed. Commissione Nazionale). Bologna, Zanichelli, 1926–1954; index, 1961. 16 vols. Vol. 1, p. 64. Letter No. 16, written in French to General Della Rocca and dated 9 February 1858.

    This collection of letters, with the exception of a few to E. D'Azeglio and to Salmour, falls entirely within the period 1856–61. Hereafter it is referred to as *Carteggi Cavour.*

    The volumes are divided as follows:

    Vols. 1–4:  Il Carteggio Cavour—Nigra dal 1858 al 1861.
        1. *Plombières.*
        2. *La campagna diplomatica e militare del 1859.*
        3. *La cessione di Nizza e Savoia e l'annessione dell'Italia centrale.*
        4. *La liberazione del Mezzogiorno.*

    Vols. 5 and 6: La Questione romana negli anni 1860–61.

    Vols. 7, 8 and 9: Cavour e l'Inghilterra, Carteggio con V. E. D'Azeglio.
        7. *Il Congresso di Parigi.*
        8. and 9. *I confliti diplomatici del 1856–61 con l'aggiunta del carteggio tra Cavour e i coniugi Circourt.*

    Vol. 10. Carteggio Cavour—Salmour.

    Vols. 11–15:  La liberazione del Mezzogiorno e la formazione del Regno d'Italia.
        11. *Gennaio–Luglio 1860.*
        12. *Agosto–Settembre 1860.*
        13. *Ottobre–Novembre 1860.*
        14. *Dicembre 1860–Giugno 1861.*
        15. *Appendici.*

    Vol. 16: Indice generale dei primi quindici volumi.

79. *Scritti Mazzini.* Above (see Note 12). Vol. 10, p. 85.

80. MASSARI, GIUSEPPE. *La Vita ed il Regno di Vittorio Emanuele II di Savoia, Primo Re d'Italia.* Milano, Treves, 1878. 2 vols. Vol. 1, pp. 365–67. Massari presents an uncritical view of Vittorio Emanuele, but at the same time he is the source of so many of the anecdotes about the king that his book is still important.

81. DE BAZANCOURT, CÉSAR. *La Campagne d'Italie de 1859, Chroniques de la Guerre.* Paris, Amyot, 1859. 2 vols. Vol. I, p. 75. Dated Genoa, 12 May. De Bazancourt was the official French historian of the war, "appelé par ordre de L'Empereur à l'armée d'Italie."

82. DE BAZANCOURT. Above. Vol. 2, p. 85. Dated Milan, 8 June 1859.

83. VISCONTI VENOSTA. *Ricordi di Gioventù.* Above (see Note 40), p. 604 (in Chap. 23).

84. CHIALA, LUIGI (ed.) *Politica Segreta di Napoleone III e di Cavour in*

*Italia e in Ungheria (1858–1861).* Roux, Torino, 1895, p. 61; quoting from Kossuth, *Souvenirs.*

85. *Lettere di Massimo d'Azeglio a sua moglie, Luisa Blondel* (ed. Giulio Carcano). Milano, Rechiedi, 1870. p. 499. Dated Turin, 29 July.

86. quoted by HANCOCK, W. K. *Ricasoli and the Risorgimento in Tuscany.* London, Faber and Gwyer, 1926; p. 290. Citing *Lettere e Documenti di Barone Bettino Ricasoli* (ed. Gotti and Tabarrini), Vol. III, p. 390.

87. *Scritti Mazzini.* Above (see Note 12). Vol. II, p. xlviii–li.

88. ABBA, GIUSEPPE CESARE. *Da Quarto al Volturno, Noterelle d'uno dei Mille.* Bologna, Zanchielli, 1964. p. 56. Entry dated: Dal Feudo di Rampagallo. Sera. (12 May). The book is often entitled simply *Noterelle d'uno dei Mille.*

    Abba volunteered to serve under Garibaldi, hoping to satisfy two ambitions: to strike a blow for the unification of Italy and to write the epic poem of the Sicilian expedition. The poem, based on his notes, was published in 1866 and entitled *Arrigo, Da Quarto al Volturno.* It had little success. The notebook, polished and made grammatical, was published in 1880, and was an immediate success.

89. *Lettere Cavour.* Above (see Note 67). Vol. 4, cxxi; written in Italian; dated Turin, 15 April 1860.

90. ABBA. *Noterelle.* Above. p. 175. Entry dated Castrogiovanni, 10 luglio.

91. GARIBALDI. *Scritti,* IV, p. 273.

92. quoted by MACK SMITH, DENIS. *Cavour and Garibaldi 1860: A Study in Political Conflict.* Cambridge University Press, 1954. p. 59.

93. *Carteggi Cavour.* Above (see Note 78). Vol. 4, p. 98. Letter No. 992, written in Italian and dated 22 July 1860. Chiala in *Lettere edite,* above, Vol. 4, cccxi, gives a shorter and more pungent version.

94. *Carteggi Cavour.* Above. Vol. 4, p. 49. Letter No. 935, written in French and dated Paris, 30 June 1860.

95. *Carteggi Cavour.* Above. Vol. 4, p. 186. Letter No. 1079, written in French and dated 29 August 1860. Also in *Lettere Cavour.* Above. Vol. 6, p. 582.

96. GARIBALDI. *Scritti,* IV, p. 296. No two reports of the speech give the same words. Cf. the version in GALTON, below, p. 26.

97. GALTON, FRANCIS (ed.). *Vacation Tourists and Notes of Travel in 1860.* London, Macmillan, 1861. p. 27. From the "Notes" provided by W. G. Clark which run pp. 1–75.

98. BLAKISTON, NOEL (ed.). *The Roman Question,* Extracts from the Despatches of Odo Russell from Rome, 1858–1870. London, Chapman and Hall, 1962. p. 118.

99. *Carteggi Cavour.* Above. Vol. 4, p. 212. Letter No. 1115, written in Italian and dated Naples, 11 September 1860.

100. *Carteggi Cavour.* Above. Vol. 4, p. 70. Letter No. 961, written in French and dated 12 July 1860.

101. *Carteggi Cavour.* Above. Vol. 4, p. 144. Letter No. 1039, written in French and dated Turin, 9 August 1860. Also in *Lettere Cavour.* Above. Vol. 3, p. 321.

102. GALTON. *Vacation Tourists.* Above (see Note 97). p. 66.

103. KING, BOLTON. *The Life of Mazzini.* London, Dent (Everyman), 1911; p. 359. To Mr. Peter Taylor, dated 11 September 1860. Letter appears

in Appendix A which published for the first time thirteen of Mazzini's letters.

104. *Discorsi Cavour.* Above (see Note 58). Vol. 9, p. 258. Debate of 11 October 1860.
105. *Discorsi Cavour.* Above. Vol. 11, p. 260. Debate of 11 October 1860.
106. *Discorsi Cavour.* Above. Vol. 11, p. 262. Debate of 11 October 1860.
107. *Carteggi Cavour.* Above. Vol. 13, p. 63. Letter No. 2091, written in Italian and dated 8 October 1860. Also in *Lettere Cavour.* Above. Vol. 4, p. 34.
108. Same as above.
109. quoted by TREVELYAN, G. M. *Garibaldi and the Making of Italy, June–November 1860.* London, Longmans, 1911, 1948; p. 282. Citing British Parliamentary Papers VII, pp. 125–27.


PART IV

110. *Discorsi Cavour.* Above (see Note 58). Vol. 11, p. 346. Debate of 27 March 1861.
111. *Discorsi Cavour.* Above. Vol. 11, p. 347. Debate of 27 March 1861.
112. GARIBALDI. *Scritti,* IV, p. 353.
113. *Discorsi Cavour.* Above. Vol. 11, p. 378. Debate of 18 April 1861. Also in Garibaldi *Scritti* IV, p. 374.
114. MARIO, JESSIE WHITE. *Garibaldi e i suoi tempi.* Milano, Treves, 1884; p. 675. Mario gives Cialdini's letter and Garibaldi's reply complete.
115. *Discorsi Cavour.* Above. Vol. 11, p. 456. Debate of 29 May 1861.
116. *Scritti D'Azeglio.* Above (see Note 31). Vol. 3, p. 399; written to Senator Carlo Matteucci in Italian, dated Cannero, 2 August 1861; published in the French paper *La Patrie.*
117. GARIBALDI. *Scritti,* V, p. 40.
118. MARIO, JESSIE WHITE. *The Birth of Modern Italy, Posthumous Papers* (ed. Duke of Liatta-Visconti-Arese). New York, Scribners, 1909. p. 329. Sometimes cited simply as *Posthumous Papers.*
119. quoted by MACK SMITH, DENIS. *Italy, A Modern History.* Ann Arbor, University of Michigan, 1959. p. 74.
120. quoted by ADAMS, JOHN CLARKE and BARILE, PAOLO. *The Government of Republican Italy.* Boston, Houghton Mifflin, 1961. p. 31. They cite Einaudi, Luigi. *Cronache economiche e politiche,* Turin, Einaudi, 1960. Vol. III, Preface. But they took their quotation from a resumé of the preface reported in *La Stampa,* 10 May 1960, p. 5.
121. GARIBALDI. *Scritti,* V, p. 229. This is how the text was published in the Turin newspaper, *Diritto,* on 25 April 1861. Hibbert (q.v.) in his biography of Garibaldi gives an almost identical text as published in the *Evening Standard,* 20 April 1865.
122. GARIBALDI. *Scritti,* V, p. 246.
123. quoted by JEMOLO, ARTURO CARLO. Church and State in Italy, 1850–1950. Oxford, Blackwell, 1960. p. 124.
124. PIRRI, PIETRO. Above (see Note 70). Vol. XXV, p. 269. Dated Florence, 8 September 1870.

125. CROCE, BENEDETTO. *The History of Europe in the Nineteenth Century* (trans. Henry Furst). New York, Harcourt Brace, 1933; Harbinger paperback, 1963. p. 225.
126. MORAVIA, ALBERTO. *Man as an End. a Defense of Humanism* (trans. Bernard Wall). New York, Farrar, Straus & Giroux, 1965. p. 248.

# SUGGESTIONS FOR FURTHER READING

These are limited to books in English and, further, to those touching directly on the Italians and their actions. To have included suggestions on the first or third Napoleon or Franz Josef opened too large a field.

A word about the modern Italian historians. Because they are writing for an audience already familiar with the basic documents of the Risorgimento, they are apt not to quote the documents at length, and so, with the exception of Piero Pieri and Pietro Pirri, they did not appear in the preceding notes. Further, because they mostly have not been translated, perhaps just because their works do suppose a close acquaintance with the Risorgimento, they do not appear in the following list, which is limited to works in English. Those who can read Italian, however, should begin by examining the writings of Adolfo Omodeo, Walter Maturi, Luigi Salvatorelli, Antonio Gramsci and Rosario Romeo. For those who cannot read Italian, Charles F. Delzell has provided a glimpse of the points of view of some of them in his *The Unification of Italy, 1859–1861*, listed below.

## BIBLIOGRAPHIES

These all offer a description of the works listed with comment.

*The American Historical Association Guide to Historical Literature*, ed. George F. Howe et al. New York, Macmillan, 1961. The section on Italy, pp. 526–48, is by Catherine E. Boyd.

*Italy in Modern Times: an Introduction to the Historical Literature in English*, by Charles F. Delzell. Washington, The American Historical Association, 1964. No. 60 of a series, "Service Center for Teachers of History."

*The Risorgimento*, by Agatha Ramm. London, Routledge and Kegan Paul, 1962. No. 50 in the "General Series" published by the Historical Association.

"Italian Historical Scholarship: a Decade of Recovery and Development, 1945–55," by Charles F. Dezell. *The Journal of Modern History*, Vol. XXVIII (December 1956), pp. 374–88.

"The Historiography of the *Risorgimento* since 1920," by Kent R. Greenfield. *The Journal of Modern History*, VII (March 1935), pp. 49–67.

(This article, though now dated, is still interesting as an attempt by a non-Italian historian to evaluate the rather slanted work of some fascist historians.)

ABBA, GIUSEPPE CESARE. *The Diary of one of Garibaldi's Thousand* (trans. E. R. Vincent). London, Oxford University Press, 1962. A translation of *Da Quarto al Volturno, Noterelle d'uno dei Mille;* first published in 1880; Bologna, Zanchielli, 1964.

ACTON, HAROLD. *The Bourbons of Naples, 1734–1825.* London, Methuen, 1956.

——. *The Last Bourbon of Naples, 1825–1861.* London, Methuen, 1961.
(Histories from a dynastic and pro-Bourbon point of view.)

——. *The Last Medici.* London, Methuen, 1932; rev'd. edn., 1958.
(Covering the period 1642 to 1743.)

ADAMS, JOHN CLARKE and BARILE, PAOLO. *The Government of Republican Italy.* Boston, Houghton Mifflin, 1961.
(Gives an account of the constitutional changes as Italy in 1946 shifted from a kingdom to a republic.)

ALBRECHT-CARRIÉ, RENÉ. *Italy from Napoleon to Mussolini.* New York, Columbia University Press, 1950. Columbia Paperback, 1960
(Summary history until the rise of Fascism after World War I.)

ALFIERI, VITTORIO. *Memoirs* (anon. trans. revised by E. R. Vincent). London, Oxford University Press, 1961. A translation of *Vita,* first published in 1806; Asti, Casa d'Alfieri, 1951.

——. *Of Tyranny* (trans. Julius A. Molinaro and Beatrice Corrigan). University of Toronto Press, 1961. A translation of *Della tirannide;* first published in Italy in 1800; included in *Scritti politici e morali,* Asti, Casa d'Alfieri, 1951.

——. for an analysis of his work and its influence, See MEGARO.

AZEGLIO, MASSIMO D'. See D'AZEGLIO.

BARILE, PAOLO. See ADAMS, JOHN CLARKE.

BARR, STRINGFELLOW. *Mazzini, Portrait of an Exile.* New York, Henry Holt, 1935.

BEALES, DEREK. *England and Italy, 1859–1860.* London, Nelson, 1962.
(A study of English policy toward Italian unification in the crucial year.)

BECCARIA, CESARE. *Of Crimes and Punishments* (trans. Jane Grigson). London, Oxford University Press, 1964. A translation of *Dei delitti e delle pene;* first published in 1764; Milan, Rizzoli, 1950.
(One of the most influential books of the eighteenth century. In the English edition above it is published jointly with Manzoni's *The Column of Infamy,* but only the latter's title appears on the binding.)

BERKELEY, G. F.-H. & J. *Italy in the Making, 1 January 1848 to 16 November 1848.* Cambridge University Press, 1940.

BLAKISTON, NOEL. See RUSSELL, ODO.

BRANCACCIO DI CARPINO, F. *The Fight for Freedom: Palermo, 1860* (trans. John Parris). London, The Folio Society, 1968. A translation of *Tre Mesi nella Vicaria di Palermo nel 1860.*
(Patriotism among the young nobles of Palermo.)

CARBONE, GEORGE. "The Long Detour: Italy's Search for Unity," in *Studies in Modern European History in Honor of Franklin C. Palm,* pp. 49–80. New York, Bookman Associates, 1956.
(A discussion of Carlo Cattaneo's idea of a federation of Italian states rather than a unified kingdom under the House of Savoy.)

CAVOUR. ———. for his life, see THAYER, WHYTE and MARTINENGO CESA-
RESCO.
———. for his policy with regard to Garibaldi, see MACK SMITH.
CESARESCO. See MARTINENGO CESARESCO.
CLARK, W. G. See GALTON, FRANCIS.
CLOUGH, SHEPARD. *The Economic History of Modern Italy.* New York, Co-
lumbia University Press, 1964.
(Though the book's emphasis is on the period after the Risorgimento,
its opening chapters discuss the economic problems of unification.)
COLQUHOUN, ARCHIBALD. *Manzoni and his Times.* London, J. M. Dent, 1954.
(The chapter on life and thought in Milan before the French Revolu-
tion is especially good.)
CONNELLY, OWEN. *Napoleon's Satellite Kingdoms.* New York, Macmillan,
1965.
(Among the five kingdoms studied, two were in Italy: the Kingdom
of Italy in the Po valley and the Kingdom of Naples. There is also a
chapter on "The First War of Italian Independence" under Murat.)
CROCE, BENEDETTO. *History of Europe in the Nineteenth Century* (trans.
Henry Furst). New York, Harcourt Brace, 1933; Harbinger paperback,
1963.
(An "idealist" view of history with a favorable judgment on the
Risorgimento.)
DANDOLO, EMILIO. *The Italian Volunteers and Lombard Rifle Brigade, Being
and Authentic Narrative, 1848–1849.* London, Longmans, 1851. A trans-
lation of *I Volontari ed i Bersaglieri Lombardi;* first published Torino,
Ferrero e Franco, 1849.
DAVIS, JAMES CUSHMAN. *The Decline of the Venetian Nobility as a Ruling
Class.* Baltimore, Johns Hopkins Press, 1962, No. 2, Series LXXX of
Johns Hopkins University Studies in Historical and Political Science.
(A study of how a "closed" ruling class passed, and probably must
pass, out of power.)
D'AZEGLIO, MASSIMO. *Things I Remember* (trans. E. R. Vincent). London,
Oxford University Press, 1966. A translation of *I miei ricordi;* first pub-
lished posthumously, 1868. Milan, Feltrinelli, ed. Legnani, 1963.
For a biography, see MARSHALL.
DELZELL, CHARLES F. (ed.), *The Unification of Italy, 1859–1861. Cavour,
Mazzini or Garibaldi?* New York, Holt, Rinehart and Winston, 1965.
(One of the "European Problem Studies." Delzell gives extended quotations from historians of differing points of view in answer to such questions as "Cavour and Garibaldi: collaborators or rivals?" and "Cavour's
use of plebiscites: desirable or regrettable?" The pamphlet, 120 pp., has
an excellent "Suggestions for Further Reading.")
DE ROBERTO, FEDERICO. *The Viceroys* (trans. Archibald Colquhoun). London, MacGibbon & Kee, 1962. A translation of *I vicerè;* first published
in 1894; Milan, Garzanti, 1959.
(One of the first and great novels of the Risorgimento betrayed. Less
self-pitying than Lampedusa's *The Leopard,* wider in scope and centered
on a family in Catania rather than Palermo.)

DOLCI, DANILO. *Waste, An Eye-witness Report on some aspects of Waste in Western Sicily* (trans. R. Munroe). London, MacGibbon & Kee, 1963. A translation of *Spreco*. Turin, Einaudi, 1960.

(Much of the book consists of transcriptions of tape recordings made of Sicilians recounting their problems with a Mafia and with the government. Many of their words are very moving; their problems, very depressing, and very little different from what they were in Garibaldi's time.)

FERRERO, GUGLIELMO. *The Gamble, Bonaparte in Italy, 1796–1797* (trans. Bertha Pritchard and Lily C. Freeman). London, Bell, 1939, 1961. A translation of *Aventure;* Paris, Plon, 1936.

(Particularly interesting for its analysis of the politics of Napoleon's campaign and the attitude of the Italians to the French in Italy.)

FOGAZZARO, ANTONIO. *The Little World of the Past* (trans. W. J. Strachan). London, Oxford University Press, 1962. A translation of *Piccolo mondo antico;* first published in 1895.

(One of the great Italian novels. It tells of a young couple in alpine Lombardia in 1859, just before the war with Austria. They lose their child and have different responses to the tragedy, reflecting their different religious beliefs. One is liberal and freethinking; the other, Catholic.)

GALTON, FRANCIS (ed.). *Vacation Tourists in 1860*. London, Macmillan, 1861.

(Contains in pp. 1–75 the account by W. G. Clark, Tutor of Trinity College, and Public Orator, Cambridge, of what he saw of Naples and Garibaldi in 1860.)

GARIBALDI. For biographies or studies of particular aspects, see MACK SMITH, TREVELYAN and HIBBERT.

GERSCHENKRON, ALEXANDER. "Rosario Romeo and the Original Accumulation of Capital," an essay in *Economic Backwardness in Historical Perspective*, pp. 90–118. Cambridge, Mass. Harvard University Press, 1962.

GLADSTONE, WILLIAM E. *Two Letters to the Earl of Aberdeen on the State of Prosecutions of the Neapolitan Government*. New York, Nichols, 1851.

GOODWIN, A. (ed.). *The European Nobility in the Eighteenth Century*. London, Black, 1953.

(Contains an essay on the nobility of Lombardia by J. M. Roberts.)

GOZZI, CARLO. *Useless Memoirs of Carlo Gozzi* (trans. John Addington Symonds, revised by Philip Horne). London, Oxford University Press, 1962. A translation of *Memorie inutili di Carlo Gozzi;* first published in 1798; Bari, Laterza, 1910.

(A Venetian life extending from 1720 to 1798 when the author, though not dead, became silent. The emphasis falls on the theatrical world of Venice in the period 1750–75.)

GREENFIELD, KENT ROBERTS. *Economics and Liberalism in the Risorgimento, A Study of Nationalism in Lombardy, 1814–1848*. Baltimore, Johns Hopkins Press, 1934, 1965.

(A detailed analysis of agriculture, commerce and journalism undertaken to reveal the sources of the sudden and effective revolt of the Cinque Giornate.)

GREW, RAYMOND. *A Sterner Plan for Italian Unity, The Italian National Society in the Risorgimento*. Princeton University Press, 1963.

(A history of the society, its organization, work and decline, and also of the intellectual and social forces that gave rise to it.)

GRIFFITH, GWILYM O. *Mazzini: Prophet of Modern Europe*. London, Hodder and Stoughton, 1932. New York, Harcourt Brace, 1932.

HALES, E. E. Y. *Pio Nono, a Study in European Politics and Religion in the Nineteenth Century*. London, Eyre & Spottiswoode, 1954.

(Pro-clerical in point of view.)

————. *Mazzini and the Secret Societies*. London, Eyre & Spottiswoode, 1956.

(From his youth through 1836.)

————. *The Catholic Church in the Modern World, a Survey from the French Revolution to the Present*. London, Eyre & Spottiswoode, 1958.

————. *Revolution and Papacy, 1769–1846*. London, Eyre & Spottiswoode, 1960.

————. *Napoleon and the Pope, the Story of Napoleon and Pius VII*. London, Eyre & Spottiswoode, 1962. Published in the U.S.A. by Doubleday as *The Emperor and the Pope*.

HANCOCK, W. K. *Ricasoli and the Risorgimento in Tuscany*. London, Faber & Gwyer, 1926.

(One of the first books to examine the social and economic aspects of the Risorgimento, and also a delight to read.)

HENDERSON, NICHOLAS. *Prince Eugen of Savoy*. London, Wiedenfeld and Nicolson, 1964; New York, Frederick A. Praeger, 1965.

(Prince Eugene, the noblest member of the House of Savoy, led the Habsburg forces in Italy during the War of the Spanish Succession, and several chapters describe the war in Italy and how it affected the Italian states and their subjects.)

HERIOT, ANGUS. *The French in Italy, 1796–1799*. London, Chatto & Windus, 1957.

(The book is dense and without notes or a bibliography, but it gives a good picture of its subject.)

HIBBERT, CHRISTOPHER. *Garibaldi and His Enemies, the Clash of Arms and Personalities in the Making of Italy*. London, Longmans, 1965.

(A biography of the man on his return to Italy in 1848 and only indirectly concerned with the social, economic and spiritual sides of the movement.)

JEMOLO, ARTURO. *Church and State in Italy, 1850–1950* (trans. David Moore). Oxford, Blackwell, 1960.

(The translation is of an abridgement of *Chiesa e Stato in Italia negli ultimi cento anni;* Turin, Einaudi, 1948. The abridgement, which concentrated on the end of the period covered, was entitled *Chiesa e Stato in Italia dal Risorgimento ad oggi,* and published in 1955.)

KING, BOLTON. *A History of Italian Unity, 1814–1871*. 2 vols. London, Nisbet, 1898.

(The standard history for many years, by one of the early liberal historians emphasizing the political side of the movement.)

LAMPEDUSA, GIUSEPPE di. *The Leopard* (trans. Archibald Colquhoun). London, Collins, 1960; New York, Pantheon, 1960.

(A novel in which the author, a Sicilian aristocrat, through the person of his ancestor, regrets the Risorgimento. See DE ROBERTO.)

LEE, VERNON (VIOLET PAGET). *The Countess of Albany.* London, W. H. Allen, 1884.

(From her marriage in 1772 to "Bonnie Prince Charlie," the pretender to the British throne, until her death in 1824, she was a figure of her times and because of her connections with Alfieri and, later, Foscolo, she was present at the Risorgimento's early literary beginnings.)

————. *Studies of the Eighteenth Century in Italy.* London, 1881.

(Although the author's style, full of little judgments, is now out of fashion, her work is still an excellent evocation of Italian culture of the period. The "Studies" are on "The Arcadian Academy," "The Musical Life," "Metastasio and the Opera," "The Comedy of Masks" (Commedia dell'Arte), "Goldoni and the Realistic Comedy," "Carlo Gozzi and the Venetian Fairy Comedy."

LEOPARDI, GIACOMO. *Leopardi's "Canti"* (trans. John Humphreys Whitfield). Napoli, Scalabrini, 1962. First published individually from 1819 until his death in 1837 and posthumously; Milan, Mondadori, 1962.

(Probably the most successful translation of the *Canti,* with Italian text on opposite page.)

————. *Selected Prose and Poetry* (ed. and trans. Iris Origo and John Heath-Stubbs). London, Oxford University Press, 1966.

For a biography, see ORIGO.

LEWIS, NORMAN. *The Honoured Society, the Mafia Conspiracy Observed.* London, Collins, 1964.

(The Mafia from 1943 to 1963, giving a vivid and depressing picture of economic bondage in western Sicily, which differs little from what it was in Garibaldi's day.)

MACK SMITH, DENIS. *Cavour and Garibaldi 1860, a Study in Political Conflict.* Cambridge University Press, 1954.

————. *Garibaldi.* New York, Knopf, 1956; London, Hutchinson, 1957.

(A short life.)

————. *Italy, a Modern History.* Ann Arbor, University of Michigan Press, 1959.

(Covering the period 1861–1945)

————. Articles are: "Cavour's attitude to Garibaldi," *Cambridge Historical Journal,* 1949, p. 360. "The Peasants' Revolt in Sicily" (in English) in *Studi in Onore di Gino Luzzatto,* Vol. 3, 1950. "The Prehistory of Fascism," *Occidente,* 1954, p. 512. "Cavour and Parliament," *Cambridge Historical Journal,* 1957, p. 37. "Italy," *The New Cambridge Modern History,* Vol. X, 1830–70, 1960.

————. *A History of Sicily.* Vol. 1, Medieval Sicily, 800-1713; Vol. 2, Modern Sicily, After 1713. London, Chatto & Windus, 1968.

MANZONI, ALESSANDRO. (Trans. Archibald Colquhoun) *The Betrothed, a Tale of Seventeenth-Century Milan.* London, Dent, 1951; a translation of *I Promessi Sposi;* first published in 1827 and revised continually until republished definitively in installments in 1840–42; Milan, Casa del Manzoni, 1942.

————. For a biography see COLQUHOUN.

————. For critical studies on his language and on *I Promessi Sposi,* see REYNOLDS and WALL.

MARIO, JESSIE WHITE. *The Birth of Modern Italy, Posthumous Papers* (ed.

Duke of Liatta-Visconti-Arese). New York, Scribners, 1909.

(A passionate supporter of Garibaldi and an eyewitness of many events; but sometimes blinded by her prejudices.)

MARSHALL, RONALD. *Massimo d'Azeglio, An Artist in Politics, 1798–1866.* London, Oxford University Press, 1966.

MARTIN, GEORGE. *Verdi, His Music, Life and Times.* New York, Dodd, Mead, 1963.

(Patriotism in music. Verdi was possibly the greatest artist to emerge from the Risorgimento.)

MARTINENGO CESARESCO, EVELYN. *Cavour.* London, Macmillan, 1898.

(An excellent, short life of Cavour.)

MAZZINI, GIUSEPPE. *Mazzini's Letters* (trans. Alice DeR. Jervis). London, J. M. Dent, 1930.

————. For his life, see KING, GRIFFITH and BARR.

————. For his thought, see SALVEMINI.

McCLELLAN, GEORGE B. *Venice and Bonaparte,* Princeton University Press, 1931.

(An account of the last years of the Republic of Venice.)

MEGARO, GAUDENCE. *Vittorio Alfieri, Forerunner of Italian Nationalism.* New York, Columbia University Press, 1930. No. 336 of the Columbia University Studies in History, Economics and Public Law.

MILLER, ANNA. *Letters from Italy in 1770 and 1771.* 2 vols. London, Dilly, 2nd edn. 1777.

NEUFELD, MAURICE F. *Italy: School for Awakening Countries, the Italian Labor Movement in Its Political, Social, and Economic Setting from 1800 to 1960.* Ithaca, N.Y., Cornell University, 1961. No. 5 of Cornell International Industrial and Labor Relations Reports.

NICOLSON, HAROLD. *The Congress of Vienna.* London, Constable, 1946; paperback, University Paperbacks, 1961.

NOETHER, EMILIANA PASCA. *Seeds of Italian Nationalism, 1700–1815.* New York, Columbia University Press, 1951. No. 570 of the Columbia University "Studies in History, Economics and Public Law."

ORIGO, IRIS. *Leopardi, a Study in Solitude.* London, Hamish Hamilton, 1935; revised edn., 1953.

PACKE, MICHAEL ST. JOHN. *Orsini, the Story of a Conspirator.* Boston, Little, Brown, 1957. Published in England as *The Bombs of Orsini.* London, Secker and Warburg, 1957.

(Though Orsini is most famous for his conspiracy in Paris against Napoleon III, the book also gives an excellent picture of conspiratorial life in Italy during the preceding quarter-century.)

PELLICO, SILVIO. *My Prisons* (trans. I. G. Capaldi). London, Oxford University Press, 1963. A translation of *Le mie Prigioni;* first published in 1832; Milan, Mondadori, 1961.

PIO NONO. For biographies or studies of particular aspects, see HALES, RUSSELL and JEMOLO.

PIOZZI, HESTER LYNCH. *Observations and Reflections made in the course of a journey through France, Italy and Germany.* Dublin, Chamberlaine, etc., 1789.

RAMAGE, CRAUFURD TAIT. *Ramage in South Italy* (ed. Edith Clay). London, Longmans, 1965. An abridgement of *The Nooks and By-ways of Italy,*

*Wanderings in search of its ancient remains and modern superstitions;* first published in 1868.

(The time of Ramage's wandering was 1828, not long after the Carbonaro revolution, and he traversed Italy south of Naples, Calabria, Basilicata and Apulia. He spent more time talking to persons than visiting ruins, and some of the conversations reveal a great deal about the life of the time. Among others, he talked with the man who had been Murat's goaler and who gave a vivid account of the former king's execution.)

RATH, R. JOHN. *The Fall of the Napoleonic Kingdom of Italy (1814).* New York, Columbia University Press, 1941. No. 484 of the Columbia University Studies in History, Economics and Public Law.

REYNOLDS, BARBARA. *The Linguistic Writings of Alessandro Manzoni; a Textual and Chronological Reconstruction.* Cambridge, Heffers, 1950.

ROBERTSON, PRISCILLA. *Revolutions of 1848.* Princeton University Press, 1952; paperback, Harper Torchbook, 1960.

(The revolution discussed include those in France, Germany, Austria and Italy and those in Milan, Rome and Venice are discussed in detail.

ROMANI, GEORGE T. *The Neapolitan Revolution of 1820–1821.* Evanston, Ill., Northwestern Univ. Press, 1950. Northwestern University Studies, Social Studies Series No. 6.

RUSSELL, ODO. *The Roman Question, Extracts from the despatches of Odo Russell from Rome, 1858–1870* (ed. Noel Blakiston). London, Chapman and Hall, 1962.

SALOMONE, A. WILLIAM. "The *Risorgimento* between Ideology and History: the Political Myth of *Rivoluzione Mancata,*" in *The American Historical Review,* Vol. LXVIII, No. 1 (October 1962), pp. 38–56.

SALVADORI, MASSIMO. *Cavour and the Unification of Italy.* Princeton, D. Van Nostrand, 1961.

(An Anvil paperback. The history is very short, less than a hundred pages, and is followed by "Readings" which are documents of the Risorgimento or excerpts from other historians, some of which are interesting and hard to find elsewhere.)

SALVEMINI, GAETANO. *Mazzini* (trans. I. M. Rawson). London, Jonathan Cape, 1956.

(Not a life, but an analysis of Mazzini's thought.)

SENIOR, WILLIAM NASSAU. *Journals Kept in France and Italy from 1848 to 1852 with a Sketch of the Revolution of 1848* (ed. M. C. M. Simpson). 2 vols. London, King, 1871.

SHARP, SAMUEL. *Letters from Italy in the years 1765 and 1766.* London, Henry and Cave, 3rd edn. 1767.

SMITH, DENIS MACK. See MACK SMITH.

SMYTH, HOWARD McGAW. "The Armistice of Novara: a Legend of a Liberal King," in *The Journal of Modern History,* Vol. VII (1935), pp. 141–82.

———. "Piedmont and Prussia: The Influence of the Campaigns of 1848–49 on the Constitutional Development of Italy," in *The American Historical Review,* Vol. LV (April 1950), pp. 479–502.

STENDHAL. *Rome, Naples and Florence* (trans. Richard N. Coe). London, Calder, 1959.

(Stendhal traveled through Italy in 1816 and 1817 and visited many more cities than the three in his title.)

STILLMAN, W. J. *The Union of Italy, 1815–1895.* Cambridge University Press, 1909.

(Stillman was one of the first historians to suggest that the Risorgimento, somehow, had failed. His history contained an answer to this point in an epilogue written by Trevelyan who suggested that Stillman had hoped for too much and was too easily discouraged.)

THAYER, WILLIAM ROSCOE. *The Life and Times of Cavour.* 2 vols. Boston, Houghton Mifflin, 1911.

(Still the standard life in English. Written from a liberal, anticlerical point of view and exalting Cavour, particularly over Mazzini, more than might most historians today.)

———. *The Dawn of Italian Independence, Italy from the Congress of Vienna, 1814, to the fall of Venice, 1849.* 2 vols. Boston, Houghton Mifflin, 1892.

(An almost entirely political history.)

TREVELYAN, GEORGE MACAULAY. *Garibaldi's Defence of the Roman Republic (1848–9).* London, Longmans, 1907; new edn. 1949.

———. *Garibaldi and the Thousand (May 1860).* London, Longmans, 1909; new edn. 1948.

———. *Garibaldi and the Making of Italy (June–November 1860).* London, Longmans, 1911; new edn. 1948.

(This trilogy is the great work in English on Garibaldi, although presenting him only at his best. More recent historians have been able to add or to correct a fact here or there and, because treating the man's entire life, may give a better rounded picture of him. But probably no one yet has surpassed Trevelyan in presenting Garibaldi at his best in superb narrative history.)

———. *Manin and the Venetian Revolution of 1848.* London, Longmans, 1923.

———. Articles are: "Englishmen and Italians," *Clio, a Muse and Other Essays.* London, Longmans, 1913, 1949. The "Epilogue" in the revised edition of STILLMAN, W. J., *The Union of Italy, 1815–1895;* Cambridge University Press, 1909.

TREVES, GIULIANA ARTOM. *The Golden Ring, the Anglo-Florentines, 1847–1862* (trans. Sylvia Sprigge). London, Longmans Green, 1956.

(The Risorgimento as seen by such English living in Florence as the Brownings, W. S. Landor and Leigh Hunt.)

VERDI. See MARTIN.

VERGA, GIOVANNI. *Little Novels of Sicily* (trans. D. H. Lawrence). Oxford, Blackwell, 1925.

(Twelve stories about Sicilian peasants in Garibaldi's time. One, *Liberty,* is based on the revolutionary excesses at Bronte described in Chapter 41 of this book.)

———. *Cavalleria Rusticana* (trans. D. H. Lawrence). New York, Dial Press 1928.

(More stories, mostly of Sicilian peasants, of which *Rosso Malpelo,* perhaps, is a masterpiece.)

VISCONTI VENOSTA, GIOVANNI. *Memoirs of Youth, Things Seen and Known, 1847–1860* (trans. William Prall). Boston, Houghton Mifflin, 1914. A translation of *Ricordi di gioventù;* first published in 1900.

(Life in Milan during the Cinque Giornate and the period of depression following it through annexation to Sardinia. Also an account of a trip, in 1853, to Rome, Naples and Sicily.)

WALKER, D. S. *A Geography of Italy*. London, Methuen, 1958; new edn. 1967.

(Technical, but revealing much about how Italy developed and why.)

WALL, BERNARD. *Alessandro Manzoni*. New Haven, Yale University Press, 1954.

(A short book, 64 pages, of which much is a summary with comment on *I Promessi Sposi*. But the surrounding remarks are excellent, both on Manzoni and on his times.)

WEBSTER, CHARLES. *The Congress of Vienna*. London, British Foreign Office, 1919; recently, Thames and Hudson, 1963.

WHYTE, ARTHUR JAMES. *The Evolution of Modern Italy*. Oxford, Blackwell, 1944.

(A political history of the period 1715–1920 with emphasis on the post-Risorgimento years.)

———. *The Political Life and Letters of Cavour, 1848–1861*. Oxford, University Press, 1930; rep't'd. 1959.

———. *The Early Life and Letters of Cavour, 1810–1848*. Glasgow, Oxford University Press, 1925.

WOODWARD, E. L. *Three Studies in European Conservatism, Metternich, Guizot, the Catholic Church in the Nineteenth Century*. London, Constable, 1929; Cass, 1963.

(A harsh judgment on Pio Nono.)

# TABLES
# OF
# SUCCESSION

---

# THE HABSBURG-LORRAINE LINE
## (The Austrian Succession)

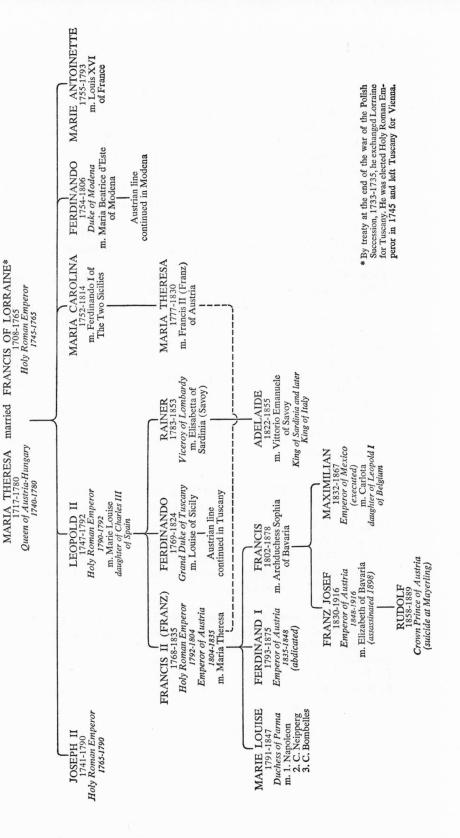

MARIA THERESA   married   FRANCIS OF LORRAINE*
1717-1780                                  1708-1765
*Queen of Austria-Hungary*              *Holy Roman Emperor*
*1740-1780*                              *1745-1765*

**JOSEPH II**
1741-1790
*Holy Roman Emperor*
*1765-1790*

**LEOPOLD II**
1747-1792
*Holy Roman Emperor*
*1790-1792*
m. Marie Louise
*daughter of Charles III*
*of Spain*

**MARIA CAROLINA**
1752-1814
m. Ferdinando I of
The Two Sicilies

**FERDINANDO**
1754-1806
*Duke of Modena*
m. Maria Beatrice d'Este
of Modena

Austrian line
continued in Modena

**MARIE ANTOINETTE**
1755-1793
m. Louis XVI
of France

**FRANCIS II (FRANZ)**
1768-1835
*Holy Roman Emperor*
*1792-1804*
*Emperor of Austria*
*1804-1835*
m. Maria Theresa

**FERDINANDO**
1769-1824
*Grand Duke of Tuscany*
m. Louise of Sicily

Austrian line
continued in Tuscany

**RAINER**
1783-1853
*Viceroy of Lombardy*
m. Elisabetta (Savoy)

**MARIA THERESA**
1777-1830
m. Francis II (Franz)
of Austria

**MARIE LOUISE**
1791-1847
*Duchess of Parma*
m. 1. Napoleon
   2. C. Neipperg
   3. C. Bombelles

**FERDINAND I**
1793-1875
*Emperor of Austria*
*1835-1848*
*(abdicated)*

**FRANCIS**
1802-1878
m. Archduchess Sophia
of Bavaria

**ADELAIDE**
1822-1855
m. Vittorio Emanuele
of Savoy
*King of Sardinia and later*
*King of Italy*

**FRANZ JOSEF**
1830-1916
*Emperor of Austria*
*1848-1916*
m. Elizabeth of Bavaria
*(assassinated 1898)*

**MAXIMILIAN**
1832-1867
*Emperor of Mexico*
*(executed)*
m. Carlota
*daughter of Leopold I*
*of Belgium*

**RUDOLF**
1858-1889
*Crown Prince of Austria*
*(suicide at Mayerling)*

* By treaty at the end of the war of the Polish
Succession, 1733-1735, he exchanged Lorraine
for Tuscany. He was elected Holy Roman Emperor in 1745 and left Tuscany for Vienna.

## HOUSE OF SAVOY

Vittorio Amedeo II                          1675–1730 (abdicated); died 1732
   became King of Sicily in 1713 and, exchanging Sicily for Sardinia,
   King of Sardinia in 1720.

Carlo Emanuele III                          1730–1773
Vittorio Amedeo III                         1773–1796
Carlo Emanuele IV                           1796–1802 (abdicated); died 1819
Vittorio Emanuele I                         1802–1821 (abdicated); died 1824
Carlo Felice                                1821–1831
   The last three kings, all sons of Vittorio Amedeo III, died without
   male heirs, and the succession passed to a cadet branch of the House,
   technically called Savoy-Carignano.

Carlo Alberto                               1831–1849 (abdicated); died 1849
Vittorio Emanuele II                        1849–1878
   became the first King of Italy in 1861 but continued to style himself
   Vittorio Emanuele *Second* in order to preserve the numbering of the
   Savoy line.

Umberto I                                   1878–1900 (assassinated)
Vittorio Emanuele III                       1900–1946 (abdicated); died 1947
   became Emperor of Ethiopia, 1936–1943, and King of Albania,
   1939–1943.

Umberto II                                  1946–1946 (abdicated)
   went into exile after the Italian people voted in a plebiscite, on
   2 June 1946, to replace the monarchy with a republican form of
   government.

## THE BOURBONS OF NAPLES
## THE KINGDOM OF THE TWO SICILIES

Carlo III di Borbone                        1734–1759 (abdicated); died 1788
   seized the kingdom from the Austrian Habsburgs and then left The
   Two Sicilies in order to succeed his half brother as King of Spain.
   His number, "the third," commonly used, refers to his position in
   the Spanish Bourbon line.

Ferdinando I                                1759–1825
   sometimes known as Ferdinando IV of Naples or, more rarely, as
   Ferdinando III of Sicily. During his reign Joseph Bonaparte was
   King of Naples, 1806–1808 and Joachim Murat, 1808–1815.

Francesco I                                 1825–1830
Ferdinando II                               1830–1859
Francesco II                                1859–1860 (deposed); died 1894

## DUCHY OF PARMA

| | |
|---|---|
| Filippo de Borbone | 1748–1765 |
| Ferdinando | 1765–1801 |
| Marie Louise | 1814–1847 |
| Carlo II | 1847–1849 (abdicated) |
| Carlo III | 1849–1854 (assassinated) |
| Roberto | 1854–1860 (deposed) |

The Regent for Roberto, a child throughout his reign, was his mother, Luisa Maria di Borbone. Note: All the dukes are Spanish Bourbons except for Marie Louise, who was Habsburg-Lorraine. Parma was part of France, 1801–1814.

## DUCHY OF MODENA

| | |
|---|---|
| Ercole III | 1780–1797 (deposed) |
| Francesco IV | 1814–1846 |
| Francesco V | 1846–1859 (deposed) |

Ercole III was the last of the male line of the d'Este family. On the Treaty of Campoformio, 1797, he lost his duchy, and on his death, 1803, his brother-in-law Ferdinand of Habsburg-Lorraine (d. 1806) became titular duke. Francesco IV was Ferdinand's son.

## GRAND DUCHY OF TUSCANY

Francis of Lorraine     1737–1765
    lived in Vienna and governed by foreign regents.
Leopoldo I     1765–1790 (abdicated); died 1792
    lived in Florence until, in 1790, he succeeded Joseph II as Holy Roman Emperor
Ferdinando III     1790–1824
Leopoldo II     1824–1859 (deposed); died 1870
    Note: The French deposed Ferdinando III in 1800 and absorbed Tuscany into France in 1807. In the interim, the Spanish Bourbons of Parma reigned in Tuscany as French dependents:
    Luigi (son of Ferdinando of Parma)     1801–1803
    Carlo (Carlo II of Parma)     1803–1807

## POPES

Clement XIII, 1758–1769

Clement XIV, 1769–1774 (suppressed the Jesuits)

Pius VI, 1775–1799 (died at Valence)

Pius VII, 1800–1823 (elected at Venice; taken prisoner by Napoleon, first to Savona and then to Fontainebleau; returned to Rome; revived the Jesuits.)

Leo XII, 1823–1829

Pius VIII, 1829–1830

Gregory XVI, 1831–1846

Pius IX, "Pio Nono," 1846–1878 (the "liberal" pope; forced to flee Rome; returned, supported by French troops; became in 1870 the first "prisoner of the Vatican.")

Leo XIII, 1878–1903

Note: *A pope's reign dates from his coronation, not from the instant of his predecessor's death or from his election.*

## PRIME MINISTERS OF THE KINGDOM OF ITALY

| | |
|---|---|
| Camillo di Cavour | January 1860 to June 1861 |
| Bettino Ricasoli | June 1861 to February 1862 |
| Urbano Rattazzi | March 1862 to December 1862 |
| Luigi Carlo Farini | December 1862 to March 1863 |
| Marco Minghetti | March 1863 to September 1864 |
| Alfonso La Marmora | September 1864 to June 1866 |
| Bettino Ricasoli | June 1866 to April 1867 |
| Urbano Rattazzi | April 1867 to October 1867 |
| Luigi Federico Menabrea | October 1867 to November 1869 |
| Giovanni Lanza | December 1869 to July 1873 |

# INDEX

Abba, Giuseppe Cesare, 1838–1901: in Garibaldi's Thousand, 542, 545, 549, 601; descriptions of Sicily quoted, 543-544, 557; description of attack on Bronte quoted, 558; at meeting of Garibaldi and Vittorio Emanuele, 619; on Garibaldi's last review, 624-625; on Garibaldi's departure, 629

Abruzzi: proclaims Garibaldi dictator, 596; civil war in, 657

Acquila, Luigi, Conte d', 1824–1897, uncle of Francesco II, 566

Acton, Harold, 1904–, cited, 127-128, 399

Acton, John, 1736?–1811, British diplomat in Naples, 44, 112, 113, 116-117; letters from Ruffo quoted, 121-122

Acton, John, 1834–1902, Catholic scholar, 678

Addams, Jane, 1860–1935, on Mazzini, quoted, 237

Adige river, 308, 310

*Alba*, journal, 264

Albani, Giovanni Francesco, Cardinal, 1649–1721, *see* Clement XI

Albani, Giovanni Francesco, Cardinal, 1720–1803, 135

Albany, Louisa Maximiliana Caroline Stuart, Countess of, 1753–1824, 55, 160, 163; letter from Foscolo quoted, 191

Alberoni, Giulio, Cardinal, 1664–1752, 12, 52

Albert, Prince Consort of Great Britain, 1819–1861, 485

Albrecht, Archduke of Austria, in war for Veneto, 690, 691

Alcamo, Sicily, 545

Alessandria: revolution attemptetd in, 202, 203; Austrian army in, 204; Mazzini plans revolt in, 242

Alexander I, Tsar of Russia, 1777–1825, 140, 149, 174, 185

Alexander II, Tsar of Russia, 1818–1881: letter to Franz Josef quoted, 432; protests against Garibaldi's Sicilian expedition, 551-552

Alfieri, Contessa, niece of Cavour, 651, 652

Alfieri, Vittorio Amedeo, Conte, 1749–1803, 53-59, 63, 427; interest in French Revolution, 67, 72, 73; Foscolo's play dedicated to, 95

Works. *Cleopatra*, 56; *Della tirannide*, 54, 57, 58; *Timoleone*, 121; *Vita*, quoted, 54

Alta Italia, Kingdom of, 321, 325, 327, 329

Altamura, captured by Ruffo, 120

Altifiumara, fort, 573-574

America, *see* United States

Ancona, 594, 595, 606

Annemasse, Ramorino attacks, 244

*L'Annessione*, newspaper, 560

*L'Antologia*, 220-221

Antonelli, Giacomo, Cardinal, 1806–1876: Secretary of State under Pius IX, 387, 401-403, 520; criticism of, 402; and civil marriage bill, 416; orders attack on Perugia, 500; warns Pius IX against alienating Napoleon III, 593; in negotiations on Rome as capital, 636; bribe offered to, 639, 640; on Ricasoli's proposals for Church, 696

Anviti, Luigi, Conte, murdered, 516

Arcola, battle of, 84

Artois, Charles Philippe, Comte d', *see* Charles X

Aspromonte, 575, 579; Garibaldi wounded in battle, 664-665

Austerlitz, battle of, 149

Austria: intellectual backwardness, 24; war against France, 75; war in Italy, 83, 91; Treaty of Campoformio, 91-92, 97-99; in coalition against France, 117, 140, 149; becomes Austrian Empire, 150; war with Napoleon, 167-168, 172, 180-181; Napoleon's partition of, 172

territory restored after fall of Napoleon, 182; treaty of alliance with Naples, 187; Italian territory after Congress Of Vienna, 187-190, map, 189; relations with Naples, 201-202; Italy ruled by, 204, 207-208, 212; government under Francis II and Metternich, 205-207

war with Italy, 1848, 307, 308, 310-313, 318-326; occupation of Italy, 329-330, 367; Sardinia resumes war, 341-343; Venice attacked, 368-374; Italian feeling against, after revolutions, 379-380; treaty with Sardinia, 384-386

in Crimean War, relations with Russia, 430-432; break with Russia, 432; in Congress of Paris, 449-454

prepares for war, 488-490; ultimatum to Sardinia, 490-491; war with Italy and France, 1859, 492-508, map, 495

protest against Garibaldi's Sicilian expedition, 541, 551-552; soldiers in Papal army, 593; war with Prussia possible, 687

offers Veneto in return for neutrality, 688; Veneto transferred to France by secret treaty, 688; war with Italy for Veneto, 688, 690-692, map, 689; peace treaty and cession of Veneto, 692-693

Avezzana, Giuseppe, 353

Azeglio, Massimo Taparelli, Marchese d', 1798–1866, 402, 407, 440, 484, 631, 640

early life, 256-257; as moderate, advises against rebellion, 256-257; interview with Carlo Alberto, 258; order of the day praising Pius IX, 313, quoted, 314

Prime Minister of Sardinia, 385, 386, 391;

Azeglio, Massimo Taparelli, Marchese d' (*Cont.*)
in Parliament, 412-414; attitude toward Cavour, 415, 417; and civil marriage bill, 416-417; ministry resigns, 417; popularity of, 420

on Law on the Convents, open letter quoted, 441; letter to Vittorio Emanuele (Spagna letter) quoted, 443-444; in Paris and London, 448; refuses to attend Congress of Paris, 449; on Austrian ultimatum, quoted, 490

in war of 1859, 501; on Cavour's order to abandon Romagna, quoted, 509-510; refuses arms to Garibaldi's expedition, 539

on civil war in Italy, quoted, 658; "Ulysses meeting Nausicaa," painting, 658; on Turin riots, 670; Taparelli his brother, 677; attitude on Roman Question, 707-708; death, 707

*Writings. Degli ultimi casi di Romagna,* 259; *I Lutti di Lombardia,* 277, 420, quoted, 278; *I miei ricordi,* quoted, 258; *La Politique et le droit chrétien,* 519-520; *Questioni urgenti,* 707; *Scritti,* quoted, 278, 314, 658

Azeglio, Roberto, Marchese d', 1789-1862, brother of Massimo, 284, 286, 384; wife of, quoted, 285-286

Bagnara, 575

Balbo, Cesare, Conte di Vinadio, 1789-1853: *Delle speranze d'Italia,* 262; *Il Risorgimento,* journal published with Cavour, 273; Vittorio Emanuele consults on ministry, 417

Bandiera, Attilio (1810-1844) and Emilio (1819-1844), revolution attempted, 248-249, 255, 349; Garibaldi's followers at tomb of, 601

Batavian Republic, 140

Bava, Eusebio, General, 1790-1854, 323, 324

Beauharnais, Eugène de, 1781-1824, viceroy of Kingdom of Italy, 148, 151, 156-157, 180

Beccarìa, Cesare, Marchese di, 1738-1794: with *Il Caffè,* 49, 50; *Dei delitti e delle pene,* quoted, 152-153

Belgiojoso, Lodovico, Conte, 1728-1801, 47, 52

Belgium, independence of, 233

Benedict XIV, Pope (Prospero Lambertini), 1675-1758, 34

Bentinck, Lord William, 1774-1839, 186, 281

Bergamo: in war with France, 90; volunteers from, with Garibaldi, 537

Bernini, Ferdinando, *Storia di Parma,* 263, quoted, 11, 39

Bernis, François de Pierre de, Cardinal, 1715-1794, 63

Bersaglieri, 345; in battle of Goito, 308; attack Garibaldi on Aspromonte, 664-665

Bersaglieri Lombardi, in defense of Rome, 353-355, 358, 359

Bertani, Agostino, 1812-1886, 557, 587; recruits for Garibaldi's army, 575-576; advice on annexation of Sicily, 584; in government of Naples, 602, 603; resigns, 606

Berthier, General Louis Alexandre, 1753-1815, conquest of Rome, 103-104

Bismarck, Otto Eduard Leopold von, 1815-1898: commercial treaty between Prussia and Italy, 687; Prussian-Italian alliance signed, 687; in war for Veneto, 688; preliminary peace with Austria, 692; in Franco-Prussian war, 715; Mazzini offers volunteers for war, 715

Bixio, Nino, 1821-1873, Garibaldi's lieutenant, 353; in Sicilian campaign, 543, 557, 558; in battle of Calatafimi, 544, 545; in capture of Palermo, 547; crossing of Strait of Messina, 577, 578; address at tomb of Bandiera brothers, 601; in Parliament when Garibaldi speaks, 645, 647

"Black cardinals," 175, 180

Bodoni, Giambattista, 1740-1813, printer, 38

Bologna, 64, 66; republic established, 85-86; Carbonaro revolution of 1831, 229, 230; United Italian Provinces established in, 234; provisional government in, 235, 237-238; captured by Austrians, 354; University professors will not swear allegiance to government, 669

Bonaparte, Joseph, 1768-1844, 79, 103; Grand Elector, 147; King of Naples, 151, 152, 157-158; King of Spain, 151

Bonaparte, Louis, 1778-1846, King of Holland, 151

Bonaparte, Lucien, 1775-1840, 133

Boncompagni di Mombello, Carlo, Conte di Samporo, 414

Bonnet, Nino, helps Garibaldi to escape, 365-366

Borjès, José, in service of Francesco II, 658

Bourbon dynasty: in Spain, 6; in Italy, 14, 15, 37; in War of the Polish Succession, 14, 15; after revolutions of 1848-1849, 382, 383, 396; hostility to Napoleon III, 552; disintegration of government, 565-567, 672-673

Braschi, Luigi, Duke, 1745-1816, 63, 65, 88

Brazil, Garibaldi in, 250

Breganze, Giacomo, advice on Mazzini's education, 214

Brescia, 90

Brigandage: civil war and, 668, 671-672; in modern times, 674

Britain: in War of the Spanish Succession, 6, 18; Mediterranean possessions, 7-8; wars with France, 18; Voltaire and Montesquieu admire, 18-19; war in Mediterranean area, 107; in coalition against France, 117, 149, 180

policy on Italy, 201; Reform Bill, 231; Roman Republic not recognized, 350; reforms praised by Cavour, 390; Bull of Restoration from Pius IX, 405; popular feeling against Pius IX, 405; commercial treaty with Sardinia, 407, 409

Crimean War, 429-432; Sardinian treaty of alliance, 437-440; loan to Sardinia, 438; Congress of Paris, 449-454

Austria favored in war with France and Italy, 485, 488, 489; "Italy for the Italians" policy, 516, 518, 521; program for unification of Italian states, 523, 524; policy on cession of Nice and Savoy to France, 527-528; protest against Garibaldi's Sicilian expedition, 541, 551; takes no action against Garibaldi, 552, 573

Russell's dispatch on united Italy, 623; Kingdom of Italy recognized, 652; Garibaldi's visit to, 682-686; neutral in war for Veneto, 688

Brofferio, Angelo, 1802-1866, 388, 461; on Cavour, quoted, 389; speech for Law on the Convents, quoted, 436-437; speech against Cavour, 456; *Liberi Comizi,* society, 533

Brondolo, Forte di, 369, 370

Bronte, Sicily, Garibaldi's forces capture, 558

Buol-Schauenstein, Karl Ferdinand, Count, 1797–1865, Austrian Minister for Foreign Affairs, 432; decree confiscating property of political exiles, 425-426; character of, 426-427; in Congress of Paris, 450, 452-454; and Franz Josef's tour of Italy, 461-464; Cavour's correspondence with, 463-464; on proposed war, quoted, 485; and Austrian ultimatum to Sardinia, 490

*Cacciatori delle Alpi,* Garibaldi's force, 501, 502, 642, 647
*Il Caffè,* journal, 49
Calabria: guerrilla war against Napoleon's rule, 157-158; Bandiera brothers attempt revolution, 248-249
Calatafimi, battle of, "Here we make Italy—or die," 544-545; monument to Garibaldi, 545, 732
Calderari (Braziers), 200
*Camorra,* underworld organization, 556, 672
Campoformio, see Treaty of Campoformio
Canova, Antonio, 1757–1822, 63
Cantù, Cesare, 1804–1895, on Cinque Giornate in Milan, quoted, 303, 323-325
Caprera, Garibaldi at, 460, 625, 641
Capua, 126; captured by Sardinian army, 622
Caracciolo, Francesco, Commodore, 113, 121; execution of, 125-126
Carafa, Ettore, execution of, 128
Carbonari, 199-200, 202, 203; enter Naples, 200; public whippings of, 203; as underground movement, 204; in Lombardo-Veneto, 207, 211; Pellico in, 209-211; uprising in Milan planned, 210; police action against, 210-211; secret societies encouraged by, 212; Mazzini joins, 213; revolution of 1831, 230-231; in Ravenna, persecuted, 230; new state as objective, 232; Mazzini disillusioned with, 236; *La Giovine Italia* compared with, 238, 239; Pius IX grants amnesty to rebels, 260; in parade honoring constitution, 286
Carducci, Giosué, 1835–1907, *Il Piemonte,* 268
Carlo, Prince of Capua, brother of Ferdinando II, 1811–1862, 227
Carlo II (Carlo Ludovico), Duke of Parma, 1799–1883, 274; in war with Austria, 308; abdication, 396
Carlo III, Duke of Parma, 1823–1854, 396; assassinated, 433
Carlo Alberto, King of Sardinia, 1798–1849: as regent for Carlo Felice, 203; Carbonaro leaders try to influence, 210; becomes King, 228; character of, 228
  in constitutional revolution of 1821, 228-229; Mazzini's Open Letter to, 229-230, 238; Mazzini's followers arrested, 240-241; Mazzini plans assassination, 241-242; Mazzini's expedition reported to, 243
  moderates attempt conciliation with, 257-258; Azeglio's interview with, 258; undecided on reforms, 267-268; refuses audience with deputation from Genoa, 283; Sardinian constitution granted, 284, 285, 386-387; reviews parade honoring constitution, 287
  in Milan revolution, 304, 305; proclamation to Lombardo-Veneto, *L'Italia farà da sè,* 307, 320, 321; in war with Austria, 307, 308, 310-312, 318-326; King of Alta Italia, 321, 327; attacked in Milan, 323-325; Garibaldi offers services to, 330

reaction against, after armistice, 331-332; negotiates with France for aid, 339-341; resumes war with Austria, 341-342; abdication, 342-343; death, 343
Carlo di Borbone (Don Carlos, Carlo III), 1716–1788, 12, 13; Duke of Parma, 12-14; in War of the Polish Succession, 14; King of the Two Sicilies, 14, 16, 281; Parma art treasures taken by, 15, 37; Church reform supported, 34; Naples University encouraged, 35-36; abdication, 40-41; King of Spain as Carlos III, 40-41; rules Naples in youth of Ferdinando I, 41, 42; treaty with Maria Theresa, 42
Carlo Emanuele III, King of Sardinia, Duke of Savoy, 1701–1773, 15, 28
Carlo Emanuele IV, King of Sardinia, 1751–1819, 115, 183
Carlo Felice, King of Sardinia, 1756–1831, 203-204, 228, 229; Mazzini exiled by, 235; Cavour imprisoned by, 268
Carlos II, King of Spain, Naples, Sicily, and Duke of Milan, 1661–1700, 3-5
Carnot, Lazare, 1753–1823, 146
Carrara, appeal for annexation to Sardinia, 479, 481
Casanova, Giovanni Giacomo, 1725–1798, 27, 38
Casati, Gabrio, Conte, 1798–1873, 332; in Milan revolution, 299-301, 304
Caserta, Vittorio Emanuele fails to attend review at, 624
Cassano, rebellion against Napoleon, 157-158
Castelfiardo, battle of, 595, 596
Castellani, Venetian faction, 280
Castellazzo, Luigi, and code of Mazzini's National Italian Committee, 421-422
Castelli, Michelangelo, 1810–1875, 332, 652; on opposition to Cavour, quoted, 272-273; begs Cavour not to desert cause, 489-490
Castiglia, Gaetano, arrested in Milan, 210
Catholic Church, see Roman Catholic Church
Cattaneo, Carlo, 1801–1869: in Milan revolution, 299-300, 304, 306; United States of Italy as objective, 312; idea of federation used in 1946 constitution, 671
Cavaignac, Louis Eugène, General, 1802–1857, 340, 381
Cavour, Camillo Benso, Conte di, 1801–1861, 273, 381, 384, 385
  early life, 268-272; liberalism, 268-271; farms, 271, 272; love affair, 271; organizations founded by, 272; Radicals oppose, 272; Sardinian constitution demanded, 283; as journalist, 286; nephew killed in battle, 332, 652; on renewal of war with Austria, quoted, 341
  in Parliament of Sardinia, 388-390; speech on Siccardi Laws, 388-390, quoted, 390; Minister of Commerce and Agriculture, 391; Minister of the Navy and Minister of Finance, 407; economic revolution in Sardinia, 407-409; commercial treaties, 407-408; in reorganization of Parliament, *Connubio,* 412-414; resigns from ministry, 414-415; Azeglio's attitude toward, 415, 417; travels in Britain and France, 415
  as Prime Minister, 417-418; popular attitude toward, 420, 427, 446-447; protests confiscation of property of political exiles, 425-426
  in Crimean War: asks for Sardinian par-

Cavour, Camillo Benso, Conte di (*Cont.*)
ticipation, 428-432; treaty of alliance with
France and Britain, 437-440

and Law on the Convents: negotiations
with Pius IX, 435; law in Parliament, 435,
436, 441-442, 444; Church documents circulated, 438; "Bishops' bribe," 442

in Paris and London, 448-449, 455; in
Congress of Paris, 449-456; speech on Congress to Chamber of Deputies, quoted, 455-
456

reactions to, after Congress, 456-458, 470;
Buol's correspondence with, 463-464; Mazzini's followers disapprove of, 464-465; cannot arrest Mazzini, 468; La Farina's contacts with, 469; on attempted assassination
of Napoleon III, 472-473; reply to Walewski
on demand for action against radicals, quoted,
474; laws on penalties for conspiracy and
revised jury system, 474, 476-477; Mazzini's
attack on, quoted, 477-478; hatred of Mazzini, 478

interview with Napoleon III on French alliance in war with Austria, 478-480; prepares for war, 481-485, 487-491; King's
speech, *grido di dolore*, written, 483-484;
nervous collapse, 489-490; receives Austrian
ultimatum, 490-491

urges Francesco II to form alliance against
Austria, 494; with Napoleon III, discussions,
499, 503; learns of peace arranged by Napoleon III, 504-505; protests against peace
treaty, 505-508; resigns, 506; interview
quoted, 508; resists treaty of Villafranca,
509-510; in retirement at Leri, 510; hopes
for unity of Italy, 521

recalled to office, 522; program for union
of states with Sardinia, 522-524; policy on
cession of Nice and Savoy, 522-524; signs
treaty ceding Nice and Savoy to France,
528; excommunicated for efforts toward
union of states, 528; defends his policies in
Parliament, 530-531; foreign governments
protest to, 551-552; advises Vittorio Emanuele on letter to Francesco II, 554; in annexation of Sicily, 559-562

plan for invasion of Papal States, 576-
577, 581-582; letter from Prince Napoléon
quoted, 577; in invasion of Papal States, 590,
593-595; Pius IX criticizes in allocution, 596

Pallavicino interviews him on Garibaldi,
605-606; annexation of states to Sardinia,
bill introduced, 606-607; speech on passage
of bill, quoted, 609-610; Rome declared capital of Italy, 610-611; on Venice in united
Italy, 611; diplomatic actions on Vittorio
Emanuele's march through Naples, 617-618;
arrangements for meeting of Vittorio Emanuele and Garibaldi, 618; reaction to Russell's
dispatch, 623

appointments in united government, 629-
630; parliamentary government established,
632-633; resigns, is reappointed Prime Minister, 634-635; Roman Question, negotiations on, 635-641; speech on Rome, quoted,
637-638; last speech, quoted, 650-651; illness, 650-651; death, 652; burial, 652

a loss to Italy, 654-655; constitutional government according to his ideas, 659; plan
for division of Italy into regional units, 668;
criticism of Azeglio's views, 707

*Personal.* appearance and character, 273,
389; bust of, by Vela, 456; devious methods, 582; as monarchist, 458; Verdi admires,
655-656

comments on: by Manin, 464-465; by
Metternich, 456; by Pallavicino, 464

*Relations with Garibaldi.* Garibaldi's interview with, 460-461; Garibaldi's *Cacciatori
degli Alpi* organized, 501; Garibaldi blames
him for cession of Nice, 528, 530; Garibaldi's Sicilian expedition, 532, 535, 538-
540; Garibaldi sees him as obstacle, 534,
538; Garibaldi's advance toward Rome, position on, 570-573, 575-577; Garibaldi demands his dismissal, 597-598, 604; letters
on Garibaldi quoted, 598-599; tries to stop
Garibaldi's advance on Rome, 599; failure
of attempts at conciliation, 605-606; threat
of civil war as his victory over Garibaldi,
606; reference to Garibaldi in speech on annexation bill, 609; Garibaldi blames him for
Vittorio Emanuele's insult at Caserta, 624;
Garibaldi's army disbanded, 642-643; Garibaldi's speech against him, 645-650; reconciliation attempted, 650; Italian attitude toward both, 681

*Writings and publications,* 274; letters
quoted, 269-270, 341, 572, 581, 598-599,
618, 635; *Discorsi,* quoted, 390, 414, 455-
456, 618, 638, 648, 651; *Il Risorgimento,*
273

Cavour, Gustavo Benso, Conte di, elder brother
of Camillo, 436

Celestine V, Pope, 1215-1296, 317

Centurioni (formerly Sanfedisti), 255

Championnet, Jean Etienne, General, 1762-
1800, 111, 114, 120-121

Charles VI, Holy Roman Emperor, 1685-1740,
6-8, 11, 14, 97; rule of Italy, 9; duchies of
Parma and Milan ceded to, 15; death, 15;
Pragmatic Sanction, 47

Charles X, King of France (Comte d'Artois),
1757-1836, 78, 231, 554

Charybdis, whirlpool, 568, 579

Chateaubriand, François René, Vicomte de,
1768-1848, 145, 154

Chiodo, General, successor of Gioberti as Prime
Minister, 338

Christian Army of the Holy Faith (Sanfedisti),
118-119

Chrzanowski, Wojciech, General, 341, 342

Cialdini, Enrico, General, 1811-1892: presents
Cavour's plan to Napoleon III, 581; in invasion of Papal States, 595; meets Garibaldi
at Teano, 620; Garibaldi's command transferred to, 622; open letter criticizing Garibaldi, 649-650; sends troops against Garibaldi, 664; in war for Veneto, 690, 691; opposes Lanza's budget bill, 713, 714

Cimarosa, Domenico, 1749-1801, 129

Cipriani, Leonato, Conte, 1812-1888, Governor-general of Romagna, 510, 515

Cisalpine Republic, 85, 97, 102, 141; constitution under Napoleon, 143-144; becomes
Italian Republic, 144, 149

Cispadane Republic, 85, 86, 89, 90, 92, 97

Civil marriage bill: in Sardinia, 416-418; in
Italy, 680

*La Civiltà cattolica,* 677

Clarendon, George Villiers, Earl of, 1800-1870:
in Congress of Paris, 450-454; speech against
Austria, 453-454; on Buol's blunder, 464;
on British policy toward Italy, 527; letter

to Napoleon III on Garibaldi in England, 684

Clark, W. G.: Garibaldi's entry into Naples, description quoted, 586, 588-589; on decline in Garibaldi's popularity, quoted, 603

Clement XI, Pope (Giovanni Francesco Albani), 1649-1721, 23

Clement XII, Pope (Lorenzo Corsini), 1652-1740, 11

Clement XIV, Pope (Lorenzo Ganganelli), 1705-1774, 60, 63

Clotilde, daughter of Vittorio Emanuele II, 1843-1911, marriage with Prince Napoléon (Plon-Plon), 478, 480, 482, 484, 491

Cobden, Richard, 1804-1865, in Venice, 265

Collegno, Marchese di, aide-de-camp of Carlo Alberto, 228-229

Communications: time required for, 276-277; telegraph, 494

*Il Conciliatore,* 208-209, 210, 220

Confalonieri, Federico, Conte, 1785-1846, 220; arrested and imprisoned, 208-211; funeral, 266

Confalonieri, Teresa, Contessa, 1787-1830: intercedes for her husband, 211; brother of, 299

Congress of Italian Scientists, 265

Congress of Paris, 449-456

Congress of Reggio, 86-87

Congress of Vienna: treaties, 182, 184-185; Austrian territory in Italy established, 187-190, map, 189

Conneau, Henri, 1803-1877, physician, intermediary between Napoleon III and Cavour, 451-452, 478

*Connubio* in Sardinian Parliament, 414, 477

Consalvi, Ercole, Cardinal, 1757-1824, 136, 138, 164, 181, 224; Napoleon expels, 175; at Congress of Vienna, 184, 188, 195, 196; letter to Pacca quoted, 188

Constitution of Italy: suggested, 51; Sardinian *Statuto* as basis of, 286, 658-659; 1946, regional divisions, 670-671

Copernicus, Nicolaus, 1473-1543, *De Revolutionibus,* on Index until 1835, 678

Corsica, 79, 237

Corte, Celestino, in battle of Goito and capture of Rome, 308

Cosenz, Enrico, 1812-1898: General in Garibaldi's army, 565; crosses Strait of Messina, 579; in advance on Naples, 580, 587; advice on annexation of Sicily, 584

Cosenza, 382, 400

Cotrone, captured by Ruffo, 119

Council of Italy, Vienna, 48, 50

Courier, Paul-Louis, 1773-1825, letters quoted, 157-158

Cowley, Henry, Lord, 1804-1884, 489

*Crepuscolo,* periodical, 395, 464

Crimean War, 428-430; Sardinian treaty of alliance with France and Britain, 437-440; Sardinian expedition, 446-447; Congress of Paris after, 449-456

Crispi, Francesco, 1819-1901: Garibaldi's political advisor, 559-561, 602; secretary to Garibaldi, 561; prepares for plebiscite on annexation of Sicily, 561-563; Prime Minister of Italy, 1895, 562; in government of Naples, 609; argument with Pallavicino, 612-615; resigns, 615; in Parliament when Garibaldi speaks, 645, 646; diary quoted, 701

Croce, Benedetto, 1866-1952: cited, 657; on

Risorgimento, quoted, 722

Cuoco, Vicenzo, 1770-1823, 129-130

Custoza: battle of, 1848, 322; battle of, 1866, 691

Dabormida, Giuseppe, Conte, 1799-1869, Minister of Foreign Affairs in Sardinia, 510, 522

Dall' Ongara, Francesco, 1808-1873, biography of Ricasoli, cited, 527

Damas, Comte Roger de, General, 1765-1823, 110, 111

Dandolo, Emilio, 1830-1857: banished from Rome, 461; death and funeral, 485-487
  *I Volontari ed i Bersaglieri Lombardi,* 359, quoted, 355, 358-359

Dante Alighieri, 1265-1321, 261, 317, 640, 721; quotation from, on bust of Cavour, 456

Da Ponte, Lorenzo, 1749-1838, quoted, 98

David, Jacques Louis, 1748-1825, 63

Declaration of Human Rights, French, 72

Depretis, Agostino, 1813-1887, 633; pro-dictator of Sicily, 584; advice to Garibaldi on annexation of Sicily, 584-585; resigns in dispute over annexation, 601

Despuig, Monsignor, Spanish envoy, 136

Diderot, Denis, 1713-1784, *Encyclopédie,* 23-24

Doblhoff, Baron, in Vienna, 291

Dolfi, Giuseppe, 1818-1869, political leader in Florence, 514

Döllinger, Ignaz von, 1799-1890, 404, 709; speeches on Church, 676-677

Dunant, Jean Henri, 1828-1910, founder of Red Cross, 502

Durando, Giacomo, General, 1807-1894, 441; speech on Crimean War, quoted, 439-440

Durando, Giovanni, General, 1804-1869, 313, 314

Economic problems: poverty as cause of crime, 671-672; reclamation projects suggested, 672; emigration as answer to poverty, 673; program after World War II, 673-674; taxes and finance, 710-712

Edict of Nantes, revocation of, 19

Edward, Prince of Wales, later Edward VII, 1841-1910, praises Garibaldi, 685-686

1848 revolutions, see Revolutions of 1848

Einaudi, Luigi, on emigration, quoted, 673

Elisabetta, Queen of Spain (Elisabetta Farnese, wife of Philip V), 1692-1766, 11-13, 15, 16, 41, 52

Elizabeth, Empress of Austria, wife of Franz Josef, 1837-1898, 462

Ely, Marchioness of, represents England at birth of French Imperial child, 452

Emilia: formed by joining Romagna, Modena, and Parma, 515; offers to unite with Sardinia, 515-516; Defensive League with Tuscany, 516-517; union with Sardinia, negotiations on, 522-523; plebiscite, 524-527

*Encyclopédie,* 23-24

Enghien, Louis, Duc d', 1772-1804, 145

England, see Britain

Espinasse, Charles Marie Esprit, General, 1815-1859, 473

Este, Ercole III, Duke of Modena, 1727-1803, 84

Este, Rinaldo d', Duke of Modena, 1655-1737, 11

Etna, Mount, 557, 558

Etruria, Kingdom of, 140-141

Eugene, Prince of Savoy, 1663–1736, 5
Eugénie, Empress of the French, 1826–1920: marriage, 418; birth of her son, 452, 453; assassination attempted, 472; opposes war with Austria, 482, 503; flees to England, 716
Eugenio Emanuele, Prince of Carignano, 1816–1888, 515

Fabbri, Edoardo, Conte, 1778–1853, 333
Fanti, Manfredo, General, 1808–1865: leads attempted invasion of Papal States, 517; commands invasion of Papal States, 590; dislikes Garibaldi, 618; Garibaldi's command transferred to, 622; with Vittorio Emanuele, 624; in army of united Italy, 629–630; Garibaldi's army disbanded, 642–643; in Parliament when Garibaldi speaks, 644–647
Farini, Luigi Carlo, 1812–1866: on Pius IX, quoted, 316; on papal government, letter to Gladstone quoted, 403; correspondence with Cavour, 509; dictator of Modena, 510; requests union of Modena and Parma with Sardinia, 515; plebiscite arranged, 524; opposes Bertani's volunteers for Garibaldi, 576, 577; presents Cavour's plan to Napoleon III, 581; Cavour's letters to, on meeting of Vittorio Emanuele and Garibaldi, quoted, 618, 624; takes civil government from Garibaldi, 624; in government of united Italy, 629–630; unsympathetic with Neapolitans, letter quoted, 630; Prime Minister, appointment, 667; resignation and death, 668
Farnese, Antonio, Duke of Parma, 1679–1731, 11-13
Farnese, Elisabetta, *see* Elisabetta, Queen of Spain
Farnese, Enrichetta d'Este, wife of Antonio Farnese, 11, 13
Farnese, Francesco, Duke of Parma, 1678–1728, 11
Faro, Sicily, 573, 577
Ferdinand I, Emperor of Austria, 1793–1875, 224, 275, 305; in student revolt, 290, 292; constitution of Lombardo-Veneto granted, 295; letter from Pius IX quoted, 315; flees to Innsbruck, 319; offers peace terms to Carlo Alberto, 319; pardons rebels in Lombardo-Veneto, 329; abdication, 338-339
Ferdinand VI, King of Spain, 1713–1759, 40
Ferdinando, Duke of Genoa, son of Carlo Alberto, 1822–1855: in war with Austria, 311, 322, 325; death, 440
Ferdinando, son of Leopoldo II of Tuscany, 513
Ferdinando I, Duke of Parma, 1751–1802, 39, 140
Ferdinando I, King of the Two Sicilies, 1751–1805: youth, 41-42; marriage, 42; dominated by his wife, 43-44; in coalition against France, 73; in war between France and Italy, 80; Nelson aided by, 107-108; welcomes Nelson, 109; Nelson advises, 110, 112-113, 116; attack on Rome, 110-111; declares war on France, 112; flight to Palermo, 112-114, 116; returns to Naples, 117; orders to Ruffo, 121, 122; burial of Caracciolo ordered, 126; in festivities honoring Nelson and Hamiltons, 126-127; decline of Naples under his rule, 129-130; signs Treaty of Florence, 140; agreements with Napoleon, 141; exiled to Sicily, 151
   restored to kingdom, 186, 187; marries his mistress, 187; treaty of alliance with Austria, 187; problems of restored government, 198-200; appoints his son Francesco as vicar-general, 200-201; at Laibach conference, 201-202; Metternich's comment on, 203; death, 224-225
Ferdinando II, King of the Two Sicilies, 1810–1859, 225-228; government begins, 225-226; marriage, first, 226, second, 227-228; relations with his brothers, 227; revolt suppressed, 248, 275; constitutions of Naples and Sicily granted, 281, 282, 285; in war with Austria, 308, 320-321; offers palace to Pius IX, 336; rules without constitution, 336-337, 367, 382
   called *Bomba*, 381; recovers Sicily, 381-382; constitutional government abolished, 382; Gladstone accuses him of injustice and tyranny, 397-399; fear and distrust of people, 399-400; Clarendon criticizes, 454; assassination attempted, 465, 603; learns of Mazzini's expedition to Sapri, 466; death, 493-494
Ferdinando III, Grand Duke of Tuscany, 1769–1824, 73, 188
Fesch, Joseph, Cardinal, 1763–1839, letter from Napoleon quoted, 154
Feudalism, 27-29, 47-48; abolished, 72-74
Filangieri, Carlo, General, 1784–1867, 382
Filangieri, Gaetano, 1752–1788, 35
Filippo di Borbone, Duke of Parma, 12, 16; reforms supported by, 37-39; death, 39
Flags: Cispadane Republic, red, white, and green, 86-87; Italian Legion at Montevideo, 254; of Mazzini's followers, motto on, 242-243; of Carlo Alberto's troops in 1848, shield of Savoy on tricolor, 311; of Naples, Bourbon lilies, 382; Garibaldi's banner in Sicily, 542
Florence: Guerrazzi, dictator, overthrown, 346-348; anti-Austrian feeling, 379-380; capital of Italy transferred to, 669-670
Floridia, Sicily, report on voting problems quoted, 562
Foote, Captain Edward James, 1767–1833, 122-124
Foscolo, Ugo, 1778–1827, 94-95, 159; opposes Napoleon, 159-163; Garibaldi admires, 161, 251, 683, 731; conspires to keep Kingdom of Italy as republic, 182; exiled, 190-191; letter to Countess of Albany quoted, 191; Mazzini influenced by, 213, 214; Leopardi compared with, 217; languages spoken by, 221; Garibaldi lays wreath on his tomb, 685; buried in Santa Croce, Florence, 727
   *Writings. Dei Sepolcri*, 160-162, 368, 456, 685; Garibaldi quotes, 251, 683; *Ultime lettere di Jacopo Ortis*, 159, 223
France: Lorraine ceded to, 15; wars with England, 18; intellectual development and social criticism, 18-19; religious problems, 19; Church in, 65
   Revolution, *see* French Revolution; National Assembly, 67-70; States General, 67; coalition against, 73, 78; constitution, 73; laws, 74-75, 134, 146; war against Austria and Prussia, 75; National Convention, 75-76
   Directory, 76-77; in Napoleon's Italian campaign, 81, 82, 86-89, 99; as dictatorship, 101-102; campaign against Rome, 101-104; Consulate, 77, 133-134, 144-145
   war in Italy (Napoleon's campaigns), 78-100; conquest of Italy, 101-107; Ferdinando I at war with, 110-112; England leads coali-

tion against, 117; Church and State separated, 142; reaction against, after fall of Napoleon, 195-198
  revolution of 1830, 233; revolution of 1848, 288-290; Italian distrust of, 307; Sardinia seeks alliance with, 339-340; Paris riots, 1848, 340; Louis Napoleon becomes President, 340-341; Roman Republic not recognized, 350, 351
  attack on Rome, 352-354, 357-361; commercial treaty with Sardinia, 407, 409; Louis Napoleon's *coup d'état* of 2 December 1851, 410-412; Louis Napoleon becomes Emperor as Napoleon III, 418-419
  in Crimean War, 429, 431; Sardinian treaty of alliance, 437-440
  war with Austria in Italy, 492-508, map, 495
  Garibaldi's Sicilian expedition, reaction to, 541; Francesco II asks for aid, 552-553, 555; aids Papal States in invasion, 593, 595; in war for Veneto, 688
  army withdrawn from Rome, 694, 695; *Legion d'Antibes* for defense of Papal State, 698, 702; army ordered back to Rome, 701, 705; Franco-Prussian war, 714-716; Second Empire ends, Third Republic declared, 716-717
Francesco I, King of the Two Sicilies, 1777–1830: vicar-general of Ferdinando I, 201, 202; as King, 225
Francesco II, King of the Two Sicilies, 1836–1894: birth, 226; becomes King, 494; and Garibaldi's Sicilian campaign, 549, 566; foreign governments refuse to help, 551-552; asks Napoleon III for aid, 552-553, 555; letter from Vittorio Emanuele quoted, 553-554; seeks alliance with Sardinia, 555; constitutional government revived, 555-556; character of, 556
  Cavour sets conditions for abandoning Sicily, 572; abdication recommended, 579; leaves Naples, 585-586; troops at Capua, 596, 602; battle of the Volturno, importance of, 608; protests against Sardinian invasion of Naples, 617; government in exile, 632, 634, 672-673; civil war incited, 657-658
Francesco IV, Duke of Modena, 1779–1846, 188; as King of united Italy, proposed, 233-234; Parma territory ceded to, 274
Francesco V, Duke of Modena, 1819–1875, 264, 308, 396
Francis I, Holy Roman Emperor, 1708–1765, 15, 16
Francis II, last Holy Roman Emperor, 1768–1835, 107, 110, 203; in coalitions against France, 73, 149; in war with Italy, 80, 81, 86, 91, 96; in Treaty of Campoformio, 97-99; refuses to return papal territories, 136; and Pius VII, 138-139; in Treaty of Lunéville, 140; Emperor of Austria, title adopted, 150-151
  war with Napoleon, 167-168, 172; Marie Louise, daughter, marries Napoleon, 174-175; territory restored after fall of Napoleon, 182; forbids Maria Carolina to enter Vienna, 186
  King of Lombardo-Veneto, 188, 204, 207; Italian opinions of, 190; in government of Italy, 204, 207-208, 211; character and opinions, 204-207; Contessa Confalonieri intercedes with, 211; censorship encouraged, 220; death, 224

Franco-Prussian war, 714-716
Fransoni, Luigi, Archbishop of Turin, 390-391
Franz, Kaiser, *see* Francis II
Franz Josef, Emperor of Austria, 1830–1916, 342; becomes Emperor, 338-339; character of, 392-393; Italy ruled by, 392-393; visits Lombardia, 396; approves of Napoleon III, 411; becomes absolute monarch, 411; suggests that Vittorio Emanuele renounce constitution, 412; punishment of Mazzini's followers, 422-424, 426; orders confiscation of property of political exiles, 425; becomes his own Prime Minister, 426
  in Crimean War, negotiations with Nicholas I, 431-432; treaty with France and Britain, 433; letter from Alexander II quoted, 432; in Congress of Paris as mediator, 449
  tour of Italy, 461-463; policies antagonize Italians, 464; and Austrian ultimatum to Sardinia, 490
  in war with Italy, 1859, 493, 494; at battle of Solferino, 502-503; peace treaty (Treaty of Zurich), 503-506; discontent in Austrian Empire, 519; withdraws from proposed congress on Treaty of Zurich, 520-521
  protests against Garibaldi's Sicilian expedition, 551-552; aid to Pius IX in invasion of Papal States, 593, 595; Warsaw meeting, 608, 610, 617; rejects Italian offer to buy Veneto, 687
*Fratelli d'Italia*, patriotic hymn by Mameli, 286, 353; in Verdi's *Inno delle Nazioni*, 655
Freemasonry, 22-23, 44, 199
French Revolution: public reaction to, 53, 67; confiscation of Church property, 67-70; Declaration of Human Rights, 72; four periods of, 72-77; feudalism abolished, 72-74; new laws, 74-75; National Convention (Reign of Terror), 75-76; Directory, 76-77; Consulate, 77; in Metternich's philosophy of government, 205-207
Frugoni, Carlo, poet, 1692–1768, 38

Gaeta, 126; Pius IX in, 336; Napoleon III intervenes in Sardinian action at, 622, 634
Gaisruck, Archbishop of Milan, later Cardinal, 204, 259-260, 267
Galiani, Ferdinando, 1728–1787, 35
Galileo Galilei, 1564–1642, 20-22; *Dialogue of the Two Greatest Systems of the World*, on Index until 1835, 404, 678
Gallo, Marzio Mastrilli, Marchese di, 1753–1833, 110
Galotti, General, at Reggio, 578-579
Garibaldi, Anita, ca. 1821–1849: Garibaldi meets, 251-253; appearance, 252; marriage, 253; in Brazilian battles, 253-254; returns to Italy, 275; joins her husband, 330; in retreat from Rome, 362, 364, 365; death and burial, 365-366, 732
Garibaldi, Giuseppe, 1807–1882
  joins La Giovine Italia, 245; naval service, 245-246; in Genoa conspiracy, 245-246; sentenced to death *in absentia*, 246
  in South America, 250-255; in Brazilian rebellion, 250; tortured by Argentine dictator, 251; shipwrecked, 251; meets Anita, 251-254; marriage, 253; Italian Legion in Montevideo, 254-255, 275; offers aid to Pius IX, 263; leaves for Italy, 275
  1848–1849: returns to Italy, 330; offers services to Carlo Alberto, 330; in service of

Garibaldi, Giuseppe (*Cont.*)
  Milan, 331; proclamation quoted, 331; in Constituent Assembly, 349, 353; defense of Rome, 353-355, 357-359; escape from Austrians, 365-366, map, 363; retreat from Rome, 361-366, map, 363; in Sicily, 382
  in Caprera, 460; as follower of Manin, 460-461; Cavour's interview with, 460-461; refuses to join Mazzini's expedition to Sapri, 465; joins *Società Nazionale Italiana*, 470; accepts command of volunteers in war with Austria, 481
  campaign against Austrians, 1859, 501-502; welcomed by crowds, Visconti Venosta's description, 501-502; in Defensive League of Emilia and Tuscany, 516-517; manifesto praising Vittorio Emanuele, 517; asks if Nice will be ceded to France, 522; angry with Cavour for cession of Nice, 528, 530
  Sicilian expedition, 1860, 532-550, map, 543; Mazzini proposes expedition, 532-533; refuses to lead Sicilian revolt in 1859, 533; resigns as President of *Società Nazionale Italiana*, 533; *Società Nazionale Armata* attempted, 533-534; second marriage, failure of, 534; decides to go to Sicily, 536-537; embarkation from Quarto, 537-538; unification of Italy under King, his purpose announced, 537, 538; *Italia e Vittorio Emanuele*, 538; Vittorio Emanuele favors expedition, 540; expedition against Papal States, failure of, 540-541
  landing in Sicily, 541-542; battle of Calatafimi, "Here we make Italy or die," 544-545; Palermo captured, 546-550; truce at Palermo, 549-550; orders march to Catania, 556-557
  annexation of Sicily to Sardinia, problem of, 558-563, 601, 612, opinion quoted, 561, decision against, 584-585; government in Sicily, corruption charged, 560-562; plebiscite on annexation ordered, 561-563; battle of Milazzo, 564-565; Messina surrendered, 566-567
  crosses Strait of Messina, 568-569, 573-579, map, 574; correspondence with Vittorio Emanuele, 569-570, 597-598; capture of Naples planned, 570, 571; invasion of Papal States planned, 570, 571, 576; advance on Naples, 580-587, map, 583; enters Naples, 587-589, speech quoted, 588; Abruzzi proclaims him dictator, 596; annexation of Naples to Sardinia, problem of, 596-597, 604; dictator of Naples, 597, 602; proclamation to Palermo on annexation, 597; demands dismissal of Cavour, 597-598, 604, letter quoted, 598
  attack on Rome, 1860: plans, 597, 599-600, 608, opposition to, 599-600; in Palermo, speeches to crowds, 601-602; popularity declines in Naples, 603; Vittorio Emanuele and Cavour, disagreements with, 605-606; civil war seen as denial of brotherhood, 606; order of the day on Sardinian army, 606; battle of the Volturno, 607-608; invites Vittorio Emanuele to come to Naples with army, 608, 612; Sardinian Parliament passes resolution of thanks, 611; quarrel among political advisors, 611-615; plebiscite in Sicily votes for annexation and for him, 616
  meets Vittorio Emanuele at Teano, 619-621, map, 620; transfers his command, 622-624; review at Caserta, Vittorio Emanuele does not attend, 624-625; loyalty to Vittorio Emanuele, 625; rewards not what he wanted, 625; returns to Caprera, 625, 629, 641
  advises dictatorship for Italy, 632; hopes for expedition to Venice or Rome, 633, 642; Lord John Russell writes to, 642; army disbanded, 642-643; in Parliament, 643-644; speech against Cavour, 645-650; Cialdini's criticism, 649-650; retires after meeting Cavour, 650
  hostile to government after Cavour's death, 655, 681; Lincoln offers him command in Union army, 657; interview with Vittorio Emanuele, 658; tour of Italian cities, 660; speech at Milan quoted, 660; expedition to Dalmatia proposed, 660-661; popular enthusiasm for, 660-662; followers arrested, 661; protests against Rattazzi, 661
  prepares for attack on Rome, 661-663; *Roma o morte,* slogan, 662; leads army to Calabria, 663; wounded in battle on Aspromonte, 664-665; popular sympathy for his wound, 666, 667; released after battle, 666; convalescence, 667; land reform and education programs, 674-675
  visit to England, 682-686; reception in London, 683-684; tribute to Mazzini, speech quoted, 684; expedition to Galicia suggested, 685, 686; protest against convention on withdrawal of French army from Rome, quoted, 686; considers fighting for Juárez in Mexico, 686; asks for appointment as dictator of Naples and Sicily, 687
  in war for Veneto, 690, 691, 693; prophecy of revolt in Sicily fulfilled, 694; election campaign, 1867, 697; new religion of peace and brotherhood, his ideal, 697, 699; Rome as capital, his objective, 697-698; at Geneva congress of International League of Peace and Liberty, 699-700
  arrested by Rattazzi and returned to Caprera, 700; Vittorio Emanuele plans his arrest, 701, 702; escapes from Caprera, 701-702; in Florence, recruits volunteers, 702; captures Monterotondo, 702; defeated at Mentana, 703-704, map, 703; claims immunity as citizen of United States, 704; imprisoned, 704; returned to Caprera, 704; accuses government and Mazzini of treachery, 704
  after Mentana, a trouble-maker watched by government, 706-707; resigns from Parliament, 707; a prisoner on Caprera, 715; offers his services to Third Republic of France, 717; does not attend Mazzini's funeral; final tribute to Mazzini, 728; army in the Vosges, 731; last years at Caprera, 731; death and burial, 731-732; his spirit remains in Italy, 732
  *Personal.* Genoa associated with, 33; Foscolo admired, 161, 731; Foscolo quoted, 251, 683; Italian not his native language, 221, 642; appearance, 252, 355; described, 542, 543, 619, 621, 644; attitude toward Sicilians, 546, 549, 557-558; a popular hero, 549, 550; Calabrian peasants call him second Jesus, 579; letters asking favors, attention to, 641-642; speaking technique, 662; effect on people and governments, 685-686
  comments on: by Cavour, 598-599; by Edward, Prince of Wales, 685-686; by Gia-

como Medici, 534; by Ricasoli, 649; by Tennyson, 683
  *Relations with Cavour, see* Cavour, Relations with Garibaldi
  *Relations with Mazzini, see* Mazzini, Relations with Garibaldi
  *Writings.* letters quoted, 642-643, 650, 687, 698; *Memorie,* 250, quoted, 251-253, 365, 538
Garibaldi, Giuseppe, armies of: Italian Legion in South America, 254-255, 275; volunteers follow Garibaldi to Italy, 330; in defense of Rome, 353; in retreat from Rome, 362, 364; *Cacciatore delle Alpi,* 501, 502, 642, 647; The Thousand, 537, 541, 546, 557; Sicilians, 546-547, 564-565; Bertani's volunteers, 575-576; for attack on Rome, 600-601; disbanded, 642-643
Garibaldi, Menotti, 1840-1903: birth, 254; keeps bullet that wounded his father, 666; in England, 682
Garibaldi's Hymn, 630, 683
Gasperi, Alcide de, 1881-1954, 681
Geneva, Mazzini's expedition from, 242-245
Genoa, 33, 80; Mazzini plans capture of, 242, 245; expulsion of Jesuits demanded, 283; constitution for Sardinia demanded, 283-284; republican revolt in, 345; commercial expansion, 409, 669; Mazzini tries to capture, 467-468; Garibaldi's embarkation watched, 537; Mazzini, tomb and memorials, 727-728
Genoa, Republic of: government, 32-33; Corsica ceded to France, 79; rebellion in, 96; as Ligurian Republic, 96, 115, 140, 149; transferred to Sardinia, 183, 198
Genovese, Abbate Antonio, 1712-1769, 35
German Empire, foundation of, 687
Germany: Church in, 65; Napoleon's changes in, 150
Ghibellines, 261
Ghisleri, Marchese, 138, 139
Giacomo, Fra, Cavour's parish priest, 652, 653
Giardini, Sicily, 577-587
Gibilrossa, pass of, Sicily, 546, 547
Gioberti, Vincenzo, 1801-1852, 261-262; *Il Primato,* 261; federation of Italian states under pope, proposal for, 312; Prime Minister of Sardinia, 337-338
Giordani, Pietro, poet, 1774-1848, 216
*La Giovine Europa,* Garibaldi's ship, 250
La Giovine Italia: foundation of, 236, 238; Carbonari compared with, 238, 239; united Italy as aim of, 238; Mazzini's plans for, 239-240; failure as political instrument, 246; Bandiera brothers in, 249
*La Giovine Italia,* Garibaldi's ship, 250
*La Giovine Italia,* Mazzini's journal, 238-239, 246; articles quoted, 240
Giuliano, Sicilian bandit in 1950s, 674
Giulini, Cesare, Conte, 395
Gladstone, William Ewart, 1809-1898: denounces government of Naples, 397-399; *Two Letters to the Earl of Aberdeen,* 398, 451, 552, quoted, 399; letter from Farini quoted, 403; and Garibaldi's visit to England, 685
Goethe, Johann Wolfgang von, 1749-1832, 63, 65, 75
Goito, battle of, 308
Goldoni, Carlo, 1707-1793, 30
Gorani, Giuseppe, Conte, quoted, 32
Gozzi, Carlo, 1720-1806, 28-31; *Useless Mem-*

*oirs,* quoted, 29, 93-94
Gray, Thomas, 1716-1771, 53
Great Britain, *see* Britain
Gregorovius, Ferdinand, 1821-1891, cited, 402
Gregory XVI, Pope (Bartolommeo Alberto Cappellari), 1765-1846, 224, 234, 248; rebellions suppressed by, 255-256; death, 259
Gualtieri, Duke of, argument against taxes, quoted, 711-712
Guelfs, 261; neo-Guelf movement, 262
Guerrazzi, Francesco Domenico, 1804-1873, 346; *L'Assedio di Firenze,* 346; dictator of Florence, overthrown, 346-348; disapproves of treaty with France and Britain, 440
Gyulai, Ferencz, General, 1798-1868: Austrian commander in Italy, 424, 490; in war of 1859, 492-493, 496-499

Habsburg dynasty: Spanish, 3-6; in Italy, 6, 9-10, 15, 16, 42, 45, 47, 49-50, maps, 10, 46; Austrian Empire, 150; after Congress of Vienna, 190; after revolutions of 1848-1849, 379-380, 396; domination ends, 552
Hales, E. E. Y., cited, 640
Haller, in sack of Rome, 104
Hamilton, Emma, Lady, 1765?-1815, 107, 112; friendship with Maria Carolina, 107, 116; welcomes Nelson at Naples, 109; in Palermo, 116-117; with Nelson on *Foudroyant,* 123; letter from Maria Carolina quoted, 124; Maria Carolina's gifts to, 127
Hamilton, Sir William, 1730-1804, 107, 114; welcomes Nelson at Naples, 109; in Palermo, 116-117; letters to Ruffo quoted, 124; honored by Ferdinando I, 127
Helvetian Republic, 140
Henry VIII, King of England, 1491-1547, 38
"Here we make Italy—or die," 544-545, 732
Herzen, Alexander, 1812-1870, Garibaldi's speech at dinner with, quoted, 684
Hofer, Andreas, 1767-1810, 172
Hofstetter, Gustav von, 364
Hohenlinden, battle of, 140
Holy Roman Empire, end of, 150-151, 190
Howe, Samuel Gridley, 1801-1876, 404
Hudson, Sir James, 1810-1885, British minister to Sardinia, 430, 524, 617, 660; on Cavour's reaction to Russell's dispatch, 623
Hugo, Victor, 1802-1885, 289, 411
Hungary: Maria Theresa's difficulties with, 47; Church reforms opposed in, 66; rebellion led by Kossuth, 339, 368, 371, 374; discontent in, 519, 552

Illyria, Kingdom of, 188
Illyrian Provinces, 172, 174, 180, 188
Immaculate Conception of the Blessed Virgin Mary, Dogma of, 401, 709
*L'Indicatore Genovese,* 220
*L'Indicatore Livornese,* 220
Inquisition, 34, 39
International League of Peace and Liberty, Garibaldi at congress in Geneva, 699-700
Isabella II, Queen of Spain, 1830-1904, 714
Ischia, Garibaldi at, 686
*L'Italia,* journal, 264, 273
*Italia del Popolo,* journal, 312, 474, 477, 478
*Italia e Vittorio Emanuele,* Garibaldi's slogan, 538
*L'Italia farà da sè,* 307, 320, 321, 415

Italian language: Piedmont dialect, 7, 268; hope of nation united by, 35; at Austrian court, 45; variety of dialects, 221-222; Tuscan dialect, 221-223, 635; literary use, 222; in Sardinia as official language, 427

Italian Legion, *see* Garibaldi, Giuseppe, armies of

Italian Republic (formerly Cisalpine Republic), 144; becomes Kingdom of Italy, 148, 149

Italy: Habsburg holdings, maps, 10, 46; intellectual development, 21-24; scientific and industrial backwardness, 21-22; feudalism in, 27-29, 47-48; in 1780, 45, map, 46; Habsburg rule of, 47-50; Home Rule demanded, 50-51; constitution suggested, 51

Napoleon's campaigns in, 78-100; republics, 85-86, 114, Latin names of, 85; French conquest of, 101-107; Napoleon's changes in, 151-155; in 1813 under Napoleon, map, 173; in 1815 after Congress of Vienna, 187-190, map, 189

Austrian rule of, 204, 207-208, 211; censorship and police state, 207-208, 219-221; Metternich calls it "a geographical expression," 221, 275; revolution of 1831, 234 revolutions of 1848, 280-285, 297-306; war with Austria, 1848, 307, 308, 310-313, 318-326; after 1848 revolutions, 374-375, 379-381; four kingdoms proposed by Napoleon III, 479

war with Austria, 1859, 492-508, map, 495; Confederation proposed in treaty of 1859, 505; civil war possible, 605-606 unification of, 629-635, maps, 630, 631; *see also* Italy, Kingdom of (after 1860)

Italy, Kingdom of (1805), 148, 152; Napoleon crowned as King, 148-149; after Treaty of Pressburg, 151; Napoleon opposed in, 156-159; Austrians occupy, 180-181; conspiracy to form republic, 182-183

Italy, Kingdom of (after 1860): Rome as capital, 610-611, 635-641, 656, 695-697; beginning of government, 629-635, maps, 630, 631; parliamentary government established, 632-633; voters, qualifications for, 632-633; Kingdom proclaimed, 633-634; Parliament, first session, 633-634; after death of Cavour, 654-655; civil wars, 657-658, 668, 671-672; constitutional government, Cavour's ideas on, 658-659; division into provinces, 668-669; capital transferred from Turin to Florence, 669-670; regional feeling persists in, 670-671; constitution of 1946, regional divisions, 670-671; Commission of Inquiry, report on civil war and brigandage, quoted, 671-672; government program of public works and reclamation suggested, 672; military action against brigands, 672; southern problem, *Questione Meridionale*, 673-675; Church and State, problems of, 675-681, 695-697; principles survive problems, 681

commercial treaty with Prussia, 687; alliance with Prussia, 687-688; war with Austria for Veneto, 688, 690-692, map, 689; peace treaty and cession of Veneto, 692-693 parliamentary elections, 1867, 697; Roman Question, attitudes on, 707-708; monasteries suppressed, 710-711; taxes and finance, 710-712; tax riots, 712; Lanza's budget bill, 713-714

plan for taking Rome, 715-718; Rome oc-

cupied, 718-719; Law of Guarantees, 720-722

Jansenists, 62; controversy with Jesuits, 19, 23; Mazzini influenced by, 213

Jemappes, battle of, 75

Jemolo, Arturo, cited, 640

Jerusalem as issue in Crimean War, 429

Jesuits: controversy with Jansenists, 19, 23; educational activities, 21, 22; accusations against, 38, 63; in Parma, 38, 39; suppression of, 60-61; revival of, 197; opposed in Milan, 204; in Genoa, expulsion demanded, 283; recalled in Naples, 382; in Sardinia, 386; Pius IX favors, 401, 709; Garibaldi expels from Sicily, 546; property confiscated in Naples, 603; influence in Rome, 639

Jews: in Naples, 34; in Rome, 65, 195

Joseph II, Holy Roman Emperor, 1741-1790, 43, 47, 48; Italy ruled by, 49-50, 392; Church reorganization, 61-62, 66; death, 66-67; feudalism abolished, 73

Joséphine, Empress of France, 1763-1814, 81, 174

Jourdan, Jean Baptiste, General, 1762-1833, 81

Juárez, Benito, 1806-1872, Garibaldi considers fighting for, 686

Karl, brother of Ferdinand I, 338, 339

Karl (Charles), Archduke, brother of Francis II, 81, 86, 168

Kléber, Jean Baptiste, 1753-1800, 132

Kossuth, Ferencz Lajos, 1802-1894, 339, 508

Lacaita, Joseph, agent of Cavour, 573

La Farina, Giuseppe, 1815-1863: with Manin, 469-470; contacts with Cavour, 469; prepares for war, 481; message on Sardinian aid to Sicily, 535; sends muskets for Garibaldi's expedition, 539; in Sicily as representative of Sardinia, 559-563; corruption of Garibaldi's government, charges on, 560-562; deported from Sicily, 561, 571; sent to Sicily, flees for life, 630; letters to Cavour quoted, 630, 631

Laibach, conference at, 201-203

La Marmora, Alessandro, 1799-1856, 446, 506

La Marmora, Alfonso Ferrero, Marchese di, 1804-1878: Minister of War in Sardinia, 391; letter from Vittorio Emanuele quoted, 435-436; prepares for war, 481; president of Sardinian ministry, 510; resigns, 522; believes Garibaldi wants to undermine monarchy, 664

Prime Minister, appointment, 670; congratulates Wilhelm I on accession, 687; offers to buy Veneto from Austria, 687; Prussian-Austrian alliance signed, 687; orders mobilization of army, 688; commands army in war for Veneto, 688, 690-691

Lamartine, Alphonse de, 1790-1869, 289, 340; Manifesto to the Powers, 289-290, 307, quoted, 289

La Masa, Giuseppe, 1819-1881, 536

Lambruschini, Luigi, Cardinal, 1776-1854, 259-260

Lamoricière, Christophe, General, 1806-1865, 593-595

Lanza, Ferdinando, Neapolitan viceroy in Palermo, 547; orders bombardment of Palermo, 548; truce with Garibaldi, 549-550

Lanza, Giovanni, 1810-1882: Prime Minister,

appointment, 712; refuses to form coalition government, 713; budget bill, 713-714; in Franco-Prussian war, policy, 714, 715; plan for taking Rome, 715-718; transfers government to Rome, 721

Lateran Treaty, 1929, 720, 733

Law of Guarantees, 720-722

Law on the Convents, 433-445, 640

*Légion d'Antibes*, 698, 702

Leipzig, battle of, 180

Leo XII, Pope (Annibale Francesco della Genga), 1760-1829, 224, 230-232

"Leoben, preliminaries of," 91-92, 96

Leopardi, Giacomo, Conte, 1798-1837, 214-220; parents, 214-215; Giordani visits, 216-217

    *Writings*, 217-220; *All'Italia*, 218-219; *Sopra il monumento di Dante che si preparava in Firenze*, 217-218; *To Angelo Mai*, 218; *Zibaldone*, quoted, 215

Leopold, Prince of Hohenzollern-Sigmaringen, 1835-1905, 714-715

Leopold I, Holy Roman Emperor, 1640-1705, 5

Leopold II, Holy Roman Emperor (Leopold I, Grand Duke of Tuscany), 62, 67, 73

Leopoldo II, Grand Duke of Tuscany, 1747-1792, 220, 264; Azeglio expelled by, 259; Lucca ceded to, 274; Metternich's advice to, 274; Tuscan constitution granted, 284; in war with Austria, 308; republicans force his acceptance of plans, 334; flees to Gaeta, 337; return expected, 346-347; returns with Austrians, 348, 367; popular feeling against, 379-380; pro-Austrian and reactionary policies, 397; expelled by revolution, 498-499; Tuscan Assembly rejects, 513

Liberal Catholic movement, 675

*Liberi Comizi*, 533

Ligurian Republic, 96, 115, 140, 149

Lincoln, Abraham, 1809-1865, offers Garibaldi command in Union army, 657

Lissa, naval battle of, 691-692

Livorno, 346, 347; Mazzini tries to capture, 467-468

Lombardia: union with Sardinia proposed, 312, 319; united with Sardinia, 321, 524; soldiers from, in defense of Rome, 353, 354

Lombardo-Veneto, Kingdom of, 188, 198; Austrian rule of, 204, 207; constitution granted, 295; in war with Austria, 307, 308; Austrian military occupation of, 392-393

Louis XIV, King of France, 1638-1715, 18, 19, 40

Louis XV, King of France, 1710-1774, 12

Louis XVI, King of France, 1754-1793; States General called by, 67; constitutional position of, 73; execution, 76, 107

Louis XVIII, King of France, 1755-1824, 182, 185

Louis Napoleon, *see* Napoleon III

Louis Philippe, King of France, 1773-1850, 231, 233, 241, 554; refuses to oppose Austrian intervention in Italy, 234, 236; deposed by revolution of 1848, 288-289

Louise Elizabeth, Duchess of Parma, wife of Filippo di Borbone, d. 1759, 16

Lucca: government of, 31-32; becomes republic, 115; after Congress of Vienna, 188; ceded to Tuscany, 274

Luigi di Borbone, 1773-1803, 141

Luisa Maria di Borbone, Duchess of Parma, wife of Carlo III, 1819-1864, 433

Macerata, revolt against priestly rule, 196, 204

Machiavelli, Nicolò, 1469-1527, 57, 58, 261, 721, 722

Mack, Baron Karl, General, 1752-1828, 110-111, 149

MacMahon, Patrice, General, 1808-1893, in battle of Magenta, 497

Maffei, Andrea, 1798-1885, 394-395

Maffei, Clara, Contessa, 1814-1886, 655; salon, 394-395, 404, 421, 461, 729

Magenta, battle of, 497

Maistre, Joseph de, 1754?-1821, on Church and State, 197

Malghera, Forte di, 327, 369-370

Malines, Catholic Congress of, 675-676

Malta, 188; French seizure of, 108, 110

Mameli, Goffredo, Marchese, 1827-1849, 353; *Fratelli d'Italia*, patriotic hymn, 286, 353, 655; death, 359

Mamiani, Terenzio, Conte della Rovere, 1799-1885, 318, 333

Manara, Luciano, 1825-1849: in Milan revolution, 305; Bersaglieri Lombardi in defense of Rome, 354, 355, 358, 359; death, 359

Mancini, Pasquale, 1817-1888, 616

Mangaldo, Angelo, commander of Civic Guard in Venice, 294-295, 299

Manin, Daniele, 1804-1857: home rule in Venice, movement for, 264-266, 279-280; arrested, 279-280; released by mob, 292-294; Civic Guard organized, 294; Arsenal captured, 295-298; president of Venetian Republic, 299, 328; asks for resistance against Austria, 367-368; in siege of Venice, 370-373; resignation and exile, 373-374

    on Austrians in Italy, quoted, 380; Cavour meets, 415; disapproves of treaty with France and Britain, 440; open letter to House of Savoy, "If not, no!" quoted, 447-448; on Congress of Paris, series of letters, 457-458; Cavour's comment on, 458; attack on Mazzini, 458-459; death of his wife and daughter, 459; Garibaldi as follower of, 460-461; national party, attempts to create, 460-461, 468-469; on Cavour, 464-465; death, 470; body returned to Venice, 710

Manin, Giorgio, son of Daniele, 1831-1882, 545, 710

Manin, Lodovico, last doge of Venice, 1726-1802, 92-93

Manteuffel, Otto Theodor, Baron von, 1805-1882, 454

Mantua: in Napoleon's campaign, 83, 84; in war with Austria, 308; trials of Mazzini's followers, 421-423

Mantua, Duchy: in Cisalpine Republic, 97; in Kingdom of Lombardo-Veneto, 188

Manzoni, Alessandro, 1785-1873, 380; *I Promessi Sposi*, 221-223, 267; Azeglio his son-in-law, 257, 420; Verdi's *Requiem* composed for, 395, 729; ode quoted by Garibaldi's followers, 575; on united Italy, 625-626; death and burial, 728-729; life summarized, 728-729

Marches, the, 594; Sardinian invasion of, 589, 598, 605; plebiscite for annexation to Sardinia, 616

Maria Adelaide, Queen of Sardinia, wife of Vittorio Emanuele II, 1822-1855, 438

Maria Amalia, Duchess of Parma, wife of Ferdinando I, 1746-1804, 39, 42

Maria Carolina, Queen of the Two Sicilies, wife of Ferdinando I, 1752–1814: marriage, 42; Maria Theresa's advice to, quoted, 42-43; children, 43; dominates her husband, 43-44; opposes French in war, 80, 107, 116; friendship with Lady Hamilton, 107, 116; admires Nelson, 109; flight to Palermo, 112-113; letter to Ruffo, 122; letter to Lady Hamilton quoted, 124; gifts to Lady Hamilton, 127; exiled to Sicily, 151; on marriage of Napoleon and Marie Louise, 174, 186-187; at Vienna to protest against Bentinck, 186; death, 187

Maria Cristina, Queen of the Two Sicilies, wife of Ferdinando II, 1812–1836, 226, 228, 494

Maria Sophia, Queen of the Two Sicilies, wife of Francesco II, 1841–1925, 585

Maria Teresa, Queen of Sardinia, wife of Carlo Alberto, mother of Vittorio Emanuele II, 1801–1855, 437

Maria Teresa, Queen of the Two Sicilies, wife of Ferdinando II, 1816–1867, 227-228, 493-494

Maria Theresa, Empress, 1717–1780: heiress of the Habsburgs, 12, 15; marriage, 15, 16; daughters, 39, 42; treaty with Carlos III, 42; letters to Maria Carolina quoted, 42-43; children of, control of Italy, 45, map, 46; as Empress, 47-48; Italy ruled by, 47-50, 190

Marie Louise, Empress of the French, 1791–1847: marriage, 174-175; in Vienna with Maria Carolina, 187; Duchess of Parma, 188, 234, 274; death, 273-274

Marinovich, Austrian officer at Venice Arsenal, 296-297

Mario, Alberto, 1825–1883, on Garibaldi at Teano, 621-622

Mario, Jessie White, 1832–1906, 622; description of Garibaldi's bullet wound, quoted, 666

Marlborough, John Churchill, Duke of, 1650–1722, 6

Maronceilli, Pietro, arrested with Pellico, 209, 210

Marsala: Garibaldi lands at, 541-542; Garibaldi's speech at, *Roma o morte*, 662

Martinengo Cesaresco, Contessa, cited, 639

Martini, Austrian commandant at Venice Arsenal, 296, 297

Marx, Karl, 1818–1883, irritated by enthusiasm for Garibaldi, 683

Masi, Ernesto, on Pius IX, 316

Massa, appeal for annexation to Sardinia, 479, 481

Mathilde, Princess, comment on Napoleon III, 476

Maximilian, Archduke of Austria, later Emperor of Mexico, 1832–1867, 464, 686

Mazarin, Jules, Cardinal, 1602–1661, 51

Mazzini, Giuseppe, 1805–1872

    early life, 212-214; parents, 213-214, 221; joins Carbonari, 213; banished from Sardinia after Open Letter, 229, 238; arrested, 235; in prison at Savona, 235, 236

    in France, 235, 237-238; finds Carbonari unsatisfactory, 236; La Giovine Italia, foundation of, 236, 238-239; infiltration of Sardinian army planned, 240-241; condemned to death *in absentia*, 241; love affair and birth of son, 241; assassination of Carlo Alberto planned, 241-242; expedition from Geneva, 242-245; flag, motto for, 242-243;

expelled from Switzerland, 246
    in England, 1837–1848, 246-247; as propagandist, 250; opposes papel leadership, 262; admires Pius IX, 263
    1848–1849: returns to Italy, 312; proclamation after Salasco armistice, 330; in Rome, 345, 348, 360; as Triumvir (dictator) of Rome, 351-353; in defense of Rome, 354, 355, 361

    National Italian Committee, proclamation on loan, 394; Cavour opposed to, 415, 440; secret committees, members arrested, 421-422; trials of his followers at Mantua, 421-423; uprising attempted in Milan, 423-425; blamed for murder of Carlo III, 433; denounces treaty with France and Britain, 440; Manin's attack on, 458-459; change in public opinion of, 459-460, 468

    expedition to Sapri, 465-467; attempted capture of Livorno and Genoa, 467-468; French action against, 474; attack on Cavour, quoted, 477-478; Cavour's hatred of, 478

    urges invasion of Papal States, 517, 576; Sicilian expedition proposed, 532-533; incites rebellion in Sicily, letter quoted, 535; Bertani's volunteers encouraged, 576; resigned to failure of his dream for Italy, 603-604; letter to Peter Taylor quoted, 604; asked to leave Naples, 613; advises followers to vote for annexation, 616

    in England, 629, 682; Cavour's last speech refers to, 650-651; hostile to government after Cavour's death, 655, 681; meets Garibaldi in England, 683, 684; Rome as capital, his objective, 698; Universal Republican Alliance, failure of, 714; in Franco-Prussian war, offers volunteers, 715-717; interned at Gaeta, 716, 718; death and burial, 727-728; reputation, positive and negative, 728

    *Personal.* Genoa associated with, 33; Jane Addams praises, 237; popular opinion of, 259, 459-460, 468; influence on Gioberti, 261; Asproni's comment on, 603

    ideas: duty, 236; political action secondary, 237; regeneration of Italy, 236; social program, 360

    *Relations with Garibaldi.* correspondence, 250; praises Garibaldi's exploits in South American, 250; Garibaldi blames him for defeat in Rome, 354, 460; warns Garibaldi of French treatment, 502; calls Garibaldi weak, tool of king, 517; influence on Garibaldi overestimated, 604; advises Garibaldi to offer annexation of Naples, 604; Garibaldi refuses to disassociate from him, 605-606; urges Garibaldi to attack Rome, 608; Garibaldi asks him to stay in Naples, 613; Garibaldi's tribute to him in London, quoted, 684; Garibaldi's letter on Roman Question, quoted, 698; Garibaldi blames him for defeat at Mentana, 703, 704; Garibaldi's final tribute, 728

    *Writings and publications.* L'Apostolo Repubblicano, 250; *La Giovine Italia*, 238-239, quoted, 240; *L'Indicatore Genovese*, 220; *Italia del Popolo*, 312, 474, 477, 478; Open Letter to Carlo Alberto, 229-230, 238, quoted, 229; Open Letter to Pius IX, 263; *Scritti*, quoted, 212-213, 220, 240, 360, 477-478, 535; *Young Italy's Letter to General Ramorino*, 245

*Mazzini*, Garibaldi's ship, 250
Medici, Cosimo III de', Grand Duke of Tuscany, 1642–1723, 7, 11, 21
Medici, Giacomo, 1817–1882, Garibaldi's lieutenant, 353; on Garibaldi, 534; in battle of Milazzo, 564; signs treaty at Messina, 567
Medici, Gian Gastone de', Grand Duke of Tuscany, 1671–1737, 3, 12, 15; death, 10–11; guardian of Carlo di Borbone, 13; education encouraged by, 22
Medici, Luigi, minister of Kingdom of Naples, 198
Melito, Garibaldi's landing at, 578
Menabrea, Luigi Federico, 1809–1896: Prime Minister, appointment, 702; capture of Garibaldi, 702, 704; defends action against Garibaldi, 704–705; ignores Roman Question, 707–708; resigns, 712; Lanza does not include him in coalition government, 713
Mentana: Garibaldi defeated at, 703-704, map, 703; results of, 704–707
Mercadante, Saverio, 1795–1870, 120, 249, 349
Mérode, Frédéric de, 1820–1874, 593, 596
Messina: bombarded by Ferdinando II (*Bomba*), 381; surrendered to Garibaldi, 566-567
Messina, Strait of, 568–569; Garibaldi's crossing of, 568–569, 573–579, map, 574
Metastasio, Pietro, poet, 1698–1782, 45, 53, 59
Metternich, Klemens von, 1773–1859, 175, 198, 221, 224; and Treaty of Schönbrunn, 172-174; in Congress of Vienna, 188, 196; will not recognize Naples as constitutional monarchy, 201; Congress of Troppau called, 201; on Ferdinando I, 203
    in government of Italy, 204, 211; philosophy of government, 205–207; censorship encouraged, 220, 221; "Italy is a geographical expression," 221, 275; Mazzini's plans reported to, 243; Carlo Alberto's relations with, 257; orders to Gaisruck in election of Pius IX, 259-260; orders Austrian troops in Italy, 264, 274–275; advice to Leopoldo II, quoted, 275; on Milan tobacco riots, quoted, 278; refuses aid in Sicilian revolution, 282-283; resigns, 290, 292
    predicts radicalism in Italy, 335; Schwarzenberg's letter to, on Franz Josef, quoted, 393; praises Cavour, 456; death, 493
*Mezzadria*, 671
Mignet, François, 1796–1884, 143
Milan: patrician class in, 48; captured by allied troops, 117; economic importance under Napoleon, 152; under Austrian rule, 190, 207; demonstrations for reform, 266-267; Tobacco Party, 277-279; revolution of 1848, 299-306; Cinque Giornate, 300-306, map, 302; republicans in, 312; in war between Italy and Austria, 322-323; Carlo Alberto attacked in, 323-325; Austrian occupation, 329-330, anti-Austrian feeling, 379; demonstration on Franz Josef's birthday, 393; Mazzini attempts uprising in, 423-425; Franz Josef in, 462-463; Napoleon III enters in triumph, 497-498; Manzoni's house, 729
Milan, Duchy: Habsburg rule of, 15, 45, 47, 51; feudalism of noble families, 47-48; Heraldic Tribunal, 52; in war with France, 80, 82, 92; in Cisalpine Republic, 97; in Kingdom of Lombardo-Veneto, 188; union

with Sardinia proposed, 312; united with Sardinia, 321; Garibaldi in service of, 331
Milazzo: battle of, 564-565; surrender of, 566-567
Miller, Lady Anna, 1714–1781, quoted, 32
Mincio river, 308, 310
Minghetti, Marco, 1818–1886, 452; on Pius IX, 314; Prime Minister, appointment, 668; plan for division of Italy into regional units, 668; capital transferred from Turin to Florence, 669-670; dismissed, 670; convention with Napoleon III for withdrawal of army from Rome, 669-670, 686
Miollis, Sextius-Alexandre-François, General, 1759–1828, 167-169, 171; letter from Napoleon quoted, 168
Mislimeri, Sicily, 546, 547
Modena, Duchy, 45, 97; becomes republic, 85; Carbonaro revolution of 1831, 229, 230; Austrian troops in, 264, 329; Parma territory ceded to, 274; in war with Austria, 308; united with Sardinia, 321; after revolutions of 1848, 396-397; occupation by Sardinia planned, 480, 498; union with Sardinia requested, 499, 515
Mombello, Napoleon's headquarters, 95
Montalembert, Charles, Comte de, 1810–1870, 709; speeches at Catholic Congress of Malines, 675-676; Pius IX condemns his views, 678
Monterotondo, Garibaldi captures, 702
Montesquieu, Charles Louis de Secondat, Baron de la Brède et de, 1689–1755, 19, 23, 36, 56, 57, 409
Montevideo, Garibaldi's Italian Legion in, 254-255
Montezumolo, Marchese, 630, 631
Montferrat, Marquisate of, 7
Moravia, Alberto, on Risorgimento, quoted, 723
Mordini, Antonio, pro-dictator of Sicily, 601
Moreau, Jean Victor, General, 1763–1813, 81, 140, 145
Moro, Domenico, 1822–1844, with Bandiera brothers, 249
Mundy, Admiral Sir Rodney, Garibaldi's farewell to, 625
Munich congress, Döllinger's speeches on Catholic Church, 676-677; Pius IX criticizes, 678
Murat, Joachim, 1767–1815: letter from Napoleon quoted, 168; Grand Admiral, 147; King of Naples, 151, 152, 158, 168, 180-181; campaign of 1815, 185-186, 190; tries to regain his kingdom, 198-199; executed, 199
Murat, Napoléon Lucien Charles, 1803–1878, 465
Mussolini, Benito, 1883–1945, 722, 733

Naples: University of, 34-36, 44; San Carlo opera, 36; under Ferdinando I, 44, 129-130; Ruffo's army captures, 120-122; terms of French surrender, 122-124; republican prisoners executed, 127-128; intellectual and cultural decline, 129-130; Carbonari in, 200; Austrian army in, 204, 207; revolution in, 321; trial of conspirators in bomb plot, 397-398; riots against police, 556
    Garibaldi plans capture of, 570, 571; Garibaldi's advance on, 580-587, map, 583; Garibaldi enters, 587-589; Garibaldi as dictator, 597, 602; dissatisfaction with Kingdom of Italy, 671

Naples, Kingdom of, 14; feudalism in, 27-28; Church property in, 33; attempt to revive Inquisition, 34

in war between France and Italy, 80, 107; French conquest of, 106-107; war with French, 110-112; Parthenopean Republic established, 114; Ferdinando I exiled, 151; under Napoleon's rule, 151-152; Bourbons attempt to recover, 157

Ferdinando I returns, 186, 187; treaty of alliance with Austria, 187; Murat tries to regain his kingdom, 198-199; Carbonari in, 199-200

as constitutional monarchy, 200-202, 281; relations with Austria, 201-202; Sicily as rival of, 281; constitution granted, 281, 282, 285; soldiers in defense of Venice, 369; after revolutions of 1848-1849, 381-382

constitutional government ended, 382; Gladstone denounces injustice and tyranny, 397-399; army opposes Garibaldi's forces in Sicily, 541, 544-550, 553, 564-567; constitutional government revived, 555-556; army in Garibaldi's advance on Naples, 580, 582

annexation to Sardinia: proposed, 596, 602, 604; by assembly or plebiscite, dispute on, 612-615; plebiscite votes for, 615-616

Napoleon I, Emperor of the French, 1769-1821

Italian campaigns, 78-100; Italian background of, 79; marriage, 80-81; on army at Nice, quoted, 81; popular admiration of, 83-84, 95-96; Pope attacked by, 87-89; political principles, 89-90; Venice conquered, 92-94; public reaction against, 98-99; invasion of England planned, 100, 102; Egyptian campaign, 102, 108; returns from Egypt, 132, *coup d'état* of 18 and 19 Brumaire 1799, 132-133

First Consul, election, 133-134; assassination attempted, 134; relations with Church, 134-135, 141-143, 154-155, 164-171, 175-181; crosses the Alps, 139; defeats Habsburg armies, 140; in Italy, good and bad effects, 141; concordat with Pius VII, 1801, 141-143; president of Italian Republic, 144; Consul of France for life, 144-145

Emperor, election, 146-147; coronation, 147-148; King of Italy, coronation, 148-149; changes in Germany, 150; changes in Austria, 150-151; changes in Italy, 151-155; letter to Cardinal Flesch quoted, 154; opposed in Italy, 156-159; Foscolo opposes, 159-163; education controlled by, 162-163; Church opposes, 164-171

war with Austria, 167-168, 172; letter to Miollis quoted, 168; letter to Murat quoted, 168; excommunication, bull of, 168, 175; divorce from Joséphine, 174, 175; marriage with Marie Louise, 174-175; on separation of Church and State, 177; Russian campaign, 178; meets Pius VII, 178-179; letter to Pius VII quoted, 178; concordat with Pius VII, 1813, 179-180

military defeats, 180; at Elba, 182; Hundred Days, 185; at St. Helena, 185; Medal of St. Helena commemorating service with, 472

Napoleon II, Duke of Reichstadt (L'Aiglon), 1811-1832, 187, 418

Napoleon III (Louis Napoleon), Emperor of the French, 1808-1873

President of France, 340-341; sends army to Rome, 352; Italian attitude toward, 409-410, 420-421; *coup d'état* of 2 December 1851, 410-412; relations with Sardinia, 412, 415, 419; Rattazzi meets, 415

becomes Emperor, 418-419; marriage, 418; in Crimean War, 429; possible ally of Italy, 447, 472; Vittorio Emanuele visits, 448-449; in Congress of Paris, 449-453; birth of his son, 452, 453; supports young Murat's effort to win Kingdom of Naples, 465; assassination attempted, 472-473; suppression of Italian radicals, 473-474; letter from Vittorio Emanuele quoted, 474-475

plans war with Austria in Italy, 475, 478-480, 482-483; in Orsini's trial, 475-476; proposes marriage of Prince Napoléon with Princess Clotilde, 478, 480, 482; proposes French alliance with Sardinia, 478-480; Cavour's interview with, 478-480; four kingdoms of Italy, plan for, 479; Vittorio Emanuele's speech, *grido di dolore*, revised, 483; tries to postpone war, 487-489

war with Austria in Italy, 1859, 492-503; proclamation to French troops, quoted, 494; commands allied armies, 494, 496-498; battle of Magenta, 497; proclamation at Milan, quoted, 497-498; battle of Solferino, 502-503; peace treaty (treaty of Zurich), 503-507; Italian reactions to, 506-508, 531; objects to union of Sardinia with other states, 515; sensitive to British opinion, 516, 518, 521; plans for congress on Treaty of Zurich, 517-518, 521

negotiations for Nice and Savoy, 518, 521, 523-524; *Le Pape et le Congrès*, pamphlet, 519-521, 596; asks Pius IX to give up Legations, 520; treaty on cession of Nice and Savoy, 527-528

Francesco II asks him for aid against Garibaldi, 552-553, 555; international action against Garibaldi proposed, 573; Cavour's plan for invasion of Papal States presented to, 581; attitude of Pius IX toward, 591-592, 594, 596; in invasion of Papal States, 593-595; opposed to Garibaldi's attack on Rome, 599-600; intervenes in Sardinian action at Gaeta, 622; withdraws fleet from Gaeta, 634

Rome as capital of Italy, reaction to, 636-637, 656-657; recognizes Kingdom of Italy, 652; calls for action against Garibaldi's volunteers, 663; convention on withdrawal of his army from Rome, 669-670, 686, 694; Clarendon's letter on Garibaldi in England, 684; neutral in war between Prussia and Austria, 687; suggests congress on Veneto, 688; Austria transfers Veneto by secret treaty, 688

orders army back to Rome, 701; Italian judgment of, 706; proposes congress on Roman Question, 707; in Franco-Prussian war, 715; imprisonment and end of Second Empire, 716; death, 728

Napoléon Joseph Charles Paul Bonaparte, Prince (Jérôme Napoléon, Plon-Plon), 1822-1891, 504, 506; marriage with Princess Clotilde, 478, 480, 484, 491; letter to Cavour quoted, 577

National Italian Committee: Mazzini's proclamation on loan, 394; members arrested, 421-

422; members tried at Mantua, 421-423; code, 421-422

National Italian Party: Manin attempts to create, 460-461, 468-470; becomes *Società Nazionale Italiana*, 470

Nelson, Horatio, Viscount, 1758–1805, 78, 121; Mediterranean campaign, 107-108; battle of the Nile, 108-109; welcomed at Naples, 109; letters to his wife quoted, 109, 126-127; urges Ferdinando I to attack Rome, 110; Ferdinando I influenced by, 112-113, 116; with Hamiltons in Palermo, 116-117; repudiates agreement on surrender of Naples, 123-124; orders execution of Carcciolo, 125-126; celebrations honoring, 126-127; death, 149; Duke of Bronte, title, 558

Netherlands: as Batavian Republic, 140; Bull of Restoration from Pius IX, 405-406

Netherlands, Austrian, 86, 140; ceded to France, 92, 97

Newman, John Henry, Cardinal, 1801–1890, sermon quoted, 317

Nice, province: incorporated into France, 140, 339; Napoleon III demands, 480; Napoleon III plans secret treaty for, 518, 521; Cavour's proposals and maneuvers of Napoleon III. 522-524; ceded to France by treaty, 527-528, 531; plebiscite, 529-530

Nicholas I, Tsar of Russia, 1796–1855: in Crimean War, 429, 431-432; Franz Josef negotiates with, 431-432; Warsaw meeting, 608, 617

Nicola, Carlo di, diary quoted, 114, 128, 151

Nicolotti, Venetian faction, 280

Nigra, Constantino, 1828–1907, Sardinian ambassador to France, 505

Nile, battle of the, 108-109

Novarra: battle of, 342, 344; in war of 1859, 496

Nyon, Mazzini's followers in, 243

O'Donnell, Austrian vice-governor at Milan, 300-301

Orlov, Nikolai, Count, 1827–1885, in Congress of Paris, 452-454

Orsini, Felice, 1819–1858: attempted assassination of Napoleon III, 473; trial, 475-476; letter quoted, 475-476; execution, 476

Orvieto, 605

Oudinot, Nicolas, Duc de Reggio, General, 1791–1863, leads attack on Rome, 352-354, 357

Pacca, Bartolomeo, Cardinal, 1756–1844, 176, 224; Secretary to Pius VII, 167; arrested, 168-170; released, 180; letter from Consalvi quoted, 188; at Rome in charge of administration, 195

Padua, Franz Josef in, 462

Paganini, Nicolò, 1782–1840, 213

Paisiello, Giovanni, 1741–1816, 129

Palermo: revolution of 1848, 280-282, 374; revolt of 4 April 1860, 535-536; Garibaldi captures, 546-550; revolt in 1866, 694

Palestro, battle of, 496

Palffy, governor of Venice, 295; Manin released by, 292-294; surrenders to Venetian rebels, 298

Pallavicino, Emilio, Colonel, 1823–1901, leads Bersaglieri against Garibaldi, 664-665

Pallavicino, Giorgio, Marchese, 1796–1878: intercedes for Castiglia, 210; Garibaldi writes

to, 460; Manin's efforts supported, 460, 468-470; fears Cavour more than Mazzini, 464; Garibaldi requests him as pro-dictator of Naples, 597; delivers Garibaldi's demands to Vittorio Emanuele, 604-605; fails to conciliate Cavour and Garibaldi, 605-606; argument with Crispi, 612-615; asks Mazzini to leave Naples, 613; resigns, 615

Palmerston, Henry John Temple, Viscount, 1784–1865, 552; Cavour attempts to influence, 452, 455; refuses to arrange peace terms between France and Austria, 503; "Italy for the Italians" policy, 516, 518; on Garibaldi's expedition in Sicily, 551; and Russell's dispatch, 623; and Garibaldi's visit to England, 682, 684-685

Pantaleone, Diomede, 1810–1885, memorandum on Rome as capital of Italy, 636, 637

Papal States, 33, 64-65; Parma claimed as part of, 38; parts returned to Pius VII, 139, 141; Napoleon's incorporation of, 152, 154, 165, 168; Legations returned to pope, 188, 196; failure of government in, 230-233; rebellion in, 255-256; peasants indifferent to reform, 262

  under Pius IX, 315-316, 318, 333, 335, 401-406; in Roman Republic, 350; French and Austrian occupation, 367; in war of 1859, 500-501; invasion planned by Defensive League of Emilia and Tuscany, 517; as obstacle to united Italy, 521; Garibaldi's unsuccessful expedition against, 540-541; Garibaldi plans invasion, 570, 571, 576

  Cavour's plan for invasion, 576-577, 581-582; Sardinian invasion, 585, 590-595, map, 594; loss of, 634; Patrimony of St. Peter as remnant of, 695, 701, 708

Pareto, Ernesto, Marchese, 385

Parini, Giuseppe, poet, 1729–1799, 50, 53

Paris: riots in 1848, 340; enthusiasm for Sardinians in Crimean War, 446-447; Congress of, 449-456; congress on Treaty of Zurich proposed, 517-518, 520-521

Parma, 153; works of art taken by Carlo di Borbone, 15, 37; works of art transferred to government, 669

Parma, Duchy, 11, 15, 16, 45, 233; end of Farnese family in, 9, 11-13; renaissance of, 37-39; Church property in, 37-38; in war with France, 82, 86; incorporated into France, 152; Marie Louise as Duchess, 188, 234, 274; Carbonaro revolution of 1831, 229, 230; Carlo II cedes territory to Modena, 274; in Kingdom of Alta Italia, 321; Austrian occupation, 329; after revolutions of 1848, 396; union with Sardinia proposed, 396, 499, 515; dictatorship offered to Vittorio Emanuele, 499

Parthenopean Republic, 114, 120

Pastrengo, battle of, 311

Patrimony of St. Peter, 596, 636, 694

Paul III, Pope (Alessandro Farnese), 1469–1549, 11, 233

Pavia: Napoleon captures, 82-83; University of, 162; theatre boycotted, 393-394

Peace of Paris: First, 182, 184; Second, 185

Pélissier, Jean Jacques, General, 1794–1864, General, 447

Pellico, Silvio, 1789–1854, 220, 261; arrested and imprisoned, 208-211; *Le mie prigioni*, quoted, 209-210

Pepe, Guglielmo, General, 1783–1855, 202, 369, 371; leader of Carbonari, 200; in war with Austria, 321

Persano, Carlo di, Admiral, 1806–1883, 597; letter from Cavour quoted, 572; in battle of Lissa, 691–692

Perugia, 65; sacked by Swiss Guards, 500-501

Peschiera, 308; siege of, 310; surrender of, 319

Petrarch, 1304–1374, 721

Philip V (Philippe de Bourbon), King of Spain, 1683–1746, 5, 6, 14; marriage, 11-12; sons, 12, 40

Piedmont: French occupation of, 140; incorporated into France, 149, 183; recovered by Italy, 183, 198; revolution attempted, 202-203; constitution celebrated, 285-287; republicans in, 337; Sardinia called, 427; resentment of other Italians for, 668-669; industrial development, 669

Pietri, Pierre, 1809–1864, Cavour's interview with, 508

Pilo, Rosolino, 1820–1860, Sicilian revolutionary, 536, 546

Pio Nono, *see* Pius IX

Piozzi, Hester Lynch Thrale, 1741–1821, Ferdinando I described by, 41-42

Pisa, University of, 21, 22, 79

Pisacane, Carlo, 1818–1857, 557; leads Mazzini's expedition to Sapri, 465-467, 533; *Historical, Political, and Military Essays on Italy,* 467

Pius VI, Pope (Angelo Braschi), 1717–1799, 62-63, 118, 233; protests against reforms of Joseph II, 61; reforms attempted by, 65; condemns French action against Church, 69-70; attacked in Napoleon's campaign, 87-89; deposed, 104; death, 131; burial, 132, 135-136

Pius VII, Pope (Luigi Barnaba Chiaramonti), 1742–1823, 136-138; Christmas homily, 137, 676; difficulties with Francis II, 138-139; concordat with Napoleon, 1801, 141-143; Napoleon's conflict with, 143, 154, 164-169, 175-181; coronation of Napoleon as Emperor, 147-148; refuses to crown Napoleon as King of Italy, 148; excommunicates Napoleon, 168-169, 175; arrested, 169-171; Paris council of bishops visits, 176-177; Brief to the Bishops of the Empire, 177; moved to Fontainebleau, 178-179; Napoleon visits, 178-179; concordat with Napoleon, 1813, 179-180; released from imprisonment, 181; refuses to sign Congress of Vienna treaty, 185; reactionary government of Rome, 195-196; religious orders encouraged, 197; Austrian garrison admitted, 204; death, 224

Pius VIII, Pope (Francesco Xaverio Castiglioni), 1761–1830, 224, 234

Pius IX, Pope (Giovanni Maria Mastai-Ferretti), 1792–1878
as Archbishop, protests against Centurioni, 255; election of, 259-260; amnesty granted to Carbonari, 260; as leader of reform, 260-263, 275; effects of his reforms, 264-265, 267

1848–1849: demonstrations for, in Milan, 278-279; *Motu Proprio,* 284-285, 402, quoted, 285; in war with Austria, 308, 313-316; allocution against unification of Italy, 313-314, 316-317, 320, quoted, 314; letter to Emperor Ferdinand quoted, 315; Papal States, government of, 315-316, 318, 333, 335; imprisoned by republicans, 335; es-

capes to Gaeta, 335-336; Gioberti offers troops for re-establishment, 337; Constituent Assembly condemned, 349; governing power abolished by Constituent Assembly, 350; appeal to France, Spain, Austria, and Naples, 350; Queen Victoria's letter to, 350; sympathy with, 350-351; French attack on Rome to restore, 352-353; allocution, April 1849, 360

returns to Rome, 1850, 361, 401; announces end of his liberal reforms, 367; in Naples, blesses population, 382-383; demands release of Fransoni, 390; government after return to Rome, 401-406; Vatican as residence, 401; Dogma of the Immaculate Conception of the Blessed Virgin Mary, 401, 709; encyclical, *Quanta cura,* 401; government criticized, 403-404; Bull of Restoration for Britain, 405; Bull of Restoration for Netherlands, 405-406; letter from Vittorio Emanuele on civil marriage bill, 416-417

and Law on the Convents: Cavour's negotiations, 435; allocution against Law, 438; documents quoted, 438-439; letter from Vittorio Emanuele quoted, 439; excommunicates Vittorio Emanuele and his ministers, 444

godfather of son of Napoleon III, 452, 453; orders medal commemorating capture of Perugia, 501; peace treaty of 1859 proposes Italian Confederation with him as President, 505; *Le Pape et le Congrès,* pamphlet by Napoleon III, 519-521, 596; temporal power questioned, 519-520; Napoleon III asks him to give up Legations, 520; excommunicates Cavour, Vittorio Emanuele, and others, 528; Francesco II asks his approval of revived constitution, 556

Sardinian invasion of Papal States, reaction to, 590-592, 634; interview with Odo Russell, 591-592; attitude toward Napoleon III, 591-592, 594, 596; volunteer army, 591, 593, 596; his liberalism analyzed, 592-593; allocution condemning Sardinia and France, 596

Rome as capital of Italy, reaction to, 610; negotiations with Cavour, 635-641; allocution on Roman Question, 637; on Cavour's death, 652-653; rejects Ricasoli's attempted negotiations, 656

Montalembert's views condemned, 678; Munich congress criticized, 678; Syllabus of Errors, 679-680, 697; decree, *Non expedit,* 680, 697

demands return of Church provinces and property, 707; religious events of his reign, 708-709; Vatican Council announced, 709; refuses Vittorio Emanuele's proposal for annexation of Rome, 717-718; last public appearance in Papal Rome, 718; spiritual freedom and temporal power, belief in, 719; calls himself a prisoner, 720; Law of Guarantees condemned, 721; lifts ban of excommunication on Vittorio Emanuele, 729-730; death and burial, 730; historical judgment on, 730-731

Pius XI, Pope (Achille Ratti), 1857–1939, 733

Plebiscites: in Emilia and Tuscany on union with Sardinia, 523-527; in Nice and Savoy on cession to France, 529-530; on annexation of states to Sardinia, proposed, 607, 612; in Naples, Umbria, Marches, and Sicily for union, 615-616; in Veneto for union, 692; in

Rome on annexation, 719
Po valley: Napoleon's campaign in, 83; as economic unit under Napoleon, 152; in war with Austria, 1848, 308, 310, 318-319, map, 309; campaign of 1859, map, 495
Poerio, Carlo, 1803–1867, trial and imprisonment, 398
Polesine, secret societies suppressed in, 208
Ponza, prisoners freed, 466
Pope: declining power of, 60, 63-64; Papal States neglected by, 65-66; attacked in Napoleon's campaign, 87-89; proposed removal of Papacy to France, 152; infallibility, dogma of, 716; Law of Guarantees on rights and privileges, 720
Pragmatic Sanction, 47
Proclamation of Moncalieri, 385
Prussia: war against France, 75, 180; in Austrian relations with Naples, 201, 202; protest against Garibaldi's Sicilian expedition, 541, 551-552; protest against Sardinian invasion of Naples, 617; commercial treaty with Italy, 687; foundation of German Empire, 687; war with Austria possible, 687; alliance with Italy, 687-688; Franco-Prussian war, 714-716

Radet, Etienne, General, 1762–1825, 169-171
Radetzky, Johann Joseph, Count, Field Marshal, 1766–1858: in Milan tobacco riots, 278; in Milan revolution of 1848, 300, 301, 303-305; in war between Italy and Austria, 308, 310, 319-325; in occupation of Italy after armistice, 329, 337, 338; in Sardinian war with Austria, 341-342; offers terms of surrender, 343, 344; Venice attacked, 369; triumphal entry into Venice, 374; ball in his honor boycotted, 379; military occupation of Lombardo-Veneto, 393; in trials of Mazzini's committee members, 421-423, 426; orders punishment for Milan uprising, 424; Franz Josef gives him Palazzo Reale in Milan, 464
Railroads, 276, 409; Turin to Genoa, 409, 430; in war of 1859, 496
Ramorino, Girolamo, General, 1790–1849: fails to lead Mazzini's expedition from Geneva, 242-245; in Sardinian army, 1849, 341, 342
Rampagallo, Sicily, Garibaldi at, 544
Rattazzi, Urbano, 1808–1873, 428, 430, 444; in Sardinian Parliament, 413; president of Chamber, 414, 417; meets Louis Napoleon, 415; resigns from ministry, 476-477; Minister of the Interior, 510; in Parliament when Garibaldi speaks, 644-647
    Prime Minister, 1862, appointment, 658-659; plan for using Garibaldi, 660-661; orders arrest of Garibaldi's followers, 661; Garibaldi's march on Rome opposed, 663-664; resigns, 667
    Prime Minister, 1867, appointment, 698; protests on French volunteers for defense of Papal State, 698; Garibaldi arrested and sent to Caprera, 700; policy on Rome, 701; resigns, 701; defends action against Garibaldi, 705
Rattazzi bill (Law on the Convents), 433-445
Ravenna: papal government in, 230-231; rebellion suppressed, 255-256
Rayneval, Comte de, report on papal government, quoted, 403
Rechberg und Rothenlöwen, Johann Bernard, Count, 1806–1899, 518-519

Red shirts: Italian Legion at Montevideo first to wear, 255; in Sicilian expedition, 541; and cross of Savoy, meeting at Teano, 621
Reggio, Garibaldi captures, 578-579
Religious orders: Law of the Convents on, 433-445; in Sardinia, 434; monasteries suppressed, 710-711
Revel, Genova di, General, Minister of War, 700; quoted, 699; resigns, 701
Revolutions of 1848, 276-277, 374; in France, 288-290; in Italy, 280-285, 297-306; Vienna student revolt, 290-292
Ricasoli, Bettino, 1809–1880: Minister of the Interior in Tuscany, 509; character of, 509; dominates Tuscan government, 511-513; promotes union of Tuscany with Sardinia, 513-515; Cavour offers support, 524
    plebiscite arranged by, 524-527, 563; instructions on voting, quoted, 526; Cavour's letters to, 539-540, 572; on Vittorio Emanuele, 570, 600; on Sardinian government, 631-632; position as Prime Minister offered to, 635; in Parliament, speeches on Garibaldi, 643-645; on Garibaldi's debates, 649; Cavour tells him of reconciliation with Garibaldi, 650
    Prime Minister, appointment, 656; attempts negotiations on Rome, 656; resigns, 658, 659; moral tone irritates deputies, 659; disapproves of division of Italy into provinces, 668-669; Prime Minister in absence of La Marmora, 688; sends army to Palermo revolt, 694; further negotiations on Rome, 695-697; resigns, 697
Righetti, minister under Pius IX, 384
Rimini: Manifesto of, 256; uprising in, 256, 257, 259
Riso, Francesco, leads revolt in Palermo, 535, 548
Risorgimento: background of, 3, 6-8, 14, 16, 51; beginning of, 1748, 17; intellectual development, 24; Italian republic as objective, 33, 36; French Revolution as influence on, 72; as opposition to Napoleon, 161, 163; Italian language unified by, 221, 222; name first used, 273; first battle of, 308; after revolutions of 1848, 401; historians' judgment of, 538-539, 633, 722-723; after death of Cavour, 654-655; principles survive problems, 681; end of, with annexation of Rome, 721-722; success of, 722-723
*Il Risorgimento*, journal, 273, 283
Rivarola, Agostino, Cardinal, 1758–1842, 230
Rivoli, battle of, 84
Rocca, Enrico della, aide to Vittorio Emanuele, 475, 620, 622
Roccaromano, Duke of, opposes French forces, 111
Rodio, Marchese di, execution of, 157
Roger-Duclos, Pierre, 1747–1816, 133
Rolle, Mazzini's followers in, 243
*Roma o morte*, Garibaldi's slogan, 662
Romagna: papal government in, 259; soldiers from, in defense of Rome, 353, 354; united with Parma and Modena as Emilia, 515
Roman Catholic Church: science and, 20-21; reformation of, as objective, 33-34, 38; property owned by, 33, 37-38; proportion of population in, 33; decline of faith in, 60, 63-64; Papacy, declining power of, 60, 63-64; Joseph II, reforms of, 61-62, 66; in France, 65; in Germany, 65; in French Rev-

Roman Catholic Church (*Cont.*)
olution, confiscation of property, 67-70; in Napoleon's Italian campaign, 87-89

Napoleon's relations with, 134-135, 141-142, 154-155, 164-171, 175-181; Sacred College of Cardinals, conclave at Venice, 135-136; concordat of 1801, 141-143; Church and State separated in France, 142; Napoleon opposed by, 164-171; catechism on Napoleon introduced in France, 166; Papal government removed to Paris, 171; "black cardinals," 175, 176, 180; bishops, council in Paris, 176-177; concordat of 1813, 179-180

revival after fall of Napoleon, 196-197; religious orders encouraged, 197; failure of government in Papal States, 230-233, 404-406; in Sardinia, Church and State, 386-388, 416-418, 433-445; obscurantism, 404; books, publication discouraged, 404; public disrespect for priests, 404-405; Law of the Convents, 433-445; clergy and Church property in Sardinia, 434-435

Rome as capital of Italy (Roman Question), 610-611, 636-639, 695-697; Church and State in Kingdom of Italy, 675-678; Montalembert's speeches, 675-676; Döllinger's speeches, 676-677; Taparelli's views, 677-678; Pius IX defends Church, 678-680; Ricasoli's proposals, 696-697; Roman Question after French reoccupation, 707-708; religious events under Pius IX, 708-709; bishops seize Church property, 713-714; Rome annexed to Italy, 718-721; Law of Guarantees, 720-722

Romano, Don Liborio, 1798-1867, prefect of police in Naples: bargain with *Camorra*, 556; recommends retirement of Francesco II, 579; message to Garibaldi on dictatorship, 580; reply to Francesco II, 585; welcomes Garibaldi to Naples, 586, 587; Garibaldi continues him in office, 597

Rome: artistic renaissance under Pius VI, 62-63; poverty of, 64-65; French attack on, 101-103; sack of, 1798, 104-105; Ferdinando II attacks, 110-111; Papal government removed from, 171; reactionary government of Pius VII, 195-197; as city separated from Italy, 317-318; after Salasco armistice, 332-333

French attack on, 1849, 353-354; siege of, 354-361, map, 356; surrender of, 361; "Third Rome," hope for, 361

as capital of Italy (Roman Question): Cavour's declaration, 610-611; negotiations of Cavour and Pius IX, 635-641; Ricasoli attempts negotiations, 656, 695-697; French army withdrawn, 694, 695

attack on, by volunteers, 700-701; French army returns to, 701, 705; Papal army and French forces defend against Garibaldi, 702-703; Roman Question after French return, 707-708; people refuse to rise in defense, 707, 708; as Papal city, 708; French troops withdrawn for Franco-Prussian war, 715

Italian government plans for taking, 715-718; occupied by Italian forces, 718-719; plebiscite on annexation, 719; government transferred to, 721

Rome, Republic of (1798), 105-106

Rome, Republic of (1849): plans for, 348; established, 350; not recognized in Europe, 350-351; Constituent Assembly: proposed, 334-335, established, 348, 349, composition of, 353; ended by surrender of Rome, 361

Rosselli, Pietro, commander-in-chief in defense of Rome, 357

Rossi, Pellegrino, Conte, 1787-1848: minister under Pius IX, 333-334; murder of, 334, 592, 679

Rossini, Gioacchino Antonio, 1792-1868, 156; *William Tell*, 220, 371, 472

Rothschild, House of, 483

Rouher, Eugène, 1814-1884, 705

Rousseau, Jean-Jacques, 1712-1778, 23

Rovere, Conte della, *see* Mamiani, Terenzio

Rubicon river, 364

Ruffini, Jacopo, 1805-1833, suicide, 241

Ruffo, Fabrizio, Cardinal, 1744-1827, 117-118; Christian Army of the Holy Faith (Sanfedisti), 118-119; leads army to Naples, 119-121; letters to Acton quoted, 121-122; urges moderation in French surrender of Naples, 122-124; letter from Hamilton quoted, 124; slighted after surrender, 127; at conclave of Sacred College of Cardinals, 135

Russell, John, Lord, 1792-1878, Foreign Secretary of Britain, 516, 552; Vittorio Emanuele asks for his moral support, 617; dispatch to Vittorio Emanuele, quoted, 622-623; writes to Garibaldi, 642

Russell, Odo, British diplomat, 482, 491, 696; interview with Pius IX, quoted, 591-592; on demands of Pius IX, 707

Russia: in coalition against France, 117, 122, 140, 180; in Austrian relations with Naples, 201, 202; in Crimean War, 428-432; break with Austria, 432; suggests congress on Italian problem, 487; protest against Garibaldi's Sicilian expedition, 541, 551-552; neutral in war for Veneto, 688

Sacred College of Cardinals, conclave at Venice, 135-136

Sadowa, battle of, 691

Salasco armistice, 325, 327, 329; end of, 341-342

Salerno, Garibaldi at, 582, 584, 585

Salvemini, Gaetano, 1873-1957, quoted, 236-237

Salvotti, commissioner in Milan, 210

San Domingo, 145

Sanfedisti (Christian Army of the Holy Faith, Ruffo's organization), 118-119

Sanfedisti, gangs employed by Church, 231, 234, 248; name changed to Centurioni, 255

San Marino, Republic of, 189, 364

Sant'Antonio, Uruguay, battle of, 255

Santa Rosa, Pietro di, 1805-1850, 390-391

Santucci, Vicenzo Cardinal, in negotiations on Roman Question, 636, 637

Sapri, Mazzini's expedition to, 465-467

Sardinia, Kingdom of, 15, 28, 34; Genoa transferred to, 183; revolution attempted, 202-203; Mazzini plans infiltration of army, 240-241

constitution (*Statuto*), 283-285, 386-387, 658-659; war with Austria, 307, 308, 318-319, 322; Milan and Lombardia, proposed annexation of, 312; Lombardia offered to, 319; Milan, Lombardia, Parma, and Modena united with, 321; republican movement opposed, 337-338; war with Austria resumed, 341-343

constitutional government under Vittorio Emanuele, 367, 374, 383-386; industrial and commercial development, 381; treaty with Austria, 384-386; Church and State, 386-388, 416-418, 433-445; Siccardi Laws, 388-390, 640; economic revolution under Cavour, 407-409; commercial treaties, 407-408; Louis Napoleon's relations with, 412, 415, 419; press law, 412; Parliament reorganized, *Connubio*, 412-414, 477; civil marriage bill, 416-418; Cavour becomes Prime Minister, 417-418; property of political exiles confiscated, 425-427; called Piedmont, 427

in Crimean War, 428-431; treaty of alliance with France and Britain, 437-440; British loan, 438; expedition and battle of Tchernaja, 446-447

Law on the Convents, 433-445, 640; clergy and Church property, 434-435; ministry resigns, 442; in Congress of Paris, 449-454; Austrian ultimatum to, 490-491; war with Austria, 1859, 492-508

Tuscany offers to unite with, 513-516; Emilia offers to unite with, 515-516; union of states. Cavour's proposal and maneuvers of Napoleon III, 522-525; plebiscites in Emilia and Tuscany on union, 523-527; Parliament, representatives from other states in, 527, 531; Nice and Savoy ceded to France by treaty, 528, 531; Sicily favors alliance with, 533; attitude toward Sicilian revolt, 535; annexation of Sicily, problem of, 558-563, 584-585, 597, 600, 601, 612, 614

invasion of Papal States planned, 576-577, 581-582; Papal States invaded, 585, 590-595, map, 594; invasion of Umbria and the Marches, 589, 598, 605

annexation of Naples: proposed, 596, 602, 604, by assembly or plebiscite, dispute on, 612-615, plebiscite votes for, 615-616; annexation of other states, Cavour's bill on, 606-607, 609-610; invasion of Naples, foreign governments protest, 617-618

Sarnico, Garibaldi's followers arrested at, 661

Savoy, Duchy, 4, 28

Savoy, House of, 7, 15, 16, 28, 183; in war between Italy and Austria, 311, 321; relations with Church, 386; Manin's open letter to, 447-448

Savoy, province: incorporated into France, 140, 339; Napoleon III demands, 480; Napoleon III plans secret treaty for, 518, 521; Cavour's proposals and maneuvers of Napoleon III, 522-524; ceded to France by treaty, 527-528, 531; plebiscite, 529-530

Schwarzenberg, Prince Felix Ludwig, 1800–1852, Prime Minister of Austria, 338-339, 342, 392, 426; description of Franz Josef, quoted, 393

Scilla, fort, 579

Secret committees, Mazzini's, 421-423; *see also* National Italian Committee

Secret societies, 199-200, 208, 211; suppressed by order of Francis II, 208; unification of Italy, plans for, 233; disillusioned by failure of Mazzini, 248, 257

Segesta, temple of, 545

Sella, Quintino, Minister of Finance, 1827–1884, 713

Siccardi, Giuseppe, Conte, 1802–1857, 388

Siccardi Laws, 388-390, 640

Sicily (island): Ferdinando II attacks, 381-382; Mazzinian uprising in, 461, 465; Neopolitans hated in, 532, 533; Garibaldi refuses to lead revolt in 1859, 533

Garibaldi's expedition, 1860, 532-550, map, 543; Cavour's role in, 538-540; Vittorio Emanuele favors, 540; foreign governments protest, 541-542, 551-552; Abba's descriptions of, quoted, 543-544, 557; Sicilians ignorant and superstitious, 545, 563; Sicilians in Garibaldi's army, 546-547, 564-565

annexation to Sardinia, problem of, 558-563, 584-585, 600, 601, 612, 614; surrendered to Garibaldi, 566-567; plebiscite decides for union with Sardinia, 616; land reform in 1960s, 674

Sicily, Kingdom of, 28; revolution attempted, 202; revolution of 1848, 280-282; constitution granted, 281-282, 285; alliance with Sardinia favored, 533; *see also* Two Sicilies, Kingdom of the

Sieyès, Emmanuel Joseph, 1748–1836, 132-133

Sinope, Russian victory at, 429

Siracusa, Leopoldo, Conte di, brother of Ferdinando II, 1813–1860: viceroy in Sicily, 227; advice to Francesco II, 553, 579; Cavour's contacts with, 572

Sismondi, Simonde de, 1773–1842, 160; writes for *La Giovine Italia*, 239

Smith, D. Mack, cited, 538, 582, 599, 730

*Società della Nazione Armata*, 533-534

*Società Nazionale Italiana*, 478, 597; foundation of, 470; prepares for war, 481; program, Italy united as kingdom, 499; Garibaldi resigns as President, 533; in Garibaldi's Sicilian expedition, 532, 537, 559, 561; recruits for Garibaldi's forces, 575

Society of Italian Unity, 383

Solario della Margarita, Clemente, Conte, 1792–1869, 268, 272; speech against Law on the Convents, 437; criticism of Cavour, 456

Solferino, battle of, 502-503

Somma, Franz Josef visits, 396

Sottocornola, Pasquale, 1822–1857, in Milan revolution, 304

Spain: Spanish Empire, 3-4, 47, map, 5; protests against Sardinian invasion of Naples, 617; Prince Leopold proposed as regent, 714-715

Spalato (Split), naval battle near, 691-692

*Squadre*, Sicilian peasants in revolt, 536, 548

Stendhal (Henri Beyle), 1738–1842, 154, 219

Stuart, Charles Edward (the Young Pretender), 1720–1788, 55

Stuart, Henry Benedict Maria, Cardinal York, 1725–1807, 135

Subalpine Republic, 85, 115

Sutherland, Granville George, Duke of, 1815–1891, in Garibaldi's visit to England, 682-684

Swiss Confederation, 7

Switzerland: as Helvetian Republic, 140; Mazzini's followers expelled, 243

Talamone, Garibaldi at, 540

Talleyrand, Charles Maurice de, 1754–1838, 177

Tanucci, Bernardo, 1698–1783, Prime Minister of Naples, 40, 41, 43, 44

Taparelli, Father, brother of Azeglio, 1793–1862, views on Church, 677-678

Tariff, 19; Cavour's treaties reduce, 407-408

Taylor, A. J. P., cited, 538

Taylor, Peter, Mazzini's letter to, quoted, 604

Tazzoli, Enrico, 1812-1852, in Mazzini's secret organization, 421-422

Tchernaja, battle of, 446-447

Teano, meeting of Garibaldi and Vittorio Emanuele, 619-621, map, 620

Tegethoff, Wilhelm von, Admiral, 1827-1871, 691

Telegraph in war of 1859, 494

Tenca, Carlo, 1816-1883, 395; *Crepuscolo*, periodical, 395, 464; censorship avoided, 395-396; refuses to publish account of Franz Josef's visit, 461-462; Franz Josef forbids printing of foreign news, 464

Tennyson, Alfred, Lord, 1809-1892, Garibaldi visits, 683

Thayer, William Roscoe, 1859-1923, cited, 482, 639, 648

Thousand, The, Garibaldi's army, 537, 541, 546, 557

Thouvenel, Edouard, 1818-1866, Foreign Minister of France, 521, 524, 598

Thucydides, Strait of Messina described by, 568

Tillot, Guillaume du, 1711-1774, reforms in Parma, 37-39

Tobacco Party in Milan, 277-279

Tolentino: Napoleon's peace terms with Pope, 88; battle of, 186

Tonello, Michelangelo, agent of Ricasoli in Rome, 696

Torre Cavallo, fort, 573

Tortona, Napoleon captures, 83

Toulon, siege of, 78-79

Traetta, Tommaso, musician, 1727-1779, 38

Trafalgar, battle of, 149

Transpadane Republic, 85, 86, 92

Treaties of Congress of Vienna, 182

Treaties of Utrecht, 6-8, 184

Treaty of Amiens, 140

Treaty of Campoformio, 91-92, 97-100, 265

Treaty of Florence, 140

Treaty of Fontainebleau, 182, 185

Treaty of Lunéville, 140, 149

Treaty of Pressburg (Bratislava), 151

Treaty of Schönbrunn, 172

Treaty of Tolentino, 233

Treaty of Zurich: terms arranged at Villafranca, 504, 506; resistance to, 508-510; signed, 510-511; effects of, 516, 517; congress on, proposed, 517-518, 520-521

Trentino—Alto Adige, 688, 693, map, 689

Trevelyan, G. M., 1876-1962, cited, 354-355, 582, 654

Trieste, 172, 688, 693, map, 689

Troppau, Metternich's Congress at, 201

Trouvé, French diplomat, 107; letter quoted, 95

Troya, Carlo, 1784-1858, 400-401; on Ferdinand II, quoted, 400

Tschudy, Swiss general, 111

Turgot, Anne-Robert-Jacques, 1727-1781, 23

Turin: reactionary government in, 197-198; revolution attempted, 202; parade celebrating constitution, 285-287; reaction against Carlo Alberto, 331, 332; capital of Italy transferred from, to Florence, 669-670; riots protesting transfer of capital, 670

Turkey: in coalition against France, 117, 122; in Crimean War, 428-432

Türr, Stefan, 1825-1908, general in Garibaldi's army, 584, 615

Tuscan dialect, 221; Manzoni's use of, 222-223; in united Italy, 635

Tuscany, Duchy: end of Medici family in, 9-11; Habsburg rule of, 15, 45; intellectual stagnation in, 21-22; Church in, 34; in war between France and Italy, 80; as Kingdom of Etruria, 140-141; incorporated into France, 152

constitution granted, 284; republicans in, 337, 345; Austrians reoccupy, 347-348; after revolutions of 1848, 397; Leopoldo II expelled by revolution, 498-499; dictatorship offered to Vittorio Emanuele, 499; Ricasoli dominates government, 511-513

union with Sardinia offered, 513-516; Defensive League with Emilia, 516-517; union with Sardinia, negotiations of Cavour and Napoleon III, 522-523; plebiscite, 524-527; peasants, attitude toward union, 525, 527

Two Sicilies, Kingdom of the, 14, 281; Habsburg claim to, 42, 45; French conquest of, 106; in war between France and Italy, 107-108; Austrian military occupation, 212; *see also* Sicily, Kingdom of

Ulloa, Girolamo, Colonel, 1810-1891, 369, 370

Ulm, battle of, 149

Ultramontanism, 197

Umberto I, King of Italy, 1844-1900, 730

Umbria, 594; Sardinian invasion of, 589, 598, 605; plebiscite for annexation to Sardinia, 616

United Italian Provinces, 234

United States: American Revolution, influence in Italy, 51, 277; minister at Turin, reports of, 551, 571; Lincoln offers Garibaldi command in Union army, 657; emigration from Italy to, 673; Garibaldi believes he is citizen of, 704

Universal Republican Alliance, 714

Urbino, 65

Uruguay, Garibaldi's Italian Legion in, 254-255

Valmy, battle of, 75

Varignano, Garibaldi imprisoned at, 704

Vatican: Pius IX resides in, 401, 721; Law of Guarantees on rights of Pope, 720

Vatican Council, 401, 708-709; opening, 713-714; dogma of Pope's infallibility, 716

Vela, Vicenzo, 1822-1891: bust of Cavour, 456; *Spartacus*, statue, 447

Velletri, celebration at, 106

Veneto, 688, map, 689; La Marmora offers to buy from Austria, 687; Austria offers in return for neutrality, 688; Austria transfers to Napoleon III by secret treaty, 688; war between Italy and Austria for, 688, 690-692; ceded to Italy, 692-693; plebiscite, 692; *see also* Lombardo-Veneto

Venice: Risorgimento supported in, 33; Teatro La Fenice, 79-80, 266; Naval Academy, 248 home rule, agitation for, 264-266, 279-280; Nicolotti and Castellani, 280; Civic Guard, 294, 296-298; Arsenal captured, 295-298; republic established, 299, 312, 321; home rule proposed, 319; in Kingdom of Alta Italia, 321, 327; protest against Salasco armistice, 327-328; isolated from rest of Italy, 345

resistance against Austria, resolution on,

367-368; Austrian attack on, 368-374; bombardment, 371-372; cholera, 372; surrender, 373-374; Franz Josef in, 462

in unification, as issue, 609-610; Cavour's position on, 611, 633-634; Garibaldi's proposed action on, 660-661; war for, *see* Veneto; fails to rebel against Austria, 693-694; Vittorio Emanuele's state visit, 709-710; Manin's body returned to, 710

Venice, Republic of, 4; feudalism in, 28-29; in eighteenth century, 29-32; Church in, 33-34; in war with France, 90-91; Napoleon's conquest of, 92-94; ceded to Austria, 97-99

Venice, Republic of (1848): established, 299, 312, 321; revived, 328; resistance to Austria continued, 367-369; Austrian attack on, 368-373; surrender, 373-374

Verdi, Giuseppe, 1813-1901: patriotism in music, 348-349, 655; Contessa Maffei's friendship with, 395, 655; VERDI acrostic as patriotic symbol, 485; admires Cavour, 655-656

*Compositions. Un Ballo in Maschera*, 485; *La Battaglia di Legnano*, 348-349; *Ernani*, 260; *Inno delle Nazioni*, 655, 663; *Macbeth*, 266; *I Masnadieri*, 395; *Requiem*, 395, 729; *I Vespri Siciliani*, 446-447

Veri Italiani, 239, 242

Verona, 305, 310, 329

Verri, Alessandro, journalist, 1741-1816, 49, 50

Verri, Pietro, journalist, 1728-1797, 49, 50

Vico, Giambattista, 1668-1774, 35

Victoria, Queen of Great Britain and Ireland, 1819-1901: letter to Pius IX, 350; Vittorio Emanuele visits, 448; favors Austria in war with France and Italy, 485; disapproves of Garibaldi, 683, 684, 685

Vienna: as seat of power in Italy, 24; student revolt in, 290-292; second revolt in, 319; revolution, October 1848, 338

Vienna, Congress of, *see* Congress of Vienna

Villafranca, peace treaty arranged at, 504, 506, 508-510; *see also* Treaty of Zurich

Villamarina, Salvatore, Marchese: in Congress of Paris, 451; on value of Russell's dispatch, 623

Vimercati, Ottavio, Conte, 1815-1879, 343

Visconti Venosta, Giovanni, 1831-1906, 625; *Memoirs of Youth*, quoted, 322-323, 406, 501-502; Rome described, 404-405; papal government criticized, 406; Garibaldi described, 501-502

Vittorio Amedeo II, Duke of Savoy, King of Sicily and Sardinia, 1666-1732, 6-7

Vittorio Amedeo III, King of Sardinia, 1726-1796, 57; in coalition against France, 73, 78, 183; in war with France, 79, 82

Vittorio Emanuele I, King of Sardinia, 1759-1824: Republic of Genoa given to, 183; reactionary anti-French government, 197-198; abdicates in favor of Carlo Felice, 203

Vittorio Emanuele II, King of Sardinia later King of Italy, 1820-1878

in war with Austria, 311, 322; Carlo Alberto abdicates in favor of, 342-343; accepts terms of surrender to Austria, 343-344

constitutional government, 367, 374; liberal opinions and policies, 383-384; treaty with Austria, 384-386; Proclamation of Moncalieri, 385; an honest king, *Il Re galantuomo*, 386; Cavour appointed to ministry,

391, 407; Franz Josef advises him to renounce constitution, 412; distrust of Rattazzi, 413; letter to Pius IX on civil marriage bill, 416-417; Cavour appointed Prime Minister, 417

in Crimean War, favors Sardinian participation, 430-432, 446-447; treaty of alliance with France and Britain, 437-438

Law on the Convents, 435; letter to La Marmora quoted, 435-436; letter to Pius IX quoted, 439; letter from Sardinian bishops quoted, 441-442; letter from Azeglio quoted, 443-444; signs bill, is excommunicated, 444

death of his mother, Maria Teresa, 437; death of his wife, Maria Adelaide, 438; death of his brother, Ferdinando, 440; death of his son, Vittorio Emanuele, 444; Manin's open letter, 447; in Paris and London, 448-449; ignores Franz Josef's visit, 463; letter to Napoleon III quoted, 474-475; speech, *grido di dolore*, 483-484, quoted, 484; supports preparation for war, 487-488

in war of 1859, 496-499, 501, 503; at battle of Palestro, 496; dictatorship of Tuscany offered to, 499; other dictatorships offered, 499; peace arranged without his consent, 504-506; signs preliminaries of peace, 506

forms new ministry, 509, 510; Tuscan offer of union presented, 514-515; Modena and Parma present offer of union, 515; recalls Cavour, 522; attitude on cession of Nice and Savoy, 522, 523, 528; excommunicated for efforts toward union, 528

Garibaldi's Sicilian expediton, 532, 538, 540; letter to Francesco II quoted, 553-554; annexation of Sicily, problem of, 558-599; correspondence with Garibaldi quoted, 569-570; Garibaldi's advance toward Rome, position on, 570; Abruzzi petitions for annexation of Naples to Sardinia, 596

Garibaldi demands dismissal of Cavour, 597-598, 604, letter quoted, 598; offended by Garibaldi's demands, 605; Garibaldi invites him to come to Naples with army, 608, 612; proclamation "To the People of Southern Italy," 614; enters province of Naples, 616-617; asks Russell for moral support, 617; meets Garibaldi at Teano, 619-621, map, 620; Russell's dispatch quoted, 622-623; does not attend review at Caserta, 624-625; inadequacy for role in kingdom, 624-625, 631; Garibaldi's loyalty to, 625; visits Palermo, insults Sicilians, 630-631

opens first session of Italian Parliament, 634; proclaimed first King of Italy as Vittorio Emanuele II, 634; objections to Cavour as Prime Minister, 635; tries to prevent Garibaldi's speech in Parliament, 643; reconciliation of Cavour and Garibaldi attempted, 650; Ricasoli appointed Prime Minister, 656; Garibaldi's interview with, 658; Rattazzi appointed in place of Ricasoli, 658-659; appointments of Farini and Minghetti, 667-668; dismisses Minghetti, appoints La Marmora Prime Minister, 670; suggests Garibaldi should lead expedition to Galicia, 685, 686; Garibaldi asks for appointment as dictator of Naples and Sicily, 687

in war for Veneto, 690, 692; attitude toward attack on Rome, 701; plans arrest of Garibaldi, 701, 702; attitude toward Napo-

Vittorio Emanuele II (*Cont.*)
    leon III, 706; visit to Venice, 709-710; fa-
    vors generals in government, 712; as con-
    stitutional monarch, understands his role,
    713; in Franco-Prussian war, objects to neu-
    trality, 716; letter to Pius IX on annexation
    of Rome, quoted, 717; opens first Parliament
    in Rome, 721; death, 729; Pius IX lifts ban
    of    excommunication,    729-730;    historical
    judgment on, 730
*Vocabulario della Crusca*, 222
Voltaire (François Marie Arouet), 1694-1778,
    18-19, 23
Volturno, battle of the, 607-608

Wagram, battle of, 172
Walewski, Alexandre, Count, 1810-1868, 474,
    480, 488, 489; in Congress of Paris, 450-
    454; retired, 521
War of the Austrian Succession, 15-17
War of the Polish Succession, 14
War of the Spanish Succession, 5-6, 18

Washington, George, 1732-1799, Alfieri's plays
    dedicated to, 54
Waterloo, battle of, 185
Wellington, Arthur Wellesley, Duke of, 1769-
    1852, 290
Whyte, Arthur J., cited, 434, 475
Wilhelm, Regent of Prussia, later Emperor Wil-
    helm I, 1797-1888: protests against Gari-
    baldi's Sicilian expedition, 551-552; Warsaw
    meeting, 608, 617; first Emperor of Ger-
    many, 687; in war for Veneto, 688
Winckelmann, Johann Joachim, 1717-1768, 63
Windisch-Gratz, Alfred Candidus Ferdinand zu,
    General, 1787-1862, 338-339
Wiseman, Nicholas, Cardinal, 1802-1865, 405
Woodward, E. L., cited, 402
Würmser, Dagobert Siegmund, Count, 1724-
    1797, 83

Zambianchi, Callimaco, leads expedition against
    Papal States, 541
*Zelanti*, 224